THE NEW
Milton Cross'
MORE STORIES
OF THE
GREAT OPERAS

THE NEW
Milton Cross'
MORE STORIES
OF THE
GREAT OPERAS

by Milton Cross and Karl Kohrs

───◆◆◆───

Revised and Expanded
by Karl Kohrs

Doubleday & Company, Inc.
GARDEN CITY, NEW YORK

ACKNOWLEDGMENTS

For generously making available the use of opera scores, libretti and background information on the operas added to this edition, the author is deeply indebted to the following:

Mrs. Roger H. Andrews, Port Chester, N.Y.; Dr. Hillel Ausubel, Librarian II, New Rochelle (N.Y.) Library; Arthur Backgren, New York City; M. Henri Bernier, instructor in French, Collegiate School, New York City; Mrs. Esther Duffy, librarian, Music Division, Greenwich (Conn.) Library; Mrs. Vivian Farrell, New York City; Richard Gaddes, general manager, Opera Theater, St. Louis, Mo.; Mrs. Kathryn Kohrs, Port Chester, N.Y.; Dr. Lewis Paul Kohrs, author and librarian, San Diego (Calif.) Library; Eugene Moon, Theodore Presser Company, Bryn Mawr, Penn.; Miss Sheila Porter, New York City Opera; Miss Marie Puente, Langhorne, Penn.; Mrs. Marie Rich, editor, and Miss Jeanne Kemp, assistant editor, *Central Opera Service Bulletin,* New York City; Francis Robinson, Tour Director and Consultant, Metropolitan Opera, New York; Miss Julia Spangler, of the staff of Tito Capobianco, general director of the Verdi Festival, San Diego (Calif.) Opera; Addice Thomas, production coordinator, the Washington Opera, Kennedy Center, Washington, D.C.; Don Walker, instructor in French, Collegiate School, New York City; Robert Willett, New York City; Mrs. Cathy Zumoff, Cornell University, Ithaca, N.Y.

CONTENTS

FOREWORD

In the more than three decades since the *Milton Cross' Stories of the Great Operas* was published, opera has undergone a transformation from the "Golden Age" to the "Space Age" with its built-in electronic concomitants. Vocally and histrionically the concept of opera as an art form has broken out of the traditional pattern, has been streamlined and—to use a term that will raise the hackles of the traditionalists—"popularized."

For better or worse, the accent today is no longer primarily on the clarion vocalization of the Golden Age stalwarts (sometimes, admittedly, at the expense of dramatic verities). Today's audiences demand more sophistication, more adventuresome elements in the pit as well as on the stage. In short, modern opera calls for singing actors rather than acting singers.

It is in response to this trend that American singers—or singers trained in America—have made a major contribution to the cause of opera. The training of these young singers principally has been in the regional opera houses of Santa Fe, St. Louis, Cincinnati, San Diego, Minneapolis, New Orleans, Baltimore—and in the top-echelon ensemble company, the New York City Opera. The nation's three international houses—the Metropolitan, Chicago Lyric and San Francisco Opera—maintain the status quo with international casts and conventional staging.

Training today is on realism in acting—eschewing the "lurch and stagger" style of histrionics. The singer does not perform "with one eye on the conductor." Inevitably, this has led to some caviling to the effect that opera has been taken away from the singer and handed over to the stage director.

But the fact is that these companies—which are among the more than nine hundred organizations devoted to operatic productions—provide today's proving ground for American singers. By this time it is a truism that Americans no longer are obliged to go to Europe to find their places in opera. For the gifted and talented there is plenty of work in the United States.

Interest in contemporary opera, the Central Opera Service reports, is at an all-time high. Its survey indexed nearly 1,000 such works—398 operas by American composers written between 1967 and 1975; 565 operas by non-American composers in about the same period. Typical of works in the modern idiom include Thea Musgrave's *The Voice of Ariadne*, Joseph Tal's *Ashmedai*, Leon Kirchner's *Lily*, Arnold Schoenberg's *Moses and Aaron*, Hans Werner Henze's *The Young Lord*, Samuel Barber's *Antony and Cleopatra*, Benjamin Britten's *Death in Venice*, Dominick Argento's *Miss Havisham's Fire*. Whether they will be permanently absorbed into the repertory only time will tell.

But there is a curious paradox. Revivals of classic operas—*La Favorita, Le Prophète, I Lombardi, Esclarmonde, Roberto Devereux, La Sonnambula, Tancredi* (to name a few)—play to S.R.O. audiences. And the bel canto revival which began in the fifties and continued on into the sixties and seventies—starring such specialists as Berganza, Caballé, Callas, Horne, Sills, Simionato and Sutherland—is a memorable chapter in operatic history. *Plus ça change, plus ç'est la même chose.*

With striking success, television has brought opera "live from the stage" into the living room. That story virtually begins with a color videotape of the final dress rehearsal of the Metropolitan Opera's production of *Il Barbiere di Siviglia*. It was taped November 4, 1968, by the Japanese Broadcasting Corporation and was hailed as presaging a new era in opera. A decade later, TV cameras were firmly focused on the operatic stage. Technical improvements now make it possible to film the stage at regular performances, with no cameras in sight and without the intrusion of extra lighting.

Among television's outstanding contributions today are the "Great Performances," "Live from Lincoln Center" and "Live from the Met" series. A fund-raising telecast of *La Bohème* with Luciano Pavarotti and Renata Scotto brought $1 million from grateful viewers.

Early predictions of a "new era" in opera were borne out in more ways than one. Not only did telecasts expand audiences from thousands to millions, but this expansion of interest had a remarkable effect on—of all things—the American economy. A survey by the Central Opera Service disclosed that in the 1975-76 season companies and workshops spent about $100 million. The value of goods and services provided by secondary sources indirectly activated by opera productions virtually doubled this figure. The $100 million injected into the American economy generated the greatest number of operatic performances enjoyed by the largest audiences in the history of opera.

The reader will note that in the present edition the category of "Concert Operas" has been absorbed into the regular alphabetical listing of operas. Whether presented in concert form or in staged productions, they are part and parcel of the "grand opera" tradition.

The twenty-four additional operas in this expanded edition (combined with the forty-five operas of the third edition) include contemporary and classic works that have been successfully performed during the past two decades and are currently in the repertoire.

It is hoped that the expanded scope of the fourth edition will in turn expand the knowledge about opera for those who treasure this art form —whether in classic or modern idiom—as an enduring source of inspiration and pleasure.

KARL KOHRS

THE NEW
Milton Cross'
MORE STORIES
OF THE
GREAT OPERAS

ADRIANA LECOUVREUR
by Francesco Cilèa
(1866–1950)

Libretto by
ARTURO COLAUTTI

Adapted from the play *Adrienne Lecouvreur,* by the French drama-
tists Augustin Eugène Scribe and Ernest Wilfried Legouvé

CHARACTERS

Adriana Lecouvreur, leading actress of the Comédie Française	Soprano
Maurizio, Count of Saxony	Tenor
Michonnet, stage manager of the Comédie	Baritone
Prince de Bouillon	Bass
Princess de Bouillon	Mezzo-soprano
Abbé de Chazeuil	Tenor
Quinault ⎤	Bass
Poisson ⎥ members of the Comédie	Tenor
Mlle. Jouvenot ⎥	Soprano
Mlle. Dangeville ⎦	Mezzo-soprano
Major-domo	Tenor
Lady's maid	Mezzo-soprano

Ladies and gentlemen, actors, stagehands, servants
Characters in the ballet: Paris, Mercury, Juno, Pallas, Venus

Place: Paris
Time: March 1730
First performance: Teatro Lirico, Milan, November 6, 1902
Original language: Italian

Adriana Lecouvreur is the fourth of five operas composed by Cilèa, a
contemporary of Puccini, Leoncavallo and Mascagni and one of the
leading Italian musicians of his day. The opera is based on incidents in
the lives of actual people prominent in the theatrical world of eighteenth-century Paris. It is the story of the tragic love affair between

Adrienne Lecouvreur, the leading actress of the Comédie Française during the earlier years of Louis XV (1710–74), and Count Maurice de Saxe, who later became Marshal of France.

Adriana and *L'Arlesiana,* Cilèa's third opera, are the only two of the composer's works which have survived in the repertoire. The 1907–8 season of the Metropolitan Opera in New York opened with *Adriana.* In the cast were Caruso, Cavalieri, Scotti and Journet. In 1963 the opera was revived at the Met for Renata Tebaldi. She also sang the leading role (opposite Franco Corelli) at the opening performance of the Metropolitan Opera's 1968–69 season on September 16, 1968. The opera was given in a Metropolitan Opera Saturday afternoon broadcast on February 2, 1978, with Montserrat Caballé in the title role, and in subsequent performances that season.

Like his contemporaries, Cilèa was a melodist, and *Adriana* is outstanding for its lyrical qualities. It has been pointed out, however, that the composer has a tendency to repeat melodic themes associated with the individual characters, which makes for a certain monotony. Yet this fault is compensated for by the richness and beauty not only of the arias but of the concerted numbers as well.

There is no overture. The curtain rises immediately.

ACT ONE

The Green Room of the Comédie Française, where two plays are about to be performed: Racine's tragedy *Bajazet,* and Régnard's comedy *Les Folies Amoureuses.* Mlle. Jouvenot, Mlle. Dangeville, Quinault and Poisson are putting on their costumes and giving last-minute touches to their makeup. Meanwhile they are driving Michonnet, the stage manager, nearly frantic with their demands for attention. Their voices blend in a spirited ensemble ("Michonnet, della biacca!") which reflects the backstage tension at curtain time.

In a lively refrain ("Michonnet su! Michonnet giù!") the stage manager complains about his lot. Worse than a lackey's, he grumbles—listening to griping actors, running their errands, trying to keep peace backstage. . . . He would give it all up if it weren't for the hope of becoming a *sociétaire* ("di socio proprietario"), a full-fledged member of the Comédie, and retiring on a pension—plus the fact that his job keeps him near that glorious creature Adriana, with whom he is hopelessly in love.

He is jolted out of his reflections as Quinault, practicing gestures with a scimitar he uses in his role, almost runs him through. The ensemble becomes more agitated as tension rises and the players begin snapping at each other.

They are interrupted by the entrance of the Prince de Bouillon and the Abbé de Chazeuil. As the two are announced by Michonnet, Poisson observes that the Prince is the current heart interest of La Duclos (Adriana's stage rival) and a dabbler in chemistry as well as in love ("di chimica dilettante e d'amore")—a significant remark in the light of later events. In a continuation of the ensemble, the Prince and Chazeuil fatuously compliment the players, who respond in kind. In a brief duet, the visitors, with spurious gallantry, commend the two actresses for their irresistible charm. Then, as they both turn to leave, they ask Michonnet where La Duclos is. Dressing, Michonnet answers, to which Jouvenot and Dangeville spitefully remark that "undressing" would be more accurate. Ignoring this sally, the Abbé remarks that the theater is packed. Michonnet tells him that is to be expected when Adriana and La Duclos are to appear in the same play. This brings more ribald comment from the two envious supporting players.

At this point, to the accompaniment of an imposing chord in the orchestra, Adriana appears. She is costumed in oriental fashion for the role of Roxane in *Bajazet* and is wearing a magnificent necklace, a gift from the Queen.[1] Oblivious to everyone, Adriana declaims the lines of her role over sustained chords in the orchestra: "Del sultano Amuratte m'arrendo all'imper." Dissatisfied with her reading, she repeats the passage.

When the Abbé and Bouillon exclaim loudly in admiration, Adriana responds in the first of the opera's well-known arias—"Io son l'umile ancella." She is nothing more than the humble servant of that glorious art which can touch the heart of mankind, she sings, merely the instrument which gives voice to poetry. Her name is Sincerity. Her voice itself is but a fragile breath which will die away. The aria ends on a high pianissimo note.

Bouillon, impressed, asks what more she would seek. Truth alone, Adriana replies simply. She adds that she has learned nothing about her art from anyone—except from her faithful friend and adviser Michonnet ("Umile cor devoto"). Michonnet, brought close to tears, protests that no credit is due him.

The stage callboy interrupts the scene and the actors prepare to go on. There is an excited murmur of voices in the background, signaling that the play is about to begin. As the Abbé and Bouillon leave, they again ask about La Duclos. Michonnet tells them she is in her dressing room hastily writing a letter. Bouillon asks sharply: "To whom?" Jouvenot and Dangeville break in to remark flippantly that the note is cer-

[1] Queen Marie of France. Born Marie Leszczynska, daughter of Stanislas I Leszczynski, King of Poland (1677–1766). She was married to Louis XV when he was fifteen years old. He had become King at the age of five.

tainly not for him, because La Duclos knows he already is here. When Bouillon and the Abbé are alone, the Prince, with a meaningful look at the Abbé, declares he must have that letter. The Abbé asks how he is to get it. Handing him a purse, Bouillon curtly tells him to proceed. They leave.

During a brief orchestral interlude Adriana, absorbed in her role, continues studying her lines while Michonnet stares at her longingly, trying to get up enough courage to speak his mind. "At last we are alone," he murmurs ("Eccoci soli, alfin!"), and this phrase introduces a touching musical dialogue in quasi-recitative.

For five long years, he sings, he has been tormented by his love for Adriana. She is young and beautiful—while for him, alas, the Maytime of life is past. Shall he confess his love now, or wait until tomorrow? But then it will be a day later still. This thought propels him to a decision.

Hesitantly, he begins by telling Adriana that he has good news: His uncle, the pharmacist in Carcassonne, had died and left him a legacy of ten thousand francs. Half amused, Adriana is duly impressed. Then, in mock seriousness, she commiserates with him ("Tanto peggio") as he wonders what he is to do with all that money. In any case, Michonnet goes on rather desperately, this stroke of fortune has given him an extraordinary idea: to get married. "Excellent!" Adriana exclaims, adding somewhat wistfully that she wishes she could ("Ah, se potessi anch'io!").

Beside himself with joy, Michonnet murmurs that now he must tell her ("Allora, glielo dico"). But before he can speak Adriana remarks, with a troubled expression, that she seems to be losing her touch—as last night's performance of *Phèdre* proved. She was too concerned over the fact that there had been no further news following the report of the battle in Courland. "News of whom?" Michonnet asks. "The man I love," Adriana answers ("Il mio cavalier").

Michonnet's joy turns to despair as she goes on to explain (mistakenly) that her beloved is a lieutenant of Count de Saxe ("Era unsemplice alfiere").[2] He has been at the front in Courland, where a battle has been raging. There had been no word of him for a long time, Adriana says, but yesterday she saw him. And tonight, she adds joyfully, he will see her as Roxane. Then, with touching concern, she asks Michonnet about his own plans for romance and a wedding. "That can wait," he answers bitterly. He leaves as three knocks are heard—the traditional signal in French theaters for the raising of the curtain.

Adriana watches him go, then turns again to the study of her role.

[2] Maurice, Count of Saxony (Maurizio), was the son of Stanislas II Augustus (1732–98), Elector of Saxony and King of Poland. The Count had pretensions to both thrones.

Suddenly there is an excited burst of music, then the voice of Maurizio calling Adriana's name. The lovers rush into each other's arms to the accompaniment of an impassioned theme in the orchestra. Impetuously Maurizio tells Adriana that he could no longer wait for her appearance, and so made his way backstage. When Adriana chides him for being reckless he launches into the well-known aria "La dolcissima effigie," in which he extravagantly acclaims her as his soul's inspiration.

In ensuing dialogue, Adriana asks if he has spoken to the Count de Saxe about his promotion. Maurizio evasively replies that the Count promises—but does nothing. When Adriana says she will somehow contrive to speak to the Count on this matter, Maurizio warns her that Saxe is a dangerous man, a devil with women ("È un uom pericoloso").

Adriana turns to go onstage and Maurizio protests that she is deserting him. Repeating the theme of his aria, Adriana assures him that tonight she will act for him alone. Their voices blend as they repeat their avowals. As they are leaving, Maurizio tells her he will be in the "third box on the right." Adriana gives him a bunch of violets as a token of her love.

Prince de Bouillon and the Abbé now reappear. The Abbé hands Bouillon a letter with the remark "Corpus delicti!" This introduces a musical colloquy in which the two plan the strategy that is to entrap the clandestine lovers. The Abbé explains that he got the letter (written by La Duclos in her dressing room) by the simple expedient of bribing her maid with one hundred louis. In spoken recitative, the Abbé reads the message aloud to the infuriated Prince: "Stasera alle undici, laggiù nel solito villino, presso la Senna . . . per un affare d'alta politica"— "Tonight at eleven, at the villa near the Seine, on a matter of political importance." His very own villa, the Prince rages. What is worse, the letter is signed "Constancy," the nickname he himself gave to Duclos. The Abbé relishes the irony.

Examining the address—"third box on the right"—the Abbé suddenly recalls that he saw Maurice de Saxe enter it. Quite obviously, the two men agree, Saxe is the secret lover. Forthwith, they begin plotting to trap the guilty pair ("Un gaio festino"). Meanwhile, unknown to the two men, Jouvenot, Dangeville, Quinault and Poisson return to the Green Room, hide in the background and overhear the entire plot, which is revealed in the continuation of the duet.

The Prince will invite the entire cast to a gay supper party at his villa. There the lovers will be surprised in their "nest," and the next day all Paris will smack its lips over the scandal. The Prince orders a servant to take the letter to "Box Three—confidential." At this point an ensemble builds up as the four players comment on the situation ("Quanto è burlevole!") and incidentally disclose additional information about the intrigues at the villa.

It seems that, while La Duclos has the Prince as her "patron," she has another ally—the Princess herself. The conniving actress has given the key to the love nest to the Princess, who brazenly entertains her own lover there. And now, an anonymous letter ("Ma già una lettera") making an appointment at the villa, written for the Princess by La Duclos, has been sold by the actress' maid to the Prince. The ensemble (calling to mind the quintet in *Carmen*) comes to a crackling finish as the players maliciously speculate on what will happen, while the Prince and the Abbé discuss their plot to bring the guilty lovers together. The scene comes to an end as Michonnet orders them to take their places in the wings for their next cues.

Stationing himself in the wings where he can watch Adriana, Michonnet listens enthralled to the monologue of Roxane. He fumes at the audience for not applauding louder for his idol's divine performance. In a plaintive refrain, "E dir che così bene," he laments that her superb acting is for someone else, not for himself. But, even so, when he listens to her voice he forgets. . . . Even the props, he gasps suddenly, striking his forehead. Frantically he begins looking for the letter which Jouvenot, in the role of Zatime, must hand to Adriana in the next scene.

At that moment, Maurizio strides in cursing because some "political matter" ("Maledetta politica!")—as stated in the letter just handed to him in his box—will prevent his seeing Adriana after the performance. Over an agitated orchestral accompaniment, the byplay involving the prop letter now follows. Maurizio reflects that his being summoned to the villa means that the Princess has mentioned his political plans to the Cardinal. Now he is torn between love and duty. He decides to wait for Adriana's exit.

Michonnet, at last finding the prop letter—a blank piece of paper—lays it on a table and, when Quinault walks by, asks the actor to give it to Jouvenot. Quinault, unco-operative as usual, ignores the request. Maurizio snatches up the paper and scribbles a message to Adriana. When Jouvenot rushes in calling for her prop letter, he hands her the piece of paper with a bow. Highly pleased with his improvised strategy, Maurizio sings in an impassioned refrain ("Adriana avrà due mie") that Adriana will know why they cannot meet as planned—ruefully adding that this is what Courland has cost him. His voice blends in a ringing phrase with that of Michonnet, who enthuses over Adriana's fabulous art as she plays the letter scene. Adriana's genuine shock and dismay at reading Maurizio's message in the prop letter brings thunderous applause from the unsuspecting audience at the closing curtain.

A brief ensemble follows as the actors troop into the Green Room, followed by Bouillon, the Abbé and other members of the audience. The players, though furiously jealous of Adriana's triumph, join in hailing her as she enters ("Ad Adriana onor!"). Pale and distraught, she is on the verge of collapse. As Michonnet revives her with smelling salts she murmurs brokenly that she saw Maurizio in the theater.

Bouillon invites all to the midnight supper party in honor of Adriana's success. She at first declines but decides to go when the Prince tells her that the Count of Saxony will be there. With that he hands her the key to the villa. Aside, Adriana sings that she will speak to the Count about Maurizio. In a choral phrase, all on stage voice their pleasure over the revelry in store at the midnight party. The curtain falls.

ACT TWO

A small salon in the villa La Grange Batelière on the banks of the Seine not far from Paris. From the terrace a flight of steps leads to a broad esplanade extending to the river's edge.

In the salon the Princess de Bouillon is waiting for her lover. A brief pulsating theme in the orchestra underscores her anxiety and impatience. In one of the opera's most dramatic arias, "Acerba voluttà, dolce tortura," she gives voice to her conflicting emotions of love, anguish and fear. A clock strikes in the distance. The Princess springs to her feet and listens intently. Every echo, every shadow of night mocks a lover's impatience, she sings ("Ogn'eco, ogn'ombra").

Finally she goes to the doors at the back, flings them open and stares at the starry sky. In the brilliant climax of the aria she implores the wandering Star of the East never to set until she is in her lover's arms ("O vagabonda stella d'Oriente"). As the music dies away on a serene phrase the Princess sinks down on a divan.

A moment later Maurizio bounds in through the doors at the back and kneels before the Princess. She greets him somewhat irritably. Maurizio explains that he was delayed because he was trying to elude two mysterious men following him. Glancing at the bunch of violets pinned to his uniform, the Princess pointedly asks if a certain sweet-scented posy might not have been the reason for his being late ("Il ritardo cagionato"). With a courtly gesture, Maurizio instantly hands her the flowers.

A long duet then ensues as the Princess informs Maurizio that she pleaded his cause (as Pretender) so fervently that Her Majesty was moved to tears ("Con la Regina a lungo favellai"). The Cardinal,[3] however, is still undecided. She goes on to warn the Count that he has enemies. Maurizio sharply interjects that he has never yet been vanquished, adding that he will flee the country rather than risk imprisonment in the Bastille as royal Pretender and plotter.

[3] André Hercule de Fleury (1653–1743), French cardinal and statesman.

At that the Princess upbraids him for daring even to think of casting her love aside and deserting her ("Ed io dovrei lasciarvi"). When Maurizio protests that he must put royal duty before love, the Princess becomes suspicious. In jealous fury she accuses him of being in love with someone else. Admitting as much, Maurizio tries to assure her that he still is devoted to her. When he flatly refuses to name her rival, the Princess warns him she will tear the mask from the woman's face.

Then, in a ringing aria, "L'anima ho stanca," Maurizio implores her (somewhat fatuously) to show him mercy instead of hatred in this hour of his anguish. Even though love is ended, their friendship must last forever. In rage and scorn the Princess cries that love is flame, friendship ashes ("Amore è fiamma, e cener l'amistà").

Suddenly the two are startled by the sound of carriage wheels outside. Panic-stricken, the Princess rushes to the door, then gasps that her husband is stepping out of his carriage. Maurizio, promising to save her, pushes her into an adjoining room.

An instant later, Bouillon and the Abbé burst in and confront Maurizio, gloating over the success of their plot. As the dialogue continues in trio form over a crackling orchestral accompaniment, they gleefully inform him that they caught a glimpse of the lady—a slim-waisted creature all in white. With a shrug, Maurizio answers that there was no such person present. Bouillon retorts that he knows everything. Losing his temper, Maurizio promptly challenges the Prince to a duel. The latter immediately backs down, remarking that it was all a joke. The Prince, says the Abbé, is in the Count's debt. "La Duclos," adds Bouillon in explanation. He has grown tired of her, he goes on, and now that the Count is her lover, he himself is free.

Suddenly everything becomes clear. Maurizio realizes—to his vast relief—that Bouillon and the Abbé assumed they were trapping him in a rendezvous with La Duclos, not the Princess. The Prince holds out his hand and the Count takes it gladly.

Adriana now appears and Bouillon hurries to welcome her. Leading her into the room he introduces her as "the great Sultana" to the Count de Saxe. The Abbé dryly comments that one merely need say "Adriana." A theme associated with Adriana sounds prominently in the orchestra at this point. As Adriana, in stunned surprise, stammers Maurizio's name, the Count, aside, warns her not to betray herself. Bouillon pompously announces that this great actress wishes to speak to the Count de Saxe about a certain young officer. Adriana quietly observes that, under the circumstances, the young officer no longer is in need of her assistance.

The Prince abruptly reminds the Abbé that he is to make preparations for the midnight supper party. Aside, he tells the Abbé that their prey is in the trap, and there she will stay. As the Abbé leaves, the

Prince declares that no one is to leave the villa until daylight. He then leaves to search the grounds.

One of the opera's finest duets ("Eri degno d'un trono") now follows as Adriana and Maurizio confront each other. Still incredulous, she asks him if he really is the renowned Count de Saxe. In the opening phrases of the duet she sings that even as "lieutenant" he was worthy of a throne. In an answering refrain ("Tu sei la mia vittoria") Maurizio apostrophizes her as his victory and his crown. In each other's arms, their voices blend in the passionate climax of the duet.

Hearing voices outside, Maurizio frees himself from Adriana's embrace. A moment later Michonnet enters with the Abbé. He is trying to get permission to leave the villa, contrary to the Prince's orders. He has urgent business with La Duclos, he explains—he must ask her if she will consent to play a certain new role ("Per una parte nuova").

With an affable leer, the Abbé tells Michonnet there is no need to go to fetch her, because she already is at the villa. Adriana gasps in surprise. Enjoying the effect, the Abbé, in a phrase insinuatingly sung on one note, explains in mythological terms ("questa è Citera") that here in "Cytherea,[4] Venus has arranged a tryst with Mars."

Adriana asks if the Abbé means the Count. Despite Maurizio's angry command to keep quiet, the Abbé obstinately insists that La Duclos is in the other room. Adriana starts for the door but Maurizio bars her way. In a flash, Michonnet enters the door and slams it behind him. In an ensuing refrain ("Adriana, ascolta") Maurizio explains that he came to the villa solely for political reasons. He swears on his honor that it is not La Duclos who is hiding in the room. Then he asks Adriana to stand guard at the door and under no circumstances allow the Abbé to enter. Moreover, she herself must promise not to attempt to find out who the lady really is. Adriana promises. Maurizio rushes away. Adriana sings ("Sull'onor suo giurò") that, as he swore on his honor and cannot lie, so she too will keep her word.

Suddenly Michonnet emerges from the room completely bewildered and stammers to Adriana and the Abbé: "What a blunder! It is not Duclos after all!" ("Che granchio!"). This introduces a dialogue in trio form, in 6/8 waltz tempo, which underscores the seriocomic mood of the scene. When the two ask Michonnet who is in the room, he sheepishly admits that he never saw her.

It was pitch-dark in there, he complains ("tenebre peste"), and as he groped about, a needle pricked his hand. In a falsetto imitation of a woman's voice Michonnet relates that a voice asked who he was and whom he was seeking ("Chi siete?"). The "unknown" told him she was

[4] The Greek island near which, according to mythology, the goddess Venus rose from the sea.

not the one, then offered to make it worth his while if he helped her to escape secretly.

Adriana and the Abbé laughingly ask Michonnet what happened next. Nothing to do but leave, says Michonnet with a shrug. Thereupon the Abbé picks up a candelabra from the table and starts for the door of the room. Adriana, resolutely barring his way, pointedly reminds him that this is someone else's secret ("É d'altri un segreto"). The Abbé asks slyly: "The Count's secret . . . or the Prince's?" With a knowing laugh, Adriana replies that the Prince's friend is innocent ("La bella è innocente"). Saying he will so inform the Prince, the Abbé leaves to the accompaniment of a descending chromatic figure in the orchestra.

A brief colloquy follows over sustained chords in the orchestra. Michonnet asks Adriana what she intends to do. Save the person in that room, she answers. Michonnet vainly tries to dissuade her, then is made even more unhappy when she says she is taking the risk not on his behalf but to keep her promise to the Count. Resignedly, Michonnet agrees to stand guard at the door.

As a slow waltz rhythm begins in the orchestra, Adriana blows out the candles one by one until the salon is in almost complete darkness. Going to the door, she knocks three times. When there is no answer she calls out: "Open, Madame, in the name of Maurizio!" ("Apritemi, Signora, nel nome di Maurizio!"). This marks the beginning of the dramatic duet which concludes the act.

Slowly the door opens and the figure of the Princess clad in white becomes dimly visible. She asks Adriana why she has come. To save you, Adriana replies. When the other tells her that all escape has been cut off, Adriana hands her the key previously given her by Bouillon. This, she says, will unlock the garden gate. She warns that she cannot give explicit directions because this house is unfamiliar to her. "I know it well," the Princess says. "There is a secret panel here."

After a moment's search she finds the panel and pushes it open. But before making her escape she insists that she must see her rescuer's face. Adriana curtly warns her not to try. Growing suspicious, the Princess, aside, murmurs that she has heard that voice before ("Ma questa voce l'udii sovente").

Here a rather menacing theme in the orchestra reflects the mounting tension of the scene as the Princess demands to know the identity of the person who is so vitally concerned with her fate at this point. Someone who trusts her, Adriana answers with simple candor. Instantly the Princess realizes that it is Maurizio. The duet surges to a powerful climax as the two women, both claiming the love of the same man, pour out their jealous rage and scorn.

At the height of the quarrel servants bearing torches are seen outside. When the Princess cries that her husband is coming, Adriana contemptuously dares her to stay. Going toward the door, she shouts to the servants to bring in the lights. Terror-stricken, the Princess rushes to the secret panel and vanishes through its opening.

Adriana turns, finds her rival gone. In wild anger she cries that the coward has fled ("Fuggita! Vile!"). As the orchestra blares out the closing theme of the duet, Bouillon, the Abbé and the players from the Comédie pass along the terrace at the back. Suddenly Michonnet rushes in holding a bracelet which the Princess dropped as she fled. This he hands to Adriana, at the same time trying to comfort her. Tormented by the thought that Maurizio probably fled the villa with her rival, Adriana collapses in despair.[5]

ACT THREE

The grand ballroom of the Prince de Bouillon's palace. At one side is a small stage. At the Abbé's direction, servants are completing preparations for the Princess' reception. After a spirited orchestral introduction, during which the Abbé officiously orders the servants about, the Princess enters costumed for the ball. In an ensuing monologue ("Ah! quella donna!") she moodily ponders how to learn the identity of her rival—she who came to her rescue and yet is stealing away her lover. In tones of suppressed fury she recalls the sound of the rival's voice—caressing yet menacing ("Oh quella voce che carezza").

Her reflections are interrupted by the Abbé, who fawns on her and comments extravagantly on her beauty—with particular reference to her voluptuous bosom. She acknowledges the compliment with amused sarcasm. In a brief, mocking refrain ("Dite che il dio d'amore") the Abbé sings that even though the god of love has given her a heart of marble, he will gladly play Pygmalion to her Galatea.[6]

The Princess, though amused, dismisses his madrigal as nonsense, and says that the Prince has no use for mythology. The Abbé significantly remarks that Bouillon prefers chemistry ("Un chimico, s'intende"). This banter is interrupted by the entrance of the Prince

[5] This detail of the plot is not explained in the stage action of the abridged version of the opera. In another version Bouillon and the Abbé enter shortly after Adriana has sung her final phrase. The Abbé takes the Prince into the room to prove to him that La Duclos was not hiding there. Michonnet then enters, gives Adriana the bracelet and tells her he saw the Count leave with the "unknown." Bouillon and the Abbé re-enter. La Duclos was not in the room and the Prince is satisfied. At his invitation, all leave for the supper party in another part of the villa. Only Adriana remains.

[6] In the Sonzogno score, the Princess, unimpressed by the Abbé's flattery, remarks that he would serve her better by finding out who Maurizio's new light-o'-love is. This the Abbé promises to do.

himself, followed by servants. At that moment the Princess asks the Abbé to bring her a box of powder. He hands her one of several the Prince has just placed on a nearby table, explaining—for some reason—that he was obliged to move the boxes out of his laboratory.

With a startled exclamation, the Prince snatches the box away from the Abbé, saying that the powder is deadly poison. He describes its properties in a sardonic refrain ("Candida lieve, come la neve"). That glittering, snow-white poison, he sings, is a favorite with traitors bent on revenge, or of heirs impatiently waiting for a bequest. A bit of it sprinkled on a ring or a glove, or dropped in tea or wine, achieves lethal results.

The Princess shows intense interest. Can it be, she asks, the famous *poudre de succession?* It is, says the Prince, adding that he has been asked by the Cardinal de Fleury to analyze it. "As a renowned chemist, of course," the Abbé puts in fawningly. The Prince sternly refuses to allow the Princess to examine the box, which he then carries out of the room.

In a brief byplay, the Princess, with deliberate emphasis, asks the Abbé if he really believes this mysterious powder has the deadly qualities attributed to it. Smirking, the Abbé replies that he has another kind of poison in mind—and she alone can cure him of its effects. The Princess abruptly changes the subject.

She has made a wager, she declares, and wishes the Abbé to help her win it. She must find out the name of the Count de Saxe's new love. La Duclos, of course . . . the Prince was certain, the Abbé lies. Knowingly, the Princess observes that the Abbé is much too clever to believe that.

At that point the Prince returns with Michonnet, who thanks Bouillon for having extended a "favor" to Mlle. Lecouvreur. In angry suspicion the Princess wonders, in an aside, what that "favor" might consist of—money? . . . diamonds? . . . The Prince and Michonnet leave to get ready for the party.

The Princess tells the Abbé that this very night she will win her wager. She challenges him to guess who among her acquaintances is likely to be the mysterious rival. At this juncture the Major-domo announces the Duchess d'Aumont. Aside, the Abbé murmurs that *she* is the woman. The Princess quickly whispers: "Make her say one phrase— 'Someone who tells me all'" ("Chi mi confida tutto"). Then, with elegant courtesy, she greets the Duchess.

The other guests now crowd in and an ensemble develops as greetings are exchanged. It is announced that there is to be a ballet, *The Judgment of Paris,* and that La Lecouvreur will recite. The ladies exclaim with pleasure when the Prince announces that the hero of the hour, the Count de Saxe, will be present.

Feigning surprise, the Princess asks if he is not still in the Bastille, imprisoned for gambling debts.[7] Somebody must have paid them, the Prince declares, adding that there is talk of a love affair. In any case, he goes on, the Count is free and already has fought a duel with the man who betrayed him—a certain Count Kalkreutz.

The Major-domo now announces Mlle. Lecouvreur, who is welcomed with great dignity by the Prince ("Venite. D'ammirar più da presso"). As Adriana modestly acknowledges his fulsome greeting ("Io son confuso") there is a startled exclamation from the Princess, to whom the actress' voice has a vaguely familiar sound. She notes with satisfaction that Adriana is not wearing the diamond necklace given her by the Queen.

The scene continues mainly in the form of a duet between Adriana and the Princess. While Adriana expresses her gratitude for the homage paid her by so brilliant an assemblage, the Princess comments in spiteful asides, waiting for the right moment to discover the identity of her rival ("Io lo saprò"). The Prince announces that the entertainment is to wait until Maurizio arrives. Staring intently at Adriana, the Princess remarks that they may wait in vain: It is reported that Maurizio has been badly wounded in the duel with Count Kalkreutz. With a gasp of horror, Adriana collapses fainting on a divan. Revived by Michonnet, she stammers that she was suddenly overcome by the heat and the glaring lights. Yet even in her confusion she notes the icy look on the face of the Princess ("il gelo di quello sguardo").

There is a stir of excitement as Maurizio is announced. Adriana, about to rush to him, is restrained by Michonnet, who warns her not to betray herself. Welcoming the hero, Bouillon tells him of the report that he had been wounded in the duel with Kalkreutz. With a careless laugh, Maurizio answers that he disarmed him with the first sword stroke.

The ensuing dialogue consists mostly of asides sung to the accompaniment of a graceful waltz tempo. Maurizio tells the Princess he returned only to see her ("Per voi qui venni"), but says he cannot accept her help in paying his gambling debts (a favor he mistakenly gives her credit for). Adriana, seeing the two whispering together, wonders fretfully if the "unknown" could have been the Princess. Maurizio, becoming aware of Adriana's presence, greets her casually. Bouillon interrupts to ask him to tell the guests about his military triumphs in Courland—

---

[7] Maurizio's imprisonment, and the reasons for it, are never satisfactorily explained. As far as can be deduced from the three versions of the libretto, his imprisonment occurred after the scenes at La Grange Batelière—ostensibly for the gambling debt he owed Prince Bouillon. However, the duel he fought with "the man who betrayed him" implies political reasons for his arrest. That leaves unexplained how Adriana's settlement of the gambling debt with the aid of the diamond necklace could have effected his release.

particularly the story of the assault on Mittau ("non ci narraste ancora").

Protesting that he has forgotten all about his exploits, the Count promptly launches into the story to the accompaniment of a vigorous martial theme ("Il russo Mèncikoff"). He tells how the Russian commander Menchikov led an assault on his palace. The defenders were outnumbered fifteen to one, but—like Charles XII at Bendera—he did not pause to count friend or foe. After three days of siege the attackers were ready to put the palace to the torch. Maurizio himself rolled out a barrel of gunpowder, lit the fuse and pushed it toward the oncoming horde. One hundred Cossacks were blown sky-high and the battle was over.[8] The assemblage hails the hero in a choral phrase.

The Prince then announces the performance of the ballet, *The Judgment of Paris*. To the accompaniment of elegant, pastoral music, the story is told in dance with choral interludes. Paris, attired as a shepherd, is given one of the golden apples of the Hesperides by the god Mercury, with instructions to bestow it upon the most beautiful of the goddesses. Juno, Pallas Athene and Venus—jealous rivals for the prize—each try to convince Paris of their rightful claim to the prize. When Venus flings aside her cloak and reveals her beauty, Paris rises to confer the trophy upon her.

But at this point the ballet myth departs from the original. Paris approaches the Princess de Bouillon and, kneeling at her feet, presents her with the golden apple. The three goddesses pay their tribute to her, then dance away with the nymphs.

The musical dialogue, with occasional ensemble passages, now continues over a graceful orchestral accompaniment. At the same time there is a sharp exchange between Adriana and the Princess. First, the Abbé points to one of the ladies and whispers that she is the mysterious rival. The Princess disdainfully rejects his assertion. Turning to Adriana, she remarks that perhaps Mademoiselle knows the name of Count de Saxe's beloved ("La bella del Conte"). At court, she continues, there was some gossip about an actress. At the theater, Adriana retorts, the talk was about an amorous noblewoman. To the huge enjoyment of the other women, the sparring goes on about a "secret midnight rendezvous."

At this point the Abbé brings matters to a head by asking for proof. The Princess mentions a charming posy given a certain hero; Adriana

[8] A fictionalized account of an actual event. Charles XII of Sweden, defeated at Poltava in 1790, found asylum in the palace of a Turkish potentate at Bender (or Bendera) and spent several years there in exile. Relations between host and guest, however, apparently deteriorated, and at one point the Turks besieged Charles's headquarters. He defended his refuge as described by Maurizio in the operatic version.

tells of a beautiful bracelet lost by someone in hasty flight. Both women try to conceal their discomfiture at these revelations. In chorus, the onlookers exclaim that the situation is as delightful as a Chinese puzzle or a Spanish romance.

"Not so," Adriana cries; "the situation is typically French" ("No, la vita francese!"). Showing the bracelet around, she explains that it was recently handed to her. As the women admire it in chorus, the Princess glares at Adriana. The Prince comes forward, examines the bracelet and exclaims that it belongs to his wife. There is general consternation. In a brief choral passage the guests take due note of the furious glances exchanged between Adriana and the Princess.[9]

Adriana and the Princess now are convinced of each other's identity. With forced politeness the Princess invites Adriana to recite. The actress flares up angrily at her patronizing tone, but controls herself at a word of caution from Michonnet. With deliberate malice the Princess suggests she recite the monologue from *Ariadne abbandonata* (*Ariadne Forsaken*).[10]

Stung by the implied insult in the play's title, Adriana glares at the Princess. The Prince hastily suggests that she recite the great speech from *Phèdre,* the role in which the actress scored one of her greatest triumphs.[11] Suddenly deciding, Adriana answers: "E *Fedra* sia!" Over a dark, sinister theme in the orchestra, Adriana declaims, in spoken tones, the passage in which the legendary Phèdre, wife of Theseus, voices her remorse for her illicit love for her stepson Hippolyte ("Giusto Cielo! che feci in tal giorno?"). With loathing and dread she anticipates the moment when her husband will return to his home, where his wife and his son are guilty lovers.

Adriana notices that the Princess and Maurizio are whispering together, and her voice rises in anger and intensity. Almost losing control, she speaks the final lines of furious denunciation directly to the Princess: "So il turpe mio . . . nè compormi potrei comme fanno le audicissime impure, cui gioia è tradir una fronte di gel, che mai debba arrossir!" ("I know my own infamy, but I cannot face it calmly, as do shameless women who glory in treachery while they display an icy countenance that cannot blush!").

Her final accusation rings out in a majestic climax. Shaken with fury, Adriana stands glaring at the Princess, who contemptuously joins the guests in their shouts of "Brava!" In an aside to the dumfounded Mi-

[9] In the Sonzogno edition (1903).

[10] Probably from the play *Ariana* by Thomas Corneille (1625–1709), brother of the renowned French dramatist Pierre Corneille (1606–84).

[11] The play by the French dramatist Jean Baptiste Racine (1639–99), based on Greek mythology.

chonnet, Adriana murmurs fiercely that now she has had her revenge ("Son vendicata"). She asks leave of the Prince, who escorts her to the door. Gazing after her malevolently, the Princess, aside, says she will pay out her rival. Seeing Maurizio start for the door, she harshly orders him to remain. As Adriana passes, he manages to whisper: "Tomorrow." The curtain falls.

ACT FOUR

A small sitting room adjoining the bedroom in Adriana's house. It is late afternoon in March. There is a brief prelude on a melancholy theme (strikingly similar to the introduction to the fourth act of *La Traviata*). Michonnet is shown in by Adriana's maid, who whispers that Adriana is still sleeping. In recitative ("So ch'ella dorme") Michonnet observes wryly that Adriana wouldn't be an actress if she weren't asleep while the rest of the world is awake. "When she does awake," he tells the maid, "tell her I am here."

Then, in a melodious aria, "Taci, mio vecchio cuor" (recalling Colline's farewell to his overcoat in *La Bohème*), he melodramatically bids his poor old heart to beat no more with hopeless passion. Let it be like this faithful friend, he goes on, looking at his watch, which also has grown tired of ticking. As for Adriana, she is not sleeping. She is sick. Her sickness is love, the same malady which has afflicted him—but too late. Michonnet scribbles a note and hands it to the maid when she reappears. This, he says, is the medicine Adriana needs.

A few moments later Adriana enters. Her demeanor is one of utter dejection and defeat, but she greets Michonnet with obvious pleasure ("Amico mio!"). This marks the beginning of a moving duet in which the two commiserate with each other about the pangs of unrequited love.

Adriana complains that she cannot sleep. Nothing matters now—the theater, fame, a career—all are illusions. Gazing at her tenderly, Michonnet asks: "But what about the one who loves you?" When Adriana asks who that could be, Michonnet blurts out that it is he himself. Seeing her startled expression, he loses courage and adds lamely that he means merely that he loves her like a father.

Touched by his devotion, Adriana looks at him in mingled tenderness and pity. But suddenly she is haunted by the memory of her encounter with the Princess at the ball. She can remember only the look of hatred on the Princess' face, she cries, as she listened to the closing lines from *Phèdre* ("che mai debba arrossir!"). Then, as though demented, Adriana seizes a shawl, throws it around her shoulders and rushes toward the door, shouting that she must have revenge on this courtesan who has stolen her beloved. Michonnet bars her path, then gently forces her into a chair. Adriana bursts into hysterical sobs. Although she refuses to take a sedative he offers her, she gradually grows calmer. Michonnet reminds her that she is not alone in her suffering. He too, he says, has endured the pain of unrequited love ("Non soffri sola"), but in any case he did not die from it. In the closing phrases of the duet they agree that love is madness, a worse torture than burning or freezing—but one survives somehow.

There is an abrupt change of mood as Adriana's four fellow players come to pay her a surprise visit in honor of her birthday ("La vostra festa"). Adriana greets them in delighted astonishment. Laughing and joking, they hand her their presents—candy, a portrait, a bit of lace. Looking on, Michonnet mutters that there is something more to this than simply a birthday party. Then he announces he has a present of his own, and hands Adriana a small case. She opens it and gasps in surprise. In the case is her diamond necklace, the Queen's gift. Adriana had given it to Prince de Bouillon as "ransom" to free Maurizio from the Bastille. The players exclaim admiringly over its beauty. In answer to Adriana's question, Michonnet shyly explains that he redeemed the gems from Prince de Bouillon with the legacy left him by his uncle. Profoundly moved, Adriana takes both his hands in a gesture of gratitude ("Nobile cor!"). Michonnet furtively wipes away a tear.

With exaggerated solemnity, Quinault and Poisson announce that they have a request to make ("Di tutti i soci") in behalf of all the members of the Comédie Française. In unison the two men, Jouvenot and Dangeville sing the titles of Adriana's four celebrated roles—Phèdre, Roxane, Chimène, Mira—and ask her to return to the stage as queen of her art.

As though suddenly inspired, Adriana replies in a ringing aria ("Sì, tornerò!") that she will indeed return. The sacred fire still burns within her heart. Through the high calling of her art she will show that he who loses as a lover can triumph as an artist. Her companions applaud her vociferously. Eagerly Adriana asks for backstage news of the theater. With great relish the players inform her that La Duclos has left the Prince, then elaborate upon the situation in an impudent quartet ("Una volta c'era un Principe").

There was, it seems, a certain elderly Prince who sought to win a young lady's hand by guile and trickery. But she paid him back in his own false coin by having a romance behind his back with a young, handsome lover. The moral of the story (expressed in a pianissimo phrase which ends the quartet) is that false coin can only buy false love ("A fals'oro falso amor").

The general merriment is interrupted by the entrance of the maid, who brings in a small casket covered with crimson velvet. With it is a note. Adriana, reading it quickly, murmurs that it is from Maurizio. In an aside, she asks Michonnet to get the others out of the room. He invites them into the adjoining room for a drink, ushers them out, then returns.

Adriana opens the casket, then suddenly staggers back as though overcome. She gasps that a strange odor rose from the casket—almost like the cold mist of death. Michonnet scoffs at this grim fancy, then asks what is in the casket. Adriana takes from it a faded bunch of violets. She cries out in dismay as she recognizes the posy she gave to Maurizio ("I fiori offerti"). In a brief refrain ("Oh, crudeltà . . . L'avesse negletto") she voices her anguish. If he had even crushed the flowers under his foot, she sobs, it would have been kinder than adding insult to injury by sending them back.

Michonnet tries to comfort her by saying that Maurizio never would do such a thing—this is a woman's trick. Taking up the flowers again, Adriana pours out her grief in one of the loveliest arias in the opera, "Poveri fiori." Yesterday, she sings, these poor flowers bloomed in all their beauty. Today they are withered and dead—like the vows of a faithless lover. And now she will give them one last kiss of love and death, Adriana goes on, raising the posy to her lips. Thus, everything is ended ("Tutto è finito"). Crushed by despair, she throws the flowers into the fireplace.

It is not the end, Michonnet protests, because Maurizio will come to her—perhaps even in the next few moments. He then confesses that he himself wrote Maurizio and told him the whole story . . . he hopes he did not do the wrong thing. Adriana is overwhelmed by his kindness and loyalty. At that moment, Maurizio's voice is heard outside. Adriana cries out that this must be a dream, and rushes to the door. Watching her in sadness and resignation, Michonnet murmurs ironically: "To think that I myself brought my rival here!" ("E dir ch'io stesso chiamato ho il mio rivale!"). He leaves to join the players in the other room.

In the next moment Maurizio bursts into the room. Adriana first tries to hide her emotions under an assumed air of indifference. She asks him coldly why he has come ("Che mai qui vi sprona"). This marks the beginning of the concluding duet of the opera.

Imploring her forgiveness ("Perdona l'oblio d'un istante"), Maurizio tells her he was misled by lies and trickery, but now he knows Adriana alone rules his heart. But Adriana bitterly tells him to go back to the woman he really loves. Maurizio responds that he has learned the price of this woman's treachery, and despises her.

Unrelenting, Adriana tells him that now it is too late. In a phrase repeating the love theme of the opera, Maurizio tells her it was her hand alone that rescued him—and now he offers his own hand and his royal name in marriage. Shaken and bewildered, Adriana replies that her head is not worthy of a royal crown ("No, la mia fronte"). She can wear only the motley of the stage.

In a passionate refrain ("No, più nobile") Maurizio sings that she is more regal than any queen because, through her art, she rules over the hearts of mankind. Adriana rushes into his arms. They bring the duet to a blazing climax, singing that not even death can destroy their golden dream ("vince la morte nel sogno d'or"). They stand locked in each other's arms as the love theme dies away in the orchestra.

Suddenly Adriana reels back as though about to faint. As Maurizio steadies her, she gasps that she has been made ill by the odor of the flowers he sent her. To his utter confusion she goes on to say she threw the flowers into the fire because they had died—just as his love for her had died. She clutches her side in a paroxysm of pain, then begins raving in delirium. Staring at Maurizio, she asks him who he is. She imagines she sees him in his box at the theater with her rival. For a moment her reason returns, then she collapses in a faint. Maurizio calls distractedly for help.

Michonnet comes rushing in and together the men manage to revive Adriana. When Michonnet asks what brought on this seizure, Maurizio tells him Adriana apparently became delirious as the result of smelling the flowers ("Fiutò dei fior"). In a horrified whisper Michonnet voices his suspicion that the flowers had been sprinkled with the poisonous powder by her rival ("Un velen . . . Quella rivale?"). Maurizio cries out in despair as the terrible realization dawns upon him.

Bending over Adriana, he sobs that her eyes are glazing over in death. As he desperately calls her name she opens her eyes. Summoning her ebbing strength, she implores Maurizio to save her ("Salvatemi!"). She does not want to die, she sings in an exultant phrase, because the one she loves has claimed her as his bride. Then, convulsed by pain, she gasps that a serpent is gnawing at her heart.

In wild delirium she starts up and begins declaiming as though in the theater. Imperiously she commands the "profane ones" to stand aside, for she is the goddess Melpomene ("Scostatevi, profani, Melpòmene son io"). Over a poignant theme high in the strings, Adriana sings that she is winging her way like a tired white dove to the Light ("Esso la Luce"), the purifying light of love. Before her is the gate to immortality—the portal which opens to joy eternal. Adriana's voice dies away in a sigh and she falls back lifeless into the arms of Maurizio and Michonnet. In wild despair Maurizio cries out: "Adriana! Morta!" The curtain falls.

ANNA BOLENA

by GAETANO DONIZETTI
(1797–1848)

Libretto by
FELICE ROMANI

Enrico (Henry VIII), King of England	Bass
Anna Bolena (Anne Boleyn), his wife	Soprano
Giovanna (Jane Seymour), Anna's lady in waiting	Mezzo-soprano
Rochefort (Lord Rochford), Anna's brother	Bass
Lord Richard Percy, Anna's first love	Tenor
Smeton (Smeaton), the Queen's page	Contralto
Hervey, the King's officer, Governor of the Tower of London	Tenor

Lords, courtiers, ladies in waiting, huntsmen, soldiers

Place: England—the first act in Windsor, the second in London
Time: 1536
First Performance: Teatro Carcana, Milan, December 26, 1830
Original language: Italian

Donizetti's twenty-third opera was long considered by his contemporaries as his masterpiece, and enjoyed that distinction at least until he composed the operas acknowledged as his greatest—*L'Elisir d'Amore, Lucia di Lammermoor* and *Don Pasquale.*

Anna Bolena was the first opera Donizetti wrote in his own individual style, rather than in imitation of Rossini, who had strongly influenced his earlier works. It is recorded that he composed the opera—completing the score in one month—at the Lake Como villa of the renowned eighteenth-century *bel canto* soprano Giuditta Pasta, who created the role of Anna. After its sensationally successful premiere it was heard all over Europe. In England the legendary basso Luigi Lablache scored his greatest success in it.

Although it vanished from the operatic repertoire—possibly because of the tragic nature of the plot—*Anna Bolena* has had successful re-vivals during the past decade or so. A La Scala production in 1957 by Count Luchino Visconti was hailed as one of the finest restorations of recent times. What was probably its first American performance was given that same year in concert form by the American Opera Society. The Society presented it again in November 1966. It was given in Eng-lish by the Santa Fe Opera Company during its 1959 season, and by the Dallas Civic Opera in 1968. In recent years it has been staged by the New York City Opera with Beverly Sills.

The opera's plot, a page out of English history, closely follows the course of events during the reign of the notorious Henry VIII. The chief deviations are Anna Bolena's madness and the betrothal of Anna and Richard Percy—events which have no historical basis.

The long and stirring overture states the principal themes of the opera.

ACT ONE

[*Scene One*] At Windsor Castle, the chief topic of gossip among the courtiers and others of the Queen's court is the marital discord between Enrico and Anna. In an opening chorus ("Nè venne il Re? Silenzio!") the courtiers discuss the rumor that the King has rejected Anna and is infatuated with another woman. Although Anna is acutely aware of the King's wavering affections, she does not know who her rival is.

Giovanna enters. In an aside (the cavatina "Ella di me, sollecita"), she wonders apprehensively why the Queen has summoned her. Does she perhaps suspect that her own lady in waiting is her rival for the King's affections?

Anna enters with Smeton and her attendants to await the arrival of the King. She notices the expressions of concern on the faces of those in her entourage and, in recitative ("Si taciturna e mesta"), asks the rea-son. She confesses that she herself is troubled by an unknown fear. To dispel the gloom she asks the page to entertain the company with a bal-lad. Smeton obliges with a plaintive love song (romanza: "Deh! non voler costringere"). But when he sings a phrase alluding to "first love," Anna abruptly silences him. There is a stir of alarm in the court. Then, almost to herself, Anna sings about a first love that was hers long ago (cavatina: "Come innocente giovane").

Asking Giovanna to approach, the Queen tells her that there is a les-son to be learned from her sorrow: The power and glory of the throne can break a proud spirit (aria: "Non v'ha sguardo"). Again Giovanna wonders if the Queen knows her guilty secret. Saying wearily that there is no point in waiting any longer for the King, Anna retires with her retinue. Giovanna remains alone.

Torn between her loyalty to Anna and her ambition to be Queen, Giovanna reflects on the Queen's ominous words (recitative: "Oh! qual parlar fu il suo!"). Suddenly there is a knock on a secret door to the chamber, and a moment later Enrico cautiously enters. A long duet ensues ("Vederci alla faccia del sole"). The King declares that these clandestine meetings must come to an end: He has decided to proclaim his love for Giovanna to all the kingdom. When she replies that in order to win her love he must make her his Queen, Enrico agrees—but adds resentfully that Anna imposed exactly the same conditions solely to win the throne. Trying to justify his repudiation of Anna, he declares that she was guilty of loving another before she married him—and even after. When he proffers Giovanna his kingdom, she flatly refuses until he reluctantly promises not to punish Anna for her supposed infidelity.

[Scene Two] Richard Percy, recalled from exile by Enrico, arrives at Windsor and is warmly greeted by Lord Rochefort. Percy eagerly asks about Anna. Divining his thoughts, Rochefort reminds him that she is now the Queen, and if he dared reveal his true feelings toward her it would doom them both. In the cavatina "Da quel dì che, lei perduta" Percy describes the anguish he suffered in exile, knowing that he had lost Anna forever. Yet he clings to the hope that even now she will give him one word of comfort. As a fanfare announces the King's return from the hunt, Rochefort again vainly warns Percy not to invite disaster.

Enrico comes in escorted by huntsmen and his palace guards, with Hervey at their head. Anna appears with her retinue. The King greets her with mocking cordiality, then notices Percy, who is standing apart. As Enrico welcomes him back to court, Anna gasps in surprise, murmuring that she did not know he had been pardoned.

Percy kneels before Enrico, thanks him for his pardon and reaches out to kiss his hand. The King brusquely withdraws it, remarking with sinister emphasis that thanks are due someone else who interceded for him: the Queen herself. Impetuously, Percy kneels and kisses Anna's hand. Aware of the King's eyes upon her, she makes a supreme effort to control herself.

Calling Hervey to him, Enrico, in an aside, tells him to watch Percy's every move from this moment on. Hervey assures him that he will set the trap for Percy. Enrico's order, in recitative ("Questo dì per noi"), leads into the fiery quartet (Enrico, Anna, Percy, Rochefort) and chorus which conclude the scene. Anna laments that her love for Percy can never be requited; Percy, heedless of Rochefort's warning, exults that Anna's very presence has restored his hope and courage; Enrico—for reasons of his own—virtually forces Percy to agree to remain at the castle. As the King leaves with his huntsmen, he remarks that he is now in search of another kind of quarry.

[*Scene Three*] Smeton steals into the Queen's apartment. He takes from inside his shirt a portrait miniature of Anna which he had purloined and which he now plans to return before the theft is discovered. Gazing at it avidly, he pours out his frustrated love in the cavatina "Ah, pare che per incanto."

Hearing footsteps outside, Smeton thrusts the portrait back inside his shirt and hides behind the draperies. Anna, nervous and excited, hurries in followed by Rochefort. At her brother's insistence she consents—against her better judgment—to permit Percy to see her. Assuring her he will stand guard over their tryst, Rochefort leaves and a moment later Percy enters.

A long and dramatic duet follows ("La fronte mia solcata"). Warning him that they are both courting death by daring to meet in this fashion, Anna desperately begs Percy to forswear her love and flee England. Crying that death is better than a life without her, Percy draws his sword and turns the point toward his heart.

At that moment Smeton springs from his hiding place and wrests the weapon aside. Raging, Percy turns on the page with sword poised, whereupon Smeton draws and prepares to lunge. With a shriek of terror, Anna falls fainting. Rochefort rushes in exclaiming that Enrico is approaching.

The King strides in, sees Percy and Smeton at sword's point and bellows for his guards. Glaring at the two adversaries, the King snarls that their guilty looks have trapped them, and the Queen as well. Shouting that he is ready to die to defend the Queen's innocence, Smeton tears open his shirt in a melodramatic gesture of sacrifice. With that the portrait falls to the floor. There is a stunned silence as Enrico picks it up. Here, he says with evil relish, is the final proof. Percy stares at Smeton in baffled fury.

Anna revives and staggers to her feet. Thrusting the portrait close to her face, Enrico cries that here is the accuser. A tumultuous ensemble then ensues ("In quegli sguardi impresso"). The more Anna protests her innocence, the more ferocious the King's accusations become; Percy voices his utter despair over Anna's apparent betrayal of his love; Smeton, Rochefort and Giovanna reproach themselves for inadvertently casting suspicion on the guiltless Queen. At the conclusion of the ensemble, Enrico peremptorily orders Anna and the three men to the Tower.

ACT TWO

[*Scene One*] An apartment in the Tower of London, where Anna is imprisoned. Before she enters from her chamber, her ladies in waiting ask in a mournful chorus ("O dove mai ne andarono") why those who once sought the Queen's favors—Giovanna among them—have not come forward to help her now.

When Anna appears they try to console her with assurances of their loyalty. Hervey enters to inform the Queen that her ladies in waiting have been called as witnesses before the Council of Peers. They leave with him. Sinking to her knees, the Queen sings a brief but eloquent prayer ("Dio, che mi vedi in core"). She asks to know what shameful thing she has done to merit so cruel a punishment.

Giovanna enters and kneels beside her, and then follows the duet which is one of the great climactic numbers of the opera. Taking note of Giovanna's looks of mingled guilt and dread, the Queen asks if she brings yet more terrible news. Giovanna tells her that the King will see to it that she is found guilty by the servile Council of Peers, and so destroy her. To save her life, she must confess to adultery, which will void her marriage and leave the King free to marry her rival. Horrified, Anna flatly refuses so to debase herself.

Giovanna implores Anna to listen to reason—to take the advice of the woman who is fated to replace her. In wild anger, Anna demands to know if this woman has the effrontery to send the Queen's own lady in waiting to her sovereign with this vile counsel. She calls down a terrible curse on the interloper ("Sul suo capo aggravi un Dio").

Cringing before Anna's fury, Giovanna finally confesses that she herself is the guilty rival. As the Queen stares at her in stunned disbelief, Giovanna goes on to say that it was love, not ambition, that made her surrender to Enrico.

Anna magnanimously forgives Giovanna, saying that the King alone is guilty of this monstrous act of treachery and lust. Shaken by remorse, Giovanna sings that the Queen's forgiveness and pardon are worse punishment than her rage. At the conclusion of the duet, Anna rises and goes to her room, leaving Giovanna sobbing bitterly.

[*Scene Two*] Outside the chamber where the Council of Peers is hearing the evidence against Anna, Hervey and the courtiers discuss Smeton's testimony. Enrico enters and the courtiers withdraw. The King and Hervey sardonically comment on the fact that the hapless Smeton, believing he could save the Queen's life, swore that she committed adultery. Thus he has drawn the net tightly around all the conspirators.

Anna and Percy are brought in and the dramatic confrontation scene follows in trio form. Anna entreats the King to destroy her if he must—but not dishonor her name with a baseless charge of adultery ("A' piedi tuoi mi prosto"). She accuses him of corrupting Smeton and forcing him to lie about her. Percy swears that Anna has never been unfaithful ("Il ver parlati; ascolta"). Enrico's only answer is that Anna and her lover are doomed.

Finally, Percy, goaded beyond endurance by the King's vindictiveness, stuns him with the assertion that Anna is his bride and that the royal marriage has no legality ("Sposi non siam"). In a towering rage, Enrico orders Anna and Percy to be taken immediately before the Council of Peers. There, he shouts, Anna will be forced to confess her illicit love—and that confession will doom them both. The two are led away.

In a brief soliloquy in recitative, Enrico expresses his disbelief in Percy's claim to Anna and concludes they are both lying to save themselves. But if the story is true, he muses, the law will have its way and he still be avenged: Anna's child will bear the stain of illegitimacy.

Giovanna enters. The King greets her ardently and salutes her as his Queen. But she answers that she cannot accept either his love or his throne unless he shows mercy to Anna, whom she herself betrayed. If she could expiate that sin, she goes on, she would spend her life fasting and praying in the darkest corner of the earth. In a dramatic aria, "Per questa fiamma indomita," Giovanna pleads for Anna's life. Enrico storms that now he loathes Anna more than ever because she has caused Giovanna this anguish. Relentlessly he reiterates his decision: Anna must die.

[*Scene Three*] The prison section of the Tower of London, where Percy and Rochefort await execution. Hervey enters and tells them that Enrico has pardoned them. When they learn that Anna is to die, Percy scornfully rejects the offer of pardon and Rochefort follows suit. In an eloquent aria, "Vivi tu, te ne scongiuro," Percy implores Rochefort to accept the reprieve and find a haven where sorrow and injustice do not exist. Rochefort declares that he will die with his friend. Guards lead both men away.

Anna's ladies in waiting enter and sing a chorus of lamentation ("Chi può vederla"). They gaze at her in grief and pity as she enters, half mad with terror and despair, her clothing in disarray. In her delirium she imagines it is the day of her marriage to the King, and she begs forgiveness of Percy. Lamenting her lost love, she sings a plaintive song, "Al dolce guidami castel natio." She asks to be taken back to the pleasant castle where she spent her youth—there to enjoy again one precious hour of youth.

Percy, Rochefort and Smeton are brought in for a final farewell.

Smeton, tormented by remorse, kneels before Anna and cries that he alone is to blame: Because he had hoped to win her love, he accused her of adultery in the belief that the King would repudiate her but spare her life.

Anna, her mind wandering, raises Smeton to his feet and asks wistfully if the strings of his harp are broken. Profoundly moved, the three doomed men pray for the repose of her soul. Suddenly there is a drum roll, the boom of cannon and the ringing of bells. The crowds outside are acclaiming the new Queen. With a prayer of forgiveness on her lips ("Non impreco in quest'ora tremenda"), Anna is led to the scaffold.

ANTONY AND CLEOPATRA

by SAMUEL BARBER

(1910–   )

Libretto by

FRANCO ZEFFIRELLI

Adapted from William Shakespeare's play of the same name

CHARACTERS

Cleopatra, Queen of Egypt	Soprano
Octavia, sister of Caesar and Antony's second wife	Lyric soprano
Charmian ⎱ Cleopatra's attendants	⎧ Mezzo-soprano
Iras ⎰	⎩ Contralto
Antony, triumvir of Rome	Bass
Caesar, triumvir of Rome	Tenor
Agrippa ⎫	⎧ Bass
Lepidus ⎬ Roman senators	⎨ Tenore buffo
Maecenas ⎭	⎩ Baritone
Enobarbus, Antony's companion in arms	Bass
Eros, armor-bearer to Antony (Young Man's Voice)	Tenor or high baritone
Dolabella, friend to Caesar	Baritone
Thidias, ambassador from Caesar	Tenor or high baritone
Canidius ⎫	⎧ Baritone
Demetrius ⎬ officers to Antony	⎨ Low tenor
Scarus ⎪	⎪ Bass
Decretas ⎭	⎩ Bass
Mardian, a eunuch	High tenor
A Rustic	Baritone or bass
Messenger	Tenor
Soothsayer	Bass
Alexas, attendant of Cleopatra	Bass
A soldier of Antony	Tenor
A captain of Antony	Tenor
A soldier of Antony	Baritone or bass

Three guards in Antony's camp ⎱
Two watchmen   ⎰   Basses

People of the Empire, attendants of Cleopatra, senators, guards, watchmen, soldiers

Place: Alexandria in Egypt, and Rome
Time: Circa 30 B.C.
First performance: Opening of the new Metropolitan Opera House, Lincoln Center, New York City, September 16, 1966
Original language: English

The world premiere of *Antony and Cleopatra* marked one of the most significant events in the modern history of opera: the opening of the new forty-five-million-dollar Metropolitan Opera House in Lincoln Center, New York City. Samuel Barber, the American composer, was commissioned by the Metropolitan Opera Association to write the work for the opening. The commission was under a grant from the Ford Foundation and the production was made possible by a gift from Francis Goelet, of New York City, a patron of the opera.

This spectacular production was staged by the Italian director Franco Zeffirelli, who also adapted the text of Shakespeare's play for the libretto and designed the sets and costumes. Mr. Zeffirelli had previously staged Verdi's *Falstaff* for the Metropolitan in 1964 with outstanding success.

Antony and Cleopatra is Samuel Barber's second opera. His first, *Vanessa,* with a libretto by Gian-Carlo Menotti, was premiered at the old Metropolitan in 1958 and won a Pulitzer Prize. Mr. Barber wrote the role of Cleopatra specifically for the American soprano Leontyne Price. "Every vowel," said Mr. Barber, "was placed with Leontyne Price in mind."

Although given a brilliant production with a huge cast, the opera was not an unqualified success. It was given only eight performances during the 1966–67 season of the Metropolitan. Critics found it skillfully wrought and occasionally interesting, but with the music subordinate to the staging. It is atonal and difficult to sing—as the composer himself concedes. While there are echoes of Wagner and Mahler, the vocal line is angular and quasi-recitative. There are no arias in the conventional sense of the term. All the scenes are bridged by instrumental interludes.

There is no overture. The curtain rises immediately.

ACT ONE

[*Scene One*] Rome. Milling around a huge symbolic golden pyramid is a shouting, jeering throng of Romans, Greeks, Jews, Persians, Africans and soldiers. In a harshly dissonant chorus ("From Alexandria this is the news") they voice their anger over the reports of Antony's wild revels with Cleopatra in Alexandria—to the utter neglect of his duties as one of the triumvirate of Rome. In a furious chant they repeat: "Let his shames drive him quickly to Rome." The chorus rises to a climax as the mob shouts: "Antony, leave thy lascivious wassails."

The mood of the scene momentarily changes as the people, in insinuating tones, express the hope that Cleopatra will treacherously enslave Antony with her seductive charms and rob him of his honor as the price of his libertinage ("Salt Cleopatra, soften thy wan lips"). In the next moment, the denunciations break out again, rising to a feverish pitch on the repetition of the phrase "Leave thy lascivious wassails."

At this point the sides of the golden pyramid unfold like the petals of an enormous flower, disclosing Antony and Enobarbus in Cleopatra's palace in Alexandria.

[*Scene Two*] The dialogue ensues in quasi-recitative. Antony declares that he must free himself once for all from Cleopatra's spell and leave Alexandria. In leaving, Enobarbus observes brusquely, we kill our women, who cannot endure separation. When Cleopatra hears of this, he goes on, she will certainly die. Cynically he adds that she seems to have a penchant for dying. Antony is momentarily bemused by thoughts of Cleopatra but abruptly shakes off the spell and reiterates his decision to leave. Enobarbus exits.

Heralded by a chorus of attendants, Cleopatra enters with Charmian, her lady in waiting. She is so overcome by the realization that Antony is determined to leave her that she calls on Charmian to support her. When Antony approaches to help her she repulses him, telling him to make his farewell and go, for now it is too late for words. Gazing passionately at her, Antony reminds her of the bliss of their love, which was like eternity—never ending. Cleopatra replies in poignant phrases that without Antony there is only oblivion. Though still resolved to leave, Antony sings that for them there can be no parting.

[*Scene Three*] The Senate in Rome. In the chamber are Caesar, Lepidus, Agrippa, Maecenas, Antony, Enobarbus and other senators. There is a fanfare of trumpets as the Senate convenes. The senators hail Antony. In an ironic byplay, he and Caesar, observing protocol, invite each other to be seated first. The two immediately plunge into matters of state. Antony rather arrogantly remarks that Caesar seems unduly concerned about certain happenings in Alexandria. Caesar angrily upbraids him for breaking his promise of assistance with arms.

As tempers rise, Maecenas, Enobarbus and the other senators try to placate the two triumvirs, but Antony sharply warns them not to interfere. He even lashes out at Enobarbus when he objects to the wrangling. Finally controlling himself, he tells Caesar he will try to make amends. Caesar, in turn, declares that he would go to the ends of the earth to find a way to patch up their differences.

Suddenly Agrippa steps forward with an extraordinary suggestion for settling the problem. If Octavia, Caesar's sister, will marry Antony, the union will provide a bond between the two triumvirs. Caesar is taken aback, but Antony expresses interest in the idea. The senators, shaking their heads, leave the chamber during a brief musical interlude. A rhythmic theme in the bass bridges to the next scene.

[*Scene Four*] Cleopatra's palace. With the Queen are Charmian, Iras and Mardian, a eunuch. An oboe solo, languorous yet plaintive, sets the mood. Cleopatra, thinking of Antony, calls for music to calm her restless thoughts. Two ballerinas are escorted in by Mardian. He dutifully tries to entertain the Queen with an inane ditty ("Now the master's gone away") and then dances with the ballerinas. They play Egyptian cymbals, antique clappers and tambourines. Cleopatra, bored to distraction, first suggests a game of billiards, then decides she will go fishing ("Give me my angle, we'll to the river").

She and Charmian fall to musing about the happy days spent with Antony, fishing and drinking and making love. Cleopatra recalls how she playfully made him wear her crown and mantle while she buckled on his sword. Beguiled by these thoughts, she asks Charmian to give her mandragora[1] to drink so that she can fall asleep and dream of her lover. Under the influence of the potion she abandons herself to thoughts of Antony. "O Charmian, where think'st that he is now?" At the conclusion of the brief but passionate refrain the dancers carry the Queen out on her luxurious couch.

[*Scene Five*] Caesar's palace in Rome. Caesar, Antony, Octavia, Maecenas, Enobarbus and people of the court.

In a recitative passage, Antony assures Caesar of his loyalty and cooperation. Caesar leads Octavia, his widowed sister, forward and presents her to Antony. In lyrical phrases he sings that he bequeaths to Antony a sister who, as his bride, will unite their kingdoms and their

[1] A narcotic plant.

hearts. Gazing fondly at Octavia, Antony sings that "the April's in her eyes."

Octavia suddenly turns and whispers mysteriously into Caesar's ear. In answer, he assures her that he still will be with her in his thoughts, even though they now will be parted as brother and sister. He leaves her and Antony together. Antony tells Octavia that, to his regret, his military duties sometimes will take him away from her side. In his absence, Octavia replies, she will pray to the gods for his safety. The court, looking on, murmurs with a certain ironic effect: "Happily, amen." Rather sententiously, Antony asks Octavia not to hold his past faults against him. Henceforth, he says, everything will be "done by the rule." Enobarbus, watching him, repeats with heightened irony the phrase sung by the chorus: "Happily, amen."

[*Scene Six*] Cleopatra's palace in Alexandria. With her are Iras, Charmian, ladies of the court and attendants. Standing before her is the Messenger who brings the news of Antony's marriage to Octavia. The scene is introduced by a rising chromatic phrase that explodes in the orchestra to underscore Cleopatra's fury. She greets the Messenger with a curse, lashes at him with a whip, then threatens him with even worse punishment.

Cowering under her blows, the Messenger protests that, after all, it was not he who arranged the marriage. In a capricious change of mood Cleopatra offers the Messenger an entire province if he will say that the report of the marriage is not true. When the hapless man truthfully replies, "He's married," the Queen lunges at him with a knife. The Messenger dodges out of reach and crouches in a corner of the room. At this point Charmian intercedes, reminding Cleopatra that the Messenger has done no wrong.

Controlling herself for the moment, Cleopatra commands the Messenger to come forward, then resumes her inquisition. Calm and enraged by turns, she demands details—and the Messenger tells her exactly what she wants to hear: Octavia is unattractively short, her voice is unpleasantly low, she does not walk—she creeps—she was a widow, she is about thirty, with a plain round face, brown hair and a low forehead.

In an amusing ensemble, the ladies of the court parrot the Messenger's answers. Finally appeased, Cleopatra tosses the man a bag of gold and dismisses him. Exhausted by her outbursts of jealous fury, the Queen asks Charmian to help her to her chamber. The music subsides into silence. The brief interlude bridging into the next scene rises to a feverish pitch, symbolizing Cleopatra's frustrated, passionate desire for Antony.

[*Scene Seven*] Aboard a Roman galley. Drinking and talking at a table at the very front of the stage are Caesar, Antony, Lepidus, Dolabella, Maecenas and Enobarbus. Torchbearers light up the scene as Roman soldiers, half drunk, make their way aboard. With them come dancers and slave girls. A rhythmic "stick dance" begins in which the dancers strike the deck in a steady drumbeat which continues to throb throughout the entire scene. The music and the action gradually crescendo to an orgiastic pitch.

At its height, a remarkable musical dialogue ensues among the company drinking at the table. Over the pounding rhythm of the stick dance the singers improvise their own sung recitative. Befogged with wine, Lepidus, Antony and Maecenas fall into a discussion about the crocodile. This serpent of the Nile, Lepidus begins, is bred out of mud by the sun. Thereupon Antony launches into a solemn, nonsensical discourse on the crocodile, which, he explains, is as broad as its breadth, high as its height, moves with its own motion and transmigrates its soul when it dies. Plied with more wine by Maecenas, Lepidus listens until he collapses in a drunken stupor. A servant carries him away. While Antony is holding forth about the crocodile, a mysterious offstage voice sings an invocatory phrase to Cleopatra: "Salt Cleopatra, soften thy lips."

As the drinking continues, Enobarbus urges the company to join the bacchanalian dance. Antony jumps up on the table and sings the drinking song, "Come thou monarch of the vine." All the men on the stage join in the refrain in a two-part chorus: "In thy vats our cares be drowned." Caesar, though unsteady on his feet, calls a halt to the revelry, reminding the others that serious business waits to be done. He bids them goodnight and leaves. The men settle down at the table, where Antony already is fast asleep.

Enobarbus, Dolabella and Maecenas begin speculating about Antony and Cleopatra. When Dolabella insists that Octavia's beauty has captured Antony's heart, Enobarbus flatly contradicts him. Antony, says he, will go back to his "Egyptian dish," then adds in Shakespeare's trenchant phrase: "Age cannot wither her, nor custom stale her infinite variety." Enobarbus then describes the first meeting of the two on the Queen's resplendent barge with its poop of beaten gold and its purple, perfumed sails. This refrain ("When she first met Mark Antony") is one of the few passages in the opera resembling the conventional aria.

Now begins the fantastic dream sequence. As an offstage chorus softly repeats Enobarbus' words, Cleopatra's barge materializes in the background. The music takes on an otherworldly, Debussyan quality. In sensuous phrases against a flowing choral background, Cleopatra sings of her longing for Antony ("Where's my serpent of old Nile?"). As the music rises to a climax, the barge slowly recedes. Antony, suddenly awakening, stares at the phantom ship. In a passionate outburst he sings

that he will go to Egypt, for there his "pleasure lies." He rushes toward
the vision with outstretched arms as the curtain falls.

ACT TWO

[*Scene One*] Caesar's palace in Rome. With him are Octavia, sena-
tors and military officers. The music begins with a repetition of the
figure heard at the opening of Act One. Caesar is furiously denouncing
Antony for disgracing Rome by enthroning himself in Alexandria with
Cleopatra at his side. There he made her Absolute Queen of Syria,
Cyprus and Lydia. The chorus comments in a running accompaniment.

Octavia, refusing to believe this report, insists that Antony is in
Athens on a mission of state. Caesar informs her that on the contrary,
he is indeed with Cleopatra, again enslaved by her wit, charm and beguiling companionship. Octavia cries out in despair. The Romans, in an
intensely dramatic choral passage ("He hath given up his empire"),
enumerate the kings whom Antony has enlisted to make war on Rome.
Octavia laments that now her heart is torn between two friends turned
enemies.

Touched by her grief, Caesar sings that the gods themselves will see
to it that justice is done. Overhearing him, the crowd screams: "Justice!
Justice!" In a violent outburst, Caesar rages against Antony's insulting
treatment of his beloved sister and his arrogant usurpation of power. He
calls on his forces to fight to the last ditch. The music crescendos into a
blazing fanfare of trumpets which bridges into the next scene.

[*Scene Two*] Cleopatra's palace garden in Alexandria. Charmian
and Iras, who are there with Mardian, tell the servant Alexas to bring in
the Soothsayer to tell their fortunes. The ensuing dialogue is mostly in
trio form, set off by a striking figure in the bass—repeated ascending
quadruplets in an insistent rhythm. The Soothsayer's auguries meet with
mocking banter from Charmian and Iras. The scene ends with the two
women cynically offering up a prayer to the goddess Isis in behalf of
their fortunes. Mardian suddenly warns them that Antony and Cleopatra are approaching. The women leave with the Soothsayer.

To a sensuously flowing accompaniment, Antony and Cleopatra are
talking of love. Their avowals are interrupted by Enobarbus, who
rushes in with the news that Caesar has captured Toryne.[2] Antony
expresses shocked surprise that Caesar has advanced so rapidly. Then
in a ringing phrase ("tomorrow, soldier") he declares to Enobarbus
that he will fight by land or sea—or redeem his honor with his own
blood. With that he rushes away to prepare for battle.

[2] Presumably a town in ancient Greece. Its exact location is untraceable.

No sooner has he gone than Cleopatra whirls on Enobarbus and upbraids him for trying to prevent her from joining Antony on the battlefield. But in a further effort to dissuade her, Enobarbus says her presence might distract Antony from his military problems. Even now, he adds, there is trouble enough. Antony's reckless conduct is the talk of Rome. There, in fact, it is being gossiped that the war is being waged by a eunuch and the women of Cleopatra's court. Stung to fury by this insult, Cleopatra curses Rome ("Sink Rome, and their tongues rot") and vows to join Antony as Enobarbus protests in vain. She storms out of the room followed by Enobarbus as the music continues in a martial tempo. It subsides into a tranquil theme as the scene changes.

[*Scene Three*] Antony's camp at night. A company of soldiers stands guard. The entire scene is in the form of an ensemble as the soldiers converse about the coming battle and about the sound of ghostly music that seems to be coming out of the ground and filling the air. It is a sign, one soldier says, that the god Hercules, Antony's mentor, is abandoning him to his own fate. In awed tones the soldiers comment on the mysterious sounds as they withdraw to the accompaniment of a foreboding chromatic passage.

[*Scene Four*] Antony's tent. He and Cleopatra are seen inside. It is dawn. Antony, declining Cleopatra's suggestion to sleep a little longer, calls to Eros, his armor-bearer, to bring his battle dress. Cleopatra laughingly helps him buckle on his armor. In an aside, she reflects that if Antony and Caesar could decide this war in a single fight, then Antony . . . She leaves the rest of the thought unspoken and instead salutes Antony as her "brave lord." He exultantly hails the dawning day of battle.

There is a fanfare of trumpets as Antony's officers, Canidius, Demetrius and Scarus, enter with a group of soldiers. They express alarm as Antony announces his decision to fight by sea. The officers warn that his ships are unseaworthy and manned by "muleteers." It will be no disgrace, they assure him, to refuse to fight Caesar with a fleet. But Antony, urged on by Cleopatra, obstinately repeats that he will fight by sea. Enobarbus joins the others in trying to turn him from this rash course ("Trust not in rotten planks"). The army, he declares, is trained to fight and conquer on land. Cleopatra steps forward and cries that she has "sixty sails," a fleet better than Caesar's.

At this point the soldiers, swayed by Antony and Cleopatra and defying their officers, burst into a challenging chorus, "By sea, we will fight by sea!" Taking Cleopatra in his arms, Antony kisses her in farewell, then cries exultingly: "What-e'er becomes of me, this is a soldier's kiss!" A stormy orchestral interlude follows, during which the scene changes to the battlefield at Actium. The Egyptian army is seen in battle formation at the feet of the towering figure of the Sphinx.

[*Scene Five*] In a rousing chorus ("On to our ships") the Egyptians hail the order to go aboard and man the galleys. At the conclusion of the chorus, which ends on an "open fifth" chord with stunning effect, the army rushes into battle. A moment later comes the din of the sea battle. The clamor is heard over a striking pianissimo passage in the orchestra, punctuated by the clangor of metal on metal. In the distance, Cleopatra's fleet can be seen in full flight, headed for Alexandria.

Enobarbus suddenly staggers in, crying in despair that he can no longer bear to watch the sixty ships of Cleopatra's demoralized fleet sail away in defeat. He is joined by Canidius, Decretas, Scarus and Demetrius. In an ensuing ensemble ("Cleopatra, in the midst of the fight") they rage against this shameful debacle. Worst of all, Antony broke off the battle at its height and followed after Cleopatra in disgraceful panic. Shaken by the disaster, the officers turn to Enobarbus with the despairing question: "What shall we do?" Enobarbus can only answer: "Think, and die!" They wander aimlessly out of sight.

An ominous drumbeat begins in the orchestra, building up to a climax of harsh, dissonant chords. As the drumbeat continues, Antony approaches with Eros and a group of wounded soldiers. Surveying the desolation of the battlefield, he voices his despair in a bitter refrain: "The land bids me tread no more upon it." In shame and anger he sings that now he, who once did as he pleased with half the world, must grovel before the upstart Caesar. There is nothing left, he tells the weeping Eros, but death. Plunged in gloom, he bids his wounded soldiers farewell.

A moment later Caesar enters with his triumphant army. Antony, he proclaims harshly, can expect nothing from him. As for Cleopatra, he will grant her pleas—providing she will either banish Antony from Egypt or put him to death. Commanding his soldiers to carry this message to his vanquished rivals, Caesar dismisses his army. An interlude of martial music follows as the soldiers leave.

[*Scene Six*] Cleopatra's palace in Alexandria, where Thidias, a wily and experienced diplomat, has come to lay down Caesar's terms of surrender. With Cleopatra as she meets the ambassador are Charmian and Iras. The Queen tells Thidias to inform Caesar that she is ready to surrender her crown to the conqueror. Following his orders to win Cleopatra over by flattery, Thidias requests the privilege of kissing her hand. Cleopatra offers it with a knowing smile, remarking that Caesar's father himself had rained kisses upon it when he came to ask for kingdoms.

Just at that moment Antony strides in with a number of his soldiers.

Seeing Thidias in the act of kissing the Queen's hand, he flies into a rage and orders the ambassador to be whipped for his insolence. The soldiers drag Thidias away.

When Cleopatra placatingly asks Antony why he is angry with her, he turns on her in furious denunciation. Let her go to Caesar, he shouts, who can show her to the mob in Rome like a victor's trophy. And then let Octavia take a wronged wife's revenge by raking her rival's face with her nails. Accusing the Queen of selling him to Caesar, the "Roman boy," Antony rushes from the room.

On the verge of collapse, Cleopatra gasps for help. Charmian and Iras counsel her to lock herself in her monument (her tomb), then send word to Antony that she has died. At once the Queen prepares to go. She orders Mardian to tell Antony that she has killed herself and that her last word was "Antony." Then Mardian is to report back to her how Antony reacted to the news. She quickly leaves with the two women.

[*Scene Seven*] The battlefield. It is night. Enobarbus is seen standing alone, staring up at the sky. He is stricken with remorse for having deserted Antony and gone over to Caesar after Antony's defeat at the Battle of Actium. In a moving soliloquy, "O bear witness, night," he calls on the moon to mark how bitterly he repents his perfidious actions. A soldier interrupts to tell him that Antony, in a gesture of forgiveness, not only has sent back the treasures Enobarbus had left behind but has added gifts of his own. When Enobarbus sardonically offers the soldier the entire store of treasures, the latter reminds him that Antony still is a "Jove" despite his ruin.

Turning away, Enobarbus resumes his self-accusation ("O sov'reign mistress of true melancholy"). Let the moon distill the poison damp of night upon him . . . let his heart shatter itself upon the flinty hardness of his crime. He will seek a ditch in which to die. Enobarbus' outpouring of grief and remorse comes to a climax in a poignant refrain, "I am alone the villain," which is particularly striking for its melodic line. He asks only for Antony's forgiveness, let the world condemn him as it will. The refrain ends on a lyrical phrase: "O Antony, Antony!" The quiet closing measures of the accompaniment underscore Enobarbus' sorrow.

[*Scene Eight*] Antony's ruined tent on the battlefield. It is night. Antony is seen with Mardian and Eros. The dialogue ensues over a somber, brooding figure in the bass. Mardian brings the news of Cleopatra's death, then leaves. Antony quietly resolves to "overtake" the Queen in death, and the scene that now follows is one of the most gripping in the opera.

Antony asks the unsuspecting Eros if he remembers the oath he swore when he was made a freedman: to slay his master if ordered to do so. Realizing what Antony means, Eros recoils in terror. But the fatal command comes. Instantly, Eros makes a decision. Drawing his sword, he asks Antony to turn his face away. Then, crying out, "Thus do I escape the sorrow of Antony's death," he kills himself. Antony gazes at the boy's body in sorrow and utter despair, then falls on his own sword—but fails in his attempt to die.

In his agony, he calls on his guards to strike him dead, but not one of them will obey his command. Suddenly Alexas dashes in asking for Antony. When the guards point to him, Alexas cries that Cleopatra sent him. Antony gasps in stunned disbelief. Though fatally wounded, he orders the guards to carry him to Cleopatra's monument—the last service they will be asked to perform for him. Offstage a men's chorus comments in a brief unison phrase that "the star has fallen." The curtain falls.

ACT THREE

Cleopatra's monument (the tomb in the shape of a pyramid). She is seated on a throne at the top. Near her on either side are Charmian and Iras. The scene opens with a brief trio passage in which the women declare that they will never leave the monument. Alexas enters to tell them that Antony, dying, is being brought to the monument by his guards. When he appears, Cleopatra greets him in mingled exultation and sorrow—"O Antony, my man of men!" She asks the women to help Antony up the steps to her—she herself does not dare to leave the throne for fear of capture.

But Antony stops them with an imperious gesture. Quietly he sings that he is asking death to wait only until he can imprint the last of many thousand kisses upon Cleopatra's lips. When she again desperately entreats the women to help him, Antony himself urges them to hurry. Momentarily deranged by her frenzy, Cleopatra mocks Antony's struggle in the grip of death. To the accompaniment of an upward-rushing chromatic theme in the orchestra, the onlookers finally lift Antony into the Queen's arms. Their voices blend in a phrase of triumph, with Antony crying out: "My old serpent of the Nile!"

Now within moments of death, Antony asks for wine. Reviving briefly, he tells Cleopatra not to lament, for he has lived out his life as the greatest prince of the world. He will die nobly—a Roman vanquished only by a Roman. Then, as Cleopatra looks on in horror, Antony falls back dead.

Wild with grief, the Queen cries out: "Noblest of men, woo't die? Hast thou no care of me?" This marks the beginning of a powerful trio in which Cleopatra, Charmian and Iras lament the death of Antony. It concludes with a softly sung phrase: "Noblest of men, past the size of dreaming."

For a long moment the three women, numbed with grief, sit staring into space. A flourish of trumpets breaks the silence, then Caesar enters with his train. Cleopatra kneels before him, but Caesar at once asks her to rise. She replies that the gods have willed that she should make obeisance before the "sole sire of the world." Caesar magnanimously assures her that her wishes as Queen will be respected, but sternly warns her not to take Antony's course.

The two take each other's measure. When Caesar, with elaborate courtesy, says he will take his leave, Cleopatra remarks with subtle irony: "And may through the world—'tis yours!"

As guards carry Antony's body away, Caesar takes the dead man's sword in his outstretched hands and delivers his sorrowful eulogy—"The breaking of so great a thing." He grieves that a malign fate has divided him from his friend and companion in arms. He and his court then leave the scene in a stately procession. One of his emissaries, Dolabella, remains behind.

At this point a brief but significant dialogue ensues. As though divining Caesar's intention to take Cleopatra to Rome as a prize of war, the three women make a pact to die together and thus cheat him of his triumph. Cleopatra contemptuously observes that the conqueror plies her with words ("He words me, girls"). She whispers her own decision to Charmian as Iras murmurs that their day has come to its end. They will die gloriously, after the fashion of the Romans, the Queen adds ironically.

Dolabella speaks up and confirms Cleopatra's suspicions that Caesar indeed intends to lead her as his captive to Rome. She thanks Dolabella for warning her. Then in an impassioned refrain ("Nay, 'tis most certain") she voices her anger and disdain at Caesar's effrontery in assuming that he could lead proud Egyptians through the streets like strumpets for the amusement of the Romans. Imperiously calling for her royal robes and her crown, she sings that she sees herself again on her royal barge, welcoming Antony.

A guard now brings in an old farmer, who has been admitted to the monument by prearrangement. Alone with him, the Queen indicates the basket of figs he is carrying and asks him if it also contains the "pretty worm of the Nile." He has it, the old man answers, adding that it has already killed many men and women. Only yesterday a woman died of its bite. She spoke very highly of the worm, the old man says. He sets down the basket and leaves as Cleopatra dismisses him.

As Iras brings in her robe and crown the Queen begins her dramatic farewell—"Give me my robe, put on my crown." She hears Antony call, she sings, and must hurry. Calling Charmian and Iras to her, she kisses them in farewell. Iras collapses and mysteriously dies. Cleopatra, looking down at her tenderly, murmurs: "Have I the aspic on my lips? Dost fall?" The Queen muses that death is like a lover's pinch, which hurts but is desired. Charmian, crouched beside her, gives expression to her grief in a poignant phrase. Cleopatra takes an asp from the basket and holds it to her breast, then takes another and applies it to her arm. In mingled pain and exaltation she cries out, "O Antony," and falls back dead.

Charmian, gazing into Cleopatra's face, sings softly that death now has possessed a woman without peer in the world. Tenderly she straightens the crown on the Queen's head. A guardsman enters saying that Caesar has sent for the Queen. Charmian holds an asp to her breast and gasps that Caesar's messenger was too slow. Her voice soaring over a chorus which now begins offstage ("She looks like sleep"), Charmian sings that this day's work has been well done—"fitting for a princess descended of so many royal kings." Then she dies.

Soldiers and townspeople crowd upon the stage and the chorus swells to a majestic climax. The words they sing are actually from Caesar's final speech in Shakespeare's play:

> . . . she looks like sleep,
> As she would catch another Antony
> In her strong toil of grace. . . .
> . . . Take up her bed,
> And bear her women from the monument:
> She shall be buried by her Antony:
> No grave upon the earth shall clip in it
> A pair so famous. . . .
> . . . Our army shall
> In solemn show attend this funeral,
> And then to Rome.

L'ASSEDIO DI CORINTO

(*Le Siège de Corinthe—The Siege of Corinth*)

by GIOACCHINO ROSSINI

(1792–1868)

Libretto by

LUIGI BALOCCHI and ALEXANDRE SOUMET

A revised version of *Maometto II*, a two-act libretto by the Duca di Ventignano

CHARACTERS

Mahomed II (Mahomet), Emperor of the Turks	Bass
Cleomene (Cléomène), Governor of Corinth	Tenor
Neocle (Néoclès), a young Greek officer	Tenor
Omar, Mahomed's adviser	Bass
Pamira (Palmyre), Cleomene's daughter	Soprano
Ismene, her confidante	Mezzo-soprano
Jero (Hiéros), Keeper of the Tombs	Bass
Adrasto, a young Greek soldier	Tenor

Turks, Greek soldiers, serving-women, people of Corinth

Place: Corinth, the ancient city in southern Greece
Time: 1459
First performance: as *Maometto II*, San Carlo, Naples, December 3, 1820; as *Le Siège de Corinthe*, Salle Le Peletier (Opéra), Paris, October 9, 1826
Original language: Italian

L'Assedio di Corinto, the thirtieth of Rossini's thirty-six operas, was the first of his works to be presented in Paris, where it was sung in French. This opera was a reworking of *Maometto II,* which Rossini had composed in 1820 for Naples; for Paris, in 1826, the two acts were expanded to three. In that form, the opera received its first staged performance in Italian in 1828. The plot originally stems from a play by the French dramatist Voltaire, entitled *Mahomet, ou Le Fanatisme* (1742). The plot has to do with the final days of Corinth, destroyed in 1459 by the Turks under Mahomed II.

When Rossini went to Paris he took up the study of French prosody in order to rewrite his opera specifically for the French language. He wrote the role of Neocle especially for Adolphe Nourrit (1802–39), who is renowned as the most accomplished singing actor among all the dramatic tenors in the history of opera.

The opera was an immediate success and became permanently established in the early nineteenth-century repertoire. It received its hundredth performance in Paris in 1839, and was presented throughout Italy until about 1870. The first New York performance was in 1883. In the present century it was revived at the Maggio Musicale Fiorentino in 1949, with Renata Tebaldi as Pamira—a role which she also sang in Rome in 1951.

One of the most recent staged revivals abroad was at La Scala in April 1969, under the baton of Thomas Schippers, when Beverly Sills, as Pamira, and Marilyn Horne, as Neocle (the tenor role rearranged for mezzo), sang with sensational success. In New York, the American Opera Society scheduled the work for performance in November 1969, and it was produced at the Metropolitan Opera in the 1974–75 season, with Beverly Sills, Shirley Verrett and Justino Díaz.

Before the rise of the curtain there is a sinfonia in the effervescent Rossinian style, interwoven with several themes heard later in the opera.

ACT ONE

[*Scene One*] The vestibule of the Palace of the Senate in Corinth. Cleomene, Neocle and Jero are gathered there with the Greek warriors and the populace. In the opening chorus the people comment on Cleomene's grave and anxious demeanor as the city awaits the first attack of Mahomed II and his army. They try to console him by reassuring him of their loyalty ("Signor, un sol tuo cenno").

In an ensuing aria "Del vincitor, superbo di Bisanzio," the Governor voices his despair over the cruel destiny of Corinth and his people at the hands of the ruthless invader. The people commiserate in a brief response ("In cosi reo periglio"). Neocle then steps forward and in a ringing aria, "Guerrieri, a noi s'affida," exhorts the warriors to defend Greece with their lives. Let them remember, he sings, that the choice is victory or slavery. Cleomene, Jero and the warriors join the call to arms, after which the warriors leave.

[*Scene Two*] In a recitative passage beginning "E salva amor la patria," Cleomene informs the populace that the first onslaught of the Turks has been beaten back, and Corinth is saved. Again he urges his people to swear on the altar of the fatherland either to triumph or to die. During the general rejoicing over the news of victory, Neocle reminds Cleomene that he has promised Pamira to him as his bride ("Tua figlia m'è promessa").

[*Scene Three*] Pamira enters. Greeting her affectionately, Cleomene commits her to the protection of Neocle ("T'appressa o figlia"). Neocle exultantly sings that Pamira's love will inspire him to heroic deeds in the coming battles. But Pamira stuns both her father and the young officer by declaring that she has given her heart to one "Alamanzor of Athens." Cleomene angrily reminds her that she has been promised to Neocle, and warns her not to flout paternal authority in this matter. Pamira, however, although torn between obedience to her father and her secret love, refuses to capitulate. The three express their various reactions to the dispute in a long trio, "Destin terribile." They entreat the gods to witness their shame and sorrow over this unfortunate turn of events.

[*Scene Four*] With the invading Turkish army closing in on the walls of Corinth, terror reigns in the city. In a dramatic chorus ("Di morte il suon") the people wail that the air is filled with the sounds of approaching death. Cleomene, in a solo passage, proclaims that he himself will lead the Greek soldiers to victory or death.

Turning to Pamira, he warns that if he is slain in battle the guilt will be hers as a traitor to her country. Brandishing a dagger, he shouts that this will exact payment for her crime. Terror-stricken by his fury, Pamira promises to remain faithful to the Greek cause ("La data fè rammento"). Her refrain builds into a trio with Cleomene and Neocle, then into an ensemble, "La gloria della patria."

[*Scene Five*] An open plaza in Corinth, where the Turkish invaders are confronting the Greek soldiers, who are now standing at bay. In a fiery chorus, "Dal ferro del forte," the Turks threaten the Greeks with annihilation unless the city surrenders.

[*Scene Six*] Mahomed enters with his followers. Flushed with victory, he bids his soldiers make the most of their triumph ("Cessi vittoria di mia voce al suono"). In an ensuing obbligato to the chorus ("Duce di tanti eroi") he boasts of his success and exhorts his men to fight on to greater glory.

[*Scene Seven*] Omar, the Emperor's general, reports that victory is indeed assured, but adds that some of the Greeks are still holding a passage leading to the main fortress. Meanwhile, one of them has been taken captive. Mahomed orders him to be brought before him. Turning to Omar, the Emperor remarks that the present situation recalls his conquest of Athens under the name of "Almanzor." There he came face to face with a beautiful woman ("qual si'offriva donzella"), and now the memory of her beauty banishes all thoughts of revenge as a conqueror.

[*Scene Eight*] Cleomene is brought before Mahomed, and a dramatic confrontation ensues in recitative. Excoriating the Governor as a treacherous rebel ("Capo all'oste ribelle"), the Turk commands him to surrender the city at once. When Cleomene defiantly refuses, Mahomed consigns him to the dungeons.

[*Scene Nine*] Pamira, who meanwhile has entered, sees her father with his captors and bewails the unhappy fate that has overtaken them both ("Oh padre! Ingrata sorte!"). She turns supplicatingly to Mahomed, then staggers back in surprise, recognizing him as the suitor she has known as "Almanzor." As she gasps out his name, Cleomene is stupefied by the realization that the man his daughter loves is the archenemy of the Greeks.

Gazing ardently at Pamira, Mahomed begs her to marry him, promising to restore peace to Corinth if she accepts him ("Giorno sarà di pace"). Pamira is about to consent—realizing that thus she can save her people from their doom—when Cleomene again reminds her that she is promised to Neocle. Again Pamira—determined to sacrifice herself—refuses to obey her father. In baffled fury, Cleomene curses her ("Spietata figlia").

The closing ensemble of the act now develops. Mahomed reiterates his fervent pleas and assurances of mercy toward the Greeks; Pamira, in an agony of indecision, laments the cruel dilemma in which she is trapped ("Deh, tace a me fatale"); Cleomene expresses his anguish over her ingratitude and disobedience; the Greek women voice their sympathy for Pamira ("Tristo il giorno"); Mahomed's followers exult over their Emperor's irresistible power.

ACT TWO[1]

[*Scene One*] A square in Corinth. In a recitative ("Da ferri sciolta") and aria ("Sì; m'avvalora il Dio") Cleomene, who had managed to es-

[1] In the Italian-language Ricordi score (1891) Act Two begins with a recitative ("Cielo! che diverrò? destin crudele!") and a brilliant aria ("Dal soggiorno degli estinti") by Pamira. This is followed by a duet between Pamira and Ismene ("Oh ciel! che fia chi mai s'avanza"), in which they are joined by the chorus of women ("Bella pace scenda almeno"). In the only available English translation of the libretto, these numbers are omitted.

cape his captors, calls down the wrath of the gods on his daughter and Mahomed—who is not only his archfoe but the seducer of his daughter as well. In bitter wrath he vows to fight on to the end for Greece.

[*Scene Two*] The pavilion of Mahomed, where Pamira is awaiting him. Tormented by remorse, she gives way to her emotions in a recitative ("Di ostili tende non è questo") and aria ("Dall'asilo della pace"). Guilt-ridden over her repudiation of Neocle, she sings that her unreasoning love for Mahomed is far more fatal than the assaults of the enemy. She prays to the spirit of her mother for strength to resist Mahomed's blandishments.

[*Scene Three*] The Emperor appears and again importunes Pamira, offering her all the fruits of victory. This marks the beginning of the long duet which comprises the entire scene ("Ti calma alfine"—in the Ricordi score: "Sgombra il timor").

When Pamira still resists, Mahomed adds the promise to show mercy toward her father. Although somewhat moved by the intensity of her protests ("Ciel, qual crudele deliro!"), Mahomed continues his entreaties, imploring her to be his Queen. In utter despair, Pamira cries that only death can end her torment.

[*Scene Four*] Overriding all Pamira's objections, Mahomed has gone ahead with preparations for the wedding. Pamira, grief-stricken but resigned, is greeted by the nuptial chorus, "La festa dell'Imene," the burden of which is that she will find happiness in marriage ("Un fortunato Imene"). The nuptial altar is then brought to the center of the scene to the accompaniment of the invocatory chorus, "Divino profeta."

[*Scene Five*] Suddenly Neocle's voice is heard outside, shouting Pamira's name. The throng stares in consternation as Omar enters leading Neocle bound in chains. Glaring at him in fury, Mahomed asks him what he wants ("Audace schiavo"). Death or vengeance, Neocle retorts defiantly ("O morte, o vendicarmi"). Then with withering scorn he goes on to say that while the women of Corinth are fighting side by side with their men, Pamira abandons herself to the caresses of the tyrant who would destroy her country. The very flowers in her hair, Neocle storms ("Pugnar tu li vedesti"), are stained with the blood of the Greeks.

Mahomed, momentarily taken aback, turns to Pamira and asks her who this man is. Suddenly and dramatically, she makes the decision that saves Neocle's life. She answers: "He is my brother" ("È mio germano"). A fiery trio ensues ("Si mai gradita"). Neocle, utterly bewildered by Pamira's quixotic action, implores her not to betray her father and her people by marriage with their mortal enemy. Mahomed, declaring that Pamira will be his bride, orders Neocle to be unchained and to witness the nuptials. Pamira cries that she can still hear her father's curse.

Omar and Ismene rush in with the news that the Corinthians have sounded the call to the final battle. (At this point in the staged version, the rear wall of the set opens to show Corinth in the distance, its ramparts crowded with women and soldiers. In a stormy chorus, "L'oltraggio m'è guida," the Greeks hurl defiance at the enemy. Then the voices of the Turks swell the ensemble as they threaten the beleaguered Greeks with fire and death.)

The ensuing action is dominated by a duet between Mahomed and Pamira ("Tu sol puoi, Pamira"), in which the Turk delivers his ultimatum: One word of consent from her will save Corinth; if she remains silent the city will perish. Resolutely Pamira answers that she will perish with it. Neocle applauds her courage in a fervid refrain. Declaring that she will now go back to Corinth and die there with her countrymen, Pamira asks Neocle to go with her.

Beside himself with fury, Mahomed bids them go—and go to die ("Ite a morir, abbene"). Before sunrise, he roars, every Greek will be exterminated and Corinth will vanish from the earth. The Greek chorus of defiance and the chorus of the Turks threatening disaster bring the act to a close.

ACT THREE

[*Scene One. The Tombs of Corinth*] With the avenging Turks now about to breach the city walls, Neocle and Jero lead the citizens to the refuge of the tombs. Neocle hails this abode of death as their final sanctuary ("Avanziamo, questo è il luogo"), while Jero laments the tragic fate of Greece. Pamira and Ismene, with the other women, offer a prayer ("Signor, che tutto puoi") beseeching the gods to punish those who desecrate their altars.

This is followed by Neocle's incredibly long and difficult aria, "E fia ver, mio Signor." He implores the gods to avert the doom of Greece and to forestall the sacrilege of the Turks. He resolves to rescue Pamira from the lustful embrace of the tyrant—to free her so that she may immolate herself with her people. On this day, he sings with mystical fervor, death will release her from this loathsome earth and her soul will join the soul of her mother.

[*Scene Two*] A room in the Governor's palace. Here Cleomene welcomes back Neocle, who he supposed had been slain by the Turks. Joyously he embraces him as a son who brings him the consolation his own daughter denies him. Pamira still ignores him, Cleomene says, and disdains all family ties. When Neocle tells him she saved his life, the Governor answers that she stained his own with infamy. Even if she now comes repentant, he bursts out, he will plunge a dagger into her heart.

[*Scene Three*] Pamira appears and humbly asks forgiveness of her father. Neocle tries to intercede for her. Cleomene at first flatly rejects her expressions of penitence ("Perfida a che ne vieni"). But when Pamira tells him she has kept faith with Neocle and has spurned Mahomed, Cleomene's wrath melts away. Embracing the two, he gives them his paternal benediction. This leads into an impassioned trio ("Celeste Provvinenza, il tuo favor"), in which they implore the protection of the gods.

[*Scene Four*] An open square near the tombs, where the people are gathered with Cleomene, Jero, Ismene and the Greek warriors. Jero reports that the Turks are storming the city ("Tutto percorsi il marziale recinto"). Cleomene hails the final hour of death and glory and invokes the blessing of the gods ("A questa morte sacra"). All kneel as Jero performs the ritual of preparation for death: the placing of palm garlands and white veils on the heads of the faithful. Then, in a dramatic aria, "Nube di sangue intrisa," over a choral accompaniment, he foretells the doom of Greece at the hands of her enemies. He bids the people fight on in the spirit of the ancient hero Leonidas, King of Sparta, who died gloriously at Thermopylae. The people respond that the very name inspires them with new courage. The chorus comes to a thunderous conclusion on the phrase "sì il sepolcro cangiarsi in altar—andiam!"

[*Scene Five*] As the siege nears its climax, Pamira, Ismene and the other Greek women are gathered in an open square to await the outcome. In recitative ("L'ora fatal s'appressa") Pamira sings that the fatal hour is at hand, then in an ensuing refrain ("Giusto ciel! in tal periglio") she exhorts the women to have the courage to die for Greece. Confusion and terror mount as the clamor of battle comes closer.

[*Scene Six*] Mahomed and his soldiers burst in with savage shouts of triumph. Resolutely facing the attackers, the women defy them to do their worst: If destiny has ordained the doom of the Greeks, then let their conqueror beware his own fate ("Se i Greci tutti, miseri fur spenti, di noi paventi il vincitor").

Mahomed, motioning his followers back, cries that in this moment of victory, revenge will be tempered with mercy. As he strides forward to take Pamira in his arms, she stabs herself, crying that first this dagger will pierce her heart ("Arresta! O questo ferro mi squarcia il sen"). She falls dead at Mahomed's feet. There is a gasp of horror from the crowd. In the background, Corinth is seen in flames, and from the distant ramparts comes the despairing cry of the vanquished defenders: "O patria!"

AUFSTIEG UND FALL DER STADT MAHAGONNY
(*Rise and Fall of the City of Mahagonny*)
by KURT WEILL
(1900–50)

Libretto by
BERTOLT BRECHT

Based originally on five *Mahagonny Songs* from Brecht's book of poems, *Hauspostille*

CHARACTERS

Speaker	
Fatty the Bookkeeper	Tenor
Trinity-Moses	Baritone
Leokadja Begbick	Contralto
Pennybank-Bill	Baritone
Jim Mahoney	Tenor
Jake (Jakob Schmidt)	Tenor
Alaska-Wolf-Joe	Bass
Jenny	Soprano
Tobby Higgins	Tenor

Place: The City of Mahagonny . . . legendary . . . anywhere
Time: Circa 1920s
First performance: Neue Theater, Leipzig, March 9, 1930
Original language: German

Mahagonny (pronounced MahaGONNY) is a word coined by Bertolt Brecht to designate a legendary city which exists beyond the confines of time and space. In the opera, the word is first uttered by Mrs. Begbick when she proposes the founding of "Mahagonny," which means a "city of nets."

Here, human values are inverted—or perverted: good is evil, evil is good. Anyone can do anything he pleases—but the cardinal sin is not paying one's debts, for which the penalty is execution.

The seeds of Kurt Weill's full-length opera were planted in his score for *Das kleine Mahagonny,* in collaboration with Brecht. Then came *Die Dreigroschenoper (The Threepenny Opera),* and finally *Mahagonny.* It is a baffling work replete with contrasts: tough, tender; lyrical, harshly dissonant; brutal, compassionate; cynical, sentimental.

There is spoken dialogue in a kind of *opéra-comique* vein, and even some set pieces that might be called arias (Mrs. Begbick's description of Mahagonny, Act One; Jim Mahoney's harangue to the audience, "You may do it," Act One; Jenny's sardonic credo, "If someone's going to kick, it'll be me," Act Two; Jim's tragic monologue, "When the sky gets light," just before his execution, Act Two). There are ensembles in the impudent jazz rhythms of the 1920s—leading off with the haunting "O moon of Alabama," first sung by Jenny and the six girls at the beginning of Act One.

Basically, the opera symbolizes the disillusionment that pervaded Europe after World War I. Social values became a mockery. The philosophy expounded operatically by Weill and Brecht ran head-on into current political dogma: the Nazis picketed the first performance in Leipzig, the Marxists raged that it was "capitalist propaganda." It ignited what Weill's widow, Lotte Lenya, called "the worst theater riot in history." A political *cause célèbre* it may have been, but *Mahagonny* remains—as Gustave Kobbé notes in *The Complete Opera Book*—an opera for opera singers.

The Leipzig premiere was performed by opera singers who, it was agreed, were not oriented to Weill's style of composing for the stage. This required singing actors. Accordingly, *Mahagonny* was produced in Berlin in 1931 with a cast of singing actors, with Lotte Lenya as Jenny. That same year, Miss Lenya assembled a cast for the recording of the opera. The accompanying libretto, in an English translation by Guy Stern, is the one followed in the story of the opera presented here.

Subsequent to the Leipzig and Berlin productions, there were numerous performances in Europe—with interest stimulated, incidentally, by Weill's immensely successful *Threepenny Opera.* The first Metropolitan Opera performance was given on November 16, 1979.

ACT ONE

A dilapidated truck clatters to a stop in a desolate region (presumably somewhere in the western U.S.A.). As the three disheveled occupants clamber out, the Speaker reads a "wanted" bulletin describing them: Leokadja Begbick, Trinity-Moses and Fatty. They are fleeing from the police.

In spoken dialogue, the three discuss their plight: the truck has broken down, they can't go any farther; they can't go back because the police are after them. Trinity-Moses says he has heard that gold has been discovered "up the coast." That's too far away, Fatty observes, and they would never get there.

At that point, Mrs. Begbick offers her own solution to the problem, to wit: the rivers "up the coast," they say, are rich in gold—and so, obviously, are the people there. It is easier to separate gold from men than from rivers. Well then, they will stay here and found a city where that can be accomplished. It shall be called "Mahagonny, the city of nets." In an ensuing arioso ("It is to be like a net"—"Sie soll sein wie ein Netz") she describes this creation.

It will be a net that will catch "edible birds" (such as prospectors from the Gold Coast) of all descriptions. It will offer them irresistible pleasures: a seven-day "no work" week; no restriction of any kind; boys and girls, gin and whisky; prizefights every third day. At the center of the city will be the Here-You-May-Do-Anything Inn.

Mahagonny, the paradise of total freedom, will flourish because the rest of the world is evil—there is no peace, no harmony, nothing to rely on. Concluding her discourse, Mrs. Begbick ties a piece of linen to the end of a fishing pole. This banner, she explains, will be raised so that ships from the Gold Coast will be able to find Mahagonny. In a vigorous trio ("But this entire Mahagonny"—"Aber dieses ganze Mahagonny"), the three salute the *raison d'être* of their sybaritic haven.

The Speaker then reports that Mahagonny has grown rapidly into a city, and that the first "sharks" (Brecht's own term for those who will be caught in the "net") are moving in. Thereupon Jenny enters with six girls, all carrying suitcases. Sitting down on the suitcases they sing in unison the famous "Alabama Song," the best-known number of the opera. It was the outstanding number of *Threepenny Opera*, in which it was sung in Brecht's beguiling "pidgin English." The final refrain is sung in harmony with Jenny's voice as an obbligato.

The Speaker proclaims that the fame of Mahagonny has spread far and wide. In a solemn, choral-like response ("We live in the cities"), men behind the scenes contrast the dismal aspect of modern cities to the golden paradise of Mahagonny. Trinity-Moses and Fatty, in an antiphonal waltz refrain, hymn the joys of living among the Mahagonny folk.

The Speaker next reports that discontented and unhappy people from all over the world are flocking to Mahagonny. As the orchestra breaks out into a catchy jazz rhythm, Jim, Jake, Bill and Joe—back from Alaska—come in with suitcases. They are excited about arriving in Mahagonny, where the air is cool and fresh, and where there are women, horses, whisky and poker. What is more, they have plenty of money.

As the four go on their way, the Speaker explains that one of them is Jim Mahoney. The story of how he came to the City of Mahagonny, and what happened to him, will now be told.

The four men are then seen on a Mahagonny pier, where they are examining a posted price list of the attractions of the city. A moment later, Mrs. Begbick enters with her own list of visitors, accommodations, prices, and so on. After she checks off Jimmy Mahoney and Jake (Jakob Schmidt), Jim introduces Pennybank-Bill and Alaska-Wolf-Joe. To oblige the men, Mrs. Begbick says, current prices will be lowered. The men promptly begin bargaining for the girls. Meanwhile, Trinity-Moses has helpfully set up a display panel of desirable prospects.

Staring avidly at the girls themselves, the men sing that they have come from Alaska, where they spent seven years in the cold felling trees. Now they have plenty of money to pay for what they want ("we pay cash if we like it"—"wir zahlen bar, wenn's uns gefällt!"). To the accompaniment of a tango rhythm, Jake tries to strike his own bargain with Mrs. Begbick for a girl, offering $30. Mrs. Begbick taunts him for being cheap ("Think it over, Mr. Jakob Schmidt"—"Ach, bedenken Sie, Herr Jakob Schmidt"). Ignoring the jibe, Jake offers $20, whereupon Jimmy, looking fondly at Jenny, says he will take her at that price.

As the others leave, he courteously asks Jenny her name. Jenny Smith from Havana, she replies, adding that there she did whatever people asked of her. The two then casually discuss the details of love-making. In a refrain over a theme in the English horn, Jenny sings that she has learned to be what a man likes her to be. Jim gently answers that he likes her just as she is. Jenny seductively mentions incidental favors: would he like her hair combed forward or back . . . shall she wear anything under her skirt. Jim gives her *carte blanche*.

The mood of the scene suddenly changes when the Speaker warns of an impending crisis. Mrs. Begbick rushes in to report to Fatty and Trinity-Moses that people have become disillusioned with Mahagonny and are leaving the city in droves. Fatty and Trinity-Moses then join her in a long trio of lamentation ("Alas, this Mahagonny"—"Ach, dieses Mahagonny"). In a lugubrious refrain, the two men moan that the city is a failure. Mrs. Begbick wails that the exodus has climaxed nineteen years of a wasted life. Nothing worthwhile has been caught in the City of Nets. There is no money—and that spells ruin of Mahagonny's prized commodity: sex.

Well then, Mrs. Begbick decides, we will turn back—back in space to the miserable cities, back in time through those luckless nineteen years of her life.

The world is waiting for you, Fatty remarks casually, then reads a newspaper report that police in Pensacola are looking for a certain Leokadja Begbick. Crime, Fatty and Trinity-Moses remind her unctuously, evidently does not pay.

The scene changes to the Mahagonny pier, where Jim, totally disenchanted with the city, is preparing to leave. Jake, Bill and Joe try to dissuade him, but he stubbornly refuses to listen. He has made up his mind, he says, because he saw a sign: *Forbidden here!* This edict violates the first law of Mahagonny: freedom.

A remarkable ensemble ensues. In spoken tones over a theme in the strings, the men first try to argue Jim into staying. He answers simply: "But something is missing" ("Aber etwas fehlt")—which he repeats like a litany to every proposal the men make. In a lyrical interlude ("Beautiful is the approach of evening"—"Wunderbar ist das Heraufkommen"), they sing of the salubrious delights of the city Jim insists on leaving.

He merely repeats that something is missing—not to mention the fact that the Mandalay Bar is closed. The men begin to lose their tempers at his obstinacy and virtually threaten him with hanging unless he agrees to "act like a human being." Jim retorts that he is not interested in becoming that species, then says he has decided to drive to Georgia. The three men are nonplussed, but manage to turn him around and escort him back into the city.

In the next scene, Bill, Jim, Jake, Joe and other men of Mahagonny are lounging in front of the Here-You-May-Do-Anything Inn listening to the tinkly, out-of-tune barroom piano. Jake sighs contentedly that such music is "eternal art." Jim's thoughts turn to Alaska, and in a tuneful but mocking ballad with a choral accompaniment he sings about the seven years in the Alaska forests.

But then he begins brooding about coming to Mahagonny—that highly touted bastion of freedom—after years of suffering and hardship, only to find fraud, corruption and wretchedness. Springing up, he flies into a rage, insults Mrs. Begbick, then whirls on the crowd with his hand on the knife in his belt.

Pandemonium breaks out as Jenny and the six girls implore Jim to spare their lives, while the men roar that they will throw out "those dumb boys—the Jimmys from Alaska." The entreaties and outcries build into a powerful fugal chorus. Beside himself with rage and frustration, Jim leaps up on a table, screaming that nobody ever will be happy in Mahagonny.

The clamor stops abruptly as the lights go out and the Speaker reports that a "typhoon-hurricane" is moving toward Mahagonny. The fugal chorus resumes as the people express their terror.

The following scene is called "The Night of the Hurricane." It is introduced by the Speaker, who says enigmatically that in "this night of horror a simple woodcutter by the name of Jim Mahoney found the laws of human happiness." The foreboding mood of the scene is accentuated by a striking chorus. It is virtually a paraphrase of the unison chorale sung by the Two Men in Armor in *Die Zauberflöte*, in which the men of Mahagonny exhort the people to have courage in the face of the hurricane. In direct contrast comes Jenny's fatalistic refrain, like a dirge: "O moon of Alabama, we now must say goodbye."

Jim alone is calm and unafraid. In an interspersed refrain ("That's the way the world is"—"So ist die Welt") he ruefully observes that even the horror of a hurricane is no match for the destructive fury of a man bent on getting what he wants. A choral refrain from the distance sardonically echoes his thought as the men sing that man needs no hurricane ("We need no hurricane"—"Wir brauchen keinen Hurrikan")—he can provide his own disasters. To which Mrs. Begbick adds that a hurricane is bad, a typhoon is worse, but the worst of all is man.

Jenny approaches Jim and tries to lure him into making love to her. He rebuffs her, then steps to the footlights to harangue the audience in the number which sums up the amoral philosophy of the City of Mahagonny: "You may do it" ("Du darfst es"). You may lie, cheat, steal, rob, rape and murder for the sake of your own well-being and the future of mankind. In any case, the hurricane is about to strike. There is little time left, so do as you please.

Fatty, Trinity-Moses and Mrs. Begbick rush in to report that Pensacola has been devastated. Mrs. Begbick triumphantly adds that all the police on her trail died in the ruins. As the ensemble builds to a climax, all sing that they too will die in the hurricane. Jim defiantly urges everyone to do what is forbidden—singing rousing songs, for instance. He sets the example by singing what is considered one of the two best numbers in the opera (the other is Jenny's "Alabama Song").

Its hedonistic theme is that "as you make your bed, so you will lie on it" ("Wie man sich bettet, so liegt man"). The others repeat the song in a lusty chorus.

Again the lights go out, leaving visible only a map projection with a superimposed arrow that moves slowly toward Mahagonny, indicating the path of the hurricane.

ACT TWO

As the lights go up during an interlude of "storm music," men and women are seen waiting on a highway outside the City of Mahagonny. Behind them, on the map projection, the arrow continues to move inexorably toward the city. As the thunderous orchestral crescendo keeps pace with the oncoming hurricane, four radio bulletins interrupt to report its progress: . . . moving at 120 miles per hour toward Atsena[1] . . . hurricane has destroyed Atsena . . . hurricane only three minutes away from Mahagonny.

[1] Fictitious. Presumably a coastal city in the path of the storm.

Transfixed with horror, the people stare at the map. Suddenly the arrow swerves around Mahagonny, then continues on its path. As the radio bulletin describes its detour, the people burst into a chorus of thanksgiving, sung over harp arpeggios in canon form ("O wonderful rescue"—"O wunderbare Lösung"). The Speaker announces that henceforth the motto of Mahagonny will be "You may do it." It is the law of the hurricane (which does whatever it pleases) and it is the fundamental law of the city.

The precepts of this law are enunciated by a male chorus standing at the footlights: first, Gluttony; second, Lovemaking; third, Boxing; fourth, Boozing. In Mahagonny, *You may do it.* Jim and the men sit down at tables laden with meats. At the center is Jake, symbolizing *Gluttony,* solemnly chanting to a zither-accordion accompaniment that he has already eaten two calves.

The men urge him to eat a third calf. Gorging himself and gasping, "Give me more," Jake falls down dead. Looking down at him, the men reverently take off their hats and sing in a mocking requiem: "Behold! Schmidt has died . . . a man without fear"—"Sehet, Schmidt ist gestorben." Replacing their hats, the men introduce the second precept: *Lovemaking.*

On a raised platform in a small room, Mrs. Begbick sits between a man and a girl. The men of Mahagonny are seated below. Mrs. Begbick admonishes the man seated beside her to make himself presentable for lovemaking ("spit out that gum . . . wash your hands"—"spucke den Kaugummi aus, wasche zuerst deine Hände"). Repeating her admonition, the men strike up the "Song of Mandalay" in a seductive rhythm that somehow accentuates the erotic implications of the theme . . . "hurry, boys . . . Love can't wait" ("Jungens, macht rasch"). Mrs. Begbick obliges with a related comment of her own in a torch-style refrain about sex versus money. The music dies away as the scene fades into darkness.

When the lights go up, Jim and Jenny are seen seated on two chairs apart from each other. In one of the most touching numbers of the opera, they sing in metaphorical terms of the courtship of two cranes ("Look at those cranes sweeping wide"—"Sieh jene Kraniche in grossem Bogen"). In the gentle concluding phrases of the duet they sing that the cranes are lovers, like themselves—and, for lovers, time stands still.

The third precept, *Boxing,* brings an abrupt change of mood. The men again step to the footlights and in a raucous chorus they recapitulate the four precepts of Mahagonny's free society. They make way for Fatty, who sets up a boxing ring. Joe enters and announces—to the consternation of Fatty and the others—a K.O. match between himself and Trinity-Moses. When the men warn Joe that this will be "murder," he stoutly answers that he is betting on himself all the money he earned in Alaska. Looking at Jim, he adds that he hopes those who value brains over brawn will bet on Alaska-Wolf-Joe.

In an ensuing duet, Jim and Joe sentimentally recall their seven winters in Alaska. As a pledge of friendship, Jim promises to bet on Joe. Joe and Trinity-Moses climb into the ring, the referee introduces them ("Trinity-Moses, 200 pounds, Alaska-Wolf-Joe, 170"), and the fight begins. Like all fight fans, the onlookers yell advice and call for mayhem. A woman screams; someone shouts that the fight is fixed.

After a brief exchange of blows, Joe goes "down for the count." The referee announces that "the man is dead." As the crowd laughs in savage glee, Jim and Trinity-Moses look down in pity and concern at the defeated fighter. In a brief chorus the men sing that in Mahagonny anything is allowed. And so, on with the next precept: *Boozing*.

The bar of the Inn. Sprawled with their feet on the tables, the men are drinking. In the foreground, Jenny, Bill and Jim are playing billiards. Jim calls to Mrs. Begbick to serve the men another round. They break into a nonsensical ditty explaining that for boozing and poker in Mahagonny one needs five dollars a day. Win or lose—here it always pays off in pleasure.

Mrs. Begbick interrupts to ask Jim to pay up. Now completely drunk, he confides to Jenny that he has no money and that they had better run for it. With that, he and Jenny and Bill climb up on the billiard table and pretend that it is a ship, with a curtain rod for a mast. Staggering around the "deck," Jim announces that he is sailing back to Alaska because he no longer likes Mahagonny. The men delightedly hail him as a great navigator.

Playing their bizarre charade to the hilt, Jim, Jenny and Bill now conjure up a typhoon. The men groan with "seasickness" and bawl out a deliberately banal chorus about the "stormy night" to keep up their courage. Finally Jim calls out that they have reached Alaska—where, he says, he will find peace at last.

Mrs. Begbick and Trinity-Moses bring him back to reality by demanding the money for the drinks. When Jim calmly replies that he hasn't any, the crowd turns on him in scorn and anger. Even Jenny and Bill refuse to help him. Trinity-Moses orders the men to tie him up.

As they do so, Jenny approaches the footlights and, in one of the principal arias of the opera, she soliloquizes about her past ("Gentlemen, my mother once stamped me"—"Meine Herren, meine Mutter prägte"). Branded by her own mother as a whore, she has made her way by sheer instinct for survival in a cruel world: ". . . if someone's going to kick, it'll be me . . . if someone's getting kicked, it'll be you" ("wenn einer tritt, dann bin ich es . . . wird einer getreten, dann bist du's!").

She sums up her philosophy of life in the cynical refrain heard earlier: "as you make your bed, so you will lie on it." Trinity-Moses tells the crowd that Jimmy has committed a "hanging crime"—he can't pay his bar bill. As Jim is led away, the men reprise the "five-dollar" chorus about Mahagonny. Marching past the footlights to the familiar refrain of "You may do it" they leave the Inn.

The scene is a forest, just before dawn. Jim is seen lying on the ground, one foot tied to a tree. In the ensuing soliloquy ("When the sky gets light"—"Wenn der Himmel hell wird") he prays that the "damned day" may never come, that night will never change to dawn.[2]

ACT THREE

A so-called court of justice in Mahagonny. Under a tent there is a small lecture-hall type of amphitheater facing a table and three chairs. In the center sits the judge, Mrs. Begbick; on either side, the defense attorney, Fatty, and the prosecuting attorney, Trinity-Moses—who has been hawking tickets to the trial at $5.00 apiece. In the prisoner's dock sits Tobby Higgins, on trial for "premeditated murder while testing an old revolver."

In an uproarious travesty of judicial procedure Trinity-Moses demands that justice take its course against this monster of depravity—and acquit him. Behind the attorney's back, Higgins and Mrs. Begbick have been exchanging hand signals as to how much of a bribe the judge will accept to settle the case. When they finally come to terms, Mrs. Begbick orders the injured party to come forward. Silence; no one moves. The judge's verdict is acquittal. In a brief refrain the jurors intone: "Dead men tell no tales" ("Die Toten reden nicht").

Enter Jim, handcuffed. Aside, he asks Bill for $100 to pay for conducting his case. Bill, although assuring Jim of his everlasting friendship, refuses to give him any money. Meanwhile, Trinity-Moses accuses Jim of every crime in the calendar. Mrs. Begbick, exasperated because Jim ignores her hand signals to indicate a bribe for acquittal, reads the indictment against one Jimmy Mahoney. Fatty keeps interrupting to ask, "Who is the injured party?"

The first charge is that Jim seduced a girl named Jenny. She thereupon identifies herself as the "injured party." Next, Jim sang a happy song (forbidden) during the hurricane—thus corrupting the spirit of Mahagonny. Bill, as a court spectator, promptly interrupts to defend Jim as "one who has discovered the laws of human happiness." Thereupon all the men roar for acquittal.

[2] This remarkable aria, with its mood of mingled despair and resignation in the face of doom, bears a striking resemblance to the soliloquy of Billy Budd, the protagonist of Britten's opera, in irons during the night before his hanging.

Trinity-Moses reads the next charge: the accused, hoping to win a lot of money, bet on his friend in a boxing match that caused his death. At that, the men shout alternately for execution and for acquittal. Now, Trinity-Moses declares, comes the most serious charge of all: Jim has not paid for three bottles of whisky and a curtain rod.

Fatty calls for a verdict. Mrs. Begbick reads off the sentences and penalties as follows:

Causing the murder of a friend: two days' arrest.

Destroying peace and harmony: two-year suspension of civil rights.

Seduction of a girl named Jenny: ten years in the dungeon.

Failure to pay debts: death.

In a brief trio, Mrs. Begbick, Fatty and Trinity-Moses declaim that these crimes are the most heinous on the face of the earth. Their denunciation brings a burst of wild cheering from the spectators.

The Speaker announces that many people, disappointed with Mahagonny, long to go to a better city—Benares, for example. But Benares has been struck by an earthquake.

Perched on barstools, Jenny, Mrs. Begbick, Fatty, Bill and Higgins lament in an outrageously out-of-tune chorus that there is no bar, no whisky, no telephone, no fun. Then let us go to Benares, they go on in a sodden chant. When they suddenly remember that Benares has been flattened by an earthquake, their lamentations rise to a doleful climax: "Where shall we go?"

The Speaker now announces the execution and death (*sic!*) of Jimmy Mahoney. It will be a grim spectacle, he warns, but nobody seems willing to raise money to save Jimmy from the electric chair. In a brief but touching duet, he and Jenny bid each other farewell. Jim fondly notes that she is dressed in white—like a widow. "I am your widow," she replies quietly. Jim commends Jenny to the care of his one remaining Alaska friend, Bill—who takes her in his arms. Jim walks toward the electric chair as the men, in a staccato chorus, reprise the refrain about the four Mahagonny precepts.

Trinity-Moses asks Jim if he has any final words. He gives his answer in a mournful *andante* refrain—"Don't be misled, there is no return" ("Lasst euch nicht verführen, es gibt keine Wiederkehr"). Its fatalistic theme is that life must be savored to its fullest, no matter what the consequences. His listeners repeat these sentiments in a brief chorus.

Seated in the electric chair, Jim casually asks Mrs. Begbick if she knows there is a God. We have an answer for that, she rejoins, and then follows a blasphemous representation of God visiting Mahagonny. It is in the form of a playlet, with Trinity-Moses playing God. While Jim is being prepared for execution, the chorus chants that God came to Mahagonny in the midst of whisky.

At the climax of the chorus, Trinity-Moses-God contemptuously consigns all the "rascals" to Hell. Laughing derisively, Jenny, Bill, Higgins and Fatty retort that they can't be dragged down to Hell because they have always been there. Jimmy is executed.

The stage darkens as the Speaker reports that huge protest marches are heralding the doom of the "city of nets." All join in reprises of refrains heard throughout the opera—"no peace reigns . . . we need no hurricanes . . . as you make your bed . . . if someone's going to kick." Men and girls parade in carrying Jimmy's personal belongings—hat, cane, watch, revolver, checkbook, shirt. In the background is seen Mahagonny enveloped in flames.

Jenny and the girls sing a final reprise of "Moon of Alabama." Led by Bill, a procession enters with placards bearing slogans of dissent and rebellion—and ironically calling for "the continuation of the golden age." Meanwhile, the music has taken on the remorseless thudding rhythm of a march to the scaffold. To its accompaniment the entire assemblage chants a final requiem of hopelessness and despair: "We cannot help ourselves—nor you—nor anyone"—"Können uns und euch und niemand helfen." The curtain falls.

THE BALLAD OF BABY DOE
by DOUGLAS MOORE
(1893–1968)

Libretto by
JOHN LATOUCHE

CHARACTERS

Horace Tabor, mayor of Leadville	Baritone
Augusta, wife of Horace Tabor	Mezzo-soprano
Mrs. Elizabeth (Baby) Doe, a miner's wife	Lyric soprano
Mama McCourt, Baby Doe's mother	Contralto
William J. Bryan, candidate for President	Bass-baritone
Chester A. Arthur, President of the United States	Tenor
Father Chapelle, priest at the wedding	Tenor
An old silver miner	Tenor
A clerk at the Clarendon Hotel	Tenor
Mayor of Leadville	Tenor
Stage doorman at the Tabor Grand	Tenor
Bouncer	Baritone
Albert, a bellboy	Baritone
A footman	Baritone
A Denver politician	Baritone
Sarah, Mary, Emily, Effie, old friends of Augusta	Two sopranos, two mezzo-sopranos
Sam, Bushy, Barney, Jacob, cronies and associates of Tabor	Two tenors, two baritones
Four Washington dandies	Two tenors, two baritones
Kate, dance hall entertainer	Soprano
Elizabeth, aged twelve	soprano part
Silver Dollar, aged seven	silent part
children of Horace and Baby Doe	
Meg, dance hall entertainer	Mezzo-soprano
Silver Dollar (grown-up)	Mezzo-soprano
Samantha, a maid	Mezzo-soprano

Dance hall girls, Baby Doe's family and foreign diplomats at the wedding, miners and their wives

Place: Leadville, Colorado; Denver; Washington, D.C.
Time: 1880 to 1899
First performance: Central City Opera House, Central City, Colorado, July 1956
Original language: English

This opera by the late contemporary composer Douglas Moore has established itself in the repertoire as a truly American opera. Its characters are drawn from American history. It is the drama of an ambitious young American, the two women who dominated his life and a silver mine that made him fabulously rich—and ruined him.

Horace Tabor trekked from Vermont to Colorado in the 1890s with his young wife Augusta, there discovered the "Matchless Mine" and then met and fell in love with Baby Doe, the wife of a miner. At the pinnacle of his success, the U. S. Government abandoned the silver standard, and his fortune vanished. Before he died in 1899, Tabor asked Baby Doe to promise that she would never sell the Matchless Mine. Baby Doe kept that promise—until the day in 1935 when she was found frozen to death at the entrance to the abandoned mine.

The music of *The Ballad of Baby Doe,* though in the contemporary idiom, is not atonal. Richly melodic, with strong rhythmic patterns, it ranges from sentimental folk tunes of the Victorian era to passages of striking dramatic power in the best tradition of grand opera.

ACT ONE

[*Scene One*] Outside Tabor Opera House, Leadville, Colorado, 1880. At left, the Clarendon Hotel; at right, a saloon. The curtain rises after a brief orchestral introduction. Shouts and laughter are heard in the saloon, then a pistol shot. Suddenly an old miner comes lurching out of the saloon, propelled by a kick from the Bouncer. He picks himself up and begins singing about finding a silver mine—the "Matchless Mine," he calls it—which is why he is celebrating.

The Bouncer comes out and warns the miner to be quiet—there is to be a concert at Tabor's new opera house next door. Continuing in a catchy, impudent refrain, the miner sings that Horace Tabor wants to buy his mine. The saloon girls, followed by the Bouncer, come out and join the miner in a mocking chorus of praise of Tabor and his "opry house." The Bouncer vainly tries to quiet them. Catching hold of the drunken miner, they whirl him around from one to the other until he finally lurches away, still bawling about his Matchless Mine. Shrieking with laughter, the girls follow the Bouncer into the saloon.

A moment later Tabor comes out of the opera house followed by four of his cronies. In a vigorous refrain ("It's a bang-up job") he sings boastfully about his opera house, its glittering chandeliers, brass and mahogany trim, and tapestries from Europe. Fawning around him, his four cronies—Sam, Bushy, Barney and Jacob—comment in chorus.

Tabor sings that his wife Augusta deserves credit for the opera house because she was determined to bring "culture" to Leadville. He and his cronies josh each other about still being "pay dirt" miners at heart even though they are dressed in swallow-tailed coats and top hats. A colorful scene follows as the girls troop out of the saloon, join the chorus and dance with Tabor and the miners. In a lusty ensemble they sing, "Gophers, dig them holes! Dig away to save your souls!"

At the height of their capers, the doors of the opera house swing open and Augusta comes out with her friends—the wives of Tabor's four cronies. For a moment they stand in shocked surprise at the antics of the miners and the saloon girls. Then Augusta launches into a tirade against Tabor for allowing this undignified behavior, exclaiming: "Horace, have you taken leave of your senses?"

She berates Tabor and the miners for leaving the opera house in the middle of the concert and thus embarrassing the ladies. Their uncouth behavior, Augusta storms, has made a mockery of her efforts to bring some refinement to this money-grubbing town.

Tabor tries to placate her—reminding her, incidentally, that the money from the saloon helped build the opera house. Meanwhile, the saloon girls, somewhat abashed, quietly go back into the saloon. A bell signaling the end of the intermission puts an end to the argument. Augusta, followed obediently by the ladies, stalks back into the opera house. Tabor stands looking after her.

As a graceful waltz theme begins, Baby Doe, followed by a Welsh servant, enters and approaches Tabor. She asks if he can direct her to the Clarendon Hotel—she has just come from Central City and is a stranger in town. With a bow, Tabor introduces himself, points in the direction of the Clarendon and gallantly welcomes her to Leadville. Their dialogue continues over the waltz music.

With another courtly bow, Tabor says he hopes they will meet again. At that moment, Augusta calls to him from the door of the opera house. As he goes inside with her, Baby Doe sings in a climactic phrase, "Indeed, we'll meet again!" The waltz theme goes on in the orchestra as the curtain slowly falls.

[Scene Two] Without interruption, the rhythm of the music changes and the curtain goes up. The scene is outside the Clarendon Hotel later that evening. Augusta and her friends and Tabor and his cronies enter on their way to the hotel following the concert. They are in the formal dress of the 1890s. In a brief chorus ("What a lovely evening!") they comment in stilted, poetic phrases on the music. The friends leave. Augusta and Tabor thank them and bid them goodnight. When they are alone, Augusta remarks that the evening has been tiring—although Adelina Patti "sang divinely." She goes inside. Tabor sits down on the hotel steps and lights a cigar.

Kate and Meg, two saloon girls, enter. They do not see Tabor, half hidden in the shadows. In a short duet, they gossip about Baby Doe, with catty comments about the airs she gives herself. Their conversation reveals to Tabor that Baby Doe has a husband—"Harvey Doe, up in Central City." The girls' voices, repeating Baby Doe's name, fade as they go on their way. Tabor, looking after them, reflectively murmurs Baby Doe's name.

Then the light comes up in the large front window of the hotel to reveal Baby Doe seated at the piano. Here she sings the aria "Willow, where we met together," a plaintive song, embellished with coloratura passages, about a lover who has gone, leaving his beloved alone and weeping.

As Baby Doe finishes the aria on a high, soaring phrase, Tabor, still sitting in the shadows, applauds. Baby Doe comes to the window and exclaims in surprise. The two look at each other, both deeply moved and now aware of their destiny. Tabor says that "Baby Doe" is the prettiest name he has ever heard. Baby Doe answers: "The fabulous Horace Tabor . . . eyes afire with dreaming." Then Tabor sings to her in an ardent refrain, "Warm as the autumn light." He tells her that her singing has brought back the memory of all the beautiful things in life he had forgotten as the years went by. The aria rises to a passionate climax as he repeats her name, then tenderly kisses her hand.

A harsh dissonance in the orchestra breaks the spell, and then comes the voice of Augusta calling to Tabor from an upstairs window. Tabor, his eyes still on Baby Doe, answers quietly, "Anything you say," then turns and goes into the hotel.

[Scene Three] The living room of the Tabor apartment in the hotel. Augusta stands at the window looking out at the deepening twilight. Samantha, the maid, is lighting the lamps. She and Augusta converse in quasi-recitative. Augusta admonishes Samantha to be more careful about dusting, wonders why Tabor has not arrived, then fusses over the messy state of his desk.

Shuffling through the papers there, she suddenly finds a check. She exclaims in irritation as she sees it is made out to Jake Sands to buy another mine. Pocketing the check, Augusta continues shuffling through the papers and suddenly comes upon a pair of white lace gloves. She examines them in puzzled surprise. A gift from her husband, of course, but why? Their wedding anniversary? No . . . that is not until next April . . . and they will have been married twenty-seven years.

Samantha picks up a card which has fallen from between the gloves and hands it to Augusta. As the music echoes the theme of Tabor's song to Baby Doe, Augusta reads the card. It is a tender love note—"I send these lacy nothings." Augusta turns the card over and reads: "Baby Doe." A violent orchestral passage underscores Augusta's fury and dismay. She asks Samantha if she has seen this woman . . . she is young and pretty, no doubt? The maid nods, then quietly leaves the room.

Augusta, staring at her hands, gives way to her grief and anguish in a wild outburst—"Look at these hands!" Age and toil have wrinkled them and made them ugly, she cries, and all for Tabor's sake. She has worked at his side through the years to build a life together. No, Augusta sobs, these hands are not pretty now . . . not like hers.

Tabor suddenly enters, goes to his desk and starts rummaging through his papers. Watching him with icy calm, Augusta asks him what he is looking for. Now follows a long, bitter scene of accusation and recrimination. Tabor furiously accuses Augusta of prying into his personal affairs. Augusta retorts that indeed she would like to know more about his personal affairs. He shouts that she is nagging him, holding him back, trying to make him "knuckle under."

But Augusta has been waiting for her moment of revenge, and now it has come. With a sneer she asks Tabor if he would prefer that she whisper "sweet nothings" the way some brazen women do, Baby Doe, for instance. With that she holds up the pair of white gloves.

Beside himself with rage, Tabor demands the gloves. Augusta, now aware that she has the upper hand, pours out her contempt, deriding him for making a fool of himself over a young girl. Tabor retorts that this girl is generous and kind, and has given him the tenderness that his coldhearted wife has denied him. Stung by this accusation of coldness, Augusta warns her husband that she will drive "that woman" out of town. Tabor, alarmed by her threat in spite of his rage, entreats her not to ruin both their lives by a senseless act of revenge. As Augusta storms out of the room, the duet ends in a violent, climactic phrase, underscored by a harsh orchestral fanfare.

[*Scene Four*] The lobby of the Clarendon Hotel, where the clerk is seen busy at his desk. There is a brief orchestral introduction in a perky, nervous rhythm. Then Baby Doe appears, carrying a hatbox, followed by a bellboy with her bags. She tells the clerk she has decided to go to Oshkosh, Wisconsin, to visit with her family. Ignoring the clerk's look of startled surprise, Baby Doe goes over to a writing desk in a

corner of the lobby. In an aside, the clerk tells the bellboy to find
Horace Tabor at once and tell him that Baby Doe is leaving town. And
that, he adds, means trouble.

In a poignant aria, Baby Doe sings the words of the letter she is writing to her mother—"Dearest Mama, I am writing." She relates that her
husband Harvey has left her and that she is alone in Leadville. But,
after all, she never loved him. They weren't suited to each other.

She recalls that her mother once told her that someday she would
meet a man who would treat her like a princess and give her the things
her beauty deserved. Now, she writes, she has met that man. They both
know they are meant for each other . . . but this is not to be. And so
they must part forever. As the tender letter theme is reiterated by the
orchestra, Baby Doe reads what she has written, then signs her name.

To the accompaniment of a somber theme in the bass, Augusta suddenly appears. The two women confront each other and a long and dramatic colloquy ensues. Augusta warns Baby Doe that there will be serious trouble if she does not end her affair with Horace Tabor. As a waltz
theme begins in the orchestra, Baby Doe answers with quiet candor—"I
knew it was wrong." Horace Tabor stood by her when she was in trouble, Baby Doe sings, and gave her help when she needed it most. They
did nothing to be ashamed of. He is a kind man, she goes on, and a
strong man—and above all an unusual man. And unusual men have unusual ways, she observes. She tells Augusta that she is leaving, then
pleads with her to try to understand this man. It is a privilege to serve
him—but at the same time he must not be denied his freedom.

Balked by Baby Doe's calm reasonableness, Augusta resorts to sneering that Tabor is nothing more than an overgrown child and a weakling.
All his success, she says, was pure luck. The mine that he found by
mere chance was so rich that even he, wastrel that he is, could not have
spent all the money it made. It was she—Augusta—who saw to it that all
the profit was not wasted on drinking and carousing. Condescendingly,
she remarks that she is glad Baby Doe has come to her senses at last
and has decided to leave. With that she says goodbye and sweeps out of
the room as a mockingly heroic theme sounds in the orchestra.

No sooner has she left than Tabor appears. He and Baby Doe rush
into each other's arms, Tabor crying out, "You're not going, my heart!"
In a passionate duet they pledge their devotion to each other, then go
up the stairs together as the curtain falls.

[*Scene Five*] Augusta's parlor in Denver, a year later. She herself is
in conversation with her four women friends, all seething with righteous
indignation. An ensemble follows in which the five women gossip maliciously. The women ask Augusta what she intends to do about Tabor
and "that woman" who flouts all standards of decency. Augusta only

keeps reiterating "nothing at all" in almost identical musical phrases with the sinister effect of a fate motive. One juicy bit of gossip is that Tabor secretly is trying to get a divorce with the help of a corrupt judge. With remorseless determination, Augusta vows that she will never let Tabor out of her grasp.

Like a chorus of witches, the four friends urge her to revenge ("tell the truth . . . shout the scandal from the housetops"). They repeat this in minor thirds with baleful effect as the curtain falls.

[*Scene Six*] A suite in the Willard Hotel in Washington, D.C., 1883. On a table heaped with flowers and gifts there towers a wedding bell of white roses surmounted by a heart of red roses pierced by an arrow of violets. Mama McCourt, Baby Doe's mother, is fussing with the decorations. Her husband, sons and another daughter are sitting stiffly on gilt chairs. At one side are four dandies, stylishly dressed, mincing young men. Everyone is waiting for the bridal couple—Horace Tabor (now Senator) and his new wife Baby Doe.

A lively ensemble follows over a restive orchestral accompaniment in alternating 7/8 and 4/4 tempo which paces the give-and-take of the dialogue. Mama McCourt flutters about, telling everybody how beautiful Baby Doe is and inviting the guests to help themselves to champagne. In brief choral passages, the four dandies comment superciliously on the proceedings or express their opinions about "high protective tariff rates." Mama McCourt brags about her "little Lizzie's" wedding gown, which cost Horace Tabor more than seven thousand dollars. The four dandies snobbishly turn their backs on Mama, remarking that nobody of any importance showed up at the wedding.

The priest who officiated at the wedding appears and is tearfully greeted by Mama. He unctuously comforts her with the usual banalities, observing that she has not lost a daughter but has gained a son. Suddenly there is a stir of excitement as a footman announces Senator and Mrs. Horace Tabor. They are saluted with a mock-operatic *maestoso* chorus.

Tabor, beaming and pompous, with Baby Doe on his arm, urges everyone to join the celebration. Greeting the dandies, he asks what the latest news is from Capitol Hill. "Bimetallism," they reply in chorus. Mama, overhearing, says she thinks that would be fun and innocently asks if the ladies can try it.

At this point the four dandies sound the first warning note of future disaster as they tell Tabor that the "silver standard is doomed." When they add that gold is the coming thing, Tabor flares up angrily. Quieting him with a gesture, Baby Doe launches into a rather florid aria in which she compares the worth of silver and gold ("Gold is a fine thing"). While gold is the sun, she sings, silver is the moon—and she herself is a child of the moon. Silver, she exults in a soaring phrase, is the stuff of dreams.

Tabor then boastfully shows the guests a case of glittering jewelry—the very ones, he says, which Queen Isabella of Spain pawned to finance Columbus' discovery of America. These, he proclaims, are what silver can buy. The onlookers gasp in admiration, while Mama McCourt fatuously expresses the wish that Harvey Doe could be present now. When the priest casually asks who Harvey Doe is, Mama then and there blunders into the damaging disclosure that both Tabor and Baby Doe have been divorced. In icy tones the priest asserts that he was not told of this, then stalks out of the room. In suppressed excitement, the guests whisper, "Scandal!" They repeat the word in a dramatic crescendo passage.

Just as they start to leave, the footman announces the arrival of the President of the United States, Chester A. Arthur. He toasts the bride, with the guests joining in a brief waltz chorus which closes the act.

ACT TWO

[*Scene One*] A balcony off the ballroom of the Windsor Hotel in Denver. It is the evening of the Governor's Ball in 1893, ten years after the marriage of Tabor and Baby Doe in Washington. After a brief introduction in waltz tempo, the curtain rises to show the dancers through the windows of the hotel.

Augusta's four friends come out and an ensemble ensues which is joined later by the four cronies. The women first gossip in their usual spiteful fashion about Baby Doe, then express their sympathy for Augusta, now rejected and alone. The cronies come out and begin to argue with their wives. They try to defend Tabor and Baby but the women scorn their arguments. With malicious assurance they predict that Baby will leave Tabor "when something better comes along."

As a waltz tempo begins in the orchestra, Baby Doe and her mother come out, fanning themselves. Seeing the four women and their husbands, Baby Doe greets them cordially. Without a word, the four women turn their backs and go inside, followed by their shamefaced husbands. Baby ironically remarks on the sudden chill in the air, but Mama fumes over the insolent behavior of the wives.

Then in a long and moving aria Baby Doe compares her own happiness with the wretched frustration of those who scorn and criticize her. Their lives are bleak and empty, she sings, because they do not know what love is. Her own life is precious and warm because she is enveloped by a love that will last forever. And this, Baby sings in a triumphant climax, is something "they will never, never know."

Suddenly a butler appears and hands her a calling card on a tray. In suppressed excitement she sends her mother to find Tabor. A moment later she turns to face Augusta, a forbidding figure in a black ball gown. Augusta is strangely humble as she explains that she has come only to say something that must now be said. Baby Doe, she goes on, has been too happy for her own good. It has made other people hateful and jealous because it has made their own loveless lives more unbearable by contrast.

Baby, at first suspicious, feels a sudden rush of pity for this lonely, despairing woman and expresses regret for any wrong she has done her. Augusta absolves her of any blame, then discloses her real reason for coming. It is to warn her that Horace Tabor faces certain ruin. Tomorrow the President of the United States will sign a bill devaluating silver —and that means that Tabor's fortune will vanish.

Baby Doe refuses to believe her and cries that Horace knows what is best and that nothing can harm him. Vainly Augusta tries to convince her that, with the price of silver steadily diminishing, Horace's wealth is a thing of the past. But he is blind to everything but his love of silver, she goes on, which is like his love for Baby Doe. In the ringing climax of her pleading, Augusta begs Baby to persuade Tabor to sell his Matchless Mine.

At that moment Horace enters. Confronting Augusta, he accuses her of trying to turn Baby Doe against him—as she has half the town. Both Baby and Augusta try to reason with him but he storms that this talk of ruin is a lie. Crying that Tabor will never see her again, Augusta rushes out of the room. As Baby starts to follow, Tabor takes her in his arms and begs her not to desert him. The Matchless Mine will never fail them, he cries.

In a touching gesture of faith, Baby takes off her necklace and ring, thrusts them into his hands and tells him to bet her treasures on the Matchless Mine. Inspired by her confidence in him, Tabor asks her to promise always to hold onto the mine. Baby Doe resolutely replies: "Always, I promise!"

[Scene Two] A club room in Denver, 1895. Tabor's four cronies are playing poker. In dialogue partly spoken and partly sung, they discuss Tabor—how he keeps harping on silver and won't change with the times. They comment disparagingly on his chances in the coming election.

The four fall silent as Tabor enters to join the game. He announces he has a proposition to offer them and asks their support against McKinley and the anti-silver gang. If they will back him up, he continues, he will risk everything he has to win the fight. But the cronies only eye him silently and shake their heads. Tabor's pleading becomes desperate. The wind is sure to blow their way again, he cries, because a great champion of humanity and free silver is on their side—William Jennings Bryan. Thereupon the cronies denounce Bryan as a faker and ridicule Tabor for his faith in him.

Goaded to fury, Tabor accuses his erstwhile companions of deserting him ("turn tail and run then!"). Let them forget that silver made them what they are, he roars, and let them crawl before their new masters. There still are free men who will stand their ground and fight. With an angry shout, he sends cards and chips flying from the table with a sweep of his hand, then strides out.

[*Scene Three*] Matchless Mine, 1896. Miners' wives are decorating a speaker's stand in front of the mine entrance. On the stand is a lectern and a huge photograph of Bryan. As the women work, they wordlessly sing a brisk marching tune. Baby Doe enters with her two children. She explains to them that flags are flying and people are shouting because the great William Jennings Bryan is coming to make a speech. He is a very great man, she says, a man who can charm the birds off the trees.

The martial music grows louder and soon a parade appears, led by Tabor. Mounting the platform, he exhorts the crowd to vote for Bryan and the silver standard. The crowd responds with a cheering chorus, "We want Bryan!" The mayor then tries to introduce Bryan, but his voice is lost in the clamor. Bryan finally silences the throng with an imperious gesture, then launches into a flowery speech on the theme historically associated with his name: "Never shall we worship before the Calf of Gold!"

He goes on in resounding, cliché-laden phrases, praising the pioneer spirit of the silver miners and Horace Tabor in particular. As he speaks, Tabor's little daughter, carrying a bunch of roses, pulls at his coattails. Finally taking notice of her, Bryan interrupts his speech to take her in his arms and thank her for the tribute. Reaching into one of the bags of silver ore banked around the lectern, he sprinkles some of it on the child's head and christens her "Silver Dollar." Then to the accompaniment of massive orchestral chords he brings his speech to a fervid climax—"Renew the ancient covenant between man and God!" Cheering him wildly, the crowd forms a procession. Several men lift Bryan to their shoulders and lead the parade away.

[*Scene Four*] Augusta's parlor, November 1896. She is standing at the window listening to the voices of newsboys shouting: "Republican landslide . . . Bryan defeated." Augusta cringes at the sound.

Samantha brings in Mama McCourt. The ensuing dialogue reveals the extent of the disaster which has befallen Tabor. With Bryan's defeat and the abandonment of the silver standard Tabor has lost everything. When Mama appeals to Augusta for help—for the sake of the children—

Augusta coldly reminds her of Tabor's words: "I want nothing from her." Mama implores her to forgive Tabor, now a ruined man, but Augusta relentlessly refuses to help. Defeated and hopeless, Mama leaves.

Alone, Augusta gives way to her despair in a deeply moving soliloquy, "Augusta, how can you turn away?" Memories of her life with Tabor come back in a flood of anguish. She sings that she cannot understand why—now when he needs her most—she cannot bring herself to help him. In a descending phrase of complete desolation she murmurs, "But—I cannot go."

[*Scene Five*] The stage of the Tabor Grand Theater, April 1899. The curtain rises as a plaintive melody sounds in the orchestra. Tabor, in workman's clothes, walks slowly out on the stage, ignoring the stage doorman, who tries to stop him. Quietly Tabor identifies himself and the doorman apologizes for not having recognized him. Here begins the fantasy which brings the opera to its poignant climax.

Staring trancelike into the gloom of the deserted theater, Tabor begins: "I wanted to take a long, long look around." He recalls how he built the opera house, repeating the musical phrases he sang in Act One when he boasted to his cronies about his accomplishment. Suddenly a spotlight reveals the pompous figure of a man holding a glittering watch fob. Tabor hears the speaker's voice—"the citizens of Denver present this watch fob of purest gold." It should have been silver, Tabor murmurs, not gold. The doorman stares at him in alarm, then mutters that he must go for help. The figure of the speaker vanishes.

Tabor stands lost in his fantasy of the past. He sees again the green hills of the Vermont farm where he was born, hears a woman call to him in shrill, querulous tones. In his dream he confuses this voice with Augusta's. An ominous hooded figure appears. Tabor rushes toward it with a happy cry of "Maw!" The apparition slaps him violently, then berates him for being a worthless no-account "like your Paw."

Reeling from the blow, Tabor still tries to embrace the woman, who suddenly throws back her hood. It is Augusta, now as a young girl. Tabor recalls the days of his courtship of the girl who was named for Augusta, Maine. He was an ambitious young man then, working for Augusta's father and determined to "be somebody." A ghostly chorus chants: "To be somebody, marry the boss's daughter."

The fantasy continues with Tabor's vision of his journey to the West with his bride . . . he and his four cronies digging for silver . . . Augusta forcing him to sign "the pledge" . . . saloon girls . . . the wild life in Leadville . . . the discovery of the fabulous silver mine that made him rich . . . Tabor, the leading citizen of Leadville . . . builder of the opry house, monument to Tabor. . . . The music swells to a blazing fanfare of trumpets.

Suddenly it subsides into dark, foreboding chords as Augusta's voice intones, "You are goin' to die, Horace Tabor, and you die a failure." Remorseless, accusing, the voice foretells his doom, but Tabor shouts defiantly that Baby Doe will save him. Augusta answers that even his own children will repudiate him. Instantly Tabor is confronted with a vision of Silver Dollar as a half-naked, drunken cabaret girl raucously singing. The music rises to a frenzied climax as Tabor, with Augusta glaring at him malevolently, utters an agonized cry for help. The vision of Augusta fades. Tabor stands dazed and exhausted.

The doorman comes in followed by Baby Doe, who rushes to Tabor and takes him in her arms. She wears a black cloak with a hood covering her hair. Shaken by his terrible dream, Tabor at first does not realize it is Baby Doe. He puts his hands to her face and murmurs that he can feel tears. Thinking it is Augusta, he gasps defiantly: "You cannot divide us."

Baby Doe gently reassures him. His life ebbing away, Tabor sinks to the floor. Baby Doe kneels beside him and covers him with her cloak. As the light gradually fades, Tabor's body is enveloped in darkness. Baby Doe begins the aria which ends the opera: "Always through the changing of sun and shadow." Singing that she and her love will walk through eternity together, she slowly pushes back her hood, revealing her hair. It is snow-white.

The light comes up, bringing the shaft of the Matchless Mine into view. Baby Doe's final words die away on a serene major chord. The curtain falls.

BENVENUTO CELLINI

by HECTOR BERLIOZ

(1803–69)

Libretto by
LÉON DE WAILLY and AUGUSTE BARBIER

Based on the *Autobiography* of Benvenuto Cellini

CHARACTERS

Balducci, Papal Treasurer	Bass
Teresa, his daughter	Soprano
Benvenuto Cellini, a goldsmith	Tenor
Ascanio, his apprentice	Mezzo-soprano
Francesco ⎱ artisans in Cellini's workshop	⎰ Tenor
Bernardino ⎰	⎱ Bass
Pope Clement VII	Bass
Fieramosca, sculptor to the Pope	Baritone
Pompeo, a professional assassin	Baritone
Innkeeper	Tenor

Artists, apprentices, artisans, masquers, carnival actors, monks, townspeople, servants

Time: 1532
Place: Rome
First performance: Grand Opéra, Paris, September 3, 1838 (also given as September 10)
Original language: French

NOTE: The role of "Clement VII" was in the Berlioz original. Because of French censorship it was changed to "Cardinal Salviati," the censors having objected to the depiction of a pope on the stage. In most productions, the character is designated as Cardinal Salviati.

This opera, the first of three Berlioz wrote, has a strange history. It was a complete failure at its Paris premiere, as well as at its London premiere two weeks afterward. Given fifteen years later in London, with Berlioz conducting, it was a qualified success. By that time the composer had established himself as one of the most gifted orchestral virtuosos of his day, and his ideas were championed by such eminent musicians as Franz Liszt and Robert Schumann.

Liszt, in fact, revived *Benvenuto Cellini* at Weimar in 1855, and Hans von Bülow conducted the opera in Hanover in 1879. Then it vanished from the operatic repertoire. The first American performance was given at Philharmonic Hall, New York, on March 22, 1965, by the Concert Opera Association under the baton of Thomas Scherman.

The stirring overture states some of the opera's most important themes. It begins in a mood reflecting the restless, rebellious spirit of the hero-artist with a theme based on the love duet of Cellini and Teresa in Act Three.

A following section is marked by a pizzicato theme in the basses which foreshadows the aria sung by Pope Clement VII at the beginning of Act Three. The main section of the overture, in sonata form, carries the impetuous "Cellini" theme along with that of the drinking song. The coda reiterates the Clement VII theme. Running through the entire overture is the effervescent gaiety of the Mardi Gras carnival.

ACT ONE

A room in Balducci's home. Late evening. Balducci is complaining to his daughter, the seventeen-year-old Teresa, that he cannot understand why Pope Clement insists on calling a troublemaker like Cellini to Rome as his official sculptor ("En vérité, c'est bien étrange"). This fellow Cellini is a wild-eyed revolutionary and is obviously up to no good. In any case, a sensible, competent artist, Fieramosca, already is available in Rome. Teresa, who seems completely disinterested, watches her father silently as he leaves the room, shaking his head.

No sooner has he gone, however, than she rushes to the open window and listens to a chorus of masquers in the street. They are singing in anticipation of Mardi Gras, which will begin on the following evening— Shrove Tuesday, 1532.

Suddenly a bouquet of flowers is thrown through the window. Picking it up, Teresa finds a note from Cellini, her lover. She realizes then that the singers were Cellini and his friends and apprentices. In a melodious cavatina, "Entre l'amour et le devoir," she reflects on how she is torn between her love for the sculptor and her filial duty. Then, over a sprightly waltz theme, she sings that she will put off any decisions on the matter until she is older and wiser—like her parents.

At the conclusion of the song, Cellini enters. In the aria "Ô Teresa, vous que j'aime" he tells her how much he loves her—and at the same time makes it clear that he objects to her being pledged to his rival, the sculptor Fieramosca.

While the two are busy with their love-making, Fieramosca himself comes mincing in on tiptoe, unobserved. He is carrying a huge bouquet of flowers. A trio in tarantella rhythm ensues. While Fieramosca makes simpering avowals of love, Cellini and Teresa—still unaware that he is in the room—ridicule his prowess as a lover and an artist. Unfortunately for the lovers, Fieramosca overhears their plan to run away together to Florence.

As the trio ends, Teresa hears the angry voice of her father outside. At her cry of alarm, Fieramosca darts panic-stricken into Teresa's bedroom. When Balducci comes storming in, flinging open the door, Cellini hides behind it. Scowling at Teresa, Balducci demands to know why she is still up at this late hour. She stammers that there is a strange man in her bedroom. With a bellow of rage Balducci rushes into her room, and while he is gone Teresa helps Cellini escape. Balducci comes back dragging the hapless Fieramosca.

Pandemonium breaks loose as Balducci and Teresa shout for their servants and neighbors to help them rid the premises of this "libertine" who has forced his way into their home. In a tumultuous closing ensemble ("Ah! maître drôle! Ah! libertin!") Fieramosca frantically protests his innocence; Balducci and Teresa denounce him as a lecherous intruder; neighbors and servants, adding their imprecations, comically threaten the cowering young man with dust mops, brooms, meat cleavers and pokers.

ACT TWO

[*Scene One*] The courtyard of an inn. Cellini, alone, sings the aria "Une heure encore," in which he meditates on whether his first duty is to his art or to his beloved Teresa. His reflections are interrupted by the entrance of a noisy crowd of his apprentices and friends, including two of his fellow artisans, Francesco and Bernardino. Cellini joins them in a lusty drinking song, "Si la terre aux beaux jours se couronne."

A comic byplay follows as the innkeeper comes bustling out. To the amusement of the crowd, he whines that he will not serve these rascally young artists another drop of wine until they have paid what they owe him ("Que voulez-vous? La cave est vide"). Luckily for the indigent debtors, Ascanio suddenly shows up with a bag of gold. In the aria "Cette somme t'est due," he announces that he has come from the papal palace with the advance payment to Master Cellini for the statue of Perseus commissioned by Pope Clement.

The others stare in awe as Cellini—whose mind is on getting away to Florence with Teresa as soon as possible—rather casually takes the purse of gold. Counting the money, he exclaims angrily that Balducci has fobbed him off with a miserable fee quite unworthy of a creative artist.

Then and there, Cellini decides to pay Balducci out for the insult. He tells his friends that tonight at the carnival there will be a pantomime performed by the great Cassandro and his troupe, in which Balducci will be burlesqued by the character of King Midas. Cellini adds that he is certain Balducci and Teresa will be in the audience ("Je sais que Balducci quittera sa demeure"). When the cannon sounds to signal the end of Mardi Gras at dawn on Ash Wednesday, and all the lights are extinguished, says Cellini, he will take advantage of the confusion and abduct Teresa. Disguised in a white monk's habit, he will easily be able to carry out his plan.

But—as before—Fieramosca overhears Cellini's plotting. In desperation he goes for advice to his friend Pompeo, a professional assassin. This worthy obligingly suggests that they double-cross Cellini by disguising themselves in monk's habits and carrying out their own abduction of Teresa. The audacity of the scheme terrifies Fieramosca, but Pompeo confidently assures him that if it comes to swordplay he is more than a match for the likes of Cellini.

Fieramosca, trying to bolster his faltering courage, boasts in a mock-heroic aria ("Ah! Qui pourrait me résister") that he will win Teresa by vanquishing his hated rival with a single sword thrust. He and Pompeo then leave to prepare for their escapade.

[*Scene Two*] The Piazza Colonna at the height of the carnival. At one side is the stage upon which the pantomime will take place. There is a brief orchestral prelude which echoes the theme of the trio in Act One.

Balducci and Teresa enter and stand near the stage. A moment later Ascanio, in brown monk's garb, and Cellini, in white, enter and converse in undertones about their plot. The simultaneous conversation of the four merges in a quartet. This builds into an ensemble as the citizens, led by Francesco and Bernardino, gather to express their delight at the prospect of seeing the wonderful pantomime called *King Midas or the Donkey's Ears*.

The performance, in *commedia dell'arte* style, begins with an overture in a melodramatic vein. To the accompaniment of descriptive orchestral sound effects, the traditional characters such as Arlequin and Pasquerello go through their antics. They bow in exaggerated humility to King Midas—an obvious caricature of Balducci with the ears of an ass—who bestows a crown upon Pasquerello. Balducci, infuriated, leaps up on the stage and chases the actors off. The crowd roars with laughter.

Then suddenly Cellini and Ascanio enter from one side of the piazza just as Fieramosca and Pompeo come in from the other side. The two rivals are dressed in white monk's habits. They promptly challenge each other and a fight breaks out—Cellini duels with Pompeo, Ascanio with Fieramosca. Ironically, the encounter takes place against a background of moving figures with lanterns—trysting young lovers among the carnival crowd. There is a sudden, ominous silence in the orchestra. Cellini lunges at Pompeo and kills him on the spot. There is a gasp of horror from the crowd, then all throw themselves on Cellini. Tearing himself free, he rushes away just as the cannon shot booms out and all the lights are extinguished.

ACT THREE

[*Scene One*] Cellini's studio. His goldsmith's furnace is offstage in the rear. It is early the following morning. Teresa rushes in with Ascanio, who is still in his monk's robe. They call out Cellini's name, then hide when Francesco and Bernardino appear. The two artisans urge the foundry workers to their tasks. The latter respond in chorus in a melancholy folk song refrain ("À l'atelier rentrons sans plus attendre"), during which Francesco and Bernardino exit into the foundry.

Ascanio, doing his best to console Teresa—who is now in tears at not finding Cellini—sings a sprightly ballad ("Mais qu'ai-je donc") recalling the goings on at the Mardi Gras carnival. Teresa smiles through her tears as he imitates her own voice as well as those of Cellini, Fieramosca and Balducci.

The two pause to listen to a group of monks outside chanting a prayer to the Virgin Mary. They both sing an obbligato in the form of a hymn, "Sainte Vierge Marie." As their voices die away on a reverent phrase, Cellini bursts in. He is still in his monk's habit.

In an ensuing recitative and air ("Ma dague en main protège par la nuit") he describes how he escaped from the crowd after the fatal duel, then joined a procession of monks to throw his pursuers off his trail. When he tells Ascanio he intends to flee to Florence with Teresa, Ascanio reminds him of his promise to the Pope to finish the statue of Perseus.[1] Cellini snaps that the statue—and the Pope—can go to the devil. He orders Ascanio to inform the apprentices that the foundry will be closed.

Ascanio leaves, but rushes back in with the news that Balducci and Fieramosca at this very moment are outside the door. It bursts open,

---

[1] One of the most renowned sculptures of medieval Italy and today one of the art treasures of Florence. The bronze statue of the helmeted Perseus, holding aloft the severed head of Medusa as he stands with one foot on her body, is in the Loggia della Signoria.

and the two stride in. Cellini and Ascanio stand shoulder to shoulder to hide Teresa from her father.

A turbulent ensemble now follows. Balducci demands to know where Teresa is, roaring that by this time she no doubt has been dishonored. To preserve what is left of her reputation, she must marry Fieramosca at once. Thereupon Cellini bellows that he will tear his rival limb from limb if he dares touch the girl. All at once there is a dead silence. In the next moment the figure of Pope Clement VII looms in the doorway. The scene continues with a dramatic sextet, "À tous péchés pleine indulgence."

The Pope demands to see the statue he has commissioned. When Cellini confesses that it is not yet finished, the Pope sternly declares he will turn the work over to another artist. Infuriated, Cellini shouts that he would not allow "Michelangelo himself" to touch his masterpiece. Seizing a hammer, he lunges toward the mold to smash it to bits, but is restrained by the Pope's guards. In measured, menacing tones ("Je vais entrer à l'atelier") the Pope delivers an ultimatum: Cellini will be pardoned both for his crime of murder and for his insult to His Holiness only if the statue is finished by nightfall. If he fails he will pay with his life. Cellini hastily assures the pontiff that he will require no more than another hour to finish the work. Pope Clement turns and stalks into the foundry, followed by his retinue, leaving Cellini in the hands of four papal guards.

Cellini, thus prevented from escaping, reflects on the course of events in one of the most dramatic arias in the opera, "Sur les monts les plus sauvages." He sings that he would gladly exchange his hectic, stormy life as an artist for the peaceful serenity of a shepherd's existence.

[*Scene Two*] Cellini's foundry, with the furnace in the center. The sculptor is frantically at work, assisted by Francesco and Bernardino. Fieramosca, obviously relishing Cellini's dilemma, warns him that the mold is beginning to congeal because there is not enough metal. Francesco and Bernardino express their dismay.

Inspired by desperation, Cellini shouts to Ascanio and the apprentices to throw into the furnace every bit of metal in the studio—including even some of his completed masterpieces. Cellini works with furious energy. With the casting finally completed, he inscribes on the base of the statue the famous inscription: "Si quis te laeserit, ego tuus ultor ero" ("If anyone harm you, I will be your avenger"). He sings the words on a single note over a sustained chord in the orchestra. Then with his mallet he carefully taps the mold as all in the studio stand transfixed. The mold falls away, and Perseus emerges in all its golden magnificence.

Pope Clement, the apprentices, artisans, friends and townspeople (joined by Fieramosca and Balducci in grudging admiration) hail the crowning achievement of Benvenuto Cellini's genius in a thunderous finale, "Gloire à lui! Les métaux ces fleurs souterraines."

BILLY BUDD

by BENJAMIN BRITTEN

(1913–76)

Libretto by

E. M. FORSTER and ERIC CROZIER

Adapted from the story *Billy Budd, Foretopman,* by Herman Melville, based on an actual incident aboard the U.S. brig-of-war *Somers* in 1842

CHARACTERS

Edward Fairfax Vere, Captain of *H.M.S. Indomitable*	Tenor
Billy Budd, foretopman	Baritone
John Claggart, Master-at-Arms	Bass
Mr. Redburn, First Lieutenant	Baritone
Mr. Flint, Sailing Master	Bass-baritone
Mr. Ratcliffe, Second Lieutenant	Bass
Red Whiskers, an impressed man	Tenor
Donald, a sailor	Baritone
Dansker, an old seaman	Bass
The Novice	Tenor
Squeak, a ship's corporal	Tenor
Bosun	Baritone
First Mate	Baritone
Second Mate	Baritone
Maintop	Tenor
The Novice's friend	Baritone
Arthur Jones, an impressed seaman	Baritone
Four Midshipmen	Boys' voices
Cabin Boy	Spoken

Officers, sailors, powder monkeys, drummers, marines

Place: Aboard *H.M.S. Indomitable,* a "seventy-four" (guns) man-of-war
Time: During the French wars of 1797
First performance: (four-act version) Royal Opera House, Covent Garden, December 1, 1951 (first revised version in two acts) BBC broadcast, November 3, 1961
Original language: English

Britten's sixth work for the musical stage was composed to fulfill the commission for a full-length opera for the Festival of Britain in 1951. It is a powerful musical drama played out against the historical background of the "tall ships"—the mighty British men-of-war that plied the seas during and after the French Revolution. The action takes place on one of them, the *Indomitable,* commanded by Captain Vere—called, in Melville's original, "Starry Vere."

What ignites this action is the threat of *mutiny:* rebellion against the brutality of life on board: impressment,[1] floggings, verminous food, wretched quarters and the like. Billy Budd, convicted of mutiny, swung from the yardarm like many another rebel. But his fate involves, in a larger sense, a philosophical concept: the cosmic struggle between good and evil, innocence and depravity. At opposite poles are Captain Vere, a martinet but a reasonable man; Foretopman Billy, an elemental innocent; and Master-at-Arms Claggart, satanic, "depraved according to nature," as Melville quotes Plato.

The action is expressed mainly in recitatives, which bridge into powerful choral climaxes. There are only occasional monologues or soliloquies that might be termed arias in the conventional sense. Basically—as pointed out by musicologist John Warrack—the opera's musical image is framed by two chord structures: B-flat major and B minor. They represent the two irreconcilable motivating forces of the opera—the pristine goodness of Billy Budd and the monstrous evil of Claggart.

ACT ONE

PROLOGUE

Captain Edward Fairfax Vere, alone in his study. Now an old man, he muses over his long and eventful life at sea ("I am an old man"). Over a gentle, melancholy theme in the strings, he recalls that he has known much goodness and much evil as well. Yet even after the long years since 1797, he is tormented by the terrible decision he was forced to make as captain of his ship, with the power of life and death in his hands. Was his verdict just? Who is condemned: the Captain . . . or the sailor who was hanged? All this happened, Vere sings as the light fades, when he was Commander of the *Indomitable,* so long ago.

[*Scene One*] Main deck and quarterdeck of the *Indomitable.* Working parties, under command of the Bosun, Sailing Master and Mates, are holystoning the deck. Voices of the officers urging the men to their

---

[1] Impressment: illegal seizure of men for duty as seamen, an accepted practice on the high seas during the nineteenth century. One of the major causes of the War of 1812 was Britain's refusal to recognize naturalized American sailors, seizing four thousand by 1810, and impressing most of them into British service.

task with curses and blows are heard over the singing of the men—"O heave! O heave away!" A bullying First Mate lashes a man with a rope. Four Midshipmen, hands on their dirks, sarcastically remind the hapless deckhands that life aboard a man-of-war is not child's play.

Among the men is the Novice, a young boy on his first voyage, confused and frightened. He accidentally bumps into the Bosun, then has the further bad luck to slip and fall when the Bosun gives him the order to "make fast to braces." Thereupon the Bosun orders Squeak, a sniveling ship's corporal, to list the Novice for "twenty strokes." The Novice frantically begs for mercy as Squeak drags him away. The First Mate warns the sailors that anyone else who wants the "cat" need only "go slipping."

The crew leaves, dragging the holystones. A sailor in the maintop calls out that the ship's boarding party is returning from a passing merchantman with three "recruits"—impressed seamen. As the Sailing Master reports the arrivals, a table and chairs are set up on the main deck, where the officers are to question the impressed men and assign them to their duties.

During a colloquy in recitative ("We seem to have the devil's own luck"), the Sailing Master grumbles about the rabble found for impressment—nothing but disease-ridden scum of the streets and jails . . . pimps, lackeys and lickspittles.

Ratcliffe comes aboard followed by the three seamen under guard—Red Whiskers, Arthur Jones and Billy Budd. The officer reports that they were taken from the British merchantman *Rights o' Man*—without resistance.

As they line up for questioning, John Claggart appears. Glowering at them, he begins. The first man, Red Whiskers, refuses to give his name until Claggart threatens him with his rattan. When he protests that his seizure was illegal, Claggart again threatens him with a beating. Red finally answers that he is forty-eight years old, a butcher by trade, and that his home is in Bristol. He continues growling under his breath until silenced by Claggart, then is assigned to the forepeak.

The next man, Arthur Jones, meekly submits to questioning. He answers that he is thirty-four years old, a weaver from Spitalfields. He too is assigned to the forepeak. When he is led away the officers again complain about the sorry specimens of humanity they are obliged to take on as crewmen.

Claggart orders Billy Budd to come forward. In contrast to the other two, he speaks up with disarming candor: his name is Billy Budd, able seaman . . . doesn't know his age . . . can't read, but can sing. Never mind the singing, Claggart growls. The other officers are impressed by Billy's good looks and his straightforward bearing. Fine recruit, they agree. But on further questioning, they discover a "flaw": he stammers. Shaking their heads regretfully, the officers ask Claggart his opinion of this specimen. As though judging an animal, he replies that here is one find in a thousand . . . a beauty . . . a pearl of great price.

Thus—stammer and all—Billy meets the test and is forthwith signed on as foretopman. Delighted, he thanks the officers profusely and expresses his satisfaction in a ringing refrain—"Billy Budd, king of the birds!" He exults that he will be happy high in his perch above the deck "among the sea hawks." Then, looking seaward, he shouts goodbye to his shipmates aboard the merchantman—"Farewell, *Rights o' Man!*" The officers gasp in dismay. With the bloody mutinies of Spithead and The Nore fresh in their minds, the very phrase itself has a sinister connotation. It smacks of incitement to *revolution*—the infection that spread from Paris to the French Navy (the "floating republic"), thence to the British Navy.[2] Ratcliffe orders Billy to go below; then he and the other officers warn Claggart to keep an eye on this young fellow—fine chap, but dangerous . . . with all that "Rights o' Man" talk. The Master-at-Arms vindictively answers that he has heard—and understands.

As the officers leave he muses with bitter contempt over their stupidity in assuming it necessary to warn him—Claggart, of all people—about this upstart ("I heard, your honor"). His brief aside seethes with hatred of this honest, comely youngster who represents everything Claggart despises. In answer to his call, Squeak, the ratlike corporal who is his spy, comes scurrying up on the main deck.

Claggart tells him to keep an eye on "that man." When Squeak misunderstands, Claggart berates him for being too stupid to know he means Billy Budd. He orders the spy to do anything he can to provoke Billy and get him into trouble. His efforts, Claggart assures him, will be duly rewarded. Thanking him, Squeak slinks away.

A sailor, a friend of the Novice, approaches to tell Claggart that the Novice is in such agony after the flogging that he cannot walk. Let him crawl, Claggart sneers. The Novice appears, delirious with pain, supported by several sailors. He moans that he is "lost . . . done for . . . forever on an endless sea." The sailors repeat his phrases in a chantlike rhythm. His friend gives him what comfort he can, telling him his bruises will soon heal.

Billy, Dansker, Red Whiskers and Donald come up just in time to see the sailors drag the stricken Novice away. Billy stares in horror at the boy's lacerated back ("Christ! the poor chap!"). Red, in cold rage at the sight, swears he will never submit to flogging. Dansker and Donald, hard-bitten seamen, make it plain to him that he too is likely to get the "cat"—fifty . . . maybe a hundred strokes. Hurts, they add laconically.

[2] Spithead: the roadstead south of England, between Portsea and the Isle of Wight. The Nore: the name given to the Thames estuary east of Sheerness. The Nore outbreak was called the Great Mutiny.

The two fall to joshing, half seriously, about the nicknames given the new recruits: "Whiskers" and "Beauty." The former objects indignantly to the monicker, whereupon Donald tweaks his beard. Billy, however, good-naturedly accepts Dansker's appellation of "Beauty."

As bosun's whistles signal the change of watch, Claggart enters with other officers and sailors. Orders to go aloft are shouted. Confronting Billy, Claggart roughly snatches a brightly colored scarf from Billy's neck, sneering that such fancy regalia has no place on a man-of-war. Addressing Billy with vicious emphasis as "Beauty," he warns him to watch his behavior.

When Claggart and the officers leave, Billy turns to Donald and naïvely expresses surprise at Claggart's apparent interest in him. Donald answers in an ominous whisper: "That's Jemmy Legs—steer clear of him." The warning is lost on Billy, who goes on to ask about the Captain. We call him "Starry Vere," says Donald, and then he and Dansker launch into enthusiastic praise of the Captain ("He's the best of them all!"). This builds into a lusty ensemble as the sailors hail Starry Vere as the hero who will lead them in victory over the hated French, "who killed their own King."

Catching their spirit, Billy himself extols Starry Vere as the Captain he would gladly die for. The ensemble rises to a strident climax as all on deck join in the chorus of praise. It is abruptly cut off as the Bosun strides in and orders everybody belowdecks.

[*Scene Two*] Vere's cabin. Evening, a week later. Vere, reading Plutarch, muses that the Greeks and Romans, and he himself, were bedeviled by the same problems. In quiet desperation, he prays. Closing his book, he sends a Cabin Boy to call in the First Lieutenant and the Sailing Master for a glass of wine. The three toast the King.

Then Vere announces that the ship is now approaching Cape Finisterre (off the northwest Spanish coast), in enemy territory where they may finally go into action. Redburn and Flint welcome the news and assure Vere that the entire ship is standing ready to come to grips with the "Frenchies." The scene continues in a crackling duet as Redburn and Flint join, to a dancelike rhythm, in deriding the French ("Don't like the French!"). In a burst of chauvinistic fervor they loudly acclaim the virtues of England ("British brawn and beef"). Vere, smiling indulgently at their patriotic ardor, proposes another toast: *"To the French— down with them!"*

The harmonies suddenly take on a darker hue as Redburn wonders if there is any danger that the infamous French revolutionary doctrines will spread to England. Vere sums it up in one ominous word: *mutiny.* The two officers react in surprise and rage ("Spithead, The Nore, the floating republic"). Then Vere bursts into a tirade ("The Nore—what had we there?") against the godless French, whose spurious notions of liberty and justice spread like poison through the Royal British Navy and precipitated the mutinies.

Vere calls for constant vigilance to ward off rebellion aboard the *Indomitable*. Redburn and Flint agree that Claggart is the man to handle the situation—with special attention to the young fellow who prates about the "rights of man" and other dangerous nonsense. Vere, however, discounts possibility of trouble from that quarter. Such talk, he remarks mildly, is merely a matter of youthful high spirits.

As if to vindicate his faith in the loyalty of his crew, the sound of singing comes up from belowdecks ("Blow her away"). Vere listens for a moment, then quietly observes that when there is happiness there is little likelihood of discontent. In a tone of fatherly concern he adds that the service owes much to these seamen. Torn from their homes, forced into arduous duty, they still obey orders and work with a will. All the same, Redburn and Flint remark skeptically, some of these fellows will bear watching.

Ratcliffe enters to report that landfall has been made and that the ship is now in Cape Finisterre. There's work ahead, Vere tells the officers as they take their leave. He takes up his book and, in phrases sung on a single repeated note ("At the Battle of Salamis"), he reads aloud to himself. As the sound of chanteys again rises from belowdecks, Vere closes the book and listens with obvious pleasure. The singing continues as the scene changes.

[*Scene Three*] The berth deck, with a series of gun bays in which seamen have stowed their kit bags and slung their hammocks.

In one of the bays, Billy, Donald, Red and Dansker join with the other sailors in continuing the chantey, "Blow her to Hilo, Riley." They gather closer as the four lead them in their traditional favorites: "We're off to Samoa," "We're towing to Malta," "We're off to Savannah," "We're off to Nantucket," "We're off to Bermuda." The raffish lyrics are set to catchy, rhythmic tunes.

Billy urges Dansker to sing along, but the seaman answers that he is too old for singing—and for dancing and women as well. All he longs for now, he adds, is a plug o' baccy. With characteristic generosity Billy offers to lend him a chew, then walks over to his kit bag to get his supply. Watching him, Dansker shakes his head, muttering that the lad's trouble is that he is too good.

Suddenly the scene of camaraderie erupts into violence. Billy catches Squeak rifling his kit bag and begins to stammer angrily. The other sailors notice this and realize something is amiss. Billy drags the squirming corporal into the open and curses him for meddling. The sailors join Billy in accusing Squeak of thievery. One of them shouts that Squeak has a knife. Quick as a flash, Billy twists his knife arm and the weapon clatters to the deck. Squeak struggles free. Billy chases him around the deck and knocks him down.

At that moment, Claggart and two of his corporals appear. His angry command cows the sailors into silence. Catching sight of Dansker, he orders him to explain. Playing down the incident, Dansker answers noncommittally that Billy found Squeak near his kit bag and dragged him away . . . Squeak pulled a knife . . . Billy knocked him down. . . .

Claggart, instantly aware that Squeak has botched his scheme to compromise Billy, orders him put in irons. When the spy tries to say he was only following instructions, Claggart orders him gagged as well. Smiling evilly, he turns to Billy with a compliment for having done "handsomely" in the encounter. With that he orders the deck cleared and lights out, then begins pacing slowly back and forth. In the gloom, a Cabin Boy stumbles against him; Claggart savagely strikes him with his rattan. The boy screams in pain.

From the distance comes the chanting of the sailors, burdened with the wistful longing for home ("Into the harbor, carry me home"). It is an ironic antiphony to Claggart's malevolent soliloquy which now follows ("O beauty, O handsomeness, goodness!"). A satanic apostrophe to all the world's evil, it is Claggart's "Credo"—like Iago's in *Otello*. It is the most extended single utterance in the opera comparable to the aria form.

In deepening tones of menace over a sinister accompaniment, Claggart curses the fate that has brought him face to face with goodness, love and the joy of living. The peace that he found in his own "natural depravity"—the peace of Hell—is now shattered, and he who shattered it must be wiped from the face of the earth. Nothing can save him from the doom which he—John Claggart, Master-at-Arms on the *Indomitable* —has fashioned out of envy, hate and despair. The soliloquy dies away in a ferocious whisper.

On the companionway, Claggart comes upon the hapless Novice. With deceptive gentleness he asks the lad if he will do a job for him. Demoralized by the flogging, the Novice answers that he will do anything asked of him. Claggart promises to protect him if he fails—as Squeak has failed. In a pitiful boast, the Novice assures Claggart that he is much cleverer than the likes of Squeak—they always told him so at home.

Preparing to close the trap, Claggart asks the boy if he would betray a shipmate—a disloyal shipmate—by pretending to join him in a mutiny. Here Claggart holds out a handful of guineas, saying: bribe him, and if he takes the bait, come and tell me. When the Novice asks who the victim is to be, Claggart rasps: Billy Budd.

In surprise and horror, the Novice gasps: "Not that one. He's *good!*"

At the sound of the word, Claggart strikes him again and again in a paroxysm of rage. Finally, at the threat of more flogging the Novice abjectly promises to do the job. Claggart hands him the coins and stalks away.

Beside himself with terror and despair, the Novice cries out against the fate that doomed him to this accursed ship and the betrayal of a shipmate he loves ("Why had it to be Billy?"). Goaded by fear of punishment, he faces up to the situation and resolutely goes to the gun bay, where Billy is asleep in his hammock.

Deep in his dreams ("It's dreaming I am . . . fathoms down"), Billy responds drowsily as the Novice whispers his name. Finally awake, he climbs out of his hammock and follows the boy to a vacant gun bay, where the frightened youngster tries his hand at treachery.

First he reminds Billy that he and his shipmates are victims of the press-gangs—forced into navy service, forced to submit to floggings, backbreaking labor, stinking food. It's gone too far, he goes on, and there's a gang aboard that wants to call a halt . . . but they need a leader. Thrusting out the handful of guineas, the Novice asks Billy point-blank if he will help.

Beginning to understand, Billy becomes enraged and struggles to stammer a reply. Unable to speak, he raises his fist. The Novice scrambles out of reach and disappears. Now Dansker, who had heard Billy's stammering outburst, asks him what happened. The Novice, Billy replies incredulously, offered him a handful of guineas to lead a mutiny. He showed the scoundrel his fist, Billy adds, and he left—guineas and all.

Dansker, who realizes what is happening, looks at him without a word. Puzzled by his silence, Billy asks if there is anything he wants—another plug of baccy, perhaps. . . . In answer, Dansker somberly warns Billy to beware of Jemmy Legs. But Billy lightheartedly scoffs at the thought that the Master-at-Arms has any ill will toward him: why, he even smiled . . . called him a "handsome fellow" . . . acted like a friend.

The scene continues in duet form as Billy, in his naïve optimism, sings that everybody likes him, he likes his shipmates ("And the life suits me"). His exuberance contrasts emotionally and musically with Dansker's grim interjections. Billy triumphantly sings that he has heard that he is in line for promotion to captain of the mizzentop. Over Dansker's dolorous litany ("Beauty, you're a fool"), Billy sings joyously of a shining world where friendship is supreme. On this fusion of contrasting themes the act comes to a close.

ACT TWO

[*Scene One*] Main deck and quarterdeck, a few days later. Vere is there with his officers, looking gloomily out over a gray misty sea. He observes that the mist will delay contact with the enemy and notes, with some concern, that the men are getting restive because of long inaction. At this point Claggart approaches, cap in hand to indicate he wishes to speak to the captain.

Deliberately obsequious, he begins by saying that his obligation to his Captain, as an honorable officer, forces him to speak on a matter he would rather not discuss. Vere, with his mind on the impending battle, testily tells him to get on with it. Although he would rather keep silent, Claggart goes on servilely, he must report that there is great danger aboard.

He is interrupted by a cry from the lookout aloft that an enemy ship has been sighted. The entire ship stirs into feverish action. Officers and sailors exult that they are closing in on the enemy ("The French at last"). Over an agitated accompaniment orders are shouted; the men turn to the task of preparing the ship for battle. There are conflicting estimates of the size of the ship and her distance from the *Indomitable*.

Vere finally identifies the Frenchman as a "seventy-four, new-rigged." He gives orders for pursuit ("Man the braces, Mr. Flint") and the commotion increases. Gunners run to their stations; the Bosun and the Sailing Master bellow at the men hauling sail; young chattering powder monkeys run forward with charges. A detachment of marines marches smartly to battle stations. Everywhere the cry goes up: "This is what we've been waiting for! Now for deeds!"

The guns are ready, but the wind is dying and the Frenchman is drawing out of range. Hoping for a breeze, the gunners are pleading for a chance to fire. On the quarterdeck, Vere remains calm and urges patience. Finally he orders a trial shot from the "long eighteens." There is a tremendous explosion offstage. But from the maintop comes the disappointing report: "Short by half a mile." Then the cry goes up that the wind is dropping. A miasma of gloom and frustration settles over the ship; the men curse the gathering mist.

Vere regretfully tells his officers that "the chase is foolish," then gives orders to dismiss. Grumbling, the men leave their stations. Noticing their morose demeanor, the officers apprehensively comment that now there may be trouble: the restless waiting will go on again, fomenting discontent. This will call for vigilance ("We must keep watch").

All the officers leave the quarterdeck except Redburn, Flint and Ratcliffe, who withdraw to the background. Vere himself stands alone, deep in thought. Claggart reappears, cap in hand. When Vere orders him to speak ("Be brief, for God's sake"), Claggart launches into his contemptible report ("As brief as my theme allows").

There is a dangerous man aboard, he begins, a man fit for the crimes of Spithead and The Nore. A common seaman he is—but sly and clever —who is stirring up (Claggart pauses for effect): *mutiny*. Vere demands proof, whereupon Claggart shows him the handful of guineas. With these, Claggart lies, the mutineer tried to corrupt an innocent boy. This mutineer, Vere asks, who is he? William Budd, Claggart replies.

Vere flatly refuses to believe the story. In a striking musical interlude, he and Claggart argue the matter. The Master-at-Arms sneers about Billy's "masculine beauty," while Vere defends him as a promising foretopman. As for the so-called evidence of mutiny, the Captain sharply reminds Claggart that the penalty for giving false witness is hanging. Finally losing patience, Vere sends for Billy and tells Claggart he is to confront the man with his accusations. He dismisses the Master-at-Arms.

The three officers then approach the Captain and report that the gathering mist has favored the escape of the French ship. The murky shroud that envelops the quarterdeck is symbolic of the confusion and frustration that weigh upon Vere as he pleads, in a lyrical phrase, for "the light of clear Heaven, to separate evil from good."

[*Scene Two*] Vere's cabin, where he is waiting for Billy. The music continues during the change of scene, with a French horn theme underscoring the Captain's opening soliloquy ("John Claggart, beware"). You are evil, he sings. The boy is good—and you shall fail.

Billy enters, aglow with boyish expectation, certain that the Captain has summoned him to tell him of his promotion—or even make him his coxswain. Impetuously he exclaims: "I'd serve you well indeed!" Vere, deeply moved by his devotion, wonders if this indeed is the sly plotter who is fomenting mutiny.

Obviously distressed, Vere forces himself to tell Billy that he has been summoned not for promotion but for questioning. Still radiating confidence, Billy stands to attention as Claggart is admitted. The inquisition begins as the Captain explains the proceedings ("Master-at-Arms and foretopman"). Staring malevolently at Billy, Claggart intones the indictment: *insubordination . . . aiding the enemy . . . bribing with French gold . . .* MUTINY.

Reeling back in horror, Billy can only stammer incoherently. Vere puts a hand on his shoulder to steady him. Suddenly losing all control, Billy, screaming, "Devil," strikes Claggart violently on the forehead. The man crumples to the floor and lies there motionless. Foreboding chords thunder in the orchestra as Vere, with an agonized cry ("God o' mercy!") kneels down and raises the lifeless body. On the verge of panic, he orders Billy into a small stateroom off the cabin, then frantically calls for his officers. In a dramatic soliloquy ("The mists have cleared") he sings that while he now must consign Billy to certain doom, it is he himself who is condemned to utter ruin. Redburn, Flint and Ratcliffe rush in. Vere tells them that Billy has murdered the Master-at-Arms.

In the ensuing ensemble ("Great God! For what reason?"), the officers and Vere express their reactions—Ratcliffe urges mercy, Flint calls for hanging, Redburn demands an immediate trial, Vere thinks only of a "doomed angel." The orchestra underscores the dialogue with thudding tympani and sonorous brasses.

The Captain immediately establishes a drumhead court, with Ratcliffe presiding, and with the Captain himself as sole witness. Vere describes the fatal scene as it occurred in his presence; Billy confirms his testimony. Stoutly affirming his loyalty to his King, he shouts that the accusation of mutiny is a foul lie. His tongue "would not work" when he tried to answer Claggart, he goes on, and he could only reply with the blow that killed the Master-at-Arms.

Vere, asked for more corroborating evidence, answers that he has nothing more to say. He controls himself with an effort as Billy begs him to intercede, and stands motionless as the boy is led back to the stateroom.

Over a portentous theme in the orchestra, the three officers discuss the momentous decision they now must make in accordance with the Articles of War, the King's Regulations, the Mutiny Act. Then there is Claggart, the most hated man on the ship. There is Billy, whom everybody loved. To a somber theme in the brasses, the officers reiterate, like a chant of doom: "We've no choice." When they finally appeal to Vere for advice, he curtly asks for a verdict. They answer: guilty . . . death by hanging from the yardarm. Vere concurs, orders Claggart's burial with full military honors, sets the hour for Billy's execution at one bell in the morning. The court is adjourned. Vere remains alone, deep in thought.

Then crashing discords break out in the orchestra as he begins a dramatic monologue ("I accept their verdict"). He gives way to remorse and haunting self-guilt: it is through him at last that beauty and goodness will be destroyed. In an anguished phrase sung on a single note he cries out that he, Captain of the *Indomitable,* is "lost with all hands on an infinite sea." The phrase is underscored by the savage blare of trumpets and the keening of flutes. Going to the door of the stateroom, Vere sings despairingly that he is the messenger of death. The music gradually subsides into a mood of quiet serenity.

[*Scene Three*] A bay of the gun deck, where Billy is in irons between two cannon. It is shortly before dawn the following morning.

In a profoundly moving ballad, "Through the port comes the moonshine astray," Billy muses quietly on his impending fate. He is calm and resigned. All is up, he sings, but he hopes he won't be sent aloft on an empty stomach. Perhaps a messmate will bring him a last drink and a biscuit. . . . He takes comfort in knowing that Donald will stand by as he walks the plank. Then, he goes on in descending *sotto voce* phrases, he'll go fathoms down to dream his last dream.[3]

Dansker interrupts his reverie to bring him a mug of grog and a biscuit. Billy thanks him warmly ("Dansker, old friend") but worries that this act of kindness may get him into trouble. The old seaman tells him there is talk belowdecks of trying to rescue him—because his mates love him. Billy vehemently objects to this rash move and urges Dansker to head off their plans. Then his thoughts wander to the failure of the chase —how the French ship escaped in the accursed mist. Perhaps, he says, there'll be a fair day, and you can still catch him.

He bids Dansker goodbye. Holding up his manacled hands, he begins his farewell soliloquy ("Can't shake hands"). In a kind of mystical transport he recalls the tragic events that spawned his doom. To the accompaniment of muted drumbeats and sonorous trombone phrases he accepts the decree of Fate: he was destined to strike down Jemmy Legs; Starry Vere ("God bless him") was destined to strike down Billy Budd.

As he sings farewell to *Rights o' Man* and his shipmates, Dansker leaves unnoticed. In serene but triumphant phrases Billy sings that he is strong and he is content—hanging doesn't matter: "That's all, and that's enough."

[*Scene Four*] The main deck and the quarterdeck. It is four o'clock in the morning and dawn is breaking. To an orchestral tumult of clashing discords, fanfares and drumbeats, officers and crew assemble. Finally Billy, flanked by a marine guard detail, is marched in. Second Lieutenant Ratcliffe steps forward and reads the Articles of War, then the sentence of death. The words are intoned on a single repeated note until the final descending phrase: "death . . . by hanging from the yardarm."

Suddenly Billy's voice rings out, clearly and exultantly: "Starry Vere, God bless you!" His benediction is echoed with savage intensity by the seamen.

Ratcliffe snaps shut his book. A marine barks an order and Billy is marched toward the mainmast (offstage). All eyes are riveted on him.

---

[3] This ballad is a setting of part of the poem, "Billy in the Darbies," with which Melville ended his story. Melville wrote of it: "the general estimate of his nature . . . eventually found rude utterance from another foretopman, one of his own watch, gifted, as some sailors are, with an artless poetic temperament. . . . The lines . . . finally got rudely printed in Portsmouth as a ballad. The title given to it was the sailor's."

Captain Vere takes off his hat. Then follows a terrifying ensemble effect: a sinister growling wells up from the packed throng on deck and surges up like the thunder of surf in a hurricane.[4] Rebellion flares in the eyes of the sailors as they glare up at the quarterdeck.

The officers stir apprehensively, but Vere stands motionless. Ratcliffe, Flint and Redburn harshly rap out the order for "Down all hands." Almost instinctively the men obey and slowly clear the deck. The clamor of the music dies into a major chord as the light slowly fades.

EPILOGUE

Captain Vere alone in his study, as in the Prologue. Haunted by memories, he relives the terrible ordeal of murder and retribution so many years ago ("We committed his body to the deep"). Even now he is tortured by remorse as he confesses to himself that he could have saved Billy's life. And yet . . . the very man he condemned saved his Captain's soul because of "a love that passeth understanding."

Reverently he repeats the words of Billy's farewell: "but I've sighted a sail in the storm, the far-shining sail. . . ." And so now he can return at last in peace to that summer of 1797—centuries ago—when Edward Fairfax Vere commanded the *H.M.S. Indomitable.*

The curtain falls.

[4] Melville wrote: "The silence at the moment of execution . . . was gradually disturbed by a sound not easily to be verbally rendered. Whoever has heard the freshet-wave of a torrent suddenly swelled by pouring showers in tropical mountains, showers not shared by the plain; whoever has heard the first muffled murmur of its sloping advance through precipitous woods, may form some conception of the sound now heard."

CAPRICCIO

"A conversation piece for music in one act"

by RICHARD STRAUSS

(1864–1949)

Libretto by

CLEMENS KRAUSS and RICHARD STRAUSS

Based on the libretto of an old Italian "opera parody" by Abate
Giovanni Battista Casti (1724–1803), with music by Antonio Salieri

CHARACTERS

The Countess Madeleine	Soprano
The Count, her brother	Baritone
Flamand, a composer	Tenor
Olivier, a poet	Baritone
La Roche, the theater director	Bass
Clairon, an actress	Contralto
Monsieur Taupe, the prompter	Tenor
An Italian singer	Soprano
An Italian tenor	
A young dancer	
Major-domo	Bass
Eight servants	Four tenors, four basses

Three musicians

Place: A château near Paris
Time: About 1775—during the period when the German composer
Christoph Willibald von Gluck began his reform of opera
First performance: Munich, October 28, 1942
Original language: German

Capriccio is not an opera—the composer himself did not call it that. As
his subtitle indicates, it has to do with a musical conversation among a
group of witty and sophisticated artists in a fashionable eighteenth-cen-

tury salon near Paris, and as such it has no plot. It is a blend of solos, ensembles and spoken dialogue in the Singspiel pattern.

The salon discussion centers on the rather esoteric question of the relative importance of words and music, and the participants eventually come to the conclusion that this problem is solved only when words and music are give their respective values in the creation of a work of art. But it is by no means a pretentious intellectual exercise. With superb artistry, Strauss has presented his "conversation" with deep human feeling and enchanting lyricism.

Capriccio is Strauss's fifteenth and last work written for the stage. What is called his "last opera"—written in conventional form—is *Die Liebe der Danaë,* which he completed some three years prior to *Capriccio.*

It was during that period, in fact, that Strauss read the libretto of Casti's "opera parody," which had been sent him by the German writer Stefan Zweig. But Strauss decided he did not want to write simply another opera—he was interested in "something unusual, a treatise on dramaturgy, a theatrical fugue." Accordingly, he discussed his plan with Clemens Krauss, director of the Munich State Opera. The upshot of it was that the two men fashioned *Capriccio* from the Casti libretto. It was given its premiere under Krauss's direction.

Since then it has been in the repertoire of most of the important opera houses in Europe, where it has enjoyed great popularity. While it has been performed less frequently in America, it has always met with success. Its first performance in this country was given by a cast of graduate students of the Juilliard School of Music in New York City in May 1954. Its first professional performance was given by the New York City Opera Company on October 27, 1965.

Although the work is scored for a fairly large orchestra, its full volume is reserved for a few climactic moments in the action, with voices and accompaniment always kept in dynamic relationship. The overture itself is played by a string sextet; it states the leading musical themes heard later throughout the work.

The entire action takes place in the salon of the young widowed Countess Madeleine. At the rear, tall glass doors lead to the terrace, beyond which is a park. At one side is a door leading to the dining room; another door downstage leads to the Countess' chamber. At the other side, a door leads to the stage of the private theater. In the salon, chairs and divans are casually arranged. Candles in wall sconces light the scene.

[*Scene One*] It is early afternoon on the Countess' birthday. Flamand, a composer, and Olivier, a poet, are standing near the door listening to the string sextet which Flamand composed for the occasion, and which serves as the "overture." (Throughout the action, the music continues without interruption from scene to scene.) Near the center of the room, La Roche, the theater director, is asleep in an armchair.

Flamand comments that the Countess looks enchanting as she listens from her room with eyes closed. Olivier, nodding toward La Roche, asks if he too is "enchanted." The two men speculate as to whether the Countess is charmed by words or by music, and in the process they both disclose that they are in love with her.

Olivier insists that words come first, then music: "prima le parole—dopo la musica." Flamand argues the contrary. They sing the Italian in echoing phrases. Finally they compromise: It is a matter of words *and* music.

As the music of the sextet dies away, La Roche wakes up and remarks that one sleeps best to soft harmonies. Half in mockery, Olivier wonders why an artist's fate must be in the hands of a man like this—pity poor Gluck! La Roche retorts that, without a theater director, an artist's creations are nothing but paper ("Ohne mich sind eure Werke totes Papier"). At the mention of Gluck, a brief phrase from his *Iphigenia in Aulis* sounds in the orchestra.

An argument ensues in trio form. Flamand and Olivier champion Gluck's reforms leading to emphasis on subject matter, while La Roche insists that nothing surpasses Italian opera, with its glorification of vocal art.

When Flamand and Olivier deride the bad librettos of the old Italian school, La Roche cites the successes of Piccini and Goldoni.[1] The latter, he says, once remarked that the new operas were "heaven for the eyes, but hell for the ears." The argument grows more heated as Flamand and Olivier ridicule the trivial farces performed for the masses. La Roche insists that the people want flesh-and-blood human beings, spectacular scenery and beautiful women on the stage—not static figures out of the dead past.

The mention of women brings up the name of the actress Clairon, who is expected at the rehearsal of La Roche's play. The controversy over aesthetics is forgotten as the three discuss the beauty and talent of this famous actress.[2] It is brought out that Olivier is currently her admirer—but now the Count seems destined to take his place. La Roche suddenly notices that the Countess is leaving her room, and now the

[1] Niccolò Piccini (1728–1800), Italian composer and Gluck's rival. Carlo Goldoni (1707–93), Italian dramatist and librettist.

[2] Mlle. Clairon (1723–1803). Real name, Claire Josèphe Hippolyte Léris de la Tude.

stage must be prepared for the rehearsal. The three hurry into the theater.

[*Scene Two*] Countess Madeleine enters with her brother, the Count. They converse in one of the principal duets of the opera, which begins as the Countess sings that the flood of musical sounds transported her to an enchanted land ("Der Strom der Töne"). In the ensuing dialogue, they discuss music versus poetry, the Countess' romantic interest in the poet and the composer and the Count's probable adventure with Clairon. The duet comes to a richly melodious climax as the two sing that truth, beauty and happiness—the greatest treasures in life— are easily lost, but as easily won ("Leicht zu verlieren").

[*Scene Three*] La Roche comes back with Flamand and Olivier to announce that the program in honor of Madeleine's birthday is about to begin. First, he says, there will be a symphony by Flamand, then a play by himself and finally a dazzling production by the entire company— which will include singers from the Italian opera. This is greeted with disparaging remarks from Flamand and Olivier about the probable quality of that portion of the performance.

Any further argument, however, is interrupted by the arrival of the actress Clairon. Her carriage is seen through the doors of the terrace, and the Count hurries out to meet her. The Countess remarks that the renowned tragedienne is dressed in ordinary traveling costume. Olivier compliments La Roche on having persuaded Clairon to appear in the play; Flamand remarks that if she could sing she would be completely irresistible.

[*Scene Four*] The Count brings in Clairon, whom he presents to the Countess with suave formality. The Countess greets her with studied courtesy, while La Roche melodramatically acclaims her as the embodiment of "Andromaque, Phèdre, Medea, Roxane."

Clairon modestly acknowledges the compliment, then asks Olivier if he has finished the drama she and the Count are to enact. He answers that only this morning he was inspired to write a beautiful sonnet. The Count then shows her the poet's manuscript, and the two begin reading their lines in spoken dialogue. It is a highly dramatic scene in which two lovers bid each other farewell before the lover departs for the battlefield. Its climax is the sonnet, which is read by the Count ("Kein Andres, das mir so im Herzen loht").[3]

At the conclusion of the reading, Clairon enthusiastically commends

[3] In reality, the German translation of a poem by Pierre de Ronsard (1524–85), a French lyric poet.

the Count on his histrionic talent. Then she ceremoniously hands the manuscript to La Roche and commands him to produce the drama on the spot. La Roche tells her that the theater is ready, then turns to go. When Olivier starts to follow, the director advises him to wait—he is too tenderhearted to allow the author to be present while his work is being prepared for the stage. With that La Roche goes into the theater, followed by Clairon and the Count.

The Countess watches her brother with a knowing smile. Turning to Olivier, she says that the lover in his play expressed himself ardently indeed. The words, Olivier answers, were addressed to the wrong person—and he will now correct that error. He thereupon fervently repeats the sonnet to the Countess herself. As she listens, Flamand goes to the clavichord and begins to improvise a melody to fit the words of the sonnet over a graceful waltz theme ("Und trüg ich's fünfmal hundert tausend").

Saying that so lovely an avowal should not be proclaimed publicly, the Countess takes the manuscript from Olivier. Flamand, exclaiming that he already can hear the music which the words inspire, takes the manuscript from the Countess and rushes into the adjoining room to compose.

[*Scene Five*] Olivier protests that now Flamand will ruin the sonnet with his music. Perhaps the music will make the words more beautiful, the Countess says, then provocatively asks the poet if he has anything to say to her in prose—now that they are alone.

A lyrical colloquy in an elegant waltz tempo follows as Olivier declares his love ("Meine Prosa verstummt") and the Countess responds. When Olivier entreats her to affirm her position on the issue of "words or music," she answers that she cannot decide. Music enchants her, she explains, but she also cherishes the intellectual beauty of words. Well then, Olivier sings, concluding the duet, name the victor. At that moment, Flamand rushes in with a sheet of music in his hand, hears Olivier's words, and cries: "Here he is!"

[*Scene Six*] Sitting down at the clavichord, Flamand sings the sonnet in one of the opera's most beautiful arias, "Kein Andres, das mir so im Herzen loht." This in turn leads into a magnificent trio as the Countess and Olivier express their reaction. The Countess ponders whether words give birth to music or music gives life to words. Olivier laments that the composer's "ear-tickling" sounds have robbed his verses of their symmetry. The poet's words, then, are merely the steps on which the composer climbs to victory.

At the end of the trio Olivier demands to know to whom the sonnet now belongs: to himself or to Flamand. "If you will allow me," the

Countess answers graciously, taking the music from Flamand's hand, "it is mine."

At this point, La Roche comes in and says he needs Olivier's help in making certain cuts in his play. He and the poet go back into the theater.

[*Scene Seven*] Now it is Flamand's turn to declare his love for the Countess. First he asks her to decide which will win the prize: music or poetry. Then he pours out his love in an impassioned aria, "Diese Liebe, plötzlich geboren."

He describes how, this very afternoon, love suddenly awakened as he watched her reading a book in the library, where he had entered unobserved. When she left, he had picked up the book she had put down opened and had read the words of Pascal: "In love, silence is better than speech" ("In der Liebe ist Schweigen besser").[4] For a long while he had sat there in the deepening twilight, and in that silence he became a changed man. Now, he sings, he asks only one word from her to crown his rapture. The Countess promises that he will have his answer in the library at eleven o'clock tomorrow morning. Exultantly singing her name, Flamand impetuously kisses her arm and rushes away.

During an orchestral interlude, the Countess, deeply moved, reflects on Flamand's avowals. From the theater come the sounds of the rehearsal, punctuated by occasional laughter. Stirred out of her reverie, the Countess rings and orders her Major-domo to serve chocolate.

[*Scene Eight*] The Count enters, full of enthusiasm over Clairon's acting—and her praise of his own performance. But he scoffs at the Countess' implication that he is falling victim to Clairon's charms. Her own situation, says the Countess, is more serious: Both Olivier and Flamand already have made violent declarations of love to her. It all came about after Flamand had set Olivier's sonnet to music—and what is more, the Countess adds, half in jest, the net result of all this may even be an opera. The Count mockingly compliments her on her role as the Muse. As for himself, he says, he prefers words to music. With equal mockery, his sister wishes him luck with Clairon.

[*Scene Nine*] Clairon, La Roche and Olivier enter from the theater and are joined a moment later by Flamand. After a brief discussion about the progress of the rehearsal, La Roche announces that there now will be a variation in the day's entertainment—by way of a dancer and two Italian singers. At a sign from him, the entertainers come in followed by three musicians with violin, cello and cembalo. First on the

---

4 Blaise Pascal (1623–62), French philosopher.

program is the ballet dancer, who performs three dances—a passepied, gigue and gavotte. The musical dialogue of the onlookers continues throughout the dances.

As they watch the passepied, La Roche informs the Count (who is obviously fascinated) that the beautiful dancer is his latest discovery, for whom he predicts a brilliant career. During the gigue, Clairon and Olivier, in a private quarrel, break off their love affair once for all. At the end of the gavotte, the company applauds the dancer, who goes back into the theater. La Roche remarks to Flamand that in the realm of the dance, at least, music is not the primary element, merely a contribution. Flamand dryly retorts that without music nobody would lift a leg.

This exchange leads into a remarkable section called the Fugue, which is virtually the climax of the opera and which embodies the philosophical concepts underlying the "words versus music" controversy. The section is subtitled "Discussion on the theme: Words or Music." It is a striking example of Strauss's ability to fuse the rhythms of words and music. The fugal theme which dominates the entire section takes its rhythm from the pulse of the opening phrase, "Tanz und Musik stehn im Bann des Rhythmus" ("Words and music are governed by rhythm").

One by one, those in the salon expound their theories. Flamand and Olivier each asserts that his art is supreme, while La Roche insists that music and poetry are nothing more than servants of the stage. He elaborates on his theory in a vigorous refrain in which he declares that the theater's ruling goddess is Fantasy, and all arts serve her. The Countess and Clairon champion the director's viewpoint.

Flamand sings (like the Composer in *Ariadne*) that music is the most sublime of the arts. Olivier argues that words alone can express pain—music is powerless to do so. At that point the Countess brings the debate up short by asking the poet how he can believe that to be true at a time when a "genius" (Gluck) has demonstrated that it is possible to write a "musical tragedy."

Thereupon the Count remarks sardonically that with one more step they will be standing on the edge of the abyss: opera! To derisive comments about the silly conventions of classical opera, the Count adds that opera is an absurdity ("Eine Oper ist ein absurdes Ding").

As the Count speaks these words there is an extraordinary musical effect. The key suddenly changes to A-flat major to introduce an intermezzo in Strauss's most ingratiating musical vein. The melody has its source in the last song of a set of twelve written by Strauss in 1918 and published (1918) in a limited edition of 120 copies under the title

Krämerspiegel (*Shopkeeper's Mirror*).[5] The talk continues about the trend of opera, the boring recitatives and the deafening racket of the orchestra, which drowns out not only the words but the singers themselves.

Finally, La Roche cries dramatically that *bel canto* is at death's door. Thereupon the Countess suggests that he bring in the Italian singers so that the company may hear an example of the dying Italian vocal art. La Roche promptly calls in the Italian soprano and the tenor, and announces that they will sing a duet from an Italian opera with words by Metastasio.[6]

The two singers launch into a duet ("Addio, mia vita"), a parody of the florid, overblown operatics of the pre-Gluck Italian school. While the words have to do with parting and death, the gay, lighthearted accompaniment points up the superficiality of this musical form.

Bored with the performance, the Countess invites the singers to have something to eat. The servants seat them at a small table to the rear of the salon, where the two eat ravenously. Meanwhile, the Count asks Clairon if he may accompany her back to Paris. She gives him permission. The Countess asks La Roche finally to reveal the details of his spectacular production in honor of her birthday.

The director announces that his stupendous "azione teatrale" will be divided into two parts. The first presentation will be *The Birth of Pallas Athene*. This is greeted by the company with sarcastic comments which build up into the first part of an octet, called the "Laughing Ensemble." La Roche and his production become the targets of their ridicule. Meanwhile, the two Italians, stuffing themselves with food, watch the scene and at the same time notice that the director is beginning to lose his temper. While the tenor frets about collecting their fee, the soprano helps herself to the Spanish wine and gradually becomes tipsy.

The Countess, realizing the situation is getting out of hand, tells La Roche that his grandiose production is far beyond the capabilities of the ordinary stage. She begs him not to take the criticism of his productions too seriously. And now, she asks, what is the second part of his show to be?

It will be *The Fall of Carthage,* La Roche informs her, and then goes on to describe this great drama, with its realistic scenery, crowds of actors, lightning, thunderbolts, and a real ship sinking in flames. This sets off the second part of the octet, called the "Quarreling Ensemble." Flamand and Olivier rail at La Roche for offering tawdry theatricals in-

[5] Mentioned in the introductory essay by E. Roth (© 1959) to the Angel recording (35669–70–71) of *Capriccio*.

[6] Pietro Antonio Domenico Bonaventura Metastasio (1698–1782), celebrated Italian poet and librettist.

stead of real drama. They warn him that the day of cheap melodrama is
over, and they will have nothing more to do with his fraudulent arts.

The Count, enjoying the squabble, comments that now the protagonists of the "noble arts" are quarreling among themselves, with the
hapless La Roche—the traditionalist—caught in the cross fire of their attacks. The Countess expresses alarm over the scathing criticism leveled
at the director and implores Flamand and Olivier to desist. La Roche
protests that he is being judged unfairly and demands a chance to defend his principles.

The voices of the Italian singers blend with the ensemble in a comic
parody of their "Addio" duet, in which they sing farewell to their
chances of collecting their fee ("Addio, mio dolce acconto"). Clairon
assures the two that the director will make good his word. He is a man
of action, accustomed to fighting for his rights. When his adversaries
have talked themselves out, he will have his revenge.

Then, as though in proof of her warning, La Roche turns on Flamand and Olivier in furious denunciation. His outburst, part recitative
and part aria, is the longest individual number in the opera. He
launches into his diatribe by asking how these "champions of the
Muses" ("ihr Streiter in Apoll") dare to mock a leading authority in
the theater. He sneers at their amateur attempts at poetry and music,
branding it too superficial to touch the human heart. It is men like himself, he goes on, who uphold the sacred tradition of the theater, who
have discovered the talent that brings splendor and majesty to the stage.

La Roche climaxes his peroration in a powerful refrain in which he
declares that, because he has given his life for the glory of the theater,
he will become one of its immortals ("Ich streite für die Schönheit").
And on his tombstone men will read the epitaph: "Here lies La Roche,
the unforgettable" ("Hier ruht La Roche, der unvergessliche").

Overwhelmed by his eloquence, the others burst into applause.
Clairon impetuously throws her arms around his neck and kisses his
cheek. The Italian soprano, now completely befuddled with wine and
overcome with emotion, bursts into tears. In comical exasperation, the
tenor, reminding her that the director is not dead yet, upbraids her for
making a scene, then drags her away. Shaking with laughter, the Count
shouts, "Bravo!"

The Countess steps forward and in a solo passage ("Verlasst die Ir-
rwege") declares that it is now the duty of the poet and the composer
to combine their talents in a work of art which will be worthy of the director and his eloquent defense of his theater. In an aside to Clairon,
the Count murmurs that his sister is (perish the thought) commis-
sioning an opera.

In a theatrical gesture, Clairon takes the hands of Flamand and Olivier and leads the men to the Countess to pay her homage as the "God-

dess of Harmony." The Countess gravely acknowledges the tribute. Sustaining Clairon's ceremonial mood, Flamand, Olivier and La Roche join with her in the "Homage Quartet" ("Was hebt sich göttergleich").

The only dissenting voice is that of the Count, who cynically observes that, willy-nilly, he is about to be afflicted with an opera. The Countess explains that her brother's musical tastes run to triumphal marches and that in his opinion opera composers are nothing but "word killers."

La Roche officiously orders the project to begin and announces the rules of procedure: There is to be no meddling with the aria; the singers must be heard over the accompaniment; verses must be repeated so that they can be understood. Flamand scoffs at these conventional restrictions on creative effort and calls for new ideas. La Roche tartly advises him not to exaggerate his own importance, then says they must first decide on a subject. Olivier and Flamand in turn suggest *Ariadne auf Naxos* and *Daphne;* themes from Strauss's own operas on these subjects are heard in the orchestra. Fuming impatiently that this is "mythology" all over again, La Roche insists on a subject that involves human beings —in short, themselves.

Thereupon the Count says he has an extraordinary suggestion: Write down the events that have occurred in this château this very day, set them to music, and there you have a contemporary opera. They themselves will be the characters in the drama. The novelty of the idea takes the others completely by surprise, and an animated discussion follows in an ensemble in quasi-recitative. All finally express their enthusiasm for the plan.

The discussion ends as Clairon says she must return to Paris. She takes leave of the Countess, who retires to her room. Flamand and Olivier accompany her to the door and remain standing there in the same positions as in Scene One.

[*Scene Ten*] La Roche brings the two Italian singers from the theater and escorts them out. On the way, he promises the tenor that he will be paid his fee tomorrow. Clairon and the Count leave together. Flamand turns to Olivier and with grave courtesy sings an inversion of the phrase heard at the beginning of the action: "prima le parole, dopo la musica." With equal chivalry, Olivier responds: "No, first the music— but born of the words."

Staring at the Countess' door, the composer and the poet give voice to their thoughts in brief, quiet phrases over a variation of the theme heard at the beginning of the first scene. Each one is thinking of his secret rendezvous with the Countess in her library at eleven o'clock the following morning. It is then that they will learn which has won her heart: the music (and thus Flamand) or the words (and thus Olivier). Their reflections are interrupted when La Roche comes bustling in saying they must leave for Paris at once. As before, he plies them with advice on how to write the opera. The three leave together.

[*Scene Eleven*] This scene consists of a delightful ensemble in which eight servants, who enter to put the salon in order, comment on the day's events. In subdued tones they discuss the behavior of the Countess and her guests—who all talked at once and made a wonderful lot of noise ("Das war ein schöner Lärm").

The Italian singer, says one servant, had a tremendous appetite—she gobbled up all the cake. Another wonders what the director's long oration was about. It is duly explained that the director is trying to reform the theater, and hopes to do so before he dies. They are all mad, the servants sing together, and they are all play acting. But behind the scenes the servants know what is going on: The Count is having a new love affair, while the Countess herself cannot decide which one of two men she is in love with. To settle the matter, a servant goes on to say, she is having them write an opera for her. Several of the others argue that there is nothing to be learned from opera because nobody ever understands the words. They insist that it is much more interesting to watch tightrope dancers or a marionette show. One of the servants suggests they entertain the Countess with a pantomime of their own.

Their chatter is interrupted by the Major-domo, who comes in and orders them to get on with their work. They are to set the table for supper, after which they will be free for the evening. In great good humor the servants conclude the ensemble, softly singing that an evening without guests will be a pleasure ("Welch Vergnügen, ein Abend ohne Gäste!"). When they leave, the Major-domo lights a candelabra. Suddenly he hears a quavering voice from the theater calling, "Director!"

[*Scene Twelve*] A gnomelike figure emerges from the shadows. Staring in surprise, the Major-domo asks him who he is. The wizened little man replies that he is the invisible ruler of a magical kingdom underground. Impatiently reminding him that he is quite visible at the moment, the Major-domo asks him his name. "I am Monsieur Taupe, the prompter," the other answers finally. He is a man of importance in the theater, he goes on, and rules this realm from his box. When he falls asleep, the actors stop talking and the public wakes up. It logically follows, then, that it is sleep that makes him indispensable to the theater. But this time, he whimpers, he slept too long and now his director has gone back to Paris without him. Amused but sympathetic, the Major-domo invites Monsieur Taupe to the kitchen and assures him that he will arrange to have a carriage ready to take him to Paris. As the prompter thanks the Major-domo and follows him out, the music softly subsides into the lyrical theme of Strauss's *Krämerspiegel* song heard earlier as the Count commented on the absurdity of opera.

[*Scene Thirteen*] As the intermezzo continues, the deserted salon darkens and moonlight floods the terrace outside. After a few moments the Countess, elegantly gowned, enters the steps out on the terrace, where she stands in deep thought. The Major-domo and two servants enter and light the candles. The Countess comes in from the terrace and asks where her brother is. He escorted Mlle. Clairon to Paris, the Major-domo replies, and will not return this evening. She will dine alone, the Countess says. She reflects for a moment on the Count's romantic dalliance, then asks the Major-domo if there are any other matters.

He informs her that Olivier will visit her tomorrow to learn how the opera he and Flamand are writing is to end. With a start of surprise, the Countess asks, "Tomorrow . . . when and where?" In the library at eleven o'clock, the Major-domo answers. He bows and leaves.

With a gasp of dismay the Countess repeats the Major-domo's words: "Morgen mittag um elf!" ("Tomorrow morning at eleven!"). The phrase introduces the great monologue-aria which concludes *Capriccio*. She realizes that she asked Flamand to meet her at the same place at the same time. This, she murmurs, will be a disaster ("Es ist ein Verhängnis"). The sonnet, Madeleine sings, has made poet and composer inseparable—although Flamand will be surprised to see Olivier in the library instead of herself. But now . . . how is the opera to end? Will music or words prevail—or, to put it another way, which lover will she choose?

Placing the music on the stand, she seats herself at her harp and begins singing the sonnet as Flamand sang it to her ("Kein Andres, das mir so im Herzen loht"). After several verses she breaks off to exclaim that the love of poet and composer has caught her in a trap from which there is no escape. Then she sings the sonnet to its conclusion. At this point a theme from Flamand's sextet, heard in the overture, sounds in the orchestra.

Suddenly Madeleine catches sight of her image in the mirror. Half in mockery, she entreats the reflection to tell her what her heart has decided. In a sudden, passionate outburst, she cries that she wants an answer—not this ironic glance ("Ich will eine Antwort, und nicht deinen prüfenden Blick!"). Then, recovering her composure, Madeleine, in the soaring climax of the aria, implores the image of herself—a woman ardently in love with poet and composer—to help her find an ending for their opera. Is there, she sings softly but with passionate intensity, one that would have meaning?

As themes of Flamand's sextet again sound in the orchestra, Madeleine smiles mischievously at her reflection, waves her fan flirtatiously, then makes an elaborate curtsy. She turns and walks into the dining room past the Major-domo, who had entered a moment earlier to announce supper. He stares at Madeleine, looks back at the mirror, then shakes his head in utter bewilderment. A horn call echoes softly and mysteriously in the orchestra. The curtain falls.

CARMINA BURANA
Cantiones Profanae
(*Secular songs for soloists and chorus*)

by CARL ORFF
(1895–   )

Based on the *Songs of Benedictbeuern,* a collection of verses written and sung by the goliards, vagabond poets of the twelfth and thirteenth centuries.

Although *Carmina Burana* is not an opera, it has become a part of the concert opera repertoire and is usually presented with its dramatic action—inherent in the music—provided by a ballet. The drama of *Carmina Burana*—like that of Berlioz' *Symphonie fantastique*—is admittedly cerebral, yet it belongs to the stage. Written by a man who is considered one of Germany's foremost composers of music for the theater, it is one of the most remarkable choral works of the present day.

Carl Orff went back to the Middle Ages for the inspiration of *Carmina Burana*. He set to music the poetry of the goliards, the picaresque nomads of Europe who sang of pagan joys and the sheer delight of living. Irreverent, witty, earthy and rebellious, the goliards nevertheless were influenced in their songs and verses by the prosody of the ancient Catholic Latin hymns. In much the same way as they satirized church ritual, Orff parodied Gregorian chant in his musical settings. There are echoes of the *Dies Irae* in the opening chorus, for example, and in one or two instances the Gregorian psalm tone is adapted note for note.

The prime source of goliard poetry is a manuscript discovered in 1803 in the monastery of Benedictbeuern in Bavaria about forty miles from Munich, Orff's birthplace. This manuscript provided the material for *Carmina Burana*. It was Orff's first major work and was completed in 1936.

The score consists of musical settings of twenty-five poems (the chorus, "O Fortuna, velut Luna" begins and ends the work); most of the lyrics are in Latin, some in Low German. There is an extraordinary variety of rhythmic patterns—including flamenco, French and Italian dances of the Middle Ages and the simple rhythms of Bavarian folk song.

The work is orchestrated for eight percussion players, with a percussion section of three glockenspiels, xylophone, castanets, wood blocks, small bells, chimes, celesta, two pianos, six tympani, tambourines, two side drums and bass drum.

Following are brief descriptions of the twenty-five musical settings.

Fortuna Imperatrix Mundi
Fortune, Empress of the World

1. "O Fortuna, velut Luna." Chorus. Fortune, as evanescent as moonlight, bestows her blessing on man—then as quickly takes it away. A powerful rhythmic thrust characterizes this sardonic chorus of homage to Fate.

2. "Fortune plango vulnera." Chorus. The three verses describe how Fate capriciously strikes down her victims in the very moment of triumph. The song ends with a symbolic warning to a king: Let him beware, for on Fortune's wheel is inscribed the name of Hecuba, goddess of revenge.

I
Primo Vere
In Springtime

3. "Veris leta facies." Small chorus. In unison passages sung in plain-chant style, altos are paired with basses, sopranos with tenors. It is an expression of pagan joy over the return of spring.

4. "Omnia sol temperat." Baritone solo. Also in the Gregorian mode, it is another evocation of spring, when the god of love rules in all hearts.

5. "Ecce gratum." Chorus. Beginning with a solemn four-note Gregorian phrase, it suddenly swings into an impudent staccato rhythm reflecting the abandoned gaiety in anticipation of the return of summer and the season of love.

Auf dem Anger
On the Lawn

6. Dance. Orchestral interlude somewhat in the manner of the French and Italian dances of the Middle Ages.

7. "Floret silva." Chorus and small chorus. Sung partly in Latin and partly in Low German, it is a plaintive yet lilting lament of a maiden for her lover who rode away on horseback.

8. "Chramer, gip die varwe mir." Solo sopranos and chorus. Sung in Low German in the manner of a Bavarian folk song, with hummed

choral interludes. A young girl asks a shopkeeper for rouge to paint her cheeks to make her more attractive to the young men.

9. Reie. A round dance—orchestral interlude. This introduces two brief choruses in folk-song style, lyrics in Low German: "Swaz hie gat umbe" and "Chume, chum, geselle min." Both, of course, have to do with the longing of the girls for the boys, and vice versa.

10. "Were diu werlt alle min." Chorus. Sung *allegretto* in unison, this is a delightfully flippant variation of a lover's lament: If all the world belonged to him, he would gladly give it up to hold the Queen of England in his arms.

II
In Taberna
In the Tavern

11. "Estunas interius." Baritone solo. One of the principal arias in the score, it is written in the style of true *bel canto* opera. Driven to despair by the aimlessness and frustration of his life, a man abandons himself to thoughts of lust and depravity.

12. "Olim lacus colueram." Tenor solo and chorus. A brief but spectacularly difficult aria, beginning on a high A natural and rising to a D above high C. It is the parodied lament of a beautiful swan, captured and roasted black upon the spit for the feast.

13. "Ego sum abbas." Baritone solo and male chorus. This is sung in unctuous Gregorian style, interrupted by raucous orchestral outbursts, by the drunken Abbot of Cucany, who describes how he meets in the tavern with his cronies for the dice game. Whoever plays against him loses everything—including his garments.

14. "In taberna quando sumus." Male chorus. A roaring chorus, mostly in unison, in which the Abbot's companions drink a toast to everyone from "the sinful brethren" to the Pope, then recite the litany of those who find their joy in wine—which includes everybody "by the hundreds and thousands."

III
Cour d'Amours
The Court of Love

15. "Amor volat undique." Soprano solo and boys' chorus. This section is dominated by an undulating figure in thirds. The *ragazzi* sing of the all-pervading presence of the god of love; the soprano reflects upon the plight of the young girl who has no lover.

16. "Dies, nox et omnia." Baritone solo. A young man complains that he is the most wretched of mortals because the heart of his lady-

love is made of ice. A short but difficult aria with an extremely high tessitura—a B natural above the staff in the bass in one of the coloratura passages. In performance, this is usually sung by a tenor.

17. "Stetit puella." Soprano solo. A beguiling melody in flamenco rhythm. The song describes a young girl in a red dress which rustles provocatively as she walks.

18. "Circa mea pectora." Baritone solo and chorus. Another lover's lament, with three verses in waltz tempo sung in Latin while the chorus responds in Low German.

19. "Si puer cum puellula." Sung by three tenors, a baritone and two basses. A striking ensemble on a Gregorian theme (marked *allegro buffo*) sung in unaccompanied triads with solo interpolations. Its theme is a passionate description of two young lovers.

20. "Veni, veni, venias." Double chorus. A lover's exuberant ode to his mistress. The choral response of "Hyrca, hyrce, nazaza trilliviros" has the effect of a demonic incantation.

21. "In trutina." Soprano solo. In a simple melody of Puccinian lyricism, a girl reflects amorously on the temptations of love.

22. "Tempus est iocundum." Soprano and baritone solos with chorus and boys' chorus. One of the most elaborate numbers in the score, it is a pagan hymn to spring, describing how the vernal urge turns the thoughts of youths and maidens to the delights of love.

23. "Dulcissime." Soprano solo. A passionate expression of surrender to the god of love, sung in the form of a brilliant coloratura phrase.

24. "Ave formosissima." Chorus. A hymn to Venus, written in imitation of a majestic Lutheran chorale, in which the goddess is compared to two celebrated heroines of medieval poetry—Blanziflor and Helena, mythological sorceresses.

25. The foregoing leads directly into the finale of *Carmina Burana,* "O Fortuna, velut Luna," a repetition of the opening chorus.

CENDRILLON
(*Cinderella*)
by JULES MASSENET
(1842–1912)

Libretto by
HENRI CAIN

Based on the fairy tale "Cinderella or the Little Glass Slipper," by
Charles Perrault, French dramatist (1628–1703)

CHARACTERS

Pandolfe, father of Cendrillon by his first marriage	Bass or baritone
Madame de la Haltière, his second wife	Mezzo-soprano
Noémie ⎱ her daughters	Soprano
Dorothée ⎰	Mezzo-soprano
Cendrillon (Lucette/Cinderella)	Mezzo-soprano
The Fairy Godmother	Coloratura soprano
Master of Ceremonies	Baritone
Dean of the Faculty	Tenor
Prince Charming	Dramatic soprano*
The King	Baritone
Prime Minister	Bass or baritone
Herald	Spoken

Servants, fairies, elves, spirits, courtiers, doctors, ministers, the
populace

Place: Legendary
Time: Legendary
First performance: Opéra-Comique, Paris, May 24, 1899
Original language: French

Henry T. Finck, the British musicologist and critic, once observed that
Cendrillon, Massenet's fifteenth work, was not an opera, but a fairy tale

* The role is sometimes sung by a tenor.

set to music. As such, its official title is: *Conte de Fées en Quatre Actes et Six Tableaux*. It is Massenet's setting of the timeless fairy tale of Cinderella, and thus it is numbered among the more than five hundred versions of the story known in Europe alone.

Cendrillon naturally brings to mind Rossini's setting of the story, which differs both musically and dramatically from Massenet's work. Rossini's opera vanished from the repertoire by 1860; *Cendrillon* was acclaimed at the Opéra-Comique in 1899, where it ran for sixty successive performances. Then it too disappeared from the stage for decades. Surprisingly, however, both enjoyed successful twentieth-century revivals: *La Cenerentola* in 1953–54 performances by the New York City Opera; *Cendrillon* in 1979 performances by the Opera Company of Ottawa, Canada, and by the Washington Opera Company at the John F. Kennedy Center.

Why did these striking works disappear from the stage for so many years? Two fundamental reasons have been offered: 1) both demand singers of extraordinary musical and dramatic versatility; 2) both require elaborate and expensive stage machinery for the many scene changes. A more esoteric reason is that public tastes changed. When the nineteenth century moved into the twentieth, the harsh realities of wars and economic disruptions were reflected operatically in the trend toward *verismo*. Fairy tales, as well as the larger-than-life dilemmas of gods and goddesses, no longer beguiled the public.

Yet in direct contradiction to all this is the fact that revivals of such works as *La Cenerentola* and *Cendrillon*—teeming with melody, imagination and naïve charm—are finding increasing favor with opera lovers everywhere.

Both have their roots in operatic history. The basis of *La Cenerentola* actually was *Cendrillon* (1810), composed by Nicolo Isouard (1775–1818), of Malta, a composer and organist who from about 1800 produced operas in Paris at the rate of about two a year. *Cendrillon* was the twenty-sixth of his thirty-nine operas (one of which was *Il Barbiere di Siviglia*, 1796).

Perrault's story (as noted) was the basis of Massenet's opera. Perrault, incidentally, also was famous for his *Contes de Ma Mère l'Oye* (*Mother Goose Tales*) for children. When Massenet was in London for the first performance of his *Le Cid* (circa 1886) he discussed with librettist/painter Henri Cain (1859–1937) the idea of setting Perrault's story. Cain forthwith fashioned the libretto of *Cendrillon*.

While both operas retain the charm of the legend, Rossini's approach is more worldly and cynical. He eschews the magical elements—the glass slipper, the pumpkin turned into a carriage, the midnight transformation and so on. He satirizes the vanities of the nobility with brilliant comic thrusts, whereas Massenet treats their pomposities with telling but gentle mockery. At the same time, his ephemeral choruses of fairies, spirits and elves overlay the action with what a critic of Massenet's day called "a fine powder of sound."

There is a brief prelude in a mock-heroic vein reflecting the self-importance of those in the household of Madame de la Haltière.

ACT ONE

The home of Madame de la Haltière. At right a large fireplace. There is an insistent ringing of bells. Men and women servants rush aimlessly about in a panic because Madame is calling. In an agitated chorus ("On appelle, on sonne") they ask each other what to do.

There is a sudden silence as Pandolfe enters and is puzzled by the obsequious manner of the servants. They assure him that he is a kind master, but grumble about his tyrannical wife ("Mais c'est madame! ah, madame!").

Impatiently dismissing them, Pandolfe launches into a long soliloquy ("Du côté de la barbe est la toute-puissance"). He wonders what possessed him to leave a quiet home in the country, living contentedly as a widower with an adorable little daughter, come to Paris and marry a harridan of a countess—whose "wedding gift" to him was a pair of obnoxious females who are now his stepdaughters.

He laments that his beloved "Lucette" (Cendrillon) is scorned and mistreated, left to remain alone at home while her haughty steprelations enjoy themselves at a ball. Then Pandolfe, beginning to get angry, vows he will soon show who is master in his own house. Suddenly hearing his wife's voice, he scuttles away terrified.

Madame, Noémie and Dorothée sweep in and discuss the prospects for the evening in a chattering trio. Madame admonishes the two to be on their mettle because this very evening they are to meet the King. The feather-brained daughters, beside themselves with excitement, ask what they must do.

Copy me in everything, Madame tells them. Stand up straight, be gracious but not overbearing—and don't try to be clever. Noémie and Dorothée comically rehearse their ballroom behavior and are duly complimented on their devastating charm. Madame assures them that "you will be very beautiful this evening" ("Faites-vous très belles ce soir").

A hilarious scene follows as milliners, tailors and hairdressers arrive to primp the three women for the ball. As they go to work, the servants withdraw to one side to look on, convulsed with suppressed laughter and making snide comments about the women as they preen themselves. Madame and her daughters assure each other that they indeed will be the talk of the ball. The beauty and fashion attendants loudly concur, then are shown out by the servants.

Pandolfe struts in, proudly showing off the peacock finery of his formal evening attire. He gets little reaction from Noémie and Dorothée, who parade before him to dazzle him with their own costumes. He in turn favors them with a casual compliment. Aside, he sings that he has high hopes for his future plans—which for the moment he will keep to himself. Surreptitiously pointing to his wife, he gleefully observes that she is obviously going crazy. Glaring at him, Madame warns that they will be late for the ball. As they prepare to leave, Pandolfe laments that he must leave Cendrillon alone in the house as usual.

In a sparkling "patter" trio—"We've distinction, we've position" ("De la race, de la prestance")—Madame and her daughters revel in their superior social accomplishments, which will certainly cause a stir at the ball. Pandolfe ironically echoes these sentiments as he follows them out.

The scene changes to show Cendrillon brooding by the fire. In one of the principal arias of the opera—"Ah! but my sisters are happy!" ("Ah! que mes soeurs sont heureuses!")—she reflects pensively on her sad lot in life. While her sisters indulge themselves in a mad whirl of court life —meeting handsome princes and noble marquises—she has nothing but her work and her dreams. She spies a cricket on the hearth and commiserates with him as another creature who is lonely and without hope.

But now there is work to do, she exclaims, rousing herself, although it is useless to try because the music of the ball she cannot attend keeps humming in her head. Nevertheless, she busies herself tidying up the house, then sits down to rest. Gazing out of the window, she murmurs that the moon and the stars are smiling down from the sky. One could close one's eyes and dream wondrous dreams. . . . In a repetition of a tender phrase of her aria, she sings quietly "All empty hopes resigning, Cinderella"—("Résigne-toi, Cendrille")—then falls asleep.

The dream sequence now begins as the Fairy Godmother appears, bends over the sleeping girl and sings tenderly: "Dearest child, I hear your plaint" ("Douce enfant, ta plainte légère"). She calls on the spirits and elves to entertain Cendrillon and dress her for the ball, so that she will be the "most admired" ("Elle soit la plus belle et la plus admirée"), and will reign as queen of the ball. The Fairy Godmother instructs the elves to fashion the ball gown of stars, moonbeams and rainbow gems, and to sprinkle its folds with perfumed love potions.

As Cendrillon, still in her dream, exclaims in delight, the Fairy Godmother orders the elves and spirits to prepare the carriage which is to take Cendrillon to the palace. Over an enchanting gossamer accompaniment, the fairyland chorus exhorts tiny woodland creatures to bring jewels of moonlight and dew to adorn the sleeping girl.

Gradually awakening, Cendrillon sees in a mirror the image of herself in glittering finery. Joyously she thanks her Fairy Godmother. But the Fairy Godmother warns her that at the stroke of midnight she must leave the ball and hurry home ("Écoute bien. Quand sonnera minuit"). Cendrillon promises. She is about to leave with her fairy entourage when she suddenly stops in distress, fretting that her steprelations will recognize her at the ball.

With that the Fairy Godmother hands her a tiny glass slipper. It is a talisman which will make "Lucette" a complete stranger in the eyes of Madame and her daughters. Now then, the Fairy Godmother sings commandingly, off with you to the ball, "my princess of princesses!" ("Voici ton carrosse, princesse!"). In ecstasy, Cendrillon sings that for once in her life she will have her fill of pleasure—and will have the heady thrill of making the high-and-mighty Madame and her precious daughters jealous.

ACT TWO

At the court, brilliantly decorated for the ball. The Prince, bored and disconsolate, is wandering aimlessly about. Throughout the following scene, three musicians, with lute, viole d'amour and crystal flute, play in the style of eighteenth-century salon music. First, however, there is a majestic fanfare which introduces the Master of Ceremonies and a group of courtiers, who salute the Prince. They are followed by doctors and ministers.

In an ensuing ensemble all express their puzzlement over the Prince's crestfallen demeanor. The Dean of the Faculty, quoting Latin in a nasal tenor, admonishes the Prince to heed the advice of his learned retainers. According to a royal decree, the Prime Minister then proclaims, everyone must be merry at the ball. When the Prince steadfastly ignores them all, they slowly leave, shaking their heads and murmuring, "Pauvre Prince!"

Alone, the Prince abandons himself to self-pity in a rather lugubrious aria ("Coeur sans amour, printemps sans roses!"). His heart is without love, the spring is without roses. He longs for someone he can love and cherish; for her he would give up all the regal splendor of the court.

As he ends his soliloquy, the King and his court enter to a resounding instrumental and choral fanfare that slyly parodies the courtly eighteenth-century pageantry. At the ball, the King informs the Prince, he will meet the daughters of the nobility. He is to choose the one who suits his fancy, and marry her. Such is the royal decree.

Then follows the glittering spectacle of the ballet, one of the most spectacular scenes in the opera, on which Massenet lavished his extraordinary skill in orchestral and ensemble writing. Here again, through the music runs a vein of subtle mockery of the self-aggrandizement typical of eighteenth-century court fetes. It begins with a beguiling Viennese waltz, then climaxes in interpretations of the Florentine, a dance native to the region of the Italian city, and the rigadoon, a dance of Provence.

At the conclusion of the ballet, Madame, her daughters, the Master of Ceremonies and the Prime Minister enter to a flippant orchestral flourish deliberately in contrast to their stuffy dignity. The Master of Ceremonies and the Prime Minister remind Madame and her daughters that they are now in the presence of the Prince, and it is up to them to display their charms to the utmost.

Noémie and Dorothée are feverishly excited and their mother tries desperately to calm them. When she tells them that the great moment has arrived—the Prince is here—Dorothée wails that she is about to faint.

At that moment Cendrillon enters and the crowd gasps in astonishment at her beauty, while Madame and her daughters glare at her contemptuously. The Prince himself stares at her as though hypnotized. The reactions of the assemblage are expressed in an ingenious interchange of musical phrases: while the crowd exclaims, in a descending musical phrase, over this "wonderful adventure" ("Ô la surprenante aventure"), Madame, Noémie and Dorothée, echoing the same phrase, denounce Cendrillon's appearance as a "horrid misadventure" ("Ô la décevante aventure!"). When the Prince meanwhile comes closer to Cendrillon the assemblage withdraws at a sign from the King. Madame, her nose in the air, hurries her daughters out, then returns to drag away Pandolfe, who has been gaping openmouthed at Cendrillon.

Then ensues an enchanting duet, the first colloquy between Prince Charming and Cendrillon. Enthralled by her beauty, the Prince sings that she is a lovely dream whose name he asks to know. To him, Cendrillon responds, she will remain the Unknown, who will truly vanish forever in the mists of his own dream. The Prince fervidly protests that he will die rather than lose her.

With infinite tenderness she sings that he is indeed her Prince Charming, in a reiterated phrase echoed bar by bar by the oboe with striking effect. She would rather die than cause him pain, Cendrillon goes on . . . he has captured her heart and she will cherish this moment forever. In passionate ecstasy the Prince cries: "I will love you forever!" ("Je t'aime et t'aimerai toujours!").

Suddenly the first stroke of the midnight chime is heard. Cendrillon gasps in dismay. The Prince takes her in his arms and implores her to stay ("Je t'aime! Reste!"). Listening for the chime Cendrillon struggles out of his arms and runs away. When he tries to follow, the Fairy Godmother, veiled, appears, stops him with a gesture, then vanishes. In utter despair the Prince bursts out: "My Unknown! My heavenly Unknown!" ("Inconnue! Ô céleste Inconnue!").

ACT THREE

[*Scene One*] Cendrillon rushes into the house, exhausted by the ordeal of running through the darkness in order to be home before the midnight chimes stop ringing. In a long monologue ("Enfin, je suis ici") she tells of the terrors of the night: how in her panic she lost her precious glass slipper . . . how she saw in the ghostly moonlight monstrous creatures with sightless eyes pointing accusing fingers at her. She lost her way but frantically ran on and on, determined to keep her promise to her Fairy Godmother ("Marraine! Marraine!").

Overcome with anguish, she sinks sobbing in front of the fireplace, grieving over the lost splendor of the ball and the tender words of Prince Charming, which she will never hear again. Her joy has turned to cinders, she murmurs, again confiding her sorrow to the cricket on the hearth. Hearing a babble of voices outside, she jumps up and escapes to her room.

Madame, Noémie and Dorothée come storming in, followed by the cowering Pandolfe. In a crackling ensemble the three harpies pounce on the feckless husband as a softhearted clod who has been made a fool of by a wretched waif masquerading as a princess. When Pandolfe timidly ventures to say that the child has a gentle charm, Madame turns on him with withering contempt ("Fi donc! Monsieur, je le conteste").

Let him remember, she fumes, that her family tree numbers four chief justices, professors, a doge, princes, bishops by the dozens, an admiral, a cardinal, six abbesses, many nuns, several kings' mistresses (all of royal blood)—not to mention hordes of smaller fry—all of whom can hold their heads higher than the nonentities of his own miserable family tree.

Noémie and Dorothée dutifully endorse these sublime observations, while Pandolfe sighs he would gladly trade an illustrious family tree for ordinary peace of mind. Cendrillon quietly enters and expresses concern over Pandolfe's woebegone expression. Family matters, he explains with a shrug, are still the same.

Stung by his sarcasm, the three women launch into their own version of what happened at the ball ("Écoute-nous, tu vas savoir"). A scheming young female, togged out in bogus finery, had the effrontery to flirt with the *Prince,* of all people! But her insolence appalled the court, and she fled in shame before the ball was half over. Pandolfe tries to protest this slanderous nonsense but the three women furiously shout at him to keep quiet.

Cendrillon, scarcely believing what she has heard, timidly asks what the Prince himself had to say to all this. The Prince, Madame answers venomously, said that this trollop was fit only for hanging. Cendrillon, as though stricken, turns pale and is about to faint. Pandolfe catches her in his arms. Then in an uncharacteristic outburst of anger he roars at the astonished women to get out. Hysterical with rage, the three, cursing him, rush away.

Holding his fainting daughter in his arms, Pandolfe tenderly comforts her ("Ma pauvre enfant chérie"). In quiet bitterness he sings that it was his accursed ambition that drove him to come to Paris as the husband of a vain social climber with two witless daughters.

Now, he goes on in a brief but moving aria ("Viens, nous quitterons cette ville"), they will leave this cruel city and go back to the farm where they had lived before his ill-starred second marriage.[1] There they will live in happy seclusion. Cendrillon, enthralled, already fancies herself gathering flowers to the song of nightingales. She thanks her father for reviving her spirits; he leaves to make plans for their journey.

In an ensuing soliloquy ("Seule, je partirai, mon père") Cendrillon sings that she will not burden her loving father with her own sorrow. Evidently believing what Madame and her daughters told her about the ball, she is certain that Prince Charming has repudiated her love. Now she is once more a lonely outcast by the fireplace, her dream of love shattered. She takes down a small branch from the mantelpiece and kisses its drooping leaves as a symbol of the love that has withered away.

Her thoughts turn to her childhood, when she knelt at her mother's knee to seek the protection of maternal love. Her mother comforted her and sang the Angelus like a lullaby ("C'est l'angélus. Dors, mon petit ange"). Cendrillon breaks into sobs at the memory. The scene darkens; there is thunder and lightning. In a sudden spasm of despair she springs up, crying that she will go to the enchanted oak tree and die there.

[Scene Two] The scene changes to the Fairy Godmother's home: a huge oak in the middle of a heath, its gnarled branches covered with flowering broom. Beyond is the sea. It is a clear moonlit night. To a shimmering accompaniment (akin to Mendelssohn's A Midsummer Night's Dream) the Fairy Godmother, looking down from the branches of the oak, joins her voice with the invisible choir of spirits singing of the magic of the summer night.

But then the Fairy Godmother calls attention to two lovers wandering sad and lonely across the darkening moor. Bidding the spirits to heed their lamentations, she commands them to build a wall of sweet

[1] This is one point at which Massenet's version differs markedly from the conventional plot of the fairy tale.

clover between the lovers ("Fermez-vous, muraille embaumée!") so that they will be near yet invisible to each other.

In an ardent duet Cendrillon and Prince Charming address their prayers to the invisible Fairy Godmother ("Je viens à vous"). Cendrillon implores pardon for whatever wrong she may have done to her Godmother; the Prince begs the Fairy Godmother to end his suffering and restore his dream of love. Still unaware of each other's identity, each in turn asks the Fairy Godmother to have compassion on the love-smitten mortal on the other side of the wall.

Finally, when Cendrillon hears the Prince's passionate avowals of love, she exclaims that now she knows he is indeed Prince Charming. When he in turn asks who she is she replies: "I am Lucette, and I adore you" ("Je suis Lucette qui vous aime"). The duet rises to a lyrical climax in a scene of mutual recognition as the Fairy Godmother causes the intervening wall of flowers to disappear.

As a token of his love, the Prince hangs his heart—"a chaste and bleeding trophy" ("Je suspendrai mon coeur, pur et sanglant trophée") —on the branches of the oak. Thereupon Cendrillon appears and the lovers rush into each other's arms. At a gesture from the Fairy Godmother, they sink to the ground. Lulled by the muted voices of the spirits, they are soon deep in magic slumber.

ACT FOUR

[*Scene One*] The terrace of Cendrillon's home, where she lies asleep. It is a spring morning. Pandolfe sits beside his daughter's couch. In a quiet refrain ("Ô pauvre enfant! Depuis que l'on t'a ramenée") he recalls how he found her—after months of hopeless searching—unconscious under a great oak tree beside a stream. At first, he muses, he thought she was dead—but Death did not dare to claim a mortal so beautiful.

Cendrillon opens her eyes and gently chides Pandolfe for watching constantly over her without ever resting. He assures her that she will soon be well, whereupon she insists that he tell her everything that happened while she was asleep ("Dis-moi la vérité!"). "You laughed and cried, and uttered strange words," Pandolfe replies. "You murmured about a Prince Charming and his fond avowals . . . about an enchanted oak . . . a bleeding heart . . . and a glass slipper. . . ." With an amused chuckle he adds: "You chattered on that your royal carriage was drawn by elves!"

In sudden disillusionment, Cendrillon murmurs: "Then it was all a dream . . . a beautiful dream, Papa?" Pandolfe answers: "Yes . . . only a dream." In an echoing phrase, she sings sorrowfully: "Mon papa! j'ai rêvé!"

The mood and the scene change to freshness and gaiety as a group of young girls urge everyone to open doors and windows wide to greet the April morning ("Ouvre ta porte et la fenêtre"). They gather under the balcony of Cendrillon's terrace to greet her. Refreshed and happy, she responds, then comes down to the garden to join Pandolfe.

Suddenly Pandolfe exclaims in dismay as he hears the voice of Madame in the distance. Flatly refusing to listen to her "bawling and bellowing" on this beautiful April morning, he leads Cendrillon away. A moment later Madame and her entourage come bustling in. In a pompous monologue, she announces that today the King has convoked an assemblage of princesses from the far corners of the earth. They will honor him in a splendid processional.

But toward the last, Madame goes on as though seeing a vision, there will come three "unknowns" who will win the unstinted plaudits of the onlookers. And these three—literally descended from the clouds at the behest of Prince Charming himself—are Madame de la Haltière and her daughters, who will make the proper obeisance to His Majesty the King.

A fanfare of trumpets announces the King's herald. All rush out at his summons, with Madame elbowing everybody out of the way. Unnoticed, Cendrillon steals in and listens attentively to the herald's proclamation: Prince Charming has summoned all princesses to try on the glass slipper lost by an unknown princess at the ball. Unless he finds the owner, the Prince certainly will die of despair.

At those words, Cendrillon gasps that now she knows that everything that has happened was not a dream ("Mon rêve était donc vrai!"). She implores her Fairy Godmother to allow her to see her adored Prince once more. Meanwhile, the processional of the princesses, mingled with the acclamations of the crowd, continues to the crescendoing music of the "March of the Princesses," the most spectacular ensemble of the opera.

[Scene Two] The scene changes to the Court of Honor of the King's palace, where the princesses are waiting to appear. The Prince himself, pale and distraught, orders the glass slipper to be displayed so that the owner—without whom he swears he cannot go on living—can appear to claim it. Looking at the princesses, he gallantly assures them that they are all very lovely indeed—but where is she who has his heart? Stricken with grief and longing, he sinks weakly back into his chair to the consternation of the King and the court.

Suddenly the voice of the Fairy Godmother is heard in the distance. To the astonishment of the throng she appears and leads the Prince over to Cendrillon, who has emerged from the throng. Ecstatically the Prince cries: "'Tis she! 'Tis my Lucette!" ("C'est elle, c'est ma Lucette!").

Only your poor Cendrillon, she murmurs in answer. Then in a repetition of the phrase heard in her scene with the Prince in Act Two, she adds: "And you are Prince Charming, 'tis true" ("Vous êtes mon Prince Charmant"). With that she hands him his heart, which he had hung on the branches of the enchanted oak. Keep it, he answers ardently, handing it back to her. The Fairy Godmother, her arms outspread in a symbolic gesture, unites the lovers as all hail their "future queen" ("Honneur à notre souveraine!").

A stirring orchestral outburst announces the arrival of Pandolfe, Madame and her daughters, the Dean of the Faculty, the Master of Ceremonies and the Prime Minister. Cendrillon rushes over to Pandolfe. But before he can move toward her, Madame elbows him aside and takes Cendrillon in her arms, caressing her and calling her "daughter." The crowd is stupefied at this brazenly spurious show of affection, and all stare incredulously as she cries: "Lucette, que j'adore!"

Pandolfe turns to the audience. With cynical amusement he sings: "All ends well, you see . . . we've done our best to give you a glimpse of fairyland" ("Ici tout finit bien. La pièce est terminée. Pour vous faire envoler par les beaux pays bleus"). As a plunging triad reverberates in the orchestra, the curtain falls.

LA CLEMENZA DI TITO

(The Clemency of Titus)

by WOLFGANG AMADEUS MOZART

(1756–91)

Libretto by

PIETRO METASTASIO and CATERINO MAZZOLÀ

CHARACTERS

Titus Vespasian (Tito), Emperor of Rome (A.D. 79–81)	Tenor
Vitellia, daughter of Aulus Vitellius, deposed Emperor of Rome	Soprano
Sextus (Sesto) ⎱ young Roman patricians	Contralto
Annius (Annio) ⎰	Mezzo-soprano
Servilia, sister of Sextus	Soprano
Publius (Publio), captain of the Praetorian Guard	Bass

Senators, Praetorians, lictors, guards, foreign envoys, soldiers, Roman people

Place: Rome
Time: A.D. 79
First performance: National Theater, Prague, September 6, 1791
Original language: Italian

Tito, Mozart's last opera, is an *opera seria,* a genre which Mozart long had planned to apply to operatic composition. His attempts began with *Mitridate* (1770), reached their apogee in *Idomeneo* (1781), then ended with *La Clemenza di Tito.*

A strange succession of events led to the opera's composition. Mozart had been working on *Die Zauberflöte* when he received a commission (tantamount to a command) from Leopold II, Emperor of Bohemia, to write a serious opera for his coronation festivities in Prague.

Meanwhile, Mozart had received a mysterious message from an "unknown" person to write a *Requiem Mass*—coupled with a handsome offer for the completed work.[1] Mozart accepted, but explained that he

[1] The "unknown" was eventually identified as Count Walsegg, an amateur musician, who wanted a Requiem in memory of his wife.

was obliged first to complete a previous commission. Now, broken in health, exhausted from overwork, he became obsessed with the idea that he actually would be writing his own Requiem. His premonition was correct: he did not live to finish the great *Requiem Mass*.

But still to be done was the opera commissioned by King Leopold. Somehow, Mozart got a libretto from Metastasio. Then he, his wife, and his colleague, Franz Xaver Süssmayr, boarded the post chaise for Prague in September 1791. En route, Mozart composed the twenty-six set numbers of the opera, while Süssmayr wrote the connecting secco recitatives. In this fashion *La Clemenza di Tito* was completed in eighteen days.[2]

The first performance in Prague was coolly received, but subsequent performances fared better. *Tito* was the first Mozart opera given in London (1806). The U.S. premiere was via NBC radio in 1940; the first stage performance, Tanglewood, Massachusetts, 1952. That same year it was performed by the Little Orchestra Society conducted by Thomas Scherman at Town Hall, New York City. There were subsequent performances at the Juilliard American Opera Center, New York City (January 1971), Covent Garden (1976) and the Salzburg Festival under the baton of James Levine on August 4, 1976. The New York City Opera staged three performances during its Fall 1979 season.

Even though Mozart wrote *Tito* in the last year of his life—he died at the age of thirty-five on December 5, 1791—his prodigious talent did not fail him. Hampered by a pompous, outmoded libretto, working against a "deadline"—which always inhibited his creative impulses—he still emerged with a brilliant score that bears the stamp of his genius.

The overture is dominated by a curving four-note figure interposed by a series of descending triads. These harmonic patterns are heard later during the course of the opera. Throughout, Mozart adopted an easy, uncomplicated style, with thin but ingenious orchestrations that do much to offset the effect of the stilted libretto.

The plot itself is structured on two basic premises: a) the resolve of Vitellia, in love with Tito, to have revenge on him when he decides to

---

[2] It should be pointed out that the libretto itself went through a number of transformations—cuts, additions, interludes, recitatives and so on.

Presumably, Metastasio's original libretto was in three acts. The introductory note to the Edition Peters piano-vocal score (German-English © 1953) states that the starting point of this "new" edition is "the dramatic masterpiece of Metastasio." The title page reads: "Opera Seria in Three Acts." In this version it was performed at the Salzburg Festival in 1949.

However, virtually all productions of the opera from the time of its premiere in 1791 to the present have been based on the two-act version reconstructed by Mazzolà from Metastasio's original libretto.

marry another—which sets in motion the rebellion against the Emperor; b) the determination of Tito to show clemency and compassion, no matter what the provocation. In the end he pardons all who have conspired against him.

ACT ONE

[*Scene One*] In Vitellia's house. In recitative, Vitellia berates Sesto ("Ma che? sempre l'istesso"), who is madly in love with her, because he keeps complaining that the burning of Rome, which she has ordered to divert attention from her plot to murder the Emperor Tito, will not accomplish its purpose. Meanwhile, she goes on in jealous anger, Tito—with whom she in turn is in love—has chosen as his consort Berenice, daughter of Agrippa I of Judaea. Sesto, trying to placate her, first protests her plans for revenge, insisting that Tito is a gentle monarch beloved by all.

The argument continues in a duet ("Come ti piace imponi"). Sesto swears he will do anything Vitellia asks. Tito must die, Vitellia storms, because he stole the kingdom that rightfully should be hers. Sesto—determined to win her favor by whatever means—sings that her hatred fans his own desire for revenge, and the duet climaxes with their mutual avowals of vengeance.

Annio enters and tells Sesto that Tito wishes to see him at once. Vitellia sarcastically urges Sesto to lose no time because the Emperor must devote all his precious time to Berenice. Angered by the jibe, Annio retorts that, as a matter of fact, Tito has banished Berenice from Rome. Yet—characteristically—Tito had no harsh words of farewell, Annio goes on. There were no reproaches. Still the fond lover, the Emperor bravely bid adieu to his Empress.

Musing that perhaps Tito still has an affection for her, Vitellia tells Sesto that her plans have been altered: it is not yet the hour for vengeance. The hapless Sesto, tortured by his love, frets over her apparent indifference toward him. In an ensuing aria ("Deh, se piacer mi vuoi") Vitellia, by way of keeping Sesto in her power, tells him that if he wants her love he must not harbor suspicions of her fidelity. He must not torture her with his own doubtings. He who is faithful, she goes on sententiously, will find others faithful; he who fears betrayal will find himself betrayed. With that exhortation, Vitellia leaves.

Annio reminds Sesto that he has promised the hand of his sister, Servilia, to him in marriage. For this union, he will also need Tito's blessing, and he asks Sesto to petition the Emperor accordingly. Sesto assents. In a brief but vigorous duet ("Deh, prendi un dolce amplesso"), the two clasp hands and swear eternal brotherhood.

[*Scene Two*] After a brief martial interlude, the scene opens on the Forum, where there is assembled a large throng of priests, senators, Praetorians, foreign envoys and citizens. In a rousing chorus ("Serbate, oh Dei custodi") they ask the gods to bless their mighty ruler, Emperor Tito.

Publio steps forward, and in extravagant terms begs Tito to accept gifts from his subjects to help build a temple in his honor ("Te della patria il Padre"). Tito modestly replies that he desires nothing more than the love and respect of his people. He will therefore dedicate these gifts to another purpose. Romans, listen, he goes on. Vesuvius has spewed fiery lava on fields and towns. Thousands have perished; the survivors are left without food or shelter. The gifts of his people will be used to help the unfortunate victims of the cataclysm—and this shall be his temple. His words are greeted by another outburst of homage from the crowd.

As all leave the Forum, Annio urges Sesto to petition Tito in behalf of his betrothal. Sesto begins—rather indiscreetly—by asking Tito how he could have decided to banish the Empress Berenice. That matter, Tito answers sharply, is not to be mentioned. Henceforth, he declares, he will bow to the wishes of his people and choose a Roman maiden for his consort. What is more, Sesto's blood will be mingled with royalty because the Emperor has decided to make Sesto's own sister, Servilia, his Empress. Sesto and Annio gasp in consternation.

Sesto desperately tries to forestall Tito's decision by saying that his plebeian sister is utterly unworthy of so exalted an honor. Annio adds, in equal desperation, that there surely must be a consort more worthy of the Emperor than Servilia. Completely oblivious to the dismay of Sesto and Annio, Tito thanks the two for bringing the beautiful Servilia to his attention. In a melodious *andante* aria ("Del più sublime soglio") he sings that only the joy of giving the poor and needy the gifts proffered by his loyal subjects can ease the onerous burdens of the throne.

[*Scene Three*] The home of Servilia. In a brief aria, Servilia reflects on the blessings of love, tenderness and devotion bestowed on mankind —yet one must be prepared to suffer misfortune in silence. As though to give tragic meaning to her words, Annio enters and tells her she has been chosen by Tito as his consort. In anguish he cries out: "O Empress, fare thee well!" Servilia, shaken by grief, laments the bitter destiny that will separate them forever. In an ensuing duet ("Ah perdona al primo affetto") they give way to their despair, but vow that their love will endure forever.[3]

[3] In some versions, Servilia's aria is omitted, and the entire scene—up to the duet —is presented in recitative dialogue.

[*Scene Four*] Vitellia's house. Alone, Vitellia rages over Tito's rejection of her in favor of Berenice as his Empress, and swears that she will yet have her revenge ("Ancora mi schernisce?"). At that moment Sesto enters. She answers his affectionate greeting with withering scorn when she learns he has not set fire to the Capitol nor murdered Tito as part of her plot. Revenge me, she goes on sardonically, and I will be yours. Then she taunts him further by remarking that since Tito is still alive, she might return to him as his mistress. Would that, she asks venomously, arouse Sesto's jealousy—and inspire him to carry out her orders?

Groveling before her, Sesto assures her that Rome will soon be in flames—and his sword in Tito's heart. Vitellia ridicules his empty promises and contemptuously orders him out of her sight. Sesto, in the throes of love, responds in a long, sentimental aria ("Parto, ma tu ben mio") that he will do whatever she asks of him; in return, he asks only for her love. Sesto turns and walks out of the room as Vitellia sneers at him for being a weakling.

Alone again, Vitellia murmurs that though she has failed to win Tito back, she is sending someone who will consummate his destiny. Annio and Publio rush in to tell her that the Emperor wishes to see her at once. Vitellia gasps in surprise—and for a terror-stricken moment wonders if Tito knows about the conspiracy.

Beside herself with fear, Vitellia cries out for Sesto ("Vengo . . . aspettate . . . Sesto!"). This leads into the dramatic trio which concludes the first act. Vitellia, tortured by guilt, rants that she is going mad. Annio and Publio sing that this sudden turn of events has completely demoralized Tito's rejected favorite. The trio climaxes with a soaring coloratura flourish.

ACT TWO

[*Scene One*] The Palatine gardens. The scene opens with dialogue in recitative. Publio warns Tito that revolt is brewing in Rome. The Emperor scoffs at the report, saying that such rumors only serve to poison the minds of the people. But what of justice for the perpetrators, Publio asks. Rigorous justice, Tito replies with characteristic magnanimity, would turn the world into a wasteland.

Suddenly Servilia rushes in and throws herself at Tito's feet ("Di Tito al piè"). Startled, the Emperor exclaims: "Servilia Augusta!" To his further astonishment, she begs him not to address her by so exalted a title. Then she confesses that although the Emperor wishes to honor her as his consort, her heart still belongs to Annio. But if her Sovereign still desires her, she goes on, she will be obedient to his wishes—and Annio will renounce her love. Profoundly moved, Tito praises her for her candor. Her willingness to sacrifice Annio's love for the throne to gratify the wishes of her Sovereign, he says, is worthy of the highest commendation. He declares that he himself will marry the lovers. Their devotion to each other will set an example to all Romans. A duet ensues in which Servilia effusively thanks Tito for relinquishing his claim on her as his consort, while he exhorts her to treasure their friendship that was born in truth.

[*Scene Two*] A plaza in Rome with a view of the Capitol. In a dramatic soliloquy, Sesto gives way to his tormenting feelings of guilt and remorse for conspiring against Tito—"the noblest, the greatest, the most human ruler in the world." Cursing himself for being a traitor, he cries that if he must carry out Vitellia's foul plotting, he hopes that he himself will fall dead before he can strike down Tito. He wonders how he can avoid this monstrous deed. But now it is too late: the revolt has begun and Rome is already in flames.

Sesto implores the gods to protect the Emperor ("Deh conservate oh Dei"). This marks the beginning of one of the major ensembles of the opera. As he rushes madly away, Annio, Servilia and Publio come in exclaiming over the awesome spectacle of the city in flames. They wonder what vile traitor has committed this crime. From the distance come the terrified shouts of the populace. The choral outbursts, sung on "Ah!", and increasing in volume as the crowds draw nearer, build up the tension of the scene. Here the chorus, singing antiphonally with the soloists, itself becomes a factor in the drama.

Vitellia now adds her voice, calling for Sesto, denouncing herself for the catastrophe she has inflicted upon Rome. Then Sesto rushes in. On the verge of madness, he begs the earth to swallow him to hide his crime of regicide. At that, Vitellia turns on him savagely, warning him not to betray himself. The ensemble rises to an overpowering climax as all lament that the night of doom has fallen, and call down a curse on the conspirators. The people rush away in panic. Only Sesto remains.

Still haunted by remorse, he groans that he would flee—but he cannot flee from his own conscience. His guilt will dog his footsteps forever. Crushed by despair, he tries to fall on his sword. At that moment, Annio bursts in, thrusts aside the blade and tells him that Tito wishes to see him at once . . . he needs his friend in Rome's crucial hour. Sesto refuses to believe Tito is alive.

He himself, he reveals, saw the assassin approach. To purge himself of his guilt and save Tito's life he sprang forward to deflect the sword-thrust. But it was too late: he saw the assassin plunge the sword into the Emperor's back. But it was *not* the Emperor, Annio tells the incredulous Sesto. It was another—an unknown—who put on the royal mantle and thus sacrificed himself for Tito.

Holding the bloodstained mantle, Sesto groans that he alone is the traitor, and now must flee to escape his doom. He is about to rush away when Annio coolly points out that, as yet, nothing is known of the conspiracy: if he (Sesto) tries to escape, he will be under suspicion. With that he takes the incriminating mantle from Sesto.

In a following aria ("Torna di Tito a lato") Annio urgently advises Sesto to make a full confession to Tito, beg his forgiveness and assure him of his loyalty.

[*Scene Three*] There is an orchestral interlude in a foreboding minor key during the change of scene to Tito's palace. There, Publio tells the Emperor that it was Lentulus who actually led the rebellion in an effort to dethrone the Emperor. To that end, he purloined an imperial mantle, attempted to incite the people to revolt and set fire to the Capitol. An overzealous member of his faction mistook him for Tito and tried to assassinate him. Lentulus, Publio reports, is now at the point of death.

Tito, appalled, asks how this monstrous evil could happen in his own court. Treachery, Publio replies, is rampant in your very house—and here is proof. With that he hands Tito the bloodstained mantle. He leaves.

In one of the longest and most dramatic arias in the opera, Tito philosophizes in bitterness and despair on the perfidy, cruelty and overwhelming evil that corrupt human actions. No ray of hope pierces the black cloud of horror that envelops him—his spirit gropes in the blackness of eternal night. His gloomy reflections are interrupted by the approach of Sesto. Tito beseeches him, as his friend, to explain why he has deserved this infamy—why all Rome has turned against him. . . .

No longer able to bear his guilt, Sesto is about to confess his part in the plot when Vitellia rushes in and cuts him short. Kneeling, she melodramatically thanks the gods that her Emperor's life has been spared. Aside, in a fierce undertone, she orders the luckless Sesto to keep quiet.

Annio and Servilia enter. Annio tells Tito that the fire in the Capitol was set deliberately and was part of a plot against his life. Tito thanks him for the warning, but then, in an irrational outburst, accuses Annio himself of plotting his death. Annio, of course, is completely baffled. Sesto only makes matters worse by trying to defend Annio, while Vitellia desperately tries to silence Sesto before he can implicate her in the conspiracy. Tito, fuming with anger, declares that the matter will be turned over to the Senate, which will deal with the plotters in its own way. With that he storms out of the room.

The confrontation develops into a long quartet in which Sesto, Vitellia, Servilia and Annio express their totally confused reactions to the dilemma. Sesto still moans about his guilt; Servilia assures Annio of her undying love; Annio begs her not to question his actions—because he himself does not know the answers; Vitellia laments the cruel punishment of fate. The ensemble ends with a cry of despair from the four: "O bitter pangs of death!" Annio and Servilia are led away by the palace guards.

Vitellia, brushing aside Sesto's ardent embrace, urges him to escape while there is still time—to save both their lives. In the next moment Publio strides in and orders Sesto to surrender his sword. Lentulus has confessed, he says, has implicated Sesto, and now the Senate is about to render a verdict. Sesto, murmuring, "This is the end," embraces Vitellia in farewell.

A trio follows. Sesto bids Vitellia to remember her lover's sighs as a gentle breeze caressing her cheek ("Se al volto mai ti senti"); Vitellia sings that this parting will break her heart; Publio sings that though he shares the anguish of the lovers, he must not give way to pity: Sesto must follow him to hear his doom. He leads Sesto away.

Alone, Vitellia, still obsessed with thoughts of revenge on Tito, broods over the disaster: Sesto is doomed; the conspiracy has failed. Was it for this that she plotted to regain the crown rightfully hers? The thought that Tito has usurped her rightful place—as the deposed Emperor's daughter—on the throne goads her to fury. Vitellia abandons herself to mingled thoughts of revenge and remorse in a brilliant recitative ("Ecco il punto, o Vitellia") and rondo ("Non più di fiori vaghe catene discenda Imene").[4]

ACT THREE

[*Scene One*] Tito's study. In chorus, members of Tito's court dutifully thank the gods that Tito has been saved from danger ("Ah grazie si rendano"). As they withdraw, Publio enters to announce that the populace is assembling in the Colosseum to witness the brutal contest between the condemned traitors and the wild beasts that will tear them to pieces. The people impatiently await the Emperor's appearance.

Tito hesitates, still refusing to believe that Sesto is guilty. Publio then produces the clinching evidence: the bloodstained cloak, he says, belonged not to Annio but to Sesto. Tito is appalled at Sesto's apparent perfidy. Annio brings in the death sentence imposed by the Senate and gives it to Publio, who in turn hands it to Tito for his signature. Tito dismisses the two.

Alone, he bursts out in bitter wrath against Sesto's heartless treachery ("Che orror! che tradimento"). He takes up his pen to sign the death warrant, but lays it aside. He decides to give the condemned man at

---

[4] In its intensity—although lacking in dazzling fioritura—this aria is in the pattern of the great Queen of the Night aria in *Die Zauberflöte*. As previously noted, Mozart interrupted work on *Zauberflöte* to complete *Tito*.

least another hearing. At his summons, Sesto is led in by Publio, and the confrontation follows in trio form.

It begins as Sesto sings that he does not recognize the face of the Emperor—it is distorted by terror ("Quello di Tito è il volto!"). Tito in turn sings that guilt has altered the very features of his faithless friend. Publio comments that the Emperor's anguish proves how deeply he has been hurt by Sesto's betrayal. Sesto, torn by remorse, begs for death to end his torment.

Tito dismisses Publio and the guards. In an ensuing recitative interlude ("Ah, Sesto, dunque è vero?") he entreats Sesto to explain what impelled him to conspire against the Emperor who loves him. Was it lust for power . . . was it remorseless ambition? When Sesto evades answering—determined not to implicate Vitellia—Tito implores him to speak as friend to friend—not as an errant subject to his monarch. When Sesto's only reply is that he deserves death as a traitor, Tito shouts in exasperation and anger: "Then you shall have it! Your ingratitude deserves it!" ("Sconoscente! e l'avrai!"). With that he leaves abruptly.

In a long aria, Sesto, on the brink of doom, turns his thoughts to Vitellia. He reflects on his love for her, his suffering because of her contempt for his cowardice and indecision, and his remorse for not having carried out the plot as she directed. Perhaps she would not condemn him, he muses, if she realized how much he loves her. The guards lead him away.

In an eloquent recitative interlude ("Dove s'intese mai più contumace infedeltà?") Tito wrestles with his conscience. He is torn between the desire to avenge himself on Sesto for his betrayal, and the horror of shedding the blood of a friend. If he now condemns Sesto, the world will say Emperor Tito is tired of mercy. But does forgiveness imply weakness . . . ? Then Tito comes to a decision: Sesto shall live, even though he is a traitor ("Viva l'amico! benchè infedele"). He tears up the death warrant.

If history will censure him, he muses, let it be for mercy, not for cruelty. He summons Publio to tell him he is now ready to go to the arena. Sesto is guilty, Tito declares, and adds—with irony that is lost on Publio —"his fate has been decided" ("Sì, Publio, è già deciso").

Then Tito, in his principal aria in the opera ("Se all'impero, amici Dei"), expounds to Publio his philosophy of kingship: if to govern demands ruthlessness and cruelty, then let the gods either take away his scepter or give him a heart of stone. But he intends to rule his people through love, honor and compassion—never through fear and blind obedience.

The Emperor leaves. Publio is about to follow when he encounters Vitellia. He tells her Sesto has confessed that he alone is guilty. Realizing that Sesto has kept faith with her, Vitellia is tortured by the thought of his love and sacrifice. Inspired by his courage, she decides to confess her guilt to Tito and absolve her lover.

[*Scene Two*] In front of the Colosseum. The populace, assembling for the spectacle in the arena, hails Tito in a chorus of extravagant homage ("Che del ciel, che degli Dei"). Inside, Sesto is led before Tito, who denounces him for the crime for which he now must die. The Emperor is about to pronounce the death sentence when Vitellia rushes in and throws herself at his feet. As Tito stares at her in disbelief she confesses that she herself plotted the rebellion, she enticed her lover into being her accomplice and the guilt is hers alone. Now she asks for the death sentence she deserves.

Overwhelmed by these litanies of crime, treachery and guilt, Tito asks the gods where he can find one truly faithful heart ("E quando troverò, giusti Numi, un'anima fedel?"). Evil events seem to conspire to make him a cruel and ruthless ruler. But he will be true to his own code of honor, he declares resolutely. Thereupon he pardons Sesto, Vitellia and all others implicated in the rebellion ("e la vita, e libertà"). Moreover, he gives Vitellia to Sesto as his bride. As for himself, he pledges his life to Rome.

The lovers—still scarcely able to believe they have been pardoned—join in fervent expressions of gratitude for the Emperor's magnanimity and compassion. This leads into the final chorus of acclamation of the Emperor Tito ("Eterni Dei, vegliate sui sacri giorni"). It rises to a climax over a blazing fanfare. The curtain falls.

[5] Notable for an obbligato written for basset horn—a tenor clarinet seldom in use today.

LE COMTE ORY

(*Count Ory*)

by GIOACCHINO ROSSINI

(1792–1868)

Libretto by

EUGÈNE SCRIBE and CHARLES DELESTRE-POIRSON

CHARACTERS

Raimbaud, a rascally friend of Count Ory	Baritone
Alice, a peasant girl	Soprano
Ragonde, confidante of Countess Adèle	Contralto
Count Ory, a notorious philanderer	Tenor
Tutor of Count Ory	Bass
Isolier, page to Count Ory	Mezzo-soprano
Countess de Formoutiers (Adèle)	Soprano
Cavalier (ensemble role)	Tenor

Cavaliers, knights, ladies-in-waiting, nuns, pages, villagers

Place: Castle of the Countess in Touraine
Time: Circa 1200, during the Crusades
First performance: Académie Royale, Paris, August 20, 1828
Original language: French

Le Comte Ory is probably the only opera that began on the vaudeville stage. Answering Rossini's request for a libretto, Scribe and Delestre-Poirson revised a vaudeville sketch they had written some twelve years earlier. They expanded its length by prefacing it with an act which became Act One of *Le Comte Ory*. Rossini then set it to music, using four numbers from his *Il Viaggio a Reims* (*The Voyage to Reims*), produced in Paris in 1825.

The opera was a great success in Paris, where it remained a staple of repertoire; by 1884 it had been staged there four hundred times. During the mid-1800s it was given in London, with the following subsequent revivals: Florence Festival (1952), Edinburgh Festival (1954), Städtische Oper, Berlin (1957), Piccola Scala, Milan (1958), Sadler's

Wells, London (1963/1972), Opera Theatre of St. Louis (1977), Santa Fe Opera (1978). The New York City Opera staged six performances during its Fall 1979 season—two on tour at the Chandler Pavilion, Los Angeles, California.

There is a brisk prelude in martial tempo, with sly dynamic effects, dominated by a vigorous theme stated by full orchestra.

ACT ONE

Outside the castle of the Countess Adèle. There is a drawbridge and a pathway leading to a nearby hermitage. Raimbaud appears to announce to a group of villagers that a hermit has arrived at the castle gates to offer advice to whomever asks for it.

Alice mischievously suggests that perhaps he will give the village girls some hints on how to win and hold a mate. Rebuking her for her impertinence, Raimbaud orders her to set up a table for the peasants—with plenty of wine. The peasants express their delight.

A sustained phrase in a change of key (also used with marked effect in the prelude) accompanies the entrance of Ragonde. She reproves the peasants for their noisy demonstrations while the mistress of the castle is mourning the absence of her brother, away on the Crusades. The Countess, she goes on, has decided to ask the hermit, famed for his wisdom, to find a cure for her melancholia. In chorus, everyone agrees that this is the logical course to take.

Count Ory enters. He is disguised as a hermit and assumes the mien of an elderly ascetic. In a cavatina ("Que les destins prospères") with a stratospheric tessitura (three high C's and an F above high C) he promises one and all to solve their problems, adding that he is particularly useful to maidens looking for husbands. Thereupon he invites all the ladies to the hermitage for further discussion. They express their undying gratitude in chorus.

As the Count preens himself on his first round of success with the feverish bevy of females, Ragonde informs him that the ladies of the castle have vowed to have nothing to do with men until their husbands and lovers return from the Crusades. Meanwhile, they are literally wasting away for lack of connubial sustenance. The Countess, Ragonde adds (to the delight of Count Ory), is particularly in need of his brand of therapy. Reiterating their thanks to the hermit, the village girls leave.

The Tutor and Isolier now enter. The Tutor, in a bad humor, morosely looks around and wonders where he is. At the Castle Formoutiers, Isolier tells him, adding in an aside that he himself is madly in love with the Countess. The Tutor frets that he has been ordered by Count Ory's father, the Duke, to keep an eye on his son—and that young hellion has been leading him a merry chase. An honorable assignment, Isolier remarks encouragingly, a tribute to your intelligence.

Inconsolable, the Tutor launches into an elaborate *andantino* aria of lamentation. Once, he sings, he was a respected scholar. Now, as the hireling of the Duke, he has been reduced to the status of an *oeil privé*—a "private eye"—to tag after his errant son. Once a distinguished intellectual, he has become the butt of an insolent young fop's japery. He ends the aria in a phrase expressing his utter humiliation.

His doleful reflections are interrupted by the girls, who return from the hermitage with ecstatic praise for the all-knowing hermit. Eyeing them skeptically, the Tutor observes that their romantic prattle means only one thing—Count Ory is in the vicinity. Accordingly, he asks the girls how long the hermit has been at the hermitage. Seven days, they answer. That confirms his suspicions, the Tutor reflects: the Count had absconded for exactly a week. In one of Rossini's inimitable ensembles, the Tutor mulls over this defection of his ward, while the girls comment derisively on his efforts to thwart the gallant young Count.

When the girls leave, he detains Alice to ask her where the hermit is. He will soon be here, Alice answers, to advise the Countess about her "symptoms." The Tutor leaves, promising to return to expose Count Ory's duplicity. Isolier, however, can only think of the joy of seeing his beloved Adèle.

At that moment, Count Ory, disguised as the hermit, stealthily enters. Isolier, who of course does not recognize him, decides to ask his advice about his own romantic problems. To the Count's chagrin, he introduces himself as Count Ory's page, and offers to pay the hermit for his counsel. In a jaunty duet, Isolier explains that he wants desperately to get inside the castle to see a certain beautiful lady—who insists on keeping their relationship strictly platonic. To complicate matters, she is awaiting the return of her brother from the Crusades. Until he arrives, she—and the ladies of her retinue as well—have vowed to allow no man to enter the castle. Count Ory can scarcely believe his ears: this upstart page is actually his rival for Adèle!

To his further surprise, Isolier confides that he has a plan for breaching the castle walls, so to speak. He will dress as a female pilgrim and enter with a group of nuns to ask for alms. Splendid, the Count murmurs admiringly—and decides to adopt the same strategy. The duet climaxes in a typical Rossinian crescendo as the two relish the thought that they have outwitted each other.

The Countess comes out of the castle with Ragonde and ladies of the court. Villagers gather to watch. She approaches the hermit; in an ensuing aria ("I live alone in sadness"—"En proie à la tristesse") she pours out her troubles. Her longing and sadness are driving her mad, she sings plaintively. In a choral accompaniment, the villagers commiserate with her. She implores the hermit to use his magic to ease the pain in her heart.

There is but one cure, the hermit says. It is his own infallible formula: fall in love. But she has forsworn love, she protests, and would rather die than break her vow. Thereupon Count Ory adroitly follows up his advantage. With all the authority of a pontiff, he releases her from her vow—"In love you shall live!" ("Que l'amour éclaire votre vie"). The Countess is beside herself with joy. In the cabaletta of her aria she declares her love for Isolier in rippling coloratura phrases sung over the choral accompaniment of the villagers.

But Count Ory hastens to warn her that this amorous page is a lecherous scoundrel as disreputable as his master, Count Ory. The Countess, shocked, allows the pious hermit to lead her toward the castle. Suddenly they are confronted by the Tutor and a group of his friends. Among them is Raimbaud, who is trying to mingle unobtrusively with the group.

To the general consternation, the Tutor points to the hermit and identifies him as Count Ory. He adds to the uproar by pointing out Raimbaud, Count Ory's friend and a rogue in his own right. When the Count, trapped, admits his identity, the principals express their amazement in a mock-heroic septet ("Indeed, it's shocking to discover"— "Quel choc de découvrir") in which the assemblage joins.

At its conclusion, a messenger hands Ragonde a letter announcing that Adèle's brother and his Crusaders will soon be home. Count Ory and Isolier quake with fright as the Countess reads the letter aloud. With deliberate sarcasm she invites them both to stay to greet the returning heroes. The people burst out in a tremendous chorus of rejoicing—one of the major ensembles of the opera.

In interspersed duets, the Count and Isolier sing that they will have their revenge and that their turn will come another day. The Tutor and Raimbaud scorn their threats. The Tutor expresses fear of the Duke's wrath when he hears about his son's latest scandalous escapades. The assemblage expresses various sentiments in the choral climax to the act.

ACT TWO

A large room in the castle where the Countess, Ragonde and the ladies of the court are awaiting the return of the Crusaders. After a brief *andante grazioso* introduction, the Countess and Ragonde—later joined by the ladies—sing that they are quite contented here without the disturbing presence of men ("Far from all men, here it is quiet"—"Dans le séjour calme et tranquille")—a delightful touch of feminine illogic. But the Countess frets that Count Ory may again try to shatter the serenity of their self-imposed "widowhood" with his lecherous designs.

Suddenly there is a clap of thunder and the ladies scream in terror. Over an accompaniment of turbulent "storm music" the Countess assures the quaking ladies that the storm will soon pass. She bids them remember that there are poor souls outside—helpless, homeless and at the mercy of the elements.

At that moment, through the clamor of the storm comes the doleful chanting of the pilgrims ("Lady, far we wander"—"Madame, au loin nous errons") making their way to the castle. As the frightened women sing a prayer for the safety of the Crusaders ("Great Lord, grant us thy aid in mercy"—"Dieu tout-puissant, aide-nous de ta grâce"), the Countess sends Ragonde to welcome the pilgrims.

As the ladies leave, Ragonde returns in great excitement to report that the pilgrims are a group of young women who have been pursued all over Europe by that fiend of a Count Ory. There are fourteen in all, not exceptionally pretty. But then, Ragonde adds with malice aforethought, the Count does not always insist on the *crème de la crème* when stalking his quarry.

In any case, she goes on, the poor girls are terror-stricken and beg for protection. One of them has asked permission to speak to the Countess. Thereupon a "pilgrim"—Count Ory in a nun's habit—is ushered in. The Countess eyes her askance, observing dryly that she is certainly no beauty. Invited to speak, Count Ory, trying to disguise his voice, begins with outrageous flattery. The dialogue continues in a scintillating duet.

While the Countess denounces the scoundrelly Count Ory, he plies her with spurious compliments and—forgetting himself—ardently kisses her hand. When she recoils in distaste, he exclaims that it is known that Count Ory loves her madly. The very idea is disgusting, the Countess retorts.

The duet continues in Rossini's best farcical vein. Irked by Adèle's disdain, the Count vows that he will yet win this "frightful delightful" wench. She expresses her contempt for scheming, devious rascals like Count Ory. Thus the duet comes to a dashing climax.

Looking out of the window, the Countess says she sees "fellow pilgrims" approaching. "My men," the Count explains, then hastily corrects himself: "My girls." The Countess hospitably offers to serve them refreshments. A moment later the Tutor, Raimbaud and the Count's cavaliers troop in, absurdly dressed in women's clothing. They roar out a lusty chorus in praise of folly—specifically, their own masquerade.

In a recitative aside, Count Ory explains to the Tutor that his page, Isolier, is at the bottom of this silly business. It was his scheme to have the Count and his followers masquerade as women to get into the castle —forbidden to men. Once inside, the Count confides, he and Isolier discovered that they were in love with the same woman: namely, Countess

Adèle. The Tutor rants against Isolier's tactics, but the Count candidly admits that they helped him personally.

As the men reprise the "chorus of folly," refreshments are brought in for the pilgrims. Looking disdainfully at the fruit and milk, they shout: "Where's the wine?" Thereupon Raimbaud enters holding aloft a bottle of wine. Then in a long and robust aria (too long to explain in recitative, he interpolates) he regales the company with a cock-and-bull story about how he discovered the secret door to the wine cellar.

There before his eyes were bottles of every description: champagne, red wines, white wines, heavy wines, light wines. Then, just as he was leaving with his arms full of liquid loot, his thievery was discovered by the concierge and the servants, who bawled: "Arrest him!" In a crisis of this kind, Raimbaud orates, there is but one logical thing to do: run. He did, and here's the wine. He hopes that every one will swallow his story as easily as they swallow the wine.

Count Ory, the Tutor and the cavaliers call for a toast to Raimbaud and also to the *former* owner of the wine—the absent brother of their gracious hostess, Countess Adèle. There is a thunderous chorus in response. Suddenly Count Ory warns that someone is approaching. He quickly orders the men to hide the bottles, behave like ladies and try to look sober. Ragonde passes by. For her benefit, Count Ory, a cavalier, Raimbaud and the Tutor solemnly intone a chorus of supplication.

No sooner is she out of sight than the drinking chorus is resumed—but only briefly. Again the Count calls out a warning, and there is a frantic scramble to hide the bottles. This time it is the Countess, who appears to assure the tired "pilgrims" that they will be made comfortable for the night. Switching to his role as a pilgrim, Count Ory thanks her profusely. She leaves, and then the pilgrims unsteadily make their way out of the room.

A moment later the Countess reappears with Ragonde and a lady-in-waiting just as a bell rings. Ragonde reports that the visitor is a page. The Countess angrily demands to know what man would dare enter her castle. Isolier walks in and brashly announces: "I am that man." He explains he has been sent by the Duke to inform the Countess that her brother and all his men will arrive at the castle at midnight.

In brief trio interludes, Adèle, her lady-in-waiting and Ragonde joyously greet the news. Isolier pointedly remarks that the Duke has always held that husbands should send word of their arrival before they reach home—to avoid complications. The Countess observes that there are others here who will be happy to learn of the Crusaders' return: the fourteen unfortunate girls who were harried by Count Ory. Thereupon Isolier stupefies the three women by disclosing that those poor innocents are really Count Ory's cavaliers masquerading as women.

Ragonde moans that she will never be able to explain to her husband on his return why the castle—sealed against men by stern vows of chastity—harbored fourteen cavaliers! Isolier, relishing his triumph over Count Ory, blandly assures the three women that everything will be satisfactorily explained in due course.

What follows is an operatic bedroom farce that only Rossini could bring off. The stage darkens as the orchestra begins a *misterioso* theme. First Count Ory steals in, hoping for a tryst with Adèle. In the dark he encounters Isolier, who is here for the same reason. The Countess sings that the magic of the night both frightens and fascinates her. The three voices blend in an intriguing trio ("The night and all this silence"—"À la faveur de cette nuit obscure")—probably the most famous number in the opera.

The Countess hears a noise and asks who is there. In a girlish falsetto, Count Ory answers that it is "little Rosina," who begs to be allowed to sleep in the Countess's room because she is afraid of the dark. Knowing it is the Count, Isolier suppresses an angry exclamation.

In the dark, Count Ory grasps Isolier's hand, thinking it is Adèle's. With his free hand, Isolier takes Adèle's as he sings, aside, that the Count will soon regret his mistake. At the same time, Count Ory, in his natural voice, exults over the success of his conquest. Adèle, becoming impatient, sharply suggests that "little Rosina" return to her own room.

At that, "Rosina-Count" sings passionately that he will never leave his beloved, ardently kisses Isolier's hand, then finally manages to embrace the furious Adèle herself.

But all this implausible trysting comes to a sudden stop when martial music is heard outside. The Countess mockingly warns the flustered Count that the Crusaders returning to their women will put an end to his philandering. To Isolier she sings that now at last all fears and uncertainties are over.

In the continuation of the trio, she and Isolier happily anticipate the return of the Crusaders, while the frustrated Count Ory laments that this night everything has gone awry. The trio ends in a surge of mixed emotions on the theme: "The men return again!"

As is usual in bedroom farces, the rival lovers discover each other as daylight dawns. Count Ory curses his page as a traitor. Isolier warns him that his father, the Duke, has been informed of his son's latest caper and will ask some questions. Count Ory falls to his knees before Adèle and implores mercy for himself and his cavaliers. Looking down at him contemptuously, Adèle advises him to make his escape before the various husbands arrive and toss him out of the window.

Isolier (who has won the game and can afford to be magnanimous) offers to help the Count escape through a secret passageway. The hapless Count sums up his ignominy in a bad pun: *Foiled by a page out of my own book!* Sadder—and presumably wiser—the erstwhile gay seducer beats a retreat. Led by Countess Adèle, Isolier and Ragonde, all in the scene hail the return of the victorious Crusaders. The curtain falls.

LE COQ D'OR

(*The Golden Cockerel*)

by Nikolai Andreyevitch Rimsky-Korsakov

(1844–1908)

Libretto by

VLADIMIR BIELSKY

Based on a fairy tale by Pushkin

CHARACTERS

The Astrologer	Tenor
King Dodon	Bass
Prince Guidon ⎱ sons of King Dodon	⎰ Tenor
Prince Aphron ⎰	⎱ Baritone
General Polkan, commander-in-chief of the King's armies	Bass
Amelfa, the royal housekeeper	Contralto
The Queen of Chemakha	Soprano

Boyars, townspeople, soldiers, slaves, dancers

Place: Mythical
Time: Legendary
First performance: Zimin's Theater, Moscow, September 24, 1909
Original language: Russian

Le Coq d'Or, the last of some fifteen operas by Rimsky-Korsakov, is a delightful mixture of fantasy, symbolism and political satire. The fact that it portrays a monarch as a lazy, capricious individual is said to have provoked the disapproval of the censor, who banned the production until certain changes had been made. The first performance did not take place until after the composer's death. Besides making extraordinary demands on the vocal resources of the artists, the opera requires singers who can dance and dancers who can sing. In some presentations it is given with the singers seated at the sides of the stage, while dancers pantomime the action.

There is a brief prelude in which we hear the musical phrase imitating the crowing of the Golden Cockerel and the theme characterizing the Queen of Chemakha.

PROLOGUE

The Astrologer, holding a magic key, appears before the curtain and addresses the audience ("Ya, koldoon. Naookoy taynoy"). As a magician endowed with extraordinary gifts of enchantment, he declares, he is about to conjure up an ancient fairy tale. None of it is true, he says, but it contains a lesson that is worth remembering. With these words the Astrologer disappears.

ACT ONE

The council hall of King Dodon's palace. Dodon is seated on a magnificent throne and at his side are his two sons, Prince Guidon and Prince Aphron. Before the King, seated in a semicircle, are the boyars[1] and General Polkan, commander of the King's armies. The soldiers who are posted as guards are sound asleep. Dodon, who appears troubled and anxious, complains of his arduous duties as ruler of the kingdom ("Ya vas sdyes zatem sozval"). Just as he has decided to take a rest from the cares of state, a neighboring king takes up arms against him. No sooner has he dispelled the threat of invasion from the north and south than the enemy strikes from the coast. It is all very disheartening, Dodon wails, and he could weep with anger. Now, he declares, he wants some constructive advice from his councilors.

Guidon at once rises to say that he has been thinking about the problem all night long and has finally arrived at a solution ("Noch vsew doomal do zari"). The trouble is, he says, that their own soldiers are too close to the enemy—they are face to face with the foe across the border. Withdraw the troops, he advises, post them around the capital, and lay in plentiful supplies of food and wine. While the enemy is expending himself in destroying the surrounding villages, their own troops can make good use of the time by training. When the enemy has finally exhausted his power in comparatively minor depredations, Dodon's forces can annihilate him in a surprise assault. The boyars loudly hail Guidon's superior strategical wisdom, but the Prince modestly deprecates their praises.

The only dissenter is General Polkan, who growls that there is a possibility the enemy may attack the capital first. Imagine what would hap-

[1] Privileged members of Russian aristocracy, next to the ruling princes. The class was abolished by Peter the Great (1682–1725).

pen, he remarks, if their beloved sovereign should get in the way of a bullet. There is general consternation. Dodon angrily declares that Polkan should be jailed for such treasonable utterances. The King then calls on Prince Aphron for suggestions.

As usual, Aphron begins, his brother is completely wrong about everything. At those words Guidon advances menacingly on Aphron, while Dodon implores the two not to waste time quarreling. Aphron then explains *his* plan ("Chto lookavit"), which, he says, is naturally the only logical one. Dismiss the troops, he counsels, and send them home. This will lull the enemy into a false sense of security. Then, exactly a month before the day on which the foe will make an assault on the capital, the army is to be quickly called up again to deliver a surprise attack which will catch the foe off his guard and put him to rout. Dodon, overjoyed at this magnificent display of military reasoning on the part of his youngest son, fervently embraces him, while the boyars acclaim his genius.

But Polkan again protests. As the enemy is notorious for his lack of consideration, he observes sardonically, he probably will neglect to notify the King as to the day on which he proposes to attack the capital. Dodon and the entire court turn on poor Polkan and denounce him for his miserable, unsoldierly objections, after which they ignore him completely.

When the King asks for further advice on the problem, one of the boyars remarks that it is a pity that some of the official fortunetellers of the kingdom have gone to their reward. A violent argument develops as to the best method of foretelling the future—counting beans, reading the dregs of a cup of kvass, or divining the stars. When the dispute is at its height, the Astrologer comes in. An impressive figure in a white shako and a long blue robe decorated with stars, he carries an astrolabe and a bag. As the boyars stare at him openmouthed, the Astrologer walks over to the throne and bows respectfully to King Dodon.

In an ensuing aria ("Slaven bood velikiy tsar") he explains the purpose of his visit. He has heard of the King's dilemma and has brought with him a fabulous bird which will protect the King and his realm from all harm. It is a Golden Cockerel. Placed upon a high perch, the Cockerel will stand guard day and night and crow a warning when danger threatens. The moment the foe appears, the Cockerel will shake his golden comb, turn in the direction from which the enemy is approaching, and utter his warning cry, "Kiricoocoo!"

As the boyars crowd around, the Astrologer reaches into his bag and brings forth the Golden Cockerel, which flaps its wings, crows, and proclaims that it will stand guard. Beside himself with joy, Dodon orders the bird to be placed on the highest perch available and then asks the Astrologer how he can reward him for this priceless boon. He need only ask, Dodon exclaims, and it will be granted. The Astrologer replies that worldly treasures do not interest him ("Mudretczam dari nye lestni"). All he desires is Dodon's promise in writing that he may have anything he asks. Bridling at this implied reflection on the value of his word, Dodon refuses, loudly assuring the Astrologer of his good faith. Bowing, the Astrologer leaves. Dodon dismisses the boyars.

As the Cockerel crows and exhorts the King to take his ease, Dodon settles down to pleasant reflections ("To to stchastye! Rooki slojha"). How convenient it will be, he muses, to take a nap whenever he pleases and rule his kingdom without lifting a finger. Meanwhile he will enjoy himself with music and dancing. Descending from his throne, he goes to the open door of the council chamber and stretches himself out in the sun.

The housekeeper, Amelfa, enters, urges the monarch to banish all cares of state, and offers him a variety of delicacies. Nibbling away at them, Dodon tells Amelfa to see to it that he does not fall asleep sitting up. She is to awaken him later if it becomes absolutely necessary. He then decides that he wants his parrot. After talking to the bird for a few moments he becomes bored, and Amelfa takes the parrot away. At her command the servants bring in an enormous bed made of ivory and covered with luxurious furs. Dodon lies down on it and immediately falls asleep, while Amelfa sits at his side and brushes the flies away from his face. The atmosphere of slumber gradually pervades the entire palace. Amelfa herself finally falls asleep at the side of the bed. The Cockerel crows softly, while an unseen chorus sings in brief, drowsy phrases.

The silence is shattered a few moments later by the shrill warning crow of the Cockerel. Pandemonium breaks loose as panic-stricken people storm into the palace, shouting that the enemy is at the gates of the capital. Polkan dashes in, arouses Dodon, and finally makes him understand that danger is threatening. Dodon jumps up and begins haranguing the crowd, appealing to them in the name of patriotism to put all their treasures and goods at the disposal of the army ("Noo, rebyatushki, voyna!").

Guidon and Aphron rush in. The King embraces his sons and urges them to hurry off to battle. They plead for a little more time to prepare, however, saying that the soldiers can do the fighting in the meanwhile. Polkan fumes that the Cockerel is making the air hideous with his crowing and is spinning madly about on his perch. Now he stops and faces eastward, Polkan wails, and in that sector the defenses are the weakest. He then advises sending all the old men as well into battle.

Dodon calls excitedly for his armor and his great red shield. The servants drag in the rusty, dust-covered armor and laboriously try to help the King put it on. He frets about its being too tight for him. His shield is eaten through with rust, he complains; the sword is too heavy; he cannot get his breath. He calls for a horse—a gentle one. When it is led forth, the servants, by dint of much pushing and tugging, finally get him into the saddle. At intervals the shrill warning of the Cockerel cuts through the din.

Ordering Polkan to go before him, Dodon starts off to war. Amelfa, much distressed, calls after him that he has forgotten to eat. The King answers that he can eat on the way. As Dodon rides away with Polkan the people hail him as their glorious leader and warn him not to go too near the enemy. The curtain falls.

ACT TWO

A narrow pass in a desolate mountain region. Lying everywhere are the bodies of hundreds of warriors killed in battle. Black carrion birds are perched on the corpses, among which are those of Guidon and Aphron. Their two horses stand with heads lowered over the bodies of their masters. A gray mist swirls over the scene and a cold wind is blowing. It is night.

The remnants of King Dodon's army, marching in double file across the battlefield, comment on the grisly scene in a mournful chorus ("Shepchet strakhi noch nemaya"). They speak of the evil birds of prey sitting on the corpses in the ghostly light of the moon, and of the icy wind that walks among the dead, sorrowing over their fate.

The soldiers stand silently as King Dodon and Polkan ride up. Suddenly they come upon the slain princes. Dismounting, King Dodon throws himself on the bodies of his sons and gives way to his grief and anguish in a poignant refrain ("Chto za strashnaya cartina"). He sobs that his two beloved sons lie here on ground soaked with their own blood, each slain by the other's sword in the confusion of battle. Crying that both his brave falcons have been snared, Dodon raises his arms and calls upon the mountains and valleys to weep with him in his sorrow. The soldiers utter phrases of lamentation. Dodon cries that henceforth he himself will lead his armies into battle so that the lives of young men will not be needlessly sacrificed.

Polkan, philosophically observing that what is done is done, announces to the soldiers that they must now annihilate the enemy to avenge King Dodon's misfortune. The soldiers swear that they will fight —as soon as they find the enemy. Pacing up and down, Dodon rages that the treacherous blackguards who inflicted this loss upon him must be run down and destroyed.

Meanwhile the rising sun dispels the mists and brings into view a large, brilliantly colored tent. Peering at it, Polkan declares that it is probably the tent of the enemy commander-in-chief and orders his soldiers to attack it at once. Unwilling to do any more fighting, the soldiers hang back, reluctantly loading their weapons. The cannoneers suggest that it would be safer first to fire from a distance. Polkan agrees, and then the cannoneers wheel an absurd-looking cannon into position, load it, and aim.

Just as Polkan is about to give the order to fire, a ravishingly beautiful young woman emerges from the tent, followed by four slaves carrying musical instruments. She is resplendently gowned and wears a white turban with a long feather. Turning toward the sun, she raises her arms in a gesture of invocation and sings the beautiful "Hymn to the Sun" ("Otvet mnye zorkoye svetilo"). In phrases of exotic beauty she implores the sun to tell her of her native land. She asks if the roses and the lilies still bloom in all their loveliness, if the maidens still go down to the river's edge at dusk to sing of the forbidden delights of love, and if they still go to meet their lovers in the cool, soft darkness with tender promises and warm kisses on their lips. The aria dies away on a lovely minor strain.

Dodon, who has been listening as though spellbound, pokes Polkan in the ribs and tells him to take due note of the lady's beautiful singing. The general suggests with a wink that if she invites them to stay and rest awhile they certainly should accept. The two walk hesitantly toward the young woman. When Dodon asks her name she answers in alluring phrases that she is the Queen of Chemakha and that she is on her way to conquer his nation ("V svoey vole ya devitcza"). The idea, says Dodon, is rather quaint, for in order to fight a war one must have an army. The Queen replies that she does not need an army—she conquers with beauty alone. She claps her hands, and two slaves bring wine for Dodon and Polkan. Dodon warily invites her to drink first. Looking at him seductively, the Queen asks if he could possibly imagine that anyone as beautiful as she would poison him. Greatly embarrassed, Dodon drinks and Polkan does likewise.

The slaves bring out a carpet and arrange seats of pillows for the Queen's guests. At a signal from Polkan the soldiers retire and begin dragging the bodies from the battlefield in the background. After a moment of uncomfortable silence Polkan clumsily attempts to make conversation by asking the Queen if she slept well. She assures Polkan that she slept soundly but adds that she was awakened at dawn by the sound of someone sighing passionately. The air was heavy with a choking perfume, and then she heard a voice tenderly calling to her. With a crude attempt at humor Polkan asks if she looked under the bed.

The Queen tartly answers that it was dark and then goes on musing over the mysterious nocturnal visitor. Polkan's persistent scoffing over what he calls romantic nonsense finally arouses the Queen's ire, and she requests Dodon to send this annoying boor away. Dodon angrily orders

Polkan to sit behind the tent. The general hurriedly obeys. He is seen occasionally sticking his head out in an effort to hear what is being said.

Moving close to Dodon, the Queen murmurs in his ear that she wishes to talk to him privately about several matters ("Oo menya k tebe yest dyelo"). This marks the beginning of a long colloquy that is carried on to the accompaniment of a flood of sensuous and exotic music. Dodon begins to show some alarm over the Queen's provocative looks and gestures. She begins by remarking that she often wonders if she is really as beautiful as people say she is. When she asks Dodon his opinion he can only stammer incoherently. It is a pity, says the Queen, that he must look upon her when her beauty is hidden by her garments. In a voluptuous melody ("Sbroshoo choporniya tkani") she describes how, when she retires, she lets her robes fall from her and gazes at herself in the mirror to see if perhaps any blemish mars her loveliness. Then she removes her combs, and her hair streams over her body in a black torrent. So that she may enjoy refreshing sleep, the Queen continues, she bathes herself in dew. She concludes with a more detailed description of her charms, all of which leaves Dodon gasping and a little pale. When the Queen asks him if he is ill he controls himself with an effort and mutters that it is merely his liver.

Deliberately tantalizing him, the Queen sings a song which concludes with an invitation to enter her tent. Perhaps the old man would at least like to look inside, she murmurs. Dodon hastily assures her that he really is not as old as he looks. In caressing tones the Queen says that she has tired herself with singing and asks Dodon to favor her with a song. If he has ever been in love, she sighs, he surely must have sung. Assuring her that his repertoire is endless, the fatuous Dodon strikes up a ridiculous ditty—fortunately very brief ("Boodoo vek tebya loobit"). The Queen applauds him in cynical merriment.

As the conversation continues the Queen's mood of ironic mockery gives way to melancholy, and in another sensuous refrain she voices her longing for her homeland ("Da, doyedesh do vostoka"). As though seeing a vision, she describes an enchanted island, where her white palace gleams through the cypress trees. There on her throne she reigns in solitary splendor. No one is near, and yet, by means of her magic power, she can summon a host of young friends who will amuse her with laughter and gaiety. But then everything fades into the shadows, and she is left to weep alone in her palace on that fabled and mysterious island.

Lamenting over these painful memories, the Queen cries that she can no longer bear her grief and loneliness. She longs for a man who will put an end to the aimlessness of her existence by possessing her and ruling her life. Thereupon Dodon loudly declares that her troubles are over, for he is the very man who is qualified to be her lord and master.

Pretending to be delighted with the idea, the Queen asks him to dance with her by way of celebration. Dodon protests that he is out of practice, but the Queen continues to coax. She makes him look more ridiculous than ever by draping a scarf around his shoulders and placing a fan in his hands. But Dodon, noticing the soldiers looking on, refuses point-blank to make a fool of himself in front of his army. When the Queen, however, threatens to dance with Polkan, Dodon changes his mind and begins prancing about in an awkward attempt at dancing.

Slave girls come out of the tent and begin a slow, sinuous dance, in which the Queen joins. Weaving and swaying before the posturing Dodon, the Queen mocks and gibes at his clumsiness. The King is oblivious to her taunts, however, as he begins whirling madly about to keep pace with the quickening tempo of the music. Laughing hysterically, the Queen finally sits down to watch his foolish antics.

At length Dodon falls exhausted at her feet. After a moment he rises and, completely under her spell, offers his entire kingdom, including himself. He implores her to come with him, saying that he will spare nothing to make her happy. They will lie at their ease all day long, he promises, with nothing to do but eat sweetmeats and listen to fairy tales. The Queen answers that she will go, provided that boor of a general is given a sound beating for his insolence. Dodon promptly offers to have him beheaded.

The Queen immediately prepares to depart. At her call the slaves hurry out of the tent, dress her for the journey, and bring out all her belongings. The soldiers also prepare to march. Dodon calls for the Queen's golden chariot. As he and the Queen seat themselves in it the Queen ironically commands her slaves to sing the praises of the royal bridegroom.

The procession at last moves off, with the slaves chanting a mocking chorus of praise in which they hail Dodon as a sorry humbug with the gait of a camel and the features of an ape ("Sestry kto khromayet ryadom"). As soldiers and slaves join in shouts of acclaim, the curtain falls.

ACT THREE

The capital of Dodon's realm, with the palace in the background. Although the sun is blazing down, black thunderclouds loom on the horizon. An ominous, oppressive calm pervades the streets. The Golden Cockerel is seen perched motionless on his spire. People are crowded in the street in front of the palace, gaping at the couriers who rush in and out. There is an air of intense excitement as the city awaits the royal procession.

In an agitated chorus ("Strashno, bratiki") the people talk among themselves. Some take heart from the fact that the Golden Cockerel is silent on his perch, while others murmur in frightened tones about the sullen clouds on the horizon and warn that a violent storm will soon strike the city.

Amelfa appears on the steps of the palace. Crowding around her, the people anxiously inquire if there is any news of the King. At first she impatiently orders them to be off, but finally, to quiet their clamor, she tells them what has happened ("Vot kackye vesti"). Their monarch, she proclaims, has sent word that he has conquered four kings—named Hearts, Spades, Clubs and Diamonds, respectively—and has saved a beautiful princess from the jaws of a dragon. He is bringing her to the city to be their Queen.

Someone asks about Guidon and Aphron. They were put in irons and executed by their father, Amelfa replies. The crowd asks why they were put to death. They quarreled, Amelfa tells the people, adding contemptuously that their own heads may be lopped off next. As the people bow and scrape before her a fanfare is heard in the distance. Looking down at the throng, Amelfa sardonically exhorts all to caper and dance about for joy over the King's return. They needn't, however, expect any favors or mercy, she adds.

There is a tremendous uproar as the procession appears, led by the strutting warriors. Then comes Queen Chemakha's fantastic retinue, made up of a grotesque array of freaks—dwarfs, giants, horned people, some with dog heads, people with a single eye in their foreheads, and so on. They are followed by male and female slaves carrying enormous quantities of treasure.

Finally the golden chariot appears with Dodon and the Queen. Dodon has lost his air of fatuous pride and seems apprehensive. He keeps looking at the Queen, who ignores him and gazes disdainfully at the crowd. The people greet their monarch with a rousing chorus ("Dolgo jhit tebe, Oorra!"), in which they assure him that they will stand on their heads, if necessary, to amuse him. It was only to serve him that they were born at all, they shout.

Just as Dodon is about to descend from the chariot the Astrologer appears. He walks slowly toward the chariot, the crowd respectfully making way before him, while the Queen stares at him as though hypnotized. Dodon greets him cordially and asks what he wants. With his eyes on the Queen the Astrologer replies to Dodon's greeting and then suggests that they now settle their bargain ("Tsar velikiy yeto ya! Razotchemsya kack droozya"). He reminds Dodon that he promised him anything he desired in return for bringing him the Golden Cockerel. Now, says the Astrologer, he desires Queen Chemakha.

Dodon promptly flies into a rage, shouting that he has no patience with such silly requests. Why—of all things—should he ask for the Queen? The Astrologer quietly replies that he desires to know the delights of love and wishes to marry. Dodon fumes that he may have anything else—knighthood, a horse from the royal stables, half his kingdom—but not the Queen. When the Astrologer repeats the request Dodon loses his temper completely and orders the guards to take the Astrologer to prison. When he turns back to protest this injustice, Dodon, in a burst of rage, strikes him dead with his sword. There is a terrific clap of thunder as the Astrologer falls. Laughing sardonically, the Queen observes that such is the fate of all disobedient serfs.

Looking down at the body, Dodon wonders if this bloodshed will bring misfortune on their marriage. Nothing more than an argument at the wedding feast, perhaps, says the Queen casually. Reassured, Dodon tries to kiss her, whereupon she pushes him away and denounces him as a miserable, doddering fool whom the very earth itself detests. She warns him that his own doom is not far off. Smiling vacantly, Dodon remarks that she is joking. There has already been one jest, the Queen says grimly.

As they descend from the chariot the Golden Cockerel flies from its perch. Crowing harshly, it hovers over Dodon, crying that it will peck the King's head. The people cower in fear. Suddenly the Cockerel hurtles downward and kills Dodon with a blow of its beak. There is a tremendous crash of thunder and the scene is plunged into darkness. Out of the blackness comes the Queen's malicious laughter. When the light returns, both the Queen and the Cockerel have vanished.

In astonishment and stupefaction the people look at the body of King Dodon. Falling to their knees, they break into a dramatic chorus of lamentation ("Oomer tsar. Oobit serdechniy"). The King is dead, they cry, their happy, fearless King—wisest of monarchs, who ruled while he lay at his ease in his palace. When angered by his subjects, he punished sternly but justly, and when his anger passed he smiled on all, and his smile was like the sunlight. In hopeless despair the people ask each other how they will live without a king. As they bow to the ground, shaken by sobs, the curtain falls.

EPILOGUE

The Astrologer steps once more before the curtain. The story, he says, is ended ("Vot chem konchilasya skazka"). The spectators, however, need not take its tragic conclusion too much to heart, for the truth of the matter is that of all the people in the play only the Queen and he himself were real. The others were mere phantoms. So saying, he vanishes.

THE CRUCIBLE
by ROBERT WARD
(1917–)

Libretto by
BERNARD STAMBLER

Based on the play of the same name by Arthur Miller

CHARACTERS

Betty Parris	Mezzo-soprano
Reverend Samuel Parris	Tenor
Tituba	Contralto
Abigail Williams	Soprano
Ann Putnam	Soprano
Thomas Putnam	Baritone
Rebecca Nurse	Contralto
Francis Nurse	Bass
Giles Corey	Tenor
John Proctor	Baritone
Reverend John Hale	Bass
Elizabeth Proctor	Mezzo-soprano
Mary Warren	Soprano
Ezekiel Cheever	Tenor
Judge Danforth	Tenor
Sarah Good	Soprano

Chorus of girls: Betty Parris (mezzo-soprano), Ruth Putnam (coloratura), Susanna Walcott (contralto), Mercy Lewis (contralto), Martha Sheldon (soprano), Bridget Booth (soprano)

Place: Salem, Massachusetts
Time: 1692
First performance: New York City Opera Company, New York, October 26, 1961
Original language: English

As the work of three contemporary Americans, as well as in the locale of its plot, *The Crucible* is a native American opera in every sense of the word. It began as a play written by the dramatist Arthur Miller and successfully produced on Broadway. Its composer, born in Cleveland, Ohio, studied and taught at the Eastman School of Music and the Juilliard School of Music. The librettist, a native New Yorker, was formerly head of the Academic Department of Juilliard.

Sung by a cast of young American singing actors, *The Crucible* was given its world premiere by the New York City Opera during its 1961–62 season, and was unanimously acclaimed by critics as a milestone in the annals of American opera. At the close of the 1961–62 season it was awarded the Pulitzer Prize for Music and the New York Music Critics Citation. Since that time it has become established in the repertory of regional opera companies throughout the country.

The plot of this opera is based on a bizarre chapter in American history—the infamous witchcraft trials in the Puritan settlement of Salem, Massachusetts. A powerful mixture of religion and sex, it is a story about innocent people trapped by accusations made by individuals temporarily deranged by mass hysteria. The demonic quality of Robert Ward's music reflects the madness which obsessed the impressionable young women whose screaming charges of witchcraft doomed their neighbors.

The score, in the modern idiom, is atonal, but a melodic line predominates. There are no arias in the conventional sense, although certain passages begin as arias and lose their identity as such when they merge with the ensemble. There is no overture. The curtain rises immediately.

ACT ONE

A spring morning in 1692. The house of The Reverend Parris in Salem. He is kneeling at the bed, on which his daughter Betty is lying motionless, scarcely breathing. Parris watches her silently as a keening, sinister figure sounds high in the strings. The servant Tituba, a Negress, enters and anxiously asks if her Betty is going to die. Parris angrily orders her out of the room, then in panic-stricken tones implores his daughter to awaken. She does not move.

As he bends over her, Abigail, his niece, bursts into the room. She tells Parris that a neighbor girl, Susanna Walcott, has come from the doctor with the message that he is unable to prescribe a cure for Betty. In an ominous, unaccompanied phrase, Abigail adds that the doctor advises looking for "unnatural causes."

When Parris flares up at this, Abigail, in growing excitement, warns him that the townsfolk are gossiping about witches . . . and perhaps he'd better go out and explain. "Explain that I found my daughter and my niece dancing in the forest like pagans," Parris breaks in wrathfully.

His outburst is underscored by a remarkable orchestral effect—an ascending unison passage interspersed with harsh open fourths.

Under Parris' relentless questioning Abigail admits that she and Betty danced under the trees, with Tituba making strange gestures over the fire. But she vehemently denies the preacher's accusation that they danced naked. Over the pulsating 12/8 rhythm of the accompaniment, Parris demands an explanation. For three years, he says, he has tried to win his stubborn congregation over to reason and respect. Now she—Abigail—has made a mockery of his efforts through her folly. His future is at stake. There is one thing he must know: Why did Elizabeth Proctor discharge her as a servant? What is more, why is it that Mrs. Proctor no longer comes to church, giving as the reason that she does not want to sit next to "something soiled"?

Abigail retorts that Goody Proctor is bitter because she—Abigail—refuses to work for her as a slave. If she wants a slave, the girl goes on, let her send to Barbados for one. In rising anger Abigail cries that her name is as good as any woman's in Salem. Elizabeth Proctor, she screams over a descending chromatic passage, is a liar.

There is a knock at the door. Parris, ordering Abigail to stay at Betty's bedside, goes to the door to greet Ann and Thomas Putnam. They ask about Betty, then, over dark, sustained chords in the orchestra, they tell Parris that their daughter Ruth is suffering from the same affliction. But it is not a sickness, Ann says, it is the devil's touch: Ruth's eyes are open but she sees nothing . . . she walks, she eats . . . She has been robbed of her soul.

It is witchcraft, Putnam cries, then tells Parris he has sent to Beverly for the Reverend Hale, who knows how to deal with witches. Parris, outraged at the suspicion that he is harboring witchcraft in his own house, asks the Putnams if they would have him howled out of Salem. Ann hysterically wails that once the devil took only babies—now he takes young women. Putnam sobs that Ruth, the last of their eight children, is dying before their eyes and not even the doctor can help.

At that moment, Rebecca and Francis Nurse enter, followed by Giles Corey. They too inquire about Betty. Before Parris can answer, Ann tells them that their daughter Ruth also has been stricken and that it is the devil's work. Parris says quickly that no one knows the cause of the illness. Putnam reminds him that he has sent to Beverly for the Reverend Hale. Giles sarcastically observes that perhaps the Reverend Hale will make Betty fly again—the way neighbor Collis saw her soar like a bird over the treetops.

Putnam turns on him angrily for jesting at a time like this, then pompously quotes the Bible to the effect that witches must not be suffered to live—and there are witches this moment in Salem. His words are underscored by an equally pompous fanfare in the orchestra.

Yes . . . call them witches and hang them all, Giles sneers. Then Thomas Putnam can take over their land. Putnam turns on Corey in fury and a violent quarrel breaks out as he threatens to bring Corey before the law for slander. This is the devil's work, Putnam says, and the Bible will bear him out. Corey retorts that even the devil can quote Scripture to his purpose. Thereupon Putnam accuses Giles of twisting the Scriptures—the way John Proctor does.

"Twisting, that's the word for you," Giles bursts out in a dramatic refrain. He reminds Putnam that his own father stole half his neighbor's land and called it his Christian duty. And now his son cries "witch" so he can steal the rest of it. As for John Proctor, he is an honest, upright man whose reputation is safe from the likes of Thomas Putnam.

At this point, Rebecca Nurse sharply intervenes. Quarreling will not help, she sings. This introduces an aria in which Rebecca tries to dispel the bitterness that is alienating the neighbors. The bustling music subsides into a serene melodic line as she reassures the parents that the girls will recover. As the mother of eleven children and twenty-six times a grandmother, she observes, she understands the silly games children sometimes play. One of them is an ancient sport: "Bedevil the old ones." But the "old ones" must be patient. As Rebecca sings, John Proctor enters unnoticed and listens intently.

Thomas Putnam impatiently interrupts Rebecca, fuming that there is no time for all this nonsense. None at all, Rebecca agrees gravely. In a flowing, Puccinilike melody she sings that love alone is the cure for this childhood malady. A child is a runaway thing, and love is the only lure that can bring the runaway home.

As the aria ends on a quiet phrase, John Proctor steps forward with a word of approbation. The others voice surprise at seeing him. Meanwhile, Abigail, who has been in Betty's bedroom on the floor above during this scene, comes forward as she hears Proctor's voice. Unnoticed by those below, she stares down at Proctor, then begins pacing back and forth in feverish excitement.

Now the quarreling breaks out again. Proctor sharply asks Putnam why he sent for Reverend Hale without official permission of the congregation. Because it was necessary, Putnam snaps. Rebecca again intervenes, exhorting all to trust in prayer rather than in Reverend Hale. Here an ensemble builds up as Putnam, Proctor, Giles and Parris—ignoring Rebecca—lash out at each other with bitter recriminations. As the quarrel rages, Abigail, watching from the floor above, grows wilder and more abandoned in her movements. Her body undulates as though goaded by passionate desire.

In towering fury, Proctor roars that neither Parris nor Putnam will be allowed to bring ruin to Salem with their threats of hellfire and damnation. He, John Proctor, will see to it that all the townspeople have an equal voice in deciding between right and wrong. Whirling on Putnam, Proctor cries out: "You wear no halo!" Parris screams: "Blasphemy!"

Rebecca, thrusting herself between the men, fiercely commands them to stop quarreling. Their feuding will "tear the town apart," she warns. This brings the men to their senses and the dispute subsides. Parris unctuously asks all to forget their differences and join in singing a psalm. Proctor, growling that soul searching is more important than psalm singing, stalks out of the room, with Giles Corey following.

Parris announces the grim Puritan hymn: "Jesus, my consolation." He is lustily joined by Ann Putnam, Rebecca, Thomas Putnam and Francis Nurse. Abigail, now quieter, comes to the head of the stairs and sings with them until she notices that Betty is beginning to writhe and moan on the bed.

At this point, separate action continues simultaneously in two scenes —one in the bedroom, the other in the parlor below. The orchestral accompaniment is so divided that each scene has its own music. While the elders roar out the psalm, Betty's movements become more violent. Abigail vainly implores her to be quiet and tries to hold her down.

Suddenly, with a wild shriek, Betty tears herself free and dashes to the window with her arms spread in a flying motion. Abigail screams for help. A rising chromatic passage in the orchestra accentuates the terror of the moment.

The psalm singing breaks off abruptly and the singers scramble up the stairs. The men clumsily try to quiet Betty. Rebecca pushes them aside, takes the hysterical girl in her arms, and calms her with a soothing gesture. During the uproar, Reverend Hale enters and goes upstairs. He carries a heavy book. Going to the bed, he begins asking questions with a ponderous air of authority. Ann Putnam whimpers that Betty is possessed and cannot hear the Lord's name. Not only that, she tried to fly—fearsome proof of the devil's work. Parris, with a desperate look at Hale, declares that one cannot be certain of this. Hale solemnly agrees.

In an ensuing refrain, "For much in the world seems devil's work," Hale pontificates on the mysteries of witchcraft. It is all revealed here, he sings as he opens his book—all the evil secrets of the demon world. This book is the weapon which will crush Satan, once he has been hunted down, Hale goes on with fanatical fervor. He raises Betty to a sitting position and in caressing tones commands her to awaken. When the girl gives no sign of hearing, he releases her and begins to question the elders about what happened. Ann tells him Betty was stricken after she, Ruth and Abigail danced secretly in the forest. Tituba was there— and Tituba knows conjuring. Parris insists that no one can be sure about such things.

But *she* can be sure, Ann Putnam bursts out. That is why she sent Ruth to Tituba—to find out from her who murdered Ruth's seven sisters. There is a gasp of horror from the listeners. When Rebecca protests against implicating Tituba in this terrible crime, Ann answers that it is for God alone to judge the guilty. Hale orders Tituba to be brought before him, then questions Abigail. She admits that she and the girls were dancing but again denies Parris' insinuation that they were naked. When Parris interjects a question about "toads in a kettle," Abigail mischievously explains that a little frog jumped in. At that Hale bluntly asks her if she made a compact with the devil. Suddenly fear-stricken, Abigail screams a denial.

Then, over a sinuous, rhythmic theme in the orchestra, Abigail accuses Tituba of bewitching her and the other girls. Tituba, bewildered and confused, denies the accusations. This introduces a dramatic ensemble as Ann, Parris, Putnam and Hale express reactions of terror and revulsion. Abigail, reveling in the havoc she is causing, now changes her story and describes how Tituba came to her as she was lying naked and tempted her with pagan songs. Ann wails that the Negress surely is the devil's own because she made the girls drink the witches brew of babies' blood. Rebecca, who alone is untouched by the frenzy, sings that it is God, not the devil, who can help them now, and that they are dealing with hysterical girls, not witches.

Parris and Putnam, convinced that the girls are possessed, implore Hale to remove the curse. Aside, Nurse voices his suspicions of Hale's motives, and his own conviction that this is a matter of dealing with poor, silly girls who need only "love and charity" to cure them of their illness.

The ensemble is sung over a rising and falling harmonic figure in the orchestra, accentuated with eerie effect by one chromatic passage high in the strings. At the climax of the ensemble the orchestral pattern changes to a succession of powerful chords rising in half tones with increasing intensity. The sinuous, flowing rhythm takes over again as Hale continues questioning Tituba. He demands to know if she spoke with the devil and threatens to whip her if she does not tell the truth. Tituba defiantly protests her innocence. With malicious insistence, Parris and the Putnams urge Hale to make her confess.

Tituba, in her panic and fear, has a momentary vision of the gibbet to which she is being condemned. During this, the triplet figure in the orchestra continues as remorselessly as the inquisition by Hale and Parris. At last, cornered and desperate, the woman lashes out at her tormentors. In a dramatic refrain ("Oh, how many times, Mister Parris") she sings that the devil has told her many times to cut Parris' throat—and the Putnams' as well. But she refused to kill even though the devil tempted her with offers of a new dress, "big black wings," and a chance to fly back to Barbados—and freedom. For a moment Tituba is lost in her fantasy, then her mood abruptly changes.

In menacing phrases of rising octave intervals she sings that the devil told her that white people as well as black are in his power. Then she saw the witchlike figure of an old woman. Ann Putnam asks excitedly: "Were it Sarah Good?" Tituba obediently answers: "It were Sarah Good." Ann gives a wild cry of triumph, then babbles that Sarah Good was a midwife to her and seven babies died in her arms. Reverend Hale sings that Tituba's confession has broken Lucifer's power. Betty sits up slowly on the bed as all in the room watch her in surprise and relief. They join in singing "Jesus, my consolation" as a hymn of thanksgiving.

Abigail's voice rises in an obbligato over the ensemble as she gives way to her mingled sexual and religious ecstasy. While these neighbors piously rejoice because Tituba's soul is saved, Abigail sings that she herself drank the devil's brew, danced before him naked and became his bride. In a soaring phrase she beseeches God to forgive her sin as the hymn comes to a roaring climax. The curtain falls.

ACT TWO

The kitchen of John Proctor's house eight days later. Doors upstage center and left, fireplace right. A musket hangs above the fireplace. Prominent on the mantelpiece is a poppet, a small rag doll. The curtain rises after a brief orchestral introduction. Elizabeth Proctor is preparing dinner.

John Proctor enters and a long musical dialogue ensues, beginning with Elizabeth's greeting: "What keeps you so late?" John answers that he has been busy with his planting. He is grateful for the return of spring and tells Elizabeth that on Sunday they will walk through their fields and enjoy the flowers. But he becomes aware that his wife is preoccupied and moody, listening absently to what he is saying. She curtly informs him that Mary Warren insisted on going to Salem, where, she said, she was to be an "official of the court." This is Deputy Governor Danforth's court, Elizabeth goes on. He is a ruthless judge, and will hang anyone who is charged with witchcraft and does not confess.

When Proctor scoffs at the idea of hanging, Elizabeth tells him that Abigail foments hysteria—real or pretended—among the other girls. If they fall into a fit when a suspect is brought into court their victim is promptly flung into jail. Elizabeth begs John to go to court and expose this vicious fraud—he must testify that Abigail herself confessed the fraud to him in his own house.

Hesitatingly, Proctor says he will think it over. Elizabeth pointedly asks him if he would scruple if Abigail were not involved. Thereupon Proctor launches into an angry tirade ("Let you not judge me"). He has had quite enough of her jealous suspicions, he sings, and it is useless to try to reason with her. Then, unwittingly betraying himself, Proctor goes on to say that if he accuses Abigail of fraud, she will retaliate by branding him an adulterer. He adds that he could not prove in court that she confessed to fraud because they were alone when she admitted it. Elizabeth gasps in dismay at this startling revelation. In anger and shame, Proctor storms at her not to judge him.

Elizabeth answers in one of the principal arias in the opera, "I do not judge you, John." In sustained, melodic phrases she sings that only his heart can judge him, then recalls the love they had for each other before their dreams were shattered. With increasing emotion she declares that Abigail will not dare accuse him of adultery for fear of damning herself. She bids him think of the innocent people who will be doomed if he keeps silent. Let Abigail dream of a promise made in bed—where promises are easily made. In the climax of the aria Elizabeth exhorts Proctor to break that promise and tear Abigail out of his heart. This he must do, she cries in passion and despair, for she has vowed to be his only wife—"or no wife at all!"

Shaken by her violent outburst, John goes to Elizabeth with outstretched arms in a conciliating gesture, but she recoils and turns away. Plunged into despair, Proctor sits down at the supper table, stares dejectedly at the food before him, then pushes it aside. Dark, heavy chords reverberate in the orchestra during this action.

The brooding silence is broken by the entrance of Mary Warren, who tries to sneak up the stairs to her room without being seen. A staccato phrase in the orchestra signals her presence. Suddenly noticing her, John angrily asks why she went to Salem without his permission. When he threatens to whip her she bursts into tears. Between her sobs she tells the couple that not fourteen but thirty-nine women have been thrown into jail and that Judge Danforth has sentenced Goody Osborn to the gallows. Then follows an eerie recital of what happened in court.

Sarah Good won't hang, Mary explains, because she confessed she was in league with the devil. Then poor Goody Osborn was brought in. She was such a sorry sight, Mary goes on, that at first she could not bring herself to accuse the old woman. But when Goody kept on denying her guilt, Mary says her scalp began to tingle and she heard a voice scream. And that voice was her own, Mary cries half deliriously. Grating dissonances in the orchestra underscore the tinge of madness in her story.

Aghast at this senseless folly, Proctor thunders that Mary is never to go back to court again to help hang innocent women. Mary whimpers that they will not hang if they confess. It is God's work—if the devil is in Salem he will be driven out. Proctor snatches a whip from the wall and lunges toward the girl, who cowers in terror.

Pointing to Elizabeth, Mary cries that she saved her life. Instantly realizing what she means, Elizabeth demands to know who accused her.

Mary refuses to answer. Convinced that it was Abigail, Elizabeth desperately entreats Proctor to go to Salem.

At that moment there is a loud knock on the door. Proctor opens it to admit Ezekiel Cheever, Reverend Hale and a group of townspeople, all carrying muskets. Hale announces that they have a warrant for Goody Proctor. In a recitative passage, Cheever reads the charge sworn out by Abigail Williams: While she was at supper with Judge Danforth, Reverend Hale and Uncle Parris she felt a stab of pain. Examining her, Parris found a needle stuck into her belly. A voice whispered that Elizabeth Proctor had done this with the help of her witch's poppet.

Over repeated phrases in descending chromatics, Elizabeth protests that she has no poppet, whereupon Hale declares that puts an end to the matter. But Cheever, with vindictive relish, points to the poppet on the mantelpiece. He takes it down, examines it and exclaims that a needle is stuck in the doll's belly. Utterly bewildered, Elizabeth asks what that means. "Your murder of Abigail Williams," Cheever replies gloatingly.

Elizabeth bursts out that Abigail herself is a murderess who should be "ripped out of this world." In savage triumph Cheever repeats her words, declaring that the court must hear of this threat. Shouting that he will give Cheever something to tell the court, Proctor drags Mary forward. In answer to his question, the fear-stricken girl admits the poppet is hers, that she stuck the needle into the doll's belly and that Abigail saw her do it.

Hale, realizing that the witch hunt has taken a sinister turn, gravely tells Elizabeth that she must answer in court to the charge. He assures her that Judge Danforth, though stern, will see that justice is done. Proctor, wild with anger, storms that he will not let Elizabeth go, then tries to drive the men out of the house. Restraining him, Elizabeth resolutely tells him she must go. Quietly she orders Mary to take care of the house in her absence, then in a poignant phrase asks John to "bring her home soon." The men lead her away.

Proctor whirls on Mary, glares at her for a moment, then snatches his musket from over the mantelpiece. For one terrible moment he seems ready to kill her on the spot. Controlling himself, he slowly lowers the gun and speaks with cold ferocity. The ensuing refrain ("You will go to that court with me"), with its clamorous dissonances punctuated by Mary's terror-stricken protests, builds up to the violent climax of the act.

When Mary cries that if she tells her story of the poppet Abigail will kill her and ruin his life with her disclosure of adultery, Proctor answers that then they will slide down together into their own hell. But whatever happens, the innocent Elizabeth will not be allowed to die for him. On the verge of madness, he seizes Mary by the throat and hurls her to the floor, shouting that God's icy wind will blow upon them as they walk naked in their sin. As staccato chords crash like hammer blows, the curtain falls.

ACT THREE

[*Scene One*] Early morning, two days later. A moonlit clearing in the forest, with a corner of Parris' house visible. A brief orchestral introduction sounds a romantic theme with a sinister undertone. Abigail, with a cloak thrown provocatively over her nightgown, enters with Proctor. The entire scene which follows is in the form of a musical dialogue, beginning with Abigail's languorous phrase: "John, I knew you'd come back to me."

Thrusting herself into his unwilling embrace, she amorously sings that she has been waiting for him night after night, and that now at last they are free to be lovers again. Roughly pushing her away, Proctor answers that indeed they are *not* free: Elizabeth is in jail, accused by Abigail herself, and Salem is under Abigail's curse. It is *they* who must be freed.

At that Abigail craftily changes her tactics as an impudent theme ripples in the orchestra. With her mystical powers, she sings, she freed these "psalm-singing hypocrites"—who said she danced for the devil—from their own corruption. And someday they will thank her for it. Outraged, Proctor curses her and threatens to whip her.

By way of answer, Abigail, in a voluptuous gesture, lets the cloak drop from her shoulders, presses her body to Proctor's and gazes avidly up into his face. In a passionate refrain ("I look only for John Proctor") she entreats him to leave his sickly wife so that together they can do God's holy work of ridding Salem of corruption. Proctor scorns her as a fraud and warns that he will expose her trickery. Wild with anger, Abigail sneers that he can do as he likes, then adds venomously that if Elizabeth dies it will be her own husband who killed her. Snatching up her cloak, she rushes away.

[*Scene Two*] The next morning. The town meetinghouse, now used as a courtroom. Townspeople are seated; Cheever, the court clerk, is at his desk. During an orchestral interlude Giles Corey and Francis Nurse enter together, then Mary Warren and John Proctor. The crowd makes way as Abigail leads the other girl accusers into the courtroom. Cheever rises and declares the court in session. To a fanfare, Judge Danforth enters with Thomas Putnam and Reverend Hale. The people rise respectfully and stand with bowed heads as Danforth gives the invocation: "Open Thou my lips, O Lord." It begins as a simple hymn tune but grows in dignity and power as the Judge asks the Lord's help in purging the land of the festering plague of witchcraft.

As the business of the court begins, Giles Corey is called to the witness stand. Cheever, in recitative over an ascending chromatic passage, reads Corey's deposition. It sets forth that Thomas Putnam prevailed on his daughter Ruth to "cry witch" on Rebecca Nurse and Martha Corey for the sole purpose of taking over the property to which the two women held title. Putnam indignantly denies this. Corey interjects that if his wife is guilty she will of course hang and her property will be forfeit. But who, he asks, has the money to buy? Nobody but Putnam.

Judge Danforth demands proof. Giles thereupon testifies that when Putnam told Ruth to accuse Martha Corey he said that this would bring him Martha's property as a gift—and three townsmen heard him say it. When Danforth orders Giles to name them he defiantly refuses. They would rot in jail like the others, he says. Danforth rebukes Corey for daring to criticize the court. Putnam unctuously remarks that only a man in league with the devil would withhold information. Thereupon Danforth orders Corey arrested for contempt. The court is in a fever of excitement.

Giles, wild with fury, leaps at Putnam and seizes him by the throat. The others pull him off as Danforth pounds his gavel to restore order. In harsh tones he orders Corey to be taken to a cell and tortured by "pressing" until he reveals the names of the townsmen. There is a gasp of horror from the crowd at the brutality of the sentence.

As Corey is led away, Parris rises to say that John Proctor has brought a statement from Mary Warren. From this point on the dialogue continues over a steady 6/8 rhythm which seems to reflect the inexorable progress toward doom to be meted out to those enmeshed in the charges of witchcraft.

Over Parris' protests, Proctor bluntly tells Danforth that the girls have nothing to do with witchcraft and that their so-called supernatural powers are fraudulent. Parris and Putnam angrily contradict him. Asked for proof, John says Mary will swear that she and the girls are faking—and Mary promptly does so. Taken aback, Danforth berates her for telling lies in his court. Mary responds in a mystical phrase, singing that she can lie no more, for she is "with God."

The Judge begins to question Abigail about Mary's statement that she, Abigail, saw her stick the needle into the poppet as a hex symbol of murder. Skillfully avoiding a trap, Abigail replies that Mary is lying. When Proctor denies this, Danforth sharply asks if he is trying to involve "this child" in murder. She is no child, John answers vehemently. Disturbed, the Judge turns again to Mary, drawing from her the admission that the girls all pretended to be possessed when they made accusations of witchcraft, and that she herself never saw any "spirits." Confronting Abigail, Danforth, warning that those who trifle with human lives risk the terrible vengeance of the Lord, asks her if she saw these "spirits."

Assuming an air of outraged innocence, Abigail cries out that her only reward for trying to rout the devil and his crew is to be vilified in this court. With malevolent emphasis, she warns Danforth that he himself may fall victim to the demons.

In the next instant she stares upward with a look of horror, hugs her arms together and begins singing in a wailing voice—"a wind . . . I freeze . . . and cold winds blow"—then turns to glare at Mary. This introduces a brief ensemble passage as the other girls, picking up their cue, repeat the phrase like an incantation. Abigail, playing her role to the hilt, kneels in prayer. John strides over to her and pulls her to her feet by her hair. She shrieks in terror.

The court erupts in pandemonium as Proctor brands her a whore and confesses his adultery with her. Now you know, he shouts, why Elizabeth is accused—because he turned this girl out of his house as a harlot. Danforth abruptly orders Parris to bring in Elizabeth Proctor, then directs Abigail and John not to face the witness. Brought before the Judge, Elizabeth looks distractedly about. Danforth brusquely commands her to look only at him and tell him why she discharged Abigail. Insisting that it was because the girl was a bad servant, Elizabeth resolutely refuses to confirm that her husband committed adultery. The Judge impatiently orders her to be removed. Turning to face her, John shouts that he has confessed and implores her to tell the truth. Elizabeth cries out in despair as she is led away. The court is in an uproar.

Only Reverend Hale comes to John's defense, begging Danforth not to condemn another innocent victim. He himself, he goes on remorsefully, is haunted by the fact that he signed Rebecca Nurse's death warrant. As for this trial, he says, it is solely a matter of private revenge. Hale reiterates his belief in Proctor's confession and denounces Abigail as a fraud.

Here begins the demonic scene which builds into the closing ensemble of the act. Abigail, realizing she is cornered, abandons herself to a simulated frenzy, crying, "Yellow bird, begone." Mary stares at her in panic, while Proctor shouts to Danforth that the girls are shamming again. The contagion quickly spreads not only to the other girls but to Ann, Danforth, Parris and Putnam. Gaping upward, they sing meaninglessly about the "bird coming down, down, down." Mary, losing all control, joins Abigail in a hysterical wailing obbligato.

Proctor, Hale and Francis Nurse, trying to make themselves heard above the din, vainly protest that this exhibition of witchcraft is a monstrous lie. Proctor rushes over to Mary and tries to restrain her. Dodging out of his reach, she launches into a wild tirade, accusing him of being "the devil's man." He came to her the other night, she sings, clawed at her back with his icy fingers and forced her to sign the devil's book. But now, she screams, she loves God and will no longer obey John Proctor.

At that the throng in the courtroom, caught up in mob hysteria, bursts into a frenzied shout of "Allelujah!" Mary, sobbing uncontrollably, throws herself into Abigail's protecting arms. The two are joined by Ann Putnam in their witch's chant. Abigail, Mary and Ann and Reverend Hale and Francis Nurse stand apart as the spectators turn on John Proctor, howling: "He's the devil's man, beware." At the climax of the chorus, Hale and Nurse, overcome with horror at the scene, rush away. The curtain falls.

ACT FOUR

The fall of 1692. A large, gloomy room in the Salem jail. Tituba and Sarah Good, awaiting execution, are sitting huddled together in the light of flickering torches on the wall. The Negress sings a plaintive refrain, like a spiritual: "The Devil say he's a-comin' to set his people free." Sarah Good chimes in with a mournful, wordless obbligato. The devil will give them big black wings, Tituba chants, and then they'll fly to Barbados, where there's singing and feasting all night long.

As her chant dies away, Cheever lurches in carrying a lantern and a bottle. He pushes the two women out of the room, giving Sarah the bottle as she reaches for it. A moment later, Abigail, wearing a hooded cloak, enters and gives Cheever a bag of money. He walks over to the heavily barred door of John Proctor's dungeon cell, calls to the prisoner, unlocks the door and leaves it ajar. As he staggers out, Proctor appears. He is gaunt and haggard from months of torture. Abigail steps swiftly to the door. In suppressed excitement she shows him clothing and money and tells him that now he is free. Proctor remains motionless, staring into space. Abigail desperately implores him to hurry—a boat is waiting at the Salem dock and there is no time to lose. In a passionate phrase she sings that they will sail away to a sunny land where they will be lovers forever.

Without a word, Proctor closes the cell door and drags himself back into the darkness. Abigail reels back in stunned surprise, then with a gesture of resignation turns to leave. Cheever, leering at her, attempts to embrace her as she passes. Fighting him off, Abigail rushes away sobbing. Cheever breaks into satanic laughter.

At his call Tituba and Sarah Good again emerge from the shadows. Cheever snatches back his bottle and drinks. Tituba, in a mournful reprise of her chant, sings that the devil has broken his promise—he is going to let them rot and die in Salem town.

Suddenly there is a loud drum roll. Danforth and Reverend Hale enter. As the Judge orders Cheever to bring in Elizabeth Proctor, Hale agitatedly warns him that trouble is brewing. The town of Beverly, revolted by the witch trials, has thrown out the court. Orphans of those executed wander about the streets; farms are left unattended and even the cattle roam wild. No one in the terror-stricken community is safe from the vicious attacks of the witch-ridden girls.

At that point Parris bursts in crying that Abigail has disappeared after rifling his money box. When Hale says that now the case against the Proctors has collapsed, Danforth angrily declares that they will either confess or hang. The fear-stricken Parris protests that the townspeople will not tolerate these hangings—only this morning he found a dagger thrust into his door as a warning of impending revenge.

Hale implores the Judge to postpone the hangings. With remorseless emphasis Danforth retorts that to smash a rebellion he would hang and quarter ten thousand men. He will not be thwarted in carrying out God's law. Elizabeth is brought in and Danforth gestures to Hale to speak to her. Warning her that her husband is doomed to die at sunrise, Hale pleads with Elizabeth to persuade him to confess to witchcraft to save his life—even if he lies to do it. Elizabeth quietly replies that she can promise nothing, but that she will speak with him. Puzzled and infuriated by her calm defiance, Danforth snarls that this woman is beyond understanding: In the face of disaster she sheds no tears.

As somber chords reverberate in the orchestra, Proctor is brought in. Danforth, Hale and Parris move away as Elizabeth and John face each other and speak over a tender, lyrical theme. John inquires about the children. Mary Warren brought her word that they are well, Elizabeth says. She goes on to tell him about the trials: a hundred or more have confessed—but not Rebecca Nurse or Giles Corey. Giles spoke only two words to the torturers who piled the crushing stones on his chest: "More weight." Shaken with horror, Proctor asks Elizabeth if she would forgive him if he lied to save his life.

She answers that it was her own lie that doomed him—and her own failure as a wife that drove him to adultery. Now, she cries in a passionate outburst, she will abide by his decision and share his fate, whatever it may be. Crushing Elizabeth in his embrace, Proctor triumphantly shouts to Danforth: "I want my life!" The Judge and the others rush forward exultingly hailing his decision. Their voices blend briefly with a backstage chorus.

But suddenly the mood of the scene changes. Danforth hands John a pen and a written confession and asks him to sign. As Proctor stares at it in bewilderment, Rebecca Nurse is brought in. She totters forward, catches sight of the document and gasps in dismay. Danforth tells her

Proctor has confessed and urges her to do the same. "It is a lie," Rebecca answers without hesitation.

Thereupon Danforth treacherously attempts to trick John into implicating Rebecca and other accused women in his confession. John curtly answers that he can only be responsible for his own sins. Hale hands him the pen and beseeches him to sign, while Danforth in vindictive fury demands a signed confession so that the village will have proof. In a majestic refrain, "God does not need my name nailed upon a church door," Proctor hurls his final defiance. He has confessed, he sings, and that is enough. He will not stain the name of his sons with his own black sins. He has forfeited his soul, but he will not forfeit his good name.

Beside himself with fury, Danforth thrusts the document into Proctor's hands with a final warning. Proctor, ignoring the distracted pleading of Hale and Parris, tears the confession to shreds. Now at last, he shouts, he sees some goodness in John Proctor. As Elizabeth rushes into his arms, he exhorts her not to quail before these tormentors but to show "a stony heart that will sink them." He kisses her in farewell.

To the strains of a funeral march, the gates of the blockhouse slowly open, showing the gallows outside. Supporting Rebecca, Proctor begins his walk to the scaffold as Danforth screams for the hanging. The chorus of villagers, "Weep for them," rises in a great surge of sound. As it dies away, the voice of Elizabeth soars in a phrase of anguish and triumph: "He has his goodness now. God forbid I take it from him."

The blockhouse gates close to a thunderous drum roll. Reverend Hale falls to his knees sobbing a prayer. Elizabeth stands motionless, the rising sun flooding her upturned face. The curtain falls.

LA DAMNATION DE FAUST

by HECTOR BERLIOZ

(1803–69)

Libretto by

BERLIOZ and M. GANDONNIÈRE

Based on a translation of Goethe's *Faust* by Gérard de Nerval

CHARACTERS

Marguerite	Mezzo-soprano
Faust	Tenor
Méphistophélès	Baritone
Brander	Bass

Students, soldiers, peasants, dancers, demons

Place: Hungary and Germany
Time: Middle Ages
First performance: Opéra-Comique, Paris, December 6, 1846
Original language: French

Although Berlioz himself entitled his *Faust* an *opéra de concert,* it has often been staged as a five-act opera. The work began in the form of nine songs with lyrics as translated from Goethe by Nerval. These Berlioz grouped into eight scenes, which he subsequently incorporated into *Faust*.

Berlioz' version of the Faust legend differs somewhat from those of Gounod and Boito. His Faust does not sell his soul to the devil outright; he bargains at first only for the sensual pleasures with which Méphistophélès tempts him. In the end, he offers his soul to save Marguerite, then—a victim of the devil's treachery—rides to hell.

The two original performances in 1846 (December 6 and 20) were failures which cost Berlioz ten thousand francs of his own money. He recouped his losses, however, with successful performances of the first two parts of *Faust* in Russia in 1847.

Although never intended to be presented as an opera, it subsequently received a number of successful stage productions in Europe, including

England and South America. *Faust* was staged for the first time as an opera by Raoul Gunsbourg in Monte Carlo on February 18, 1893. It was first heard in America, in the concert version, under Leopold Damrosch in New York on February 12, 1880. The operatic version was given by the Metropolitan on December 7, 1906, with four additional performances during the 1906-7 season. Most performances in recent years have been given in the original concert form.

ACT ONE

[*Scene One*] The curtain rises immediately on a pleasant landscape outside Faust's study. Weary after a night of poring over his books, he muses on the enchantment of the returning spring ("Le vieil hiver a fait place"). Following this aria there is a brief orchestral interlude with rhythms of a peasant dance and a martial air.

[*Scene Two*] Faust listens to the singing of the peasants ("Les bergers quittent leurs troupeaux")—the "Ronde de Paysans." He comments enviously on their carefree gaiety and their lusty enjoyment of life.

[*Scene Three*] Another part of the plain, with a fortress in the distance.[1] Watching soldiers march out of the fortress, Faust sings that the specter of war now looms over this pleasant land, with the sons of the Danube marching into battle ("Mais d'un éclat guerrier"). The army continues to advance to the strains of the "Rákóczy March." At first Faust is inspired to patriotic fervor by the military pageantry, but then he is haunted by the realization that victory is won only at the cost of suffering and death.

ACT TWO

[*Scene Four*] Faust's study in north Germany. A cavernous fireplace dominates the room, and curled up on the hearth is a poodle. In a despondent mood, Faust laments that the solitude of the forest has failed to bring him the peace of mind he longs for ("Sans regrets j'ai quitté"). Overwhelmed by despair, he seizes the flask of poison on his table. Just as he raises it to his lips he hears the Easter hymn ("Christ vient de ressusciter"). Its majestic strains restore his courage, and he expresses the renewal of his faith in a jubilant obbligato to the chorus ("Ô souvenirs! Ô mon âme tremblante"). Overcome by emotion, he falls to his knees and joins in the concluding "hosanna" of the hymn.

[1] This scene is set in Hungary because Berlioz wanted to introduce a Hungarian musical theme—which he did in the form of the famous "Rákóczy March" ("Marche Hongroise"), the dominating music of the scene.

[*Scene Five*] The poodle in front of the fireplace vanishes. In its place crouches Méphistophélès. Rising, he takes note of Faust on his knees and sarcastically commends him for his piety ("Ô pure émotion! Enfant du saint"). A scene in recitative ensues. Eying him suspiciously, Faust asks the devil why he has come ("Qui donc es-tu?"). To show him, the devil replies, that there are other things in life besides the dull study of philosophy—for example, pleasure, power and fortune. In behalf of such pursuits, Méphistophélès adds, he is at his service. Faust accepts the offer on one condition: that he will be granted one moment in time when he can say, "This moment, stay. I am happy" ("Si jamais je dis au moment qui passe: Arrête-toi"). The devil assents with an ironic bow, and then the two rush away.

[*Scene Six*] Auerbach's tavern in Leipzig, where Méphistophélès has brought Faust to sample the pleasures of carousing. They listen as students on a spree roar out a drinking song ("À boire encore"). The leader of the crowd, Brander, obliges with a rollicking ditty about a rat ("Certain rat, dans une cuisine")—the "Chanson de Brander."
It is the story of the rat that grew sleek and plump in the kitchen until the cook slipped poison into his soup. Thereupon he squirmed and moaned as though "in the throes of love"—as the song's cynical refrain goes. Finally, to escape his misery, the rat jumped into the oven, where the kitchen maid saw to it that he was properly roasted. In a sardonic coda the drinkers sing a fugue on the theme of Brander's song, vocalizing on an "Amen."
Méphistophélès steps forward and sneeringly compliments the students on the devotional quality of their choral efforts, then asks leave to respond with a song of his own. This he does with the famous "Song of the Flea" ("Une puce gentille"). The flea was the favorite of a wealthy prince, who one day ordered his tailor to measure the insect for a resplendent court costume. Impressed with his sartorial importance, the flea called in all his brothers and sisters from the provinces and persuaded the prince to confer royal titles upon them. The resident lords and ladies of the court not only were obliged to tolerate the interlopers but were forced to scratch in secret so as not to offend their sovereign. Méphistophélès ends his song with a satirical guffaw, and then he and Faust disappear.

ACT THREE

[*Scene Seven*] A meadow on the banks of the Elbe, to which Méphistophélès has transported Faust. He is lying on a bed of roses. In a sensual incantation ("Voici des roses") the devil conjures up an idyllic vision for Faust's benefit. Gnomes and sylphs encircle him in a sinuous dance as they invite him to find happiness in dreams ("Dors, heureux Faust"). At the conclusion of the chorus Marguerite emerges from among the roses as Méphistophélès tempts Faust with a vision of her.

ACT FOUR

[*Scene Eight*] A street near Marguerite's home. Soldiers and students crowd in. The soldiers sing that cities and women are equally difficult to conquer ("Villes entourées")—but both eventually surrender. Then the students strike up a Latin song, "Iam nox stellata velamina pandit" ("Under night's starry vault there is time to drink and love"). The two groups join in an ingenious choral ensemble, after which they leave the scene.

[*Scene Nine*] Méphistophélès comes in with Faust and shows him Marguerite's house. Stealing alone into her room, Faust voices his amorous thoughts in the beautiful aria "Merci doux crépuscule!"

[*Scene Ten*] Suddenly Méphistophélès rushes in and warns that Marguerite is approaching. Trembling with ardor and excitement, Faust hides behind the draperies. As the devil leaves he remarks cynically that he and his sprites will oblige with a nuptial serenade.

[*Scene Eleven*] Marguerite enters. In recitative she wonders why the air has a strange heaviness. She has a premonition of evil, yet is beguiled by thoughts of her lover-to-be . . . will a kind Fate bring him to her? Braiding her hair, she sings the plaintive medieval song about the King of Thule ("Autrefois un roi de Thulé").
The King had received a golden chalice from his Queen as she lay dying, and this he treasured as his most precious possession. As he neared the end of his life he gave away all his lands and wealth, keeping only the chalice. One day he called his barons together for a feast in an ancient castle by the sea. There he drank a final toast from the chalice, then hurled it into the breakers. As it sank out of sight the King grew pale and shuddered in his death throes. Marguerite's voice trails off as she falls asleep.

[*Scene Twelve*] Méphistophélès suddenly materializes. Summoning his demons and will-o'-the-wisps, he commands them to dance in order to charm Marguerite into his power. To a shimmering accompaniment, the "Minuet of the Will-o'-the-Wisps" follows, introducing the dream sequence.
Standing on the steps of a church, the devil draws Marguerite to him

with the gestures of a sorcerer. He conjures up a vision of Faust which alternately appears and then vanishes. As the girl raises her arms supplicatingly, the cross on the church lights up. Méphistophélès cowers back and hides his face behind his cloak. Finally Marguerite staggers toward the church and falls fainting on the steps. The demons burst in and circle about her in a frenzied dance. At a magical sign from Méphistophélès the dream fades. Marguerite is seen asleep in her chair. Then the devil sings an insulting "moralizing" serenade ("Chantons à cette belle une chanson morale") about the unfortunate consequences of an innocent maiden's tryst with her lover.[2] The demons chant a suggestive refrain. The devil makes them disappear as Faust approaches.

[*Scene Thirteen*] Marguerite awakens, sees him, and rushes into his arms. Then follows the passionate duet "Ange adoré, dont la céleste image," one of the most beautiful numbers in the score.

[*Scene Fourteen*] As the lovers stand in a blissful embrace, Méphistophélès rushes in exclaiming that the neighbors are converging on the house. With them is Marguerite's mother, whom the village gossips have informed that a stranger has stolen into her home and is making love to her daughter.

Pretending great concern over Marguerite's safety, the devil cries that "this angel" must be saved at all costs ("Il faut sauver cet ange"). This marks the beginning of a stormy trio. Faust and Marguerite lament that their dream of love has been shattered. Méphistophélès curses the intruders. The trio blends with the chorus of the townspeople maliciously taunting "Mother Oppenheim." Mingled with their derisive laughter, the ensemble rises to a furious climax.

ACT FIVE

[*Scene Fifteen*] Marguerite's room. In the romanza "D'amour l'ardente flamme" she abandons herself to thoughts of Faust—his gentle smile, his beautiful eyes, his enchanting voice and the fiery ecstasy of his kisses. In sorrow and longing she waits for his return. From behind the scenes come the voices of the soldiers and students in a reprise of their chorus. With a final despairing cry Marguerite leaves.

[*Scene Sixteen*] Faust alone in a forest. Enchanted by the beauty of the scene, he sings a majestic invocation to Nature, "Nature immense,

---

[2] This is a variation on the theme of the serenade sung by Gounod's Méphistophélès, who cynically advises the maiden not to yield to her lover until the wedding ring is safely on her finger.

impénétrable et fière." Méphistophélès appears and watches him unob-served. In a sinister refrain ("Cette âme à moi librement donne") he muses that he still cannot claim Faust's soul because he has not yet said to a moment in time: "Stay. I am happy"—the stipulation of his bar-gain.

A passage in recitative follows. Making himself known, Méphis-tophélès informs Faust that Marguerite is in prison, doomed to die for the murder of her mother: she gave her an overdose of the sleeping po-tion Faust himself had provided so that he and Marguerite could tryst undisturbed.

Faust turns on the devil in fury, accusing him of treachery and order-ing him to save the girl. Instantly Méphistophélès hands him a docu-ment. Sign it, says the devil, and he will save Marguerite. Scarcely look-ing at the paper, Faust forthwith signs away his soul. Now sure of his victim, Méphistophélès deliberately suggests that it may already be too late. Shaken by terror, Faust calls on Time to stop ("Temps, arrête-toi")—thus inadvertently sealing his fateful bargain.

In savage exultation, Méphistophélès calls for his horses ("Hola! Vortex, Giaour!"), and then begins the fearsome "Ride to Hell" [*Scenes Seventeen and Eighteen*]. Storm winds howl, hideous monsters roar, huge black birds beat their wings on Faust's head. At the side of the road, terror-stricken peasants pray for mercy.

[*Scene Nineteen*] As the riders near the abyss, the chorus of the damned greets Méphistophélès, chanting in diabolical gibberish ("Iri-miru Karabrao! Tradioun Marexil firtrundixe"). When he tells them that Faust has finally signed the pact that damned his soul, the demons hoist the devil on their shoulders with a chorus of fiendish triumph. Then all are engulfed in the flames of hell.

In a brief epilogue, earthly voices are heard recalling the horror of the scene ("Alors l'Enfer se tut")—the shrieking demons, the wail of lost souls in torment.

[*Scene Twenty*] Heaven, where the Blessed Spirits welcome the soul of Marguerite (the "Apotheosis"). In a majestic closing chorus ("Re-monte au ciel, âme naïve") they sing that this innocent soul has been forgiven the mortal sin committed in error, and that one day Faust him-self may be granted divine mercy.

DIALOGUES DES CARMÉLITES
(*Dialogues of the Carmelites*)
by FRANCIS POULENC
(1899–1963)

Libretto by
GEORGES BERNANOS

Derived from a novel by Gertrud von le Fort (*Die Letzte am Schafott—The Last One on the Scaffold*) and a scenario by The Reverend Father Bruckberger and Philippe Agostini. Opera adaptation authorized by Emmet Lavery.

CHARACTERS

The Marquis de la Force	Baritone
Blanche, his daughter (Sister Blanche of the Agony of Christ)	Soprano
The Chevalier, his son	Tenor
Madame de Croissy, Prioress of the Carmelite Convent (Mother Henriette of Jesus)	Contralto
Madame Lidoine, the new Prioress (Mother Marie of St. Augustine)	Soprano
Mother Marie, Assistant Prioress (Mother Marie of the Incarnation)	Mezzo-soprano
Sister Constance of St. Denis (a very young nun)	Soprano
Mother Jeanne of the Child Jesus (Dean of the Community)	Mezzo-soprano
Sister Mathilde	Mezzo-soprano
Mother Gerald ⎫	⎱
Sister Claire ⎬ older nuns	⎰ Choristers
Sister Antoine, Portress ⎭	
Sisters Catherine, Felicity, Gertrude, Alice, Valentine, Anne of the Cross, Martha, St. Charles	Choristers
Father Confessor of the Convent (Chaplain)	Tenor
First Commissioner	Tenor
Second Commissioner	Baritone
Thierry, a valet	Baritone
Javelinot, a physician	Baritone

Public officials, officers, guards, prisoners, citizens

Place: Paris and environs
Time: 1789–94
First performance: La Scala, Milan, January 26, 1957 (in Italian)
Original language: French

Dialogues of the Carmelites is the operatic setting of a heroic drama played out against the dark and bloody background of the Reign of Terror in Paris. It is the story of the incredible valor of sixteen Carmelite nuns who took the vow of martyrdom that led them to the guillotine in the Place de la Révolution on July 17, 1794.

They have their counterparts in history. Their fate is described in the diary of Mother Marie of the Incarnation—the only member of the Order who was not executed.

Named for the Biblical Mount Carmel in Palestine, the ancient Carmelite Order still exists, with some seven hundred convents throughout the world.

Dialogues is one of three stage works of Francis Poulenc, an outstanding member of "Les Six," a group of talented musicians who represent the modern French school of composition.[1] They led French music away from nineteenth-century romanticism into veristic naturalness and simplicity.

Poulenc began his illustrious career as a composer of music hall operettas, sentimental songs based on circus tunes and street ditties, and even jazz. Witty, sophisticated and elegant—yet at the same time a skillful technician—he never eschewed his innate gift for the melodic line. The composer insisted that his operas be sung in the language of the country where they were given. Hence the La Scala world premiere in Italian. Subsequent premieres in "native" languages included: Paris, San Francisco, NBC television, Cologne, Covent Garden, Vienna—1958; New York City Opera—1966; Metropolitan Opera—1977.

ACT ONE

The library of the Marquis de la Force in Paris, 1789. Double doors at left, smaller door at right, window at back. During a brief crisp

---

[1] The other two works in that category are: *Les Mamelles de Tirésias* (*The Breasts of Tiresias*) and *La Voix Humaine,* a one-character (soprano) operatic tour de force.

"Les Six": Poulenc, Darius Milhaud, Georges Auric, Arthur Honegger, Germaine Tailleferre, Louis Durey—all of whom came under the influence of Erik Satie, the *enfant terrible* of the musical scene, whose iconoclastic ideas were credited with setting musical impressionism on a new path.

orchestral introduction the curtain goes up to reveal the Marquis dozing in a chair. (The entire scene continues in quasi-recitative, with certain melodic interludes.)

The Marquis is aroused when his son, the Chevalier, strides into the room asking brusquely: "Where is Blanche?" His father reproves him for disturbing his midday nap. The Chevalier apologizes, then explains that he is worried about Blanche because Roger de Dames, a family friend, reported he had seen the girl's carriage stopped by a howling mob of peasants. The Marquis merely shrugs: a minor incident . . . excitable but harmless peasants. . . . But then he confesses that he himself is haunted by all this talk of rebellion.

Over an increasingly agitated accompaniment he recalls ("C'était le soir") how a mob, panicked by a fireworks explosion, closed in on his own carriage years ago. He and his wife escaped, thanks to the quick action of their coachman—but not before a stone had smashed a carriage window. For a long moment the Marquis stares into space. That night, he goes on quietly ("quelques heures plus tard"), his wife died after prematurely giving birth to Blanche.

The Chevalier asks forgiveness for his rude intrusion. His concern, he says, is not so much for Blanche's safety as for her strange outlook on life—it is not like a young, pretty girl to be a prey to morbid fears. The Marquis pooh-poohs these apprehensions, remarking that a young girl has a right to her moods. The truth is, the Chevalier responds gravely, that Blanche is being destroyed by her own fears—just as the worm destroys the fruit ("Le mal est entré en elle").

At that moment Blanche herself enters, returning from the convent. With deceptive lightheartedness, she twits her brother for taking things so seriously, then casually dismisses the attack on her carriage. Her father and brother commend her for her bravery. When she asks permission to retire to her room, the Marquis advises her to take extra candles—she always had been afraid of the dark. He recalls something she often said: "Every night I die; every morning I am born again" ("Je meurs chaque nuit").

With mystical intensity, Blanche sings that there is only one day of Resurrection—Easter—but every night is like the Agony of Christ (this is the personal symbol of her Carmelite sisterhood). The two men look at each other, completely mystified. The Chevalier and Blanche leave. A moment later the Marquis hears Blanche scream in fear. Thierry, the valet, rushes in, exclaiming that Blanche must have been frightened by shadows. He is followed by Blanche, who is hysterical. Finally controlling herself, she asks the Marquis's permission to become a nun ("j'ai décidé d'entrer au Carmel").

The Marquis gasps in disbelief, then gently tries to reason with her. But in a dramatic refrain ("Oh! mon père, cessons ce jeu") she sings that she can no longer bear the strain of facing the world. God is guiding her, and now she must renounce the world so that He will restore her to grace. Exhausted by her emotions, she sinks to her knees. Deeply moved, the Marquis strokes her head.

Without pause the scene changes to the parlor of the Carmelite convent at Compiègne. Madame de Croissy, the Mother Superior, and Blanche are talking together. The Superior, old and fatally ill, nevertheless sharply catechizes the novice: what impelled her to join the Order . . . do its stringent rules frighten her? Blanche candidly answers that she is seeking a life of heroism. The life of a Carmelite, the Superior observes dryly, is not designed to make heroism easy. That is an illusion—and illusions, she warns in an unaccompanied phrase, are the most dangerous form of our desires. Here, she adds pointedly, you will be deprived of them. Then with sudden intensity she declares that the purpose of the Order is neither to mortify the flesh nor safeguard virtue. Its only reason for being is *prayer*.

Severe trials are yet to come, the Superior continues, in which God will test not her strength but her weakness. Blanche, now in tears, sobs that she is crying for joy, not sorrow: if these admonitions were even harsher, she still would put her trust in the Superior. Remember, the latter counsels, the Order does not protect—*we* protect the Order ("c'est nous qui gardons la Règle").

Finally, the Superior asks what name Blanche will choose as novice. Blanche replies: "Sister Blanche of the Agony of Christ" ("m'appeler Soeur Blanche de l'Agonie du Christ"). In an unaccompanied phrase, the Superior sings: "Go in peace, my child."

The scene changes to the workroom of the convent, where Blanche and Sister Constance are busy at their daily tasks. They chatter about their household problems . . . the food ("lentils again!") . . . there is no bread . . . Mother Jeanne burned her fingers while ironing. . . . To a dancing 2/4 rhythm, Constance recalls her happy days in her native village in Brittany, singing and dancing with the friendly peasants. She loved them all, she sings winsomely, because they all loved her.

But Blanche dispels her mood by asking her how she can be gay when their Mother Superior is on her deathbed. Constance answers that she would gladly die in place of the Superior—but then . . . when one is old . . . perhaps it is time. . . . The two begin naïvely philosophizing about death. Perhaps, Constance observes, dying could be as amusing as living. Blanche resents her flippancy, and the two come close to quarreling. Impulsively, Constance proposes that they should ask God to take both their lives in place of their Mother Superior's.

Blanche is shocked at this sacrificial impulse—but she is completely dumbfounded when Constance confesses that she has always known that she and Blanche are destined to die together, and on the same day ("et que nous mourrions ensemble"). When Blanche berates her for uttering such ridiculous nonsense, Constance humbly asks her forgiveness.

A series of bell-like chords accompanies the scene change to a cell in the convent infirmary. Mother Marie of the Incarnation (the Assistant Prioress) sits at the bedside of the dying Mother Superior. The Superior frets about her helplessness . . . about dying all alone, with no one to console her. She wonders how much longer she has to live. She reflects that she has been with the Order for forty-two years—every day of which she has thought about death.

Her thoughts turn to Blanche, the newest member of the Order, who causes her more worry than any of her other daughters. By strange coincidence, Blanche chose the same name she herself assumed as a novice long ago—*Sister Blanche of the Agony of Christ*. In a sudden resurgence of her failing strength the Superior, in a tone of command, commends this novice to the care of Mother Marie—"and you will answer for her before God" ("Vous me répondrez d'elle devant Dieu"). More gently, the Superior adds that this obligation will call for patience and firmness—qualities Marie has, Blanche has not.

After a long, tense silence there is a knock at the door. Blanche enters and kneels at the bedside. The Superior affectionately tells Blanche that she, as newest member of the Order, is closest to her heart —like the child of one's old age. There will be many trials ahead . . . she will be the poorest of the poor, but her courage must never falter. She must remain submissive in the hands of God. Now then, the Superior sings tenderly, for the last time: goodbye. Grief-stricken, Blanche leaves.

The accompaniment stirs to a brisk tempo as Dr. Javelinot enters. The Superior asks for another dose of the medicine which has relieved her pain, but the doctor tells her that she cannot stand another dose. With a show of spirit, the Superior says that she must revive long enough to say goodbye to her charges—it is a custom of the convent. The doctor quietly but firmly refuses.

The refusal agitates the Superior to the point of delirium. An insistent 2/4 rhythm in the orchestra intensifies the effect of her outbursts. She scoffs blasphemously at Mother Marie's plea to concern herself only with God. Let Him concern himself with *me,* she rages. Then she sneers at the hapless Sister Anne—who has come to her bedside—for giving way to her grief. She conjures up a vision of the convent chapel, desecrated and bloodstained. Desperately she tries to sit up, clawing at her face to tear away "the mask of despair" ("arracher ce masque avec mes ongles").

Over the bell-like theme heard at the beginning of the scene, Mother Marie orders that the nuns are not to see the Superior, but are to go about their duties as usual. As the Superior tries to give an order to

Marie, she falls back with a strangled cry. At that moment Blanche enters as though walking in her sleep. Marie tells her that the Superior—despite her order to the other nuns—has summoned her beloved novice to her bedside for a final farewell.

Blanche approaches and kneels. As the Superior—her mind wandering on the brink of death—gasps out Blanche's name, Marie, aside, angrily resents the novice's intrusion. Suddenly, with a piercing cry—"fear of death" ("peur de la mort")—the Superior falls back dead. Horrified, Blanche murmurs that "our Reverend Mother was about to ask" . . . ("La Révérende Mère désirait" . . .). She remains sobbing on her knees as the convent bells chime softly.

ACT TWO[2]

The chapel of the convent, where the Superior lies in state. It is night; the room is lighted only by six tall candles. Blanche and Constance stand watch over the catafalque. An orchestral interlude sets the religious mood of the scene.

The two nuns chant a portion of the Requiem Mass: *Qui Lazarum resuscitasti a monumento foetidum.* Constance then leaves to call replacements for the watch. Alone, Blanche stares for a moment at the body; trembling with fear, she hurries to the door, only to come face to face with Mother Marie. In confusion and fright Blanche tries to make excuses for leaving. At first Marie sharply rebukes her, but then is touched by her distress. Over a tenderly melodic refrain ("Non, mon enfant, de grâce!") she tells Blanche to go to her cell and get some rest. Tomorrow, she adds, it will be easier to ask God to forgive her for failing at her task.

In the next scene Blanche and Constance are carrying flowers and a flowered cross to the Superior's grave. Constance, chattering away as usual, remarks that the cross seems much too large for the Superior's poor little grave. Will the next Prioress, she wonders, love flowers? In any case, she hopes it will be Mother Marie. Blanche, still smarting from Mother Marie's reprimand, snaps that Constance evidently thinks God will give her anything she asks for.

To her further irritation, Constance begins philosophizing about this problem of dying ("Pensez à la mort de notre chère Mère"). The good Lord, she decides, made a mistake in consigning their beloved Superior to so mean a death. It was much too small for her—like an ill-fitting garment really made for another person. Now, that other person will enjoy a comfortable, befitting death. After all, she goes on as Blanche stares

2 In some versions, continuation of Act One.

at her in utter bewilderment, we do not die for ourselves, but for others. Or for *each other,* she adds in a flash of clairvoyance.

The scene shifts to the vaulted chapter room. A large crucifix hangs on the center wall. Large door at left, smaller one at right. Under the crucifix is the Mother Superior's chair. The nuns are assembled for the ceremony of obedience to the new Prioress—Madame Lidoine. At rise of curtain, the ceremony is being concluded. Each nun kisses the Superior's hand; some seat themselves on benches along the wall. Last to enter are Blanche and Constance.

Mother Marie of St. Augustine explains the obligation of obedience ("Mes chères filles") in a long discourse which continues in alternating 3/4 and 2/4 rhythms. She mourns the death of her beloved predecessor . . . stresses the cardinal virtues of goodwill, patience and forbearance. Her voice rises in intensity as she warns against the self-indulgence of welcoming martyrdom as a benign fate ("Méfions-nous même du martyre"). The first duty is prayer. Martyrdom is its highest reward.

Concluding, the Prioress asks pardon for being carried away by her own feelings. With a kind of wry humor she adds that she will leave it to Mother Marie of the Incarnation to "end this little talk" (aware of her assistant's flair for taking charge of things). Marie self-importantly exhorts the nuns to take the Prioress's admonitions to heart, then leads them in chanting the *Ave Maria.* The Carmelites leave.

Suddenly the doorbell rings violently.[3] The visitor is the Chevalier de la Force, who says he must see his sister Blanche before he goes abroad. Under the circumstances, the Superior decides, the convent visiting rules may be abridged. Blanche will be sent for; Mother Marie will be present, unobserved, during the interview. Brother and sister confront each other through the interview grille in the parlor.

Then follows the dramatic duet in which the Chevalier tries, without success, to persuade Blanche to leave the convent and Paris before the storm breaks. At first he reproaches her for her apparent indifference to his visit ("Pourquoi vous tenez-vous ainsi"). Her father is worried over her safety, he tells her.

Blanche quietly assures him that she is quite happy—and is not afraid —for she puts her trust in God. The Chevalier tries to reason with her gently—as though talking to a child. Bridling at this, she declares that it is her sacred duty to remain where she is. With that she turns away. In the face of her resolution, her brother bows to the inevitable. With a despairing goodbye, he starts toward the door.

Blanche, suddenly afraid in spite of herself, implores the Chevalier not to leave her in bitterness ("Oh! ne me quittez pas"). She begs him to realize that now they are fellow-soldiers in a battle that each must

---

[3] Beginning of Act Two, Scene One in the two-act version.

face with courage. Her brother looks at her in sorrow and compassion, then leaves. Overcome by despair, Blanche leans weakly against the grille. Mother Marie enters. Having overheard the entire interview, she is aware of Blanche's distress, yet she sternly admonishes her to control herself. Blanche wails that everyone treats her like a child . . . they offer only pity—and that she is too proud to accept. To conquer pride, Marie says gently, one must have courage. She leads Blanche away.

To a somber theme in the orchestra, the scene changes to the sacristy of the convent, where the Chaplain is meeting with the nuns. He informs them ("Mes chères filles") that the revolutionaries have forbidden him to perform his religious duties. This, then, has been his final Mass. In farewell, he leads them in a closing chant: *Ave verum corpus natum*. When Blanche expresses fear for his safety he reveals that he has been ordered to go into hiding—but he plans to remain near the convent. He blesses Blanche as he leaves.

Mother Marie bolts the door after him. Watching her, Constance bursts out indignantly against the French for not coming to the defense of their priests. The Superior observes that when there is a shortage of priests there is always a plentiful supply of martyrs to restore the balance of grace ("Quand les prêtres manquent"). To which Mother Marie remarks rather cynically that the Holy Ghost obviously revealed the truth through their late Superior. So that France again will have priests, the Carmelites need only offer themselves as martyrs.

The Superior rebukes her, replying that it is not the privilege of the Carmelities to decide on martyrdom. ("Ce n'est pas à nous de décider"). The nuns look at each other in consternation.

The doorbell jangles again, and the Chaplain steps in through the smaller door in the room. From outside comes the sinister muttering of the revolutionary crowd on the way to the City Hall. Caught between the crowd and the soldiers, the Chaplain explains, he had no choice but to come back. The clamor outside grows louder. Mindful of what will happen to the nuns if he is discovered with them, the Chaplain disappears through the door.

There is a thunderous pounding on the door—underscored by staccato chords in the orchestra—which soon begins to break apart under the blows. The Superior calmly orders Constance to open it. Two Commissioners of the Revolution stalk in. With insolent self-importance, one reads the edict of the Legislative Assembly . . . "whereas" . . . "wherefore" . . . and so on ("Ainsi qu'en a décidé"): premises occupied by religious groups are to be vacated immediately, and sold.

Mother Marie quietly asks the Commissioner to permit the nuns to exchange their habits for suitable layman's clothing. The Commissioner sneers that there is no longer any need for their absurd garments. A uniform, Marie retorts, does not make a soldier fight—neither do Carmelites become martyrs because they wear a nun's habit. When death is everywhere, the Commissioner scoffs, dying means nothing. When life is desecrated, Marie replies scornfully, living means nothing.

To her astonishment, the Commissioner's mood suddenly softens. Things would have gone badly, he says confidentially, if anyone else had heard her words. Then he confides that for two years he was a sacristan. Now, he adds ironically, he must perforce run with the wolves. But he promises to keep the Revolutionary patrol from spying. Meanwhile, he warns guardedly, beware of one Blancart, the blacksmith . . . *an informer!*

During a long silence, the Commissioners leave. Over a melancholy theme in the orchestra (strikingly like that of the Simpleton's lament in *Boris Godunof*) Mother Jeanne enters and tells the nuns that the Superior must leave at once for Paris. She catches sight of Blanche, who had been crouching behind the other nuns. Pitying her distress, she hands the girl a statuette of Christ with the hope that it will give her courage. Just as Blanche takes it, there is a savage shout from the mob outside. Startled, Blanche drops the figurine. It shatters on the stone floor. Desolately, Blanche murmurs: "Now nothing is left but the Lamb of God" ("Il ne nous reste plus que l'Agneau de Dieu!").

ACT THREE[4]

There is a brief introduction in the stately triple rhythm of the saraband (an ancient Spanish dance) which continues under the ensuing dialogue. The scene is the chapel, which has been pillaged by the mob. The grille of the sacristy is torn loose. A nun stands watch near the door. The others are huddled around Mother Marie, with Blanche and Constance side by side. Mother Jeanne and Sister Mathilde are seated on the other side of the chapel. The Chaplain, who had ventured outside and again had barely escaped the mob, reappears; his clothing is spattered with mud, the sleeve of his jacket torn. Asked by Mother Marie to speak to the nuns, he suggests that she herself is better qualified at this moment.

Acquiescing, Marie decisively proposes that the Carmelites take the vow of martyrdom ("Mes filles, je propose . . . le voeu du martyre"). The nuns' response is silence—which does not go unnoticed by Mother Marie. Mother Jeanne complains that these special vows often cause dissension. Well then, Marie offers, let us decide by secret vote. If there is even one against, I will withdraw my proposal.

The nuns agree to the vote, but some whisper, with a glance in Blanche's direction, that one of their number undoubtedly will vote no.

4 In some versions, continuation of Act Two.

Blanche herself seems at the point of collapse. During this scene, Constance watches her with intense concentration. The Chaplain, who has donned his vestments, asks the nuns to go behind the altar one by one to vote. When they have complied, the Chaplain whispers to Marie. One vote against, she intones. Some of the nuns nod knowingly.

Constance cries out that it was she who voted no. There is a gasp of astonishment from the nuns. But in the next breath the girl says she agrees with the majority and beseeches the Mothers to allow her to take the vow. Blanche, sobbing, buries her face in her hands. The Chaplain decides in Constance's favor, then bids the nuns to come to the altar two by two, with the youngest—Blanche and Constance—first, to take the vow. After her avowals, Blanche manages to steal away unobserved.

In a brief interlude, three officers assemble the nuns (now in ordinary dress and carrying their few belongings) to tell them the conditions of their freedom ("Citoyennes, nous vous félicitons"). Addressing them as "fellow citizens," they commend the women for their cooperation. But there must be no more convent living . . . no more dealings with the enemies of the Republic—the priests and other minions of the Pope. From now on, the officers warn, they will be closely watched. They turn and leave abruptly.

The Superior says the Chaplain is to be warned not to say Mass under these dangerous circumstances. Marie sarcastically asks if this precaution is in the true spirit of their vow. Ignoring the jibe, the Superior tells the nuns they must answer to God for their vows—she herself will answer for all of them. The Carmelites leave the convent, free to find refuge wherever they can.

To an agitated theme in the orchestra, the scene changes to the library of the Marquis de la Force. The place is a shambles, the luxurious furnishings in torn disarray. A small stove, on which a stew is cooking in a large pot, stands in the fireplace. In the middle of the room is a folding bed. Blanche is now a wretched servant in her father's house, requisitioned by the revolutionaries.

The door is flung open and Mother Marie enters. She curtly informs Blanche that she has come to take her to a place of safety. At first Blanche flatly refuses to go. She says that although she is mistreated here she feels safe—no one would think of looking for her among these miserable ruins. Suddenly she notices that the stew is burning. That will mean punishment, she cries frantically. Marie resourcefully pours the stew into another pot, then tries to calm the sobbing girl.

Inconsolably, Blanche weeps that everyone despises her because of her fears . . . . everyone is against her—and she despises herself. And now the final blow: her father was guillotined a week ago. In wild anguish, Blanche throws herself on the bed.

In ringing tones Mother Marie declares that the only misfortune is not in being despised but in despising oneself. Bending over the girl, she intones with intensity: "Sister Blanche of the Agony of Christ!" As if inspired, Blanche rises from the bed with a fervent cry: "My Mother!"

Thereupon Marie gives her an address—"Mlle. Rose Ducor, 2 Rue St. Denis"—where she will be completely safe. Marie adds that she herself will be waiting there. Blanche forlornly replies that she cannot go. Marie ends the argument: "You will go, my sister."

From another room a woman's rasping voice calls out an order. Blanche rushes away to obey. Deeply troubled, Mother Marie leaves. An interlude in spoken dialogue follows. Blanche learns from an old man and two old women she meets on a street near the Bastille that the Carmelites have been arrested.

Scene: A large prison cell in the Conciergerie, where the Carmelites are crowded together. The Superior sits on a broken-down chair. Daybreak.

To an accompaniment in a rather calm 2/4 rhythm, the Superior tries to cheer the nuns by pointing out that they have survived at least the first night of imprisonment ("Mes filles, voilà que s'achève")—always the hardest. Tomorrow they will be free—as they always are in their hearts—but under a new kind of discipline. She praises them for their courage in taking the vow of martyrdom—which she herself now embraces. Whatever happens, she adds, she will share their fate. Then they will be free of all earthly fears, Mother Jeanne interjects. With touching simplicity, the Superior says that on the Mount of Olives, Christ Himself knew the fear of death.

Constance speaks up to ask where Blanche is—then answers her own question by saying confidently that she will return. How can you be so certain, the Superior asks. In naïve confusion, Constance replies that she had a dream. The nuns burst into laughter.

The door flies open and the jailer strides in. Over a sinister rhythm in the orchestra, he reads the names of the sixteen doomed Carmelites sentenced to death by the Revolutionary Tribunal. The charges: unlawful assembly . . . sedition . . . crimes against the people of France . . . ("toutes les prévenues susnommées sont condamnées à mort"). Instead of an expected thunderous chord on the word "death," Poulenc here achieves a startling effect with a sudden triple pianissimo arpeggio.

Casually rolling up his document, the jailer leaves. The Carmelites bow their heads in silence. Over sustained chords in the orchestra the Superior softly sings that she had hoped that her daughters would be spared this ordeal ("Mes filles, j'ai désiré de tout mon coeur"). Now there is nothing left but to die. For the last time, she goes on with infinite compassion, she must place her daughters under strict obedience, with her eternal blessing.

In an interlude before the curtain, the Chaplain tells Marie that all the Carmelites have been condemned. Shaken by anguish and remorse, Marie cries that she too took the vow of martyrdom and certainly must join her sisters in death. God will decide who is to redeem that pledge, the Chaplain tells her gently; she has to answer only for herself. They leave.

The Place de la Révolution, where the tumbrels have transported the Carmelites through the jeering crowd. As the women unhesitatingly walk to the scaffold (which is out of sight), the Chaplain, wearing a cap of Liberty, surreptitiously intones the absolution and makes the sign of the cross.

Then the Carmelites, in defiant exaltation, begin the majestic hymn to the Virgin Mary, *Salve Regina*. One by one they disappear to the horrifying thud of the guillotine. Now only two are left—Constance and Mother Jeanne. Again the terrible, rasping crash—and only Constance is left.

At that moment, Blanche elbows her way through the throng and runs toward the scaffold. Constance greets her with a radiant smile, then steps forward singing: "O dulcis Virgo . . . Ma . . ."

As the crowd gapes in stunned silence, Blanche mounts the scaffold. Resolutely and calmly she sings lines from the *Veni Creator: Deo Patri sit gloria et Filio qui a mortuis surrexit ac Paraclito. In saeculorum saecula. In saeculorum* . . . A long silence, finally broken by a single minor chord. The curtain falls.

DIDO AND AENEAS
by HENRY PURCELL
(1659–95)

Libretto by

NAHUM TATE

Based on Vergil's *Aeneid*

CHARACTERS

Dido, or Elissa, Queen of Carthage	Soprano
Belinda, her lady in waiting	Soprano
First Woman	Soprano
Second Woman	Mezzo-soprano
Sorceress	Mezzo-soprano
First Witch	Soprano
Second Witch	Soprano
Spirit	Soprano
Aeneas, a Trojan prince	Tenor or high baritone
A sailor	Tenor

Chorus of courtiers and people, witches, sailors

Place: The ancient city of Carthage on the northern coast of Africa
Time: Antiquity
First performance: London, about 1689
Original language: English

Henry Purcell is considered the greatest composer of the early classical period in England, a creative artist who brought the music of the Elizabethan age to its finest flowering. He wrote the music for some thirty-five dramatic works, many of them masques, which were spectacles staged for the entertainment of royalty. Outstanding among his stage works, besides *Dido and Aeneas,* are *King Arthur, The Witch of Endor, The Fairy Queen* (based on Shakespeare's *A Midsummer Night's Dream*) and *Dioclesian.*

Much of the history of *Dido and Aeneas* has vanished with the past.

It has been established that Purcell composed it for a school for girls in London, where it was first performed about 1689. But—unaccountably— there is no record of its performance for the next two hundred years. The opera was staged in 1895 by students at the Royal Academy of Music for the bicentenary of the composer's death.

In recent times it has been revived with increasing frequency in concert and stage performances, sometimes with ballet to give more movement to the essentially static nature of the plot. It was presented in a modified concert version by the American Chamber Opera Society in New York in 1954 under the baton of Arnold U. Gamson and has since had other performances in various parts of the United States. It was revived by the New York City Opera during its Fall 1979 season on a double bill with *Le Bourgeois Gentilhomme.*

The plot of the opera is based on episodes in the *Aeneid* of Vergil. Dido, the reputed founder of the ancient city of Carthage, gives refuge to Aeneas after his flight from Troy during the Trojan War. They fall in love—only to become the victims of a conspiracy brewed by a malevolent sorceress and her witches. An evil sprite in the employ of the sorceress falsely informs Aeneas that the god Jove has commanded him to sail at once to Italy. Aeneas reluctantly obeys and leaves Carthage, whereupon Dido stabs herself on a funeral pyre.

The stately overture, dominated by a theme in rising and falling triads, sets the somber mood of the legend.

ACT ONE

[*Scene One*] Dido's palace at Carthage. The Queen and Belinda enter with their entourage. In a spirited chorus Belinda and the court exhort Dido to shake off her sorrow for the moment ("Shake the cloud from off your brow"). Belinda reminds her that Fortune still smiles on her and that her empire is growing.

But Dido, inconsolable, answers that she is tormented by a secret grief and that peace of mind is utterly strange to her ("I am prest with torment"). Belinda guesses her secret: she is yearning for Aeneas, who is expected at the palace. They are fated to become lovers, and their love has a two-fold destiny: to save Carthage and to restore ruined Troy.

In a recitative passage ("Where could so much virtue spring?") Dido muses over Aeneas' manly virtues and heroic conquests—he is gentle in peace, yet fierce in war. Belinda and the other women of the court assure the Queen that she has nothing to fear from this great hero.

Aeneas appears and declares his love for Dido. For her, he proclaims, he will defy Destiny itself. He begs her to accept his avowals—if not for his sake, for the sake of the future of Carthage. Belinda surreptitiously urges Aeneas to be ardent in his wooing, for Dido's eyes betray her love even though her lips deny it ("Pursue thy conquest, Love"). The scene ends as the chorus hails the triumph of love and beauty. This is followed by a brief ballet called the "Dance of Victory."

[*Scene Two*] The cave of the witches. Introduced by a foreboding theme in the orchestra, the sorceress summons her witches and commands them to put Carthage to the torch. They respond in wild chorus ("Harm's our delight"). The sorceress exults that before sunset they will destroy the hated Queen of Carthage and her royal lover as well.

When the witches ask how this is to be accomplished, the sorceress explains that Aeneas is destined to go to Italy. At the moment, she goes on, he and Dido are idling their time away in hunting. When they return, the sorceress' own mischievous sprite, disguised as the messenger Mercury, will inform Aeneas that Jove has commanded him to set sail this very night.

The witches express their glee in a spiteful, snarling chorus (sung to "ho-ho-ho"), then sing that they will first conjure up a storm to force the lovers to break off the hunt and hasten back to court. Deep in the recesses of their cave, the witches promise, they will prepare hideous charms to work against the lovers. They symbolize their evil machinations in an ensuing "Dance of the Furies." This closes the act.

ACT TWO

A clearing in the forest at Diana's spring. Dido, Aeneas and Belinda enter with their train to rest from the hunt. Dido is silent and downcast. In a lyrical refrain repeated by the chorus ("Thanks to these lonesome vales") Belinda sings about the beauty of this secluded spot. In an ensuing aria Dido sings that Diana often comes to bathe in this spring—here, where the unfortunate Actaeon met his fate.[1]

Aeneas, exulting over the spoils of the chase, triumphantly holds aloft a boar's head impaled on his spear. Dido, however, can think only of the approaching storm, which is vividly depicted by rising and falling chromatic phrases in the orchestra. As the storm breaks, Belinda and the chorus urge everyone to flee back to the palace because there is no shelter in the open woods. Just as they are about to rush away, the false Mercury appears in Aeneas' path. He tells him Jove is angry over his amorous dalliance and has commanded him to set sail immediately for Italy. Dido meanwhile goes with the others.

Saying he will obey at once, Aeneas laments that he must leave Dido

---

[1] Actaeon, the hunter of Greek mythology who surprised the goddess bathing. She changed him into a stag and he was torn to pieces by his own hounds.

just when she has surrendered to him ("But ah! What language can I try"). Crying that he would rather die, he rails against the gods for separating him from his beloved.

ACT THREE

Aboard Aeneas' ship which is about to weigh anchor, the sailors sing a lusty chorus ("Come away, fellow sailors"). Unobserved by them, the sorceress and the witches come forward and balefully sing that their plot thus far has succeeded: Dido is about to be torn from her lover. They burst into savage laughter. In a solo interlude the sorceress gloats that their next duty will be to destroy Aeneas and his ships. Tonight Elissa (Dido) will perish and tomorrow Carthage will be in flames. The witches and sailors join in a dance of wild abandon.

Dido and Belinda approach Aeneas' ship. Crushed by despair, the Queen sings that the gods themselves have conspired against her (Recitative: "Your counsel all is urged in vain"). Aeneas appears. He tells Dido that he cannot explain why the gods have decreed that he must leave her. The Queen turns on him in bitter sarcasm, commending him for his "crocodile tears," and for blaming the gods for his own desertion of her. Contemptuously she tells him to go back to his "promis'd empire" and to leave her alone.

Stung by her disdain, Aeneas cries that he will defy Jove himself for her love ("In spite of Jove's commands"). This builds into a dramatic duet as Dido pours out her scorn and Aeneas vows he will not leave her. Quailing before her wrath, Aeneas resignedly leaves.

Alone, Dido gives way to her despair in the famous aria "When I am laid in earth." At its conclusion she stabs herself and dies. The opera ends with an eloquent chorus of lamentation: "With drooping wings, ye Cupids come."

ERNANI

by GIUSEPPE VERDI

(1813–1901)

Libretto by

FRANCESCO MARIA PIAVE

Based on Victor Hugo's drama, *Hernani*

CHARACTERS

Ernani, an outlaw (Don Juan of Aragon)	Tenor
Elvira, niece and ward of	
Don Ruy Gomez de Silva	Soprano
Don Carlo, King of Spain	Baritone
Giovanna, waiting woman to Elvira	Mezzo-soprano
Don Ruy Gomez de Silva, grandee of Spain	Bass
Don Riccardo, lieutenant to Don Carlo	Tenor
Iago, esquire to Don Ruy	Bass

Outlaws, knights, ladies, courtiers, women in waiting

Place: Aragon and Castile in Spain; Aix-la-Chapelle in France
Time: About 1519
First performance: Teatro La Fenice, Venice, March 9, 1844
Original language: Italian

This opera has as its theme the revolt against the tyranny of Charles V of Spain (1500–58; Holy Roman Emperor 1519–56), which was the core of Victor Hugo's revolutionary drama. The theme of the uprising stirred the Italian people to patriotic fervor in their own mid-nineteenth-century rebellion against the tyranny of the Hapsburgs.

Hugo, in his *Hernani* (written in 1830), had expressed what the censors considered dangerously subversive sentiments—not to mention his exploiting the idea of conspiracies against a reigning monarch. This aroused the anger of the Austrian authorities, particularly because they were having their hands full trying to keep the Italian populace quiet during the occupation of Venice. In *Ernani,* Verdi had woven the conspiratorial elements of Hugo's drama into his own plot.

A scene in the original libretto brought down on the composer's head the wrath of the Austrian chief of police, who demanded that the scene be withdrawn. Verdi and his librettist finally placated the censors by toning down the conspiratorial implications.

But the revolutionary spirit still pervaded *Ernani* and aroused audiences to violent political demonstrations. The Venetians, for example, considered the great chorus in Act III, "Si ridesti il Leon di Castiglia" ("Rise up, Lion of Castile"), a patriotic tribute to the city they loved. All over Italy that chorus came to symbolize the sufferings of a nation under the heel of the hated Austrians. On more than one occasion it touched off clamorous demonstrations.

At the first performance of *Ernani* in Rome in 1849, the audience, joining in another great Act III chorus, "A Carlo Quinto sia gloria e onor" ("Glory and honor to Charles V"), substituted the words "Glory and honor to Pio Nono," a reference to Pope Pius IX, who was Pope from 1846 to 1878. The popular belief was that this new Pope would lead a movement for unification of Italy. Thus the volatile Italians turned a night at the opera into a political free-for-all.

After its premiere in Venice, *Ernani* became an operatic sensation, and within nine months was taken up by fifteen other theaters. It was the first Verdi opera to be heard in London, and was the first grand opera ever to be heard in San Francisco, where it was given by an Italian troupe about 1851. The San Francisco Opera gave its own premiere of the opera on September 13, 1968.

The role of Elvira was a favorite with such legendary prima donnas as Adelina Patti and Marcella Sembrich. Mme. Sembrich sang the role for the first time in the first Metropolitan performance on January 28, 1902, with Antonio Scotti and Édouard de Reszke. Although given infrequently thereafter, *Ernani* was revived in 1921 and remained in the Metropolitan repertoire for three successive seasons. Metropolitan revivals include performances in 1965, when it proved popular with opera audiences. The opera was scheduled for the opening performance of the Metropolitan Opera's 1970–71 season.

As the composer's fifth opera, *Ernani* belongs to his "first period." The four acts bear the subtitles "The Bandit," "The Guest," "Clemency," and "The Masker."

There is a brief prelude which states two important themes heard later in the opera.

ACT ONE
(*The Bandit*)

[*Scene One*] A rugged, wild region in the mountains of Aragon, the hideout of the fugitive bandit Ernani—in reality Don Juan of Aragon—

and his followers. The rebel mountaineers and bandits are seen eating, drinking, playing cards or cleaning their weapons. They sing a lusty drinking song in praise of their wild, free life in the mountains.

Ernani appears and silently watches them. He is moody and preoccupied. Noticing him, his comrades ask him why he is so sad, and then try to cheer him by assuring him of their loyalty. In an aria, "Come rugiada al cespite," preceded by a brief recitative, Ernani tells them what is troubling him. Elvira, the woman he loves, is being held a virtual prisoner in a neighboring castle by her uncle, Don Ruy Gomez de Silva—who, Ernani says, "will drag her to the altar." In a striking staccato chorus, "Quando notte il cielo," the bandits promise to help him abduct Elvira. Cheered by their comradely spirit, Ernani sings that reunion with Elvira will make him forget the bitterness of his exile. As the chorus comes to a rousing close, he leads his men toward the castle.

[Scene Two] Elvira's apartment in Silva's castle. It is night. Restless and troubled, Elvira, in recitative ("Sorta è la notte"), expresses her loathing of Silva, who relentlessly pursues her, imploring her to marry him. But the more Silva insists, the more she thinks of Ernani and the deeper her love for him grows. In the brilliant aria "Ernani, involami," she voices her longing for him. If Ernani could take her away from Silva's hated caresses, she sings, they could both be happy—even in an alien land. Her aria is interrupted by a chorus of her women in waiting, who come in with wedding gifts. Ironically, they sing that many a girl in Spain envies Elvira as the bride-to-be of Silva.

In spite of herself, Elvira is touched by their naïveté, but she sings that without Ernani any thought of love is a mockery. Not even the most priceless jewel could banish the hatred of Silva from her heart. Elvira brings the aria to a dazzling finish over the accompaniment of the chorus, then she and the women leave the room.

Suddenly Don Carlo enters, in disguise, followed by Giovanna. He curtly orders her to tell Elvira that he is waiting to see her. Alone, he laments that Elvira spurns his love in spite of all his devotion and kingly power—and all because of a common bandit who is his rival. Yet, he murmurs, he will try once more to win her. At that moment Elvira returns, and a dramatic duet follows, beginning with Elvira's angry exclamation: "Sire!—fia ver? Voi stesso."

Although Don Carlo, in a passionate outburst ("da quel dì che t'ho veduta"), begs for her love, Elvira furiously orders him to leave her. Royal pomp and splendor mean nothing to her, she cries, and she will never yield. In rising anger, Don Carlo seizes her arm and tries to force her to come with him. At that Elvira snatches Don Carlo's dagger from his belt, then warns him that if he does not leave her instantly she will plunge the dagger into his heart and into her own ("Mi lasciate, o d'ambo il core").

Staggering back in horror, Don Carlo shouts for his henchmen. But instead of their appearance, a secret door in the chamber is flung open and Ernani strides in, announcing sardonically: "As one of your henchmen, here I am" ("Fra quei fidi io pur qui sto"). This signals the beginning of a fiery trio. The two men recognize each other instantly. Confronting his archenemy, Don Carlo rages that he, as King of Spain, could doom Ernani as a rebel, but out of sheer pity for so despicable an outlaw he will give him a chance to flee for his life.

"So you know me," Ernani retorts. "You whose father killed my father and robbed me of all I own!" Now, he goes on, he despises this King more than ever, because he is also his rival in love. With that, Ernani draws his sword and Don Carlo draws his.

Instantly, Elvira steps between the two men with dagger upraised. She bitterly rebukes both men for their effrontery in claiming her for themselves. One more word, she cries, and she will plunge the dagger into her heart—she belongs neither to the King nor to the lover. These words and Ernani's defiance blend in a striking unison passage, and then Don Carlo's voice joins to bring the trio to a ringing climax.

As the three stand glaring at each other, Silva comes in followed by Giovanna and lords and ladies of the court. In fury he demands to know what these two interlopers are doing in his home—and, what is worse, in the same room with his bride-to-be. Turning to the onlookers, he rages that they can see for themselves how the sanctity of his home has been violated.

Then in a moving aria, "Infelice! e tuo credevi," he accuses Elvira of betraying his trust and his love . . . old age and death itself would be better than this cruel disgrace. In a sudden change of mood he whirls on Don Carlo and Ernani, crying out that this insult must be avenged. He calls for his sword. Continuing the aria in a vigorous martial tempo ("Infin che un brando vindice"), Silva sings that there is one weapon left to him—his sword, which alone can wipe out infamy. Although his soul recoils from this monstrous disgrace, he will meet it bravely. The lords and ladies of the court, commenting on Silva's courage, bring this cabaletta to a stormy climax.

Ernani and Don Carlo try to speak, but Silva cuts them short, saying swords alone can answer. And the first to answer, he adds, glowering at the King, will be Don Carlo.

At that moment Iago, esquire to Silva, enters and announces Riccardo, standard-bearer to the King. The members of the court, suddenly realizing that the King of Spain is standing before them, express their surprise in a tremendous choral outburst: "Oh cielo! è desso il Re!"

Then follows a typically Verdian ensemble in which all onstage give voice to their thoughts at the same time. It also serves to move the plot forward. The chorus begins in a hushed undertone, unaccompanied. Don Carlo bids Riccardo notice how Silva has suddenly restrained his anger in the presence of his King, and this observation is echoed by the chorus. Elvira and Ernani voice fears for each other's safety. Ernani implores her to flee with him; she sings that now she can only choose between him and the dagger she holds. Silva himself sings that in the presence of his King he cannot harbor suspicions of betrayal.

At the thunderous conclusion of the ensemble Silva kneels before the King and asks pardon for his inhospitable actions. Don Carlo instantly grants it. Silva then asks him why he entered the castle in disguise. The wily Don Carlo, in an aside to him, answers that he had come to ask Silva's advice about a successor to the Holy Roman Emperor Maximilian, who recently had died. The truth is, of course, that Don Carlo himself wants to win Elvira.

He asks the unsuspecting Silva if he may stay as a guest, and Silva readily assents. At this Elvira and Ernani exclaim in dismay, realizing that both Silva and the King now can thwart their plans to escape. But Don Carlo, who wants Ernani out of the way, uses his kingly prerogative to order him out of the castle. In reply, Ernani defiantly accuses the King of plotting his father's death and warns that he, Ernani, will exact vengeance for the deed.

Elvira implores him to flee—"Fuggi, Ernani, ti serba al mio amore!" This marks the beginning of the great ensemble which closes the act. At its end, Don Carlo angrily motions Ernani to leave. He goes with a gesture of farewell to Elvira, who looks at him despairingly, then goes to her apartments. Silva escorts Don Carlo from the room.

ACT TWO
(*The Guest*)

The great hall of the castle of Don Ruy Gomez de Silva. Family portraits in richly carved frames hang on the walls. The hall is thronged with nobles, knights and ladies gathered for the nuptial ceremony of Silva and Elvira. The scene opens with a chorus hailing the bridal pair, "Esultiamo! Letizia ne inondi!"

The massive central door opens and Silva, in the magnificent robes of a grandee of Spain, is ushered in by Don Iago. He tells his esquire that he will grant an audience to a pilgrim who has just come to the castle gates. Ernani is led in, disguised in the rough garb of a monk, the hood partially hiding his features. In recitative, Silva tells the stranger that he is welcome—that here "the guest is lord."

Elvira, in her bridal finery, enters with her attendants. In an hour, Silva announces proudly, this beautiful woman will be his bride. Ernani gasps in surprise, then throws back his pilgrim's hood and reveals his identity. He will be the first, he storms, to offer a bridal gift—his own head.

As Elvira watches in stunned disbelief, Ernani turns furiously on Silva, shouting that he is Ernani, a dispossessed nobleman now hunted down like a beast of prey. Yet it is his hatred of his enemies that gives him courage to go on. Elvira sings distractedly that he will be doomed ("Ohimè, si perde"), and then the music continues in trio form. Ernani sings that even his own men would be accused of treason if they dared protect him. Elvira reiterates her warning of doom. Silva vainly tries to assure Ernani that as a guest the ancient law of hospitality will protect him here in the castle ("In queste mura ogni ospite").

As proof, Silva calls for his halberdiers to man the castle walls and ensure the safety of his guests. He leaves with his retinue and Elvira follows. At the entrance she pauses and turns to Ernani with a pleading look. Ernani, glaring at her, calls her a traitress ("Tu . . . perfida!"). Elvira begs him not to question her fidelity, for she had been told Ernani had been slain. Snatching up the dagger she had taken from the King earlier, she cries that she would have used this dagger at the altar to prove she had kept faith with the man she loves. Moved by this avowal, Ernani takes Elvira in his arms and together they pledge their love ("Ah, morir potessi adesso!").

As their duet ends in a quiet, passionate phrase, Silva enters. He halts for a moment in shocked surprise, then advances on the couple with drawn sword. At that moment Iago enters and announces that Don Carlo and his troops are at the castle gates demanding entrance. Sheathing his sword, Silva orders the gates to be opened. Ernani exultantly cries that fate has spared him, but Silva warns that proper vengeance will be forthcoming at the time of his own choosing. In a powerful unison passage ("La vendetta più tremenda"), Elvira and Ernani sing that death will be better than parting. Their voices blend with Silva's in the trio which brings the scene to a close.

Silva strides to a portrait of himself on the wall, thrusts it aside to reveal a secret door. He motions Ernani to enter, closes the panel, then stands waiting for Don Carlo. Elvira leaves, weeping. Don Carlo enters with Riccardo, his lieutenant, and a group of knights, and a dramatic dialogue ensues in quasi-recitative. The King demands to know why the castle is so heavily guarded. Without waiting for a reply, he goes on to say that he suspects certain noblemen of plotting against the regime— and they will be dealt with accordingly. Silva protests that he is loyal. In rising anger, the King fumes that even though an incipient rebellion has been headed off, the bandit Ernani still hides in this castle. Give him up, Don Carlo shouts, or he will order his soldiers to level "all eleven towers" of this castle to the ground.

Silva calmly asks if the King expects him to betray a poor pilgrim who came asking only shelter for the night. "Yet you would dare betray your King," Don Carlo thunders. The Silvas, Don Ruy answers in cold scorn, are not betrayers. Don Carlo rages that now it will be either Silva's sword or Ernani's. Quietly Silva replies: Take mine. Ordering Riccardo to take Silva's sword, the King commands his soldiers to search the castle. Aside, Silva murmurs that his castle—like himself—will keep faith with his guest.

Face to face, Silva and Don Carlo express their thoughts in a powerful duet "Lo vedremo, o veglio audace." Don Carlo sings that now it will be shown how long Silva's defiance will last—when the issue is his life or Ernani's. Don Ruy, pointing to his portrait, sings that never will men look at it and say that *this* Silva was a betrayer.

The colloquy ends when the King's soldiers return, swords in hand. In a staccato chorus, "Fu esplorata del castello" (a foreshadowing of the "Zitti, zitti" chorus in *Rigoletto*), they report that they found no trace of the bandit. Pointing to Silva, they urge the King to punish him for shielding this outlaw. Don Carlo ominously responds that perhaps torture will bring the desired results.

At this point, Elvira enters and, overhearing the King's threat, throws herself at his feet and begs for mercy. Don Carlo, taken aback at her anguished plea, suddenly turns to Silva. In menacing tones he delivers his ultimatum: either give up Elvira to him or surrender Ernani. Staggering toward the portrait which hides the secret panel, Silva asks the King to kill him then and there rather than force him into betrayal. Relentlessly, Don Carlo repeats his ultimatum. In mingled despair and triumph, Silva leads Elvira to the King, then cries out that he still has kept faith with his guest.

Here begins another of the opera's dramatic ensembles, blending the voices of Don Carlo, Silva, Elvira, Riccardo and Giovanna. The soldiers, looking on, sing that they will carry out the King's commands. Don Carlo declares his love for Elvira ("Ah! vieni meco, sol di rose"). Silva swears vengeance. Riccardo assures Elvira that now her sorrow will turn to happiness. Giovanna laments Elvira's misfortune, while Elvira herself sings that now all hope is gone.

At the conclusion of the ensemble, Don Carlo leads Elvira away, with the King's soldiers and members of the court following. All leave except Silva, who for a long moment stands motionless, arms folded. Then, breaking from his reverie, he sings that only heaven can protect the King from the hatred he bears him ("Vigili pure il ciel sempre su te"). Striding over to one of the suits of armor ranged along the wall, he snatches up two swords, measures them one against the other. With both in one hand he steps quickly to the secret portrait panel and presses a spring. The panel flies open, revealing Ernani.

Then and there, Silva challenges Ernani to a duel. When Ernani protests that he will not fight a man of Silva's years, the old man furiously demands that he cross swords. Ernani replies that he would gladly fight —and die—if he could see Elvira once more. Silva tells him he is doomed, because Don Carlo has taken Elvira away as hostage. No, not as hostage, Ernani cries out, for Don Carlo really wants Elvira for himself—he is their rival in love. He implores Silva to allow him to share his revenge on the King. But Silva, beside himself with rage, shouts that Ernani must be the first to die.

Well then, Ernani says, if there is no other way, he will die, but not now. He takes his hunting horn from his belt and hands it to Silva, saying that if Silva still claims the life of Ernani after they have accomplished their revenge, he will return to pay the forfeit at the sound of the hunting horn. With terrible intensity he sings the fateful words: "Ecco il pegno: nel momento in che Ernani vorrai spento, se uno squillo intenderà, tosto Ernani morirà" ("When the horn sounds, Ernani will forfeit his life"). This he swears on the memory of his dead father. Both men then repeat the oath in ringing phrases ("Iddio m'ascolti, e vindice").

Silva summons his cavaliers, who rush in and pledge their allegiance. Together, Silva and Ernani order them to mount their horses and dash in pursuit of the fugitive King and Elvira ("In arcion, cavalieri"). The cavaliers join the two men in the stirring chorus of vengeance which concludes the act ("Per te spirano, sangue, vendetta").

ACT THREE
(Clemency)

The tomb of the Emperor Charlemagne in Aix-la-Chapelle, the city where the Electors are gathered to choose the new Holy Roman Emperor. Don Carlo and Riccardo are seen in front of the tomb. In recitative, Don Carlo reveals that he has learned of a plot to kill him and he has decided to hide in the tomb itself to find out the identity of the conspirators when they gather here for their rendezvous. He orders Riccardo to report the decision of the Electors. If they choose Don Carlo as Emperor, Riccardo is to signal their choice with three cannon salvos and then return—bringing Elvira with him.

Alone before the tomb, Don Carlo invokes the spirit of Charlemagne in an impressive soliloquy, "Gran Dio! costor sui sepolcrali marmi." He broods on the futility of striving for honor, power and possessions. All these are nothing ("Con voi nel nulla"). And yet, he sings in the ensuing cavatina ("Oh de' verd' anni miei"), he knows that destiny has accorded him one moment of godlike power. Don Carlo turns, unlocks the door of the tomb and slowly enters.

To the accompaniment of a staccato theme in the orchestra the conspirators enter, muffled in cloaks and carrying torches. They are led by Silva, Ernani and Iago. In hushed tones they sing that here at the tomb of the great Charlemagne they will uphold the cause of the Catholic League and save Spain from the usurper ("Per la lega santo ardor"). In a dramatic gesture they throw down their torches, plunging the scene into darkness as they sing that they need no light to guide their blows for freedom.

Silva announces that Don Carlo's assassin will be chosen by lot. At his command the plotters write their names on slips of paper and place them on top of a nearby tomb. When all have signed, Silva picks up one of the slips and reads the name: Ernani. In a ringing phrase Ernani exults over his good fortune and the soldiers shout that if he fails in his mission they will avenge him.

But Silva calls on Ernani to yield the assassin's task to him, saying that in return he will release Ernani from the pledge to forfeit his life at the sound of the hunting horn. Ernani resolutely refuses, crying out that first his own thirst for revenge must be satisfied. Brandishing their swords, the soldiers burst into the famous unison chorus "Si ridesti il Leon di Castiglia." Hailing the heroic spirit of the Lion of Castile, they sing that, just as Spain once rose up against the Moorish oppressors, so they will fight for freedom to the last man. At the fiery conclusion of the chorus, a cannon shot booms out. The conspirators stand transfixed. Then there is a second shot, and the door of Charlemagne's tomb is flung open. A third shot—and Don Carlo strides forth, crying in a thunderous voice: "Carlo Quinto, o traditor!" ("Traitors! It is Charles the Fifth!").

As the conspirators shrink back in fear and confusion a huge crowd emerges from the tomb, led by the Electors. They are followed by pages carrying the crown, scepter and other imperial insignia. Seen among the throng are Elvira and Giovanna. Don Carlo peremptorily orders the nobles among the conspirators to be executed, the others imprisoned. Thereupon Ernani steps forward, identifies himself as Don Juan of Aragon and claims his right to stand with the nobles ("Io son conte").

As Don Carlo glares at him, Elvira rushes forward, throws herself at the King's feet and begs for mercy ("Ah, Signor, se t'è concesso"). Don Carlo looks down at her for a moment in furious anger. Then, restraining himself, he turns his gaze to the tomb of Charlemagne and begins the great aria "Oh sommo Carlo." In majestic phrases he sings that, as successor to the mighty Emperor, he will emulate the monarch and pardon those who plotted to destroy him. As a crowning gesture he leads Elvira to Ernani and gives them both his blessing as lovers. This introduces the stirring ensemble which closes the act, "A Carlo Quinto sia gloria e onor," in which all hail the magnanimity of the new Emperor.

ACT FOUR
(*The Masker*)

The scene is a masked ball at the palace of Don Juan of Aragon (Ernani). During a gay chorus a mysterious masked figure in domino costume enters, looks around as though searching for someone, then leaves. As the guests also leave, Elvira and Ernani enter. For a brief moment they sing of their happiness in a duet which ends in a phrase of passionate intensity, "Fino al sospiro estremo."

But in the next instant the mood is shattered by the distant sound of a hunting horn. Ernani, knowing what it means, recoils in horror. As Elvira anxiously asks what is wrong, the horn sounds again, nearer this time. Momentarily losing control, Ernani imagines he sees the face of a devil grinning mockingly at him. Recovering, he tells Elvira that it was only the pain of an old wound returning and asks her to go for a doctor. When she leaves he murmurs that the specter of the grinning devil was only a figment of his imagination. He starts to leave—and comes face to face with the masked figure.

In menacing tones the stranger repeats the words of Ernani's pledge—the pledge which dooms him: "Ecco il pegno: nel momento in che Ernani vorrai spento, se uno squillo intenderà tosto Ernani morirà." With that he tears off his mask. It is Silva.

Despairingly Ernani begs for a reprieve. In reply, Silva offers him the choice of a dagger or a cup of poison. In hopeless resignation Ernani reaches for the dagger just as Elvira rushes in. Here begins the fiery trio which brings the opera to its close, "Ferma, crudele, estinguere."

Elvira desperately pleads for mercy. Ernani cries that her pleas will be in vain and that now all he needs is the courage to die. Silva remorselessly demands fulfillment of the pledge. Wildly calling Elvira's name, Ernani stabs himself. Elvira falls fainting over his body. Looking down at them, Silva, in ferocious triumph, sings that the demon of revenge has done his work well. The curtain falls.

ESCLARMONDE

by JULES ÉMILE FRÉDÉRIC MASSENET
(1842–1912)

Libretto by
ALFRED BLAU and LOUIS DE GRAMONT

Based on an ancient French romance

CHARACTERS

Phorcas, Emperor of Byzantine	Bass
Esclarmonde, his daughter	Soprano
Parséis, her sister	Mezzo-soprano
Chevalier Roland, Count of Blois	Tenor
Chevalier Énéas, a Byzantine knight,	
fiancé of Parséis	Tenor
Cléomer, King of France	Bass
Bishop of Blois	Baritone
Byzantine herald	Tenor

Envoys, dignitaries, knights, soldiers, guards, monks, priests, penitents, executioners, townspeople, children

Ballet: spirits of air, water and fire

Place: Byzantium, an ancient city on the Bosporus, and France
Time: Mythical, and fourteenth-century France
First performance: Opéra-Comique, Paris, May 14, 1889
Original language: French

The seventh of Massenet's twenty-five operas, *Esclarmonde* is a mélange of oriental fantasy and medieval history. For his own purpose, Massenet translated a tale of knightly derring-do into some unforgettable music. He was acknowledged as a master of instrumentation and musical technique—a fine craftsman with a facile, melodious style.

His use of bass, clarinet and contrabassoon, in the Wagnerian manner, gave much of his music an impressive sonority. His *Esclarmonde* was known among professional musicians as a "small French *Tristan,* a small French *Parsifal*—but French to the core."

The opera was a spectacular success and ran for ninety-nine performances between May and December 1889. After that its popularity
waned—with isolated performances in Brussels, St. Petersburg and New
Orleans (1893). It was not heard again in the United States until its
brilliant revival by the San Francisco Opera Association in 1974. It is
this production that was given by the Metropolitan Opera during the
1977-78 season.

The composer dedicated the opera to Sibyl Sanderson, originally
from Sacramento, California—an extraordinarily beautiful singer with
an extraordinary voice (a three-octave range from low G to G above
high C). While she was studying in Paris, Massenet heard her sing at a
dinner party and was immediately captivated by both her voice and her
charm. He later told her: "You have justified my faith in you, because
it was for you that I wrote *Esclarmonde*." (He also wrote *Thaïs* for
her.)

Sanderson created the role of Esclarmonde in her debut at the
Opéra-Comique and followed this (according to another version of the
opera's history) with one hundred consecutive performances.

But the years took their toll of Massenet's star, and her voice gradually deteriorated. Her Metropolitan Opera debut as Manon was not an
unqualified success. She became ill after her subsequent return to Paris,
where her career was tragically cut short. She died on May 15, 1903, at
the age of thirty-eight.

PROLOGUE

The basilica at Byzantium.[1] At back, the iconostasis (entrance to the
sanctuary in the Orthodox Eastern Church), its golden doors closed.
The Emperor Phorcas is seated on his throne, attended by dignitaries,
warriors, guards and incense bearers.

To the accompaniment of majestic chords in the brass, with organ interludes, Phorcas addresses the assemblage ("Dignitaires, guerriers,
sous ces augustes voûtes"). He announces that, although he is a supreme magician, he must obey a higher destiny. Therefore, he will abdicate his throne to his daughter Esclarmonde and confer upon her his
magic powers.

To safeguard these powers she must remain veiled until her twentieth
year. Then, at a tournament of knights in Byzantium, the winner will
claim the hand of Esclarmonde. He orders the doors of the iconostasis
opened. Esclarmonde, veiled, appears like a Byzantine idol, a gem-
encrusted crown glittering on her head. The assemblage hails her in a

[1] Later Constantinople, now modern Istanbul.

vigorous chorus ("Ô divine Esclarmonde!"). At her side are her sister Parséis and ladies-in-waiting.

Phorcas, handing Parséis his scepter and crown, tells her that she alone will know the place of his retreat ("Toi seule, ô Parséis"), then proclaims her as royal guardian over her sister. Esclarmonde descends from the sanctuary and faces her father. Sadly bidding her farewell ("Hélas! chère Esclarmonde, il faut nous séparer"), he bids her raise her veil so that he may see her face for the last time. He is dazzled by her beauty. Dropping her veil, she moves slowly back to the sanctuary. Phorcas remains, with Parséis in his arms. The throng pays homage to Esclarmonde as Empress ("Sublime Impératrice!").

ACT ONE

Byzantium. A terrace of the Empress Esclarmonde. She is resting on a couch. An orchestral interlude sets the mood of her reflections. She thinks longingly of Roland—a hero whom she has never met, but whose name burns strangely in her heart ("Roland! Comme ce nom me trouble étrangement").

Parséis enters, and a dialogue continues in duet form ("Ô ma soeur! Ma tendre souveraine"). Why, Parséis asks her sister, are you so unhappy? Esclarmonde frets that her father's decree has isolated her from mankind. She is as solitary and powerless as an idol—and thus must wait until a tournament decides her fate as a mortal woman. Parséis reminds her that her father made her not only an Empress, but a magician as well. And so she has the power to choose any king or knight she likes for a husband.

Thereupon Esclarmonde confesses that she is in love with the knight Roland, Count of Blois ("Un héros fameux par ses exploits"). He passed through Byzantium once. She saw him then—proud and handsome—while a veil cruelly hid her own face from him. She hopes he will be the victor in the tournament. But now, she adds forlornly, he is far away in France.

But you are a sorceress, Parséis says, in a significant single-note phrase. Use your magic to bring Roland to you. Esclarmonde answers sadly: to love is not enough . . . one must *be* loved. The duet concludes as the two women bewail the torment of unrequited love.

A fanfare outside announces the arrival of Énéas, returning from the wars in France. He kneels in homage to Esclarmonde. Then Parséis, observing that the Empress has had enough of homage, asks him to tell of his exploits in France ("Parlez-nous simplement de vos lointains voyages").

In a stirring martial refrain ("En l'honneur de vos divins yeux"), Énéas gallantly answers that he fought his best in her honor. Among the thousands he fought, Énéas goes on, there was but one who could have defeated him: Roland. Esclarmonde and Parséis gasp in surprise. Énéas relates that, in combat, Roland easily could have run him through ("Vainqueur, dans sa colère"). Instead, he extended his hand in a brotherly gesture, and they swore eternal friendship. Now, as reward for his chivalry in the lists, Roland is to be proffered the hand of Bathilde, daughter of Cléomer, King of France.

Esclarmonde starts violently, gasping that now Roland is lost to her forever. Parséis, aware of her distress, asks Énéas to leave. Before he goes, he tenderly asks to be reassured of her love. Watching him, Esclarmonde murmurs wistfully: "they are happy." This phrase ("Ils sont heureux") marks the conclusion of the preceding dialogue, which has been sung in trio form.

In a sudden frenzy, Esclarmonde tears away her veil, crying that she can resist no longer ("je ne résiste plus!"). Énéas's news of Roland has decided her: this very night she will use her sorcery to transport him to a magic island where they will consummate their love. Though she will remain veiled, her fiery passion will make her his queen forever.

With that, Esclarmonde, in a tempestuous aria underscored by a theme stated by the French horn, invokes the spirits of air, sea and fire to bring Roland to her ("Esprits de l'air! Esprits de l'onde! Esprits du feu!"). As the aria climaxes in a soaring high D, spirit voices join to intone the name of Roland. Esclarmonde and Parséis jubilantly cry out that they see him.

The following scene dissolves into the vision—described in a duet by Esclarmonde and Parséis over a galloping rhythm in the orchestra—of King Cléomer and Roland boar hunting in the forest of Ardennes ("Dans la forêt des Ardennes"). The blare of hunting horns vividly depicts the chase. The vision unfolds, showing Roland stepping from a boat to the shore of an enchanted island as the music subsides into a mood reflecting the calm of the sea.

As the scene darkens into night, Esclarmonde invokes the spirits to carry her to the island where her beloved awaits her. Bidding farewell to Parséis, she says she will return at dawn. Her voice dies away in evocative phrases as she disappears.

ACT TWO

[*Scene One*] The enchanted island in moonlight. To music that sparkles like that in *A Midsummer Night's Dream,* or in the Windsor Park interlude in *Falstaff,* a bevy of spirits dances on the seashore. Roland appears, wondering what has brought him to this mysterious place ("Où suis-je? En quel lieu de la terre"). Dancing around him, the spirits lead him to a grassy bank, where he falls asleep.

To a limpid, curving theme over a muted brass chorale, Esclarmonde appears. Gazing fondly down on the sleeping knight, she passionately sings that now she will enfold her lover in her arms. She hymns the night in a brief refrain ("Ô Nuit! Nuit vénérée"), then bends over and kisses Roland on the forehead. He awakens wondering if the being he sees is still a figment of his dream ("Quelle forme vers moi se penchait").

This introduces an impassioned duet, which in a way is a lyrical echo of the famous duet in Berlioz's *Les Troyens*—"Nuit d'ivresse et extase infinie," sung by Dido and Aeneas. Roland, of course, does not recognize Esclarmonde, who tells him simply that she is the woman who loves him and wants to be his wife ("Oui, je t'aime et je veux être à toi").

But this can be, she warns, only if he neither sees her face nor asks her name. If he agrees to these conditions, she will be his; if not, she will vanish. When Roland fervently implores her to stay, Esclarmonde surrenders herself to his embrace. Together they hail the nuptial rites ("Hymen! voici le divin moment"), joined by the voices of the spirits.

[*Scene Two*] A room in an enchanted palace. The music continues without pause into an orchestral interlude. Roland lies on a couch; Esclarmonde, veiled, stands near him. The duet of the previous scene continues as Roland rhapsodizes over this night of love ("Hélas! ma bien aimée!"). Though he does not know her real name, he sings, he knows that she is called the Adored One ("Tu t'appelles l'Adorée!"). Ardently—but firmly—Esclarmonde reminds him of his oath; Roland swears he will keep the faith.

But now it is dawn, Esclarmonde sings, and they must part. Roland must go forth to battle with the Saracen chief, Sawegur, who is laying siege to King Cléomer at Blois. It is Roland's first duty to rescue his people from the clutches of the savage invader. The duet ends on a soaring unison note.

As he is about to leave, a group of virgins, guardians of the sacred sword of St. George, materializes in the background. One carries the sword. The music takes on a martial rhythm as Esclarmonde takes the sword and hands it to Roland. In a majestic refrain ("Cette épée a du ciel reçu le privilège") she sings that this blessed weapon will assure victory in combat—but it will shatter in the hands of the knight who breaks his oath. As trombones sound the sword motif, Roland grasps the weapon by the hilt and holds it aloft so that it forms a cross. In ringing tones he salutes its awesome power ("Ô glaive! à ton aspect je m'incline").

Esclarmonde and Roland bid farewell—reminding each other not to forget a promise and an oath. Esclarmonde leaves. Roland turns to watch her go, then raises his sword, point upward. The scene closes in a thunderous orchestral climax.

ACT THREE

[*Scene One*] Blois, on the river Loire in France, now under siege and in smoking ruins. Gathered with King Cléomer in a desolate square, the citizens, in a powerful chorus ("Ô Blois, misérable cité!"), lament the fate of their city. They implore their king not to yield to the demands of the ruthless Sawegur. Only a miracle can save Blois, Cléomer tells them. Now the Saracen demands a tribute of one hundred virgins as the price of peace. Again a cry of despair comes from the panic-stricken populace.

At that moment a procession appears, led by the Bishop of Blois accompanied by monks and choir boys bearing the cross. They chant the *Kyrie Eleison*. Following them are the penitents. In a stately refrain ("Mettez en Dieu votre espérance") the Bishop exhorts the kneeling townspeople to put their trust in God. Suddenly the sound of trumpets announces the arrival of the Saracen envoy from Sawegur. He arrogantly asks Cléomer for his answer to Sawegur's demands. In baffled rage and desperation, Cléomer and the people cry: "Who will save us now?"

To a blazing fanfare, Roland strides forth out of the crowd with the answer: "I!" The people cheer him joyously. Roland defiantly tells the Saracen envoy to inform Sawegur that a knight of Blois challenges him to combat. Urging the populace to have courage, he sounds a call to battle. He rushes away, followed by all except the women and children and the Bishop. Cléomer climbs up on the ramparts, while the Bishop asks the crowd around him to pray for victory ("Implorons le Seigneur et tombons à genoux!"). The people chant a response.

Offstage sounds of battle rise to a climax as the victorious Roland and his warriors burst in. He is hailed in a tumultuous chorus ("Victoire! Roland est vainqueur!").

King Cléomer then offers Roland the hand of his daughter Bathilde as reward for his valor ("Noble héros, je veux aujourd'hui même"). To the stunned surprise of the King, the Bishop and the people, Roland refuses. He gives no reason, saying only that he is sworn to silence. Cléomer, furious, leaves. The Bishop follows, first observing in a cryptic phrase ("Je saurai ce qu'il ne veut point dire") that he will soon discover the real reason for Roland's refusal of Bathilde as his bride. A sinister figure in the bassoon underscores his comment. While the people continue to cheer their hero, Roland, aside, expresses fervent longing for the bride whose face he has never seen.

[*Scene Two*] An orchestral interlude with a prominent theme in the cellos is played during the scene change to Cléomer's palace. At rear, an alcove closed by curtains of brocaded gold. A window at back, wide door at right. Roland is standing at the window. It is evening. The orchestral interlude leads into Roland's melodious aria ("Le peuple délivré"). He muses that the acclaim of the populace cannot quench his burning desire to be with his unknown bride.

Suddenly the Bishop appears, and a dramatic confrontation occurs. He begins unctuously with a blessing, then launches into his inquisition. Why, he asks, did Roland refuse Bathilde as his bride? I am sworn to secrecy, Roland replies, and I will keep my oath. Alternately wheedling and threatening Roland with eternal damnation, the Bishop tries to learn Roland's secret.

Despite his resolution, Roland becomes frightened at the Bishop's threat of doom. He confesses that his soul is no longer his own. It belongs to a woman—a being from another world—and he is her husband ("Une fée est ma femme, et je suis son époux!"). She became his bride on an enchanted island, he explains.

Losing his ecclesiastical composure, the Bishop shouts that Roland has been enslaved by the devil ("Du démon abhorré"). A devil, answers Roland with simple logic, would not have asked him to save France from the Saracen. The significance of this is lost on the Bishop, who can only raise his hands in a gesture of absolution. He leaves as Roland sinks to his knees, asking God's mercy.

At that moment he hears a voice calling his name. It is sung in a cadenza-like coloratura phrase with a trill on high D. Roland springs up. In a fervid aria ("C'est sa voix, sa voix qui m'appelle!") he exults that his beloved has kept her oath and is returning to him. At its conclusion Esclarmonde emerges from the alcove; Roland rushes into her arms.

Without warning, the Bishop, the priests and the executioners storm into the room intoning an ominous chant of exorcism ("Au nom du Père!"). It brings to mind the cathedral scene in *Faust*, when Méphistophélès pronounces Marguerite's doom. The Bishop tears the veil from Esclarmonde, who screams in shame and horror. Roland staggers back, dazzled by her beauty. She turns on him in a furious outburst ("Roland! tu m'as trahie"), denouncing him for betraying her. Then, in sorrow and resignation, she sings that Roland has seen her for the first and last time—he has lost her forever ("Mais c'est pour la première et la dernière fois").

As the priests and executioners, at the Bishop's command, lunge forward to seize Esclarmonde, they are hemmed in by the spirits of fire and shrink back in terror. When Roland raises his sword to defend Esclarmonde, it shatters in his hand. She screams a curse ("Parjure!

sois maudit!"), then disappears, to the malevolent chanting of the priests.

ACT FOUR

A clearing in the forest of Ardennes. At one side is the vine-covered entrance to a cave. Wood nymphs and spirits dance in a sprightly ballet. To the sound of a trumpet, four heralds appear to announce the tournament that is to take place in Byzantium. Then a Byzantine herald steps forward and proclaims that the victor will win the hand of Esclarmonde. The heralds and the dancers then vanish into the forest.

Énéas and Parséis appear. Bewildered and lost, they are vainly searching for Esclarmonde. Énéas assures Parséis that the Emperor Phorcas, her father—who has retreated to the nearby cave as his final home—will solve the mystery of Esclarmonde's disappearance.

To the accompaniment of a dark-hued theme in the bass, Phorcas emerges from the cave, walking as though in a trance. He voices his anguish over the destiny of Esclarmonde. To his astonishment, he sees Énéas and Parséis. His daughter tells him of the forbidden romance of Esclarmonde and Roland and implores him to have mercy on his erring daughter.

But Phorcas storms that Esclarmonde must be punished. There is a violent clap of thunder; Énéas and Parséis cower in terror at the entrance of the cave. The Emperor commands the spirits to bring Esclarmonde to him at once. She appears, moving like a sleepwalker. As her mind clears, she recalls the terrible ordeal with the Bishop and the executioners, and Roland's betrayal ("Ah! je me souviens! Honte sans pareille!"). Calming, she recalls, to a *Tristan*-like theme in the orchestra, the happiness of her nuptial night with Roland.

There is an abrupt change of mood as she looks about her, sees her father, and desperately begs his forgiveness. But Phorcas is relentless. In a trio, Énéas and Parséis join him in warning Esclarmonde that the law is inflexible—she must renounce Roland ("Obéis, Esclarmonde, à l'inflexible loi"). If she refuses, he is doomed.

At first she protests: she will not condemn her lover to death—she will condemn herself first. Phorcas, Énéas and Parséis remorselessly exhort her to obey the law. As they leave, Roland enters, shaken by the prospect of the ordeal he now must undergo. He and Esclarmonde come face to face. Kneeling, Roland implores her pardon. Pardon—yes —she answers, but because of his betrayal she must renounce his love. In anguish he cries: "This is madness! You speak of forsaking me! You wish me to forget you!" ("Folie! Tu parles d'abandon! Tu veux que je t'oublie!").

But in the next moment they are in each other's arms, passionately singing that nothing matters except their love ("Nous nous aimons et rien n'est vrai que notre amour!"). They are about to flee when the spirit voices, to a thunderous accompaniment, repeat the inexorable decree: Renounce your lover ("Renonce à ton amant").

In helpless terror, Esclarmonde cries out to Roland that she must leave him forever. "Then," Roland shouts despairingly, "you do not love me!" In the stormy climax of this scene, the voices of Roland, Phorcas and the spirits shout: "Answer!"

Esclarmonde sobs brokenly: "I no longer love you" ("Je ne veux plus t'aimer") and throws herself into her father's arms. As the spirit voices, in savage triumph, intone that the crime is expiated ("Le crime est expié!") Phorcas and Esclarmonde vanish. Roland falls fainting.

He revives at the sound of the trumpet announcing the tournament at Byzantium. Resigned to his fate, he cries that now he will find the death he seeks ("Ô mort! je t'appelais"). He turns and runs to join the procession of knights riding to the tournament.

EPILOGUE

The basilica in Byzantium, as in the first scene of the opera. Musically and dramatically, the first scene also is repeated to the point where Phorcas commands the victor of the Byzantium tournament to be brought before him. Roland enters. He is in black armor, his visor down.

When Phorcas asks his name so that he can receive the victor's reward—the hand of Esclarmonde and the throne—Roland simply answers no. But Esclarmonde recognizes his voice and suppresses an exclamation of joy. Raising his visor, Roland identifies himself thus: "My name is Despair. I am called Sorrow!" ("Mon nom est Désespoir! Je m'appelle Douleur!"). So far as rewards are concerned, he adds, he is not interested. While Esclarmonde exults at his refusal, the court stares at him incredulously. Turning away, Roland sings that, for him, there is only one being whom he cherishes. Beyond that—nothing.

Esclarmonde is scarcely able to control herself. Then, at a word from Phorcas, she lifts her veil. There is a tremendous shout of acclaim from the crowd, hailing her as the Empress Esclarmonde. At the sound of her name Roland turns and greets her with an impassioned phrase: "It is you whom I adored!" ("Toi! c'est toi que j'adorais!").

This marks the beginning of the brief but fiery duet of recognition and reconciliation, climaxed by the final chorus of homage to the two royal lovers—("Ô divine Esclarmonde! Ô valeureux héros! l'univers vous acclame en frémissant d'amour!"). The curtain falls.

LA FANCIULLA DEL WEST
(*The Girl of the Golden West*)
by GIACOMO PUCCINI
(1858–1924)

Libretto by

CARLO ZANGARINI and GUELFO CIVININI

Based on David Belasco's drama
The Girl of the Golden West

CHARACTERS

Minnie		Soprano
Jack Rance, sheriff		Baritone
Dick Johnson (the outlaw Ramerrez)		Tenor
Nick, bartender at the Polka saloon		Tenor
Ashby, a Wells Fargo agent		Bass
Sonora		Baritone
Trin		Tenor
Sid		Baritone
Handsome	miners	Baritone
Harry		Tenor
Joe		Tenor
Happy		Baritone
Larkens		Bass
Billy Jackrabbit, an Indian		Bass
Wowkle, Billy's squaw		Mezzo-soprano
José Castro, a Mexican from Ramerrez's gang		Bass
Jake Wallace, a wandering folk singer		Bass
A post rider		Tenor

Men of the California mining camp

Place: At the foot of the Cloudy Mountains in California
Time: 1849–50
First performance: Metropolitan Opera House, New York City,
December 10, 1910
Original language: Italian

On a visit to New York in 1907, Puccini saw David Belasco's Broadway production of *The Girl of the Golden West*. Impressed by its dramatic power, the composer invited Belasco—whose *Madam Butterfly* had formed the basis of Puccini's previous opera—to collaborate on an operatic version of the melodrama of the forty-niners.

The opera was given one of the most memorable premieres in the history of the Metropolitan, with Enrico Caruso, Emmy Destinn and Pasquale Amato in the cast, Arturo Toscanini conducting, and Puccini and Belasco standing in the wings. Despite its brilliant premiere, the opera lasted only four seasons at the Metropolitan, a "weak libretto" being blamed for its indifferent success. It has been revived periodically, however, to considerable acclaim.

In its use of recitative and in the symphonic quality of the orchestral accompaniment, *Fanciulla* represents somewhat of a departure from Puccini's earlier style of composing.

There is a brief but dramatic orchestral introduction, which states one of the romantic themes of the opera.

ACT ONE

The interior of the Polka saloon. It is sunset and the room is partially in darkness. Sheriff Jack Rance, smoking a cigar, is sitting near the fireplace. Larkens, a young miner, is seated on a cask, his head in his hands. He takes an envelope from his pocket, walks over to the counter, puts a stamp on the envelope and drops it into the mailbox. Then he sits down again dejectedly.

From outside come the voices of miners calling to each other, then snatches of a song, "Là lontano, là lontan." Nick the bartender starts lighting the lamps and then, during a brief orchestral passage, the miners come trooping in from camp.

There is noisy byplay as they josh each other, call for drinks, and sit down to play cards. Someone asks about Minnie, the proprietress of the saloon. During all the talk and banter, Larkens continues to brood. Glancing at him, Rance asks Nick what is wrong with the boy. "Homesick—as usual," says Nick. "He's dreaming of his mother in Cornwall." Somberly, Rance remarks that the boy is cursed with gold fever in this godforsaken country ("Che terra maledetta"). Then with a gesture of impatience he asks why Minnie has not appeared. Nick shrugs in answer. Frowning, Rance walks into the adjoining dance hall.

Meanwhile, the miners go on with their card games. Billy Jackrabbit, the Indian, sidles up to the counter, steals some cigars and scurries out. Nick bawls that anybody who wants to dance can go into the dance hall, which adjoins the bar. The miners jeer good-naturedly because there are no women to dance with.

When Nick comes by with cigars, Sonora, aside, asks if there is any message from Minnie. "Yes," Nick tells him slyly, "she says *you* are her favorite." Overjoyed, the gullible Sonora passes out cigars. A moment later Nick tells Trin exactly the same story, whereupon Trin calls for drinks all around.

Suddenly above the barroom clamor comes the sound of a plaintive song, "Che faranno i vecchi miei." The men pause and listen. As Nick calls out that the singer is Jake Wallace, the men become strangely quiet, moved by the homesickness expressed in this refrain, in which the singer muses about his aged parents far away, hoping and longing for their son's return. Strumming his banjo, Jake enters singing. He stops in surprise at the faces turned toward him in silence. Softly the miners echo a phrase of his song. And here begins one of the most affecting choruses in the opera—"Al telaio tesserà." Moved close to tears by memories of home, the miners express their feelings in phrases of simple tenderness, in sharp contrast to their raucous behavior of a few moments before. As the song dies away into anguished silence, Larkens, bursting into tears, gets to his feet. In abject despair he cries that he wants to go home ("Non reggo più"), that he is sick to death of this brutal existence. He begs for help to get back home. The miners promptly take up a collection and pour the money into his hands. Larkens sobs his thanks and then leaves as the miners hum the closing phrases of the chorus.

As some of the miners resume their game of faro, there is a sudden burst of violent action. Handsome accuses Sid of cheating. Crowding around him, the miners, in a staccato chorus ("Al laccio il ladro"), shout that they will hang the scoundrel then and there. Sid whines for mercy.

At that moment, Rance strides in from the dance hall and restrains the miners with a contemptuous gesture. Coldly he asks why death should seem so terrible ("Cos'è la morte?"), then adds that he knows of a worse penalty. He calls for Sid's cheating card, and a miner hands him the two of spades. Pinning it above Sid's heart, the sheriff sneers that he will wear it like a flower. And if he dare take it off, Rance growls, hang him. With bellows of rage, the miners brutally kick Sid out of the barroom. Then, as though nothing had happened, Rance and the others go back to their card game.

At this point Ashby, the Wells Fargo agent, enters. First calling for whisky and asking about Minnie, he announces that he is finally closing in on the bandit he has been hunting for three months. This fellow, he warns, is at the head of a dangerous band of thieves ("La banda di ladri"), and the miners should be on their guard. With that, Ashby, groaning that he is dead tired, flings himself down on a bunk in the corner of the room and covers himself with a cloak.

The men drink a toast to Minnie. With an arrogant smile Rance murmurs, "Missis Rance, quite soon" ("Mistress Rance, fra poco"), a remark which sets off a brief but violent quarrel. Sonora taunts Rance that Minnie is only making a fool of him. The sheriff warns Sonora that he will take no insults from a drunken miner ("è il whisky che lavora"). Sonora whips out his pistol, whereupon Rance rushes at him and the two start fighting.

Before the miners can intervene, Minnie bursts into the room, thrusts the two men apart and snatches Sonora's pistol away from him. The others step back. There is a sudden silence, then they hail Minnie with a shout. Confronting Sonora, Minnie angrily berates him for causing trouble. He, and the other men as well, shuffle in embarrassment. Rance sulkily retreats to a corner. Minnie sharply warns the men that if there is any more of this nonsense she will discontinue her school. Like guilty schoolboys, the miners clumsily try to placate her by offering her flowers, a length of ribbon and a silk handkerchief. Minnie's anger melts away as she smiles her thanks.

Ashby now joins the group and clinks glasses with the lady. The dialogue continues in a kind of quasi-recitative. Ashby plays the gallant for Minnie's benefit. Noticing Rance sitting alone, she favors him with a greeting. She settles Sonora's barroom bill as he pays off with a bag of gold. Ashby, talking to Rance, expresses concern because so much of the miners' gold is kept unguarded in the saloon when there are so many outlaws around. He recommends the security of the Wells Fargo bank.

At length Minnie takes a Bible out of a box at the end of the bar, then sits down with the miners to continue their "Scripture lesson." A droll and charming scene underscored with striking musical ingenuity ensues as she asks: "Dove eravamo?" ("Now, where were we?"). Opening the Bible to the "Fifty-first Psalm of David," she asks her pupils to recite. The burly miners respond like schoolboys.

First, Harry describes King David ("Era un re dei tempi antichi") as a "reg'lar hero" who slew a giant with the jawbone of an ass. In the "second lesson" Minnie explains to the mystified Joe that hyssop, a plant that grows in the Orient, also can grow in men's hearts. Then in a simple but moving refrain she reads the familiar verses beginning "Wash me and I shall be whiter than snow," and explains its message: In all the world there is not one sinner who cannot be redeemed through love.

The calm mood of the scene suddenly is broken by the sound of hoofbeats outside. It is the post rider bringing the mail—along with a warning that an outlaw has been seen in the neighborhood. The rider hands a letter to Ashby, who reads it with astonishment. He asks the messenger if he knows a certain Nina Micheltorena. Before he can answer, Minnie, with noticeable relish, declares that this Nina is a Spanish hussy ("È una finta spagnuola") who spends all her time flirting with the men. Ask them, she adds mischievously, looking at the miners. They shrug in embarrassment.

Aside in recitative, Ashby tells Rance that he will have the outlaw Ramerrez swinging at the end of a rope by nightfall. He explains that Nina Micheltorena will lure him to the Palmetto saloon at midnight, and then . . .

A brief choral interlude follows in which the miners, reading their letters, express their reactions to the news from home: Handsome's girl, Kitty, has married the old clockmaker . . . Happy's parrot died calling his name . . . Harry reads about wars and other disasters . . . Joe howls in grief because his grandmother has died. As the others try to comfort him he wipes away his tears and calls for whisky. The miners drink and then go into the dance hall. Only Rance remains, his eyes on Minnie.

Nick comes in to say that a stranger—a San Franciscan, he thinks—is at the door asking for whisky and water. Minnie, amused at this unusual drinking order, tells Nick to bring the stranger in. As the bartender goes out, Rance impulsively tries to embrace Minnie, then asks her to marry him. She bluntly tells him that she is not interested in his proposal. When he persists in his attentions she warns him away by brandishing her pistol. Rance controls himself with an effort, then sits down at a table and picks up a deck of cards.

In a curious change of mood, Minnie asks him why he is angry with her—when she has given him an honest answer to his proposal. Rance replies in a melodious refrain, yet in words of despair and self-mockery. When he left home, he sings ("Minnie, dalla mia casa son partito"), no one cared—he left unloved and unloving. He was born with a gambler's poisoned heart, and gold alone gave him what he was looking for. And now, he adds sardonically, he will give a fortune for a kiss.

Minnie remarks that real love is very different, then goes on in a predominantly minor refrain ("Laggiù nel Soledad") to recall her own luckless childhood in Soledad, where her father kept an inn. There he dealt cards at the gaming tables while her mother cooked and tended bar. Sometimes, when both parents sat at the card table heaped with money, Minnie would creep under the table looking for stray coins. There she would notice her mother's pretty feet snuggled up to her father's. And now, Minnie concludes in a soaring phrase, remembering how deeply her mother loved her father, she herself will never marry a man unless she truly loves him.

The scene is interrupted as Nick enters followed by Dick Johnson (who is really the outlaw Ramerrez), who tosses his saddle into a corner and then announces that he is the man who asked for whisky and water. Face to face, he and Minnie instantly realize that they have met before. Both try to hide their mutual astonishment.

Rance, with deliberate malice, asks Johnson if by any chance he might be looking for a certain Nina Micheltorena. Johnson brushes the question aside and simply identifies himself as "Johnson from Sacramento." Rance, fuming with rage, strides to the other side of the room.

In a brief colloquy in quasi-recitative ("Vi ricordate di me?"), Minnie and Johnson recall how they met on the road to Monterey. As they talk affectionately, Rance, beside himself with jealous fury, walks up to the bar and knocks Johnson's glass off it with a sweep of his hand. Again he demands to know why Johnson has come to the camp, but the latter merely looks at him in contemptuous silence.

Rance rushes to the entrance of the dance hall and calls the miners into the barroom, telling them that the stranger refuses to explain his business. When the men threaten Johnson Minnie intervenes, saying she will vouch for him. The miners promptly start shaking hands with him while Rance, pale with anger, walks away.

As a waltz rhythm begins in the orchestra, Johnson offers his arm to Minnie to escort her into the dance hall. Minnie demurs, saying she has never danced, but the men urge her on. They all join in a wordless, lilting waltz tune, stamping their feet and clapping their hands in time to the music. All of them leave except Sonora, Trin, Handsome, Harry and Rance.

Nick enters and asks for Minnie. A moment later Ashby and a group of miners burst in, pushing José Castro, one of Johnson's gang. Kicking him to the floor, they tie him up and then shout for a hanging. The music of the waltz continues as an ironic accompaniment to their violent outcries. Castro, catching sight of Johnson's saddle, thinks his leader has been captured. Desperately playing for time, Castro tells the men that he knows where Ramerrez is and can lead them to him.

After a brief discussion the men storm out to saddle their horses. Johnson comes out of the dance hall and Castro manages to tell him that he allowed himself to be captured to throw the pursuers off the trail. The gang is hiding close by, he says, and will soon give a signal, a whistle. If all is ready, Johnson is to whistle in return. Rance and several of the men come back in. Glaring at Johnson, who watches with assumed indifference, the sheriff orders the men to untie Castro and take him away.

Nick starts closing the saloon, putting out the lights. Minnie enters from the dance hall as Nick leaves the barroom. The agitation of the music gradually subsides into serene chords as Johnson and Minnie stand facing each other. Here, *andante sostenuto,* begins the duet "Mister Johnson, siete rimasto." Johnson, touched by Minnie's charm-

ing naïveté, comments that it is strange to find her in a place where anyone could walk in and rob her—even of a kiss. Minnie replies that she
has handled that kind of a situation before—and still can. With growing
interest, Johnson asks her more about her life, remarking that she deserves something better than this. Minnie answers that she wants nothing better ("Mi contento, a me basta"). She lives alone, goes her own
way and is afraid of nobody. With disarming candor she tells Johnson
that she feels quite safe with him.

In ringing phrases Johnson sings that, even though he is a stranger to
himself, he too has enjoyed his solitary life to the fullest. Yet somehow
he knows that here is a woman who has still to enjoy all that life has to
offer.

Minnie, strangely disturbed, answers ("Io non son che una povera
fanciulla") that he is talking to her—a common good-for-nothing—in a
new and beautiful language she does not understand. To a surging
orchestral accompaniment, Johnson cries that her heart understands it
and that now they both know it is the language of love.

There is a sudden interruption as Nick enters to warn that an outlaw
gang is skulking around the camp. A moment later a shrill whistle
sounds outside. Johnson realizes it is the signal. Minnie makes an involuntary move toward him, as though seeking his protection.

As the action continues from this point, the music again takes up the
symphonic pattern of the duet. Minnie says her fears now are only for
the safety of the keg which contains a fortune in the miners' hard-won
gold. The miners usually take turns in guarding it, but tonight they are
on the trail of the outlaw. Whoever wants that gold, Minnie exclaims,
will have to kill her to get it. When Johnson asks why she would risk
her life for someone else's gold, she tells him.

These poor men ("Povera gente"), she says, have left home, wives
and children to live here like dogs, to wrest the gold from the earth with
backbreaking labor, then send it home to support their families. It is for
such men, Minnie declares, that she would die guarding the contents of
that keg.

Deeply moved, Johnson swears he will protect her and the gold. But
now, he says, he must go. He asks if he may come to her cabin for one
more goodbye. Yes, Minnie answers . . . and then perhaps he can explain to her what she, a good-for-nothing "with thirty dollars' worth of
education," might have been. She tries to laugh, but breaks down sobbing.

As the closing love theme of the duet soars through the orchestra,
Johnson tenderly comforts her ("No, Minnie, non piangete").[1] Nothing
matters, he says, but goodness of heart. Looking into her eyes, he sings

---

[1] To heighten the effect here, Puccini added a chorus humming the theme backstage.

quietly, "e avete un viso d'angelo" ("you have the face of an angel").

Johnson abruptly turns away, picks up his saddle and rushes out of the door. The music stops and there is a profound silence. Nick tiptoes in and puts out all the lights except one, which dimly lights the room. As though in a dream, Minnie murmurs softly: "Un viso d'angelo!" The curtain falls slowly.

ACT TWO

Minnie's cabin on the mountainside. The cutaway stage set shows the loft above the single room. Toward the rear of the room is a canopied bed; at one side is a fireplace. Wowkle, the Indian girl, is seated cross-legged on the floor with her papoose cradled on her back in typical Indian fashion. Rocking back and forth, she sings a plaintive lullaby, "Il mio bimbo." Billy Jackrabbit enters, greets Wowkle with an Indian grunt, then goes over to the table, on which there are glasses and a plate of cream cakes. When he reaches for the cakes, Wowkle sharply tells him not to touch them.

The two begin talking about getting married, and about the baby. Tomorrow, Billy says, they will go to church and sing. Nestling close to him, Wowkle begins singing a doleful hymn tune, "Come fil d'erba"—the grim text from the fortieth chapter of the Book of Isaiah. Billy chimes in, then irreverently remarks that they will get married and have plenty of beads and whisky.

Suddenly Minnie enters carrying a lantern. Hurrying about excitedly, she straightens out the room and gives orders to the Indians. She begins dressing up for Johnson's visit, first trying on a pair of slippers only to discover that they are too tight. As she is primping in front of the mirror, there is a knock on the door. Johnson enters, bundled in a fur coat. In charming confusion, Minnie stammers a welcome. Johnson gallantly compliments her on her appearance, then tries to embrace her. Annoyed by his familiarity, Minnie fends him off. A swift chromatic passage played by the flutes underscores her momentary irritation.

Taken aback, Johnson begs to be forgiven, but teasingly adds that he is not the slightest bit sorry. Minnie's annoyance vanishes. Then, rather pensively, she asks him why he came to the Polka—did he perhaps take the wrong road, thinking he was going to see Micheltorena? Anxious to change the subject, Johnson again tries to embrace her and again she rebuffs him. Looking around the room, Johnson remarks that it is curious that she should prefer to live alone like this in the mountains.

In a lilting refrain ("Oh, se sapeste"), Minnie describes how exciting her life really is—galloping through the fragrant meadows on her pinto or drifting in her boat down the river past banks of wildflowers, then home again to her Sierras—so high they seem to touch the hand of God.

In the winter she is busy teaching at the "Academy," her school for the miners. Over a rhythmic, flowing accompaniment, the two philosophize about literature, love and men and women in general.

Under the spell of Minnie's charm, Johnson impulsively asks for a kiss, but she adroitly keeps him at a distance. Outside, the blizzard howls furiously. Minnie dismisses Wowkle, telling her she may stay in the barn for the night. Alone in the cabin, Minnie and Johnson passionately embrace as the music storms to a climax. A violent gust of wind tears the door open and snow swirls into the room. Oblivious to the storm, the lovers remain locked in each other's arms.

The clock strikes, breaking the spell. Relinquishing their embrace, the two stare at each other as though hypnotized. In a sudden change of mood, Johnson harshly warns Minnie not to listen to anything he says. Bewildered, Minnie exclaims that she gave her heart to him the first moment they met. Johnson abruptly says goodbye and starts to leave.

Warning him that it will be impossible to get through the snow, Minnie urges him to stay. At that moment three shots ring out. Johnson is alarmed, but Minnie merely shrugs. Perhaps they have caught the outlaw Ramerrez . . . what does it matter . . . Gazing at Johnson passionately, she cries, "Resta! È destino!" Then, in the great unison duet "io non ti lascio più," Minnie and Johnson sing that they belong to each other and will live and die together.

Freeing herself from Johnson's arms, Minnie says that now they must say goodnight. Johnson stretches out on the bed, Minnie wraps herself in a bearskin robe and lies down in front of the fireplace. After a few moments she breaks the silence with a question: "Did you ever know Nina Micheltorena?" From behind the bed curtains: "Never." Then, "Buona notte," and silence again.

They are roused by a knock on the door and Nick's voice is heard outside. Johnson, pistol in hand, faces the door. As Nick calls out that Ramerrez is on the trail, Minnie forces Johnson to hide behind the bed curtains. In the next moment Nick, Rance, Ashby and Sonora burst into the room, and, in recitative, they break the news to Minnie: Mister Johnson, her gallant partner from Sacramento, is really the outlaw Ramerrez. He came to rob the Polka. Minnie furiously denies his intention, then demands to know who told them that Johnson is Ramerrez.

Rance, with malicious enjoyment, answers: "Nina Micheltorena." He is her lover, the sheriff goes on, and when she was questioned at the Palmetto she showed the men his picture to prove it. With that he hands Johnson's picture to Minnie. With a forced laugh, she remarks that Johnson keeps charming company.

Recovering her composure, she thanks the men and bids them goodnight. As they leave, Rance, with a sneer, warns her to be on her guard. In a voice edged with fury and contempt, Minnie orders Johnson to come out. Stricken with shame, he admits he came to rob the Polka, but when he saw who his victim would be . . . Minnie cuts him short, branding him a liar and a thief. Struggling to hold back her tears of rage, she orders him out.

Johnson desperately begs her to allow him at least one word before he goes ("Una parola sola"). This is the beginning of the magnificent aria in which Johnson discloses his dark and bitter past—the wretched life that made him an outlaw. Yes, he says, he is indeed Ramerrez and he has been living under a curse. When his father died the only heritage he left his family was a gang of murderous outlaws. To escape this miserable existence, he left home for a life of banditry. Then destiny led him to Minnie. At that moment, inspired by love, he resolved to make a new start in life—to turn from crime to honest work. His only prayer was that Minnie would never know about his past. But this prayer God has not answered, Johnson says somberly as the aria ends in a minor key.

In bitter despair Minnie answers that she can forgive him everything except his betrayal with a kiss—her first kiss of love. Now nothing matters. Go, she cries. Johnson walks out like a man going to his execution.

A moment later a shot cracks out, then there is the thud of a body falling against the door. Minnie frantically tears the door open, and Johnson, holding his side, staggers in. He makes a weak effort to go outside again, but Minnie forces him to climb the ladder to the loft and hide.

As he falls there exhausted, Minnie takes away the ladder and runs to answer a knock on the door. Rance, brandishing a pistol, strides in. Minnie feigns surprise when he shouts that Johnson is in the house, and sarcastically urges him on when he begins searching. In baffled fury Rance stops looking, then suddenly and violently catches Minnie in his arms, shouting that he is madly in love with her. Wrenching free, Minnie snatches up a whisky bottle and raises it to strike.

Rance staggers back. Stretching out his hand, he cries that he knows she loves Ramerrez, but he will never have her. A drop of blood falls on his hand. Rance looks up at the ceiling with a ferocious cry. Minnie desperately tries to divert his attention, but is foiled when the blood keeps dripping down on the handkerchief with which Rance is wiping his hand.

Spying the ladder, Rance places it under the trap door, draws his pistol and orders Johnson to come down. Minnie begs him not to shoot. Johnson climbs slowly down the ladder and with Minnie's help drags himself to the table. There he sinks into a chair and, fainting from loss of blood, slumps forward with his head on his arms. Watching him, Rance sardonically asks if he would like to play poker—he can have his choice: the gallows or the pistol.

Outraged at the sheriff's cruelty, Minnie entreats him to stop tormenting his victim ("Basta, uomo d'inferno!"). Then suddenly she has an inspiration. To a sinister rhythm in the orchestra, she makes a deal with Rance. We are three of a kind, she tells him—he a gambler, Johnson a thief, she herself the owner of a gambling house. Well then, they will settle matters in the way they know best: in a game of poker. If Rance wins, Minnie and Johnson will be at his mercy. If Minnie wins, Johnson belongs to her. The best two hands out of three will win.

Rance, crying that he is sure to win, gazes avidly at Minnie. Here the famous card game begins, to the accompaniment of an ominous theme which continues throughout. Unseen by Rance, Minnie slips several cards into her stocking. She wins the first hand, Rance the second. They cut cards for the final hand. Stalling for time, Minnie tells the sheriff she is sorry for what she said in anger. Rance gloats over the prize which will soon be his.

Suddenly Minnie gasps that she feels faint and asks Rance to bring her a drink. When he goes to a shelf for the bottle and a glass, Minnie hides the losing hand in her bodice, then takes the winning cards from her stocking. By the time Rance comes back to the table Minnie is waving the cards and screaming that she has won with "three aces and a pair" ("Tre assi e un paio!"). Rance slams his cards on the table, glares at her for a moment, then stalks out of the cabin in cold fury.

Over a surging orchestral climax, Minnie bursts into hysterical laughter. Seeing Johnson still unconscious at the table, she bends over him sobbing as the curtain falls.

ACT THREE

A forest clearing in the Sierras, the rendezvous of the Wells Fargo posse which is pursuing Johnson. It is dawn. Rance, Ashby and Nick are huddled near the campfire. Nick and Rance curse the day Johnson crossed their path. The sheriff bitterly regrets his bargain with Minnie—and also that he kept his word and did not reveal Johnson's hiding place to the posse. Nick ironically compliments him on behaving like a gentleman.

Rance moodily wonders what attracts Minnie to an upstart scoundrel like Johnson. In a comically melodramatic phrase ("Amore! Paradiso ed inferno"), Nick observes that love alone is the cause of all the trouble. It is heaven and hell. It is a disease that afflicts the whole world—and Minnie worst of all.

The scene is interrupted by the sound of shouting in the distance. Ashby leaps to his feet, unties his horse and starts toward the trail in the background. As the babble of voices sounds nearer, an agitated chromatic passage sweeps through the orchestra like a portent of fateful events. Looking down the trail, Ashby shouts that the outlaw will not escape this time.

The posse comes running in armed with pistols, knives and clubs. There is a tremendous uproar. The orchestral accompaniment changes to a sinuous theme in the bass. Led by Ashby, the posse rushes away to continue the search. Rance and Nick remain. Glaring in the direction of Minnie's cabin, Rance sings that now it will be her turn to weep—just as he did when she mocked at his love ("Or piangi tu, o Minnie"). From the distance come the voices of the miners in brief echoing phrases, almost like a wail.

Some of the miners now come by shouting that the outlaw is surrounded. Rance mutters that even though Johnson has the devil on his side, he—Sheriff Rance—will pay him out. The miners come storming back with the news that Johnson was captured but escaped. From this point on, the scene builds into the climactic ensemble of the opera. The voices of the individual miners—Joe, Handsome, Happy and Sonora—describing the progress of the chase to Rance blend with those of the other miners as they ask for news. At one point, Billy Jackrabbit appears with a rope, which he slings experimentally over a branch.

Watching him, several miners sing that they will teach the outlaw to dance at the end of a rope ("Lo faremo ballare"), then break into the familiar refrain "Dooda, dooda, day!" Rance sings despairingly that even though he himself kept his bargain with Minnie, his word of honor will not save Johnson now. Almost unnoticed in the confusion, Nick drags Billy Jackrabbit to one side. Thrusting some gold into the Indian's hands, Nick orders him not to make the noose until he is told. No tricks now, Nick warns, pointing his pistol at Billy's head.

A moment later Johnson is dragged in by the cursing, yelling miners. He is pale and disheveled, but still defiant. Ashby turns the prisoner over to Sheriff Rance, pompously declaring that justice must be done. The agent rides off, ironically wishing Johnson luck. The men now gather around Johnson in kangaroo court formation and the trial begins. It is set forth in musical terms in one of the most remarkable ensembles in opera, opening as Rance, savoring his moment of revenge, lights a cigar, blows a cloud of smoke in Johnson's face and says: "E così, Mister Johnson, come va?"

Johnson contemptuously tells him to get on with the hanging. Inflamed by Rance, the miners burst into a chorus of vituperation, accusing Johnson of robbery, plunder and murder. They lay all the crimes of the region at his feet—the killing of post rider, the massacre of a squadron in Monterey. But worst of all, they shout, was the crime of stealing Minnie away from them. Now they will make him pay for his caresses.

Johnson replies that while he has been a thief, he is not a murderer.

He is not afraid of death, he cries, and offers to cut his own throat to prove it. He asks only to say one more word—one word about the woman he loves. The men are surprised into momentary silence. Rance lunges at Johnson, checks himself, looks at his watch and says he will give the prisoner two more minutes. Sonora steps forward to quiet the crowd, insisting that Johnson has the right to speak.

Johnson thanks him and then makes his plea in the great aria "Ch'ella mi creda." He asks his captors never to let Minnie know how he died, but to tell her instead that Johnson has gone far away to lead the better life she taught him how to live. He will never return, he sings, but he will never forget Minnie, the one and only flower of his life.

As he finishes, Rance again lunges at Johnson and this time strikes him brutally in the face, an act which brings a mutter of angry protest from the miners. Johnson gets up and strides toward the tree where Billy Jackrabbit is standing with the noose in his hands. The crowd follows in awed silence. Six men, pistols drawn, range themselves on either side of the tree.

Suddenly from the distance comes a piercing shout and the sound of hoofbeats. Everyone stops in his tracks and stares down the trail. Then there is a tremendous shout: "Minnie!" Rance, screaming like a madman, rushes forward to go on with the hanging. Minnie, brandishing a pistol, rides up followed by Nick. Leaping from her horse, she rushes over to Johnson and defies Rance and the crowd to touch him. Rance tries to goad the miners on, but as they press closer Minnie screams that she will kill Johnson and herself if they move one step nearer.

Sonora, throwing himself between Minnie and the crowd, shouts at the men to leave her alone. Livid with rage, Minnie denounces them for turning against her ("Non vi fu mai chi disse"). Bitterly she reminds them that not one of them ever said "Stop" when she made sacrifices in their behalf, patched up their quarrels and helped them when they needed help. Now, she goes on, she claims as her own another man she has helped—to whom she has shown the way to a new life. The robber he once was has died. They cannot kill this man again.

Sonora interrupts to say that it is not the theft of gold that matters, but the theft of her heart. Instantly Minnie's anger vanishes and she thanks Sonora for being the first to forgive. Then, as the miners shuffle guiltily, she approaches them one by one, recalling how she tried to teach them that love and forgiveness could redeem the very worst of sinners. As a gesture of faith and trust, Minnie tosses away her pistol. Some of the miners weep unashamedly. Finally won over, the men sing that Minnie deserves their mercy ("Minnie merita tutto").

Speaking for all, Sonora says that Minnie's words have come from God Himself ("Le tue parole sono di Dio"). With that he cuts the rope binding Johnson's hands and helps him to his feet. He leads him over to Minnie, then turns away, choking back a sob.

The lovers slowly leave the scene as the farewell chorus of the opera begins—"Addio, mia dolce terra." Weeping, the miners watch them until they are out of sight, singing *sotto voce* that they will never return. From the distance the voices of Minnie and Johnson drift back like an echo . . . "Addio, mia California." The curtain slowly falls.

LA FAVORITA

by GAETANO DONIZETTI

(1797–1848)

Libretto by

ALPHONSE ROYER and JEAN-NICOLAS-GUSTAVE VAËZ

Adapted from the drama *Le Comte de Comminges,* by F. T. de Baculard d'Arnaud

CHARACTERS

Alfonso XI, King of Castile	Baritone
Leonora di Gusman (or Guzman)	Soprano
Inez, her confidante	Soprano
Fernando, a young novice of the Monastery of St. James of Compostella; afterward an officer	Tenor
Baldassare, Superior of the Monastery	Bass
Don Gasparo, the King's Minister	Tenor

Courtiers, guards, monks, ladies and gentlemen of the court, attendants

Place: Castile, Spain
Time: Circa 1340
First performance: Grand Opéra, Paris, December 2, 1840
Original language: French

Donizetti composed *La Favorita* (*La Favorite* in the original French version) during his two-year stay in Paris after he had left Naples in 1839. It is about the fifty-sixth work in his prodigious operatic output that totaled approximately seventy works (counting revisions, etc.) from 1818 (*Enrico di Borgogna*) to 1844 (*Caterina Cornaro,* his last opera).[1]

[1] Pratt's *New Encyclopedia of Music and Musicians* (revised 1954) lists four "posthumous" works: *Poliuto,* 1848; *Rita,* 1860; *Gabriella di Vergy,* 1869; *Il Duca d'Alba,* 1882. These dates presumably refer to first stage presentations. Kobbé's *New Complete Opera Book* (© 1919-22-35) reads—"In 1882, thirty-four years after Donizetti's death, there was produced in Rome an opera by him entitled *Il Duca d'Alba.*"

La Favorita actually began its life as *L'Ange de Nisida,* a three-act opera that had been performed at the Théâtre de la Renaissance in Paris. In reworking the score, Donizetti borrowed a tenor aria from his uncompleted *Le Duc d'Albe (Il Duca d'Alba).* Known as "Ange si pur," it became "Spirto gentil" in the first Italian translation, and is one of the best-known tenor arias in operatic literature.

The opera reached Italy for the first time as *Leonora di Gusman* (or *Guzman*) at the Teatro Nuovo, Padua, in June 1842, then was staged at La Scala and in New Orleans in 1843. It was first heard in New York in 1845. As *Leonora,* it was heard at the Metropolitan in 1895. As it went through various translations, the names of characters were changed: Alfonso to Louis VII of France; Leonora to a Greek girl named Elda. Other titles included: *Riccardo e Mathilde, Daila, Elda,* and *Die Templar in Sidon.*

La Favorita was not an immediate success; certain critics found it mediocre—even condemned it. At first Donizetti could not even find a publisher. But after several performances it caught on, and soon became an established favorite not only in the French provinces but all over Europe during the next year. The composer at length found a publisher who paid him 12,000 francs for the score. By the end of 1841 it had become so popular that the publisher paid a young, struggling composer— one Richard Wagner—an advance of 500 francs against a total fee of 1,100 to make six different transcriptions from the score.

Through the years there have been many revivals the world over. In one, 1864, the famous mezzo-soprano, Rosine Stoltz sang the leading role she had created in Paris twenty-four years before. In the United States there have been revivals in Philadelphia, Chicago, New Orleans and San Francisco. Prior to the performance of *La Favorita* at the Metropolitan February 21, 1978, the last performance by that company was on December 29, 1905, with a glittering Golden Age cast headed by Edyth Walker, Enrico Caruso, Pol Plançon and Antonio Scotti. The first Metropolitan broadcast ever was on March 14, 1978, with a cast headed by Shirley Verrett, Luciano Pavarotti, Bonaldo Giaiotti, Sherrill Milnes, Alma Jean Smith and John Carpenter.

As a product of Donizetti's later years, *La Favorita* ranks with the finest of his operas. The late Arturo Toscanini said of it: *"La Favorita* is all beautiful; the last act—every note is a masterpiece."

The overture establishes the mood of the opera by stating themes associated with the emotional climaxes of the plot. Thematic fragments of the principal arias are fused into a concluding fanfare.

ACT ONE

The Monastery of St. James of Compostella. Monks are chanting as they file through the courtyard. Baldassare notices that the young novice, Fernando, seems preoccupied. When he asks the reason, Fernando responds in the romanza "Una vergine, un angiol d'amore." He explains that as he prayed in the chapel a surpassingly beautiful woman knelt beside him. He frankly confesses that the sight of her drove all other thoughts from his mind ("Ah! da quel giorno che insiem le soavi"). He declares he has fought in vain against the allure of this tormenting image.

A dramatic duet ensues. Baldassare is shocked at Fernando's passionate outburst ("E fia vero?"). He cannot believe that the novice he has favored as his successor has yielded to worldly temptation. But Fernando ignores his remonstrances and cries out: "I love her!"

Baldassare warns him not to profane his holy vows, and demands to know the name of this creature who is seducing him ("ma rispondi, chi è dessa la bella"). Again Fernando's answer is: "I love her!" In a towering rage, Baldassare orders the novice to leave the monastery ("Vanne dunque, frenetico, insano")—and may God have mercy on him.

The duet continues as Fernando, completely oblivious to Baldassare's threat to banish him, sings that the smile of this angel ("Angiol caro, soave, beato") will be like the lodestar to a mariner, guiding him to the safe haven of his hope. Baldassare thunders that he will pay a dire penalty for scorning his holy vows, and that remorse will torment him until the end of his days.

Turning to go, Fernando asks the Superior for his blessing. Baldassare harshly refuses, yet voices the hope that heaven's vengeance will not strike down one who has repudiated his faith.

The scene changes to the island of Leon, where King Alfonso has provided a luxurious hideaway for his mistress, Leonora. In a melodious chorus ("Bei raggi lucenti") Inez and the ladies of Leonora's entourage sing of the delights of this retreat.

Looking toward the sea, Inez bids the women be silent as a boat approaches the shore. It is bringing a lover ("l'amoroso suo destin"). In lyrical phrases Inez and the women sing that they will meet him when he steps blindfolded (at Leonora's orders) from his boat ("Ed al giunger tuo disvela"), then guide him to a bower perfumed with jasmine and orange ("degli aranci e gelsomin") where his beloved awaits him.

When Inez, first removing the blindfold, escorts Fernando to Leonora, he plies the confidante with questions: Why does she keep silent about the woman she serves—the woman he loves . . . ? Inez answers simply: "She is here. Ask her yourself" ("Ella ver noi s'avanza").

To a majestic fanfare, Leonora enters, and now follows the long duet in which she explains that their love can lead only to sorrow and that they are fated to part. Fernando will not believe her. He protests that he has broken his holy vows to be near her, and for her love he will face death itself. Ardently he asks her name. That he must never know, she replies ("Nol dimandar").

When Leonora reiterates that their love is doomed, Fernando, with a hint of jealousy, asks if there is someone else who claims her affections. She protests that it is destiny alone that foredooms their future together. Resolving to put an end to the matter, Leonora hands Fernando an army commission which she says will be his passport to a glorious career ("di queste cifre ti volea far dono"). But first he must promise to abandon her forever.

In a vigorous refrain ("Fia vero? lasciarti"), Fernando vehemently rejects the thought of leaving her, but Leonora insists that they must part. The duet is interrupted as Inez enters to announce that King Alfonso is approaching. Panic-stricken, Leonora thrusts the parchment into Fernando's hands and tells him to leave at once. In the soaring conclusion of the duet, he swears he will never leave her, while she resigns herself to their parting.

In recitative, Fernando ruefully reflects that he can never aspire to a woman so high in rank above him. He is a mere plebeian—and his rival is none other than King Alfonso. But his spirits rise when he realizes that in his hands is the proof of Leonora's devotion—the army commission, his most coveted goal. In a martial refrain ("Sì, che un tuo solo accento") he sings that he in turn will prove his worth on the field of honor—he will be both a hero and a faithful lover. His exultant phrases bring the act to a close.

ACT TWO[2]

The royal gardens of King Alfonso's palace. An introductory fanfare announces the presence of the King, who is in conversation with his Minister of State, Don Gasparo. In a brief colloquy they discuss the victory of Fernando over the Moors. When Gasparo fawningly gives Alfonso credit for the triumph, Alfonso replies that the victory is Fernando's. He will be rewarded for his courage at ceremonies in Seville this very day. At this point, Gasparo informs the King that Baldassare is on his way to ask for explanations of the King's tangled marital

---

[2] In some versions, continuation of Act One.

affairs. With cool sarcasm, Alfonso remarks that obviously someone has been talking. Gasparo leaves.

Alone, Alfonso voices his defiance of the Church and his court and passionately declares his love for Leonora in a ringing aria, "Ma de' malvagi invan." For her, he sings, he will defy all his enemies and even renounce his throne because destiny has linked his fate with hers. He recalls Gasparo and orders him to prepare a banquet in Leonora's honor.

Leonora enters with Inez, from whom she learns about Fernando's brilliant victory over the Moors. In a despairing phrase, she sings that for Fernando, all is glory; for her, only dishonor ("a lui la gloria . . . a me l'infamia!").

Alfonso enters, notices Leonora's downcast expression and asks the reason. In a melancholy refrain ("Quando le soglie paterne varcai") she responds that he has betrayed her into thinking that she would become his wife. For this promise she left her father's honorable house . . . for this promise she has incurred the contempt of the court as the mistress of a King.

Alfonso vainly urges her to think only of the joys of this luxurious retreat. Leonora replies that while there is splendor all around her, sorrow and remorse gnaw at her heart. Now she asks only to be allowed to leave this bower of dishonor.

Alfonso assures her that he will prove to all the world that he loves only her. Leonora protests that she is too lowly a person to "mate with a monarch" ("È vil Leonora, è grande troppo il Re!"). The duet comes to a lyrical conclusion as the two reflect on the emotions that have driven them to this impasse. Alfonso then bids Leonora to lay her troubles aside and enjoy the banquet and ballet he has ordered for her pleasure.[3]

At the conclusion of the ballet, Gasparo bursts in with the news that one of the King's trusted friends is plotting against him. He shows Alfonso a letter addressed to Leonora. Alfonso reads it incredulously, then whirls on Leonora demanding to know who dares write her in such passionate phrases. One whom I love, Leonora answers calmly. When Leonora refuses to disclose his name, Alfonso storms that he will wring the answer from her by torture. Leonora begs for mercy.

At that moment, Baldassare strides in. A dramatic recitative follows. The Superior denounces the King for his sinful liaison with Leonora ("Io son quello, io son che vengo"). In majestic defiance, Alfonso de-

---

[3] This ballet has been described as marking a high point in the development of French Romantic ballet. It was danced in a *pas de deux* by Lucien or Marius Petipa (accounts vary) and Carlotta Grisi, one of the foremost Romantic ballerinas and a cousin of Giulia and Giuditta Grisi, legendary nineteenth-century opera stars.

clares he is King and his word is law in the realm ("Io sì, lo voglio . . .
è sacro il mi voler").

Over a stately 9/8 rhythm, Baldassare excoriates Alfonso for deserting his lawful queen ("Ah, paventa il furor"). This builds gradually
into a quartet as Gasparo, Leonora and Alfonso express their reactions
—Leonora bewails her inevitable doom; Alfonso is haunted by remorse;
Baldassare intones his dire warning. Their voices are joined with those
of the people of the court.

During an interlude underscored by ominous chords in the orchestra,
Baldassare, holding up the seal of a papal bull, thunders that the curse
of the Church will strike the guilty lovers unless they part by tomorrow
—and part forever. The court is in turmoil. Alfonso first defies the papal
interdiction, insisting that he is still ruler in his own kingdom. Leonora
gives way to her shame and remorse.

Baldassare, invoking the papal injunction ("Lo stemma è questo del
Superior"), declares that Alfonso's crime will bring down his kingdom
in ruins. The court curses the plotter who menaces the safety of the
kingdom. Alfonso continues to defy Baldassare, but finally wavers.
Voicing these various sentiments, the principals and the ensemble bring
the second act to a tempestuous close.

ACT THREE[4]

A room in the court of the Alcázar. After a brief prelude, Fernando
enters, having returned from his victory over the Moors, and now hailed
as the savior of the Alcázar. He is impatient to see his beloved Leonora
again ("A lei son presso alfine!"). He reflects that he left Alfonso's
court as a mere officer and has returned as a hero. Although the King
has summoned him to receive his reward, he can think only of Leonora.
Fernando sees Alfonso approaching and leaves.

Alfonso and Gasparo enter. Currying favor with the King, Gasparo
asks what punishment awaits the miscreant responsible for the disastrous situation at court. Alfonso contemptuously ignores the question
and orders Gasparo to imprison Inez as Leonora's accomplice in this intrigue. Dismissing the Minister, he turns to welcome Fernando with
praise for his victory.

For his valor, Alfonso tells him, he can have anything he asks for.
Fernando modestly replies that serving his King is honor enough. As for
a reward, he desires only the hand of the noble lady whom he adores.
Granted, Alfonso says; name her. Fernando turns and sees Leonora.
There she is, he cries, in all her beauty ("vedila, più bella!"). Alfonso
stares in stunned surprise and gasps out her name. Leonora, distraught,

---

[4] Act Two in some versions.

murmurs that now her guilt will be discovered ("l'amante! rea comparir gli innante!").

With menacing calm, Alfonso tells Leonora that Fernando has confessed his love for her and has asked for her hand in marriage. That will be granted, he says, then adds with fierce intensity: "But you will leave Spain tomorrow" ("Doman tu dei partir"). Then in a striking refrain ("A tanto amor, Leonora") Alfonso sardonically voices the hope that the lovers will be happy and that the curse of Fernando's duplicity will not blight their future. The irony of Alfonso's acquiescence of course completely escapes Fernando, who is blissfully unaware of the relationship between the King and Leonora.

The scene continues in trio form. Leonora hopes that her own shameful deception will be hidden from her lover. Fernando thanks Alfonso for his magnanimity. The latter, in suppressed bitterness, sings that revenge will yet be his. He commands the two to be at the church within an hour for the marriage rites, then leads Fernando away.

Alone, Leonora reflects in anguish on her dilemma. It is at once a blessing and a curse, she sings in recitative ("Fia dunque vero"). She will marry the man she loves, yet that marriage will bring him only shame and dishonor. Then she gives way to her tormenting thoughts in one of the most famous mezzo-soprano arias in opera: "O mio Fernando," with a range of A-natural below the staff to A-natural above.

She sings that, as a bride, she would gladly bring to him her unsullied love—but she vows to tell him the bitter truth. She realizes that she will incur Fernando's terrible anger, which will strike like lightning. Yet she dares hope for some shred of compassion ("se fia scemo il tuo disdegno"). Overcome by despair, she cries for death. Her prayers for mercy have failed, and now she is resigned to her doom ("non avrà perdono in ciel"). Her final words are underscored by a crashing chord, followed by throbbing clusters of descending semiquavers.

In recitative, Leonora calls Inez and requests her to go to Fernando and tell him, once for all, the truth: she is Alfonso's mistress. If he rejects her, she will be resigned to her fate; if he pardons, she will be his slave forever ("prostrata ognor servirlo"). But he must learn everything —and from her lips alone, Leonora declares as she leaves.

Just as Inez turns to go, she is confronted by Gasparo, who tells her she is under arrest on Alfonso's orders. He thereupon places her in the custody of a group of female guardians. In a melodious—if implausible—interlude ("Già nell'augusta cella") they blithely hymn the joys of the impending matrimony.

Alfonso's court is assembled for the nuptials, with Fernando standing before the King to receive his honors. For vanquishing the Moors, Alfonso intones ("A ognun fia noto"), he confers upon this hero the title of Count Zamora and the second title of Marquis of Montreal ("Conte, e Marchese di Montreal t'eleggo"). From this point the situation develops musically and dramatically into one of the major ensembles of the opera.

Gasparo taunts the courtiers for naïvely believing that this is how a King rewards a hero—when in truth it is a cynical payment for foul deception. (The courtiers are unaware of the trick played on Fernando: Inez, intercepted by Gasparo, never delivered Leonora's message.)

Leonora appears in her bridal finery, trying desperately to remain calm. Fernando, oblivious to everything, greets her ecstatically. The entire assemblage bursts into a reprise of the nuptial chorus ("Già nell'augusta cella"). In a jeering antiphony ("Oh viltade! obbrobrio insano!") Gasparo and the courtiers give vent to their jealous rage over Fernando's honors and revile him for his apparent infamy. May dishonor be his mate ("ch'egli abbia sol compagno il disonor"), they sing in the furious climax of the scene.

The hapless Fernando, still without any warning of impending disaster, joyously invites the courtiers to share his high spirits. They reply with scathing references to the price he has paid for his honor. Fernando flares up at this insult, but—still uncomprehending—offers his hand in friendship. The men contemptuously turn their backs on him and storm away.

Fernando is about to rush after them with a challenge to fight when Baldassare and Gasparo enter. As the Superior embraces his "spiritual son" he overhears Gasparo's ironical interjection: "And husband of Leonora" ("Lo sposo di Leonora"). Baldassare now realizes that Fernando does not know the truth. He joins the courtiers—who have returned to gloat over the luckless Fernando—in confronting him with the appalling reality: "Your bride is the mistress of the King" ("La destra or dando alla bella del Re!").

Fernando gasps in horror and dismay. Ignoring Baldassare's warning to leave before the King arrives, he shouts that he will have revenge. When Alfonso enters with Leonora, Fernando, in a paroxysm of fury, accuses him of contriving his disgrace. He tells the King to take back his glittering badges, treacherously bestowed at the price of a soldier's honor ("Al prezzo dell'onor!"). This scene builds into the tumultuous climax of the opera. Alfonso recoils at Fernando's repudiation. Fernando spurns the King's explanations. In a thundering choral accompaniment the people of the court voice their consternation and disbelief. Baldassare implores Fernando to come away with him and forget this day of catastrophe.

Finally, Fernando hurls the badges of his promotion to the ground, stamps on them, then breaks his sword and dashes the fragments at Alfonso's feet. He shouts that the sword he wielded in his sovereign's defense now lies in shards of shame ("il brando profanato . . . lo spezzo innanzi a te!"). Leonora implores the King to be merciful, then tries to assure Fernando that she will atone for her crime of deceiving him. She calls in vain for Inez—who holds the key to this debacle. Gasparo, with vicious satisfaction, tells her Inez is in prison. Leonora now knows that her message to Fernando was never delivered.

As the ensemble thunders to its conclusion, Baldassare leads the stricken Fernando away.

ACT FOUR[5]

The Monastery of St. James, where Baldassare has brought Fernando to resume his vows. There is an introduction in a majestic theme which is taken up by the monks calling to prayers ("Compagni, andiam"). Baldassare enters. In a moving refrain ("Splendon più belle in ciel le stelle") he reflects on the serenity of this retreat—where his son can forget his ordeal of shame and dishonor and find peace of mind at last. The chorus of monks takes up the theme.

In a colloquy in recitative between Baldassare and Fernando it is revealed that Alfonso has divorced his legal wife because of his infatuation for Leonora. To escape his vindictiveness, the Queen has sought refuge in the monastery. Meanwhile, a young novice, travel-worn and exhausted, has appeared at the monastery gates.

Fernando sadly reflects on the ruin of his dreams of love and glory ("Favorita del Re"), then gives way to his emotions in the great aria "Spirto gentil" ("Ange si pur" in the original French).[6] He laments that his love for Leonora has cost him his happiness and his honor—a phantom that has left him only grief.

Baldassare interrupts his sorrowful reflections to lead him to the chapel, where Fernando says he will pray for the Queen.

When they leave, Leonora enters. Despairingly she sings Fernando's name. She hopes that—somehow—she will be able to kneel at his feet and implore his forgiveness.

Suddenly, over the sound of the organ, she hears Fernando chanting with the monks in the chapel. But it is not a serene prayer that she hears. In ironic contrast to the devotions of the monks, he is calling for heaven's vengeance on the woman who has so basely betrayed him ("E l'implacato duol"). Leonora moans that now all is lost; she feels that death is near. Her lamentations bring Fernando out of the chapel, where he is surprised to discover the kneeling figure of the novice. It is

---

[5] In some versions Act Three.

[6] Known the world over, this aria is, in a sense, responsible for the opera's surviving in repertoire for more than 150 years.

only when she looks up at him, begging him not to curse her, that he realizes that the supplicant is Leonora herself.

Glaring down at her, Fernando orders her to leave the monastery ("Ah va, t'invola, e questa terra"). Her presence must not profane this holy place. As for himself, he wants only to remain here and die in peace. As for her, let her return to the perfumed bower of her royal lover.

In a last despairing effort at reconciliation, Leonora reveals the fatal mistake that has destroyed them both ("D'ambo sul capo un solo error ricade"): the interception of Inez's message. And that is why their marriage is a shameful mockery.

On her knees before Fernando, Leonora sings her heartrending pleas for mercy ("Pietoso al par del Nume"). This marks the beginning of the duet that brings the opera to a close. Though profoundly moved, Fernando first reiterates that they must part forever. But Leonora's plea for pardon strikes him to the heart, and his love for her surges back in a resistless flood. Clasping her in his arms, he cries out: "I love you . . . nothing can condemn our faith in each other" ("io t'amo! Vieni, io m'abbandono alla gioia!"). He promises that they will seek refuge in some haven where they can share their love forever ("Fuggiam, fuggiamo insieme!").

But Leonora protests that he must remain true to his holy vows and devote his life to God ("A Dio ti volgi"). From the chapel comes the chanting of the monks. Yet even as Fernando implores her to leave with him, she collapses and dies in his arms.

To his anguished cry for help, Baldassare and the monks rush in. Looking down at Leonora, Baldassare, unaware of her identity, calls for the obeisance of silence to this unfortunate novice. Finally he sings to the monks: "Pray for our brother who was departed ("per lui pregate fratelli Iddio!"). In utter desolation Fernando murmurs: "And tomorrow, pray for me!" ("Avrò doman la prece anch'io!"). The curtain falls.

DIE FRAU OHNE SCHATTEN

(*The Woman Without a Shadow*)

by RICHARD STRAUSS

(1864–1949)

Libretto by

HUGO VON HOFMANNSTHAL

CHARACTERS

Emperor of the Southeastern Islands	Tenor
Empress	High dramatic soprano
Nurse	Dramatic mezzo-soprano
Spirit Messenger	High baritone
Guardian of the Temple Threshold	Soprano or falsetto singer
Apparition of a Young Man	High tenor
Voice of the Falcon	Soprano
A Voice	Alto
Barak the Dyer	Bass-baritone
His Wife	High dramatic soprano
One-eyed brother ⎫	High bass
One-armed brother ⎬ brothers of Barak	Bass
Hunchback ⎭	High tenor
Voices of six children	Three sopranos, three altos
Voices of the Watchmen	Three high basses

Royal servants, beggar children, slave girls, attendant spirits, voices of spirits

Place: The legendary Empire of the Southeastern Islands
Time: Universal
First performance: Vienna Opera, October 10, 1919
Original language: German

This operatic amalgam of fantasy and reality is a product of Richard Strauss's later period as a composer. Although overblown and pretentious to a certain degree, with a libretto burdened with abstract symbolism and somewhat confusing allegory, the opera contains some of Strauss's finest music. In its use of leitmotivs it is Wagnerian, and in the scope of its music and drama it is truly a "superopera." The "woman without a shadow" is a woman without children—the woman who repudiates motherhood. The central theme of the opera is that through true marriage, love and sacrifice the shadowless woman can be brought to the fulfillment of her destiny: the giving of life.

The premiere marked the first great evening of the post-World War I Vienna Opera.

Although given frequently in Europe, *Die Frau ohne Schatten* did not achieve immediate popularity in the United States. It was given its American premiere at the San Francisco Opera on September 18, 1959. Its next presentation in this country, however, made history. It was performed on October 2, 1966, at the new Metropolitan Opera House in Lincoln Center, New York City, in one of the most elaborate productions in the annals of the Metropolitan. Received with tremendous acclaim, it played to sold-out houses during the 1966–67, 1968–69, 1970–71 and 1977–78 seasons.

There is no overture. The curtain goes up immediately.

ACT ONE

[*Scene One*] A terrace overlooking the imperial gardens of the Emperor's palace. At one side, dimly lit, is the entrance to the royal bedroom, where the Emperor and the Empress are sleeping. The Nurse, crouching in the shadows, is guarding the bedroom.

A powerful three-note theme sounds in the orchestra. Then the Nurse sings that a light is rising over the lake ("Licht über'm See"), and wonders if it heralds the approach of Keikobad, the all-powerful monarch of the shadowless spirit world. She sings that she has been watching all night long in pain and sorrow over his child, the Empress.

The Spirit Messenger steps out of the shadows. Clad in armor, he is bathed in a ghostly bluish light. It is not Keikobad, he announces ("Keikobad nicht"), but his Messenger. Here begins a long musical dialogue in which the significance of the shadow is made clear. The Messenger reminds the Nurse that he is the twelfth to have visited her in a year to ask the fateful question: "Does the Empress cast a shadow?" ("Wirft sie einen Schatten?"). A single note, repeated in sextuplets, underscores his question. If so, the Messenger goes on, the Nurse and everyone else are doomed.

In suppressed triumph the Nurse answers that there is no shadow—the light passes through the Empress' body as though she were made of glass. The Messenger berates her for her carelessness in allowing the girl to fall, as a human being, into the hands of the Emperor.

Trying to defend her actions, the Nurse says that the girl inherited from her own mother a longing to be human. And it was her own father who gave her the power to transform herself into a gazelle, which the Emperor then captured. How could she, the Nurse asks tartly, pursue a gazelle?

Abruptly the Messenger asks to see the Empress. Shaking her head, the Nurse replies that the Emperor is with her. To the accompaniment of the "Huntsman" theme in the orchestra, she explains that the Emperor is a hunter and a lover—but nothing more. Although he has been with his wife for twelve months, at dawn he is off to the hunt and does not come back until nightfall. His nights are her days; his days are her nights.

After twelve long months, the Messenger declares, the Emperor now has only three short days left to be with the Empress. Then she must return to her father Keikobad. "And I with her," the Nurse exclaims joyfully. In a foreboding phrase foretelling the fate of the Emperor the Messenger says: "He will be turned to stone!" ("Er wird zu Stein!"). But she herself will meet Keikobad, the Nurse says, and will bow before him. Warning her to remain on guard for the fateful three days, the Messenger vanishes.

The Emperor, dressed for the hunt, comes in and calls to the Nurse. The Empress is sleeping, he says, and the Nurse is to answer her call when she awakes. Then in a long dramatic monologue ("Heute streif' ich bis an die Mondberge") he sings that today he will go hunting in the moon mountains—where he first found the Empress. She was in the form of a gazelle and cast no shadow. Her beauty set his heart on fire.

Now if he could only find his red Falcon, the Emperor cries—the Falcon who caught his gazelle. As she bounded away, the Falcon swooped down and struck her between the eyes. She fell. The Emperor leaped toward her with his spear poised for the kill. At that instant the gazelle was transformed into a woman—and he held his beloved in his arms. Yet in this feverish moment, the Emperor continues, he was shaken with fury because the Falcon had struck down his bride. He hurled his dagger at the bird and wounded it. The Falcon's look haunts him still.

Casually the Nurse asks him how long he will be away on the hunt. Probably three days, the Emperor answers. Tell the Empress, he goes on in a fiery refrain ("wenn ich jage, es ist um sie"), that when he goes hunting it is for her sake alone, for she is the prize of all prizes. He rushes away.

The Nurse dismisses the servants who had come in with the Emperor, and a moment later the Empress comes out of her room. She asks if her beloved has gone ("Ist mein Liebster dahin?"). This marks the beginning of a brilliant aria. Had she not awakened, she sings, she might have dreamed herself back into the body of a bird or a gazelle. She laments that she has lost the talisman that could transform her, because she gladly again would be the quarry to be hunted down by the Emperor's Falcon.

Suddenly she looks up, sees the red Falcon, and exclaims joyfully over his return. Then in alarm she cries that blood is dripping from his wounded wing and tears are gushing from his eyes. Anxiously she asks the Falcon why he weeps.

The Falcon theme, repeated on a single note accented by appoggiaturas, strikingly imitates the call of a bird. "Why should I not weep?" the unseen Falcon sings ("Wie soll ich denn nicht weinen?"). "The Empress casts no shadow, and so the Emperor must be turned to stone." Terrified, the Empress recalls that on the lost talisman a curse was engraved. The voices of the Empress and the Falcon blend as they reiterate these thoughts.

In desperation the Empress asks the Nurse where she can find a shadow ("wo find' ich den Schatten?"). A long musical dialogue now ensues. The Nurse sternly answers that the Emperor has failed to accomplish what had been decreed: He has not given the Empress a child and she casts no shadow. For this failure he must pay the penalty. As the Empress begs the Nurse to help her find a shadow the Nurse relentlessly reminds her of the terms of the contract. Moreover, if the Empress wants a shadow, she herself must go and get it. And to find it, the Nurse adds softly, but with malevolent emphasis, she must go down into the world of mankind ("Bei den Menschen").

The harsh "Mankind" theme sounds in the orchestra in minor thirds as the Nurse goes on to say that the breath of man is the breath of death. Its very purity reeks of corruption. And now they must descend from their own realm among the stars to mingle with these vile earthly creatures and endure their stupidity for the sake of finding a shadow.

The Empress cries that she must have that shadow and demands to be led down to earth. Still trying to dissuade her, the Nurse warns that dawn is breaking—the human dawn. The light is the earth's sun, which these wretched beings use to cast their shadows. Thus the day dawns over this monstrous realm where mindless hordes with blank faces and unseeing eyes struggle for survival. Does the Empress still wish to go to this loathsome place—or shall they relinquish the shadow?

Undaunted, the Empress replies that she must go—there is an overpowering urge within her that makes her do the very thing that fills her with horror. Well then, says the Nurse, go they will ("Hinab denn mit uns"). From this point the dialogue continues in duet form as the two plan their journey. At its conclusion the curtain falls, while the orchestra continues with a vivid musical description of the descent of the Empress and the Nurse to the earth. A number of leitmotivs are interwoven, including the cry of the Falcon and the "Mankind" theme. The interlude goes on without pause into the next scene.

[*Scene Two*] Barak the Dyer's house, which also serves as his workshop. The Dyer's three brothers—One-eyed, One-armed, and Hunchback—are quarreling savagely. Underscoring their imprecations is the "Mankind" theme. Suddenly the Dyer's Wife rushes in and stops the quarrel by dousing the three with a bucket of water. The brothers turn on her in violent denunciation, railing at her for being a meddling outsider. Once there were thirteen children in this family, they shout, but even then there was always something to eat for any hungry beggar who came to the door. And yet this "upstart beauty" dares abuse the members of the family.

At the height of the altercation the Dyer appears in the doorway. Turning on him in fury, the Wife screams at him to get the brothers out of the house—either they go or she goes. Driving them out, Barak orders them to prepare the animal skins he has brought home to take to market.

Trying to placate his wife, Barak reminds her that these brothers once were healthy children without deformities. This is their home, as it has always been. Where else should they go? When the Wife makes a spiteful reference to the "thirteen children" and their platefuls of food, Barak declares that if they had thirteen children of their own he would see to it that they too had enough to eat. Now, as her husband, he demands to know when she will give him children. Impulsively, Barak touches her shoulder in a tender gesture of affection.

Rudely shaking him off, the Wife sneers that she knows what "husband" means—it means that she has been bought for the sole purpose of being a slave to him and his house. But now, she adds harshly, there is an end to it—she will be slave no longer.

The argument continues in duet form. The Dyer recalls that the godmothers, according to custom, spoke incantations over the Wife's body to assure her fruitfulness—and he has reason to be grateful for these portents of good fortune. The Wife retorts that spells muttered by bleary-eyed hags have no power over her.

Oblivious to her ill temper, Barak kneels before the pile of skins he brought in and begins sorting them over. There is a brief orchestral interlude based on the theme of "Barak's Goodness." Watching him contemptuously, the Wife sings that for two and a half years she has been his wife ("Dritthalb Jahr bin ich dein Weib") and still he has not made her a mother. Now she has lost interest in motherhood, and he himself can put his desire for her out of his mind.

Barak recoils at her cruel words but patiently explains that he is not angry with her. He will wait for the blessings which are sure to come. Here the theme of "Barak's Patience" gives orchestral emphasis to his words. The Wife gibes angrily that no "blessings" will come to this house. Rather, they will shake the dust of this wretched place from their feet. Ignoring her bitterness, Barak picks up the bundle of skins and leaves for the market place.

A moment later there is a flash of light which reveals the Nurse, in a robe of black and white patches, and the Empress, dressed as a servant girl. The Wife stares at them in bewilderment. Kneeling before her and kissing her foot, the Nurse launches into mocking flattery of the Wife's matchless beauty ("Schönheit ohnegleichen"). Addressing her as "Princess," she asks if the fellow who just left with a pack on his back is one of her lackeys.

"The man is a dyer and my husband," the Wife tells the Nurse coldly, "and that you know as well as I do." Unabashed, the Nurse continues her outrageous blandishments, saying that the Wife's body is "as slender as a palm tree." The Empress breaks in to exclaim that she will kiss the shadow this charmer casts. The Nurse pretends to be distressed because the Wife must languish here alone and bear children. Stung by their mockery, the Wife sobs that they are making a fool of her before God and man.

Playing out her evil masquerade, the Nurse begins to lead the Empress away, exclaiming that the Wife knows the "secret" and is only making fun of her visitors. Completely bewildered, the Wife asks what she means. The "secret," the Nurse answers, is her shadow—which she can sell for whatever price she asks. But who, murmurs the Wife, would buy a poor crooked shadow like hers?

In a dramatic refrain ("Alles, alles, du Benedeite") the Nurse tells her that eager buyers will give her anything she wants if only she will surrender her shadow. She can have slaves, silken garments, palaces, throngs of lovers, imperishable beauty. With that she snatches a jeweled tiara out of the air and places it upon the Wife's head. The latter wails that she does not even have a mirror to see her own image.

The Nurse puts her hands over the Wife's eyes, then the two women vanish. The scene changes at once into a luxurious boudoir, with a bevy of beautiful slave girls waiting to attend their mistress. They hail her as princess in a flowing, wordless chorus sung with the effect of gentle laughter.

As it fades away, the Nurse leads in the Wife, now wearing a loose wrap, with the tiara glittering in her hair. She sits down in front of a large mirror and gasps in delighted astonishment as she sees her image.

The voice of the Empress is heard asking the Wife if she will give up her shadow for this image. Before she can answer, the voice of a Young Man sings that for such an image he would give up his life and his soul into the bargain. Lost in wonder, the Wife sings that this is all a waking dream.

The scene suddenly changes back to the Dyer's house. The Wife, once more in her tattered clothes, clings to the Nurse in terror. How, she asks, can she cast off her shadow and give it away? The Nurse, exchanging a significant glance with the Empress, sitting nearby, craftily leads the Wife into admitting that she is satiated with the idea of motherhood without ever having been a mother. Henceforth, she declares, she will deny her husband his wish to have children. The Nurse has now won her point.

In a long aria beginning with the "Renunciation of Children" theme ("Abzutun Mutterschaft") the Nurse commends the Wife on her decision. For this renunciation she will be glorified among women. Then the Nurse explains how she and the Empress will help the Wife in her resolve to thwart her husband. For three days they will stay in the Dyer's house as servants and deliberately upset the routine of domesticity. For this service, the Wife will give them her shadow. Then she will be free to enjoy the dream of delight they showed her before—the slave girls, a palace garden, tons of gold.

The Wife warns that Barak is coming home and will want his supper —and his bed, which she will deny him. Tomorrow, then, the Nurse says, she and the Empress will arrive at noon disguised as poor relations. She is to greet them only after midnight, then permit them to leave secretly for a while. Now, the Nurse announces briskly, there is work to do.

With that she conjures up a fantastic array of legerdemain. As a gust of wind sweeps through the room, five fishes come flying through the air and land in the frying pan, under which the fire blazes up. Half the double bed breaks away and becomes a single cot. The Nurse and the Empress disappear. As the Wife stares uncomprehendingly, children's voices are heard as though issuing from the frying pan. Plaintively they beg to be let in. Here the music states the "Unborn Children" theme. The Wife fumes over the whining voices coming from the fire and looks around for water to douse the flames. The voices, chiding her for her hardheartedness, die away.

To the accompaniment of the theme of "Barak's Suffering," the Dyer enters bent under the weight of a huge basket. He sniffs the odor of frying fish and asks the Wife why she does not sit down to eat. "Here is your dinner," she snaps. "I am going to sleep." Pointing to the single cot, she tells him there is his bed. Barak looks at it in dismayed surprise. In spoken phrases, the Wife then announces that tomorrow her two cousins will move in. They will sleep at her feet and will work here as her maids. So be it.

Shaking his head sadly, Barak sits down on the floor and begins eating a slice of bread. He muses that he had been forewarned that at first his wife would act strangely—but this behavior is hard to bear. Now he cannot even enjoy his meal.

Then from the outside comes the chorus of the Watchmen, sung in unison over a majestic choralelike accompaniment. In ironic contrast to the bitter mood of the foregoing scene, they exhort husbands and wives ("Ihr Gatten in den Häusern dieser Stadt") to hold marriage sacred, for they are entrusted with the seed of life. Gazing at his sleeping wife, Barak softly asks if she can hear the Watchmen. He listens intently as they sing that husbands and wives are the bridge over which the dead cross the abyss to return to life. With a deep sigh of resignation, Barak lies down to sleep. The curtain falls.

ACT TWO

[*Scene One*] Barak's house. The Empress, in her role as servant girl, helps Barak pack up his load of skins. Then the Nurse sarcastically urges him to return home quickly to the Wife who cannot bear his absence. At the moment, the Wife is sitting to one side, still wearing the tiara. The Empress goes over to her, kneels before her and holds up a mirror; the Wife admires her image. When Barak leaves, the Nurse goes to the Wife and asks if she is to call the "one who is now expected"—the one for whom she has adorned herself ("Wie ruf' ich den, der nun herein soll?").

When the Wife replies that she adorns herself for no one but the image in the mirror, the Nurse deliberately tempts her with a romantic description of a youth who is burning with desire for her. At first skeptical, the Wife recalls that one day a young man did indeed come toward her in a crowd . . . but she does not remember the street where it happened, much less his name.

The Nurse, stealthily picking up a broom and using it as a wand, mutters an incantation and commands the Wife to close her eyes. Here the "Phantom Lover" theme echoes in the orchestra. When the Empress exclaims in shocked amazement over this trickery the Nurse assures her that it is all to her advantage. Are men really so corrupt, the Empress asks. Men, replies the Nurse sardonically, are monsters.

Eyes closed, the Wife muses over the youth, whom she recalls as in a dream, thus betraying her secret desires. Then suddenly, at the Nurse's command, the Young Man materializes as the "Phantom Lover" theme again sounds insinuatingly in the orchestra. Apparently a lifeless dummy, he is supported by two small dark creatures, who vanish immediately. Opening her eyes, the Wife murmurs that he is the young man she met . . . and yet he is not. The Phantom appears to come to life and approaches her. She shrinks back from his touch, crying that she wants only to run away and hide.

Excitedly the Nurse urges the two to take advantage of this magic moment. Her words are echoed by a ghostly chorus. The Empress laments because these two meet—the love thief and the housewife—one with a heart and the other without. In sudden alarm, the Nurse warns that Barak is approaching. She throws her cloak over the Phantom, who disappears.

Barak and his brothers come storming in, followed by a crowd of beggar children. The Dyer is carrying a huge bowl; One-eyed is playing a bagpipe; Hunchback, with a wreath on his head, drags in a cask; One-armed carries in another large dish. The four are in high spirits, and Barak jovially greets his wife as "Princess" and invites her to the feast. She turns her back on him.

The three brothers strike up a lusty refrain in praise of their successful shopping spree on this lucky day ("O Tag des Glücks"). The beggar children, crowding in the doorway, echo their phrases. But the gay mood of the scene is suddenly shattered as the Wife bursts out in a venomous diatribe against Barak ("Wahrlich, es ist angelegt"). All this merrymaking, she sings, is a coarse insult to sensitive feelings. He who hungers for bread is given a stone . . . he who longs to taste the food of dreams is thrown the leavings from the table of the rich. There is nothing left to him but his tears. Here the "Discontent" theme is heard briefly in the strings. Overcome by rage and self-pity, the Wife sits down sobbing in a corner, burying her face in her hands.

Trying to ignore her outburst, the genial Barak invites all to enjoy the feast. He observes that, although the Wife has a sharp tongue and a bad temper, she still is blessed because of her pure heart and her youth. Then he orders the servant girl (the Empress) to offer the Wife some delicacies. As she obeys, the Wife screams at her to keep away. Again she sobs about her cruel misfortune.

At this point a long ensemble begins with a trio passage sung by the three brothers ("Wer achtet ein Weib"). While no one heeds a wailing woman, they sing, they realize that she always has been a long-suffering wife. Then they sing again about their lucky shopping day and the feast that is being prepared. When Barak invites everyone to share, the beggar children join the chorus to praise his generosity. Meanwhile, the Wife continues her lamentations. This chorus, in which variations of the themes of "Bitterness and Mockery" and "Barak's Suffering" are briefly intermingled, brings the scene to a close. The music continues in an interlude in which the theme of "Barak's Suffering" is again heard, then the notes of the Falcon's call.

[*Scene Two*] Outside the Emperor's falcon house deep in the forest. Moonlight shines through the trees. The Emperor rides up on his horse, dismounts and hides behind a tree from where he can see the door of the house. This entire scene is given over to the Emperor's intensely dramatic monologue "Falke, Falke, du wiedergefundener," sung over a symphonic accompaniment. The Emperor implores the Falcon to tell him why he has been led to this place. The letter from his wife explained that she would be secluded here for three days—but the house is empty. The Emperor wonders if the Falcon has misled him.

Then he sees the Nurse and the Empress come stealing through the trees and into the house. Watching in dismay, the Emperor cries that the scent of mankind clings to the Empress. Certain that he has been betrayed, he resolves to kill her. He draws an arrow from his quiver, then unsheathes his sword. But unable to drive himself to murder, he moans despairingly, "Du bist nicht, der sie töten darf" ("It is not for you to kill her"). Begging the Falcon to lead him from this accursed place, the Emperor rushes into the forest with an anguished cry as the music storms to a climax, ending suddenly with the Falcon's call. The next scene follows without pause.

[*Scene Three*] Barak's house, where he is at work over his skins, with the Wife and the Nurse watching him impatiently. The Wife—as usual—complains because Barak will be late getting to market. He replies that he has been working hard since morning without much to show for it. When he asks the Wife to bring him a drink she snarls that there are servants here to do that.

The Nurse pours a drink and slips a drug into it, and Barak gulps it down. A few moments later he says he is sleepy, whereupon the Wife resumes her remorseless nagging. Mumbling that he will take his goods to market later on, Barak falls fast asleep on the floor. The Wife's bad temper now begins to annoy even the Nurse. Sharply ordering her to be quiet, she informs her that Barak has been given a sleeping potion. Panic-stricken, the Wife tries in vain to rouse her husband.

He will sleep until morning, the Nurse says casually, adding that in the meantime many happy hours are in store. She offers to bring the person for whom the Wife is waiting. Angry and suspicious, the Wife spurns all the Nurse's suggestions. She goes on talking mysteriously about a person of her own choosing who will come to her from a strange place without any help from the Nurse.

Despite her objections, the Nurse again summons the Apparition of the young man. The dialogue continues in trio form as the Young Man, the Wife and the Nurse talk in abstract terms about death and unrequited love. Suddenly the Young Man falls to the floor as though in a faint. As the Wife bends over him he tries to seize her hand. She shrinks back in terror. Seeing the Nurse and the Empress stealing toward the door, the Wife screams at them to help her. "If the dead are living," she wails, looking from the Young Man to Barak, "then the sleepers may well be dead." She manages then to awaken Barak. The Nurse turns back and throws the cloak of invisibility over the Young Man, remarking that when the wind changes she will recall him.

A long colloquy now ensues between the Wife and Barak. She berates him for falling asleep instead of guarding his home and his wife from intruders. Alarmed, he calls to his brothers for help, while the Wife continues her torrent of abuse. Gathering his tools together, Barak murmurs that something is happening to him that he does not understand . . . his best mortar is broken . . . he wonders if he no longer understands his trade.

There is one "trade" he never has understood, the Wife remarks sarcastically. Thinking of how she resisted the temptations of the Phantom Lover, she adds that if Barak knew what had happened he would scarcely dare move for fear of shattering so precious a treasure as her faithfulness. Barak, utterly bewildered, mutters that he hears but cannot understand.

This is not the first time she has spoken and he has not understood, the Wife sneers. But the day will come, she goes on ominously, when she will leave this house and never return. She is, after all, not a captive bird in a cage. For her, home will be somewhere else.

During an ensuing orchestral interlude in which the theme of "Bitterness and Mockery" is prominent, the Wife leaves with the Nurse while the Empress gathers up the rest of the scattered tools. Barak sits staring blankly into space. Then, as if in a dream, he asks: "Who's there?" The Empress answers: "Your servant, my lord."

[Scene Four] The scene curtain falls and, after an agitated orchestral interlude, rises on the Emperor's bedroom in the falcon house. On the bed the Empress is tossing restlessly in her sleep. The Nurse is asleep at the foot of the bed. In her sleep the Empress murmurs that the man's eyes have a tormented look before which even cherubim would quail. Suddenly sitting bolt upright, she cries: "Barak, I have sinned against you!" ("Dir, Barak, bin ich mich schuldig!"). Still in sleep, she falls back.

During an orchestral passage her dream materializes. One wall of the room disappears. In its place is a huge cave with a bronze door in one side. Tombstones show up in the flickering light of torches. From the distance comes the call of the Falcon. The Emperor enters, as though following the bird, and passes in front of the bronze door. There is a sound of rushing water. An unseen chorus intones: "To the water of life . . . to the brink of death . . . beware!" Then comes the voice of the Falcon calling that the woman casts no shadow and so the Emperor must be turned to stone ("Die Frau wirft keinen Schatten"). The Emperor leaves through the bronze door and the cave disappears.

The Empress awakes, still in the grip of her dream. She cries that the Emperor's body is stiffening . . . he can no longer speak. Everything is her fault, she wails, and she has even destroyed Barak . . . whatever she touches she kills . . . if only she herself could be turned to stone.

[*Scene Five*] During a brief orchestral interlude the scene changes to Barak's house. He is sitting on the floor. As the room gradually darkens the three brothers enter, murmuring in awe that something strange is happening. The Nurse, who has returned with the Wife, warns that some supernatural power is at work here. But she assures the Wife that what she desires will come to pass.

This introduces a long ensemble sung by the Wife, the Nurse, the Empress, the three brothers and Barak. The Wife sings ("Wie ertrag' ich dies Haus") that she cannot endure a house where darkness falls in the middle of the day and even the dogs howl in fright. The Empress muses on the behavior of the "sons of Adam" and expresses guilt over the fact that her presence among humans only adds to their troubles. Yet she is thankful that destiny has led her to the Dyer, whose sterling qualities as a man have made her visitation worthwhile. The three brothers sing that the sun darkens and the waters of the river stand still—strange things are happening that they do not understand. Barak wonders why some mysterious dark power seems to hold him in its grip. The Nurse continues to promise the Wife that her desires will be fulfilled.

The ensemble is interrupted as the Wife, enraged by Barak's outwardly calm demeanor, launches into a furious tirade ("Es gibt derer, die bleiben immer gelassen") underscored by the "Bitterness and Mockery" theme. There are some people, she storms, who face life with a calm that nothing can disturb. Glaring at Barak, she rages that such people are beneath contempt.

She goes on to taunt her trusting husband with her infidelity. While he went to market, she tells him, she entertained a stranger. At first the thought of her husband spoiled her pleasure, but then she found a way to thrust him out of her mind. Once for all, she has rejected her unborn children—his and any other man's as well. To seal this act she has sold her shadow—and for a magnificent price.

Barak leaps to his feet and stares at her in horror. In spoken tones he gasps that this woman has gone mad, then orders the brothers to stir up the fire so that he can look into her face. As the flames rise, the brothers scream that the Wife casts no shadow.

At this point the ensemble is resumed. The Nurse calls to the Empress to seize the shadow for herself. Now the deed is done, she adds maliciously. Finally roused to fury, Barak shouts that he will drown this brazen wench. The Empress cries that she does not want the shadow because it is stained with blood. Trying to restrain the raging Barak, the brothers warn that there must be no blood on his hands. They curse the Wife and implore Barak to chase her out of the house. The Nurse cries triumphantly that at last the shadow is theirs—and now, he who calls for blood must have a sword. At this instant Barak raises his arm in a gesture of swearing an oath of vengeance. A glittering sword flies through the air and into his outstretched hand. He lunges at his wife as the brothers desperately try to hold him back.

For a moment, the Wife stands paralyzed with fear. Then with an anguished cry she flings herself toward Barak, sobbing that her faithlessness was a lie and that her own lips betrayed her. Here and now, she goes on, she sees a man she never saw before—Barak, a stern judge and a noble husband. If she must die for something that never happened, then let him kill her quickly.

Shaking off the brothers, Barak raises the sword to strike. It flies out of his hand. A moment later the room splits apart and Barak and his Wife disappear into a yawning gulf. Water roars into the room through great cracks in the walls. The brothers flee through the open door to escape the torrent, while the Nurse drags herself and the Empress to a place of refuge. The scene is plunged into darkness. To a fanfare of trumpets the Nurse invokes the infernal powers. The curtain falls.

ACT THREE

[*Scene One*] A subterranean vault divided by a thick wall. Barak sits on one side, his wife on the other, with neither aware of the other's presence. The wailing theme of the "Unborn Children" sounds in the orchestra. Begging the voices to be quiet, the Wife expresses her remorse in a touching monologue which begins as she again denies she deceived her husband ("Ich hab' es nicht getan!"). She longs desperately to see him again, to make him understand that although she enticed her would-be lover into her house she did not violate the sanctity of marriage. In despairing tones she calls out Barak's name.

On the other side of the wall, Barak sings of his love for his Wife, whose young heart has been entrusted to his care. The voices of the two then blend in a tender duet ("Mir anvertraut"). It ends in a swift change of mood as Barak recalls the terrible moment when he was about to murder his wife. Now all he desires, he sings in pianissimo phrases, is to tell her: "Do not be afraid." This passage brings to mind the love duet in *Tristan und Isolde*.

A sudden shaft of light pierces Barak's cell and lights up a staircase at the back. As a rising major chord passage sweeps through the orchestra, a Voice commands the Dyer to climb. When he does so, the Wife implores him in ringing phrases ("Komm zu mir") to come to her. To see him once more she would gladly die by his sword. Then, commanded by the Voice, she also hurries up the stairs.

[*Scene Two*] During a surging orchestral interlude marked by a series of ascending chords, the scene changes to a stone terrace rising above a river. Steps lead up to a bronze door where Keikobad's Messenger is waiting with attendant spirits. Moored at the foot of the steps is a boat in which the Empress lies sleeping, with the Nurse seated beside her. As the Messenger and attendant spirits disappear through the bronze door the Nurse rouses the Empress. A long dialogue follows. In angry impatience the Nurse urges the Empress to leave this accursed place ("Fort von hier").

When the Empress protests that the boat will not move, the Nurse tells her to climb out so that they may take the road that leads away from this evil region. But the Empress, looking up, exclaims that she sees a gateway—one she has seen before. From somewhere on the mountain comes a trumpet call sounding the "Keikobad" theme. In great excitement the Empress sings that this is a summons from her father. She will go to him to intercede for her husband the Emperor, who now stands before the judgment seat.

Craftily the Nurse tries to dissuade the Empress from entering the gateway—which leads to Keikobad's temple—promising her a shadow ("Ich schaff' dir den Schatten"). She reminds her that the light still can be seen through her childless body, even though the Wife's miserable shadow clings to her. The Nurse says she even will help the Empress find the one she loves—the Emperor—if only she will come away from this fearsome threshold. To cross it, she warns, is worse than death.[1] When the Empress demands to know what lies beyond the threshold, the Nurse replies, "The water of life." No, the Empress cries, it leads to the brink of death. Then she angrily accuses the Nurse of deliberately misleading her and keeping from her the meaning of supernatural mysteries. But for herself, the Empress declares, everything is clear: she must and will go to her husband. As though in a trance, she sings that she must taste of this water of life. Is it, perhaps, blood from human veins? As she moves toward the portal, the Nurse throws herself in front of her, crying out that the water of life is a monstrous delusion. Whoever drinks of it is doomed to unspeakable disaster.

Desperately the Nurse begs the Empress to heed her warning.

---

[1] It may be noted that at this point the plot of the opera moves into the realm of symbolism. Actions and utterances of the characters cannot be explained in terms of everyday reality.

Though Keikobad is her father, he is a heartless tyrant who will punish her horribly for falling in love with a mortal. To him, there is no fouler crime than trafficking with the accursed creatures of earth.

The Empress answers in one of the most brilliant arias in the opera—"Aus unsern Taten steigt ein Gericht"—introduced by a blazing fanfare of trumpets. We will be judged by our deeds alone, she sings, and we must obey only the call of the heart. And now she and the Nurse will part forever, because the Nurse knows too little of what is in men's hearts. They pay a terrible price for their guilt—but, phoenixlike, they rise out of death into life. She belongs to them, the Empress sings. Looking at the Nurse in mingled contempt and pity, she adds, "You are not my kind!" With that she turns toward the temple door, which opens to admit her, then closes. The Nurse, beside herself with anger and frustration, screams a curse on all mankind.

Now the voices of Barak and his Wife are heard. They are wandering over the mountain searching for each other. In an ensuing trio, the Nurse continues her maledictions, while Barak and his Wife despairingly cry out for each other. Suddenly Barak comes upon the Nurse and asks her if she has seen his Wife. With deliberate malice, the Nurse points in the wrong direction—then does the same thing when she meets the Wife a few moments later. To add to their confusion, she first tells Barak to avenge himself because his Wife is cursing him, then tells the Wife that her husband is about to murder her. In helpless confusion, Barak and his Wife wander away.

The Nurse, as though suddenly transfixed by a vision, cries out for her "child"—the Empress. She sees her drinking the lethal golden liquid, the water of life, and hears the scream of agony torn from her throat. Wild with fear, the Nurse flings herself on the temple door, screaming "Keikobad!" Her cry is echoed by unseen voices. In answer, Keikobad's Messenger appears and harshly orders her to leave the threshold—at once and forever.

On the verge of madness, the Nurse protests that it was the Messenger himself who gave the Empress into her care ("Mir anvertraut"). She followed instructions, but the Empress rejected her. Keikobad must believe this. The Messenger cuts her short, saying that the Empress is now with Keikobad. As for her—the Nurse—no one needs her.

The scene darkens and a violent thunderstorm breaks. At this point an ensemble begins. The Nurse wildly implores Keikobad to listen to his faithful servant ("Deine Dienerin schreit zu dir"). The voices of Barak and his Wife again are heard as they call to each other. The Messenger denounces the Nurse for daring to utter the name of Keikobad. As punishment for her failure and her arrogance she will be banished to the world of men which she so despises. With that the Messenger pushes her violently into the boat, which drifts away. Screaming a final, savage imprecation ("Fressendes Feuer in ihr Gebein"—"May fire devour their bones"), the Nurse vanishes.

[*Scene Three*] As the wailing voices of Barak and his Wife are heard once more over a brief interlude dominated by the "Retribution" theme, the scene changes to a templelike hall. At the back is a curtained niche. The Empress enters, and attendant spirits go to meet her, bidding her to meet her destiny with courage. To the accompaniment of a solo violin the Empress walks slowly to the niche and calls to her father— "Vater, bist du's?" This introduces the beautiful aria in which the Empress confesses that though she surrendered herself to human love, she did not buy a shadow. Now she asks where she can find a shadow of her own.

As though in reply, a fountain of golden water gushes up near her. Gazing at it thoughtfully, the Empress sings that she does not need the water of life, for she has something stronger to sustain her: love. The Guardian of the Threshold appears and beseeches her to drink. Then the shadow of the Wife will be hers. Refusing, the Empress asks what then will happen to the Wife.

Suddenly she hears Barak calling to his Wife. Excitedly the Empress exclaims that this human being also is a symbol of her failure, because to protect herself from mortal guilt, she invoked supernatural powers. As for the water of life, it is stained with blood, and she will not drink. To a swirling harp glissando, the fountain subsides.

In ringing phrases the Empress proclaims that she belongs to the world of men ("Mein Platz ist hier in dieser Welt"). There is her guilt, there she will remain. She calls on her father to pass sentence. The light in the niche grows brighter, finally revealing the Emperor turned to stone, with only his eyes showing any sign of life. As variations of the "Empress" theme flare in the orchestra, the Empress calls out in spoken phrases that the curse has struck—thus the Emperor has been punished for her sins. In imitation of the Falcon's cry, foreboding voices intone that the woman casts no shadow; therefore the Emperor has been turned to stone. With a cry of anguish, the Empress falls to the ground.

The golden fountain bubbles up again. The Guardian of the Threshold reappears and, bending over the Empress, again tempts her to drink. One sip . . . and then not only will the Wife's shadow be hers forever, but the Emperor will return alive to her arms. From the distance come the plaintive voices of Barak and his Wife pleading for mercy—for if the Empress now drinks of the water of life their doom will be sealed. Struggling against her desire to drink the life-giving water, the Empress begs Keikobad to let her die rather than tempt her further. As the voices of Barak and his Wife fade away, the Empress raises herself to her knees beside the fountain and utters a final tormented cry: "Ich will nicht!"

The fountain disappears. As light begins to flood the scene, a shadow appears on the ground in front of the Empress. The Emperor, now restored to life, rises from his throne. In an ensuing aria ("Wenn das Herz aus Kristall zerbricht") he explains the miracle that has taken place. When a crystal heart is shattered by a plea for mercy, unborn children hasten to receive the gift of life. Man and wife are redeemed and can now fulfill their destiny. This he learned, the Emperor sings, when he was in the grip of the deathly spell which turned him into stone.

[*Scene Four*] From the distance come the voices of the unborn children calling to "Father and Mother." As the Emperor and the Empress comment on their happiness their voices blend with those of the children in a triumphant chorus. At its conclusion the scene changes, during an orchestral interlude, to a sunlit landscape through which a golden torrent flows. The Emperor and the Empress gaze on the scene from a height.

The Dyer's Wife now appears, singing that if she cannot find her beloved husband she wants only the sentence of his sword. Barak, on the other side of the stream, calls out that he will protect her forever. In the next moment they catch sight of each other and Barak exclaims that he sees his wife's shadow. Magically, the shadow becomes a golden bridge upon which the two rush into each other's arms. The chorus of unborn children hails their reunion.

Jubilantly Barak sings that now, inspired by the promise of future children, he will work as no one ever worked before ("Nun will ich jubeln"). This marks the beginning of the magnificent quartet which concludes the opera. The Emperor sings that the sound of children's voices is the sound of humanity. The Empress and the Dyer's Wife rejoice in the fact that they both have shadows because they have been rewarded the gift of humanity after a trial by fire. The unborn children sing that all trials are over and that happiness reigns supreme. After a soaring climax the music subsides into a serene major chord as the curtain falls.

GIOVANNA D'ARCO

by GIUSEPPE VERDI

(1813–1901)

Libretto by

TEMISTOCLE SOLERA

Adapted from *The Maid of Orleans,* a play by Schiller

CHARACTERS

Carlo (Charles VII), King of France	Tenor
Giovanna (Joan)	Soprano
Giacomo (Jacques), her father	Baritone
Delil, an officer of the King	Tenor
Talbot, commander of the English army	Bass

Officials of King Carlo's court, French and English soldiers, grandees, heralds, pages, halberdiers, deputies, magistrates, guards, angels, demons

Place: France
Time: Circa 1429
First performance: La Scala, Milan, February 15, 1845
Original language: Italian

At the time Verdi began the composition of *Giovanna D'Arco,* he had already achieved operatic fame with *Nabucco, Ernani* and *I Due Foscari.* Asked to write an opera for La Scala, he turned to a version of the Joan of Arc story fashioned by the librettist Solera from the drama by Johann Christoph Friedrich von Schiller.

For operatic purposes, Solera virtually ignored the historical background of the story. Joan, for example, is betrayed to the English by her own father—not by a treacherous countryman, as history records. Moreover, in Solera's libretto, she dies on the battlefield instead of at the stake. But Verdi, as could be expected, compensated for many of the plot's inadequacies through the power of his music, which brings the otherwise static characters to life. Some of the music concededly is routine, some of it simple to the point of naïveté. Yet there are passages of true Verdian eloquence.

Giovanna was only moderately successful, and there were comparatively few performances following the premiere. A bizarre revival was staged at Palermo in 1847, when it was provided with an entirely new libretto to satisfy the police censors. Joan was changed to a compatriot of Sappho, and the opera retitled *Orietta of Lesbos*. After that, however, the original rarely showed up on the operatic stage.

Oddly enough, contemporary revivals have met with remarkable success, prompting critics to ask why this early evidence of Verdi's genius has been so undeservedly neglected. *Giovanna* received its American premiere by the American Opera Society in New York on March 1, 1966; in May of that year it was performed in London at the Royal Academy of Music.

There is a long opening sinfonia, reminiscent of the harmonic style of Beethoven, which establishes the tragic mood of the opera. This is followed by a lyrical *andante pastorale* scored for flute, oboe and clarinet.

PROLOGUE

At the court of King Carlo in Domremy, people of the court and a throng of citizens express their mingled rage and despair over France's evil fate at the hands of the invading English ("Qual v'ha speme?"). Carlo enters. In recitative ("Amici, v'appressate") he announces his abdication and releases all his subjects from further allegiance to him. In the ensuing cavatina ("Sotto una quercia") he relates how the Maid appeared to him in a vision and requested him to lay down his helmet and sword in a certain spot in the nearby forest. By this act of abnegation, she explained, he will save France from divine punishment.

Carlo describes the spot in the forest as it appeared in his vision and asks his listeners if anyone has seen it. They earnestly entreat him not to go there ("Per poco uditeci, fermate!"). Brushing aside their warning, the King goes into the forest and finds the designated spot. A descriptive orchestral interlude accompanies the scene change to the secluded retreat where Giovanna comes to pray for guidance in her destined role as the savior of France.

Meanwhile Giacomo, deeply distressed by his daughter's mysterious behavior, has concealed himself in a cave nearby to find out for himself if Giovanna secretly communes with angels or demons. In a dramatic recitative ("Gelo, terrore m'invade") he expresses his forebodings. Suddenly Carlo enters, and Giacomo watches him as he lays down his helmet and sword.

Giovanna appears. Unaware that she is being observed by her father and the King, she sinks to her knees, and in the beautiful cavatina "Oh, ben s'addice questo" she prays for strength to face her ordeal. She promises to forswear all earthly love if the divine spirits will answer her prayer. The chorus of angels and demons is heard in reply ("Tu sei bella")—the angels exhorting her to be steadfast, the devils tempting her with profane pleasures.

Carlo approaches and Giovanna greets him joyously. Snatching up his helmet and sword, she promises him victory, and in the ensuing cabaletta ("Ah! son guerriera!") she hails the sacred cause of France.

Then follows an interlude in the form of an unaccompanied trio in which the three principals voice their respective reactions (beginning with Giovanna's phrase: "A te, pietosa Vergine"). The cabaletta then continues, after which Giovanna leaves with Carlo. Giacomo laments that his worst fears have been realized.

ACT ONE

[*Scene One*] The camp of Talbot's army, which has been defeated by the French troops led by King Carlo and Giovanna. In a sorrowful chorus the English bemoan the disaster on the battlefield ("Ai lari! alla patria!"). They express their superstitious horror over the supernatural powers that enabled the Maid to lead the French to victory. The vanquished troops curse their foe ("Perduta Orleano").

The camp is suddenly thrown into an uproar as Giacomo staggers in, glaring wildly about him. Driven to the verge of madness by the shame of Giovanna's liaison with King Carlo, Giacomo begs Talbot, through an interpreter, to be allowed to fight with the English ("Questa rea che vi percuote"). In a ringing aria, "Franco son io, ma in core," he sings that, French though he is, he will help defeat the monarch who has dishonored his daughter. He promises to turn Giovanna over to the English.

Talbot acknowledges the offer ("Vien! di guerra in forte"). Giacomo pours out his rage and grief over Giovanna's apparent perfidy in the aria "So che per via." The soldiers commend him for his courage and self-sacrifice ("Nobile vecchio affretatti"), then hail the opportunity to avenge their defeat ("Vien la vendetta").

[*Scene Two*] The court at Rheims. Giovanna, alone, muses in recitative over the mysterious destiny that has brought her to this fateful moment ("Qui! dove più s'apre"). Then, in one of the opera's most moving arias, "O fatidica foresta," she voices her intense longing for home and family. The tender love of those dear to her, she sings, is stronger even than the divine will which commands her to be the savior of France.

She is about to leave when Carlo enters. When she tells him of her decision to return to her home and leave France to her own destiny, he entreats her to stay ("Dunque, o cruda, e gloria e trono"). This marks the beginning of a long, impassioned duet. Carlo sings that she must not leave him, because she has brought him not only victory but love as well. Now her divine mission is to crown him in the cathedral and thus restore him to the throne of France.

Giovanna, powerless to resist him, finally confesses her love, even though she realizes she is courting her own doom. The unseen chorus of evil spirits rises in gloating triumph ("Vittoria! plaudiamo a Satana").

ACT TWO

Outside the Cathedral of Rheims during Carlo's coronation. The throng pays homage to the King in the "Triumphal March" ("Da cielo a noi chi viene"). At the doors of the cathedral, Giacomo waits to confront Giovanna when she emerges with Carlo after the ceremony. In the dramatic romanza "Speme al vecchio era una figlia," he prays that his daughter still may expiate her sins through the ordeal of divine punishment. The doors swing open and Giovanna comes out followed by King Carlo. The throng bursts into a majestic chorus of acclaim, "Te, Dio, lodiam." Carlo pays homage to Giovanna for her heroic defense of France ("Non fuggir, donzella"), declaring she is worthy to be revered with St. Denis as the savior of her country.

Thereupon Giacomo rushes forward and launches into furious denunciation ("M'odi, o re"). He accuses both the King and Giovanna of blasphemy, then charges that his daughter holds secret rendezvous with Satan, who has endowed her with infernal powers. He demands that she confess her guilt then and there, but Giovanna remains silent. There is a crash of thunder; Giacomo cries that thus heaven bears witness to the truth of his charges.

A fiery trio follows ("No! forme d'angelo"): Carlo defends Giovanna, who protests her innocence; Giacomo, in a final desperate entreaty, grasps his daughter's hand and begs her, in the name of God, to admit her guilt ("Dimmi, in nome del Dio"). The vast throng, suddenly seized by mass hysteria, bursts out in condemnation of Giovanna ("Sì! la colpa è manifesta"). Her guilt has been proved, they shout, cursing her as a witch ("Fuggi, o donna maledetta"). They demand that she be handed over to the English to be burned at the stake.

ACT THREE

[Scene One] The English camp, where Giovanna lies chained during the attack by the French. In an eloquent prayer ("Oh, qual mi scuote") she asks for deliverance from the enemy, then admits having broken her vows of chastity by yielding to the temptation of carnal love.

As she prays, Giacomo approaches and listens spellbound. Overwhelmed by her repentance and convinced at last of her ultimate innocence, he rushes forward and impetuously strikes off her chains. Giovanna fervently embraces him, and then father and daughter express their happiness over their reconciliation in a lyrical duet, "Amai, ma un solo instante," one of the climactic moments of the opera. In its outline it foreshadows the famous Violetta-Germont duet in *La Traviata*.

Inspired with new courage, Giovanna asks her father for his sword ("La tua spada!") and rushes out to lead the French again to victory. Giacomo, following, urges her on with a battle cry: "Ecco! Ella vola!"

[*Scene Two*][1] Giovanna, mortally wounded in the battle, is borne back to the fortress—now recaptured—to die. With her fading strength, she holds aloft the banner of the French emblazoned with the fleur-de-lis. Gazing down at the Maid, King Carlo pours out his grief in one of the opera's finest arias, "Quale più fido amico." In mystic ecstasy, Giovanna sings that she sees the vision of the Virgin bending over her with words of divine consolation and forgiveness ("S'apre il cielo . . . Discende la Pia"). Her voice blends with Carlo's and Giacomo's in a final elegiac trio, and at its conclusion Giovanna falls back lifeless.

All on the scene fall to their knees and in wonder and sorrow pay homage to the Maid who brought victory and salvation to France ("Oh, prodigio! d'insolito raggio"). Blending with this closing ensemble is the chorus of the mystical voices which inspired Giovanna—the celestial and infernal spirits—now joining in a paean of redemption.

---

[1] Because of the unavailability of an authorized English translation of the libretto, the closing scene of the opera is presented here in an abridged description.

GIULIO CESARE

by GEORGE FREDERICK HANDEL

(1685–1759)

Libretto by

NICCOLÒ FRANCESCO HAYM

CHARACTERS

Romans

Giulio Cesare (Caius Julius Caesar)	Bass-baritone
Curio, a Roman tribune	Bass
Cornelia, wife of Pompey	Contralto
Sesto (Sextus Pompey), her son	Tenor

Egyptians

Cleopatra, Queen of Egypt	Soprano
Tolemeo (Ptolemy), her brother, King of Egypt	Bass
Achillas, Egyptian general commanding Ptolemy's forces	Bass-baritone
Nirenus, confidant of Cleopatra	Bass

Romans, Egyptians, soldiers, slaves, ladies in waiting

Place: Egypt, after the Battle of Pharsalus
Time: 48 B.C.
First performance: King's Theater, London, February 20, 1724
Original language: Italian

This opera was written during the period when Handel was at the height of his fame in London as an operatic composer and conductor. It was one of twenty operas he wrote during his association with the Royal Academy of Music.

Of all those works, it perhaps comes closest to being "grand opera" in, say, the Verdian sense. Full of vivid action, *Giulio Cesare* abounds in musical utterances that have trenchant emotional thrust. It offers a fusion of the lyric with the dramatic. In the main, the action centers around Cleopatra's manipulation of the destinies of Caesar and Ptolemy, and how she thus changed the course of Egypt's history.[1]

Premiered with a cast including the famous castrato Senesino (Francesco Bernardi), the soprano Francesca Cuzzoni and the basso Giuseppe Boschi, the opera was a resounding success. After the peak of its popularity had passed, it was revived in 1730 and again in 1787. But with the passing of the vogue for baroque opera in the latter half of the eighteenth century, *Giulio Cesare* disappeared from the stage.

In America, a staged revival of the opera by the New York City Opera Company in 1966 and 1968, with Beverly Sills and Norman Treigle in the leading roles, was outstandingly successful. Subsequent productions have proved popular with the American public.

The brief overture begins with a *maestoso* theme leading into an *allegro* expressive of the turbulent course of events which make up the plot of the opera.

ACT ONE

[*Scene One*] A broad plain along the Nile, near a bridge. In a brief martial chorus the Egyptians hail the advancing Roman troops. Caesar strides forward and addresses the throng as the conquering hero ("Presti omai l'Egizia terra"). In an ensuing recitative he utters the historic phrase: "I came, I saw, I conquered." He then tells how he defeated Pompey, who too late had sought the aid of King Ptolemy.

During his discourse, Cornelia and Sextus approach and kneel in abject humility before Caesar. Cornelia makes an eloquent plea for mercy, entreating Caesar to sheathe his sword and bring peace to the land. Caesar tells her he comes in the spirit of forgiveness and asks her to bring Pompey to him as a friend.

At this point Achillas enters attended by slaves, one of whom carries a large covered vessel. He removes the cover, revealing the severed head of Pompey. Caesar and the throng gasp in horror; Cornelia falls fainting into Sextus' arms. Achillas imperturbably explains that this trophy is presented by Ptolemy as "proof of his allegiance."

Caesar bursts out in furious denunciation of Ptolemy for this foul deed ("Empio, dirò, tu sei") against a vanquished foe. He commands Achillas to inform Ptolemy that he will seek him in his palace before nightfall, then angrily orders the general out of his sight. Caesar himself leaves hurriedly, followed by the throng.

[1] At Pharsalus, in the Grecian province of Thessaly, Caesar routed the army of Pompey during the Roman civil war. Pompey fled to Egypt, where he was beheaded by Ptolemy.

Cornelia gives voice to her bitter grief in the aria "Priva son d'ogni conforto," after which she leaves with her ladies in waiting. Sextus, in horror and fury, calls on the avenging Eumenides to strike down the murderer of his father ("Svegliatevi nel core, furie d'un alma offesa").

[*Scene Two*] A gallery in the palace of Ptolemy. Cleopatra enters with Nirenus, whom she orders to take her to Caesar. She remarks that her beauty will gain more from the conqueror than the bloody trophy presented to him by Ptolemy. A moment later her brother enters and angrily accuses her of trying to usurp the throne. When she answers that she claims only what is rightfully hers, Ptolemy caustically advises her to concern herself with needle and thread instead of crown and scepter. Contemptuously branding him a "boudoir hero," Cleopatra sweeps out of the room.

Achillas comes in and describes Caesar's horror and anger when he saw the head of Pompey. The treacherous general goes on to say that when Caesar comes to the palace tonight, that will be the moment to slay him. Or better still, Achillas adds craftily, he himself will do the deed—if Ptolemy will promise him Pompey's widow as his bride. But Ptolemy, while gloating over the prospect of doing away with Caesar, hedges on the promise to his general, whom he curtly dismisses. Alone, he gives voice to his murderous intentions in the ringing aria "L'empio, sleale, indegno."

[*Scene Three*] At a monument to Pompey in Caesar's camp. It is in the form of an urn flanked by weapons and trophies. Standing before the urn, Caesar reflects on Pompey's fate—yesterday a conqueror who held the world in the palm of his hand, today . . . dust and ashes ("Alma del gran Pompeo").

As he stands there brooding, Cleopatra enters, dressed in a simple gown. Kneeling before Caesar, she identifies herself as "Lydia," one of Cleopatra's serving maids. She begs him to protect her from the lecherous advances of Ptolemy. Caesar assures her that when he sees Ptolemy this very evening, he will intercede in her behalf. With a fervent phrase of thanks, Cleopatra leaves. In a lyrical arietta, "Non è si vago e bello," Caesar muses on "Lydia's" beauty and charm. He too leaves.

A moment later Cleopatra returns with Nirenus, who compliments her on capturing the mighty conqueror's heart on their first meeting. In answer, Cleopatra remarks that now she dares Ptolemy, with all his ruthless power, to take the throne. As for herself, the goddess of love will lead her there. She orders Nirenus to bring Caesar to her chambers after he has seen Ptolemy. There, she murmurs voluptuously, she will proffer the hero a love feast that will make him her slave forever.

Seeing Cornelia approaching, Cleopatra and Nirenus hide. The widow, dressed in deep mourning, goes to Pompey's monument and kneels before it. Still crushed by grief, she sings the moving aria "Nel tuo seno," lamenting that she has lost her greatest treasure. Looking up, she sees a dagger among the trophies displayed. She seizes it, crying that it is destined for Ptolemy's heart. At that moment Sextus steps from behind the monument. He snatches the dagger from his mother, declaring that it is a son's duty to avenge his father's murder. But to whom, he wonders, can they turn for help?

Thereupon Cleopatra and Nirenus emerge from their hiding place. Again identifying herself as "Lydia," Cleopatra tells Cornelia that not only will she herself help, but she will summon certain persons who know how to bring the guilty one to justice. In a brief arietta ("Cara speme questo core") Sextus enthuses over the possibility of accomplishing his revenge. He and Cornelia leave.

In wild exultation, Cleopatra relishes the thought of bringing Ptolemy to book for his crimes, and abandons herself to her emotions in the brilliant aria "Tu la mia stella sei." She thanks the gods for aiding her plans. Midway in the aria her mood suddenly changes to tenderness as she thinks of Caesar ("Qual sia di questo core") . . . she sought a throne and found a loving heart. Cleopatra ends the aria on a passionate phrase.

An intermezzo follows during a change of scene. It is from the Concerto Grosso in G minor.

[Scene Four] The palace of Ptolemy, where a reception in honor of Caesar is in progress. Ptolemy, Achillas and various Egyptian dignitaries are watching the dancing girls. In a lusty refrain ("Belle dee di questo core") Ptolemy urges the guests to enjoy the entertainment.

Caesar and his retinue enter. There is an ironic exchange in recitative between Caesar and Ptolemy, bristling with veiled insults. The two monarchs, with their adherents, sit on either side of the hall. Caesar, watching the Egyptians narrowly, comments about Ptolemy in a remarkable aria, "Va tacito e nascosto." He describes him to his courtiers as a relentless hunter, with weapons at the ready, on the trail of his prey. He will not pause until he has destroyed his victim.

After the aria there is an orchestral interlude during which an ominous byplay takes place. As Caesar and his retinue slowly withdraw, a group of Egyptians stealthily follow. When Caesar turns to look back, they stop in their tracks, then advance on him again as he goes on. The effect is of a hunter stalking a human quarry.

Cornelia and Sextus arrive. In bitter irony, Cornelia commends Ptolemy for his magnanimity toward Pompey. Sextus, cursing Ptolemy, lunges at him with a sword. Instantly the boy and his mother are surrounded by Egyptian guards. Ptolemy orders Sextus imprisoned. He tells Cornelia she will be consigned to his harem, where she will be taught proper respect for the emperor.

Achillas, sidling up to Cornelia, slyly asks her to be his bride, promising her freedom if she consents. Cornelia rebuffs him with furious contempt. When Sextus, overhearing, shouts that his mother would die rather than consort with an Egyptian, Achillas orders him to the dungeon. Clasping her son in her arms, Cornelia desperately pleads for mercy. They bid each other farewell in a poignant duet, "Son nata a lagrimar."

ACT TWO

[*Scene One*] The palace of Cleopatra. It is a starry night. Nirenus escorts Caesar to Cleopatra's chambers, where he gazes in astonishment at the luxurious furnishings. Cleopatra enters, regally dressed. Approaching Caesar, she gives expression to her amorous feelings in the beguiling aria "V'adoro, pupille," sung over muted strings. Caesar listens in hypnotic fascination.

But the romantic spell is broken when Nirenus bursts in exclaiming that soldiers are at the doors shouting that Caesar must die. He begs Caesar to make his escape. At this point Cleopatra discloses her real identity and cries that weapons cannot harm the Queen of Egypt. Caesar is thunderstruck. Assuring him that she will thwart his enemies, Cleopatra rushes away. A moment later she reappears, declaring that even her power as Queen cannot stem the fury of the invaders. But when she entreats Caesar to flee, he draws his sword and shouts that Caesar knows no fear. In the great aria "Al lampo dell'armi" he voices his defiance. As he rushes out, cries of "death to Caesar" are heard. Sinking to her knees, Cleopatra implores the gods for his protection in the stately aria "Se pietà di me non senti."

[*Scene Two*] In Ptolemy's harem, Cornelia expresses her hopelessness and shame in the arietta "Deh piangete, oh mesti lumi." Nirenus rushes in with the unwelcome news that Ptolemy is on his way to the harem to speak with her. Even more disturbing is the news that Sextus, with the help of Nirenus, bribed his jailers to free him and is coming to kill Ptolemy.

With deceptive gentleness, Ptolemy attempts to persuade Cornelia to submit to his desires. She turns on him with furious scorn. Enraged, he warns that her refusal only serves to inflame him further ("Si spietata, il tuo rigore"), and that he is determined to have his way with her. At the conclusion of the aria he forces Cornelia to her knees.

At that moment Sextus rushes in with drawn sword and springs toward Ptolemy. But before he can strike, Achillas and his soldiers burst in. One of the soldiers wrenches the sword out of Sextus' hands. At the same time, Achillas thrusts another sword toward Ptolemy and warns him to prepare for battle. He tells him that Caesar, cornered by the Egyptian soldiers, leaped from the palace balcony into the sea and was drowned. Cleopatra, at the head of the Roman troops, is on her way to the palace to avenge Caesar's death.

Then Achillas asks Ptolemy if he will now make good his promise to give him Cornelia as his bride. Ptolemy harshly tells him to get out of his sight, and turns away. Watching him go, Achillas swears revenge. Tossing Sextus the sword wrested from him earlier, the general leaves. When Sextus laments that he has failed in his attempt at revenge and is not worthy to be called his father's son, Cornelia bids him not to lose courage and exhorts him to fight on. Regaining his confidence, Sextus declares he will never rest until the murder is avenged ("Langue offeso mai riposa").

ACT THREE

[*Scene One*] The curtain rises to the sound of battle music. The scene is Ptolemy's encampment on the seacoast near Alexandria. In his headquarters, Ptolemy stands gazing at Cleopatra, who is being guarded like a captive by soldiers. With savage satisfaction, Ptolemy boasts that he still is King and conqueror, despite the fact that Achillas betrayed him with the false story of Caesar's death. When Cleopatra defiantly answers that it was not he, but blind Fate, that caused her defeat, Ptolemy orders her to be put in irons. He leaves.

Dejected and alone, Cleopatra gives way to her despair in the aria "Piangerò la sorte mia," one of the opera's finest numbers. At a sign from her guards, she walks slowly away.

[*Scene Two*] A spot on the shore near the encampment, where Caesar, staggering from exhaustion, is seen approaching from the water's edge. In recitative, he recalls how he was rescued from the sea . . . once more he has escaped death. But now, he muses, where shall he begin again . . . where are his legions . . . where are his weapons? He continues his reflection in the aria "Aure, deh, per pietà," imploring the sea to restore him to strength, to good fortune and to his beloved.

As he stands facing the sea, Sextus comes in leading Achillas, who is mortally wounded. A dramatic scene in recitative ensues. With his life ebbing away, the general makes his dying confession. First he asks Sextus to go to Cornelia. He is to tell her that it was he—Achillas—who plotted the murder of Pompey. It was because he loved her and wanted her as his bride that he also joined the plot against Caesar. As reward,

Ptolemy had promised him Cornelia, but the King treacherously broke his word. In revenge, Achillas says, he betrayed Ptolemy by inciting his own soldiers against him.

Drawing a signet ring from his finger, Achillas tells Sextus to take it to a nearby cavern, where a hundred armed soldiers are concealed. When he shows them the ring they will obey him without question, and will accompany him through a secret underground passage into the city. There they will find Cornelia as a prisoner of Ptolemy. They are to rescue Cornelia and then slay the King. Thus, Achillas gasps, his revenge will be complete and he will die in peace. With that the general falls back dead.

Caesar, who had approached unobserved just as Achillas handed Sextus the ring, now strides forward. Identifying himself, he asks Sextus for the ring. Sextus staggers back in surprise. Caesar tells him that he himself will lead the hidden soldiers to the rescue of Cornelia and of Cleopatra as well. In a ringing aria, "Quel torrente, che cade dal monte," he sings that vengeance, like a mighty torrent, will sweep his enemy to destruction.

[*Scene Three*] Ptolemy's tent on the battlefield, where Cleopatra is held prisoner with her ladies in waiting. She sorrowfully tells them that their days of serving her are over, because she has been condemned to death by this monstrous tyrant—her own brother, who has usurped her crown.

Suddenly, shouting and the clash of weapons are heard outside. In the next moment the entrance curtain of the tent is ripped away and Caesar strides in. Cleopatra stares at him in terror and unbelief, convinced she is seeing a ghost. When he assures her he is not a phantom, but has come to set her free, she rushes to him with a joyous, passionate cry. Caesar tells her that the final, decisive battle is at hand . . . Mars has commanded and he obeys. He will fight for Egypt and for the world itself, inspired by the fire she has kindled within him.

They clasp each other in an impassioned embrace. Cleopatra hails her hero in a dazzling aria, "Da tempeste il legno." Her ladies in waiting adorn her with the royal mantle symbolizing her rightful claim to the throne as Queen of Egypt.

[*Scene Four*] The banks of the Nile, as in Act One. Roman and Egyptian soldiers are arrayed on either side of the scene, with the tribune Curio at the head of the Roman troops. To a blazing martial fanfare, Caesar rides up in his chariot as Egyptian dignitaries escort Cleopatra from her tent. Caesar steps from his chariot to greet her. In recitative, Curio acclaims Caesar as Egypt's liberator. The latter thanks him for his loyal service and assures him that the fame of his troops has spread throughout the world.

Cornelia and Sextus come forward and kneel to receive a cordial greeting from Caesar. Sextus announces that he has slain the tyrant Ptolemy and that now his father is avenged. Caesar says that Pompey was indeed fortunate in having so noble a son. Turning to Cleopatra, he places a golden crown on her head and hails her as Queen of Egypt.

A ballet—the "War Dance," in which youths are vanquished by temple virgins in a simulated battle—is performed before the assemblage. Then Caesar leads Cleopatra forward and the two apostrophize their happiness in a lyrical duet, "Caro! Bella! Più amabile beltà." At its conclusion the throng hails the couple in a mighty chorus of triumph, "Ritorni omai nel nostro core."

GUILLAUME TELL
(*William Tell*)
by GIOACCHINO ROSSINI
(1792–1868)

Libretto by

ÉTIENNE DE JOUY, HIPPOLYTE-LOUIS-FLORENT BIS
and ARMAND MARRAST

Based on the play *Wilhelm Tell*, by Friedrich von Schiller

CHARACTERS

Guillaume Tell ⎫	Baritone
Arnold ⎬ Swiss patriots	Tenor
Walter Fürst ⎭	Bass
Hedwige, Tell's wife	Mezzo-soprano
Jemmy, his son	Soprano
Melchthal, Arnold's father	Bass
Gessler (or Gesler), Governor of Swiss Cantons	Bass
Rudolph, captain of Gessler's bodyguard	Tenor
Ruodi, a fisherman	Tenor
Leuthold, a shepherd	Bass
Mathilde, a Hapsburg princess	Soprano

Peasants of the three cantons—Schwyz, Uri and Unterwald—shepherds, shepherdesses, ladies of Mathilde's court, hunters, soldiers and guards of Gessler, pages

Place: Switzerland
Time: Circa A.D. 1200–1300
First performance: Grand Opéra, Paris, August 3, 1829
Original language: French

Guillaume Tell involves one of the most extraordinary episodes in the history of opera. Rossini, thirty-seven years old, had composed thirty-nine operas in nineteen years. After he composed *Tell* in 1829, he stopped composing operas.

Personal considerations aside (nervous disorder, physical exhaustion, etc.), Rossini had his own artistic reasons for deciding that *Guillaume Tell* was to be his final work in that genre. He had reached the conclusion, after his succession of comic operas, that *opera seria* was more important than *opera buffa*. He also was aware that a new form of opera was finding favor with the public, which had lost interest in classical mythological plots, and was demanding realism.

This new vogue reflected the political ferment in Europe. The plot of *Tell* supplied the elements that brought opera closer to contemporary life: the people's revolt against tyranny. The story of *Tell* unfolds against the background of the struggle of the Swiss people to regain their freedom after being subjugated by the Austrian Empire.

Rossini took exceptional pains with the opera—the first one he wrote exclusively for the French stage. It is acknowledged as his masterpiece, although flawed by a clumsy and overlong libretto.[1] It was mildly received by the Parisian public but acclaimed by the press. During Rossini's lifetime, it received more than five hundred performances at the Paris Opéra. Meanwhile, in an Italian translation, it was heard throughout the world.

Guillaume Tell was in the repertoire of the Metropolitan Opera during its 1884–85 season. Subsequent revivals were given there on January 5, 1922 (Martinelli, Ponselle, Sundelius, Danise, Mardones), and on March 21, 1930 (Lauri-Volpi, Fleischer, Pinza, Danise, Petrova).

The world-famous overture, characterized as a symphonic poem in miniature, opens with a serene pastoral theme which is interrupted by a kettledrum roll heralding the approaching Alpine storm. A furious *allegro* depicts the storm itself. After the storm passes, the music again subsides into a pastoral mood as the English horns sound the *ranz des vaches*—the call that Swiss herdsmen blow on Alpine horns to call cattle from lower to higher pastures in June. The overture concludes in a spirited fanfare sounded principally by hunting horns.

ACT ONE

William Tell's chalet near Lake Lucerne. Tell, standing at one side leaning on his spade, is deep in thought. Jemmy is practicing with his bow and arrow; Hedwige is sitting before the house, plaiting a basket.

[1] In fact, Rossini was beset by libretto problems. He first engaged Jouy, but rejected his libretto and called in Bis as well as Marrast. Originally in five acts, *Tell* was cut down to three by omitting Act Three and condensing Act Four and Act Five into one act. The opera later was usually staged in four acts as presented here.

Toward the rear, peasants are decorating three small chalets being made ready for three newly wedded pairs.

In the opening chorus the peasants gratefully hail the beautiful morning that presages a day of cloudless skies ("Quel jour serein le ciel présage"). They turn to watch Ruodi, a fisherman, approach in his boat. In a spirited refrain ("Accours dans nacelle") he invites his sweetheart to come for a ride. But the mood of the music momentarily darkens as Tell sings that while this happy youth is thinking only of love and pleasure, dark clouds of tyranny are overshadowing the land. Ruodi's lighthearted song merges ironically in a quartet with Tell, Hedwige and Jemmy. They decry his heedless courage in ignoring the dangers that lurk both for him and his trusting maiden.

From the distance comes the sound of the *ranz des vaches*. To the peasants, it is a signal that the day's work is over, and now they can enjoy their leisure. The village patriarch, Melchthal, enters leaning on the arm of his son Arnold. The peasants greet him respectfully ("Salut, honneur, hommages"). Tell, Hedwige, Jemmy and the peasants request the patriarch to give his blessing, in traditional fashion, to the three couples who are plighting their troth on this festive day. Melchthal graciously responds ("Pasteurs, que vous accéder"), and this cues in a resounding chorus of homage ("Aux chants joyeux"), built mainly on the theme of the *ranz des vaches*.

In recitative, Tell invites Melchthal and Arnold to his chalet. Moved by Tell's affectionate greeting to Hedwige and Jemmy, Melchthal turns to Arnold and asks why he has not yet made plans to marry and thus enjoy the happiness of a home and family of his own. His father and the others leave.

Alone, Arnold bitterly reflects that such happiness can never be his. He is hopelessly in love with Mathilde, a princess of the hated Austrians —and thus he is betraying not only his country, but his own father as well.[2] Like all his countrymen, Arnold cannot forget history: the Austrians had been traditional enemies of the Swiss since they had seized power over Switzerland more than one hundred years before.

At the same time, he ruefully recalls that by an ironic twist of fate he rescued this princess—herself a symbol of tyranny—from drowning in a raging mountain torrent. And for her love, to compound his shame, he has enlisted in the Austrian Army, completely repudiating his love for his own country. Suddenly a fanfare of hunting horns announces the approach of Gessler, his court and his soldiers.

Exulting that now he will meet his beloved Mathilde, Arnold is about to rush away when he is stopped by Tell. A dramatic colloquy ensues

[2] In some versions of the libretto, Mathilde is identified as Gessler's daughter; in others, as his sister.

("Où vas-tu?"). Noticing Arnold's agitation, Tell asks the reason. Arnold replies that he is concerned about the approach of the Austrians. Watching him closely, Tell concludes that Arnold is pretending—and this is confirmed in Arnold's aside: "Ah! Mathilde, my soul's idol!" ("Mathilde, idole de mon âme!").

Still trying to justify his actions, Arnold tries to warn Tell of the danger in resisting the Austrians. Dramatically he points to the chalet where Hedwige and Jemmy are waiting ("Songe aux biens que tu perds!"—"Think of what you will lose!"). Tell answers that he knows the risks—but it is better to die than to live as slaves. In a continuation of the duet, Arnold, wavering, sings that he will renounce his love, but not his country and his family.

It needs only Tell's well-timed cry of "Melchthal! Melchthal!" to transform Arnold into a fervent patriot who will forswear his love for Mathilde to fight for his father and the freedom of Switzerland. The duet climaxes as the voices of Arnold and Tell merge in a phrase of defiance: "Death I swear the foe!" ("Malheur à nos tyrans!").

A choral ensemble follows ("Oh light of heaven"—"Ciel, qui du monde") as the peasants hail the three bridal couples, who enter in procession and kneel before Melchthal. Performing the nuptial rites, he exhorts them to be faithful to each other and to their country. Over an ominous horn phrase, Tell breaks in to warn that Gessler and his company are coming nearer. At this point, Arnold disappears. Tell urges the people not to quail before Gessler's taunts, and to stand firm against the threats of the Austrians.

Meanwhile, he has noticed that Arnold has left, and concludes that the young man fears the consequences of his betrayal. Saying that he will go to look for him, he tells Hedwige to take charge of the wedding festivities. The merriment, he adds, will hide from Gessler the fact that revolt is brewing. The peasants join in a joyful nuptial chorus ("Hyménée, ta journée"), which is followed by a ballet.

In an ensuing ensemble, the peasants pay homage to Jemmy as Tell's brave son. Jemmy and Hedwige are happily surprised. A company of archers begins a march around the stage. The peasants burst into a defiant ensemble ("Children of hardy Nature"—"Enfants de la nature"). They sing that the swords and lances of the invader will be no match for the arrows of simple but hardy peasants whose courage is as firm as their beloved mountains.

The merrymaking comes to an abrupt stop as the shepherd Leuthold staggers in, disheveled and carrying a bloodstained ax. To the shocked peasants he gasps that he is being pursued by Gessler's soldiers. One of them tried to abduct his only daughter, the shepherd goes on, and he killed the attacker with a blow of his ax.

Leuthold, now fleeing for his life, cries that if he can get across Lake

Lucerne he will be safe from his pursuers. When he appeals to Ruodi, the fisherman protests that it would be certain death to cross the lake at this time. Leuthold turns on him in fury, denouncing him for refusing to help a neighbor whose life is at stake.

At this point Tell returns with the news that he cannot find Arnold. Then he hears Gessler's search party shouting for Leuthold, and at the same time the shepherd begs him to save his life. When Leuthold tells him that Ruodi refused to row him to safety, Tell declares that he himself will ferry the hapless shepherd across the lake. Bidding a hasty farewell to his tearful wife and Jemmy, he and Leuthold prepare to embark just as the Austrian soldiers close in.

As a foreboding rhythm throbs in the orchestra, the Swiss kneel and offer a prayer for the safety of Tell and Leuthold ("Dieu de bonté"). This introduces the long and powerful ensemble which concludes the act. The prayer is interrupted when the Austrians burst in, led by Rudolph, captain of Gessler's bodyguard, who warns that there will be no mercy for those who defy their Austrian rulers.

Rudolph angrily demands the name of the miscreant who helped their quarry escape, as Gessler's soldiers warn the Swiss that the lives of their wives and children are at stake. The Swiss reply that they will not betray the one who befriended them. Their defiance is underscored by Melchthal, who majestically confronts Rudolph. Tell your master, he declares, that there are no traitors or spies in these mountains. At that, Rudolph, in a towering rage, threatens the Swiss with "pillage and slaughter" ("Que de ravages"). Undaunted, the Swiss, although surrounded now by Gessler's soldiers, continue to shout their defiance. At the climax of the scene, Gessler's guard seize Melchthal. The unarmed peasants make a desperate effort to free him, but are driven back by the spears of the soldiers. They finally drag the patriarch away.

ACT TWO

A clearing in a pine forest high up in the Swiss mountains. A stirring fanfare introduces a hunting chorus ("Quelle sauvage harmonie") sung by lords and ladies of Gessler's court, and by hunters bearing the trophies of the chase. In the distance they hear the fanfare that signals that the hunt is over. All leave the scene except Mathilde, who has slipped away from her companions to be alone with her thoughts of Arnold.

After a prelude notable for its unique clusters of triplets in thirds and fifths, Mathilde reflects on her lover ("Elles s'éloignent enfin"). She is sure that he has followed her here, and her beating heart betrays her abiding love for this simple yet noble mountaineer. Then she gives way to her emotions in one of the arias for which the score is famous: "Sombre forêt, désert triste et sauvage" ("Oh gloomy forest, solitary wilderness"). She sings that she prefers the serenity of this retreat to the hectic glitter of the court. Looking up, she sees Venus, the star of love, and prays that it will be her guide.

Arnold appears. In a duet ("Oui, vous l'arrachez à mon âme"), they greet each other in mingled joy and despair while giving way to their overwhelming passion for each other, even though they realize their love is hopeless: the gulf between them is too deep. Yet Mathilde urges Arnold to seek glory on the field of battle—in the service of the Austrians—and sings that her love will inspire him to great deeds ("Retournez aux champs de la gloire").

Mathilde suddenly warns that she hears footsteps. Telling Arnold to meet her at dawn in the nearby chapel of Our Lady, she hurries away. Arnold turns to confront Tell and Walter Fürst, a young and rather overzealous patriot. A somewhat acrimonious exchange follows. When Tell offers a mock apology for interrupting this woodland tryst, Arnold angrily infers he has been spying. Walter interjects that there are far better ways of serving their cause than trysting. But our cause is no longer Arnold's, Tell declares, because he has secretly joined the Austrians. Arnold is stung to fury by the accusation.

It is for the love of Mathilde—daughter of their worst enemy—that this man has turned traitor, Tell goes on relentlessly. Recoiling at this insinuation, Arnold storms that he will not fight for a country that is no longer his—a country torn by hatred and strife and not worth defending. He will leave it forever, he cries, to seek glory and honor elsewhere.

In a powerful aria ("Quand l'Helvétie est un champ de supplice"), Tell denounces Arnold for his betrayal. Then he stuns him with the news that the very tyrant he has sworn to serve has executed Melchthal for treason. In anguish and remorse, Arnold reproaches himself for having deserted his father in the hour of his death ("Ses jours qu'ils ont osés proscrire"). This leads into a trio in which Tell and Walter sing that Arnold's remorse and horror have banished all thoughts of his traitorous love for Mathilde and have spurred him to avenge his father's murder.

When Arnold declares he will seek out Gessler at once to punish him for his crimes, Tell counsels him to bide his time. The hour of vengeance will soon be at hand: even now Swiss patriots are assembling in a secret place, their only weapons spades and plowshares. At the appointed hour they will strike the blow for freedom. In a continuation of the trio, the three men join hands and sing that sacred Freedom will inspire them to victory.

Soon they are joined by the men of the cantons of Unterwald, Schwyz and Uri. They enter stealthily to the accompaniment of a martial theme which is the music of the "Gathering of the Cantons." Then the scene builds into the thunderous ensemble that climaxes the act.

They sing that they will have their revenge on Gessler for his cruel tyranny, and then drive the Austrians out of Switzerland forever. The ensemble ends with a soaring choral phrase: "Aux armes!"

ACT THREE

[*Scene One*] Interior of the shrine of Our Lady, a ruined chapel on the grounds of Gessler's palace at Altdorf, where Mathilde and Arnold have met for their final farewell. In a recitative passage, Arnold tells the princess that he must renounce her love and his dreams of glory to avenge his father's murder. To Mathilde's horror, he reveals that it is Gessler who ordered his father's execution. In a moving aria, "Pour notre amour plus d'espérance," Mathilde sings that now nothing is left of their love but hopelessness and despair.

Their rendezvous is interrupted by an outburst of shouting and the blaring of trumpets from the direction of the palace. Mathilde warns Arnold that Gessler is summoning his court for festivities. She implores her lover to flee: to be discovered here would mean certain death. As for herself, she sings dolorously, she cannot remain to share his love in this alien land—and so . . . this is farewell forever ("adieu, c'est pour toujours!"). The duet ends with this despairing phrase.

[*Scene Two*] The scene changes to a plaza in front of Gessler's palace, where preparations are being made to celebrate the centenary of Austrian rule over Switzerland. At stage center is a flagpole surmounted by Gessler's hat, a fatuous symbol of his power. A chorus of soldiers lustily hails the mighty ruler ("Gloire au pouvoir suprême").

Gessler pompously warns that there are reports of civil disobedience in the land, which will not be tolerated. Then at his order the soldiers force the Swiss to march past the flagpole and bow to the hat as a gesture of submission to Austrian rule. Adding insult to injury, he commands them to sing and dance in celebration of the Austrian victory over the Swiss a hundred years ago. Then follow a ballet, with choral accompaniment, and a military review.

At the conclusion, Rudolph suddenly confronts Tell, demanding to know why he has not bowed to the hat. Tell retorts that though his people have been degraded, he himself will never bow to a tyrant. When Gessler angrily asks who dares defy him, Rudolph identifies Tell as the notorious malcontent who helped Leuthold, the murderer, to escape. Gessler forthwith orders Tell to be seized and bound in chains. Jemmy rushes sobbing to his father, who embraces him tenderly.

An agitated quartet develops as Tell excoriates Gessler as a heartless oppressor; Gessler and Rudolph curse Tell as a traitor, while Jemmy assures his father that if he dies his son will die with him. In an aside, Tell sends Jemmy to his mother with a message: she is to tell the Swiss in the three cantons that every beacon is to be lighted at nightfall as a signal for revolt.

Suddenly Gessler has an evil inspiration. When Tell asks only that Jemmy's life be spared, Gessler coldly replies that his son's fate lies in his own hands. This patriot, he sarcastically tells the crowd, is renowned as an archer. Very well, then. Let an apple be placed on the boy's head. If the arrow finds its mark, he will be freed. If not, this rebel will die with his son.

As pandemonium breaks out, Tell falls to his knees and implores Gessler not to impose this terrible ordeal. In savage triumph, Gessler sneers that he has finally brought this proud rebel to his knees. Tell almost loses courage, but rallies when Jemmy, with childlike trust, says he is not afraid, because he knows his father's skill. Resolutely, Tell calls for his crossbow and arrows. He selects one, conceals another in his jacket. At this point, one of Mathilde's pages slips away and runs toward the palace.

Tell, desperately trying to control himself, asks Gessler if he may embrace his son once more. Gessler assents. Quietly, Tell instructs the boy to kneel, not to move a muscle—and to pray ("Sois immobile . . . invoque Dieu"). He takes careful aim, shoots and the apple flies from Jemmy's head. The Swiss shout with joy; Gessler curses in fury and frustration. Jemmy runs to his father and embraces him. As he does so, the second arrow falls out of Tell's jacket. Gessler sees it and asks, in an unaccompanied phrase: "For whom was the second arrow?" ("À qui destinais-tu ce trait?"). There is a crashing chord in the orchestra. "For you," Tell replies. Gessler understands: he himself would have been the target, had Tell's first arrow killed his son. Raging, Gessler condemns both Tell and Jemmy to death.

Just as he pronounces the sentence, Mathilde and some of her court rush in. Confronting Gessler, she warns him not to condemn an innocent boy, and that she will answer for this child's life in the name of the King of Austria himself. As the Swiss express their gratitude for Mathilde's intercession, Rudolph reminds the infuriated Gessler that he can still wreak his vengeance on Tell himself.

Well then, Gessler snarls, he will make an example once and for all of this insolent rebel: he will be thrown into the dungeon at Küsnacht, across the lake, where he will be eaten alive by venomous snakes. All on the scene cry out in horrified protest at this gruesome sentence. This builds into another of the opera's great ensembles. Mathilde reiterates her vow to save Jemmy; Gessler and his soldiers rail against Tell as their archenemy; Tell and his adherents curse the tyrannical Governor.

ACT FOUR

[*Scene One*] Arnold's ancestral home in the mountains, where he has come to spend a quiet hour with memories of his happy boyhood before he is plunged into the violence of the impending revolt. But his memories are tinged with bitterness: it was at this pleasant retreat that his father was branded a traitor, then dragged to his doom by Gessler's soldiers. Arnold recalls the bittersweet past in the aria "Asile hérédi-taire."

His reflections are interrupted by the shouts of the Swiss revolu-tionaries, mobilized for the attack on Gessler's forces, calling for venge-ance. They explain that William Tell has been imprisoned, and ask Ar-nold's help in freeing him. Arnold tells them that his father had foreseen this crucial hour and had secreted a cache of arms in his home. In fiery exultation he calls on the Swiss to follow him to Altdorf, where they will seal Gessler's doom ("Amis, secondez ma vengeance"). Ar-nold's voice soars over the chorus in one of the most spectacular arias in opera. With Arnold leading them the soldiers rush off.[3]

[*Scene Two*] On the shores of Lake Lucerne, below Tell's chalet. A violent storm is churning up the waves on the lake. Neighbor women offer their sympathy to Hedwige, who is trying to see Gessler to beg for mercy for her husband and her son. She gasps in surprise when she hears the voices of Jemmy and Mathilde. They joyfully embrace. Jemmy discloses that through Mathilde's efforts Tell will soon escape from the prison.

In an ensuing trio ("Je rends à votre amour"), Mathilde assures Hedwige and Jemmy of Tell's safe return, and the two express their gratitude for her help. To give them even greater comfort, Mathilde promises to be hostage for Tell until he is freed. Jemmy leaves to light the beacon that is to be the signal for the final revolt. Mathilde and Hedwige, joined by the neighbors, sing a prayer for Tell's safety ("Toi, qui du faible est l'espérance").

[3] This aria involves an interesting bit of operatic history. In one phrase—"Trom-pons l'espérance homicide, arrachons"—it rises from middle G, through A, B-flat and B-natural to a sustained high C. The Paris Opéra tenor Gilbert-Louis Duprez (1806–96) was the first to sing a high C "from the chest," a feat which won him the accolade of the greatest tenor of his day. Rossini's reported comment: "It sounded like the squawk of a capon whose throat is being cut."

As a sidelight on the relative merits of the "chest tone" and the "head tone," it is told that Adolphe Nourrit, a contemporary rival of Duprez, took the high C-sharp in the Mathilde/Arnold duet in Act Two ("Oui, vous l'arrachez à mon âme") "easily in head voice." Duprez omitted it altogether.

At its conclusion Leuthold rushes in with the news that Tell has escaped and is about to make the dangerous crossing of the lake. A vivid orchestral interlude depicts the rising fury of the storm. Finally the boat touches shore and Tell is fervently greeted by Hedwige and Jemmy, who hands him his crossbow and arrows. At that moment Gessler and his soldiers appear, shouting that the rebel will not escape them. As Gessler approaches, Tell raises his crossbow, takes careful aim and shoots. With an arrow through his heart, Gessler plunges backward into the lake. His soldiers flee in terror.

Walter Fürst and a detachment of Swiss come storming in. Walter says they have seen the beacon of revolt and are ready to deal with Gessler. Pointing to the lake, Tell says: "There is his tomb" ("Dans le lac . . . sa tombe"). There is a chorus of cheers from the throng. But Tell warns them not to rejoice too soon: Altdorf is still in the hands of Gessler's troops, who will surely seek revenge for his death.

At that moment Arnold appears at the head of the rest of the Swiss forces. Holding aloft the banner that flew before Gessler's castle during the centenary celebration, he announces that Altdorf fell before the onslaught of the Swiss. As the throng acclaims the good news, Arnold, aside, grieves that his father is absent on this day of liberation.

The storm has passed and the mountains are bathed in sunshine under a clear blue sky. Tell exhorts the people to give thanks for their hard-won freedom. In a soaring ensemble, the Swiss hail William Tell as their liberator. The curtain falls.

HÉRODIADE

(*Herodias*)

by JULES MASSENET

(1842–1912)

Libretto by

PAUL MILLIET and HENRI GRÉMONT

Based on Gustave Flaubert's novelette *Herodias*

CHARACTERS

John the Baptist	Tenor
Herod Antipas, Tetrarch of Judea	Baritone
Phanuel, Herod's chief adviser, soothsayer and astrologer	Bass
Vitellius, Roman Proconsul	Baritone
Chief Priest	Baritone
A Voice	Tenor
Salome, daughter of Herodias	Soprano
Herodias	Mezzo-soprano
A young Babylonian girl	Soprano

Israelites, Canaanites, Pharisees, guards, Ethiopian slaves, dancing girls, populace

Place: Jerusalem
Time: A.D. 30
First performance: Théâtre de la Monnaie, Brussels, December 17, 1881
Original language: French

Hérodiade, Massenet's fourth opera (he wrote twenty-five in forty-seven years), has the same central characters as Richard Strauss's *Salome*—but there the similarity ends. Where Strauss's depraved princess lusts for the head of John the Baptist, in Massenet's opera it is Herodias who demands his head—because he had denounced her as Jezebel.[1]

---

[1] The wife of Ahab, who introduced pagan worship, persecuted Elijah, and instigated murders. Her name became a symbol of evil and depravity. (II Kings, Chapter 9.)

Moreover, Massenet's Salome loved the Prophet with passionate devotion—as contrasted to the necrophiliac obsession which transformed her Straussian counterpart into a demon. Further, where the Wilde-Strauss plot generally follows the episode of Herod, Herodias, Salome and John in Chapter 6 of the Gospel of St. Mark and Chapter 14 in the Gospel of St. Matthew, Massenet's opera deviates entirely from those biblical accounts.

Abandoned by her mother, Salome had arrived in Jerusalem with a caravan of Jewish merchants. In the desert she had met John, who befriended her. She did not know Herodias was her mother. On seeing Salome, Herod fell violently in love with her, goading Herodias to lethal jealousy. Herod, in turn, became madly jealous when Salome confessed her love for the Prophet. The result was that Salome and John were doubly condemned to death.

Reprieved, Salome begged Herodias to spare John. Then she saw the executioner enter with a bloody sword in his hand. Dagger in hand, she sprang at Herodias, who screamed: "I am your mother!" Salome plunged the dagger into her own body. Herodias collapsed over the body of her daughter.

Premiered in Brussels, *Hérodiade* was a brilliant success. So popular was Massenet at the time that four hundred Parisian opera buffs traveled to Brussels for the performance. The opera was produced in Paris February 1, 1884, with such superstars as Jean and Édouard de Reszke (John and Phanuel, respectively), Victor Maurel (Herod), Zelia Trebelli (Herodias) and Fidés-Devriés (Salome). In a 1903 revival in Paris, Emma Calvé sang Salome. She also appeared on occasion as Herodias. In 1904, *Hérodiade* was given as *Salomé*, the title change having been ordered by the Lord Chamberlain for reasons of his own. The first American performance was at the New Orleans Opera February 13, 1892; first New York performance, Manhattan Opera House, November 8, 1909, with Lina Cavalieri as Salome.

The brief overture, which opens with serene arpeggios, is dominated by an insistent figure (later associated with John the Baptist) which is finally restated in a full-orchestra climax.

ACT ONE

[*Scene One*] A court in the palace of Herod in Jerusalem. It is dawn. There is a milling crowd of townspeople and slaves, mingled with merchants and traders hawking their wares—a typical scene in an oriental marketplace. In the opening chorus ("Alerte! Levez-vous! Le palais est ouvert!") the crowd notes the opening of the palace gates and the beginning of another day of marketing. The slaves sing of the treasures brought to Herod the Tetrarch by the Jewish caravan—gold, silver, incense, perfumes. During the bargaining a fight develops.

At the height of the uproar Phanuel appears and angrily restores order; the crowd melts away. Alone, Phanuel gloomily reflects on the factional strife that divides the Israelites and leaves them at the mercy of the Roman conquerors ("Le monde est inquiet"). He watches sadly as the merchants and traders leave the courtyard.

To the accompaniment of a triplet passage in the orchestra, Salome appears and hesitantly approaches Phanuel, who stares at her in surprise. He asks why she has come to Jerusalem. Aside, he wonders if this innocent child really knows "of what blood she is born." Salome explains that—as usual—she is seeking her mother. A voice told her to come to Jerusalem, but her mother is not here. And so again, she sighs, she is all alone.

But in a sudden change of mood, Salome exclaims that there is someone here who will help her: the Prophet ("Le Prophète est ici!"). Then follows the lovely aria "Il est doux, il est bon," in which she pours out her love for John the Baptist. He is gentle and kind, she sings, and when he spoke she found sublime peace. In passionate ecstasy she sings that she can no longer live without him.

Phanuel listens entranced by her innocence and ardor, then gently assures her that she can count on his friendship and bids her let her faith be her guide. He looks on her with tender concern as she says farewell; then he himself leaves.

An agitated theme stirs in the orchestra as Herod strides in, distraught and excited. He exclaims that Salome has fled the palace ("Elle a fui le palais") and that the thought of her seductive charms is driving him mad. In an impassioned refrain ("Déesse ou femme au charme séducteur") he gives way to his sensual desire for this beautiful creature—"goddess or woman"—imploring her to return ("Salomé! je te veux. Reviens!").

To the accompaniment of a furious triplet outburst in the orchestra Herodias storms in, crying that she was accosted by a half-naked wild man with blazing eyes who denounced her and called her Jezebel ("Venge-moi d'une suprême offense!"). Herod impatiently asks if she knows who this man is. "John the Baptist," Herodias screams—then demands his head.

As Herod recoils, she frantically begs him not to refuse her this request ("Ne me refuse pas!"). This marks the beginning of a tempestuous aria in which Herodias plays on Herod's sympathy as a wronged wife. She reminds him that for his love she abandoned her child and her family. She recalls the happy days of their courtship on the banks of the Tiber, conjuring up the vision of the goddess Diana blessing their union. Although Herodias climaxes her aria in feverish supplication, Herod coldly rejects her pleading. He reminds her that John the Baptist is a powerful friend of the Jews, who rely on him for help.

When Herodias sneers at him for making excuses, a furious quarrel breaks out. Herod thunders that he intends to remain master in his own empire, and orders her out of his sight. Herodias vows she will accomplish her revenge in her own way. In a foreboding phrase (it ranges from high A-flat to B-natural below the staff) she sings: "John, I shall strike thee down!" ("Jean, je te frapperai!").

At that moment John himself stalks in, echoing her threat with icy deliberation. Both Herod and Herodias cry out in terror. A turbulent trio ensues as John fiercely reiterates his denunciation ("Jézabel, pas de pitié"), while Herod and Herodias implore him to have mercy. Finally, shaken by the Prophet's maledictions, the two stumble blindly into the palace. The thunderous accompaniment subsides into a menacing theme stated deep in the bass as John contemptuously watches them go.

Salome enters, rushes over to John and with a joyous cry of greeting throws herself at his feet. Gazing down at her compassionately, he asks why she has come. In a rapturous aria ("Ce que je veux te dire est que je t'aime") she pours out her love for him.

John tries in vain to calm her, but her impassioned entreaties grow more intense. Almost yielding to her embrace, he begs her to leave him. Impulsively, Salome loosens her hair and wraps it around his knees in a gesture of voluptuous abandon.

Realizing that Salome is helpless in the grip of her emotions, the Prophet exhorts her to love him—if she must—with a pure and holy love that leaves no room for profane desires. But as her voice blends with his in the climax of the duet, Salome sings that even though she hears his admonition, she has only to look into his eyes to know that she will love him forever.

ACT TWO

[*Scene One*] Herod's apartments in the palace, where he is being entertained by the provocative dancing of slaves and women of his court. In a sinuous chorus ("Roi, t'assoupir sur ta couche") they bid him forget the cares of the throne and abandon himself to dreams of love and glory.

But the seductive movements of the dancers only serve to remind him of the charms of Salome. His libidinous thoughts torment him as he stares unseeing at the Babylonian ballet. At its conclusion a young Babylonian woman offers him an amphora of magic wine. It is a love potion, she sings, which will bring him a vision of the one who has inflamed him with desire. For a moment Herod hesitates, but then is overpowered by the thought of Salome.

Murmuring, "Sweet illusion, fade not again" ("Ne t'enfuis pas, douce illusion!"), he drinks. As promised, the potion produces a tantalizing vision which he describes in one of the most famous baritone arias in opera: "Vision fugitive."

When the Babylonian woman offers him more wine, Herod suddenly becomes suspicious: perhaps it is poisoned. . . . Then recklessly he drinks down the wine and hurls the amphora from him. Delirious, he imagines he is leading Salome to the couch. Begging her to come closer, he falls down on the couch in a drunken stupor.

Just at that moment, Phanuel enters, walks over to the couch and stares down at Herod in mingled pity and contempt. Here is a king, he murmurs sardonically, a man who rules an empire. A woman appears, seduces him. And now, here lies the monarch: a sodden, delirious ruin.[2]

Herod suddenly awakens. Although still befuddled, he recognizes the soothsayer and implores him to set him free from the torment of his dream. Exasperated, Phanuel brusquely tells Herod he is obviously losing his mind: while he babbles about a woman ("Une femme t'occupe"), his kingdom is in a turmoil of fear, mutiny and revolution. He himself, Phanuel goes on, tried to rouse the Israelites to action, but they cringe before the power of Rome.

Herod, who now has regained his senses, boasts that the people are with him still. They bow to you as king, Phanuel remarks, but their real hero is John the Baptist. Well and good, Herod retorts, adding that he will use this John to lead the revolt against the Romans. Once they are gone, the Prophet and all other dangerous radicals will be drawn and quartered. But their temples will remain, Phanuel interjects. With ferocious emphasis Herod shouts: "I will tear them down!" ("Je les renverserai!"). In ironic contrast, from the distance comes a chorus of Israelites hailing Herod as their liberator. Herod relishes this as confirmation of his power.

[Scene Two] The great square in Jerusalem. Here the populace has gathered to swear fealty to Herod, who will free them from the tyranny of Rome ("Roi! que ta superbe vaillance"). This marks the beginning of one of the great ensemble numbers of the opera. Herod, standing on the steps of the palace with Israelite envoys, tells the people that the moment has come to drive out the hated Romans ("Ô peuple, le moment est venu"). When he calls on them to join him in the "holy war," they respond, in a resounding continuation of the ensemble, that they will fight to the death ("Oui, la mort ou notre indépendance!").

Thereupon Herod asks the envoys what military aid they will supply.

---

[2] Foreshadowing, in effect, the scene in Verdi's *Otello*, when Iago stands over the prostrate Moor intoning: "Ecco il Leone!".

They report: "fifteen thousand of horse with footmen and weapons . . . five score of chariots" ("quinze mille chevaux, des hommes, des armes, cent chariots").

Suddenly from the distance comes the fanfare of Roman trumpets, and at that moment Herodias appears at the top of the palace steps. Silencing the people with a wave of her hand, she derides them for their display of defiance of Rome just when Rome's dreaded Proconsul himself has arrived to call them to account. The people cry out in terror: "Vitellius!" The envoys groan that now all is lost. Herodias, aside, tries to give the quaking Herod some measure of courage, and vows that she herself will outwit the Romans.

From the fear-stricken Israelites comes a chorus of lamentation as the Romans approach with trumpets blaring ("Les Romains! L'airain retentit!"). Vitellius is borne in on a huge litter by Ethiopian slaves, and accompanied by his entourage carrying torches and banners surmounted by the imperial golden eagles of Rome. Herod, shaking with fear, and Herodias, proud and haughty, advance to welcome the Proconsul.

Scowling, Vitellius rises from his litter; the crowd abjectly bows before him, with eyes averted. The Proconsul wonders if their servility masks a plot against Rome. He loudly warns that any evidence of subversion will bring dire punishment. The individual reactions to this threat are voiced in a powerful ensemble: the terror of the Israelites, the arrogant warning of Vitellius, the boasting of the Romans, the defiance of Herodias, and the whimpering of Herod, whose braggadocio has long oozed away.

Only Phanuel, in this crucial moment, thinks of John the Baptist and sings that now the Prophet's hour is at hand . . . God has not forgotten him. The ensemble climaxes in a thunderous outburst that keynotes the scene: "Qu'ils tremblent!" ("Beware!").

Vitellius steps forward. In a show of magnanimity, he asks, in the name of mighty Caesar, what is the wish of the Israelites. When the people recover from their surprise at this question they ask the restoration of their Temple and the right to reverence their High Priest as a precept of Jewish faith. Rome will grant the petition, the Proconsul tells the stunned Israelites—if they promise not to revolt. There is a shout of acclamation from the populace.

As Vitellius, Herod, Herodias, Phanuel and the entourage are about to go into the palace, hosannas are heard in the distance. To the general consternation, a throng of Canaanite women and children appear, escorting John the Baptist and Salome. Over an accompaniment of majestic chords, the Canaanites hail the Prophet in the familiar words of the *Benedictus* of the Mass: "Blessed is he that cometh in the name of the

Lord" ("Gloire à celui qui vient au nom du Seigneur").[3] The theme is a variation of the one heard prominently in the overture.

Herodias fumes as she watches Herod, who stares at Salome as though hypnotized. Vitellius, awed in spite of himself at the obeisance made to John, ironically asks who this hero can be. Herod exclaims that he is the Prophet of God. Herodias, with treacherous emphasis, warns Vitellius that this man wields great power over the Israelites.

John, majestic and commanding, strides forward. In ringing tones he proclaims that God alone rules, and that temporal power will be shattered at His command ("Toute justice vient du ciel"). The Proconsul and Herodias retreat into the palace. Herod, his lecherous gaze riveted on Salome, is led away by Phanuel. The voices of the Canaanites, Israelites and Romans merge in the choral climax of the act.

ACT THREE

[*Scene One*] Before Phanuel's house. The soothsayer stands gazing up at the stars. He soliloquizes about their power over mankind's destiny in one of the most striking arias in the opera: "Stars, that have so long burned in boundless space" ("Astres étincelants que l'infini promène"). First, looking down on the sleeping city, he muses that its people, satiated with their hedonistic pleasures, ignore the Prophet's warning of doom ("Dors, ô cité perverse!").

Meanwhile he will consult the stars for an answer to a troublesome question: Who is this John the Baptist? Is he a mortal or a god? Why do his warnings strike fear into the hearts of kings and peasants alike? Staring into the heavens, Phanuel cries: "Stars that have so long shone, speak!" ("Astres étincelants, parlez!").

Suddenly Herodias emerges out of the shadows and rushes up to Phanuel. Hysterically she commands him to name the planet that controls the destiny of the creature who has stolen Herod's love. Since Herodias commands it, Phanuel answers quietly, she will hear. He begins by saying he has long observed her own planet ("J'ai souvent contemplé ton astre"). This marks the beginning of a dramatic colloquy. Phanuel explains that the planets of Herodias and her rival are now in conjunction, which means that two earthly beings are united—not by fate but by love. There is evil in these planets, Phanuel goes on with a note of terror in his voice, and there are bloodstains on the planet of the Queen.

But there is yet another planetary sign, says Phanuel—a symbol of the Queen's motherhood. But where is her child? Sternly, the soothsayer commands Herodias to remember. She cannot remember, she answers

---

[3] *Benedictus qui venit in nomine Domini.*

dolorously, but she longs desperately to hold this child in her arms
again.

Her anguish turns to delirious joy when Phanuel promises she will indeed see her child again. With that he points to the Temple. There
stands Salome. "Behold," Phanuel cries, "there is your daughter!" In an
unaccompanied phrase, Herodias screams: "No! My daughter is dead!"
Phanuel furiously denounces her as a heartless, evil creature who may
well call herself a woman—but never a mother.

[Scene Two] A brief prelude in a serene religious mood introduces
the scene: before the Sanctuary of the Temple, where Salome is keeping
vigil. John has been imprisoned in the dungeon underneath the Sanctuary. In ironic contrast to Salome's mood of despair, a chorus in praise
of Herod and Herodias is heard in the distance ("À tous deux richesse
et bonheurs"). Salome curses the Israelites for their subservience to a
King who himself vacillates between tyrannizing his own people and
meekly bowing to the power of Rome.

But then her thoughts turn to John, and in an ensuing aria ("Charme
des jours passés") she recalls the day she first met the Prophet . . .
how his words gave her happiness and courage. She prays that if he now
must die God will allow her to die with him. Crushed by grief, Salome
collapses before the doors of the Sanctuary.

[Scene Three] Meanwhile, Herod, who has descended to the dungeon in the hope of enlisting John's help in his plotting against the
Romans, bitterly reflects that the conquerors have torn power out of his
hands and made a mockery of his reign. But he vows to have his
revenge—and to that end he will use the Prophet to defy the power of
Rome.

Suddenly Herod catches sight of a shadowy figure crouched in front
of John's cell. When he discovers it is Salome, he is beside himself with
joy ("Rêves réalisés"). This introduces the bizarre scene in which
Herod, frantic with desire, tries to force himself on Salome—alternately
beseeching her, then demanding that as his slave she must submit to
him. Revolted by his clumsy advances, she finally makes him understand that she has given her love to John the Baptist—a man whose
power puts Caesar himself to shame.

In fury and frustration Herod shouts that he will put both Salome
and John to death ("Et je vous livrerai tous les deux au bourreau!").

As the ancient chant of the Jews—Schmah Israël Adonai—is heard in
the Sanctuary, Salome sinks down in front of the great veil which conceals the Holy of Holies (having finally eluded Herod and made her
way out of the dungeon).

[*Scene Four*] The Temple doors open and the Jews enter for the traditional ritual observance, which is followed by the Sacred Dance.

After the ceremonies, Vitellius, Herod, Herodias, Phanuel and the court, along with the Romans and the Temple priests, range themselves on the Temple steps and face the populace. Vitellius pompously reminds the Jews that they—along with the rest of the world—benefit from Rome's largesse. Including Caesar's chains, Herod remarks in a sarcastic aside. The Temple priests, currying favor with Vitellius, exhort him to condemn this radical, John the Baptist, who incites the Israelites to rebellion. The Proconsul turns to Herod. Relishing his discomfiture, Vitellius craftily observes that, since John is a Galilean, it is his (Herod's) responsibility to judge him. The servile priests again clamor for John's condemnation as the false Messiah.

Though trapped by the Proconsul's subterfuge, Herod still clings to the hope that he will be able to use John's power to overthrow the Romans, and thus secure his throne. He orders John to be brought before him. Escorted by Temple guards, John strides in. The populace, awed by his majestic appearance, comment in a brief choral phrase ("Le voilà!").

Herod and Herodias sneer that this man is no longer the insolent rebel, but a false prophet who will be forced to answer for leading the Israelites astray. John himself sings that he will speak as God's advocate. The inquisition begins.

Herod respectfully asks him his name. "I am John," he replies, "son of Zacharias."

"Is it true," Herod asks, "that your preaching has incited the people to revolution?"

John answers: "I preach peace on earth, goodwill toward men—and freedom for all" ("La liberté!").

At the word "freedom," pandemonium erupts and then builds into the major ensemble scene of the opera. Herod, Herodias and Vitellius scream imprecations; the Israelites exultantly reiterate the cry of "freedom." But Herod now decides to play his trump card. Silencing the crowd, he asks John if he will join him in overthrowing the power of Rome. With regal disdain, John replies that God does not concern himself with the trivial ambition of kings.

At that, the clamor breaks out again and the ensemble roars on. There are cries of "Death to the traitor!" "Crucify him!" At the height of the uproar, Salome rushes in and throws herself into John's arms, crying that if he dies she will die with him ("laissez-moi partager sa mort"). Herod curses as he realizes that the Prophet—whose life he might have spared—is truly his rival for Salome's love.

Looking up at John, Salome sings that she belongs to one whose life has been devoted to the love of all mankind ("C'est Dieu que l'on te nomme"). Her refrain continues as an obbligato to the ensemble as the people comment in awe on her willingness to share the Prophet's doom.

In jealous fury, Herod denounces John as a traitor, and declares that this holy prophet is the lover of Salome. He shouts: "Let them both die! This is my decision!" ("Frappez-les! car ma voix les condamne!"). Herodias, aside, murmurs that a strange fear strikes her heart.

Facing the seething mob, John, with mystical fervor, challenges the Israelites to slay him—as they have slain many of their prophets ("Frappez donc! frappez les apôtres"). Then in thunderous tones he foretells the doom of Rome: a city plunged into eternal night, where not one stone will be left standing upon another.

But the populace, inflamed with mindless hatred, ignores the Prophet's warning and clamors for the death of John and Salome ("Qu'ils meurent!"). This marks the beginning of the mighty ensemble which concludes the act.

ACT FOUR

[Scene One] A brief prelude sets the somber mood of the scene: the dungeon under the Temple. In quiet resignation, John prays for strength to face his doom. Sonorous chords underscore his reflections, which he reveals in another of the opera's great arias—"Adieu donc, vains objets qui nous." He sings that he can face eternity without fear—but then the tantalizing thought of Salome brings a surge of passionate emotion. He implores God to deliver him from the torment of his carnal desires. "Why, O God," he cries, "dost thou allow this love to test my faith?" ("Ô Seigneur, tu souffres que l'amour vienne ébranler ma foi?").

As though in answer to his question, Salome enters the dungeon. John stares in disbelief, then greets her with a cry of mingled joy and despair: "'Tis thou in this dismal place!" ("C'est toi! dans ce sombre lieu!").[4] They cling to each other in an impassioned embrace, and then ensues the duet in which they abandon themselves to their love. John interprets their meeting as a sign that God Himself has granted him this final moment of happiness. Salome reiterates in voluptuous ecstasy: "John, I love thee!"

They are still locked in each other's arms when the Chief Priest and Ethiopian slaves enter. The priest tells John that his fatal hour has come. To Salome he says that Herod has reprieved her and that she is to come to the palace. With that the slaves literally tear her from John's arms and drag her away as she screams in despair. John resolutely follows the Chief Priest.

---

[4] As Radames to Aïda: "Tu—in questa tomba!"

[*Scene Two*] The Great Hall of the palace. The Romans are celebrating their victories and the invincibility of the Empire in a typical saturnalia. In a brawling chorus—"Nous sommes Romains!"—they hail the glorious triumph of the Caesars. Vitellius, Herodias, Herod and the court enter to watch the ballets which are to climax the festivities. Exotic dances are performed in turn by Babylonian, Phoenician and Gallic women.

The applause of the spectators is cut short when Salome rushes in and wildly begs to be allowed to die with the Prophet ("Le bonheur de mourir avec celui"). She appeals to Herodias as a mother—still unaware that she herself is the Queen's daughter. As Herodias listens, guilt-stricken and spellbound, Salome reveals the tragic story of her abandonment ("Lorsque m'abandonnait").

It was then, she sings, that the Prophet befriended her and gave her the strength to go on in the search for her mother. Profoundly moved, Herodias muses that the child she lost might well have been as beautiful as the one kneeling before her. But it is the sound of Salome's voice that finally convinces Herodias that she is indeed her daughter. In a sudden transport of rage Salome bursts out that—for the sake of a shameful marriage—her mother abandoned her ("Pour un hymen infâme"). She screams the words like a curse; Herodias gasps in terror.

Salome's voice soars over the ensemble commenting on this hectic scene as she begs the Queen to spare John's life. But Herodias remorselessly answers that the Prophet is to die. At that moment Salome turns and sees the executioner approaching, a bloody sword in his hand. Drawing a dagger from her girdle, she flings herself on Herodias, crying: "You have slain him . . . now you shall die!" ("Il est mort de ta main!"). Herodias shrieks: "Spare me! I am your mother!"

Dagger upraised, Salome intones with terrible deliberation that if this detestable Queen is indeed her mother, she will now give back the blood her mother gave her. Whereupon she plunges the dagger into her own body. Herodias, throwing herself upon the body of her daughter, wails in anguish and despair: "Ma fille!"

The curtain falls.

LES HUGUENOTS

by GIACOMO MEYERBEER

(1791–1864)

Libretto by

EUGÈNE SCRIBE and ÉMILE DESCHAMPS

CHARACTERS

Count de Nevers, a young Catholic nobleman	Baritone
Tavannes ⎫	Tenor
Cossé ⎪	Tenor
Méru ⎬ Catholics, friends of Nevers	Bass
Retz ⎪	Bass
Thoré ⎭	Bass
Raoul de Nangis, a Huguenot nobleman	Tenor
Marcel, a soldier and Raoul's servant	Bass
A servant of Count de Nevers	Tenor
Urbain, page to Marguerite de Valois	Mezzo-soprano
Marguerite de Valois, Queen of France, espoused to Henry IV of Navarre	Soprano
Valentine, daughter of Count de St. Bris and betrothed to Count de Nevers	Soprano
Count de St. Bris, a leader of the Catholics	Baritone
Bois-Rosé, a Huguenot soldier	Tenor
Maurevert, a Catholic nobleman	Bass

Catholics, Hugenots, soldiers, ladies and gentlemen of the court, students, townspeople, monks, gypsies, dancers

Place: Touraine and Paris
Time: August 1572
First performance: Grand Opéra, Paris, February 29, 1836
Original language: French

Les Huguenots, which was spectacularly successful and which established Meyerbeer as the foremost operatic composer of his day, deals with the violent and bloody struggle between the Catholics and Protestants in France during the sixteenth century. It is based on events leading up to the St. Bartholomew's Day massacre, around which the climax of the opera is built. Like *L'Africaine,* it is usually sung in Italian, its title being *Gli Ugonotti.*

The prelude is dominated by the powerful theme of the great Lutheran chorale, "Ein' feste Burg" (*A Mighty Fortress*). It continues through several variations of rhythm and harmony, after which the music leads directly into the first act.

ACT ONE

The banquet hall in the castle of Count de Nevers, a prominent Catholic party leader, in Touraine, where Nevers has gathered a group of his friends—Tavannes, Cossé, Méru, Retz, Thoré, and other noblemen—for an evening of gay entertainment. The banquet has not yet begun. Greeting his friends, Nevers strikes up a refrain of careless gaiety ("Ne' bei dì di giovinezza"—"Des beaux jours de la jeunesse"), hailing the days of youth and folly. The others join him in a lusty chorus. Tavannes approaches him and asks why the banquet is being delayed. Nevers explains that he is awaiting another guest, a young nobleman who has recently received a commission in the Lancers through the aid of Admiral Coligny (head of the Huguenot party). This news brings a scornful exclamation of "Huguenot!" from the guests.

Nevers, however, entreats the noblemen to look upon the newcomer as a brother, thus following the example recently set by the rulers of France. He reminds them that the Protestant Admiral Coligny and Catherine de' Medici, the Catholic Queen Mother, have agreed to forget their differences and live in eternal peace. The noblemen comment sardonically on the probable implication of the word "eternal." As they are discussing the matter Cossé exclaims that a stranger is approaching. Saying that he is Raoul de Nangis, Nevers hurries to meet him. The others meanwhile make cynical references to the visitor's solemn "Calvinist" demeanor.

Raoul answers Nevers's greeting in a dignified refrain ("Sotto il bel ciel della Turrena"—"Sous le beau ciel de la Touraine"), in which he voices his appreciation of the fact that he, a humble soldier, is privileged to meet the nobles of Touraine. He bears himself with such gallantry and forthrightness that he wins the grudging approval of the noblemen. After introducing him to the others, Nevers invites all to the banquet table. As the feasting begins the men sing a long and vigorous chorus in praise of youth, wine, and merrymaking ("Piacer della mensa"—"Bonheur de la table").

After the chorus Nevers, seated next to Raoul, remarks on the latter's preoccupied manner and suggests that perhaps he is in love. He himself,

Nevers reveals, is to be married the next day. In a mock-tragic tone he laments that now he must forsake all the adoring court beauties who have besieged him with their attentions. Thereupon Tavannes suggests that all the guests tell the stories of their amours. Nevers invites Raoul, as the guest of honor, to begin the round of stories. The noblemen are vastly amused when Raoul admits that though he is very much in love he knows neither the name nor the title of the lady whom he adores.

Raoul recounts how one day, when he was riding near Amboise, he saw a crowd of rough students about to attack the occupant of a luxurious equipage. He rushed up, quickly routed them, and then was rewarded with a dazzling smile of thanks from the enchanting creature whom he had rescued. From that moment, he exclaims, he has been di er slave. Raoul voices his ardor in the graceful aria, "Bianca al par hermine"—"Plus blanche que la blanche hermine." He recalls that as he gazed on this lovely being, fair as a lily, he murmured that even if he were never to see her again he would carry her image forever in his heart. Her smile, he continues in ecstasy, seemed to speak of love. The noblemen voice their approval of his romantic sentiments in a choral phrase.

The conversation is interrupted by the entrance of Marcel, Raoul's servant and a fanatical Huguenot. Striding to his master, he chides him for consorting with Catholic infidels and excitedly urges him to leave their evil presence. Raoul tries to calm him and then apologetically explains that Marcel is a rough old soldier who is as brave as he is religious. He was reared, says Raoul, according to the stern laws of Luther and taught to hate the Pope, and he never loses an opportunity to express himself on the subject. Quietly ordering Marcel to keep silent, Raoul turns back to the table. Nevers proposes a toast. Just as they are about to drink, Marcel, muttering that he must protect his master from damnation, roars out the Lutheran chorale "Ein' feste Burg" ("O tu, che ognor in guardia stai"—"Seigneur, rempart et seul soutien").

More amused than annoyed at the interruption, Nevers asks Raoul the meaning of the song. Raoul, greatly embarrassed, explains that it is a chant sung by the Huguenots to ward off evil. The noblemen good-naturedly allow Marcel to finish his hymn, after which Cossé remarks that the old soldier reminds him of an adversary he encountered during the Battle of Rochelle. He remembers that meeting well, he goes on, fingering a sword cut on his cheek. Looking at him, Marcel admits it was he who inflicted the wound. Raoul is alarmed over Marcel's lack of diplomacy, but Cossé gaily laughs the matter off and invites Marcel to drink with him.

Marcel, of course, refuses, whereupon Nevers suggests that if he will not drink perhaps he will sing. Marcel replies that he will oblige the company with the battle song of the Protestants at Rochelle—a song against Papists, bigots, and women—one that was sung to the accompaniment of the "piff, paff, piff, paff" of bullets. He then sings the famous *chanson huguenote* ("Finita è per i frati"—"Pour les couvents c'est fini"), describing how the Protestants will put monks and priests to rout, strike them down without mercy, and destroy their altars. The second stanza concerns itself with the punishment to be meted out to women. They, too, must perish by sword and gun, so that their evil charms will no longer ensnare honest men. As Marcel sings the recurring "piff, paff" phrases he pantomimes the motions of firing a gun. The song ends in a fierce crescendo.

As the noblemen applaud Marcel's song a servant approaches Nevers and informs him that a very beautiful lady is waiting in the garden to see him. Nevers, remarking that he would not leave his drinking if the King himself were to summon him, casually asks if the visitor is one of the ladies of the court. The servant replies that she is a stranger. In that case, says Nevers to his guests, who have been listening avidly, he will go at once, for this may mean a new conquest. Urging the noblemen to continue the banquet, he tells them he will return shortly with full details about the fair stranger.

In a lively ensemble ("L'avventura è singolare"—"L'aventure est singulière") the guests speculate on this newest adventure of Nevers's and comment on his consistent good fortune with the ladies. Tavannes suggests that they go quietly to the windows at the back, which overlook the garden, and spy on Nevers during his interview. All rush to the windows except Raoul and Marcel, who withdraw to one side of the room and speak quietly together. Noticing that Raoul has not joined the group at the window, Méru approaches him and jestingly asks if his stern Huguenot principles do not permit him to look at a pretty face. Smiling, Raoul answers that he will oblige him by looking.

He gazes outside and then recoils with an exclamation of dismay. Excitedly he tells Marcel that Nevers's visitor is the very lady whom he rescued from the students. Disillusioned at finding the woman he idealizes in a rendezvous with so notorious a cavalier as Nevers, Raoul declares that his love for her has turned to hate. The noblemen derisively comment that another trusting lover has been deceived. Raoul tries to rush out but is restrained by the other guests.

They cease their conversation when Méru warns that Nevers is returning. Nevers comes back into the room and, as the guests talk among themselves, he reveals, in an aside, what has transpired. The visitor was Valentine, his betrothed, lady-in-waiting to Queen Marguerite. At the request of the Queen, she came to ask that their nuptials be canceled. Nevers adds that though he courteously acquiesced, as any cavalier would, he is burning with rage over the matter. Meanwhile the noblemen come forward and, in a mocking chorus ("Al gran conquistator"—

"Bonheur au conquérant"), acclaim Nevers as an irresistible conqueror of womankind.

At the conclusion of the chorus Urbain, Queen Marguerite's young page, appears. When Nevers asks whom he seeks, Urbain replies in the florid cavatina "Lieti Signor, salute!"—"Nobles Seigneurs, salut!"[1] He informs the noblemen that a gracious and beautiful lady has sent him with a message for one of them. Never has any cavalier been so highly favored, he avows. Ending the aria in a brilliant cadenza, Urbain brings forth the letter.

Taking it for granted that the letter is for him, Nevers reaches for it, remarking that it is rather boring to be constantly importuned by adoring ladies. He is considerably taken aback when the page informs him that the letter is for a certain Raoul de Nangis. Raoul, equally astonished, takes the letter and reads it aloud. It informs him that a royal carriage will shortly be waiting for him. He is to permit himself to be blindfolded and conducted to the carriage, which will bring him to the writer of the letter.

Looking at Nevers and the other noblemen, Raoul observes that this is undoubtedly an attempt to have some sport at his expense. He adds that he will see the adventure through and then casually hands the letter to Nevers. Examining it, Nevers exclaims that it bears the seal of the Queen. His manner toward Raoul instantly changes from condescension to almost fawning respect. He assures Raoul of his firm friendship, saying that he has his best interests at heart ("Voi sapete ch'io sono"—"Vous savez si je suis un ami"). This introduces the finale of the act. The other noblemen crowd around Raoul with effusive congratulations and declarations of friendship.

Urbain also comments on the kind fate which has bestowed such good fortune on Raoul, who still does not know what to make of the sudden change in attitude on the part of his host and the noblemen. Marcel expresses his happiness by roaring out several bars of a *Te Deum* and by proclaiming that Samson has overcome the Philistines. After the thunderous climax of the chorus, Raoul is led away by Urbain and the curtain falls.

ACT TWO

The garden of the castle of Marguerite de Valois at Chenonceaux. Queen Marguerite is seated in her pavilion, attended by Urbain and her maids of honor. In a long and brilliant aria ("Ovago suol della Turrena"—"Ô beau pays de la Touraine") she reflects happily on the beau-

[1] This cavatina is also known by the phrase which follows the opening cadenza—"Nobil donna e tanto onesta," or "Une dame noble et sage."

ties of Touraine. Here among the plashing fountains, the lovely flowers, and the pleasant woodland glades all care is cast aside and thoughts of love fill every heart. The maids of honor echo her sentiments in a graceful chorus. In the last part of the aria Marguerite declares that she would be content to relinquish her regal power and preside only over this peaceful retreat.

At the conclusion of the aria Valentine approaches. Urbain, who is in love not only with all the maids of honor but with the Queen and Valentine as well, breathes an amorous comment on Valentine's beauty. When the Queen asks her about Nevers, Valentine replies that he readily agreed to release her from the nuptial contract. Marguerite tells her that she has already arranged another alliance. Raoul de Nangis, she says, will be here today. When Valentine expresses some reticence in meeting him, Marguerite says that she herself will see him first.

The maids ask the Queen's permission to bathe in the nearby stream. When permission is given they sing a melodious chorus about the joys of bathing in the cool and sparkling waters ("Giovin beltà su questa riva"—"Jeunes beautés sous le feuillage") and then retire to the bank of the stream. Noticing Urbain stealing close to watch them, Marguerite reprimands him and sends him away. In a few moments, however, he returns. The Queen is about to rebuke him again for his amorous spying when he announces that a cavalier is approaching. As the maids exclaim in fright over the possibility of being seen at their bath, Urbain assures them that all is well, for the cavalier is blindfolded. Marguerite announces that it is Raoul. Valentine protests that she cannot stay, and leaves despite Marguerite's request that she remain.

While the Queen is waiting for Raoul, Urbain sings a gay cavatina ("No, caso egual giammai"—"Non, vous n'avez jamais, je gage") in which he recalls his thrilling adventure of escorting a handsome, blindfolded cavalier through the streets of the village to the castle. Crowds followed them, while the village girls, all agog, strewed flowers in the stranger's path. The maids of honor, having finished their bathing, crowd around Urbain and chatter in excited wonder over his remarkable story.

As the page ends the cavatina with a flashing cadenza, the maids see Raoul approaching and sing admiringly of him in a lively chorus ("Desso è qua"—"Le voilà!"). Dismissed by the Queen, the maids and Urbain withdraw, with many a backward glance at the mysterious cavalier.

When Marguerite and Raoul are finally alone she commends him for keeping the appointment and tells him he may remove the blindfold. Complying, Raoul utters an exclamation of wonder over the beauty of the woman before him. A long, florid duet ensues as Raoul, unaware that she is the Queen of France, addresses her in phrases of extravagant

praise ("Beltà divina, incantatrice"–"Beauté divine, enchanteresse").
He cries that he is burning with a desire to serve her. Smiling, Marguerite says that she will require some proof of his sincerity. Kneeling at her feet, Raoul swears that his sword and his very life are hers to command. Moved by his ardor, Marguerite reflects, aside, that if she were so minded she could make a conquest at this moment. She resolves, however, to keep faith with Valentine. The duet continues to a thrilling climax as Raoul reiterates his pledge of devotion, while Marguerite declares that she will deny herself the pleasure of a romantic conquest for the sake of Valentine's future happiness.

At the conclusion of the duet Urbain once more appears. He informs Marguerite that the ladies and gentlemen of the court have come to pay their respects to their Queen. Raoul is surprised and embarrassed when he realizes that he had been pouring out his heart to the Queen of France herself, but Marguerite reassures him with a smile. She then tells him of her plan to arrange a marriage between him and Valentine, daughter of Count de St. Bris, a leader of the Catholics, for the purpose of uniting the Catholics and the Huguenots and putting an end to their bloody strife. When Raoul consents, Marguerite declares that he will henceforth be a member of her court. Urbain plaintively murmurs that the Queen bestows favors on everyone but himself.

During the playing of a minuet the people of the court appear, led by St. Bris and Nevers. Catholics and Huguenots separate into two groups. Marguerite announces that they are to witness a nuptial union which she herself has arranged and then introduces Raoul. The people acclaim the Queen in a brief choral passage, during which a courier arrives and hands her several messages. Reading them, Marguerite informs St. Bris and Nevers that her brother, King Charles IX, requires their presence in Paris at once on important state business. Before they go, however, Marguerite adds, all noblemen–Catholics and Huguenots alike–must swear by the marriage that is soon to take place that they will forever keep the peace. Surrounding the Queen, St. Bris, Nevers, Raoul, and the nobles, holding forth their hands, take the oath in a tremendous chorus ("Per la fè, per l'onor"–"Par l'honneur, par le nom"). They swear by the King, their swords, and their faith that they will keep sacred the vows of peace. In a brief, unaccompanied quartet sung by Raoul, Nevers, St. Bris, and Marcel, the first three ask the blessing of Heaven on the peace that has now been established. Marcel, however, ignores the vow and confines himself to praying that his master may be protected from these infidels. Marguerite and the others then add their prayers for peace.

At a sign from the Queen, St. Bris leaves to bring Valentine. A moment later, as Marguerite announces that the bride will be presented, St. Bris comes forward escorting Valentine whom he leads toward Raoul.

Seeing her, Raoul staggers back in astonishment, recognizing her as the lady whom he saw with Nevers in the garden on the night of the banquet. Crying out that he has been betrayed and deceived, Raoul furiously declares that he will never marry her.

The reactions of the court to Raoul's outburst are expressed in a powerful ensemble ("Oh delir, oh demenza"—"Ô transport, ô délire"). Marguerite, Urbain, St. Bris, Nevers, and the Catholic faction denounce him for his outrageous insult to Valentine, who laments that he has rejected her without reason. Marcel commends his master's courage, his sentiments being echoed by the Huguenots. Raoul himself declares bitterly that neither Valentine's smiles nor tears will ever deceive him again.

In an interlude Marguerite implores Raoul to explain his actions. It is a matter of honor, Raoul answers, adding that the reason is his secret. Turning on him in fury, St. Bris and Nevers swear revenge. They draw their swords, whereupon Raoul draws his. Marguerite signals a guardsman to disarm Raoul and then angrily reminds St. Bris and Nevers that they have no time to waste in quarreling, for the King expects them in Paris today. When Raoul declares that he will go with them, St. Bris sneers that the scoundrel who can thus win the Queen's favor is indeed fortunate. Marguerite sternly silences him, while Raoul retorts that it is St. Bris whom the Queen is protecting. If he had not been deprived of his sword, Raoul threatens, St. Bris would already have paid for his insults with his life.

The ensemble continues to its great climax with St. Bris, Nevers, and Raoul hurling denunciations, while Catholics and Huguenots threaten each other with dire vengeance. Occasionally the stentorian voice of Marcel is heard in the phrases of the Lutheran chorale. At the conclusion of the chorus St. Bris and Nevers carry away the fainting Valentine. Raoul tries to follow them but is restrained by guardsmen. There is great uproar and confusion as the curtain falls.

ACT THREE

The Pré-aux-Clercs, an open space on the banks of the Seine in Paris. At one side is a tavern. At the other, the entrance to a chapel. It is a holiday, and a crowd of townspeople sing a chorus about the joys of feasting and taking their ease ("Quest' è giorno di festa"—"C'est le jour du dimanche"). A company of boisterous Huguenot soldiers, drinking at the tavern, then strike up the well-known *Rataplan* Chorus, clapping their hands to simulate drumbeats. They are led by the soldier Bois-Rosé, who first sounds a note of defiance to the Catholic foes and then voices a pledge of allegiance to the Calvinist cause. The rest of the chorus is devoted to praise of the embattled Huguenot warriors and is climaxed by a shout of acclaim for the Protestant leader Admiral Coligny.

Preceded by a group of Catholic women chanting an *Ave Maria*, St. Bris, Nevers, Valentine, and the people of the court appear in a nuptial procession moving toward the chapel. Having been spurned by Raoul, Valentine is to marry Nevers. As the procession passes, Marcel strides up and asks if St. Bris is there. The townspeople warn him that he must not try to speak to the count and must bow as a sign of respect. Marcel retorts that he makes obeisance only to God. The Huguenot soldiers shout their approval of his sentiments and break out again with their defiant *Rataplan*. The enraged townspeople denounce them for their disloyalty and lack of respect. Signs of a brawl gradually develop.

Just as soldiers and citizens advance threateningly toward each other, a gypsy troupe comes along and changes the mood of the scene with a gay chorus ("Da me chi vien"—"Venez! Venez!"). They move about among the throng, trying to sell their wares and offering to tell fortunes, after which they entertain the crowd with a gypsy dance. At the conclusion of the dancing the crowd settles down to feasting and drinking.

Nevers, emerging from the chapel with St. Bris and Maurevert, another nobleman, says that Valentine will remain in the chapel to pray for a while. He will return later and escort her as his bride to his castle. St. Bris remarks that this marriage will compensate him for Raoul's insult to his daughter. As Nevers leaves, Marcel approaches St. Bris with a letter from Raoul. The soldier explains that the Queen and Raoul—as well as himself—came from Touraine to Paris this morning. St. Bris exclaims in surprise as he reads the letter, in which Raoul challenges the count to meet him on the meadow of Pré-aux-Clercs at nightfall. Marcel leaves when St. Bris assures him that he will be at the appointed place. The count tells Maurevert that he will keep the meeting a secret from Nevers, for his son-in-law is not to risk his life. Declaring that there is no need for St. Bris to risk his own, Maurevert tells the count that there are other ways to punish this miscreant. The two men go back into the chapel to discuss plans for dealing with Raoul.

With the ringing of the curfew, the people gradually disperse. After they have gone St. Bris and Maurevert reappear from the chapel, having made arrangements for ambushing Raoul. As they leave, Maurevert assures St. Bris that his friends will be near to aid him. No sooner have they gone than Valentine rushes out of the chapel. In great agitation, she exclaims that she has heard her father and Maurevert plotting Raoul's murder. She must save him, not only for the sake of her love for him, but for the sake of her father's honor.

As she is wondering how she can warn Raoul, Marcel appears, saying to himself that he will remain here to share his master's fate. A long and dramatic duet ensues ("Nella notte io sol qui veglio"—"Dans la nuit où seul je veille"). Peering through the gloom, Marcel declares that he will keep watch all night for the enemies who will surely be gathering here. Valentine, heavily veiled, approaches him with an entreaty for help. Marcel draws his sword, but sheathes it again when she speaks Raoul's name. Valentine then tells him what he already knows—that Raoul is to fight a duel in the meadow with St. Bris. But she adds the warning that he must not come alone, for there is a plot against his life. Though he has scorned her, she says sadly, she still loves him and would gladly die for him.

Marcel fears it is too late to warn Raoul, for he has already left his home to go to the scene of the duel. Marcel prays for his safety, while Valentine gives way to despair, lamenting that she is torn between her love for Raoul and her duty toward her father. Marcel exhorts her to have courage, assuring her that her devotion will be well rewarded. Reiterating these sentiments at great length, they finally bring the duet to a close. Valentine goes back inside the chapel, while Marcel stands guard outside.

Raoul and St. Bris now arrive with their seconds. Marcel warns his master that there is a plot against his life, but Raoul scoffs at the thought. The six principals—Raoul, St. Bris, Cossé, Tavannes, Retz, and Méru—then sing a ringing sextet in which they swear to abide by the rules of honorable dueling ("De'dritti miei ho l'alma accesa"—"En mon bon droit j'ai confiance"). They prepare to fight, while Marcel voices his despair over the fact that he can do nothing to save his master from the treachery that will strike him down. In the continuation of the ensemble the principals declare that no one is to enter the field except the combatants and that the victor will show no mercy to the vanquished. At its conclusion Raoul and St. Bris raise their swords but are stopped by a warning cry from Marcel.

Drawing his sword, he rushes toward the back, shouting that intruders are lurking near by. Thereupon Maurevert and two armed men appear. Maurevert accuses the treacherous Huguenots of appearing in force to aid Raoul, while Marcel calls down the wrath of Heaven on the perfidious Catholics for the same reason. At that moment he hears the voices of the Huguenot soldiers in the tavern, singing their *Rataplan* Chorus. Dashing to the tavern, he pounds on the door, crying, "Coligny! Coligny!" This brings the soldiers streaming out of the tavern. St. Bris and his adherents meanwhile shout for the Catholic students, who rush out of another part of the tavern. Huguenot and Catholic women appear suddenly and join the men of their respective factions.

The two groups insult and defy each other in a roaring chorus ("Siamo qui"—"Nous voilà"), and then fierce fighting begins. The uproar is brought to a sudden halt by the appearance of Marguerite on horseback, attended by her retinue and guardsmen. With majestic anger she denounces the two groups for breaking the peace they swore to keep. When she asks who is to blame for starting the quarrel, St. Bris and Raoul hotly accuse each other of treachery. Marcel interrupts to declare that a lady informed him that the noblemen had plotted to assassinate Raoul when he arrived to fight St. Bris. There is the lady, he announces dramatically, as a veiled figure comes slowly out of the chapel.

Rushing up to her, St. Bris tears aside her veil, recoiling in horror as he recognizes his daughter. As he upbraids her for betraying him, Valentine implores the Queen for mercy. Turning to the Queen, Raoul, utterly bewildered, asks the meaning of Valentine's secret interview with Nevers. Marguerite explains that she met the nobleman only to break off her engagement to him at the request of her Queen.

She is interrupted by St. Bris, who insists that Valentine is to be the bride of Count de Nevers. There are expressions of consternation from the crowd. Looking toward the river, St. Bris calls attention to the approach of a gaily decorated nuptial barge bringing Nevers and the bridal party. In a ringing refrain ("Ma che! ascolta te, del sposo trionfante"—"Mais écoutez de l'époux triomphant") St. Bris exults that the glorious houses of Nevers and St. Bris will now be united.

Nevers comes ashore, approaches Valentine and ardently greets her, saying that everything is in readiness for the nuptials. Hostilities are momentarily forgotten as the gypsies appear, dance about Valentine and Nevers, and offer gifts and flowers. They join the people of the court in singing a bridal chorus ("Il destin che dal ciel"—"Au banquet où le ciel"). Lighting torches, the gypsies then escort the bridal party to the barge. The gay chorus continues, underscored, however, by the ominous theme of the ensemble sung by the Huguenots, who reiterate their warnings of vengeance.

Valentine laments that she is bound in marriage to a man she hates, while Raoul cries in fury and despair that the woman he loves has been given to his detested rival. Marcel tries to comfort him. As he and Raoul sadly watch the glittering barge move away, the curtain falls.

ACT FOUR

A hall in the castle of Count de Nevers. At the back is a large window overlooking the street. At one side is a door leading to Valentine's room. It is St. Bartholomew's Day, August 25, 1572. Valentine comes in. Overwhelmed by sorrow and haunted by thoughts of Raoul, she voices her grief in a tender aria ("In preda al duol"—"Parmi les pleurs"). She sings that the realization of Raoul's love for her is her only solace. Her reflections are interrupted when Raoul suddenly enters the room. He has come, he says, to see her once again before he dies.

Valentine warns that St. Bris and Nevers are on their way here at this very moment. Distractedly she urges Raoul to flee, but he replies that he will have it out with his foes here and now. Finally she persuades him to conceal himself behind the curtains of a window at the rear.

St. Bris, Nevers, and the gentlemen of the court come in. St. Bris announces that the time has come to reveal the plot which Catherine, the Queen Mother, has ordered to be put into effect against the Huguenots. Turning to Valentine, he asks her to leave the room, but Nevers requests that she be allowed to remain. Her devotion to the cause, he says, gives her the right to share the secrets of state.

In a vigorous refrain ("Di guai crescenti ognor"—"Des troubles renaissants") St. Bris asks assurances of the nobles that they will aid in delivering the country out of the hands of the Huguenots. When they reply, he explains the royal decree: the Huguenots are to be put to the sword at once—this very day. Nevers asks who has condemned them. Heaven itself, St. Bris replies. And who, Nevers inquires, is to strike the first blow? In answer, St. Bris points to Nevers and the other noblemen. There is a rousing choral interlude as the noblemen, led by St. Bris, call on Heaven to aid them in destroying their foes ("D'un sacro zel l'ardore"—"Pour cette cause sainte").

Only Nevers is silent. When St. Bris asks him why he does not join in the pledge of devotion to the cause, Nevers replies that he will not stain his father's sword with contemptible murder. Defying St. Bris, he breaks his sword across his knee and hurls the pieces at the count's feet. Valentine steps quickly to his side, commends his bravery, and urges him to leave with her. But St. Bris, declaring that Nevers obviously has repudiated the Catholic cause, orders him taken into custody. As Nevers is led away, Valentine, at a sign from her father, goes to her room.

St. Bris then gives the orders: the Catholics are to station themselves at strategic points throughout the city. Some are to meet outside the Hôtel de Nesle, where the Huguenots will be gathered to celebrate the nuptials of Queen Marguerite and the Huguenot Henry of Navarre. Coligny is to die first. At the first sound of the bell of St. Germain the Catholics are to poise for the attack. When the bell tolls the second time they are to fling themselves upon the Huguenots and put them to the sword. Valentine, reappearing at the back of the room and hearing her father's words, wails in despair that though Raoul now knows of the plot he cannot make his way out of the castle in time to warn his friends.

While St. Bris is speaking three monks come in carrying baskets of white scarves. Now follows the famous scene which is known as the "Benediction of the Swords." The men draw their weapons and hold them aloft. In a powerful unison refrain St. Bris leads the monks in blessing the swords and the cause in which they are drawn ("Nobili acciar, nobili e santi"—"Glaives pieux, saintes épées"). The noblemen answer in a tremendous burst of sound. As they ferociously cry that they will show no mercy in striking down the infidels, St. Bris gives each man a white scarf stamped with a cross, which is to serve as an identifying badge in the combat. After rising to a blazing climax, the voices sink to a dramatic whisper as the men caution each other to keep silent. The music dies away on ominous chords and not a sound is heard as the nobles and monks steal out of the room.

When all have gone, Raoul emerges cautiously from his hiding place, looks around, and then rushes to the door. He finds it locked. At that moment Valentine comes back through the door leading to her room. Now there ensues the famous duet, "O ciel! dove vai tu?"—"Oh ciel, où courez-vous?" one of the most magnificent numbers in the opera.

Valentine asks him where he will flee. Raoul says he will not flee but will go to warn his friends that assassins are near. Valentine cries that among his enemies are her father and her husband. Justice must be done, Raoul answers grimly. But the attack is being made at Heaven's command, Valentine avers. With bitter scorn Raoul asks if the faith to which she confesses requires men to murder their brothers. He is about to leave, exclaiming that the hour of the attack is almost at hand. Valentine implores him not to go for the sake of his own safety.

Desperately clinging to him, Valentine finally cries out that she cannot let him go because she loves him. Despite his anxiety and agitation, Raoul greets her confession of love with feverish ecstasy. Passionately he entreats her to flee with him, but Valentine begs him to stay and save his life. Suddenly the bell of St. Germain tolls the signal for the alert. Tearing himself from Valentine's arms, Raoul cries that he cannot stay while death is poised to strike down his friends. In terror and despair, Valentine continues her entreaties, while Raoul conjures up visions of streets running red with the blood of the Huguenots.

Then the bell tolls the second time, signaling the beginning of the massacre. Raoul draws Valentine to the window and opens it to let her look down on the fearful slaughter taking place in the streets below. Valentine faints in his arms. Placing her gently in a chair, Raoul utters a despairing prayer for her protection and then leaps out of the window. Reviving momentarily, Valentine opens her eyes and sees him. She collapses as the curtain falls.[2]

ACT FIVE

[*Scene One*] The Great Ballroom of the Hôtel de Nesle, where the Huguenots are celebrating the marriage of Queen Marguerite and Henry

[2] In some versions the opera ends at this point.

of Navarre. There is an interlude of ballet. The tolling of the signal bell is heard faintly above the sound of the music. The festivities come to an abrupt halt as Raoul, disheveled, his clothing drenched with blood, rushes in shouting the terrible news of the massacre. Frenziedly he calls the Huguenots to arms ("All'armi, amici miei"—"Aux armes, mes amis") telling them that the Catholics have put the Protestant churches to the torch, murdered Coligny, and plundered his home. The Huguenots respond in a fiery chorus ("L'armi impugnamo"—"Courons aux armes") in which they swear to avenge their dead. At its conclusion the men draw their weapons and prepare to follow Raoul. There is wild disorder as the curtain falls.

[*Scene Two*] The cloister of a Huguenot church, partially in ruins as the result of the fighting, where many Huguenots have taken refuge. Shouts and gunfire sound in the distance. Marcel, Raoul, and Valentine appear. Raoul exclaims over Marcel's wounds. The old soldier says that the church is surrounded by their foes and there is nothing left but to die. Raoul turns to leave, saying that he must go back to the fighting, but Valentine restrains him.

She suggests that he tie a white scarf around his arm and go with her to the Louvre, where he will be safe under the protection of the Queen. When Raoul asks what he must do to save his life, Valentine answers that he must turn Catholic. Then, she says, she can freely give him her love. Flatly refusing to betray his faith, Raoul asks about Nevers. Valentine tells him that her husband has been slain. Again Valentine implores Raoul to go with her, but a quiet word from Marcel strengthens his resolve not to yield. In a dramatic and poignant refrain ("Così, io ti vedro perir"—"Ainsi je te verrai périr") Valentine makes her final plea. So great is her love, she cries to Raoul, that she will risk eternal damnation by renouncing her faith for his. After the aria she asks Marcel to consecrate their union with his blessing. As they kneel before him and he raises his hands, the Huguenots softly intone the Lutheran chorale. In a brief trio ("Nell'unir vostre man"—"Savez-vous qu'en joignant") Marcel asks the lovers if they will remain true to their vows. Valentine and Raoul devoutly respond.

The tender and tragic mood of the scene is shattered by the harsh voices of the oncoming Catholic soldiers, calling on the Huguenots in the church to yield or die. From within the dark recesses come answers of defiance. There are sounds of a brief but fierce encounter, followed by a terrible silence. Listening, Marcel murmurs that the Huguenots will never sing again.

An impressive trio follows ("Ah, vedete il ciel"—"Ah! voyez! le ciel") as Marcel, Valentine, and Raoul, inspired by the heroic defiance of their people, join in expressions of religious ecstasy over a vision of heaven and bid farewell to earth. The Catholic soldiers finally burst in and call on them to recant or die. Oblivious to everything in their joy, Valentine, Marcel, and Raoul sing the phrases of the chorale and then, in ringing tones, hurl their defiance at the soldiers. As they are dragged away the curtain falls.

[*Scene Three*] A street in Paris. A crowd of Catholic soldiers stampedes by, shouting for revenge. As they go on their way Marcel and Valentine appear, supporting Raoul. They have managed to escape their captors, but, in fleeing, Raoul has been mortally wounded. St. Bris approaches through the darkness at the head of his soldiers. When he demands that the three identify themselves, Raoul, despite Valentine's desperate efforts to keep him quiet, shouts, "Huguenots." St. Bris gives the order to fire. Rushing over to the group as they fall, St. Bris cries out in anguish as he recognizes his daughter. Gasping that she will pray for him in heaven, Valentine falls dead beside the bodies of Marcel and Raoul.

As the soldiers gather around, savagely clamoring for further revenge, Marguerite's equipage appears. She is returning from the nuptial ball and is on her way to the Louvre. Transfixed with horror, she gazes upon the bodies and then tries vainly to silence the bloodthirsty shouts of the soldiers as the curtain falls.

IDOMENEO, RE DI CRETA

(Idomeneus, King of Crete)

by WOLFGANG AMADEUS MOZART

(1756–91)

Libretto by

ABBÉ GIAMBATTISTA VARESCO

Based on a French opera by André Campra and A. Danchet

CHARACTERS

Idomeneo, King of Crete	Tenor
Idamante, his son (originally soprano role)	Tenor
Ilia, daughter of Priam, King of Troy	Soprano
Electra, daughter of Agamemnon, King of Argos	Soprano
Arbace, counselor to Idomeneo	Tenor
High Priest	Tenor
Voice of Neptune	Bass

Retinues of Idomeneo and Idamante, Cretans, warriors from Crete and Argos, Trojan prisoners, priests of Neptune, dancers

Place: The island of Crete
Time: Shortly before the end of the Trojan War, circa 1200 B.C.
First performance: Munich, January 29, 1781
Original language: Italian

Mozart composed *Idomeneo* in 1780 when he was commissioned to write an *opera seria* for the Munich Carnival of 1781. At the time, he was cathedral organist in Salzburg, and a libretto was furnished him by the Abbé Varesco, chaplain to the Archbishop of Salzburg. The opera is the fifth of Mozart's eleven full-length works for the stage. With its theme of classic tragedy, it is the only one which may correctly be called "grand opera"—as contrasted to the other stage pieces, which fall into the category of *opera buffa,* in which the serious elements of the plot are balanced by situations of comic relief. *Idomeneo* is *opera seria,* a form in which Mozart was intensely interested.

The plot is the story of Idomeneo's return from the Trojan War after years of absence. While the characters involved are from Greek mythology, they are not presented in the frame of historical perspective. As these figures of classic tragedy move through the opera they emerge as a tapestry of human emotions with a quality transcending time.

Although *Idomeneo* has music of grandeur and nobility, it never became a part of operatic repertoire. Written toward the end of the vogue for *opera seria,* it was an anachronism. It has been said that this work—like *La Clemenza di Tito,* Mozart's other *opera seria*—was a museum piece the moment it was put on the stage. Following its Munich premiere it was given only once more during Mozart's lifetime.

A notable revival in this century was under the direction of Richard Strauss, who revised the libretto and rescored the opera for the Munich Festival of 1930. Subsequently it was performed at Glyndebourne in 1951, and in America at Tanglewood, Massachusetts, in 1949 (Goldovsky Opera Company); the New York premiere was given by the Little Orchestra Society in 1951, and the Academy Opera Theater presented it in Brooklyn in 1966.

The overture, with its opening unison passage in D major, establishes the intensely serious mood of the opera. A gradual change to a minor key foreshadows tragedy. In the concluding section a brief characteristic theme emerges in the form of a descending figure for woodwinds, and this is heard several times during the opera. The overture leads directly into Ilia's recitative, which begins without a chord.

ACT ONE

Ilia's apartment in the palace of Idomeneo. In a long recitative ("Quando avran fine omai") she bewails the misfortune which has followed her since the destruction of Troy, where her father, Priam, was slain. She recalls how she was carried away as a captive by the Cretans, then how she was rescued from drowning by Idamante during a storm on the voyage to Crete.

Now she is torn between her love for Idamante and sorrow for her family, lost in the holocaust of Troy. Her grief is even more bitter because she believes that Idamante does not return her love. She is convinced that he is enamored of Electra, who came to the palace as an exile from Argos following the murder of Clytemnestra. Ilia gives voice to her conflicting emotions in the ensuing aria, "Padre, germani, addio," marked by its violent outburst on the word "Grecia" (Greece), on which she lays the blame for her woes.

At the conclusion of the aria Idamante appears with his retinue. He tells Ilia that his father's ships have weathered a terrible storm and are nearing the Cretan coast. Even now, Arbace, Idomeneo's counselor, is searching the shore for him and his men. In gratitude to the gods, Idamante goes on, he will free the Trojan prisoners. Then only one "prisoner" will be left—he himself, who has been captured by Ilia's charms. He elaborates on this thought in the aria "Non ho colpa."

The Trojan prisoners are brought in and they hail their release in a resounding chorus, "Godiam la pace." Electra enters and furiously upbraids Idamante for showing clemency to the enemies of Greece. Her tirade is interrupted by Arbace, who rushes in with the news that another storm has overtaken Idomeneo's fleet and that he has been drowned. Shaken by the news, Idamante calls on his retinue to follow him to the seacoast in search of survivors.

Electra, remaining behind, broods in jealous rage over Idamante's infatuation with Ilia. In the aria "Tutto nel cor vi sento" she calls on the Furies to assist her plans for revenge.

The action now shifts to the storm-wracked seacoast where the wreckage of Idomeneo's ships lies scattered on the sands. The fear-stricken people kneel and pray to the gods to have mercy on those in the grip of the storm ("Pietà! Aiuto o giusto Numi!"). After the prayer they leave the scene, while from the distance come the cries of the sailors, also praying for help.

As their voices die away, Idomeneo appears with a group of his followers, whom he sends on to find help. Left alone, he bitterly reproaches himself for the sinister bargain he made with the sea god Neptune to save his life: he promised to offer up as a sacrifice to Neptune the first mortal he would meet. In the aria "Vedrommi intorno" he reveals his torment at the thought of shedding the blood of an innocent victim. To his horror he sees a figure coming toward him. It is the first mortal he has seen—the unwitting sacrifice. The King curses the gods for their vindictive cruelty toward mankind.

Idamante approaches and generously offers the shipwrecked stranger his assistance. They do not, of course, recognize each other as father and son, yet each senses something vaguely familiar about the other. After several searching questions, they suddenly realize who they are. Idamante joyfully tries to embrace his father, but the horrified King—realizing that his own son will be the victim of his vow to Neptune—warns him not to come near. Stunned by the rebuff, Idamante expresses his bewilderment and anguish in the aria "Il padre adorato ritrovo." The two go their separate ways in utter dejection as the scene ends.

The Cretan warriors and sailors who survived the shipwreck now appear to the accompaniment of a spirited march and are met by the Cretan women, who dance with joy. All join in an exuberant chorus of thanks to Neptune and the sea gods who serve him ("Nettuno s'onori"). This long choral movement is known as a *ciacconna,* the Italian equivalent of the *chaconne,* a device favored by French composers to bring an act to an exciting climax.

ACT TWO

Idomeneo's palace. The act begins with a long dialogue between the King and Arbace. Idomeneo relates that Neptune, jealous of his success in the Trojan War, threatened to destroy him and his fleet, then forced him to agree to sacrifice a mortal to save himself. That mortal, the King says, is his own son.

When he begs Arbace to help him out of this dilemma, the counselor suggests sending Idamante to accompany Electra back to Greece—thus putting him beyond the consequences of his father's ill-fated bargain. Idomeneo profusely thanks Arbace for his advice. Seeing Ilia approaching, the counselor leaves.[1]

In recitative, Ilia and Idomeneo confide in each other. When she expresses her gratitude for the kindness shown her by Idamante, the King answers that his son is carrying out his father's own wishes. In the beautiful aria "Se il padre perduto" Ilia sings that even as a captive she is fortunate: she has acquired a second father and a second homeland.

When she leaves, the King, reflecting on her words, realizes that Ilia has become reconciled to captivity simply because she is in love with Idamante. Thus the tragedy of his vow is threefold: Ilia's happiness as well as his own will be destroyed by Idamante's death. In the great aria "Fuor del mar" Idomeneo laments that Neptune spared his life only to confront him with a more merciless destiny.[2]

Electra approaches. Having learned from Arbace that Idamante is to accompany her back to Greece, she fervently thanks Idomeneo for his magnanimous decision. When he leaves to make final arrangements she expresses her joy at being united with Idamante in the aria "Idol mio, se ritroso altro amante." She also relishes the thought that she has taken him away from Ilia.

The aria leads directly into a brief march which introduces the barcarole "Placido è il mar," sung by the sailors and people as they are about to embark. Electra is joined by Idamante, Idomeneo and their retinues as they prepare to board ship. In the farewell trio which follows ("Pria di partir, o Dio!") Idamante and Electra thank the King for

---

[1] At this point in the original there is an aria for Arbace ("Se il tuo duol"), which is usually omitted. Its theme is that it will be to Idamante's advantage to remove him from the scene. Mozart wrote the entire scene to provide a recitative and aria for the tenor Panzacchi, who created the role of Arbace.

[2] This aria was written as a special favor to Anton Raaff, who, at the age of sixty-five, created the title role.

his benevolence. Idomeneo exhorts his son to fulfill his destiny. In an aside, Idamante expresses his secret grief over parting from Ilia.

Just as the ship is about to sail, a howling storm bursts over the sea. The people voice their terror in an agitated chorus ("Qual nuovo terrore!"). Imploring Neptune to have mercy, they demand to know who among them has incurred the sea god's wrath with evil-doing.

Idomeneo steps forward. In a recitative passage he cries that it is he who has sinned, and he calls on Neptune to punish him alone. He entreats the god not to claim an innocent victim. At that moment an immense sea monster rears up from the waters of the harbor. In the turbulent chorus which concludes the act ("Corriamo, fuggiamo quel mostro") the panic-stricken people urge all to flee for their lives.

ACT THREE

The garden of Idomeneo's palace. Ilia soliloquizes about her longing for Idamante in the tender aria "Zeffiretti lusinghieri," exhorting the breezes to carry her message of love to him. A moment later he enters and dialogue in recitative follows. Idamante tells Ilia that he is hopelessly in love with her, while at the same time he is almost mad with despair over his father's strange behavior toward him. Now, he goes on, he must go forth to slay the monster Neptune has loosed upon the Cretans—and he hopes the encounter will result in his own death.

Entreating him not to give up hope, Ilia cries that she loves him, and that if he dies she herself will die of grief. This leads to the ecstatic duet "S'io non moro a questi accenti," in which the two pledge their undying love.

As they embrace at the conclusion of the duet, they are discovered by Idomeneo and Electra. In the ensuing recitative, Idamante again implores his father to explain why he continues to treat his own son like an enemy. The King, unable to bring himself to disclose the real reason, advises Idamante, for his own sake, to flee the country. When Idamante asks him at least to show compassion toward Ilia, an innocent captive, Electra is consumed by jealous fury. She is driven to distraction when Ilia—unaware of the irony—turns to her for comfort and advice.

In resignation and despair, Idamante finally says he will obey his father and leave. Sorrowfully he bids Ilia to remain and live in peace. As for himself, he will go wandering alone ("Andrò ramingo e solo"). This phrase introduces the magnificent quartet which the musicologist and critic Edward J. Dent called the most beautiful ensemble ever composed for the stage.

Ilia sings that she is determined to die with her lover; Electra seethes with hate and revenge; Idomeneo cries for death to release him from his disastrous vow. The quartet's overriding theme is expressed in the ensemble phrase "soffrir più non si puo" ("to suffer more is not possible"). It ends in a mood of profound tragedy as Idamante repeats the opening measures: "Andrò ramingo e solo."

Suddenly Arbace rushes in shouting that an angry crowd, led by the High Priest of Neptune, is outside demanding to speak to the King. Suspecting the reason for the uproar, Idomeneo nods understandingly to Arbace, then goes out followed by Electra and Ilia.

Staring after them, Arbace is assailed by ominous thoughts about the future of Crete, which he describes in a recitative ("Sventurata Sidon") and an aria ("Se cola ne' fati è scritto"). He fears that the present misfortunes presage the doom of the kingdom. If Crete is guilty, then let her pay the penalty. He begs the avenging gods to spare the King and his son, offering himself as a sacrifice in their stead.[3]

The scene now shifts to a large square in front of the royal palace. Idomeneo, attended by Arbace and his retinue, is seated on his throne. Confronting him are the High Priest and the clamoring throng.

In majestic anger the High Priest tells the King that the savage monster is destroying the city—the streets are running with blood, thousands of his subjects have been swallowed alive by the hideous creature. And yet, the Priest thunders, the King is deaf to their piteous cries for help. In behalf of the people, he calls on Idomeneo to name the person who is to be sacrificed to appease Neptune's wrath. The Priest's excoriation is underscored by a powerful descending figure in the accompaniment.

Thereupon Idomeneo cries out that the sacrificial victim is his own son, Idamante. Pandemonium reigns as the High Priest and the crowd express their horror in a thunderous chorus, "O voto tremendo! spettacolo orrendo!"

During a brief but stately march the scene changes to the Temple of Neptune. Before it stands a gigantic statue of the sea god. On the scene are Idomeneo, with his court, and the High Priest and the people. The temple priests enter in a procession for the ritual of sacrifice. Idomeneo begins the ceremony with a solemn prayer to Neptune ("Accogli o re del mar") in which the priests join. The people hail the King in a brief choral phrase ("Stupenda vittoria").

The ceremony is interrupted by the blare of trumpets mingled with shouts of triumph. Arbace rushes in and tells Idomeneo that Idamante has slain the sea monster and that the people are saved. But Idomeneo is aghast at the news, realizing that Neptune, who sent the monster to ravage the city, now will exact an even more terrible revenge.

Escorted by the royal guard, Idamante enters, dressed in a white sacrificial robe with a wreath on his head. A dramatic colloquy in recitative now ensues. Idamante declares he is willing to be sacrificed in

---

[3] This scene, which Mozart also wrote for Panzacchi, is usually omitted.

fulfillment of his father's vow, which finally was revealed to him. Over the King's anguished protest that he cannot slay his innocent son, Idamante says the will of Jove must be obeyed. Then he commits Ilia to his father's care, saying that her love will replace that of the son he has lost. In an ensuing aria, "No, la morte io non pavento," he sings that he will welcome death, knowing that his beloved will live in peace.

Just as Idomeneo steels himself to proceed with the sacrifice, Ilia rushes in. Throwing herself at his feet, she begs him to offer her as the sacrificial victim. She cries that Idamante is innocent—his life must be spared because on him depends the future of Crete. She herself, she goes on, is a Phrygian, a natural enemy of Crete, and therefore deserving of death. As Idomeneo and Idamante vainly try to dissuade her, Electra looks on in jealous rage. Ilia, deaf to all pleas, turns toward the sacrificial altar, but Idamante restrains her.

At this juncture there is a crash of thunder and the giant statue of Neptune begins to sway. To the reverberating accompaniment of trombone chords, a sonorous oracular voice, apparently emanating from the statue, begins to pronounce judgment ("Ha vinto amore").

The oracle proclaims that through the triumph of love King Idomeneo has been pardoned for his sacrilege. But as a king, he cannot be forgiven for repudiating his vow. Therefore he must abdicate in favor of Idamante, who will ascend the throne with Ilia as his bride.

As the voice of the oracle falls silent, Ilia and Idamante rush into each other's arms, and there are expressions of joy and relief from everyone. In sharp contrast, Electra now comes forward and gives vent to her jealous fury in the opera's most spectacular aria, "D'Oreste, d'Ajace ho in seno i tormenti." She sings that rather than see Idamante in the arms of her rival she will follow her brother Orestes down into hell and there share with him the torments of the damned. She begs the Furies to tear out her heart. Bringing the aria to a fiery climax, Electra rushes away.

To the accompaniment of a sweeping phrase in the violins, Idomeneo ascends the throne for the last time. In an eloquent recitative he makes his final declaration: his fateful vow has been rescinded, Neptune has been appeased and now there will be peace forever in Crete. Then he formally presents Idamante and Ilia to their subjects.

In an ensuing aria, "Torna la pace al core," Idomeneo sings that he has been rejuvenated by the spirit of youth, like an ancient tree that bursts into leaf in spring. The people pay tribute to their new monarch and his bride in a mighty chorus ("Scenda Amor, scenda Imeneo"), a hymn of praise to the gods of love and marriage.

L'INCORONAZIONE DI POPPEA

(*The Coronation of Poppea*)
by CLAUDIO MONTEVERDI
(1567–1643)

Libretto by
GIOVANNI FRANCESCO BUSENELLO

Based on Book XIV of the *Annals* of Publius Cornelius Tacitus, a Roman historian

CHARACTERS

Poppea, a courtesan	Soprano
Nerone (Nero)	Tenor
Arnalta, Poppea's old nurse	Contralto
Drusilla, lady in waiting to Ottavia	Soprano
Ottone (Otho), Poppea's former lover (in Tacitus, her husband)	Bass
Seneca, elder statesman and Stoic philosopher	Bass
Ottavia (Octavia), the Empress	Soprano
Valetto, a page in Ottavia's service	Tenor
Damigella, a maidservant in Ottavia's service	Soprano
Liberto, captain of the guard	Baritone
Lucano (Lucan), a Roman poet, friend of Nerone's	Tenor
Littore (Lictor), a minor Roman official	Bass
Primo Soldato	Tenor
Secondo Soldato	Tenor
Pallade (Pallas Athena), goddess of wisdom	Soprano
Amor, god of love	Soprano

Senators, consults, tribunes, soldiers, disciples of Seneca, servants, people of Rome

Place: Rome
Time: Circa A.D. 55
First performance: Theater of SS. Giovanni ed Paolo, Venice, in the autumn of 1642
Original language: Italian

As the work of a musician who invented a basic system of harmony and who was called the founding father of opera, *L'Incoronazione di Poppea* represents the cornerstone of opera as an art form. Monteverdi adapted the madrigal form to operatic creation by making the music as important as the words, thus giving the voice a greater range of expression. He had laid the foundations with *L'Orfeo* (1608), which required an unheard-of orchestra of thirty-six musicians in support of the vocal line.

His contribution to the development of this genre reached its culmination in *Poppea*—the first opera to use a historical subject for its plot. It was Monteverdi's last work, written when he was seventy-five years old. Of his seven operas, only *Poppea* and *L'Orfeo* have survived. His other works, however—hundreds of madrigals, motets, masses and choral pieces—are treasures of the world's musical heritage.

As to the plot of *Poppea*, it is concededly one of the most amoral and immoral in the history of opera. Vice triumphs over virtue, evil over good, cruelty over compassion. Nero and Poppea are the incarnation of corruption, and in their lust and selfish ambition they destroy all who cross their paths. Yet these hapless mortals work out their destinies in music of extraordinary eloquence and majestic power.

A masterpiece of Italian drama in the seventeenth century, *Poppea* established a tradition. It was played in the principal opera houses of Italy and was chosen to inaugurate the first public opera house opened in Naples in 1651. With a revival of interest in Monteverdi's music in the late nineteenth and early twentieth centuries, the opera was produced in Paris during that era.

Occasionally appearing in modern repertoire, *Poppea* was performed in an abridged version at Glyndebourne in 1962. In America there have been performances in Dallas and workshop presentations at universities. The Chicago Lyric Opera produced the work in November 1966. It was presented in its original form (a prologue and three acts) at Caramoor, Katonah, New York, in June 1968 by the New York City Opera under the baton of Julius Rudel and subsequently during the company's 1977–78 season.

The opera opens with an imposing sinfonia with its theme sounded forth in majestic chords, reflecting the panoply of the imperial Roman court.

ACT ONE

[*Scene One*] Poppea's house outside Rome. It is early morning. Two guards lie asleep before the door. Ottone, returning from the wars, enters and in the aria "E pure io torno" expresses his joy over the prospect of seeing his beloved Poppea again. He sings that he is drawn to her as though by some magnetic force. But his ardor turns to despair when he suddenly catches sight of the two soldiers. Recognizing them as Nerone's bodyguards, he realizes that the Emperor has displaced him as Poppea's lover. Crying to the gods to witness his anguish, he rushes away.

His lamentations awaken the guards, who bawl out the customary challenge—which of course does not bring an answer. In an ensuing duet ("Sia maledetto Amor") the two launch into a comical tirade about their military duties. They fervently curse everyone who is in love —particularly Nerone and Poppea for keeping them up all night on guard duty. They curse the vileness of Rome and wind up with a double curse on the army.

The two deplore Nerone's shameful humiliation of his Empress. What is worse, they go on, Rome is being threatened on all sides by enemies—but the Emperor only laughs and goes on making love. Finally, however, they agree that under the circumstances it is wisest to see nothing they are not supposed to see. Their voices sink to a whisper as they warn that the Emperor is approaching.

Nerone enters with Poppea and a long, impassioned duet follows. Poppea seductively implores the Emperor not to leave ("Signor, deh, non partire"). Nerone, surfeited for the moment, says he must go, warning her that their rendezvous must be kept secret until he can free himself from the Empress. But when in the next moment he tells Poppea that he will return to be with her forever, she bids him go with her blessing. The duet ends on amorous phrases of avowal.

[Scene Two] Inside Poppea's house. Savoring her triumph, Poppea sings that her hopes are high because the god of love himself will lead her to the throne ("Speranza, tu mi vai"). Arnalta comes in and tries to warn her that Ottavia knows of her liaison with Nerone and may exact a terrible revenge. Poppea blithely answers that the god of love and the goddess Fortune both are on her side. Arnalta sardonically observes that she must be mad indeed to put her trust in a blind boy and a capricious old woman.

[Scene Three] Ottavia's apartment in the palace. Tormented by jealousy and shame, the Empress abandons herself to bitter reflection in the recitative and aria "Disprezzata regina." Queen of an empire, she is the object of scorn and ridicule as the wronged wife. She laments the unhappy lot of her sex: fated to be enslaved by marriage, destined to suffer the pain of childbearing only to bring into the world tyrants, brutes and murderers.

In her anguish and frustration, Ottavia curses the gods for allowing

Nerone to go unpunished—then suddenly expresses horror at her own blasphemy. In a phrase of hopeless resignation, she asks leave to bury her misery in silence.

Drusilla, noting her mistress' distress, naïvely tries to console her with some practical advice: now that Nerone has been taken from her by Poppea, the Empress is free to choose someone worthier of her. This alone, Drusilla says, will assuage her grief. Ottavia answers that she will bear her burden of sorrow as befits the dignity of an empress.

Seneca comes in with Valetto and in sententious phrases ("O gloriosa del mondo Imperatrice") gives Ottavia the benefit of his counsel. Urging her not to quail before misfortune, he declaims that adversity makes one immune to the blows of fate. The Empress acidly observes that his eloquence is no balm for a wounded heart.

Valetto, exasperated by Seneca's pomposity, turns on him with a flood of stinging rebuke ("Madama, con tua pace"). Asking Ottavia's leave, he warns the philosopher that if he persists in offering the Empress oratory instead of assistance he himself will make a bonfire of his precious books and singe his beard into the bargain. The threat makes no impression on Seneca. Ottavia leaves, followed by the page.

As the philosopher stands deep in thought, Pallas Athena appears before him. In a foreboding refrain ("Seneca, io miro in cielo") she foretells his doom: the planets are in evil conjunction, and before another day dawns he will hear the warning of his fate. Seneca replies that he is not afraid to die—after the turbulent ordeal of life he will welcome the peace of death. The vision of the goddess fades.

Nerone strides in and informs Seneca that he has decided to dethrone the Empress, then marry Poppea and make her his Queen. A dramatic colloquy ensues. Seneca implores the Emperor not to defy the laws of Rome and bring the wrath of the Senate and the people down upon his head. Nerone contemptuously retorts that he cares nothing about public opinion.

The philosopher's persistent talk of "reason" and "conscience" gradually drives Nerone to hysterical fury. In a final effort to bring him to his senses, Seneca reminds him that he is Emperor of Rome and that it is unworthy of him to be swayed by the charms of a woman. Thereupon Nerone furiously denounces him as a presumptuous old meddler and rushes away. Looking after him, Seneca murmurs that he knows only too well what the consequence of the Emperor's mood will be: when lust for power supplants reason, disaster is sure to follow.

[*Scene Four*] Inside Poppea's house. She and Nerone are in each other's arms. With tantalizing guile, Poppea asks if her modest charms are pleasing to him ("Come dolci, Signor"). This marks the beginning of a voluptuous duet. Completely under her spell, he promises to share the Empire with her and bestow upon her the title of "Illustrious Empress." He cries that the royal diadem, all Rome, even Italy itself are mere baubles unworthy to be offered so glorious a queen.

Now confident of her mastery over Nerone, Poppea removes the last obstacle in her path. His trusted counselor Seneca, she says, has let it be known that he is the real power behind the throne—it is he who wields the scepter. In sudden fury Nerone shouts for the Lictor and orders him to go at once to Seneca with this message: he is to die this evening. Then turning back to Poppea he sings that today she will see what love and Nerone together can accomplish ("Ciò che può far Amore").

[*Scene Five*] Poppea's house. Ottone abjectly entreats Poppea not to desert him. She tells him flatly that she is rejecting his love in favor of a kingdom, then leaves him with a gesture of disdain. Ottone loudly bewails his misfortune. At this point Drusilla enters and takes due note of his self-pitying lamentations. In the ensuing duet ("Già l'oblio seppelli gli andati") she offers him the consolation of her love. He gratefully accepts and swears eternal fidelity. But when she leaves he murmurs that while Drusilla's name is on his lips, Poppea's is in his heart.[1]

[*Scene Six*] This scene is an interlude in the form of an amusing duet between Valetto and Damigella. The love-smitten page describes his emotions in rather simple-minded terms ("Sento un certo non so che"). Damigella twits him about his childish prattle ("Astutello garzoncello"), observing that if he really fell in love he probably would lose his mind completely.

[*Scene Seven*] Seneca's garden. In a recitative passage, the philosopher muses on the blessing of solitude ("Solitudine amata"), which releases the soul from the thrall of earthly corruption. His meditation is interrupted by the Lictor, who asks his pardon for bringing evil tidings. Seneca replies that he knows what the message is: he will obey the Emperor's command, and by this evening he will be dead.

A moment later his friends and disciples throng into the garden, and he announces that his final hour has come ("Amici, è giunta l'ora"). In a stirring chromatic chorus ("Non morir, Seneca") the people beg him not to die. Though moved by their entreaties, he asks them to leave, then orders his servants to prepare his bath. There, he sings in farewell, his innocent blood will flow like a river ("come sangue innocente io vo").[2]

---

[1] End of Act One in the original.

[2] According to history, Seneca committed suicide by cutting his wrists in his bath.

ACT TWO

[*Scene One*] Nerone's apartments in the palace. Celebrating the death of Seneca, Nerone and his friend, the decadent poet Lucano, stage a drunken orgy. In a duet ("Cantiam amorose canzoni") they hail Poppea as a woman whose talent for love-making is equaled only by her lust for power.

[*Scene Two*] Ottavia's apartment in the palace. A dialogue in recitative takes place in which the Empress orders Ottone to kill Poppea. When he recoils in horror, she warns him not to disobey. He is to disguise himself as a woman to conceal his identity. Ottone cries that he cannot murder in cold blood, whereupon the Empress threatens to accuse him before Nerone of improper conduct toward her. As he well knows, she adds, that will mean unspeakable torture. Terror-stricken, Ottone agrees to carry out her plan.

[*Scene Three*] In an exultant refrain ("Felice cor mio") Drusilla expresses her joy at having won Ottone as her lover. But at the climax of her song he rushes in, almost beside himself with fear and anxiety, and tells her of Ottavia's murderous command. Still bemused by thoughts of romance and oblivious to Ottone's distress, she gaily repeats the phrases of her love song. When he begs her to be silent and listen, she assures him that he can count on her aid without fail. As for the disguise—she not only will give him her garments but will dress him with her own hands.

[*Scene Four*] Poppea's bedroom (or the palace garden). Elated at the news of Seneca's death, Poppea sings a jubilant hymn to the god of love ("Amor, ricorro a te") as her mentor in her campaign for the throne. When Arnalta enters she happily assures the nurse that she will share her good fortune. Noticing that Poppea is overwrought, Arnalta urges her to rest. She sings her to sleep with a hypnotic lullaby which, with its undulations from major to minor, is one of the most striking numbers in the opera.

A moment after she leaves, Amor appears. He observes that it is well that Poppea, with eyes closed in sleep, cannot see her murderer approaching. In the ensuing aria, "O sciocchi frali mortali," he muses that slumbering mortals thus think themselves safe from all harm. Fortunately for them, Amor keeps a sleepless vigil. And now he, that same little god, will save this sleeping mortal from the evil fate designed for her.

To the accompaniment of a menacing arpeggio, Ottone, dressed in

Drusilla's clothes, creeps toward Poppea's bed. In quasi-recitative he sings that she will never awaken to discover that her murderer is the lover she rejected. Just as he raises his dagger, Amor springs forward and furiously denounces him as a vile assassin. As a god, he cries, he will not waste his arrows on so ignoble a mortal, but will leave him to the hangman's noose. Ottone rushes away.

Poppea awakens and catches sight of the fleeing figure in woman's clothes. Her cries of "Drusilla" bring Arnalta to her side. The nurse shouts for the servants, ordering them to pursue and kill the would-be murderess. They dash away as the music rises to a surging climax. At this point there is another seriocomic touch characteristic of the opera. Amor struts forward and boastfully asserts that it was he alone who saved Poppea because he has willed her to be Empress.

[*Scene Five*] A street in Rome.[3] Drusilla, unaware of what has happened, gloats over the fact that her rival for Ottone's love soon will be eliminated. Suddenly she is surrounded by a shouting throng led by Arnalta and the Lictor. The nurse screams that there is the assassin, who has tried to escape detection by changing her clothes. When Drusilla asks what crime she has committed, Arnalta accuses her of trying to murder Poppea. Drusilla only then realizes with horror that Ottone's fateful disguise has implicated her in the conspiracy.

At that moment Nerone enters and Arnalta repeats her accusations. When Drusilla protests her innocence, the Emperor orders her to be tortured until she confesses and names her accomplices. Impelled by her love for Ottone, she suddenly decides to shoulder the blame and blurts out that she alone plotted the murder. As Nerone savagely orders his soldiers to torture her to the utmost, Ottone rushes in. Over Drusilla's frantic protestations he shouts that he is guilty and begs the Emperor to put him to death.[4]

Nerone, however, consigns him to exile in the desert, with forfeiture of all his titles and his fortune. Turning to Drusilla, he proclaims that he will reward her valorous determination to share her lover's guilt by granting her pardon. Drusilla replies that she asks nothing more than to live and die in exile with Ottone. She thanks Fortune that the Emperor has recognized the power of love in a woman's heart. Angry and exasperated, Nerone orders the lovers out of his sight.

Then he stuns the throng with the proclamation that he has banished Ottavia from the throne and has condemned her to perpetual exile. She

[3] Act Three in the original.

[4] In the original, Ottone confesses that Ottavia commanded him to murder Poppea. Nerone seizes upon this as an excuse to punish the Empress with banishment.

is to be taken to the nearest seacoast, put aboard a flimsy boat and left to the mercy of the wind and waves.

Poppea enters as he speaks the final words of his decree. With gloating satisfaction she commends his decision as wise and just. Taking her in his arms, Nerone declares that today he will make her his Empress and invest her with crown and royal purple. Poppea responds with a passionate declaration of love ("Idolo del cor mio"), which marks the beginning of a fervid, sensuous duet.

[*Scene Six*] Ottavia, bereft of her throne and doomed to perpetual exile, bids a poignant farewell to Rome, fatherland and friends in one of the opera's greatest arias, "Addio Roma, addio patria, addio amici." Bold dissonances in the accompaniment underscore the intensity of her grief.

[*Scene Seven*] This scene is another example of the interludes of comic relief which heighten the contrasting impact of the opera's underlying tragedy. In the aria "Io, che son la nutrice" Arnalta gloats over the caprice of fortune which has made her the confidante of the Empress of Rome. Now all those who once scorned her as a humble nurse will bow and scrape and murmur, "Your Ladyship." Born a servant, she will die a lady. She reflects, however, that if she were to be reincarnated she would prefer the reverse: after all, those who live a life of ease leave it regretfully; those who live in misery and hardship welcome the release of death.

[*Scene Eight*] The climactic Coronation Scene is introduced by a stately fanfare, and then the populace hails Nerone and his new Empress in a resounding chorus, "Con il consenso universal." At its conclusion the crowd disperses, leaving Emperor and Empress alone on a darkening stage. In a transport of triumph and sensual ardor, their voices merge in a final duet—the great passacaglia which crowns the opera—"Pur ti miro, pur ti stringo."

L'ITALIANA IN ALGERI
(*The Italian Girl in Algiers*)
by GIOACCHINO ROSSINI
(1792–1868)

Libretto by

ANGELO ANELLI

Based on the legend of Roxelana, favorite slave of Suleiman II, known as "the Magnificent," sultan of Algiers, circa 1520

CHARACTERS

Mustafa, Bey of Algiers	Bass
Elvira, his wife	Soprano
Zulma, personal slave of Elvira	Mezzo-soprano
Haly (Ali), Mustafa's bodyguard, captain of the Algerian pirates	Bass-baritone
Lindoro, young Italian slave of Mustafa	Tenor
Isabella, an Italian beauty from Verona	Mezzo-soprano
Taddeo, suitor of Isabella	Baritone

Eunuchs of the harem, Algerian pirates, Italian slaves, pappataci, harem women, sailors

Place: Mustafa's palace on the seashore in Algiers
Time: Thirteenth century
First performance: Teatro San Benedetto, Venice, May 22, 1813
Original language: Italian

Rossini's operatic harem romp, a work bubbling with wit and frivolity, is his ninth opera and the one that put him in the front rank of musicians of his day at the age of twenty-one. He considered the libretto by Angelo Anelli the best buffa work he had thus far encountered in his meteoric career; he said he wrote the opera in eighteen days.

L'Italiana, acknowledged as Rossini at his comic best, took the fun-loving Venetians by storm. But the composer took the accolades in stride. The story goes that after the spectacular first night, he remarked:

"I thought that after hearing my opera the Venetians would treat me like a crazy man; they turned out to be crazier than I am."

After scoring in other cities in Italy and in Europe, the opera reached New York in 1832 and established itself in the repertoire. It was performed four times during the Metropolitan Opera season of 1919–20. In subsequent revivals in recent years it was sung by such *bel canto* specialists as Giulietta Simionato, Teresa Berganza and Marilyn Horne. Miss Horne headed the cast of the Metropolitan's new production on November 10, 1973.

The overture, of course, is a staple of the orchestral repertoire. It foreshadows the irrepressible gaiety that infuses the opera from beginning to end. The first theme imitates the bombastic proclamations of Mustafa—when he can make himself heard over his chattering harem. A second theme portrays the elegant, mischievous charm of Isabella. The overture winds up with one of the famous Rossinian crescendos.

ACT ONE

[*Scene One*] An anteroom between the palace apartments of Mustafa and Elvira. She is seated on a sofa and is attended by Zulma and an entourage of eunuchs. In the opening chorus ("Serenate il mesto") the eunuchs commiserate with Elvira, born to the suffering that is the lot of womankind. In solo interludes, she bewails her misfortune. Zulma advises her not to try the Bey's patience too far—he is dangerous when aroused. The eunuchs solemnly comment that in present circumstances there is not much hope for the lady.

Everyone starts in alarm as Mustafa is announced. He stalks in to staccato chords in the orchestra, then launches into a blustering coloratura aria ("Delle donne l'arroganza"), sung over a choral accompaniment and the fear-stricken interjections of Elvira and Zulma. The Bey informs the world at large that he is a woman tamer without peer and more than a match for feminine wiles.

When Elvira sobs that she will do anything to please her lord and master, the Bey roars at her to stop her infernal whimpering and go away. As the ensemble builds up, Elvira's wailing grows louder and Mustafa's temper gets worse. Meanwhile the eunuchs loudly praise the Bey as the paragon of virility whose very presence makes women swoon.

In ensuing recitative, Mustafa orders everybody out of his sight except Haly, who is directed to bring in the Bey's favorite Italian slave, Lindoro, immediately. As things stand, he goes on irritably, Elvira is boring him to death. Getting rid of her is bad—but keeping her is worse. And so he has decided to marry her off to Lindoro, a promising young fellow who is an ideal candidate for the job of husband. But he is not a Turk, Haly points out. What of it, Mustafa retorts. A submissive, obedient creature like Elvira is just the type for this splendid young Italian. But this is against Moslem law, Haly protests. *I* am the law, Mustafa bellows. Then he fumes about his harem—these females are driving him crazy with their everlasting billing and cooing. What he wants is one of these beautiful Italian creatures—a haughty, high-spirited signora who will be worthy of his prowess as a great lover.

Haly asks for time until the next ship arrives. Today, the Bey answers peremptorily, is Monday: if you do not produce an Italian by Friday—off with your head. That will not be necessary, Haly murmurs as he follows Mustafa out.

Lindoro enters. In a melodious cavatina ("Languir per una bella") he pours out his anguish over being separated from his beloved Isabella and from his homeland. The aria, with its romantic French horn obbligato and replete with above-the-staff roulades, rounds out the picture of a moonstruck lover.

As he revels in his misery, Mustafa bursts in with the great news: he is about to present Lindoro with a wife. Thunderstruck, Lindoro asks how he can marry without first being in love. You Italians, Mustafa scoffs—always thinking about love! Doesn't money mean anything? Not everything, Lindoro replies hastily, trying to squirm out of the trap. What then *do* you want, Mustafa demands. A loving woman who will be my soulmate, Lindoro answers sentimentally. Good, says Mustafa, I have the perfect woman for you. This leads into a duet ("Se inclinassi a prender moglie") in which the two discuss the qualifications of an ideal wife. One woman in a hundred, Lindoro observes skeptically. Mustafa (determined to promote Elvira) reiterates that the woman he has in mind will meet every test. Still trying to escape the connubial trap, Lindoro ticks off his requirements: modesty, charm, tenderness, eyes like stars, ravishing figure, flawless complexion and so on and so on. Mustafa tops him on every item. Lindoro keeps refusing, Mustafa keeps insisting, and thus the duet climaxes in a blaze of vocal pyrotechnics.

[*Scene Two*] A rocky section of the Barbary coast not far from the palace, where a ship has been driven ashore in a storm which is now abating. On deck, a scene of wild confusion. Soon Haly's pirate ship approaches. Staring at the wreck, he and his crew gloat over their prize ("Quanta roba"). They gape at the sight of the beautiful Isabella ("Ma una bella") and sing that this booty certainly will please their great Bey. Haly orders everybody off the wreck. Isabella, with queenly dignity, makes her way to shore through the openmouthed throng of pirates.

Surrounded by her captors, Isabella laments her cruel fate as a castaway in a cavatina ("Cruda sorte"). At first she recalls the terror of the storm, and wonders if she will ever see her beloved Lindoro again. But then her courage returns. In the ensuing cabaletta ("Già saper pratica") she sings that this is the moment for determination, not despair. After all, her captors are only men—and she knows how to deal with the breed. They are all alike, with one thing on their minds, and they are putty in the hands of a beautiful woman. And so: *avanti!*

Haly and his pirates find Taddeo among the survivors and drag him ashore. He abjectly begs for mercy. When Isabella tells Haly that this creature is her "uncle," Taddeo has wit enough to agree, and explains that he is obliged to remain with her as her protector. Their ship was driven off course, he goes on, after they had sailed from Verona.

Ah-ha, Italians, Haly exclaims delightedly, who will be more than welcome at the palace of the Bey. Best of all, the beautiful lady herself will be made queen of the harem. With that stunning news, Haly leaves, driving the captured sailors and slaves before him.

Taddeo groans that now indeed all is lost—he will be tortured in Turkish fashion as a captive; she will be the mistress of a sultan. Isabella shrugs: *sarà quel che sarà*. Her casual acceptance of the situation irritates Taddeo, and the two fall to quarreling ("Ai capricci della sorte"). In this duet, Isabella sings that she can bear misfortune more easily than callous rudeness from a man. Taddeo retorts that he is not one to be treated like an infatuated schoolboy lover—what is more, he knows exactly what kind of a trap he is being led into. Tempers rising, they begin calling each other names: stubborn donkey . . . shameless hussy . . . lackey . . . crafty female. . . . So the shouting match continues.

Then suddenly—emotionally and musically—the mood changes. Isabella wonders how she can escape a fate worse than death ("Ma in man de' barbari"). Taddeo is certain he will be impaled in accepted Turkish fashion ("Ma se all lavoro"). Seeing no way out of their predicament, they decide to call a truce. The hectic tempo of the duet subsides into a serene rhythmic phrase. Then the two address each other as in a formal introduction: *Donna Isabella . . . Messer Taddeo . . . La furia or placasi*—"Let us make peace again."

Then in a vivacious continuation of the duet ("Ah! no, per sempre uniti") they resolve to face their fate bravely as "niece" and "uncle." When Taddeo frets that he does not trust the Bey, Isabella assures him that she is quite capable of handling the situation in her own way.

[*Scene Three*] The anteroom in the palace, as in Scene One. In recitative, Zulma, Elvira and Lindoro discuss the situation. Lindoro insists that he does not want to marry Elvira—who quite logically reminds him that she is currently the wife of the Bey. But Zulma points out that it is the Bey who gives the orders in the palace—and his orders are that Lindoro is to marry Elvira.

Mustafa enters. Good news, he tells Lindoro. A ship is sailing for Italy in an hour; he has ordered the captain not to sail until Lindoro comes aboard—on the condition that he takes Elvira with him. Lindoro decides to capitulate—and, anyway, he may be able to make Elvira his legitimate wife once they are both in Italy.

When Elvira tearfully protests that she cannot leave Mustafa, he brusquely tells her to stop crying, and be off. Whereupon he turns his attention to Haly, who enters to tell him about capturing a beautiful Italian—the very woman he is looking for. He orders Haly to summon his harem: he will favor them with a demonstration on how to deal with an Italian woman. As an afterthought, he reminds Elvira and Lindoro not to miss the boat.

In an ensuing aria ("Già insolito ardore") he revels in the thought that this impending conquest is inflaming his desire and will add glory to his name as an irresistible Don Juan. As for Elvira: go—and take Zulma with you ("Voi partite, m'annoiate"). With that he leaves with Haly and his entourage.

[*Scene Four*] The magnificent hall of the palace. The finale of the act, a masterpiece of ensemble writing, opens with a pompous chorus of eunuchs ("Viva il flagel delle donne"), hailing the potentate who alone knows the secret of changing distaff tigers into tender, loving lambs. At its conclusion Haly, in a stentorian unaccompanied phrase, announces Isabella ("Sta qui fuori la bella Italiana"). Mustafa is stunned by her beauty.

Then follows a hilarious duet in which Isabella and Mustafa—each singing to themselves—express contradictory thoughts about each other. Isabella ridicules the Bey as a fat, panting caricature of a lover, and decides she knows exactly how to go about making a complete fool of him. Mustafa relishes the thought of possessing this delicious morsel of femininity.

Suddenly Taddeo bursts in. Pushing Haly aside, he announces that he is Isabella's uncle and is here to protect her. When he sees Isabella and Mustafa virtually in each other's arms, he staggers back in astonishment. Beside himself, he even appeals to Mustafa for help, addressing him comically as *Signor, Monsieur,* and *Euer Gnaden.* When Haly derides him as a blockhead, Mustafa casually orders: off with his head. At this point, Isabella intercedes. Taddeo, she says, really is her uncle. Mustafa gallantly relents and allows Taddeo to keep his head.

The voices of Isabella, Taddeo, Haly and Mustafa blend in a quartet ("Caro, capisco adesso") expressing their various reactions—Isabella outrageously flattering Mustafa, who responds with fatuous endearments, Taddeo as usual bemoaning his fate, Haly voicing his contempt for the cringing Taddeo.

Over the accompaniment of a minuet rhythm (one of the most captivating themes in the opera), Elvira, Zulma and Lindoro now enter to bid farewell to Mustafa ("Pria di dividerci da voi"). The minuet continues in ironic contrast to an interruption as Isabella and Lindoro suddenly recognize each other. Dumbfounded, they wonder what will happen now ("Che mai sarà?").

Then follows a remarkable ensemble known as the "Septet of Amazement." It begins as Mustafa comments ("confusi, stupido") on the surprise and confusion that seem to have overcome Isabella and Lindoro. The others—Elvira, Taddeo, Haly, Zulma—join to express their amazement at this unexpected turn of events.

Midway in the uproar there is a moment of stunned silence as Isabella steps forward. Staring at Elvira, she asks Mustafa who this woman is ("Dite: chi è quella femmina?"). My wife, Mustafa replies, adding casually that since he no longer wants her he is marrying her off to his favorite slave, Lindoro. Infuriated, Isabella exclaims she will not tolerate this kind of barbaric practice. Either Elvira remains as lawful wife, or she—Isabella—will leave at once. What is more, she demands the services of Lindoro as her personal slave. When Mustafa protests, she accuses him of not loving her. Completely outmaneuvered, Mustafa moans that this woman is driving him crazy. Zulma, Elvira and Lindoro gleefully comment that Isabella has made an ass of the mighty Bey.

As all the others—including the women of the harem, the slaves and the eunuchs—express their reactions, the scene builds into one of the most bizarre ensembles in the opera. They sing that they are drowning in a sea of confusion, then begin to imitate the sounds they hear going on inside their addled heads: crows cawing, hammers pounding, bells ringing, cannons booming.[1] This brings the act to a roaring climax.

ACT TWO

[*Scene One*] The anteroom of the palace, as in Act One. In an opening chorus, Elvira, Zulma and Haly, with the eunuchs and slaves, comment derisively on Mustafa's surrender to Isabella ("Uno stupido, uno stolto"). Elvira grudgingly admires the beautiful Italian who has defeated the great sultan at his own game. In an ensuing recitative, the three conclude that Isabella's devious tactics may yet serve to bring Mustafa to his senses and leave him content to be a good husband.

The Bey himself enters and orders the women to inform Isabella that

[1] Use of this choral technique to generate musical pandemonium is in an *opera buffa* tradition that goes back to the time of Pergolesi.

she is to have coffee with him in his room. When Elvira warns him that his beautiful Italian may be too clever to fall into that kind of a trap, he boasts that she already adores him and will be only too happy to have a tête-à-tête. In any case, the Bey adds, he will persuade her blockhead of an uncle to assist him in this affair. Leaving, he orders Haly to call Isabella. She herself enters lamenting that not only has she been shipwrecked and made captive in a harem, but her Lindoro has deceived her.

When he comes in and remarks on her woebegone expression she accuses him of deserting her to become the husband of Elvira. Escort, Lindoro corrects her, *never* a husband. He fervently assures her of his undying love, and to prove it he will devise some means of escape. They plan to meet later in the garden. Isabella leaves to have "coffee" with Mustafa.

In the following cavatina ("Ah, come il cor di giubilo") Lindoro sings of his joy in being reunited with his beloved. As he leaves, Mustafa enters with Taddeo. They are followed by the eunuchs and two ferocious-looking Moors carrying a Turkish costume and a saber.

Mustafa, aside, tries to convince himself that Isabella really loves him. Taddeo interrupts his reflections, imploring for mercy. Frightened out of his wits, he is certain that he is being led to his execution. Mustafa tells him to calm down: instead of impalement he is to be honored with the title of "Kaimakan," lieutenant of the Bey and official protector of the Mussulman (Moslem). The title, the Bey explains, is bestowed to honor him as uncle of the beautiful Italian who is to become queen of the harem. Taddeo thanks him profusely. The eunuchs hail Taddeo in a mock-heroic chorus—"Viva il grande Kaimakan!"

Suspecting that he is being maneuvered into a trap, Taddeo stammers that he is too much of a dolt to qualify for so exalted a position. No matter, Mustafa answers; his only duty will be to smooth the way into Isabella's good graces. Aside, Taddeo murmurs that now he has succeeded only in digging his own grave ("Messer Taddeo, che bell'impiego è questo").

The two Moors now dress Taddeo in a bizarre Turkish harem costume—complete with turban and saber. Awkwardly trying to adjust himself to this regalia, he continues to stammer excuses. He cowers when the Bey glares at him in annoyance. Finally deciding he would rather "swat flies and fan the Bey" than be impaled, Taddeo promises he will do his best as Kaimakan ("Non vi voglio disgustar"). The eunuchs reprise their mocking chorus of acclaim.

[*Scene Two*] Isabella's apartment in the palace. Richly dressed in Turkish fashion, she is seated before a large mirror. Elvira, Zulma and Lindoro, at one side, stare wonderingly as Isabella preens herself in her

Oriental finery. Deliberately playing the imperious queen, she orders her "slave," Lindoro, to serve coffee—for three. When Elvira humbly interjects that Mustafa will object to a third person, Isabella sharply rebukes her for kowtowing to a bullying husband.

In Italy, she adds, things are different. She orders Elvira to wait in her room until she is called for. Then she will be given a lesson in dealing properly with a man. If only she had such courage, Elvira mutters as she leaves. Isabella continues primping in front of the mirror.

As a lilting theme sounds in the orchestra, Mustafa, Taddeo and Lindoro steal in at the back of the room unobserved (they think) by Isabella. This action introduces the delightful scene of Isabella's "playacting." In honeyed phrases ("Per lui che adoro, che il mio tesoro") she expresses her passionate longing for her "lover." To herself—in an allegro passage unheard by the eavesdroppers—she vows to teach the conceited lord of the harem a trick or two about women ("aspetta, tu non sai chi sono ancor").

Each of the three swains, of course, assumes that Isabella's blandishments are meant for him alone, and they react accordingly: Mustafa explosively sighs, "Darling!"; Taddeo rages over her fickleness; Lindoro wonders if all this is part of their own plot, or if Isabella is a faithless hussy. Meanwhile, Isabella relishes the idea of making fools of all three, and then the scene builds into a sparkling quartet. Having accomplished part of her designs, Isabella leaves.

The three deluded admirers withdraw to another part of the palace, where Mustafa tells Taddeo to bring in Isabella. He instructs him that he is to leave as tactfully as possible as soon as he hears a sneeze ("quando io starnuto levati tosto"). This leads into the uproarious "sneezing quintet," which begins when Mustafa pompously introduces Taddeo to Isabella as her personal Kaimakan ("Sir Taddeo, Kaimakan, io presento"). Almost choking with laughter at Taddeo's ridiculous costume, Isabella manages to acknowledge the honor.

Taddeo and Lindoro now fall in with the plot. With a knowing look at Isabella, Taddeo tells her that as her Kaimakan his first duty is to "preserve the status quo." Lindoro assures the Bey that Isabella is making herself as attractive as possible to please him alone. On cue, Isabella ardently murmurs, "Darling!" Mustafa sneezes resonantly; Taddeo and Lindoro respond with "Gesundheit!" Taddeo curses Mustafa under his breath, but makes no move to leave as instructed. Another sneeze . . . Taddeo again ignores the signal.

Beginning to lose his temper, Mustafa lets go with a barrage of sneezes, to no avail. Isabella and Lindoro double up with laughter; Taddeo vows to stay even if Mustafa bursts. The uproar subsides momentarily as Isabella calls for coffee and sends a slave to recall Elvira. While the four are being served by Lindoro, Isabella tries to intercede

with Mustafa on Elvira's behalf. He snaps that he wants nothing to do
with this stupid woman, then explodes in exasperation as the four implore him to be kind to his wife ("Andate alla malora"). Denouncing
them all as traitors, he shouts that he is not being taken in by their skulduggery.

The ensemble continues in quintet form over an accompaniment in
swirling thirds in a polonaise rhythm. The Bey's anger and impatience
transmit themselves to the others, who sing that all this nonsense is
driving them out of their minds. Thus the ensemble winds up in a
bristling climax as Mustafa storms from the room, followed by the
others.

[*Scene Three*] Haly comes in and sings an amusing aria ("Le femmine d'Italia"), a kind of patter song in which he compares Italian
women with others he has met during his world travels. In his Le-
porello-like "catalogo" (here freely translated) he describes them thus:
in London, majestic; Dublin, domestic; San Francisco, gracious; Paris,
flirtatious; Moscow, vivacious—and so on. But the best by far, he concludes, are the Italian women.[2]

A scene in recitative follows in which Taddeo and Lindoro develop
their plot against Mustafa—and, incidentally, try to hoodwink each
other. Taddeo reveals that he is not Isabella's uncle, but the man she really loves. Lindoro chuckles to himself over this delusion. But when
they see Mustafa approaching they leave off their double-talk and con-
centrate on their victim.

Mustafa waddles in, still fuming over being made sport of by a gaggle
of conniving "friends," and sarcastically asks Taddeo if his niece assumes he is as gullible as an Italian. On the contrary, Taddeo assures
him, she loves his lordship very dearly. Lindoro quickly concurs. The
fact is, he adds, that Isabella thinks so highly of him that she has ordered a banquet in his honor and will confer on him the coveted title of
"Pappataci."

"Pappataci! What an honor!" Mustafa exclaims. "And *what* is 'Pappataci?'" Lindoro gravely informs him that it is so prestigious a title
that it cannot be inherited ("A color che mai non sanno"). It can be bestowed only on the man who has proved himself a great lover. Taddeo
adds that now the palace has a Pappataci *and* a Kaimakan—an unbeata-
ble combination. The Bey, profoundly impressed, is loud in his praise
of the devastating charm of Italian women.

Taddeo and Lindoro then point out that the duties of a Pappataci are
indeed difficult—but pleasant—to wit: eat, drink and then go to sleep

[2] In interpolating this aria (often omitted) Rossini followed the operatic custom
of his time: giving every leading singer a chance to be heard on his own.

("ber, dormire e poi mangiare"). Beaming in anticipation, Mustafa repeats the rules, with the two conspirators flippantly echoing his phrases.

In a recitative interlude, Zulma tells Haly that Isabella is playing up to Mustafa for the sole purpose of reconciling him with Elvira. To that end, she plans to honor him with a banquet and a title—which will melt whatever resistance he has left. It will be worth the trouble, Zulma remarks, if it teaches the Bey a lesson.

[*Scene Four*] In the anteroom of the palace. Taddeo and Lindoro marvel at Isabella's clever ruse: while distracting Mustafa's attention with festivities, she has arranged to have the captive Italian sailors and slaves ready to escape on the ship waiting in the harbor. Isabella herself enters, followed by the Italians, who lustily sing that, like true sons of Italy, they are armed and ready to fight for freedom ("Pronti abbiamo e ferri e mani"). Noticing Taddeo and Lindoro looking on skeptically, Isabella chides them for doubting the success of her plan. They will soon learn, she declares, how a woman's courage can turn defeat into victory.

Then in a remarkable change of mood she exhorts the Italians to think of their homeland ("Pensa la patria") and to act with bravery and determination in the name of Italy's new spirit of freedom. The aria, sung over the chorus of sailors and slaves, has a dignity in sharp contrast to the frivolous spirit of the opera.[3] When Taddeo sneers at these patriotic sentiments, Isabella roundly berates him for his cynicism. Yet in the next moment she impulsively turns to Lindoro, assuring him of her love. She goes on to express her joy over the prospect of returning to Italy, while the sailors and slaves sing that they will trust her to lead them to freedom. Her dazzling roulades sung over the choral accompaniment bring the ensemble to a typical Rossinian climax.

Taddeo, apparently oblivious to Isabella's rebuke, witlessly marvels that she is risking her life for the sake of his love. Mustafa appears. Taddeo tells him that Isabella is preparing for his investiture in the order of Pappataci, in which other distinguished Pappataci are to participate.

The latter arrive to a pompous fanfare scored mainly for horns.[4]

[3] "Pensa la patria" brings to mind the famous chorus in Verdi's *Nabucco,* likewise a fervid expression of longing for homeland and freedom. Like Verdi, Rossini was a patriot. In 1841 he wrote that the unification of Italy inspired the music of "Pensa la patria."

[4] A mischievous Rossinian instrumental ploy implying the symbolism of cuckoldry. The horn symbolism was a staple joke of *commedia dell'arte:* a cuckolded husband appeared wearing horns. In the context of the opera, the reference to "horns" has a double meaning. "Pappataci" has been variously translated: *pappa—*

They hail the initiate in an absurd parody of a ceremonial hymn ("Dei Pappataci s'avanza il coro"). Hail the Pappataci, and let only horns resound, they bawl at the top of their lungs ("I corni suonino"). Taddeo and Lindoro, helpless with laughter, comment sardonically on the spectacle of the fat-bellied, jowly participants. With ponderous seriousness, Mustafa acknowledges the investiture ("Frati carissimi").

Isabella steps forward. Over a *maestoso* theme in the orchestra she solemnly informs the Bey that, with all the ladies swooning over his manliness, he must swear obedience to Pappataci. Thereupon she orders Taddeo to read the oath from a scroll. He intones the lines on a single repeated note, which Mustafa parrots after him: *Di veder e non veder, di sentir e non sentir, per mangiare e per goder, di lasciare fare e dir* ("What I see I shall not see, what I hear I shall not hear, while I eat and drink with glee, let nothing interfere").

Mustafa and Taddeo seal the oath with the phrase, "Pappataci Mustafa." This, incidentally, involves a nine-note bass clef skip from G above the staff down to F, including a trill.

The other Pappataci then call for the final test, which Taddeo again reads from the scroll: *Giuro in oltre all'occasion, di portar torcia e lampion, e se manco al giuramento, più non abbia un pel sul mento* ("I'll never stop eating and drinking, and if I fail to keep my oath my beard will be forfeit").

Isabella announces that the test of eating and drinking is about to begin, with Mustafa and Taddeo setting the pace. While they are both stuffing themselves, Isabella and Lindoro passionately reaffirm their avowals. Noticing their embraces, Mustafa becomes somewhat suspicious, but Taddeo—still unaware of what is happening—admonishes the Bey to be true to his oath and keep on eating ("mangia e taci"). Mustafa happily obeys.

The ensemble continues in quartet form to the accompaniment of rising and falling phrases in thirds. As Isabella urges Mustafa to eat more and more, Taddeo and Lindoro concede that Isabella's gulling of Mustafa is sheer genius. Meanwhile, the Bey continues to play Pappataci to the limit of his digestive apparatus.

The quartet ends suddenly to give way to a graceful theme in the violins. At that moment a ship appears in the background, with the Italian sailors and slaves aboard. They strike up a tuneful barcarole ("Son l'aure seconde"), singing that there is a following breeze and that the time has come to sail to their beloved homeland.

---

to gorge; taci—silence. Thus, Mustafa is ordered to eat and keep quiet. Other meanings: a complaisant, indulgent husband, or—in a more subtle connotation—cuckolded. The dictionary definition of *pappataci* is—Complaisant husband; one who takes what he gets without questioning.

Hearing the voices, Taddeo looks up and sees Isabella and Lindoro, arm in arm, go aboard the ship ("Andiam, mio tesoro"). Realizing that he and the Bey had been duped, he tries to warn Mustafa, who imperturbably concentrates on eating. Taddeo is now in an agony of indecision: should he remain to be impaled, or sail with the lovers and play the ass as supercargo? Desperately he pleads for advice. Isabella and Lindoro calmly advise him to make up his mind: the ship is about to sail. Taddeo finally scrambles aboard.

Haly, Zulma and Elvira burst in, shouting to Mustafa that his prize is escaping, along with the other captured Italians ("L'Italiana se ne va")· Mustafa sees the ship, then bawls for his soldiers, slaves and eunuchs. Thanks to Isabella's ministrations as hostess at the banquet, they all are hopelessly drunk. As they reel toward the ship, the Italians, standing armed at the gunwales, warn that anyone who tries to board will be shot. At that, Mustafa's minions stagger away.

Mustafa philosophically accepts defeat, ruefully admitting to Elvira that Italians are more than a match for him ("Sposa mia, non più Italiane"). She tenderly assures him that she will always be a loving wife ("buona vostra moglie ognor sarà").

All on the scene burst into the exuberant closing chorus—"Buon viaggio, stian bene, potete contenti"—goodbye and good luck. They hail "La bella Italiana," who has taught husbands and wives what a strong-willed beautiful woman can accomplish. The curtain falls.

JENUFA

(*Her Ward—Její Pastorkyně*)

by Leoš Janáček

(1854–1928)

Libretto by the composer

Based on the drama of the same name by Gabriella Preissova

CHARACTERS

Grandmother Buryjovka, housekeeper at the mill	Alto
Laca Klemen ⎱ stepbrothers, Buryjovka's grandsons	⎰ Tenor
Steve Buryja ⎰	⎱ Tenor
Kostelnitchka Buryjovka, a widow,	
Buryjovka's daughter	Soprano
Jenufa, Kostelnitchka's stepdaughter	Soprano
The Miller	Baritone
The Mayor	Bass
His wife	Mezzo-soprano
Charlotte, their daughter	Mezzo-soprano
Maidservant	Mezzo-soprano
Barena, servant girl at the mill	Soprano
Jano, a cowherd	Soprano
A woman	Alto

Villagers, musicians, young people

Place: A village in eastern Moravia
Time: Early nineteenth century
First performance: Czech National Theater, Brno (Brünn), Moravia, January 21, 1904
Original language: Czech

The Moravian composer Leoš Janáček, along with Antonin Dvořák and Bedřich Smetana, formed the historic triumvirate of artists who expressed in music the intensely nationalistic spirit of the Czechoslovakian people. Janáček himself was a specialist in folk music and developed specific theories about the effect of national speech rhythms on musical expression. He employed these theories in his operas—notably *Jenufa*—to infuse them with rugged peasant vitality that gives voice to elemental emotions in uninhibited flow of melody.

Jenufa is essentially an example of Czech *verismo*. The drama on which it is based had its source in an actual occurrence described in court records—a fact which recalls the origin of Leoncavallo's *Pagliacci*. Janáček spent ten years writing *Jenufa*, never losing faith in its worth as an expression of the true Czech spirit. He dedicated it to the memory of his daughter, Olga, whose illness and death at the age of twenty-one shadowed the years of his work on the opera.

The third of the composer's ten operas, *Jenufa* at first was slow in finding favor with the public. After its premiere in 1904 it virtually disappeared from the repertoire, but following its revival in Prague in 1916, *Jenufa* brought Janáček international fame. Translated into German, it was given in Vienna in 1918 with Maria Jeritza in the title role.

Its first performance in America was at the Metropolitan, also with Jeritza. There was little interest in the work at the time and it was dropped from the repertoire. Subsequently, it was performed by the Chicago Lyric Opera Company in 1959, then in 1966 by Thomas Scherman and the Little Orchestra Society in New York in concert form.

A recent performance of *Jenufa* in this country was that given by the Hamburg State Opera Company at the Metropolitan, Lincoln Center, New York, on June 26, 1967. The leading male role of Laca was sung by the American tenor Richard Cassily, formerly a member of the New York City Opera Company. The Metropolitan staged *Jenufa* again in a new production in November 1974.

There is a brief but vigorous overture dominated by a broad, sweeping theme in 6/4 tempo over a pizzicato in the basses. A xylophone obbligato gives the effect of the clacking of the mill wheel, which is part of the background of the opening scene.

ACT ONE

A rustic mill in an isolated section of eastern Moravia. In front of the mill is a footbridge over the millstream. At right a peasant hut with a porch; at left another hut. There are bushes about, and a number of fallen trees. Jenufa stands near the millstream, looking off into the distance; Grandmother sits on the porch peeling potatoes. Laca, seated on a tree trunk, is carving a whip handle out of a branch.

Jenufa, waiting for Steve, her lover, frets because he has not returned, and sings that last night she was haunted by terrible fears ("Už se večer chyh"). Overcome by anxiety, she kneels and prays to the Vir·

gin Mary ("O panno Maria"), at the same time revealing her agonizing secret: if Steve is called up for military service, they cannot be married —and thus her shame will become known. She is soon to have a child by Steve. Jenufa ends her prayer with a plea for mercy.

Grandmother breaks in to complain that Jenufa is idling instead of helping an old woman whose eyesight is failing. With that, Laca comments in an ironic refrain ("Vy stařenko"), sung over a repeated triplet figure in the orchestra. With some bitterness he remarks that there are many things Grandmother no longer can see—she mistakes him for the Miller, for one thing.

He is well aware, he goes on accusingly, that he is not her grandson. She always ignored him and favored Steve when they were children. But all he wants now, Laca sings, is his inheritance of twelve hundred gulden, and then he will go where he pleases.

Jenufa's voice blends with Laca's as she chides him for his disrespect toward Grandmother. In jealous irritation, Laca says that no one can expect Jenufa to keep her mind on her work when all her thoughts are on Steve. Wincing at his resentful look, Jenufa turns to Grandmother and tries to placate her. In a tender, melodic passage ("Stařenko, nehnĕvejte se!") she sings that she will make amends for Laca's rudeness.

Going toward the porch, she happens to notice that her rosemary plant is withering and needs watering. With a sigh, Jenufa sings that if it should wither, all the luck in the world would wither with it ("A kdyby mi uschla"). This meditative phrase, softly dying away, emotionally foreshadows Jenufa's tragedy. It is a striking illustration of how Janáček used the repetition of words or brief phrases—typical of Czech folk music—to produce a psychological effect.

Jenufa's thoughts are interrupted by a shout from Jano, the young cowherd, who rushes in excitedly waving a piece of paper. He exclaims that he has learned how to read, and entreats Jenufa to write out another lesson for him. She promises to do so, and also to teach him how to write. Jano skips happily away. Grandmother commends Jenufa for helping the villagers, adding that she has a man's head on her shoulders and should have been a teacher. Jenufa answers ruefully that, as for her poor head, she lost it long ago.

An ensemble scene now follows. The Miller enters and notices Laca trying to carve out his whip handle. When Laca complains that the knife is dull, the Miller takes a whetstone from his pocket and offers to sharpen it. Laca meanwhile teases Jenufa by flicking her scarf from her head with his stick. When she remonstrates, he sneers that she would not mind if Steve did the same thing. Exasperated, Jenufa runs into the house.

Gazing longingly after her, Laca admires her beauty and the Miller adds his words of approval. With malicious satisfaction, Laca says that he deliberately put worms in the flowerpot to wither the rosemary—just the way Jenufa's marriage to Steve will wither away. The Miller upbraids him angrily for his spitefulness, then taunts him for being in love with the girl. Laca scoffs at this. At any rate, he says, if Steve was drafted today, that will end everything between him and Jenufa.

But Steve was not drafted, the Miller declares. Jenufa, who at that moment has come out of the house, overhears and gives a cry of joy. The scene continues briefly in quartet form as the four express their reactions. Jenufa rejoices; Grandmother and the Miller comment on Steve's never-failing good luck; Laca fumes over the "injustice" of the situation. Kostelnitchka appears, is told the news about Steve, then goes into the mill. The Miller hands Laca his knife, saying he is unable to sharpen it. He leaves.

Now from the distance come the voices of the recruits singing to the music of the band. In a boisterous chorus ("Všecí ženija") they sing that only those who want to marry are afraid of war. He who has money can stay home; he who has none must go. The recruits swarm in, along with a shouting throng of mill hands and small boys. Finally Steve appears, followed by four fiddlers. Jenufa joyously greets him.

Celebrating his escape from the draft, Steve is roaring drunk. When Jenufa reproaches him, he answers in a blustering refrain ("Jà napily? To ty mně, Jenufa?"). How could she dare accuse Steve Buryja, who owns a mill and a farm, and who is a prime favorite of all the girls? One even gave him a bouquet, Steve boasts, showing Jenufa the flowers, then tossing them away. Turning to the fiddlers, he throws money to them with both hands and orders them to play Jenufa's favorite song—"It's a long way to Nove Zamky" ("Daleko široko"). This chorus is one of the finest examples of Janáček's technique in the use of native folk song, combining music with the basic rhythms of speech.

The chorus has to do with a legendary tower built of young men. It was crowned, symbolically, with the body of the girl's lover transformed into a golden dome. When the dome tumbled down, the lover's sweetheart caught it in her lap. The chorus is interrupted at intervals by a wild peasant dance called the "odzemek." Steve, seizing Jenufa around the waist, drunkenly tries to dance with her.

Suddenly Kostelnitchka stalks grimly through the crowd and silences the musicians with a wave of her hand. She turns on Jenufa with a torrent of reproof ("A tak bychom slí celým životem") for wasting her time collecting "cast-off coins." She climaxes her diatribe with a stern warning that she will prevent Jenufa's marriage unless Steve promises to stay sober for one year.

The recruits, staring at her in awe, comment on her stern visage. Kostelnitchka, ignoring them, threatens Jenufa that if she heeds Steve instead of her stepmother, God Himself will punish her. Grandmother tries to intercede on Steve's behalf, while Laca contemptuously looks on, secretly relishing the discomfiture of his stepbrother and rival.

As Kostelnitchka leaves, she drops her shawl. Laca, with exaggerated courtesy, snatches it up and hands it to her. She coldly acknowledges the gesture. The festive atmosphere of the scene evaporates as Grandmother orders the musicians and the recruits to leave. In a kindlier tone she advises the crestfallen Steve to go home and sleep off the effects of his drunken brawling. Then she turns to comfort the sobbing Jenufa in a phrase which introduces a lyrical quartet in a minor key—"Every young couple must endure some sorrow" ("Každý párek si musí"). The voices of the others—the Miller, Jenufa and Laca—blend with Grandmother's in the theme of consolation. The mill hands, also repeating the words, sing a melodious choral accompaniment as they follow the others from the scene.

Jenufa and Steve are left alone, and a dramatic colloquy ensues in quasi-recitative. Quietly, but with desperate earnestness, Jenufa implores Steve to show decent concern for her plight and warns him not to provoke her stepmother any further. Things will be bad enough, she cries, when the birth of the child will reveal her sin. Now that he has been released from the draft, Steve must marry her.

Resorting to bluster to hide his fright, Steve retorts that Kostelnitchka is hounding him unjustly . . . she is mean and suspicious. His intentions are honorable, he insists. After all, he adds boastfully, he is Steve Buryja, the prime favorite of all the girls.

Infuriated by his arrogance, Jenufa seizes him by the shoulders and storms that she alone has claim upon him. If he fails her now, she warns, she will commit suicide. Alarmed by this threat, Steve promises Jenufa that he will never desert her ("Však tě snad nenechám tak"). Grandmother, who has been listening to the two young people arguing, urges them to desist. Again she advises Steve to go home and rest. Making the most of the situation, Steve melodramatically sings that Jenufa is the most beautiful of all girls, then strides away. Grandmother goes into the house; Jenufa sits down on the porch and takes up her work, her head bowed in despair.

Laca enters. With an angry gesture he tosses his stick away and stands for a moment looking at Jenufa. Here begins the duet which leads into the ensemble concluding the act. With his knife still in his hand, Laca moves closer to Jenufa and gloatingly comments that Steve's courage deserted him in the face of Kostelnitchka's anger ("Jak rázem všecko"). Even so, Jenufa retorts, he is a hundred times the better man. Stung by this thrust, Laca picks up the bouquet Steve had thrown away and reminds Jenufa that it came from one of the girls who had smiled at her lover. Jenufa answers that she is proud to have even this token of his love ("Takovou kytkou"). For a moment, Laca stares at her in disbelief. Then in jealous fury he shouts that Steve, the lover she considers "a hundred times the better man," is interested only in her rosy cheeks.

Suddenly Laca looks at the knife in his hand. In an ominously quiet phrase, he murmurs that it could make those same cheeks rosier still. A xylophone passage in the orchestra gives a macabre emphasis to his words. With the knife in one hand and the bouquet in the other, Laca stalks toward Jenufa, who shrinks back in terror. At that moment, Barena, the servant girl, appears and watches the scene, paralyzed with fear.

Laca, raging, asks Jenufa what price she is willing to pay for this gift of flowers. He seizes her in a violent embrace. With a scream of terror, she struggles to escape. Trying to restrain her, Laca gashes her cheek with his knife. The action continues to the thunderous accompaniment of rising and descending sextuplet figures.

Gasping in pain, Jenufa holds her apron to her wounded cheek as Barena stands by helplessly wringing her hands. Laca, shaken by remorse and despair, takes Jenufa in his arms, crying that he has loved her since they were children. Jenufa wrenches herself free and stumbles blindly into the house.

The screaming and confusion bring Grandmother and the Miller rushing to the scene. Barena hysterically tells them what has happened. The Miller dashes into the house, then emerges shouting that Kostelnitchka must be summoned to dress Jenufa's wound. Laca, numbed with horror for a moment, rouses himself and walks slowly away. The Miller roars after him: "You madman, you did this deliberately!" The curtain falls.

ACT TWO

There is a brief orchestral prelude with an undulating theme in a minor key. The curtain rises on the living room of Kostelnitchka's farmhouse, six months later. Jenufa, her face disfigured by a livid scar, sits at a table sewing. She is pale and obviously despondent.

Kostelnitchka, who has been sitting nearby, opens the door to the adjoining room to let in more warmth. Looking concernedly at Jenufa, she asks why she spends so much time praying to the Virgin Mother. For help in her misery, Jenufa answers sadly. In a quasi-recitative passage, Kostelnitchka reflects on the events of the past months ("Už od té chvile"). When Jenufa finally confessed that she was carrying Steve's child, her stepmother brought her to her own house, where she kept Jenufa hidden until the child was born. To explain her absence for six months, Kostelnitchka told the neighbors that Jenufa had gone to visit relatives in Vienna.

As for Steve, Kostelnitchka says bitterly, he shows not the slightest interest in his child. Jenufa interrupts to hurry to the door of the adjoining room, exclaiming that she heard the child cry. Her tender solicitude is reflected in the gentle, flowing theme which sounds in the orchestra.

Kostelnitchka upbraids Jenufa for making a fuss over the child, saying it would be more to the point if she prayed to be relieved of this unwelcome burden. When Jenufa protests that her baby has not cried once since he was born, Kostelnitchka snaps that the child's constant whimpering is driving her to distraction. She turns on Jenufa with a flood of ill-tempered reproach.

Exhausted by the bickering, Jenufa murmurs that she wishes to go to bed. With a sinister glance at her, Kostelnitchka pours out a drink from a small pan on the stove and hands it to Jenufa, saying it will help her sleep. To the accompaniment of a lyrical theme in the orchestra, Jenufa drinks the potion, bids her stepmother goodnight and walks slowly into the other room. Kostelnitchka closes the door behind her as the music dies away.

Alone, Kostelnitchka gives way to her pent-up anger and hatred in a dramatic soliloquy ("Ba, ta tvoje okenička"). For twenty weeks, she fumes, this gallant lover of her daughter has not dared come near the house. But today he will be here, because she made him promise to come, and so the matter will be settled once for all. And then there is this child, a pale, helpless wretch like his father . . . she hates the one as much as the other.

In harsh, disjointed phrases, Kostelnitchka sings that she prayed the child never would be born. Her prayers were in vain—the child is a week old and still alive. In suppressed fury she murmurs that now she must face the humiliation of begging Steve to marry Jenufa.

There is a knock at the door. Kostelnitchka quickly locks the door of Jenufa's room, then admits Steve. Eyeing her suspiciously, he asks her why she has sent for him. In answer, Kostelnitchka points to the door of Jenufa's room. Alarmed, Steve asks if something has happened to her. Telling him that Jenufa and the child are well, Kostelnitchka angrily berates him for neglecting his son. Steve whines that he often thought of the baby, but stayed away because he did not want to face Kostelnitchka's accusations. And besides, he adds callously, Jenufa has lost her beauty—and for that he is not to blame.

Kostelnitchka flings open the door of Jenufa's room and points inside. "There is your son," she cries. "His name is Steve . . . I christened him myself!" Momentarily overcome by pity and affection, Steve then and there offers to support the baby and Jenufa on the condition that his fatherhood is kept secret.

Thereupon Kostelnitchka turns on him in furious denunciation ("Odivej se také na ni") for bringing shame upon Jenufa, then desert-

ing her like a coward. Her anger changes to desperate entreaty as she
falls to her knees and begs him not to abandon those who belong to him
by the sacred law of parenthood. Momentarily overcome, Steve buries
his face in his hands.

But suddenly he tears himself away from Kostelnitchka, crying that
marriage would only bring tragedy both to Jenufa and himself. Puzzled,
Kostelnitchka asks why. Steve's answer, in an agitated refrain ("Proto,
že se ji bojim"), is deliberately evasive until he finally blurts out the
truth. First he insists he is afraid of Jenufa because she has changed
from a gay young girl into a sad and unfriendly creature. Besides, the
disfiguring wound on her cheek completely banished his love for her.

Then, to Kostelnitchka's consternation, he tells her he also is afraid
of her. She seems like a witch who is constantly spying on him. But in
any case, he goes on with brash candor, he cannot marry Jenufa because he is engaged to the Mayor's daughter, Charlotte. Kostelnitchka
recoils with a scream of fury as Steve dashes out of the door.

As she glares after him, Jenufa's voice is heard from her room in an
eerie wail over an insistently repeated note in the orchestra. Tormented
by a dream, Jenufa cries that a huge rock is falling on her. Kostelnitchka listens, realizes that Jenufa is still asleep, then again abandons
herself to the torturing thoughts of Steve's treachery. She rages that she
longs to throw the body of Steve's wretched offspring at his feet and
force him to acknowledge it as a symbol of his guilt. Her baleful outburst is given emphasis by a piercing dissonance high in the strings.
Then, spent by her fury, she murmurs desolately: "Now who will save
her?"

At that moment, Laca enters unobserved and overhears her. For a
moment he is taken aback. Quickly recovering, he comes forward and
casually asks Kostelnitchka if Steve and Jenufa have made their plans
for marriage. They did not even talk together, the stepmother replies
gloomily. Laca, in sudden excitement, asks her if she now will give
Jenufa to him—as she had promised. He swears he will never leave her.

Thereupon Kostelnitchka tells him the grim truth: Jenufa never went
to Vienna, but was hidden here in this house while she gave birth to
Steve's son. Although stunned by this disclosure, Laca asks if he now
will be obliged to take both Jenufa and the child. The child is dead,
Kostelnitchka replies. Steve knows, she adds, and she will have revenge
upon him for his perfidy. As though the thought suddenly occurred to
her, Kostelnitchka asks Laca to leave immediately to find out when
Steve and Charlotte are to be married. As she virtually pushes him out
of the room, Laca promises to "be back in a moment."

Now follows Kostelnitchka's great soliloquy, one of the climactic moments in the opera, in which she plans the murder of Jenufa's child
("Co chvila . . . a ja si mán"). In hushed, fear-stricken tones she sings

that the "moment" in which Laca said he would return will be for her an eternity of agony. Feverishly she tries to decide on a course of action. Shall she hide the baby? No . . . alive, it soon would be discovered—and her daughter's shame still would live on. Suddenly she comes to a decision: she will give the child back to God ("Já Pánubohu chlapce zanesu"). The phrase is sung to the accompaniment of a semiquaver figure in the orchestra which musically reflects her growing dementia. In spring, when the ice melts, there will be no trace of the body, Kostelnitchka babbles, thinking of the millstream. And so, this sinless child will go back to heaven. . . .

Half crazed by her sense of guilt, Kostelnitchka imagines she sees accusing eyes staring at her. She stabs a forefinger into the air, crying that this is how they will point to Kostelnitchka when they learn of her monstrous crime. Then with insane cunning she steals into Jenufa's room, picks up the child and wraps him in her shawl. As a menacing theme thunders in the orchestra, she pauses and looks down at the baby. Dementedly she cries: "He was born in sin—like the black soul of Steve!" Clasping the child to her breast, Kostelnitchka rushes out of the house, locking the door from the outside.

A moment later Jenufa enters and begins the scene which brings the opera to the peak of tragedy. Still under the influence of the drug given her by Kostelnitchka, she calls dazedly for her stepmother ("Mamičko, mám těžkou hlavu") and stares vacantly around the room. Like a sleepwalker she goes to the window, opens the shutters and gazes up at the sky. In disjointed phrases she sings about the stars and the moon, and then her thoughts turn to Steve. If only he would come to see his little blue-eyed boy . . .

The thought of her baby sends her rushing back into her room with a cry of alarm. In a frenzy she tears away the bedclothes, searching for the child. Momentarily deranged, she implores unseen neighbors not to harm the boy, and sobs that she and Steve alone are guilty. With a wild scream of terror she rushes to the door and tries to tear it open.

At that moment her reason partially returns and she becomes calm. Making a supreme effort to collect her thoughts, Jenufa tells herself that ". . . this is Mother's room . . . the door is locked . . . Mother has taken little Steve to the mill to see his father . . . but now I must pray for him. . . ." Kneeling before a picture of the Virgin Mary, she sings the beautiful prayer "Zdrávas královno" ("We greet thee, O Queen"). She concludes the prayer with a feverish plea for the safe return of her baby.

Suddenly the door bursts open and Kostelnitchka staggers in. She is haggard and shivering with cold. Jenufa eagerly asks if Steve has seen his child and if he will bring the boy back and stay with her. In answer,

Kostelnitchka tells the girl that she has been out of her mind with fever for the past two days, and during that time the baby died.

Jenufa crumples to her knees and buries her face in her stepmother's lap. A theme of indescribable sorrow sweeps through the orchestra as she sobs in her anguish: "Mother, my heart is breaking" ("Mamička, srdce mi bolí"). It is one of the most profoundly moving moments in the opera.

Unmoved by her grief, Kostelnitchka coldly tells her to thank God for being free of her burden at last. Jenufa asks her if she has sent for Steve, as she had promised. The scoundrel deserves nothing but curses, Kostelnitchka replies fiercely. When he finally came to see his son, she goes on, she begged on her knees for his help—but his only answer was to offer money. In frantic self-justification, Kostelnitchka repeats Steve's words: he was afraid of Jenufa because of her scar, afraid of Kostelnitchka because she was a witch . . . and now he is going to marry Charlotte, the Mayor's daughter. There is a striking musical effect here as Jenufa, in repeated phrases almost like an obbligato to her stepmother's theme of accusation, sings a prayer asking forgiveness for Steve.

Kostelnitchka, now aware that Jenufa no longer has any strength left to resist, urges her to bestow her affections on Laca, a decent young man who can be trusted. Seeing him approaching at that moment, she adds hastily that he knows the entire story and is willing to forgive.

In response to Laca's affectionate greeting, Jenufa thanks him warmly for his kind thoughts of her ("Děkuji ti, Laco"). From this point the dialogue continues in duet and trio form. When Jenufa mournfully says that she has reached the end of her life, Laca asks her point-blank if she will marry him. Kostelnitchka, trembling with excitement, entreats Jenufa to accept his proposal.

Chiding her stepmother for her presumption, Jenufa reminds Laca that now she is a woman without money and without honor . . . a woman unworthy of pure love. Does he then, she asks, still want her as his wife?

In answer, Laca takes her in his arms and passionately declares his love. Jenufa, overcome with happiness, responds in a lyrical phrase that now they can face the good and bad in life together. Kostelnitchka gives them her blessing.

But as she does so, a sinister theme begins to sound in the orchestra. It continues with increasing intensity as Kostelnitchka launches into a denunciation of Steve as the cause of all the past misfortune. Losing all control, she curses Steve, the woman he will marry and herself. As she collapses in a chair, a violent gust of wind wrenches a window open. Over a descending chromatic passage in the orchestra, Kostelnitchka, mad with fear, wails that she hears a howling from the river. She throws herself into Laca's arms. Jenufa, slamming the window shut, exclaims that the wind is icy. In a phrase which rises to a maniacal scream, then drops to a gasp of horror, Kostelnitchka cries: ". . . as though Death is trying to enter here!" The curtain falls to a clamorous fanfare.

ACT THREE

Kostelnitchka's room, as in Act Two. A white tablecloth is spread over the table, on which is a pot of rosemary, a bottle of wine, glasses and a plate of cakes. Jenufa, in her Sunday dress, is seated at the table, prayer book in hand; a maidservant is arranging her shawl. Laca is standing nearby. Also in the room are Grandmother and Kostelnitchka, who is restlessly pacing back and forth. She is pale and worn.

A scene in quasi-recitative follows as the Mayor and his wife arrive for the wedding festivities and are greeted by Jenufa, Laca and Kostelnitchka. As greetings are exchanged, Kostelnitchka grows more excited and distraught, and acts irrationally. One moment she exclaims that today Jenufa will be betrothed to a good and upright man; in the next, she presses her hands to her head and wails that she has not been able to sleep. When Jenufa assures her that she soon will be well again, Kostelnitchka hysterically protests that a long life would be a horror. Staring wildly, she cries: "What then?" Abruptly coming to her senses, she quietly wishes Jenufa well on her wedding day.

A lively discussion now ensues about Jenufa's wedding dress, which the Mayor's wife considers much too simple and severe for the occasion. When Kostelnitchka remarks rather tartly that even royal brides prefer to dress simply these days, the Mayor's wife sniffs that she would never think of going to the altar in anything but her best finery. The discussion ends when Kostelnitchka invites everyone into Jenufa's room to look at the trousseau—which, the stepmother says proudly, she herself made.

Jenufa and Laca, remaining behind, exchange confidences in an ensuing duet which begins when Jenufa remarks wryly on the comments about her wedding costume. Laca shyly hands her a bouquet, which she pins to her jacket, murmuring that Laca deserves a better bride than she. Brushing aside her self-denigration, he assures her that his only wish is to atone for all the sorrow he has caused her. He confesses he was jealous and envious of Steve, but because of her love he has banished these evil thoughts. In fact, Laca says, he has invited Steve and his bride-to-be to the wedding.

At that moment Steve and Charlotte arrive and the scene continues briefly in quartet form. Steve is ill at ease, and Charlotte speaks for him in a brief refrain ("Pánbůh rač dát dobrý den"). It is Steve's fault they are late, she explains. Today they will only be onlookers, but their turn at the altar will come. She wishes the bridal couple luck, and Steve self-consciously joins her. At Jenufa's urging, the two young men shake hands.

The four continue chatting until the others re-enter, which leads into a short ensemble passage. While the Mayor complains good-naturedly about the ordeal of inspecting the trousseau, Kostelnitchka, in an aside to Laca, says that it was only because of him that she consented to Steve's presence at the wedding. It was Jenufa's wish too, Laca replies quietly.

Meanwhile, Barena and a group of village girls come by to extend their good wishes, which they do in a spirited chorus ("Nepozvali jste nás"). They sing that even though they weren't invited, they want to add some merrymaking to the occasion. They follow with a typical peasant folk song ("Ej mamko, maměnko moja!"). Its theme is a light-hearted conversation between a mother and daughter—about marriage, of course. At its conclusion, Barena hands Jenufa a bouquet. She thanks the girls warmly as they leave.

Laca warns that the wedding party must be at the church promptly at nine o'clock. The Mayor announces that it is now time for the nuptial blessing. Laca and Jenufa kneel before Grandmother. She intones the blessing ("Tož já vám zehnám") over a hushed minor theme in the orchestra expressed in a repeated chromatic figure. At its conclusion, Grandmother adds softly to Laca: "Remember me with love."

The Mayor then calls on Kostelnitchka to give her blessing, remarking banteringly that she probably "will do it like a parson." But just as she raises her hands, there is a babble of voices outside, with shouts of ". . . some beast has murdered the child!" Kostelnitchka gasps in terror. This marks the beginning of the opera's powerful climax.

Jano bursts in with the news that a child's body has been found in the millstream by the men who were cutting ice. He begs the Mayor to look at the body. The Mayor rushes out, followed by all but Steve, Kostelnitchka and Grandmother. Over the accompaniment of a driving figure in descending chromatics, Kostelnitchka frantically calls for Jenufa to help her. Grandmother tries to calm her. Steve, panic-stricken, dashes for the door, but is met by Charlotte, who sends him sprawling back inside. Jenufa is heard outside, screaming that the child is her son. Laca drags her into the house and tries desperately to quiet her. The Mayor follows, holding the baby's blanket and red cap, which were found with the body. Staring at them, Jenufa, mad with grief, wails that her poor child does not even have a coffin or a wreath.

The townspeople, shouting that Jenufa has killed her child and should be stoned to death, crowd threateningly into the room. Jenufa implores Steve to flee. As the Mayor stands irresolute, Laca confronts the throng and roars that he will kill anyone who touches Jenufa. Awed by his furious defiance, the people stare at him in sudden silence.

Kostelnitchka drags herself to her feet and in dramatic, unaccompanied phrases begins her terrible confession. As her listeners gasp in horror, she tells how, to save her daughter's honor, she kept Jenufa in her house until the baby was born, so that no one would know. She explained Jenufa's absence by saying the girl was in Vienna. Then one night she gave Jenufa a sleeping potion, took her sleeping child to the millstream and pushed him under the ice. And from that moment on, she knew she was a murderess. In stricken tones, Kostelnitchka adds that she told Jenufa her baby had died while she lay unconscious from fever.

Jenufa bursts out in a wild cry of rage. Charlotte, who has been listening stunned with horror, whirls on Steve and cries that he is to blame for this disaster. Hysterically she runs to her mother and demands to be taken home, saying she would rather die than marry Steve. He himself buries his face in his hands and stumbles blindly away.

Laca, in agonized self-accusation, moans that it is he who is to blame because he disfigured Jenufa and caused Steve to reject her. With dramatic suddenness, to the sound of a serene major chord in the orchestra, Jenufa steps forward. Lifting Kostelnitchka to her feet, she says quietly that now there has been enough of shame and disgrace. Kostelnitchka, screaming that she will kill herself before the police come for her, rushes toward the adjoining room. But she stops abruptly, muttering that the police would hold Jenufa responsible for her death.

In ringing phrases, Jenufa sings that at this moment she understands everything. Turning to the crowd, she entreats them not to condemn. They must forgive this woman, because the Redeemer Himself will not deny her mercy. Laca is outraged at Jenufa's magnanimity. In a final dramatic entreaty ("Odpust' mi jenom ty"), Kostelnitchka implores forgiveness. She loved herself more than her daughter, she sings, and is no longer worthy to be called "Mother." Yet now she receives strength from the very one whose life she has ruined—strength to face the ordeal of expiation. Turning to the Mayor, she orders him to take her away. As he does so, and the others follow, Jenufa murmurs: "God be with you."

Facing Laca, Jenufa calmly tells him that all the others have gone and now he too must go ("Odešli . . . Jdi také!"). This marks the beginning of the magnificent duet which concludes the opera. Jenufa sings that, after what has happened, marriage would be impossible. She blesses Laca, adding that he is the best man she ever has known. She long ago forgave him the senseless crime of slashing her face. Like herself, she says, he sinned because he loved.

Laca's answer is a question ("Ty odejdeš do světa"): will she go in search of a new life without taking him with her? Jenufa warns that she will have to testify in court and bare her shame to the world. Laca passionately declares that for her love he will endure anything—nothing matters so long as they have each other. As Jenufa ecstatically sings his name, he enfolds her in his arms. The music surges to a lyrical climax as the curtain falls.

LA JUIVE
by JACQUES HALÉVY
(1799–1862)

Libretto by

EUGENE SCRIBE

CHARACTERS

Éléazar, a wealthy Jewish goldsmith	Tenor
Rachel, his daughter	Soprano
Albert, sergeant at arms of the Emperor's archers	Baritone
Prince Léopold	Tenor
Ruggiero, provost of the city of Constance	Bass
Town Crier	Baritone
Cardinal Brogni	Bass
Princess Eudoxia, niece of the Emperor and wife of Prince Léopold	Soprano

Townspeople, soldiers, Jews, ladies and gentlemen of the court, dancers, an officer, a major-domo

Place: The city of Constance
Time: 1414
First performance: Grand Opéra, Paris, February 23, 1835
Original language: French

Although Halévy was somewhat overshadowed by Meyerbeer, his contemporary, he was an eminent musician in his own right and was highly respected by other composers of his day. Halévy composed more than thirty operas, but *La Juive,* which established his fame, is the only one which has survived in modern operatic repertoire.

There is an elaborate overture, which states several important themes of the opera—principally the strongly contrasting themes symbolic of Éléazar's steadfast loyalty to his faith, and the power of the Christian church.

ACT ONE

A square in the city of Constance. At one side is the entrance of a large church. Opposite is the shop and home of Éléazar, the goldsmith, and his daughter Rachel. The doors of the church are open, and a number of people unable to get inside are kneeling at the entrance and on the steps. Inside the church the choir is heard chanting a *Te Deum*. One of the worshipers outside looks across the square at Éléazar's shop and angrily remarks that the Jew is working on a Christian festival day.

As the others murmur against this desecration in a brief choral phrase, Éléazar appears at the door of his shop and gazes defiantly at the throng. Rachel appears at his side and entreats him to return inside so that he will not further provoke the crowd. As the Jew and his daughter retire, the concluding phrases of the *Te Deum* peal forth.

Unnoticed by the people at the church, a man in a long cloak strides across the square. He encounters Albert, sergeant at arms of the Emperor's archers, who recognizes him as Prince Léopold and expresses astonishment at seeing the Prince on what is apparently a secret visit to the city. The Prince cautions him to be silent, saying that Emperor Sigismond must be kept in ignorance of his presence in the city at least until nightfall.

Léopold then asks the reason for the great crowd at the church and the general air of festivity. Albert explains that the Emperor has called together the council of nobles and prelates, following the defeat of the heretic John Huss and his adherents. The Emperor's aim, says Albert, is to rally all Christians under the banner of one faith, the better to stem the onslaught of all infidels throughout the world. Now that the Hussites have fallen, Albert continues, Emperor Sigismond has ordered the people to give thanks. Albert and Léopold then leave the square. The people raise their voices in an exultant chorus of thanks for the victory ("Hosanna, plaisir, ivresse").

At the conclusion of the chorus, Ruggiero, provost of Constance, announces that a royal edict will be read by the Town Crier. In dramatic recitative ("Monseigneur Léopold, avec l'aide de Dieu") the Crier proclaims that Prince Léopold, with God's help, has put down the Hussite rebellion. In recognition of the victory, the Emperor and Cardinal Brogni declare this a day of Christian festivity and thanksgiving in the churches. Wine shall flow from the fountains in the square and the people are to rejoice. The crowd acclaims the beneficence of the Emperor and the Cardinal in powerful choral phrases.

During a moment of silence the sound of hammering is heard. When Ruggiero asks who dares work on this sacred day some of the people in the crowd tell him that the offender is Éléazar, the rich goldsmith.

Thereupon Ruggiero orders his guard to bring Éléazar before him, declaring that the Jew must be punished for his insolent disregard of proprieties. With Rachel clinging to his arm, Éléazar is dragged from his shop by the guardsmen. When Rachel distractedly asks what her father has done to deserve punishment Ruggiero denounces Éléazar for working on a church festival day. Éléazar retorts that he is an Israelite and owes no respect to the God of the Christians. He has every reason to hate them, he shouts, for it was the Christians who burned his two sons at the stake before his very eyes. Ruggiero, infuriated by Éléazar's defiance, tells him that he will suffer the same fate, for the Emperor has decreed death for heretics.

The proceedings are interrupted by the approach of Cardinal Brogni. Bowing obsequiously before him, Ruggiero informs him that he has arrested two heretics for profaning the festival day by working. The Cardinal asks the Jew his name. When Éléazar replies, Brogni remarks that the name seems familiar. Éléazar recalls that when Brogni was in Rome, before he took holy orders, he had a wife and daughter. Brogni sharply orders him to be silent, murmuring that their loss was a tragedy he wishes to forget. Now, he says, he lives only to serve God.

Éléazar, still angry and defiant, asks the Cardinal if he remembers banishing him from Rome. As Ruggiero fumes over the Jew's audacity Brogni quietly asks Éléazar's pardon, tells him he is to go free, and expresses the hope that they will henceforth be friends.

In a majestic refrain ("Si la rigueur et la vengeance") Brogni, addressing the crowd before him, declares that hatred and bitterness must give way to compassion and mercy. An ensemble develops as Rachel voices her relief at hearing the Cardinal's plea for tolerance, while the people praise his kindness. Éléazar, however, grimly resolves that he will never allow himself to be drawn into friendship with the Christians. Ruggiero, gazing at him in scorn and contempt, asserts that goodness is the refuge of the weak and that the soul triumphs by the sword alone. Brogni concludes by exhorting the people to remember the admonition of the Holy Scriptures: forgive your enemies.

The Cardinal and Ruggiero retire, Éléazar and Rachel return to their home, and the crowd disperses. When the square is quiet Léopold appears and looks cautiously around. Stepping quickly into the shadow of the balcony of Éléazar's house, he sings a tender serenade ("Loin de son amie vivre sans plaisirs"), in which he expresses the joy of being reunited with his beloved after a long absence. In the second stanza he sings that the charms of other scenes were lost upon him because the one he loved was not at his side. He thought only of the day when he could return to her arms. After his serenade Rachel comes out on the balcony. Her song blends with Léopold's as she sings of the happiness of hearing his voice again, while he rejoices over returning to her.

Leaving the balcony and coming out of the house, Rachel eagerly greets Léopold, addressing him as "Samuel." (For the sake of carrying on his romance Léopold has taken the name of Samuel and has told Rachel that he is a Jewish artist.) Léopold tenderly asks Rachel if she still loves him. She fervently reassures him, saying that she is happy in her love, for they have the same religion and the same God. Samuel's art, she goes on, means more to her than all her father's treasures. Eagerly Léopold asks when he may see her again. Tonight, at the Feast of the Passover, Rachel answers, because at that rite all Israelites are welcome at her father's house. With that she sends Léopold away and hurries inside.

In a few moments the people crowd into the square, eager to begin the feasting and drinking. Surrounding the fountains, which shortly begin to flow with wine as promised in the royal proclamation, they begin the chorus introducing the magnificent finale of the act ("Hâtons-nous, car l'heure s'avance"). Urging each other to make the most of this joyous occasion, they drink to the Emperor, the Cardinal, and the members of the council, and then dance around the fountains to the rhythm of a spirited waltz. The dancing stops when the royal procession is seen approaching, and the people hail the dignitaries in a continuation of the chorus.

Éléazar and Rachel thread their way through the jostling throng toward the steps of the church, from which vantage point they hope to watch the procession, which is being held to celebrate Prince Léopold's victory over the Hussites. Just as they reach the steps they are espied by Ruggiero, who promptly calls the attention of the crowd to the fact that Jews have dared to profane the steps of the church by their presence. In an angry chorus ("Au lac, oui, plongeons dans le lac") the people shout that they will throw the Jews into the lake as punishment for their impiety. Éléazar pours out his scorn and contempt for their threats, while Rachel vainly tries to quiet him. At the height of the altercation Albert rides up and orders Éléazar and Rachel to be seized.

Léopold suddenly appears. At a sign from him Albert calls off his soldiers, who, on seeing the Prince, draw back respectfully. Rachel is dumbfounded at seeing the man she knows as Samuel, an artist and a Jew, wielding unquestioned authority over the royal soldiers. As he rushes to her she entreats him not to intervene lest he fall victim to the fury of the mob. Meanwhile the attention of the people has been distracted by the approaching procession. They acclaim the glittering pageant of cavaliers, warriors, and dignitaries of Church and State in a vigorous chorus ("Le cortège, le voici, plaçons-nous").

The voices of Rachel, Éléazar, Léopold, and Albert are heard in interludes as they express their reactions to the situation. Rachel prays that it may be made clear to her why Samuel has suddenly appeared as a powerful leader of the Christian forces. Clinging to his daughter, Éléazar implores her to flee with him from the scene of their persecution and shame. Léopold confides to Albert that Rachel must never learn the mystery of his dual identity, saying that if she were to learn the truth it would shatter her love for him.

As the Emperor and the Cardinal appear, followed by their retinues, the chorus swells to a thunderous climax, a *Te Deum* mingling with shouts of acclaim for the Emperor. Léopold suddenly pushes through the crowd and then vanishes. Utterly bewildered, Rachel watches him go. Éléazar, standing at her side, scornfully regards the throng, which moves by, singing and shouting, as the curtain falls.

ACT TWO

A room in Éléazar's home, where the Feast of the Passover is being celebrated. Éléazar, Rachel, and Léopold are seated with a group of Éléazar's friends around a large table. Led by Éléazar and Rachel, the Jews chant the ritual prayer ("Ô Dieu, Dieu de nos pères"). In an impressive refrain ("Si trahison ou perfide") Éléazar prays that the wrath of the Hebrew God may fall on all traitors to the faith. He then calls on all to partake of the unleavened bread. As it is being distributed Éléazar offers another eloquent prayer for guidance and strength ("Dieu, que ma voix tremblante"), in which he asks that the enemies of Zion may be confounded.

To her surprise and dismay Rachel sees Léopold secretly throw away the bread which has been given him. Her attention is diverted at that moment by a knock at the door. Men's voices demand admittance in the name of the Emperor. At Éléazar's command the ritual vessels and candles are hurriedly concealed and the table taken away, after which the Jews leave through a door at the rear of the room.

Léopold is about to go into an adjoining room with Rachel when Éléazar detains him, saying he may need his help. Rachel goes into the other room, while Léopold takes his place before an easel standing at the rear, keeping his back to the entrance door of the house. When all is in order Éléazar opens the door to find a woman standing there. Motioning her servants to withdraw, she enters, glances at the man standing before the easel, and asks who he is. Recognizing the voice of his wife Eudoxia, Léopold utters a suppressed exclamation of consternation and dismay. Éléazar quietly answers that the man is an artist in his employ. He will be dismissed if the lady so desires, the Jew adds. Smiling, Eudoxia says that there is nothing secret about her visit. She then identifies herself as the niece of the Emperor, whereupon Éléazar kneels respectfully. Ordering him to rise, Eudoxia says that she has been told that he has a rare piece of jewelry ("Tu possèdes, dit-on, un joyau magnifique"). This marks the beginning of a long dialogue in trio form. Éléazar replies that the jewelry in question is a costly gold chain set with precious stones which was once worn by the Emperor Constantine himself.

Eudoxia tells him that she wishes to purchase it as a gift for her husband, Prince Léopold, who won the glorious victory over the Hussites. He returns today, she goes on, and then ecstatically reflects on the bliss of being reunited with him. At these words Léopold gives way to remorse over the thought that he is destroying the happiness of two women through his faithlessness and deception. Éléazar murmurs that though he has cursed the Christians there is much solace in the prospect of adding to his wealth through the sale of the desired gift.

At length he brings forth the chain, and Eudoxia admires its magnificent workmanship. She readily agrees to pay the price Éléazar asks—thirty thousand florins—saying that the person for whom it is intended is well worthy of so superb a gift. Éléazar increases Léopold's discomfiture by murmuring to him, aside, that those in love greatly benefit those who sell. Eudoxia orders Éléazar to engrave the chain with Prince Léopold's coat of arms and her own and tells him to deliver it without fail the next day. Éléazar promises to do so.

The trio is concluded as Eudoxia repeats her expressions of happiness over Prince Léopold's homecoming, and Léopold bitterly reproaches himself for his duplicity. Éléazar mingles expressions of contempt for the Christians with rejoicing over his good fortune. As the ensemble ends with a brilliant flourish, Éléazar escorts Eudoxia to the door and goes out with her.

Rachel, who has not heard the foregoing conversation, reappears from the other room and takes this opportunity to ask Léopold to explain his strange actions before the church and at the Passover feast. Warning that her father is returning, Léopold promises to tell her later. Éléazar re-enters, sees the two whispering together, and suspiciously asks what is troubling them. Without waiting for a reply he tells Léopold to go to his home and orders Rachel to join him at evening prayers. A brief trio follows ("Si trahison ou perfide"), in which Éléazar and Rachel repeat the sentiments expressed during the Passover feast, while Léopold muses over the punishment that may be visited upon him for his treachery.

After Léopold leaves and Éléazar goes into the other room to begin his prayers Rachel voices her fear and confusion in the dramatic aria "Il va venir! et d'effroi . . . je me sens frémir." She awaits her lover's return with foreboding, not happiness, because distrust and uncertainty envelop her like a dark cloud. Even though she may deceive her father, she reflects, the eyes of God see all her sinful actions. Despairingly she cries that though she should flee to avoid this fateful meeting her strength has failed her.

At the conclusion of the aria Léopold returns. Noticing his look of unhappiness and guilt, she upbraids him for his mysterious and suspicious behavior. To her surprise and horror, her lover confesses that he is a Christian. A dramatic duet follows as Rachel turns on him in anger and scorn ("Lorsqu'à toi je me suis donnée"). In bitter despair she reproaches herself for dishonoring her father by yielding to the love of a Christian. Léopold cries that he has risked his honor and his fortune for her sake. When Rachel reminds him that they can never marry, for the penalty is death, Léopold passionately entreats her to flee with him. They will forget that they are Jew and Christian and will live only for their love.

Rachel recoils at the thought of leaving her father and struggles against Léopold's feverish entreaties. Finally, overwhelmed by her passion for him, she joins him in rapturous expressions of love and devotion. As they declare that the same destiny awaits them both, Éléazar comes unnoticed from the other room and overhears them.

When they turn to leave the house he strides forward and bars their way. In grim tones he asks Rachel where she would go to escape a father's curse. A stormy trio now ensues ("Je vois son front coupable") as Éléazar declares that their guilt is written in their faces and that they will be relentlessly punished for the sin of loving without a father's blessing. Rachel and Léopold voice their terror over his wrath. Turning on Léopold, Éléazar denounces his perfidy, shouting that if he were not of his own race he would strike him dead. Thereupon Léopold tells him to strike the blow, for he is a Christian.

Wild with rage, Éléazar rushes toward Léopold with upraised dagger. Rachel interposes herself between the two men, crying that she is as guilty as Léopold. With poignant eloquence she implores her father to forgive them and to pronounce his blessing on their love. Moved by her pleas, Éléazar finally tells Léopold that he may take Rachel as his bride.

Léopold now confesses that he cannot marry her. Horror-stricken, Rachel and Éléazar ask him why he refuses, to which Léopold answers that the laws of heaven and earth forbid him to marry. Éléazar wildly curses him for his treachery. Rachel, desperate and bewildered by his refusal, vows that she will yet find out his secret. Léopold can only repeat his expressions of remorse and self-reproach. After the trio comes to a stirring climax Léopold hurries away. Éléazar sinks sobbing into a chair. Snatching up the cloak which Léopold has left, Rachel throws it around her shoulders and rushes out to follow him as the curtain falls.

ACT THREE

[*Scene One*[1]] A room in the Emperor's palace. It is the day of the fete in honor of Prince Léopold's return. Eudoxia enters and, in joyous reflection over the return of her hero, expresses her emotions in a long and fervent aria ("Assez longtemps la crainte et la triste"). At its conclusion a major-domo announces that a pale and distraught young woman is waiting outside and earnestly requests to see the Princess.

The visitor proves to be Rachel, who, determined to learn the secret of Léopold's refusal to marry her, has trailed him to the palace. She is still unaware, however, of his actual identity. With revenge in mind, she asks Eudoxia to allow her to serve as slave in her court for one day—the day of the fete. Startled at the bizarre request, Eudoxia at first refuses, then finally gives her consent. Their voices blend as Rachel sings that Eudoxia's kindness has given her a measure of solace, while the Princess comments to herself that Rachel seems to be buoyed by a strange new hope.

After Rachel leaves, Léopold appears. Noting his anxious, preoccupied air, Eudoxia tries to cheer him by singing a gay and alluring bolero ("Mon doux seigneur et maître"). As she concludes the song a fanfare is heard without. Léopold asks why the trumpets are sounding. Eudoxia informs him that it is the signal for the opening of the fete honoring him as conqueror of the Hussites.

[*Scene Two*] The gardens of the Emperor's palace, where the royal fete is in progress. The Emperor is seated under a canopy with Cardinal Brogni, Eudoxia and Léopold. After an opening chorus sung by the people hailing the festal day ("Ô jour mémorable"), the major-domo announces that there will be a presentation of the ballet pantomime, *The Enchanted Tower*. The pantomime depicts the assault on an enchanted Moorish castle by cavaliers. In a picturesque struggle the cavaliers strike down the wicked Moors, rush inside, and shortly emerge escorting a group of beautiful ladies whom they have rescued from captivity. During the performance the Emperor and his retinue leave.

Following the ballet, the people sing a vigorous chorus in homage to Prince Léopold ("Sonnez, clairons, que vos chants de victoire"), over which Eudoxia sings a brilliant obbligato by way of expressing her own happiness as the wife of the illustrious hero.

At the conclusion of the chorus, Éléazar, accompanied by Rachel, is escorted to the dais, carrying a golden casket containing the jewel-en-

[1] In some versions this scene is omitted, Act Three beginning with the scene of the fete.

crusted chain. Seeing Léopold at Eudoxia's side, Rachel starts back in surprise. Eudoxia takes the chain from the casket and proudly presents it to Léopold, saying that, as his royal wife, she confers the gift in the name of the Emperor.

Revelation of the fact that Léopold is the husband of Eudoxia brings a cry of tragic rage from Éléazar and Rachel. Rushing up on the dais, Rachel tears the chain out of Léopold's hands and gives it back to Eudoxia, storming that he is unworthy of the honor. She denounces him as the vilest of betrayers—one who has committed a crime for which the Christian law demands death. He has given his love to a Jewess, and that Jewess, she cries dramatically, is herself. Léopold cries out in terror and despair, and his words mark the beginning of a powerful ensemble ("Je frissonne et succombe"). All join in expressions of incredulous horror, while Rachel begs to be allowed to share Léopold's fate. Brogni and Ruggiero, who has meanwhile appeared at the Cardinal's side, ask each other in dismay if the law must inflict its punishment even on their Prince. Éléazar resigns himself to death. The onlookers, calling on God in terror and bewilderment, lament this day of impiety and evil.

Supporting Rachel, Éléazar turns to the royal group on the dais and asks them to prepare the scaffold. In sneering defiance he demands to know if the miscreant is to be spared because of his royal station. Rising, Brogni looks at Léopold, who stands with bowed head. His silence, the Cardinal declares after a moment, is evidence of his guilt. Stretching his hands toward the Prince, Rachel and Éléazar, Brogni pronounces upon them the terrible anathema of the Church ("Vous qui du Dieu vivant outragez la puissance"). Cursing them, Brogni turns to Léopold and proclaims that he is banished from the Church and will be denied absolution. The bodies of the criminals will be left unburied, and no prayers will be said over them. Against them the doors of heaven are shut forever. In a continuation of the chorus the people comment on the grim words of doom. Eudoxia and Rachel both cry out that they would gladly die in Léopold's stead. Éléazar furiously dares Brogni to do his worst, while Léopold implores the Cardinal to spare the Jews. The people grimly intone that the guilty ones must pay the supreme penalty for their impious crime. As the ensemble concludes in a tremendous flood of sound the curtain falls.

ACT FOUR

A gloomy Gothic room which serves as antechamber to the council room. Guardsmen are stationed about. Eudoxia comes in and hands one of the guards a slip of paper, saying that it is a writ from the Cardinal giving her permission to speak to Rachel. As the guards go to bring Rachel, Eudoxia murmurs that she still loves the Prince and is determined to save him even at the cost of her own life. Rachel is brought in and the two women stand face to face. The guards retire. A long and dramatic dialogue follows, during which the voices of the women blend in duet interludes. As Rachel gazes at Eudoxia with proud contempt, the Princess tells her that the judges have condemned Léopold. Rachel alone can save him now, Eudoxia says. The Jewess sardonically comments on the justice dispensed by the Christian tribunal.

The Princess desperately entreats Rachel to testify that Léopold is innocent and thus save his life. Rachel scornfully rejects the plea, declaring that her heart is broken and that her only wish is to die with the man who betrayed her. Though he has ruined her life, she says, she still loves him. Footsteps sound outside, and Eudoxia cringes in terror, crying that Léopold is being led before the council to hear the death sentence. Rachel exclaims in horror, and then the two voices blend in dramatic phrases of prayer ("Dieu tutélaire"), which bring their conversation to a close. Both conclude with passionate declarations of love for the Prince.

Cardinal Brogni appears, followed by guards who are to take Rachel before the council. Eudoxia leaves. When Brogni informs Rachel that she is about to face her judges she tells him that she will make a confession which will save the man she loves. Brogni asks if the confession will save her own life as well. Her life is forfeit, Rachel answers, adding that she has only one desire—to save Léopold. As guards lead her away Brogni grieves over the fact that one so young must die ("Mourir, mourir si jeune!"). This is the introductory phrase of the long duet which ensues as Éléazar is brought before him. Just before Éléazar appears, Brogni murmurs that the father may yet be persuaded to save his daughter from death.

When Éléazar is led in Brogni warns him that Rachel is now before the council and tells him that he can save her by repudiating his faith. Éléazar retorts that he would rather die than bow to the will of the Christian God. Brogni says that the God of Christian judgment is stern and implacable, to which Éléazar replies that there is no God but the God of Jacob. But He has deserted His people, Brogni observes. Though some fall in the strife, Éléazar answers firmly, the God who led the Maccabees will still lead His people in triumph. Thus, then, says Brogni resignedly, Éléazar prefers to die.

Yes, Éléazar replies, but before he dies he will have his revenge on *one* Christian. With that he points a shaking finger at the Cardinal. As Brogni stares in surprise, Éléazar recalls to him the sacking of Rome, years before, when Brogni's wife and daughter fell victims to the mob and his palace was burned. Brogni asks him not to speak of that terrible day when everything he held dear was lost.

Not everything, Éléazar remarks grimly. A certain Jew, he goes on, saved Brogni's daughter from the flames and brought her up as his own child. This Jew he knows well, Éléazar says. In anguished phrases ("Ah! j'implore en tremblant") Brogni entreats him to tell him the name of the man who has his child. In a repetition of the musical theme Éléazar asks with savage irony by what right Brogni begs mercy of his victim ("Et de quel droit viens-tu?"). In the fiery conclusion of the duet Éléazar shouts that the secret will die with him on the scaffold, while Brogni, frenzied by the Jew's refusal to impart his secret, abjectly begs Éléazar to take pity on him. Shaken by anguish, Brogni staggers to the door of the council chamber and goes inside.

Alone, Éléazar gives way to conflicting emotions of triumph and despair in the magnificent aria "J'ai fait peser sur toi mon éternelle haine." Now that he has doomed his archenemy to eternal, tormenting grief, he muses, he is willing to die. But it is Rachel, after all, who will pay with her life for the satisfaction of his revenge, for if he revealed his secret to Brogni the Cardinal would most certainly free her. In a tender strain ("Rachel, quand du Seigneur la grâce tutélaire") he reflects on his love for his daughter. It is as if he heard the voice of Rachel herself—Rachel, so young and lovely—beseeching him to save her. Reflecting that he has only to speak one word to save her, he resolves to forego his revenge.

At that moment he hears the harsh voices of the throng outside, demanding death for the Jews. Goaded to fury and defiance by their taunts, Éléazar cries that Rachel must not be allowed to live her life among these vile Christians who howl for his death. In feverish exultation he calls on his God to give him strength to take his daughter with him to his doom ("Dieu m'éclaire, fille chère"). In the final phrases of his soliloquy he prays that God may pardon him when He gives his daughter the martyr's crown. As the guards appear to conduct him to the council the curtain falls.

ACT FIVE

A large square in another part of Constance, where the accused are to be put to death. In the foreground is a huge tent, from which the nobles and prelates are to witness the executions. Beyond, at one side of the square, is an enormous caldron filled with boiling water. The crowds packed on all sides of the square sing a rather macabre chorus, the burden of which is that they are looking forward to the day's entertainment —the spectacle of Jews being boiled alive ("Quel plaisir! quelle joie! contre eux que l'on déploie"). After the chorus, Brogni, Ruggiero, and dignitaries of Church and State march in solemn procession to the tent to the accompaniment of a majestic *marche funèbre*. A group of penitents leads in Éléazar and Rachel.

Ruggiero proclaims that Éléazar and Rachel must die. Léopold, through the Emperor's intervention, will suffer not death but banishment. When Éléazar comments sardonically on this example of Christian justice, Ruggiero declares that Léopold's life was saved by the testimony of a witness that he was innocent.

Éléazar asks who gave this testimony. Stepping forward, Rachel answers that it was she. Éléazar is stunned by her words. At Ruggiero's command she turns to the populace and in a firm voice asserts that she swore falsely to Léopold's guilt ("Devant Dieu qui connaît"). The throng shouts savagely for her death. Ruggiero denounces the two Jews for conspiring against the Prince.

As the Cardinal and the people intone a prayer for the souls of the condemned, Rachel cowers in her father's arms. Torn by anguish, Éléazar, looking from his daughter to Brogni, tries to decide if he should allow Rachel to go to her death or abandon her to the Christians. Coming close to Éléazar, Brogni once more implores him to tell his secret. Without answering, Éléazar turns away. Suddenly the executioner gives the death signal and Rachel is led toward the platform above the boiling caldron. Frantically Éléazar calls to Rachel, who stops and faces him. Going close to her, he asks if she wishes to live. Calmly and dispassionately Rachel asks how that can be. By renouncing her faith and embracing Christianity, Éléazar answers. Pointing toward the caldron, Rachel quietly says that her God awaits her there. In a brief, exultant phrase ("C'est le ciel qui m'inspire") Rachel and Éléazar welcome death and the martyr's crown. The prayers of the people sound softly.

As Rachel mounts the platform Brogni again approaches Éléazar and in tones of desperate entreaty asks if his daughter, saved from the flaming ruins in Rome, still lives. Glancing at Rachel, Éléazar answers yes. In feverish joy Brogni asks where she is. "There!" Éléazar cries in a terrible voice, and at that instant the executioner hurls Rachel into the caldron. Groaning in agony, Brogni sinks to his knees, burying his face in his hands. With a look of sardonic triumph on his face Éléazar goes to his death. As the people exult that at last they have been revenged on the Jews, the curtain falls.

KÁT'A KABANOVÁ

(Katya Kabanova)

by LEOŠ JANÁČEK

(1854–1928)

Libretto by

VINCENC CERVINKA

Based on the play *The Storm*, by the Russian playwright Aleksandr Nikolaevich Ostrovski (1823–86)

CHARACTERS*

Váňa Kudrjáš, *Vanya Kudrash,* a teacher	Tenor
Gláša, *Glasha,* a servant	Mezzo-soprano
Dikoj, *Dikoy,* a rich merchant	Bass
Boris Grigorjevič, *Grigorievich,* his nephew	Tenor
Fekluša, *Feklusha,* servant of the Kabanov family	Mezzo-soprano
Marfa Ignatěvna Kabanová, *Kabanicha,* widow of a rich merchant	Contralto
Tichon, *Tikhon,* her son	Tenor
Kát'a Kabanová, *Katya,* his wife	Soprano
Varvara, adopted daughter of the Kabanov family	Mezzo-soprano
Kuligin, a friend of Kudrjáš	Bass

Villagers, peasants

Place: Kalinov, a small Russian town on the Volga
Time: Circa 1869
First performance: Brno (Brünn), Moravia, Czechoslovakia, October 23, 1921
Original language: Czech

In *Katya Kabanova,* Janáček's seventh opera, the composer brought into confrontation the mores of the old and new in the Slavonic society

* Czech spellings are followed here, in italics, by the Anglicized forms of the Russian spelling in the original play.

of the nineteenth century. The conflicting forces are represented by the principal characters: Kabanicha and Dikoj, of the older generation—stubborn, bigoted and domineering; Varvara and Kudrjáš, of the younger generation—flouting tradition and chafing under the taboos imposed by their elders. At the core of this impasse are the unhappy Katya and Boris. They too are young, but they are in effect anachronisms because they are subservient to the older generation. In the end, they are trapped in what has been described as the "tragedy of adultery."

As he did in *Jenufa,* Janáček fused his music with the natural rhythms of Czech speech (to which he devoted years of study as a folklorist), lending extraordinary vitality and conviction to the vocal and instrumental contour of his opera.

Throughout the work, stark dissonances underscoring the vocal line dissolve into music of striking lyrical beauty. To intensify the dramatic impact, the composer frequently utilizes such "esoteric" keys as C-flat and D-flat minor. Overall, the opera unfolds principally in declamatory patterns characteristic of Czech folk songs, which Janáček, as a profound student of his native language, fashioned with unerring skill.

Subsequent to its premiere, *Katya* was performed in German in Prague in 1922; in England (Sadler's Wells), 1951; in New York, 1960; at the Edinburgh Festival by the Prague Opera, 1964; in Florence (the Italian premiere) by the Belgrade Opera, 1957; in Paris, 1968. The first English version heard in America was given by the San Francisco Opera Company, September 17, 1977, and later entered the repertoire of the New York City Opera. A concert version, in the original Czech, was given by the Opera Orchestra of New York under the baton of Eve Queler at Carnegie Hall, February 25, 1979.

The overture begins with a muted, foreboding theme which soon crescendoes into a harshly dissonant movement foreshadowing the emotional turmoil of the characters in the opera.

ACT ONE

[*Scene One*] A park overlooking the Volga in the Russian village of Kalinov. At one side is the home of the Kabanovs. Kudrjáš, seated on a bench, is musing over the beauties of the Volga. Gláša, coming out of the house, reacts indifferently to his enthusiastic comments about the view.

From one side comes the sound of voices raised in argument. That means, Gláša says, that the merchant Dikoj is, as usual, browbeating his poor nephew, Boris. As the voices come closer, she scurries into the house; Kudrjáš too hurries away to get out of range. Dikoj loudly berates his nephew for being a lazy lout who comes hanging around the house instead of working. When Boris asks what he is to do, Dikoj roars at him to go to the devil. Boris slinks away.

Seeing Gláša in front of the house, Dikoj asks where Kabanicha is. Somewhere in the park, she answers curtly. With a snarl, Dikoj stalks away. Meanwhile, Kudrjáš, taking Boris aside, asks him why he continues living with his uncle and knuckling under his insults.

Boris glumly replies that he has no other choice, then divulges a bit of family history. His grandmother resented his father because he married a noblewoman—who, in her turn, intensely disliked her husband's family. The couple moved to Moscow, where they reared Boris and his sister and had a happy family life. But both parents died of cholera there. The grandmother, who died later in Kalinov, willed a legacy to the orphans—provided they would remain on good terms with their uncle, Savël Prokofjevič Dikoj.

Boris further explains that his sister was kept in Moscow by their mother's family—and thus spared the domestic tyranny of Dikoj. Were it not for her, Boris adds, he would spurn the inheritance, and he himself escape the clutches of his bully of an uncle.

Their colloquy is interrupted by the entrance of Fekluša, coming back from church with the Kabanov family. Kudrjáš, who dislikes the family, starts to leave. Boris restrains him. There is a brief duet interlude in which Fekluša fatuously extols the Kabanovs for their generosity and piety, while Kudrjáš cynically derides their ostentatious almsgiving to the beggars while mistreating their own peasants.

Just as Boris is complaining that he is wasting his time in this remote village, he sees Katya approaching with Tichon, Kabanicha and Varvara. In suppressed excitement, he confides to Kudrjáš—over reiterations of the "Katya" theme in the orchestra—that he is madly in love with this woman—idiot that he is! Kudrjáš sternly warns him not to risk a liaison with a married woman and court disaster for them both. But Boris, beside himself with ardor, drags Kudrjáš behind a corner of the house where they can watch Katya unobserved.

At the door, Kabanicha asks Tichon if he will drive to the market in Kazan. Unless, of course, she adds spitefully, he prefers to stay home with his wife instead of helping her. Cringing as usual, Tichon answers that he will gladly obey. When Katya offers her services, Kabanicha sharply tells her to stop meddling and taking her husband's side against his own mother. Hurt and angry, Katya rushes into the house. Varvara, looking on, sarcastically murmurs that this is a fine place for a sermon on marital behavior.

Kabanicha continues her remorseless badgering, deriding Tichon for prating about loving Katya and being too indulgent with her. He probably wouldn't mind, she adds insultingly, if Katya took a lover. This stings Tichon into a futile attempt to silence her. Screaming, "Idiot!" Kabanicha storms into the house.

Stunned by her cruelty, Tichon turns to Varvara, whimpering that, after all, Katya herself is to blame for these misunderstandings. Exasperated by his spineless capitulation, Varvara furiously upbraids him for not taking Katya's part. Without a word, Tichon stumbles away. Varvara sings reflectively that Katya is indeed weak and defenseless—yet charming. Wistfully she adds: "How I long to help her!"

[Scene Two] A room in the Kabanov house. Doors to right and left; also at left an alcove, where Katya and Varvara are embroidering.

The ensuing scene is in the form of a long duet. It begins when Katya suddenly lays aside her sewing and asks rhetorically: "Do you know what is very strange?" ("Viš, co mi napadlo?"). Why is it, she goes on as Varvara stares at her in perplexity, that people can't fly like the swallows? She stretches out her arms to imitate flying. Varvara dismisses this as childish nonsense.

Once she herself was as free as a bird, Katya sings, as though in a trance, but all that is over now. Here she feels caged and no longer carefree. She recalls that at home her mother treated her like a doll without a soul—and so she lived her own secret life. Early in the morning she would bathe in the fountain, then water every single flower in the house and in the garden.

Later she would go to church. In rising ecstasy Katya sings that there she felt transported to paradise ("Bývalo mi, jak bych, stupala do ráje"). She saw no one, heard no voices. The other worshipers stared at her as she knelt sobbing at the beauty of the sunshine that streamed through the church windows and burnished the ramparts of the great cathedrals of her vision.

Suddenly her mood changes. Fear-stricken, she grasps Varvara's hand, crying that some sinful power is dragging her into the abyss of Hell. Varvara, terrified by her mad outburst, asks if she is ill. No . . . not ill, Katya moans, but tormented by shameful desires. She cannot sleep . . . someone whispers voluptuous words into her ear, and she feels herself surrendering to passionate embraces.

As though waking from a dream, Katya stares at Varvara and wonders aloud why she has been confiding this mad fantasy to an innocent maiden. Varvara, glancing furtively around, confesses that her own sensual fantasies are even more sinful.

Desperately, Katya cries out that hers is the deadliest sin of all: she loves another man ("když miluji jeného"). Perhaps, Varvara murmurs seductively, you might meet him. Katya recoils in horror at the thought, crying: "No . . . no . . . God forbid!"

At that moment Tichon enters dressed in traveling clothes; Gláša and

Feklusá bring in his luggage. Katya throws herself into his arms and desperately implores him not to go away—or, if he must, to take her with him. Impossible, Tichon answers, freeing himself from her embrace. He must obey his mother, and go alone. Despairingly Katya sings: "You do not love me any more" ("Což pak už mne nemas rad?"). Tichon vehemently protests that he loves her—but that love is a slavery from which one must escape—even from one's wife.

As though seeking absolution from her secret guilt, Katya overwhelms Tichon with passionate avowals. As he stares at her uncomprehendingly, she warns him that if he leaves her here alone, something dreadful will happen. To his further consternation, she demands that he make her swear a fearful oath ("žádej o de mne nějakou strašli vou přísahu"), which she intones with sinister deliberation in phrases sung on a single repeated note: *When you are away, under no circumstances will I look at or speak to any stranger; and I will think of no one but you.*

Falling to her knees, she beseeches Tichon to bind her to her oath. If she breaks it, she cries, may she never see father or mother again, and may she die in sin. Raising her to her feet, Tichon denounces her oath as desecration itself.

Kabanicha bustles in and tells Tichon that everything is ready for his journey. She reminds him not to forget the usual custom: to instruct his wife how to behave in his absence. Moreover, she demands that this be done in her presence to assure that his instructions will be obeyed. Kabanicha intones the rules one by one, and the hapless Tichon dutifully parrots her words: *Honor my mother; show her the respect you would show your own mother; don't be lazy; don't sit staring out of the window; don't make eyes at the young men.*

Allowing the two a few moments alone, Kabanicha goes into the house. When she returns with Gláša and Varvara she peremptorily orders Tichon to kneel down. He kisses her hand. Now, she commands, say goodbye to your wife. When Katya ardently kisses Tichon, his mother remarks venomously: "Shameless wench! Just as though he were your lover!" ("Nestydatá! Loučiš se smlencem!"). Crestfallen, Tichon hurries away as the music crescendoes to a *maestoso* fanfare of minor chords.

ACT TWO

[*Scene One*] A working alcove in the Kabanov house, where Kabanicha, Katya and Varvara are embroidering. It is late afternoon. The ensuing dialogue is sung over a rather insinuating theme in a persistent 3/2 rhythm.

Kabanicha is nagging Katya mercilessly. Why, she asks, is she not like other devoted wives who weep alone while their husbands are absent . . . ? Katya answers honestly that it is not her nature to feign sorrow. If you really loved your husband, Kabanicha says maliciously, there would be no need to pretend. With that she storms out of the room.

Varvara seizes the opportunity to tell Katya that Gláša will make up their beds for the night in the garden, then tells her of the plot to outwit Kabanicha. The Old One always keeps the door in the garden wall locked. But, Varvara explains gleefully, she has purloined Kabanicha's key and substituted a false one. Here is the key, she says triumphantly, thrusting it into Katya's hands.

And now, she goes on as Katya gasps in surprise, she will tell Boris. As Katya takes the key she reproaches Varvara (halfheartedly) for leading her astray. Scoffing that there is no time for that kind of prattle, Varvara leaves.

Now follows one of the most moving interludes in the opera—in itself a masterpiece of subtle musical characterization. Staring at the key, Katya wrestles with her conscience as the alluring love motif sounds in the orchestra. Singing that the key is searing her hand like a live coal, she resists the impulse to throw it out of the window.

Hearing Kabanicha's voice outside, Katya hides the key in her dress, then stands anguished and irresolute: she has the key—an instrument of Fate. Is it so sinful to think about one's beloved . . . why should I lie about loving him? I would be lying only to myself. . . .

Half mad with desire, Katya cries again and again over the tormenting love theme: "I must and will see him!" ("Jen když ho uvidim!"). May the night come soon, she murmurs as she hurries away.

There is an abrupt change of mood as Kabanicha, carrying a lamp, comes in followed by Dikoj, who is drunk. When she impatiently tells him to go home and sleep it off, he whines that nobody understands him. Somebody probably has been asking you for money again, Kabanicha remarks sarcastically.

Thereupon Dikoj relates in drunken detail how, during Lent, the devil himself sent a moujik to cut wood for him. He cursed the poor peasant, but then knelt at his feet and begged his forgiveness. That proves, he burbles self-pityingly, sidling over to Kabanicha with a clumsy attempt at a caress, that it is his nature to be softhearted. Grimacing in distaste, she pushes him away.

[Scene Two] A ravine overgrown with bushes. Above, the garden wall of the Kabanov property, with a small door, from which a path leads down the slope. A summer night. There is a brief prelude reiterating the familiar love motif, mingled with certain foreboding harmonies.

Kudrjáš enters carrying a balalaika. He sits down and sings a simple Russian folk song, one of the most engaging numbers of the opera: "Early in the morning in the garden" ("Po zahrádce děvucha"), on the theme (naturally) of a young swain courting his beloved.

As he finishes his song he sees Boris approaching. The latter explains that he has come because a young woman told him he is to meet someone here. Realizing what is happening, Kudrjáš warns him to go away. Boris, oblivious to everything except the prospect of meeting Katya, pours out his love for her in an impassioned refrain describing the moment when he first saw her praying in church ("kdybys je viděl, jak se modli"). Watching him, Kudrjáš shakes his head, murmuring that now warnings are useless.

Suddenly Varvara steps through the garden door, gaily singing that her "Vanya" (Kudrjáš) is bringing presents to his "Czarina." The two greet each other affectionately. As they walk away down the path, Varvara calls to Boris that Katya will soon be with him. She adds: "Come to the Volga."

Alone, Boris soliloquizes about lovers meeting in the night—just as he himself is doing. He feels his heart pounding and wonders what he will say to Katya. Suddenly she walks through the garden door, eyes on the ground as the love motif surges in the orchestra. Ardently singing her name, Boris impulsively reaches for her hand, but she shrinks back, imploring him not to touch her ("Nedotýkej se mne"). Then ensues the magnificent love duet, one of the great moments of the opera.

Haunted by guilt, struggling vainly against her fierce desire for Boris, Katya sings that she can never atone for the sin of loving him. Crying that she no longer has a will of her own, she throws herself into his arms. She begs for death, but Boris chides her for thinking of death when life is so wonderful.

The mood of the scene changes to one of carefree gaiety as Varvara and Kudrjáš return. Varvara diplomatically suggests that the lovers stroll down to the Volga, as they did, adding that Kudrjáš will call them back in time to forestall any discovery of the lovers' rendezvous outside the garden door.

Kudrjáš grudgingly compliments Varvara on her mischievous plotting against Kabanicha, but is apprehensive about being discovered. Varvara pooh-poohs his fears, remarking that the Old One always sleeps soundly. What is more, she has been busy talking to Dikoj. And there, she adds flippantly, are two monsters who understand each other. In any case, Gláša also is keeping watch and will sound the alarm.

At intervals, from the near distance, come the impassioned voices of Katya and Boris. They blend with those of Varvara and Kudrjáš in a remarkable quartet of contrasting moods: Katya and Boris, suffused with passion and guilt; Varvara and Kudrjáš, equally amorous, but gay and lighthearted.

At a warning word from Varvara, Kudrjáš calls to the other pair that it is "time to go home." They themselves climb slowly toward the garden door, singing together a peasant ditty about a lass who would rather stay out all night than go home to bed. When Katya and Boris appear, Varvara lightly taunts them for being unable to part from each other. Katya, with head bowed, climbs slowly up the path. Boris remains below watching her. Their emotions are expressed in an orchestral climax of three powerfully evocative phrases.

ACT THREE

[*Scene One*] A run-down building—presumably an old mansion—with colonnades and vaulted ceilings, surrounded by an overgrown lawn. In the distance a promenade on the banks of the Volga. It is late afternoon, and a storm is threatening. Kuligin and Kudrjáš come in seeking shelter from the storm. Other passersby also hurry in.

A brief agitated prelude presages the advancing storm. The two men examine the traces of huge portraits on the walls. Kuligin points out one he recognizes as that of Ivan the Terrible. In quasi-recitative they reflect ironically that Russia has never lacked tyrants—there is one in every family. As though to confirm the observation, Dikoj comes stamping in grumbling about the rain. The people bow obsequiously. Spying Kudrjáš, Dikoj roars at him to keep away—he has been seeing too much of him lately.

Ignoring his bullying tone, Kudrjáš mildly asks if he has ever heard of Franklin's invention: the lightning rod. As Dikoj hides his ignorance behind a derisive sneer, Kudrjáš tries to explain that Franklin's rod is a protection against lightning, which is an electrical phenomenon. Dikoj blusters that lightning is God's way of punishing evildoers. He violently denounces Kudrjáš as a pagan Tartar who dares defy Almighty God with his silly gadgets.

In reply, Kudrjáš calmly quotes the Russian poet Derzhavin: "Though worms devour my body, my Spirit commands the lightning" ("Mé tělo rozpadne se v prach, však rozum hromem svlád!").[1] This brings another wild outburst from Dikoj. Bellowing that the stupidity of these peasants can drive one into sin, he lurches out of the building.

Meanwhile, the storm has passed and everyone leaves the building. Varvara comes in, and a moment later Kudrjáš returns with Boris. Varvara beckons to Boris and tells him they are in deep trouble: what is to be done with Katya? Tichon has returned unexpectedly and Katya is be-

[1] Gavril Romanovich Derzhavin (1743–1816), Russian poet/statesman.

having like a demented woman. Deathly pale, she wanders about the house as though searching for something, and imploring her mother to help her. There is disaster ahead, Varvara goes on somberly, because Katya probably will confess everything to Tichon.

As Boris gasps in terror, Varvara tells him that Kabanicha, suspecting something, sits watching Katya like an animal stalking its prey. Varvara suddenly warns that Katya and Kabanicha are approaching; Boris and Kudrjáš quickly hide. There is an ominous rumble of distant thunder.

Katya, in hysterics, rushes in and wildly calls to Varvara. Visitors who have sauntered into the building look at her curiously as Varvara tries to calm her. Katya moans that she is afraid of the lightning. In brief choral interpolations, the people intone—like a chorus in a Greek tragedy—that there is no escape from God's punishment for the sinner.

Kudrjáš and Boris reappear—to Katya's dismay—just in time to be confronted by Kabanicha, Tichon and Dikoj. Racked by guilt and remorse, Katya kneels before Kabanicha and pours out her confession: "Look down on a wretched sinner" ("Hřišná jsem před Bohem, před vám!"). Shaking off Varvara's restraining hand, she shouts that she spent ten nights with her lover.

In mingled anger and despair, Tichon commands her to name the man. Losing all control, Katya cries: "Boris Grigorievich," and collapses into Tichon's arms. There is a violent clap of thunder as the storm breaks out again. With rancorous self-satisfaction, Kabanicha murmurs to Tichon: "Son, did I not always tell you . . . ?" ("Synku dočkal jsi se!"). As Tichon screams Katya's name like a curse, she suddenly revives, tears herself from his arms and dashes madly out into the storm to the accompaniment of savage harmonies in the orchestra.

[*Scene Two*] A secluded spot on the bank of the Volga. It is night. Tichon enters, followed by Gláša carrying a lantern. They are searching for Katya.

Tichon, outraged, yet still in love with his errant wife, groans that she deserves to be beaten to death—or buried alive, as his mother suggests. But he loves her, and would not harm a hair of her head. He and Gláša leave to continue their search. Following them come Kudrjáš and Varvara. Kabanicha had locked her in her room, Varvara says, but she managed to escape. Now, she asks Kudrjáš, what shall we do? Run away, he replies promptly—run away to gay Moscow. Happy and excited, they run off together.

There is a moment of silence. Then from the distance come the voices of Tichon and Gláša calling to Katya. She herself enters and approaches the riverbank as though walking in her sleep; a melancholy, wandering theme in the orchestra seems to reflect her hopelessness. On the verge of madness she thinks about Boris . . . about her shameful confession that has destroyed them both. The voice of Kuligin breaks in on her reflections with a brief, careless refrain. He passes by, stares at her, then goes on his way.

With an effort she recalls the past . . . how Boris caressed her and spoke fervent words of love. Now it is night. Everywhere people are going peacefully to sleep—but for her, sleep is like sinking into the grave. Hearing singing in the distance, she murmurs that it sounds like a funeral. She shrinks back involuntarily as a drunk staggers by leering at her. Plunged again in the confusion of her thoughts, she reflects that women like her once were put to death.

Now people stare accusingly at her . . . why don't they throw her into the Volga . . . ? But they only cry, "Live! Live with the torment of your sins!" In a paroxysm of anguish she clutches at her breast, wailing that the pain in her heart is more than she can bear. Overcome by grief and remorse, she stumbles to the river's edge. Over the clamor of the orchestra her voice rises in a frenzied scream: "My star . . . my fate . . . my beloved . . . answer me!" ("Ži vote mîy, radosti moje, duše má jak tě mám rada!").

Boris appears, calls her name. They rush into each other's arms as the orchestra thunders out the love motif. Then gradually they become calmer, and the music subsides into a serene interlude. Katya implores Boris to forgive her for rashly confessing their secret love. Hesitantly he tells her that his uncle has banished him to Siberia.

Under the stress of emotion, Katya's mind begins to wander. First she begs Boris to take her with him because people are staring at her, Kabanicha locks her up, Tichon beats her. In the next moment she tells him he must go alone. Over the singing of a wordless chorus symbolizing the voice of the Volga, she tenderly asks Boris to give alms in memory of her to every beggar he meets. Turning to go, Boris laments the bitterness of parting.

When he is out of sight Katya moves closer to the water's edge. There is an orchestral imitation of warbling birds as she sings that the birds will flutter among the flowers—scarlet, blue, yellow—that will adorn her grave. It will be so quiet . . . so beautiful, she murmurs, but now I must die. Crossing her hands over her breast, she leaps into the Volga.

The scene erupts into confusion. Kuligin, on the opposite bank, shouts that a woman has jumped into the river. Other passersby, some carrying lanterns, call for help. Dikoj and Gláša appear; Dikoj pushes off in a nearby boat. Tichon comes rushing to the riverbank and is held back by his mother. Whirling on Kabanicha, he screams that she has murdered his wife. She recoils in fury, her reaction underscored by an upward-flaring chromatic phrase in the orchestra.

At that moment Dikoj clambers up the riverbank with Katya's lifeless body in his arms. As Tichon despairingly wails her name, Dikoj places the body on the ground, saying with cruel irony: "This was your Katya" ("Zde máte svou Katěrinu!"). Tichon collapses on her body. Dikoj strides quickly away.

Kabanicha steps forward, bows with exaggerated courtesy to the horrified people crowding around, then says sardonically: "Thank you, good people, for your services" ("Děkuji vám dobři lidé za úslužnost!"). As the curtain falls slowly, a majestic, requiem-like phrase is wordlessly intoned by an unseen chorus. The music comes to a stop in a violent, thudding chord.

KHOVANCHINA
(*The Khovanskys*)
by MODEST PETROVICH MOUSSORGSKY
(1839–81)

Libretto by the composer and
VLADIMIR VASSILIEVITCH STASSOV

Based on the drama of the same name by Aleksandr Pushkin

CHARACTERS

Prince Ivan Khovansky, commander of the Streltsy (Archers)	Bass
Prince Andrei, his son	Tenor
Prince Vassily Golitsin	Tenor
The Boyar Shaklovity	Baritone
Dossifé, patriarch of the Old Believers	Bass
Marfa, a young widow, member of the Old Believers	Mezzo-soprano
Scribe	Tenor
Emma, a young girl from the German quarter of Moscow	Soprano
Varsonoviev, henchman of Golitsin	Baritone
Kouzka, a Streltsy	Bass
First ⎫	Bass
Second ⎬ Streltsy	Tenor
Third ⎭	Tenor
Streshniev, a herald of the Czar's guards	Tenor
Susanna, an older woman, member of the Old Believers	Soprano

Archers, Old Believers, ladies in waiting and Persian slaves in the court of Ivan Khovansky; bodyguards of Peter the Great; the populace

Place: Moscow, and on the estate of Prince Khovansky, near the city
Time: 1682
First performance: Kononov Theater, St. Petersburg, February 21, 1886 (amateur production). Official premiere given at the Maryinsky Theater, St. Petersburg, November 7, 1911
Original language: Russian

Khovanchina (variously spelled *Khovanstchina, Khovantschina, Chovantchina*) was Moussorgsky's last opera (1885) and the successor to *Boris Godunof*. Although the composer's work on this immense drama was cut short by his death, he left an almost complete vocal score. The opera was revised for stage performance and orchestrated by Moussorgsky's friend Nikolai Rimsky-Korsakov.

There is a marked difference in musical style between this opera and *Boris*. For example, the conventional form of recitative in *Boris* is replaced in *Khovanchina* by broad, intensely melodic passages. Moussorgsky regarded this elaboration as his own discovery, which he called "melody justified by meaning." In the opera's great choruses—particularly those sung by the Old Believers—he utilized some of the liturgical melodies of the ancient Russian Church. They were adapted from manuscripts of masses dating back to the Middle Ages.

The action of *Khovanchina* has its roots in the history of Old Russia; it deals with the struggle between the ancient beliefs and the radical influences of Peter the Great (1682-1725). It was Moussorgsky's idea to dramatize this turbulent period in Russia's history—to portray the clash between the old regime and the new, the conflict of Eastern and Western ideas, the confrontation of orthodoxy and iconoclasm.

In the opera, Old Russia is represented by Prince Ivan Khovansky and his son Andrei, along with their followers (the Streltsy), and by Dossifé, leader of the Old Believers (the orthodox adherents of the Old Russian Church), and his disciple, Marfa. The radicals are represented by Prince Golitsin and his henchman, Varsonoviev, both of whom were identified with the faction of Czar Peter the Great. That monarch, by the way, gave the opera its title: He coined "Khovanchina" as a term of contempt for the Khovansky princes who hatched a revolt against him.

Actually, the central figures in the action are Marfa and Dossifé. Moussorgsky presents Marfa in basically human terms—a woman torn between overpowering sensuality and religious fervor. Dossifé symbolizes the fanatical mysticism of Old Russia. These two people embody the three fundamental ideas of *Khovanchina:* the Russian soul and its torment, the history of Russia and the problem of sin and its expiation.

Yet in the larger sense *Khovanchina* is an opera of the Russian people—as Moussorgsky said: "It is the Russian people I want to paint." The hero is not a person, but a nation. In the music itself, the composer revealed where his sympathies lay. The sectarians and the serfs, for example, are given rich, sweeping melodies in their choral utterances. The non-Russian Western elements are delineated in a deliberately gauche, superficial style. With the soul of the Russian people as its protagonist, *Khovanchina*—like *Boris*—is a genuine musical folk drama.

Although *Khovanchina* was heard infrequently during the years following its premiere, it was eventually given in major opera houses all over the world. Probably the most widely known music from the score is that of the two orchestral excerpts—the Prelude to Act One and the Entr'acte preceding Act Four, both of which are in the symphonic repertoire.

The opera's American premiere, in Russian, took place at the Hammerstein Metropolitan Opera House in Philadelphia on April 18, 1928. Its first hearing in New York was on March 7, 1931, at the Mecca Temple (later the City Center), where it was presented by a company called The Art of Musical Russia. The opera was given its first performance at the Metropolitan Opera House in New York on February 16, 1950. It was sung in English by a cast including Risë Stevens (Marfa), Lawrence Tibbett (Khovansky), Charles Kullman (Golitsin) and Jerome Hines (Dossifé). The role of Dossifé was created at the opera's premiere in St. Petersburg by the great Russian basso Feodor Chaliapin. The work is often sung in Italian and in French.

During the past several years *Khovanchina* seems to have enjoyed a revival of interest, and it reappeared in some of the principal opera houses in Europe. The Bolshoi Opera, in Moscow, presented a televised production on March 20, 1969, and that same year it was sung in Turin, Lausanne and East Berlin. In America, the Chicago Lyric Opera opened its 1969 season with a new production of *Khovanchina*.

The Prelude, during which the curtain rises slowly, was entitled "Dawn on the Moskva River" by the composer and is a musical landscape painting of Moscow at sunrise. It is dominated by a typically Russian melody which is heard in five variations—much in the manner of traditional Russian singers, who vary the melody with each succeeding stanza.

ACT ONE

Red Square, Moscow. At one side is a stone pillar on which is a brass plate with an inscription; a chain fastened to the pillar stretches across the square. On the other side of the square is the Scribe's hut. Kouzka, a Streltsy (archer), is sleeping near the pillar. It is dawn.

There is a sound of church bells mingled with a fanfare of trumpets. A detachment of Streltsy, coming from night guard duty, crosses the square, and the men awaken Kouzka. In a robust unison chorus ("Je marche sur Ivangorod"—"Me ne andrò verso Ivangorod"), they boast of their exploits in defending a portion of the city.

As they mill about, the Scribe emerges from his hut, sharpening his quill. The Streltsy bow in mock solemnity, hailing him as "Worshipful Writer to the Council." Laughing derisively, they then go on their way. The Scribe, shaking his head, laments the evil days that have fallen on

Russia, but in the next breath murmurs that, for himself, business is not bad.

Shaklovity enters and calls to the Scribe; dialogue in quasi-recitative follows. The Boyar orders the old man to write a letter he is about to dictate, warning him beforehand of fearsome torture if he ever dare reveal its contents ("Si tu braves tous les tourments"—"Si ti regge il cuore a soffrir"). The Scribe is momentarily terrified but forgets his fear when Shaklovity hands him a purse. As he begins the letter, a passage in the orchestra suggests the motion of the writer's hand. It is similar to that heard in *Boris* when the monk Pimen is writing in his cell.

The letter, addressed to "mighty Czars, Grand Dukes and Princes" ("Aux tsars souverains"—"Agli imperatori"), states that Prince Ivan Khovansky and his son Andrei are plotting a rebellion against the Empire. As the Scribe reads back what he has written, a group of Russians passes by. In a brief mocking chorus ("Il était une commère"—"C'era una comare") the peasants comment slyly on the connivery that is afoot.

After they leave, Shaklovity continues dictating the details of the Khovansky plot ("l'effroi sur la Russie"—"chiamare per l'immensa Russia") over a descriptively sinuous accompaniment: The traitor means to incite peasants and soldiers alike against the Czar, enlist the aid of the Old Believers,[1] then place his son, Prince Andrei, on the throne.

Suddenly the Streltsy are heard returning. Shaklovity wraps himself in his cloak and conceals himself while the Scribe, wailing in terror, stuffs the letter in his pocket. The Streltsy, roaring out a unison chorus of dire threats against their enemies, pass through the back of Red Square.

Shaklovity emerges and dictates the conclusion of the letter, which states that when peace is restored the writer's name will be revealed. Taking the letter, he again brusquely warns the Scribe to keep silence. The latter, irritated by the Boyar's insolent manner, turns on him angrily. Shaklovity, though somewhat taken aback by the outburst, advises the Scribe never to try to learn the name of the writer of the letter. Curiosity, he adds pointedly, is the devil's work. With that he glides away.

Gazing after him, the old Scribe sardonically wishes him a pleasant journey ("Douce soit ta route!"—"Facile ti sia la via!"). In the ensuing refrain he sings that his own wits are more than a match for this fellow who gives himself such high and mighty airs. Accordingly, he has signed the incriminating document with the name of Ananiev. He is dead—and the dead can feel no disgrace.

[1] The fanatical sect which clung to traditional beliefs and refused to accept the reforms of Patriarch Nikon in 1654. They broke away from the Orthodox Church when a revision of the Bible was introduced.

The people and the Streltsy now crowd into the square to hail Prince Ivan Khovansky, singing the first of the great choruses for which the opera is famous: "Gloire au grand prince Ivan"—"Gloria al padre e onor!" This powerful number, with its phrases in open fifths giving the effect of raw peasant vitality, is sometimes called the "White Swan" ensemble. The peasants hail Khovansky by that title ("au blanc cygne"— "al cigno candido").[2]

In an unaccompanied phrase, the Streltsy command the populace to listen to His Highness the Prince. Arrogant and proud, Ivan strides forward and addresses the throng in the form of a rhetorical question ("Vous, mes enfants"—"O figli miei"): Is it not true that the treacherous boyars[3] are spreading ruin not only in Moscow, but in all of Russia? Have we not pledged ourselves to destroy the enemies of the people? In answer, the peasants and soldiers again sing the "White Swan" chorus. After its thundering climax, the crowd follows Khovansky and his soldiers from the scene, the voices dying away in the distance.

Suddenly an agitated theme breaks out in the orchestra, and Emma comes rushing in pursued by Prince Andrei, who tries to embrace her. Fending him off, she distractedly implores him to leave her alone ("Grâce, trop faible"—"Grazia! Lasciate mi"). When he leers that the dove can never escape the falcon, she furiously denounces him as the villain who murdered her father, drove her lover into exile and scorned her mother's pleas for mercy. In desperation, Emma begs Andrei to kill her. But her protestations only inflame his desire, and he passionately entreats her to yield to him.

As Emma struggles to elude the Prince, Marfa steals behind a pillar and watches the scene. She ironically repeats the Prince's amorous phrases. In complete panic, Emma screams for help. With that Marfa comes forward and throws herself between the girl and Andrei, who staggers back in surprise.

With majestic dignity, Marfa turns on the hapless Prince with a flood of denunciation. So this, she begins ("Ah! oui, prince"—"Ah, tal fede, mio principe"), is how you repay me for my devotion . . . has a noble Prince nothing better to do than dally with the affections of an innocent maiden?

Andrei furiously orders Marfa to leave. Turning to Emma, he tells her to ignore this meddling strumpet ("Ignores-tu, ma chère enfant"— "Udisti mai, bellezza mia") and listen instead to the story about a handsome young man and the mistress he no longer loves. He solved the problem of getting rid of her in a very practical manner.

Thereupon Andrei springs at Marfa with an upraised dagger. Quick

---

[2] Adapted by Moussorgsky from a traditional Russian wedding song.

[3] Also spelled "boyard." They were privileged members of the Russian aristocracy, next to the ruling princes. The class was abolished by Peter the Great.

as a flash, she draws a dagger from underneath her cloak and parries the blow. In an unaccompanied phrase, she sings quietly that two can play at this game. In any case, she goes on, this is not the way in which a certain Prince will meet his fate—it will not be her hand that will send him to his doom.

Marfa's voice blends with Emma's and the Prince's in a trio passage. The Prince curses that the devil himself sent Marfa to torment him. Emma bewails the fact that while Marfa saved her life, she is powerless to save Marfa's. Marfa herself, as though in a trance, sings that she hears the voice of Fate and can see the shining portals of the blessed.

At this point Ivan Khovansky returns with the Streltsy and the people, who sing a reprise of the "White Swan" chorus. Over the ensemble, the voice of Emma is heard in a brief but anguished prayer for help. Ivan catches sight of Prince Andrei with Emma and exclaims in surprise. Struck by Emma's beauty, Khovansky orders his bodyguards to take her to his palace. Thereupon Andrei plants himself in front of the girl and defies his father to take her away from him. Furious at the Prince's defiance, Ivan bellows to his guards to take the girl. Andrei, with equal fury, commands them not to touch her. In helpless confusion, the men ask whom they are to obey.

As Ivan and Andrei rage at each other with increasing violence, Dossifé appears with a group of Old Believers. With commanding authority he strides between the two men and demands to know the reason for their frenzy ("Possédés du diable"—"Ravvedervi!"). As the two recoil in surprise, Emma throws herself at Dossifé's feet and implores him to save her. He turns to Marfa and orders her to take the terror-stricken girl home.

Whirling on the two Princes, the patriarch pours out his wrath in a brief but dynamic aria, "Le règne des ténèbres s'étend"—"La tenebra impera trionfa." He accuses them of bringing the Church of Russia to disaster through their pride, treachery and unbelief. Turning to the Old Believers, he exhorts them to cling to their orthodoxy even if it means martyrdom. Humbly, but with intense conviction, Dossifé calls on all true believers to hold fast to their faith ("Orthodoxes, soyez notre appui!"—"Ortodossi, aiutatetci!").

Wild with fury over Dossifé's accusations, Prince Ivan orders the Streltsy to place the patriarch and the Old Believers under arrest and imprison them in the Kremlin. To a fanfare of trumpets he then proclaims Andrei as the head of the Streltsy. As he leaves with his guards, the people stare in utter bewilderment. Andrei, still shaken by the quarrel with his father, follows slowly. As the Old Believers are led away, Dossifé leads them in a beautiful prayer, "Ô Seigneur! Que la Force ennemie"—"Dio Signor! Non far prevaler." They respond with an unaccompanied choral refrain, the so-called "Aeolian Chorus"[4]: "Dieu, délivre-nous"—"Dio possente." Their hymn dies away in the distance as the curtain falls.

ACT TWO

The summer home of Prince Golitsin[5] in Moscow. The Prince is sitting at a candlelit desk reading a love letter from the Czarevna, his royal mistress. Before the rise of the curtain there is a brief introduction in a foreboding minor key. This theme accompanies Golitsin's aria as he reads the letter ("Tendre frère Vassienka"—"Mio diletto Vassienka").

Although the letter is full of impassioned phrases, the Prince is wary of the Czarevna's avowals ("Doit-on croire au serment d'une femme"— "Credere devo al giuro di donna"). He reflects that she is ambitious and capricious—and if he suddenly fell out of favor with her it might well cost him his head. Be careful, Prince, he murmurs softly as the aria ends.

Golitsin's thoughts are interrupted by the entrance of his henchman, Varsonoviev, who tells him that the "sorceress" he sent for has arrived. When the Prince angrily upbraids him for calling the woman a sorceress, Varsonoviev servilely apologizes for this slip of the tongue.

He then brings in Marfa, who looks around cautiously as she approaches Golitsin. She remarks that the suspicious glances of the servants aroused her fears of an ambush. Golitsin says apprehensively that in these dangerous times no one knows what disaster the future may bring. Marfa then reveals that she is well aware of Golitsin's reason for summoning her: She has a reputation as a seeress, and she is to tell his fortune.

Marfa asks for a bowl of water. It is set before her, and then begins the Divination Scene, with Marfa's great aria, "Forces mystérieuses"— "Forze recondite," one of the most memorable scenes in the opera. The aria is introduced by a strangely dissonant passage which heightens the effect of superstitious dread.

In quasi-recitative, Marfa invokes the spirits of dead mariners to lift the dark veil of the Prince's future. Staring into the bowl, she intones that now the vision becomes clearer: She sees the Prince hemmed in by treacherous "friends" who smile as they plot his doom. Then she launches into the prophecy itself ("Bientôt va venir une disgrâce"—"T'in-

---

[4] Aeolian: refers to one of the ancient systems of musical scales. Another used in this opera is the Phrygian, in the brief chorus of the Old Believers in the last act.

[5] Counselor (and lover) of the Czarevna Sophia. He is representative of Western-oriented Russia—as opposed to the Khovanskys, symbolic of feudalism, and Dossifé, symbolic of mystical Russia.

combe funesto il bando"). It is declaimed in a minor key, in the steady rhythmic pattern of a typical Russian folk song.[6]

The Prince's destiny, Marfa sings somberly, is disgrace and exile. His fate is sealed—and neither his wit nor his wisdom will save him. Stripped of wealth and honor, he will suffer deprivation. In lonely, bitter exile he finally will learn the truth.

Listening in mingled horror and anger, Golitsin bursts out: "Go!" With a baleful glance at him, Marfa slowly withdraws, again searching with her eyes every corner of the room. Varsonoviev glides in. Golitsin, *sotto voce,* orders him to see to it that the woman is drowned in the nearby lake. Marfa, at the door, overhears this and rushes away.

Alone, Golitsin gives way to his despair in the great soliloquy "Et voilà mon avenir fatal"—"Ecco il giudizio del destino mio!" He broods over the ruin of all his hopes and ambitions for a better Russia. He had won the confidence of the boyars and had strengthened Russia's ties with other nations. His victory over the Poles had inspired foreign respect. Finally, he had restored to his people the lands torn from them by greedy invaders. And now his reward is oblivion. In an agonized phrase ("La rouille des Tatars"—"Addentro t'ha la ruggin tartara") he cries that the shadow of the Tatar lies long over this holy land.

As he sits staring into space, Ivan Khovansky enters without being announced. Golitsin looks up. For a moment the two leaders of the opposing factions in Russia—sworn enemies—face each other. Then Golitsin curtly invites his visitor to be seated. With a sneer, Khovansky remarks that, under the circumstances, taking a seat presents a problem ("M'asseoir! Le pourrais-je!"—"Seder! Che problema!"). This introduces a long and bitter dispute between the two men, carried on over a powerfully stated unison passage in the orchestra.

It begins as Ivan Khovansky, with mocking courtesy, asks where he is to sit—now that Prince Golitsin, with his treacherous scheming, has reduced the Khovanskys to the level of serfs ("Maintenant nous n'avons plus de place"—"Privi siam dei nostri posti ormai"). Perhaps his place is on the door mat, he adds sardonically.

It is strange, Golitsin retorts sarcastically, that the rich and powerful Khovansky should suddenly be concerned about the fortunes of other nobles. Be that as it may, Ivan answers, Prince Golitsin, in his ruthless disregard of the honor of the boyars, no doubt is following the precept of the Tatars themselves: "All men are created equal." That being the case, heads may be lopped off indiscriminately. Infuriated by this sally, Golitsin flares up momentarily, then controls himself with an effort.

In a calmer tone he goes on to say that he was forced to adopt harsh

[6] The tune of the prophecy reappears in an orchestral variation when Golitsin is taken into exile; also when Marfa warns Andrei, in the final scene, that death is near.

measures with the boyars ("J'ai pu blesser les boyars"—"Ho forse offesi i boiardi"), but those measures were necessary. At the same time, no punishment was meted out to Ivan Khovansky, leader of the Guards and the most powerful man in Moscow, before whom all must bow their heads. And now this grandee complains of being slighted!

Goaded to fury by Golitsin's stinging sarcasm, Khovansky roars that he will listen to no more slanderous accusations ("Arrête, prince!"—"Ah, basta al fin"). At that moment Dossifé enters and stands listening, his eyes fixed on Khovansky. Golitsin, noticing the patriarch, bows ironically to Prince Ivan. Oblivious to everything in his rage, Khovansky goes on to remind the other that he is of royal Tatar blood and need not submit to contempt and insult. Moreover, he asks, how can Golitsin boast of his generalship when half his army died of privation even before his latest campaign began.

This thrust rouses Golitsin himself to violent anger, and the two men advance threateningly toward each other. But once more Dossifé steps forward in the role of peacemaker, exhorting the raging noblemen to calm themselves ("Ô princes, calmez-vous"—"Ponete all' ira il fren"). The scene continues in trio form over reverberating chords in the orchestra. Dossifé tells the princes that their personal quarreling will never save Russia. They must turn to God for help and put their trust in the ancient faith.

Khovansky falls silent but Golitsin obstinately argues with the patriarch. When the latter insists that the people must be taught according to the traditional customs and beliefs, Golitsin scornfully says he has no use for the old ways. Dossifé cries that this attitude is the result of insidious foreign influence. The radicals and reformers have so terrorized the people that they are fleeing their homes and hiding in the forests.

At this point Khovansky unctuously remarks that time and again he has tried to reason with this headstrong Prince to convince him that he must return to the old ways. In spite of his efforts, he adds, Golitsin destroyed the repository of ancient wisdom, *The Book of Pedigrees*.

Before Golitsin can reply, the voices of the Old Believers are heard in the distance chanting that they have triumphed over heresy ("L'hérésie nous l'avons flétrie"—"Vinta abbiamo l'eresia"). The conversation of the three men continues over the chorus. A moment later the Old Believers and a crowd of townspeople, carrying lighted tapers, pass by outside, singing as they go.

Scowling at them, Golitsin asks who these people are. They are men of deeds—not words, Dossifé replies pointedly. They have remained true to their old faith. With angry contempt, Golitsin brands them ineffectual dissenters. Khovansky, relishing the other's discomfiture, remarks that the traditionalists may yet save Russia.

Suddenly Marfa bursts into the room, falls on her knees before Golit-

sin and begs him to save her life. The Prince curses her as a witch. As
the others stare in consternation, Marfa turns to Dossifé and tells him
what has happened ("Au jour tombant je sortais"–"Me ne tornavo").
When she left the Prince's house at dusk a serf followed her. As she
passed the "Marsh" near Belgorod the man seized her, saying he had
been ordered by Prince Golitsin to drown her. Just then a group of Petrovsky, the Czar's personal guards, came by and saved her.[7] The realization that the Czar's troops are in Moscow brings expressions of alarm
and dismay from Ivan and Golitsin, as well as from Dossifé. In the general confusion Marfa and her accusations are forgotten.

Excitement flares as Varsonoviev comes charging in, crying that the
Boyar Shaklovity is at the door. Striding forward, Shaklovity announces
that the Czarevna has issued a proclamation accusing the Khovanskys of
conspiring against the Empire ("Seigneurs! la tsarevna vous fait"–"O
principi! La tsarevna ordina"). Dossifé tells Ivan that now all hope is
lost. Turning to Shaklovity, he asks what the Czar's own reaction is to
the plot. With obvious relish, the Boyar answers: "He calls it 'Khovanchina.' "[8] There is general consternation as the orchestra thunders out
the theme heard in the five variations in the Prelude. The curtain falls.

ACT THREE

The massively timbered barracks of the Streltsy in a suburb of Moscow. Opposite is the home of Prince Ivan Khovansky. As the curtain
rises, the chorus of the Old Believers is heard in the distance, again
chanting their hymn of triumph over the heretics. It swells to a great
crescendo as the procession passes through the Streltsy quarter, then
gradually dies away as the Old Believers move out of sight.

One of the last in the procession is Marfa, who unobtrusively remains
behind. As the bass theme associated with the Old Believers continues
in the orchestra, she sits down on an embankment near Prince Andrei's
house. There, in one of the opera's most beautiful arias, "Moi, jeunette,
j'ai parcouru"–"Ha percorsi la gióvane," she sings of her love for the
Prince. This aria, actually a Russian folk tune, is introduced by a tender
phrase in descending triads. The folk melody is sustained throughout
the aria in a throbbing 6/4 tempo.

The song portrays Marfa's passionate longing for her lover in the
symbolic terms of a love-smitten maiden stumbling through brook and
briar in the night to the home of her beloved. But there she knocks in
vain. Her faithless lover has deserted her. Ending the aria on a menac-

---

[7] The motive of the Prelude, describing the peaceful dawn in Moscow, is heard
during Marfa's story. It is here symbolic of her relief at being saved.

[8] Thus the Czar contemptuously characterized the treason of the Khovanskys.

ing phrase, Marfa sings that she will avenge herself on her lover for his cruelty ("sa vengeance éclatante et cruelle!"—"or ti resta la gretta settaria!"). [9]

But while Marfa is giving expression to her amorous longings, Susanna, one of the Old Believers, steals in and listens to her song. A stern, self-righteous member of the sect, she warns Marfa that she will be damned eternally for her carnal thoughts ("Blasphème! Point de pardon"—"Grave peccato inespiabil fai"). This introduces a long and dramatic duet.

The old woman, shocked and outraged, upbraids Marfa for her "shameless singing." Tormented by memories of her love affair with Prince Andrei, Marfa answers that she will not hide the truth about the past. If Susanna had ever known a man's ardent kiss, Marfa goes on, she would not now presume to condemn another woman for yielding to the soul-consuming fire of love ("Si tu comprenais"—"Ah, se intender mai potessi"). Susanna grows almost hysterical as Marfa's words stir to life her own long-suppressed desires ("Est-ce le diable qui me trouble?"—"O che il demonio sé mi trae?").

In a passionate frenzy Marfa turns toward Prince Andrei's house and implores him not to forget her ("Rappelletoi ma chère âme"—"Pensa, ricorda, diletto mio"). Losing all control, Susanna furiously accuses Marfa of corrupting her with visions of carnal love ("Tu as voulu me tenter"—"Tu m'hai tentata"). For this she will denounce her to the Old Believers and have her burned at the stake.

As the old woman hurls her imprecations, Dossifé comes out of Andrei's house and Marfa bows low before him. Quietly she tells him that Susanna is condemning her because she has told the truth about her sinful past. Dossifé sternly rebukes Susanna for her self-righteous cruelty toward an unfortunate sister. When she defies him, the patriarch loses his temper and roars that she is the devil's own offspring ("Bélial s'empare de ton esprit"—"Belial é il solo tuo Signor!"). Wrathfully he orders her out of his sight. Susanna scurries away in terror.[10]

A moving duet ensues as Dossifé turns to Marfa with words of comfort and encouragement ("Ah! mon enfant si chère"—"Ah, creatura mia!"). Marfa reveals that Prince Andrei has betrayed and abandoned her, but she confesses that her tormenting desire for him gives her no respite. If it is wrong to love, she cries in despair, then let her be put to death so that her soul may be saved.

Dossifé, profoundly moved by her anguish, tells her he himself has

[9] This aria is built upon three themes: two refer to Marfa's despairing love for Andrei. The third is associated with her prophecy in the Divination Scene.

[10] In some productions the character of Susanna does not appear. Then the next scene between Marfa and Dossifé follows immediately after Marfa's aria.

sinned and is in need of forgiveness. Trust in God's mercy, he counsels her, and do not be afraid of loving. With that the patriarch gently leads her away.

The Boyar Shaklovity now appears. Though notorious as a scoundrel and a plotter, he is haunted by a premonition of Russia's doom. He expresses his forebodings in one of the opera's principal arias, "Ah, malheureuse Russie"—"Ah, che destino maligno." He ponders whether the Empire will at last fall victim to her enemies. She has survived the depredations of the Germans, as well as the tyranny of the Tatars—but she is still the prey of other evil forces. Shaklovity climaxes his aria with a prayer for Russia's deliverance from the clutches of merciless enemies ("des mains de mercenaires, arrache la Russie!"—"O Dio, ribenedici questo suol, esaudimi!").

As he stands for a moment plunged in gloom he hears the sound of a brawling chorus of the Streltsy in the distance. Let the "Khovansky lambs" sing while they may, he murmurs sardonically, for their song soon will be ended. He turns and disappears.

The Streltsy, some of them still drunk after a night of carousing, come stampeding in and roar out a mighty chorus—mostly about their prowess in drinking and fighting. One of the most stirring numbers in the opera, it is in the best tradition of Russian male ensembles.

At the climax of the chorus they are interrupted by an excited crowd of women—most of them the wives of the Streltsy themselves. The men fall back as the women, in a shrill ensemble ("Ah! les vauriens maudits"—"Ah, maledetti beoni"), rail at them for behaving like drunken brutes. Hurling insults at each other, the men and women bring the chorus to a turbulent conclusion.

The uproar comes to a sudden stop as the Scribe comes rushing in, obviously beside himself with terror. The Streltsy crowd around him, trying to find the reason for his panic ("Quelle espèce d'âne?"—"Che ti piglia, scemo?"). Over an agitated theme in the orchestra, the Scribe finally tells the incredulous Streltsy that while he was busy at his letter writing in the suburb of Kitaigorod ("J'étais au travail près de Kitaigorod"—"A Kitaigorod ero per ufficio") he heard mounted troops approaching. When they came to the Streltsy quarter, he goes on, the troops began to attack women and children.

Ignoring the jeering disbelief of the Streltsy, the Scribe reports that suddenly the Petrovsky joined the troops in the attack and routed the Streltsy, who were defending their quarter. At this news there are outcries of terror from the women and the Streltsy. The Scribe makes his getaway unnoticed.

Kouzka comes forward to urge the others to ask Prince Ivan Khovansky if this alarming report is true, or if the miserable Scribe is lying for reasons of his own. Thereupon the women and men surge toward the Prince's house and make their plea in a brief chorus ("Père, montretoi!"—"Padre, vien a noi!"). When Khovansky comes out of his house with a paternal greeting, the Streltsy implore him to lead them in a counterattack against the Petrovsky.

But the Prince's reply ("Qu'il vous souvienne du temps"—"Vi ricordate, o figli") takes them by surprise. Recalling how they once fought a bloody battle to drive the traitors out of Moscow, Ivan declares that now things have changed: They must submit to the will of the Czar Peter. With a pompous "farewell," Khovansky goes back into the house.

Fear-stricken and completely bewildered, the Streltsy and their women pray for deliverance from their enemies ("Que l'ennemi s'éloigne"—"Ci guarda dai nemici"). The curtain falls slowly.

ACT FOUR
(Part I)

The luxuriously furnished dining hall in the house of Prince Ivan Khovansky outside Moscow. The Prince, seated with guests at his banquet table, is listening to the song of his serving girls ("Sur la verdoyante rive"—"Sulla riva del ruscello"). Their song, a typical Russian folk tune in a minor key, is about a young lover who bathed in the brook before he went to meet his sweetheart.

Khovansky interrupts the singing, complaining that the song is much too sad for this festive occasion. At his prompting the girls strike up a lively ditty ("Tard au soir quand tout sommeille"—"Vigilavo a tarda sera") which they call "Haiduchok."[11] The chorus is interrupted by the entrance of Varsonoviev, who warns Prince Ivan that his life is in danger.

Khovansky scornfully rejects the possibility that he could be attacked on his own estate. He curtly dismisses Varsonoviev, then calls for his Persian dancers, who entertain him and his guests with the "Dance of the Persians," familiar as a concert number.

A few moments after the dancers leave the scene, Shaklovity enters and obsequiously approaches Prince Ivan. He informs the Prince that the Czarevna is calling a meeting of the Guard Council to discuss the crucial state of affairs in Russia, and she urgently requests the Prince to be present. Ivan at first flatly refuses to go, but Shaklovity, playing upon the Prince's exalted opinion of his own statesmanship, persuades him to attend.

Calling for his most resplendent robe of state and his jewel-encrusted

[11] A name once given to the Hungarian infantry. The song itself has the rhythm and character of the czardas.

staff, Khovansky commands his serving maids to sing in his honor. They oblige with a stately chorus ("Il nage fier le cygne blanc"—"In contro al cigno"). In resounding unison phrases—interspersed with the salutation "Ladou," almost like an incantation—they hail him as the glorious White Swan who now goes to meet his snowy mate.[12] The irony of this paean becomes violently apparent in the next few moments. As Prince Ivan turns and strides majestically toward the door, Shaklovity plunges his dagger into his back. Khovansky, with a terrible cry, falls dead. The serving maids rush away screaming in terror.

Shaklovity, glaring down at the Prince's body, repeats with savage mockery the refrain of the serving maids: "Aye, all glory to the snow-white swan, Ladou, Ladou!" The curtain falls.

ACT FOUR
(Part II)

The square in front of the Cathedral of Vassily Blyenye (St. Basil) in Moscow, where a crowd is gathered. A troop of cavalry, armed with sabers, rides in and forms ranks in front of the church, their backs to the entrance. The people quickly move to the opposite side of the square. Soon a carriage escorted by soldiers passes through the square; the onlookers, craning their necks, chatter excitedly. In the carriage is Prince Golitsin, on his way to exile. As the procession moves out of sight, the people slowly follow with heads bowed. In a brief choral phrase ("Que le Sauveur t'absolve!"—"Iddio ti dia perdon!") they implore God's mercy on the departing Prince.[13]

For several moments the square is empty. Then Dossifé appears with Marfa, to whom he describes the succession of tragic events which have shaken Russia: Prince Golitsin exiled, Prince Ivan Khovansky murdered, the destiny of Prince Andrei hanging in the balance—in Moscow certain factions even have hailed him as Czar. The patriarch relates these events in a recitative passage ("Tel du Destin l'arrêt s'est accompli"—"Compiuto s'e il giudizio deldestin").

Marfa herself has news of further disaster. The Grand Council has ordered "foreign troops" to slaughter the Old Believers. In fanatical excitement, Dossifé cries that the hour has come for the final immolation of the faithful. He exhorts Marfa to win Prince Andrei to the faith, so that he may die with them and save his soul. Assuring her that she will receive a crown in heaven as her reward, Dossifé hurries away. Alone,

[12] This chorus was described by Oskar von Riesemann, Moussorgsky's biographer, as "almost the only example of continuous 17/4 time (6/4+5/4+6/4) time in music."

[13] This phrase is sung over an orchestral variation of the theme of Marfa's prophecy about Golitsin.

Marfa, in a transport of religious fervor, exults in the expectation of martyrdom.

To the accompaniment of a quivering theme in the orchestra, Prince Andrei bursts in and angrily demands to know where Emma has been kept hidden. Marfa tells him that the girl is now far away from Moscow —and probably reunited with the man from whom Andrei himself had once separated her. Wild with rage, Andrei curses Marfa as a witch and shouts that he will call his guards and have her executed on the spot.

In quiet defiance, Marfa answers him in one of the most intensely dramatic passages in the entire opera, "Tu ne comprends guère, prince" —"Né presagio, sire," sung in a variation of the theme of her prophecy. Over the steady beat of a single note accentuated by a harsh, open-interval figure in the bass, she warns Andrei that he is sealing his own doom by ignoring the call of his destiny. But Andrei, his thoughts still on Emma, pays little heed.

Marfa goes on to remind him that the corpse of his father, murdered by traitors, still lies stark and unburied in his home, with wind and wolves for a deathwatch. Meanwhile, these selfsame traitors are hunting down his son.

But Andrei, now beside himself with fury, refuses to believe her ("Non, je ne te crois pas"—"Non, vo' credere a te") and accuses her of trying to destroy him with her witchcraft. One word from him, he rages, will bring his guards to lead her to the stake.

"Call your guards," Marfa says quietly. Staring incredulously at her for a moment, the Prince sounds his horn. Suddenly the great bell of the cathedral begins tolling, and then a bizarre procession comes into view. The Streltsy, carrying axes and blocks for their own beheading, march in followed by their wives—who now, strangely enough, apparently have turned against them.

There is a gasp of horror from Andrei, who abjectly begs Marfa to save him from sharing the fate of the Streltsy. Assuring him of safety, she leads him away. Meanwhile, the women, in a frenzied chorus ("Non, pas de grâce"—"Morte, agli empi, morte!"), scream for death without mercy for the hapless Streltsy, who kneel in prayer before their execution blocks.

But the scheduled execution is thwarted by the arrival (in a fantastic turn of the plot) of the Czar's guards (the Preobajensky), who enter to a blazing fanfare followed by a majestic, hymnlike march.[14] They are led by the herald, Streshniev, who proclaims that the Czars Ivan and Peter have pardoned the Streltsy. They are to go in peace to their homes and pray that the glorious Empire may continue to prosper. In

[14] This march tune is the same as that of the familiar hymn "Glorious Things of Thee Are Spoken," by Franz Josef Haydn.

honor of this royal gesture of magnanimity, the Preobajensky are to parade before the Kremlin.

The Streltsy, stunned by their reprieve, rise silently and watch the Czar's men leave to the accompaniment of the march tune. The curtain falls.

ACT FIVE

The hermitage of the Old Believers in a pine forest not far from Moscow. A bright moon glimmers through the trees. Dossifé enters slowly to the accompaniment of a serene unison passage in ascending and descending eighth-note patterns, descriptive of the sighing of the wind through the pines. In one of the opera's most impressive arias, "Là, en cet endroit"—"Qui in questo luogo," he reflects that here in this peaceful spot the Old Believers will meet their final doom. He recalls how he has struggled to keep his flock unwavering in its faith. The way has been hard, but now the time is at hand for their eternal reward. He prays that their unshakable devotion will inspire men for ages to come. Sinking to his knees, Dossifé ends the aria in a quiet invocatory phrase.

One by one the Old Believers appear, Marfa among them. In dolorous tones, Dossifé tells them that their cause is lost ("Perdue est notre cause"—"Perduta è la causa"). They are now at the mercy of their enemies. Prince Ivan Khovansky is murdered, Prince Golitsin banished, Prince Andrei himself is hiding in the hermitage to escape those who have marked him for death. Now the Antichrist has come among them, but they must be prepared to die rather than yield. In a brief choral phrase the Old Believers reassure the patriarch of their steadfastness.

Dossifé bids them put on their white ceremonial robes, light their tapers and wait for the hour of immolation. As the bell of the hermitage begins to toll, the Old Believers defy the power of the Antichrist and hail their redemption "by flame and fire." After the chorus they return to the hermitage with Dossifé, while Marfa remains alone.

She gives way to her anguish over Andrei's treachery toward her, but prays that she may have the strength to save his soul through her abiding love. As though mocking her agony of spirit, she hears Andrei's voice in the distance singing of his longing for Emma ("Où donc est ma liberté?"—"Dove sei, o libertà?"). But when he appears a moment later, calling Emma's name, Marfa rushes to his side. She pours out her love in a sweeping aria ("Souviens-toi des jours"—"Ah, fa che ti souvenga") in which she gives expression to her mingled feelings of religious ecstasy and sensual desire. Offering Andrei her last embrace, she ends the aria with a fervid "Alleluia!"[15]

---

[15] This scene, which Moussorgsky called the "requiem of love," was said to be one of the things in the opera that pleased him most.

Dossifé, clad in a ceremonial shroud, emerges from the shadow of the pines proclaiming that the trumpet of doom has sounded. The fanfare of the approaching Poteshny guards is heard in the distance. For the second time, Andrei beseeches Marfa to save him.

Over the sound of a funeral march, Marfa replies ("Entends monter" —"Non odi tu") that the troops—the executioners—are upon them, and now there is no place to hide. Destiny has decreed that they are to be forever united in death. As she thus pronounces Andrei's doom, the Old Believers, carrying their tapers, assemble and begin building a pyre. Taking Andrei by the hand, Marfa leads him up to the pyre. Repeating the passionate avowal expressed in her aria ("Souviens-toi des jours de notre amour"—"Ah, fa che ti sovvenga l'ora dell'amor"), she sings that now they will rekindle the fire of their love in the devouring flames.

They both then mount the pyre, followed by the Old Believers, who sing the invocatory "Phrygian Chorus," "Ô Dieu de gloire"—"Dio della gloria." In a solo over a descending chromatic passage in the brass, Dossifé exhorts the faithful to have courage, for they shall see God. Snatching a taper, Marfa ignites the pyre. The harsh fanfare of the Czar's guards comes nearer.

As the flames billow upward, the doomed victims join in a mighty plea for pardon of their sins ("Ô Maître, toi, mon aide"—"O Signor! Nostro padre").[16] Soaring over the chorus comes Marfa's final passionate entreaty to Andrei, "Remember our moments of bliss!" But Andrei, engulfed with the others in the flames, cries out: "Emma!"

To a clamorous fanfare, the Czar's guards rush in, then stagger back in horror at the holocaust. As the theme associated with the Poteshny resounds in the orchestra, the curtain slowly falls.

[16] This final chorus was composed by Nikolai Rimsky-Korsakov from Moussorgsky's rough draft of the scene.

THE LAST SAVAGE

(*L'Ultimo Selvaggio—Le Dernier Sauvage*)
by GIAN-CARLO MENOTTI
(1911–   )

Libretto by the composer

CHARACTERS

The Maharajah of Rajaputana	Bass
The Maharanee	Contralto
Kodanda, the Prince, their supposed son	Tenor
Sardula, a servant girl	Soprano
Abdul, a peasant	Baritone
Mr. Scattergood, an American millionaire	Bass-baritone
Kitty, his daughter	Soprano
Two Indian scholars	Tenors
Two American tailors	Tenor, baritone
An English tailor	Tenor
A Roman Catholic priest	Bass
A Protestant minister (a Negro)	Baritone
A rabbi	Tenor
A Greek Orthodox priest	Tenor
A philosopher	Baritone
A physician	Baritone
A painter	Tenor
A poet	Tenor
A scientist	Tenor
A composer	Baritone
A concert singer	Soprano
A businesswoman	Soprano

In India: Hunters, Indian nobility, ladies in waiting, attendants

In Chicago: Journalists, military and civil authorities, politicians, society women, debutantes, various guests

Place: In India and Chicago, U.S.A.
Time: Present
First performance: Opéra-Comique, Paris, October 22, 1963, in French, as *Le Dernier Sauvage*
Original language: Italian

The Last Savage, Gian-Carlo Menotti's ninth opera, was his first full-length work in *opera buffa* form. He had been fairly successful in this form with his first opera, the one-act *Amelia Goes to the Ball* (1934), and again wanted to try his hand at comedy. Accordingly, in about 1947 he began sketching out a plot for an opera. First called *The Last Superman,* it was about a young American girl, a student of anthropology at Vassar, who went to the Himalayas in search of a cave man as a research subject. There she found her "primitive," brought him to Chicago to expose him to civilization, then ended up by marrying him and living with him in a cave in India—complete with refrigerator and television.

The opera is a penetrating but good-natured satire on the foibles and pretensions of modern society, as contrasted to the serenity of life close to nature which mankind has sacrificed for the sake of becoming "civilized." Menotti, of course, gives the simple life the best of it. Accordingly, he eschewed harsh dissonances and other "far-out" musical elements, writing out of the conviction that there is in people an instinctive desire for, and sensitivity to, simple melody. He preferred, as he said, to adhere to the lyric tradition of Rossini, Donizetti and Cimarosa. The score abounds in melody and bubbles with humor. It is eclectic—but the artistry which infuses the music is Menotti's own.

Menotti wrote the libretto in Italian, and it was given in its original form as *L'Ultimo Selvaggio* in Venice on May 15, 1964. The first American performance, in an English translation by George Mead, was given at the Metropolitan on January 23, 1964.

There is a lively overture in a brisk tempo, which mingles jazz and conventional rhythms. Opening with a C-major chord, it states several leading themes of the opera.

ACT ONE

[*Scene One*] A room in the palace of the Maharajah in the foothills of the Himalayas. The Indian potentate and Mr. Scattergood are examining various documents. A long musical dialogue takes place in which the two discuss the possibility of marriage between the Maharajah's son, Kodanda, the Crown Prince, and Scattergood's daughter, Kitty. They begin by enumerating their respective possessions—motor cars, airplanes and wives ("How many motor cars?"—"Quante automobili?").

The Maharajah piles up an impressive total—twenty-two cars, thirty-two airplanes, twenty-seven wives (one official), ninety-six little cities and six big ones. Scattergood can boast of a paltry six cars, three airplanes, one wife (all the law allows), châteaux, chalets and villas in

Europe and Peru, a ranch in Arizona, six buildings and eight sky-scrapers in Chicago and New York. All this is sung in quasi-recitative over an accompaniment in a rollicking tempo.

Having duly taken inventory, the two conclude that marriage between their two children would be a commendable idea. The only obstacle is that Kitty and the Crown Prince are stubborn and flatly refuse to get married. Scattergood suggests that the Maharanee might be helpful. She is too stupid for that, the Maharajah snorts, adding that the one thing to her credit is that she bore him his only son.

"What!" Scattergood exclaims. "Only one son from twenty-seven wives!" In a brief refrain ("It seems rather improbable"—"E già, pare impossibile") the Maharajah blandly explains that twenty-six of the wives turned out to be sterile, but the Maharanee vindicated his man-hood by bearing him a son without delay. The boy, he says, is blue-eyed and fair-haired (doesn't resemble his father) and it may well be that one of his ancestors was pure Anglo-Saxon.

At this point the Maharanee herself appears. Enormously fat, she waddles in supported by Sardula and another servant girl, sinks into a heap of cushions and begins munching almonds.

Looking at her with casual contempt, the Maharajah observes that she is pear-shaped, but at least she gave him an heir. He goes on to describe her in derisive terms in a hilarious aria, "Look her over"—"Ma la guarda." This is a mountain of a woman, he sings, a Rock of Gibral-tar, a tuba, an entire band. Yet she is as logical as the dome on the nave of a cathedral. She neither reads nor writes, never walks and sel-dom talks. Her favorite diversion, next to stuffing herself with sweets, is playing the stock market. Scattergood, fascinated, murmurs that she is obviously a smart woman.

Asking her advice, says the Maharajah, is a waste of time, but he in-vites Scattergood to go ahead. Awed by the woman's vast bulk, he tim-idly approaches and with a nervous stammer asks what she thinks of the marriage plans. Like a massive idol, she stares at him for a long mo-ment, then replies in sepulchral tones. Her advice is brief and to the point: if he will see to his daughter, they will do the same with their son. Both Scattergood and the Maharajah hail this solution as a stroke of genius.

Scattergood starts to leave, saying he must find his daughter. The Maharajah protests his going in the heat of the day and leads him back to his chair. With a clap of his hands he summons servants, whom he orders to call the Crown Prince and to tell the American girl that her father wishes to see her.

An orchestral interlude in 5/4 time follows, during which several ma-sons, working with lightning speed, erect a wall separating the Maharaja-jah and Scattergood and dividing the stage into two parts. After the masons have left, Crown Prince Kodanda enters and announces that he knows why he has been called ("Father dear, I already know"—"Padre mio, indovino perché").

This introduces a remarkable ensemble which blends the voices of the characters on either side of the wall (in the manner of the *Rigoletto* quartet). Kodanda at once declares he will have nothing to do with the marriage proposals. His father denounces him as an ungrateful son. A family argument develops briefly as the Maharanee blames her husband for spoiling the Crown Prince. Kodanda implores his parents to spare him the fate of marriage to the American girl. Arguing in pantomime, the three move upstage.

On the other side of the wall, where Scattergood is sitting staring into space, Kitty enters. She is dressed in an explorer's costume. Noting her father's woebegone expression, she asks what is troubling him ("Papa, what's wrong?"—"Papa, che c'è?"). Musical dialogue ensues. Scattergood's explanation is that times are bad and that his ulcer is bothering him. But Kitty, realizing what really is on his mind, warns him—just as Kodanda did on the other side of the wall—that she will have nothing to do with any plans for marriage.

Then in a kind of parody of an operatic *secco* recitative ("I have traveled here to India"—"Siam venuti apposta in India") she says she has come to India for the sole purpose of finding the "last primitive cave man." As this is to be the subject of her Ph.D. thesis, she does not intend to interrupt her scientific studies by getting married. She is convinced that this prehistoric man has survived and is somewhere in India —and she will be the one to find him.

Kitty and her father withdraw upstage and the scene shifts back to the other side of the wall. From this point on the ensemble continues in sextet form involving the four principals plus Sardula and the Maharanee. It begins as the Maharajah and Scattergood, in echoing phrases, entreat their offspring to heed parental advice. Kodanda reiterates that he is not interested in American women—their skins are too white. He would much prefer a girl like Sardula. The Maharanee gasps in dismay at the idea of his marrying a servant girl.

Sardula herself chimes in to advise Kodanda that his wife should be an American girl with oil wells. Half jestingly, the Crown Prince ticks off other marital possibilities—German, French, Greek, Italian. The women reject them out of hand for various reasons. They have only one suggestion, which they repeat in thirds like a chant: "But this American girl fits to perfection"—"L'Americana invece è perfetta").

The three now withdraw as Kitty and Scattergood move into the scene. Insisting that she will not marry until she finds her "wild man," Kitty assures her father that this discovery will make her famous. This is her destiny, she sings, and to accomplish her mission she will stay in

India "forever." For want of a better answer, Scattergood plaintively remarks that the future is uncertain and that all he asks is to die in peace. Kitty climaxes her part of the argument on a high coloratura phrase.

Kodanda, Sardula and the Maharanee now resume the battle. Again the women insist he must marry a rich girl. Again they reject Kodanda's candidates: English or French (too mannish and too clannish, respectively). In the identical musical phrase sung before, they repeat their chant: "But this American girl fits to perfection."

Kodanda thereupon launches into a discourse on the relative wifely qualifications of American and Indian women. He does not deny that American women are attractive, but they complain too much. He prefers a simple, tenderhearted native girl—the kind of woman he can understand. He concludes his discourse on a lyrical phrase.

The Maharajah steps in at this point to upbraid his son for being somewhat stupid: After all, this is to be a marriage of convenience. This introduces a new phase of the discussion on both sides of the wall. In a last-ditch effort to win the battle, the Maharajah and Scattergood call attention to the deplorable state of world affairs. In India—reformers, constitutions, revolutions! In America—billion-dollar budgets, Democrats, taxes, Senate investigations! Under the circumstances it is difficult to amass another million. Kitty and Kodanda must not miss their golden opportunity, the fathers declare. They must marry *now*. The upshot of all this is that the two suddenly agree to be married. The parents and Sardula shout a joyful "Bravo!"

But in the next instant their hopes are dashed. Kodanda says he will marry only if Kitty gives up anthropology. Kitty announces she will marry only after her mission is completed. Kodanda points out that it would be a disgrace for an Indian Crown Prince to marry a girl hunting an ape man. Kitty asks her father how he could reasonably expect her to face Vassar without a scientific trophy. And so the question remains: What is to be done? The others shrug helplessly.

At this point there begins a brilliantly contrived concerted number, introduced by the phrase "Now, another question"—"Senta che furba è questa," in which the six principals ponder the situation. The parents and Sardula sing that, under the conditions as stated, their problem is to find this prehistoric man. Kitty declares she would do anything to please dear Papa—but it must be done her way. She is not interested in being a rich man's wife and is determined to dedicate her life to science.

Kodanda observes that he knows any number of charming women who are mad about him—he does not have to waste his time on a conceited Vassar girl. In any case, he adds, his only true love is Sardula. The sextet ends with a flourish on the phrase "That is the problem as of

now"—"Il gran problema è tutto qua." Kitty and Kodanda leave by
their separate exits.

The Maharajah claps his hands to recall the masons and orders them
to remove the wall immediately. This they do as quickly as they built it,
while the music that accompanied the building is played backward.
Face to face again, the Maharajah and Scattergood gloomily admit their
plans have failed. The dilemma is unchanged: no wild man, no marriage. The men decide once more to ask the Maharanee's counsel. In
her usual oracular fashion she delivers her answer: If a genuine savage
cannot be found, they will have to invent one. The men applaud her ingenuity.

Thereupon Sardula edges forward and says she knows of someone
who could play the role to perfection. As the others stare in surprise she
explains that this likely prospect is a handsome young peasant from the
hills who has been courting her for the past two years. As it happens, he
is here at this very moment because today is her birthday and he came
to bring her a present. The Maharanee orders her to bring him in at
once.

As Sardula runs off there is a brief byplay between the Maharanee
and Scattergood which has an important bearing on the plot later on.
Looking at him intently, the Maharanee asks if they have ever met before. When Scattergood says no, she insists his face is familiar. The
matter is dropped as Sardula reappears, pushing her young man ahead
of her. A majestic fanfare accompanies his entrance. Awed by his phy-
sique, the parents stare at him. Self-conscious and embarrassed, he stares
back.

In answer to the Maharajah's question, he says his name is Abdul.
An ensemble then follows in which Abdul is persuaded to play the role
of a prehistoric savage and is instructed on how to carry out the masquerade. When he protests he knows nothing about acting, the others
assure him he is perfect for the part. Sardula impatiently urges him to
accept. The Maharajah explains what he is to do. He is to let his hair
and beard grow and hide in the jungle like a wild man. When he finally
is "discovered," he is not to speak, but only to emit ferocious, apelike
growls. To illustrate, the Maharajah thumps his chest and imitates a
Tarzan howl. With an understanding nod, Abdul says: "Like Hollywood." The Maharajah beams approvingly.

Then Abdul is told that after he is taken to the jungle he is to allow
himself to be captured by a "lady from Chicago." He then will be exhibited in public for two or three weeks as a prize specimen of prehistoric man. For this caper he will be well paid—the American will take
care of that, the Maharajah adds complacently. Scattergood gasps. His
Highness looks at him expectantly.

Afraid to refuse, Scattergood offers one thousand dollars. Mistaking

Abdul's bewilderment for dissatisfaction with the offer, Scattergood raises it to ten thousand. Abdul, in helpless confusion, protests that it is not a question of money—and furthermore, he is not interested in being an actor. Scattergood offers fifty thousand. The Maharajah generously suggests making it an even hundred thousand. As Scattergood groans over the figure, the Maharajah leads Abdul to a table, scribbles out a contract, then reads it in spoken words. It stipulates that Abdul is to receive one dollar in advance, ninety-nine thousand, nine hundred and ninety-nine dollars when the job is finished.

The ensemble continues in quasi-recitative interspersed with concerted passages. Unable to reason with his determined benefactors, Abdul turns to Sardula with a pleading look. She, of course, tells him to be practical and not to refuse all this "lovely money" which is being thrust into his hands. The parents are aghast at the thought of anyone refusing to accept one hundred thousand dollars.

Losing his temper completely, Abdul furiously rejects the whole idea. At that point, Sardula resorts to her ultimate weapon: tears. If he cannot support her, she wails, how can they be married? Sardula, of course, wins the day—with the help of the others, who loudly berate Abdul for being a coldhearted monster. Abdul consents to sign the contract if Sardula will promise to marry him. Instantly her demeanor changes to passionate affection. The Maharajah and the Maharanee compliment Abdul on his decision and assure him that once he signs the contract he can live like a king for the rest of his life. Reiterating these various sentiments, the principals bring the scene to a close.

[*Scene Two*] There is a long orchestral introduction dominated by a sinuous rhythmic figure. It is late afternoon in the court of the palace. The Maharanee is dozing in a corner as Sardula reads her the latest stock market quotations. From the distance comes the sound of a women's chorus ("O my hunter, far away"—"Dove erri, O cacciator"). They sing about the hunter whose sweetheart assures him that she will be waiting for him with her lamp to light his way safely home.

As the refrain dies softly away, Sardula stops reading, sees that the Maharanee is fast asleep and starts to tiptoe out of the room. Suddenly Kodanda appears, blocks her way and tries to embrace her. A brief scene in quasi-recitative follows. Struggling to free herself, Sardula angrily reminds Kodanda that she is engaged to another man—and, what is more, he himself is engaged to that American girl.

Kodanda contemptuously dismisses the thought of marrying "that anthropologist" and tells Sardula that he is madly in love with her. Sardula retorts that he will marry the anthropologist whether he likes it or not. It is all arranged—even if she doesn't find the primitive man. But Kodanda only becomes more ardent and vows he will tame her. She defies him, which only serves to make him more persistent. The theme of conquest and resistance continues in duet form. It reaches a climax when Sardula tears herself from Kodanda's arms, then slaps his face and runs away. Crestfallen, Kodanda stares after her.

A moment later there is a distant fanfare of hunting horns. This awakens the Maharanee, who orders Kodanda to assemble the court. As the fanfare swells, a great throng crowds upon the scene—men and women of the court, visiting princes and their retinues, a band of hunters, porters carrying the spoils of the chase. Then come the Maharajah, Scattergood and Kitty, all in hunting costume. Finally, four porters carry in a huge cage. In it sits Abdul disguised as a savage.

In a delightful spoof of the conventional operatic "triumphal chorus," the crowd hails the success of the hunt ("These are the mighty hunters"—"Che i cacciatori"). The focus of attention, of course, is the strange creature in the cage. The crowd speculates as to whether he is a demon from the moon, half man or half beast, or a Hollywood star. The chorus rises to a mighty crescendo of wild guesses, with one and all finally wondering if this captive could be the Abominable Snowman.

Kitty steps forward and, in recitative, orders her trophy to be exhibited as evidence that she has not been chasing phantoms at her father's expense. In an ensuing aria, the first in the opera ("Just look at him"—"Guardatelo"), she triumphantly declares that here is living proof that she has discovered the surviving member of a prehistoric race. She bids the crowd to take note of his muscular build, but warns them not to come too close. Kitty says she is convinced that beneath that savage exterior is a human being of true nobility who will respond to kindness and patient understanding. She herself will teach him the arts of civilization, and the world of science will honor her for her accomplishment. The crowd acclaims her vociferously, while Kodanda laments that now he is fated to marry her.

The Maharajah, calling for silence, commands the scholars of his court to come forward and render a scientific opinion about this fabulous creature. Aside, he warns them that any adverse remarks will cost them their heads.

An amusing colloquy follows as the First and Second Scholars discuss the prehistoric specimen in pompous, pseudoscientific terms. They begin by agreeing that he obviously is not oriental, then experimentally address him in German, English, French and Italian. Abdul roars obligingly. They decide that he belongs to an unknown race—possibly a direct descendant of Pithecanthropus erectus. Their final conclusion is that his speech is monosyllabic and a trifle unrefined.

The Maharajah, bored with their chatter, curtly dismisses them. As the crowd again acclaims this scientific wonder, Scattergood steps forward and urges Kitty and Kodanda to set the wedding date. Thereupon

Kitty causes general consternation by disclosing the next step in her anthropological research. This specimen, she explains, will require intensive study. Accordingly, she proposes to tame him, then take him to the zoological gardens in New York.

At this there are expressions of dismay from the parents and Sardula, while the onlookers voice their approval of Kitty's decision. This introduces an ensemble. Scattergood fumes that Kitty's plan is outright treason; she denies any ulterior motive. Sardula wonders how far this bizarre experiment will go. Kodanda sees a ray of hope—perhaps this turn of events will free him of the obligation to marry Kitty. The Maharajah and the Maharanee resign themselves to letting Kitty have her way, thus wrecking their hopes for marriage.

At this point it is agreed that there must be an official answer to Kitty's proposal, and the crowd calls on the Maharajah to decide. He steps forward, calls for silence, then pauses uncertainly. The Maharanee whispers in his ear, whereupon his harassed expression gives way to a happy smile. Turning to Kitty and Kodanda, he proclaims that their problem has been solved: They are to remain engaged, but the wedding will be postponed for six months. The two young people enthusiastically agree to the plan. The Maharajah promptly invites everyone to a banquet in honor of Kitty. It will be a magnificent feast, he promises, with dandelion soup for the Indians and toasted lions for the Christians. During a brief interlude of martial music all follow the Maharajah into the palace.

The Maharanee detains Scattergood for a moment. In a repetition of the musical phrase she sang in Scene One, she repeats her mysterious question—this time asking if he has ever been in Singapore. As puzzled as before, Scattergood answers no. And also as before, the Maharanee murmurs that his face is so familiar. They both go into the palace.

Abdul, alone in his cage in the deepening twilight, gives way to his gloomy forebodings in a long dramatic soliloquy preceded by a recitative ("Ah, see where my love for her has brought me"—"Guard un po in che guaio me son messo"). Here he is, he reflects bitterly, a captive slave in a cage, trapped by love. What is worse, he probably will be taken to America. Ruefully he admits he alone is to blame for his predicament because he allowed a woman to make up his mind for him.

In the ensuing aria, "Only for you"—"Solo per te," he laments that for Sardula's love and the lure of money he bargained away his freedom and his happiness. In the dramatic climax of the aria he bids farewell to the forests, fields and mountains of his beloved native land—these treasures which money cannot buy. A thunderous phrase in the orchestra underscores his despair. The aria is a fine example of Menotti's gift for simple, classic melody.

Abdul's malancholy reflections are interrupted by Sardula, who tiptoes in carrying a lantern. He greets her by complaining bitterly about his fate. She tries to soothe his feelings by telling him she has brought him something to eat, along with bandages and disinfectant for his cuts and bruises. When he fumes about being taken to America she offers him some practical advice: Get civilized in a hurry, collect your fee, then come back and marry Sardula.

With that she cautiously enters the cage and sits down next to Abdul. In a charming duet ("My handsome hunter") the two plan their future life together. Thanks to that beautiful money, it will be one long, glorious holiday . . . wining and dining like kings . . . servants by the score . . . no boring household duties. Perhaps they will raise a family, twenty children or so . . . there will always be music and dancing . . . nothing as dull as farming for them. Enchanted by their dream of affluence, they climax the duet with an ardent declaration of love. A noise outside puts an end to their tryst. Sardula snatches up the lantern and scampers away. The curtain falls.

ACT TWO

[Scene One] Kitty's boudoir in her father's penthouse in Chicago a few months later. Lounging on a sofa, she is talking on the telephone. Abdul, still in his cave man costume with his hands chained together, is having his measurements taken by three tailors. An ensemble in quartet form follows as Kitty describes Abdul to a friend over the telephone, while the tailors argue about the proper attire for him. Kitty is inviting "all Chicago" to a party—"artists, scientists, and the clergy"—where she will present her primitive man to society.

The tailors, gasping at Abdul's chest measurement—fifty inches—wrangle over the color of his suits. By the time they have discussed the relative merits of zippers versus buttons and are caviling about the sartorial tastes of American versus British tailors, Kitty has completed her telephoning. Driven to distraction by the squabbling, Abdul explodes. Denouncing them as stupid clowns, he bellows at them to leave him alone. In uproarious confusion, the tailors snatch up their materials and scramble for the door. When one of them turns and sticks out his tongue, Abdul lunges at him with a roar of anger. Kitty seizes a whip and cracks it like a lion tamer. Abdul stops in his tracks and glares at her.

Ordering him to lock the door, Kitty informs him that the next step in his education will be a lesson in the art of love. Stepping back suspiciously, Abdul asks what she means by "love." A complicated subject with a complicated object, Kitty explains casually. Abdul tells her curtly he will have none of it, whereupon Kitty lashes at him with the whip. Abdul begs for mercy. Then, to the accompaniment of a languorous theme (somewhat like the love motive in *Tristan*), she gives him his first lesson in the art of kissing, going into seductive detail. After the first try, she concedes that, for a primitive, he is quite adept at this esoteric art. Getting into the spirit of the "lesson," Abdul assures her that he can do even better.

Realizing that the situation may get out of hand, Kitty hastens to explain that "civilized" love is another matter: it demands more poetry. Nevertheless, she continues with the next lesson—the art of embracing. For best results, she informs Abdul, there must be soft lights, sweet music and whisky. With that she leads him to the sofa, stretches out voluptuously and pulls him down beside her. For a moment, Abdul is repelled by this brazen exercise in civilized love-making, but then he surrenders to her embrace. They remain in each other's arms as the scene fades.

The romantic mood is sustained by the orchestral interlude which continues without pause.

[*Scene Two*] The garden of the Maharajah's palace, where Kodanda is discovered alone. Like Abdul, he is brooding over his uncertain future. In recitative, he reflects on his life as an only son and heir to a throne. And now, he muses, Sardula is beginning to fall in love with him—which complicates matters still more. Committed as he is to marry Kitty, what can he offer Sardula?

Kodanda ponders this question in one of the most melodious arias in the opera, "No, I dare not ask"—"Chiedere non so." His reasoning is that, so long as he does not know how she would answer his declaration of love, he still can live in hope. But if she answered no, he would not care to live. In the dramatic concluding phrases of the aria he sings that this doubt is both a torment and a pleasure.

[*Scene Three*] The living room of Scattergood's penthouse. On a platform at one end of the room is a large table. Before it, chairs are arranged as for a lecture. Abdul, impressive in a dark blue suit, stands at the window gazing at the Chicago skyline. It is five o'clock in the afternoon.

To the accompaniment of an agitated theme in the orchestra, Scattergood comes hurrying in. Dialogue in recitative follows. Scattergood informs Abdul that after tonight's reception his job will be finished, and he can go back to India. Handing him his plane ticket, Scattergood adds that his chauffeur will rush him to the airport immediately after the party. As to his fee, he says, showing Abdul a huge roll of bills, it's much too bulky to carry around, but he will find it in his pocket when he leaves.

Abdul mutters that he will be happy to go back to India. Scattergood dryly observes that he will be equally happy, because he was beginning to be concerned about these long "private lessons" with his daughter. Stung by the insinuation, Abdul bursts out that this "tutoring" has torn him apart emotionally and left him in a state of complete confusion.

With a placating gesture, Scattergood launches into one of the principal baritone arias of the opera, "You are free now"—"Tu mi piaci." Sung in a vigorous tempo, it is a brilliant example of Menotti's skill in fusing words and music. It is Scattergood's sardonic litany of the multiple blessings of civilization, of which he, as one of its products, is a helpless victim. With cynical relish he enumerates them: from dictaphones to doctors, from stenographers to sleeping pills. He urges Abdul to make his escape from civilization while he still is free—free from lunches, conventions, stock market fluctuations, "those damned initials, P.T.A., UN, NATO," insurance men, politicians, pensions, and contributions to Spoleto.[1] Scattergood concludes this spectacular aria with a dramatic reiteration of his warning: "Save yourself today!"—"Tu salvati che puoi!"

Kitty, wearing a cocktail gown, now enters and asks her father what is delaying the party—the guests are getting impatient. Let them in, Scattergood says, sarcastically cautioning his daughter not to make any high-flown speeches because these "leeches" are interested exclusively in drinking. Kitty peremptorily orders Abdul to the platform, then opens the doors. The guests, most of them brandishing cocktail glasses, burst in on a wave of senseless chatter. Ahead of them is a frenzied group of photographers, who lunge toward Abdul aiming their cameras. The crowd enters during a descriptively discordant orchestral interlude as Scattergood, at the door, does his best to maintain his dignity as a welcoming host.

What follows is a devastating satire, set to music, on the exhibitionistic tomfoolery of the typical "intellectual" cocktail party. When the guests finally seat themselves and the uproar momentarily dies down, Kitty addresses the assemblage in a deliberately flamboyant aria, "Let me present to you"—"Io vi presento." Beginning with a coloratura phrase ("Ladies and gentlemen"), it is a mocking imitation of the conventional operatic aria, complete with recitative and cantabile.

Kitty solemnly bids her audience to look upon this man who only six weeks ago was a savage prowling the jungle. Because of her knowledge of Freudian psychology, anthropology, parabiology and philology (plus a few flicks of the whip), she was able to tame and train this creature. Today he is as civilized as any member of the audience. He has faultless manners, knows the value of a dollar and is not afraid of television. All

[1] Menotti's private joke about the Festival of Arts in Spoleto, Italy, which he founded.

this goes to prove, Kitty declares, that she is unquestionably the world's greatest anthropologist. The audience wildly applauds her.

From this point on the scene builds into a long and complex choral ensemble. The guests express their admiration for Kitty's achievement and marvel that this erstwhile primitive's manners are as impeccable as their own. Abdul fumes that the behavior of these representatives of civilized society is more than he can bear. Kitty repeats the concluding phrases of her aria in a coloratura obbligato to the chorus. The score calls for an ending on a high E-flat.

Scattergood, pounding a gavel in true board chairman style, pompously calls upon the various distinguished groups present to come forward and identify themselves for Abdul's benefit, to give him some idea of how an enlightened society functions. First he calls on the clergy.

The members of the ministerial group, vociferously contradicting each other, begin explaining who God is. The Philosopher chimes in to assure Abdul that God does not exist—and neither does he. The Physician elbows close to warn Abdul about the fatal effects of tobacco. A fluttering covey of ladies presses forward to gaze at Abdul admiringly and invite him to dine with them—individually. Members of the working press, representing the newspapers, radio and television, demand to know what he thinks of Chicago, the U.S.A. and American women. The hapless Abdul only stares impassively at the clamoring mob. When some protest, in a brief concerted passage, that he is acting like a temperamental Hollywood star, Kitty entreats them to be patient with him.

Next, a chorus of debutantes approaches with the information that they are out to capture rich husbands. They need not be clever—merely rich; if not rich, perhaps they will serve as lovers. The debutantes are elbowed out of the way by the politicians, who bellow that Abdul's salvation lies in voting, respectively, for communism, Democrats, Republicans, Conservatives, a dictator and a king. Each politician warns Abdul not to believe the others. They are all liars.

Then it is the turn of the military officers and city officials. The military threatens Abdul with arrest if he tries to escape; the civic authorities remind him that the local law requires every savage to have an elementary school education.

Abdul next is favored with an exhibition of the creative talents of an avant-garde painter, a poet and a composer. The painter produces a masterpiece on the spot by splashing his canvas with multicolored paint squirted from an iron tube. There is a burst of frenzied applause. The poet recites an incomprehensible bit of free verse entitled "I." More applause.

The composer, carrying a tape recorder, steps forward with three instrumentalists and a soprano, who are to perform his latest opus. He first explains he has succeeded in creating "lots of sound" while avoiding anything that would make musical sense. Announcing he will demonstrate a "perfect example of the new electrododecaphonic style," he turns on the tape recorder and gives the cue to the instrumentalists and the singer. For this performance Menotti has written some eleven measures of excruciating dissonances (he once described this as "my first dodecaphonic composition"), over which the soprano screeches a two-line ballad in German: "Tag ohne Schmerzen/ Ist wie Nacht ohne Kerzen."[2] This brings more hysterical applause from the guests, who embrace the composer.

The final display in this extravaganza is provided by the scientist, who exhibits a boxlike contrivance bristling with push buttons, dials and knobs. This clever invention, he announces, has won him the Nobel Prize and it represents the ultimate solution to all cosmic problems. Simply by pushing a button, one can destroy the universe.

Again the audience madly applauds. Abdul despairingly asks Kitty how she can endure this lunacy. It simply shows, she replies imperturbably, how complicated and exciting life can be.

At this point the reception explodes into headlong pandemonium, with each guest bellowing louder than the others for Abdul's attention. A "career woman" pushes a contract under his nose, shrieking at him to endorse a new perfume called "Essence of Wild Man." With the others reiterating their own claims and demands, the ensemble surges to a frenzied climax.

Suddenly Abdul, losing control of himself, bursts out in a wild scream of rage. The guests stare at him in stunned silence. Turning to Kitty, he cries that although he loves her he cannot endure this maniacal civilization of which she is a part. In rising anger he denounces her for deceiving him and tells her to find another victim for her selfish adventures. Let her keep her idols, he roars, he will end his life as a self-respecting peasant. With that he springs from the platform and fights his way to the door, bowling over everyone in his path and tearing down a mobile hanging from the ceiling as he goes. As it comes crashing down, the panic-stricken guests scream in terror. The curtain falls to the accompaniment of a thunderous orchestral climax. This scene has been compared to the famous brawl in Act Two of *Die Meistersinger*.

ACT THREE

A month later, in a clearing deep in the Indian jungle. At one side, almost hidden by foliage, is the entrance to a cave. Abdul, clad in a leopard skin, is sprawled under a tree.

In a spoken soliloquy, he reflects on the incredible train of events of

[2] Roughly translated: "Day without pain is like night without candles."

the past months, trying to fathom the reason for the fantastic behavior of the "civilized" people he encountered. They talked endlessly about freedom, love and money . . . yet they seemed to long desperately for the serenity he himself is enjoying at this moment in the jungle.

He lacks only one thing, he muses: love. His thoughts turn amorously to Kitty, but he slaps himself in the face to end this reverie. When he again lapses into thinking about Kitty's kisses, a monkey in the tree above him shatters that dream by pelting him with coconuts. Rubbing his head, he mutters that he has paid the penalty for wasting his time daydreaming. Hearing a sudden noise in the jungle, Abdul vanishes into the cave.

After a brief orchestral interlude, a company of servants and soldiers of the Maharajah straggles into the clearing carrying picnic baskets, suitcases and other gear. They are part of the searching party organized by the Maharajah to hunt down and recapture Abdul.

In a doleful, minor chant ("Long is the journey"—"Lungo è il cammino") they complain about the endless journey they are forced to make at the whim of rich people. They are followed by Kitty and Scattergood in hunting costume. A passage in recitative ensues. Scattergood fumes that they have been hunting this wretch Abdul for three weeks all in vain. He blames Kitty for the entire fiasco and denounces Abdul as a brazen fraud.

If she will forget him, Scattergood says beseechingly, it not only will make her poor father happy but will save him from paying this savage the ninety-nine thousand, nine hundred and ninety-nine dollars he still owes him. But Kitty obstinately insists that she must find Abdul and learn the truth from his own lips. She will not believe he deliberately deceived her, she adds, bursting into tears. The servants and soldiers again break out in their lugubrious refrain, chanting that death lurks behind the green mask of the forest.

Heralded by an orchestral interlude in a stately martial tempo, the Maharajah arrives followed by the Maharanee, Sardula, Kodanda and the rest of the royal entourage. Showing impatience with the general air of gloom, he commands everyone to join him at lunch in the tent which servants are setting up. Then His Highness rasps out an order to the soldiers to continue the search for Abdul until they find him. If they do not find the fugitive immediately, he warns, he will execute them all for a crime against the state. With that he stalks into his tent, followed by the crowd.

Meanwhile, some distance away, Sardula is reclining under a tree. Kodanda steals up behind her and closes his hands over her eyes. She gently frees herself and then they kiss passionately. A brief colloquy follows. Kodanda says he has come to a decision: he will marry Sardula if she will have him. Taken by surprise, she asks what is to be done about Abdul. Forget him, is Kodanda's succinct advice—if a tiger hasn't eaten him, "our little Kitty" will. Sardula giggles at this, then reminds Kodanda that his father is waiting for him. He goes into the tent.

Alone, Sardula gives expression to her perplexing thoughts about Abdul in the aria "How shall my lips deny it?"—"Che gli dirai quel giorno?" The theme of it is that she does not know how she can find the words to tell Abdul she no longer loves him. At the conclusion of the aria she walks slowly into the tent.

A moment later Scattergood comes bustling out with the Maharanee waddling after him. The two sit down on stools placed under a tree by a servant. The scene which follows in recitative unravels the plot of the opera in terms of high comedy. The Maharanee begins by reiterating her apparently pointless question: "Where have I seen you before?" This time she mentions Egypt. Scattergood casually answers that he had traveled there. With a startled shriek, the Maharanee babbles that now it all comes back to her: Scattergood was the handsome young tourist ("you looked like Rudolph Valentino") who made love to her in the shadow of the pyramids beside the Nile. With that she throws herself into his arms, crying that she is about to faint. Staggering under her weight, Scattergood groans in dismay.

To his utter consternation she reveals that there was a sequel to their romantic adventure—a sequel in the person of Kodanda, who is their own son. Then, Scattergood stammers incredulously, his daughter Kitty is Kodanda's sister. In a brief "patter" duet, they sing that this love match they have been promoting actually would be an incestuous relationship which must be broken off at all costs.

The Maharanee promises to head off the marriage on the condition that the Maharajah never will find out about his wife's indiscretion. As Scattergood swears eternal silence—and sighs in relief—she frightens him out of his wits by hinting, with ponderous coquetry, that perhaps it is not too late to revive their romance.

He is rescued from the Maharanee's amorous clutches by the entrance of a group of servants who have dragged Abdul out of his cave at the end of a rope. In a brief chorus ("See what we've got"—"Eccolo, l'hanno acchiappato") they describe how they fought to subdue this dangerous savage. Abdul struggles furiously to free himself and the servants finally untie him.

The Maharajah, Kodanda and Kitty come rushing out of the tent. Abdul falls to his knees and in a dramatic refrain ("Won't you hear me"—"Ascoltatemi vi prego") implores them to give him his freedom. He has kept his part of the bargain, he cries, and now he asks only to be left in peace. In chorus, all the others assure him they do not mean to harm him—they have come simply to pay him the rest of his fee, as per agreement. Holding out a huge roll of bills, Scattergood declares in a recitative passage that as an honest American he will now pay Abdul the balance still owed him.

From this point, the scene continues in a succession of ensembles, duets and arais to the finale of the opera. When Abdul, as before, protests that he has no use for money, his would-be benefactors exclaim that this is impossible. But Kitty comes to his defense, praising him as a "superman" who is above any such crass considerations as money. Impulsively throwing her arms around his neck, she declares that all she wants is his love.

Abdul tries to restrain her ardor, reminding her that he is still engaged to Sardula. He and Kitty turn to her questioningly. With simple candor Sardula confesses she no longer loves Abdul because her heart has changed. With that she bursts into tears. In a brief ensemble the others try to comfort her, while Abdul tells her that his heart too has changed. Hearing this, Kitty again impetuously embraces him. Suddenly the Maharajah, who has been staring at these bizarre goings-on as though hypnotized, bursts out in exasperation to demand what it all means. Scattergood's efforts to explain only irritate him more, and he roundly berates the millionaire for condoning all this nonsense. But he is somewhat mollified when he hears Abdul try to convince Kitty that, though he loves her madly, nothing could drag him back to face those "fiends of hell" in Chicago whom she calls her friends.

Thereupon Kitty, in mock-heroic phrases underscored by a majestic cantabile in waltz tempo, proclaims that for his love she will renounce civilization and live with him in a cave. She tells the others they may as well go home, because she has decided to live in the jungle with the man she loves. Her resolve ("And I shall stay"—"Io resterò") is sung in a ringing dramatic phrase which soars to a high D sharp. (The comparison here with the scene between Radames and the High Priest Ramfis at the third-act curtain in *Aida* is irresistible.)

There is a bellow of rage from the Maharajah, who demands immediate action from Scattergood on his daughter's about-face. Prompted by an approving glance from the Maharanee, he answers that he is in favor of Kitty's decision and will not stand in her way. Furiously reminding Scattergood that their investment is at stake, the Maharajah growls that this is what happens when one deals with Americans.

To make matters worse, Kodanda, leading Sardula, kneels before him and asks his paternal blessing. His Highness roars that he will have him shot for his impudence. The Maharanee intervenes, advising her husband not to stand in the way of true love. The others add their entreaties, reminding him that love has nothing to do with logic. Now in a towering rage and completely frustrated, the Maharajah shouts that everyone except himself has gone crazy.

A septet ensues in which the principals sum up their various reactions

("Ah, how fortune waits in hiding"—"Ah, il destino che sorprese"). The four young people rejoice that they have been united with their true loves at last; the Maharajah laments that all his plans have ended in disaster—with his stupid son choosing a servant girl and Kitty a jungle savage. Scattergood marvels that he, a respectable citizen, has a love child in India, a romantic secret which the mighty Maharajah never will discover. The Maharanee reflects over her good fortune in being re-united with the charming lover of her Nile adventure. The septet ends in a rousing operatic climax as all intone the moral of the tale: Wise men gamble only on the present; only fools gamble on the future.

The Maharajah, fuming that he wants nothing more to do with children or marriage, strides toward his tent. He declares that henceforth he will devote his precious time to his stamp collection. The Maharanee, Sardula and Kodanda follow him inside.

A scene now follows between Kitty and her father. Scattergood again tries to dissuade her from her absurd notion of living in the jungle. Kitty blandly assures him that life will not be as primitive as he imagines: He is to leave Abdul's money with her, then send out a butler and a cook from Chicago. Her father, aghast at the idea, warns her that Abdul probably will kill her when he discovers her scheme. Kitty flippantly observes that a woman has nothing to fear from a man who is a lover, and that it would be nonsense to think of her surrendering completely. Roaring with laughter, Scattergood remarks that sex appeal is the downfall of every superman.

Kitty asks him to send some housekeeping necessities to the cave without unduly disturbing Abdul, then to send more money later to make the place livable. It will all be quite delightful, she says airily—and as for husband Abdul, if he wants to play Samson she'll gladly play Delilah. Kitty sings the name in a soaring coloratura phrase.

During a brief orchestral passage, the Maharajah and his entourage emerge from the tent, which is then dismantled and carried away. His Highness, whose wrath has subsided into a mood of benevolence, bids Kitty an affectionate farewell ("The sun is going and we must go"—"Tramonta il sole e si deve partir"). This marks the beginning of another richly melodic septet in which all, with a certain mocking sentimentality, take leave of each other with the hope that heaven will protect them from their individual follies. They leave Kitty and Abdul with exaggerated gestures of farewell.

During a serene orchestral interlude the scene darkens into twilight. Over the sound of jungle mutterings and twitterings are heard the distant horn calls of the Maharajah's party.

The lovers, lying down on a bed of moss, blend their voices in an impassioned duet, "See how the dying sun"—"Ecco sul verde mar." They sing of the tranquil magic of the jungle and the enveloping friendliness of the forest. Civilization is far away, and in this green enchanted world of their own they ask for nothing more than the beauty and wonder of their love.

Abdul bends over Kitty and passionately embraces her as the theme of the duet fades into silence. Suddenly a mischievous figure sounds softly in the orchestra. With her free arm, Kitty gestures surreptitiously toward the forest. Out of the shadows come servants, who silently carry into the cave a bathtub, a refrigerator and a television set. The curtain falls.

I LOMBARDI ALLA PRIMA CROCIATA

(*The Lombards at the First Crusade*)

by GIUSEPPE VERDI

(1813–1901)

Libretto by

TEMISTOCLE SOLERA

CHARACTERS

Arvino	} sons of Folco, a Milanese nobleman	{ Tenor
Pagano		{ Bass
Viclinda, wife of Arvino		Soprano
Giselda, her daughter		Soprano
Pirro, esquire of Arvino		Bass
Prior of the city of Milan		Tenor
Acciano, tyrannical Governor of Antioch		Bass
Oronte, his son		Tenor
Sofia, wife of Acciano		Soprano

People of Milan, priests, retainers of Folco, Moslem envoys, Crusaders, knights, soldiers, Moslem and Lombard women, Turks

Place: Milan, Antioch (ancient capital of Syria), and the Palestinian country near Jerusalem
Time: A.D. 1099
First performance: La Scala, Milan, February 11, 1843
Original language: Italian

I Lombardi is a saga of the First Crusade, military expeditions of the eleventh, twelfth and thirteenth centuries launched by Christians to wrest the Holy Land (Palestine) from the Saracens (Moslems). The "Lombards" of the title are two brothers, Arvino and Pagano, descendants of Teutonic tribes who invaded Italy in A.D. 568 and established the Lombard kingdom. It was finally overthrown by Charlemagne in 774.

With fanatical zeal, the Crusaders invaded the Turkish Empire, battled the Saracens at Antioch (now the Turkish city of Antakya), then pushed their way some 350 miles southward and finally captured Jerusalem, the sacred objective of their campaign. This is the historical background of the plot fashioned for Verdi by his librettist Solera.

Verdi's fourth opera promptly got him into trouble with the censors. The Archbishop of Milan frowned on certain references to religious rituals (such as baptisms or conversions) and alerted the Chief of Police. That worthy, who happened to be an opera buff, saved the situation for Verdi and the La Scala management (who refused to change the libretto) by an adroit compromise: he advised substituting "Salve Maria" for "Ave Maria" in Giselda's prayer in Act One, Scene Two: "Salve Maria! di grazia il petto."

Actually, this dispute was only part of the matter. There were political overtones. The Austrian authorities, who were in complete control of Italy, were wary of the reactions of the volatile Italian public to the implications of rebellion in the resounding Risorgimento-like choruses in Act Three. They echoed the politically incendiary sentiments of the famous "Va, pensiero" chorus in *Nabucco*.[1]

I Lombardi, however, was warmly received (without incident) by the Italians. The La Scala premiere was followed by performances in London (1846); New York (1847)—the first Verdi opera to be performed there; Paris (1847), in French as *Jérusalem;* La Scala (1850)—retranslated as *Gerusalemme*. Between that period and the mid-1950s there were numerous performances throughout Europe.

In the first production of *I Lombardi* in the United States in the twentieth century, the opera was revived (in Italian) with outstanding success in June 1979 by the San Diego Opera Verdi Festival at the Civic Theatre under the directorship of Tito Capobianco.

ACT ONE
(*The Revenge*)

A brief prelude on a rather foreboding theme suddenly erupts into a *vivace* fanfare which introduces the opening chorus.

[*Scene One*] The plaza in front of the Cathedral Sant'Ambrogio in Milan. From within comes the sound of an exultant chorus. The crowd outside comments on the ceremony ("Oh, nobile esempio"), which has to do with the return of the Lombard Crusader, Pagano, from banishment to the Holy Land.

The background of the situation is explained in the ensuing ensemble

[1] *Il Risorgimento:* Italy's great national movement for liberation, reform and unification from the latter part of the eighteenth century to circa 1870. Verdi's choruses are an expression of the deep-rooted patriotism of the Italian people.

("Però di Pagano nell'occhio travolto"). Many years ago, Pagano and Arvino were in love with Viclinda. She married Arvino and bore him a daughter, Giselda. One day Pagano, in a fit of jealous rage, wounded Arvino, and was forthwith banished to the Holy Land to expiate his crime. The ceremony in the cathedral is apparently in observance of his return as a repentant offender.

Pagano comes out of the cathedral and prostrates himself in prayer ("Qui nel luogo santo e pio"). Arvino embraces him in a gesture of pardon, and the crowd shouts approval of his magnanimity. This leads into the first of the opera's great ensembles, beginning with Giselda's refrain ("T'assale un tremito!") in which she voices suspicion (shared by Viclinda and Arvino) of Pagano's rather ostentatious gesture of repentance.

In a conspiratorial colloquy with Pirro ("Pirro, intendesti. Cielo non fia che"), Pagano swears he will exact revenge for his banishment. The renegade esquire, who has turned against Arvino, assures him of his support. Their voices blend with the ensemble. The Prior of Milan now proclaims the appointment of Arvino as leader of the First Crusade ("Or s'ascolti il voler cittadino"). Then, in a surging chorus ("All'empio, che infrange la santa promessa"), the entire assemblage calls down maledictions on those who threaten the holy Crusade for an assault on the infidels.

All leave the scene except Pagano and Pirro; Pagano listens moodily to the chorus of nuns sounding majestically from the cathedral ("A te nell'ora infausta"). He confides to Pirro that a frustrated love affair drove him to his misdeeds. In an ensuing aria ("Sciagurata! hai tu creduto") he gives way to his feelings of remorse—but still tries to justify his actions.

Pirro tells him that his followers are now ready to help him carry out his plans for revenge. Then follows the striking *Coro di Sgherri* (chorus of assassins), sung *sotto voce* in a style that foreshadows the famous "Zitti, zitti" chorus in *Rigoletto*. In the following cabaletta Pagano relishes the prospect of revenge ("O speranza di vendetta").

[*Scene Two*] A room in the palace of Folco in Milan. In recitative, Arvino, Viclinda and Giselda again voice their apprehensions over Pagano's "repentance." Arvino and Viclinda leave. Giselda, falling to her knees, sings the profoundly moving prayer "Salve Maria! di grazia il petto," imploring protection in this hour of fear and uncertainty. Ending the prayer in a soaring phrase—"ne aggravi l'ultima sera"—she leaves.

A moment later, Pirro stealthily leads Pagano to the door of Arvino's room, whispering that Viclinda is there alone. Just as they disappear, that section of the palace bursts into flames. Pagano emerges with Viclinda struggling in his arms, but stops short when he hears the voice of

Arvino ("Io l'ascolto"). Horrified, he realizes that in the attempted abduction he has slain his own father, not his hated brother.

As he stands transfixed, people of the palace, alarmed by the fiery confusion, rush in. Here begins the long and powerful chorus—one of the major ensembles of the opera—in which all curse Pagano for his treachery—"Orror! Mostro d'averno orribile!" In the frenzy of his remorse, Pagano joins in his own condemnation—"Farò col nome solo il ciel." He is prevented by the guards from turning his sword against himself, and is forthwith again condemned to exile. The chorus rises to a blazing climax in the finale of the act.

ACT TWO
(*The Man of the Cave*)

[*Scene One*] The palace of Acciano in Antioch, where the Governor is receiving a delegation of Moslem ambassadors. In a furious chorus ("Deh scendi, Allhà terribile, i perfidi a punir!") they call down the vengeance of Allah on the invading Crusaders. Swearing revenge, they storm away.[2]

Oronte enters with his mother, Sofia. In recitative, he confesses his forbidden love for Giselda, a Christian—and now a captive of his own father. Sofia, herself a secret Christian, sympathizes with her son. Oronte pours out his love for Giselda in a lyrical aria—"La mia letizia infondere"—often compared with the famous tenor aria "Quando le sere al placido," in *Luisa Miller*. In the cabaletta ("Come poteva un angelo"), he apostrophizes Giselda's perfection. The cabaletta ends in duet form as Sofia joins him in expressing these sentiments.[3]

[*Scene Two*] A cavern in a mountain height overlooking Antioch. Standing at the entrance, the Hermit (Pagano) reflects on impending events. In recitative followed by an eloquent prayer ("Ma quando un suon terribile") he expresses the hope that he may soon be able to help the invading Crusaders capture Antioch from the Saracens—and thus redeem himself. The accompaniment is marked by rhythmic pulsations of rising and falling arpeggios.

As he concludes his prayer, he sees a man in Moslem garb approaching. It is the treacherous Pirro—who meanwhile has renounced Christianity and become a Moslem. Totally unaware, of course, that he is talk-

[2] Verdi scored the sudden contrasting pianissimo/fortissimo passages in this chorus to heighten dramatic effect—a device he used effectively in male choruses of his later operas.

[3] In the original score there is a second version, *Cabaletta Nuova*, with more elaborate vocal embellishments.

ing to Pagano, he explains that he is a Lombard who unwittingly helped a Crusader in the murder of his own father. Now, haunted by the guilt of parricide, he seeks solace from a holy man ("Oh ferma! ascolta, per pietade!"). To ingratiate himself further, Pirro craftily discloses that the Crusaders are about to attack Antioch. He himself is in command of the city's defenses—and he himself will assist the Crusaders in breaching the city walls. For this service to the holy cause, the Hermit exults, they both will receive divine pardon.

A distant blare of trumpets heralds the advance of the Crusaders. The Hermit exclaims that now the hour of triumph has come; then he and Pirro vanish within the cavern. As the trumpet fanfare crescendoes, the Hermit, now in full armor, reappears and thereupon confronts Arvino at the head of his Crusaders.

Now follows a stirring, typically Verdian tenor/baritone duet—a colloquy with overriding irony as its theme. Like an arrogant conqueror, Arvino begins questioning the Hermit ("Sei tu l'uom della caverna?"), but his manner softens as the Hermit answers him with quiet dignity. Almost humbly, Arvino asks the Hermit's help in rescuing his daughter Giselda from captivity of the Moslems ("un branco musulmano ha la figlia a me rapita").

Though face to face, Arvino unaccountably does not realize that the man whose intercession he is asking is his sworn enemy—his own brother and the murderer of his father. Pagano treacherously assures him that this very night ("O Lombardi fratelli: questa notte porrete le tende") the Lombards will conquer the city. In response to his challenging declaration, the Crusaders burst into a fiery *allegro vivace* hymn of hate against the Saracens ("Stolto Allhà! sovra il capo ti piomba").

[*Scene Three*] The harem in Acciano's palace in Antioch, where the hapless Giselda has become the latest addition to the sultan's harem. In a jeering chorus ("La bella straniera") the other harem women cynically bid her forget the misfortune of captivity and make the most of her position as the sultan's current favorite. Frightened and confused, Giselda again finds refuge in prayer ("O madre, dal cielo soccorri al mio pianto"). The serene *cantabile* theme rises gradually to a brilliant coloratura climax.

Suddenly Giselda is startled by a cry for help from the harem women, who come rushing in pursued by the soldiers of the Crusaders. With them is Sofia. When she and Giselda manage to evade the rampaging soldiers, she tells the girl that Acciano and Oronte have been slain by the Crusaders ("Sposo e figlio mi caddero ai piedi"), and accuses Arvino as their murderous leader.

At that moment Arvino himself strides in and Giselda gasps in horror. On the verge of madness she denounces her father for the slaughter in hushed phrases of suppressed fury ("No! giusta causa non è d'Iddio" —"God himself would not allow the earth to be so drenched in blood"). This introduces her dramatic aria—"I vinti sorgono, vendetta"—which in turn leads into the powerful ensemble climaxing the act—"Che fai? la misera."

ACT THREE
(The Conversion)

[Scene One] The Valley of Jehoshaphat, the King of ancient Judah (Judea), in southern Palestine. In the distance are the Mount of Olives and Jerusalem.

The scene opens with a resounding chorus of Crusaders, knights and pilgrims on their way to Jerusalem ("Gerusalemme, la grande, la promessa città!"). It expresses their intense longing for the goal of all their desires: the Holy City, the ultimate homeland. As their voices die away in the distance, Giselda appears. She is grieving for Oronte, believing that he died in the slaughter at Antioch.

She looks up to see a man—apparently a Lombard—standing before her. To her surprise and joy he reveals himself as Oronte ("Ah no! d'Oronte stai fra le braccia!"). He confesses he is ashamed of having resorted to disguising himself as a Lombard to escape from the beleaguered city in order to see her again. They rush into each other's arms and pledge their love in an impassioned duet ("Errante andai di terra in terra"). In its fiery climax, Giselda prays that her mother will forgive her for giving her love to a Saracen ("Madre, perdona! un'anima redime un tanto amor!"), while Oronte himself vows to become a Christian for the sake of Giselda's love ("Per te, Lombarda vergine, tutto abbandono").

Suddenly they hear the shouts of the warriors in the Crusaders' camp sounding the call to battle ("All'armi"). The voices of Giselda and Oronte soar above the chorus in a striking unison obbligato as they sing that only death can part them ("Ah! vieni, sol morte nostr'alme divida").

[Scene Two] Arvino's tent. Alone, Arvino rages over Giselda's perfidy in fleeing Antioch to be with Oronte, the Saracen enemy, and thus bringing dishonor on his name ("All'obbrobrio di mia casa nata"). His bitter reflections are interrupted by a group of his soldiers who rush in to inform him that Pagano has been seen in the camp ("Più d'uno Pagano ha notato"). Over the martial rhythm of the chorus, Arvino bursts out in fury against his brother ("Sì! del ciel che non punisce") while the soldiers clamor for revenge ("Vendetta feroce persegua l'in-degno").

[*Scene Three*] A cave on the banks of the River Jordan. There is a prelude in the form of an elaborate violin solo with a concerto-like ac-companiment. The solo continues as an obbligato throughout the ensu-ing scene.

Giselda is seated at the bedside of Oronte, who has been mortally wounded while attempting to escape. In wild despair she inveighs against God for inflicting this unjust punishment upon her and her lover ("O Dio de' padri miei!"). Suddenly the Hermit appears at the entrance to the cave. Hearing Giselda's lamentations, he demands to know who dares rail against God. Oronte, near death, warns Giselda to show re-spect to the holy man ("Uom d'Iddio t'appressa a me!"). Looking down on the dying Saracen, the Hermit, in a sonorous phrase intoned on a single note ("Sorgi! il ciel chiami in vano"), assures him he need not appeal to Heaven in vain. With that, he baptizes Oronte "with the sacred water of Jordan . . . the Water of Life" ("l'acque sante Gior-dano sian lavacro a te di vita"). A stately theme interwoven with surg-ing harp arpeggios sounds like a benediction in the orchestra.

This leads into a beautiful trio in one of the most moving death scenes in all of Verdi's operas ("Qual voluttà trascorrere"). Giselda implores Oronte not to die; he tries to answer in *mezza voce* phrases as he gasps for breath ("T'accosta! Oh nuovo incanto"). As the Hermit intones that the final hour has come, Oronte dies in Giselda's arms.

ACT FOUR
(*The Holy Sepulcher*)

[*Scene One*] A cave near Jerusalem. Giselda lies there asleep. A ce-lestial chorus ("Componi, o cara vergine") sounds in the background. Giselda suddenly sits up, inspired by a vision of Oronte in heaven—she even imagines she hears his voice. In a long and brilliant aria ("Qual prodigio! Oh! in nera stanza") she expresses her ecstasy over being united in spirit with her lover.

[*Scene Two*] The camp of the Crusaders and pilgrims near the Tomb of Rachel.[4] The Crusaders are preparing an assault on Jerusalem, the Holy City, goal of the First Crusade. The scene opens with a mighty chorus—"O Signore, dal tetto natìo"—another Risorgimento hymn of yearning for homeland and freedom. After a tumultuous climax, the chorus ends in a sustained pianissimo phrase, like a sigh of despair ("fa

---

[4] The wife of the Hebrew patriarch Jacob.

la sabbia d'un arido suol"). The people are almost overcome by the march under a scorching sun in a hostile, arid land.

But their spirits are revived as the Crusaders respond to the call to arms sounded by Arvino and the Hermit, who are to lead them in the assault ("Guerra! S'impugni la spada"). Then follows the great Battle Hymn, "Inno di Guerra e Battaglia."

[*Scene Three*] After a brief prelude in a martial tempo, the scene changes to another part of the Crusader camp. Arvino and Giselda are attending the Hermit, gravely wounded in the assault, and raving in delirium. Trying to calm him, Arvino, taking his hand, tells him that a friend, "Arvino," is guarding him ("Presso d'Arvin tu sei").

Mention of the name shocks the Hermit out of his delirium. He cries that he is stained with blood ("D'Arvin quest' è pur sangue!"). Hell itself, he raves, opens at his feet ("Oh Averno, schiuditi ai piedi miei") because this is the blood of his own father ("Sangue è del padre"). Arvino recoils in horror when he realizes that the dying Hermit is Pagano.

In an ensuing duet ("Ti calma! Vedi, tu sei fra noi") Giselda and Pagano join in entreating Arvino to forgive his brother's crime. Embracing Pagano, Arvino sings that he now absolves him of his guilt ("Anche l'uom t'assolverà"). Raising himself, Pagano voices his gratitude, then begs for a last look at the Holy City ("Me felice! Or sia concessa a' miei sguardi la città!").

In the background are seen the ramparts of Jerusalem, over which waves the banner of the First Crusade, emblazoned with the cross. The throng of Crusaders and pilgrims bursts into the thunderous closing chorus of the opera—"Te lodiamo, gran Dio di vittoria"—"Praise to God, who has given us the victory!" The curtain falls.

LUCREZIA BORGIA
by GAETANO DONIZETTI
(1797–1848)

Libretto by
FELICE ROMANI

Based on Victor Hugo's play *Lucrèce Borgia*

CHARACTERS

Donna Lucrezia Borgia, Duchess of Ferrara	Soprano
Don Alfonso, Duke of Ferrara	Bass
Gennaro, a young soldier of unknown birth	Tenor
Maffio Orsini, a young nobleman, friend of Gennaro	Mezzo-soprano
Rustighello, confidential follower of the Duke	Tenor
Gubetta ⎱ secret agents of the Duchess	⎰ Bass
Astolfo ⎰	⎱ Bass
Jeppo Liverotto ⎫	⎧ Tenor
Don Apostolo Gazella ⎬ friends of Gennaro	⎨ Tenor
Ascanio Petrucci ⎪	⎪ Bass
Oloferno Vitellozzo ⎭	⎩ Bass
A servant	Tenor
A cupbearer	Baritone
An offstage voice	Baritone

Nobles, guards, spies, maskers, brigands

Place: Venice and Ferrara
Time: Early sixteenth century
First performance: La Scala, Milan, December 26, 1833
Original language: Italian

Lucrezia Borgia, a landmark in operatic evolution, marked a turning point in the history of Italian opera. As in *Anna Bolena,* composed three years earlier, Donizetti moved away from the *opera seria* of the eighteenth century to the new idiom of the nineteenth century as exemplified by Verdi. *Lucrezia Borgia,* in fact, has been described as standing midway between Rossini and Verdi. Of the two operas in Donizetti's transitional period, *Lucrezia Borgia* marked his furthest musical advance into the nineteenth century.

With his international fame virtually established by *Anna Bolena,* Donizetti added to his operatic laurels with *Lucrezia Borgia,* which many considered his masterpiece. It held the stage during the nineteenth century but was long absent from the contemporary repertoire. Its single performance at the Metropolitan was given December 5, 1904, with such distinguished Golden Age singers as Caruso and Scotti. The most recent U.S. stage revival was the highly successful one by the New York City Opera in a new production on March 18, 1976. It was followed by five more performances that season.

The opera, incidentally, is notable for the "trouser role" of Maffio Orsini (the nobleman friend of Gennaro). It was a favorite with nineteenth-century mezzos—including Mme. Ernestine Schumann-Heink, famous for her recording of the "Brindisi," Orsini's drinking song in Act Two.

The plot of the opera does not coincide with historical facts. The real Lucrezia Borgia (1480–1519) was the daughter (by a mistress) of Cardinal Rodrigo Borgia, later Pope Alexander VI. During three marriages she bore an illegitimate child. In 1501, at the age of twenty-one, she married Alfonso d'Este, later Duke of Ferrara. She became known as a patroness of the arts and devoted her life to education and charity. Her predilection for poisoning people is dramaturgic fiction.

PROLOGUE

Terrace of the Grimani Palace in Venice. At back is the Giudecca Canal, and beyond a silhouette of Venice in the moonlight. A festival is in progress. Elegantly dressed men and women, some masked, are strolling about. Among them are Gennaro and his friends—Orsini, Gazella, Petrucci, Vitellozzo and Liverotto—and Gubetta, a secret agent of the Duchess Lucrezia. They join in a gay ensemble about the delights of Venice ("Bella Venezia!") and anticipate going to Ferrara to the palace of the Duke Alfonso, fourth husband of Lucrezia Borgia.

When Gubetta casually mentions her name, there is a sudden chill in the mood of the young men. Orsini sharply warns Gubetta never to mention her name ("Non la nomar giammai"). This woman, he says, poisoned his brother. The others also express their hatred of her. But Gennaro jibes at Orsini as a teller of tales. Remarking that he is not interested in stories about the Borgia, he goes over to a marble bench and lies down.

Orsini, nevertheless, goes on ("Nella fatale di Rimini"). During a battle, he relates, he himself fell wounded, and Gennaro rescued him.

The two men swore eternal friendship. But then a giant of a man in black appeared and warned them to flee from the Borgia ("Fuggite i Borgia, o giovani"), for where she is there is death ("dov'è Lucrezia è morte"). Then he vanished.

But the maskers dispel this dark mood of evil omen and urge everyone to dance ("Senti. La danza invitaci"). Orsini comments that the memory of the giant's warning still haunts him. He looks at the sleeping Gennaro and envies his peaceful rest. The others conclude the chorus and then stroll away.

Lucrezia, masked, steps out of a gondola, approaches Gennaro and looks tenderly down at him ("Tranquillo ei posa"). Gubetta, who had remained behind, watches her and steals closer. When she turns and discovers him, he explains that he has come to guard her from possible insults of unfriendly Venetians. Lucrezia replies that although she is aware that she is loathed in Venice, she still considers herself safe ("E insultata sarei"). She asks Gubetta to leave her alone with Gennaro.

As he goes, Don Alfonso and Rustighello enter to spy on the mysterious figure at Gennaro's side. In the aria "Com'è bello! Quale incanto," Lucrezia marvels at Gennaro's comely features. Moved to tears, she takes off her mask to dry her eyes. The Duke and Rustighello recognize her, and their suspicions are confirmed. Alfonso orders Rustighello to trick Gennaro into coming back to Ferrara—where he can be dealt with accordingly. The two leave.

Lucrezia continues her adoration of Gennaro in an impassioned cabaletta, "Mentre geme il cor sommesso." When she impulsively kisses his hand he awakens and stares at her in astonishment. Overcome by her beauty, he sings that surely no man could resist her ("No, per mia fede!"). He confesses then and there that he loves her, but adds that there is someone he loves even more: his mother. He has never seen her, he goes on, but now—why, he does not know—he feels he must tell this beautiful stranger his sad story ("È funesta istoria").

He tells his story to the accompaniment of a flowing waltz tune much like a Neapolitan folk song. He grew up in Naples believing he was the son of a humble fisherman ("Di pescatore ignobile"). But one day he was abducted by a mysterious warrior who gave him a horse, some weapons and a letter.

This letter, Gennaro relates ("Era mia madre—ahi misera!"), was from his mother, who implored him never to ask her name. With that he hands it to Lucrezia. To her utter stupefaction, she realizes that the letter is her own, and that the ardent young man before her is her own son. Almost losing control, she bursts into tears, but she decides not to reveal her identity. She entreats Gennaro always to cherish the memory of his mother ("Ama tua madre, e tenero"). Touched by her compassion, he answers that he will always love his mother ("L'amo e sem-brami"), and thus the dialogue continues in a lyrical duet.

The rendezvous is interrupted by Orsini and his friends. Lucrezia tries to flee, but Gennaro holds her back, demanding to know who she is. "Someone who loves you," she cries desperately, replacing her mask and trying to struggle out of his arms. Orsini strides forward, declaring that he knows this woman. Gennaro shouts that he will allow no one to insult her.

Then in a tumultuous ensemble ("Chi siam noi sol chiarirla ne piace") Orsini and his friends identify themselves as Lucrezia's victims. One by one, Orsini ("Maffio Orsini, signora, son io"), Vitellozzo, Liverotto, Petrucci and Gazella intone the litany of her monstrous crimes —brothers, uncles, cousins betrayed, looted of their property or murdered. Lucrezia is terror-stricken; Gennaro gasps in disbelief. The men, now joined by the festival maskers, savagely denounce the woman as the incarnation of evil ("Ella è donna che infame si rese").

When Gennaro furiously demands to know who this loathsome creature is, Lucrezia beseeches him not to listen to her accusers ("Non udirli, Gennaro"). Finally losing control, she tears the mask from her face. In a thunderous unison phrase, the onlookers cry: "It is the Borgia woman" ("È la Borgia"). Gennaro staggers back in horror; Lucrezia's voice rises in a piercing wail of despair.

ACT ONE

[Scene One] A square in Ferrara. It is night. At one side, the balcony of a palace. On the wall beneath it is a marble crest emblazoned with the name BORGIA in gilded bronze. Opposite is the entrance to Gennaro's house, its windows lighted.

Alfonso and Rustighello, wearing long cloaks, enter and look up at the windows ("Quello è suo tetto"). From the house come sounds of revelry. In their ensuing duet ("E in esso ancora il vuole") the two men discuss the situation. Alfonso sings that Lucrezia has demanded that he bring Gennaro to the palace. He can enter, the Duke adds grimly, but he will never leave the palace alive. This drunken brawl will be his last, because he now will be paid out in full for daring to court Lucrezia ("Vien, la mia vendetta"). In foreboding phrases the two men sing that the lagoon is always ready for its victims.

As they leave, Gennaro and his friends noisily emerge from his house. They lustily bid their host goodnight, but he himself seems preoccupied with thoughts of his mother. Orsini invites him to a party at the Princess Negroni's palace. When Gubetta steps forward and invites himself, the others eye him suspiciously.

Noting Gennaro's thoughtful mien, Orsini twits him about thinking too much about the Borgia woman ("Ammaliato t'avria forse la Borgia?"). Gennaro angrily retorts that he detests this creature ("chi abhorra al par di me costei"). Thereupon, to show his contempt, he strides to the heraldic shield under the palace balcony and with his dagger strikes off the "B" in BORGIA. "Read it now," he shouts defiantly ("Leggete adesso"). Amid jeering laughter his friends reply: "ORGIA!"

Gubetta alone does not laugh. This little caper, he sings somberly, will demand its price. Gennaro impudently replies that he is quite ready to take the blame for the desecration. He re-enters his house as his friends leave, laughing and joking. Astolfo and Rustighello enter. In a brief recitative, they comment that each is on his way to a fateful errand involving Gennaro: Astolfo to take him to the Duchess; Rustighello to take him to the Duke. One way leads to a party, the other to death ("L'una a festa, l'altra a morte").

At Rustighello's signal, a group of brigands steals in. Then follows a remarkable conspiratorial chorus in the vein of the Assassins' Chorus in *Macbeth* ("Chi v'impose unirvi a noi?") or that of the courtiers ("Zitti, zitti") in *Rigoletto*. At its conclusion they start to batter down Gennaro's door to take him prisoner.

[*Scene Two*] A room in the Ducal Palace. At back, a huge door; to the right, glass-paneled doors; at left, a secret door. There is a table with a velvet cover.

Alfonso and Rustighello enter. The prisoner, Rustighello says, is waiting. In a refrain underscored by an insistent six-note theme, the Duke gives him his orders ("Or bada. A questa in fondo segreta sala"): Rustighello is to bring from an adjoining room a gold and a silver flask. The gold one contains the lethal Borgia wine ("Vin de'Borgia è desso"). Then he is to wait outside for further orders. Alfonso dismisses Rustighello as a servant announces Lucrezia.

Obviously distraught, she sings in a menacing single-note phrase ("A voi mi trae vendetta") that she demands revenge on the scoundrel who not only has insulted the name of Borgia but has defaced the family escutcheon. "I want him killed," she says, "and in my sight." Only too willing to abet Lucrezia's plans for revenge, Alfonso swears he will grant her request, then orders Gennaro to be brought in. Lucrezia gasps in dismay. A dramatic colloquy in recitative follows.

When Gennaro demands to know why he has been taken prisoner, Alfonso replies that he is suspected of having desecrated the Borgia escutcheon. Before Genarro can answer, Lucrezia interjects that he is not the perpetrator. But despite her desperate protests, Gennaro insists he is guilty.

At her request he is led away, and then Lucrezia frantically begs Alfonso to spare the life of this innocent young man ("di quel giovane illeso la vita"). Alfonso blandly reminds her that he has sworn to grant her request for the youth's death, and that he will not break his oath ("la mia fede vi diedi, o signora").

This leads into a fiery duet, followed by a trio which builds into the great Act One climax of the opera. In the face of Lucrezia's desperate entreaties, Alfonso accuses her of following Gennaro to Ferrara because she is in love with him. When the Duke scorns her denials of a liaison, Lucrezia, in one of the spectacular arias of the opera—"A te bada, a te stesso pon mente"—warns him of dire consequences if he refuses mercy (an obvious reference to the fate of her previous victims). The aria ends in a dazzling coloratura climax.

Alfonso, flouting her threats, answers that he knows only too well the Borgia tradition of reprisal ("chi sei tu, se il volessi, potrei"). But now she is in *his* power, and now she must choose: Is Gennaro to die by the sword or by poison? Driven to a decision, Lucrezia begs Alfonso to spare Gennaro death by the sword. If he must die, let it be by poison. In a descending phrase of despair, she sings that she will leave the wretched youth to his fate ("L'infelice al suo fato abbandono"), then collapses on a chair.

Gennaro is brought in. Alfonso tells him that he will be pardoned in deference to Lucrezia's wishes. Cynically he adds that Italy should not be deprived of so brave a soldier. Gennaro, unaware that Alfonso in reality is pronouncing his doom, profusely thanks the Duke in lyrical phrases ("Pur, poichè dirlo è dato").

Lucrezia is thunderstruck at Gennaro's apparent perfidy in currying favor from the Duke. Gennaro rather fatuously observes that perhaps he really deserves mercy: it was he himself who once saved the life of the Duke's father when he was surrounded by enemies. Alfonso ironically offers him a purse of gold to join his army, but Gennaro demurs that Venice has the first claim on his loyalty.

Thereupon Alfonso, in a spurious gesture of friendliness, invites Gennaro to join him in a drink of wine. Lucrezia, knowing what the invitation will mean, is beside herself. In suppressed fury she curses Alfonso as a heartless monster ("ne avresti orror con me"). Meanwhile, Gennaro, in a lyrically ironic counterpoint ("Meco benigni tanto"), enthuses over Alfonso's magnanimous pardon.

At a sign from the Duke, Rustighello brings in the flasks. The Duke pours his wine from the silver one, then hands the gold one to Lucrezia to serve Gennaro. As the men raise their glasses, Alfonso mockingly sings, "V'assista il ciel, Gennaro" ("Heaven help you, Gennaro"). Gennaro courteously responds to the toast. They drink. With a look of evil triumph at Lucrezia, Alfonso goes out with Rustighello.

When Gennaro kneels before Lucrezia in gratitude, she whispers in a

fierce undertone that he has drunk poisoned wine ("Infelice. Il veleno
bevesti!"). This marks the beginning of the tempestuous duet which
concludes the act. Handing him a vial, she tells him it contains an antidote that will save his life ("Una goccia, una sola"), then implores him
to flee at once.

Gennaro, suddenly suspicious, accuses her of plotting his own death:
perhaps this "antidote" is worse than the poison ("Forse una morte più
orrenda"). In vain Lucrezia tells him she acted only to save his life,
then warns him that Alfonso has sworn to kill him as his rival.

Finally, kneeling before him, she beseeches him to drink the antidote
and save his life for the sake of the mother he loves ("Bevi, e fuggi, t'en
prego"). Moved at last by her pleas, he drinks. In joyous relief, Lucrezia guides Gennaro through a secret door—even while he himself
warns her that if she has betrayed him, he will have his revenge ("Ti
punisca"). Alfonso and Rustighello re-enter just as Lucrezia falls fainting on a chair.

ACT TWO

[*Scene One*] The courtyard facing Gennaro's house. It is night; light
shines through one of the windows. As a melancholy theme sounds in
the French horns, Rustighello and the brigands, searching for Gennaro,
cautiously approach the house. In a hushed chorus ("Rischiarata è la
finestra") they sing that the light in the window means that Gennaro is
still in Ferrara—and thus vulnerable to the Duke's revenge. Hearing
footsteps, the brigands withdraw with a hushed reprise of their conspiratorial chorus.

The music changes to a brisk tempo as Orsini appears and knocks at
Gennaro's door. He answers, and a duet in quasi-recitative ensues as
Orsini invites him to a party at Princess Negroni's palace. When Gennaro says he must leave immediately for Venice, Orsini protests that
they had promised each other that they never would be separated. Gennaro agrees to stay, although he fears for his life ("Minacciata è la mia
vita"). Unnoticed by the two, the brigands, waiting to seize Gennaro,
lurk in the background. Rustighello restrains them: they must wait until
Orsini is out of the way.

The duet continues. Gennaro, still hesitant, admits he is afraid of betrayal. Losing patience, Orsini derides him for his suspicions ("Quale in
re credulità"): the Borgia pretended to save him simply to test his affection for her. As for the Princess Negroni and the Duke, they are noble
people who can be trusted. Unconvinced, Gennaro decides to leave,
then changes his mind. In the conclusion of the duet ("Teco sempre, o
viva, o mora") the two reiterate their resolve never to be separated.
They leave.

Rustighello and the brigands rush in to follow Gennaro. Rustighello warns them not to act hastily, because at this moment their quarry is on his way to the Negroni palace—and running headlong into the trap. In a sinister chorus ("È tenace, è certo l'amo") the brigands sing that, in effect, the hook to catch this fish has been well baited. A kettledrum roll sounds ominously as they slink away.

[*Scene Two*] A banquet hall in the Negroni palace. At a lavishly set table are the Princess Negroni, Orsini, Liverotto, Vitellozzo, Gazella and Petrucci—the nobles all accompanied by beautiful women. Gubetta and Gennaro sit opposite each other. A scene of abandoned gaiety follows as all join in a lusty drinking chorus ("Viva il Madeira").

Orsini loudly proclaims that he has written a new toast. The festive mood of the scene suddenly darkens as Gubetta laughs derisively ("S'egli è insultarti il ridere"), then deliberately picks a quarrel with Orsini. When he snatches up a knife, the others intervene and call for peace. The adversaries quiet down, observing that they will meet tomorrow and fight like gentlemen ("di batter vi doman da cavalieri").

A cupbearer enters with "Syracusan wine" ("Vin di Siracusa")—which of course is the deadly Borgia concoction. All the nobles quaff heartily except Gubetta, who surreptitiously tosses his wine over his shoulder. Gennaro notices, and apprises Orsini of the gesture, but the latter shrugs it off. Stimulated by the wine, the men call for a song. Orsini obliges with a robust ballad, the "Brindisi" ("Il segreto per esser felice"), the general theme of which is, "We don't give a damn for tomorrow." All present roar out the refrain.

Suddenly there is a startling interruption: from outside comes the tolling of a funeral bell and a foreboding chant of doom—"La gioia de'profani." The revelers listen in stunned silence, but Orsini defiantly resumes his ballad. The others again join in but stop abruptly when the death chant is repeated. Panic erupts when the lights grow dim. The men scramble toward the doors, only to find them locked. Gubetta watches them contemptuously.

Then the huge door at the back swings open. Lucrezia stalks in accompanied by armed guards and black-robed monks. In the room behind her may be seen five coffins flanked by funeral tapers. In ferocious triumph, Lucrezia sings: "I am Borgia ['Sì, son la Borgia']. In return for your 'favors' to me in Venice I now offer you a feast in Ferrara. Your insults will be avenged ['Dell' ingiuria mia piena vendetta ho già']: the poison will kill you, and these 'couches' will be your last resting place." She points to the five coffins.

Thereupon Gennaro springs forward shouting that five coffins are not enough: there must be a sixth ("non bastanti cinque"), because he is resolved to die with his friends. When Lucrezia cries that he now has been poisoned a second time ("Sei di nuovo avvelenato"), he holds up the antidote vial. In desperate entreaty she bids him drink . . . there is only enough left for him. Well then, Gennaro cries, we shall all die ("Allor, signora, morrem tutti").

Snatching up a knife from the table, he lunges toward Lucrezia crying that she will be the first to die—and by his hand ("Voi primiera di mia mano"). Lucrezia screams, "Stop! You are a Borgia. Do not spill your own blood!" ("Ferma—un Borgia sei—il tuo sangue non versar"). Gennaro stops with knife upraised.

In one of the great arias of the opera—"Ah, di più non domandar"— Lucrezia again begs Gennaro to drink the antidote for the sake of the mother who loves him. But in his blind fury Gennaro rages that the Borgia not only murdered his friends but robbed him of a mother's love.

"But your mother lives! She speaks to you now" ("Vive, e a te favella"), Lucrezia sings. The truth dawns on Gennaro, but it is too late: the poison finally takes effect. He gasps, "Mother, I am dying" ("Madre! Io moro"), and dies at her feet.

Alfonso, Rustighello and people of the court rush in. Alfonso sternly asks: "Where is he?" Looking down at Gennaro's body, Lucrezia answers in a striking musical phrase: "Desso! Miralo"—"Look . . . there he is." Then she gives way to her anguish in the magnificent aria "Era desso il figlio mio." As all on the scene comment on the tragedy, Lucrezia collapses with her son's body cradled in her arms. The curtain falls.

LUISA MILLER
by GIUSEPPE VERDI
(1813–1901)

Libretto *by*
SALVATORE CAMMARANO

Based on the drama *Kabale und Liebe,* by the German poet-dramatist Johann Christoph Friedrich von Schiller

CHARACTERS

Count Walter	Bass
Rodolfo, his son (first disguised as Carlo)	Tenor
Miller, an old soldier	Baritone
Luisa, his daughter	Soprano
Federica, Duchess of Ostheim, Count Walter's niece	Contralto
Wurm, steward to Count Walter	Bass
Laura, a peasant girl	Mezzo-soprano
A peasant	Tenor

Ladies attending the Duchess, pages, servants, archers, men-at-arms, villagers

Place: A Tyrolean village
Time: Seventeenth century
First performance: Teatro San Carlo, Naples, December 8, 1849
Original language: Italian

Luisa Miller, Verdi's fifteenth opera, is a blood-and-thunder melodrama which contains to a satisfying degree the familiar elements of grand opera—emotional upheaval, display of passion, intrigue, star-crossed lovers—all set to broad, sweeping melodies and thunderous choral climaxes.

It has been described as Verdi's first outstanding success since *Ernani,* and as a work that prepared the way for his later triumphs. In this opera the composer shifted his area of plot interest from the larger-than-life world of kings, courtiers, statesmen and epic battles to the *verismo* portrayal of individual human beings in situations involving the play of elemental emotions. Verdi was fortunate in having a libretto based on the soundly constructed drama by Schiller.

Subsequent to its premiere in Naples, where it was acclaimed, it was given in Spain, France, Russia, Hungary, Turkey, South America and England, with performances in Italian, French, German, Hungarian and English. In London (1858), however, it failed. Its first production in America was at the Castle Garden Theater in New York City on July 20, 1854. The Metropolitan Opera Company staged it on December 21, 1929, with Rosa Ponselle in the role of Luisa. Although favorably received, it was given only a limited number of performances. It was absent from the operatic repertoire in this country until its revival during the Metropolitan's 1968–69 season. It was presented in a Metropolitan Opera Saturday afternoon broadcast on December 11, 1971.

The overture, considered one of the best Verdi ever wrote, is dominated by variations on the theme of a dramatic refrain sung by Rodolfo at the conclusion of Act Two.

ACT ONE
(*Love*)

[*Scene One*] After a brief introduction the curtain rises on a picturesque Tyrolean village. At one side is the cottage where Luisa and her father live. Opposite is a small church. Visible in the background is the castle of Count Walter. Villagers gathered to celebrate Luisa's birthday greet her in a spirited chorus ("Ti desta, Luisa, regina de' cori") as the queen of their hearts.

Miller, Luisa and her friend Laura appear and thank the peasants for their good wishes. But Luisa, looking around anxiously, frets because a certain young man she has been expecting is nowhere to be seen. Her father tries to reassure her. At the same time he voices certain misgivings about this young man, who calls himself Carlo. He is a complete stranger, not only to Count Walter but to everyone else in the village. Miller hopes his daughter will not be deceived in her love for him.

Luisa answers her father in one of the opera's principal arias, "Lo vidi, e'l primo palpito," the burden of which is that from the first moment she saw Carlo her heart throbbed in rhythm with his. Fate has destined them to be united in eternal love. The aria ends in a brilliant cadenza. As the villagers crowd around to present her with garlands of flowers, Carlo (Rodolfo in disguise) makes his way through the throng and hands her his own bouquet. Luisa exclaims in delight. Miller looks on with concern; the villagers comment on the tender scene.

A long ensemble now ensues, beginning with an ardent duet in which

Luisa and Carlo pledge their eternal love ("T'amo d'amor ch'espri-
mere"). Over the choral accompaniment sung by the villagers, Miller's
voice blends in trio form as he expresses his premonition of disaster that
may overtake this love affair ("Non so qual voce"). Laura's voice is
added to form the quartet which dominates the ensemble. As it approaches its climax the clock in the church tower strikes the hour. With
telling dramatic effect, the chorus suddenly is hushed to a whisper as all
go into the church singing that the voice of heaven itself seems to be
sounding to crown this day of happiness with worship. The ensemble
then concludes with a repetition of the opening theme.

All except Miller enter the church. As he himself is about to go in,
Wurm, the Count's steward, appears and calls to him. A long colloquy
follows. The two men converse in recitative over a foreboding orchestral figure. In a jealous rage, Wurm reminds the old man that it has
been a year since he promised Luisa's hand in marriage. But up to now
this promise has not been kept.

Miller protests that he made the promise only on condition that Luisa
really assured him that she was in love with Wurm. Thereupon the
steward upbraids Miller for failing to exercise a father's rightful authority over his child. In a majestic aria, "Sacra la scelta è d'un consorte,"
Miller replies that a girl's choice of a husband is a sacred privilege that
cannot be dictated—it is hers alone. He is no tyrant, Miller sings, but a
kind and loving father who would not presume to rule his daughter's
heart.

Wurm sneers that this father will pay the penalty for being a foolish,
indulgent old man. When Miller demands an explanation, Wurm stuns
him with the disclosure that the supposed "Carlo" is none other than
Rodolfo, the son of Count Walter. With that he stalks away. Shocked
and dismayed, Miller cries that his heart in broken ("Ei m'ha spezzato
il cor!").

He continues his lamentation in another powerful aria, "Ah, fu
giusto il mio sospetto!" Now his foreboding of disaster is justified: His
innocent daughter, this precious gift of heaven, may be betrayed and
her honor sullied. In the ringing climax of the aria he prays that a father's love may yet save her from ruin. Overwhelmed by despair, he
turns and walks away from the church door.

[*Scene Two*] A room in Count Walter's castle. The Count and
Wurm enter through a door at the back. They are followed by several
servants, who remain standing at the door. There is a brief conversation
in recitative between the two men. Walter fumes in anger when Wurm
informs him that Rodolfo has been courting Luisa. Deliberately goading
him, Wurm remarks that the boy is headstrong. Walter, abruptly an-

nouncing that the Duchess d'Ostheim will arrive shortly, tells Wurm to summon Rodolfo. The steward and the servants leave.

Alone, the Count gives way to the secret fear that is haunting him. He cries that Rodolfo will never know what his happiness has cost his father. Then, in an intensely dramatic aria, "Il mio sangue," he expresses the mingled emotions of anger and guilt that are tormenting him. He would give his life's blood, he storms, to bestow power and position upon his son—but Rodolfo only answers his father's efforts with ingratitude and defiance. For Rodolfo's sake, he himself has committed a crime and now is ridden by guilt. Over a surging chromatic figure in the orchestra, Walter voices his terror of eternal punishment. A ringing cadenza concludes the aria.

Rodolfo enters. Controlling himself with an effort, the Count greets him with a show of affection. He tells Rodolfo that Federica, the Duchess d'Ostheim, his future bride, is on her way to the castle. Rodolfo greets the news with half-concealed expressions of alarm and distress. His father goes on to say that, because Rodolfo and Federica have known each other from childhood, this marriage will be an ideal one. In fact, says the Count, when he made the offer of marriage, the Duchess was overjoyed ("Come l'offerta"). Then in continuing recitative he discloses the sequence of events which have led up to the present situation.

Federica's father had forced her to marry the Duke, who later was slain in battle. But all this time she had cherished a secret love for Rodolfo, and when the King of Lamagne himself asked her to marry him she refused because of that love.[1] When Rodolfo protests that he has no desire for power or position, his father upbraids him for his lack of ambition and peremptorily commands him to obey.

A fanfare announces the arrival of the Duchess and her entourage. The people of the court greet her in a chorus of extravagant praise ("Quale un sorriso"). Moved by her warm welcome, she embraces the Count. Presenting Rodolfo to her, he tells her that his son wishes to speak with her alone. Meanwhile he himself will prepare for the royal hunt. All except Federica and Rodolfo leave at a sign from the Count. Rodolfo starts to speak, addressing her as "Duchess" ("Duchessa"). She interrupts to say that, despite all the enticements of court life, her only wish is to be "Federica" to him.

A long and impassioned duet now ensues ("Dall'aule raggianti di vano splendore"). The splendor and luxury of the court, she sings, never have diminished her yearning for her native land here in the Tyrol. Kneeling before her, Rodolfo (aware of the effect his rejection of her will have) begins by saying that, although they shared the joys of childhood, the later years have changed things. Alarmed at his troubled

[1] Lamagne: presumably a mythical kingdom; geographic location not identifiable.

look, Federica asks him to explain. He confesses that he loves someone else.

As Federica recoils, thunderstruck, Rodolfo entreats her to pardon him for causing her this grief ("Deh! la parola amara"). He declares he would rather die than lead her to the altar when his heart belongs to another. The Duchess turns on him in jealous fury and scorn. Let him take her life instead of his own, she bursts out ("Arma, se vuoi, la mano"), and she still will pardon him with her dying breath. But a jealous heart, she warns, knows neither pardon nor pity. Rodolfo implores her forgiveness. As the two reiterate these emotions, the duet rises to its blazing climax. In the throes of anger and despair, Federica and Rodolfo rush away in opposite directions.

[Scene Three] The interior of Miller's house. At one side are two doors, one leading to Miller's room, the other to Luisa's. On the wall next to Miller's door hangs his campaign sword along with a military decoration. Through the window of a passageway at the back can be seen part of the village church.

From the distance comes the music of a rousing hunting chorus ("Sciogliete i levrieri"). The hunters call for the dogs to be unleashed and the horses spurred to follow the quarry. There is a brief interlude as Luisa comes out of her room and goes to the window. Anxiously she wonders why Carlo has not left the hunt and returned to her as he had promised. The chorus continues, then dies away as the hunting party rides on.

Suddenly Miller bursts in and throws himself into a chair. He is distraught, and Luisa asks him what has happened. Her father cries out that his worst suspicions have been confirmed: Her lover has deceived her ("Sei tradita"). As Luisa gasps in disbelief, Miller tells her he has just learned that Carlo actually is Rodolfo, the son of Count Walter. (This phrase is sung over a single note insistently repeated in the orchestra, a striking dramatic effect.) What is more, Miller goes on, Rodolfo is to marry a duchess, who this day arrived at the castle. Luisa distractedly begs her father to say no more.

Pacing in fury about the room, Miller suddenly stops and stares at the military decoration hanging on the wall next to his sword. In a menacing, ascending phrase ("Per questa d'onore assisa") he swears on the badge of honor that he will have revenge. Luisa cries out in terror.

Rodolfo, who had appeared in the doorway just in time to hear Miller's words, now strides into the room. Miller lunges at him, but Luisa throws herself between the two men. In a ringing phrase over dark, sustained chords in the orchestra Rodolfo declares that even though his true identity now is known, his heart has not changed. Then in a dramatic gesture he pushes Luisa to her knees in front of her father and kneels beside her. In a passionate outburst ("Son io tuo sposo") he sings that, as her father and God Almighty are witnesses, he is Luisa's betrothed. Miller, deeply moved, warns him of the Count's wrath when he learns of this. With fierce intensity Rodolfo declares that he knows a dreadful secret ("A me soltanto e al cielo") which, when he reveals it, will make the Count beg for mercy.

Luisa suddenly exclaims that someone is entering the house. Rushing to the door, Rodolfo comes face to face with his father. He demands to know why he has come ("Tu, signor, fra queste soglie!"). This marks the beginning of the fiery ensemble which concludes the act.

The Count thunders that he has come, with a father's authority, to put an end to this squalid intrigue. Rodolfo shouts that he will not tolerate this insult to the woman he loves. This "pure" love, Count Walter sneers, has been bought and paid for. In mounting fury, Rodolfo draws his sword, but then sheathes it and steps back. He will spare the life of the man who gave him his own, he storms—and now the score is even ("La vita mi donasti"). Luisa collapses in the arms of her father, who roars that he will avenge this vile affront to a soldier's honor. Beside himself with rage, Count Walter snarls that this fool will rue his insolence, then shouts for his archers.

His men come rushing in followed by Laura and the villagers. Despite Rodolfo's frantic protests, the Count orders the archers to bind Luisa and her father in chains. As Miller curses him, Luisa kneels before the Count and begs for mercy. Thereupon Miller roughly pulls her to her feet. In furious defiance, he thunders that his daughter will kneel only to God—never to a tyrant ("Fra mortali ancora oppressa").

Rodolfo, torn between love and filial duty, sings that despite his devotion to Luisa, he still must remain loyal to his father. The Count relentlessly reminds him that his word is law ("Tu piegarti, tu"). Turning on Luisa and her father, he warns them of dire punishment to follow. The voices of the four blend in a quartet passage. Luisa's entreaties rise in a soaring obbligato ("Ad immagin tua creata"). With the archers and villagers singing that the Count must be obeyed, the voices crescendo into a typically overpowering Verdian chorus.

At its climax, Rodolfo draws his sword and, planting himself in front of Luisa, defies anyone to touch her ("Da questo acciar svenato"). At that, Count Walter pushes Luisa toward the archers, at the same time daring Rodolfo to strike him. Placing the point of his sword on Luisa's heart, Rodolfo shouts that he will kill her rather than see her fall into the hands of such murderous ruffians. Here Verdi wrote one of the most memorable tenor passages in the opera. Rodolfo's phrase of defiance— "Ah, pria che l'abbiano"—rises at its climax to a high C flat. Glaring at him, the Count sardonically asks why he does not make good his threat. Rodolfo's wild rage abruptly changes to icy calm. In a *sotto voce* phrase rising in half steps with an effect of terrible menace ("Trema! svelato agl'uomini") he whispers to his father that he now will reveal how Walter acquired the title of Count. With that he rushes out of the room.

Walter, staggering back in horror, calls after him. Crying that he will grant Luisa her freedom, he stumbles blindly from the room. Luisa sinks half fainting to her knees. Expressing their consternation in a thunderous phrase, the villagers crowd around her. The archers rush away as the curtain falls.

ACT TWO
(*Intrigue*)

[*Scene One*] The interior of Miller's cottage. As the curtain rises, Laura and the villagers crowd in calling for Luisa. She comes out of her room, looks into the anxious faces of the throng and asks what has happened. The villagers explain in an ensuing chorus ("Al villaggio dai campi"), which is another fine example of Verdi's remarkable instinct for dramatic choral effects. They sing that as they came through the mountain pass they saw the archers lead away an old man in chains. Realizing that the man is her father, Luisa expresses her despair in an obbligato phrase over the choral accompaniment. The villagers exhort her to have courage.

She frantically tries to rush away to the castle to intercede for her father, but Laura restrains her. At that moment Wurm appears. Ordering the villagers to leave, he informs Luisa that her father has been imprisoned for threatening Count Walter ("Ei, del Conte vassallo"). Such defiance from a vassal is a serious crime; his life hangs in the balance. As Luisa pleads for him, the treacherous Wurm tells her that there is one way she can save her father's life. The Count, he says, will spare Miller if she will send Rodolfo a letter which he—Wurm—will now dictate. With that he leads Luisa to a table and hands her a pen.

Over an ominous orchestral figure of octave skips, Luisa, hypnotized by fear, writes as Wurm begins with the words "Wurm, io giammai." For an instant she recoils, then forces herself to continue. Wurm dictates that she only pretended to love Rodolfo because of his wealth and royal position—it was selfish ambition alone that drove her on. And now, to escape Rodolfo's avenging anger, she will flee with her real lover.

In sudden fury, Luisa flings down the pen to protest this outrage ("Lo speri invano!"). In an ensuing aria ("Tu puniscimi, o signore"), one of the most dramatic in the opera, she sings that she will endure God's punishment without a murmur if only he will deliver her from the clutches of the monsters who demand that she save her father's life at the price of her honor.

With icy contempt, Wurm remarks that if she does not wish to agree to the terms she is free to go. He turns as if to leave. In desperation, Luisa finishes the letter and hands it to him. Wurm reads it over, then with gloating satisfaction states the final terms of his fiendish bargain. The first: Luisa is to swear on her father's life that she wrote the letter voluntarily ("Sul capo del padre"); the second: She is to go to the castle and confess to the Duchess d'Ostheim that she is in love with Wurm ("Un sol cenno ancor t'è prescritto"). This marks the beginning of one of the principal duets in the opera.

Wurm relentlessly presses his advantage. When Luisa, trapped, implies her consent to his diabolical scheme, Wurm, with an evil smile, assures her that her father will be freed. Luisa bitterly denounces him for his sadistic cruelty ("A brani, o perfido"), then demands that her father be released at once so that he at least can comfort her in her own hour of doom.

In cynical mockery Wurm promises her that time will solve all these problems—he still hopes that she willingly will become his bride. On these mingled expressions of fury, anguish and vengeful cruelty, the duet brings the scene to its close.

[*Scene Two*] A room in Walter's castle. Musing alone, the Count reveals that Rodolfo has been driven close to madness by his father's command to marry the Duchess. But there is no turning back now, the Count mutters. His reflections are interrupted by the entrance of Wurm. A long duet follows, in which a crucial turn of the plot is disclosed. In recitative, the two discuss the next step in their machinations. Luisa agreed to all the conditions, Wurm says with malicious relish, and will come secretly to the castle today. They will somehow contrive to place her incriminating letter in Rodolfo's hands. Looking intently at the Count, Wurm asks what caused his change of heart during his argument with Rodolfo over Luisa. A terrible threat from his son, the Count replies.

In mysterious, guilt-ridden tones he goes on to explain ("L'alto retaggio non ho bramato"): For Rodolfo's sake he schemed to gain control of the old Count's estates and wealth—and in so doing committed a monstrous crime. Wurm (well aware of how deeply he himself is implicated) uneasily reminds Walter that he aided his plans by finding out that Rodolfo was determined to marry Luisa—a marriage which would have disinherited him, thus thwarting his father's designs. As the duet continues, the two recall how they ambushed the old Count in the forest and murdered him.

While Walter gives way to guilt and remorse, Wurm boasts that their crime never will come to light. Everyone, he says with a show of bravado, believes their version of the affair: The old Count was slain by brigands. Walter whirls on him with a cry of desperation: "No, not everyone!" ("Non tutti!"). In hushed, fear-stricken phrases, Walter tells him that Rodolfo, walking in the forest, heard the fatal shots. Rushing to the spot, he found the old Count still alive. Before he died, he named his assassins.

Wurm, now beside himself with terror, wails that he is lost. From this point on the duet rises to a frenzied climax. Walter answers that Wurm is not alone in his guilt—the devil himself has chained them together in their doom ("Congiunto non t'ha Satano a' miei destin?"). Wurm, staring wildly around, shouts that his life no longer is safe in this haunted castle. The duet concludes with a ringing unison phrase.[2]

A moment later Walter announces the Duchess Federica and motions Wurm to leave. Recovering his composure, the Count informs Federica that Rodolfo has overcome his infatuation for Luisa. As proof, he adds, Luisa herself is being brought to the castle to explain the situation. Thereupon Walter opens a secret door and admits Luisa accompanied by Wurm. The latter presents her to the Duchess. In an aside, he whispers a warning to Luisa about the danger facing her father.

Looking at her, Federica muses admiringly on Luisa's comely appearance and her expression of candor and honesty. Luisa secretly laments that the happiness she expected will now be accorded another woman ("A costei sarà concesso"). From this point the scene builds into a long dramatic ensemble.

Federica asks Luisa point-blank whom she loves. In quiet desperation, Luisa answers that her lover is Wurm. He acknowledges her confession with an ironic bow. Federica asks sharply: What of Rodolfo? He came in disguise, Luisa replies—why, she never knew, but there were no words of love between them. The Duchess' face brightens, while Luisa's darkens with jealous rage.

The inquisition continues. Noticing the angry look in Luisa's eyes, Federica intuitively demands to know if she is lying. The two men watch her tensely, wondering if she will break under the strain. When the Duchess commands Luisa to speak, Walter, in a vicious undertone, warns her to speak for the sake of her father. In a stricken voice, Luisa answers that she can only repeat what she has said before: she has always loved Wurm ("Lo stesso da Luisa udrete ognor"). Aside, she wonders if her uncontrollable jealousy is driving her mad ("Come celar le smanie").

Here begins one of the most remarkable ensembles to be found in any of the earlier Verdi operas. It is sung unaccompanied to the very end of the scene in staccato unison phrases alternately loud and soft,

---

[2] This number has been described as the first of the great Verdian bass-baritone duets, foreshadowing "Solenne in quest'ora," from *La Forza del Destino*.

vividly reflecting the emotional upheaval of the situation. Luisa laments that she is being devastated by jealousy and despair ("Ahimè, l'infranto core"). The Duchess exults in her conquest over her rival ("Un sogno di letizia"). Walter and Wurm, relishing the success of their evil conspiracy, sing that fortune has smiled on them ("Pinto ha di vivo giubilo"). They vow to keep the hapless Luisa in their power. At the conclusion of the quartet there is a tremendous orchestral fanfare.

[*Scene Three*] The hanging gardens of Count Walter's castle. At the back is the door to Rodolfo's apartment, from which he enters with Luisa's note in his hand. A peasant follows him in. Rodolfo orders the man to explain how he managed to get the note.

Luisa, the peasant says, earnestly begged him to take the note secretly to Wurm—and at all costs to keep the knowledge of it from Rodolfo. He adds slyly that he decided instead to bring the note here because he suspected some intrigue, and considered the possibility of a reward. Rodolfo throws him a purse and dismisses him.

In stunned disbelief, Rodolfo cries out that Luisa cannot be guilty of such perfidy. Yet here is the letter in her own handwriting. His father, then, knew: underneath that tenderness is a black, deceitful heart . . . her love is a wretched illusion. Rodolfo portrays his disillusionment in one of the opera's finest arias, "Quando le sere al placido." He recalls the moment when he first looked into Luisa's eyes, heard her avowal of love and pressed his lips to hers. But even then she perjured herself and betrayed him. The aria ends in a cry of anguish—"Ah! mi tradia!"

As Rodolfo turns to leave, he is suddenly confronted by Wurm. The two stand face to face for a moment, then Rodolfo hands the other the letter. When Wurm has read it, Rodolfo takes it back. Now, he says in cold fury, the hour of death has come for both of them. He holds out two pistols and curtly invites Wurm to take his choice. As Wurm staggers back in consternation, Rodolfo bursts out that they will die together. He takes aim, but before he can fire, Wurm dodges aside and fires into the air. Rodolfo, in blind fury, lowers his pistol with a scream of "Coward!"

The sound of the shot brings Walter and his men-at-arms rushing into the gardens. Wurm pushes his way through the crowd and vanishes. With a despairing cry, Rodolfo falls to his knees before his father. The Count, in a deliberate pretense of sympathy, tries to calm him. He has repented his severity, he says, and no longer will stand between his son and his chosen love. Rodolfo, although surprised at this change of heart, laments that it is all too late—Luisa has deceived him. Now he asks only for death. Not death, the Count interjects, but revenge.

Uncomprehending, Rodolfo asks what he means. His father thereupon urges him to marry Federica to show his contempt for his betrayer.

Desperate and confused, Rodolfo first refuses, then consents. Following up his advantage, Walter goads him on by appealing to his pride. Finally, exhausted by his emotion, Rodolfo resignedly sings that he is ready for either the altar or the tomb and will bow to his fate ("L'ara o l'avello apprestami!").

Touched by his grief, the soldiers and villagers, in an accompanying chorus ("Del genitor propizio"), exhort him to trust in his father's love. The Count himself unctuously counsels him to forget the one who so cruelly betrayed him. This ensemble brings the act to a close. As the curtain falls, Walter leads Rodolfo away.

ACT THREE
(Poison)

A room in Miller's house. Luisa is writing at a table on which are a lighted lamp, a basket of fruit and a cup of milk. At one side of the room, Laura and a group of peasants who have come to comfort Luisa stand gazing sadly at her. Through an open window at the back can be seen the village church, lighted up.

In a brief chorus ("Come in un giorno") the peasants comment on how, in one short day, sorrow has left its mark on Luisa. Laura entreats her to take some food to restore her strength. Gently refusing, Luisa asks her visitors to respect her grief.

Earthly food, she sings melodramatically, never again will pass her lips ("A questo labbro"); she will soon taste of celestial joys. (A descriptive arpeggio in the orchestral underscores this thought.) Suddenly she sees the lights of the church through the open window and asks what is happening. Laura informs her that there is a special ceremony at the church at which the new Count is being invested with his title as lord of the estates. Turning to the peasants, Laura sings that Luisa would die if she were told that at this very moment preparations are being made for the wedding of a certain royal couple. As the peasants comment softly in chorus, Miller enters. Luisa throws herself into his arms. Laura leads the peasants away.

The remainder of the scene is taken up with a long recitative and duet, another of the principal numbers in the opera, which foreshadows the great baritone and soprano duets in later works such as *Traviata* and *Rigoletto*.

It begins as Miller expresses his concern over Luisa's pallid, sorrowful mien ("Pallida, mesta sei"). He goes on to say that he has heard the entire story from Wurm, and now knows how much his daughter has sacrificed to save her father. Luisa tells him she has indeed renounced her true love—then adds meaningfully to herself: "But only on this earth."

She hands her father the letter she has just written and entreats him to see that it reaches its destination. Alarmed, Miller begins reading in half-spoken recitative: "Orribil tradimento ne disgiunse, o Rodolfo." The letter asks Rodolfo not to believe this monstrous deception. She is bound by an oath to reveal no more. But there is a home—far beyond the reach of lying and deceit—where they can be together forever. He is to meet her there at midnight.

Miller trembles violently. The letter falls from his hands. In a stricken voice he asks: "Where is this home?" ("Quella dimora saria?"). Luisa replies quietly: "La tomba." Miller utters an anguished cry as an ascending chromatic figure erupts in the orchestra. Then Luisa, as though in a trance, sings that the tomb is a rose-strewn bed—a sweet resting place for those whose lives are pure ("La tomba è un letto"). Only for those who are evil is the tomb a place of darkness and horror; for guiltless, loving hearts it is the gateway to eternal peace.

In agonized protest, Miller cries that she dare not take her own life—there is no pardon for suicide ("Pel suicida non v'ha perdono!"). Tormented by grief, Luisa bursts out: "Is not love to blame?" ("È colpa amore!"). Sobbing, Miller throws himself into a chair and launches into a refrain of bitter reproach ("Di rughe il volto, mira"). A father's love for his child, he sings, should be returned to comfort him in his old age. But as for him, his only reward is a harvest of tears—he himself will be the first to enter the tomb prepared for him by an ungrateful child.

Stricken with remorse, Luisa tears up the letter and promises her father to abandon thoughts of suicide. They embrace joyfully as they sing in a climactic phrase ("Ah! in quest'amplesso l'anima oblia") that in their devotion to each other they can forget their sorrow. With sudden urgency Luisa says they must leave this place at once—there is great danger here. She tells her father to get some rest; they will leave at dawn. Miller starts for his room, then turns and embraces Luisa. Together they sing the beautiful concluding theme of the duet—"Andrem, raminghi e poveri." As fugitives, they will wander wherever Fate will lead them, begging for their bread if they must. But father and daughter will never part, and the Lord will bless them.

Miller slowly goes to his room. A moment later Luisa hears the sound of organ music from the church. Kneeling, she sings quietly that this will be her last prayer in her beloved home ("Ah! l'ultima preghiera"). Tomorrow she will pray among strangers. The serenity of the prayer theme brings to mind Desdemona's prayer in *Otello*.

As Luisa remains kneeling with bowed head, Rodolfo, enveloped in a cloak, appears in the doorway. In an undertone he orders the servant who is with him to inform his father that everything is ready for the wedding ceremony and that he will await him at Miller's home. Then, glaring at Luisa, who is still unaware of his presence, he murmurs ominously that she prays—and it is time to pray. He takes a vial from his pocket and pours some of its contents into the cup of milk on the table.

At that moment Luisa sees him and springs to her feet. Holding her note to Wurm in his outstretched hand, Rodolfo harshly asks if she wrote it. Gasping for breath, Luisa answers yes. As though struck, Rodolfo collapses into a chair, clutches his throat and calls for a drink. Luisa quickly hands him the cup of milk. The liquid is bitter, Rodolfo exclaims. Suddenly realizing that he drank from the cup into which he poured the poison, he asks Luisa to taste. He watches her in fascinated horror as she drinks, then murmurs dolorously: "Tutto è compiuto"—"Everything is accomplished." The two stare at each other in terrible, deathlike silence, which is shattered after a long moment by a crashing chord in the orchestra.

Rodolfo tells Luisa to go. Another lover, he says, is waiting for her, another bride is waiting for him at the altar. But they will wait in vain, he adds somewhat irrationally. With that he leaps to his feet, begins pacing furiously back and forth, then flings away his sword. This sword with which he once defended the innocent, he rages, now is useless. As he chokes with anger, Luisa again offers him the cup of milk, saying it will restore him. In bitter mockery he remarks that his betrayer well knows what she is offering him.

When Luisa recoils at this brutal jibe, Rodolfo exhorts her to leave him, singing that he cannot comprehend how a creature so beautiful can have the heart of a demon ("Ah! lungi quel volto lusinghier"). Losing control, he breaks down weeping. Luisa, trying vainly to calm him, says that there is more reason for his tears than for his anger ("Piangi, il tuo dolore"). Rodolfo replies that these tears are the dews of death. The duet is suddenly interrupted by the sound of a clock striking.

Taking Luisa's hand, Rodolfo sings that now has come the last hour between them and eternity ("Donna, per noi terrible"). Warning her not to perjure herself now, he demands to know if she really loved Wurm. Distractedly she tries to evade answering. Again cautioning her not to lie, Rodolfo storms that before the lamp goes out she will be face to face with the Almighty. Thrusting the empty cup before her, he tells her that they have both drunk the fatal poison. Luisa totters as though about to faint. Rodolfo carries her to a chair.

Recovering, Luisa sings that death has released her from her oath, and she can now reveal the truth. She then tells how, to save her father, she wrote the letter of renunciation as Wurm dictated it ("Avean mio padre"). Now she will die innocent. The dreadful realization of his fatal mistake dawns upon Rodolfo. Half crazed by remorse, he calls down a terrible curse upon himself and his father ("Maledetto il dì ch'io nacqui"). God, he rages, created him in a moment of anger. Luisa implores him to spare her the horror of outraging Almighty God at the moment of death.

At the fiery climax of the duet, Miller rushes in. Rodolfo, retrieving his sword, shouts that he will now expiate the crime of being Luisa's assassin. He pauses as he hears Luisa say that she feels the calm of death. Throwing down his sword, Rodolfo rushes to her. He turns to Miller and says that all hope is gone—Luisa has drunk poison. For a moment Miller stands transfixed, then takes Luisa in his arms. In a serene refrain ("Padre ricevi l'estremo") she bids farewell to her father and Rodolfo. Their voices blend with hers in a moving trio as they pour out their grief. Luisa dies in her father's arms.

Count Walter, the villagers and the men-at-arms rush in and crowd around Miller and Rodolfo, who are kneeling beside Luisa's body. Rodolfo looks up and sees Wurm standing in the doorway. Screaming that death will be his punishment, Rodolfo seizes his sword, lunges at Wurm and kills him on the spot. He whirls to face Count Walter and in the next moment falls dead at his feet. His father stares down at his body sobbing: "Figlio!" The throng thunders a cry of horror as the curtain falls.

LULU

by ALBAN BERG

(1885–1935)

Libretto by the composer

Based on two tragedies by the German dramatist Frank Wedekind: *Erdgeist* (*Earth Spirit*) and *Die Büchse der Pandora* (*Pandora's Box*)

CHARACTERS

Lulu	High soprano
Dr. Ludwig Schön, a newspaper publisher	Baritone
Alwa, his son, a composer	Tenor
Dr. Goll, a medical health officer	Speaking role
Walter Schwarz, an artist	Lyric tenor
An Animal Trainer ⎱ Rodrigo, the Athlete ⎰	Basso buffo
Schigolch, an old man posing as Lulu's father	Bass-baritone
The Prince, an African explorer	Tenor buffo
The Schoolboy	Soprano
Countess Geschwitz	Dramatic mezzo-soprano
Director of the theater	Basso buffo
Theater checkroom girl	Alto
A servant	Mimed

Place: A town in Germany; Paris, London
Time: Circa 1920
First performance: Stadttheater, Zürich, June 2, 1937
World premiere of three-act version: Paris Opéra, February 24, 1979
Original language: German

Berg began work on *Lulu* in 1929, seven years after the completion of *Wozzeck*. He had finished the first two acts and about one third of the last act at the time of his death in 1935. However, in 1934, the composer had made an orchestral suite which he called the *Lulu Suites* consisting of five symphonic excerpts from the opera. This was first performed in November of 1934.

Lulu is a relentlessly realistic study of a woman—an amoral, passionate creature who lived and loved according to the laws of her own demonic nature. Within that world of her own, she experienced ecstasy and despair, triumph and defeat, trust and betrayal. It was her destiny to destroy those she loved—and then at the last to wreak her own destruction as the victim of a monstrous act of violence.

As a disciple of Arnold Schoenberg (to whom he dedicated the opera), Berg adapted that composer's astringent twelve-tone idiom to a warmer, more fluid harmonic structure to delineate the complex emotions of the characters in *Lulu*. Although predominantly a twelve-tone score—and certainly not an opera in the conventional sense—*Lulu* has moments of intense lyricism and rich instrumentation evocative of Verdi and Wagner. In his musical pattern, Berg selected certain identifying forms of the various characters: for Lulu, a single twelve-tone series; for Dr. Schön, the sonata; for Alwa, the rondo; for Countess Geschwitz, the pentatonic (five-tone) scale.

In constructing the work for the stage, Berg had to combine Wedekind's *Erdgeist* and *Büchse der Pandora* to conform to the dramatic requirements of an opera. To solve the problem, he devised a film sequence, with musical accompaniment, which was to serve as a bridge between the first half of the opera (based on *Erdgeist*) and the second (based on *Büchse*). This manner of staging, with rear-projection films and slides, is generally followed in performances today.

The world premiere of the three-act version under the direction of Pierre Boulez was the sensation of the 1978–79 Paris opera season. In the cast were: Teresa Stratas, Lulu; Toni Blankenheim, Schigolch; Franz Mazura, Dr. Schön; Gerd Nienstedt, the Athlete. The American premiere of the complete opera was given by the Santa Fe Opera Company July 28, 1979, with Nancy Shade in the title role. The Canadian premiere, with Karen Armstrong as Lulu, was scheduled by the Canadian Opera Company for its 1980–81 season in a new English translation by Arthur Jacobs.

Subsequent to the premiere of the two-act version (with epilogue) in 1937, *Lulu* established itself in the repertoire. It was given regularly in Germany by the Hamburg State Opera, which gave the first performance in New York (in German) at the Metropolitan Opera House June 6, 1967. In September and October of 1967 it was presented (in English) by the American National Opera Company under the baton of Sarah Caldwell in Indianapolis, St. Louis, Buffalo, Madison (Wisc.), Chicago and Brooklyn. The Metropolitan Opera produced the truncated version in its 1976–77 season, and the three-act version in 1980–81.

There is no overture. The curtain rises immediately on the Prologue.

PROLOGUE

The entrance to a circus tent. At one side stands a clown carrying an enormous drum. In front of the entrance is the Animal Trainer (Ringmaster), dressed in top hat, frock coat, white trousers and riding boots; he has a whip in one hand and a revolver in the other. He addresses the audience in a long monologue ("Hereinspaziert in die Menagerie") in which he invites the "proud ladies and gentlemen" to gaze upon the inhabitants of the menagerie. These he sardonically describes in terms of derogatory human attributes: the rapacious tiger, the greedy bear, the exhibitionistic monkey, the venomous reptile.

Then the Trainer calls backstage and orders August, a stagehand, to bring forth his prize specimen, the serpent. The stagehand comes in with Lulu in his arms. She is dressed in the Pierrot costume for the opening act. Here is a creature, the Trainer proclaims in the manner of a sideshow barker, who was born for seduction and murder. When Lulu glares at him for this gratuitous insult, he tries to makes amends. There is really nothing extraordinary about this creature at the moment, the Trainer says, but there may be some surprises later on. At his command, the assistant carries Lulu offstage. As she passes the Trainer, he pats her hips and murmurs that she is his greatest treasure.

Then in stentorian tones he invites the audience to witness a breathtaking spectacle: he will place his head between the jaws of the beast—the name of which they doubtless know.

ACT ONE

[*Scene One*] The studio of the Artist (Schwarz). Lulu, in her Pierrot costume, holding a shepherd's crook in her hand, is posing on a dais. The Artist stands at his easel in front of her half-finished portrait. Dr. Schön, hat in hand and with his overcoat on, is sitting on an ottoman watching the Artist. From behind a Spanish screen in front of the door of the room comes the voice of Alwa. He asks if he may come in, then appears.

Casually greeting his father and then the Artist, Alwa goes over to the portrait. With great enthusiasm he exclaims that he wants to engage Lulu as his leading lady in his opera. Lulu demurely remarks that she could not dance well enough to play the role. Dr. Schön interrupts to ask Alwa why he came to the studio. To ask him to attend the rehearsal of his opera, Alwa replies. As Schön rises to leave, Lulu asks Alwa to reserve a box for her at the opening performance.

Alwa and his father pause to inquire why Lulu's husband is not present. Evading the question, Lulu pointedly requests Dr. Schön to convey her greetings to his fiancée. Deliberately ignoring the remark, Schön turns back to the portrait and criticizes the Artist's work. Then he and Alwa leave.

No sooner have they gone than the Artist, with brush and palette still in his hands, rushes to the dais with a passionate cry. Lulu fends him off, warning him that her husband will arrive at any moment. This marks the beginning of a tumultuous duet.

There is a noise outside, and the two listen apprehensively for a moment. Then the Artist goes back to his easel. Suddenly he throws down his brush and palette, exclaiming that he cannot go on. Lulu, exasperated by his behavior, orders him to continue painting, but the Artist, losing control of himself, lunges toward her. She hurls the shepherd's crook in his face and rushes toward the door with the Artist in pursuit. Dodging him, Lulu scurries up a stepladder at the rear of the studio. Ecstatically she cries that from this height she can see all the cities of the world ("Ich sehe über alle Städte"). The Artist, now in a frenzy, tries to pull her down and in so doing knocks over the ladder. In falling, it shatters a piece of sculpture. Staring at the wreckage, the Artist shrieks that he is ruined. Then he again tries to seize the girl.

Evading his grasp, Lulu staggers toward the couch, on which she collapses. The Artist swiftly locks the door of the studio, then kneels beside Lulu and covers her hand with kisses. Eyes closed, she warns him that her husband will soon arrive. Oblivious to the warning, the Artist cries out that he loves her. Lulu, with eyes still closed, murmurs as though in a dream that she once loved a student with 175 scars. But the Artist amorously babbles on, first calling her "Nelly," then "Eva." Reminding him that her name is Lulu, she pushes him away with a gesture of revulsion. As he tries to continue his violent love-making, the voice of Lulu's husband is heard outside. Panic-stricken, Lulu begs the Artist to hide her. When he starts toward the door she holds him back, crying that her husband will kill them both.

In the next moment the husband (Dr. Goll, the medical health officer) batters down the door and lunges into the room. Glaring madly at Lulu and the Artist, he rushes toward them brandishing his cane and screaming a curse. Suddenly he gasps for breath, then falls to the floor dying of a stroke. With a gasp of horror, the Artist kneels and tries to lift the body, calling on Lulu to help him. Shrinking back in fear, Lulu refuses. The Artist hurries out to call a doctor.

Alone, Lulu voices her thoughts in a brief monologue called the "Canzonetta" ("Auf einmal springt er auf"). Crouching near the door, she wonders if her husband perhaps will suddenly spring to his feet. Softly she calls to him by her nickname for him: "Pussi." She waits, as though expecting him to answer. Then she warily circles the body, singing that her husband's eyes are following her every step. Gingerly touching the body with her foot, she cringes back. In almost childlike awe she says that now he is really dead . . . the dance is over. He has deserted her—and now what is she to do?

The Artist returns saying that the doctor is on his way. Lulu casually observes that her husband is past all medical help and is quite obviously dead. Shocked at her callousness, the Artist upbraids her. Taking her by the hand, he leads her to the couch and begins questioning her to the accompaniment of a rising and falling chromatic theme in the orchestra ("Kannst du die Wahrheit sagen?"). He asks if she knows how to speak the truth . . . if she believes in a Creator . . . if she has ever loved.

As though in a trance, Lulu answers every question with "I don't know." Then suddenly coming to her senses, she asks the Artist what it is that he really wants to know. Completely baffled by her inexplicable behavior, he roughly orders her to change her clothes. With a surprised glance at him, Lulu goes into the other room.

Staring down at the dead man, the Artist addresses him in a brief dramatic refrain ("Ich möchte tauschen mit dir"). He would gladly change places, he sings. He will give her back, he goes on irrationally, along with his own youth as well. This happiness is more than he can bear—it fills him with hellish terror. In a sudden frantic outburst, the Artist begs the dead man to awaken, then swears that he never touched his wife. Becoming calmer, he sings that his only wish was to bring her a bit of happiness.

His monologue is interrupted as Lulu enters from the adjoining room holding up the top of her dress at the back. She asks him to hook it up because her hand is shaking. The Artist complies as the curtain slowly falls. The music continues into a long orchestral interlude, part of which is in canon form—the theme is that associated with the Artist's hopeless passion for Lulu. There is no pause in the accompaniment as the curtain rises on the next scene.

[Scene Two] An elegantly appointed salon in Lulu's home. She is now married to the Artist. On one wall hangs the portrait of Lulu as Pierrot. She herself is lying on a chaise longue, gazing at her reflection in a hand mirror. She rubs her forehead thoughtfully, then puts the mirror aside with a petulant frown.

The Artist enters, carrying his brush and palette and a packet of letters. Lulu smiles in greeting. Spoken dialogue follows. The Artist hands Lulu a letter which she identifies from the perfumed envelope as from "the Corticelli." She slips the letter into her bosom. The Artist excitedly tells her that his portrait of her as "the Dancer" has been sold for fifty thousand marks. And that, he adds exultantly, makes the third painting he has sold since he and Lulu were married.

He hands Lulu another letter, which she reads aloud. It announces the engagement of Charlotte Marie Adelaide, daughter of Counselor Heinrich Ritter von Zarnikov, to Dr. Ludwig Schön. The Artist remarks rather cynically that the eminent doctor at long last has made up his mind to announce his engagement publicly. After all, what could possibly stand in the way of marriage for a man of his importance? In silence, Lulu folds the letter and puts it aside. When the Artist says that they must send Dr. Schön a congratulatory note, Lulu enigmatically observes that they already have congratulated him. "You may do so again if you wish," she casually tells her husband.

Saying it is time to get to work, the Artist kisses Lulu and tells her she looks particularly attractive this morning. He kneels and impetuously takes her in his arms. The doorbell rings; he curses the interruption. Lulu tells him not to answer the bell, but the Artist reminds her that it may be the art dealer. "And even if it were the Emperor of China," Lulu murmurs languorously. The implication is lost on the Artist, who goes out to answer the door.

During a brief orchestral passage, Lulu abandons herself to her amorous thoughts and lies with eyes closed. The mood passes, and she sits up. The Artist returns and tells her that the visitor is only a beggar, for whom he has no small change. Again saying he must get to work, the Artist goes into the adjoining room.

Straightening her dress and arranging her hair, Lulu goes to the door and admits the beggar—who actually is Schigolch, a bedraggled, asthmatic old man. The music of the long soliloquy which ensues is designated as "chamber music for a woodwind ensemble." It is throughout in a deliberate, dragging tempo, reflecting the labored speech of the old man.

Looking around, Schigolch remarks rather querulously that he expected the Artist to be a "different" sort of a fellow. He then admits that he has come for money—two hundred marks, or perhaps three hundred. . . . Shrugging resignedly, Lulu gives him the money. Schigolch, neglecting to thank her, compliments her on her new home—taking particular note of the luxurious rugs. Rather amused, Lulu remarks that she likes to walk on them barefoot. The old man leers, then suddenly gasps for breath; Lulu offers him a drink. Recovering himself, he notices her portrait and exclaims: "It is really you!"

In a rather aimless way, Schigolch begins plying Lulu with questions: How does she spend her time . . . is she still studying French? When Lulu, in growing impatience, sharply asks why all this matters to him, he obsequiously answers that his only concern is that his "little Lulu" will never suffer privation. He caresses her knee suggestively. Pushing his hand away, she says that not "within the memory of man" has she been called "Lulu"—and it also has been a long time since she danced.

Schigolch asks, puzzled: "What, then, are you now?" In a spoken phrase, Lulu replies bitterly: "An animal."

The doorbell rings, and Lulu gets up quickly. Schigolch, aware that he must leave, rises with a painful effort. Helping him to the door, Lulu accompanies him outside. For a moment the stage is empty. An orchestral passage in discordant, rising chromatics underscores the scurrilous character of the old man. This chromaticism is associated with Schigolch throughout the opera.

Lulu returns with Dr. Schön, who is obviously angry and excited. He asks what her father is doing in her house ("Was tut denn Ihr Vater?"), then adds spitefully that if he were her husband he would never allow that wretch inside the door. This marks the beginning of a long duet (designated in the score as "sonata") which later builds into one of the most climactic scenes in the opera.

Coolly ignoring Schön's show of temper, Lulu asks why he has come. Thereupon Schön tells her she must stop visiting him. If Walter (the Artist) were not so naïve, Schön goes on, he long ago would have become aware of her deceitfulness. Lulu answers contemptuously that Walter, like all lovers, is blind. He knows her only as a woman who satisfies his desires.

There must be an end to this, Schön bursts out. Lulu's answer is a shrug. Goaded by her indifference, Schön furiously reminds her of what he has done for her: Twice he found her a husband . . . and even found a position for her current spouse. More than that, he has made it possible for her to live in luxury. Whatever she may feel about the situation, Schön goes on, he no longer wants anything to do with it. During this tirade, his voice blends with that of Lulu's as she blandly repeats that, so far as her adoring husband is concerned, she exists solely for his pleasure.

When Lulu asks why he has decided to break off their relationship, Schön tells her he has become engaged—and he wishes to bring his bride into a home that is without shame. She is indeed enchanting, Lulu says mockingly, but there is no reason why they themselves should not continue to meet.

Schön retorts furiously that they will never meet again—except in the presence of her husband. Lulu repeats the word "husband," and instantly her demeanor changes. With quiet intensity she answers Schön in a spoken passage over a sinister theme in the orchestra ("Wenn ich einem Menschen auf dieser Welt angehöre"): If she ever belonged to anyone in this world, it is to him alone. He took her in—a petty thief who tried to steal his watch—gave her food and made a home for her. No one else in the world has ever shown her such love and care.

With desperate insistence, Schön begs Lulu not to stand in the way of his marriage. He implores her to give him his freedom for the sake of his important position in the business world. And what is more, she must no longer be seen going in and out of his house at all hours. Growing angry, Lulu sarcastically assures him that she has no objections to his marriage, but warns him that he cannot discard her at his own convenience. Furthermore, she adds, she is not in the slightest jealous of this "child." Schön retorts that his bride-to-be is not much younger than herself.

The quarrel is interrupted by the entrance of the Artist. Noting the hostile expressions on the faces of the two, he asks what is wrong. Lulu and Schön glower at him in silence. Taking Lulu's arm, the Artist tries to lead her toward the studio, but she impatiently draws away from him. Indicating Schön, she says that he has grown tired of her. With that she hurries into the studio. Schön, in an aside, murmurs that now the matter must be settled once for all.

Puzzled and suspicious, the Artist confronts Schön. The ensuing colloquy is partly sung and partly spoken. Schön begins by reminding the Artist that he married "half a million" ("Du hast eine halbe Million geheiratet"), that he has won recognition as an artist and now has a secure position in the world. Obviously struggling to get to the point, Schön exhorts the bewildered Artist to assume more responsibility as a husband. He must not entrust her to someone else, Schön adds meaningfully.

Beginning to understand Schön's insinuations, the Artist is dumbfounded. Schön, insidiously plotting his revenge upon Lulu, unctuously assures the Artist that he has come not to cause a scandal but to avert one. When Walter hotly interrupts that Schön has never understood Lulu, Schön declares that he cannot allow him to go on in his blind innocence. The woman, he says, does have qualities of respectability—she has, in fact, improved enormously since he first knew her.

That was when she was twelve, Schön explains in answer to Walter's startled question. Thereupon he proceeds to detail Lulu's past in a mélange of lies and innuendo. He first saw her as a flower girl in front of a cafe, took her into his home and put her in the care of a woman he engaged to rear her. Walter mutters that Lulu spoke only of an "aunt" who raised her. Deliberately ignoring the remark, Schön goes on to say that it was through him that Lulu met her first husband, Dr. Goll.

Relentlessly continuing, Schön says that Lulu—determined to become his wife after Dr. Goll's death—did her utmost to come between him and his present fiancée, whom he met as a widower. Stunned and incredulous, Walter says brokenly that Lulu told him nothing of all this and swore to him that she had never been in love before. With deliberate cruelty, Schön observes that one cannot apply conventional standards of behavior to a person of "Mignon's" origin.

At the name "Mignon," Walter looks at Schön questioningly. He soon learns that while he himself affectionately called Lulu "Eva," she was "Mignon" to Schön and "Nelly" to Goll. When Schön admits that he never knew her real name, the Artist bitterly remarks that perhaps she alone knows.

Schön's next disclosure—for Walter's benefit—is that Lulu's father, contrary to her story that he died in an insane asylum, actually was in the Artist's own studio this very day. When Walter scoffs at this, Schön points to the two liquor glasses on the table as mute evidence of the "father's" visit. In despair, Walter cries that everything is a lie.

The dialogue continues in duet form with mounting dramatic intensity. Schön, having reduced the Artist to a state of helpless confusion, urges him to take a firm hand with Lulu—she requires "authority." Walter sobs that Lulu swore by her mother's grave that she had never been in love before. Schön sardonically answers that Lulu never knew her mother, much less her mother's grave.

Collapsing on a chair, the Artist cries that there is a terrible pain in his chest. Looking down at him, Schön, with cruel irony, exhorts him to take good care of Lulu—"after all, she is yours" ("Wahr' sie Dir, weil sie Dein ist"). Overwhelmed by shame and despair, Walter screams in anguish. Schön remorselessly urges him to act at once—or lose the woman he loves.

Suddenly calm, Walter gets to his feet and says he will now have a talk with Lulu. Taking his hand in a spurious gesture of encouragement, Schön guides Walter out of the room. Closing the door after him, he murmurs with evil satisfaction that this was a hard bit of work. Then, in sudden alarm, Schön realizes that the Artist did not go into his studio, but into the adjoining room. At that moment agonizing groans come from the other side of the door.

Schön rushes to the door and finds it locked. As he frantically tries to force it open, Lulu bursts out of the studio in a state of hysterical excitement. Schön shouts at her to fetch a hatchet from the kitchen. Lulu, regaining control of herself, says that Walter no doubt will open the door himself—once he has finished weeping. Schön, furious with her, orders her to do as she is told.

The doorbell rings. Exclaiming that he must not be found in the apartment, Schön tiptoes out and closes the door behind him. Lulu glides to the locked door of the adjoining room and crouches there listening. Schön reappears with Alwa, who is excitedly telling him that a revolution has broken out in Paris. Ignoring him, Schön hammers on the locked door and shouts to the Artist to open it. Again he orders Lulu to bring the hatchet. Alwa, completely oblivious to the uproar, babbles that no one in the editorial office knows what to write about the Paris revolution.

Lulu finally returns with the hatchet, with which Schön and Alwa break open the door. The two stagger back in horror. Lulu looks into the room and recoils with a shriek of terror. She runs to Alwa, who has collapsed upon the sofa, and begs him to take her away. He pushes her into the studio as Schön, wiping his brow, goes into the room. A moment later he emerges, shaken by what he has seen. Gesturing toward the room, he cries, in a symbolic phrase: "There lies my betrothal, bleeding to death."[1] Alwa shouts that Schön has brought this curse upon himself, then denounces his father for his wretched treatment of Lulu.

Lulu reappears, dressed in traveling clothes. When Schön asks her what she will tell the police, she coldly answers that he can do the talking. Cursing the Artist, Schön goes to the telephone and reports the details of the suicide: ". . . cut his throat with a razor . . . persecution complex . . ." As he talks, there is a brief exchange between Lulu and Alwa about Walter's tragic act.

Completing the telephone call, Schön comes forward, saying that now at last he can retire from the world. The three are startled by the ringing of the doorbell—the police have arrived. As Schön starts toward the door Lulu tells him there is blood on his hands. She sprinkles perfume on her handkerchief and wipes off the blood. When Schön reminds her that the blood is her husband's, she casually remarks that it will leave no trace. Outraged at her cruel indifference, Schön screams: "You monster!" Lulu answers imperturbably: "But you will marry me." Going toward the door, she murmurs affably: "Have patience, children." The curtain falls.

[Scene Three] Before the curtain rises there is an orchestral interlude and at its conclusion a jazz band is heard. This ragtime, which forms the basis of the melodrama of the opening part of the scene, continues throughout the ensuing dialogue. In the dressing room of a theater, Lulu is preparing to dance in a pantomime. Alwa, pouring champagne into two glasses, is speaking to Lulu, who is putting on her costume behind a screen.

Alwa says that never before has he seen a theater audience so excited. Lulu asks him if he has seen his father in the theater, then tells him that the Prince will be there to see her perform. His Highness, she explains, wants to marry her and take her to Africa. In a resplendent ballet costume she emerges from behind the screen. Alwa gasps in admiration, but suddenly clutches his hand to his chest as though in pain.

At this point the music of the jazz band stops and the orchestra takes up the accompaniment. Here for the first time is heard the "rondo"

---

[1] The key word in the phrase is "betrothal"—*Verlobung*, used here in an esoteric sense to describe Schön's awareness of disaster.

theme associated with Alwa. Deliberately tantalizing Alwa, Lulu asks if he remembers the first time she came to his room. Alwa replies in a passionate refrain ("Sie trugen ein dunkelblaues Kleid"). He recalls that she wore a dark blue dress and that she seemed to be an other-worldly being far beyond his reach. He adored her more than his own mother. He remembers that when his mother died he threatened to fight his father in a duel unless he married Lulu immediately.

She tells Alwa that his father had told her of the incident. But now, she goes on (over the music of the jazz band, which resumes at this point), Dr. Schön must be prepared to recognize her as a successful actress—he insisted she go on the stage so that she could be seen by some patron of the arts rich enough to marry her.

When Alwa vehemently protests that no one must take her away from him, Lulu meaningfully answers that she knows—even without looking—that there are those in the audience who are considering that very possibility. She reminds him that, after all, it is in his stage work that she is on display before the public. At the sound of the call bell, she turns to go onstage. In a brilliant coloratura phrase, Lulu sings that the thought of her appearance onstage is like an icy chill that courses through her body. Alwa shakes his head uncomprehendingly as he watches her leave.

Alone, he muses in a recitative passage that this woman is an ideal subject for an opera: Scene One, the health officer—impossible; Scene Two, the Artist—still more impossible; Scene Three—but why go on? His reflections are interrupted by the entrance of the Prince. Intro-ducing himself, His Highness launches into a fatuous discourse about Lulu ("Würden Sie es für möglich halten"). He has been studying her spiritual qualities, he declares, as reflected in her dancing, and has come to the conclusion that she symbolizes the joy of living. As a wife she would make any man supremely happy. In an aside he adds: "As *my* wife."

His monologue is interrupted by the frantic ringing of the call bell. There is an uproar outside and then the door bursts open and Lulu staggers in. She falls into a chair. An attendant explains that she fainted in the middle of her dance. Lulu, who seems to have lost control of her-self, gasps that Dr. Schön and his fiancée were in the audience.

A moment later Schön himself strides in and furiously confronts Lulu, accusing her of using the ballet to revenge herself upon him. An agitated sextet ensues, blending the voices of Schön, Lulu, Alwa, the Prince, the attendant and the stage manager. Schön fiercely orders Lulu to return to the stage and finish her dance. Lulu defiantly refuses to dance before his fiancée. The Prince and the stage manager express their consternation. Lulu protests that she is too exhausted to go on, and the attendant implores Schön to allow her a few moments' rest. When Alwa asks the stage manager to continue the performance with the next number until Lulu can recover, Schön storms that she has a contract and must dance in spite of everything. Lulu finally agrees to do so after she has rested. At a sign from Schön, all the others leave.

Whirling on Lulu, Schön again irrationally accuses her of using her role as an instrument of sheer revenge ("Wie kannst du die Szene gegen mich ausspielen?"). This introduces the long, intensely dramatic scene (designated as a "sonata") which concludes the act. It is a scene in which Lulu quietly but remorselessly destroys Schön's will to resist and reduces him to helpless despair. Her weapons in turn are sarcasm, flattery, cajolery, seductiveness.

She taunts him with hints of a liaison with the Prince, who is to take her to Africa. With a sneer she advises him to hurry back to his innocent bride-to-be. When Schön, goaded to the edge of madness, raises his fist, Lulu insolently dares him to strike her. The man rushes to the door, screaming that he must escape, then breaks down sobbing that he does not know where to go. Watching him with venomous satisfaction, Lulu voices her triumph in a phrase that soars to the topmost range of the voice (the musical notation is F above high C): "This is a moment of indescribable joy—the tyrant is weeping!" ("Mir tut dieser Augenblick wohl. . . Der Gewaltmensch weint!").

Completely demoralized, Schön asks Lulu what he is to do. She thereupon hands him paper and pen and tells him to write as she dictates. As though hypnotized, Schön obeys. This "letter scene" is in the form of a canon: as Lulu dictates, Schön repeats the words as he writes them down. The letter informs Dr. Schön's fiancée that he is breaking off their engagement because he is no longer worthy of her. His message is being dictated by the woman who wholly dominates his life.

Schön, sobbing abjectly, signs his name. Lulu harshly dictates a postscript warning his fiancée not to try to save him. In utter despair, Schön cries out that the hour of execution has come. Lulu, ignoring him, arranges her ballet costume and goes out to the stage. The curtain falls to the accompaniment of thunderous chords.

ACT TWO

[*Scene One*] A luxurious salon in Dr. Schön's home. He and Lulu are now married. Clad in negligee, she is sitting in an armchair. Nearby, seated on the ottoman, is the Countess Geschwitz, a handsome woman in mannish attire. Dr. Schön is standing at left. The opening recitative is dominated by the pentatonic music identifying the Countess. Making a social call, she says she is looking forward to seeing Lulu at the ball for women artists. She makes it clear to Schön that a man would be persona non grata. Looking admiringly at Lulu's portrait, the Countess inquires about the artist. Both Lulu and Schön are evasive and embarrassed. Sensing their discomfiture, the Countess takes her leave. Lulu accompanies her out of the room.

Left alone, Schön abandons himself to bitter reflection in a brief monologue in arioso style ("Das mein Lebensabend"). Here he is, in the evening of his life, after thirty years of striving, in a house ridden with evil. He is not safe in his own home . . . there may be spies behind the draperies. Drawing his revolver, he stares apprehensively at the windows. Stealthily he pulls the drapes aside but finds no one there. Staggering back, he bursts out that he is going mad. He looks around with an expression of utter revulsion. Hearing Lulu's footsteps outside, he hides his revolver.

Though obviously preoccupied with thoughts of the Countess, Lulu asks Schön if he will take her for a drive. He answers impatiently that he must go to the stock exchange. Deliberately enticing him, Lulu comes close and gazes up at him amorously. In an insinuating phrase ("Ich fürchte: Vieles") she sings that the one thing she is not afraid of is his love for her. Unable to resist her, Schön pushes her gently toward the bedroom.

The stage is momentarily empty. Then the Countess Geschwitz enters, cautiously looks around and hides behind the fire screen. A moment later Schigolch comes limping in, gasping for breath and complaining about the "slippery floors" in the house. A bizarre scene follows.

The Athlete (Rodrigo) appears on the balcony at the rear of the room holding the young Schoolboy by the arm. As he drags him down the steps, the boy struggles to free himself from Rodrigo's grasp. The ensemble which now builds up is constructed on the chromaticism characterizing Schigolch.

From the leering comments made by the old man and Rodrigo, it becomes clear that this youngster has fallen into Lulu's clutches and is hopelessly in love with her. In fact, he tells the two that he has written a poem to her. They comment in cynical amusement. Schigolch, staring lecherously at the boy, remarks that his eyes have enslaved Lulu. Turning to Rodrigo, the old man sings: "We are finished!" The two clink glasses and with sardonic formality drink a toast to each other.

Lulu, dressed in a revealing gown set off by a corsage of orchids, makes a dramatic entrance. The Schoolboy gapes open-mouthed at her; she leans provocatively over him for a moment, inviting him to smell the orchids. Schigolch and the Athlete ask her if she is expecting the Prince ("Sie erwarten wohl den Prinzen?"). Showing her irritation at the question, Lulu turns and goes up the stairs to the balcony. In a continuation of the ensemble, both Schigolch and Rodrigo admit—to the utter bewilderment of the Schoolboy—that they wanted to marry Lulu. It also now becomes clear that Schigolch is not her father—as he has pretended. In fact, he tells Rodrigo that Lulu never had a father.

She appears just in time to overhear his remark. Smiling, she admits it is true and that she is a "wonder child." The ensuing action verges on farce. When Schigolch and the Athlete express concern about Dr. Schön, Lulu calmly assures them that he is at the stock exchange. As Rodrigo is bragging about how he will toss the Doctor into the air if he shows up, the manservant announces Alwa. Cursing him, Rodrigo scurries behind the draperies; the Schoolboy ducks under the table; Schigolch, taking the key to the balcony room from Lulu, starts crawling slowly up the stairs.

Alwa, in a dinner jacket, immediately begins talking to Lulu about his opera, then notices Schigolch on the stairs. Startled, he asks Lulu who he is. She glibly answers that he is an army comrade of Dr. Schön's who was wounded in the war. Alwa asks if his father is at home and Lulu tells him he is at the stock exchange. The servant, entering with a bottle of champagne and glasses, stares brazenly at Lulu. Alwa notices the look and angrily asks him what is wrong. Lulu tries to make light of the matter. The servant, obviously unable to control his feelings, rushes out.

Lulu hastily brings Alwa's thoughts back to himself with insinuating flattery, saying that what she admires most about him is his strength of character ("Was ich immer am höchsten"). He is the only person in the world, she tells him, who has protected her without robbing her of her self-respect. Alwa, of course, falls victim to her blandishments. With a show of modesty, he admits his intuitions have been correct. During this conversation, Schön appears on the balcony, glares down at his son, then withdraws.

Alwa masks his amorous thoughts behind a façade of high-sounding phrases—none of which, obviously, swerve Lulu from her intention to make him her next victim. With tantalizing candor she assures him that it is because of his regard for her that she can give herself to him without reservation. Alwa is completely swept away.

The dialogue is interrupted by the entrance of the servant, who is still in a state of uncontrollable agitation. Alwa sharply asks him if he is ill; Lulu again intervenes. Schön reappears and looks down balefully at the hapless servant, who walks out unsteadily balancing his tray.

Alwa, losing control of himself, begins making violent love to Lulu, quite unaware that Schön and the Athlete emerge to watch the scene briefly. Finally Alwa throws himself into Lulu's arms crying: "Mignon, I love you!"[2] Stroking his hair, she speaks in an eerie, haunting half whisper: "I poisoned your mother."

---

[2] This phrase ("Mignon, ich liebe Dich") marks the midpoint of the "Alwa Rondo," which has been described as the lyrical focus of the entire opera. It is Berg's expression of his personal affection for the extraordinary character he created in Lulu.

The two are completely oblivious to the sinister pantomime in progress behind them. Rodrigo, looking out from behind the draperies, sees Schön. The latter takes aim at him with his revolver. Rodrigo frantically points to Lulu and Alwa, but Schön holds his aim on him. Before Rodrigo can dodge back behind the draperies, Lulu catches sight of him and then sees Schön on the balcony. She leaps to her feet with a gasp of fright. Pocketing his revolver, Schön comes down the stairs with a newspaper in his hand. He strides over to Alwa, who is still on his knees and staring at Lulu as though in a trance.

Grasping his son by the shoulders, Schön pulls him to his feet and shouts that revolution has broken out in Paris. Alwa shows no sign of having heard what he said. Schön dementedly babbles that no one in the editorial department knows what to write about the situation. With that he drags Alwa out of the room.

The Athlete, panic-stricken, tries to escape up the stairs but Lulu bars his way, warning that Schön will kill him. In desperation, Rodrigo dodges behind the draperies a moment before Schön, revolver in hand, reappears. Confronting Lulu, he furiously denounces her for dragging him into the mire of her own corruption ("Du Kreatur, die mich durch den Strassenkot"). This marks the beginning of a scene designated as a "five-strophic aria."

At the height of his tirade, Lulu interrupts to ask with infuriating insolence what he thinks of her dress. Beside himself with anger, Schön roars at her to get out before she drives him to killing his own son. Suddenly he thrusts the revolver at her and commands her to kill herself. Almost playfully, Lulu points the gun at him and inadvertently fires a shot into the ceiling. At that moment the Athlete darts out from his hiding place, bounds up the stairs and vanishes.

Schön, catching sight of him, demands to know if Lulu has hidden any other men in the house, then begins to search the room. He discovers the Countess Geschwitz behind the fire screen. As she begs Lulu to save her, Schön roughly drags her into the other room and slams the door, snarling after her: "Now you will have to stay until the end."

Exhausted by his rage, he flings himself down beside Lulu, thrusts the revolver into her hands and says there are enough bullets left for her to make an end of things. Lulu quietly tells him he can do so himself by divorcing her.

That would indeed be the end ("Das wär' noch übrig"), Schön retorts with savage irony, and would leave the way clear for his successor to her affections. But how, he asks, can divorce be the end for two people who are fused together as one? Frantic with rage, he tries to wrest the revolver from her.

Now aroused and frightened by his violence, Lulu tears herself away from him and in a ringing refrain known as "Lulu's Song"—the "coloratura Lied"—("Wenn sich die Menschen") she speaks out in her own defense. If men have killed themselves for her, she sings, their rash actions do not demean her. He knows as well as she why they married; if he has sacrificed his old age to her, she has given him her youth in return. In a climactic phrase (again at the topmost range of the voice) she declares that she has always been true to herself—and no one ever has had reason to regard her otherwise.[3]

Schön, screaming in uncontrollable frenzy, forces Lulu to her knees and turns the revolver in her hand toward her. At that moment the Schoolboy, under the table, shouts for help. Schön whirls toward the table and at that instant Lulu fires five shots into his back and keeps pulling the trigger of the empty gun. As Schön slumps down, the Schoolboy scrambles from his hiding place and helps him to a chair. In spite of his agony, Schön gasps: "Another one!"

Lulu bends over him, but he weakly thrusts her away and calls for Alwa. He comes headlong down the stairs from the balcony. When Schön asks for water, Lulu pours a glass of champagne and brings it to him as she wails that it was she who fired the shots. The Schoolboy whimpers that she is innocent. Schön raises the glass to his lips. When Alwa, with the Schoolboy's help, lifts him to his feet to take him to the adjoining room, Schön warns his son not to let Lulu escape—because *he* will be the next one. When they reach the door, and Alwa opens it, the Countess Geschwitz rushes out. Schön collapses and dies on the threshold. Lulu, kneeling down and tenderly stroking his brow, murmurs that now it is over.

She rises and turns to go up the stairs, but Alwa bars her way. The Countess and the Schoolboy stand by helplessly. Now genuinely terrified over the debacle she has brought about, Lulu implores Alwa not to hand her over to the police. She promises to be faithful to him forever, throwing her arms around his knees in a melodramatic gesture of entreaty.

Alwa looks down at her in mingled pity and contempt. There is a clamorous pounding at the door as the police, presumably called by neighbors who heard the sound of gunfire, demand entrance. Pushing Lulu violently away, Alwa goes to open the door. The Schoolboy, in helpless terror, whines that now he will be hounded out of school. The curtain falls. The orchestral accompaniment continues without interruption into a tumultuous interlude which sustains the feverish mood of the preceding scene. The music gradually subsides to a slow, deliberate tempo; it is based on the *Erdgeist* theme and the portrait motive.[4]

[3] Berg called this Lulu's "confession of faith."

[4] Berg wrote this music to accompany the film sequence which in the opera establishes the connection between Wedekind's two dramas. Additionally, the retro-

[*Scene Two*] The room in Schön's house as in Scene One. The Countess Geschwitz is sitting in a chair, a rug over her knees. Seated near her on the ottoman is the Athlete. Alwa, deep in thought, is pacing back and forth. The three are waiting for Schigolch, who is coming from the prison hospital where Lulu has been confined as a victim of cholera. An epidemic has been raging through the city. Rodrigo—for reasons which will become apparent later—is posing as Alwa's servant.

As the scene opens, the Countess, Rodrigo and Alwa are discussing Lulu. Rodrigo wonders if the cholera has left its mark on her as it has on the Countess. The latter says that the affliction which disfigures ordinary people only makes Lulu more beautiful—and Lulu now is lovelier than she has ever been.

In any case, Rodrigo says, he intends to go on his way to his next theatrical engagement without Lulu. When the Countess expresses shocked surprise that he would permit his fiancée to travel alone, the Athlete explains in a brief refrain ("Erstens fährt doch der Alte mit"). To begin with, he sings, the old man (Schigolch) is going with her to protect her. Furthermore, he (Rodrigo) is obliged to wait for his show costumes, which include a pair of rose-colored tights. He fumes that the effect of his acrobatic costumes will be spoiled because he has gained weight while lying in a hospital bed for three months as an accomplice in the Countess' fantastic "conspiracy." The Countess expresses disgust over the Athlete's lack of consideration for Lulu.

Alwa expresses misgivings about the Countess' plan to spirit Lulu out of the hospital, but he warmly commends her for her unselfish efforts in the girl's behalf. In token of his gratitude he offers to reimburse Geschwitz for her personal expenses with a loan of twenty thousand marks. The foregoing is partly in spoken dialogue.

Before she can reply, Schigolch comes in—grumbling as usual. The musical accompaniment is an exact repeat, in slow motion, of that heard when the old man came into the house complaining about the "slippery floors" at the beginning of the act. Schigolch explains he has been busy arranging for passports for the Countess, Lulu and himself, and adds that he knows of an excellent hotel in Paris. The Countess interrupts to tell him that Rodrigo expects him to accompany Lulu alone. Probably because Rodrigo is afraid of becoming infected, Schigolch sneers. Rodrigo somewhat cynically remarks that there will be no harm in having her disinfected before their honeymoon. Alwa proffers the Countess a wallet with ten thousand marks but she refuses to take it. She and Schigolch leave for the hospital.

---

grade pattern of the harmonies reflects the misfortune that now overtakes Lulu. From the peak of social position as the wife of Dr. Schön, she plunges to the status of murderess, spends a year in prison and then is liberated to go eventually to her doom.

No sooner have they gone than Rodrigo and Alwa begin quarreling
about money. In the ensuing interval of spoken dialogue the events
leading up to the present situation in the opera are disclosed. Rodrigo
angrily upbraids Alwa for offering the Countess Geschwitz money when
he (Rodrigo) is practically penniless, having spent everything in a harebrained scheme to effect Lulu's release from prison following the
murder of Schön.

What is more, Rodrigo goes on, he is doing Alwa a favor by acting as
his servant, so that no new servants (who might report the "conspirators" to the police) need be engaged. And finally, he is willing to
risk his life to make his prospective bride (Lulu) "the greatest woman
acrobat of the age."

Alwa retorts that he knows that the Countess has paid Rodrigo every
cent she owes him—and is even now paying him a monthly salary.
Under the circumstances, says Alwa, he is somewhat suspicious of Rodrigo's professed unselfish love for the murderess. In any case, he no
doubt would have ended up a drunken beggar had it not been for the
generosity of the Countess.

Infuriated, the Athlete asks Alwa what would have happened to him
if he had not sold his father's scurrilous rag of a newspaper for two million marks. The net result of *that* windfall was that Alwa composed a
miserable opera—in which Lulu's legs are to play the "leading role,"
and which no theater in the world would think of performing.

The two are about to come to blows when the doorbell rings. Rodrigo, greatly excited, cries that now he will see his bride at last, after a
year's time. But Alwa warns him to hide. The visitor turns out to be the
Schoolboy. He tells the exasperated Alwa that he has just escaped from
the house of correction and has come to ask help in "liberating the
woman." He goes into some vague explanation about the testimony at
Lulu's trial.

He is interrupted when Rodrigo emerges from behind a curtain and
gives a deliberately awkward imitation of a servant. But he promptly
drops his masquerade when he sees the Schoolboy. Enraged, he
threatens him with a beating. Rodrigo realizes, of course, that the boy
has been romantically involved with Lulu and he is bent on revenge. He
tells the Schoolboy that "the woman" (significantly, he does not call
her Lulu) has been dead for three weeks.

When the boy refuses to believe it, Rodrigo thrusts a newspaper in
front of him and points to an item which reports that the murderess of
Dr. Ludwig Schön is a cholera victim. Rodrigo snatches the paper away
before the Schoolboy can finish reading the first sentence. He finally accepts the fact that Lulu is dead when Alwa assures him it is so. The boy
grieves for her but adds, with a cynicism far beyond his years, that he

will find some other way to go to the devil. Rodrigo, infuriated at the boy's insolence, throws him bodily out of the room.

A moment later Lulu appears on the balcony with Schigolch. She walks haltingly, leaning on the old man's arm as though barely able to support herself. The music which accompanies her entrance is a slow-motion passage corresponding to that of her first appearance in Act Two. Wearing the Countess' black dress, her face ghostly white and skeletonlike, she is a veritable apparition. The Athlete gasps in anger and dismay. He rages that such a creature could never appear in his circus act and that he intends to denounce her to the police as an impostor. Shouting that he will sue for damages enough to support him for the rest of his life, he storms away.

Lulu, Alwa and Schigolch look at each other with expressions of relief. The old man takes his leave, saying he will get the sleeping car tickets and return for Lulu in half an hour. Lulu sits down on the sofa and then her demeanor and her appearance mysteriously undergo a complete transformation. She again becomes the alluring creature of the earlier scenes. In a soaring phrase ("O Freiheit! Herrgott im Himmel!") she exults that she is free at last after two long years of imprisonment. Alwa hands her a drink.

Looking around, she asks what happened to her portrait. Alwa goes to the fireplace and turns the portrait around to face her. He explains that the Countess first thought of hanging it in her home, but then feared that the police might find it as incriminating evidence if they searched the premises. Without the slightest show of concern or regret, Lulu murmurs that now her most ardent admirer is in prison in her place.

Then in a long passage in spoken words Lulu tells Alwa the incredible story of how the Countess sacrificed herself to help her escape from prison. First she volunteered as a nurse in a Hamburg hospital during the cholera epidemic. Purloining the contaminated clothing of a dead victim, she brought the garments to the prison. Both she and Lulu were stricken with cholera and taken to the isolation ward of the prison hospital. As they lay side by side in the same room, the Countess applied makeup so that the two resembled each other. On the day Lulu was discharged from the ward as cured, the Countess put on her prison garb while Lulu donned the Countess' clothes. And now, Lulu comments with cruel amusement, the Countess is in prison as the murderess of Dr. Schön.

Alwa, dumbfounded, asks why she pretended to be desperately ill when she arrived with Schigolch. Simply to get rid of Rodrigo, Lulu answers. With sensual abandon she stretches out her arms and asks Alwa for a kiss. He takes her in his embrace and responds with fierce ardor.

With calculated viciousness, she reminds him that she shot his father. Alwa's answer is to beg her for another kiss.

For a moment he looks into her eyes. With feverish intensity he sings that, but for their innocent look, he would regard her as the cleverest harlot who ever lured a man to his doom. In a high coloratura phrase, Lulu gaily answers that she wishes she were. She asks him to flee across the border with her so that they can see each other as often as they wish ("so oft wir wollen"). The two repeat the words in parallel musical phrases.

Now hopelessly under her spell, Alwa, in the aria entitled "Hymn" ("Durch dieses Kleid"), apostrophizes Lulu's body in voluptuously erotic terms over surging glissandi in the orchestra. As he buries his face in her lap she murmurs malevolently: "Is this the sofa on which your father bled to death?" In passion and despair Alwa screams: "Silence!" The curtain falls to dark, foreboding chords as at the end of Scene Three in the first act.

ACT THREE

Up until the world premiere of the three-act version, Act Three was usually performed in the form of an Epilogue—almost all in mime—to the accompaniment of Berg's symphonic variations. It is in two scenes linked by entr'acte music in the form of four elaborately developed variations of the *Lulu Suite*.

[*Scene One*] The action takes place mainly in the glittering salons of the demimonde in Paris, where Lulu had arrived with Alwa and Schigolch, and was later joined by the Countess Geschwitz. There she becomes enmeshed with an unsavory group of underworld characters. Chief among these is the scoundrelly Marquis Casti-Piani, who not only blackmails Lulu but contrives the financial ruin of Alwa. Lulu is rescued from exposure and arrest through the efforts of the Countess Geschwitz, and then the four make their way to London.

[*Scene Two*] Lulu, now a common streetwalker, lives in wretched poverty in a slum garret. Sharing her existence there are the Countess, Alwa, Schigolch and Rodrigo, who remain loyal to Lulu despite her degradation. The Countess herself treasures her last possession—the portrait of Lulu painted by her artist-husband, Walter Schwarz.

Soon the final catastrophe strikes. Alwa is killed in a quarrel with one of the men solicited by Lulu. Not long after, Lulu is stabbed by Jack the Ripper, the last man to accompany her to her garret. The murder takes place offstage, with Lulu's dying shriek bringing the action to a horrifying climax.

Confronted by the Countess Geschwitz as he makes his escape, Jack the Ripper strikes her down. The tragedy ends with her dying words: "Lulu, my angel, let me see you once again. I am near you, I will stay near you, to eternity."

Completion of the Third Act and its musical reconstruction are credited, respectively, to Dr. George Perle and Friedrich Cerha. Dr. Perle is professor of music at the Queens College of the City University of New York, a Berg specialist and an authority on serial music. Mr. Cerha is an Austrian composer and conductor.

Dr. Perle was permitted by Berg's publisher, Universal Edition, of Vienna, to study the composer's voluminous manuscripts. Mr. Cerha had been working on the Berg scores since 1962.

Why this material had not been published in the intervening years has been explained by the attitude of Berg's widow, Helene. Berg died at the age of fifty on Christmas Eve, 1935. Mrs. Berg asserted that in "conversations" with her dead husband he told her he wanted *Lulu* to remain in its two-act form. Negotiations for the release of the Third Act material presumably were completed following the death of Mrs. Berg on August 30, 1976.

Dr. Perle said Berg had orchestrated about three fifths of the final act, with precise indications. He left a Particell (short score) with sketches and other materials, including a typescript of the Act Three libretto. Dr. Perle characterized this as the final statement of music and text that indicates every note of music, every metronome mark, every word of text and every stage direction.

MACBETH
by GIUSEPPE VERDI
(1813–1901)

Libretto by
FRANCESCO MARIA PIAVE

Based on Shakespeare's play

CHARACTERS

Duncan (Duncano), King of Scotland	Mute
Macbeth (Macbetto) ⎱ generals in	⎰ Baritone
Banquo (Banco) ⎰ King Duncan's army	⎱ Bass
Lady Macbeth	Soprano
Macduff, a Scottish nobleman	Tenor
Malcolm, son of Duncan	Tenor
Fleance, son of Banquo	Mute
Gentlewoman to Lady Macbeth	Mezzo-soprano
A doctor	Bass
Servant to Macbeth	Bass
A herald	Bass
Hecate, goddess of witchcraft	Mute

Witches, messengers of the King, Scottish nobles, peasants, assassins, English soldiers, aerial spirits, apparitions

Place: Scotland and England
Time: About the year 1040
First performance: Teatro Pergola, Florence, Italy, March 14, 1847
Original language: Italian

Of *Macbeth,* his tenth opera, Verdi wrote: "Here is this *Macbeth,* which I love above all my other operas." His affection for this work seems to have been rooted in his love for Shakespeare, which dated from his early years. Verdi himself wrote a prose version of the libretto, which he then gave to Piave to turn into verse to conform to conventional libretto requirements. The first performance in Florence was greeted with restrained enthusiasm—mainly because this opera was in many respects a departure from the conventional form. In *Macbeth,* Verdi was trying his hand at something new: music drama, in which character delineation took precedence over a mere succession of tuneful arias and concerted numbers. But the public soon "caught on"; subsequent performances were wildly acclaimed.

Verdi's abiding fondness for *Macbeth* prompted him to make drastic revisions after it had been in the repertoire almost twenty years. He rewrote most of the third act, revised two important arias, and completely changed the ending of the opera itself. The new version was presented at the Théâtre Lyrique in Paris on April 21, 1865. There it received only fourteen performances. Verdi, keenly disappointed, conceded that it was "a fiasco." Today it is usually performed in its original version, which retains its popular appeal because of its unique power and intensity of expression. *Macbeth* was presented in a Metropolitan Opera Saturday afternoon broadcast on February 3, 1973. It was staged by the Dallas Civic Opera in December 1977.

There is a brief but dramatic prelude mingling the fanfare of trumpets with swift chromatic passages. Also heard is a fragmentary refrain later associated with Lady Macbeth's sleepwalking scene in Act Four.

ACT ONE

[*Scene One*] The curtain rises on a desolate heath, its gloomy expanse visible in flashes of lightning. An eerie theme sounds in the English horns, then a harsh fanfare of brass underscores the wildness of the scene. As lightning flares and thunder crashes, the witches gather. To a staccato accompaniment, the First, Second and Third Witches being their colloquy—"Che faceste? Dite su" ("Where hast thou been, sister?").

One says she has been killing swine. Her companion tells how she came upon a sailor's wife munching chestnuts and asked her for some. The woman told the witch to go to the devil—and for that bit of insolence one sailor's wife will become a widow—her husband will drown at sea. The other witches cackle their approval of this summary punishment as they dance in a circle to the macabre accompaniment.

Suddenly there is a drum roll. The dance becomes wilder as the witches shriek that Macbeth is on his way. In a moment, he and Banquo appear. The two men comment in recitative on the day's fateful events and on the hideous spectacle of the witches ("Giorni non vidi"). Macbeth commands them to speak ("Or via parlate!"). In sonorous, prophetic tones ("Salve, o Macbetto") they hail him as Thane of Glamis and Cawdor, and as King of Scotland. They tell Banquo that he will be the father of future kings. As their voices die away in a sinister whisper, the witches vanish.

A moment later a messenger arrives and tells Macbeth he has been made Thane of Cawdor by the King. (He already had the title of Thane of Glamis.) Macbeth first exults that two prophecies already have been fulfilled, and the third promises him a throne. Yet he wonders why evil thoughts cross his brain. Banquo comments in an aside that even in a moment of triumph the forces of darkness can trap an unwary victim ("Oh, come s'empie costui"). The voices of the two men blend in a brief but fiery duet. They leave, followed by the messenger. The witches return and hail Macbeth and his destiny in another frenzied chorus ("S'allontanarono!").

[*Scene Two*] A hall in Macbeth's castle. After a short introduction of successively rising chromatic phrases (foreshadowing the duet in *Otello*), Lady Macbeth enters. Over a sustained chord, she reads aloud a letter from Macbeth describing the witches prophecy ("Nel dì della vittoria"). She reflects with satisfaction on the ambition which is spurring Macbeth ("Ambizioso spirto tu sei"), then in an ensuing cavatina ("Vieni! t'affretta! Accendere!") she ponders if he will now let scruples stand in his way.

A servant comes in to tell her that King Duncan is coming to the castle this night with Macbeth. Lady Macbeth, realizing that destiny already is at work, repeats with evil gloating: "Duncano sarà qui? Qui la notte?" Then in an aria of savage exultation she calls on the infernal spirits to assist her in plotting murder ("Or tutti sorgete, ministri infernali").

Macbeth enters. With deliberate emphasis, Lady Macbeth greets him as "Cawdor," then exhorts him not to falter in his resolve to kill King Duncan. A strain of martial music announces the arrival of the King and his retinue. Duncan enters with Macduff, Malcolm and Banquo, and all are ceremoniously greeted by Macbeth, his Lady and their court. The assemblage then leaves the hall.

Macbeth returns alone, deep in thought. Calling a servant, he orders him to tell Lady Macbeth to prepare his nightly drink and to ring a bell when it is ready. Suddenly he staggers back with a gasp of terror, then cries out: "Is this a dagger which I see before me?" ("Mi si affaccia un pugnal?"). Here follows the musical version of his famous soliloquy ("A me precorri sul confuso") in which he steels himself to the murder of Duncan and attempts to justify his act to himself.

He tries to convince himself that the dagger is only a figment of his imagination. In fear-stricken tones he implores the "sure and firm-set earth" not to hear his footsteps lest his whereabouts be discovered ("Immobil terra!").

Suddenly a bell rings. Macbeth intones over dark chords in the orchestra: "Non udirlo, Duncano" ("Hear it not, Duncan, for it is a knell/ That summons thee to heaven, or to hell"). He leaves on his murderous errand. Lady Macbeth enters to a foreboding phrase in the orchestra. Haunted by the suspicion that the plot may have gone wrong, she starts in momentary fear as she hears the shriek of an owl—the bird of evil omen. Then Macbeth bursts into the room, a bloody knife in his hand. Shaken with guilt and terror, he cries out: "Tutto è finito!"

This marks the beginning of a long duet. Macbeth, panic-stricken, tells of the murder, describing how the courtiers guarding Duncan prayed in their sleep for his protection. To that prayer, Macbeth groans, he could not say "Amen." Lady Macbeth venomously asks for more details. In growing terror, Macbeth goes on—"Allor questa voce m'intesi nel petto" ("Methought I heard a voice cry, 'Sleep no more!/ Macbeth does murder sleep'").

Lady Macbeth derides him for giving way to remorse. She tells him to take the dagger back into the room and smear the blood on the courtiers as evidence of their guilt ("Il pugnal là riportate"). When Macbeth abjectly refuses to go, she snatches the dagger from his hands and stalks toward the King's room. Macbeth stares at his bloody hands and cries out in horror and despair: "Oh questa mano! non potrebbe l'Oceano queste mani a me lavar!" ("Oh, these hands! Not Ocean's waves could wipe this blood clean!").[1] The sound of knocking within increases his terror. Lady Macbeth returns and chides him contemptuously for his cowardice: "My hands are of your colour . . . A little water clears us of this deed."

When the knocking is repeated, Lady Macbeth tells her husband that they must hurry to their chamber so that they will not be found near the scene of the crime. They leave as the music dies into silence.

Macduff comes in with Banquo, saying he had been ordered by the King to wake him early. Banquo then tells of the strange and terrible things that have happened during the night: "Oh qual orrenda notte!"

This marks the beginning of the powerful ensemble which closes the act. Both men go into the King's room, discover the murder, then rouse the household with their cries of horror. All in the castle are aghast at the news, then express their feelings in the closing chorus, "Schiudi, inferno, la bocca ed inghiotti" ("Open wide thy portals, Hell!").

[1] A paraphrase of Shakespeare: "What hands are here? ha! they pluck out mine eyes!/ Will all great Neptune's ocean wash this blood/ Clean from my hand?"

ACT TWO

[*Scene One*] A room in the castle. In a brief recitative passage, Macbeth and Lady Macbeth discuss the situation confronting them. Macbeth is moody and distraught; his wife sharply asks him why he has been avoiding her ("Perchè mi sfuggi"). The deed is done, she says, and now he is King. Moreover, Duncan's son, Malcolm, fled to England and is being accused of the murder of his own father. Now the throne is left vacant—for Macbeth.

But Macbeth recalls that the witches prophesied that Banquo would be the father of kings ("Banco padre di regi"). A short recitative follows in which Macbeth and Lady Macbeth plot Banquo's murder. Macbeth leaves to accomplish this. Alone, Lady Macbeth sings the dramatic aria "La luce langue," in which she reflects on the evil this night will bring. The darkness will hide yet another murder . . . more blood . . . but so be it. In a ferocious outburst, she exults in her power—"O voluttà del soglio!" This phrase is introduced by a powerful ascending passage in the orchestra. Concluding the aria, Lady Macbeth gloats that he who was destined to be King soon will be dead ("Cadrà fra poco esanime chi fu predetto Re").

[*Scene Two*] A park. Macbeth's castle in the distance. In the foreground, a band of assassins talk among themselves in a sinister chorus ("Chi v'impose unirvi a noi?"). It has a strong resemblance to the "Zitti, zitti" chorus in *Rigoletto*. They reveal that they have been ordered by Macbeth to kill Banquo, who will arrive with his son Fleance. In a staccato passage ("Sparve il sol"), they sing that the sun has set, bringing on the darkness that hides bloody deeds. Now Banquo's hour of doom is near. The voices die to a whisper as the assassins slink away to wait in ambush.

Banquo enters with Fleance, warning him that danger lurks in this gloomy spot. He expresses his foreboding in an impressive aria, "Come dal ciel precipita," which is introduced by a dark, tremulous passage in the strings. The two go into the park. A moment later Banquo's cries are heard as an assassin strikes him down. He shouts to Fleance to save himself. Fleance, pursued by a murderer, dashes across the park as a trumpet passage blares out a theme of doom.

[*Scene Three*] A magnificent banquet room in Macbeth's castle. Gathered there are Macbeth, Lady Macbeth, Macduff and the lords and ladies of the court. The assemblage hails Macbeth and his Lady as King and Queen ("Salve, o Re"). Macbeth toasts Lady Macbeth, who responds with the "Brindisi" ("Si colmi il calice"). She is joined by the chorus.

As Macbeth is lifting his glass with the others, one of the assassins appears at a side door. Macbeth leaves the table and goes over to him. The assassin tells him that Banquo's murder was accomplished, but that his son escaped. Macbeth, shaken by the news, returns to the table. Controlling himself with an effort, he announces that Banquo has not kept his promise to attend the banquet ("Banco falla!"). He himself will sit in the absent guest's place.

But as he goes toward the chair, he sees Banquo's ghost sitting in it. Recoiling in terror, he shouts: "Non dirmi ch'io fossi! le ciocche cruenti non scuotermi incontro" ("Thou canst not say I did it: never shake/ Thy gory locks at me!"). He sings the second phrase in a hushed descending chromatic passage.

Lady Macbeth and the guests stare at him in alarm. In an aside, Lady Macbeth sneers: "Are you a man?" Macbeth cries out: "Yes—and a brave one to face what I see before me." Glaring at the apparition, he raves: "Can sepulchers give back the dead?" ("Il sepolcro può render gli uccisi?"). As it slowly fades from sight, Macbeth becomes calm and calls for a toast to the absent Banquo. Lady Macbeth repeats the "Brindisi," with the chorus joining.

Suddenly the ghost reappears. Macbeth, now on the verge of madness, commands it to leave ("Spirto d'abisso!"), then defiantly shouts that he is not afraid. Swirling chromatics in the strings underscore his terror. Lady Macbeth, in an aside, angrily berates him for his panic. In a passage which begins *sotto voce* then rises to a frenzied outburst, Macbeth sings that the ghost cries for blood, and blood it shall have. Today, the witches will tell him what the future will bring ("Sangue a me quell'ombra chiede"). The guests look on in consternation.

This scene introduces the ensemble which builds into the intensely dramatic finale of the act. Macduff and the lords and ladies voice their horror over Macbeth's frenzied outbursts ("Biechi arcani!"). They sing that an accursed power rules over this land, where now only the guilty can remain. Soon it will become a lair of thieves and assassins. Lady Macbeth rages at her husband for his faintheartedness. Macbeth himself rants that the witches will give him the key to the future. These sentiments blend in the mighty climax of the act.

ACT THREE

A dark cave. In the center a caldron boils. Thunder and lightning.

There is an introductory chorus of incantation sung by the witches ("Tre volte miagola la gatta"). Dancing around the caldron, they sing about the "ingredients" that make up their infernal brew. A ballet follows in which they invoke Hecate, goddess of witchcraft. In pantomime, she tells them that Macbeth is approaching, then instructs them in the manner in which his doom is to be brought about.[2]

Following the ballet (or, in the original version, after the Incantation Scene), Macbeth enters with his soldiers. Ordering them to wait, he enters the cavern and commands the witches to tell him what his fate is to be ("Ch'io sappia il mio destin"). Then follows the Apparition Scene. Over dark, brooding chords in the orchestra, the witches unfold Macbeth's future.

First they ask him if he wishes to hear the prophecies from "the unknown powers" ("Dalle incognite posse") or from themselves. Invoke the powers—if they have the answers, Macbeth commands. Thereupon a helmeted head emerges from the ground. It warns Macbeth to beware of Macduff ("Da Macduffo ti guarda prudente").

Next a bloody child arises. It tells Macbeth that none born of women can harm him ("Nessun nato di donna ti nuoce").

Finally there is the apparition of a crowned child, holding the branch of a tree in his hand. It tells Macbeth that he never will be vanquished until the day he sees the Birnam Wood marching against him ("Fin che il bosco di Birnam vedrai ravviarsi e venir contro te!").[3]

Macbeth exults over these auguries of his triumph ("Oh! lieto augurio!"), then asks the witches if Banquo's sons ever will seize his throne. They warn him not to ask. Fiercely Macbeth demands an answer, threateningly brandishing his sword. Instantly the caldron sinks into the ground and then Macbeth hears the wailing of bagpipes. As he stares in surprise, a procession of eight kings marches across the stage. The eighth is Banquo, who is carrying a mirror.

In a frenzy, Macbeth draws his sword and rushes at the phantoms, commanding them to disappear ("Fuggi, regal fantasma!"). To the accompaniment of an orchestral fanfare, he counts them as they march by. In terror-stricken tones he asks the witches if these phantoms will live. When the witches answer yes, Macbeth faints. The witches, in a striking phrase sung on a single note, invoke the spirits of the air to revive the King ("Aerei spirti").[4]

The witches then disappear as Macbeth staggers to his feet. Lady Macbeth enters. In the ensuing dialogue Macbeth tells her of his talk with the witches, of the three apparitions and their prophecies, and of the vision of Banquo's sons, who are destined to become the future

[2] The ballet was written for the Paris version of the opera, presented at the Théâtre Lyrique in 1865. Verdi had revised the opera in 1864.

[3] In Shakespeare: ". . . until/ Great Birnam wood to high Dunsinane hill/ Shall come against him."

[4] In the Paris version, a chorus of spirits ("Ondine e silfidi") and a ballet follow.

kings of Scotland. Lady Macbeth curses them. She and Macbeth together vow that Macduff's wife and babies will perish in the flames of the castle of Fife, and that Banquo's son Fleance will be tracked down and killed. The duet comes to a climax in a trenchant passage that begins in tones of suppressed fury and swells to a furious cry for vengeance ("Ora di morte omai").

ACT FOUR

[*Scene One*] A desolate region on the border between England and Scotland. In the distance the forest of Birnam. A group of Scottish refugees sings a chorus of lamentation over the oppression of their country by the tyrant ("Patria oppressa!").

Macduff, standing at one side, crushed by sorrow and despair, mourns his wife and children, murdered by Macbeth ("O figli miei"). In a moving aria ("Ah, la paterna mano") he grieves because he was not with his loved ones to protect them from their slayer, then vows revenge for this foul deed.

To a flourish of drums and a fanfare of trumpets, Malcolm enters at the head of a company of English soldiers. When he learns from his men that they are in the forest of Birnam, he orders that each soldier is to cut a branch and carry it with him ("Svelga ognuno e porti un ramo"). Malcolm and Macduff, drawing their swords, then take their places at the head of the company. In a rousing chorus ("La patria tradita") they sing that they will free their country from the chains of the oppressor.

[*Scene Two*] A room in Macbeth's castle. It is night. There is a long orchestral interlude which establishes the eerie mood of the Sleepwalking Scene. A doctor and a gentlewoman are in the room. In a brief recitative, they disclose that Lady Macbeth has been walking in her sleep, and they have waited for two nights to watch her. Tonight, says the gentlewoman, she will certainly appear.

As she speaks, Lady Macbeth enters carrying a candle. She sets the candle down, rubs her hands as though washing them, then begins the great aria "Una macchia è qui tuttora . . . via, ti dico, o maledetta!"— "There is still a spot here . . . out, damned spot . . . out, I say!" At the beginning of the aria there is a rising figure in the orchestra which keeps repeating like an accusing voice, while through the shuddering accompaniment comes the moaning of the English horn. In the interpretation of Lady Macbeth's tormenting thoughts, the aria ranges from a low C flat to a high D flat, encompassing more than two octaves.

The doctor and the gentlewoman stand transfixed with horror as Lady Macbeth recalls, one by one, the murders which have stained her hands. All the perfumes of Arabia, she murmurs in her dreadful night-mare, will not wash away the smell of human blood. As she ends the aria on a high pianissimo phrase, "Andiam, Macbetto" (she imagines she hears someone knocking), the doctor and the gentlewoman intone a prayer.

[*Scene Three*] A hall in the castle. Macbeth enters raging against the thanes who have united with England against him ("Perfidi! All' Anglo contro me v'unite!"). Defiantly he recalls the prophecy that "none born of woman" can harm him. Suddenly he is overwhelmed by hopelessness and despair. In the aria, "Pietà, rispetto, amore," he sings that honor, respect and love—the comforts of a man's later years—will be denied him. His only epitaph will be curses.[5]

A gentlewoman enters and informs Macbeth that Lady Macbeth is dead. Too numbed by tragedy to grieve, Macbeth cries out in bitter scorn: "La vita! che importa? È il racconto d'un povero idiota! Vento e suono che nulla dinota!"—"What is life? It is a tale/ Told by an idiot, full of sound and fury,/ Signifying nothing!"[6]

Macbeth's soldiers rush in shouting that "Birnam Wood" is approaching. Realizing that the prophecy has come true, he curses the witches for betraying him. Calling for his sword and shield, he exhorts his soldiers to fight. They respond in a brief but stormy chorus, "Dunque all' armi!"

The scene quickly shifts to a plain, where English soldiers, each carrying a branch, are slowly advancing. Malcolm and Macduff appear. Macduff orders the warriors to discard their branches, unsheathe their swords and follow him into battle. All rush off.

After a short orchestral interlude, Macbeth dashes in pursued by Macduff, who cries that at last he has tracked down the murderer of his wife and children. Turning on him, Macbeth dares Macduff to kill him, shouting that no man born of woman can harm him—"nato di donna ucidermi non può." Roaring that he was not born, but "was from his mother's womb untimely ripp'd" ("Nato non sono: strappato fui dal sen materno"), Macduff plunges his sword into Macbeth's body.

As Macbeth falls, a group of women and children rush in, stare in horror at the dying man, then break out into lamentation over this day

---

[5] From Shakespeare: "My way of life is fallen into the sear, the yellow leaf;/ And that which should accompany old age,/ As honour, love, obedience, troops of friends,/ I must not look to have; but, in their stead,/ Curses, not loud but deep . . ."

[6] In Shakespeare, this is the conclusion of Macbeth's famous soliloquy on hearing of Lady Macbeth's death. It begins: "She should have died hereafter;/ There would have been a time for such a word./ To-morrow, and to-morrow, and to-morrow,/ Creeps in this petty pace from day to day . . ."

of bloodshed ("Infausto giorno!"). Raising himself, Macbeth begins his final aria, "Mal per me che m'affidai." In an evil moment, he sings, he put his trust in witches' prophecies—and now they have destroyed him. As his life ebbs away, he gasps that he dies "at war with earth and heaven" ("muoio . . . al cielo . . . al mondo in ira").[7]

There is a triumphant shout offstage, then Malcolm and Macduff enter with their soldiers, who drag in Macbeth's followers as prisoners. Other soldiers, thanes and the populace crowd in. Kneeling before Malcolm, Macduff says he slew Macbeth, then hails Malcolm as King ("Salve, o Re!"). All onstage repeat the acclamation, then join in the chorus which brings the opera to its fiery climax. The curtain falls.

[7] This aria's curious history was once described by Carl Ebert, manager of the Städtische Oper in West Berlin, in an interview with Harold C. Schonberg of the New York *Times*. In staging the opera in 1931, Mr. Ebert said, he was convinced that Verdi, with his infallible sense of theater, would have written a final aria for Macbeth, rather than have him die offstage—as in the Paris version. Mr. Ebert undertook a search and eventually found the missing aria at Sant' Agata, Verdi's home.

MARIA STUARDA
by GAETANO DONIZETTI
(1797–1848)

Libretto by
GIUSEPPE BARDARI

Based on the play *Maria Stuart,* by Johann Christoph Friedrich von Schiller

CHARACTERS

Elisabetta (Elizabeth), Queen of England	Soprano
Maria Stuarda (Mary Stuart), Queen of Scots	Mezzo-soprano
Anna (Anne Kennedy)	Soprano
Robert, Earl of Leicester, favorite of Queen Elizabeth	Tenor
Talbot, lay priest of the Church of England	Baritone
Lord Cecil, adviser to Queen Elizabeth	Bass-baritone

Courtiers, people of the court, soldiers, guards

Place: England—Westminster Palace and Fotheringay Castle
Time: 1587
First performance: La Scala, Milan, December 30, 1835
Original language: Italian

Maria Stuarda, Donizetti's thirty-third opera, has a bizarre history. The first rehearsals for the premiere originally scheduled for October 1834 at the Teatro San Carlo, Naples, were thrown into an uproar when the two *prime donne* playing the leading roles suddenly flew at each other in a no-holds-barred battle. Later at the dress rehearsal before an invited audience, Queen Maria Christina of the Two Sicilies was so horrified by the scene of Maria Stuarda's condemnation that she fainted. Further performances promptly were forbidden by the censors.

To salvage his opera, Donizetti adapted the music to another libretto, entitled *Buondelmonte,* with the locale of the plot in twelfth-century Florence. In that form it was premiered on October 18, 1834—with the same two warring sopranos. It was a failure.

At the 1835 premiere of the opera in its original form, the renowned soprano Maria Malibran created the title role. Although ill and in poor voice, she insisted on singing, with the result that the opera was unfavorably received. To make matters worse, there was more badgering by the censors, who objected to Maria Stuarda calling Elisabetta a "bastard."

Withdrawn after seven performances, the opera was given elsewhere in Italy. Thirty years later, in 1865, it reappeared at the Teatro San Carlo. The next recorded revival was at Bergamo (Donizetti's birthplace) in 1958. The first American performance (1964) was given in concert form by the Little Orchestra Society in New York under the direction of Thomas Scherman. Another concert presentation was given on December 6, 1967, at Carnegie Hall by the American Opera Society under the baton of Allen Sven Oxenburg. During the 1968 to 1973 seasons it was staged in Europe, London, San Francisco (1971) and New York (New York City Opera, 1972).

In the context of history, *Maria Stuarda* is a sequel to *Anna Bolena.* It involves the lethal feud between Elizabeth, the daughter of Henry VIII by Anne Boleyn, and Mary Stuart, ex-Queen of France and Queen of Scotland. The situation at the opening of the opera is that Mary has been imprisoned at Fotheringay Castle by her jealous older cousin on charges of treason. Mary defies Elizabeth at the cost of her life.

ACT ONE

Westminster Palace, where courtiers and people of the court are awaiting the arrival of Elisabetta. After a brief orchestral prelude on a plaintive theme, they express their mood of excited anticipation in the chorus "Qui s'attenda." The Queen appears, and an ensemble ensues during which she discloses her thoughts on the possibility of linking the thrones of England and France by marrying the King of France.

But in the recitative and cavatina which follow, Elisabetta hints that she is in love with someone else. She then discusses the fate of Maria Stuarda with Talbot and Lord Cecil. The lay priest entreats her to show mercy to her rival, while the crafty Lord Cecil, by innuendo, portrays Mary as a dangerous conspirator who must be eliminated.

When they have left, Leicester enters. Elisabetta informs him that he is to be her ambassador to France. She is obviously annoyed when he accepts the post with casual courtesy, but she betrays by look and gesture that her secret love is Leicester himself.

A scene now follows between Talbot and Leicester. The priest gives Leicester a letter from Maria in which she begs the Earl to use his influence to arrange a meeting between her and Elisabetta. Leicester, burning with love for Maria, vows he will risk life itself to save her;

Talbot warns him that any such rash action would bring Elisabetta's jealous wrath down upon his head. The thoughts of the two men are expressed in the recitative "Questa imago, questo foglio" and the cavatina "Si fida tanto."

In an audience with the Queen, Leicester shows her the letter from Maria. Elisabetta regards it as conclusive proof that the Queen of Scots is determined not only to usurp her throne but her secret lover as well. At the same time—seeing her chance to humiliate Maria further—Elisabetta agrees to their meeting. Leicester's impassioned pleas in behalf of her rival infuriate the Queen, but she controls herself. The dialogue begins with Leicester's refrain, "Era d'amor l'immagine," which is followed by the duet "Sul crin la rivale la man mi stendea." This number closes the act.

ACT TWO

In the park at Fotheringay, Maria and her companion Anna are enjoying a moment of freedom from confinement in the castle. As they revel in the beauty of the woods, Maria recalls the smiling landscape of her native France in the cavatina "Oh nube, che lieve per l'aria."

A chorus in the distance is heard announcing the arrival of Elisabetta with her hunting party. It has a certain foreboding quality which heightens Maria's dread of the meeting with her hated rival. Leicester appears and tells her that the Queen arranged the hunting party simply as an excuse to come to Fotheringay to see her. In the ensuing duet, "Da tutti abbandonata," Leicester counsels Maria to be respectful to Elisabetta. He adds, however, that he will have his own revenge if she refuses to show mercy. Overwhelmed by Maria's comeliness and bravery, Leicester impulsively asks her to marry him. Though profoundly moved, she gently evades a direct answer. The Earl leaves to meet Elisabetta.

The Queen arrives with Cecil and her entourage. Maria, escorted by Talbot, greets her with formal respect, and then follows the great sextet, "E sempre la stessa superba," sung by Elisabetta, Maria, Anna, Leicester, Cecil and Talbot.

At its conclusion there follows the famous "Dialogue of the Two Queens." Forcing herself into an attitude of submissiveness, Maria kneels before Elisabetta and asks forgiveness. But the Queen harshly accuses her of having violated her marriage vows and further charges her with complicity in the murder of her second husband, Henry Darnley.

Goaded to fury, Maria denounces Elisabetta as a despicable creature driven by lust and ambition and calls her the bastard of Anna Bolena ("figlia impura di Bolena"). The epithet, of course, seals Maria's doom.

ACT THREE

[*Scene One*] Westminster Palace as in Act One. Elisabetta is seated at a table facing Cecil, with Maria's death warrant before her. A dramatic duet ensues, beginning with the Queen's brilliant, florid arietta, "Quella vita a me funesta." Here she makes her decision to sign the death warrant—and also determines to revenge herself on Leicester by ordering him to witness Maria's execution.

Leicester enters, and the scene continues in a powerful trio, "Deh! per pietà suspendi." While the Earl begs Elisabetta to spare Maria's life, Cecil remorselessly demands her death. Enraged by Leicester's show of compassion for her rival, the Queen storms: "Go, worthless one—prepare the tomb for your beloved" ("Vanno indegno, prepara la tomba"). This scene marks the dramatic and musical climax of the role of Elisabetta.

[*Scene Two*] Maria's apartment in Fotheringay Castle. In the aria "Che vuoi?" she expresses her longing for Leicester. Cecil enters with Talbot and hands her the death warrant. When he asks if she wishes a minister of the Church of England to accompany her to the scaffold, Maria contemptuously dismisses him, declaring she will be true to her Catholic faith.

Alone with Maria, Talbot discloses that he is secretly a Catholic priest and can give her absolution. The poignant "Duet of Confession" follows ("Delle mi colpe lo squallido fantasma"). Half mad with fear of approaching doom, Maria imagines she sees the ghost of her murdered husband. She tells Talbot that Darnley died because Elisabetta was jealous of his love for her. As the duet continues, Maria touchingly thanks Talbot for his words of spiritual comfort ("Quando di luce rosea"). She listens with bowed head as he intones the words of absolution ("Lascia contenta al carcere").

Cecil reappears to inform her that Elisabetta will grant her a final request. Resigned and serene, Maria asks that her faithful Anna be permitted to accompany her to the scaffold.

[*Scene Three*] An anteroom off the execution chamber. Here, in a turbulent chorus ("Vedeste? vedemmo"), a crowd of Stuart supporters rages helplessly over the impending execution of their Queen. Anna enters and asks them to lower their voices lest they disturb the Queen in her final moments.

Suddenly Maria appears. She is dressed in royal black and is wearing her crown. With resolute calm she tells the courtiers that she is happy to return to God's embrace. As they gaze at her in awed silence,

Leicester bursts in and forces his way to her side. In a transport of religious ecstasy, Maria now sings the eloquent "Hymn of Death" ("Deh! Tu di un'umile preghiera").

During this scene two cannon shots have sounded to herald the approaching execution. The third shot booms out, signaling the moment of doom. Taking Leicester's arm, Maria sings her farewell in a refrain inspired by love and courage ("Ah, se un giorno da queste ritorte"). Then, with Anna and Leicester on either side, she walks with firm steps to the scaffold.

THE MOTHER OF US ALL
by VIRGIL THOMSON
(1896–   )

Libretto by GERTRUDE STEIN
Scenario by MAURICE GROSSER

Based on the life and career of Susan B. Anthony (1820–1906), women's rights activist

CHARACTERS

Susan B. Anthony	Dramatic soprano
Anne, her confidante and friend	Contralto
Gertrude S.	Soprano
Virgil T.	Baritone
Daniel Webster (1782–1852), Massachusetts senator	Bass
Andrew Johnson (1808–85), 17th U.S. President	Tenor
Thaddeus Stevens (1792–1868), anti-slavery legislator	Tenor
Jo the Loiterer	Tenor
Chris the Citizen	Baritone
Indiana Elliot	Contralto
Angel More, part angel, part ghost	Light lyric soprano
Henrietta M., a feminist of 1890	Soprano
Henry B., a poetic gentleman of the 1870s	Bass-baritone
Anthony Comstock (1844–1915), reformer and censorship leader	Bass
John Quincy Adams (1767–1848), 6th U.S. President	Tenor
Constance Fletcher (1858–1938), American novelist/playwright	High mezzo-soprano
Gloster Heming ⎱ intellectuals of 1890/1900	⎰ Baritone
Isabel Wentworth ⎰	⎱ Mezzo-soprano
Anna Hope, feminist of 1900	Contralto
Lillian Russell (1861–1922), singer/actress	Lyric soprano
Jenny Reefer, feminist friend of Susan B. and Anne	Mezzo-soprano
Ulysses S. Grant (1822–85), 18th U.S. President	Bass-baritone
Herman Atlan, a French painter of 1860	High baritone
Donald Gallup, a young college professor	Baritone
Indiana Elliot's brother, a farmer of the 1870s	Bass-baritone
Negro man and Negro woman	Spoken

"A.A. and T.T.," page boys or postilions; townspeople

Place: The United States
Time: Nineteenth century
First performance: Brander Matthews Hall, Columbia University, New York, May 7, 1947
Original language: English

The Mother of Us All (1947), as well as *Four Saints in Three Acts* (1934), established Virgil Thomson as one of the foremost composers of American opera. In both, Thomson disavowed conventional forms—not so much in his music, which for the most part is melodious and warm—as in the librettos. Devised by the American expatriate writer Gertrude Stein, they are abstract poetry set to music.

They represent—as Patrick J. Smith comments in *The Tenth Muse*[1]— the final and complete liberation of the word as a *meaning symbol,* freeing it to become primarily a sound or collection of sounds. *Four Saints in Three Acts* is a landmark in this emancipation. In the style of *dramma per musica* (drama through music, as exemplified by the great operatic reformer Gluck, for example), music and text become an amalgam of mood, emotion and thought.

Reducing words to sounds involves a new approach to the libretto form. At first hearing, the word sequence of the opera's text is virtually incomprehensible, unrelated. But the very repetition induces a hypnotic flow, and phrases imperceptibly take on a logical meaning (*Susan B.: Rich, to be rich, is to be so rich that when they are rich they have it to be that they do not listen and when they do they do not hear, and to be poor, to be poor, is to be so poor they listen and listen what they hear well what do they hear, they hear that they listen. . . .*).

In contrast to *Four Saints,* this opera is less abstract, with more narrative quality and even a semblance of plot. Stein turned to a more conventional idiom. An intriguing element in the libretto is the concept of timelessness. People of different periods in American history appear to be living at the same time: for example, John Quincy Adams, who died in 1848, makes love to Constance Fletcher, born in 1858; General Grant talks about his "comrade-in-arms" of a hundred years later, General Eisenhower.

Such deliberate anachronisms dramatize the timeless nature of this pageantry of post-Reconstruction life in America. Other characters, real or imaginary, contribute to this effect.

[1] *The Tenth Muse—A Historical Study of the Opera Libretto.* New York, Alfred A. Knopf, 1970.

It was the nineteenth-century era that Thomson suggested to Stein as a subject for a libretto when they met in Paris in October 1945. She chose Susan B. Anthony as the focus of action and experience that would reflect the life of that period. *The Mother of Us All* represents the last collaborative effort of Thomson and Stein. Subsequent to its premiere in 1947 (ten months after Stein's death) it has been given more than one thousand times in more than two hundred productions.

There is no overture. The curtain goes up to the accompaniment of a drum roll and five crashing staccato chords.

ACT ONE

[*Scene One—Prologue*] A room in Susan B. Anthony's house. She and Anne are seated at a table; Anne is knitting, Susan is pasting clippings in a scrapbook. Gertrude S. and Virgil T., as narrators, are standing near the proscenium, right and left. They speak directly to the audience; as Susan and Anne converse, the narrators interject their comments.

Susan holds forth rather peevishly on the subject of men: among other things, she remarks, they are conservative, dull and gullible—but when Susan B. Anthony talks to them, they listen. Gertrude and Virgil observe with cynical amusement that it is easy to be right when everybody else is wrong.

[*Scene Two*] A political meeting. On a platform, chairs and a table with a vase of flowers. To an accompaniment in a brisk martial tempo, Virgil harangues the crowd about the plight of the "poor persecutor"— who always ends up by being persecuted. He is interrupted by the entrance of a noisy political parade. T.T. and A.A., carrying placards reading "VOTE," are followed by Daniel Webster, John Adams, Andrew Johnson, Thaddeus Stevens and Anthony Comstock. Trailing along are Jo the Loiterer and Chris the Citizen.

Over a dirge-like theme in the orchestra, Daniel Webster—without breaking stride—declaims about evidence offered in a case he once won in court ("he digged a pit"). As he marches out, Gertrude and the crowd sing a mocking jingle to the tune of "London Bridge Is Falling Down," about Daniel with a beard. Webster re-enters a moment later and mounts the platform along with Susan, Anne, Constance Fletcher and several politicians. In a simple, hymn-like tune, Susan introduces herself. There is a byplay between Jo the Loiterer and Chris the Citizen. Jo tells Chris about his non-existent wife ("I want to tell"). After considerable rambling nonsense about a domestic quarrel over a tree in their garden, the two leave, their arms about each other.

Angel More flutters in to an appropriately harp-like accompaniment. She is the ghost of Daniel Webster's former sweetheart; tiny wings sprout from her shoulders. To anyone who will listen, she sings that she "is not a martyr any more."[2] Those on the platform begin squabbling among themselves; Constance Fletcher finally persuades them to leave the platform and take seats among the spectators, who now include Lillian Russell and Ulysses S. Grant. Grant declaims about a comrade-in-arms of a hundred years later: General Dwight D. Eisenhower; Jo the Loiterer amuses himself by teasing Angel More about a mouse. The restless crowd is finally quieted when Susan and Webster, now alone on the platform, rise to begin their debate.

Susan begins serenely with a reminder that she is not "old." Webster replies with pompous aphorisms. Actually, the ensuing debate consists of quotations from the writings and speeches of the two, without logical continuity. They argue, for example, about the question of a canal in Ohio and the sovereignty of the state of Massachusetts. The debate finally builds up to a melodramatic climax, with the two shouting at each other. In a delightful anticlimax, the irrepressible Jo still twits Angel More about the mouse.

[*Scene Three*] An orchestral interlude—aptly titled "Cold Weather" —bridges the change of mood from the previous scene. A village square in front of Susan B.'s house. At one side, the front porch. In the square are benches and tables. Townspeople are walking about. Henrietta M. exchanges a few words about the cold weather with Andrew Johnson, who then joins Thaddeus Stevens, Anthony Comstock and Ulysses S. Grant as they enter. As usual, they are arguing vociferously.

Constance Fletcher, coming out of Susan's house, tries to mollify the men, and temporarily succeeds. She is approached by John Adams, who forthwith begins to make love to her in lushly romantic terms—"Dear Miss Constance Fletcher, it is a great pleasure that I kneel at your feet" (and so on). Passersby comment mockingly.

Meanwhile, Stevens and Johnson fall to quarreling again. Among those overhearing are Lillian Russell, Herman Atlan, Jenny Reefer, Donald Gallup,[3] and Jo and Chris, all of whom deplore the men's display of temper in pointless arguments. Jenny, humming a waltz tune, begins dancing with Herman Atlan and the crowd follows suit. Finally all dance away, leaving Jo to ask Chris why everybody has forgotten Isabel Wentworth. And apparently everybody has.

[2] This brief refrain echoes a phrase in Walther's "Prize Song" in *Die Meistersinger*.

[3] The name of the Yale University librarian who edited Gertrude Stein's posthumous works.

[*Scene Four*] The same. It is dark. Susan is sitting on her porch. A prelude with discordant harmonies reflects her meditative but troubled mood. She lapses into a daydream: "I do not know whether I am asleep or awake. . . ." As her dream materializes, a Negro man and a Negro woman approach and speak to her. Susan talks to the pair about the right to vote and about women suffrage. They listen attentively but are bewildered by the vigorous expression of her convictions in an eloquent refrain—"If I believe." Next in the dream comes Donald Gallup, who admits he can be of little help to her. In the third dream, Johnson, Stevens and Webster enter and bombastically proclaim, in a parody of Gilbert-and-Sullivan patter: "We are the chorus of the V.I.P." Nothing matters to them except their own self-importance.

Looking at them contemptuously, Susan majestically reiterates her determination to fight for truth and right. Ignoring her, the three men continue their fatuous self-glorification in a trio—"When they all listen to me." As they stalk away, Jo and Chris enter and decide to ask Susan to explain the difference between rich and poor—no use asking the V.I.P.'s, Jo remarks.

The difference, Susan tells them in a simple but expressive refrain, is that the rich are so rich that they need not listen; the poor are so poor that they must. As for herself, she adds, there is neither wealth nor poverty: all that matters is the ink in her pen.

[*Scene Five*] The same. There is a brief orchestral interlude on a theme based on a revival hymn tune. Susan, still sitting alone, thinks about the impending marriage of Jo and Indiana Elliot, reflecting that even when they marry women are always alone. The wedding party arrives: Indiana and Jo in wedding finery; John Adams and Constance Fletcher; Daniel Webster and Angel More; Jenny Reefer and Anne sit next to Susan and Ulysses S. Grant.

For the benefit of all, Susan expresses her views, pro and con, about marriage—which she approves of in theory. But her listeners are occupied with other problems. Jo and Indiana become engrossed in a minor dilemma about the wedding rings; John Adams resumes courting Constance Fletcher in flowery language. Daniel Webster pontificates, as usual, about his role in performing the ceremony, then sentimentally assures Angel More of his devotion. Angel responds by singing mysteriously about joining the "invisible choir," which leaves Webster perplexed. Ulysses S. Grant startles everybody by pounding his chair on the floor and bellowing for silence. Susan restores quiet by announcing that Jo the Loiterer and Indiana Elliot are now to be joined in a "civil and religious marriage."

At that moment, Indiana Elliot's brother bursts in, shouting that he forbids this marriage. Who knows, he cries, whether Jo the Loiterer is a bigamist, a grandfather or a refugee. Pandemonium erupts. Indiana promptly disavows her brother; Susan, Anne and Jenny express skepticism about the prospects of marriage; Ulysses S. Grant again pounds his chair on the floor, roaring that he cannot tolerate noise, and demands complete silence.

The dialogue continues to the accompaniment of a waltz rhythm to the end of the act. Jo assures Grant that he can be silence personified, while Susan goes into a lengthy explanation of why she has never married. Adams and Webster again express their adoration of Constance Fletcher and Angel More, respectively. When Indiana's brother again bawls his protest to his sister's marriage, the crowd—irritated and bored by the whole proceedings—hustles him out of the square. Finally Daniel Webster raises his hands and pronounces the marriage vows. Susan sings that now Indiana and Jo are married, they will have "the Vote!" A triple-forte brass fanfare underscores the word.

ACT TWO

[*Scene One*] Susan B. Anthony's drawing room. Susan and Anne are busy with their housework, meanwhile talking with Jenny Reefer, who has come to tell Susan that the politicians want her to address their meeting. Susan demurs, saying that, in the end, the politicians will leave her to fight alone. At that moment, Jo enters excitedly, wailing that Indiana refuses to take his name as his wife. He is followed by Indiana herself, who completely ignores him and tells Susan that the men insist on her addressing the meeting.

Thaddeus Stevens and Andrew Johnson, followed by a group of adherents, now come in to add their entreaties. They sententiously remind Susan that her first duty is to "humanity." At first Susan flatly refuses, retorting bitterly that despite all her efforts they would not vote her laws. In a brief chorus ("Do come, Susan B. Anthony"), the visitors plead with her over her steadfast protests. But finally she allows herself to be persuaded, warning them that this time they will have to do more than promise: she will expect honest answers. Thaddeus and the townspeople promise to support her and thank her profusely. All follow her out.

[*Scene Two*] The same. Susan and Anne have returned from the political meeting, and Anne compliments her on the success of her speech. But Susan answers ruefully that although men can be gallant when they choose, they still are afraid: afraid of themselves, afraid of women, afraid of their neighbors, afraid of other countries, afraid of black men. When danger threatens they huddle together like frightened brutes.

Women, Susan goes on, also are afraid—but only for their children's sake. That is the difference between men and women.

And so, because of their fears, the politicians have written the word "male" into the Constitution of the United States. In a brief duet, Susan and Anne vow to fight against this legalistic denial of women suffrage, and to teach women not to be afraid to vote.

Jenny Reefer enters with a group of suffragettes and triumphantly announces that she has converted Lillian Russell to the cause. Lillian herself, exuding charm, enters to the strains of a Viennese waltz. She is followed by a group of admiring men, among whom is John Adams. With his usual mawkish sentimentality, he sings that his beloved Constance Fletcher is much more beautiful than Lillian Russell. Daniel Webster strides in, berates Susan for opposing the word "male" in the Constitution, and over a thumping rhythm, orates meaninglessly that the proud ensign of the republic shall never be polluted.

Jo and Indiana come in. Indiana announces that after all, "Indiana Loiterer" is a rather nice name—but that Jo must change *his* to "Jo Elliot." Jo plaintively sings that he must do as he is told. This wins the approval of the townspeople, who are gathering for a rally. A.A. and T.T. wave "Votes for Women" banners. In an amusing patter chorus which closes the scene ("Susan B. Anthony was very successful") the crowd congratulates Susan on her successful fight for women's rights.

[*Scene Three—Epilogue*] Some years later. At center is a statue of Susan B. Anthony, which is to be dedicated. It is concealed from the audience by an American flag. At one side, a speakers' stand; at the other a refreshment table. First to enter is Anne, guest of honor, who exults that at last women have the vote. Susan B. (invisible) echoes her in a triumphant phrase—"the word 'male' is not there anymore." Dressed in white, she crosses the stage as an unseen ghost. Virgil T. escorts Anne to the speakers' platform and sits down beside her.

One by one, the other characters enter with desultory comments about the ceremony. Henry B., glancing behind the draped flag, wonders if all women are as cold as marble; Angel More (still a wraith) murmurs about "dear Daniel Webster," after bowing to the statue. John Adams regrets that the profile of his beloved Constance Fletcher is not a part of the statuary. Andrew Johnson shuffles in, disconsolate because he has no hope left; Thaddeus Stevens, glowering at the statue, gives vent to futile rage. Daniel Webster, staring into space, passionately begs Angel More to come away with him.

Constance Fletcher, now nearly blind, is led in. John Adams greets her tenderly and kisses her hand. Indiana rushes in and to everyone's annoyance announces that she has a great deal to say about marriage. The voice of the invisible Susan answers placatingly: marriage is indeed a puzzle. Gloster Heming and Isabel Wentworth, two 1890 intellectuals, come in. Heming confesses his high-sounding name is really one he made up; Isabel observes that somebody finally found her after she had been forgotten. Anna Hope declares that, although she is a feminist, she is still a "non-believer."

Lillian Russell wanders in somewhat unsteadily, having sampled the champagne served the guests by A.A. and T.T. Anthony Comstock, shocked by her behavior, glares at her disapprovingly. General Grant, with a sneer at Comstock's self-righteousness, remarks that when a dog barks, one must listen to him.

The general confusion mounts as four young men lurch in pleasantly drunk. Herman Atlan, drunk enough to feel sorry for himself, moans that nobody loves him. Donald Gallup, Jo and Chris, however, make the most of their alcoholic euphoria. Then, in random musical phrases, the assemblage voices the word that symbolizes the triumph of Susan B. Anthony: "The VOTE!"

At that point, Virgil T. unveils the statue. There on the pedestal stands Susan herself in black bonnet and garnet velvet gown. Over a stately accompaniment she sings her valedictory: "We cannot retrace our steps." As she muses in mingled sorrow and triumph over her long life, women lay wreaths at the foot of the statue and quietly leave the scene.

In her final moments, Susan sings exultantly of her martyrdom—"not to what I won, but to what was done." The familiar music of the hymn heard earlier surges up like a majestic chorale. The stage darkens. Standing alone, Susan B. Anthony quietly repeats the phrase: "My long life . . ." The music dies away on a serene major chord. The curtain falls.

MOURNING BECOMES ELECTRA
by MARVIN DAVID LEVY
(1932–   )

Libretto by
HENRY BUTLER

Based on the play by Eugene O'Neill

CHARACTERS

Christine Mannon	Dramatic soprano
Lavinia Mannon, her daughter	Soprano (spinto or dramatic)
Jed, an old servant of the Mannons	Bass
Adam Brant, a sea captain	Dramatic baritone
Peter Niles, Lavinia's suitor	Lyric baritone
Helen Niles, his sister	Lyric soprano
General Ezra Mannon, Christine's husband	Bass-baritone
Orin Mannon, his son	High baritone or tenor

Servants (sopranos), townspeople (altos), townsmen (tenors), soldiers, sailors, dock workers

Place: A small seaport village in New England
Time: Spring and summer of 1865–66
First performance: Metropolitan Opera House, Lincoln Center, New York City, March 17, 1967
Original language: English

Mourning Becomes Electra, by the young Amerian composer Marvin David Levy (his first full-length opera), is an operatic retelling of the *Oresteia* trilogy by the Greek dramatist Aeschylus. The immediate source of the Levy opera is the trilogy by Eugene O'Neill, who himself retold the legend in terms of the doom-haunted lives of a New England family in 1865.

In the play's transition from antiquity to the nineteenth century, Agamemnon becomes Ezra Mannon; Clytemnestra, Christine; Electra, Lavinia; Orestes, Orin; Aegisthus, Adam Brant. But both in the plays and the opera the baleful theme of the legend remains the same: The plight of human beings caught in the remorseless grip of their own destinies.

The opera's three acts bear the titles of the three O'Neill plays—*Homecoming, The Hunted, The Haunted.* Librettist Butler condensed the six-hour trilogy into three hours, omitting certain secondary characters, paraphrasing the dialogue, but retaining the basic dramatic elements.

Although the music is essentially atonal, some of the passages are handled in almost conventional melodic style. In fact, Mr. Levy uses his own concept of the Wagnerian leitmotiv. Certain orchestral and vocal phrases recur—not to identify a character in the Wagnerian sense, but in association with the thought or emotion which impels the action of the moment. An ultramodern touch in the orchestration is the brief use of electronic tape for synthetic background sounds to heighten dramatic effects.

There is no overture. The curtain rises after a short orchestral introduction in which the dominant theme, briefly stated, is the one associated with Christine in fleeting moments of tenderness.

ACT ONE
Homecoming

[*Scene One*] The porch of the Mannon house, with a view between two huge decaying columns on either side. A basket of freshly cut flowers makes a splash of color against the grimness. It is late afternoon in April. Christine, with an air of nervous excitement, stares down the garden path. Over the "frustrated love" theme in the orchestra, she softly calls the name of "Adam."

A moment later Lavinia, returning from the village, rushes up to the porch. She is about to go into the house when Christine stops her. Lavinia breathlessly tells her that her father has returned from the battle front and will be home this evening. Christine seems unconcerned over this news, but then asks anxiously about Orin. He will be home in a day or two, Lavinia tells her; he suffered a head wound in battle but it is not serious.

With rather forced composure Christine informs her daughter that she has invited Captain Adam Brant for the afternoon. There is a gasp of angry surprise from Lavinia. Christine casually adds that she had met Brant by chance while visiting her father in New York, and she thought perhaps his visit here would please Lavinia. The latter asks maliciously if the flowers are in honor of the Captain, then testily reminds her mother that General Mannon also will be home this evening.

Christine spitefully comments on Lavinia's strange look of adoration when she speaks of her father, then observes that a daughter should look elsewhere for love. With vicious emphasis, Lavinia retorts: "As her mother has done!" Christine chokes back her fury as Jed enters to announce that Captain Brant has arrived. Here the dissonant theme of "frustrated love" again sounds in the orchestra. Christine, going to meet Brant, gestures to Lavinia to follow. Ignoring her, Lavinia asks Jed what he knows about Adam Brant. In a melodic but somber refrain, Jed relates that Brant is the offspring of David Mannon, Lavinia's uncle, and a servant girl named Marie Brantone. The curse that destroyed them both lives on, Jed says, and now their son has come back to the house his parents disgraced. Lavinia furiously protests that this sordid story must be a lie.

Jed leaves as Christine returns with Brant. Lavinia greets him with icy politeness—fighting down her secret passionate feelings toward him. For Christine's benefit, Lavinia says to Brant that for a moment she mistook him for her father. Chagrined, Christine goes into the house.

Ignoring Lavinia's brusqueness, Brant affably remarks that he is glad of the chance to see her again—reminding her of their secret tryst "that evening last month." The colloquy continues in half-spoken, half-sung recitative. Lavinia rudely turns aside Brant's friendly overtures. When at last he tries to embrace her, she repulses him violently, cursing him as the spawn of a servant girl. In a towering rage, Brant seizes her, storming that there is no hiding from the truth: David Mannon committed suicide. When his mother brought David's son back to the Mannon house, begging for help for her child, she was hounded to her grave by Ezra Mannon, "the upright judge," who mouthed sanctimonious prayers all the while. And now, Lavinia interjects over a menacing triplet figure in the orchestra, Adam Brant is taking his shameful revenge here in the house of Mannon.

As they stand glaring at each other, Christine rushes in asking what has happened. Lavinia turns on her in wild fury. They will no longer use her, she rages, to mask their clandestine designs, for now she knows. . . . She followed her mother to her tryst with Adam in New York. There, outside the door, she listened to their love-making. With hysterical intensity Lavinia repeats her mother's words as she pleads for Adam's kisses. Brant, shattered by Lavinia's outburst, goes toward her in an effort to calm her, but Christine restrains him with: "No, Adam, no!"[1]

---

[1] Here in the orchestration the composer makes use of one of the fundamental harmonic devices in the opera—a chord of two minor thirds set a diminished octave apart. Its powerful dissonance symbolizes the hatred and misunderstanding which alienate the characters from each other. This device is used throughout the opera.

At Christine's mention of Adam's name there is an abrupt change of mood. With grim candor, Christine declares that she loves Adam Brant. She asks him to leave her alone with Lavinia. Brant complies, and then the two women stand face to face. One of the principal duets in the opera now ensues, in which mother and daughter futilely strive to understand each other. It begins with Lavinia's half-whispered question: "What lie will you ask me to believe?"

Christine speaks despairingly of the wall of hatred between them. That hatred was spawned here in the "tomb of the Mannons," she says, during her life with a husband she could not love. Somewhat moved, Lavinia asks if she always hated Mannon. Over the theme of "dead love" in the orchestra, Christine replies that she loved him once—and tried also to love his daughter. But that daughter was only the pain he inflicted upon her. Lavinia asks: "What of Orin?"

He was born in Mannon's absence, Christine says, when she could forget his cruelty. Her son was hers and hers alone . . . with no one to stand in the way of her love for him. And now this love, Lavinia murmurs desolately, is given to Adam Brant. In a poignant phrase, underscored by a variation of the double minor-third chord, Lavinia sings that she should pity, but she cannot pity what she does not understand. Reiterating these thoughts, the two women bring the duet to a moving climax on a lingering phrase which dies softly away. In this moment Christine and Lavinia seem to have bridged the gulf between them.

With shattering suddenness, the scene again erupts into violence. As Christine turns as if to join Brant, Lavinia warns her that Mannon never will let her go. Christine screams defiantly that he cannot stop her. With equal violence, Lavinia replies that she will help her father thwart her escape. Despite her rage, Christine realizes that Lavinia's real purpose is to eliminate her as a rival for Adam's love. Goaded by this thought, she lunges at her daughter. At that moment Adam rushes in and seizes her by the arm. Spent by her fury, Christine concedes her defeat, murmuring that Lavinia has won . . . Adam will be sent away. She sardonically asks Lavinia if she wishes to be present at their last farewell.

Glaring at her, Lavinia says she is not counting on an easy victory. As she turns to go into the house she snarls a warning that she will be watching—she does not want her father to see Adam Brant here.

Brant, taking the half-fainting Christine in his arms, cries out: "I will not leave you!" Here for the first time is heard the "poison" theme, which foreshadows the murder of Ezra Mannon. It occurs again several measures later when Christine sings that "one does foolish things for love." With fierce intensity, underscored by rising chromatic figures in the orchestra, she goes on to say that she prayed that Ezra Mannon would not come back alive from the war—prayed so hard that she actually believed he never would. But she always has known, she adds darkly, that she must one day free herself.

With a furtive look around, she asks Adam, in spoken recitative, if he has the vial she asked him to buy for her. He hands it to her. Suddenly aware of her terrible resolve, Adam cries out in protest. As the "poison" theme blares again and again in the orchestra, Christine dementedly implores him to help her in her evil plotting. Everyone knows, she argues, that Mannon has a failing heart . . . if he dies they will be above suspicion. Seeing his hesitation, she plays her trump card: It must be Ezra's life or her own. Faced with this ultimatum, Brant promises to do whatever she asks.

A rising chromatic passage erupts in the orchestra, marking the beginning of their impassioned love duet. Clasped in each other's arms, they sing that the love which blossomed out of hate will bind them together forever. They will sail away to the Blessed Isles, where the sound of the surf will obliterate this nightmare of cruelty and fear. The duet rises to a ringing climax, then subsides into softly sung lyrical phrases.

Their moment of happiness is interrupted by the sound of a cannon shot and the blare of martial music in the distance. Christine exclaims this means that Ezra has returned, and tells Adam that he must leave at once. After an embrace, Adam hurries down the garden path. Watching him, Christine sings that now they are bound together in Mannon's death . . . Adam can never leave her. She goes into the house as the martial music and the babble of voices grow louder.

Helen and Peter Niles come bounding in from the garden. Calling gaily for Lavinia, they go into the house to look for her. Jed and the other servants come out to greet the townspeople now crowding on the scene. In a brief choral phrase they hail the return of the illustrious General Mannon. The General, resplendent in his uniform, enters and shakes hands with his well-wishers. The ensemble continues as the townsfolk comment that the great man's "foreign wife" does not come out to greet him, but waits for him in the shadows of this strange house. Their voices drop almost to a whisper as they look around apprehensively, then the chorus builds up again into a rousing tribute to General Ezra Mannon.

After the General acknowledges the plaudits, the crowd gradually disperses. Mannon and Jed talk together. Peter and Helen reappear with Lavinia. The young suitor reminds her that she promised to give him an answer when her father returned. But Lavinia, gazing ardently at Mannon, scarcely notices Peter. As she comes toward her father, Jed tactfully ushers Peter and Helen back into the house. Lavinia suddenly throws herself into Mannon's arms. At that moment he sees Christine at the window above the porch. As she moves away, Mannon frees himself from Lavinia's embrace and hurries into the house. A moment later he is heard calling his wife's name. Lavinia, fuming in jealous rage, stands glaring at the house as the scene fades. There is an orchestral interlude which continues without pause into the next scene. Heard prominently is a variation of the "death" motive, later expressed in Orin's phrase: "How death becomes the Mannons." As the curtain rises we hear the theme of "dead love."

[*Scene Two*] Ezra Mannon's bedroom, where the General lies asleep on a big four-poster. It is night; moonlight shines through the windows. As the "poison" theme sounds in the orchestra, Christine rises from the bed, puts on a dressing gown, then looks intently at her sleeping husband. Sinking into a chair, she begins to weep quietly.

Suddenly Ezra awakens and calls her name, marking the beginning of the long duet which culminates in Mannon's murder. Responding to her husband's call, Christine tells him that her sleep was disturbed by Lavinia's pacing up and down the hall outside all night long, like a sentry. Mannon remarks rather plaintively that at least there is someone who loves him. He raises himself, lights a candle and asks Christine if she can bear to look at him. When she turns away with a grimace he entreats her not to leave him ("Do not go, Christine"). The orchestral harmonies here and in the ensuing refrain are based on the minor-third chord, with its dissonance accentuating the misunderstanding which separates husband and wife. Mannon tells Christine that he thought of her constantly on the battlefield and prayed that he would not die before he saw her again. He admits that he has denied her the love she needed, but implores her to let him live out his "numbered days" with her.

Exhausted by his emotion, he sinks back gasping for breath. Feigning concern, Christine asks if his heart is paining him. Her question rouses Mannon to accusing anger and drives him to the verge of delirium. As Christine vainly tries to quiet him he rants that in this house, which is not his own, "they" are waiting for death to set her free. Losing control under his accusations, Christine rages that after the bitter cruelty he has inflicted on her he can never again lay claim to her love. Mannon, in a spasm of fury, lunges at her. Recoiling, Christine begins to taunt him venomously about her infidelity with Adam Brant—"a Mannon, too." Goaded beyond endurance, Mannon screams a curse, then falls back writhing in pain. Gesturing to the night table, he gasps for his medicine.

Christine picks up the bottle, sets it down again. In a swift movement she goes into her room, which adjoins the bedroom, and returns with the bottle of poison Adam brought her. She pours some of the poison into a glass of water, lifts Mannon's head and literally forces him to drink. This action takes place to the accompaniment of the serpentine harmonies of rising and falling chromatics.

In a paroxysm of agony, Mannon pushes Christine violently away from the bed. She stumbles back against the wall, where she stands transfixed as Ezra screams: "Lavinia!" The "poison" theme sounds clamorously in the orchestra. Lavinia bursts into the room, picks up the bottle of poison on the night table and goes to her father. Mannon clutches her wrists to prevent her from giving him any more of the poison, then points to Christine and gasps: "The medicine! Guilty!" Dazed and uncomprehending, Lavinia takes him in her arms. Seconds later his dead body slips from her grasp. Looking down at him, Lavinia wildly implores him not to leave her.

For a moment there is a terrible silence. Then, in ironic contrast to the horror of the scene, the jaunty music of the town band is heard in the distance. Lavinia looks up at her mother, who is staring at the bottle Lavinia still holds in her hands. She looks at her father, then back to Christine. The dreadful truth dawns upon her. Paralyzed with horror, the two women stare at each other. As the dissonant minor-third chords again blare out in the orchestra, Christine collapses fainting. The curtain falls.

ACT TWO
The Hunted

[*Scene One*] Interior of the Mannon home. The divided set shows the parlor at right; at left is the library-study, where is placed the bier of Ezra Mannon. A brief orchestral introduction begins softly. Christine is in the library receiving the condolences of the townspeople. Meanwhile Orin, in Union Army uniform, with his head bandaged, enters the parlor followed by Lavinia, dressed in deep mourning. Moving restlessly about the room, Orin asks where his mother is. Lavinia, telling him he must wait, watches him apprehensively as he touches Christine's favorite chair and murmurs that he dreamed of her sitting there to welcome him when he returned home. Several townspeople come in, pay their respects, then leave.

In a brief duet, Lavinia and Orin comment on their father's death. Staring at the portraits of the Mannons on the walls, Orin querulously asks why his father should crowd this tomblike house with one more ghost. Lavinia sharply rebukes him. He again asks impatiently for his mother.

With insidious tenderness, reflected in the curving, lyrical line of the music, Lavinia tells Orin that she has need of his strength now . . . he must put his trust in her. Their mother, she goes on, only will weaken his resolve. Orin upbraids her angrily for feuding with Christine. Their colloquy is interrupted by the approach of Christine, Helen and Peter. Orin and his mother rush into each other's arms, and in a brief duet express their happiness over their reunion. Lavinia watches them for a moment in cold anger, then goes into the library and stands at her father's bier. Helen and Peter stand in awkward embarrassment at the entrance to the parlor.

Aware of the situation, Christine becomes the gracious hostess and admonishes Orin to play the gallant to Helen. The tension eases as they exchange greetings and join in a laugh. Christine exclaims that the sound of laughter is strange to this grim old house. She and Orin urge Helen to sing the song they all remember from happier days. To encourage her, Christine begins singing: "Bring my dress of soft silk." Helen then takes up the song about the maiden with flowers in her hair, whose dearest treasure is her lover's golden ring on her finger. As Helen ends the song, Orin impulsively takes her in his arms and begins to waltz. This moment of tenderness is shattered by Lavinia's sudden appearance in the doorway. Glowering at Orin, she calls out that her father is waiting. The others stare at her in stunned surprise. Helen and Peter turn to leave. Christine, controlling herself with an effort, courteously bids them goodbye, and Orin escorts them down the hallway to the door.

Alone for the moment, Christine looks at the frowning portraits of the Mannons and sings defiantly that they cannot destroy her happiness, because her son has come back to her. As though to flout their disapproval, she waltzes about the room. Orin returns and watches her morosely for a moment. She embraces him affectionately, then half-teasingly asks if he is angry with her. In answer, he leads her to a chair, sits at her feet and begins to tell her how much he longed for her during his absence.

This marks the beginning of a lyrical duet. Christine is momentarily disturbed when Orin sings dreamily about finding his mother in the Blessed Isles. She remembers that it was there that Adam Brant had promised to take her after the quarrel with Lavinia. (The two words are sung in a repetition of the rising five-note phrase Adam sang in Act One.) In the continuation of the duet, mother and son reveal their deep affection for each other.

Ironically, the spell of their intimacy is broken by a gesture. When Christine enfolds Orin in her arms, he reaches up and amorously strokes her hair. She shrinks back in a movement of distaste, thinking of Ezra's familiar caress. The discordant minor-third harmonies which dominated her scene with her husband sound in the orchestra.

Nervous and irritated, Christine says that Lavinia, blaming her for Mannon's death, hates her bitterly. When Orin starts to say that Lavinia wrote him, Christine—shrewdly anticipating his next thought—interrupts to say that Captain Brant came only to court Lavinia. She warns Orin never to believe anything Lavinia tells him . . . he must trust only in his mother's love. Orin looks at her ardently, then in sudden fury vows he will kill Brant if he ever comes to the Mannon house again. Christine, aghast at his wild look, exclaims: "So like your father!"

Lavinia appears in the doorway. Orin kisses his mother, then walks submissively out of the room and into the library, where he stands looking down at the bier. Lavinia, ignoring her mother, watches him. In mingled grief and despair, Orin marvels "how death becomes the Mannons." This powerful, brooding phrase constitutes the "death" theme, a dominating leitmotiv of the opera. Orin repeats it in a continuation of the refrain in which he apostrophizes his father. It is his duty, he sings, to pray but not to mourn, because his father taught him that a soldier does not weep.

Blending with Orin's lamentation is the savage undercurrent of conversation between Lavinia and Christine, and thus the scene continues briefly in trio form. Lavinia demands to know why Mannon, on his deathbed, cried: "Guilty!" Again trying to turn aside suspicion, Christine answers that he had forced her to confess her love affair with Brant. Deliberately goading her, Lavinia asks if she also has confessed this to Orin. Christine retaliates by reminding her that Orin has sworn to kill Brant. Realizing she has failed in this skirmish, Lavinia storms out of the room.

She goes into the library, locks the door behind her and confronts Orin. She asks him point-blank if Christine has convinced him that his sister is insane. When Orin answers evasively, Lavinia assures him she is not mad—but what she knows could drive her to madness. Orin implores her to desist. Thereupon Lavinia takes from the bosom of her dress the bottle of poison. As the "poison" theme flares up in the orchestra she cries out that she here and now accuses her mother and her lover of murder.

Orin gasps in horror. Lavinia shouts that the two are guilty beyond doubt because Adam Brant promised Christine that they would be together forever. Here the double minor-third chords and the "poison" theme clash harshly in the orchestra. Orin tries to snatch the bottle out of Lavinia's hand. In the parlor, Christine distractedly calls Adam's name, then begins pounding frantically on the door of the library, begging Orin to let her in.

When Orin starts for the door, Lavinia blocks his path, asking if he will believe his mother's guilt when he sees her in her lover's arms. Then in a swift movement she places the poison bottle on the bier beside the body. Standing so that she hides the view of the bier from the door, she commands Orin to let their mother come in. Christine stumbles into the room, gasping that she is afraid. She cowers before Orin's ferocious glare. At that moment Lavinia moves to one side, exposing the poison. Christine staggers back with a piercing wail of anguish and terror. Lavinia snatches up the bottle, literally drags Orin from the room and slams the door after her.

Christine hurls herself against the door, screaming that the guilt is not Adam's, but hers alone. Frenziedly she prays for punishment . . . she herself will bear God's wrath, but Adam must not die. Sinking to her knees she chants the four words like a litany and continues mouthing them silently as the scene fades. An orchestral interlude bridges to the next scene. Prominent in this interlude is a foreboding four-note motive later associated with Orin's disintegrating mental state.

[*Scene Two*] The foredeck of Adam Brant's clipper ship moored alongside a dock in Boston Harbor. The captain's cabin is at stage level, with the main deck above; the scene is played on these two levels. A gangway connects the main deck with the pier. Harbor sounds, fragments of sea chanties, bells and foghorns are heard over an orchestral accompaniment which is serene and at the same time sinister.

Adam Brant appears, nervously paces the deck and peers apprehensively into the shadows on the dock. His agitation increases to the point where he strikes the gunwale with his fist. Then in a soliloquy ("Too weak to kill the man I hate") he reflects on the change that Christine has wrought in his life. Cursing his weakness and irresolution, he confesses to himself that he will never again follow the sea because this woman's consuming love has destroyed his courage and his pride. As he stares moodily into space, Christine emerges furtively out of the shadows. The "poison" theme rises briefly in the orchestra, symbolizing her haunting guilt. Brant rushes to her side and helps her across the gangway to the deck.

Christine throws herself into Brant's arms, crying: "Hold me, Adam!" This marks the beginning of the duet which later builds into the opera's principal quartet as Lavinia and Orin appear on the scene. Brant leads Christine to his cabin, where he asks her what happened after he left her home. As she begins her story—saying Lavinia heard Mannon accuse her before he died—Lavinia and Orin stealthily approach the cabin skylight on the main deck. There they crouch and listen as Christine goes on with her story. Several times during her recital Orin almost loses control of himself but is restrained by Lavinia.

Unconsciously trying to shift the blame from herself, Christine relates how Lavinia held the bottle of poison in her hand. She suppresses a scream of terror as she recalls the dreadful moment later at the bier. As Brant tries to comfort her she implores him to leave this ship at once. Suddenly realizing what she is asking him to do, she is stricken with remorse. An explosive chromatic figure in the orchestra underscores her reaction. But Brant, in sorrow and resignation, sings that now it is all too late—this ship and the sea have finished with him forever. Christine sobs that she has brought him nothing but misfortune.

To this, Brant replies in musical phrases of simple eloquence that she brings the gift of love. The refrain, with its affirmative theme, introduces the lyrical quartet in which the four principals express their profound emotions of hopeless longing, their hunger for love and their regret over the happiness they have lost forever. Here is one of the few moments of compassion and understanding in the entire opera. The duet rises to a poignant climax on a powerful minor chord.

For a brief interval there is a deep silence. Then Brant quietly assures Christine that somehow they will find a way to be together. He leads her to the deck. Lavinia and Orin withdraw into the shadows and hide. On the pier, Christine and Brant stand for a moment in each other's arms, murmuring: "We will not say goodbye." Then Brant watches as Christine hurries away.

Lavinia and Orin reappear on deck and quickly go down into the cabin, where they look around carefully. At the sound of Brant's returning footsteps Orin slips behind the door and draws a knife from his belt. Lavinia stands waiting. There is a succession of hammering discords in the orchestra. Brant enters, looks at Lavinia in stunned disbelief. Orin leaps forward and plunges his knife into Adam's body. With an expression of utter bewilderment on his face, Adam stretches his arms toward Lavinia, then crashes forward across the table and rolls to the floor. Lavinia looks down at him and shudders violently. Orin, as though in a trance, kneels beside the body. He wonders aloud if it is Adam Brant or he himself who has died on this night.

Lavinia harshly orders him to carry out the rest of their plan: This must be made to seem the work of marauders . . . a killing during a robbery. She sends him into the other room to break the locks on the cabin door to indicate a forced entry. To the accompaniment of clashing dissonances in the brass, Lavinia, overwhelmed by anguish and remorse, falls to her knees beside Brant's body. A variation of the theme of "frustrated love" wells up in the orchestra.

Orin re-enters and looks at her in astonishment. Noticing him, Lavinia rises abruptly and sacrilegiously prays that the soul of Adam Brant may repose in peace. With a look of revulsion, Orin turns and strides out of the cabin. About to follow, Lavinia looks down at Adam's body and snarls: "and burn in hell!" A brass fanfare in the orchestra underscores her imprecation.

As the cabin fades into the gloom, Lavinia and Orin make their way to the pier and vanish. The entire scene fades, with the music continuing in a somber, meditative mood. This changes abruptly into a nervous, agitated figure which builds into a violent climax just before the rise of the curtain on the next scene.

[*Scene Three*] The exterior of the Mannon home, with all the windows shuttered. It is dawn of the day after Adam's murder. Christine, in a frenzy of excitement, paces back and forth. Finally, exhausted by her emotions, she leans against one of the pillars and in a dramatic soliloquy ("Nothing . . . why am I so afraid?") gives way to her tormenting thoughts. The fear that stabs at her heart will not let her sleep, she sings, and she will never sleep until Adam comes to her. She tries to silence the imagined voices of the "Mannon dead," who are haunting her with their demand for vengeance. Defiantly she sings that she will not let them drag her to the grave to lie beside them there.

As she gasps for breath after her outburst, Lavinia and Orin come up the drive. Orin makes a wild lunge toward his mother but Lavinia manages to hold him back. He then tells Christine that they followed her last night and saw her with her lover. Covering her ears, she tries to run into the house. Orin catches her by the wrists, forces her arms apart and hurls the words into her face: "Brant is dead. My knife is in his heart!" The "poison-guilt" motive storms in the orchestra.

With a high-pitched moan of agony, Christine sinks to the ground where she lies shaken by sobs. Orin, suddenly stricken by her grief, kneels beside her and begs her not to weep. Lavinia coldly orders him into the house. Christine's moaning rises and falls softly in long-drawn phrases. About to go inside, Orin pauses. Now that Father is not here to punish, he murmurs eerily, perhaps they can open the shutters and let in the sunlight.

Lavinia looks down at Christine, whose face is an expressionless mask. "The deed had to be done," she says gently but sternly, "and now Father can rest." She tries to help Christine to her feet. At her touch, Christine's reason seems suddenly to give way completely, and she bursts into insane ranting—"Time to sleep! Blot out the stars!" This marks the beginning of her long aria, one of the most dramatic in the opera. God will not leave them alone, she cries. He sits in the dark shadow of death and destroys them with the fatal power of love. Lost in her madness, Christine imagines she sees Adam and stretches her arms toward the vision. She repeats the tender phrase he sang to her aboard his ship—"You bring the gift of love." As she begs for a "morningless and never-waking sleep," her voice rises in frenzied exultation, then sinks to a dying whisper.

Lavinia, who has been watching her mother in growing horror, makes a desperate effort to bring her back to her senses. As Christine stumbles up the steps to the door, Lavinia cries out: "Mother! You can live!" Christine in maniacal fury shrieks: "Live?" She bursts into demoniac laughter. With that she raises her hands in front of her face as though to blot out forever the sight of her daughter's hated face, then turns and staggers into the house.

Lavinia makes an involuntary move toward the door, but turns around and stands motionless. From the orchestra comes the menacing thunder of bass drums, mingled with the skeletal rattle of a xylophone and the snarling riffle of snare drums. Through the clamor comes the sound of a pistol shot. Lavinia recoils with a shuddering scream of "Justice!" From the study comes Orin's cry of horror as he finds Christine's body. He staggers out of the house and falls on his knees beside Lavinia, sobbing that he drove his mother to her death. Drawing him close in a comforting gesture, Lavinia assures her brother that she loves him and will help him forget. Orin gets up, stumbles up the steps and, still weeping bitterly, stands leaning against one of the columns.

There is general confusion as Jed, followed by servants and field workers, rushes in exclaiming that they heard a shot. Lavinia, cold and impassive, orders Jed to go for the doctor. He is to say, she goes on with menacing emphasis, that Christine Mannon killed herself in grief over her husband's death. Jed, with a grim nod of understanding, leaves. The servants and workers stare at Lavinia uncomprehendingly as the curtain falls.

ACT THREE
The Haunted

[*Scene One*] The interior of the Mannon house, as in Act Two, Scene One. A summer evening a year after the events of Act Two. The covered furniture and draped portraits give the rooms a look of emptiness and desertion.

After a brief orchestral passage, Jed enters the library and unveils the portrait of Ezra Mannon. In the parlor, a servant turns up the lights as Helen and Peter come in. Jed, in a brief refrain, wonders if the returning Mannons will preside over this house or if its sorrow still will be master. His voice blends with Helen's and Peter's as they sing the waltz theme of the song Helen sang at Christine's request on their previous visit. Peter teases Helen about being a future bride. They laugh gaily and begin waltzing together. When Jed comes in from the study Helen impulsively tries to get him to dance with her. He refuses good-naturedly. After a brief byplay, all leave to prepare for the arrival of Lavinia and Orin.

Heralded by descending chromatic harmonies in the orchestra, Orin appears in the study. Now with beard and mustache, he bears a striking resemblance to his father. He is thin and haggard, with an expression of dejection. Staring at Mannon's portrait, he murmurs: "We are home, Father." Meanwhile, Lavinia enters the parlor. She too has changed—to the extent that she is almost the exact image of her mother. She has an air of unusual vivaciousness and looks around approvingly at the preparations made for her homecoming.

But her demeanor changes when Orin, in answer to her call, comes in from the study. She looks at him apprehensively as he says plaintively that he had hoped Mother would be here. But only *they* are here, he adds, pointing to the portraits. The remarkable colloquy which now ensues discloses in part the events of the past year, and also Lavinia's desperate efforts to exorcise the demons of their guilt.

Lavinia alternately cajoles and bullies her helpless brother. She reminds him that he promised to forget the Mannons when he sailed with her to his "dream islands" to find peace. Instead, she goes on reproachfully, he insisted on returning to face his guilt and thus destroy it forever. Well then, he must now face the truth. As though hypnotized, Orin kneels before her, and she is suddenly the relentless inquisitor.

Step by step, Lavinia forces Orin to repeat after her—as though cross-examining a witness—that their mother murdered their father, that she did this to be free to join her lover, that she died by her own hand, that her death was an act of justice. Finally, he must swear that all of the foregoing is true. The torturing effect of the ordeal is underscored by the discordant arpeggios which sound during the pauses in the inquisition. Cringing before her, Orin forces out his "confession," then breaks down sobbing. Lavinia, having accomplished her purpose, takes him in her arms as a mother comforts her child and sings quietly: "It is all over now."

At the sound of footsteps in the hall outside, Lavinia helps Orin to his feet; he moves to one side of the room. Peter enters carrying a candelabra. He catches sight of Lavinia and gasps in surprise at her changed appearance. At this point Orin steps forward. His manner has changed from childish self-pity to cynical mockery. He remarks to Peter —ignoring his friendly greeting—that Lavinia was very much taken with the romantic charm of the tropical islands they visited. The brown-skinned men fascinated her, he says. Controlling her anger, Lavinia pointedly tells him that Helen is waiting for him. Orin stalks out, sneering that Peter is not likely to be as entertaining a companion as the captain of a clipper ship.

Peter, utterly bewildered, asks Lavinia what he means. She shrugs off the question, realizing that he is too naïve to cope with the situation. When he extravagantly praises her beauty, she expresses her reaction in a melodramatic aria which is a mélange of spurious emotion and deliberate seductiveness. The burden of her aria is that, through loneliness, frustration and despair, she learned at last what Peter himself always knew: that she must give her love unselfishly to him. At the conclusion of the aria she throws herself into Peter's arms and the two stand in a passionate embrace.

Helen and Orin suddenly appear in the doorway. In bitter reproach, Orin asks Lavinia if this means that he must give her up forever. To save the situation, Lavinia, as tactfully as possible, suggests that it is time to leave. Peter leads Orin away for a private talk. Helen, alone with Lavinia, voices her misgivings about Orin in a simple, moving refrain. The truth is, she says, that Orin never will allow his sister to become Peter's wife. He is haunted by fear and speaks of secret crimes. This is beyond her understanding, Helen says sadly, but her only thought is to save him from himself. She adds compassionately that God will forgive them for whatever wrongs they have done. With cruel contempt, Lavinia answers that she does not need God's forgiveness . . . she has forgiven herself. With that she turns on her heel and goes into the alcove. Helen is nonplused by her rudeness.

A moment later Orin slips furtively into the room. He is holding a large envelope, which he hands to Helen with instructions to give it to Peter. Lavinia, overhearing, steps out of the alcove. Orin angrily warns her not to interfere. Brushing him aside, she demands the envelope from Helen, who looks questioningly at Orin. Lavinia, realizing that Orin may, at this moment, slip beyond her power, insinuatingly says that her brother knows that she always will do what is best for him. Orin reacts to this with a sneer. For a moment the three stare at each other in silence.

Suddenly Orin, abjectly admitting defeat, nods to Helen, who hands the envelope to Lavinia. Turning despairingly to Helen, he tells her that the Orin she loved was killed in battle . . . she must forget him. Bursting into tears, she hurries away. Whirling on Lavinia, Orin struggles for the envelope and finally snatches it out of her hands.

In baffled fury, Lavinia demands to know what he has written. The history of the Mannon crimes, Orin replies, in which she has a place of honor as the "strangest criminal of all." Terrified, Lavinia warns him that the law can punish them both for what they had to do. Orin retorts that she alone is guilty of her mother's death. Suddenly calm, he declares that the moment has come for Lavinia to plan his death. He warns her, however, that while he lives he will not let her go.

Beginning to be frightened by his mad demeanor, Lavinia cries that she will not remain in this house where she has spent half her life in darkness . . . she will no longer be denied the joy of love. With a satanic sneer, Orin asks if she means love with the naked island men.

The next few moments of this scene are almost a repetition of the action in Act One, Scene Two, when Christine taunts Mannon into his fatal outburst of rage. With the same deliberate malice, Lavinia tells Orin that she would indeed find love with the naked islanders if she chose. Like his father, Orin loses all control. Shouting he will kill her, he seizes Lavinia by the throat, then hurls her to the floor.

Exhausted by his rage, Orin stares down at his sister with blank eyes. From this moment on, the tide of madness slowly engulfs him. In broken, low-toned phrases he entreats Lavinia to forgive him. The fateful moment has come at last, he murmurs, and now—again—one Mannon must destroy another. Lavinia beseeches him to be silent.

A look of depraved desire comes over Orin's face. Over a sinister figure of writhing chromatics in the orchestra, he sings that Lavinia must belong to him . . . they are bound together by love and guilt. Caressing her hair, he murmurs that now she is neither sister nor mother, but "a strange woman with the same beautiful hair." Suddenly, in a burst of insane passion, he tries to kiss her.

Gasping in horror, Lavinia struggles out of his arms, then screams that he is too vile to live . . . may he die and set her free. The word "die" seems to shock Orin out of his violence. Like a sleepwalker he glides to the door, where he turns and stares vacantly at his sister. Almost childishly he begs her not to cry, but in the next instant, again in the grip of his madness, he adds sardonically: "The damned do not cry." Tossing the envelope on the table, he walks into the study and locks the door.

Lavinia runs to the door, tries futilely to open it and begs Orin to let her in. Oblivious to everything, he goes slowly to the desk and takes a pistol out of the drawer. Lavinia, frantic with despair, comes back into the parlor, sees the envelope and snatches it to her bosom. In the study, Orin sinks to his knees.

In his madness, he imagines he sees his mother. He sings that he is afraid of the shadows in the hall and begs her to hide him in her arms. His voice trails away in a falsetto wail. Raising the pistol to his head, he fires.

Lavinia, screaming his name, lunges toward the door, then stops. Turning back, she puts the envelope in a drawer, which she locks. As the "madness" theme thunders in the orchestra she raises her eyes and glares defiantly into the accusing eyes of the Mannon portraits on the walls. Then, grim and erect, she stalks out of the room.

The orchestral accompaniment surges into a thundering passage of descending chromatics. The harmonies thematically underscore the brooding tragedy of the Mannon family and the finality of their doom. This effect is further intensified by a three-chord figure powerfully stated by the brasses.

[*Scene Two*] Outside the Mannon house, late afternoon three days later. The shutters are thrown back, the windows open. Lavinia enters carrying a basket of flowers. She is in deep mourning and is startlingly changed in appearance, her face a mask of tragedy. Her manner is grim, desperate and defiant.

Jed comes out of the house. Lavinia hands him the flowers, then sits at the top of the steps of the portico in statuesque immobility. Looking at her with concern, Jed urges her to come inside and give up this endless waiting. Orin is at rest, he says, and now she must sleep. Lavinia answers that in this house she never will sleep. She adds that she will marry Peter and leave this abode of death. A moment later Peter appears. Jed leaves and Lavinia rises excitedly. As she waits for him to come up the drive she leans against one of the columns and closes her eyes.

Peter is drawn and tense, his eyes downcast, his fists clenched. When he comes closer to Lavinia he makes a visible effort to shake off his black mood. She greets him without opening her eyes; he sits down on the steps and looks up at her. Then she returns his gaze and is startled by his stricken expression. Gently taking her hand, Peter tries to reassure her. They will soon marry, he says. In a flash of bitterness he adds that he will take her away from this haunted house, this ugly town and its uglier gossip.

Taken aback by his anger, Lavinia probes for the cause of his bitter mood. Peter confesses he is being tormented by the stories he has been hearing about the Mannons: Ezra Mannon's death . . . his wife's suicide . . . and then Orin's. . . . In suppressed rage, Lavinia murmurs that she hopes there is a hell for the good. Peter goes on to mention a letter Helen has told him about—a letter he should see. But most important, he adds, he is to ask Lavinia before God if she will dare marry him. When Lavinia answers with a fervent "Yes," Peter cries that now there is nothing more to fear.

Not God, not the living—only the dead are to be feared, Lavinia replies. The dead will destroy them, she adds darkly, unless he wants her enough to kill for her . . . as she has done for him. Then she feverishly begs him to carry her into the house and make her a bride before the eyes of the Mannons to "shame them into silence." The theme of "frustrated love" reverberates in the orchestra. With terrible abandon, Lavinia cries out: "Love me—Adam!" The sound of the name brings her to her senses. Laughing vacantly, she wonders why she called Peter by that name. Outraged by her shameless ardor and now aware of the truth, Peter answers: it is because she loved Adam Brant, and Orin knew. Lavinia murmurs desolately that the dead always come between them—it is useless to fight back. This is sung to a variation of the "death" theme heard during Lavinia's scene with Orin just before his suicide.

In a final attempt to confirm his suspicions, Peter demands that Lavinia show him the letter Orin wrote. Lavinia replies in spoken words: "Not while I live!" Recoiling as though struck in the face, Peter stares at her in horror and disbelief. Turning away from him, Lavinia quietly tells Peter she can never marry him. Almost tenderly she says that now he knows all he needs to know, and he must never come to the Mannon house again. Plunged into despair, Peter slowly walks away. Lavinia, nearly fainting, turns, sees he is gone, then cries out that it is not true that she loved . . . She stops abruptly, squares her shoulders and turns again toward the house.

Calling Jed, she orders him to take all the flowers out of the house, close the shutters and nail them fast . . . she does not wish to see the sun. Jed stares at her in bewilderment and reminds her that she had planned to go away. With a hollow laugh, Lavinia says there is no place to go—her home always has been here. Brusquely she orders Jed to do as he is told.

Standing alone, Lavinia begins the aria which concludes the opera, "Welcome me, House of Mannon." It expresses her renunciation of life and her surrender to the evil destiny of the Mannons. She will never leave this house, she sings over the intermingled themes of "love" and "death," nor will anyone else ever enter it again. She will live out her life with the annihilating guilt and wickedness of this house. In a ringing phrase she calls down upon herself the punishment for the crimes of all the Mannons. Her voice trails away in quavering, disconnected phrases, reflecting her withdrawal from reality.

Finally identifying herself completely with the dead Mannons, Lavinia sings: "I know you will bless me with a long and lonely life." She stands staring like a blind person into the sunlight. Jed appears at one of the windows and closes the shutters with a bang. As though on signal, Lavinia turns, walks stiffly into the house and closes the door behind her. A murmurous figure in the orchestra, similar to that heard at the very beginning of the opera, fades into silence as the curtain falls.

NABUCCO
(*Nebuchadnezzar*)
by GIUSEPPE VERDI
(1813–1901)

Libretto by

TEMISTOCLE SOLERA

Based on the Book of Jeremiah in the Old Testament

CHARACTERS

Nabucco (Nebuchadnezzar), King of Babylon	Baritone
Ishmael, nephew of Sedecia, the King of Jerusalem	Tenor
Zacharius, Chief Priest of the Hebrews	Bass
Fenena, daughter of Nabucco	Mezzo-soprano
Abigail, a slave girl, believed to be Nabucco's other daughter	Soprano
High Priest of Baal	Bass
Abdallo, an old official of Nabucco's court	Tenor
Anna, sister of Zacharius	Soprano

Hebrews, Levites, Assyrians, vestal virgins, soldiers

Place: Jerusalem and Babylon
Time: Biblical era of the captivity of the Jews
First performance: La Scala, Milan, March 9, 1842
Original language: Italian

Nabucco, Verdi's third opera, was his first great success. It not only made him a new operatic hero in Italy but spread his fame throughout Europe. This roughhewn music, with its powerful dramatic thrust, was in an idiom unfamiliar to a public accustomed to the suavities of Donizetti and Bellini, and the opera's premiere generated the wildest excitement. The score has what Italians call *ruvidezza,* translated as "rudeness, coarseness, roughness." Admittedly it has its crudities—but it is a forthright expression of the sufferings of a people. To the Italians, it was a ringing protest against oppression, particularly the famous chorus of the

captive Hebrews "Va, pensiero sull'ali dorate," which practically everyone in Italy soon knew by heart.

Before the curtain rises there is an overture, the *Sinfonia,* which majestically states several choral themes heard in the opera. One is the
chorus of the Levites in Act Two, the other the chorus of the captive
Hebrews. This overture is considered to be the first since Rossini's
William Tell to be linked with development of the dramatic action. The
fact that it was singled out for critical praise is somewhat ironical. It is
recorded that Verdi composed the overture in a cafe as an afterthought
at the suggestion of his brother-in-law.

ACT ONE

In the Temple of Solomon, in Jerusalem. Assembled in the Temple,
the Hebrews, Levites and vestal virgins lament the defeat of the city by
Nabucco in an ensemble, "Gli arredi festivi." They are panic-stricken
over the imminent arrival of the hated King of Babylon and his barba-
rous hordes. The festive hangings of the Temple, the people sing, must
be torn into shreds to symbolize their grief and shame. In a unison refrain, "I candidi veli," the Levites exhort the vestal virgins to pray for
deliverance. The vestals call on the Lord of Hosts for help and mercy
("Gran Nume, che voli"), then all the people implore their God to avert
the destruction of the Temple.

Suddenly the High Priest Zacharius strides on the scene, half dragging Fenena, daughter of Nabucco. With them is Anna, the High
Priest's sister. In a ringing cavatina, "Sperate, o figli," Zacharius bids
the Israelites take heart, because the Lord has given a precious hostage
into their hands—Fenena, the King's own daughter. He goes on to remind them that Jehovah sent Moses to protect his people in Egypt. And
because they put their trust in the Lord, not a single man of Gideon's
army perished. The High Priest exhorts the Jews not to be afraid.

At that moment there is a noise offstage and the people cry out in
alarm. Ishmael enters with a band of Hebrew soldiers and announces
that the dread Assyrian King and his mighty army are closing in on the
city. Zacharius, trying to calm the populace, steps forward to say that
the Lord will surely prevent the enemy from desecrating Zion. With that
he hands Fenena over to Ishmael, saying that she is a symbol of the
Lord's assurance. Then in a solo interlude, "Come notte a sol fulgente,"
he implores the God of Abraham to give his people victory in the coming battle. The people repeat his supplication, then follow him from the
Temple. Only Fenena and Ishmael remain.

Ishmael tries to embrace Fenena but she sternly repulses him, asking
how he dare speak of love in this hour of disaster. In recitative, Ishmael

tells her that, as a captive, she is even more beautiful to him than when he saw her in the Babylonian court where he served as ambassador for the King of Judah, his uncle. He recalls that Fenena, risking the anger of her jealous sister Abigail, there later freed him from prison. Now, in turn, he will set her free, Ishmael cries.

Fenena warns him that if he does he will betray his own people. Ishmael answers that his love is stronger than loyalty. At that moment Abigail, sword in hand, rushes in at the head of a band of Assyrian soldiers disguised as Hebrews. Ishmael and Fenena shrink back in terror as Abigail shouts that the Temple has been captured. In a stormy refrain, "Prode guerrier," she turns on the lovers with savage scorn. She derides Ishmael for his love for Fenena, then warns the girl that now nothing can save her from a sister's revenge.

Suddenly she glides to Ishmael's side and whispers that she too loves him ("Io t'amava . . . Il regno"); she offers him her kingdom and her heart. If that love is returned, she sings, she can save him and his people. Ishmael disdains her offer, replying that he has no fears for himself but is concerned only for the safety of his people. A brief trio ensues as Fenena joins to sing that her prayers are not for herself but for her persecuted people. Abigail reiterates her avowal while Ishmael continues to rebuff her.

As the trio ends, a panic-stricken throng of Hebrew men and women, Levites and soldiers swarms on the scene crying that the raging Nabucco, brandishing his bloody sword, is advancing on the Temple ("Lo vedete? Fulminando!"). The defenders have been routed and the King, astride his horse, is nearing the Holy of Holies. The people fall back in terror as Abigail and her soldiers hail Nabucco. The shouts of the invaders are heard outside. Zacharius demands to know how the enemy found the secret passage into the city. Ishmael tells him it was the work of Babylonian spies. Abigail sneers that his excuses are in vain—the King approaches. Heralded by a military band, Nabucco arrogantly rides his horse to the very threshold of the Temple. There Zacharius bars his way, warning the King not to desecrate the House of God ("Questa è di Dio stanza"). Nabucco asks impudently: "What God?" Thereupon Zacharius seizes Fenena, holds the point of his dagger against her body and warns the King that if he dares profane the Temple his daughter will die then and there ("Pria che tu profani il templo"[1]).

Momentarily awed by Zacharius' fury, Nabucco dismounts. He threatens, however, that this defiance will bring even greater destruction

[1] This phrase is almost identical to that sung by Rigoletto when he commands the courtiers to leave in Act Three of *Rigoletto*.

down upon Zion ("Tremin gli'insani"). This marks the beginning of the ensemble which concludes the act.

Fenena begs her father to show mercy to the conquered people. Ishmael and Zacharius implore God to change the heart of this cruel King and to save his victims from chains. Abigail, in soaring obbligato passages characterized by a rushing semiquaver figure, exults that now she can revenge herself on the woman who stands between her and the man she loves ("L'impeto acqueta del mio furore"). These passages are underscored by the choral accompaniment sung by the people as they beseech God for deliverance.

In a solo passage ("O venti, il capo a terra") Nabucco taunts the Jews because their God did not dare come to their aid. Goaded to murderous fury, Zacharius raises his dagger to stab Fenena, screaming that if the conqueror thirsts for blood, the first drop to be spilled will be his daughter's ("Iniquo mira!"). Ishmael leaps forward and tears the dagger from Zacharius' hand. Snatching Fenena out of his grasp, Ishmael pushes her into her father's arms, crying that now she has been saved by love.

Nabucco, in savage triumph, orders his soldiers to plunder and destroy, to burn the Temple and to spare no one—the only crime will be to show pity. Abigail sings that if she cannot tear her love for Ishmael out of her heart, at least the destruction of the Jews will slake her thirst for revenge. Zacharius and the Hebrews turn on Ishmael and curse him for his traitorous act in saving Fenena's life. These conflicting sentiments blend as the ensemble thunders to its climax.

ACT TWO

[*Scene One*] Nabucco's palace in Babylon. Abigail, holding a parchment, comes in excitedly. In a dramatic recitative and aria she traces the course of events. She sings that she has discovered a fateful document ("O fatal scritto") which reveals that she is not Nabucco's daughter but the child of a slave. Now, as the supposed daughter of a king, she is worse than a slave. Nabucco, who has gone to wage a war of extermination against Judea, has left Fenena, her hated rival, in charge of the throne. She herself has been scorned and rejected. But these fools, she muses, do not know the heart of Abigail. She will have her revenge—and it will destroy all of them ("Su tutti il mio furore"). These phrases, sung in rising half steps with octave skips, give an extraordinarily menacing effect. Fenena, Nabucco, the kingdom—perhaps even herself—will be brought to ruin before she will allow the secret of her lowly birth to be discovered.

Then, as though exhausted by her fury, she reflects in quiet despair over the time when she too could find joy in her heart—when she could share another's grief. Now who is there to restore to her one single moment of lost tenderness? These emotions are expressed in a flowing cantabile, "Anch'io dischiuso un giorno."

Her reverie is interrupted by the entrance of the High Priest of Baal followed by members of the court. He announces that the accursed Fenena has betrayed her country by ordering the captive Jews to be freed. This rabble must be curbed, he and the others sing in a unison choral passage, and for this reason they are offering the crown to her—Abigail. To clear the way for this palace revolution they already have spread the report that Nabucco has been slain in battle ("Noi gia sparso"). Now the Assyrians are calling on Abigail to save the Empire.

Realizing that her plans for revenge suddenly have come to fruition, Abigail replies in savage exultation that now she will mount the throne on bloodied steps ("Salgo già del trono aurato"). Now the Assyrians will see that the scepter truly belongs to her. What is more, she adds cryptically, they will see the King's own daughter kneeling at the feet of a slave. (This concluding phrase is sung in a striking passage of sixteenth notes descending from high C.) In a choral accompaniment to the aria, the High Priest and the court sing that Baal himself will share Abigail's revenge.[2]

[*Scene Two*] A hall in the palace. At right a door leading to a gallery; at left a door to Nabucco's apartment. It is evening. Lamps illuminate the scene. Zacharius enters, followed by a Levite carrying the Tablets of the Law. In recitative Zacharius explains that he has been chosen by the Lord to bring the message of salvation to the unbelievers. In the ensuing aria, "Tu sul labbro dei veggenti," he sings that through his lips the Lord will speak to the Assyrians and the Holy Writ will prevail over false idols. At the conclusion of the aria he and the Levites enter the door to Nabucco's apartment, now occupied by Fenena.

A moment later a group of Levites cautiously enters through the other door. In hushed tones they wonder who has sent them to this dangerous place. The answer comes from Ishmael, who, apparently unnoticed, has followed them into the room. The Levites gasp in surprise at seeing him. It was the High Priest himself who sent them here, Ishmael tells the astonished Levites. They turn on him in furious denunciation ("Maledetto del Signor!"). This is one of the most striking choruses in the opera—a square-cut melody sung in *presto* tempo, with which Verdi achieved an extraordinarily dramatic effect. He uses the same device—

---

[2] This scene, with its vigorous declamation and response, has been pointed out as being typical of the new energy with which Verdi was imbuing his operas. Its grim mood foreshadows the vindictive cruelty of the priests in *Aïda*. The difficult aria itself is noteworthy for its two-octave range.

written for male voices—in later operas, notably in the "Zitti, zitti" chorus in *Rigoletto*.

When Ishmael begs for mercy, the Levites revile him as an outcast, shouting that he has betrayed his brothers and bears the mark of Cain. Ishmael begs for death rather than this disgrace. His despairing cry, "Oh, la morte, per pietà," blends with the denunciations of the Levites. As they stand glaring at him, Zacharius and the Levite carrying the Tablets of the Law return accompanied by Fenena and Anna. The latter steps forward and asks the Levites to pardon Ishmael because the woman he saved is not an enemy but a Jewess. Fenena has been converted to Judaism. Ishmael and the Levites are stunned. Zacharius corroborates Anna's assertion.

Shouting is heard offstage, and a moment later Abdallo, an elderly official in Nabucco's court, rushes in. He approaches Fenena and tells her that Nabucco has been slain ("Donna regal! deh fuggi!"). He warns her to flee because the populace has chosen Abigail as Queen. At that point the High Priest of Baal and Abigail come storming in at the head of a shouting crowd of Assyrians. Confronting Fenena, Abigail demands the scepter. Fenena retorts that she will die rather than give it up.

Nabucco and his warriors come charging through the crowd. Thrusting himself between the two women, the King snatches the crown from Fenena's head, puts it on his own and defies anyone to remove it ("Dal capo mio la prendi"). A booming figure in the bass underscores his defiance.

A powerful ensemble begins here as Nabucco expresses the terror and confusion of the moment in a *sotto voce* phrase of suppressed fury —"S'appressan gl'istanti." His voice is joined by those of Abigail, Fenena, Ishmael and Zacharius, who repeat this theme. Finally all onstage burst into a tremendous chorus of lamentation.

Nabucco suddenly silences the crowd with a gesture. On the verge of madness, he cries out that he has cast down not only the god of the Babylonians but the God of the Hebrews as well ("S'oda or me, Babilonesi!"). Now there is no God but Nabucco. Here Verdi achieves a telling effect as each of Nabucco's recitative phrases begins a half tone higher than the preceding one.

While Nabucco's warriors hail him, Fenena, Zacharius and the Hebrews cry out in horror at the King's blasphemy. As Nabucco wildly repeats that he is God, Zacharius calls down the curse of Jehovah on him ("Insano! a terra, a terra"). Nabucco orders his soldiers to drag Zacharius to the foot of the King's statue and there put him to death. Fenena steps forward crying that she, as a Jewess, will die with him. In blind fury, Nabucco forces her to her knees and screams: "Giù! prostrati! non son più re, son Dio!" ("Bow down! I am no longer King! I am God!").

As a chromatic descending passage explodes in the orchestra, there is a crash of thunder. A bolt of lightning blasts the crown from Nabucco's head. In a horrified whisper the onlookers comment that heaven has punished the King for his insolence. There is a moment of absolute silence.

Nabucco, now a hopeless lunatic, stares vacantly before him. Then, lost in his madness, he asks, in the ensuing aria: "Chi mi toglie il regno scettro?" ("Who has robbed me of my scepter?"). He shrinks back from the horrid phantoms he sees and murmurs that the crimson sky is sprinkling his brow with drops of blood. With a final despairing cry for help, Nabucco falls in a faint. Abigail picks up the crown and sings with malevolent satisfaction that the hosts of Baal have lost none of their greatness ("Ma del popolo di Belo non fia spento lo splendor"). The curtain falls.

ACT THREE[3]

The sumptuous hanging gardens of Babylon, where Abigail is holding court. Dignitaries and courtiers are in attendance. The High Priest stands at an altar flanked by the golden statue of Baal. There is a crowd of citizens, soldiers and priests. In chorus, "E' d'Assiria una regina," they pay homage to the new Queen, Abigail. The High Priest hands her a warrant authorizing the extermination of the Jews—first of all the traitorous Fenena. Abigail studies the document, craftily pretending to be puzzled by its demands.

At that moment Nabucco, an apparition in torn robes and unkempt beard, staggers into the room. (The music here depicts him as a weak and doddering old man.) A scene in recitative follows. At first Abigail angrily commands that the old man be taken back to his cell. With sudden kingly authority Nabucco asks who dares speak in his presence. Instantly Abigail's manner softens, and she asks him to follow her. His mind wandering, Nabucco asks: "Where?" Here is the council chamber, he goes on, and here is his throne—and he well knows how to mount it. Lurching up the steps toward the throne, he stops and glares at Abigail, asking who this interloper is. Abigail swiftly rises and dismisses the court.

Here begins the great confrontation scene, which is in the form of a long and brilliant duet beginning with Nabucco's question as he faces

[3] In some stage versions this act begins with the chorus of the captive Hebrews, "Va, pensiero, sull'ali dorate," followed by Zacharius' aria foretelling the doom of Babylon—"Oh, chi piange?"

Abigail: "Donna, chi sei?" ("Woman, who are you?").[4] When she replies that she is the guardian of the throne he brands her as an imposter. Pitilessly exploiting Nabucco's confused state of mind, Abigail tricks him into signing the death warrants of the captive Jews and Fenena. In a momentary flash of sanity, the King realizes he has now doomed his own daughter. He cries out in anguish: "È sangue mio!" Remorselessly following up her advantage, Abigail says softly: "You have another daughter." But Nabucco, still in possession of his senses, tells her she is nothing but a slave and commands her to kneel before her master. Then he distractedly searches in his robes for the secret document which proves she was born a slave.

Abigail thereupon draws the document from her bosom and tears it to shreds before his eyes. In a dazzling coloratura phrase, "Tale ti rendo, o misero," she sings that thus she gives the King back his lie. Nabucco despairingly cries that his power is gone and that he is only a shadow of a king ("L'ombra son io del re"). In malicious exultation Abigail sings that her hour of glory has come ("Oh, dell'ambita gloria") and that now an empire will kneel at the feet of a slave.

A fanfare of trumpets interrupts the duet. Abigail tells Nabucco that it signals the death of the Hebrews whom he himself condemned. He shouts for the guards but Abigail tells him that these very guards are holding him prisoner—the prisoner of a slave. Totally helpless in Abigail's power, the King abjectly begs her to have mercy on a father mad with grief ("Deh perdona a un padre che delira!").[5] He will give her the throne, he sings, if she only will give him his daughter's life. In cruel triumph Abigail scorns his plea—"Esci! invan mi chiedi pace!" Now he will see how well a slave can wear the robe of royalty. This brings the duet to a fiery conclusion. In the closing passages, a chromatically descending figure depicts Nabucco's despair and symbolizes his defeat.

The scene now changes to the banks of the Euphrates, where the Hebrews are toiling as slaves in chains. Here they sing the famous chorus "Va, pensiero, sull'ali dorate," in which they voice their anguished longing for their homeland and freedom. They bid their thoughts to fly "on gilded wings" to the banks of their beloved Jordan and to Zion, ruined though it is. This great chorus, which begins in unison, has certain melancholy overtones of ancient psalms.

Listening to their lamentations, Zacharius springs to his feet and

4 The forerunner of a great line of Verdian duets—Macbeth and his wife, Rigoletto and Gilda, Violetta and Germont in *La Traviata,* Amelia and Riccardo in *Un Ballo in Maschera,* Leonora and Padre Guardiano in *La Forza del Destino,* Desdemona and Otello, etc.

5 In this portrayal of paternal love, Verdi set the pattern—so to speak—of similar characterizations in later operas, such as Rigoletto, Boccanegra, Germont and Amonasro.

berates them for their self-pitying, womanish tears ("Oh, chi piange? di femmine imbelli"). Then in a ringing aria, "Del futuro nel buio discerno," he prophesies the utter destruction of Babylon, where "not one stone will be left upon another" ("Niuna pietra ove sorse l'altera"). In choral accompaniment, the Hebrews sing that this man has inspired them with the holy fire of courage.

ACT FOUR

The throne room in Nabucco's palace, where he is seen sitting motionless in a deathlike sleep. There is a brief prelude dominated by the theme of the "Marcia Funebre" (as Verdi called it) which will be heard later in the act as Fenena is led to her execution.

Suddenly Nabucco awakes, still in the grip of a terrible dream. Hearing the funeral march, he fancies it a call to arms and shouts for his horse, his sword, his warriors. Outside, a crowd bellows the name of Fenena, then a band blares the funeral march. Rushing to a window, Nabucco sees Fenena, her hands bound, walking between two files of soldiers. Barely able to comprehend what he sees, the King gasps that Fenena is weeping. This exclamation is underscored by a poignant phrase in the orchestra. Then he hears the shout: "Fenena a morte!"

Suddenly conscious of the impending tragedy, Nabucco runs to the door of the throne room, finds to his horror that it is bolted. He is a prisoner. In terrible despair he falls to his knees and prays to the God of the Hebrews for pardon ("Dio degli Ebrei, perdono!"). He promises to raise an altar to Jehovah, to renounce his paganism, and henceforth to worship only the True and Omnipotent God. At the conclusion of the prayer he leaps to his feet and with a furious effort again tries to wrench open the door.

As he struggles, the door is flung open from the outside and Abdallo, the King's venerable official, bursts in with a group of Babylonian soldiers. Nabucco, believing them to be his captors, roars at them to leave him alone. Abdallo and the soldiers assure him that they have come to rescue him. Crying out that his mind now is clear, the King demands his sword ("Abdallo, il brando mio!"). As Abdallo hands it to him, Nabucco shouts that he will save Fenena. Over a blazing fanfare, Abdallo and the soldiers promise the annihilation of the Babylonian traitors.

Brandishing his sword, Nabucco commands the soldiers to follow him ("o prodi miei, seguitemi!"). Reason has returned, he sings, and he is King of Assyria once more; his enemies will see his crown blaze like the sun. Followed by the soldiers, he strides out.

The next scene takes place in the hanging gardens, as shown previously. Present are Zacharius, Anna, Fenena, courtiers, Hebrews, guards and the populace. The High Priest of Baal stands at the temple portico beside a sacrificial altar. On the other side stand two executioners with axes.

To the strains of the funeral march, Fenena and the condemned Hebrews are led in. Fenena approaches Zacharius and kneels before him. In a brief recitative passage ("Va! la palma del martirio") Zacharius gently bids her accept the martyr's crown and go to her reward in heaven. In a poignant aria, "Oh, dischiuso è il firmamento," Fenena serenely resigns herself to her fate.

Without warning, from offstage comes a mighty shout of "Viva Nabucco!" Just as the High Priest vainly commands the execution to proceed, the King, Abdallo and the soldiers rush in. Pointing with his sword to the golden statue of Baal, Nabucco orders his soldiers to destroy it at once. Before they can touch it, the statue crashes to the ground in a mass of rubble.

In a triumphant refrain, "Ah, torna Israello, torna alle gioie," Nabucco bids the children of Israel return to their homeland and rebuild the Temple of their God. Then he discloses that Abigail, tormented by her guilt, has taken poison. Turning to Fenena, he asks her to kneel in worship to Jehovah. Thereupon the entire assemblage joins in the great prayer "Immenso Jeova."

At its conclusion, a sudden hush falls over the throng. All watch in consternation as Abigail, half carried by two soldiers, makes her way through the crowd and stands before Nabucco. There she makes her final confession of guilt and her dying entreaty for pity ("Su me . . . morente . . . esanime"). Holding out her arms as if to embrace Fenena and Ishmael, she sings to Nabucco that these two always have loved each other and have always put their trust in the King. But now, she asks brokenly, who will absolve her of guilt? In her death throes, she cries: "Solleva Iddio l'afflitta. Te chiamo . . . o Dio . . . non maledire a me!" ("God alone can lift the burden. Oh, God, do not condemn me!").

As a tremendous fanfare resounds in the orchestra, Zacharius proclaims that henceforth the King of Assyria will be the servant of Jehovah ("Servendo a Jeova sarai de' regi il re!"). The curtain falls.

LES PÊCHEURS DE PERLES

by GEORGES BIZET

(1838–75)

Libretto by

MICHEL CARRÉ and E. CORMON

CHARACTERS

Zurga, king of the pearl fishers	Baritone
Nadir, his friend	Tenor
Leila, a Brahmin priestess	Soprano
Nourabad, a Brahmin high priest	Bass

Pearl fishermen, priests, priestesses, natives, slaves, dancers

Place: Ceylon
Time: Legendary
First performance: Théâtre Lyrique, Paris, September 29, 1863
Original language: French

Les Pêcheurs de Perles, composed twelve years before *Carmen,* met with indifferent success and for a long period suffered undeserved neglect. There is a wealth of pleasing melody in the score, with music of impressive impact and power underscoring the dramatic climaxes of the action. Although the opera as a whole may be comparatively unfamiliar, one number is universally known—the beautiful tenor aria sung by Nadir near the end of the first act, "Je crois entendre encore" (often sung in Italian under the title of "Mi par d'udir ancora"). A revival of the opera was staged by the Metropolitan in 1916, with Caruso in the role of Nadir. His recording of the aria is one of the treasures of the 78rpm era.

ACT ONE

An open sandy beach on the island of Ceylon, with huts of the pearl fishermen to the right and left. The sea is visible in the background. Toward the rear, on a rock overlooking the sea, stand the ruins of an ancient Indian temple. Gathered for a day of festivity, the fisherfolk sing a spirited chorus ("Sur la grève en feu"), during which tribal dances are performed by dancing girls. The people call on the dancers to drive away the evil spirits and then go on to sing about their destined task of braving the dangers of the sea in search of pearls.

Zurga, a leader of the fishermen, interrupts the singing and dancing to announce that on this day they must select a chieftain. He himself is elected king by acclamation, the fishermen hailing him and pledging allegiance in a brief but sturdy chorus ("C'est lui que nous voulons pour maître"). As Zurga shakes hands with the men, a newcomer is seen approaching. When he comes nearer Zurga recognizes him as his friend Nadir, a young courier and jungle hunter.

Welcomed by Zurga and the crowd, Nadir describes, in a melodious, swinging refrain, the adventures he has had, telling how he has roamed through savannahs and forests, stalking the tiger, the jaguar, and the panther ("Des savanes et des forêts"). He lives a lonely life in the demon-haunted jungles, he continues, seeing no human being for a year at a time. The men join him in the concluding phrases of his song as he shakes hands and hails them as boon companions. Zurga invites him to stay and live with the fishermen and join them in their pleasures. Nadir promptly decides to do so. The dancing then resumes, and the people repeat the refrain of the opening chorus, after which they leave the scene.

Nadir and Zurga, now alone, begin reminiscing about the past. They speak of an oath of friendship to which they both swore and assure each other that they have never broken it. When Zurga proposes a toast to the fact that they once successfully resisted temptation and have since forgotten their days of folly, Nadir gravely says they will never forget. As long as they live, he avers, they will remember their last voyage together—that night when they put into the harbor of the city of Candy and visited the Brahmin temple there. The priests were calling the faithful to worship, Nadir says softly.

In a sonorous duet ("Au fond du temple"—"Del tempio al limitar") —one of the great tenor-baritone duets in opera—the two men relive the experience that prompted them to take the oath of which they have been speaking. A veiled woman emerged from the exotic gloom of the sacred temple and walked toward them with the grace and dignity of a goddess. The worshipers, murmuring in wonder and awe, prostrated themselves before her. As she passed the two men she raised her veil for an instant, and they saw a face of ravishing beauty. She mysteriously disappeared, Nadir and Zurga following her in vain. Both were consumed by passion for her, and their rivalry made them bitter enemies for a time.

They eventually came to their senses, however, and took an oath never again to allow anything to break their friendship. Each promised the other that he would never try to find the mysterious and beautiful priestess. The duet ends in ringing phrases as they pledge each other friendship to the death ("Amitié sainte, unis nos âmes fraternelles").

As they clasp hands a fisherman appears and tells Zurga that a boat has landed nearby. Saying that he has been awaiting it, Zurga tells Nadir that its arrival has to do with an ancient custom that prevails among the pearl fishermen. Each year a beautiful virgin, whose identity is kept secret, is brought to the seashore to pray for the safety of the fishermen when they go on their dangerous quest for pearls ("Une fille inconnue et belle"). Her face hidden by a veil, she stands on the rock near the ruined temple, chanting prayers to drive away evil spirits and calm the sea. No one may look at her or come near her during her vigil.

Heralded by shouts of the crowd, a veiled woman appears, followed by Nourabad, high priest of Brahma, and four other priests. It is Leila, the Brahmin priestess whom Nadir and Zurga saw in the temple at Candy. A crowd of women go before her, scattering flowers in her path and singing a chorus of welcome ("Sois la bienvenue"). Approaching her, Zurga asks in solemn tones if she will keep the oath she has taken ("Seule au milieu de nous"). She must promise to keep her face concealed, to pray day and night at the brink of the sea, and to deny herself friend or lover. Leila swears to the oath in the name of Brahma. If she is faithful, Zurga proclaims, she will be rewarded with the most beautiful pearl that can be found in the sea. But if she betrays her oath and yields to love, he adds menacingly, she will be accursed and Brahma will demand her life as forfeit. The crowd repeats the curse which Zurga utters—"Malheur à toi!"

As Leila recoils at Zurga's warning, Nadir comes forward with an exclamation of dismay over the harshness of the penalty imposed. Leila murmurs that she recognizes his voice. Taking her hand, Zurga notices that she is trembling in fear, whereupon he urges her to renounce her oath while there is yet time. Gazing at Nadir through her veil, Leila firmly answers that she will remain to accomplish her destined task. At the sound of her voice Nadir starts toward her, but checks himself.

In a ringing ensemble Zurga, Nourabad, the priests, and the people declare that Leila has promised to be faithful. Leila responds. All kneel and offer a prayer to Brahma for protection ("Brahma, divin Brahma"). Zurga then leads Leila into the ruined temple, with Nourabad and the priests following, while the fishermen go down to the shore. Zurga returns to Nadir, shakes his hand, and then leaves.

Gazing up at the temple, Nadir wonders if the voice he heard was that of Leila or only an illusion. He reproaches himself for not having confessed to Zurga that he had been false to his oath—that after seeing Leila at the temple he had followed her to her secret retreat. There he had looked upon her and listened to her singing. In the famous aria "Je crois entendre encore" Nadir recalls the fascination of her voice as it drifted to him through the palms. He sees again the vision of loveliness revealed when the night breeze swept aside her flowing veils. The aria ends on a note of longing and tenderness as Nadir abandons himself to his blissful dream. Lost in reflection, he lies down on a mat before one of the huts and gradually falls asleep. The voices of the fishermen drift up from the shore in a soft choral phrase.

Nourabad and the priests now lead Leila out of the temple to the rock overlooking the sea. The priests light a fire in a brazier and then command Leila to sing. She sings a stately invocation to Brahma ("Ô Dieu Brahma"), which is answered by the voices of the fishermen on the shore. Nadir awakes, exclaiming that he hears the voice that once enchanted him. As he listens, Leila sings an exquisite refrain ("Dans le ciel sans voile"), which artfully conceals a message of love in phrases of prayer to Brahma. Under the starry sky, she sings, her heart and voice go out to the one she adores. The voices of the people are heard again, urging her to continue her enthralling song, and Leila's tones soar above the ensemble in a beautiful obbligato.

Springing to his feet, Nadir steals to the foot of the great rock. Leila lifts her veil for an instant and looks down at him. Crying out her name, Nadir assures her that he will remain near and defend her with his life if need be. Their voices blend in phrases of adoration over the accompaniment of the chorus as the curtain falls.

ACT TWO

The interior of the ruined temple above the sea. At the rear is a terrace overlooking the rocky cliff at the water's edge. The scene is flooded with moonlight. An unseen chorus softly chants an invocation to night ("L'ombre descend des cieux"). Leila, Nourabad, and the priests are seen on the terrace. The high priest tells Leila that the fishermen have returned to land and that her nightly vigil is over. When she apprehensively asks if she is to be left alone in the temple, Nourabad assures her that she will be safe. On one side of the temple, he says, is the rocky, inaccessible shore, while the only other approach is guarded by the priests, fully armed. He tells her that if she remains faithful she may sleep without thought of fear.

Leila replies that when she was a mere child her courage was tested in the face of death. In a dramatic refrain ("J'étais encore enfant") she relates how one night a fugitive sought refuge in her home from a band of enemies. Moved by his pleas for protection, she concealed him. When his pursuers appeared she refused to answer their questions, even though they threatened her with their daggers. The fugitive was thus able to escape, but before he left her home he showed his gratitude by giving her a golden chain, telling her to keep it in memory of the man whose life she had saved.

Her steadfastness will likewise be rewarded under the Brahmin law, Nourabad promises at the conclusion of her story. But if she fails, he reminds her grimly, torture and death await her. Exhorting her to think on her vows, Nourabad leaves with the priests. The chanting of the chorus is heard again.

Momentarily giving way to fear, Leila recovers her composure as she looks toward the terrace. Her heart tells her, she murmurs, that her lover is near. In a tender refrain ("Comme autrefois dans la nuit sombre") she rejoices that, as in days past, her lover watches over her from his hiding place in the shadows of the jungle so that she may sleep in peace. She voices her happiness in the thought that he is near. As she ends her song the strains of a guzla[1] sound from below the rocks. Then Nadir's voice is heard in a brief serenade ("De mon amie, fleur endormie"), singing of his beloved who is held captive in a palace of azure and gold in the depths of a crystal sea. Soon he appears and Leila rushes into his arms.

The duet that follows is one of the loveliest numbers in the opera ("Par cet étroit sentier qui borde un sombre abîme"). When Leila asks how he made his way over the treacherous rocks along the shore, Nadir replies that the god of love guided his footsteps. Trembling with fear, Leila implores him to flee, for death is certain if he is discovered. She tries to free herself from his embrace, crying that she must not betray her oath.

Nadir passionately sings of the nights when he listened enchanted as she sang in her secret retreat, and in an answering refrain Leila recalls the bliss of those moments. Though he had sworn never to see her again, Nadir says, he was drawn to her by the fatal power of love. Leila replies that she has waited for him during the long nights of her vigil at the sea, always knowing that he would come to her.

Suddenly she tears herself away, crying that terrible danger threatens and imploring him to remember the penalty she must pay for breaking her oath. But when Nadir answers that neither a sacred oath nor death itself can separate them now, Leila throws herself into his arms, rapturously exclaiming that she would give her life for this one moment of bliss. As they stand in passionate embrace, thunder rumbles in the distance. Gazing up at the sky, the lovers sing that they will defy the storm's wrath and Brahma's anger as well.

Warned by a sense of imminent danger, Leila begs Nadir to leave at once. Promising that he will return the next evening, he embraces her in

---

[1] Or gusla—a single-stringed instrument with a bowl-shaped body and a sounding board of skin or parchment.

farewell. At that moment Nourabad appears on the terrace and sees the lovers. Muttering that treason has been committed, the high priest rushes away. He reappears shortly, followed by priests whom he sends in pursuit of Nadir. The sounds of the storm grow louder, and from the shore come the voices of the fisherfolk expressing their fear of impending disaster and praying for protection against the fury of the tempest ("Quelle voix nous appelle?").

As Nourabad strides toward Leila, the priests drag in Nadir. The people, who have rushed up from the shore and have crowded into the temple, exclaim in horror as Nourabad points to Nadir and Leila and thunders that they have violated the sacred oath. A dramatic ensemble develops as the priests surround them with drawn daggers ("Pour eux point de grâce! Non!"). The crowd roars that no mercy must be shown and that the culprits must die. Leila resigns herself to her fate, while Nadir, vowing that he will never ask for mercy, defies the threats of the people.

The uproar is suddenly halted by Zurga, who forces his way through the angry crowd to Leila and Nadir. He reminds the fishermen that they have elected him king and have given him the power to pronounce judgment on his subjects. In an aside, Leila and Nadir murmur their thanks to him. The fishermen draw back, muttering resentfully that if it is Zurga's wish, mercy will be extended to the traitors. Turning to Leila and Nadir, Zurga quietly tells them to go.

Thereupon Nourabad strides forward, declaring angrily that at least they will know by whom they have been betrayed. With that he tears the veil from Leila's face. Staggering back in surprise as he recognizes Leila, Zurga, in terrible fury, shouts for revenge. Frenzied by the thought that Nadir has betrayed his vow of friendship, Zurga rages that neither mercy nor pity will be shown the offenders—both must die. The ensemble continues as the priests and the fishermen renew their denunciations. As the storm breaks in full fury, they kneel and intone a grim invocation to Brahma, swearing that they will exact the ultimate penalty for the sacrilege which has been committed. Nadir is led away by the fishermen and Leila by the priests as the curtain falls.

ACT THREE

[Scene One] The interior of Zurga's tent, which is enclosed by draperies. Pacing up and down, Zurga gives way to remorse and despair over having doomed Leila and Nadir ("L'orage s'est calmé"). His anger, like the storm, has spent its force, he soliloquizes, and now he realizes that he acted out of jealous hatred and a mad desire for revenge. Crying out that the terrible judgment he pronounced must surely be an evil dream, he declares that he is certain that Nadir did not betray him.

And yet he has doomed not only his dearest friend but the beautiful Leila, whom he adored. Overwhelmed by his anguish, he sinks exhausted on a couch.

Escorted by two fishermen, Leila appears at the entrance of the tent, saying that she must speak with him alone. Dismissing the fishermen, Zurga tells her to enter. A spirited duet ensues ("Je frémis, je chancelle"). Aside, Leila wonders how she can placate this fierce chieftain, while Zurga murmurs that she is more beautiful than ever in the hour of her doom. When he quietly tells her not to be afraid, she kneels at his feet and implores him to spare Nadir's life, insisting that he is innocent. She swears that it was only by chance that he found her. In an undertone Zurga says that perhaps Nadir did not break the pact they made.

Leila begs Zurga to spare Nadir so that she can more easily face her own punishment. He gave her all his love, she says tenderly, and she loved him in return. At those words Zurga cries out that he might have saved Nadir's life because of their friendship, but now he must die. In the effort to save Nadir's life by declaring her love for him, Zurga says sardonically, she has sealed his fate. Losing all control, Zurga confesses to Leila that he too loved her and that now jealousy is goading him to revenge. At one stroke he will destroy the woman who spurned him and the friend who betrayed his trust.

The duet rises to a stormy climax as Leila distractedly entreats him to take revenge on her alone. When he rejects her pleas, Leila warns that he will be haunted by remorse for this deed as long as he lives, while death will forever unite her with Nadir. Zurga rages that they will pay the penalty for their ignoble passion.

At the conclusion of the duet Nourabad and a group of fishermen appear. Shouts are heard in the distance. The hour of doom has come, Nourabad announces, and Leila declares that she is ready. Zurga orders her to go. As she leaves she takes a golden chain from around her neck and hands it to a young fisherman, telling him to take it to her mother as a token of remembrance. When Leila is led away Zurga snatches the chain from the fisherman's hands, examines it carefully, and then rushes out of the tent. The chain he holds is the one he gave Leila long ago for saving his life.

[Scene Two] A wild and desolate spot in the jungle, where a huge pyre has been built. Grouped in front of the pyre, the people watch a barbaric dance and then invoke Brahma in a fierce chorus ("Dès que le soleil"). They exult that as soon as the sun rises they will strike the avenging blow. The blood of the guilty ones will flow like wine, inspiring them with holy joy.

To the strains of a funeral march Nourabad appears, followed by Leila and Nadir, who are in chains. The high priest chants that Zurga has delivered the malefactors into the hands of the people, and the crowd repeats his words in savage exultation. Seeing a red glow spreading over the horizon, the people exclaim that dawn is breaking and that the fatal hour is at hand.

They are startled when Zurga rushes in, torch in hand. Shouting that the gods have rained down fire from heaven and that their village is being ravaged by flames, he calls on them to save their children while there is yet time. The people run toward their homes in mad disorder. Nourabad, however, remains behind and, unobserved by Zurga, Leila, and Nadir, conceals himself near the pyre.

Zurga tells Leila and Nadir that he started the fire in the village to distract the attention of the people. Saying that Leila once saved his life and that now he will save hers, he severs the chains of the captives. Nourabad steals away to inform the people of their king's treachery.

Zurga, Leila, and Nadir join in a dramatic trio ("Ô lumière sainte"). Leila and Nadir give thanks for their deliverance. Gazing at the lovers, Zurga declares that he will gladly face the death to which he has now doomed himself, for he could not bear the anguish of losing Leila to Nadir. In brief solo interludes Leila and Nadir sing rapturously of the happiness that awaits them in some paradise far from this scene of terror. The trio is resumed as Leila and Nadir exult over their release, while Zurga cries out in wonder and despair over their great love.

As shouts of the returning crowd come from the distance, Zurga leads Leila and Nadir to a secret path by which they can escape. In another brief trio passage Leila and Nadir bid farewell to Zurga, who cries that his task has been accomplished ("Plus de crainte, ô douce étreinte").

Nourabad rushes in at the head of the throng, points to Zurga, and denounces him as the arch-traitor who set the village on fire. He has destroyed their homes and threatened their lives, the high priest shouts, and then calls upon the people to pronounce the traitor's sentence. With fierce cries they hurl themselves on Zurga, drag him to the pyre and force him to ascend. A moment later Zurga, shouting that he has given Leila his life, disappears in the flames ("Adieu, ma Leila, je te donne ma vie!").

Gazing at the pyre, the crowd chants that the will of the gods has been done and that the infamous traitor has met his just doom ("C'est l'arrêt de Dieu"). Then they turn to the flaming jungle behind them and cry in fear-stricken tones that the angry gods are avenging themselves on the people. As they prostrate themselves and rise again with a thunderous cry to Brahma, the curtain falls.

PIQUE-DAME

(*The Queen of Spades*)
by PETER ILYITCH TSCHAIKOWSKY
(1840–93)

Libretto by
M. I. TSCHAIKOWSKY

Based on a story by Pushkin

CHARACTERS

Czekalinsky	Tenor
Ssurin	Bass
Hermann, a young officer	Tenor
Count Tomsky	Baritone
Prince Yeletsky	Baritone
The Countess	Mezzo-soprano
Lisa, her granddaughter, betrothed to	
Prince Yeletsky	Soprano
Pauline, Lisa's companion	Contralto
Governess	Mezzo-soprano
Mascha, Lisa's maid	Soprano
Master of ceremonies	Tenor

Chloë	⎫	persons in the Interlude,	⎧	Soprano
Daphnis (Pauline)	⎬	*The Sincere Shepherdess*	⎨	Contralto
Plutus (Tomsky)	⎭		⎩	Baritone

Tschaplitsky	⎫	gamblers	⎧	Tenor
Narumoff	⎭		⎩	Bass

Servants, governesses, townspeople, guests, gamblers, children, actors

Place: St. Petersburg
Time: End of the eighteenth century
First performance: St. Petersburg, December 19, 1890
Original language: Russian

Pushkin's strange and dramatic story about the Queen of Spades greatly interested Tschaikowsky, and he composed the opera with much enthusiasm. Written about three years before his death, the score contains few set arias or ensembles. Much of it is in recitative sung over a symphonic accompaniment.

There is a brief prelude which opens with somber chords suggestive of a "fate" motive. This is followed by themes which will be heard in arias sung by Hermann and Lisa, and these are merged into a dramatic climax.

ACT ONE

[Scene One] A public garden in St. Petersburg on a beautiful spring day. There are pleasant walks and playgrounds, and a grove is visible in the background. The park is thronged with children, maids, nurses and governesses. Several little girls, playing the game of "cat and mouse," begin singing the words of their game ("Gorew, gorew yasno"). This builds into a gay ensemble as maids, nurses, governesses and small boys sing various refrains. The maids urge the children to dance and sing and to make the most of their carefree childhood. The governesses complain that they must spend their days watching over noisy and disobedient youngsters. A group of boys playing soldiers marches by, singing a brave chorus about facing shot and shell in defense of the fatherland. Many of the small children troop after the boys, and the women leave to follow their charges.

Czekalinsky and Ssurin, two young-men-about-town, stroll in, discussing last night's card game. It lasted all night, as usual, Ssurin says. Czekalinsky mentions their friend Hermann and his strange obsession for cards. He sits at the card table watching every move of the game but never plays. Perhaps he is working out some system to win, Ssurin suggests with a laugh. Czekalinsky dryly observes that there may be another reason why Hermann does not play—he has no money.

While the two are talking they meet Hermann and his companion, Count Tomsky. Hermann, moody and preoccupied, does not notice Czekalinsky and Ssurin as they pass. When Tomsky asks why he is sad he mumbles a vague answer. Tomsky says he cannot understand why Hermann's usual gaiety has given way to melancholy. Now he sits at the gaming tables all night long, never playing, but watching the game with a strangely troubled expression.

Admitting that the cards have a powerful fascination for him, Hermann finally confesses that the real reason for his perturbed state of mind is that he is in love with a beautiful woman he has seen at the gambling house. She is proud and high-born, and he does not dare approach her. He gives voice to his emotions in an impassioned refrain ("Sravenja vsye perebiraya"), in which he compares her to an angel. He is tormented by the thought that her heart may belong to someone else. Only a kiss from her, he sighs, would soothe his anguish.

Tomsky urges him to pluck up courage and tell the lady about his love, but Hermann answers that as an officer in modest circumstances he could never hope to win her. In that case, Tomsky says, with practical logic, he had better find himself another girl. Hermann protests that there can never be another woman in his life but this beautiful creature. As the two continue on their way Tomsky advises Hermann to control his emotions lest they drive him to madness.

When they have gone strollers throng into the park and join in a tuneful chorus ("Nakonetz to Bog poslal nam"). They rejoice that the month of May, with its sunshine and laughter, has come at last, and that the biting winds of early spring have given way to warm and refreshing breezes. At the conclusion of the chorus Hermann and Tomsky reappear, still discussing the lady whom Hermann adores from afar. Tomsky asks if she has ever given him a sign of returning his affections. At times, Hermann replies, it seems as though she looks at him with an expression of mingled love and pity. But it is hopeless, and there is only one course left to him, Hermann adds melodramatically, and that is to die.

At that moment Prince Yeletsky approaches with Czekalinsky and Ssurin, who are congratulating him on his betrothal to Lisa. Tomsky adds his congratulations as he and Hermann greet the Prince. The voices of Hermann and Yeletsky blend briefly. The Prince revels in the beautiful May day which has brought him so much happiness, while Hermann, aside, reflects that what is a blessing for others is misfortune for him.

As Tomsky asks the Prince who his future bride is, Lisa and the Countess appear. Yeletsky proudly indicates Lisa. Hermann staggers back in surprise and dismay as he recognizes her, realizing that the woman he worships is to be the bride of another. Lisa and the Countess, in their turn, are startled at seeing the mysterious stranger whom they have noticed at the gambling house. Tomsky, turning to Hermann with a look of pity, quietly remarks that his problem is solved. Czekalinsky and Ssurin, talking together, remain in the background.

A brief but impressive quintet ensues ("Mnye strashno! on opyat peredo mnoy"). Lisa and the Countess exclaim over the strange coincidence of their meeting with Hermann and wonder if it bodes some misfortune. Hermann declares that the sight of the Countess fills him with a nameless fear and then laments that he has lost forever the woman he loves. Tomsky sympathizes with Hermann's suffering and then notes that Lisa seems strangely agitated upon seeing him. Prince Yeletsky also notices Lisa's apparent confusion and wonders why this sudden change has come over her.

After the quintet Tomsky approaches the Countess, who asks him about Hermann. Continuing the conversation, they walk a little distance away, while Prince Yeletsky sings ardently to Lisa of their future happiness. Glaring after them as they leave arm in arm, Hermann mutters that unseen disaster will soon blast the Prince's happiness like a bolt of lightning. A low rumble of thunder sounds in the distance as Hermann seats himself on a bench and abandons himself to gloomy thoughts.

Tomsky, having taken leave of the Countess, comes forward and is joined by Czekalinsky and Ssurin. They refer to the Countess as a rather frightening old hag, and then Tomsky asks the other two if they have ever heard the story of how the Countess, who was called the Queen of Spades, fell in love with the Jack of Spades. As Czekalinsky and Ssurin entreat him to tell the story, Hermann looks up expectantly and listens with intense interest. In a dramatic monologue ("O, tack poslushayte!") Tomsky relates that the Countess, in her youth, was a reigning beauty of Paris. Because of her all-absorbing passion for cards she was called the Queen of Spades. One of her lovers, the Count Saint-Germain, was skilled in black magic, and he taught her a secret combination of three cards which enabled her always to win. She not only cheated at cards but betrayed her husband by making love to another, to whom she told the card secret. One day when she was playing at Versailles she lost almost all her fortune, having suddenly forgotten the combination which Saint-Germain had taught her.

She looked up from the table to see a mysterious stranger gazing at her. He approached and invited her to walk in the garden with him, saying that there, in the light of the full moon, he would tell her the secret of the three cards. Having taught her the trick, the stranger—who, of course, was the devil in disguise—said that if she went back to the game and doubled her bets she would win all she had lost and a fortune besides. This proved true, and she was even able to recoup her husband's losses. But one night when she was at a game with another admirer to whom she had told the secret, the devil appeared and warned her that if she told the secret of the three cards to a third lover she would die on the spot. As Tomsky speaks the storm comes nearer, with the thunder rumbling louder and louder. Laughing over the story, Tomsky, Czekalinsky and Ssurin hurry away, leaving Hermann alone.

Soon crowds of people come running by, all scurrying for shelter from the storm, which is about to break. They sing an agitated chorus, urging all to seek cover ("Kack bistro groza nastupila"). As the storm rages about him Hermann voices his thoughts about Tomsky's story in a dramatic soliloquy ("Poluchish smertelniy oodar ti"). Repeating the devil's warning to the Countess, he suddenly gives way to his anger and jealousy. Shouting to the lightning and thunder to be his witnesses, he swears that he will win Lisa for himself. As he rushes away the curtain falls.

[*Scene Two*] Lisa's room. At one side is a glass-enclosed porch, beyond which a garden is visible. Lisa is seated at the piano. With her are Pauline and a group of girls who have come to celebrate Lisa's engagement. Lisa and Pauline sing a charming pastoral duet ("Oojh vetcher oblakov"), which is applauded by the other young ladies in chorus. Then Pauline sings a solo, a sentimental and melancholy song of unrequited love ("Podrugi miliya").

When Lisa and the others appear deeply moved Pauline makes amends for this mournful interlude by suggesting that they sing a gay folk song they all know—the song of Mashenka. Dancing about and clapping their hands to mark the rhythm, Pauline and the other girls sing a typically Russian song about a girl who scorned a rich suitor and married the lad of her choice ("Nuka svetik Mashenka"). Lisa does not join them but stands looking thoughtfully out at the garden.

The singing and dancing are interrupted by the governess, who comes bustling in and scolds the girls for their undignified conduct. Warning them to behave with decorum befitting young ladies of society, the governess stalks out, the girls meekly following. Pauline remains behind for a moment in an effort to cheer Lisa and then affectionately bids her good night.

Mascha, the maid, comes in, puts out all the lights but one, and is about to close the door to the garden. Lisa tells her to leave it open and then dismisses her. Gazing into the garden, she sings, in a beautiful aria, of the thoughts that are troubling her ("Otkooda yeti slezi"). She wonders why she is haunted by a strange longing that moves her to tears, despite the fact that she has everything her heart desires. She is loved by the Prince, who is handsome, gracious and charming. And yet when he is near she becomes frightened and bewildered, because another man seems always to be standing at his side. It is the stranger of the gambling house. In passionate phrases she confides the secret of her love to the night, singing that it is as mysterious and inscrutable as the stranger himself.

As she moves away from the door Hermann comes in from the garden. Lisa, seeing him, shrinks back in surprise and alarm. A dramatic colloquy ensues. Hermann implores her to let him speak, if only to say good-by. When she excitedly orders him to leave he draws a pistol from his pocket and threatens to kill himself. At Lisa's restraining gesture he puts the weapon away. In a passionate refrain he confesses his love for her ("Vet yeto moi posledniy smertniy tchass"). By giving her love to another, he cries, she has sealed his doom. He asks only one embrace before they part forever, and then he can go willingly to his death. As he kneels supplicatingly before her she bursts into tears. Hermann asks if her tears mean acceptance or refusal, and when her manner indicates that she has yielded to his plea, he is wild with joy.

Their conversation is interrupted by a knock on the door. The Countess' voice is heard outside. Warning Hermann that it is too late to escape, she tells him to hide behind a curtain. Composing herself, Lisa opens the door to admit the Countess and several of her maids. She demands to know why Lisa is not asleep and asks to whom she was talking. Lisa replies that she was merely reciting a few lines from *Werther*.[1] Fuming that the erratic notions of the younger generation are beyond her comprehension, the Countess orders Lisa to go to bed and then sweeps out of the room.

No sooner has she gone than Hermann emerges from his hiding place, thoughtfully murmuring the words of the devil's prophecy about the cards as related in Tomsky's story. Lisa meanwhile locks the door after the Countess. As she turns to Hermann he renews his entreaties for her love. Lisa sharply orders him to go at once, but when he says that to go is to die, she yields. Rushing into each other's arms, they pledge their love in exultant phrases as the curtain falls.

ACT TWO

[*Scene One*] The luxurious ballroom in the home of a diplomat. Guests in masquerade costumes and evening dress are dancing. A group of choristers seated on one side of the room sings an impressive number hailing the festivities ("Radostno, veselo v djen sey"). After the chorus the master of ceremonies announces that fireworks will be shown in the garden. As all the guests leave to view the display, Tomsky, Czekalinsky and Ssurin, all masked, come in. They are discussing Hermann's eccentric behavior of late. Ssurin declares that he is trying to solve the riddle of the three cards, but Tomsky insists that Hermann is not gullible enough to be taken in by anything so fantastic. Czekalinsky and Ssurin decide to have a bit of sport at Hermann's expense over the matter of the cards. They go out into the garden with Tomsky.

As servants set up the scenery for the Interlude in the center of the room Lisa and the Prince come in, both unmasked. The Prince anxiously asks Lisa the reason for her sadness, but she replies evasively. Looking at her earnestly, Yeletsky entreats her, in an eloquent refrain, to believe in his love ("Postoyte na odno mgnovenje"). Begging Lisa to confess her fears to him, he declares that he will protect her from every

---

[1] Goethe's famous romantic novel, *Die Leiden des jungen Werthers* (*The Sorrows of Young Werther*).

danger. He can no longer bear the torment of her silence, he says, and entreats her to trust in him. At the conclusion of the refrain Lisa and Yeletsky walk slowly toward the garden.

Hermann now enters wearing a costume but no mask. He is reading a note from Lisa telling him to meet her after the performance. Hermann muses that if he could solve the riddle of the cards he could quickly win his fortune and then take Lisa away with him. At that moment Czeka-linsky and Ssurin creep up behind Hermann and in whispered tones ask if he is the third lover who will bring about the Countess's death through the three cards. Then they vanish. Hermann leaps to his feet in terror, fearing that he has heard the ghostly voice of fate. The voices of Czekalinsky, Ssurin, and several other masqueraders are heard outside, repeating, "Three cards!" Hermann distractedly rushes away.

The Interlude, a pastoral play entitled *The Sincere Shepherdess,* is now performed for the entertainment of the guests. It has the classic characters of Daphnis, Chloë, Plutus and a group of shepherds and shepherdesses. They sing a chorus in the Mozartean vein ("Pod tenju goostoju"), after which a saraband is danced. Daphnis (played by Pauline) and Chloë then enter and sing a charming love duet ("Moy milenkiy drujok").

They are interrupted by Plutus (played by Tomsky), who makes an impressive entrance in a golden chariot. With him is the goddess Fortuna. Plutus descends from his chariot with a flourish and promises Chloë a dazzling array of treasures in return for her love ("Ya gori zolotiya"). But Chloë spurns him and proclaims that her heart belongs to Daphnis, trembling and fainthearted though he is. Thereupon Plutus, in a towering rage, gets into his chariot and rides away, leaving Fortuna behind. She blesses Daphnis and Chloë, and the happiness of all is chanted by the chorus ("Prishel konetz muchenjam").

After the play the guests again mingle. Hermann, walking through the crowd, comes face to face with the Countess. As they stare at each other in confusion, Ssurin, masked, walks stealthily behind Hermann and asks him if he is pleased with his bride. Ssurin disappears before Hermann can turn and see him. Frightened and bewildered by this voice apparently out of nowhere, Hermann wonders if he is going mad.

At that moment Lisa, wearing a mask, cautiously approaches, gives Hermann a key to her house and tells him how to gain access to the Countess' room. He must come at midnight, she says, because the Countess will still be playing cards downstairs. Behind the portrait of the Countess, Lisa goes on, is a secret door which leads to her own room. She tells him to come the next day, but Hermann declares that he must be there this very night. If that is his will, Lisa says submissively, she can do nothing but assent. With that she leaves. Looking after her, Hermann reflects that it is not his will but the will of fate. Exulting over

the fact that he will at last learn the secret of the three cards, he hurries
away.

There is an excited stir as the master of ceremonies announces that
the Czarina Katerina has arrived. Led by the choir, the guests hail her
in a brief but stirring chorus ("Slavsya sim Ekaterina"). As the Czarina
enters with her retinue the curtain falls.

[*Scene Two*] The bedroom of the Countess. Several small lamps
shed a dim light. At one side is a large window, in front of which is an
armchair. Near the window is a door leading to the boudoir and another
door at the rear. On the other side of the room is a large portrait of the
Countess as a beautiful young woman—the Queen of Spades—behind
which is the secret door leading to Lisa's room.

Somber chords sound in the orchestra as Hermann appears. For a
moment he wavers, wondering if this attempt to learn the Countess' secret is too fantastic to succeed. He starts toward the secret door, deciding to abandon his plan and go to Lisa's room, when he suddenly stops
and stares at the portrait as though hypnotized. The clock strikes midnight.

In a dramatic recitative he declares that the portrait has enchanted
him and that he cannot leave ("A, vot ona, 'Veneroyu moscovskoy'").
He laments that he did not know the Countess in the days of her youth
and beauty. But even now, he muses, her fatal spell is driving him relentlessly along the path of his destiny. Hearing the sound of voices outside, Hermann conceals himself behind the curtains of the bed.

The Countess enters, attended by her maids, who sing a brief chorus
urging her to rest after her tiring day ("Blagodetelnitza nasha"). They
escort the Countess into her boudoir. Lisa and Mascha come in. Lisa
reveals that Hermann is in the house and warns Mascha not to disclose
his presence. Declaring that she has made up her mind to be his bride,
Lisa says that she will obey him unquestioningly. She goes out through
the secret door, while Mascha leaves by the door at the rear.

The Countess, now in her nightdress, reappears with her maids, who
sing another chorus of their song. They try to lead her to the bed, but
she impatiently pushes them away and seats herself in the chair by the
window. She fumes at their inane expressions of solicitude as they
flutter around trying to make her comfortable. When she is settled they
withdraw to the rear of the room.

In a long recitative the Countess expresses her distaste for the
boorish society of the present day and then abandons herself to
thoughts of the past ("Ah, postil mne yetot svet"). She meditates about
the brilliant levees at the court where Madame Pompadour held sway,
and murmurs the names of the dukes with whom she danced. She recalls the songs she sang for the royal audiences. It was at Chantilly, she

remembers, that she danced with the King. Suddenly she starts as though awakening from a dream. Looking around, she sees the maids, still waiting to be dismissed. She sends them away and then gradually falls asleep, softly singing a little French song she remembered from her youth ("Je crains de lui parler la nuit").

A moment after the Countess' voice dies away Hermann emerges from his hiding place and stands before her. She wakes with a start and stares at him in terror. Assuring her that he intends no harm, Hermann tells her that he has come to learn the secret of the three cards. As the Countess rises in alarm Hermann kneels before her and in a dramatic refrain endeavors to persuade her to reveal the secret ("Yesli, kogda-nibud znali"). If there is one spark of compassion left in her heart, he cries wildly in a melodramatic appeal to her emotions, if she can recall the happiness that love for child, sweetheart or husband ever brought into her life, then she must tell him the names of the three cards.

The Countess glares at him with cold contempt. Goaded to fury by her silence, Hermann draws his pistol. Raising her hands as though to fend him off, the Countess falls back dead. Stunned with horror, Hermann stammers that his threat was only a joke and repeats his entreaties. He takes the Countess' hand, then recoils, gasping that she is dead.

Lisa suddenly comes through the secret door. Hermann rushes to her, crying that the secret of the cards is lost forever. For a moment Lisa does not understand. Pointing to the Countess' body, Hermann moans that she is dead. Lisa rushes over and kneels sobbing at the feet of the dead woman. Shaken with remorse, Hermann pleads that he did not seek her death—he only wanted the secret of the three cards. Lisa turns on him in fury and despair, crying out that now she realizes that it was not for her love that he came here but only because of his evil passion for cards. Her trust, she sobs, has been rewarded with betrayal. Hermann tries to explain. In a ringing phrase Lisa brands him a scoundrel and orders him to go. As he staggers from the room Lisa sinks unconscious at the feet of the Countess. The curtain falls.

ACT THREE

[*Scene One*] Hermann's quarters in the barracks. Moonlight shows through the windows and the moaning of the wind is heard. Hermann is seated at a table, reading a letter by the light of a candle. From the distance comes the music of a funeral march and then the sound of trumpets and drums. Over a somber theme played by the woodwinds, Hermann reads, in a spoken voice, the letter from Lisa in which she writes that she is certain that he did not intentionally kill the Countess. She is remorseful for having blamed him and asks him to meet her at the quay at midnight so that she can ask his forgiveness and end her suffering.

Hermann bitterly reproaches himself for having caused her this sorrow. He wearily rests his head on his arms and falls asleep. A ghostly chorus is heard singing a chorale ("Gospodu molussya ya"). Hermann springs to his feet in terror, exclaiming that he hears the hymn that was sung at the Countess' funeral. He recalls the grim details of the rites—the candles, the incense, the old woman lying like a pale waxen image in her coffin. He cringes in terror as he tries to drive away the vision of the Countess' face, with one eye winking at him.

Suddenly there is a knock on the window, which is flung open by a blast of wind. The candle is blown out. As Hermann rushes in panic toward the door, the ghost of the Countess stands in his path. Softly she murmurs that she cannot rest in her grave. She tells Hermann that he must marry Lisa to save her, and then speaks the names of the three magic cards—three, seven, ace. With that the phantom disappears. As though demented, Hermann dances around the room shouting the combination. Quickly putting on his uniform, he rushes out.

[*Scene Two*] The canal near the Winter Palace. The Neva quay and the Peter-Paul fortress are seen in the background. Lisa, dressed in mourning, is standing under an archway, waiting for Hermann. It is nearly midnight, and Lisa fears that perhaps Hermann will fail to meet her. In a long soliloquy she voices her anxiety and despair ("Oojh polnoch blisitsya"). At first she refuses to admit that Hermann is capable of deceiving her, but finally, overwhelmed by hopelessness, she laments that she has allowed herself to be dazzled by glittering illusions and has been lured to her destruction by a betrayer and a murderer. In the next moment she cries for her lover and reproaches herself for doubting him. Then she sobs that her dream of love is over, that the forbidden desires to which she yielded are destroying her.

As she stands weeping she sees Hermann approaching. Ecstatically crying out that he has justified her faith in him, she rushes into his arms. Their voices blend in a brief but tender duet as they sing that sorrow and despair will be forgotten in the bliss of their future ("O da minovali stradanya"). When Lisa asks where they will go Hermann answers that he must first return to the gambling house and win his fortune. As Lisa looks at him in astonishment he begins to talk wildly about how the Countess came to him today and told him the secret of the three cards. With a distracted laugh he describes how the Countess died of fright when he threatened her with his pistol. Lisa is crushed when she realizes that he was instrumental in causing the Countess' death.

Their voices blend again as Lisa reiterates that the desires to which she yielded have betrayed her into the hands of a demon. Hermann raves that nothing matters now—he knows the secret of the three cards and destiny will have its way. He babbles that he is the fatal third lover who doomed the Countess through the three, the seven, and the ace. Lisa tries to calm him, but it is too late. Completely out of his mind, he no longer recognizes her. Pushing her roughly aside, he runs away like a madman. Crazed by anguish, Lisa rushes to the quay and hurls herself into the river.

[*Scene Three*] The gambling house. Tomsky, Czekalinsky, Ssurin, Tschaplitsky, Narumoff and other guests are seated at tables, drinking and playing cards. They sing a lively chorus in praise of wine, youth and merriment ("Budem pit i veselitsya"). After an interlude at cards the Prince enters and is cordially greeted by Tomsky, who remarks that he has not seen him in his old haunts for many a year. One always returns, the Prince replies in French, and then goes on to say that he has reversed the proverb: Unlucky in love, lucky at cards. When Tomsky looks at him with a puzzled expression the Prince explains that his engagement was broken off. The rest of the story, he says, is too sad to tell.

The conversation is interrupted by the other players, who noisily demand a song from Tomsky. After much coaxing Tomsky sings a lively ditty ("Yeslib miliya dyevitzi"), in which he compares the pretty girls to birds with whom he would like to bill and coo. His listeners gaily repeat his words and then all join in a lusty chorus, the burden of which is that God made the world as round as a coin ("Tack v nenastniye dni sobiraliss oni").

After the chorus the men resume their card games. Suddenly Hermann bursts in and lurches over to a table. Observing him, Prince Yeletsky remarks to Tomsky that his foreboding has come true and asks him to serve as his second if the need should arise. Hermann announces that he will play cards, whereupon Czekalinsky, Ssurin and some of the others cynically remark that a miracle has come to pass ("Vot tchudessa on stal igrat"). This introduces an ensemble which builds up as Hermann bets on the three and the seven and wins enormous sums. Flushed with his triumphs, Hermann calls for champagne. Glass in hand, he sings that life is like a game of cards—you wager, and then you win or you lose. Only one thing is certain: in the end Death will claim his share of the stakes.

After his song he calls for another game. The Prince challenges him. Hermann stakes all he has won on a single card. The other players urge the contestants to desist from this mad gamble. Ignoring them, Prince Yeletsky looks intently at Hermann and murmurs that at last he will get even with him.

Czekalinsky deals. "Ace wins!" cries Hermann, showing his card. The Prince says quietly, "Your queen has lost." As Hermann looks at him, dumfounded, Yeletsky tells him to look at the card in his hand.

Hermann is unable to believe his eyes. Instead of an ace he holds the queen of spades. At that moment the phantom of the Countess materializes in the background, looking as she appeared in the portrait in her room. In a frenzy Hermann screams that she has tricked him by stealing his ace of hearts. Defiantly crying that he still will escape her fatal power, he plunges a knife into his breast.

The other players crowd around him. As they support him he looks up at the Prince and gasps a plea for forgiveness. In the ecstasy of death he envisions Lisa hovering over him like an angel. As he dies an unseen chorus majestically intones a prayer for his soul ("Gospodj! Prosti yemu!"). The curtain falls.

PORGY AND BESS

by GEORGE GERSHWIN

(1898–1937)

Libretto by DU BOSE HEYWARD

Lyrics by DU BOSE HEYWARD and IRA GERSHWIN

Based on the play *Porgy*, by Du Bose and Dorothy Heyward

CHARACTERS

Porgy, a cripple	Bass-baritone
Crown, a tough stevedore	Baritone
Bess, Crown's girl	Soprano
Robbins, an inhabitant of Catfish Row	Tenor
Serena, his wife	Soprano
Jake, skipper of a fishing boat	Baritone
Clara, his wife	Soprano
Maria, proprietress of the cookshop	Contralto
Sporting Life, a dope peddler	Tenor
Mingo	Tenor
Peter, the Honey Man	Tenor
Lily, the Strawberry Woman, Peter's wife	Mezzo-soprano
Frazier, a Negro "lawyer"	Baritone
Annie	Mezzo-soprano
Jim, a cotton picker	Baritone
Undertaker	Baritone
Crab Man	Tenor

Alan Archdale
Detective
Policemen ⎫ speaking parts
Coroner
Scipio

Inhabitants of Catfish Row, fishermen, children, stevedores

Place: Catfish Row, Charleston, South Carolina, U.S.A.
Time: The recent past
First performance: Boston, Massachusetts, September 30, 1935
Original language: English

Presented by the Theatre Guild, *Porgy and Bess* was given its premiere with such famous Negro singer-actors as Todd Duncan (Porgy), Anne Brown (Bess), Warren Coleman (Crown) and John W. Bubbles (Sporting Life). It opened at the Alvin Theater, New York City, on October 10, 1935.

The first European performance was in Zurich in 1945. In 1952 an all-Negro company headed by Metropolitan Opera soprano Leontyne Price made a triumphant tour of Europe. The company performed to great acclaim in Moscow in 1955–56.

Recognized as the first truly American opera to make a genuine success, the music of *Porgy and Bess* is founded on the jazz rhythms of the 1920s. Gershwin developed an idiom of his own, based on one segment of American life. While critics at first argued whether it was high-class musical comedy or low-class grand opera, the eventual consensus was that it is a folk opera of the highest order. Not all of the musical numbers (some thirty-one are indexed) can be called operatic, but all are solidly constructed on a soundly conceived harmonic basis. In certain instances, Gershwin made effective use of the Wagnerian leitmotiv technique—at least to the extent of identifying analogous situations by means of the same themes in different harmonic patterns.

In this opera the characters sing and speak in "Gullah" dialect, the language of the Negroes living in the coastal areas of South Carolina and Georgia. To assure authenticity, Gershwin spent some months in the area among the people there.

As musician and composer, George Gershwin traveled the road from Tin Pan Alley to the concert hall and the operatic stage. He supplied all or part of the music for some twenty-two Broadway musical comedies—practically all of them outstanding successes. His first successful attempt at a serious work was the famous *Rhapsody in Blue,* in 1924. The *Concerto in F* came a year later, and *An American in Paris* followed in 1928. Then he turned to opera, and *Porgy and Bess* was his last major work. It has been seen and heard by more people than any other American opera.

On July 11, 1937, George Gershwin, thirty-nine years old, died in Hollywood. He was then on the threshold of even greater fame as a potent force in American music.

There is no overture. The curtain rises after a brief orchestral introduction in a brisk jazz tempo, with scoring for xylophone, triangle, chimes and brass.

ACT ONE

[*Scene One*] Jasbo Brown's room on Catfish Row on a summer night. At the piano, Jasbo is playing a blues number in a slow, hypnotic rhythm. In the dim half light, a half-dozen couples are swaying trance-like to the music as they sing "Da-doo-da, wa-wa, O-wa-de-wa" in softly accented phrases, almost like an incantation.

The lights dim out, then come up on another group on the stage, in the center of which Clara sits with her baby in her arms. Rocking back and forth, she sings the tender lullaby "Summertime." Its languorous tempo reflects the happy-go-lucky mood of Catfish Row at this time of year when "the livin' is easy, an' the cotton is high."

Again the lights fade and then come up on still another group—Mingo and his friends shooting dice. The easy rhythms change to a driving syncopation over the beat of tom-toms. Kneeling in a circle and rolling the dice, Mingo and the other players break into a chorus sung in typical crap game jargon, "Roll dem bones." Around them, Catfish Row stirs into its usual nocturnal activity. Couples stroll back and forth, children scamper about laughing and playing games.

As conversation continues in quasi-recitative among the players, an argument develops. Sporting Life produces his own dice; Jake, rolling them, begins complaining about his bad luck. Thereupon Mingo snatches them up and shows them to Jake, who exclaims that they are the dice that "cleaned out the game last Saturday night." Sporting Life curses Mingo. The three men glower at each other.

At this juncture Serena and Robbins appear. Ignoring his wife's plea not to join the game, Robbins kneels down and begins throwing the dice. Clara comes in with her baby in her arms. Watching the game, she sings a reprise of "Summertime." In a choral accompaniment, the men sing in dice game chatter: "Seven come seven." At the close of the chorus, Jake walks over to Clara and notices that the baby is still wide awake.

Taking the child from her, he sings his own "lullaby," one of the most engaging numbers in the opera, "A woman is a sometime thing." In catchy jazz rhythm, Jake, with good-natured cynicism, warns his offspring that woman will born him, mourn him and tie him to her apron strings until some other woman comes to claim him. She in turn will take his clothes and leave him. At the climax of the refrain, the dice players join in a lusty chorus.

With a self-satisfied air, Jake hands the baby back to Clara bragging that he has put the child to sleep. As he turns back to the game there is a loud wail from the child. The players laugh derisively. Clara leaves, remarking disdainfully that her baby has better sense than to listen to Jake's foolishness.

Just as the players are about to resume, Maria, standing in the doorway of her shop, calls out that Porgy is coming. She orders the boy Scipio to open the iron gate at the end of the street to let him in. Seated in a small cart drawn by a goat, Porgy rides in like a charioteer to the accompaniment of an imposing theme which musically identifies him in the style of a Wagnerian leitmotiv. The crowd greets him noisily; the dice players welcome him as "the ol' crap shark."

From his cart, Porgy responds with a courtly "good evenin'" to the ladies present. Over a chromatic triad figure in the orchestra, he announces that his luck is riding high: he has a pocketful of money which will go to any man who "has the guts to shoot it off me."

Just as the men are about to roll the dice, one of the players calls out that Crown is approaching—and he seems to be in an ugly mood. Porgy asks if Bess is with him, which prompts Jake to taunt him about being "soft" on Crown's girl. Porgy hotly denies this. But when Maria and Serena sneer that Bess is unfit for decent company, Porgy angrily rebukes them in a memorable phrase sung over sustained chords in the orchestra: "Between the Gawd-fearin' women and the Gawd-dammin' men, that gal ain't got a chance."

Then he gives voice to his mingled bitterness and defiance in a moving refrain, "They pass by singin'." Women will have nothing to do with a cripple, he sings. They pass his door, look in, then go on their way. A cripple is fated to travel the lonesome road alone. As he ends the refrain on a melancholy phrase, Crown is heard shouting outside. A moment later he swaggers in with Bess.

First he loudly orders Sporting Life to bring him a drink, and the latter immediately hands him a pint bottle. Crown drinks and hands the bottle to Bess, who follows suit and then passes the bottle to Robbins. Crown roughly snatches it out of his hands. Throwing down his money, Crown announces he is ready to play.

Robbins is the first to throw. Mingo tauntingly remarks that Robbins' wife allows him only fifty cents to gamble with. Bess steps forward and offers to stake him to the game. Porgy takes due note of this, then pointedly offers Robbins some timely advice by way of a reprise of "A woman is a sometime thing." Bess and the dice players join him in a choral interlude.

As the game continues, with the players calling their throws in crap game jargon, the tension increases. Crown, suspicious, ill tempered and getting drunker, warns that he will stand for no cheating. Losing all his throws, he rubs the dice with a rabbit's foot for luck. Robbins sneers that he is too drunk to read the dice. Not drunk enough, Crown retorts, then asks Sporting Life for a packet of dope. Bess sharply warns the peddler not to give Crown the "happy dust," but she obediently pays the peddler for it when Crown orders her to. Peter steps between the two men with a well-intentioned warning that dice and "happy dust" do not mix. Crown threatens him with his fist, but the others restrain him. As the game is resumed, Sporting Life wins the pot. In a brief choral passage in canon form, some of the group comment that Crown is "cockeyed drunk." He cuts them short with a menacing gesture and a snarl.

Jake calls out that it is Porgy's turn to roll the dice. Eyes half closed, swaying from side to side, Porgy begins to sing "Oh, little stars, roll" like an incantation over sustained chords in the orchestra. He rolls and takes the pot as Crown glares in mounting anger. With a jeering laugh, Porgy rolls again—but this time he loses. Robbins throws next, makes his point and picks up the money.

Grabbing Robbins' wrist, Crown threatens to kill him ("Touch that money an' meet yo' Gawd!"). This marks the beginning of the opera's first big ensemble scene, which culminates in Crown's murder of Robbins. With reckless courage, Robbins defies Crown. The onlookers, all in terror of Crown and realizing what will happen, implore each other to head off the fight—but no one moves. Suddenly the two men lunge at each other. Serena, distractedly begging for help, tries to go to her husband's aid but is held back by Jake and Clara.

As the chorus rises to a frenzied climax, Crown and Robbins crouch face to face in the shafts of light streaming from windows suddenly flung open. Crown brandishes his cotton hook. Then, as an ascending chromatic passage erupts in the orchestra, he seizes Robbins and kills him with one terrible blow of the cotton hook. Robbins' body falls in front of Porgy's door. Crown stands staring at his victim as though hypnotized.

Rushing to his side, Bess urges him to flee before the police arrive. At the word "police," the onlookers, who have been watching the scene in stunned silence, vanish as if by magic. When Crown asks where she will hide, Bess casually replies that there will always be a man around to take care of her. He had better be "temporary," Crown growls menacingly. As he turns to go, Bess takes money from her stocking and gives it to him.

A moment later, Sporting Life appears. Bess asks him for "happy dust" to steady her nerves. Giving her the powder, the peddler insinuatingly suggests that she go to New York with him. There, he says, they will make a "swell team." When Bess scornfully rebuffs him he slinks away.

During an ensuing orchestral interlude, Bess tries the doors of the nearby houses, looking for a place to hide from the police. Some are locked, others are opened and then slammed in her face. She finally reaches the door of Maria's shop, where Maria answers her desperate plea for help with an insult. Despairingly, Bess asks who lives across the street. Porgy, Maria tells her, adding callously that he would be of no help to a woman of her kind—he is only a crippled beggar.

With a hopeless gesture, Bess walks slowly toward the iron gate at the end of the street. At the sound of a police whistle she stops, then turns back toward Porgy's house. She recoils in horror as she comes upon Serena, still crouched over Robbins' body. Averting her eyes, Bess hurries into Porgy's house. The curtain slowly falls as a variation of the theme of Porgy's loneliness ("They pass by singin'") begins in the orchestra and builds into a surging climax.

[*Scene Two*] Serena's room, the following night. Robbins' body lies on a bed in the center of the room. Serena is seated at the foot, with the mourners huddled around her. This entire scene is given over to one of the most overpowering ensembles in the opera. A choral adaptation of the typical Negro spiritual, it is dominated by the descending chromatic figure of its opening phrase—"He's gone, gone, gone"—in the tempo of a funeral march.

During the chanting, visitors come to pay their respects. The first of these are Porgy and Bess. Serena glares as Bess, observing the funeral custom, goes toward the bed with a gift of burial money. The widow angrily protests that she does not need Crown's money to bury her husband. Bess quietly replies that it is not Crown's money, but Porgy's. Somewhat mollified, Serena tells her to put it in the saucer with the rest of the burial collection.

One of the mourners raises her voice in fervent appeal—"Come on, sister, come on, brudder, fill up de saucer." This theme is taken up by the chorus. Peter and Lily enter and add their contributions while the mourners pray for more money to take care of the widow and her fatherless children. As the chorus of entreaty rises to a climax, there is a dramatic interruption.

A commotion is heard outside and in the next moment a detective, a white man and two policemen burst into the room. A scene in spoken dialogue ensues. Serena leaps to her feet as the other Negroes cower in fear. The detective begins a brutal inquisition, first asking Serena if her husband left any funeral insurance. When Serena answers no, the detective tells her to see to it that Robbins is buried the next day. Whirling on Peter, the detective accuses him of murdering Robbins, and warns him that he will be hanged for it. When Peter denies it, the detective draws his pistol and demands that he name the killer. Peter stammers that Crown is guilty.

Still not satisfied, the detective turns on Porgy. At first the cripple is silent, even when threatened with the pistol. Then he quietly protests that he knows nothing at all about the killing. In baffled fury, the detective orders the policemen to take Peter to jail as a material witness and keep him there until Crown is caught.

Crown is on the loose, Porgy says, and there isn't a rope long enough to hang him. So much the worse for the old man, the detective growls.

Turning to Serena, he snarls that unless Robbins is buried the next day, the Board of Health will turn his body over to the medical students. Serena's lamentations mingle with Peter's anguished cries of protest as the policemen drag him away.

Stunned and bewildered, the Negroes huddle together. Porgy, in a recitative passage, reflects on the cruel irony of the situation: Peter, an innocent man, is dragged off to jail; Crown, a killer, goes on his lawless way unpunished. The dolorous chant, "Gone, gone, gone," breaks out again, softly at first, then crescendoing to a wild outburst of grief.

As a heavy, pulsating rhythm begins in the orchestra, Serena suddenly gives way to her sorrow in the poignant aria "My man's gone now." Instead of being comforted by her husband, she wails, Old Man Sorrow will be her only companion as she travels on to the Promised Land. The mourners, swaying to the beat of the music, join in a keening accompaniment. Serena ends the aria on a descending phrase of utter despair.

Meanwhile, the undertaker enters, quietly watches the scene, then takes up the matter of funeral arrangements with Serena. When she tells him there are only fifteen dollars in the burial saucer, he observes, with professional solicitude, that that is hardly enough to bury a grown man. Remembering the detective's warning, Serena begs the undertaker to bury her husband in the graveyard to keep his body out of the hands of the medical students.

Moved by her frantic plea, the undertaker finally agrees to provide "the box and one carriage," even though it means losing money. Emptying the contents of the burial saucer into his pocket, the undertaker leaves.

The mood of the scene now changes abruptly from profound sorrow to a kind of mystical ecstasy. The transformation occurs when Bess leaps to her feet and bursts out in an exuberant phrase: "The train is at the station an' you better get aboard." The words are sung in a gradually increasing rhythm imitating the starting of a train. The mourners, responding to Bess's mood of exaltation, express their feelings in the jubilant chorus "Leavin' today."

This marks the beginning of the spectacular ensemble which concludes the act. With joyous abandon, the mourners sing of the "rollin' drivin' wheels" of the heavenly train that will carry them to the Promised Land to meet their departed brother. The chorus, impelled by the driving syncopation of the orchestral accompaniment, rises to a tremendous climax.

ACT TWO

[*Scene One*] Before the rise of the curtain, the chimes of St. Michael's Church, adjacent to Catfish Row, mingle with the voices of Jake and his fishing crew singing a wordless fragment of a sailor's ditty. The chimes strike nine. At the curtain the men are seen repairing their nets and swaying to the rhythm of the music. Jake strikes up a chanty about taking his boat out to the banks to fish ("Oh, I'm goin' out to the Blackfish Banks").

Spoken dialogue and recitative follow. Annie calls down from her window to remind the sailors about the picnic and the parade, which is due to start at ten o'clock. Clara anxiously warns Jake to keep a weather eye open for the September storms. Laughing, Jake answers he must go out in spite of hurricanes to make money for his son's college education.

Porgy, at the window of his room, strums his banjo and sings the delightful number "I got plenty o' nuttin'." It is an eloquent expression of his serene contentment with his lot in life—he has his "gal and his song" and needs nothing more. In a brief choral interlude ("Porgy change"), the listening neighbors marvel at the change which has come over Porgy since Bess has come into his life. All are happy about the couple except Serena, who observes bitterly that only a killer like Crown is a match for a woman like Bess.

A succession of episodic but musically integrated scenes, contributing to the development of the plot, now follows. In the first of these, Sporting Life enters Maria's shop. She watches him grimly as he pours a packet of dope into his palm. Just as he is about to inhale the powder, she blows it out of his hand. He turns on her with a curse. Eyeing him coldly, Maria warns him not to peddle "happy dust" in her shop.

Then in one swift movement she seizes him by the throat, forces him down on the table top and picks up a carving knife. With the knife poised at his throat, she pours out her contempt for him in what is virtually an "aria" in spoken words over an ominous, throbbing accompaniment ("I hates your struttin' style"). She vows that if he does not stop peddling dope to the people of Catfish Row she will carve him up and feed his carcass to the buzzards. Neighbors who have crowded in to watch the encounter laugh at his plight. The hapless peddler gasps in terror. Fortunately for him, Lawyer Frazier, a shyster, walks into the shop at that moment. Maria releases her victim and casually greets the lawyer.

Frazier tells her he is looking for a man named Porgy. Called from his house across the street by Maria, he is questioned by the lawyer about Bess. When Porgy declares that she is now his woman, Frazier informs him that Bess must divorce Crown to make the present arrangement "legal." In a remarkable demonstration of extralegal skulduggery, Frazier talks Porgy into buying a "divorce" for one dollar and a half. When the fraudulent document is duly signed and sealed, the shyster triumphantly observes that it has cost only one dollar and a half to change a woman to a lady. With that he struts away. The onlookers, in gleeful derision, chant "Woman to lady."

The merriment suddenly evaporates when Scipio calls out that a white man is approaching. When the stranger enters and announces he is looking for a man named Porgy, the crowd stares at him in suspicious silence. But when he adds that he comes with good news, the neighbors bring Porgy forward to meet him. Introducing himself as Mister Archdale, the visitor tells Porgy that his friend Peter will soon be back home. Peter's family once were in his service, he explains, and he has furnished bond for him. Porgy and all the others call down a blessing on Peter's benefactor.

As he is leaving, he encounters Lawyer Frazier. Knowing his man, Archdale remarks that he hopes the lawyer is "not selling any more divorces." Thereupon Porgy shows him the spurious document. Archdale sternly warns Frazier to close up his "divorce mill" or go to jail. He adds magnanimously that he will not report the lawyer this time. Cringing, Frazier mumbles his thanks.

To the accompaniment of a menacing trill high in the strings, a huge bird suddenly swoops low over the crowd. Porgy cries that it is a buzzard, a bird of evil omen. The people voice their superstitious terror in a choral phrase, "Drive him off!" In a dramatic aria, "Buzzard, keep on flyin'," Porgy defiantly sings that the buzzard's menace is powerless against two people who can share love and laughter. No longer will the creature's evil shadow darken his door, nor will he be its helpless prey. In the ringing climax of the aria, Porgy sings that for him there will be no more loneliness and despair—because Porgy is "young again." All the neighbors join him in a thunderous closing phrase: "Buzzard, keep on flyin'!"

Porgy limps to his room and the others disperse, leaving only Bess and Sporting Life. Sidling up to her, the peddler again tries to persuade her to go to New York with him. Again Bess angrily rebuffs him. Still persisting, he offers her dope and tries to pour some of the powder into her hand. Snatching away her hand, Bess cries that she is through with dope.

At that moment, Porgy, unseen, opens his door and overhears the two. Still holding the powder toward Bess, Sporting Life taunts that nobody ever is through with "happy dust." Porgy's hand emerges from the doorway and seizes the peddler's wrist in a viselike grip. Forcing Sporting Life to his knees, Porgy warns him to stay away from Bess, then sends him sprawling from the doorstep. Leering at Bess, Sporting Life remarks that when all her other men have deserted her, he and his "happy dust" still will be close by. He saunters away as Porgy curses him.

Porgy turns to Bess and begins the famous duet "Bess, you is my woman now," the best-known number in the opera. He sings that her love has blotted out the bitter, lonely past, and Bess responds that she will be his forever—"mornin' time an' evenin' time an' summer time an' winter time." The duet ends on a serene chord as they embrace.

The raucous sound of a brass band breaks the mood of the scene. The residents of Catfish Row, all in their best finery, stream out of their houses and begin dancing to the music of the band. In a rousing chorus ("Oh, I can't sit down") they look forward to a day of fun at a picnic on Kittiwah Island.

Porgy and Bess watch the gay procession follow the band on the way to the wharf. Maria, carrying a huge basket, comes by and admonishes Bess to hurry. Bess replies that she does not want to leave Porgy, but at his insistence she reluctantly joins Maria. Gazing fondly after her, Porgy turns back to his room with a joyous reprise of his song—"Got my gal, got my song."

[*Scene Two*] Kittiwah Island. The same day. The scene opens to the beat of African drums, to which the picnickers are dancing with characteristic abandon. More music is supplied by an "orchestra" composed of youngsters playing mouth organs, combs, bones and washboards. One beats out a bass rhythm on an overturned washtub. Caught up in the frenzy of the music, the picnickers burst into a wild, barbaric chorus, "I ain't got no shame." At its conclusion, Sporting Life ambles forward and entertains the crowd with one of the most engaging numbers in the opera, "It ain't necessarily so." A gem of musical wit, it is Sporting Life's saturnine commentary on some of the familiar Bible stories— David and Goliath, Jonah and the whale, Moses in the bulrushes, and Methuselah. The crowd joins Sporting Life in the closing phrases.

But one of the listeners is Serena, who is outraged at this mockery of biblical tales. Stalking through the crowd, she denounces Sporting Life and his listeners in hellfire-and-damnation terms ("Shame on all you sinners"), warning them that the Lord surely will punish them for their godless ways. As they squirm under her accusing gaze, she orders them to pack up their baskets and hurry to the boat which is about to sail back to the mainland. Gathering up their belongings, the picnickers scamper toward the wharf. Last to leave are Serena and Maria, who call to Bess to hurry.

As the two women disappear, Bess, carrying a picnic basket, appears and hastens after them. A sharp whistle from a nearby thicket stops her in her tracks. Dropping her basket, she gasps: "Crown!" This marks the beginning of the long duet which is one of the most dramatic episodes in the opera. It is sung partly in recitative, partly in lyrical interludes. Crown, who has been hiding on the island since the murder of Robbins, tells Bess he has managed to stay alive by foraging for food. When he avidly tries to embrace her, she protests that she will miss the boat back to the mainland.

Barring her way, he reminds her that he promised to come back for her at cotton-picking time. Now, he says, his friend Johnny can get them aboard the river boat to Savannah. Vainly trying to elude him, Bess tells him that she has been living with Porgy. Crown greets this with a sneer and again reminds her that any such arrangement was to be strictly "temporary." Menacingly he asks if she would prefer a crippled beggar to a man like Crown.

In tones of desperate entreaty, Bess answers that she cannot bear the thought of Porgy waiting for her in vain when the boat returns to Catfish Row. Again a mocking laugh from Crown. Resorting to feminine guile, Bess pleads that she is getting old . . . for five long years she has been at his beck and call . . . now, a strong man like Crown needs a young girl. . . . As for herself, the only man who needs her is Porgy. But Crown, wild with desire, keeps repeating that Bess is his woman. The two reiterate these assertions in duet form as the scene builds to a climax.

Bess tries to break away as the steamboat whistle sounds. Crown seizes her in a passionate embrace and kisses her to the accompaniment of a strongly accentuated orchestral theme which may be identified as the "kiss" motive. For a moment Bess fiercely resists him, then voluptuously enfolds him in her arms. In savage triumph, Crown sings, over a discordant variation of the "kiss" motive, the concluding phrase of the duet: "Wid you and me it will always be the same." Then, as an ascending chromatic figure flares in the orchestra, Crown violently pushes Bess into a palmetto thicket. She struggles to her feet and slowly backs away from him deeper into the foliage. He follows her like an animal stalking its prey. The curtain falls as the orchestra thunderously repeats —this time in strident open fifths—the closing theme of the duet.

[*Scene Three*] Catfish Row. Before dawn a week later. The fishermen are getting ready to leave. Jake enters, carrying a lantern and a net, and calls his men together. One of them remarks that he sees signs of a storm, but Jake cautions him not to scare the womenfolk with that kind of talk. Trooping out, the men sing a reprise of the chanty heard at the beginning of the act.

As their singing dies away in the distance, a piercing wail comes from Porgy's room, where Bess is lying ill and delirious. As Maria explains to Serena, Lily and Peter, anxiously listening with her outside, Bess had wandered into the palmetto jungle on her way home from the picnic and was lost for two days. Now, burning with fever and out of her mind, she imagines she is still on Kittiwah Island fighting off Crown's advances, and pleads desperately for help. Phrases of the music of that turbulent scene echo in the orchestra.

After a time, Porgy comes out and tells the others that Bess finally has fallen asleep. They discuss taking Bess to the white man's hospital, but Serena declares that she can heal the sick woman with prayer. Falling to her knees, she begins chanting with religious fervor: "Oh, Doctor Jesus!" The others also kneel and shout their responses as Serena prays that the devil may be driven out of the body of this poor sick woman. She ends the supplication with a confident "Amen." Then with calm finality she says that Doctor Jesus has taken the case; by five o'clock Bess will be well. As the music continues on a serene, *Tristan*-like theme, the others look at her in awe and gratitude.

Meanwhile, in Catfish Row, life goes on. Lily and Peter—once more the Strawberry Woman and the Honey Man—wander off on their rounds. The Crab Man comes by, makes a sale to Maria, and goes on his way chanting.

Porgy, sitting deep in thought on his doorstep, looks up startled as Bess calls his name over the theme of "Bess, you is my woman now." She appears at the door. Dressed in a nightgown, she looks haggard and exhausted. Sitting down beside Porgy, she murmurs, childlike, that it is lonely in the room without him ("I lonesome here all by myself"). This phrase marks the beginning of a long and moving duet, the theme of which is based on Porgy's aria. Porgy tells her how she wandered back to Catfish Row in a raging fever and was put to bed by Maria. Of this, Bess says with a sob, she remembers nothing at all.

Comforting her, Porgy says gently that he knows she has been with Crown, but that does not matter now—he does not want her ever to go away. Bess confesses that she has promised to go with Crown when he comes back for her at cotton-picking time. She shrinks back in fear as a look of dark anger crosses Porgy's face. Grimly but calmly he says that he will never keep a woman against her will.

In a passionate refrain ("I wants to stay here") Bess pours out her love for Porgy and reveals her haunting terror of Crown. She is unworthy of Porgy's love, she cries—but when Crown touches her with his hot hands she cannot resist him. Distractedly she begs Porgy to save her from Crown's evil spell.

Porgy answers in a ringing refrain ("Bess, you don' need to be afraid") that with him by her side she will find happiness—and he himself will take care of Crown. Over a majestic accompaniment, the duet rises to a fiery climax.

As the two go inside, Clara and Maria enter. Clara apprehensively remarks about the ominous look of the sea, which, she says, seems to be waiting for the sound of the hurricane bell. Maria scoffs at the possibility of a hurricane but betrays a certain anxiety. A restless sextuplet

figure stirs in the orchestra like a rising storm wind. This figure gradually builds into a surging chromatic passage depicting the approach of
the hurricane. People rush back and forth shouting warnings. From the
distance comes the clangor of the hurricane bell. Clara, hysterically
calling Jake's name, stumbles into the courtyard and falls in a faint. The
orchestral accompaniment, simulating the howl of the storm, rises to a
violent climax as the curtain falls.

[*Scene Four*] Serena's room. It is dawn of the following day, with
the hurricane raging at its height. Huddled in groups, the terror-stricken
Negroes pray for help and protection in the dramatic ensemble which
continues throughout the scene. During the first part, a humming chorus
takes the place of the orchestral accompaniment. The prayers inter-
mingle in a religious frenzy, with each group making its individual appeal for mercy.

The singing intensifies as the storm wind howls louder. At times the
voices sink almost to a whisper as the Negroes chant that the sky will
fall, the sun will rise in the west and the moon will set in the sea. They
shriek in fear as lightning blazes and thunder crashes, to the accompaniment of rampaging chromatics in the orchestra.

Clara, hugging her baby close, goes to a window and peeps through a
crack in the shutter. There is a sudden, startled silence as she calmly begins singing a reprise of "Summertime." When the chanting chorus is
resumed, there is a brief colloquy, like an obbligato, between Porgy and
Bess. As though thinking aloud, Bess says that no one could live
through a storm like this on Kittiwah Island. She looks at Porgy with an
expression of profound relief and adds: "I guess you got me for keeps."
Divining her meaning, Porgy replies: "Ain' I tell you dat?"

Another blaze of lightning is accompanied by a particularly violent
outburst of the storm. In rising terror the Negroes chant: "Oh, dere's
somebody knockin' at de do'!" In a momentarily amusing byplay,
Mingo and Peter urge each other to open the door to prove no one is
there—but neither has the courage. Maria finally goes toward it but
stops in her tracks at the sound of loud knocking. Several men fling
themselves against the shaking door as those in the room scream in terror. But in spite of their efforts the door is slowly pushed inward.

In the glare of the lightning, the towering figure of Crown looms on
the threshold. He sees Bess and strides over to her; the other Negroes
shrink back in fear. When he asks Bess why she has no greeting for
"her man," she replies coldly that Porgy is her man now. She flares up
when Crown answers with a cruelly insulting remark about Porgy. Now
violently angry, Crown threatens Bess.

Over the theme of "Bess, you is my woman now," Bess repeats that
she is Porgy's woman, which brings a sneering laugh from Crown.

Lunging suddenly at her, he throws her to the floor. When Porgy crawls to her defense, Crown sends him sprawling. The protesting cries of the Negroes mingle with the increasing clamor of the storm.

Serena thrusts herself in front of Crown and warns that God will surely strike him dead. With a brazen laugh, Crown answers that he and God fought it out all the way back from Kittiwah—and now he and God are friends. At this point the Negroes again take up their chanting. Momentarily struck by a superstitious fear, Crown roars at them to be quiet. Over the wailing of the chorus he babbles that those in a hurry to meet Judgment Day need only step outside into the hurricane. He blasphemously calls on God to laugh with him at these cringing mortals.

Then in insolent defiance he bursts into an earthy ditty in exuberant jazz tempo: "A red-headed woman make a choo-choo jump its track." As though to counter its vulgarity, the shocked Negroes sing a chorale-like chant: "Lord save us, don't listen to that Crown." In an ironic obbligato, Crown reprises the song, its jazz beat jarring against the solemn rhythm of the prayer.

The final notes are cut off abruptly by a scream from Clara, who is standing at the window. Bess, looking out, cries that Jake's boat is floating upside down in the river. Clara, in wild panic, pushes her baby into Bess's arms and rushes out into the storm. Bess calls for a man to go to Clara's aid, but no one stirs. Crown, making the most of the situation, sardonically asks Porgy why he does not answer when a woman calls. Porgy glares at him in helpless fury.

Shouting that he will get Clara and then come back and get Bess, Crown swaggers to the door. As he opens it, the howling wind blows out the lamp. In the darkness the terrified Negroes again sing the prayer which opened the scene: "Oh, Doctor Jesus!" It is sung to the accompaniment of an undulating sextuplet figure over an insistently repeated theme in the bass. The prayer continues to its conclusion after the curtain slowly falls.

ACT THREE

[*Scene One*] Catfish Row, the next night. Again the Negroes are gathered to mourn one of their number—this time it is Jake, who was lost in the hurricane. In one of the most beautiful numbers in the opera, "Clara, don't you be down-hearted," they offer their comfort to the grief-stricken widow.

As the singing softly continues, the scene changes to Maria's shop where she is seen at her work. Sporting Life appears on the street outside, listens to the singing, then bursts into a harsh, sneering laugh. Maria upbraids him furiously for mocking those who are grieving for their dead. In quasi-recitative, there is a sharp exchange between the

two. Why mourn over a man who is dead, Sporting Life remarks insolently, when there are plenty of men left living who like pretty women?
Maria, intuitively aware that he is thinking of Bess, reminds him that
the woman he himself has in mind already has her man. Two men,
Sporting Life observes meaningfully. This remark puzzles Maria, who
believes Crown is dead. When a woman has two men, Sporting Life
goes on, there is likely to be a "carvin'," with the police picking up the
pieces. Maria turns away in disgust; the peddler strolls off toward the
iron gate at the end of the street.

A moment later Bess appears at the window of Porgy's room with
Clara's baby in her arms. As she sings a reprise of "Summertime," the
mourners, each carrying a lantern, come out of Clara's house and go to
their own homes. The action which now follows takes place during a
long orchestral interlude dominated by an ominous quadruplet figure in
the bass.

Crown suddenly appears at the iron gate, drops to his hands and
knees and begins crawling stealthily toward Porgy's door. There, above
him, the shutter opens slowly. A hand holding a long knife emerges,
then plunges the knife into Crown's back. The knife is withdrawn and
hurled to the ground. Crown in his agony writhes almost to his feet.
Porgy leans from the window, closes his hands around Crown's throat
and holds him until he stops struggling. In one violent movement, Porgy
hurls his adversary's body to the ground. With a ferocious laugh of triumph, Porgy screams: "Bess, you got a man now, you got Porgy!" The
curtain falls to a thunderous phrase in the orchestra.

[*Scene Two*] Catfish Row, the next afternoon. The scene opens with
an orchestral interlude marked by a nervously undulating quadruplet
figure and a distorted fragment of the "Summertime" theme. The first
half of this scene is in spoken dialogue and recitative.

A detective and a coroner come to Catfish Row to question Serena
about the murder of Crown. Abetted by Annie and another neighbor
woman, Serena pretends to be very sick. Appearing at the window with
her head wrapped in a towel, and groaning with every step, she insists
she has been in bed for three days, with the other women nursing her.
She of course disclaims any knowledge of what happened, admitting
only that Crown killed her husband two months ago. The women's solemn denials, sung in trio form with seriocomic effect, drive the detective
into a fuming rage. Annie calmly closes the shutter in his face.

Balked and exasperated, the detective snarls that he nevertheless will
find a witness for the coroner's inquest. He strides to Porgy's door,
viciously kicks it open and bellows an order to come out. To the accompaniment of the syncopated theme heard at the end of the duet sung
by Porgy and Bess in Act Two, Scene One, Bess helps Porgy to the

doorstep, then stands beside him with the baby in her arms. Sporting Life glides in unobserved and stands listening.

The coroner, with a show of friendliness, begins to question Porgy about Crown. On his guard, the cripple pretends he has difficulty remembering the man. Then he is told he is being called as a witness to identify the body. Recoiling in abject terror, Porgy begs to be spared the ordeal, but the officers threaten him with jail if he refuses to go. They leave to bring policemen to assist in the proceedings.

Sporting Life walks over to Porgy and Bess, standing paralyzed with fright. Steadying herself, Bess advises Porgy to shut his eyes and only pretend to look at the body. Thereupon Sporting Life venomously remarks that when a murderer is forced to look at the body of his victim, the victim's wounds will begin to bleed. And that, he adds maliciously as Porgy screams in terror, is how the cops find the killer.

At that moment the policemen arrive. They seize Porgy and drag him away through the iron gate as he hysterically protests that no one can make him look at Crown's face. Bess cries out in despair while Sporting Life laughs sardonically. With vicious relish he tells her that, far from being merely a witness, Porgy will be locked up in jail—and probably will be hanged for Crown's murder.

Bess, now completely demoralized, is an easy prey for the dope peddler. He inveigles her into taking some of the white powder. Her senses numbed, she listens as though hypnotized as he describes how he will take her to New York and show her the exciting life of the big city. In the opera's famous blues number, "There's a boat dat's leavin' soon for New York," he urges her to come with him. He promises to buy her a mansion on upper Fifth Avenue, to dress her in the latest Paris styles, and then go "struttin' through Harlem."

Suddenly coming to her senses, Bess turns on Sporting Life in furious denunciation and orders him away. Instead of going he holds out a second packet of dope toward her. As the "Summertime" theme sounds in the orchestra, she knocks the powder out of his hand. With a shrug, he murmurs, in a phrase from "It ain't necessarily so," that he will leave the second "shot" where she can find it. Bess stares at it for a moment, then abruptly turns into the room and slams the door. Sporting Life, with an evil smile, lights a cigarette and walks away. As the curtain falls, the orchestra states the theme of his blues number.

[*Scene Three*] Catfish Row, a week later. The scene opens with an orchestral interlude descriptive of another day in Catfish Row. A young man lies asleep in a doorway, a street sweeper appears, then two workmen pass by. More people gradually appear, and a choral refrain develops as they greet each other ("Good mornin', sistuh, good mornin', brudder"). Children dance by to a carefree waltz tune ("Sure to go to Heaven").

At the end of the chorus the clang of the patrol wagon is heard in the distance. Mingo runs toward the iron gate shouting that Porgy has come home. The news of his arrival has a strange effect upon the people: instead of rushing to greet him, they gather in small groups and look apprehensively toward the gate. When he finally enters, they make an obvious effort to bid him a warm welcome. As the syncopated theme of the duet in Act Two again is heard, Porgy makes his way to one of Maria's tables and sits down.

Delighted at being the center of attraction, Porgy begins telling how he outwitted the police by keeping his eyes shut when he was told to look at Crown's body. He cautions his neighbors not to let Bess know he has returned, because he has a surprise for her. Mingo, Peter and several others surreptitiously try to leave as Porgy happily distributes the presents he has brought to celebrate his return: a mouth organ for Scipio, a feather-trimmed hat for Lily and finally a red dress for Bess. But now he begins to notice that his friends are leaving. To win their attention, he launches into the story of how he concealed his dice in his mouth, lured the other inmates of the jail into a crap game and won all their money.

When the story seems to fail to impress his listeners, Porgy impatiently calls for Bess, and becomes more and more mystified when there is no answer. He catches sight of Mingo trying to sneak away and upbraids him for his strange behavior. At the same time, he notices that almost all of his neighbors have left.

Suddenly he sees Serena sitting on his doorstep with a baby in her arms. Crawling over to her, he remarks slyly that he has been gone only a week—and here she is with a new baby. Serena, unable to face Porgy, turns to go inside. As she does so, Porgy catches sight of the baby's face and recognizes it as Bess's child—and his own.

Excited and alarmed, he calls Bess's name. When there is no answer, he turns to Maria—the only one left on the scene—and begs her to tell him what has happened. Maria answers evasively that Bess was not worthy of him. Porgy retorts that he is not interested in her opinions. In an ensuing refrain, "Oh, where's my Bess," he piteously begs for some word of her. This introduces a poignant trio sung by Maria, Porgy and Serena.

The women try to convince Porgy that Bess is a faithless creature who fell under the evil influence of Sporting Life, neglected her child and abandoned herself to dope and liquor. Deaf to their entreaties to forget her, Porgy repeats over and over that he cannot live without his Bess and implores the women to tell him where she has gone.

At the conclusion of the trio Lily appears—and it is she who finally tells him what has happened. Bess left Catfish Row, Lily tells Porgy, and Serena has taken her child to raise as her own. Overjoyed to know that Bess is alive, Porgy asks where she has gone. To New York, Lily says, "a thousand miles up north, pas' the custom house."

Suddenly resolved, Porgy calls for his goat and cart. All the neighbors crowd around, wondering what is happening. Ignoring the pleas of Serena and Maria to stay in Catfish Row with his friends, Porgy declares that he is going to "Noo York" because he must be with his Bess. He stretches out his arms, and two men help him into his cart.

In an exultant refrain he sings, "I'm on my way to a Heavenly Lan'!" He is joined by the chorus in a triumphant affirmation of his love and faith. The orchestra majestically sounds the theme of "Bess, you is my woman now" as the curtain falls.

PRINCE IGOR

by Aleksandr Porfirevitch Borodin

(1834–87)

Libretto by the composer

Based on *The Song of the Army of Igor,* a Russian poem dating from the fourteenth century

CHARACTERS

Igor Sviatoslavitch, Prince of Séversk	Baritone
Jaroslavna, his wife of his second marriage	Soprano
Vladimir Igorevitch, his son by his first marriage	Tenor
Prince Galitsky (Vladimir Jaroslavitch), brother of Jaroslavna	Bass
Kontchak ⎱ Khans of Polovtsy Gzak ⎰	⎰ Bass ⎱ Bass
Kontchakovna, daughter of Kontchak	Alto
Ovlour, a Polovtsian convert to Christianity	Tenor
Skoula ⎱ goudok (or gudok) players Eroshka ⎰	⎰ Bass ⎱ Tenor
Maid to Jaroslavna	Soprano
A young Polovtsian girl	Soprano

Russian nobility, boyars, old men, Russian soldiers, dancing girls, the populace, Polovtsian khans, companions of Kontchakovna, slaves, prisoners, guards, Polovtsian soldiers

Place: Novgorod, in Russia, and the Tartar region in Central Asia
Time: 1185
First performance: Maryinsky Theater, St. Petersburg, November 4, 1890
Original language: Russian

This dramatic and colorful opera, so imbued with the spirit of ancient Russia, has a fantastic history. Borodin, a professor of chemistry and an eminent scientist in his own right, was equally renowned as a composer who is credited with writing the first Russian music of national charac-

ter to be acclaimed outside his own country. He was one of the group
known as the "Russian Five," or the "Mighty Five"—the others being
Rimsky-Korsakov, Glazounov, Cui and Balakirev.

Although Borodin worked on *Prince Igor* for eighteen years, he left it
uncompleted at the time of his death. His friends Nikolai Andreyevitch
Rimsky-Korsakov and Alexandre Konstantinovitch Glazounov finished
the work from his notes and sketches, and orchestrated the score. In
fact, the overture and all of Act Three except the opening march were
composed by Glazounov. But the themes at the core of the opera are
Borodin's. To infuse it with the true Russian musical expression, he
delved into Russian history and folk music. The idea had been suggested to him by Vladimir Vassilievitch Stassov, the Russian nation-
alist writer and critic.

The score is richly and vigorously melodic and especially overpowering in the great choruses. Outside Russia, the opera usually has been
sung in Italian or French. *Prince Igor* is famous for its *Polovtsian
Dances,* a standard classical item in ballet and symphonic repertoire.

Prince Igor received its first production in the version completed and
edited by Rimsky-Korsakov and Glazounov in Moscow on January 30,
1898. The opera was given its American premiere, in Italian, at the
Metropolitan Opera House on December 30, 1890, with Frances Alda,
Pasquale Amato and Adamo Didur heading the cast. It was presented
during three successive seasons thereafter, then was dropped from the
repertoire. Since that time it has rarely been presented in the United
States as a complete opera, although the *Polovtsian Dances* are often
programed. An interesting contemporary sidelight is that some of the
themes from the opera were adapted for the score of the Broadway musical *Kismet,* presented in 1953.

Prince Igor was successfully revived, in an English translation, by the
New York City Opera Company during its 1968 and 1969 seasons.

The long overture states the principal themes of the opera in elaborate symphonic style, with emphasis on the sensuous melodies of the romantic episodes.

PROLOGUE

A public square in front of the cathedral in the town of Poutive. Soldiers and nobles of Prince Igor's court are about to start a campaign
against the Khan Kontchak, of the Tartar tribe of Polovtsy. As a great
throng of townspeople watches, Prince Igor, his wife, the Princess Jaroslavna, and boyars emerge from the cathedral in a solemn procession.

The crowd bursts into a mighty chorus praising the Prince for his
exploits. They hail him as "the sun in all his glory" ("Al fulgente Sol,

gloria"—"Au soleil brillant gloire"), and their acclamations include his son Vladimir along with his chief ministers. From the Don to the Danube, they sing, Prince Igor will declare the glory of Russia.

The prince cries out that the hour of decision is at hand, but at that moment the sky suddenly is darkened by an eclipse of the sun. The people, staring at the sky in terror, cry out that this is a portent of disaster ("Esser potra presagio"—"C'est le présage fatal") and implore the Prince not to undertake the campaign.

But as the eclipse passes and the sky brightens again, Igor sings that whether the sign foretells good or evil no one can escape his fate ("Il ciel espri l'oscuro"—"Au ciel s'il passe"). Meanwhile, he will go forth to fight in a just cause. In a ringing phrase he commands his forces to prepare for battle, then leaves to review his troops. The Princess and the boyars follow.

Skoula and Eroshka, two rascally gudok players,[1] now come wandering in. In a brief recitative ("Amico: in andar"—"Amis, allez là-bas") they sing that they are not interested in fighting—they would much rather spend their time in feasting and drinking. And so they have decided to stay at home in the service of Prince Galitsky. With that they toss their weapons aside and sneak away.

Following the review of his troops, Prince Igor returns with his wife. A duet ensues as he bids his followers to say farewell to their wives ("Salutiam le spose"—"Appelez nos dames"). Jaroslavna begs him not to go because there have been omens of misfortune, but Igor replies that he must go for the sake of his honor and the fatherland.

A brief quartet passage follows as Vladimir and Prince Galitsky add their voices to sing that there is no turning back now. Igor asks Galitsky, as the Princess' brother, to watch over her during his absence. The treacherous Galitsky pretends to be grateful for the duty Igor has entrusted to him. Thus, he says, he will repay the Prince for having befriended him when he was banished from his home by his own father. Igor rather impatiently shrugs off Galitsky's fawning expressions of gratitude. Jaroslavna leaves with the other women of the court.

Igor turns to an old priest and asks his blessing. The priest complies, with the chorus of the people again hailing Prince Igor and Vladimir as heroes going into battle for the glory of Russia.

[1] These two comic characters are stock figures in traditional Russian opera. They have their counterparts, for example, in the drunken monks in *Boris Godunof*. The instrument the two play, the gudok, is an old Russian three-stringed viol resembling a cello.

ACT ONE

[*Scene One*] The court of Prince Galitsky's palace in Poutivle. The populace, led by Skoula and Eroshka, now are singing the praises of Galitsky. They also comment on the latest court gossip: some gay young blades, with Galitsky's connivance, have carried off several girls for their own pleasures. To the huge amusement of the crowd, Eroshka imitates the voice of a girl begging the Prince to allow her to go home.

Galitsky himself strides in. He declares, in a brief recitative, that he does not share Igor's enthusiasm for the hard life of a soldier—his tastes run to merrymaking and a life of luxury. Then in a long and lusty aria ("Se di Poutivle principe"—"Si l'on me trouvait") he describes what life in court would be like if he ruled in Igor's place. It would be given over to pleasure—endless revelry with the most beautiful women in Russia always at hand. He climaxes the aria with a roaring invitation to drink.

A group interrupts to ask him what would happen to the Princess. She is much too serious-minded, Galitsky answers carelessly. She can go to a convent and pray for his sinful soul if she likes—just so long as she doesn't interfere with his carousing. The throng hails him delightedly.

As the Prince turns to go indoors he is met by a group of young girls who, in an agitated chorus ("Ah! che viltà"—"Ah! mécréants!"), tell the Prince that one of the girls has been abducted by his men. Galitsky casually assures them that she will be safe in his hands. When the girls beg him to have pity on the victim, the Prince angrily orders them to be off. They run away in terror. Skoula and Eroshka, watching, sardonically commend Galitsky for his firm hand with women.

These two court jesters now deliberately set out to incite the populace against Prince Igor and Jaroslavna. In recitative, they sing that the Princess has no authority in the palace now because Igor and all his palace guards are away at war. What is more, she is stingy with her wine and deserves no sympathy whatever. But with Galitsky, the two go on, things are different—he lets the wine flow like water. As if to prove their point, the servants roll out a huge cask of wine. The populace howls in glee.

Thereupon Skoula and Eroshka launch into a mock-serious song in praise of their generous patron, Prince Galitsky, "Chi cercasse un buon signore"—"Qui recherche un bon maître." They urge everyone to rally to the Prince, whose hospitality has no equal. To rouse the gullible populace still more, Skoula and Eroshka remind them how hard they are forced to labor under Igor's stern rule—joyless servitude from dawn till dusk. But under Galitsky's benevolent regime they will be asked to do nothing but sing and dance and play.

The brawling crowd responds, in the roaring chorus which closes the scene ("È ver! Si può donargli"—"Que n'est-il donc dans Poutivle"), that Galitsky is the man they want as leader. Prince Igor and his army are far away and there is nothing more to fear. In frenzied excitement the people clamor for a meeting of the Parliament to overthrow Prince Igor. Then, shouting "Glory to Prince Galitsky," the crowd storms away.

Skoula and Eroshka, reeling drunk and holding each other up, bellow out a nonsensical phrase about "going home to mama" as they stagger in the wake of the mob.

[*Scene Two*] The palace apartment of the Princess Jaroslavna. She is sitting alone, lost in thought. In recitative ("Da lungo tempo Igor"—"Depuis longtemps Igor") she laments the long absence of Prince Igor and Vladimir. She is haunted by a premonition of disaster. This introduces the aria in which she recalls the happy days before Igor rode away to battle ("Or più non va, mio desiato Igor"—"Le temps n'est plus, où mon Igor"). She hears him calling to her in her dreams, only to awaken to anguish and bitter loneliness. As she ends the aria on a poignant phrase, she buries her face in her hands, abandoning herself to her grief.

Suddenly her old nurse bustles in with the news that a group of girls has come to ask the Princess' help. These are the girls who previously had appealed to Prince Galitsky. In an excited chorus ("Noi veniam ploranti"—"Nous venons, princesse") they entreat the Princess to intercede in behalf of the girl who has been abducted. Her captor, they wail, not only derided their pleas for mercy, but threatened them as well. The girls beg Jaroslavna to punish the betrayer.

When the Princess asks them to name him, the girls are thrown into confusion. They finally summon up enough courage to reply, and do so in a striking chorus, "Principessa, la voce trema"—"Ô maîtresse, c'est d'une voix." Sung *allegro vivo* in 5/4 tempo, it reflects their hysterical fear as they disclose that the lecherous villain is Prince Galitsky himself. He has wronged them many times before, they declare. Now that he has usurped Prince Igor's power, he shows himself as a cruel tyrant who oppresses the people and spends his time in wild carousing. His followers have plundered the land; not a woman is safe in the town.

Just as they finish their chorus of accusation, Galitsky himself walks in. Screaming in terror, the girls rush away. In recitative, over ominous chords in the orchestra, Jaroslavna asks Galitsky if what the girls have told her is true. A long and heated colloquy follows as the Prince insolently replies that this whole affair is none of her business. What he wants, he adds brusquely, he takes. With a sneer he remarks that in the palace it is customary to greet a guest with wine and good cheer. Obviously, he adds, the Princess' own brother is not as welcome as the stinking rabble who fill her ears with their wretched complaints.

Exasperated by his mockery, Jaroslavna reminds Galitsky that she still is Princess in this palace and warns him that he will answer for his shameless conduct when Igor returns. Galitsky coolly retorts that at the moment he is the ruling Prince at the behest of the people of Poutivle. With infuriating arrogance he advises his sister to keep this fact in mind and not risk his anger.

When the Princess turns on him wrathfully for threatening her, Galitsky changes his tactics. He was only joking, he tells her placatingly ("Ho detto per celiar"—"C'était pour plaisanter"). He likes to see her angry, he says, because when she is angry she is more beautiful than ever. With deliberate malice he reminds her that she still is young and attractive, that her husband is far away and that living alone is dreary business. Does she not, he inquires, even have a secret lover to comfort her?

Goaded to fury by his insinuations, Jaroslavna storms that she has had enough of his insolence ("Dell'insolenze il colmo"—"Assez d'audace et d'insolence"). As rightful Princess she has the power to send him under guard to his father in Galicia, where he will receive the punishment he deserves. Jaroslavna furiously commands Galitsky to release the girl he has abducted, then orders him out of her sight.

With a contemptuous shrug, the Prince promises to free the girl—and then look about for another who will be more agreeable. He leaves to the accompaniment of a descending chromatic passage. Jaroslavna, spent by her anger, murmurs that she has no more strength left to fight.

As she sits brooding, she suddenly is aroused by the entrance of the council of boyars. She welcomes them eagerly, but they bring only news of further misfortune. In a dramatic chorus ("Fa' cuor, Principessa"—"Écoute, princesse") underscored by a somber, insistent rhythm, they sing that the fearsome Khan Gzak and his Tartar hordes have crossed the Russian frontier and are at the gates of Poutivle. But the worst news of all is that Prince Igor has been badly wounded and has been taken captive along with his brother and Vladimir, Igor's son. Overcome by horror, Jaroslavna falls in a faint. Quickly revived, she asks the boyars what now can be done to save the city from the invaders. In another vigorous refrain ("Maintes fois, luttant sans crainte"), sung mostly in unison, they assure the Princess that they have successfully defended Poutivle before and—with God's help—will do so again.

Deeply moved by their loyalty, Jaroslavna sings that the fighting spirit of the boyars has given her new hope. She bows low to them in a regal gesture of thanks.

Suddenly from outside comes the clangor of the alarm bell, followed by the terrified screams of women. As a powerful sustained chord reverberates in the orchestra, the boyars shout that the tocsin signals that the enemy is upon them ("Campane d'allarme son"—"La cloche d'alarme, hélas!"). This marks the beginning of the closing ensemble of the act.

As the red glow of the burning city begins to show through the windows of the palace, the voices of the boyars blend with those of the women in the streets below as they cry for help. Jaroslavna's voice soars above the chorus in an agonized plea to the Blessed Virgin to save the people from the wrath of an angry God who is punishing them for their sins. The boyars, drawing their swords, vow they will defend the Princess with their lives as the chorus surges to its climax. The curtain falls.

ACT TWO

The camp of Khan Kontchak of the Polovtsy. It is evening. In a sinuous, flowing chorus ("O fior languente"—"Ô fleur fanée") a group of Tartar girls sings about the beauty of the night and how its enchantment will turn their lovers' thoughts to them.

Now follows the "Dance of the Polovtsian Maidens," the first of the tribal dances which Khan Kontchak has arranged for the entertainment of his royal captives—Prince Igor, his brother and Vladimir.

After the dance, Kontchakovna, daughter of the Khan, sings a beautiful invocation to night ("O notte virginal!"—"Oh! descends des cieux bleux"), accompanied by the chorus of girls. It is also an expression of passionate longing for her lover. Her song ends on a phrase in the lower reaches of the contralto register, with the music dying gently away.

The mood of the scene abruptly changes as the Russian prisoners and their guards are seen approaching in the background. They are greeted warmly by Kontchakovna and the girls, who offer them food and wine. The prisoners thank them in a brief chorus ("Que Dieu donne aux belles filles"). They then go on their way and the women also leave the scene. The Polovtsian patrol passes by on its rounds of the camp. As the guards move on, the renegade Ovlour[2] enters to take his post standing guard.

Then to the accompaniment of quiet, sustained chords in the orchestra, Vladimir enters. In recitative ("Fugge fra brividi il Sol"—"Lentement baissa le jour") he muses that, with the sunset, the steppe is enveloped in mysterious shadows. The warm south wind stirs him to thoughts of Kontchakovna. He gives voice to his passionate longing in the ensuing cavatina ("Ah, vien, rispondi al mio sospir"—"Ah, viens,

[2] A rather shadowy figure, whose identity is not too clearly established. As a Christianized Polovtsy—and thus a traitor to his Tartar tribe—he seeks to join the Russians. To that end, he puts himself at Igor's service and engineers the Prince's escape from Kontchak's camp.

réponds au tendre appel"), one of the finest numbers in the opera. In its lyrical concluding phrase, ending on an octave interval, Vladimir entreats his beloved to come to his arms.

As an agitated theme stirs in the orchestra, Kontchakovna emerges from her tent and rushes to Vladimir's embrace. A rapturous love duet follows ("Sì! io t'adoro"—"Quel amour égale"). But at its conclusion, on a long, sustained chord, the romantic mood is suddenly broken as Kontchakovna asks if Prince Igor will give his consent to their marriage. There is no hope of that, Vladimir answers ruefully, so long as he and his father remain captives. Kontchakovna assures him that her own father would have no objections to the union. Suddenly Vladimir warns that Igor is approaching. The lovers hastily separate and leave.

To the accompaniment of a somber phrase in the orchestra, Prince Igor enters. Brooding over his defeat and captivity ("Ohimè! Nel cor mi graverà"—"Hélas! mon âme est triste"), he is haunted by memories of the past and thinks of the fateful portent of the eclipse. In another of the opera's fine arias ("Ma pur lontano in gran miraggio"—"Et puis je vois dans un mirage"), Igor laments his disgrace. He thinks of his wife, waiting in vain for him. He cries out that if God will give him his freedom he will redeem his own honor and save Russia from the invader—for there still is time. But the aria ends on a note of hopelessness as Igor sings that there is no escape from the torment of his conscience.

As he stares at the dawn which now is beginning to brighten the sky, Ovlour approaches. Saying that the dawn is a symbol of a new life, he tells Igor he will help him escape—at this very moment a horse is saddled and waiting. The Prince scorns the offer. He thanks Ovlour for his loyalty but rejects the idea out of hand. Taken aback by Igor's angry refusal, the renegade leaves.

A moment later Kontchak strides in. A long colloquy follows. The Khan jovially asks Prince Igor why he is so sad ("E sempre il ciel ti guidi"—"Que le ciel te bénisse!"). When Igor replies that it is because he is a captive, Kontchak assures him that—far from being a prisoner—he is an honored guest. The Tartar adds that he respects bravery and courage on the field of battle; he admires Igor for these sterling qualities and would like nothing better than to be his friend and ally. Kontchak impulsively offers the Prince lavish gifts—his fastest horse, his most beautiful slave girls, priceless treasures—anything to make him happy.

Igor gravely thanks the Tartar for his generosity but tells him that he can never be happy while he is a prisoner. Thereupon Kontchak offers the Prince his freedom—if he will promise not to resume the war against the Polovtsy once he returns to his homeland.

To that, Igor promptly replies that he will make no such promise. He will fight Kontchak to the death . . . he will march into the Tartar country and dip water out of the River Don with his helmet. Kontchak, philosophically accepting the situation, commends Prince Igor on his frankness. He remarks, somewhat wistfully, that if they could be allies they would hunt together like two tigers, and their armies would be invincible. With that he invites Igor to enjoy the entertainment he has prepared.

At Kontchak's command, singers and dancers appear and perform the *Polovtsian Dances*. To a stirring choral accompaniment the dances rise to a pitch of wild, barbaric abandon. A sensuous chorus of young girls is followed by a dance of savage men, with its underlying rhythm of four sharply accented descending notes, then by a movement of young men with bows and arrows symbolizing war games. A voluptuous dance follows to the accompaniment of an insinuating oriental melody. The scene comes to a blazing climax with a fanfare of trumpets and crashing of cymbals as all onstage hail the victorious leader Khan Kontchak.

ACT THREE

Before the rise of the curtain the "Polovtsian March" is played. It begins quietly, then builds into a climax in a fanfare of trumpets. The scene opens on the Polovtsy camp, where the tribesmen are awaiting the arrival of the triumphant Khan Gzak and his army. Soon the soldiers appear, some guarding Russian captives, others carrying the booty of war. Khan Gzak and his officers ride in on horseback and are greeted by Khan Kontchak. Prince Igor, Vladimir and the other Russian prisoners stand to one side, watching the scene intently. All the men in the throng hail Khan Gzak in a resounding chorus ("I trionfatori cinti"—"Nos guerriers vainqueurs"). Kontchak follows with a vigorous aria ("La clava ancor possente"—"Le glaive en main"). He exults in the victory over the Russians. The warriors break in with shouts of acclaim. Kontchak announces that a council of war will be held. He sings of the burning of the villages, of the devastation of the land, where now only wild beasts howl. Here mothers sorrow over their children lost in the trackless steppe, where the scream of the eagle calls the ravening beasts to their grisly banquet. This is sung to rising and falling chromatic figures in the orchestra. Kontchak hails Gzak as a hero, boastfully singing that both now rule the world. The warriors respond with a fierce cry of acclamation.

To a fanfare of trumpets, Kontchak invites all to share the spoils of war, then orders the most beautiful of the captive women to be brought to his tent. He declares that a war council will be held the next day to plan the campaign. The Tartars, in a savage chorus ("Al gran consiglio"—"Au grand conseil"), hail the prospect of another foray against the Russians and debate whether to sack Kiev or Poltava.

Meanwhile, the Russian prisoners observe the scene in rising anger at the bragging Polovtsy. In an ensuing ensemble, led by Igor and Vladimir, they rage over the report that Poutivle has been destroyed and their wives and children taken captive. The Russians urge Prince Igor to accept Ovlour's help in trying to escape to Russia, so that he can save the fatherland while there still is time.

To infuriate the prisoners still more, the Tartar guards burst into a chorus of praise of the two victorious khans, comparing them to the splendor of the sun and the moon ("Il vittorioso è pari al sol!"—"Kontchâk est semble au soleil!"). As the Russians angrily withdraw to their tents, the guards call for kumiss,[3] then begin drinking and dancing. The scene climaxes in a drunken orgy which leaves most of the guards sprawled asleep on the ground.

As darkness falls, Ovlour cautiously makes his way to Prince Igor's tent and calls to him softly. In quasi-recitative he discloses the plan for escape. The guards are dead drunk, he reports, and now the Prince and Vladimir can safely make their way to the river. At the signal, a whistle, they are to swim across to the other side, where horses are saddled and waiting. The Prince says he is ready to go. Ovlour hurries away.

A moment later Kontchakovna rushes to Vladimir's tent and calls out his name. An impassioned duet ensues ("L'amor tuo si dissolve?"—"L'amour fut éphémère?") as Kontchakovna asks Vladimir if it is true that he is deserting her now. She knows of his plan to escape but desperately implores him not to leave her. She will not even ask to be his bride, she sings, and would be happy to be his slave. Vladimir sorrowfully replies that, despite his love for her, his first duty is to his country. As he sings farewell, his father storms out of his tent.

A stormy trio follows. Igor angrily asks Vladimir if he intends to throw his lot with the Polovtsy and thus betray his country. Kontchakovna continues her entreaties, while Vladimir cries that he lacks the strength to resist her love. Suddenly Igor hears Ovlour's whistle and tries to drag Vladimir away. Kontchakovna holds him in her embrace; Vladimir begs his father to allow him one last kiss of farewell. Igor vainly tries to tear him from Kontchakovna's arms, then dashes away.

Kontchakovna, screaming that she will sound the alarm, strikes furiously on a sheet of iron used as an alarm bell. As the Polovtsy rush in from all sides she tells them that Prince Igor has escaped with the help of the traitorous Ovlour. Roaring in fury, some of the Tartars dash away in pursuit, while others shout that Vladimir must be executed on the spot. Kontchakovna throws herself in front of him, saying she will die with him. The Tartars retreat before her defiance. The pursuers re-

[3] A drink made from fermented camel's milk.

turn to report that the River Don is rising so fast that they cannot cross to follow the fugitives.

At that point, Khan Kontchak and the other chieftains stride in. He is surprised to see his daughter and Vladimir. The Tartars, threatening to close in on Vladimir, tell Kontchak about Igor's escape and Ovlour's treachery. Kontchak sternly orders that Vladimir is not to be harmed. Then in calm but impressive phrases he declares that the fugitive Prince is a respected foe and a brave man who has done exactly what the Khan himself would do in the same situation. Then he adds harshly: for the guards, death; Vladimir is to live.

For a moment the other chieftains stare at him in consternation, then burst into a chorus of angry protest ("È pronto ognun ad obbedir"—"À t'obéir chacun est prêt"). They are willing to follow his leadership in battle, they sing, but this prisoner is another matter. Though the old "falcon" has flown home, the young one still is in their grasp—a prime target for an arrow. The chieftains then demand that all the Russians be slain before they too escape. Kontchak imperturbably replies that now they have the young falcon they will keep him "chained"—with a mate.

Turning to Vladimir, Kontchak presents Kontchakovna to him as his bride ("Si tu di mia famiglia"—"Sois donc de ma famille")—now he no longer is an enemy but a dear son-in-law. Then to the chieftains he proclaims: "Tomorrow we march on Russia!" All the Tartars shout their approval as the curtain falls.

ACT FOUR

A square in Poutivle adjacent to the city wall. On a terrace, Jaroslavna stands alone. It is dawn. She pours out her anguish and longing in the great aria known as "Jaroslavna's Lament" ("Udirà lo sposo diletto"—"Dans la douleur est mon pauvre coeur"). It is based on the same theme heard in Act Two as the captive Prince Igor expressed his longing for his wife. She sings that she longs to fly like a bird to the banks of the Don so that she could bathe her husband's wounds. She invokes the aid of the wind that roars across the steppe, the mighty River Dnieper and the sun itself, pleading for the return of her beloved Prince Igor. The aria concludes with a cry of despair. Jaroslavna remains staring over the ramparts.

A crowd of villagers passes. In a mournful chorus ("Qual fragor selvaggio"—"Est-ce un vent d'orage") they sing that it was not the storm nor the wolves that laid their town in ruins—the destroyer was Khan Gzak. The voices die away in an unaccompanied phrase as the crowd straggles out of sight.

In quasi-recitative, Jaroslavna reflects on the desolate landscape ravaged by the Polovtsy. Suddenly she catches sight of two horsemen in the distance. An insistent rhythm in the orchestra, gradually increasing in intensity, underscores her rising excitement as she describes the two coming closer: One is dressed like a Polovtsy, the other has the bearing of a noble Russian. Then at last she discerns that the riders are Prince Igor and Ovlour. Jaroslavna greets her husband with a shout of joy and the two rush into each other's arms. Then follows the rapturous love duet, "È ver, non à illusion la tua"—"J'ai cru rêver! Mon Dieu, merci," one of the most beautiful numbers in the opera. Curiously, at the conclusion of the duet, the romantic sentiments give way to a warlike mood as Igor and Jaroslavna vow death to the khans. Gazing fondly into each other's eyes, they walk slowly to the entrance of the citadel.

Just before they enter, Eroshka and Skoula wander in unsteadily, both half drunk. To the accompaniment of their gudoks, they launch into an amusing duet ("Or fiammegia il sole"—"Le soleil rayonne!"). Unaware of the Prince and the Princess, they comment sardonically on Igor's heroic "exploits."

Now that a new "sun" (Prince Galitsky) is beaming upon the town, they bellow, there is no need to weep for Prince Igor, who is far away as a prisoner of Khan Kontchak. Rather, weep for the brave Russian soldiers whom Igor led to their doom. With Russian gold, this great Prince built bridges that never were crossed. The flooded River Kayala carried away one bridge, and with it Igor's army—and Igor's glory. Now from the Danube to the sea the Russian people curse the name of Prince Igor.

But as the two are bawling out the end of their song, they catch sight of Prince Igor and Jaroslavna at the door of the citadel. Clutching each other in terror, they babble that now they certainly will be beheaded, executed, drawn and quartered. In drunken solemnity they ponder the situation—the matter, they agree, requires great cunning. Suddenly they have an inspiration: they will ring the town alarm bell in the nearby tower, call all the people together and be the first to announce that the glorious Prince Igor has returned home.

This they promptly do. The townspeople crowd excitedly into the square, asking the reason for the alarm. When Skoula and Eroshka shout that the "Prince" has arrived, the people angrily denounce them as drunken scoundrels hand in glove with a traitor. As the crowd is about to close in on them, Skoula points to the citadel shouting: "There is Igor, son of Sviatoslav, and the Polovtsy who brought him home!"

The throng rushes toward Igor and Jaroslavna, who now come forward followed by the boyars and the elder statesmen of the Kremlin. The people hail them in the thunderous closing chorus of the opera, "Placa alfin la tetra sorte"—"Le ciel calme enfin nos peines." The curtain falls.

LE PROPHÈTE

by GIACOMO MEYERBEER

(1791–1864)

Libretto by

EUGÈNE SCRIBE

CHARACTERS

Berthe		Soprano
Fidès, mother of Jean of Leyden		Mezzo-soprano
Zacharie	Anabaptist leaders of a	Bass
Jonas	Westphalian revolt	Tenor
Mathisen		Baritone
Count d'Oberthal		Baritone
Jean (John of Leyden), innkeeper, later the false Prophet		Tenor
Peasant woman		Soprano
Anabaptist		Mezzo-soprano
Townsman		Tenor
Two officers		Tenor / Baritone

Nobles, citizens, peasants, soldiers, prisoners

Place: Dordrecht, Holland; Münster, Westphalia

Time: Circa 1534

First performance: Grand Opéra, Paris, April 16, 1849

Original language: French

Le Prophète is one of the four operas which represent Giacomo Meyerbeer at the pinnacle of his lifework as an operatic composer. They established him as the founder of nineteenth-century romantic French opera and as the most eminent composer of his time. His scores are structured on sturdy German harmony, sumptuous Italian melody and titillating French rhythms. His operatic world is larger than life, portrayed on a vast musical canvas in bold, vivid colors.

First came *Robert le Diable* in 1831—supernatural and demonic—

which made the fortune of the Paris Opéra. Five years later he created *Les Huguenots,* a stupendous musical drama based on the St. Bartholomew's Day massacre of August 24, 1572. Thirteen years later came the premiere of *Le Prophète,* which repeated the success of *Les Huguenots.* The last of this great "quartet" is *L'Africaine,* completed in 1864, the year of Meyerbeer's death. Presented in 1865, it is acknowledged as the finest work among the sixteen operas he wrote.

Le Prophète is associated with some of the greatest names of the Golden Age: Nordica, Melba, Scalchi, Brandt, Schumann-Heink, Louise Homer, the de Reszkes, Maurel, Plançon, Caruso, Didur. On January 18, 1977, a cast including Marilyn Horne, James McCracken, Renata Scotto, Jerome Hines, Frank Little, Raimund Herincx and Morley Meredith sang the opera in its first Metropolitan performance since 1928. The first Metropolitan broadcast was on January 29, 1977.

In her highly acclaimed role of Fidès, Miss Horne is successor to a long line of similarly gifted mezzos—including Pauline Viardot-García, who created the role in 1849.

The opera is broadly based on an actual uprising led by a group of Anabaptist fanatics in Westphalia circa 1534. The historical original of John of Leyden (Jean) is Jan Beukelszoon, born 1509, sometime innkeeper, merchant and tailor, who had himself crowned in Münster. That set off an orgy of cruelty and violence which demoralized the city. It was captured by imperial forces on June 24, 1535. Jan, the "false prophet," was tortured to death.

ACT ONE[1]

The village of Dordrecht in Holland. At one side, steps leading up to Count d'Oberthal's castle.

There is a brief pastoral introduction. To the piping of shepherds, peasants and laborers come in from their fields and cottages. They sing a chorale ("La brise est muette") expressing their happiness over the fine, clear weather.

Berthe enters. In a coloratura aria ("Mon coeur s'élance et palpite"), she revels in the thought that she will soon see her fiancé, Jean (John of Leyden). She turns to see Fidès approaching, and runs to her with a warm greeting. Fidès, though tired from walking from Jean's inn in Leyden, responds affectionately. Placing an engagement ring on Berthe's finger, she tells her that she has come to bring Jean's bride-to-be to him this very day ("Allez, allez, amenez là").

---

[1] In some presentations, Act One consists of Meyerbeer's original Acts One and Two. Then, Act Two combines Acts Three and Four; Act Three is the original Act Five.

Berthe demurs, wondering anxiously why Jean deigns to choose a poor orphaned peasant girl like herself—a vassal of Count d'Oberthal. Smiling, Fidès assures her that she is indeed the prize catch in the village ("Berthe est la plus gentille") and will be most welcome as Jean's helpmate at his inn. But Berthe protests that they cannot marry without permission of Count d'Oberthal. Very well, says Fidès, we will go to see him at once.

As the two go toward the castle stairs, they catch sight of three ominous figures in black at the top. Berthe explains that they are missionaries visiting the provinces. Actually, they are Anabaptist revolutionaries from Westphalia—Jonas, Zacharie and Mathisen. Raising their hands as if in benediction, they sing, in a taunting parody of a Latin psalm ("Ad nos, ad salutarem undam"), that they have come to free the peasants from the bondage of their oppressors. This, of course, is an incitement to revolt. As they descend the stairs, the throng watches them curiously.

The Latin psalm, in a vigorous 6/4 rhythm, marks the beginning of a powerful ensemble. As the Anabaptists urge the peasants to turn against their masters, their excited listeners shout that they will follow these leaders to freedom. Now thoroughly aroused, the peasants arm themselves with pitchforks, spades and cudgels and rush up the castle stairs, led by the Anabaptists.

They stop in their tracks as the castle doors suddenly swing open to reveal Count d'Oberthal surrounded by nobles and guards. Glaring at the intruders, he demands to know who dares disturb the peace of his castle. Then he notices the Anabaptists and rails at them as meddlesome Puritans. He recognizes Jonas as his former steward who stole his wine. In rising anger he commands his guards to beat the three and evict them. The guards drag them away.

Meanwhile, Berthe and Fidès timidly approach the Count, who notices the girl with obvious pleasure and asks why she has come ("Ah! celle-ci vaut mieux"). Aside, Fidès exhorts her not to be afraid. In an ensuing duet ("Un jour dans les flots de la Meuse") the two women plead their case. Berthe begins by telling the Count that when one day she tried to drown herself in the River Meuse, Jean rescued her. Fidès repeats her phrases. Now, the girl goes on, she wants to marry Jean and hopes the Count will grant her permission, as the law of liege lord demands.

Gazing avidly at her, d'Oberthal exclaims that such beauty and innocence must not be allowed to leave the castle. He firmly refuses her request. Hearing this, the peasants burst into a furious chorus of protest against this new evidence of their master's cruelty ("Ô nouvelle infamie!"). Threatened by the guards, they turn to flee, but rally when Fidès berates them for their cowardice. They advance menacingly on d'Oberthal, who first ignores them. Suddenly he turns in fury and orders them to leave ("Cédez tous, ou si non, soldats")—or face his soldiers.

The Count and his entourage go back into the castle and the doors close behind them. The cowed peasants slink away. Then the three Anabaptists reappear at the top of the castle stairs and repeat their spurious psalm of benediction. The peasants turn and kneel. In anger and frustration, they shake their fists at the castle walls.

ACT TWO[2]

Jean's inn on the outskirts of Leyden. A door at right, doors at back. Tables and chairs. Jean enters carrying several bottles which he places on the tables.

To the rhythm of a waltz, villagers outside sing of their delight in dancing ("Valsons toujours"). They dance into the inn and sit down at the tables. A generous soldier calls for a round of beer and the villagers lustily demand service from Jean. In an aside, he sings of the joy of meeting his beloved Berthe when she returns with his mother this very evening ("Le jour baisse, et ma mère bientôt"). The waltz rhythm continues throughout the following scene.

The Anabaptists enter. Jonas, looking at Jean in astonishment, remarks in an aside that the innkeeper bears an amazing resemblance to the portrait of King David in the Cathedral of Münster—a portrait, he adds, with miraculous powers. Turning to a peasant, he asks: "Who is that man?"

"Jean, our host," the peasant replies. "He is strong, brave, and knows the Bible by heart." Zacharie, with a knowing glance at the other two, comments that he is the very man they need—sent to them by the Lord ("Celui qu'à nous aider appelle le Très Haut!"). They watch Jean closely as he bids goodnight to the peasants, who dance away.

In recitative, Zacharie asks Jean why he seems troubled. Because of a strange dream, he explains. Then he describes it ("Sous les vastes arceaux un temple magnifique"). He stood in a magnificent temple, a crown on his head, with a vast throng kneeling before him and chanting: "The Messiah has come!" Yet on the temple wall he saw an inscription of doom: "Woe unto thee!"

When he turned to ascend his throne he was swept away in a sea of blood and flame. There was a mighty clamor of voices—some damning him, others crying for mercy. Jean says he awoke shaking with horror. Treacherously, the Anabaptists assure him that the dream proves he is destined to reign. But Jean strenuously rejects the idea—his only thought now is for his beloved Berthe, he sings in a tender refrain

---

[2] In some versions, continuation of Act One.

("Pour Berthe, moi, je soupire"). When the Anabaptists reiterate their predictions he impatiently asks them to leave. They go. Though suspicious of his visitors, Jean happily turns his thoughts to his coming marriage.

Suddenly Jean hears the galloping of horses and the clatter of arms. A moment later, Berthe, barefoot, disheveled and terror-stricken, throws herself into his arms. She wails that she is being pursued by Count d'Oberthal and his soldiers—having escaped while being taken to the castle ("Ah! d'effroi je tremble encore!"). Trying to calm her, Jean glances outside, then pushes her into a curtained alcove under a stair.

The Count and his soldiers storm in. The scene continues in recitative. Fuming with rage, d'Oberthal shouts that one of his captives escaped into the woods near this inn while being taken to his Harlem castle ("Loin de ces rives, au château de Harlem"). He delivers his ultimatum: if she is here, surrender her—or your mother will die before your eyes ("Ou ta mère à l'instant, à tes yeux va périr"). Jean, on his knees, begs for mercy ("Ah! cruels, prenez ma vie").

As d'Oberthal glares down at Jean, soldiers drag in his mother. Berthe emerges from the alcove. Sinking to the floor, Fidès raises her arms supplicatingly to her son. A soldier, standing over her, raises a headsman's ax. In a paroxysm of fury, Jean screams that the Count will be guilty of parricide ("Qu'il fasse sur toi seul tomber le parricide"). This climactic phrase is powerfully sung on a single repeated note. He seizes Berthe and pushes her violently into the hands of the soldiers. As they drag her away, Jean slumps into a chair and buries his face in his hands.

Fidès, rising, embraces Jean and expresses her gratitude for his sacrifice in her behalf. She sings the famous arioso "Ah! mon fils," one of the finest numbers in the opera and considered a prime example of Meyerbeer's operatic genius. At its conclusion she again embraces her son, then quietly goes into an adjoining room.

Jean rages momentarily against the Count and his hirelings, then hears the psalm of the Anabaptists outside. He welcomes them eagerly. At once they begin their carefully laid plan to ensnare him in their nefarious plotting. They will make him King, they tell him. In an insidious *sotto voce* ("Gémissant sous le joug et sous la tyrannie") Zacharie sings that the persecuted people of Germany are awaiting their Messiah. The other two join him in a conspiratorial trio ("Oui, c'est Dieu qui t'appelle"), assuring Jean that God himself has called him to wreak vengeance on the tyrants. They remind him that another loyal citizen before him saved her country from oppressors: Joan of Arc.

The ensemble continues in quartet form as Jean—now completely under the spell of the Anabaptists—sings that he is ready for action. But then Zacharie stuns him by saying that his sacred mission will oblige him to cut all earthly ties: he will never see his mother nor his home again. Jean cries that he cannot forsake his mother—his only treasure on earth. He begs abjectly for one moment to bid her farewell. The Anabaptists harshly refuse: his first duty is vengeance; his next, to accept the crown as King of a downtrodden people. Jean's resolution collapses. Despairingly he sings that if he kissed his mother now he would never leave her ("No, . . . si je l'embrassais je ne partirais pas"). Looking at him contemptuously, the Anabaptists relish their evil triumph.

ACT THREE[3]

The winter camp of the Anabaptists on the shore of a frozen lake near Münster in Westphalia. The city is under siege by rebellious peasants. There are sounds of fighting; soldiers drag in several prisoners in chains. After an orchestral introduction in a martial rhythm, the besiegers burst into a savage chorus of triumph ("Du sang que Judas succombe"), boasting that they will dance on the tombs of the tyrants. It is God Himself who demands vengeance. Kneeling, they sing a brief *Te Deum*, then take up their frenzied cry for blood. Led by Zacharie, who sings in an obbligato to the chorus, they vow to annihilate their enemies.

When the throng disperses, the Anabaptists comment on the success of their soldiers, then watch a crowd laden with provisions for the camp crossing the ice on skates. A chorus ("Voici les fermières") commenting on the graceful movements of the skaters leads into the music of a ballet—the familiar *skaters' waltz*.

The scene changes to Zacharie's tent, where Mathisen reports that he ordered Count d'Oberthal to surrender. The Count defied him because, he said, the Anabaptists burned his son's castle to the ground. Nevertheless, Zacharie remarks, he will soon surrender. Fortunately Jean—whom they have created Prophet-Emperor—is on his way to Münster.

At that moment Jonas enters with a stranger he found loitering behind the lines. It is d'Oberthal, but the others do not recognize him in the darkness of the tent. He tells them he wants to join the Anabaptists (hoping that this ruse will enable him to get to Münster without being identified) ("Laissons-lui son erreur").

This cues in a seriocomic trio ("Verse, verse, frères") sung by Zacharie, d'Oberthal and Jonas, in which they relish the prospect of storming the Münster ramparts and hanging all the miscreants—including d'Oberthal himself. Jonas then strikes a light, revealing the Anabaptists and the Count to each other. In surprise and fury, the Anabaptists turn

[3] In some versions, Act Two.

on the Count, who curses his two captors. Zacharie sardonically observes that now d'Oberthal will surely hang with the rest of the traitors.

The trio ends in a violent climax as Zacharie orders soldiers to lead d'Oberthal to the gallows. Jonas stops him to ask: "This . . . without the Prophet's sanction?" Zacharie retorts: "That is my business." Jonas follows d'Oberthal and the soldiers.

Jean enters, gloomy and preoccupied. When Zacharie asks why he—the Prophet who saved Germany as Joan of Arc saved France—is troubled, Jean quietly answers ("Jeanne d'Arc, sur ses pas") that Joan made heroes of her followers; he has made only hangmen of his own. Now, he declares over clarion chords in the orchestra, he will go no further ("je n'irai pas plus loin!").

Zacharie staggers in surprise. To his further confusion, Jean sings that he longs to see his mother. Zacharie reminds him that he had sworn never to see her again. Thereupon, Jean throws down his sword, crying that he has freed Germany, and that, for him, is the end. Zacharie threatens him with his dagger, but Jean ignores him.

He turns to see d'Oberthal, a chanting monk at his side, being led away by soldiers. To his execution, says Zacharie vindictively. Angrily Jean demands: "Who dares speak of death when I speak of pardon?" At his order, the soldiers release the prisoners. Overcome by this act of mercy, d'Oberthal contritely says he deserves to die for his crimes. He then reveals that Berthe, to save her honor, again tried to drown herself. A spy, however, reported that she had been rescued and has been seen in Münster.

He was on his way to set her free, d'Oberthal goes on, but was captured—and here he is. Quietly he says: "Strike!" With their headsman's axes poised, the soldiers close in. "Spare him," Jean commands; "Berthe will pronounce his sentence." Then he rallies his followers and prepares to lead them to the battlements of Münster to rescue Berthe.

Mathisen comes running in with the news that a mutinous rebel faction had turned against their comrades, attacked Münster, but were beaten back. A moment later, the defeated turncoats straggle in. They sing ("Par toi Münster nous fut promis") that Jean promised to lead them in conquering Münster. As a false prophet, he failed them, and now they have met with disaster. Jean furiously demands to know who instigated this counterrevolt. The three Anabaptists accuse each other.

Jean bitterly denounces those who did not keep faith with him ("Perfides, que mon bras devrait punir"). He warns that God will call them to account for their perfidy. The chastened rebels kneel as Jean leads them in a prayer for forgiveness and victory ("Éternel! Dieu sauveur qui notre faiblesse").

Trumpets sound the call to battle. Mathisen runs in shouting that the peasants are gathering under his banner and are ready to storm the battlements. Jean, in a kind of mystical exaltation, sings that, like the biblical King David, he will praise God for giving him the victory. His followers, singing that God Himself will triumph over Münster ("Ä Münster! En marche! Dieu nous suit!"), join in triumphal chorus.

ACT FOUR[4]

A square in Münster before the steps of the Town Hall, adjacent to the palace. The city is now occupied by Jean and his adherents. Citizens carrying sacks of gold and precious stones climb the steps of the Town Hall; others return empty-handed. More and more citizens gather in the square, apprehensively talking among themselves.

In a *sotto voce* chorus ("Courbons notre tête") they voice their dismay over the duplicity of Jean—once their prophet and savior, now their ruthless conqueror—having proclaimed himself Prophet-Emperor. When they see a troop of Anabaptist soldiers approaching, they dutifully chant: "Long live the Prophet!" Among themselves they chant in a perverse echo with a touch of grim humor: "Down with the Prophet!"

One of the citizens leads in Fidès, in rags and reduced to beggary. Exhausted, she sinks down on the steps, begging for alms to pay for a mass for her son, whom she believes is dead ("Donnez pour une pauvre âme"). Several citizens give her money, then are startled by a commotion in the palace. They whisper that the hour has come for the counter-revolt. Taking up their sacks, they hurry away.

In a flowing phrase musically associated with Berthe, the girl, disguised as a pilgrim, shuffles in. In another moment, she and Fidès recognize each other and fervently embrace. This meeting introduces a long duet, one of the outstanding numbers in the opera. First Berthe describes her harrowing ordeals after she was parted from Fidès ("Pour garder à ton fils"). Rather than break her betrothal vows to Jean, she again tried to drown herself. And again she was rescued—this time by a fisherman who hid her from d'Oberthal's pursuing soldiers. She came to Münster when she learned that Jean and his mother had gone there.

Berthe implores Fidès to lead her to the arms of her beloved ("Conduis-moi dans ses bras!"). The phrase is sung in a soaring cadenza. There is a moment of ominous silence. Then, over a sustained, foreboding chord in the orchestra, Fidès sobs that her son is dead ("Mon fils . . . il est mort").

The duet resumes in brief unaccompanied phrases ("Dernier espoir . . . Hélas! plus espoir"). In recitative, Fidès relates that one day she found Jean's bloodstained clothing in her cottage. A mysterious voice

---

[4] In some versions, continuation of Act Two.

called out that he had been murdered on the orders of the Prophet.[5] Enraged, Berthe cries out that God Himself will guide her to this perfidious tyrant to kill him ("Dieu me guidera"). Lamenting for Jean and crying for vengeance, the women bring the duet to its climax.

During an orchestral interlude in a martial tempo, the scene changes without pause to the Cathedral of Münster. Then follows the pageant of the coronation of Jean as Emperor. Clad in white, his head bared, he enters attended by guards and electors bearing the scepter, crown and other imperial insignia. The procession moves into the cloister.

Fidès enters alone, kneels and remains there with bowed head. From the cloister comes the sound of a Latin chant ("Dominer, salvum fac regem nostrum") sung in homage to the "Prophet-King." Fidès recoils at the sacrilege of invoking God's blessing on the scheming false prophet who murdered her son. In helpless rage she curses him. As if to mock her, the chant echoes from the cloister. In a refrain soaring over the chanting ("Ah! ma fille, ô Judith nouvelle"), she prays that Berthe herself, like "a second Judith," will strike down the Prophet in revenge.[6]

The coronation procession, led by children, reappears. The Emperor is acclaimed in a mighty chorus. Then . . . softly, as though in a dream, Jean sings that he is indeed the Emperor, chosen of God ("Je suis le fils de Dieu").

But Fidès recognizes his voice. Struggling to her feet, she cries: "My son!" Jean is about to rush to her when Mathisen stops him with the warning: "If you speak, your mother dies!" Jean, now hopelessly enmeshed in his fear of the Anabaptists and his own bizarre ambition, stares at Fidès and coldly asks who this woman is. Fidès sings that she is only a poor mother who wishes to pardon an ungrateful son ("Moi qui je suis la pauvre femme").

Jean, playing out his despicable role—abetted by the Anabaptists— denounces the blasphemy of this demented woman who claims to be the mortal mother of a Prophet ordained by God. As the Anabaptists and the people hail him in chorale interludes, Jean solves the dilemma with cunning born of desperation. At first he faces down the crowd, which begins to voice suspicion of his claim as Prophet. While some rail at Fidès as a blasphemer, others curse Jean as an impostor.

Extending his hands over the kneeling woman, Jean pretends to exorcise this wretched creature who claims the Holy Prophet is her son. Then, in a melodramatic gesture, he stretches out his arms and com-

[5] This grim masquerade was contrived by the Anabaptists to conceal from Fidès the fact that Jean and the Prophet are one and the same.

[6] The reference is to the biblical story, in the Apocrypha, of Judith, who delivered her people by slaying Holofernes, the general of Nebuchadnezzar.

mands the nobles around him to plunge their swords into his heart if Fidès declares he is her son ("Si je suis enfant . . . Punissez l'imposteur! Frappez"). There is a menacing murmur from the crowd: "Answer!"

In a striking phrase beginning on a G below the staff and rising to the G two octaves above, Fidès replies: "I have no son" (Je n'ai plus de fils, hélas!").

The throng bursts into a tremendous chorus ("Miracle du grand Prophète") hailing the Great Prophet for performing a miracle. Jean, his retinue and the people leave the Cathedral. Fidès, praying that Berthe will succeed in assassinating her ruthless ingrate of a son, tries to follow the crowd. The three Anabaptists bar her way with the points of their swords.

ACT FIVE[7]

[*Scene One*] A dungeon-like room in the Münster palace. At one side a stone stairway leads upward.

In a brief entr'acte, Jonas, Mathisen and Zacharie discuss the imminent attack of the legitimate German Emperor to drive out the usurper, the Prophet. The Emperor has promised to pardon them if they will betray Jean. This they agree to do. They leave.

Soldiers bring in Fidès. Sitting down on a stone bench she gives way to her mingled emotions of terror, anger and compassion in the famous cavatina and air "Ô prêtres de Baal," one of the most spectacular numbers in the opera. Now, she sings, the minions of Baal (the false god of the ancient Semites, whom she now equates with her faithless son) have thrown her into this dungeon. She rages at the thought of his betrayal. But in the ensuing cavatina ("Ô toi qui m'abandonnes") her mood softens; she pities and pardons him and she will wait for him in heaven.

A soldier comes down the stairway and orders her to kneel: the Great Prophet is about to appear. Beside herself with excitement, Fidès launches into the concluding air ("Comme un éclair précipité"): she prays that Truth may strike her son like lightning, redeem his soul and bring him back to God.

Jean, wrapped in a mantle, his crown on his head, comes down the stairs and faces his mother. A duet follows. Fidès first turns on Jean in furious scorn ("Arrière! Prophète et fils de Dieu!"), sardonically calling him "Prophet and son of God." He is no longer a son of hers, she rages, only a tyrant whose hands are stained with blood. Jean abjectly begs her forgiveness but she orders him out of her sight. She will forgive

---

[7] In some versions, Act Three.

him only if he repudiates those who made him King. Jean protests that he cannot desert his loyal followers.

In a sudden change of mood, Fidès clasps his hand in one of hers. With the other she points upward. Heaven will hear a mother's prayer, she sings ("à la voix de ta mère") and heaven will pardon an erring son. She opens her arms and Jean rushes into her embrace. Together they sing of penitence and pardon.

They are still in their embrace when a door in the wall opens and Berthe, dressed in white and holding a torch, comes in. Mysteriously, she walks along one wall, then stops and touches a stone. It swings open to disclose a cavern. Dumbfounded, Fidès asks the meaning of this. Berthe, strangely excited, explains that her grandfather, warden of the castle, once told her about the secret store of powder hidden in this cavern. Now . . . one touch of the torch, and the false Prophet, his followers and the palace itself will vanish in flames.[8] Fidès, horrified, gasps, "My son," and at that moment Berthe recognizes Jean.

Her ecstatic greeting ("C'est toi qui m'es rendu?") leads into a pastoral trio ("loin de la ville"), which briefly relieves the tension of the opera's denouement. Berthe, Fidès and Jean muse over the happiness they will share when this terrible ordeal will be a thing of the past.[9]

Their dream is shattered when a soldier rushes in to tell Jean that he has been betrayed and that the German Emperor's forces have seized the castle to kill the Prophet. When Berthe hears the word "Prophet," the terrible truth dawns upon her: Jean, her lover, and the false Prophet she has sworn to assassinate are one and the same.

Guilt-stricken by the thought that she—in the madness of revenge—sought to kill the man she loved, Berthe implores the earth to swallow her and hide her crime ("Ô spectre épouvantable! Ô terre entr'ouvre-toi"). This builds into a trio as Fidès and Jean join Berthe in expressing their conflicting emotions. It climaxes as Berthe, in a final gesture of expiation, plunges a knife into her breast and dies in Jean's arms. Jean sobs: "Morte! Morte!"

With Berthe's body in his arms, he orders his soldiers to lead his mother out of the room. Others follow with the body of the girl. Jean picks up his crown, which he had put on a stone table, and places it on his head. Now, he sings in recitative, he will have his revenge on his betrayers. He goes up the stairs.

[Scene Two] The scene changes to the banquet hall of the palace. At back are two tall iron gates leading out of the hall. Jean, pale and

---

[8] As part of her bizarre plot, Berthe has set a slow fire to the powder stores, timed to ignite during the forthcoming coronation banquet.

[9] Its effect is singularly like that of the Aïda/Radames duet, "Fuggiam gli ardori inospiti."

deep in thought, sits at a raised table laden with food and wine in golden goblets.

Anabaptists and guests at the coronation banquet sing the praises of the Prophet ("Gloire au Prophète"). Young girls dance a bacchanale. Jean calls two of his officers to him. Aside, in quasi-recitative ("Quand vous verrez entrer nos ennemis"), he warns them of impending catastrophe: when the forces of the German Emperor finally invade the palace, the officers must flee for their lives, for at that moment this banquet hall will be destroyed by an explosion. He bids them a friendly farewell, and with a bitter smile turns back to the revelry. Young dancing girls proffer him a goblet of wine.

Rising, Jean roars out a drinking song with savage exuberance ("Versez que tout respire"). Let all drink in frenzy and delirium, he shouts sardonically. The unsuspecting guests respond to this lethal toast.

The troops of the Emperor, d'Oberthal at their head, rush in. Together, the Anabaptists and the Count shout that now the false Prophet is in their power. At that moment the iron gates at the back clang shut. Now, Jean exults, the vile traitors will expiate their crimes, and this hall will be their tomb.

The hall erupts in a violent explosion—a fiery seal on the final vengeance of Jean and Berthe. As the hall crashes in ruins, Fidès, who had been sitting near Jean, throws herself into his arms. In a unison duet ("Ah! viens divine flamme vers Dieu qui nous réclame") they calmly face their immolation—in effect a Westphalian *Götterdämmerung*. The curtain falls.

I PURITANI
(*I Puritani di Scozia—The Puritans of Scotland*)
by VINCENZO BELLINI
(1801–35)

Libretto by
COUNT CARLO PEPOLI

After the play *Têtes Rondes et Cavaliers* (*Roundheads and Cavaliers*), by François Ancelot and Xavier-Boniface Saintine. In its general outline, the plot is based on *Old Mortality*, by Sir Walter Scott.

CHARACTERS
(*Italian version of English names as used by Bellini*)

Lord Gualtiero Valton (Walter Walton), Puritan	
Governor General of Plymouth	Bass
Sir Giorgio Valton, Puritan, his brother	Bass
Elvira Valton, Gualtiero's daughter	Soprano
Sir Riccardo Forto (Forth), Puritan, Elvira's suitor	Baritone
Sir Bruno Robertson (Benno Robertson),	
Puritan official	Tenor
Enrichetta di Francia (Henrietta of France),	
Stuart Queen, widow of Charles the First	Soprano
Lord Arturo Talbo (Talbot), Stuart Cavalier	Tenor

Soldiers of Oliver Cromwell, men-at-arms of Lord Arturo, ladies-in-waiting, lords and ladies of the court, heralds, pages, servants, villagers

Place: Plymouth, England
Time: The 1650s, during the English wars between Oliver Cromwell and the Stuarts
First performance: Théâtre-Italien, Paris, January 25, 1835
Original language: Italian

Although burdened by an implausible and rather ridiculous libretto, *I Puritani,* Bellini's tenth and last opera, contains some of his finest music. His ingratiating melodies, with their glittering coloratura embellishments, stamped him as a master of the great *bel canto* operatic writing of the seventeenth century and a peer of Rossini and Donizetti.

At its premiere the opera was a sensational success and subsequently was heard on stages all over the world. The cast was headed by four of the most renowned singers in operatic history: Giulia Grisi (Elvira), Giovanni Battista Rubini (Arturo), Antonio Tamburini (Riccardo) and Luigi Lablache (Giorgio). These four singers later toured together for many years, billed as the *I Puritani Quartet.*

It was as Elvira that Marcella Sembrich made her debut (in her first role on any stage) in Athens on June 7, 1877. She also sang the role in the first performance of *I Puritani* at the Metropolitan, on October 29, 1883. It was not given there again until February 18, 1918—with Giuseppe De Luca as Riccardo—then disappeared from the repertoire after five performances.

The opera next appeared in America on October 3, 1955, when Maria Callas sang Elvira at the Chicago Lyric Theater with Giuseppe Di Stefano, Ettore Bastianini and Nicola Rossi-Lemeni. On May 24, 1960, Joan Sutherland made a sensational success as Elvira in a revival of the opera at the Glyndebourne Festival. The inclusion of *I Puritani* arias in the concert programs of Miss Sutherland and Miss Callas very probably has been responsible for the revival of interest in the virtually lost art of *bel canto* singing. The Metropolitan Opera Company presented the opera in a new production during the 1975–76 season, starring Joan Sutherland and Luciano Pavarotti.

Inept libretto aside, *I Puritani* is rarely given today simply because it is beyond the capabilities of most singers. It requires coloratura singing not only by the sopranos but by the baritones as well—not to mention a tenor role which soars to two high Ds and three high Fs above high C.

Bellini's career was tragically cut short when he was in his thirty-fourth year and at the height of his creative powers. A few days before the performance of *I Puritani* which was to open the 1835 season at the Théâtre-Italien, the composer—who had remained in Paris since the premiere—was stricken with intestinal fever. He died in the Paris suburb of Puteaux on September 24, 1835.

It is said that during the entire performance everyone in the opera house—performers, instrumentalists and audience—wept with grief. Afterward, the cast and musicians joined in a great requiem mass directed by Rossini and Cherubini at the Church of the Invalides.

There is a brief introduction which opens with a fanfare, then leads into a plaintive, flowing melody expressive of the romantic elements of the opera.

ACT ONE

The curtain rises on a seventeenth-century castle, bristling with fortifications, in Plymouth, England.[1] Its towers are silhouetted against the early morning sky. Bruno and a company of Cromwell's soldiers are discovered; they stir into activity as a trumpet sounds. In a chorus ("Quanto la tromba squilla") they sing that the trumpet sounds the call to the battle in which they will annihilate the proud Stuarts.

Then, to the sound of organ music from inside the castle, Bruno bids the warriors sing a morning hymn of praise to the Creator. Kneeling, the Puritans join in a moving and dignified anthem: "La luna, il sol, le stelle." It dies away in a phrase of quiet reverence.

The mood of the scene suddenly changes as the villagers crowd in with a gay chorus hailing Elvira on the day of her betrothal ("Garzon, che mira Elvira"). They bring the chorus to a rousing finish, then move from the scene with the soldiers, leaving Bruno standing alone.

A moment later Riccardo enters, and dialogue in recitative follows. Riccardo says despondently that these nuptial choruses are funeral dirges to his ears because he has lost Elvira. Her father, he tells Bruno, had promised him Elvira's hand, but when he arrived at the castle with his troops he learned that she is in love with the hated Stuart Cavalier Arturo Talbo. Her father, Riccardo fumes, can do nothing to change her heart. Bruno advises him to forget his disappointment by devoting his life to the service of his country.

But Riccardo, inconsolable, expresses his despair in a melodramatic aria, "Ah, per sempre io ti perdei." He laments that he has lost Elvira forever and that nothing is left him but oblivion. The aria illustrates the vocal agility demanded of male as well as female singers in this opera. As Bruno vainly tries to turn Riccardo's thoughts to patriotism, the disgruntled suitor bids farewell to his dreams of bliss ("Bel sogno beato d'amore e contento").

The scene changes to Elvira's apartment in the castle, where she is seen in conversation with Sir Giorgio, her uncle—whom she affectionately calls her "second father." In recitative, Giorgio tells her how happy he is that today she is to be a bride.

Thinking he means she will marry Riccardo, Elvira protests in alarm and dismay that she will never be a bride. In an ensuing aria ("Sai com'arde in petto mio") she declares that if she is dragged to the altar she will die of grief.

Thereupon Giorgio informs her that the Cavalier she really loves is

---

[1] For reasons of his own, the librettist, Pepoli, located Plymouth, which is several hundred miles from the Scottish border, in Scotland.

on his way to the castle. Elvira, scarcely able to believe this news, literally weeps for joy. A long duet follows ("Piangi, o figlia, sul mio seno") in which Giorgio explains how he persuaded Elvira's father to allow her to marry the man of her choice. He finally won Lord Valton's consent, Giorgio says, by warning him that if Elvira was forced to marry another, she would die ("se ad altre nozze andrà, misera perià!").

As Elvira fervently embraces her uncle, trumpets are heard outside. Giorgio says that Arturo and his soldiers have arrived. In a brief choral phrase the soldiers announce Arturo Talbo, and the people of the castle respond with a greeting. In a ringing duet ("A quel nome" . . . "A quel suono") Elvira and her uncle express their mutual joy over the fortunate turn of events. In a choral accompaniment the people pay homage to the brave Cavalier.

The next scene takes place in the great hall of the castle. To the accompaniment of a spirited introduction in 6/8 tempo, Lord Arturo enters from one side accompanied by esquires and pages carrying nuptial gifts. From the other side come Elvira, Lord Valton and Sir Giorgio. They are followed by ladies and gentlemen of the court, and peasants carrying garlands of flowers. The company salutes the forthcoming nuptials in a majestic chorus, "Ad Arturo, A Elvira! Onor!"

In an interlude, Arturo steps forward with a gallant tribute to his bride ("A te, o cara, amor talora"). She responds with an avowal of her love. As the ensemble builds to its fiery climax the voices of the lovers soar above in an obbligato of brilliant coloratura phrases.

All then leave the hall, with only the principals remaining. In an aside to Bruno, Lord Valton reminds him of the order he has given: anyone who leaves the castle without Valton's permission will be put to death. Dialogue in recitative follows. Turning to the lovers, Lord Valton tells them they must go to the altar without him. He then gives Arturo a note admitting him to the nuptial temple and asks Giorgio to accompany the bridal pair at the ceremony.

At that moment Enrichetta enters escorted by Bruno. Valton tells her she has been called before the English Parliament in London. Enrichetta asks him why she must go. Evasively, Valton replies that he must do his duty. Arturo, aside, asks Giorgio if this woman is an adherent of the Stuarts ("E de' Stuardi amica?"). Giorgio explains that she has been Valton's prisoner for many months and is believed to be a spy for the Stuarts.

Exclaiming that this summons means her doom, Arturo gives her a pitying look. Enrichetta gazes at him beseechingly. Valton bids Elvira to prepare for her nuptials, orders Bruno to saddle his horse, then tells Enrichetta that they must leave at once. Before he goes he gives his paternal blessing to Elvira and Arturo. He exits with the others, leaving Enrichetta and Arturo alone.

Turning to Enrichetta, Arturo urges her to put her trust in him and assures her that he will help her in every possible way. When he asks the reason for her fear she replies that her death now is only a matter of time. Arturo shudders. When Enrichetta asks him why, he answers that he trembles not only for her—whoever she may be—but for himself as well. Moreover, he is haunted by the memory of his father, who died for his loyalty to the Stuarts. But no matter who she is, Arturo goes on, he is determined to save her.

It is too late, Enrichetta says, then identifies herself as the daughter of King Henry and the wife of Charles the First of France. Like them, her fate will be the headman's ax ("È tardi! figlia a Enrico, e a Carlo sposa"). Thunderstruck, Arturo kneels in homage to his Queen.

This colloquy leads into a dramatic duet. Arturo vehemently declares he will help her escape or die in the attempt. Enrichetta begs him not to risk his life for her, but to think of Elvira, who even now is waiting for him at the altar. Arturo implores her not to mention the name of his beloved lest the thought of her swerve him from his purpose ("Non parlar di lei che adoro"). Enrichetta desperately insists that she is resigned to her fate—her life is over, but his is still before him. Arturo cries that he will save his Queen or die with the name of his beloved on his lips. He ends his declaration on a ringing phrase of defiance. At that instant, in startling contrast to the grim mood of the scene, Elvira's voice is heard in a joyous coloratura phrase expressive of her happiness.

A moment later she appears with Giorgio. Crowned with a wreath of roses and wearing a pearl necklace, she carries the wedding veil given her by Arturo. In a lilting refrain ("Son vergine vezzosa") she sings about her bridal finery. Looking on admiringly, Enrichetta, Arturo and Giorgio comment on her childlike joy over being a bride. Their voices blend with hers in a quartet ("Se miro il suo candore") which continues until the end of the scene.

During an interlude, Elvira—like a child playing a game—asks Enrichetta if she may put the wedding veil on her head "in a new fashion" ("il velo in foggia nuova"). Amused, Enrichetta consents. In a continuation of the quartet, Elvira gleefully admires the effect; Giorgio and Arturo asks Enrichetta to indulge Elvira's childish whim; Enrichetta herself comments that the veil will hide the sorrow in her face.

Lord Valton and his retinue interrupt the ensemble briefly to remind Elvira that the hour of the wedding is drawing near. At the conclusion of the quartet, Elvira leaves with her father, after being assured by the other three that Arturo will place the wedding veil on her own head at the proper time. Giorgio follows her, and Enrichetta and Arturo again are left alone.

As Arturo, looking around cautiously, takes from his belt the note given him previously by Lord Valton, Enrichetta, in recitative, observes that the white veil should adorn the head of a bride-to-be—but not her own ("Sulla verginea testa"). She is about to take it off when Arturo restrains her. It is heaven's will, he tells her, that the veil was placed upon her head. It will conceal her face, and thus when they leave the castle it will deceive the sentry into thinking that Arturo is escorting his bride.

Just as Arturo is about to lead her away, Riccardo appears and with drawn sword bars his path. In bitter anger, Riccardo—of course mistaking the veiled Enrichetta for Elvira—accuses Arturo of trying to steal his promised bride ("Ferma, invan rapir pretendi"), then challenges him to fight. This marks the beginning of a tempestuous musical dialogue—another example of the difficult coloratura parts Bellini wrote for male voices in the opera. Arturo draws his sword and accepts the challenge.

As the two adversaries are about to lunge at each other, Enrichetta, imploring them not to sacrifice their lives for her sake, interposes herself between them. In so doing she disarranges the veil, revealing her face. Riccardo, recognizing her as the Queen, staggers back in surprise. Arturo sardonically dares him now to make good his challenge to fight ("Tua voce altera"). To Arturo's utter amazement, Riccardo replies that he will do nothing to prevent his leaving with the Queen.

There is a brief passage in quasi-recitative. Arturo, now losing all hope of marrying Elvira, swears he will always love her. Enrichetta wonders if her good fortune is a dream, and if now she can be reunited with her son. Riccardo, glaring at Arturo, gloats that his rival will suffer even more than he himself has suffered—he will lose his beloved and his country as well. In ironic contrast, a chorus behind the scenes hails the wedding day.

Arturo, about to rush away with Enrichetta, suddenly turns to Riccardo and asks if he will swear to say nothing until they are safely outside the castle walls. Riccardo swears to it. The other two then disappear. After a few moments Riccardo goes to an adjoining balcony overlooking the castle ramparts and watches the fugitives vanish into the distance.

Lord Valton, Sir Giorgio, Bruno, Elvira and the ladies of the wedding party now enter. Elvira, looking around anxiously, asks where Arturo is ("Dov'è Arturo?"), and her question is echoed by Valton, Giorgio and the court. This marks the beginning of the tempestuous ensemble which concludes the act.

As all stare at Riccardo in consternation, he breaks the news that Arturo and the royal prisoner have escaped. Pandemonium erupts as the alarm bell of the fortress clangs and cannon are fired off. Over a clamorous orchestral accompaniment, the men and women denounce the Cavalier bridegroom as a vile traitor ("Col vil cavaliero!").

Their outcries are suddenly hushed as Elvira totters forward, staring wildly around. Shocked out of her senses, she sings in disconnected phrases that Arturo's beloved wears a white veil . . . he calls her his bride and her name is Elvira ("La dama Arturo"). Then in anguished tones she asks: "But am I not Elvira?" There is a gasp of horror from the onlookers.

In the grip of her madness, Elvira imagines she sees Arturo. With passionate intensity she implores him to come to the temple where they will be united forever ("Oh, vieni al tempio, fedele Arturo"). She repeats her avowals over a choral accompaniment.

In mounting delirium she upbraids Arturo for his betrayal and wails that the flames of rage are devouring her heart ("Qual febbre vorace m'uccide"). Then, exhausted by her outburst, she stares with unseeing eyes as the Puritans thunder out a malediction against the traitorous fugitives ("Non casa, non spiaggia raccolga i fuggenti!"). May they be denied home and haven, and may they be accursed eternally in life and in death—"eterno sia il penar." On this phrase the ensemble comes to its blazing conclusion.

ACT TWO

A large room in the castle, with side doors leading to Elvira's apartment and to other rooms. Villagers, Puritans and Bruno are gathered together discussing the misfortune which has befallen Elvira. A brief orchestral introduction states a melancholy theme which is taken up in a chorus of lamentation, "Piangon le ciglia, si spezza il cor." The villagers and Puritans sing that Elvira surely will die of unrequited love . . . she wanders over the castle grounds weeping and crying, "Pity! pity!"

Giorgio enters and all eagerly ask for news of Elvira. Sometimes she is sad, sometimes happy, Giorgio reports, and she seems to hover between reason and insanity. At the urging of his listeners, Giorgio, although protesting he is too grief-stricken to speak, describes Elvira's plight in the aria "Cinta di fiori e col bel crin disciolto." He tells how she wanders aimlessly about, wearing a chaplet of roses, her hair disheveled, repeating: "Where is Elvira?" Or, dressed in her wedding gown, she repeats her vows as though at the altar. At other times she sings sadly of love to the accompaniment of her harp, then in the agony of her grief she cries for death. The aria is sung to accompanying choral phrases as the listeners call down the avenging lightning of heaven upon Elvira's betrayer ("Si, cada il folgore sul traditor").

As the aria ends, Riccardo enters with a document and electrifies the company with the news that Arturo has been condemned to death by the English Parliament. The people express their satisfaction in a choral phrase. Riccardo continues reading the parliamentary decree to the effect that Lord Valton has been declared innocent of any conspiracy and that his honors will be restored to him. But what will honors mean to him, the people ask, when he finds that his beloved daughter is hopelessly insane?

At that, Riccardo asks Giorgio if there is any hope. In a recitative passage ("Medic'arte n'assicura") Giorgio explains that Elvira's physicians have declared that any sudden joy or sorrow might serve to shock the girl out of her madness. In a menacing phrase ("Qual mai merita, Arturo") the Puritans murmur that a dire fate surely awaits the culprit responsible for this debacle.

Riccardo steps forward and in continuing recitative ("In me duce premier, parla Cromvello") proclaims that in the name of Cromwell the Puritans must hunt down the traitor who has stained English ground with blood. And when he is brought to justice, there will be neither pity nor pardon for him. The Puritans and villagers rush away. Riccardo and Giorgio remain.

Suddenly they hear Elvira's voice. In a dolorous, wailing phrase ("O rendetemi la speme") she asks for the boon of hope or the release of death. A moment later she appears, and then follows the opera's famous Mad Scene—a dramatic and musical parallel to that in Donizetti's *Lucia di Lammermoor*.

Hopelessly out of her mind, Elvira recalls how her lover called to her "in his voice so soft and sweet" ("Qui la voce sua soave") and swore eternal fidelity. But then he cruelly deserted her, and now she asks only for a ray of hope—or death. The phrase she sang just before she entered is heard here again. Looking at the two men with the vacant stare of the demented, Elvira identifies Giorgio as her father and Riccardo—much to his despair—as Arturo. When she takes his hand and gently asks him to come to the wedding he breaks into sobs. In a tender phrase ("Ah! se piangi ancor tu sai") she tries to comfort him.

Both men, shaken by her grief and confusion, vainly try to bring her to her senses. But, lost in her dream world, she implores Arturo to join her. In a refrain of passionate entreaty ("Vien, diletto, è in ciel la luna") she brings the scene to a close. The voices of Giorgio and Riccardo blend with hers as they express their pity and compassion. As the accompaniment dies into silence, Bruno appears and gently leads Elvira away.

Then, as a rhythmic, martial theme sounds in the orchestra, Giorgio grasps Riccardo's arm as though about to confide an important secret. With intense emphasis he tells him that he must save his rival's life. When Riccardo flatly refuses, Giorgio pointedly reminds him why it was that Arturo and his prisoner managed to escape—referring, of course, to the fact that Riccardo himself made that escape possible. Bridling at this, Riccardo retorts that it is the English Parliament that has doomed Arturo ("Fu voler del Parlamento"). He himself, he adds, neither hates nor fears him—but die the traitor must.

Giorgio accuses him of acting out of jealousy and guilt ("Un geloso e reo tormento"). He warns Riccardo that if he dooms his rival, not one person but two will die. Then, Giorgio goes on in foreboding tones ("Se tra il bujo un fantasma vedrai"), the ghost of Elvira, accusing him of causing her death ("io son morte per te"), will hound him to his grave. And with her will be the avenging phantom of Arturo.

Partly out of superstitious fear, Riccardo's anger subsides somewhat. The two men, in effect, then strike a bargain: if Arturo is captured unarmed, Riccardo promises to spare his life; if he returns to give battle, Giorgio agrees to fight him to the death. And their own battle cry will be: "Country, victory and honor!" ("Patria, vittoria, onor!").

This climactic phrase brings the long colloquy to one of the opera's most famous numbers—the "Liberty Duet"—"Suoni la tromba" ("Let the trumpets sound"). Its theme brings to mind the chorus "D'immenso giubilo," the opening of Act Three of *Lucia di Lammermoor*.

In an exuberant, martial refrain, Giorgio and Riccardo sing of the glorious privilege of fighting for liberty and dying for one's country. When the trumpet sounds at dawn, they will sally forth to do battle with all perfidious tyrants and destroy their power forever. The two conclude the duet with a thunderous repetition of their battle cry.[2]

ACT THREE

A garden and a grove of trees outside Elvira's apartment in the castle. Lights in the apartment shine through the windows. There is a long orchestral introduction with a dark, brooding theme welling up in the bass.

As it diminuendos into silence, Arturo rushes in crying that at last he is saved ("Son salvo"). He exults that he has outrun his pursuers. In recitative he expresses his happiness over having returned safely from exile to his beloved country ("Oh patria! Oh amore!"), where he can again embrace his adored bride-to-be.

Unseen by Arturo, Elvira, dressed in white, passes by the window of her apartment. A moment later she is heard singing a plaintive ballad ("A una fonte afflito") about a lonely troubadour sitting beside a foun-

---

[2] In another version, Giorgio and Riccardo end the duet by repeating the terms of their bargain: if Arturo is defenseless, he will be pardoned; if he returns in arms, he must die.

tain and pining for his love. In joyful surprise, Arturo exclaims that he hears his own love song, then eagerly calls Elvira's name. When there is no answer he himself takes up the ballad, hoping this will bring Elvira to his side.

But just as he concludes the aria he is startled by the sound of a drum and a babble of voices from beyond the castle walls. In a brief choral phrase ("Agli spaldi, alle torri andiam") Cromwell's soldiers call out that they will search for the fugitive near the ramparts.

In desperation Arturo is about to hide inside the castle, but then realizes that this might well put both Elvira and himself at the mercy of his pursuers. Instead, he decides to sing his troubadour song ("Corre a valle, corre a morte"), in the hope that it will awaken in Elvira the memory of their love and thus bring her to him.[3] This verse describes the suffering and loneliness of the exile.

As he ends the serenade, Elvira appears, walking as though in a dream. Still out of her mind, she piteously calls Arturo's name. He rushes forward and kneels at her feet. At that instant Elvira recovers her senses and recognizes him. Holding her in his arms, Arturo cries that now love has reunited them and there is nothing more to fear.

Then, singing that this reunion has banished all his sorrow ("Nel mirarti un solo instante"), Arturo begins the main section of the great duet which is one of the musical pinnacles of the opera. During its course Elvira asks Arturo—to his complete bewilderment—if the prisoner with whom he escaped is now his wife. He in turn asks if she does not realize that the prisoner was none other than the Stuart Queen—who would have died at the hands of the Puritans had he not helped her escape from the castle.

When the truth finally dawns upon Elvira ("Qual lume rapido"), she abandons herself to the rapture of being reunited with her lover. The two then repeat their avowals in the magnificent finale of the duet ("Star seco ognor"[4]).

But as the two stand clasped in each other's arms, the sound of drums again is heard—a sound which shocks Elvira back into temporary insanity. To Arturo's horror, she begins to murmur incoherently about trampling on the wedding veil. Collapsing at Arturo's feet, Elvira frantically entreats him not to desert her again for the woman with whom he fled ("no, colei più non t'avra"). Outside, the soldiers are heard in a triumphant shout of "England and Cromwell" ("Anglia, Cromvello!").

[3] In another version this aria begins: "Cerca il sonno a notte scura."

[4] This phrase is sung by Arturo at the beginning of the refrain, which contains an F above high C. Elvira's answering refrain begins with "Caro, non ho parola," after which the two voices join.

As Arturo distractedly tries to bring Elvira to her senses, Riccardo, Giorgio and Bruno, followed by soldiers and villagers, burst upon the scene, with the soldiers savagely clamoring for Arturo's death ("Te alla morte condanno!").

Suddenly Elvira tears herself from Arturo's arms and staggers forward as though waking from a nightmare. The violence of the scene has produced still another shock which has restored her reason. Arturo strides to her side and in a simple yet majestic refrain ("Credeasi misera") sings that Elvira suffered because she believed he betrayed her. Now he will defy his enemies and die with her. This marks the beginning of the overpowering ensemble which concludes the opera. In a repetition of the refrain ("Qual mai funerea"), Elvira wonders what dreadful sound awoke her from her madness, and declares that she is ready to die with her lover.

As the ensemble gathers intensity, the Puritans rage that the traitor must die; the people express horror over the lovers' impending doom; Riccardo and Giorgio voice their pity for the hapless pair. Then, after clasping Elvira in a farewell embrace, Arturo suddenly whirls and faces his captors. In a reprise of the theme heard before he furiously denounces them for subjecting Elvira to this inhuman ordeal ("Arrestatevi —scostate!"). As for himself, he rages, let them do their worst. Over the chorus of soldiers shouting for vengeance, Arturo reiterates his denunciation in an obbligato which soars to a high C and beyond to two high Fs.

A blare of trumpets cuts through the uproar. Soldiers rush in and hand a message to Giorgio, who reads it with Riccardo. Together they announce that the Stuarts have been defeated, the captives have been pardoned and freedom once again reigns in England ("l'Anglia terra ha liberta"). Joyfully embracing, Elvira and Arturo join the throng in a final jubilant chorus in praise of love and victory. The curtain falls.

THE RAKE'S PROGRESS
(*Der Wüstling—Carriera d'un Libertino*)
by IGOR STRAVINSKY
(1882–1971)

Libretto by
W. H. AUDEN and CHESTER KALLMAN

Suggested by a series of engravings by the eighteenth-century artist William Hogarth (1697–1764), who satirized the social customs of his day

CHARACTERS

Trulove	Bass
Anne, his daughter	Soprano
Tom Rakewell	Tenor
Nick Shadow	Baritone
Mother Goose	Mezzo-soprano
Baba the Turk	Mezzo-soprano
Sellem, an auctioneer	Tenor
Keeper of the Madhouse	Bass

Whores and Roaring Boys, servants, citizens, madmen

Place: England
Time: Eighteenth century
First performance: Teatro La Fenice, Venice, September 11, 1951
Original language: English

Igor Stravinsky was seventy years old when he completed *The Rake's Progress,* yet the work is anything but traditional in its harmonic structure or dramatic concept. It is true that the listener hears echoes of Mozart, Bellini, Rossini and other classical composers, but one soon becomes aware of subtle musical ironies.

An aria, for example, begins in conventional form, then imperceptibly changes its character as dissonances transform its harmonic structure. An eighteenth-century arioso is unexpectedly brought into the twentieth century through the medium of the atonal pattern of the accompaniment. At the same time there are emotional passages in which Stravinsky's astringent, complex harmonies give way to simple, unabashed melody. These contrasting musical forms give the opera a stimulating freshness and an element of surprise.

The Rake is the composer's fourth opera. In 1914 he wrote *Le Rossignol,* a three-act opera; in 1917 *Renard,* a satirical chamber opera; in 1921 *Mavra,* a Russo-Italian comic opera.

The first American performance of *The Rake* was given at the Metropolitan in English on February 14, 1953. Critical reaction was mixed, and after seven performances it was dropped from the repertoire. In Europe, however, it is a staple operatic item—most of the smaller houses in Europe have produced it since World War II. It was given by the Hamburg State Opera at the Metropolitan Opera House, Lincoln Center, on June 29, 1967, during the German company's visit to America. The production was staged by Gian-Carlo Menotti.

Derived from the engravings of eighteenth-century London life by Hogarth, the plot actually is a version of the Faustian legend. To the motley assemblage of characters depicted by Hogarth, the librettists Auden and Kallman added the Mephistophelean figure of Nick Shadow. He is the devil to whom Tom Rakewell sells his soul—but not with the legendary consequences. The devil fails to collect his fee when Tom, at the last moment, is redeemed by the love of Anne, the girl he rejected and deserted.

There is a brief prelude in waltz tempo, with trumpet passages in the manner of a fanfare.

ACT ONE

[*Scene One*] The garden of Trulove's house in the country on a spring afternoon. The house is at right; a garden gate at the back. Downstage left is an arbor, where Anne and Tom Rakewell are seated.

In a lilting duet ("The woods are green") Anne and Tom sing of the magic of spring in the month of May, when the world is the special province of lovers. Trulove steals in and watches them unobserved. His voice blends with theirs in a trio as he expresses the hope that lovers' avowals will be more than empty promises ("O may a father's prudent fears"). He reflects that all too often we find out too late what really is in the hearts of others—and in our own as well. He listens with paternal anxiety as Anne and Tom, in the conclusion of their duet, pledge eternal fidelity.

Coming forward, Trulove tells Anne she is wanted in the kitchen, then turns to talk to Tom. A brief scene in recitative follows. Trulove informs Tom that, through a friend he has found a bookkeeper's position for him in London. Tom assumes an air of humble gratitude, but then says that he has other plans and cannot accept the offer. When Trulove bridles somewhat at this, Tom hastens to assure him that his daughter certainly will not marry a poor man. She may marry a poor man, Trulove answers pompously, so long as he is honest and not lazy. With that parting shot he goes into the house. Tom looks after him with a sneer.

In an ensuing recitative ("Here I stand"), followed by an aria ("Since it is not by merit"), Tom expresses his cynical philosophy of life. He has no intention of slaving away in a countinghouse to pile up wealth for others. For his part, he agrees with the learned doctors who assert that striving for good works is futile, because one's achievements are foreordained. That being the case, Tom reasons, he will put himself into the hands of his Fate.

He continues this line of thought in the aria. He is resolved to trust to Fortune and live by his wits; the world is large and his whole life is ahead of him. He ends his aria with a flippant variation of the old adage: "Wishes, be horses; this beggar shall ride!" Pacing back and forth, deep in thought, Tom makes a wish for money.

Instantly, Nick Shadow materializes at the garden gate as an insinuating glissando sounds in the orchestra. Tom turns with a gasp of surprise as Nick speaks his name inquiringly. He identifies himself; Nick, with a courtly bow, does the same, adding that he is the bearer of good news. It has to do with a long-lost relative of Tom—an uncle. The news is so good, in fact, that he should call his friends together to share it, Nick goes on. Tom promptly hurries into the house to summon Anne and her father. Nick unlatches the gate and strides into the garden.

When the others return, Nick discloses the reason for his visit in a Bellinian aria of mocking elegance ("Fair lady, gracious gentlemen"). Tom Rakewell, says Nick, had an uncle whom he—Nick—served for many years. He left England to seek his fortune in strange lands. Making money, in fact, was his sole aim in life. But at the last, when he lay dying, he realized that all his gold had bought him neither joy nor solace in his old age. He longed to go back to England, where, he believed, his wealth could bring happiness to a young man he vaguely remembered as his nephew.

Slyly pausing for effect, Nick announces that the benevolent uncle is dead. He himself has come to inform Tom Rakewell that this long-neglected relative remembered his kin on his deathbed—and Tom is now a rich man.

An exuberant quartet follows in a parody of the conventional operatic ensemble. It begins as Tom exults over the astounding success of his first wish ("I wished but once"). He thanks Nick profusely for his services. Shadow ironically thanks him in turn, and the phrase "be thanked" is taken up by Anne and Trulove to lead into the choralelike climax of the quartet. In a melodramatic refrain ("My Anne, behold") Anne and Tom rejoice in their good fortune.

Nick finally interrupts the happy proceedings by apologetically reminding Tom that the inheritance involves certain legal matters which must be attended to. In short, they must be off to London. That can wait, Tom murmurs, his head in the clouds. But Trulove and Anne urge him to settle the estate at once so that the marriage can be arranged. Tom thereupon agrees to go; Nick tells him a carriage is waiting down the road. Shadow leaves for a talk with Trulove while Anne and Tom bid each other farewell in a graceful *duettino* ("Farewell for now").

When Trulove and Nick reappear, Tom asks Shadow what his customary fee is for such valuable services. Then and there, Nick Shadow binds the unsuspecting Tom to a Mephistophelean contract: they will settle the account one year and a day from the present date for whatever sum Tom considers fair and just. Tom, of course, agrees.

In an ensuing refrain ("Dear Father Trulove") Tom assures his prospective father-in-law that he will send for him and Anne as soon as his affairs are settled. And then all London will be at Anne's feet. Trulove is pleased, but Anne seems suddenly apprehensive and turns away. Tom sings confidently that success comes to him who is clever enough to play the game and win. Anne wonders why she feels certain misgivings at this happy moment. Trulove fears that Tom's sudden good fortune only will encourage him in his sinful ways. These thoughts are voiced in a trio which brings the scene to a close. Anne, Tom and Trulove go toward the garden gate. Nick holds it open for them as they pass through, with Anne and her father singing a final "farewell." Alone, Nick Shadow turns to the audience with the phrase: "The progress of a rake begins."

[*Scene Two*] After a prelude dominated by harsh, agitated dissonances, the curtain rises on Mother Goose's brothel in London. Tom, Nick and Mother Goose are sitting at a table downstage drinking. Prominent backstage is a large cuckoo clock. Milling about are the whores and Roaring Boys, London's eighteenth-century hoodlums. In a two-part chorus ("With air commanding") in descriptively crude harmonies, the Roaring Boys boast of how they roam the streets at night unchallenged, stirring up trouble. The whores respond with a chorus acclaiming their own exploits in Cupid's campaigns. The two groups join in a lusty climax to sing a toast to Venus and Mars.

A scene in recitative follows. Nick asks Tom to explain to Mother Goose that he has been thoroughly schooled to enjoy the life of pleasure which now awaits him—this by way of proof that Nick has fulfilled his duties as Tom's "godfather." In a phrase sung on a single note, as though saying his catechism, Tom replies that he was told that his first duty is to himself, and that he must ignore the precepts of every teacher except Nature. Mother Goose and Nick comment approvingly.

Plying him with wine, the two ask him to define Beauty, Pleasure and Love. In lyrical phrases, Tom recites that Beauty is something which Youth owns, but money can buy. It has one flaw: it dies. Pleasure is the stuff of dreams—it can be anything from a hat to a cat. Then over a sinuous figure in the orchestra, he attempts to define Love. Leaping to his feet, he exclaims that the very word fills him with terror. As Mother Goose refills his wineglass, the cuckoo clock sounds the hour of one. Tom cries out that he must go before it is too late. Thereupon Nick makes a commanding gesture toward the clock, which turns backward and coos the hour of twelve in exact synchronization with the notes of a descending figure in the orchestra. Nick casually assures Tom that there is plenty of time for pleasure—he may repent at leisure.

Tom sits down and wildly gulps another drink. The whores and Roaring Boys break into a raucous chorus about the pleasures of the night ("Soon dawn will glitter"). At its conclusion, Nick rises to announce that a young friend of his, Mister Tom Rakewell, wishes to favor them with a song by way of initiation into their company.

As all applaud, Tom comes forward and sings the cavatina "Love, too frequently betrayed." It is a plaintive song in a minor key, in which Tom laments that he has been unfaithful to Anne. He implores the Goddess of Love not to desert him in his darkest hour.

In a brief refrain ("How sad a song") the whores murmur pensively that the young man is most charming in his sorrow. They offer him the solace of their kisses. Mother Goose dispels the sentimental mood by declaring that tonight she claims Tom as her prize. As though on signal, the men and women, facing each other, form a lane. Taking Tom's hand, Mother Goose leads him slowly through the lane toward a door at the back. Nick, standing to one side, watches them with malevolent satisfaction.

The whores and Roaring Boys, mingling again, sing a madrigal-like chorus in nonsensical doggerel keyed to the word "Lanterloo." At its conclusion Nick raises his glass in the direction of the door at the back. With sinister meaning, he wishes his "master" sweet dreams . . . and let him dream on, for to awake is to die. The curtain falls.

[*Scene Three*] The garden of Trulove's house (as in Scene One) on an autumn night. There is a full moon. During a brief, serene orchestral introduction, Anne, in traveling clothes, enters from the house. In recitative, she reveals that she has had no word from Tom. She sings that she will go to London to find him because she knows he needs her help. In the following aria, "Quietly, Night, O find him," Anne offers an invocation to the night. In poetic terms she implores the moon to help her find her lover. The aria ends on a descending phrase which reflects her longing and despair.

Suddenly her father calls her from the house. She turns to go inside, then pauses. For a moment she is torn between loyalty to her father and devotion to Tom. Her father is strong, she decides finally, while Tom is weak and needs her help. Sinking to her knees, she sings a brief but moving prayer for guidance, "O God, protect dear Tom."

In the next moment, Anne makes her decision. Rising swiftly, she expresses her resolve in the brilliant cabaletta which concludes the act, "I go to him." Even though Tom has cast her off, she sings, she must keep the faith, because love cannot falter or change. No matter how wretched he may be, she will not desert him now. This remarkable aria in C major begins with Mozartean simplicity. Its center section, with its distorted harmonies, reflects Anne's grief and uncertainty. Then it returns to the C-major mode, embellished with chromatic figures and roulades. Anne brings the aria to an exultant climax on a high C. The curtain falls.

ACT TWO

[*Scene One*] A room in Tom's house on a London square. The morning sun pours through the window. Street vendors are heard. Tom is having breakfast. At a particularly loud noise, he strides to the window and slams it shut. Staring morosely at the scene outside, he abandons himself to bitter reflection in a long soliloquy in the form of two arias interspersed with recitative. In the first ("Vary the song, O London, change")—sung in the florid style of eighteenth-century opera—he voices his contempt for the spurious harmonies of the city. None of its music, he sings, can fill the void in his heart.

In the ensuing recitative ("Nature, green unnatural Mother"), over a staccato rhythm in the bass, he gives vent to his loathing of the vaunted delights of "civilized" society: the food which chokes him, the wine which is bitter in his mouth . . . the witless card playing . . . the fatuous matrons and their marriageable daughters . . . the strumpets and their more obvious charms. . . . Tom breaks off his reflections with an expression of disgust, then suddenly remembers Anne. Stricken with remorse, he murmurs that he does not dare even think of her.

For a moment he sits plunged in gloom. Then again he bursts into an aria, one of furious scorn ("Up Nature, the hunt is on") for the senselessness and corruption of life in the city. He rails against the frustration of his search for the meaning of his existence. Finally, numbed by despair, he sighs in a spoken phrase: "I wish I were happy."

Instantly, Nick Shadow slips into the room. He glides over to Tom, hands him a circus playbill and asks if he recognizes the person pictured on it. Tom replies that it is Baba the Turk, the bearded lady of the circus. With amused sarcasm, he remarks that fearless heroes of the battlefield have been known to faint dead away at the sight of her. After more banter, Tom suspiciously asks Nick why he has brought up the subject of Baba.

To his utter consternation, Nick suggests that Tom marry her. In quasi-recitative over a rhythmic, skipping figure in the orchestra, Shadow cynically gives his reasons: human beings, he says, are enslaved by either their desires or their obligations. To be completely free, one must ignore both desire and duty. Marrying Baba the Turk, Nick gravely assures Tom, will symbolize his liberation.

Shadow elaborates on this specious reasoning in an ensuing aria, "In Youth the panting slave pursues." The conventional man, he sings, wastes his powers in the futile pursuit of women and success. In the end, he has nothing to show for his efforts except old age and regret. To escape that wretched fate, a man must be strong enough to will his own destiny. Only he who cannot be enslaved by passion or swayed by reason is free and beyond the law.

At the conclusion of the aria Nick looks at Tom with a quizzical expression. Tom looks back at him and begins to laugh—quietly at first, then louder and louder. Nick joins in and the two shake hands. With Shadow's help, Tom begins to dress himself for an evening's frolic. During the preparations, the two sing a duet ("My tale shall be told"), in an exuberant 6/8 rhythm, in which they anticipate the delights they will share in their conquest of Baba the Turk. It will be a story that will be told by young and old around the fire for years to come. Finally Tom, resplendent in the finery of an eighteenth-century dandy, and Nick together hail the future success of "Tom Rakewell, Esquire." Like Mephistopheles and the youthful Faust, the two rush off to begin their adventure as the curtain falls.

[*Scene Two*] A street in front of Tom's house in London on an autumn evening. The entrance is reached by a semicircular flight of stairs. At left a servants' entrance; at right a tree. As a winding figure in thirds sounds in the orchestra, Anne enters. She looks anxiously up at the entrance, then walks slowly up the steps and timidly lifts the knocker. But when a servant appears she scurries down the steps and hides against the wall under the tree until he has passed by.

In the following recitative and arioso ("O heart, be stronger") she sings that she will conquer her terror of this strange city and act with courage inspired by love. In the concluding phrases she declares that love has the power to cheat hell of its prey.

Anne shrinks back startled as a procession of servants appears carrying oddly shaped packages into the servants' entrance. Then a sedan chair is carried in, preceded by servants with torches. A young man steps out and Anne gasps in surprise as she recognizes Tom. When she rushes forward to throw herself into his arms he gently restrains her. A dramatic duet follows. Tormented by guilt, Tom beseeches her to go back to her home and never think of him again. When she replies that she will not leave without him, he implores her to listen to reason ("Listen, listen to me"). London, he sings, is a haunt of evil where it is wise to be afraid. Heedless of his warning, Anne answers that there is nothing to be afraid of because she is protected by his love. Tom bitterly protests that he no longer is worthy of her—the city has corrupted him beyond redemption. The duet ends with his anguished cry: "O Anne!"

The mood of tenderness and sorrow is shattered when Baba the Turk thrusts her head through the curtains of the sedan chair and upbraids Tom for making her wait. Anne is stunned when Tom tells her that this apparition is his wife. A trio follows, beginning with a phrase sung by Anne ("Could it then have been known"), who laments that love which blossomed in spring has died in shame in autumn. Tom voices his hopelessness and despair. Baba speculates venomously on the identity of a possible rival who shows up on her wedding day. The trio comes to an end—with a touch of irony—on the word "forever." For Anne and Tom it is a cry of despair; for Baba it is a petulant objection to being kept waiting.

Anne rushes away. Tom helps Baba alight from the sedan chair. Patting his cheek, she asks him who "that girl" was. Only a milkmaid who wanted money, Tom answers casually. With that he escorts Baba up the steps to the entrance of the house.

From the distance comes the sound of a crowd shouting a welcome to Baba the Turk. By the time she and Tom reach the top of the stairs, the townspeople throng to the scene. Tom goes into the house. Baba, veiled, stands before them in the pose of a star performer. In chorus, they beg her to show herself just once before she retires. With an imperious, theatrical gesture, Baba removes her veil, revealing her flowing black beard. The applause of the crowd mingles with a fanfare as the curtain falls.

[*Scene Three*] Tom's room (same as Scene One). Now it is cluttered with a fantastic jumble of objects—stuffed animals and birds, display cases of stones and fossils, bric-a-brac, glassware and so on. After a brief orchestral introduction, the curtain rises to reveal Baba and Tom at breakfast. Tom, obviously in a bad humor, is scowling. Baba is chattering away, scarcely stopping for breath. She babbles in the form of an amusing aria ("As I was saying") to the accompaniment of a twittering figure in the orchestra. Into Tom's unwilling ears she pours the detailed description of the souvenirs she has collected during her circus travels—musical glasses, Chinese fans, a bottle of water from the River Jordan, snuffboxes, stuffed birds . . . and so on and so on.

Eventually she becomes aware that Tom has not spoken a single word, and asks him what is wrong. When he snaps at her she affectionately puts her arms around his neck, then tries to coax him into good humor by singing, unaccompanied, a silly little song, "Come, sweet, come." Exasperated, Tom pushes her violently away and roars at her to sit down.

Thereupon Baba, bursting into tears of rage, abandons herself to a wild orgy of destruction. She gives voice to her fury in a spectacular aria which begins with the words "Scorned, abused, neglected, baited." Each word is sung a half tone higher, and at each word Baba seizes an object in her collection and smashes it to bits. Beside herself with jealousy, she accuses Tom of still being in love with her young rival. She screams that, sigh as he may, the "milkmaid" will never be his wife. Baba brings the aria to an end on a rising chromatic phrase sung on the word "never."

Suddenly Tom tears off his wig and pushes it down over Baba's face back to front. Her voice is instantly cut off at the climax of the phrase. For the rest of the scene she sits motionless and silent. Ignoring her, Tom paces sullenly back and forth, his hands in his pockets. Then, flinging himself down on the sofa, he mutters that he cannot find relief in tears—only one remedy is left him: sleep.

He falls asleep as a single sustained note sounds in the orchestra, to be followed by a mysterious skipping figure in the bass. A door silently opens and Nick Shadow peeps in. After a cautious look around he wheels in a large object covered by a dust sheet. He pulls off the sheet to reveal a weird contraption—a kind of cabinet with a hopper on top and a door in the front.

Nick takes a loaf of bread from the table and puts it into the cabinet. Next he throws into the hopper a piece of broken vase he has picked up off the floor. Then he turns a wheel. The broken china falls into the cabinet and the loaf of bread slides out of a chute. After repeating the operation to see that everything is working properly, he puts the loaf of bread back into the cabinet and takes out the piece of broken china, which he keeps in his hand. It is obvious that the machine is the clumsiest kind of a fake. Singing softly to himself, Nick replaces the dust cover, wheels the contraption to Tom's bedside, then stands looking down at him.

In his sleep, Tom murmurs that he wishes "it were true." Waking, he sits bolt upright and stares at Nick in surprise. Then in an agitated refrain he tells Shadow about his strange dream: he had invented a wonderful machine which could change stones into bread. Thus, through his genius, he was able to banish hunger from the world.

With the theatrical gesture of a magician, Nick whips the cover off the machine and asks Tom if it resembles that in his dream. It is the same, Tom gasps, then says excitedly that he needs a stone to make it work. Nick hands him the piece of broken vase; Tom drops it into the hopper, turns the wheel, and out comes the loaf of bread. Incredulous, Tom snatches up the loaf and tastes it. Overwhelmed, he sinks to his knees and murmurs in awe: "A miracle!" In a simple, quiet phrase, almost like a prayer, he wonders if this one good deed will make him worthy of Anne.

This leads into a long duet and a following recitative which conclude the act. Gazing in mystical exaltation at his magic machine, Tom sings that it will open to man the gates of paradise from which he once was driven ("Thanks to this excellent device"). Nick, sidling to the front of the stage, winks broadly at the audience and observes that any sensible person can see that his young master is a fool ("A word to all my friends"). Yet, he adds slyly, there are business opportunities here for the smart investor.

Tom takes up the duet to sing that mankind, freed at last from the thrall of hunger, poverty and pain, will shout hallelujahs in praise of this marvelous contrivance. Nick, in turn, comments cynically that idlers and the scheming poor would be eager to invest in this worthless toy—the bigger the lie the easier the victim.

Carried away by the ideal of saving humanity, Tom sings in melodramatic phrases that man now will attain his highest state of being and assume his rightful place as monarch of the universe. Nick's voice blends with Tom's in the closing measures of the duet as he urges the audience to seize the chance to profit by investing in this machine—a clever fraud which is bound to pay big dividends.

As Tom stands transported by his dream, Shadow, in ensuing recitative, brusquely reminds him that the device is not yet a reality. First it must be mass-produced, then advertised and sold. This, of course, will require capital. Brought suddenly back to earth, Tom ruefully admits that he knows nothing about such things and wonders if, after all, this noble vision is only an illusion like everything else. But Nick quickly assures him that these matters have been taken care of—he already has interested a number of reputable financiers who are impatiently waiting to get the project under way. Tom thanks him effusively, and is all for meeting the investors at once. He and Nick begin wheeling the machine out of the room. At the door, Shadow pauses to ask Tom if he will tell the good news to his wife. Tom replies harshly: "I have no wife. I've buried her." The curtain falls.

ACT THREE

[*Scene One*] Tom's house. The same as in Act Two, Scene Three, except that everything is covered with dust and cobwebs. Baba, with Tom's wig covering her face, is still sitting motionless at the table. It is an afternoon in spring.

Before the curtain rises a brief choral phrase is heard ("Ruin! Disaster! Shame!") like an ominous chant over a restlessly rising and falling accompaniment. The Crowd of Reputable Citizens then is revealed examining the objects in the room. In chorus ("What curious phenomena") they exclaim over the weird display and indicate that an auction is about to take place. From offstage again comes the chant of "Ruin! Disaster! Shame!"

The people of the crowd, looking at each other with malicious I-told-you-so expressions, now come forward and in a hushed chorus sing directly to the audience. In this chorus they disclose the extent of the catastrophe. Hundreds have been ruined by Tom Rakewell's ill-fated venture in promoting his magic machine: merchants have gone mad, widows are selling their clothing to buy food, starving children are roaming the streets, even duchesses have been driven to suicide. And Tom Rakewell alone is to blame for the debacle. At the conclusion of the chorus the people turn back to their examination of Baba's collection.

A moment later Anne enters. She looks around, then goes quickly from group to group asking if they have seen Tom Rakewell. All in turn give her vague, confusing answers: he fled to America . . . he died of fever . . . he is a Methodist, a Papist . . . he's converting the Jews . . . he is being hounded by creditors. . . . Anne runs from the room in despair. Looking after her, the crowd mutters that this poor girl probably is another of Tom's victims.

Then Sellem the auctioneer bursts into the room followed by servants who scurry about setting up a dais for him. When it is finally in place Sellem mounts it and launches into his auctioneer's routine ("Ladies, gentlemen, be all welcome"). He bellows that this will be the "ne plus ultra" of auctions. Those fortunate enough to be present are ordained to establish the divine balance in Nature: thousands lose so that other thousands may gain. He bows to vociferous applause.

Sellem then turns his attention to the objects on display and calls for bids. This he does in one of the longest arias in the opera ("Who hears me, knows me"), sung to the staccato accompaniment of single-note figures which have the effect of building up the excitement of the scene. Occasionally he is interrupted by shouted bids from the crowd, whereupon he demands higher and higher offers. In two amusing interludes he calls out the bids, then bangs his gavel in true auctioneer fashion.

Finally, with elaborately mysterious movements, he walks over to Baba. In a brief refrain, sung *mezza voce* in a deliberate waltz tempo, he calls attention to the prize offering of the day. He expertly stirs the curiosity of the crowd by speculating on what might lie behind the mask of this figure—a precious jewel . . . an oracle . . . an octopus . . . perhaps even an angel . . . ? The crowd grows wild with excitement and the bidding becomes more frantic. Scarcely able to make himself heard, Sellem begins shouting the final bids, starting with "fifty." By the time he reaches "one hundred" the uproar is at its height. Bellowing "going, going, gone," he snatches the wig from Baba's face. There is a sudden, stunned silence as the crowd gapes in disbelief.

Like an automaton, Baba instantly begins singing the cadenza exactly at the point where, in the preceding scene, she was cut off on the word "never" when Tom covered her face. Then, as though regaining consciousness, she stands up. Snatching up a veil lying on the table, she dusts herself off. Glaring at Sellem and the crowd, she furiously denounces them for stealing her treasures. When the people cower back she orders them out. Her tirade is interrupted by the voices of Tom and Nick outside, calling out like street hawkers: "Old wives for sale!" All in the room listen in bewilderment.

Here begins a long and involved ensemble which brings the scene to a close. Baba reacts angrily to the sound of the men's voices; the people exclaim in surprise. Anne rushes in and goes to the window looking for Tom. She and Baba then confront each other and Baba beckons to the girl to come closer. When Sellem tries to continue with the auction, Baba cuts him short.

Turning to Anne in a complete change of manner, Baba tells her to find Tom again and set him straight ("You love him"). This marks the beginning of a duet which is one of the most melodious in the opera. The lad is scatterbrained, Baba sings, but not entirely bad. She assures Anne that—good or bad—he still loves her.

In mingled happiness and remorse, Anne sings that it is she who has been untrue, because she doubted Tom's love. Sellem and the chorus comment sympathetically. Continuing the duet, Baba warns Anne about Tom's companion, a snake who has poisoned his victim. With that she gently dismisses the girl. When Anne anxiously asks Baba where she herself will go, Baba replies that a lady of talent has nothing to fear.

In a flowing refrain ("I shall go back") Baba explains that she will go back to the stage—her own world of good manners and wealth. She has been away too long, and now this interlude must end. In the continuation of the duet Baba reiterates these thoughts; Anne wonders if she can win back Tom's love at the expense of Baba's happiness. The voices of Sellem and the crowd provide a choral accompaniment. The people marvel at the strange turn of events while Sellem laments the ruinous interruption of his auction.

At the conclusion of the ensemble the voices of Tom and Nick again are heard outside. They sing a simple, rather charming nonsense song, "If boys had wings." As before, everyone in the room stops and listens intently. Then, as all express their various reactions, the concluding ensemble of the scene begins. Anne exclaims happily as she recognizes Tom's voice; Baba exhorts her to go to him: Sellem and the crowd cry that the archthief has reappeared—his crime is grave, and now the law is closing in.

In chorus, Baba, Sellem and the people warn Anne that she must act quickly if she wishes to save the man she loves. Anne's voice rises above the chorus in a coloratura obbligato as she expresses the hope that her love will give her the courage to save Tom. As the ensemble ends, Anne turns to Baba with a fervent "God bless you!" She rushes away. From the distance come the voices of Tom and Nick in the ending of their ditty.

Baba turns to Sellem and imperiously orders him to call her carriage. Startled out of his pompous manner, Sellem jumps to obey—apparently forgetting that the carriage was to be one of the prize items of his auction. Regally motioning the gaping crowd aside, Baba stalks to the carriage. At the door she turns and sternly informs all that the next time they see her, they will pay. She gets in and rides away to a majestic fanfare. Staring after her, the crowd murmurs that it has been a hectic day. The curtain falls.

[*Scene Two*] A gloomy churchyard at night. At front and center is a newly dug grave; behind it a flat raised tomb, with a sexton's spade leaning against it. At right is a yew tree. Before the curtain rises there is a brief, somber orchestral introduction.

Tom and Nick enter hurriedly. Nick carries a small black bag. To the accompaniment of a sinister theme in thirds, Tom looks apprehensively around. Then, over an eerie, throbbing figure in the bass, he voices his premonition of danger ("How dark and dreadful is this place"). He sings that the strange look on Nick's face strikes fear into his heart. With ominous calm, Shadow reminds him that a year and a day have passed. Now, according to their contract, it is time to settle accounts. This is sung with ironic effect to the tune of the ditty Nick and Tom sang during the auction scene.

Terror-stricken, Tom implores Shadow to be patient. Now he is a beggar, he goes on, but as soon as he is rich again he will pay every cent he owes. In a foreboding *mezza voce*, Shadow tells him he does not want his money. He wants his soul. He commands Tom to make certain that he now recognizes the person he was fool enough to hire for this fee.

There, Nick snarls, is his grave—and here are the means for his last exit. He may take his choice. Thereupon Nick takes from his bag a knife, a rope, a vial of poison and a revolver.

In wild despair, Tom begs the hills to hide him from his impending doom, or the sea to cover him. He cries out against the caprice of fate that made an unknown uncle choose him as his heir. Nick gloatingly sings that nothing now can hide his sins and that there will be rejoicing in hell when he arrives. On the stroke of midnight, Shadow declares, Tom must kill himself. Slowly he begins to count as a distant clock strikes. Tom abjectly begs for mercy. But on the stroke of nine, Nick holds up his hand. There is a deep silence.

His manner suddenly unctuous, Nick remarks that although Tom has presumed upon their friendship, Nick Shadow always is the gentleman. He will forgive Tom his breach of faith and will suggest a pleasanter way to decide his fate. They will play a game of cards. The scene continues in a dramatic recitative.

Nick asks Tom if he has a deck of cards. Taking one from his pocket, Tom remarks with grim humor that this is all that is left him in this world—or the next. Nick comments approvingly that a jest always makes the game go well. The rules, he goes on, are as follows: Nick Shadow will cut three cards. If Tom can name them, he is free. If not . . . Nick points to the contents of the black bag.

To the accompaniment of a nervous, darting figure in the orchestra, the game proceeds. Nick cuts the cards, then holds the exposed card away from Tom and toward the audience. Tom trembles with fear. Suddenly he murmurs Anne's name and instantly regains control of himself. He names the card: queen of hearts. Nick casually tosses the card aside. The clock strikes once. As Tom raises his head in a gesture of thanks, Shadow observes to the audience that this sportive gentleman gambles "the peace of hope against the guineas of despair."

Again Nick cuts the cards and again Tom, seized by terror, wonders what power can help him name the right card. Nick tauntingly remarks that, as Lady Luck has been his good friend before, he might well give her a second chance.

At that moment the sexton's spade leaning against the tomb clatters to the ground. Startled and angry at the noise, Tom, with the expletive "The deuce!" kicks the spade away. For an instant he stares at it, then in a flash of understanding he names the card: two of spades. The clock strikes again. Glaring at Tom in baffled fury, Nick sneeringly remarks that he is to be congratulated on his luck. Then in menacing tones he reminds Tom that his last chance has come. Quaking in terror, Tom hides his face in his arms and leans against the tomb.

Nick swiftly picks up one of the discarded cards, holds it up and in a brief refrain addresses the audience. The simpler the trick, he sings, the easier the deception. He explains that he has taught his guileless pupil to believe that things do not repeat themselves. But the next card will contradict this precept. It will be the queen of hearts again—and for Tom Rakewell it will be the queen of hell. He calls to Tom to name the final card.

In a brief duet passage the two sing that this time Fortune has given neither help nor hint. Nick maliciously asks the "love-lucky" Tom if he is afraid. Tom, who has been looking wildly about, suddenly turns his face away from the ground as though he had seen some unspeakable horror. He gasps that he caught sight of the imprint of cloven hoofs. The goats are back, Nick murmurs casually, now that spring's returned. In an anguished phrase, Tom voices the words "return" and "love."

Suddenly from far off comes Anne's voice calling, "Return!" In a following phrase she sings that love can cheat hell itself of its victim. Tom, without realizing what he is doing, sings the word "love" with her, then checks himself. Nick stands as though turned to stone. As a tremendous fanfare bursts out in the orchestra, Tom exultantly welcomes love—which at this moment has returned to save his life—as his queen of hearts. Thus naming the fateful card, he tears the remainder of the deck out of the still motionless Shadow's grasp. The clock strikes twelve. With a joyous cry, Tom falls senseless to the ground.

To the accompaniment of thunderous, hammering chords, Nick Shadow roars that the failure of his scheme has damned him to the torment of ice and flame ("I burn! I freeze! In shame I hear"). Then he commits his final act of revenge: with a sorcerer's gesture, he makes Tom insane. Howling in terror, Nick sinks slowly out of sight into the grave. As the hammering rhythms die away into silence, the scene is plunged into darkness. Then the action continues.

A tender theme imitative of forest murmurs begins in the orchestra. The dawn gradually brightens the churchyard, where the open grave is now covered with a mound of green grass. Tom, hopelessly mad and smiling vacantly, puts grass on his head and begins singing in a childlike voice. In a simple, poignant melody he sings that he is Adonis, beloved of Venus. As the quiet woodland theme is again taken up by the orchestra the curtain slowly falls.

[*Scene Three*] A large room fronting a row of cells in Bedlam, the famous hospital for the insane in old London. At the back is a raised platform with a straw pallet. Tom is standing before it facing a chorus of madmen, who include a blind man with a broken fiddle, a crippled soldier, a man with a telescope and three witchlike creatures. Throughout the ensuing scene the conventional harmonic patterns are broken by eerie dissonances, reflecting the mental distortions of the insane.

In a brief arioso in mock-heroic style, Tom exhorts his hearers—whom he calls "shades"—to array themselves in festive attire to welcome the goddess Venus, who has promised to visit her Adonis. The inmates respond in a derisive chorus that Venus never will keep her promise to a madman.

Crushed by their taunts, Tom sinks down on the pallet and buries his face in his hands. The others begin to dance before him in a grotesque minuet, meanwhile singing a chorus of despair, "Leave all love and hope behind." As it concludes with a phrase of utter desolation—"In a night that never ends"—a key scrapes in the rusty lock of the door. The inmates scurry to their cells, warning each other of the Keeper's whip. The Keeper enters with Anne. Pointing to Tom, who is still sitting motionless, he assures Anne that this inmate is harmless. He will answer only to the name of "Adonis," the Keeper says, and advises Anne to indulge his fancy. When he leaves, she softly calls "Adonis." Tom leaps to his feet and joyfully hails her as Venus, his Queen.

In a brief but stately arioso, he sings that he waited for her so long that he almost believed the blasphemous madmen who told him she would never appear. With great dignity he invites her to mount her throne, then leads her gently to the pallet. Kneeling before her, he implores her to hear his "confession."

Here begins the duet ("In a foolish dream") which is one of the opera's finest numbers. It is virtually in the style of a Bach aria, with intertwining harmonies of striking poignancy. It is a lyrical declaration of penitence, forgiveness and mutual love in terms of classical mythology. As it ends on a serene phrase ("Nor now no notion of 'Almost' or 'Too late'") Tom suddenly collapses on the pallet. Anne cradles him in her arms. Still addressing her as "immortal queen," he asks her to sing him to sleep.

His head on her breast, Anne sings the beautiful lullaby "Gently, little boat." Between the two verses, and at its conclusion, the inmates listening in their cells sing that the music has released them from the torment of their madness.

After a brief silence, the Keeper and Trulove enter. Saying that the story is ended at last, Anne's father bids her come home. As sustained chords sweep through the orchestra, Anne gently lowers Tom to the pallet. Looking down at him, she murmurs that though she has kept her vow of faith, he no longer needs her now. She sings goodbye and joins her father. In an ensuing *duettino* ("Every wearied body"), set in measured, Handelian rhythm, they sing that the end of life is inevitable; what God has ordained will come to pass. They slowly leave followed by the Keeper.

A moment later Tom wakes up, leaps to his feet and stares wildly around. Frantically he calls for Venus. In recitative phrases in the style of eighteenth-century opera he bids her join him in "the holy rites of love." The sound of his voice brings the other inmates rushing from their cells. As they crowd around him he shouts dementedly for Achilles, Helen, Eurydice, Orpheus, Persephone. In mingled fury and anguish he demands to know where the others have hidden his beloved Venus. In bewilderment they murmur that no one has been here.

Tom suddenly staggers back, gasping that he feels death approaching. Now in the grip of his fantasies, he implores Orpheus to strike his lyre in a hymn of sorrow . . . let nymphs and shepherds weep for the beautiful Adonis whom Venus loved. This too is sung in the classically ornate style of eighteenth-century opera. With this final expression of despair, Tom falls back dying on the pallet. Like a Greek chorus, the inmates break into lamentation for Adonis ("weep for the dear of Venus"). The curtain falls.

EPILOGUE

This is sung in front of the curtain by Baba, Tom, Nick, Anne and Trulove. Baba is without her beard and the men are without their wigs. To a lighthearted, bubbling accompaniment they comment in turn on what has happened onstage.

Anne observes that not every rake is lucky enough to have a faithful sweetheart rescue him; Baba declares that all men, good or bad, are mad; Tom warns that young men who dream they are Vergil or Caesar will wake up to find they are only ordinary rakes. Nick finally remarks that it has been rumored that he does not exist—and sometimes he wishes he didn't. Then all join to point out the moral of the tale ("So let us sing as one"): For idle hands and hearts, the devil finds work to do. Pointing at the audience, they bow and leave the stage.

IL RITORNO D'ULISSE IN PATRIA
(*The Return of Ulysses to His Homeland*)
by CLAUDIO MONTEVERDI
(1567–1643)

Libretto by
GIACOMO BADOARO

Based on the *Odyssey* of Homer

CHARACTERS

Human Fragility		Alto
Time	The Prologue	Bass
Fortune		Soprano
Love		Soprano
Penelope, wife of Ulysses		Mezzo-soprano
Euryclea (Ericlea), Penelope's nurse		Mezzo-soprano
Melantho (Melanto), Penelope's handmaiden		Soprano
Eurymachus (Eurimaco), a courtier, lover of Melantho		Tenor
Neptune (Nettuno), God of the Sea		Bass
Jove (Giove, Jupiter, Zeus), father of gods and men		Tenor
Ulysses		Tenor
Minerva, Goddess of Wisdom		Soprano
Eumaeus (Eumete), an old servant of Ulysses		Tenor
Irus (Iro), court jester, follower of the suitors		Tenor buffo
Telemachus (Telemaco), son of Ulysses and Penelope		Tenor
Antinoüs (Antinoo)		Bass
Amphinomous (Anfinomo)	Penelope's suitors	Tenor
Pisander (Pisandro)		Tenor
Juno (Giunone, Hera), wife of Jove, Queen of the Gods		Soprano

Chorus of Nereids, Sirens, courtiers, Phaeacians, etc.

Place: Ithaca, in Greece
Time: Antiquity
First performance: Venice, February 1641
Original language: Italian

The *Odyssey* relates the return of Ulysses (Odysseus in Greek) to his kingdom of Ithaca after an absence of twenty years. He had left Troy in flaming ruins after his soldiers had burst out of the wooden horse (the stratagem of Ulysses himself) and pillaged the city. Monteverdi's opera—his sixth, composed in 1641—takes up the story just before Ulysses' return to his palace.

Some doubt for a time had been expressed if Monteverdi actually had composed the opera, but subsequent research established him as the composer. Several different versions of the score are extant; the original score has a prologue and five acts. Much of the writing is in quasi-recitative, with embellishments in the baroque style of which Monteverdi was the acknowledged master. Some of it is surprisingly modern; it has been noted that the declamation and song speech are closer to contemporary opera than the idioms of Verdi or Puccini.

The score abounds in dramatic madrigal forms. As to subject matter, Monteverdi concerned himself with the destinies of gods and men—as contrasted to *L'Incoronazione di Poppea* (1642), the first opera to be written on a historical subject, with mortals as the protagonists.

Through the years there have been many revivals of the opera—either in concert form or in stage presentations. As such, it was presented in Brussels, Paris, Florence, Milan, Hamburg and at Glyndebourne. The American premiere was at the Kennedy Center, Washington, D.C., by the American Opera Society of Washington on January 19, 1974. The opera was revived (in Italian) by the New York City Opera company in New York, February 29, 1976.

NOTE: The following story of the opera is based on an English translation of the libretto by Geoffrey Dunn, realized by Raymond Leppard (Faber Music Limited, London, 1972), and a version of the score by Luigi Dallapiccola (Edizioni Suvini Zerboni, Milano, 1942).

PROLOGUE[1]

The Prologue is sung by the allegorical figures of Human Fragility, Time, Fortune and Love—each in turn expressing philosophical reflections. Human Fragility sings of his tenuous existence ("Mortal così son io") as Fortune's plaything. Time observes that his sharp teeth nibble away at mortal aspirations ("Salvo è niente dal mio dente"). Fortune, noting that he is both blind and deaf ("Mia vita son voglie"), sings that he grants mortals favors without prejudice—either for joy or sorrow. Love proclaims himself as Amor, God of Gods ("Dio de'Dei feritor"). Although he too is blind—and naked besides—he is armed with his bow and arrows, against which mortals are defenseless.

[1] Omitted in some versions.

Summing things up, Human Fragility cynically remarks that belief in these gods—blind and crippled as they are—is utter nonsense. In a delightful madrigal ("Per me fragile") the four sardonically warn mortals not to expect either help or mercy from this weary, miserable coterie of gods.

ACT ONE

[*Scene One*] The scene opens in the royal palace at Ithaca, where the lonely and grief-stricken Penelope laments the absence of Ulysses ("Di misera Regina"). At her side, her nurse Euryclea commiserates with her. She recalls how her husband punished the adulterous Helen with the burning of Troy, yet it is she—Penelope—who has suffered the most; these twenty years of separation have cost her untold agony. She gives way to her grief in anguished phrases—"Torna, Ulisse! Penelope t'aspetta!"). The long aria ends with a phrase of quiet but desperate pleading—"Torna, deh torna, Ulisse!"

[*Scene Two*] In the next scene Penelope's handmaiden, Melantho, and Eurymachus, her lover, join in an amorous duet—beginning as Melantho sings that love's desires burn like fire, but still cause the sweetest pain ("Duri, e penosi son gli amorosi"). Eurymachus responds ardently: "Bella mia graziosa Melanto!"

[*Scene Three*] The scene change is introduced by a brief dialogue between Nereids and Sirens ("Fermino i Sibili"). They caution each other to be silent when the sea god Neptune is silent. The temperamental god has calmed the sea over which Ulysses now is being borne in a Phaeacian ship to the shore of Ithaca. To the accompaniment of a brief orchestral interlude, Neptune himself appears.

He philosophizes on how the gods are to punish man for his sins— which he brings on himself ("Superbo è l'uom, et è del suo peccato"). But if Jove, father of gods and men, persists in pardoning men for their misdeeds, let him at least allow Neptune to govern his own realm without condoning the sins of men to his own dishonor ("col proprio disonor, l'uman peccato").

Overhearing, Jove reproaches Neptune for denying mortals the gift of compassion, the supreme gift of Jove himself ("Gran Dio . . . contro l'alta Bontà del Dio sovrano").

But Neptune now is in a towering rage because the Phaeacians, who had befriended Ulysses when he was stranded on their island, brought him to Ithaca and carried him, fast asleep, to the shore ("Hanno i Feaci ardite"). Then they sailed back to Phaeacia. Furious because they flouted his authority as a sea god, Neptune sings, over a foreboding unison phrase deep in the bass, that he will change their ship into a rock at the entrance to the Phaeacian harbor ("la nave loro andante farò immobile scoglio"). Jove diplomatically comments that the Phaeacians deserve Neptune's punishment.

Unaware of their impending fate, the crew sings in a brief but exuberant chorus ("In questo basso mondo") that here on earth man may do as he pleases.

Watching the ship, Neptune sings in a quiet, unaccompanied phrase that now the sea will be the richer for a new rock ("Ricche d'un nuovo scoglio"). Then, over a thunderous chord in the orchestra, he gestures with his trident. Instantly the ship turns to stone. Thus, he intones, the Phaeacians will learn not to defy the gods ("quand'ha contrario il ciel non ha ritorno").

Lying on the shore where the Phaeacians had left him, Ulysses awakens and wonders where he is ("Dormo ancora . . . che contrade rimiro?"). In a long and impressive aria he gives way to the turmoil of his thoughts: have the gods deserted him . . . has he been sleeping the sleep of death . . . ? Then he rages against the Phaeacians, who promised to bring him back to Ithaca but who treacherously abandoned him on this barren shore ("Feace mancatori . . . mi lasciaste in questa riva aparta").

Suddenly, to the accompaniment of a sprightly refrain, Minerva appears, disguised as a shepherd. A long duet ensues. When the goddess addresses him affectionately ("Caro a lieta"), Ulysses implores this shepherd lad to help a wretched outcast. What is the name of this place, he asks. Ithaca, Minerva replies, over serene chords in the orchestra. In his confused state, Ulysses does not recognize the name. In answer to Minerva's questions about his identity, he tells her everything she already knows. She advises him now to follow her instructions.

No one, Minerva tells him, knows he is in Ithaca. In the disguise of a beggar, he is to go to his palace, there to confront the shameless horde of suitors who have desecrated his home and made life miserable for Penelope.[2] Ulysses profusely thanks the goddess for her guidance and protection.

In an extraordinary aside, Minerva interrupts this dialogue to assume the role of the chorus—a stock device in Greek drama to explain the action. Over harsh, open fifths in the orchestra she recalls the flaming doom of Troy ("Io vidi per vendetta"), and how Ulysses took it upon himself to avenge the duplicity of Helen, wife of Menelaus, in eloping with Paris to Troy—which set off the Trojan War. The goddess warns

---

[2] As described in *Bulfinch's Mythology:* "More than a hundred nobles of Ithaca and of neighboring islands had been for years suing for the hand of Penelope, his wife, imagining him dead, and lording it over his palace and people, as if they were owners of both."

"the mad race of mortals" not to meddle thus with the decrees of the gods ("Quinci imparate voi, stolti mortali").

Ulysses is now unrecognizable in tattered animal skins. Minerva tells him to go to the fountain of Arethusa, where he will be met by Eumaeus, his faithful old servant. Meanwhile, she will bring Telemachus back from Sparta to be with his father on his return to his palace. Ulysses continues to rejoice in his good fortune.

[*Scene Four*] In a brief scene in the palace, Melantho tries to comfort the dejected Penelope. Her beloved Ulysses, she reminds the Queen, has been dead these many years. She herself is still young, beautiful and desirable—she needs only love to bring these gifts to fruition again and banish her sorrow ("dal piacer il tuo dolore saettato cadera"). But Penelope despondently answers that she will never love again.

ACT TWO

[*Scene One*] A woodland near the hut of Eumaeus. In recitative ("Come mal si salva un Regno"), followed by a tranquil aria ("Colli campagne e boschi"), Eumaeus reflects on the joys of simple country life as contrasted to the hectic glitter of the court. His reverie is interrupted by the boorish Irus, the court jester, who impudently remarks ("Pastor d'armenti può") that meadows are fit only for grazing beasts, not men. Eumaeus berates him as a gluttonous intruder, and tells him to be off and fill his belly, as usual ("Corri, corri a mangiar a crepare"). Irus waddles away.

Ulysses, approaching quietly, overhears Eumaeus lament the long absence of his master. He will soon return, Ulysses confides to the old servant, to claim his wife and his kingdom ("Sel del nomato Ulisse"). Overjoyed at this assurance, Eumaeus offers the supposed beggar food and the shelter of his hut. The two leave together.

[*Scene Two*] There is a brief scene aboard the ship bringing Minerva and Telemachus back to Ithaca. In a duet ("Gli dei possenti") they thank the gods for favorable winds. From the harbor at Ithaca, they make their way to the hut of Eumaeus, where Minerva cautions Telemachus to follow her instructions, for he is now in his father's country, where enemies lie in wait ("Eccoti giunto alle paterne ville").

Eumaeus fervently welcomes Telemachus ("Oh gran figlio d'Ulisse"), exclaiming that he knows that the might and splendor of the kingdom now will be restored. Telemachus thanks him for his faithfulness, but observes that the one for whom they long is still missing. Thereupon

Eumaeus tells him that this poor beggar (indicating Ulysses) has revealed that the hero will return this very day.

At that, Telemachus excitedly urges Eumaeus to hurry at once to the palace ("Vanne tu pur veloce") and inform Penelope that her son has returned home. Thinking of the plight of his mother, he chides Minerva for bringing him back to a household despoiled by a horde of rapacious suitors ("Che veggio ohimè, che miro"). His irritation is underscored by explosive chords in the orchestra. Assailed by doubt, he wonders if his father is indeed alive. Can the dead be changed into the living . . . ?

In that instant, Minerva restores Ulysses to his true self, and he thus reveals himself to Telemachus. Father and son rejoice in their reunion in an exultant duet ("Oh padre sospirato"). Then Ulysses bids Telemachus to go at once to Penelope and tell her she will soon see her husband; he in the meantime will resume his disguise.

[*Scene Three*] The scene changes to the palace, where Penelope is being importuned by three of her most persistent suitors—Antinoüs, Amphinomous and Pisander. They pay court to her in fatuous, extravagant allegorical terms in an ensemble. This develops from a trio ("Ama dunque, sì, sì") into a quartet (when Penelope gently but firmly fends off her would-be lovers—"non voglio amar"), then expands into a full-blown chorus in madrigal form ("All'allegrezze dunque").

This amorous onslaught is interrupted when Eumaeus rushes in to tell Penelope that Telemachus has returned with the news that Ulysses may be alive ("Apportator d'alte novelle"). The panic-stricken suitors realize that now they will be called to account for their debaucheries. Antinoüs sententiously reminds them that they all are guilty of desecrating the palace and that vengeance is upon them ("Compagni, udiste?"). This warning builds into a trio, during which the suitors disclose their plot to kill Telemachus.

Eurymachus runs in to tell them that the eagle of Jove has been seen hovering over the palace—a portent of certain disaster. Despite this forewarning, he and the suitors resolve that, before Telemachus appears, they will once more tempt Penelope—this time with gold—to yield her love.

[*Scene Four*] Eumaeus' hut. Minerva promises Ulysses that he shall have his revenge on the suitors, who will all be slain by the arrows from his mighty bow. Ulysses promises to follow her plan of vengeance. Eumaeus relates how the suitors turned pale with terror when they learned that Ulysses was approaching—he will soon see these cowering brutes for himself. Ulysses relishes the prospect of striking down the interlopers.

[*Scene Five*] Ulysses' palace. Telemachus describes to Penelope his adventures in searching for his father ("Del mio lungo viaggio"), then tells of meeting Helen of Troy (who obviously enchanted him). Penelope reproaches him for allowing himself to be deceived by the baleful charms of this creature. But Telemachus protests that this was no idle infatuation: it bore fruit when, in Sparta, Helen appeared to him in the form of a bird and prophesied that Ulysses would soon return home. Penelope ruefully sings that this at least plants the seed of renewed hope in her heart.

ACT THREE

[*Scene One*] The banquet hall in Ulysses' palace, where the suitors are gathered for their usual revelries. Antinoüs brutally insults Eumaeus for daring to bring a wretched beggar into the banquet hall of the nobility ("Sempre villano Eumete"). When Eumaeus mildly protests, Antinoüs orders him and the beggar out of the banquet hall. The loutish Irus echoes his insult.

Thereupon Ulysses, with mocking courtesy, begs the Queen's permission to give this fat clown his comeuppance—then tosses him over his shoulder in a brief wrestling match, to the huge delight of the suitors. As reward for his prowess, Penelope graciously extends to the beggar the hospitality of the palace ("Valoroso, mendico in corto resta").

Renewing their spurious advances, the three suitors in turn offer Penelope a royal crown, jewels, rich garments and a kingdom for her love. With cynicism lost on the palpitating lovers, Penelope thanks them—as "men of honor"—for their generosity. Watching the spectacle in disgust, Telemachus, aside, implores his father to return and drive out the usurpers.

Finally Penelope announces that she will choose her future husband in a trial of skill. Bidding Melantho to bring Ulysses' bow and arrows, she declares that whoever can bend the bow the farthest will win her heart and the kingdom. In a brief ensemble ("Lieta, soave gloria") the suitors hail the chance to win the long-sought prize. But one after another the three fail to bend the massive bow. Ulysses then steps forward and humbly asks if a beggar may enter the contest. Penelope gives him permission as the suitors laugh derisively.

Imploring the gods to aid him in this test, Ulysses attaches an arrow and easily bends the bow. Then over pounding bass rhythms in the orchestra he cries that Jove himself has ordained this vengeance ("Giove nel suo tuonar"). With that, he aims at the suitors and slays them one by one. The people of the court express their consternation in an awed whisper ("Meraviglie, prodigi") that suddenly crescendoes into a thunderous tonal outburst of terror. Gazing at his fallen victims, Ulysses intones that now he has done Minerva's bidding ("Minerva, alle morti"), as the music swells into a triumphant fanfare.[3]

Now follows an interlude of "comedy relief" in the form of a spectacular buffo aria sung by Irus. It begins with a vocalization on a note sustained for nine measures in 4/4 over a staccato accompaniment. It is in effect Irus's attenuated cry of horror at witnessing the slaughter of the suitors whom he had amused as a court jester, and who always kept him well fed. Now, he moans, there is no one to fill his empty belly ("non troversi chi goda empir del vasto ventre"). Rather than go hungry, he tearfully decides he will commit suicide and let the hungry tomb feast on his body ("vada il mio corpo a disfamar la tomba").

[*Scene Two*] Penelope is in her apartment with Melantho, Eumaeus and Telemachus. The two women lament that the carnage has brought new grief to the palace. Eumaeus tries to convince Penelope that the heroic beggar is really Ulysses in disguise, but she refuses to believe him. Telemachus substantiates Eumaeus, saying that Ulysses was thus disguised by Minerva herself. Penelope, unconvinced, bitterly retorts that this is merely a caprice of the gods in mockery of trusting mortals.

[*Scene Three*] Olympus. There is a colloquy among Juno, Jove and Neptune. Minerva tries to placate Juno, who is still outraged at the trickery of the Trojans. Now that the ruin of Troy is complete, Minerva says, it is time for the gods to think of peace—specifically Neptune, who has been furious with the Phaeacians for defiantly bringing Ulysses safely to Ithaca. Jove joins Juno (whose rage has subsided) in asking Neptune to forgive those who defied him. The sea god relents and declares that Ulysses will be forgiven his misadventures ("Viva Ulisse sicur!"). A brief chorus hails the magnanimity of the gods.

[*Scene Four*] In the palace, Telemachus and Eumaeus are nonplussed at Penelope's steadfast refusal to believe that the victorious

---

[3] The scene is described in *Bulfinch's Mythology* as follows, in part:

"The test selected was shooting with the bow. Twelve rings were arranged in line, and he whose arrow was sent through the whole twelve was to have the Queen for his prize. . . . The first thing to be done was to bend the bow in order to attach the string. Telemachus endeavored to do it but found all his efforts fruitless and . . . he yielded the bow to another. *He* tried with no better success. Another tried, and another. . . . Then spoke Ulysses, humbly suggesting that he be permitted to try. . . . He sped the arrow unerring through the rings. Without giving them time to express their astonishment, he said: 'Now for another mark!' and aimed direct at the most insolent of the suitors. The arrow pierced his throat and he fell dead. . . . All were slain, and Ulysses was left master of his palace and possessor of his kingdom and his wife."

archer who rid the palace of suitors really is Ulysses. When he himself approaches and fervently addresses her as the supreme goal of all his adventures ("O delle mie fatiche"), she rebuffs him as an impostor. He is not the first, she tells him, who has resorted to fraud to claim the kingdom of Ulysses.

At this point, Euryclea enters to offer the clinching evidence of Ulysses' identity: a scar on his knee inflicted by a wild boar ("ove scopersi del feroce cinghiale"). The nurse confesses that she saw it when Ulysses was preparing for his bath, but was commanded by him never to mention it.

Shaken, but still unbelieving, Penelope sings ("Creder ciò ch'è desio") that she has doubted everyone because she holds her bed chaste for the only man who has seen it: her husband Ulysses. Thereupon Ulysses dispels all her doubts by describing the silk coverlet on her bed, embroidered with a design—worked by her own hands—of the chaste Diana and her nymphs.

Joyously, Penelope cries that now she believes ("Or sì ti riconosco") and opens her arms for Ulysses' embrace. Their voices join in the jubilant love duet ("Scioglio di lingua") which brings the opera to its close.

ROBERTO DEVEREUX

(Elizabeth and Essex)

by GAETANO DONIZETTI

(1797–1848)

Libretto by

SALVATORE CAMMARANO

Based on François Ancelot's tragedy *Élisabeth d'Angleterre*

CHARACTERS

Elizabeth, Queen of England	Soprano
The Duke of Nottingham	Baritone
Sara, Duchess of Nottingham	Mezzo-soprano
Roberto Devereux, Earl of Essex	Tenor
Lord Cecil	Tenor
Sir Walter Raleigh	Bass
A page	Bass
A servant of Nottingham	Bass

Ladies of the Royal Court, courtiers, pages, royal guards, attendants of Nottingham

Place: England
Time: Circa 1600
First performance: Teatro San Carlo, Naples, October 29, 1837
Original language: Italian

The fifty-seventh of Donizetti's seventy operas, *Roberto Devereux* is one of the landmarks of the bel canto era—although not as successful as his other operas in this historical framework: *Anna Bolena* and *Maria Stuarda* (sequel to *Bolena*). The three works constitute a trilogy with a background of English history extending from about 1536 to 1600.

Roberto Devereux takes up the historical sequence at the point where the Earl of Essex becomes the favorite of the Queen—only to fall victim to her obsessive jealousy. Actually, in the framework of history, Donizetti's librettist played fast and loose with facts. Sara, for example, is a creation of the librettist—as is the title of "Duke" given Nottingham. In reality he was Charles Howard (1536–1624), First Earl of Nottingham and a descendant of the Third Duke of Norfolk, Thomas II (1473–1554). Nottingham's real wife was Catherine Carry, whom he married three years before Essex was born. Yet Cammarano served Donizetti's purpose well, and history's loss is opera's gain.

Despite its successful premiere in Naples, *Devereux* eventually vanished from the repertoire. It was not until 1964 that a surprising resurgence of interest in bel canto opera brought about a successful revival of the opera in Naples. This resurgence gathered momentum as more of Donizetti's works found favor with the public.

And on the crest of the bel canto revival were the brilliant performances of such specialists as Maria Callas, Joan Sutherland, Teresa Berganza, Montserrat Caballè, Marilyn Horne and Beverly Sills. During the New York City Opera's 1971 season, Miss Sills (as Queen Elizabeth) shared honors in an outstanding revival of *Roberto Devereux* with a distinguished cast that included Beverly Wolff (Sara), Herman Malamood (Devereux), Louis Quilico (Nottingham), Bernard Fitch (Cecil), David Rae Smith (Raleigh), William Ledbetter (Page) and Don Yule (Nottingham's servant). This was one of the opera's major revivals since its first performance in America at the Astor Place Theatre, New York City, January 15, 1849.

The overture, with its startling effect of several explosive chords in the opening measures, states two important themes: a variation on "God Save the Queen" and the melody of Roberto's cabaletta ("Bagnato il sen di lagrime") in the Tower.

ACT ONE

[*Scene One*] The Great Hall in Westminster Palace. The ladies of the Court are busy at their tasks. Sara, Duchess of Nottingham, sits at one side reading a book and weeping silently.

Watching her, the ladies comment on her grief-stricken demeanor, then ask the reason for her tears ("pallor funero"). She explains that she is moved by the sad tale of the Fair Rosamond ("Lessi dolente istoria").[1] When they try to comfort her she forces a smile and assures them that she nonetheless is happy. Aside, she laments that her fate is even worse than Rosamond's—she at least had the release of death ("All'aflitto è dolce il pianto").

Elizabeth enters and greets Sara with a friendly kiss. She confides that she has yielded to Nottingham's request that she grant an audience to Roberto when he is brought back from Ireland accused of conspiring

---

[1] The story of Rosamond (Rosamund) Clifford, mistress of Henry II of England and victim of the jealousy of his wife, Eleanor of Aquitaine.

against the Crown ("Alle fervide preci del tuo consorte"). She hopes there will be no evidence of another kind of betrayal. Sara interjects that Roberto has always been faithful to his Queen. To the Queen, yes, Elizabeth retorts. But to *Elizabeth* . . . ?

Sara listens in fear-stricken silence as the Queen reveals the reason for her tormenting jealousy ("Un orrendo sospetto"): suspecting Roberto's wavering affections, she sent him to Ireland to get him beyond the reach of an unknown rival—only to learn that he was enmeshed in treason. Now, Elizabeth sings, she believes he has committed an even more heinous crime—betraying her with a rival. Sara cowers in guilt and fear as the Queen declares that robbing her of Roberto would be worse than robbing her of her crown ("Il core togliermi di Roberto!").

At this point, Cecil, Raleigh and the other lords enter, and now follows the first of the opera's great ensembles. Cecil, as official spokesman, announces that Essex is charged with treason ("Nunzio son del Parlamento"), and demands that the Queen pronounce his death sentence. Elizabeth, in turn, asks further proof of his guilt.

Suddenly the Court is thrown into an uproar as a Page announces that Roberto himself asks for an audience with the Queen. Cecil and Raleigh fume in rage. Elizabeth, in a lyrical refrain ("Ah! Ritorna qual ti spero"), hopes that Roberto will return as her faithful lover. Cecil, Raleigh and the other lords spitefully comment that Essex's star of good fortune has "not yet set." The Queen sings that if he comes back as her lover, he will be absolved of any crime.

Roberto enters and prostrates himself before the Queen. Dismissing the Court, Elizabeth whirls on Essex with an accusation of guilt ("In sembianza di reo tornasti"), which marks the beginning of a fiery duet. When she charges him with plotting against the Crown, he retorts that his only reward for fighting in the Queen's behalf is execution for treason. Elizabeth rages that more than once has she protected him, as her favorite, from those who were plotting his ruin. Pointing to the ring on Roberto's finger, she reminds him that she gave him this talisman as a pledge of her protection.

Her mood softens as, in a melodious refrain ("Ah! Col pensiero io torno"), she recalls the happiness she and Roberto shared as lovers. But Essex then makes the fatal mistake of answering that, although a place near the throne holds no allure for him, he can offer proof of his loyalty to his Queen. But not proof of your love, Elizabeth rejoins with deadly emphasis.

Controlling her rage, she craftily begins her inquisition, and a complex interchange of emotions ensues. With studied calm, she asks if perhaps there is someone whose heart "beats wildly" when he is in danger. Roberto is aghast, suspecting that the Queen knows of his liaison with Sara. Having trapped him, Elizabeth relentlessly urges him to confess his love for another ("l'alma tua mi svela omai"). "I will lead you both to the altar," she adds sardonically.

When Essex denies he is in love with another woman, Elizabeth flies into a towering rage—and then and there condemns him to death ("Un lampo, un lampo orribile"). Realizing he is doomed, Essex sings despairingly that the secret of his love will die with him. The Queen's accusations and Roberto's denials merge in the climax of the duet.

Elizabeth leaves. Roberto, numbed by the violence of the Queen's wrath, sinks into a chair. He is startled out of his thoughts when Nottingham bursts in and effusively embraces him. Roberto recoils from the embrace ("Che? . . . fra le tue braccia!"). This marks the beginning of a duet in which the incriminating blue scarf is mentioned for the first time ("una cerulea fascia").[2] Nottingham says he found Sara in her room embroidering a blue scarf with a golden thread, meanwhile sobbing inconsolably ("Ieri, taceva il giorno"). He was distressed and puzzled by her tears, he goes on, and for a moment felt a stab of jealousy. But he thrust that unworthy thought from his mind because "sin can never enter the hearts of angels" ("Ah! Chè mai nel cor degli'angeli").

Cecil and the lords enter to inform Nottingham that the Queen has called a meeting of peers to announce a death sentence. Cecil glares at Roberto in vicious satisfaction. Essex quietly turns to Nottingham and asks him to leave him to his fate. In a moving refrain, the Duke assures Roberto that he will do his utmost to save him for the sake of their friendship. The ensemble continues as the lords express their approval of the verdict, while Nottingham reiterates his assurances to Roberto.

[*Scene Two*] Sara's apartment in Nottingham's house. It is the setting for the climactic confrontation of the lovers. Alone, Sara tries to rationalize her guilt ("Nel mio cor soltanto") but is haunted by the thought of Roberto's danger. Then he himself strides in wrapped in a long cloak. Obviously disturbed, he inexplicably begins to upbraid her—first for allowing him to fall in love with her, then for deceiving him ("Una volta, o crudel").

Sara explains that during his absence her father died, and the Queen virtually forced her into marrying Nottingham. She implores Essex, for his own sake, to accept the love of the Queen. When Roberto repudiates Elizabeth's amorous attentions, Sara points to the ring on his finger. There, she sings, is the pledge of the Queen's love. Contemptuously tossing the ring on the table, Essex cries that he far rather would die for the woman he really loves.

---

[2] A handkerchief (*fazzoletto*) "with the little strawberry designs" plays a similar part in the plot of Verdi's *Otello*.

Realizing the hopelessness of the situation, Sara begs Roberto to flee the country—for the sake of his life and for the sake of her honor. Roberto at first refuses to accept this solution—even though it is proof of Sara's devotion. Finally, however, giving way to her desperate pleading, he agrees to escape. Thereupon she gives him the blue scarf as the token of her love ("Vanne! Di me ramentati"). The lovers sing their farewell in an impassioned climax ("Ah! quest'addio fatale").

ACT TWO

The Great Hall at Westminster as in the opening of Act One. Lords and ladies are discussing Roberto's fate, now being deliberated in Parliament. As yet there has been no official word of the verdict, but the Court is certain that, unless the Queen intercedes, Roberto is doomed ("Senza l'aita della regina"). This scene builds into another massive Donizettian ensemble.

As foreboding chords sound in the orchestra, Elizabeth and Cecil now appear. Cecil informs the Queen that despite Nottingham's defense of Roberto the death sentence has been imposed. Sir Walter Raleigh, who has just entered, reports that Essex was apprehended and searched for incriminating evidence. Despite his struggles, this was taken from him: Raleigh hands Elizabeth the blue scarf. A somber theme, like a leitmotif, sounds in the trombones.

Quivering with rage, the Queen examines the scarf, then orders Nottingham to be brought in. Handing her the death parchment, he eloquently pleads for mercy for Roberto ("Non venni mai si mesto"). A dramatic duet ensues. In a paroxysm of fury, Elizabeth cries that Roberto has betrayed her with a rival. Nottingham protests that he has been tricked and slandered by his enemies. Elizabeth retorts that there is indisputable proof of Roberto's duplicity, and for his betrayal he must die ("Muoia, e non sorga un gemito"). In the stormy climax of the duet, she shouts down Nottingham's desperate pleas for mercy.

Roberto is brought in under guard as the "Scarf" theme again sounds in the orchestra. Glowering at him, Elizabeth thrusts out the blue scarf, then denounces him as a villain and a liar ("Un perfido"). The scene continues in trio form as both Roberto and Nottingham express their dismay over the disclosures of infidelity. The Queen rages that it would have been better if Roberto had been buried alive than to have risked the anger of the daughter of Henry VIII ("del tremendo ottavo Enrico").

Roberto realizes that Nottingham—now transformed into the outraged husband—is his mortal enemy, and expresses his fears for the unfortunate Sara ("Mi sovrasta il fato estremo!"). In blind rage, the Duke turns on Essex, sword in hand, vowing to kill him on the spot ("La spada un istante").

At that point, Elizabeth, in a tone of majestic authority, commands Roberto to name her rival ("Qual si noma l'ardita rivale")—and save his life. There is a moment of deathlike silence. Then he answers quietly: "Rather death" ("Pria la morte"). Staring at him incredulously, Elizabeth murmurs: "Yes, you shall have it" ("Sì, l'avrai").

At a sign from the Queen, the entire Court enters, and here begins the magnificent ensemble which brings the second act to its climax. In a ringing phrase ("Tutte udite") she commands the attention of the Court, signs the death sentence and hands it to Cecil. At a certain hour, she announces, a cannon shot will signal the moment of execution. With that she turns on Essex with furious denunciation, then dismisses him. Roberto cries that her cruelty will rob him of his life, but not of his honor. Nottingham, Raleigh and Cecil join in cursing him as Elizabeth storms that he will die in dishonor.

ACT THREE

[*Scene One*] Sara's apartments as in the final scene of Act One.

Ushered in by a servant, one of Roberto's soldiers hands the Duchess a letter. It is from Roberto, informing her of the death sentence. Horrified, Sara snatches up the Queen's ring and vows to return it to Elizabeth in a final plea for mercy. She is about to rush away when Nottingham appears in the doorway.

Glaring at his wife, he demands the letter. Murmuring that now she is lost, Sara obeys. A stormy duet follows as the Duke reads Roberto's final message ("Tu dunque puoi dal suo capo"). In his unreasoning anger, he believes that not only has Roberto given Sara the ring as his own pledge of love, but that she herself has compounded her infidelity by giving him the gold-embroidered scarf. In mingled shame and fury, Nottingham laments that he has been betrayed by his friend and by his wife. Sara desperately protests her innocence; the Duke shouts his accusations.

Suddenly from the distance comes the sound of a funeral march. Sara runs to the window and gasps in terror as she sees Essex being led to the Tower. Nottingham savagely exults. When Sara tries to rush out with the ring, the Duke seizes her, shouts for his guards and orders them to hold her prisoner in his house. Ranting about his double betrayal, Nottingham is deaf to Sara's anguished promise to return after she has delivered the ring, then surrender herself to his vengeance. After the furious climax of the duet, the Duke strides out. Sara collapses in a faint.

[*Scene Two*] The Tower of London. Roberto is alone in his cell. A melancholy horn solo introduces the recitative in which he confronts the terror of impending doom. He still believes the Queen's ring will save him—although he does not fear death itself. He wants only to live to redeem Sara's honor. Then he will be willing to die at Nottingham's hands. In the intensely moving aria (with its cabaletta) "Come un spirito angelico" (the theme of which is stated in the overture) he swears that Sara is chaste—and he will seal that oath with his blood.

Roberto suddenly hears the lock turning in the cell door. Now . . . the pardon, he cries. As ominous chords thunder in the orchestra, Raleigh and guards enter—bringing, not pardon, but death. Essex staggers back, incredulous. In a despairing outburst ("A morte! in terra, o sventurata!") he sings that, despite the Queen's perfidy, he will ask God's mercy on her. The angels themselves will share his grief—and "there will be weeping and sorrow for the first time in heaven" ("sì piangerà d'affanno per la prima volte in ciel"). He reiterates these sentiments in the following cabaletta ("Bagnato il sen di lagrime"), after which the guards lead him away.

[*Scene Three*] The Great Hall of Westminster, as in the opening of Act One.

Elizabeth sits alone on a sofa; on the table before her is her crown. The ladies of the Court silently watch her. Tortured by doubt, Elizabeth wonders why Sara has deserted her in this terrible hour . . . Raleigh had hurried to Sara's palace to bring her back to the Queen—possibly with news of Roberto and the ring. Now, Elizabeth sings despairingly, she is in need of solace. She is no longer a Queen—only a mortal woman bereft of her lover ("Io sono donna alfine").

In the aria "Vana la speme non fia," she gives way to her tormenting suspicions. Will her hope be in vain? Will her lover, though on the brink of death, send the royal ring to her? Will she at last see him penitent in her presence? But . . . time is flying. Will her lover still choose death to prove his love for her rival—whoever she may be? No . . . no . . . let time be stopped before the ax falls . . . let this ungrateful wretch abandon his Queen to this interloper. . . .

At the point of losing control, Elizabeth becomes aware that the ladies are watching her apprehensively. Once more the Queen, she sings proudly: "Let no mortal say: 'I have seen the Queen of England weep.'" ("Ah! non sia chi dica in terra: la regina d'Inghilterra").

Cecil and the lords enter to tell Elizabeth that Essex is now on the way to the block. Frantically she asks if he gave any sign, or some token for his Queen. None, Cecil answers. Suddenly Sara, breathless and disheveled, bursts in and throws herself at Elizabeth's feet, then holds forth the ring. When the Queen asks how she got it, Sara, on the verge of madness, does not attempt to explain, but only gasps: "I am your rival! Punish me, but spare the Earl!" ("Tua rivale! Me punischi, ma del conte salva i giorni!").

Instantly the Queen commands the courtiers to speed to the Tower with the ring. In a frenzy she offers her crown as reward if Essex is returned to her alive. As the courtiers turn to leave, a cannon shot is heard. There is a cry of horror from the crowd. In ferocious exultation, Nottingham shouts that Roberto is dead.

In towering fury, Elizabeth turns on Sara and the Duke, demanding to know why there was a delay in returning the ring. Nottingham steps forward and declares that he alone is to blame. He adds malevolently: "Blood I wanted, and blood I got" ("Sangue volli, e sangue ottenni!"). Then and there Elizabeth condemns the Duke and Sara to death ("Quel sangue versato") and orders them out of her sight.

With cynical detachment, the courtiers urge her to be calm, unctuously reminding her of her first duty to the Crown: "he who reigns does not live for himself." In abysmal despair the Queen murmurs that she no longer reigns. Suddenly she is transfixed by a horrifying vision: the execution block, awash with blood . . . a figure running through the palace holding aloft its severed head . . . in place of the throne, a tomb opening for her. . . . Ironically the courtiers reiterate their sententious aphorism.

Murmuring that she is descending to the tomb ("In quella discendo"), the Queen dismisses the Court. The lords and ladies barely hear her final words: "Let James be King of England" ("sia Giacomo il Re, Dell'Anglia Giacomo è re"). They look back to see Queen Elizabeth, a woman broken by grief and remorse, fall back on the sofa and raise Roberto's ring to her lips. The curtain falls.

RODELINDA

by GEORGE FREDERICK HANDEL

(1685–1759)

Libretto by

NICCOLÒ FRANCESCO HAYM

CHARACTERS

Rodelinda, Queen of the Lombards	Soprano
Bertaric, King of the Lombards, her husband	Baritone
Grimwald, tyrant of the Lombards	Tenor
Hadwig, Bertaric's sister	Contralto
Garibald, Duke of Turin, Grimwald's henchman	Bass-baritone
Hunolf, a soldier, Bertaric's henchman	Bass
Flavius, young son of Rodelinda and Bertaric	Mute

Men and women of the court, townspeople, nobles, guards

Place: Milan
Time: Sixth century A.D.
First performance: London, February 13, 1725
Original language: Italian

Rodelinda is a dramatic story of treachery, lust for power and the eventual triumph of good over evil in a royal court of the early Christian era. In contrast to most of Handel's opera-oratorios, this work is in a prevailingly minor key, which heightens the tragic aspects of the plot and gives impact to the play of elemental emotions. The musical design of the opera is based on the *da capo* aria, in which recitatives are followed by long, florid arias embellished with roulades, chromatic scales and arpeggios. Handel—as did other composers of the period—wrote these arias for the legendary *castrati,* those extraordinary singers who could encompass seemingly endless coloratura passages in a single long breath.

One of the leading singers in the first performance of *Rodelinda* was the great contralto *castrato* Senesino (Francesco Bernardi), for whom Handel wrote some of his finest arias. Senesino, as Handel's *primo uomo,* sang in Handel operas for more than ten years. Handel authorities agree that *Rodelinda* contains some of the composer's best music. It was given in concert form by the Handel Society of New York at Carnegie Hall on November 23, 1966.

ACT ONE

Queen Rodelinda mourns her husband, King Bertaric, believing he is dead. Grimwald, the King's archenemy, had succeeded in banishing him, then had falsely reported his death. Plotting to usurp the throne, Grimwald also seeks to marry Rodelinda. Meanwhile, he spurns Hadwig, Bertaric's sister, whom he had first courted.

The unfortunate Hadwig turns for consolation to Garibald, who is treacherously conniving against Grimwald. At first Garibald—in his turn —spurns Hadwig, but then deludes her into thinking he is in love with her. With her help he plans to get the throne away from Grimwald.

Bertaric, returning in secret from exile at the risk of his life, makes his way back to the castle, where his Queen is a virtual prisoner. With him is Hunolf. When Bertaric impetuously resolves to enter the castle, Hunolf restrains him, warning him against risking his own life—as well as Rodelinda's—by so rash an action. Kneeling at the tomb of his ancestors, Bertaric voices his despair and longing in the recitative and aria "Pompe vane di morte . . . Dove sei amato bene."

Alone in the castle, Rodelinda broods over her fate. In the aria "Ombre, piante, urne funeste," she sings that in the funeral shadows of the cypresses on the castle grounds she sees an omen of impending disaster.

Grimwald enters. Rodelinda turns on him in fury, denouncing him as a murderer and warning that he will die for his crimes ("Morrai, si l'empio tua testa"). But her anger only serves to inflame his desire, and he expresses his passion and lust in the aria "Se per te giunge a godere."

Realizing resistance is useless, Rodelinda finally consents to marry Grimwald but demands Garibald's death as the price of her surrender. She then manages to evade Grimwald long enough to meet secretly with Bertaric, who has gained entrance to the castle with the connivance of servants. Rodelinda confesses she consented to marry Grimwald only to save her husband's life. Bertaric, horrified, refuses to believe her story and denounces her seeming infidelity in the aria "Si l'infia consorte."

ACT TWO

[*Scene One*] Bertaric, still in a rage over Rodelinda's betrayal, meets with Hadwig and Hunolf to discuss how they may thwart the conspiracy of Grimwald and Garibald. Although somewhat mollified by assurances that the Queen is faithful to him, Bertaric gives way to his doubt and frustration in the aria "Con ranco mormorio."

[*Scene Two*] An intermezzo sustains the mood of rising tension and impending conflict. The curtain rises on the hall of the castle where Rodelinda and Grimwald are gathered with their retinues. Confronting Grimwald, Rodelinda makes an eloquent plea for mercy ("Spietati, io vi giurai"). Grimwald, ignoring her protestations, sings that he is bound to her by chains of love ("Prigioniera ho l'alma in pena").

In subsequent action, Bertaric and Rodelinda again meet in her apartment, where Bertaric, finally convinced of his wife's fidelity, takes her in his arms. She pledges her devotion in the aria "Ritorna, oh caro e dolce mio tesoro." At this moment they are discovered by Grimwald. Beside himself with rage, he accuses Rodelinda of betraying him with her "paramour" ("Tuo drudo è mio tesoro")—for some reason, he does not believe Bertaric is the King and Rodelinda's husband. He consigns Bertaric to a dungeon. Husband and wife bid each other farewell in one of the opera's finest duets, "Io t'abbraccio."

ACT THREE

There is a prelude and fugue before the rise of the curtain.[1]

[*Scene One*] Grimwald, tormented by the realization of his guilt, voices his terror and remorse in the aria "Tra sospetti, affetti, timori") ("In suspicion, contrition, in terror!").

[*Scene Two*] Bertaric, brooding in his cell, wonders bitterly if, after all, he has been abandoned by those he trusted ("Chi di voi più infedele?"—"Which of you did worse deceive me?").

As he ends the aria he is startled by a sudden noise. A sword is thrust through a crack in the wall and clatters at his feet. He picks it up just as a figure moves toward him in the darkness. Bertaric lunges at the intruder, only to find that he has wounded Hunolf, to whom Hadwig had given a key to a secret door in the dungeon and who had come to help Bertaric escape. Despite his wound, Hunolf leads Bertaric out of the dungeon, pausing first to tear off the king's cloak—stained with his blood—which he flings to the ground.

A moment later Rodelinda and Hadwig rush in, find the bloody cloak and of course believe Bertaric has been murdered. Rodelinda gives way to her anguish in the aria "Ahi perchè, giusto ciel."

[1] From Handel's G minor Concerto Grosso.

[*Scene Three*] The final scene takes place in a meadow outside the dungeon walls. Grimwald, now half crazed by guilt and fear, staggers in exhausted from trying to escape his imaginary pursuers. In a stormy aria, "Fatto inferno è il mio petto," he cries that the torments of hell are raging in his soul. Then, as though bereft of his reason, he stares vacantly at a group of children passing by and sings a pastoral refrain about the children who tend the meadows ("Pastorello d'un povero armento"). At its conclusion he lies back and falls asleep.

Garibald sneaks in and craftily draws Grimwald's sword from its sheath. Just as he is about to plunge it into Grimwald's heart, the latter wakes up. As Garibald staggers back, Bertaric and Hunolf burst in. Tearing the sword out of Garibald's hands, Bertaric springs at the would-be assassin, who flees in terror. Bertaric follows and kills him offstage. He returns and tells Grimwald, who is stunned at having been saved by the man whom he plotted to rob of his wife and his throne.

Rodelinda comes in with Hunolf, Hadwig and Flavius, followed by people of the court. United at last with her husband, Rodelinda greets him in a fervent aria ("Mio caro bene"). There is general rejoicing as Grimwald restores the crown to Bertaric. Then all join in the great choral finale, "Dopo la notte oscura."

LA RONDINE
(*The Swallow*)
by GIACOMO PUCCINI
(1858–1924)

Libretto by
GIUSEPPE ADAMI

Based on a libretto by A. M. Willner and Heinz Reichert

CHARACTERS

Magda de Civry, a demimondaine, mistress of Rambaldo	Soprano
Rambaldo Fernandez, a Parisian banker	Baritone
Ruggero Lastouc, a student, son of a friend of Rambaldo's	Tenor
Prunier, a poet	Tenor
Lisette, Magda's maid	Soprano
Bianca ⎫	Soprano
Yvette ⎬ friends of Magda	Soprano
Suzy ⎭	Mezzo-soprano
Périchaud ⎫	Baritone/Bass
Gobin ⎬ friends of Rambaldo	Tenor
Crébillon ⎭	Baritone/Bass
Georgette ⎫	Soprano
Gabriella ⎬ grisettes	Soprano
Lolette ⎭	Mezzo-soprano
Rabonnier, a painter	Bass
A student	Tenor
Major-domo	Bass

Students, artists, ladies and gentlemen, grisettes, cocottes, flower girls, dancers, waiters

Place: Paris and Côte d'Azur
Time: During the Second French Empire (1852–70, under Napoleon III)
First performance: Monte Carlo Theater, March 27, 1917
Original language: Italian

Puccini's eighth opera, *La Rondine* was composed after such international successes as *Manon Lescaut, La Bohème, Tosca* and *Madama Butterfly*. While it has echoes of these works, this opera is in an entirely different vein—light, lyrical and abounding in ingratiating dance rhythms. It is notable for interesting experiments in harmonization which are more sophisticated than those in *La Bohème* or *Tosca,* by way of comparison.

When Puccini was in Vienna in 1912 he heard a number of light operas and was attracted by the effervescent gaiety of the music. Interested in trying his hand at this style of composition, he began work. The writing, however, was beset by a succession of financial and political complications. First of all, two Viennese theater directors had offered him about 200,000 crowns (at the time the equivalent of $50,000) for an operetta. Puccini, who flatly refused to have anything to do with operettas, turned down the project, but the directors persisted in offering him a contract. Meanwhile, during negotiations, war had broken out between Italy and Austria, and Puccini was censured in some quarters for "dealing with the enemy."

Toward the end of the war, matters eventually came to a mutually satisfactory conclusion. The directors having compromised by accepting a "lyric comedy" instead of an "operetta," Puccini honored his contract and *La Rondine* emerged.

Puccini had first decided to write the opera in the style of genuine *opéra comique,* with spoken dialogue, but dropped the idea in favor of recitative. Incidentally, the tenor role of Prunier (created by Tito Schipa at the Monte Carlo premiere) originally was written for baritone.

Although considered one of the composer's lesser operas, *La Rondine* is a charming work with a sound plot and abundant melody. Puccini himself once said it was his favorite among all his operas. The title refers to the prophecy of the poet Prunier, who tells Magda that, like the swallow, she will one day leave her home but—also like the swallow—she will always return.

One of the outstanding interpreters of the role of Magda was the late Lucrezia Bori. In the Metropolitan Opera's first performance of the opera on March 10, 1928, she sang the role with Beniamino Gigli as Ruggero. Early in 1936 the then impresario Edward Johnson scheduled a series of performances for Miss Bori. Her performance as Magda on a Metropolitan broadcast on Saturday afternoon, March 21, 1936, marked her farewell appearance in opera.

La Rondine was presented in a revival by the Juilliard American Opera Center in December 1979.

The brief orchestral introduction is dominated by an undulating three-chord figure which continues thematically into the scene. This figure, as a theme, is one of the most important in the score. It might be called the leitmotiv of Magda's renunciation. It is heard prominently in Act Three when Ruggero brings Magda the letter from his mother, and also when Magda tells him she cannot marry him because of her past.

ACT ONE

A luxurious salon in Magda's home in Paris. At back, right, is a large veranda with windows through which the Tuileries can be seen in the deepening twilight. The portiered entrance to the salon is in the back wall, to the left. A door in the left wall leads to the boudoir. There is a fireplace with a mirror over the mantelpiece; placed about are armchairs, divans and tables. Downstage, a grand piano covered with a rich brocade on which stands a vase of red roses.

Rambaldo is seen at right rear with his friends—Périchaud, Gobin and Crébillon. Prunier, lounging against the piano, is gossiping with Yvette, Bianca and Suzy; Magda is pouring coffee, which Lisette hands around to the guests.

The scene ensues in recitative interspersed with musical dialogue in various ensemble forms. Prunier, cynical but good-humored, informs the three girls that something very serious is happening in Paris: an epidemic of love has broken out ("Una cosa assai grave"). High society has been smitten by overpowering passion.

Lisette, happening by at the moment, scoffs at this as sentimental nonsense. In these days, she remarks, one simply answers any romantic proposal with "yes," and that ends the matter. Feigning annoyance, Prunier insists that Magda dismiss this impertinent minx on the spot. With an indulgent shrug, Magda remarks that in her house outrageous behavior is more or less the rule. Lisette flounces away.

At Magda's invitation, Prunier continues his discourse on the mysterious epidemic which is raging in Paris ("La malattia diciamo epidemica"). It is caused, he explains gravely, by a dangerous microbe which strikes the heart. In a brief trio ("E un microbo sottile") Yvette, Bianca and Suzy comment in mock alarm. Prunier goes on to say that no one is immune—not even Doretta.

And who, the others promptly ask, is Doretta? When the poet tells them she is the heroine of his latest song, the girls insist that he sing it. He pretends reluctance. Magda thereupon calls for silence, then announces that the illustrious poet Prunier has deigned to favor the company with his latest masterpiece.

Seating himself at the piano, Prunier strikes a romantic pose, then plays an introductory arpeggio. As a hush falls over the company he begins his song, "Chi il bel sogno di Doretta." It is a simple yet graceful ditty about a maiden who dreamed she was being wooed by a king who promised to make her rich and happy. But she spurned him, saying that not all his gold could bring her happiness.

Magda, listening intently, slowly approaches the piano. The poet stops playing, rises and says quietly that he does not know how to end the story of Doretta. Perhaps, he adds to Magda, she can finish it. The simple story intrigues her, Magda answers, then sings a reprise of Prunier's song. One day, so her version goes, a young student kissed Doretta's lips and the madness of love engulfed her. Magda's guests, fascinated, express their admiration in a hushed, spoken phrase.

In a passionate, soaring climax, Magda—now thinking not of "Doretta" but of herself—sings of the golden dream of love that once was hers ("O sogno d'or poter amar così"). Prunier impulsively takes the red roses from the vase on the piano and scatters them at Magda's feet. The men and women crowd around with effusive expressions of approbation.

As a sinuous theme continues in the orchestra, Prunier, Magda and Rambaldo—as though aware of each other's thoughts—comment with veiled irony. Rambaldo remarks rather sardonically that the tide of passion swept him off his feet. Magda, taken aback by his unaccustomed show of feeling, says that it was the poet—not herself—who inspired these emotions.

Prunier disclaims any credit. In each soul, he declares sententiously, there lurks a romantic demon whose power is absolute ("Nel fondo d'ogni anima"). Rambaldo, looking intently at Magda, remarks that he has exorcised his particular demon with holy water. If she wishes to see him, he adds in an ironic jest, here he is. With that Rambaldo takes from his pocket a jewel case with a pearl necklace and hands it to Magda. She takes it with a gasp of surprise, then shows it around.

Rambaldo tells her he had planned to present this gift earlier, but the present occasion seems more appropriate. Annoyed at his insinuating tone, Magda retorts that he has heard her answer to him in the song she sang a moment ago. With a slight bow, Rambaldo turns and walks to the other side of the room. Prunier, watching Magda, murmurs that the "Doretta" of his song was unyielding, but her real-life counterpart probably will surrender to the lure of treasure.

Suddenly, to the accompaniment of a staccato phrase in the orchestra, Lisette enters and hurries over to Rambaldo. In a *vivace* passage reflecting her breathless haste ("quel signore giunse ancora") she tells him that the young man who has called seven times before is here again and now refuses to go away without seeing the master of the house.

Turning to Magda, Rambaldo asks if he may be permitted to introduce the son of an old family friend. She curtly reminds him that he is in his own house and can do as he pleases. Rambaldo sends Lisette to bring in the visitor.

As the orchestra takes up a syncopated waltz theme, Prunier rather peevishly again asks Magda why she does not get rid of this saucy maid of hers. Magda good-naturedly defends Lisette as a good girl who brings a ray of sunshine into her mistress' life. At this, her three friends, Bianca, Yvette and Suzy, wryly comment that hers is the kind of life they would gladly lead—especially with so lavish a provider. As for themselves, they complain, the problem is always the same: money.

In a quasi-recitative passage, Magda rebukes the girls for thinking of nothing but money ("Denaro! Nient'altro denaro!"). She is certain, she says, that—like herself—they look back fondly on the days when they were grisettes: they had no money but were rich in happiness with their sweethearts.

Bemused by her recollections, Magda begins to sing about the carefree hours she spent dancing at Chez Bullier—dancing the night away as a voice whispered magic words into her ear. Then, to the accompaniment of one of the opera's ravishing waltz tunes, Magda relates how the voice of love ("Fanciulla, è sbocciato l'amore!") yet warned her that ecstasy must be paid for in anguish. The owner of that voice was an ardent young student. After a night of dancing he ordered two glasses of bock, threw down twenty sous and told the waiter to keep the change. The girls laugh over this example of reckless extravagance, then entreat Magda to tell the rest of her story. The young man, she continues, asked her name ("Il tuo nome vuoi dir?"), but she would not tell him. Instead, they both wrote their names on the table top, then for a long time looked silently into each other's eyes.

Suddenly she became frightened and ran away, but she could not escape the throbbing music and the sound of her lover's voice. In a poignant phrase that dies away on a high note, Magda expresses her longing to relive the joy of that adventure.

As she sits lost in thought, Prunier rejoins the group. Yvette, Bianca and Suzy, disappointed with the commonplace ending of Magda's romance, mockingly discuss it with the poet. They have a most unusual subject for a poem, they tell him ("Poeta, un argomento!"): a pure, modest maiden fled in fright from a ballroom and a beer glass. Her passionate lover's curly hair and bushy side whiskers had quite turned her head—and so she ran home to her old guardian aunt. Giggling over their own joke, the three girls waltz in a circle around Prunier.

Purposely misunderstanding their nonsensical version of Magda's story, the poet remarks that an old aunt with side whiskers could never inspire him to flights of poetic fancy. But the niece undoubtedly could,

Magda says with a smile. That would depend, Prunier replies fatuously, entirely on whether she could meet a poet's exalted standards ("Può darsi . . . ma qualora"). To be worthy of him, she must be beautiful, charming, worldly and refined—in short, a combination of Galatea, Berenice, Francesca and Salome.

With pretended seriousness, Magda asks how all these feminine virtues can be discovered. Quite simply, the poet answers: every woman's character is plainly written in the palm of her hand. The women, of course, beg him to read their palms at once. Prunier declares that this procedure requires the utmost secrecy. On his orders Yvette, Bianca and Suzy set up a screen in one corner of the room. Thus out of view of the other guests, they seat themselves around Prunier; Magda is the first to stretch forth her hand. At this point the focus of the action shifts.

As the waltz theme of Magda's story sounds in the orchestra, Lisette enters, shows Rambaldo the visitor's card, then brings him in. He is Ruggero Lastouc. Although Rambaldo greets him cordially, the young man is ill at ease. Apologizing for his intrusion, he hands Rambaldo a letter of introduction from his father. As the other begins reading, the action shifts back to Prunier. Assuming a prophetic air, he tells Magda that her palm has revealed her destiny.

In a brief refrain over a series of soft chords in the orchestra, Prunier prophesies that Magda, like the swallow, is fated to leave her home for a distant land ("forse, come la rondine"), a land of sunshine and—perhaps—love. Magda asks apprehensively if this prophecy might also mean misfortune. Destiny, Prunier replies gravely, always has two faces: one smiling, the other sad.

As Prunier next reads Bianca's palm (advising her in the future to accept whoever has the most to offer), Rambaldo finishes reading Ruggero's letter of introduction and learns that he is visiting Paris for the first time. Calling to Prunier, he asks him if he can suggest where Ruggero might best spend his first evening in the city. In bed, Prunier answers flippantly. Walking over to the visitor, he condescendingly informs him that the so-called pleasures of Paris are nothing more than illusion.

Thereupon Lisette, to everyone's consternation, cries that Prunier is wrong—Paris is the most wonderful city in the world. Exasperated by her interruption, Prunier orders her to be silent. Ignoring him, Lisette hands Ruggero a pencil and a piece of paper, then asks the guests to name the most exciting night clubs in Paris for the visitor's benefit.

Over an exuberant accompaniment in polka rhythm, they call out the names: Le Bal Musard . . . Frascati . . . Cadet . . . Pré Catalan; and finally, from Lisette, Chez Bullier. Ruggero, though utterly bewildered, dutifully writes down the names. He shakes hands with Rambaldo, then turns to leave—forgetting to pick up the piece of paper. Lisette, drawing aside the portiere at the doorway for him, urges him to choose Chez Bullier. There, she sings ("Amore è là"), love reigns supreme in a realm of laughter and delight. She follows him out.

Magda, Prunier, Rambaldo and the others, who have been watching the scene from the veranda, burst out laughing. As Magda comes forward—the pearl necklace dangling carelessly from her hand—she remarks that Prunier and the others should have shown more consideration for Ruggero and spared him embarrassment. Rambaldo dryly comments that a night at Bullier's probably will make up for it—to which Bianca adds that Bullier's is famous for its miracles. Magda, repeating the name softly to herself, tosses the necklace on the nearby table.

Rambaldo, Prunier and the guests now leave. The closing action of the scene takes place to the accompaniment of a melodious waltz theme. Magda rings for Lisette, orders her to call her carriage, then countermands the order. Lisette reminds Magda that this is her night off. Told she may leave, the maid turns out all the lights in the room and hurries out.

Sitting in the faint glow of a light on the veranda, Magda softly repeats Prunier's prophecy in the same musical phrases: "Forse come la rondine . . ." ("Like the swallow, I may go to a distant land . . ."). She notices the sheet of paper which Ruggero had left on the table. Magda picks it up, then drops it as though having made a sudden decision. As a sustained chord sounds faintly in the orchestra, she whispers, "Bullier's," then runs smiling into her boudoir.

To the accompaniment of a unison figure, which is repeated in changes of key, Lisette appears. She is carrying a shawl and a gaudy hat. Tiptoeing to the boudoir door, she listens, then turns away—only to run into Prunier in top hat and overcoat with a turned-up collar. He takes her in his arms and kisses her. With a startled gasp, she tears herself away. The ensuing musical dialogue is remarkable for the fact that its curious blend of tenderness and irony is underscored by the accompanying theme itself. Prunier tells Lisette that she could not possibly imagine how much he despises her ("Tu sapessi a quale prezzo di disprezzo"). She is utterly unworthy of him—and yet he loves her.

The two then go on to argue comically about what Lisette is wearing. Prunier bluntly disapproves of her entire costume, despite Lisette's protests that she has borrowed her mistress' best frock, coat and hat. Prunier sends her to change into a costume more acceptable to him, meanwhile calling in mock despair on the nine muses to forgive him for consorting with a creature so unworthy of him.

When he is finally satisfied with Lisette's appearance, the two start for the door arm in arm and make their exit on a softly sung but melodramatic phrase: "sono te" ("I am thine!"). No sooner have they left than Magda emerges from her boudoir. She is in the simple dress of a grisette. As the tender waltz theme sounds in the orchestra she fastens a rose in her hair, drapes a shawl around her shoulders and goes toward the door. In a brief musical phrase she sings: "Who knows what Doretta dreamed?" ("Che il mistero di Doretta"). At the door she turns, goes back to the mirror and asks her reflection: "Who would recognize me now?" She leaves as the curtain falls.

ACT TWO

The ballroom at Chez Bullier. At left, a curving stairway leading down from the entrance; at right, steps lead up to a balcony. In the left wall, two large windows give a view of the street. In the ballroom, profusely decorated with flowers, is a throng of students, grisettes, courtesans, men about town and couples out for a night of fun. Flower girls and waiters move among the tables.

In the brilliant ensemble writing of this act, Puccini mingled the decadent, sophisticated gaiety of Paris with the nostalgic sentimentality of prewar Vienna. The resulting *Schwärmerei* is evoked by the irresistible waltz rhythms that dominate the entire act. There are echoes of *Rosenkavalier,* of Lehár, of Johann Strauss. But the melodies are not borrowed; they are Puccini's own. These waltzes are the composer's accolade to Vienna. He loved the city and paid a generous musical tribute to its irrepressible spirit.

The scene opens with a tumultuous ensemble (reminiscent of the Café Momus scene in *La Bohème*) blending the voices of flower girls, brash young students and other merrymakers. Imperceptibly, the action focuses on a table where Ruggero sits alone. Some of the girls begin eyeing him curiously and remark on his solemn demeanor ("Così solo! È funebre!"). Their inquisitiveness getting the better of them, they crowd around his table and ask him his name. Is it, perhaps, Armando . . . Marcello . . . Ernesto . . . Alberto . . . ? Ruggero, in mingled embarrassment and irritation, only glares at them. Finally giving him up as hopeless, the girls move away with a burst of derisive laughter.

With a sudden change in the mood of the music, Magda appears on the stairway and looks around in timid hesitation. A group of eight students, noticing her, comment that although she is poorly dressed she has the air of a lady of quality. One young man advances up the stairs and offers her his arm. Magda shrinks back in embarrassment. In a brief chorus ("Siam studenti, gaudenti") the youths introduce themselves as pleasure-seeking students endowed with every desirable masculine trait —except money. They offer to serve as her escort for the evening.

Anxious to evade them, Magda says she has an appointment. Looking around in desperation, she suddenly notices Ruggero and smothers an exclamation of surprise. Drawing their own conclusions, the students gallantly lead her to Ruggero's table. In high good spirits they give the lovers their blessing and go on their way laughing.

Magda, in charming confusion, haltingly apologizes to Ruggero for intruding on him in this manner. She only wanted to escape the attentions of the students, she explains, and will leave as soon as they are out of sight. Touched by her distress, Ruggero invites her to sit beside him. From this point on the dialogue continues over shifting rhythms in the orchestra: a sensuous, sustained figure, a staccato rhythm and an ebullient Viennese waltz.

Entreating Magda not to leave, Ruggero tells her that in her shyness and modesty she is like the girls in his native Montauban ("Così timida e sola"). They are not like the girls here. They prefer to dance to old-fashioned tunes, and to set off their beauty they need only a simple ornament—or perhaps a single flower such as she herself is wearing in her hair. Ruggero invites Magda to dance but she demurs, protesting that she cannot dance like the girls in Montauban. Saying he is certain she dances divinely, Ruggero offers his arms and draws her to the dance floor. In an aside, Magda murmurs that this adventure is like the one she had long ago ("L'avventura strana come nei dì lontani").

As the two mingle with the other dancers their voices blend in a brief duet ("Nella dolce carezza"). This introduces the splendid waltz chorus which dominates the act. While the music gradually grows wilder and more abandoned, Magda and Ruggero dance their way to the stairs and go up to the balcony. There they pause to watch the scene below and sing of the enchantment of this moment ("Dolcezza! Ebbrezza"). For a brief interval they go to the garden outside, and from a distance their voices blend with the chorus in a surging climax.

The music subsides as the crowd drifts toward the adjoining garden. Lisette and Prunier enter, with Lisette complaining over the poet's domineering attitude toward her—she cannot sneeze or turn right or left without being criticized. Prunier blandly answers that it is all a part of her education: perhaps, by some miracle, he may be able to teach her how to behave properly. Still bickering, they dance their way toward the garden.

Magda and Ruggero return and make their way back to their table, where—exhausted but beaming happily—they drop into their chairs. At this point, Magda virtually re-creates the romantic episode of her past. She says she is thirsty. Ruggero orders two glasses of bock from a passing waiter. Thereupon Magda asks if he will grant her a favor: give the waiter twenty sous and tell him to keep the change. Ruggero, puzzled, smiles at this whimsical request.

As though her thoughts were far away, Magda vaguely explains that the generous tip brings back the memory of an old aunt. Then she repeats the refrain sung by Yvette, Bianca and Suzy in the first act when they told Prunier about the frightened maiden who ran away from "a ballroom and a beer glass" ("Una fuga, una festa"). Noticing Ruggero's bewildered look, she adds softly that all this is only a fairy tale. The waiter brings the beer. Magda proposes a toast "to all your loves" ("A nostri amori"). Frowning, Ruggero sets down his glass without responding. With earnest emphasis he declares he could love one woman only—and to her he would dedicate his whole life. Impressed by his sincerity, Magda gravely echoes his words.

Fearing he has offended her, Ruggero speaks in tender reassurance. They are friends, he says, and yet he does not know her name. Still recreating the past, she says she would rather write her name than say it, singing the identical phrase in which she had told her friends of her adventure. With a small pencil Ruggero hands her, Magda writes a name: Paulette. Reading it approvingly, he writes his name beside hers on the table top. Now, Magda says softly, there will always be something of themselves in this place. Ruggero answers that these names will fade— but her enchantment will live in his heart forever.

Then, gazing into each other's eyes, they give voice to their emotions in an impassioned duet, "Perchè mai cercate," one of the opera's most lyrical moments. The duet ends not on a vocal phrase but in a long kiss as the love theme surges up in the orchestra.

Oblivious to everything, Magda and Ruggero remain locked in each other's arms. A group of night club patrons, coming chattering and laughing down the staircase, notice the two and lapse into respectful silence. In a pianissimo choral phrase ("Non facciamo rumore") they comment that such love is not a matter for laughter. With exaggerated gestures of secrecy they steal away.

Lisette and Prunier, who had come in shortly after the others, stagger back in surprise as they catch sight of Magda and Ruggero—who are still in a passionate embrace. At Lisette's startled cry when she believes she recognized her mistress, the lovers separate in confusion. Now follows a delightful scene with variations on the "mistaken identity" theme, a dramatic vignette which is played out over a flood of Puccinian melody.

To begin with, Prunier and Magda instantly recognize each other, and, unobserved by Ruggero, Magda puts a warning finger to her lips. Lisette, who keeps insisting that the woman is her mistress, is even more astounded when she recognizes Ruggero. Prunier hastily admonishes her that she has been drinking too much and has simply been deceived by the woman's remarkable resemblance to Magda. With elaborate courtesy he presents Lisette to Ruggero, telling him she is eager to know if her previous advice to come to Chez Bullier has brought him luck. In answer, Ruggero gallantly turned to Magda.

Unsuspectingly, he now introduces Magda to Prunier and Lisette as "Paulette," adding the information that Prunier is a very famous poet. Lisette, sitting down beside Magda, confidentially tells her she is the very image of her mistress. She must be a charming woman, Ruggero puts in. Just as she would be, Lisette says with naïve tactlessness, indicating Magda, if she were wearing the right clothing. "As you are, for example," Magda remarks, highly amused. Thereupon Lisette explains that all her finery costs her nothing—it is all borrowed from her mistress. To Lisette's annoyance, Prunier roars with laughter.

In an aside, Magda, with a touch of feminine malice, asks Prunier if his companion is his "Salome" or his "Berenice." The poet is stung by this jibe at his conceit. Meanwhile, Ruggero has ordered champagne and proposes a toast to love. The response is sung by all four in a unison phrase.

With glass upraised, Ruggero turns to Magda, and in the beautiful aria "Bevo al tuo fresco sorriso" sings a toast to her beauty and her laughter. In an answering phrase Magda sings that now her dream will last forever ("È il mio sogno che s'avvera"), and then the four voices blend in a glowing paean to all lovers. They are joined in a choral ensemble by the other patrons, who meanwhile have returned to the ballroom. As the great chorus rises to its climax, the four lovers are deluged with flowers thrown from the balcony and from every part of the ballroom. Several girls step out from the crowd and crown Prunier with a garland.

A moment later, as the throng is gradually dispersing, the romantic mood of the scene is suddenly shattered. The music changes to a rapid, menacing rhythm. Rambaldo appears at the top of the staircase. Prunier, catching sight of him, whispers a warning to Magda. Terrified, she asks the poet to get Ruggero out of sight. Prunier makes a reassuring gesture, then turns to Lisette to warn her of her master's presence. Before she can recover from her fright, the poet orders Ruggero to take her into the garden.

(In contrast to this moment of tension, there is an amusing byplay on the other side of the ballroom. A grisette runs away with an aging roué's top hat. He stumbles after her, forgetting to pay his check. The waiter, in turn, chases after him and triumphantly returns with the money a few moments later, to the vast amusement of the onlookers.)

Prunier, watching Rambaldo approaching down the stairs, urges Magda to leave at once. To his dismay she refuses to move. At a loss as to his next maneuver, the poet, while futilely trying to keep Magda in the background, greets Rambaldo with ostentatious cordiality. Taking his hand, he enthuses over the large emerald the banker is wearing. Rambaldo's answer is an icy stare. With a gesture of hopelessness, Prunier turns on his heel and retreats into the garden.

Face to face with Magda, Rambaldo demands an explanation. Magda replies in a poignant refrain: "L'amo! Ma voi non lo sapete." He will never know, she sings, how much she has longed for true love—and now she has found it. As for him, everything is over. Moved by Rambaldo's incredulous look, Magda grasps his hand in an impulsive gesture of pity and begs his forgiveness for hurting him. Bowing, Rambaldo coldly says he hopes she will not regret her actions. With that he turns and without looking back stalks from the ballroom.

Magda collapses into a chair and for a long time stares motionlessly into space. In the grim, cold light of dawn, now beginning to show through the windows, the ballroom with its disordered tables, over-turned glasses and wilted flowers is a tawdry reminder of the frenzied gaiety of the night. Outside, a wistful, ghostly voice sings that a cool fragrance heralds the dawn that robs the night of its magic and transforms love into an illusion ("Nella trepida luce d'un mattin").

Ruggero reappears carrying Magda's shawl. Calling "Paulette," he gently reminds her that it is dawn and they must go. Magda rises and faces him uncomprehendingly. Only then does he notice with alarm that she is deathly pale. As though waking from a trance, Magda comes toward him with arms outstretched. In mingled passion and despair she apostrophizes her dream of love in a reprise of the theme of Ruggero's aria ("Ti amo! Ma tu non sai"). Their voices blend in an ecstatic unison phrase as the curtain falls.

ACT THREE

A cottage on the Côte d'Azur, where Magda and Ruggero are in seclusion. In front, a terrace with tables and chairs. Beyond, an open field and farther off an olive grove, with a path leading down to the sea. At the back a wall, covered with ivy and climbing roses, with an opening in the middle. It is afternoon of a beautiful spring day.

As the curtain rises, the lovers are having tea on the terrace. They give expression to their bliss in a long duet in waltz tempo which begins when Magda sings that the murmur of the sea enhances the charm of this spring day ("Anche il mare respira"). At the conclusion of the duet they sit in silence for a few moments and then Ruggero turns to more practical matters—namely, money.

The bills are piling up, he tells Magda ruefully, pulling several from his pockets. Even the landlord, he says, is eying his tenants suspiciously. Ruggero discloses that he wrote his father three days ago for money but has had no reply. Perhaps, he adds with a chuckle, they will have to go begging. Magda utters an exclamation of distaste.

Shrugging off his financial troubles, Ruggero says he has a happy secret to tell—one his beloved probably can guess: he has asked his father for his consent to their marriage. Magda, nonplused, can only stammer that she had not expected such news. This should not surprise her, Ruggero says with disarming simplicity, because he has sworn to love her forever.

Taking her in his arms, he tells her of his own dream of marital happiness in the opera's best-known aria "Dimmi che vuoi seguirmi." He asks her to follow him to his home high on a hill surrounded by the serene beauty of nature. In this idyllic spot their love will come to its fruition. His mother will be there to protect her against all care and sorrow, and soon they may hear the laughter of a child. But perhaps—who knows?—their life in this haven of sun and shadow will be but a prelude to their golden future, their final golden dream. He ends the aria on a tender questioning phrase—"E chi sa?"

Overwhelmed by emotion, Magda sobs in his arms. Kissing her hair with tender reverence, Ruggero releases her and walks slowly from the scene. Alone, Magda is wracked by terror and guilt. In an agitated refrain ("Chi più dirgli?") she asks herself the agonizing question: how can she tell her trusting lover of her past? With a single word she will shatter their happiness forever . . . and yet she dare not live a lie to hold Ruggero's love. Plunged into despair, Magda goes into the cottage.

As an ascending chromatic passage erupts in the orchestra, Lisette and Prunier come hurrying in—wrangling, as usual. Lisette appears to be panic-stricken because she fears they have lost their way and will never find Magda's cottage. Prunier sneers that, as usual, she is overplaying the scene. Lisette wails that he has ruined her life.

A long and hectic argument ensues in duet form as Prunier launches into a diatribe on the general subject of Lisette's disastrous lack of talent as an actress ("Non mi stupisce"). He had been fool enough to hope, he fumes, that he could make her a star—on the assumption that she had wit enough to learn the ditties he composed for her stage debut in Nice. And what happened? The "star" vanished without a trace.

Lisette, covering her ears, moans that she still can hear the hisses that greeted her performance ("il sibilare di quella gente"). All she asks now is silence. Here, in this remote spot, she has it, Prunier remarks sardonically. As for her stage debut, he adds, he had hoped to make her forget—at least for one evening—that she is nothing more than a servant. Ignoring him, Lisette looks wildly around in comic terror, exclaiming that she hears mysterious hisses. Prunier sarcastically observes that she is obviously a victim of his highest theatrical ambitions.

Then, realizing that the girl is quite beside herself with unreasoning fear, the poet changes his tactics. He assures her that they are now at Magda's cottage and that in this lovers' retreat she is safe from the cruel taunts of the theater audience in Nice. And here, he goes on pompously, he will restore her to the kind of life she is fitted for—far from the world's strife ("fuori del mondo").

At that moment, Magda's valet comes across the terrace with some letters on a tray. Prunier asks him to inform the lady of the house that two friends from Paris have come to visit her. No sooner has the valet left than Lisette turns on Prunier in a furious outburst ("Alla fine m'hai seccato!"). She has had enough of his high and mighty airs and his nagging criticism of her, she rages. Now that he has destroyed all her dreams and illusions, she asks only that he leave her in peace. Roused to genuine anger by her accusations, Prunier retorts scornfully that gratitude never has been one of her virtues. Losing all control, Lisette screams, "I hate you!"

The two recover themselves quickly as Magda appears. Prunier tells her they have come only to ask if she is happy. Her absence, he says, is the talk of all Paris—and when he tells her friends the truth they refuse to believe him. They cannot understand how a sophisticated woman of Paris can resign herself to rural domesticity for the sake of a love affair. Magda sharply protests his insinuations.

Quickly changing the subject, she asks Prunier why he and Lisette actually have come to this place. With obvious relish he explains that the theater patrons of Nice ("Il teatro di Nizza") have decreed that Lisette is not destined to become one of the immortals of the stage. He adds, however, that his real reason for coming is to ask if Lisette may be permitted to resume her position as a maid. Magda assents, and Lisette, with a sigh of relief, says that now at last she is happy. As though to symbolize her return to the status of servant, she takes off her hat.

Then, over a repetition of the musical theme first heard during the dialogue between Prunier and Lisette near the close of Act One, Prunier speaks candidly to Magda. Lisette, he begins, is happy because she has returned to the place and station where she belongs. And this, he tells Magda, is what she herself must do: leave this dream world and go back to her own reality. Magda angrily tries to silence him. The poet tells her he is only doing his duty: he was asked to give her this message by one who understands her and can solve all her problems.

With that he abruptly turns to Lisette and bids her farewell. In an unaccompanied recitative he requests Magda's permission to ask Lisette one more question. She nods. In a stage whisper, he asks Lisette at what time she will be free this evening. At ten o'clock, she answers. Saying he will meet her then, Prunier struts jauntily away.

Turning to Magda, Lisette remarks briskly that the house is obviously in need of tidying up and that she will be glad to serve her mistress as before. She hurries out and returns shortly, dressed in her maid's uniform, and curtsies to Magda.

A moment later, as the "renunciation" theme is heard in the orchestra, Ruggero rushes in and excitedly shows Magda a letter from his mother. Magda turns pale and sways unsteadily, as though about to faint. Alarmed, Ruggero leads her to a chair, then assures her that all is well: his mother has given his bride-to-be her blessing. He hands Magda the letter. Controlling herself with an effort, she begins reading to the accompaniment of a simple yet eloquent theme.

Ruggero's mother writes ("Figliuolo, tu mi dici") that she weeps with happiness when she thinks of the gracious lady whose heart he has won and who will be the mother of his children. If she is modest and virtuous, then she is indeed truly blessed. Here, at the ancestral hearth, everyone impatiently waits to meet her son's chosen bride. Magda stops reading, her voice choked with sobs. Tearfully she reads the letter's closing phrase: "Donale il bacio mio!" ("Give her a kiss from me!").

As Ruggero kisses Magda on the forehead she tears herself away, crying in anguish that she dare not receive his mother's kiss ("No! non posso riceverlo!"). Here again the "renunciation" theme is heard.[1] This marks the beginning of the farewell duet which ends the opera. In despairing tones Magda tells Ruggero that, stained by her past, she is not worthy of entering his home as his bride. She has had other lovers, she confesses, who bought her affections with their ill-gotten wealth.

But it is he himself, she goes on, who has given her the greatest treasure of all—his steadfast love—and she cannot and will not repay him with lies. Falling on his knees, Ruggero wildly implores her not to leave him and plunge his life into ruin ("Taci! le tue parole"). Magda answers that leaving him is worse than death—but she must go because she loves him too much to betray him.

Fiercely clinging to her, Ruggero reiterates his entreaties; Magda, with desperate insistence, repeats that she will not add to her guilt by ruining his life. Suddenly calm, she takes his face in her hands and looks with passionate intensity into his eyes. Only he, she sings, has known her innermost soul ("L'anima mia che solo tu conosci"), and it will be his forever. And when this pain is only a memory, he will return to his home, she will return to her sorrow.

Gently releasing Ruggero, Magda rises. Lisette comes from the cottage, and her look shows that she understands. She goes to Magda and supports her as she begins to walk away. After a few steps Magda turns and sings her final phrase of farewell, "che sia mio questo dolore" ("let me bear our sorrow alone"). Weeping bitterly, Ruggero collapses as the curtain falls.

[1] A few measures later, a new and powerful theme takes over. It is reiterated in an extraordinary succession of changes of key, illustrative of Puccini's experiments with new harmonizations.

RUSALKA

by ANTONÍN DVOŘÁK

(1841–1904)

Libretto by

JAROSLAV KVAPIL

Based on the fairy tales of Hans Christian Andersen and Czech folk ballads

CHARACTERS

Rusalka, the Naiad	Soprano
The Watersprite, her father	Bass
Ježibaba, the Witch	Mezzo-soprano
The Gamekeeper (Forester)	Baritone
The Kitchen Boy (Turnspit)	Mezzo-soprano
The Prince	Tenor
The Foreign Princess	Soprano
A Young Hunter	Tenor
First Dryad	Soprano
Second Dryad	Soprano
Third Dryad	Mezzo-soprano

Ladies and gentlemen of the Prince's court, wedding guests, huntsmen, water nymphs

Place: Legendary
Time: Legendary
First performance: National Theater, Prague, March 31, 1901
Original language: Czech

Rusalka is a chapter out of the "Undine" legends—the stories of ephemeral creatures of underwater realms (Rhinemaidens, Lorelei, "Ruthie" of Hauptmann's *Sunken Bell,* the Sirens of *The Odyssey,* the sea nymphs of Hans Christian Andersen's tales) who ventured into the mortal world usually to their own destruction and that of men as well.

Author Jaroslav Kvapil and Dvořák fashioned the opera on the ancient French story of Melusine (Undine), the watersprite who became a human. Adapted by La Motte-Fouqué,[1] it served as the basis for many Undine operas. *Rusalka* has been called a perfect musico-dramatic work—a superb amalgam of words and music.

Dvořák, who habitually wrote in a burst of inspiration, began the opera on April 21, 1900, completed it November 27, 1900, seven months and one week later. Though none of his other eight operas won lasting acclaim, the success of *Rusalka* exceeded all expectations. By 1950 it had been performed more than six hundred times at the Prague National Theater. Dvořák did not live to see his opera performed abroad, but it won great popularity on foreign stages.

The brief prelude begins with an important melodic phrase, heard throughout the opera, associated with Rusalka and her native under-water element.

ACT ONE

A forest glade at the edge of a lake near the hut of Ježibaba, the Witch. Rusalka, deep in thought, is sitting nearby under a tree. The scene opens with a chorus of dryads ("Hou, hou, hou, stojì měsíc nad vodu") teasing the Watersprite about the moon peeping through his window. (The basic motif sounded in the prelude is heard here.) They also taunt him because he wants to get married and is trying to catch a dryad to be his wife.

Emerging from the waves, the Watersprite looks around and sings that he will yet capture one of these damsels and take her down to his splendid watery realm. But the dryads mischievously dance out of his reach. The Watersprite, watching them with tolerant amusement, sighs philosophically: "Ah, well, they are young!" ("Inu, mládi, mládi!").

Rusalka suddenly breaks in on his reflections. She is downcast and asks her father to banish her sadness, then confesses that her fervent wish is to escape from the depths and live like a human being—to enjoy the sunshine ("Chtěla bych od vás, hlubin těch zbýti"). In short, she wants to become a mortal. She reminds him that he himself has told her that the beings in the world above have souls—souls that ascend to heaven when they die.

Such souls, the Watersprite warns her, are stained with mortal sin. But full of love, Rusalka rejoins. Alarmed, the Watersprite asks if she is in love with a mortal. To his dismay she tells him that her lover visits her frequently ("Seim často přichází"). He plunges naked into the lake, she sings, to take her in his arms. But alas, she is only a wave. She

---

[1] Baron Friedrich Heinrich Karl (1777–1843), German writer, author of the romantic novel *Undine* (1811).

must become a mortal so that she can return his love with passionate kisses.

The Watersprite warns her that she will be lost forever if she yields to a human being. Her only answer is to implore him to tell her how she can join her human lover. Resignedly, her father advises her to consult the Witch Ježibaba, warning her again of the doom that awaits her ("Ztracena, do věků"—"Doomed you are for all time"). With a despairing cry he sinks beneath the waves.

Alone, Rusalka confides to the moon her secret passion for her mortal lover in what is undeniably one of the most enchanting arias in opera—"Měsíčhu na nebi hlubokém"—"O moon, high up in the deep, deep sky." At its conclusion a cloud momentarily obscures the moon. Frightened and cold, Rusalka waits for Ježibaba.

To the accompaniment of the basic motif—now harshly sounded by trombones and trumpets—the Witch emerges from her hut grumbling over being awakened. Rusalka, in the guise of a water fairy, begs Ježibaba to give her a potion to release her from the waves. The Witch obliges. Transformed into a woman, Rusalka steps ashore.

In a melodramatic aria ("Staletá moudrost tvá všechno ví"—"Your ancient wisdom knows everything") Rusalka pays homage to the Witch for her magic powers "to destroy . . . to create . . . to change men into monsters and back again . . . to concoct strange drugs. . . ." Then she begs for a drug that will give her a mortal soul. That, the Witch remarks cynically, is what everybody asks her for—but how much is Rusalka willing to pay for this miracle? Everything she has, Rusalka cries.

To the accompaniment of foreboding variations of the basic theme, Ježibaba intones the fateful terms of the bargain ("Dám ti, dám věz to rarach sám"—"I'll do it, by the devil, yes!"). First, Rusalka must surrender her transparent Naiad's veil. If she fails in her quest for human love she will be cursed forever by the underwater world she has rejected. Then, human speech will be denied her. Finally, if her lover betrays her, both will die under the curse of eternal damnation.

But Rusalka, obsessed by desire, defies Ježibaba's warning, protesting that her human soul will defend her against this evil sorcery. Then she follows the Witch into her hut, where she helps brew the magic potion. Bending over the seething kettle, Ježibaba chants the incantations ("Cury mury fuk, bilá pára vstává z luk!"—"Abracadabra, fog is lifting in the glade") as she adds the ingredients to her poisonous brew: dragon's blood . . . bile . . . a bird's heart . . . tomcat, pour that brew into her mouth . . . *from now on, not a word.* . . ."

The nightmarish scene fades. Dawn breaks over the lake; hunting horns sound in the distance. In a brief refrain, a hunter (unseen) sings about a white doe in the woods ("Jel mladý lovec, jel a jel") being pursued by the Prince. The Prince himself appears, bow in hand. He wonders about the strange, beautiful creature he has been stalking. The trail has led him to the lake, where his bow seems useless in his hands. He feels himself drawn to the lake by a mysterious force. The Young Hunter approaches to warn him against hunting the white doe at the cost of his soul.

But the Prince scorns the warning. When his hunting companions appear he sends them back to the palace, explaining that he wishes to find out for himself why he is under the spell of the lake. Just as he sits down at the water's edge, Rusalka appears before him, in a filmy gown, her golden hair cascading over her body.

The Prince gasps in surprise. Is she a woman or a vision . . . is she the white doe he has been hunting . . . or is she herself the trophy of the hunt . . . ? Rusalka, mute under Ježibaba's curse, stretches out her hands toward him. If some sorcery has closed her lips, the Prince sings rapturously, his kiss will now unlock them. Then, if she loves him, she can tell him so ("Máš-li mne ráda, zjev mi to!").[2]

Rusalka flings herself into his arms. Welling up from the lake come the lamentations of the Watersprite and the water nymphs, calling in vain for a daughter and a sister lost forever. The Prince, crying that the magic of this moment will vanish all too soon, throws his cloak around Rusalka and leads her toward the palace.

ACT TWO

The palace park. In the background, the gallery of the palace and the banquet hall.

The Gamekeeper enters with the Kitchen Boy and an amusing colloquy ensues as the two gossip about the extraordinary happenings that have thrown the palace into an uproar. The Gamekeeper asks the Kitchen Boy (who calls him "Uncle Vaněk") the latest news. To begin with, the boy says, the palace is swarming with guests and the servants are working night and day.

This is all because the Prince found a weird female creature in the forest—and he wants to marry her. She wanders around like a ghost and never says a word. A fine bride, indeed, the Kitchen Boy sniffs. The Gamekeeper sings ("Je to pravda vskutku") that this bears out the rumors he has heard: peculiar things are happening in the forest . . .

---

[2] The episode of the "white doe" has a rather interesting parallel in Act One of Strauss's *Die Frau ohne Schatten*. The Emperor of the Southeastern Islands has left his Empress asleep and is leaving early to go hunting. In a long monologue he recalls how one day while hunting in the "moon mountains" he had found his Empress: she was in the form of a gazelle.

there is a witch, and a deadly watersprite . . . at midnight, naked nymphs dance in the moonlight, and woe to anyone who looks at them. All this leaves the Kitchen Boy quaking with fear.

Then he adds more bad news: the Prince is no longer his handsome self. He wanders about in a daze . . . ignores the advice of "Auntie Háta" and the parson to turn this creature out of the palace for his own good. But there is one ray of hope, the Kitchen Boy goes on. The Prince seems to be tiring of his moonstruck bride-to-be and is now interested in a beautiful foreign princess. The Gamekeeper rejoices over this news. He and the Kitchen Boy abruptly scurry away as they see the Prince and Rusalka approaching.

Though elegantly gowned, Rusalka looks pale and distraught. In a minor refrain ("Již týden dliš mi po boku"—"A week now have you lived with me") the Prince laments that he still cannot fathom the mystery of Rusalka. She is cold in his embrace, she is without passion. Goaded by desire, he cries that he must possess her.

At that moment the Princess enters and overhears his impassioned outburst. Aside, she sings that if the Prince rejects her it will be at the cost of his own happiness and that of the mysterious interloper as well. She deliberately places herself between the Prince and Rusalka, and haughtily asks if the Prince remembers that, at the moment, he is a host as well as a lover. Embarrassed, the Prince apologizes. Looking at Rusalka with icy disdain, the Princess asks her why she has nothing to say: presumably, it is her eyes, not her tongue, that have enslaved an ardent Prince.

Rusalka recoils at the insult. The Prince, discomfited, placatingly offers his hand to the Princess, whereupon Rusalka seizes it. He snatches it away, then curtly orders her to go to her room and dress for the ball. The Princess, leaving with the Prince, sneers that she still can claim the Prince's adoration, even though Rusalka has his heart.

As the Rusalka theme heard in the prelude sounds softly in the orchestra, she herself restrains an impulse to follow him, then sorrowfully goes to the entrance of the banquet hall, where she manages to conceal herself from the guests. Night falls. In the banquet hall, the scene changes to one of festive gaiety as the guests arrive. But the rhythms of the dance are suddenly interrupted when the Watersprite emerges from the pond in front of the palace.

In a somber aria ("Ubohá Rusalka bledá"—"Pitiful Rusalka, pallid") he mourns his daughter's absence from his realm. Her sisters weep for her return—but despoiled by human love, and with the curse still upon her, she will bring back only death to the world where she belongs.

Meanwhile, in the banquet hall, the Prince moves among the guests, the Princess on his arm. Rusalka steps forward in his path, but the

Prince totally ignores her. From the background comes the lyrical chorus ("Květiny bílé po cestě"—"White blossoms along the road"). In the rhythm of a folk tune, it tells symbolically of the red roses that will adorn the bridal chamber, while white blossoms (water lilies) will quickly fade and die. The voice of the Watersprite is heard briefly as an obbligato.

Rusalka stares at the Prince, then rushes wildly toward the pond. Her speech suddenly restored, she screams to her father to save her from the bondage of human love. She has paid the price for betraying her father by being herself betrayed: her Prince loves another—a human woman.

In wild despair she sings that now her magic charms are utterly useless ("O marno to je a prázdnota je v srdci mém"—"Oh useless it is, and emptiness is in my heart"). She cannot cope with human passion . . . she is lost forever, and can neither live nor die. She sees the Prince and the Princess approaching, and again beseeches her father to save her.

In a curious blend of ardor and irony, the Princess expresses wonder over the Prince's growing passion for her, then tauntingly asks what has become of her mute rival. The Prince answers that it is she herself who has wrought the change in him with her human love. With veiled sarcasm, the Princess asks if he would be content to return to the embrace of this frigid vision clad in moonlight.

But her mockery is lost on the Prince, who takes her in his arms with impassioned avowals of love. At that moment Rusalka rushes forward and thrusts herself into the Prince's arms. Crying out that her body is as cold as ice, he pushes her away. Thereupon the Watersprite rears up out of the pond shouting that the Prince will never escape Rusalka's embrace. With that he drags her into the pond.

The Prince stares transfixed, then kneels before the Princess and abjectly begs her to save him from this monstrous apparition ("Z objeti moci tajemné spaste mne"). With a burst of derisive laughter she tells him to join his beloved in hell ("V hlubinu pekla bezejmennou"), then storms away.

ACT THREE

The glade on the shore of the lake at night. Rusalka, pale, her golden hair turned white, sits staring vacantly over the water.

In a melancholy aria ("Necit elná vodni moci"—"Thoughtless Watersprite") she reproaches her father for dragging her back to the netherworld where her own sisters now reject her. With the curse upon her, she longs only for death. The Witch comes out of her hut and cruelly derides her for having failed to win her human lover. In answer to

Rusalka's desperate plea for help, Ježibaba explains to her what she must do to expiate her sin of seeking human love ("Miláček te zavrh', přestal tě mit rád"—"Your lover has turned against you, ceased to love you").

Only human blood, the Witch intones, will redeem her from the curse. Thereupon she hands her a knife. Shaken with horror, Rusalka flings the knife into the lake. Crying that she will not redeem herself at the price of her lover's life, she plunges into the water.

From the depths comes the plaintively beautiful chorus of the water nymphs ("Odešla jsi do světa"—"You have left us for the world") warning Rusalka that she has forfeited the right to join them. Now she is doomed to wander endlessly about the world like a will-o'-the-wisp.[3]

At this point the dramatic tension is broken by a comic scene in which the Gamekeeper and the Kitchen Boy, both frightened out of their wits, approach Ježibaba's hut to ask for help for the Prince. The Gamekeeper, telling the Kitchen Boy not to be frightened, pushes him toward the hut and calls to the Witch. He explains that "Auntie Háta" sent them to her for advice. Eyeing the Kitchen Boy, Ježibaba says Auntie probably hopes to pay for her necromantic counsel by sending this urchin for her breakfast. Well and good, the Witch says—but he will need fattening up to make a good meal.

When the hapless Kitchen Boy wails in terror, the Witch cackles gleefully. She finally learns from the Gamekeeper that the Prince is gravely ill, under the spell of a beautiful water witch who disappeared before he could marry her. As Ježibaba is about to answer, the Watersprite leaps out of the lake cursing the two emissaries for lying about Rusalka and roaring that he will have revenge. The two frantically dash away followed by Ježibaba's fiendish laughter.

Night falls. In the light of the rising moon, dryads dance in the glade to the accompaniment of a delicately lilting chorus. They are interrupted by the Watersprite, who rises from the lake to tell them of Rusalka's tragic fate. Sorrowfully he sings her name, then sinks back beneath the waves. A cloud covers the moon; the dryads, suddenly frightened and cold, disappear.

The Prince bursts madly out of the forest and rushes to the water's edge, crying that he has been searching vainly for his white doe ("Bíla moje lani!"—"Where are you, my white doe?"). He frantically implores her to come to him; moonlight again floods the scene to reveal the apparition above the lake. In a serene refrain ("Miláčku, znaš mne?"—"Do you still know me, lover?") Rusalka calls to him: now she is ac-

[3] There is a marked resemblance to the incantatory chorus of witches in Act Three of Verdi's *Macbeth*.

cursed, neither woman nor nymph . . . once she was his beloved . . . now she is his death.

Lost in his madness, the Prince staggers toward the apparition, begging for the kiss that will doom him ("Libej mne, mir mi přej"—"Kiss me, give me peace!"). Rusalka takes him in her arms, and there he dies.

From the depths of the lake comes the voice of the Watersprite intoning that Rusalka's sacrifice is all in vain. Rusalka kisses the Prince for the last time. Tenderly she sings that his human goodness has finally redeemed her—and may God have mercy on his human soul ("Lidská duše, Bůh tě pomiluj!"). The curtain falls.

SEMELE

by GEORGE FREDERICK HANDEL

(1685–1759)

Libretto by

WILLIAM CONGREVE

Congreve's original work *Semele* was arranged for Handel's use—probably by Newburgh Hamilton, one of the composer's oratorio librettists

CHARACTERS

Jupiter (Jove)	Tenor
Juno	Alto
Cadmus, King of Thebes	Bass
Semele, his daughter	Soprano
Athamas, a prince of Boeotia, in love with Semele	Alto
Ino, Semele's sister	Alto
Somnus, god of sleep	Bass
Iris, a messenger from Olympus	Soprano
Apollo	Tenor

Priests, soothsayers, Loves, Graces, Zephyrs, nymphs, swains, attendants

Place: Greece
Time: Antiquity
First performance: Covent Garden, February 10, 1744
Original language: English

While musical dictionaries list *Semele* as a "stage piece" rather than an opera, it has also been referred to as the "first great full-length English opera." Handel here achieved a blend of oratorio and opera, introducing certain elements (dramatic action, *da capo* arias, recitatives) which move the work out of the realm of pure oratorio.

The English dramatist Congreve (1670–1729) in his libretto took his plot from the Greek legends as related by Ovid and Euripides. In his setting, Handel gave the mythical characters human attributes—susceptibility to the mundane emotions of pride, jealousy, remorse, fear and anger—and thus the opera emerges as a human drama of unique expressiveness. Semele, a beautiful mortal, is loved by Jupiter, and she herself aspires to godhood. Her ambition for immortality destroys her—with Juno's wifely jealousy as the instrument of her destruction.

The work is characterized by a sustained flow of Handelian melody, with majestic choruses and scenes linked by vigorous recitatives. Two of the principal arias—Semele's "O sleep, why dost thou leave me?" and Jupiter's "Where'er you walk"—are familiar in the concert repertoire.

Despite its musical distinction, *Semele* failed completely in London. Withdrawn after three performances and given only once more later in 1744, it was never revived during Handel's lifetime. For some reason, Handel had aroused the ire of the opera faction. They not only damned *Semele* as "profane," but resented what they called an oratorio being staged as an opera. Opposition went beyond a war of words: Hired hoodlums waylaid, beat up and robbed patrons who came to see the performances.

In the intervening years, *Semele* has rarely been given. In a contemporary revival, it was presented in June 1969 at Caramoor, Katonah, New York, by the New York City Opera Company under the direction of Julius Rudel.

The three sections of the long overture can be related to basic elements of the opera's action: the *maestoso* to the solemnity of the sacrificial scene; the fugue to the consequences of Juno's avenging wrath; the gavotte to the pastoral charm of scenes in Act Two.

ACT ONE

[*Scene One*] The temple of Juno. Flanking the altar is a golden statue of the goddess. Priests are seen performing a sacrificial rite, during which flames leap up from the altar and the statue bows. A priest proclaims that Juno has accepted the sacrifice; the assemblage responds with a chorus of rejoicing: "Lucky omens bless our rites."

In a recitative passage, King Cadmus and Athamas both try to persuade Semele to accept Athamas as her bridegroom. The King urges her to "hear and obey," while Athamas entreats her to give heed to "a lover's prayer."

But Semele, thinking only of her lover, Jove, is unmoved by their pleas, and in recitative ("What refuge now is left me?") she frets over her dilemma: on one hand, her father's wrath if she disobeys; on the other, Jove's anger if she yields to mortal love. She begs the god to help her ("O Jove, in pity teach me which to choose"). This larghetto refrain leads into a long aria, in baroque style, expressive of tender long-ing ("The morning lark to mine accords his note").

Athamas, assuming her avowals are meant for him, thinks of his approaching nuptials with joyous anticipation ("Hymen, haste! Thy torch prepare!"). His amorous sighing, in turn, is overheard by Semele's sister, Ino, who is hopelessly in love with him. Furious over his lack of attention to her, she bursts out: "I can no longer hide my passion!" The three others are startled by her outcry, and King Cadmus asks: "Why dost thou untimely grieve?" This marks the beginning of a beautiful quartet in which Ino turns aside the efforts of the others to console her.

At the conclusion of the number, thunder rumbles ominously and the flames on the altar are extinguished. In mingled terror and anger, the priests demand that the nuptial ceremonies (for Semele and Athamas) cease forthwith ("Cease your vows, 'tis impious to proceed"), warning of Jove's avenging wrath. Cadmus sings that while Jove thunders, Juno approves; Athamas implores her aid in winning Semele. In an aside, Semele herself swears to Jove that she loves him alone. There is a crash of thunder and the altar sinks out of sight.

[*Scene Two*] In a long duet ("Hopeless lover, turn thy eyes") Ino commiserates with Athamas over his unrequited love for Semele. She invites him to find consolation in her own arms, but his casual reaction to the suggestion goads her to jealous fury ("Insensible! Ingrate!"). In the concluding sections of the duet ("You've undone me!") they express their mutual confusion and frustration.

[*Scene Three*] Cadmus rushes in and tells Athamas to prepare him-self for disastrous news about Semele. In a feverish recitative ("Wing'd with our fears and pious haste") he relates that she has been abducted by Jove, who swooped down in the guise of an enormous eagle with flashing eyes and golden beak. While Athamas breaks into lamentation, Ino secretly gloats over the elimination of her rival. The priests and soothsayers now enter and Cadmus commands them to explain the reason for Semele's abduction.

To his surprise, they burst into a congratulatory chorus ("Hail Cadmus! Jove salutes the Theban King!"). They compliment him on the fact that the mighty Jove himself has favored him by taking his daughter to the celestial regions to be his companion.

The voice of Semele is heard in an insinuating gavotte refrain ("End-less pleasure, endless love"), as though in mockery of her father's dis-tress over her fate. She sings of her bliss in the arms of the god—whose thunder and lightning now have been tamed by her caresses. The chorus takes up this theme in a kind of parodied madrigal style.

ACT TWO

[*Scene One*] The act is introduced by a sinfonia. Juno asks Iris, the messenger from Olympus, where Jove has taken Semele. Iris answers that the rendezvous is a palace on the heights of Cithaeron, beyond the reach of mortal eyes. In an ensuing refrain ("There from mortal eyes retiring") she sings that Semele, attended by Loves and Graces, abandons herself to the delights of love.

Juno vents her fury in a stormy recitative ("Awake, Saturnia!"), one of the most dramatic in all Handel's operas. She orders the goddess to destroy Semele—let the Furies tear her to pieces. Iris warns her of the terrible monsters that guard Jove's hideaway ("Hear, mighty queen"): thousand-eyed dragons with forked tongues and brazen wings.

In a frenzied *da capo* aria ("Hence, Iris, away!") Juno commands the messenger to go with her at once to the Maeotian Lake, the abode of Somnus, god of sleep. There she will force the god to exercise his magic to seal the eyes of the dragons guarding Semele's love nest.

[*Scene Two*] An apartment in Semele's palace. Loves and Graces hover around her bed. She awakens and sings the famous aria "O sleep, why dost thou leave me?" While voicing her passionate longing for her lover, she is haunted by the thought that the joys of love are illusory and fleeting.

[*Scene Three*] Jove appears. Semele greets him amorously. He responds in a long *da capo* aria ("Lay your doubts and fears aside"), counseling her to think only of the pleasures of love, now that he has returned. In an ensuing recitative he somewhat gratuitously assures her that "I and Love are one." Semele answers with a voluptuous avowal ("With fond desiring, with bliss expiring"), in which she coquettishly observes that she too can claim that "I and Love are one." Loves and Zephyrs approvingly comment in chorus ("How engaging, how endearing").

Semele lapses into a pensive mood and Jove asks what is troubling her. Wistfully she replies that she is, after all, only a mortal, with all the misgivings and fears that beset a mortal woman. The god immediately suspects her of harboring a dangerous ambition to become immortal, and in the aria "I must with speed amuse her" he resolves to divert her from these thoughts of godhood. Again the Loves and Zephyrs voice their approval of amorous dalliance ("Now Love that everlasting boy invites").

By way of providing Semele with further distractions, Jove tells her he will bring Ino to keep her company for a while. He will then transport the sisters to Arcadia, which he describes in one of the loveliest of all Handel arias, "Where'er you walk."

[*Scene Four*] Semele and Ino embrace. Ino describes how she made the journey under the protection of Jove himself. Then in a lyrical aria, "But hark! The heavenly sphere turns round," she revels in the serene beauty of Arcadia. Semele's voice blends with hers in a pastoral duet ("Prepare then, ye immortal choir"). Loves and Zephyrs respond in a great fugal chorus ("Bless the glad earth with heavenly lays").

ACT THREE

[*Scene One*] The cave of Somnus. The mood of the scene is established in a remarkable overture with a hypnotic swaying figure in the bass. Roused from sleep by Juno and Iris, the god sings a trancelike invocation to slumber ("Leave me, loathsome light"). His voice dies away to a murmur as sleep overpowers him.

When Iris chides Somnus for his lethargy, Juno remarks that she knows what will keep him awake. Thereupon she offers him the nymph Pasithea for his pleasure. The god's response is instantaneous and enthusiastic. In a delightful buffo aria, "More sweet is that name," he savors the joys of a romantic interlude with the nymph.

Pasithea will be his, Juno promises, if he does her bidding. He is to send his minister, Morpheus, to tantalize Jove with a dream of a woman like Semele—only more beautiful. The purpose is to inflame the god's passion to the point where, when he awakens, he will grant Semele anything she asks. Then Somnus himself is to cast a spell on Ino, so that Juno may take her shape and appear thus before Semele. In an ensuing duet ("Obey my will, thy rod resign") Juno and Somnus agree on the terms of their bargain.

[*Scene Two*] Disguised as Ino, Juno enters Semele's apartment carrying a mirror, which she hands to Semele. Pretending to be dazzled by Semele's beauty, Juno asks if she has become immortal. Unsuspecting, Semele answers that she still is a mortal and is not aware of any change in herself. Juno plies her with spurious compliments. Overwhelmed by the adulation of her supposed sister, Semele, gazing into the mirror, invokes her image in the brilliant aria of self-praise "Myself I shall adore."

Juno then offers Semele practical advice on how to obtain from Jove the immortality she longs for: when he approaches her bed, she is to refuse his caresses until he agrees to discard his mortal disguise and appear in his true form as a god. Inflamed by desire, Jove will grant her wish, and thus she will become a goddess.

Completely carried away, Semele expresses her gratitude in the siciliana aria "Then let my thanks be paid." She promises that when she achieves immortality she will endow her sister with charms like her own. Juno, warning that Jove is approaching, starts to leave; Semele assures her she will follow her advice. In a sardonic aside, the goddess dismisses her as a conceited fool.

[*Scene Three*] Jove rushes in with an impetuous greeting, "Come to my arms, my lovely fair," the opening phrase of his aria. He is astonished when Semele gently but firmly fends off his advances, then launches into a petulant harangue about his insistent demands on her ("I ever am granting"). To placate her, Jove promises, in a vigorous recitative passage ("Speak your desire"), to give her anything she asks. As he swears by all the gods on Olympus, there is a menacing rumble of thunder.

Then, to his utter dismay, Semele demands that he stop masquerading as a mortal and appear before her as the god he really is. Realizing that she is pronouncing her own doom, he warns her not to insist on his granting her wish ("Ah, take heed on what you press"). Semele reiterates her demand in the opera's most spectacular coloratura aria, "No, I'll take no less." At its conclusion she rushes away.

[*Scene Four*] Remorseful and dejected, Jove ponders the fate ordained for Semele ("she must a victim fall"). He resolves to use only his "softest lightning" and "mildest thunderbolts" to mete out her doom . . . but die she must. Juno reappears briefly to gloat over her victory.

[*Scene Five*] Abandoned and resigned to her fate, Semele sings her farewell in the poignant aria "Too late I now repent." It ends in a spoken, unaccompanied phrase of despair: "I can no more." She cringes in terror as she sees Jove descending in a cloud. Semele vanishes as a thunderbolt obliterates the palace.

[*Scene Six*] Cadmus, Athamas, Ino and the priests comment on Semele's doom in a dramatic choral arioso, "Oh, terror and astonishment." In an interlude, Ino recalls, as though in a trance, her strange journey to Arcadia. The god Hermes, she sings, foretold Semele's doom and her own betrothal to Athamas. Cadmus thereupon gives the pair his paternal blessing, and Athamas voices his happiness in the aria "Despair no more shall wound me."

[*Scene Seven*] A bright cloud descends on Mount Cithaeron, and from it emerges Apollo as the god of prophecy. He proclaims that from

Semele's ashes a phoenix shall rise in the form of a god mightier than love—in short, Bacchus, the offspring of Semele and Jove. The chorus hails the new deity in a majestic prelude and fugue, "Happy shall we be."

LA STRANIERA

(*The Stranger*)

by VINCENZO BELLINI

(1801–35)

Libretto by

FELICE ROMANI

Based on the Gothic novel *L'Étranger,* by Viscount Charles Victor d'Arlincourt

CHARACTERS

Alaide (La Straniera)	Soprano
Lord Montolino	Bass
Isoletta, his daughter, betrothed to	
Count Arturo	Mezzo-soprano
Arturo, Count of Ravenstel	Tenor
Baron Valdeburgo	Baritone
The Prior of the Knights Hospitalers	Bass
Osburgo, friend of Arturo's	Tenor

Ladies and gentlemen of the court, huntsmen, peasants, servants

Place: The Castle of Montolino in Brittany
Time: Circa 1300
First performance: La Scala, Milan, February 14, 1829
Original language: Italian

The famous love affair between Bellini and Giuditta Turina-Cantu, a beautiful, cultured society girl of Milan—twenty-five years old and unhappily married to a millionaire—was said to have been the inspiration for *La Straniera.* He began work on it during the summer of 1828, when he had already made a name for himself with *Bianca e Fernando* and *Il Pirata,* and was the idol of the operatic world. Most of the score was composed while he was living at Giuditta's villa on Lake Como. The pastoral surroundings there, in fact, influenced Bellini's setting for several scenes in the opera.

La Straniera, the fourth of Bellini's ten operas, was an unqualified success. Bellini himself reported that the audience howled with enthusiasm. His main source of satisfaction, however, was that the opera established him as a composer in his own right, rather than an imitator of Rossini, for whom he had high respect as a musician.

The plot has all the melodramatic elements of the typical Gothic tale: doomed lovers, renunciation, suicide, frustrated passion—all overlaid with the brooding mystery of sorcery and witchcraft. These elements Bellini fused into the sensuous melodies that are at the core of *bel canto* art.

The opera's overture opens with a thunderous unison chord in the brass, then goes on to state several themes of leading arias and ensembles. Noteworthy is a section in the lively rhythm of a folk dance much like the Scottish reel.

ACT ONE

[*Scene One*] On the shores of the lake outside the Castle of Montolino. A chorus of peasants and people of Montolino's court hails the approaching wedding of Isoletta and Count Arturo ("Voga, il vento tace"). At its conclusion, Isoletta and Valdeburgo appear. The bride-to-be confides to Valdeburgo that she is in deep distress over Arturo's inexplicable change of heart ("Col cor trafitto"). Apparently, she says, he has fallen hopelessly in love with another woman—a sinister, wild creature known as "La Straniera," who lives alone in a hut on the shore of the lake.

In the aria "Io la vidi" she relates that only yesterday she caught sight of this witch and heard her wail in an unearthly voice: "Abandon all hope, ye who long to recapture the joys of love" ("Ogni speme è a te rapito che riponi nell'amor"). This leads into a duet in which Valdeburgo expresses his grief over Isoletta's plight and tries to console her.

From the distance comes the excited chorus of the people of the castle as they pursue La Straniera to her hut and curse her as a sorceress. As Isoletta and Valdeburgo leave, Montolino and Osburgo appear. When Montolino reveals his apprehension over Arturo's behavior ("Osburgo? Io non divido"), the latter tries to reassure him with the promise to do his best to bring the errant suitor to reason ("Tu pur col vogo").

[*Scene Two*] The interior of La Straniera's hut in the forest. Arturo enters and looks around, musing that a magic spell hovers over this place ("È sgombro il loco")—a spell he is powerless to resist. He stares wonderingly at a portrait of La Straniera, bejeweled and dressed in the robes of a queen. Hearing footsteps, he withdraws to a dark corner of the room.

Alaide enters. In the romanza "Sventurato il cor che fida" she philosophizes on the sorrows of unrequited love. Her reflections are interrupted when Arturo steps out of the shadows and impetuously declares that he has come only to serve her ("In tuo soccorso"). This marks the beginning of a duet. Alaide upbraids him for daring to come to her hut; Arturo replies that an irresistible force draws him to her. Although she confesses that she is mysteriously attracted to him, she implores him to leave. His love, she warns, will destroy them both.

[*Scene Three*] A clearing in the forest. Osburgo and his party sing a hunting chorus, "Campo ai veltri." With them are Arturo and Valdeburgo, whom the hunters had met in the forest. Flatly rejecting Osburgo's suggestion to go back to the castle for the prenuptial festivities, Arturo begs Valdeburgo to go with him to meet Alaide. He promises never to see her again if the Baron disapproves of her ("Tu di me in traccia"). This introduces a long duet in which the two argue the matter. Valdeburgo finally agrees to go.

[*Scene Four*] Alaide's hut. When Valdeburgo sees La Straniera, he greets her like a long-lost friend. Embracing her, he is about to call her by her real name when she stops him ("Cielo! Taci! Qual gioia!"). Arturo is beside himself with joy over Valdeburgo's apparent approval of Alaide. But his hopes are dashed when Valdeburgo tells him, over ominous chords in the orchestra, that he must forswear Alaide: she cannot return his love because another destiny is in store for her. Arturo gives vent to his surprise and rage in the refrain "Un dubbio atroce." Drawing his sword, he is about to lunge at Valdeburgo when Alaide interposes herself with a cry of "Ah, non partir!"

This action sets off the dramatic trio which is one of the opera's most memorable numbers. Its main theme brings to mind the theme of the tenor aria "Ecco ridente" in Rossini's *Il Barbiere di Siviglia*. Valdeburgo tries to convince Arturo that he is not his rival; Arturo forces Alaide to agree to see him at least once more ("Ecco gl'indegni insieme"). Warning Arturo again that their love is accursed, she begs the two men to leave her in peace.

[*Scene Five*] The shore of the lake near the castle. Arturo, tormented by jealousy, is certain that Valdeburgo is his rival, and when he meets the Baron by chance in the forest he challenges him to a duel. Valdeburgo, wounded, staggers and falls into the lake just as Alaide rushes in. Turning on her in fury, Arturo storms that he has just slain her real lover. Horrified, Alaide cries that Valdeburgo is her brother, not her lover. With a despairing shout, Arturo flings down his blood-stained sword and plunges into the lake to save Valdeburgo. Arturo's outcry brings people from the castle rushing to the scene, where they find Alaide crouching alone beside the bloody sword. In a wild chorus, "Un uom nell'onda," they brand her a witch and accuse her of murdering the Baron. She is dragged away as their prisoner.

ACT TWO

[*Scene One*] The great hall of the Castle of Montolino, where the trial of La Straniera is taking place. The Prior, as judge, reflects on the evidence in the refrain "Udimmo. Il tuo racconto." Before Alaide is brought in, Osburgo, as first witness, gives damaging testimony against her ("E dubitar ne puoi?").

When the accused—her face veiled—appears and the Prior asks her name, she replies: "La Straniera. A me tal nome." The Prior, recognizing her voice, smothers an exclamation of surprise. Dialogue in recitative follows. When the Prior has heard her testimony he asks if there is anyone she can call as defense witness. There is no one, Alaide answers.

At that moment Arturo bursts in, shouting that Alaide is innocent and that he alone is guilty ("Morte cadrà sul mio"). At the height of the ensuing uproar, Valdeburgo strides in. There is a stunned silence in the court, and then he declares that both Alaide and Arturo are innocent. He makes his plea for mercy in a ringing aria, "Sì, li sciogliete, o Giudici." The onlookers express their consternation in a stirring chorus.

Ordered by the court to reveal her identity, Alaide answers that she will lift her veil only to the Prior. When she does so, he staggers back in surprise, then says with deep respect: "Go, you are free. And forgive us our sins." Alaide leaves, escorted by Valdeburgo; Arturo, baffled and dejected, walks away alone. The Prior, turning on Osburgo, angrily censures him for giving false testimony against Alaide ("Tu che osasti mentir").

[*Scene Two*] A spot near Alaide's hut. Arturo has come to ask her forgiveness and to beg for her love. He is intercepted, however, by Valdeburgo, who entreats him to abandon his attempts to win Alaide. He adds the warning that Arturo will see her "only over the body of her brother" ("E osar puoi tanto"). This leads into a fiery duet, one of the most impressive numbers of the opera.

Arturo finally promises to renounce Alaide and marry Isoletta, but he makes one final request. He asks that Alaide be allowed to attend the wedding so that he may see her once more. Valdeburgo assents, then exhorts him to be mindful of Isoletta's deep love for him and to be faithful to her.

[*Scene Three*] The church on the day of the wedding. Isoletta, still haunted by thoughts of Arturo's ominous behavior, is gloomy and despondent. She gives way to her fears in the aria "Ah! se non m'ami più." In a following chorus ("Sì, vincesti, esulta alfine") her serving-women try to reassure her. A wedding hymn is then sung ("È dolce la vergine").

The wedding party arrives, with Arturo in a state bordering on frenzy. Valdeburgo, trying to calm him, assures him that Alaide has consented to be present ("Coraggio: ella ti vede"), but Arturo scarcely seems to hear. When Isoletta approaches, he glares wildly at her and behaves so irrationally that she threatens to halt the ceremony then and there. The church is thrown into an uproar. Alaide meanwhile surreptitiously comes closer to the altar. There the four principals voice their mutual confusion and despair in the great quartet "Che far vuoi tu?" At its climax, Isoletta cries that she will release Arturo from his marriage vows. Thereupon Alaide rushes forward and implores her to take courage and go on to the altar. Then she turns and, half fainting, makes her way toward the door of the church. Almost at the door, Alaide pauses and prays for mercy for all those caught up in this disaster ("Cielo pietoso").

Arturo, at the altar, suddenly turns away from Isoletta and dashes toward the door. Brandishing his sword, he orders Alaide to follow him. At her cry of terror, Valdeburgo and the Prior rush to her side. The Prior stuns the throng by proclaiming that La Straniera is in reality Queen Agnes of Brittany; it has just been learned that her rival for the throne has died and the plot against her life has collapsed. She will now resume her rightful place as Brittany's Queen. Arturo, staring at her in disbelief, dementedly cries that now the truth is known ("Ancor ti trovo"), then plunges his sword into his body. Isoletta kneels sobbing at his side.

The wedding guests comment in chorus on the tragic scene ("Pari all'amor degli angioli"). In solo passages ("Or sei pago"), Alaide laments the ironic destiny that has recalled her to the throne at the sacrifice of her own happiness. A powerful choral expression of grief and compassion ("Al ciel, lo spirto l'abbandona") brings the opera to a close.

SUOR ANGELICA

by GIACOMO PUCCINI

(1858–1924)

Libretto by

GIOVACCHINO FORZANO

CHARACTERS

Sister Angelica	Soprano
The Princess	Contralto
The Abbess	Mezzo-soprano
The Monitor	Mezzo-soprano
Mistress of the Novices	Contralto
Sister Genevieve	Soprano
Sister Lucilla	Mute
Sister Osmina	Mezzo-soprano
Sister Dolcina	Mezzo-soprano
The Nursing Sister (Infirmary)	Mezzo-soprano
The Tourières	Mezzo-sopranos
The Novices	Mezzo-sopranos
The Lay Sisters	Soprano, Mezzo-soprano

Chorus of women, children, men (behind scenes)

Place: A nunnery in a mountain region of Italy
Time: Latter part of the seventeenth century
First performance: Metropolitan Opera House, New York City, December 14, 1918
Original language: Italian

Suor Angelica is the second one-act work of the operatic triptych known as *Il Trittico*—the first being *Il Tabarro,* the third *Gianni Schicchi*. It is the story of the beautiful daughter of a Florentine nobleman, who entered a nunnery to expiate the sin of being an unmarried mother. Haunted by her guilt, and crushed by unjust punishment visited upon her by a vengeful relative, Suor Angelica commits suicide.

Ironically, of the three operas, this was Puccini's favorite. But along with *Il Tabarro* it failed to sustain the interest of the public, and both operas lasted only two seasons at the Metropolitan. *Gianni Schicchi,* on the other hand, won enduring popularity. The Italian premiere of the triptych, in Rome on January 11, 1919, with Arturo Toscanini conducting, was an outstanding personal triumph for Puccini. At the world premiere in New York, the role of Suor Angelica was created by Geraldine Farrar.[1]

In the opinion of some commentators, two elements have hindered the success of *Suor Angelica:* for a short work, it is too episodic, with too many loosely connected scenes; also, it employs only women's voices, which makes for a certain monotony.

Yet in its entirety, it is a touching work, full of sweeping Puccinian melody and melancholy tenderness. Throughout, the composer sustains an ethereal mood, combining religious ecstasy with elemental human emotions.

There is no overture. The curtain rises to a bell-like theme in the orchestra which echoes the majestic theme of the great *Te Deum* in the first act of *Tosca.*

An open space in front of a small church, with arcades to the right and left. Toward the back, at one side, a garden may be seen; on the other side, part of a cemetery. In the foreground a shrine with a fountain, and some cypresses. It is a clear evening in spring.

Over the ringing of bells, the voices of the nuns in the chapel are heard singing the *Ave Maria.* Two Lay Sisters, late for chapel, hurry toward the entrance. For a moment they pause to listen to the birds singing in the cypresses, then they go inside.

Sister Angelica, also late, walks quickly to the chapel. But before she enters she kneels down and kisses the threshold—an act of penance for being late. A few moments later her voice is heard alone in a brief phrase as she joins in the *Ave Maria*—"Prega per noi peccatori."

The chorus ends, and the Abbess comes out of the chapel followed by the nuns walking two by two. When she pauses before the shrine the sisters bow low as they pass her. The Abbess blesses them and leaves. The sisters talk together in small groups. They fall silent as the Monitor and the Mistress of the Novices come forward and confront the two who were late. They sternly reprove them for this infraction of the rules ("Sorelle in umiltà"). Sister Angelica also was late, says the Monitor,

---

[1] *Suor Angelica* is often performed as one of the operas of the triptych. As such, it was staged by the New York City Opera Company at the New York State Theater, Lincoln Center, on February 23, 1967. The Metropolitan Opera Company presented the triptych in a new production during the 1975–76 season. (See also *Il Tabarro,* page 658.)

but she made the proper penance. Because they neglected to do so, they not only must kiss the threshold but must say twenty prayers for the poor and needy. The two Lay Sisters express their contrition in a brief invocation to the Savior ("Cristo Signore") and go to their cells.

The Monitor and the Mistress then turn to Sister Lucilla and Sister Osmina and chide them for breaking other rules. For making the nuns laugh in chapel, Lucilla is ordered to work at her spinning wheel in complete silence. Osmina, caught hiding a bunch of roses in her sleeve, is told to go to her cell at once. Denying the accusation, Osmina marches to her cell and defiantly slams the door.

The remaining sisters, innocent of any infractions, are rewarded by being allowed to play and rest awhile. Sister Angelica, having made her amends, is included in this privilege. To the accompaniment of serene arpeggios she busies herself watering the flowers. Meanwhile, Sister Genevieve, in a sprightly melody, calls to the nuns to observe how the rays of the setting sun soon will turn the water of the fountain into gold. Perhaps, she sings, they will again see the miracle which has happened three times before ("Comincian le tre sere").

In answer to a young nun's question about the miracle, the Mistress of the Novices explains: on three evenings of every year ("Per tre sere dell'anno solamente") in the past, the sunset has turned the water to gold. But this has not happened for a year—and during that interval a sister has died. The nuns listen silently, absorbed in their own thoughts, as a requiemlike theme sounds in the orchestra.

Taking up the refrain, Sister Genevieve sings ("O sorelle in pio lavoro") that they must now sprinkle the fountain's golden water on the grave of the departed Sister Bianca Rosa. In mystical, symbolic phrases, Sister Angelica interrupts to express her own thoughts. Mysteriously she sings ("I desideri sono i fiori") that earthly desires bloom and die like flowers—but in death there is life eternal.

The reflective theme of the scene is carried on by Sister Genevieve, who recalls the days when she was a shepherdess. Looking upward, she wonders if it is a sin to long to hold a fleecy lamb in her arms again ("Mio, tu sai che prima"). If it is, she adds, then she asks forgiveness from the Lamb of God. Next to confess is Sister Dolcina, who admits having an insatiable craving for sweetmeats. She is reproached with gentle severity by the other nuns.

At that point Sister Genevieve turns to Sister Angelica and asks if she has any fond desires. The change of mood is reflected in the darkening harmonies in the orchestra. Angelica firmly answers "no" and goes on watering the flowers. In an ensemble phrase the sisters comment that Sister Angelica is lying. She has a desire, they sing ("Noi lo sappiamo"). Her dearest wish is to hear from her relatives—for seven long years she has had no word. She was banished from a home of wealth and nobility, so the Abbess said, and had to take the veil. The nuns look at each other questioningly, asking: "How . . . why . . . ?"

Their conjectures are interrupted by the Nursing Sister, who rushes in to ask help from Sister Angelica. The Nurse cries that Sister Chiara was stung by wasps as she was trimming a rosebush in the garden. The poor girl is now lying in her cell in great pain. Sister Angelica tells the Nurse to make a potion of herbs and flowers dipped in milk. It will be bitter, Angelica warns, but it will ease the pain. As the Nurse thanks her profusely, Angelica murmurs she is glad to be able to help.[2]

Suddenly there is great excitement as two convent attendants (tourières) arrive leading a donkey laden with gifts for the sisters. They crowd around and in a lively ensemble express their delight over the contributions—filberts, almonds, flour, butter, lentils, milk. Then one attendant stirs up more excitement by announcing that a distinguished visitor has arrived at the convent in a splendid carriage.

Angelica, rushing forward, asks in startled tones if the carriage is emblazoned with a coat of arms in ivory . . . if it is upholstered in pale blue silk. The attendant shrugs. In chorus, the nuns remark that Angelica has turned pale and is trembling. When the bell sounds to announce the visitor, they chatter excitedly, wondering who it may be. Angelica meanwhile stands apart; eyes upraised, she implores the Virgin Mother for help, as though haunted by a premonition of misfortune. Watching her, Genevieve silences the nuns with a gesture, then approaches Angelica. In a phrase of lyrical tenderness she expresses the hope that, at long last, Sister Angelica will have a visitor. Deeply moved, Angelica thanks her.

As a kind of fanfare sounds in the orchestra, the Abbess enters to announce the visitor. The nuns gaze compassionately at Angelica, who stands as though in a trance. When the Abbess calls her name, the spell seems to be broken. With a wave of her hands, the Abbess dismisses the other nuns, who go toward the fountain, where the water has turned to gold in the light of the setting sun. There they fill their watering cans and go toward the cemetery. Angelica breathlessly asks the Abbess who the visitor is ("Madre, parlate!"). She sings that she has waited for seven long years, and now . . .

The Abbess interrupts to say that the visitor is her aunt, the Princess. Angelica greets the news with a choking cry. Sternly warning Angelica that she must be obedient and submissive, because the Blessed Mother will hear her every word, the Abbess leaves. Angelica walks toward the arcade, then stops a few paces from a door in the side wall.

A moment later, as a foreboding theme sweeps through the bass, the Princess is escorted in by the portress and the Abbess. A tall, forbid-

---

[2] In the original score this scene is marked for an optional cut.

ding figure with aristocratic bearing, she stares coldly at Sister Angelica. Almost losing control, Angelica rushes toward her, but halts when the Princess stretches forth her hand in an imperious gesture. Angelica feverishly kisses it, then falls to her knees sobbing. The Princess only looks down at her contemptuously. Now follows the climactic scene of the opera, which is in the form of a long, dramatic duet.

It begins as the Princess recalls how Angelica's father, the Prince Gualtiero ("Principe Gualtiero, vostro padre"), and her mother, Princess Clara, when they both died twenty years ago, left their children in the Princess' care. Their inheritance, she sings, was left in equal shares— but the will gave her, the Princess, the power to change it in the event of some "indiscretion" on the part of the heirs. With that she hands a document to Angelica and peremptorily tells her to read it, then sign it.

Confused and frightened, Angelica timidly begs for some show of love and pity. In answer, the Princess tells her why she must sign this document—which will cancel forever all claims to her inheritance: her young sister, Anna Viola, is to be married. In phrases of poignant tenderness, Angelica asks a blessing on her sister. There is a striking change of key here from the grim minor accompaniment to the Princess' words to the major harmonies of Angelica's.

When Angelica asks whom Viola is marrying, the Princess vindictively replies that the bridegroom is a man whose love can overlook the disgrace which Angelica has brought upon her ancient and honorable name ("Chi per amore condono"). Outraged by this insult, Angelica asks how it is possible for her mother's own sister to show such cruelty. In a furious outburst, the Princess denounces Angelica for daring to invoke her mother's name. Then in a sudden change of mood, she launches into a somber, almost mystical refrain ("Di frequente las sera") in which she describes how every evening she kneels in her chapel to commune with the spirit of Angelica's mother. But when this ecstasy has passed, she goes on as the harmonies darken in the orchestra, only one thought remains: Angelica, and her need for repentance.

Angelica softly answers that she has always prayed to the Blessed Mother for forgiveness ("Tutto offerto alla Vergine")—but one thing she will not promise even her. In anguish and despair she screams: "To forget my son!" She abandons herself to her grief and hopeless longing for her baby in a tortured refrain, "Mio figlio!" Then in a frenzy she rages that the Princess must tell her what has happened to her child, or be forever cursed.

The Princess calmly tells Angelica that her son died two years ago. With an agonized cry, Angelica falls to the ground. The ensuing wordless action takes place to the accompaniment of a powerfully dramatic orchestral passage. The Princess rises as though to help Angelica, checks herself and goes over to a sacred image on the wall. There, leaning on her cane, she stands with head bowed as though in prayer. The scene gradually darkens. Angelica, racked by sobs, remains kneeling. The portress enters, places a candle on the table, then pauses as the Princess says a few words to her. She goes out and returns a moment later with the Abbess, who brings an inkwell and a quill.

Angelica stares at her, then realizes what she must do. Dragging herself to the table, she signs the document, buries her face in her hands and turns away. The Princess picks up the document and takes a step toward Angelica, who shrinks back with a gesture of horror. The Princess goes toward the door, turns toward Angelica with a look of gloating and contempt, then disappears. Angelica, wailing in anguish, falls to her knees. The gloom of night envelops the scene; in the background the nuns are seen lighting the votive lanterns on the tombstones.

Angelica now pours out her longing for her dead son in the opera's principal aria, "Senza mamma, o bimbo." As though hypnotized, she cries out for death to release her so that she can be with her son. Sister Genevieve and the other nuns move slowly toward her through the gloom like white ghosts. In a choral accompaniment to Angelica's final rapturous invocation to the Blessed Virgin, they sing that her prayers will be answered. The convent bells chime as they withdraw to their cells. Angelica, walking as though in a dream, slowly follows.

There is a brief, serene orchestral interlude, during which Angelica reappears. She is carrying an earthenware jar, which she places at the foot of a cypress tree after filling it with water from the fountain. She then gathers a small heap of twigs and leaves and sets them afire with a flint. On the flames she places the jar, then stands watching it intently for a moment. Now Sister Angelica's healing potion, she murmurs ("Suor Angelica ha sempre"), will do its work. The flowers on which she has lavished loving care will in return give her the blessed gift of poison . . . the gift of eternal peace.

Facing the cells, she begins the song of farewell, "Addio, buone sorelle." Her son is calling her, she sings, and she now will go to meet him in paradise, where they will be together for all eternity. With a cry of exultation she rushes to the shrine, kisses the cross, then picks up the jar and drinks the poison. She gasps in pain as it takes effect. The jar drops from her hands.

Her expression of serene resignation suddenly changes to one of horror at the realization of her terrible crime of suicide. In agony and remorse she screams that she is damned forever ("Ah! son damnata!"). Wildly she implores the Madonna for a sign of pardon for this deadliest of sins ("O Madonna, salvami!"). It was the love of her son, she wails, that led her to this act of madness.

Through the mists of approaching death, Angelica hears the voices of angels interceding for her ("O gloriosa virginum"). Her voice soars over the swelling chorus as she makes her final entreaty for absolution. A vision appears before her: a dazzling glow envelops the chapel as the doors slowly open. The Blessed Virgin emerges leading a small, fair-haired boy. She gently pushes him toward Angelica as the unseen chorus bursts into a triumphant phrase—"Gloriosa virginum! Salve, Maria!"

The boy takes one step toward Angelica, then another and finally another. The voices of the angelic choir fade into a lingering pianissimo. Angelica, dying, sinks gently to the ground. The curtain falls.

SUSANNAH

by CARLISLE FLOYD

(1926–   )

Libretto by the composer

Suggested by the story of Susannah and the Elders in the Apocryphal book of the *History of Susannah*

CHARACTERS

Susannah Polk	Soprano
Sam Polk, her brother	Tenor
Olin Blitch, an evangelist	Bass-baritone
Little Bat McClean	Tenor
Elder McClean	Baritone
Elder Gleaton	Tenor
Elder Hayes	Tenor
Elder Ott	Baritone
Mrs. McClean	Mezzo-soprano
Mrs. Gleaton	Soprano
Mrs. Hayes	Soprano
Mrs. Ott	Contralto

People of Hope Valley (singers, dancers)

Place: New Hope Valley, Tennessee
Time: The present
First performance: World premiere: Florida State University, Tallahassee, Florida, February 24, 1955; New York premiere: New York City Opera, September 27, 1956. That company again presented the opera at the New York State Theater on October 31, 1971.
Original language: English

Carlisle Floyd wrote his own libretto for *Susannah* and called it "a musical drama in two acts." Set in the Appalachian region of Tennessee, it is a story about simple mountain people, a chapter of Americana in operatic terms. The story involves the destinies—and the doom—of a beautiful young girl, Susannah, and a pulpit-pounding itinerant evangelist, Olin Blitch. Innocence is arrayed against lust, compassion against bigotry.[1]

Subsequent to its premieres in 1955 and 1956, *Susannah* has held its place in the repertoire of opera companies throughout the United States.

ACT ONE

A brief prelude begins with a unison phrase that crescendoes into crashing chords in open fourths and fifths. A *molto cantabile* section follows in a minor key. This in turn segues into the lively introduction to the opening quartet sung by Mrs. Gleaton, Mrs. Hayes, Mrs. Ott and Mrs. McClean.

[*Scene One*] The yard of the New Hope church in New Hope Valley on a Monday evening in mid-July. A square dance is in progress, with a fiddler and a caller in the background. Looking on are people of the community, including the church Elders and their wives. Susannah, strikingly pretty in a brightly colored dress, is the center of attention in her square. Happy and excited, she seems unaware of being the star attraction of the dance.

By way of making conversation while looking on, the four Elders' wives comment on the weather, which is hot and oppressive. The Lord always sends this kind of weather at "meetin' time," one of them remarks. Mrs. McClean moralizes waspishly that this is the Lord's way of smoking out sinners, then announces that a revival preacher is coming who will help the Lord in His work. Olin Blitch is his name, Mrs. McClean says, and she intends to assist him in dealing with the sinners. The dialogue is sung over simple, hymnlike phrases interspersed with recitative.

The women register wifely disapproval as they watch their menfolk try to step into the square dance with Susannah. Mrs. McClean maliciously calls attention to the girl "showin' herself to all the men . . . and look at the cut of her dress." . . . Her companions comment spitefully.

At this point Olin Blitch enters the scene, a swaggering figure in a plaid shirt and a ten-gallon hat. As onlookers and dancers become aware of his presence, the dancing stops and everyone eyes him suspi-

[1] The Apocryphal story of Susannah and the Elders tells how the beautiful, virtuous wife of Joachim was proved innocent, by Daniel, of adultery, the charge brought against her by Elders who had attempted to violate her. They were executed.

ciously. The Elders advance to meet him and McClean brusquely asks him who he is. Blitch identifies himself in a bombastic refrain—"I am the Reverend Olin Blitch." He is a hellfire-and-damnation preacher who has come to Hope Valley, as he proclaims, to "cast out devils and conquer sin." His monologue is sung to the tune of a gospel hymn. Their suspicions allayed, the people now welcome him in a vigorous evangelistical chorus as he shakes hands.

But it is not long before he notices Susannah with more than casual interest and inquires about her. McClean gratuitously informs him that she is a motherless child who is being raised by a brother, a shiftless drunkard. Blitch unctuously declares he will pray for both sister and brother.

With his avid gaze still on Susannah, he says he would like to "join the young folks," then makes his way to Susannah's square. The awed young people stop dancing and stare at him as he approaches her and holds out his hand. Smiling shyly, Susannah responds to his request for a dance. Eyeing the two, Mrs. McClean venomously sings: "She'll come to no good, mark my words."

[*Scene Two*] Later the same evening. The rickety porch and steps of the Polk farmhouse. On the porch are an old rocking chair, a rusty plowshare and some unpainted flowerboxes. Frayed curtains cover the windows.

After a tranquil interlude vaguely echoing a theme heard in the prelude, Susannah and Little Bat McClean enter. Although rather oafish, the boy has a sinister, furtive manner, and yet it is obvious that he adores Susannah. She herself is still ecstatically thinking about the square dance—"was there ever such a nice square dance!" Bat momentarily dispels her gay mood by asking anxiously where her brother Sam is—he is "scared o' Sam." He has been warned, he adds, to stay away from Susannah because there is "bad blood" in the family.

Susannah assures him that he has nothing to fear from Sam. Recalling the dance, Bat remarks that all the menfolk—including the preacher —were "courtin'" her. Modestly deprecating her popularity, Susannah wryly remarks that the preacher was not much of a dancer. The two fall silent as they look up at the stars. Susannah expresses her wonder and awe in one of the most lyrical interludes in the score ("Ain't it a pretty sight!").

The stars, she sings, can see beyond the mountains and she wonders what is out there. She means to find out for herself some day, and have a look at all those tall buildings and all those bright lights they tell about in the mail-order catalogues. And yet . . . she might get lonesome for the valley and the birds and the trees. . . . On this thought she ends the aria in a tranquil phrase. The accompaniment throughout is noteworthy for the use of a major-seventh figure, repeated in various keys, that synchronizes the words and the music.

Bat quietly leaves just as Sam, unobserved by Susannah, enters and repeats the phrase of her aria—"Ain't it a pretty sight!" With affectionate concern he asks her about the square dance. She had fun, she answers—despite hard looks from the Elders' wives. When Sam asks if any of the men courted her, she protests that she is "too young" for that. He teases her about "gettin' on nineteen," with the prospect of becoming an old maid.

Susannah insists that she has no intention of getting married—she would rather keep house for her brother. She is pleased when Sam says he is "proud of her cookin'," then asks him to sing her favorite song, "Jaybird," before she goes to bed. The two join in the perky folk ballad, joyously dancing together as they sing. Out of breath, they sit down and quietly gaze up at the stars.

[*Scene Three*] A woods near the Polk place the following morning. Susannah, offstage, is heard humming the "Jaybird" song over a burbling accompaniment descriptive of a stream gushing over rocks. But suddenly the harmonies break into harsh open fifths as Hayes, Ott, Gleaton and McClean appear. They are looking for the "crick" in which the evangelist Blitch can baptize his converts. As they peer through the trees, McClean suddenly shouts: "There it is!"

The four stop in their tracks and stare with lascivious concentration at the sight of Susannah bathing in the nude. As the explosive open fifths crescendo in the orchestra, they express their outrage over this "shameless wench." Then in a discordant quartet ("This woman is of the devil") they trumpet their self-righteous indignation. With their eyes still riveted on Susannah, the four furtively retreat, chanting that the "valley must be told" of this girl's scandalous conduct. As their voices die away, Susannah's lilting song again is heard in the distance.

[*Scene Four*] The same evening; the yard of the New Hope church, as in Scene One. Upstage is a long table laden with food. The Elders are at one side of the scene, their wives at the other. Young people clustered around the table seem ill at ease, making halfhearted attempts at having a good time.

The oppressive mood of the scene is reflected by a foreboding theme in the orchestra which continues through the quasi-recitative of the women. With malicious relish they gossip in "I told you so" vein that they were right all along about that wicked girl with the pretty face. Susannah herself enters carrying a covered dish. The Elders and their wives scowl at her and barely acknowledge her friendly greeting.

Smiling bravely, she explains that she has brought some fresh-cooked peas, and hopes that everybody will enjoy them. As she sets the dish on the table, she hears McClean's voice over thunderous unison chords in the orchestra: "Susannah, you ain't welcome here." Stunned, she turns to meet the pitiless stares of her tormentors. After a pathetic attempt to face them down, she runs blindly away. No one moves. A succession of massive chords surges up from the orchestra and then comes the rancorous voice of Mrs. McClean: "I wouldn't tech them peas o' her'n."

[*Scene Five*] A half hour later. Susannah, her face in her hands, is seated on the steps of her house. Little Bat enters stealthily. Suddenly aware of him, Susannah leaps to her feet as a violent chromatic phrase erupts in the orchestra. Bat stammers that there is something he must tell her: the Elders have spread the word that they saw her bathing naked in the creek, and that they are going to run her out of the church and maybe even out of the valley.

Susannah gasps that she has been bathing there all along . . . nobody has the right to spy on her. "They" say, Bat leers, that she "loves up" the young men and sends their souls to hell. Savoring this squalid tattling, Bat adds: "There's more. . . ." At that, Susannah whirls on the cringing boy and demands to know what he means.

Squirming in terror, Bat wails that "they" made him swear that she allowed him to "love her up in the worst way." Susannah screams at him to go away and never come to her house again. As he scurries off, blubbering, Sam suddenly appears in the doorway. Crushed by shame and despair, Susannah throws herself into his arms moaning that something terrible has happened. "Yes . . . I heard it all," says Sam quietly.

Trying to calm her, he sings in a quiet refrain that some people would sooner believe what is bad than what is good—and then do evil to others in the name of the Lord. Sobbing, Susannah entreats him to explain why these things are happening to her. Sam can only answer with silence. Like a hurt child yearning to be comforted, she asks him to sing the "Jaybird" song again. In the concluding measures of the act, a brief theme sounded in the orchestra ends abruptly in a violent crescendo.

ACT TWO

[*Scene One*] The front steps of the Polk farmhouse, as in Scene Five of Act One. Sam is standing in the doorway smoking his pipe. Susannah is sitting on the steps, staring into space. A brief opening orchestral phrase reflects a mood of despair and frustration.

In the ensuing colloquy, Sam tries to reason with Susannah and give her the courage to face her accusers. All "they" want, he tells her, is a public confession. There is nothing to confess, she replies—but then is tortured by uncertainty: perhaps she *is* guilty . . . perhaps she is a creature of the devil. This brings a sharp admonition from Sam.

Susannah flatly asserts that she will never leave the house again to face the obscene gestures and hear the prurient language of the men of the community. Sam angrily declares he would gladly kill them all to avenge these insults. Why, Susannah wonders, is God punishing her . . . she has never harmed anyone, not even a bird. Her distress is underscored by a variation of a *cantabile* theme in 6/4 which characterizes other emotional climaxes in the opera.

Urging her not to lose faith, Sam advises her to go to the revival meeting to show the people that she is not afraid. He adds solicitously that he does not want to leave her alone while he goes across the mountain to look after his traps. With unconscious irony, Sam gives her the choice of being alone or facing the ordeal of the meeting.

Her protests in vain, Susannah finally agrees to go to the meeting. To cheer her, Sam promises to stay sober and to return tomorrow before sundown with a "sack full o' critters" for their food. As the music dies away on a somber phrase, the two resume their places as at the beginning of the scene.

[*Scene Two*] The interior of the New Hope church on the same evening. There is a crude pulpit with an altar rail, behind it benches for the choir. The congregation is seated on rough-hewn benches under the flickering light of oil lamps. The Elders and their wives are prominently seated on the front benches. Little Bat is there with his parents. Two Elders are passing around battered dishpans for the collection. On the last bench at the rear sits a huddled figure—Susannah.

As the curtain rises, the choir is singing, *a capella,* a revival hymn with its grim inquisition: "Are you saved from sin, ready to meet your Lord?" As an obbligato comes the stentorian bellow of Blitch exhorting the faithful to dig deep into their pockets for the Lord. With the collection plates brought forward and duly prayed over, Blitch launches into his soul-saving revival spiel in spoken words and recitative over an eerie theme in the orchestra.

He does not spare his listeners. He warns them of eternal damnation if they do not come forward to be "saved." He frightens them with lurid tales of sinners who repented too late and were plunged into the bottomless pit. Finally, panting from exertion, he exhorts sinners to come to the altar for their last chance for salvation. Several shy, frightened young people come forward and kneel before him.

In a melodramatic gesture, Blitch places his hands on the heads of the penitents as the choir begins another gospel hymn—"Come, sinner, tonight's the night." In spoken words, Blitch delivers the final warning of doom: "Tomorrow might be too late!" A deafening orchestral clamor emphasizes his words.

Suddenly he silences the choir and begins speaking with ominous deliberation. There is one among us, he intones, who will not accept the Grace of the Lamb . . . he himself has prayed in vain for her soul. . . . As if on cue, the entire congregation turns and glares at Susannah. Transfixed with terror, she stares back at Blitch. Asking the choir to sing one more verse of the "invitation" hymn, he unctuously entreats Susannah to come forward and confess her sins.

As he repeats the exhortation with mounting fervor, an insidious note of cajolery creeps into his voice. Susannah, as though hypnotized, walks slowly toward him down the aisle. Looking up at him, she sees a smile of lustful triumph on his face. Recoiling, she screams, "No! No!" and rushes panic-stricken out of the church. The congregation is in an uproar. Blitch, his features contorted in anger and frustration, controls himself with an effort and loudly pronounces the benediction.

[*Scene Three*] An hour later. Susannah is on her porch, trying to forget the ordeal of the meeting by singing a melodious ballad ("The trees on the mountain are cold") about a May-December lover who deserted his sweetheart and her baby.

She gasps in dismay when Blitch appears and compliments her on her singing. When he mouths that he has come to pray for her soul she remarks tartly that she has already prayed enough for both of them. Then she lashes out against the Elders and their vicious lies . . . they even told Little Bat to lie about her. In bitter anguish she cries that the cruel gossiping of the neighbors—and of Blitch himself—has almost driven her to kill herself. With spurious concern Blitch tells her she must cleanse her heart of sin, and then she will see the light. Susannah breaks down sobbing.

Taking advantage of her helplessness, Blitch now plays upon her sympathies. He is a lonely man, he says as he draws closer to her. He needs someone to love, and he needs the love of a woman. Hesitantly putting his arm around her shoulders he asks casually if Sam will be home tonight. No, she answers blankly. Eyes closed, she makes no effort to resist the evangelist as he slowly leads her into the house.

[*Scene Four*] The interior of the New Hope church. At rise of the curtain, Blitch is seen kneeling in prayer at the altar. Guilt-ridden, he prays in abject earnestness—but in resounding biblical metaphors—to be forgiven for having defiled a young girl's body with his lust. His prayer continues over the pounding rhythm of a funeral march until he utters his final plea in the words of Christ—"And let this cup, if it be Thy Will, pass from me."

While he is still kneeling, the Elders and their wives enter and walk down the aisle, looking at him with puzzled expressions. Following them is Susannah, who sits down on the bench she had occupied at the meeting. Suddenly aware, Blitch springs to his feet, stares at the group, then fixes his eyes on Susannah. She meets his look with studied indifference.

Regaining his composure, Blitch assumes his usual evangelistic manner and brazenly asks his surprised listeners to make amends for the wrong they have done the innocent young girl sitting at the rear of the church. As before, all turn and stare at Susannah. When Blitch urges them to ask her pardon for their unjust accusations, they look back at him in mingled disbelief and contempt. Then, moving as one, they stalk out of the church. When Blitch futilely calls after them that Susannah is innocent, Mrs. McClean sardonically informs him that they will see him at the baptism.

Blitch stands in helpless confusion. Then he recoils as he hears Susannah, still sitting motionless, break into devastating, half-suppressed laughter. Shuffling up the aisle toward her, he stammers that he tried to help her—which Susannah acknowledges with icy contempt. When she starts to leave, Blitch clumsily puts a detaining hand on her shoulder. She jerks fiercely away and walks toward the door. Blitch calls after her: "Fergive!" She replies caustically: "I've fergot what that word means." Brokenly, the evangelist repeats the prayer of Christ.

[*Scene Five*] Susannah's porch at sundown of the same day. She stands leaning against a post, staring into space. Sam comes in carrying his bag of game and his shotgun. Somewhat drunk, he tries to greet his sister with a kiss, but she does not respond. When she shrinks from his embrace he irritably demands to know what has happened to her. "Everything," she replies curtly. Then over a turbulent accompaniment she pours out her terrible story.

Yes . . . she went to the meeting, just as her brother—who was out getting drunk—had asked her to. The preacher followed her home . . . and she let him stay all night. Furiously Sam asks her why. Susannah screams back that she was tired of fighting, tired of insults and accusations, too tired to care. In a paroxysm of rage, Sam curses the preacher and shouts that he will kill him before the day is over. Scoffing at his threat, Susannah goes into the house.

For a moment Sam stands motionless. Then with sinister deliberation he takes his shotgun from the rack, walks slowly down the steps into the yard, where he breaks into a run and disappears. There is silence. From the distance comes the sound of a baptismal hymn.

Inside the house, Susannah calls to Sam that supper is ready. Hearing no answer, she comes out on the porch, looks up at the empty gun rack and is transfixed by the fearsome realization of what is about to happen. From the distance comes the sound of a gunshot. Susannah collapses on her knees, sobbing that she would have killed her brother to keep him from doing what she knows he now has done.

Little Bat runs in shrieking that Sam shot the preacher while he was baptizing—"and he was prayin' for you afore he died." He warns her that the people believe that she put Sam up to killing the preacher. Now they are coming to run her out of the valley—and to hang Sam when they find him. As the boy begs her to escape while there is still time, a humming chorus indicates the approach of the crowd. Bat wildly rushes away. As the mob storms in, the humming crescendoes into an ensemble—"Git out'n the valley, Susannah."

It drones on like a death chant as McClean, Hayes, Ott and Gleaton come forward to denounce her for plotting the murder of the preacher who prayed for her soul. They are stung to fury when Susannah suddenly bursts into maniacal laughter. Followed by the mob, the Elders close in, but stop in their tracks when Susannah dodges into the house and emerges with a gun in her hands. As she menacingly brandishes the weapon, McClean and the mob try to cow her with the warning that "there'll come a reckonin' time." With a show of bravado, they raise their fists—but gradually retreat. Bursting into derisive laughter, Susannah puts the gun on the rack.

She turns to see Little Bat sneaking up on the porch. She looks at him with loathing, but with a seductive movement of her body invites him to come closer and "love her up some." When he puts his arms around her she slaps him savagely across the face.

Bat staggers back, then runs howling away with Susannah's terrible laughter ringing in his ears. When he is out of sight, her laughter stops abruptly. She moves to the doorway, where she stands silent, erect and unafraid. The curtain falls.

IL TABARRO

(*The Cloak*)

by GIACOMO PUCCINI

(1858–1924)

Libretto by

GIUSEPPE ADAMI

Based on *La Houppelande*, a story by Didier Gold

CHARACTERS

Michele, owner and captain of a barge	Baritone
Luigi, a stevedore	Tenor
Tinca, a stevedore	Tenor
Talpa, a stevedore	Bass
Giorgetta, wife of Michele	Soprano
Frugola, wife of Talpa	Mezzo-soprano

Stevedores, a street singer, milliners, an organ-grinder, two lovers

Place: Paris
Time: About 1850
First performance: Metropolitan Opera House, New York City,
December 14, 1918
Original language: Italian

Il Tabarro is the first one-act opera of Puccini's triptych *Il Trittico,* the second and third being *Suor Angelica* and *Gianni Schicchi*. It is a story of passion, violence and revenge in the *verismo* pattern of *Cavalleria Rusticana* and *Pagliacci,* concerned with tragic upheaval in the lives of simple people.

Its setting is the Paris of *La Bohème* (written twenty years earlier), but not the gay, happy-go-lucky world of the artists. *Il Tabarro* has to do with the harsh existence of working people, who can only dream of a better life they never will know.

The opera never achieved the success of *Gianni Schicchi,* and it is revived only occasionally. Yet it has a plot of great dramatic thrust and a sound harmonic structure embellished by glowing melody. Despite its comparative obscurity, it is one of Puccini's most effective works.

The entire action takes place on Michele's barge anchored at a wharf on the Seine. A gangplank connects it with the wharf. The barge is neat and brightly painted, with its flat roof surrounded by a low, white fence lined with pots of geraniums. Laundry is drying on a clothesline; a cage of canaries hangs beside the cabin door.

As the scene opens, Michele, pipe in mouth, is sitting at the helm of the barge and staring into the sunset. Giorgetta is busy taking in her wash, watering her plants and cleaning the canary cage. Stevedores are carrying sacks of cement out of the hold and loading them on a dray on the wharf. From the distance comes the long-drawn whistle of a tugboat, mingled with the moan of foghorns.

To the accompaniment of a barcarolelike rhythm in the orchestra, which continues during most of the opening scene, the stevedores sing a kind of sea chanty ("Oh! Issa! oh!"). Its theme is that they must hurry to get the day's work done, because if they are late getting home their sweethearts may wander off with some other lads.

Giorgetta, pausing in her work, asks Michele what he is thinking about as he stares into the sunset and smokes his pipe ("O Michele? Non sei stanco"). He shrugs off the question and asks if the stevedores have finished. In a brief refrain ("Han lavorato tanto") Giorgetta expresses her concern for the hard-working stevedores, then asks Michele if she may serve them a drink as a reward for their day's work. Michele commends her for her thoughtfulness and tells her to bring out a bottle of wine.

Teasing her about thinking of the stevedores instead of her husband, Michele affectionately tries to embrace her. She resists him, and when he asks for a kiss she offers only her cheek. With a sharp look at her, Michele releases her and goes below deck. The chorus of stevedores again is heard briefly.

A moment later Luigi crosses the gangplank to the barge. Obviously fatigued, he grumbles about the never-ending heat ("Si soffoca, padrona"). This marks the beginning of an ensemble which blends the voices of Giorgetta and Luigi, then Tinca and Talpa. With a passionate look at Luigi, Giorgetta remarks that the heat, like everything else, will have an end. She adds that the wine she is about to serve him will help matters. As she goes into the cabin, Tinca and Talpa, each carrying a sack of cement, stagger up out of the hold. Like Luigi, they complain about the heat and their backbreaking work.

Giorgetta reappears with a pitcher of wine and pours out drinks for the three men. Luigi gaily sings that "a good friend" has come to their assistance, and the four drain their glasses. Spying an organ-grinder passing on the wharf, Luigi throws him a coin and asks him to play. The man obliges with a number comically out of tune. Tinca and Talpa roar out the praises of wine; Tinca is rapidly getting drunk.

Looking seductively at Luigi, Giorgetta sings that the only kind of music that interests her is music one can dance to. Tinca drunkenly offers to be her partner and she good-naturedly accepts. Luigi twits the stevedore about his clumsiness, then pushes him aside and takes Giorgetta in his arms. They dance together like lovers.

Suddenly Michele emerges from the hold. Giorgetta and Luigi abruptly stop dancing. Motioning the organ-grinder to leave, Luigi throws him another coin, then follows Tinca and Talpa down into the hold. Michele approaches Giorgetta, who makes an obvious effort to appear casual.

A colloquy follows as she asks him if he plans to sail the next day. ("Dunque, che cosa credi?"). Through the music of the dialogue comes the voice of a street singer who now appears on the wharf. His plaintive cry, "Who will buy my latest songs" ("Chi vuol l'ultima canzonetta"), is in ironic contrast to the nagging conversation between Giorgetta and Michele. She tries to find out why he has decided to leave Luigi and the other stevedores behind. As for Luigi, Michele answers, it would be better for him if he stayed in Paris—and, in any case, his mind is not always on his work.

Listening with growing irritation, Giorgetta turns away momentarily and becomes aware of the sunset. In a brief refrain ("Già discende la sera") she admires its flaming beauty, but then reflects sadly that the end of another day also brings closer the end of summer. Forebodingly, she murmurs that the sun seems drenched in blood.

Her thoughts are interrupted by the approach of Frugola. Giorgetta sarcastically comments that, as usual, she probably is chasing her husband. Michele growls that she has good reason—he drinks too much. The real reason, Giorgetta retorts, is that Frugola is jealous.

From this point on, Puccini blends several musical themes into a remarkable ensemble which focuses the action of a complex scene. As Giorgetta and Michele continue their dialogue, the street singer and an itinerant harpist, on a street across the Seine, entertain a group of milliners who have just come out of their shop. The street singer favors the girls with one of his ballads, "Primavera, non cercare," a bittersweet story about a girl named Mimi whose heart was broken in a love affair. The girls, moved by Mimi's plight, buy copies of the ballad and then go on their way singing its refrain, "anche il cuore di Mimi!"

Meanwhile, Giorgetta and Michele continue their bickering. He patiently tries to discover why she is angry with him: has he mistreated or neglected her? No, Giorgetta answers—then bursts out that his brooding is driving her to distraction. She cries that she would rather be cursed and beaten—anything but this silence. Again she demands to know why he is acting so strangely. Instead of answering, Michele goes toward the prow of the barge and checks the mooring. With mocking effect, the chorus of the milliners is heard in the distance, repeating the "Mimi" refrain about unrequited love. Giorgetta, listening, murmurs that she is always happy when she is in Paris. Michele nods significantly.

The scene is interrupted by the entrance of Frugola, who comes aboard carrying a bag filled with junk she has collected. A frowzy, unkempt woman of about fifty, she shouts an effusive greeting. Michele responds with a wave of his hand, then retreats below deck. Frugola loudly asks Giorgetta if she has seen Talpa, her husband. In an ensuing refrain ("il mio uomo") she explains that, to relieve his aching muscles, she rubbed him down with rum. He absorbed enough through his pores to make him drunk.

Then she opens her sack and enthusiastically displays its contents—a fantastic jumble of odds and ends. In a refrain introduced by a swaying, harplike figure in the orchestra, she describes her wares ("Se tu sapessi"). She offers Giorgetta a comb—"good as new"—then enumerates the rest of her treasures. There are scraps of silk and lace, silver buckles, golden lockets—all souvenirs of forgotten love affairs or moments of tender passion.

When Giorgetta points to a certain package, Frugola rambles on that it contains fresh beef for her beloved cat, Corporal. With that she launches into extravagant praise of her pet ("Cuore di manzo per Caporale"). He is a very superior cat, she sings, and her only true friend. Human beings may betray her, but Corporal never will. He has a most admirable philosophy of life: being a king in a cave is better than being a slave in a palace. It is better to be satisfied with two slices of beef than to hunger for love and die of a broken heart.

Frugola's babbling is interrupted as Talpa and Luigi come out of the hold with Michele. A scene in ensemble follows. Michele asks Luigi if he will help load another cargo tomorrow ("O Luigi, domani"). Tinca and the other stevedores emerge from the hold and start to cross the gangplank. When Frugola catches sight of Tinca she begins to upbraid him about his drinking. If she were his wife, she tells him, she would nag him into sobriety. And take all the joy out of life, Tinca retorts. Only in drinking, he goes on, can one forget the bitterness of living.

Luigi, who has been listening intently to the conversation, enlarges on Tinca's point of view in one of the opera's major arias, "Hai ben ragione." Tinca is right, he sings. For the poor there is no other escape from misery. They are doomed to live by the sweat of their brows without hope of reward. The doors to a better life are forever closed against them. It is useless to struggle—the wise man accepts this as a fact of life and bows to his fate. There is only one answer—drinking, Tinca comments sardonically. Giorgetta angrily tells him to be quiet. Taken aback, Tinca slinks away.

In contrast to Luigi's bitter mood, Frugola sings lightheartedly that her dream of happiness is a cottage in the country ("Ho sognato una casetta"). Giorgetta declares that the place of her dreams is Paris—she blossoms like a flower when she breathes the air of the city ("E ben altro il mio sogno"). She laments that Michele will not leave this dismal existence aboard his barge.

Then she recalls the village outside Paris where she and Luigi grew up. It was Belleville, Luigi explains. In an ensuing duet ("Come me, l'ha nel sangue!") he and Giorgetta reminisce about the happy days of their childhood. In the climax of the duet ("Ma chi lascia il sobborgo") they sing that their memories of the gay and exciting life in Belleville are tinged with sorrow, because they know they never can return to the place which is their true home. The duet ends on a soaring unison phrase. Frugola, deeply moved, murmurs that she can understand their longing and sorrow.

Talpa dispels this nostalgic mood by inviting Giorgetta and Luigi to have supper with him and his wife. Luigi declines, explaining that he must have a talk with Michele. Talpa and Frugola leave arm in arm, repeating the plaintive refrain about the cottage of their dreams.

Alone, Giorgetta and Luigi voice their emotions in an impassioned duet ("O Luigi! Bada a te!"). When Giorgetta softly repeats his name, Luigi impulsively tries to take her in his arms. Fighting for self-control, she warns him that Michele might find them together—and he would kill them both if he found out they were lovers. But in the next moment they declare that not even the threat of death can keep them from each other's arms.

They hear Michele approaching and quickly draw apart. Luigi asks the skipper if he will take him along on the trip to Rouen. Michele scoffs at the suggestion, telling Luigi that there is no work to be had in that city. As Luigi shrugs resignedly, Michele leaves to attend to his barge duties.

No sooner has he gone than Giorgetta, tormented by anxiety and desire, asks Luigi why he wants to go to Rouen ("Dimmi: perchè gli hai chiesto"). This marks the beginning of one of the finest duets in the opera. Luigi replies that he asked to go because he cannot bear to share her with someone else. To a blazing orchestral accompaniment, they abandon themselves to their emotions and reiterate their avowals.

As they become calmer, Giorgetta tells Luigi to return later for their rendezvous. She will leave the gangplank in place; he is to wait until she gives him the signal by lighting a match—as she has done before. Its flame will be like a star in heaven, she sings, a blazing symbol of their love. The duet continues with increasing intensity. At its climax, Luigi cries that if Giorgetta spurned his love he would kill her in his jealous madness and fashion her heart into a beautiful jewel. Giorgetta, fearing that her husband is approaching, frantically signs Luigi to leave. He goes quickly. There is a suspenseful pause in the music.

Then Michele, carrying a lantern, comes out of the cabin. Looking sharply at his wife he asks why she has not gone to bed ("Perchè non vai a letto?"). Here begins another of the opera's great duets. First, in quasi-recitative, they talk about Luigi and Tinca. Giorgetta commends her husband for keeping Luigi on the crew, but urges him to dismiss Tinca, who drinks too much. Michele remarks dryly that he drinks only to keep from strangling his unfaithful wife. Giorgetta testily says she is not interested in family gossip.

As the music takes on a deeper emotional quality, Michele comes closer to Giorgetta and asks why she no longer loves him. To evade answering, she says she is tired and will go to bed—although she dreads the hot, gloomy cabin. Michele, trying to soften her mood, tenderly recalls the happier days when they shared the cabin with their baby. Shaken by the memory, Giorgetta sobs. Michele sings eloquently of the times when he held her in his arms, when he kissed her and enfolded her warm body in his cloak.

But that golden September is gone, Michele sings in somber phrases. Now their baby is dead and their lives no longer mean anything. He himself has only his old age to offer a young wife. Stricken by his pleading for her love, Giorgetta tries to end the ordeal, but Michele will not let her go. He reminds her of how much they once were in love and abjectly begs her to give him back her heart. He holds out his arms to her.

Giorgetta protests that, neither for herself nor for him, can things be the same again; life has changed them both. Michele stubbornly refuses to believe that this has come to pass. In complete despair, Giorgetta tells him she is going to bed, then hurries into the cabin. Glaring after her, Michele snarls in a savage undertone: "You harlot!" ("Sgualdrina!"). The outburst is underscored by somber chords in the bass.

At length he gets up and attends to the red and green navigating lights of his barge. In ironic contrast to his turbulent mood, two lovers passing on the wharf are heard singing that lips are made for kissing and that the precious hours of night must not be wasted ("Bocca di rosa fresca"). As their voices die away, the stillness is broken by the sound of a bugle from a distant military barracks.

Michele turns and stalks slowly toward the cabin, where he stands listening intently. In tones of despair, he murmurs: "Nulla! Silenzio!" There is a menacing drum roll and a trombone passage, dark and foreboding. This introduces the magnificent aria which is the musical climax of the opera. Tortured by suspicion and jealousy, Michele wonders who is the lover for whom Giorgetta, lying sleepless in the cabin, is waiting

("Chi l'ha trasformata?"). Is it Talpa? He is too old. Tinca? She despises that sot. Luigi? No . . . he spoke first of leaving the crew, then asked as a favor to be taken along to Rouen.[1]

The thought of his mysterious rival goads Michele to wild fury. He cries that he will seek out the guilty man . . . beat him . . . crush him . . . scream into his face: "It is you! It is you!" ("Sei tu! Sei tu!"). A terrible destiny has chained their lives together and now they both face the black abyss ("giù insiem nel gorgo più profondo!"). A rising and falling chromatic figure in the accompaniment heightens the impact of the words. The aria ends on a phrase of overpowering menace: "La pace è nella morte!" ("Only your death will bring me peace").

Exhausted by his rage, Michele sinks down beside the tiller and slowly lights his pipe. Luigi, watching from the shadows of the wharf, mistakes the flare of the match for Giorgetta's signal, runs across the gangplank and leaps aboard. His action is reflected in a hurrying rhythmic figure in the orchestra. Michele waits until the intruder comes closer. Suddenly recognizing Luigi, he springs at him like a wild animal and grasps him by the throat. Luigi screams in terror. Over a clamorous accompaniment, Michele tries to force a confession from his captive, who momentarily struggles free and whips out his knife. Michele twists his arm until the knife clatters to the deck. Now Luigi will go to Rouen as he asked, Michele howls, but as a bloated corpse in the river.

Then in a paroxysm of fury he again seizes Luigi by the throat and shouts that only a confession will free him. Luigi gasps that it is true: he loves her. Relentlessly tightening his grip, Michele forces Luigi to repeat the words. The boy's answer is cut short in the final convulsion of death. As though demented, Michele glares down at the body.

Suddenly Giorgetta, calling his name, rushes from the cabin. Michele quickly lifts Luigi's body in his arms and covers it with his cloak. Wailing that she is frightened, Giorgetta comes closer. With stony calm, Michele murmurs that he was aware that she was not able to go to sleep. Giorgetta, with a deliberate touch of coquetry, asks him to forgive her thoughtless words and rude behavior, then asks if she may sit beside him.

With sinister meaning that even now is lost on Giorgetta, Michele in turn asks: "Where? Under my cloak?" The cloak, Giorgetta answers, reminds her of something he often told her: every person carries a mysterious cloak, under which he conceals either "a secret joy or a secret sorrow."

[1] In another version of this scene (as given in the Ricordi score, copyright 1918), Michele remains seated, wraps his cloak around him and stares out over the Seine. In the aria he addresses his thoughts to the river, which he compares to endlessly flowing eternity ("Scorri, fiume eterno").

Michele leaps to his feet, flings back the cloak, and in a thunderous voice shouts: "And sometimes a crime!" ("Qualche volta un delitto!"). Luigi's body rolls grotesquely at Giorgetta's feet. She staggers back with a scream of horror.

Michele violently seizes her and, forcing her down, thrusts her face against the face of her dead lover. The curtain falls.

TANCREDI

by GIOACCHINO ROSSINI

(1792–1868)

Libretto by

GAETANO ROSSI

Based on episodes in *Gerusalemme Liberata* (*Jerusalem Liberated*), by the Italian poet Torquato Tasso (1544–95), and *Tancrède*, by the French author Voltaire (François Marie Arouet—1694–1778)

CHARACTERS

Argirio, ruler of Syracuse	Tenor
Amenaide, his daughter	Soprano
Tancredi, an exiled Syracusan knight	Contralto
Orbazzano, a Syracusan nobleman	Bass
Isaura, a noblewoman, confidante of Amenaide	Soprano
Roggiero, Tancredi's squire	Contralto

Knights, nobles, pages, people of the court

Place: Syracuse, an ancient city on the east coast of Sicily—today the site of the modern city of Siracusa
Time: Circa A.D. 1050
First performance: Teatro La Fenice, Venice, February 6, 1813
Original language: Italian

The first Rossini opera staged at La Fenice, *Tancredi* is the eighth of his thirty-seven operas and his first *opera seria*—composed when he was twenty-one years old. Its beginnings were rather hectic. The premiere and the next performance were interrupted by the illness of the two leading ladies. The first version with its "happy ending" for Tancredi and Amenaide was changed to the "tragic ending" closer to Voltaire's drama, in which Tancredi dies in the presence of Argirio and Amenaide. But this ending proved unpopular, and so the first ending was restored. The opera became an international favorite. Everywhere, opera buffs sang or whistled the phrase, "Mi rivedrai; ti rivedro," from the famous cavatina "Di tanti palpiti."

Tancredi was first heard in New York in Italian on December 31, 1825, then vanished from operatic stages for half a century. In recent times, there was a staging at the Maggio Musicale Fiorentino (Florence) in 1952, with Giulietta Simionato and Teresa Stitch-Randall, and a concert version in London in 1959. A highly successful revival was presented March 14, 1978, under the aegis of the Opera Orchestra of New York, Eve Queler conducting, with Marilyn Horne in the title role.

In *Tancredi,* Rossini carried on the tradition of casting women (as well as castrati) in heroic male roles—with the difference that he gave more prominence to legitimate male voices than his predecessors did. Thus far the role of Tancredi has been the province of mezzos or contraltos.

The overture, in Rossini's impressive *opera seria* vein, begins with a stately *andante marcato* theme. The second part is dominated by a flowing barcarolelike melody in thirds and sixths. It ends in a typical Rossinian crescendo.

ACT ONE

[*Scene One*] A hall in the palace of Argirio, where knights, Isaura and attendants are assembled. In a chorus ("Pace, onore, fede, amore") they hail the end of the civil war between the ruling Syracusan houses of Argirio and Orbazzano. In a solo interlude, Isaura confers on the knights the sacred white scarves (*sciarpe bianche*), a symbol of valor and peace.[1] Argirio and Orbazzano enter. In a brief duet ("Se amistà verace e pura") they proclaim the end of civil strife and exhort the Sicilians to swear fealty to a united Syracuse. The assemblage responds in a lusty chorus. In ensuing recitative, Argirio announces to the knights that Orbazzano, hero of the hour, will lead the united forces of Syracuse against Solimar, the Saracen who menaces Sicily. All traitors who conspire with the foe will be put to death. Orbazzano interjects that there is yet another enemy to reckon with: the exiled Tancredi.[2] Banished in childhood from Sicily, he has long harbored plans for revenge on the land that rejected him.

Overhearing, Isaura is dismayed over the fate that awaits Tancredi if he returns from exile. Her distress increases as she hears Argirio declare

[1] An investiture similar to that in Meyerbeer's *Les Huguenots* when at the "Benediction of the Swords," the soldiers received white scarves stamped with a cross as identifying insignia in combat. It was a traditional ceremony of knighthood.

[2] Tancredi was the son of Tancred, a Norman leader (circa A.D. 1100) of the First Crusade, who achieved power in Syracuse, but was later expelled by Orbazzano. Tancredi was then said to be eleven years old.

that not only has Amenaide been espoused to Orbazzano, but that Tancredi's property has been confiscated.

Summoned by her father, Amenaide enters to the strains of a welcoming chorus ("Più dolci e placide"). She responds with the brilliant cavatina "Come dolce all'alma sia," which ends in fervent expressions of longing for Tancredi. To her consternation, Argirio informs her that everything has been decided: she is to become the happy bride of Orbazzano ("La tua fè . . . Ad Orbazzano concesso"). In an aside she manages to ask Isaura about the secret letter she sent to Tancredi urging him to return to Syracuse. As a precaution, she did not mention his name or her own. Isaura whispers that the slave—who alone knows for whom the letter is intended—already is on his way.

When Argirio and Orbazzano become suspicious of her confused demeanor, she pretends that she is overcome by the unexpected good fortune of becoming a bride. Argirio, looking at her intently, observes that his daughter obviously knows what her duty is. And so, he goes on decisively, she is to be the bride of Orbazzano.

Controlling herself, Amenaide entreats her father to postpone the nuptials for one day. This brings an angry protest from Orbazzano, but Amenaide calmly assures him that she will do her duty. She leaves, followed by the two men. Isaura, alone, laments Amenaide's dilemma ("Amenaide sventurata") in a striking recitative passage sung over a single sustained note sounded in the orchestra with sinister effect.

[*Scene Two*] A seaside park near the palace of Argirio. A skiff approaches with Roggiero, Tancredi and his four knights. They bear his banner, lance and shield, which is inscribed with the heraldic device: "Faith and Honor." Roggiero steps ashore first and cautiously looks around. Tancredi and the knights follow.

In recitative, Tancredi gives way to the emotions that overcome him as he stands once more on the soil of his beloved country—the country that has ungratefully banished him ("O patria . . . dolce e ingrata patria!"). Impulsively he kneels and kisses the ground, then thinks of the joy of meeting Amenaide ("Amenaide! O mio pensier soave!"). This leads into the beautiful cavatina "Tu che accendi questo core," Tancredi's lyrical paean to his beloved. The aria's well-known middle section, "Di tanti palpiti," virtually made the opera famous throughout the world.[3]

Tancredi sends Roggiero to Argirio's castle to tell Amenaide that a strange knight wishes to speak to her. The squire is to take careful note of her reactions, but is not to reveal Tancredi's name. He himself wishes

[3] The phrase "Mi rivedrai; ti rivedro" resembles the phrase sung by Cavaradossi in Act Three of *Tosca:* "O dolci mani."

to savor her joyful surprise at meeting him again. He then orders his knights to announce that an unknown warrior offers himself as a defender of Syracuse ("di Siracusa ai difensor").

Argirio and Amenaide enter. When Tancredi and his knights warily advance to meet them, Argirio invites them to the nuptials, which are to take place at noon. Only Amenaide and Tancredi realize that this confrontation has at last brought them face to face. When Amenaide reminds her father that he agreed to postpone the nuptials for a day, he harshly answers that the ceremony cannot be delayed. New dangers threaten Syracuse: not only has the treacherous Solimar come to claim Amenaide as the price of peace, but Tancredi is approaching with vengeance in his heart. Death, Argirio declares, awaits him. Amenaide gasps in despair.

In the first of the two principal tenor arias in the score, Argirio proclaims that the Senate has condemned all traitors to death ("Della patria ogni nemico"). The brave Orbazzano will rush from the altar to the battlefront to annihilate the treacherous invaders. Warning Amenaide not to compromise her honor and to remember her nuptial vows, he leaves.

Amenaide wonders remorsefully if her letter has persuaded Tancredi to come to Sicily at the peril of his life. As she is lamenting her ill-considered action, he steps forward and calls her name. She asks why he has dared return in the face of certain death, and implores him to flee. Although disconcerted by her fear-stricken entreaties, he declares he will defy his enemies.

In an ensuing duet ("L'aura che intorno spiri") Amenaide reiterates her warning. Tancredi—unaware that she has consented to marry his rival, Orbazzano—sings that their love will triumph over fate. Amenaide tries to explain that "things have changed"—which only makes Tancredi suspicious of her reasons for urging him to leave. On these sentiments, the duet rises to a ringing climax.

Meanwhile, Roggiero enters and overhears Amenaide's protestations and Tancredi's ardent replies. What he has heard, he sings in recitative ("Che intesi! O tradimento!") confirms his worst suspicions: Amenaide has betrayed Tancredi; Orbazzano has stolen the woman he loves and his possessions as well; his own city has condemned him to death. There is nothing left but exile or doom.

[*Scene Three*] A plaza in front of a Syracusan temple, where the wedding of Amenaide and Orbazzano is to take place. Ceremonies begin with a chorus of nobles and warriors hailing the nuptials. At the edge of the throng are Tancredi and Roggiero. Tancredi, fuming with anger, swears that the wedding will not take place. Roggiero reminds him that he is among his enemies. Tancredi scoffs at the warning, saying that no one will recognize him after his absence since childhood. When Roggiero begs him to flee, Tancredi vows he will not leave before he has taken revenge not only on his rival but on the woman who has betrayed him.

The two stand apart as the wedding party enters to an orchestral fanfare. Argirio, Amenaide and Isaura are accompanied by nobles, knights and people of the court. Argirio pompously invites all to the rites, which will symbolize an era of peace in Syracuse ("Amici, cavalieri, al tempio").

Tancredi, struggling free from Roggiero, presents himself to Argirio and asks permission to join the knights in defending the city ("Concedi tu che premier nel gran Senato"). As Amenaide and Isaura look on incredulously, Argirio accepts the offer—then embraces the very knight he has condemned to death.

Glaring at Amenaide, Tancredi intones that death is better than betrayal of "Faith and Honor"—the device that adorns his shield. Amenaide recoils at the implied accusation of infidelity. As Argirio fumes because Orbazzano has not yet appeared for the ceremony, Tancredi, in a fierce aside, denounces Amenaide for pledging her love to his rival. Thereupon she resolutely declares that she will not perjure herself, then proclaims to the stunned assemblage that even if it costs her life she will not marry Orbazzano ("O padre, cavalieri, d'Orbazzano di morte a costo").

At that moment, Orbazzano himself bursts in, overhears her and furiously shouts that she shall have the death she asks for. In his upraised hand is Amenaide's letter. Orbazzano thunders that this proof of treachery was written to Solimar, the archenemy of Syracuse; the slave who delivered it was put to death. He hands the letter to the horrified Argirio, who reads it in spoken words over foreboding chords in the orchestra: *"T'affretta; in Siracusa atteso sei . . . Gloria, ed amor t'invitano . . . Trionfa degl'inimici tuoi . . . Vieni a regnar su' questo cor, su' noi."* (*"Hasten hither; thou art expected in Syracuse . . . glory and love invite thee hither. Triumph over thine enemies; come and reign within my heart, and over us"*).

This leads into a fiery ensemble ("Ciel! che intesi? O tradimento!") as all express their reactions: Argirio, torn by grief and rage, sings that Amenaide is no longer his daughter; she herself bemoans the fatal error of the letter, but still protests her innocence; Tancredi denounces her betrayal; Orbazzano warns that death awaits her. Amenaide's plea for mercy is spurned alike by her father, Tancredi, Orbazzano and the people of the court.

Isaura alone remains loyal. She manages to escape from the avenging throng in an effort to find someone who will come to Amenaide's rescue. Meanwhile, Amenaide dares her accusers to prove her guilty. Ar-

girio and Tancredi sing that the infamy of such a daughter is beyond belief. As all lament the terrible events of this fateful day ("Quale
infausto orrendo giorno"), the chorus rises to a stupendous climax.

ACT TWO

[*Scene One*] The hall in the palace of Argirio, as in Act One. The
scene opens with a colloquy between Isaura and Orbazzano, who later
are joined by Argirio and members of the Court. Amenaide has been
imprisoned and is under the sentence of death as a traitress. Orbazzano
rages against her perfidy: once her prospective bridegroom, he is now
her chief accuser. The Senate has condemned her; only Argirio's name
is lacking on the death warrant.

At the mention of his name, Argirio enters saying that he is no longer
the father of a daughter whose duplicity is unbelievable ("Io padre più!
Non sono!"). Nevertheless he invokes the law of knighthood by which a
knight may fight in the lists as champion of a condemned woman. If he
wins, her life will be spared. Amenaide spurns Orbazzano as her champion, but refuses to name another. Furious, Orbazzano calls on Argirio
to sign the death warrant ("La morte segna della rea"). He is about to
sign when Isaura interjects: "È tua figlia!" ("She is your daughter!").

Here begins the most dramatic ensemble of the opera. In a transport
of grief and shame ("O Dio! Crudel! qual nome caro e fatal"), Argirio
cries that the mention of her name racks his heart and stays his hand
from the death warrant. While Isaura and one faction of the assemblage
beg him to show mercy, another faction, led by Orbazzano, shouts that
he must put his country's honor before paternal love. Argirio gives way
and signs the warrant as the Orbazzano faction howls approval. He
staggers away followed by the knights and the court.

As before, the lone dissenting voice is Isaura's. Whirling on Orbazzano, she excoriates him for his sadistic cruelty in turning Amenaide's
own father against her. Snarling that this will be a day of doom for all
traitors, he storms away. In a brief serene refrain Isaura prays that God
may give Amenaide courage to face her undeserved fate.

[*Scene Two*] A prison cell, where Amenaide is seen in chains. A
brief introduction sets the ominous mood of the scene. In a recitative
interlude ("Di mia vita infelice") followed by a cavatina ("O ciel, tal
sorte") she reflects on her fate: on Tancredi, who does not know she
will die because she loves him; on her wretched father, who loves her,
yet is convinced of her infamy; on her innocence stained by accusation
of a monstrous crime.

In calm resignation she sings that she is not afraid to die if one day
her lover will learn that she was faithful—and perhaps will shed a tear in

her memory ("Qualche sospir dal sen"). She collapses sobbing on a bench.

Suddenly Orbazzano comes in followed by Argirio, knights and guards. He tells Amenaide that the crowd outside is clamoring for her execution. She gasps in surprise as she sees her father. He has come, he tells her, for a last embrace and to follow her to the tomb—a loving father will forgive even in the face of death ("Ad abbracciarti; a seguirti alla tomba").

When Amenaide still protests her innocence, Orbazzano accuses her of writing the letter that is a foul document of treason. She retorts that she wrote it in the hope of saving her country, not to betray it. Orbazzano orders his knights to lead her to the execution ("Colei guidate al suo destin").

They stop in their tracks when Tancredi bars their way, saying that he will be the champion of the accused ("Fermate! Io l'accusata donna"). Turning on Orbazzano, he challenges him to combat with the traditional gesture of knighthood—throwing his gauntlet at his adversary's feet. Orbazzano picks it up, demanding to know who his challenger is (in effect assuming the role of Amenaide's champion—even though spurned by her). You will know, Tancredi replies, when you fall in combat. (At this point only Amenaide knows who he really is.)

But when she acclaims him as her champion, Tancredi scorns her, still regarding her as the promised bride of Orbazzano. Argirio again gratefully embraces him, still unaware that the unknown knight is his sworn enemy. Tancredi declares he will fight for her, traitress though she may be. A ringing duet follows ("L'indegna odiar dovrei") in which Orbazzano and Tancredi sing that they cannot hate this woman, and they will fight in the lists to expunge her guilt and to restore the honor and glory of the country she has betrayed. They rush off to battle.

Isaura comes in for a final meeting with the doomed Amenaide, who asks for news of her champion. He has fought for her, Isaura says, even though he still believes she is unfaithful. As they anxiously await the outcome of the combat, Argirio enters and tells how he escorted the rivals to the lists before an immense throng of spectators ("Il tuo campion guidai"). The trumpets gave the signal, then the two knights clashed in battle. Argirio confesses he could not witness the encounter, and left the scene.

Amenaide, falling to her knees, prays for her champion ("Gran Dio! Deh tu proteggi"). On the brink of her own death, she thinks only of her valiant defender. She prays for his victory in the lists ("Giusto Dio che umile adoro") so that she may live to assure him of her innocence and devotion.

She is startled by the sound of a triumphal chorus hailing the conqueror. The crowd shouts that Orbazzano has been slain by her champion ("Estinto. Dell'eroe, che per te ha vinto"). Amenaide, beside herself with joy, expresses her happiness in soaring coloratura phrases over the chorus that climaxes the scene. Saved from death by Tancredi's victory, she leaves her cell. Only Isaura remains. In a brief recitative passage ("Quante vicende omai") she reflects on the caprice of fate that brings joy and sorrow on the same day.

[*Scene Three*] The scene opens with a stirring triumphal march as the victorious Tancredi rides through the shouting throngs in Syracuse ("O laudate, o populi"). With him in his festooned carriage is Roggiero.

The procession suddenly halts when Tancredi steps from the carriage and, to the utter consternation of his knights, announces that his destiny commands him to leave Syracuse forever ("Ma un destin crudele"). When Amenaide tries to detain him, he stares at her contemptuously, observing that he has saved her life—which should be satisfaction enough. If she still desires his death, she shall have her wish.

Here begins another of the opera's great duets. Tancredi refuses to listen to Amenaide's denial of guilt, although confessing to himself that he still loves her. She swears that she has been faithful. The duet rises to a dazzling coloratura climax as Tancredi says farewell and Amenaide sings that she will follow him. In a frenzied gesture she tears away her dress and offers him her naked bosom, crying: "E qui sfoga il tuo furor"—"Here then, take your revenge." As she sobs in despair, Tancredi turns and strides away. When Roggiero tries to follow, Tancredi motions him back.

When Tancredi and Amenaide both leave the scene, Roggiero turns to find Isaura. A brief colloquy in recitative follows. Roggiero declares he will not abandon Tancredi to his exile—he must not be left alone because of Amenaide's perfidy. Isaura exhorts him to join Tancredi and convince him that Amenaide is guiltless.

Then she discloses that she alone knows the fatal secret that has torn the lovers from each other. An oath seals her lips, but the time is near when she will speak the word that will unravel this tragic mystery. There has been too much suffering . . . too much weeping, she adds as she leaves ("Già troppo si penò, si pianse assai").

Roggiero voices the hope that Isaura's revelation will finally reconcile the lovers. In an ensuing aria ("Torni alfin ridente e bella") he reflects on the prospects of future happiness for Amenaide and Tancredi.

[*Scene Four*] A cave in a mountainside, where the self-exiled Tancredi has taken refuge. A brooding orchestral interlude reflects his hopeless mood. He wonders to what strange place his despair has led him. Only the wailing wind answers ("Dove son io? Di quei torrenti il fragore venti"). Nature itself has turned against him as he wanders on alone ("Il tristo abbandono di natura"). In the following cavatina ("Ah! che scordar non so") he sings that he cannot forget Amenaide even though she has betrayed him. Overwhelmed by grief he goes back into the cave.

Suddenly from the distance comes the chorus of knights searching for Tancredi to lead them in defending Syracuse from the onslaught of the Saracens ("Regna il terror nella città"). Led by Argirio, Isaura, Amenaide and Roggiero, they advance toward the cave. As Amenaide calls his name, Tancredi appears. Staring at her, he sardonically asks if she is on her way to join Solimar, and thus crown her treachery.

Ignoring her agonized denials he promises to heed the knights' call to arms; he will die not only for his country but for the woman who has betrayed him ("Taci, è vano quel pianto"). In the aria "Perchè turbar la calma," he upbraids Amenaide for shattering the solitude of his exile, adding disdainfully that he will abandon her to her remorse and shame. But he pauses in his diatribe when she sinks sobbing at his feet.

The knights break in with a thunderous call to battle ("Vieni al campo") with Solimar. In an obbligato, Tancredi sings that only he who has loved can measure the weight of his grief. He rushes away at the head of his knights. From the distance comes the clamor of battle and Amenaide wails that Tancredi is now sealing his own doom. Argirio leaves to join the knights.

Suddenly the tumult ceases.[4] Amenaide cries out in horror as she sees her father returning with a group of soldiers who are carrying Tancredi, fatally wounded. Argirio reports that Tancredi was victorious—but at the cost of his own blood. Dying, he repeats Amenaide's name. Wild with grief, she asks him if he still believes her guilty—and again hears him answer that she has betrayed him ("Ah! M'hai tradito!").

But in his final moments he learns the truth. Argirio tells him that the fatal letter, branded by the Senate as proof of treason, was written not to Solimar but to himself as an act of love and loyalty.

Looking up at Amenaide, Tancredi asks if she loves him. Weeping bitterly, she replies that she has always loved him. Then, he murmurs desolately, it is hard for me to die ("Che m'è grave il morir"). With his last breath he asks Argirio to place "my bloodstained hand" in that of Amenaide's and bless their union as man and wife so that he can die as the husband of the woman he loves. Tancredi dies in Amenaide's arms, murmuring: "Ti lascio . . . addio." The curtain falls.

[4] From this point, the opera as described here follows the so-called "tragic ending," closer to Voltaire's *Tancrède*. It was staged in Ferrara March 30, 1813.

LES TROYENS
(*La Prise de Troie, Les Troyens à Carthage*)
by HECTOR BERLIOZ
(1803–69)

Libretto by the composer

Largely based on the first, second and fourth books of the *Aeneid*,
by Vergil (Publius Vergilius Maro), 70–19 B.C., Roman poet

CHARACTERS

Cassandra, a Trojan prophetess, daughter of King Priam and Queen Hecuba	Mezzo-soprano
Dido, a Tyrian princess, founder and Queen of Carthage	Mezzo-soprano
Anna, her sister	Contralto
Aeneas, Trojan hero, son of Anchises and Venus	Tenor
Ascanius, son of Aeneas	Mezzo-soprano
Coroebus, lover of Cassandra	Baritone
Panthus, a Trojan priest	Bass
Iopas, a Tyrian poet	Tenor
Narbal, Dido's minister of state	Bass
Hylas, a sailor	Tenor
Hector (as a vision)	Bass

Populace, warriors, sentinels, shades, nymphs, satyrs

Place: Troy and Carthage
Time: Antiquity
First performance: (Les Troyens à Carthage) Théâtre Lyrique,
Paris, November 4, 1863
Original language: French

Les Troyens, Berlioz' third stage work, is his acknowledged operatic
masterpiece. This titanic score—in its original form comprising almost
five hours of music—is one of the most grandiose creations in the history
of opera. Sir Donald Tovey called it a "gigantic and convincing master-

piece of music drama," and Romain Rolland regarded it as the *Paradise Lost* of music.

Yet in some respects the opera was a failure. To begin with, the original proved too long for one evening. Berlioz himself wrote to a colleague: "My score is far too long." In any case, he was persuaded to divide the work into two parts: the first two acts of the original five became *La Prise de Troie;* the remaining three became *Les Troyens à Carthage.* It was the latter section which was produced for the first time in Paris.

Misfortune beset the premiere. The singers were underrehearsed and did not understand their roles; the stage mechanism was woefully inadequate for so complicated a production. Finally, the public could not understand the composer's unconventional musical treatment of his subject matter. *Les Troyens* ran for twenty-two performances, then vanished from the stage.

The opera emerged from oblivion some sixteen years later, when it was presented in concert form. The first complete version was given under the baton of Felix Mottl in Karlsruhe on December 6 and 7, 1890. A year later *La Prise de Troie* was performed at Nice and at the Paris Opéra; *Les Troyens à Carthage* was revived by the Opéra-Comique in 1892. But two decades elapsed before Paris finally heard the original opera—in a version somewhat condensed for a single evening performance in 1921.

A subsequent production of the entire work—again with minor cuts—was given by an amateur company in Glasgow in 1935. After another hiatus of some twenty years, interest in the opera revived to such a degree that some critics wondered why this masterpiece had been so long neglected. From about 1957 to the present there have been notable revivals—both staged and in concert form—in Paris, London, Glasgow, Vienna (1976) and America (American Opera Society, the San Francisco Opera [1966] and the Metropolitan Opera [1974]).

Berlioz, like Wagner, wrote his own libretto. The Trojan legend as a subject for a grand opera had been suggested to him by the Princess Carolyne von Sayne-Wittgenstein, the companion of Franz Liszt. The idea had a special appeal for Berlioz—the Vergilian epic had been a favorite of his since childhood. He focused the plot of his opera on the story of the fall of Troy and the tragic romance of Dido and Aeneas.

"In form," writes Jacques Barzun in his *Berlioz and His Century,* "both poem and score carried forward . . . the Berlioz principle: choosing musical situations and linking them by the shortest path of recitative. Between larger sections there are no links. The hearer must make the mental jumps with the composer. Yet such is the dramatic force of the music that one need not memorize a libretto. That Troy fell to the Greeks and that Aeneas abandoned Dido is really all the information one requires."

(NOTE: In the following description of the plot, acts and scenes are designated in conformity with the original score.)

ACT ONE
La Prise de Troie
The Capture of Troy

[*Scene One*] The action begins on a day in the tenth year of the Trojan War when the Trojans discover that the besieging Greek army has vanished. Gathered at the site of the enemy's deserted camp, the people—deluded into thinking that the Greeks have broken off the siege—sing the exuberant opening chorus, "Ah! quel bonheur de respirer l'air pur." They rejoice that they are again able to breathe the air of freedom after ten years of war.

They exclaim ("Que de débris!") over the weapons that litter the battlefield—swords, helmets, shields—then recoil in momentary terror as they come upon a grim object. It is the tomb of Achilles, raised by the Greeks in memory of the slain hero. But soon their attention is diverted by another Greek memento, the Wooden Horse ("Ce cheval colossal"). As the people rush pell-mell to view it more closely, Cassandra appears.

[*Scene Two*] Staring after them, she voices her tormenting forebodings in the aria "Les Grecs ont disparu." She sings that she saw the ghost of the slain Trojan hero Hector—itself a portent of catastrophe. And now the Trojans, with King Priam himself leading their drunken celebration over a supposed victory, do not realize they are doomed.

This unhappy King ("Malheureux roi!"), Cassandra intones in a continuation of the aria, will vanish into eternal night—and with him the entire race of Trojans. In anguish she cries that when she tells of the horror she foresees, no one will believe her.

[*Scene Three*] At this point Coroebus comes in and excitedly asks her to join him in the victory celebration. Shocked at his careless gaiety, Cassandra replies that the hour of doom is near. Coroebus implores her to forget her groundless fears and to come with him ("Reviens à toi"). This marks the beginning of a long duet. In vain she prophesies that soon the streets of Troy will run red with blood, that the temple virgins will be dragged naked into the streets and raped. In vain she begs Coroebus to flee before he himself is killed by the Greeks.

But her lover refuses to leave her. In hopeless despair, Cassandra finally relents. She asks for a final kiss to seal their doomed betrothal ("Et mon chaste baiser"), then faints in Coroebus' arms.

[*Scene Four*] An open space before the walls of Troy, where the victory celebration is to continue and where an altar to Pallas Athena has been set up. A triumphal procession enters, led by King Priam and Queen Hecuba. With them are their son Helenus and daughter Polyxena, Aeneas at the head of his soldiers, and his son Ascanius, who leads in a group of children. Also in the procession are Coroebus, Panthus, the priests of Jupiter and Neptune, Trojan dignitaries, magistrates and soldiers. All join in a mighty chorus of thanks to the Trojan gods for Troy's deliverance from the Greeks ("Dieux protecteurs de la ville éternelle").

Next, a mock combat of young warriors is staged for the entertainment of the King and Queen. At its conclusion the mood of the scene changes abruptly. Andromache, the widow of Hector, enters leading her young son Astyanax. Clad in white robes of mourning, she takes him to the altar as the people express their pity in a solemn choral phrase ("Andromaque et son fils! Ô destin!"). Astyanax places flowers on the altar while his mother kneels and prays. Then she escorts him to the throne and presents him to Priam and Hecuba, who give the boy their blessing.

Meanwhile, the brooding figure of Cassandra looms in the background. To herself she murmurs the sinister prophecy that Andromache is doomed to even greater disaster than that which will befall Troy. The widow and her son leave the scene as the people again comment sympathetically.

[*Scene Five*] Suddenly Aeneas makes his way through the crowd and tells Priam that he has received word of a frightful disaster that has overtaken Laocoön, the High Priest of Neptune, and his two sons ("Du peuple et des soldats, ô roi"). When a group of Trojans urged that the Wooden Horse be taken into the city as a trophy, Laocoön warned that it had been left there by the treacherous Greeks for some evil purpose—and not, as some Trojans believed, as an offering to Pallas Athena.

With that the priest plunged a lance into the horse's flank. A hollow groan reverberated. Then, without warning, two enormous serpents reared up from the sea, coiled themselves around Laocoön and his two sons and devoured them before the eyes of the horror-stricken Trojans.

The victory celebration erupts into panic, with the people crying that Laocoön's fate was a sign that the gods were angry over his sacrilegious act. The tragedy is commented on in a thunderous ensemble, "Châtiment effroyable," one of the most spectacular numbers in the opera.

Aeneas orders the Horse to be brought into Troy at once. All shout approval. The strains of the "Trojan March" are heard as the crowd rushes away. Cassandra, standing to one side, again sounds her warning —and again no one listens. She wails that she cannot bear the sight of her people singing and dancing on the brink of the abyss ("Non, je ne verrai pas la déplorable fête!"). Crying that fire and death lurk in the entrails of the Horse, Cassandra screams one final, desperate plea: "Arrêtez! Arrêtez!" The crowd surges by unheeding. As she watches the gigantic image being drawn through the gates, she moans in despair: "Le destin tient sa proie! Et Cassandre, va mourir sous les débris de Troie!" ("Fate has her prey. And Cassandra, go and die in the ruins of Troy!").

ACT TWO

[*Scene One*] Aeneas, asleep in the palace, is visited by the ghost of Hector, which warns him to flee before it is too late ("Ah! fuis, fils de Vénus!"). Troy is in ruins . . . King Priam is beyond help. Now the fate of the Trojan race is in Aeneas' hands. He is destined to lead his people to Italy, there to found a new empire which will rule the world.

[*Scene Two*] As the vision fades, Panthus, wounded and carrying images of the gods of Troy, bursts in with the news that the Greeks, springing from the Wooden Horse, massacred the Trojan soldiers, slew Priam and sacked Troy ("La ville ensanglantée"). Coroebus and armed warriors rush in and rally with Aeneas to make a last-ditch stand to save the city. In a defiant chorus ("Le désespoir dirigera nos coups") they call on Mars and the Furies to lead them into battle.

[*Scene Three*] The Temple of Vesta. A group of Trojan women, including Polyxena, are invoking the protection of the goddess Cybele ("Puissante Cybèle").

[*Scene Four*] Cassandra appears. In a vigorous aria ("Tous ne périront pas") she proclaims that not all the Trojans will die. Aeneas and his band of warriors survived the final battle, rescued some of the citizens and managed to secure some of King Priam's treasury. The Trojans are now retreating to the safety of Mount Ida.

In stricken tones Cassandra goes on to say that Coroebus was slain, and now she herself has no wish to live. She exhorts the women to kill themselves to escape the ravaging Greeks. When some of the more timid shrink back in terror, Cassandra furiously denounces them as cowards. The others, in a powerful chorus ("Complices de sa gloire"), swear they will never let the Greeks defile them and will die with Cassandra. With cries of "Italy! Italy!" they leap from the parapet of the temple or stab themselves.

As the soldiers swarm in, Cassandra plunges a dagger into her breast, withdraws it and hands it to Polyxena. Stretching her arms toward Mount Ida, Cassandra gasps "Italy!" and falls dead.

ACT THREE
Les Troyens à Carthage
The Trojans at Carthage

According to legend, Dido, a princess of Tyre, founded Carthage in north Africa, where she had taken refuge following the murder of her husband, Sychaeus, by her brother Pygmalion. At the time this section of the opera opens, the building of Carthage had been in progress for seven years.

[*Scenes One and Two*] The garden of Queen Dido's palace. The Queen is seated on her throne, with her sister Anna on one side and Narbal, her minister of state, on the other. The Carthaginians hail their Queen in a majestic chorus, "Gloire à Didon."

In a stately aria ("Nous avons vu finir sept ans à peine") Dido thanks her people for their efforts during the past seven years in building Carthage into a proud and flourishing city. In the second part of the aria ("Chers Tyriens") she exhorts them to even greater efforts to prove themselves a new race of heroes.

Dido adds, however, that at this very moment Carthage is threatened by Iarbas, the savage chieftain of the Numidians, who are marching on the city. What is worse, Dido says, this insolent barbarian is demanding her hand in marriage. Her outraged subjects swear to defend her against this interloper. Dido thanks them for their allegiance.

[*Scene Three*] Then follows a procession honoring the builders, artisans and laborers who brought Carthage into being. Led by Narbal, they pass in review before the Queen to the accompaniment of a stirring march.

[*Scene Four*] Dido and Anna are left alone and a long duet ensues, beginning with Dido's refrain "Les chants joyeux." She muses that the loyalty of her subjects has restored her happiness and has dispelled a strange fear that has been haunting her.

When Anna asks why she, the adored Queen of a beautiful realm ("Reine, d'un jeune empire"), should be afraid, Dido replies that she has been troubled by a mysterious longing. Knowingly, Anna observes that her sister is longing for love. Dido protests that she will always remain faithful to the memory of her husband ("Non, la veuve fidèle"), and points to Sychaeus' wedding ring on her finger. Anna gently reminds her that Queen Dido is still young and beautiful—and Carthage needs a king.

The duet continues in a surging flood of melody. Dido confesses that her sister's words stir a dangerous joy in her heart ("Sa voix fait naître dans mon sein"), while Anna comments that Dido cannot resist the thoughts of love that now stir her ("Ma voix fait naître dans son sein"). The duet ends as Dido impulsively calls out her husband's name, and Anna asks her forgiveness for having tempted her with thoughts of love.

[*Scene Five*] A moment later Iopas hurries in with the news that a strange fleet, seeking refuge from the storm, has anchored in the harbor. The mariners are asking an audience with the Queen. Dido tells Iopas to bid them welcome. In an ensuing aria ("Errante sur les mers") she recalls how she herself once fled from her native land to wander at the mercy of the elements without hope or haven. Remembering this, she could not now refuse help to those in a similar plight.

[*Scene Six*] Aeneas (disguised as an ordinary seaman), Ascanius, Panthus and other Trojan leaders enter to the strains of the "Trojan March." Ascanius, acting as spokesman, identifies himself and his companions as Trojans—homeless wanderers after the fall of their city. In proof, he presents Dido with symbolic gifts: the scepter of Iliona, a daughter of Priam's. Queen Hecuba's crown; and the gold-embroidered veil of Helen of Troy.

Panthus then steps forward and explains that their leader, Aeneas, is destined by the gods to sail on until he reaches Italy, where he is to found a new home for the Trojans.

[*Scene Seven*] The conversation is interrupted by Narbal, who rushes in crying that Iarbas is marching on Carthage, plundering and killing as he approaches. Thereupon Aeneas throws off his disguise. He is clad in armor, except for his helmet and buckler. Assuring Dido that he will defend her against the invader, he rallies the Carthaginians around him.

They respond in a resounding chorus ("C'est le fils de Vénus") as a soldier brings Aeneas his helmet, buckler and javelin. Confiding Ascanius to Dido's care, he leads the Carthaginians into battle with the Numidians.

[*Scene Eight*] A symphonic interlude, "Royal Hunt and Storm," now follows, with ballet, pantomime and chorus. It is a pastoral scene deep in the forest, with nymphs bathing in a pool. They hide as hunting horns are heard in the distance. A storm comes up, and hunters ride by to find shelter. Soon Dido, dressed as Diana the huntress, and Aeneas, still clad in half-armor, appear and find refuge in a grotto.

As the storm rages to its climax, a bolt of lightning splinters a huge tree and sets it afire. Sprites, nymphs and satyrs dance orgiastically around the flames. Wildly they cry "Italy! Italy!"—reminding Aeneas of his destiny. The storm gradually subsides and the woodland creatures vanish. Serene calm pervades the scene once more.

ACT FOUR

[*Scene One*] The garden of Dido's palace on the shore of the Mediterranean, where the Carthaginians are celebrating Aeneas' victory over Iarbas. Standing apart from the throng, Anna and Narbal are seen in conversation. In quasi-recitative they express concern over Dido. Captivated by Aeneas, she spends her time in feasting and hunting—to the neglect of her duties as Queen.

[*Scenes Two and Three*] Dido and Aeneas enter with Panthus and Ascanius. A victory ballet is presented. The action which follows is staged in a deliberate tableau for purposes of the plot. Dido sits on a couch, her left profile to the audience, and rests her left arm on the shoulder of Ascanius, who kneels beside her in a pose symbolic of Cupid. Aeneas sits at Dido's feet, and the others group themselves at the back of the couch.

[*Scene Four*] Dido asks Iopas to entertain her with a song. Taking up his harp, the poet obliges with a hymn to Ceres, goddess of the harvest ("Ô blonde Cérès"). But the Queen, bored and restless, stops him, saying apologetically that the music does not soothe her.

Turning to Aeneas, Dido asks him to continue his story of the fall of Troy ("Énée, daignez achever")—and particularly about the fate of Andromache. She listens intently as Aeneas recounts how Andromache had been taken into slavery by Pyrrhus, the son of Achilles, who had slain Hector ("Hélas! en esclavage réduite par Pyrrhus"). Pyrrhus fell in love with her, and his wooing erased the memory of her husband. Andromache married her captor and became the Queen of Epirus.

[*Scene Five*] Enthralled by the story, Dido sings that the example of the widowed Andromache, yielding thus to a new love, freed her from any feelings of remorse ("Tout conspire à vaincre mes remords"). Gazing passionately into her eyes, Aeneas repeats her phrase.

[*Scene Six*] This marks the beginning of the famous quintet, one of the most beautiful ensembles in the opera, blending the voices of Anna,

Iopas, Narbal, Dido and Aeneas. During the ensemble, Ascanius gently slips Dido's wedding ring from her finger. She takes it from him, but absent-mindedly leaves it lying on the couch when she rises at the conclusion of the ensemble.

All onstage turn to contemplate the beauty of the deepening twilight, expressing their emotions in a septet, another of the opera's outstanding ensembles ("Tout n'est que paix et charme"). At its close, all except Dido and Aeneas withdraw, and then follows a love duet of surpassing beauty ("Nuit d'ivresse et d'extase infinie").

It is a lyrical paraphrase of the dialogue between Jessica and Lorenzo in *The Merchant of Venice*.[1] In an undulating 6/8 tempo, the lovers sing of other lovers like themselves on an enchanted, moonlit night: Venus and Anchises, Troilus and Cressida, Diana and Endymion.

Then Dido—with a kind of mischievous irony—sings that "in such a night" the son of Venus was cold to Dido's caresses. In the same vein, Aeneas answers that Queen Dido was gently pardoned for her unjust accusations.

The lovers melt into the shadows and conclude the duet offstage. A moment later the god Mercury materializes in the moonlight. Striding up to a broken column on which Aeneas had hung his helmet and buckler, Mercury strikes the buckler three times with his caduceus— each time intoning "Italy!" Then he vanishes.

ACT FIVE

[*Scene One*] The beach at Carthage, where the sailors of the Trojan fleet have pitched their tents. Their ships are lying at anchor nearby. Aboard one of them, Hylas, a young sailor, sings a plaintive song about his longing for home ("Vallon sonore").

[*Scene Two*] Panthus and Trojan officers enter and give orders for embarkation. The priest tells the officers that Aeneas, fearing the wrath of the gods over his dallying in Carthage, will do their bidding: he will desert Dido and resume his destined quest for Italy. In an ensuing chorus ("Chaque jour voit grandir la colère des dieux") the Trojans sing that they know only too well that the gods are angry. Shrieks and groans rend the night . . . the ghosts of dead Trojans come to haunt them, all the while repeating "To Italy!" The men go aboard the ships.

[*Scene Three*] Now follows an interlude of comedy relief involving two sentinels who are marching back and forth at their post on the

[1] In Shakespeare, Act Five, Scene One: "The moon shines bright; in such a night as this,/ When the sweet wind did gently kiss the trees . . ."

beach. In salty dialogue they tick off their list of complaints: here they are in Carthage—a snug harbor where the food is good, the wine plentiful and the wenches buxom, gay and willing. And what happens? They must leave all this and start on another dangerous voyage in a harebrained search for some place called Italy. But then, they conclude resignedly, orders are orders, and soldiers must obey.

[*Scene Four*] The mood of the action changes abruptly. Aeneas enters and walks slowly toward the beach. Staring at his ships, he gives way to his gloomy thoughts in the soliloquy "Inutiles regrets! Je dois quitter Carthage!" He recalls how Dido looked at him in stunned disbelief when he told her he must leave. In vain he reminded her that not only his own destiny but that of the Trojan race is in his hands. But the look in Dido's eyes, he goes on, shattered his resolve to leave her.

In the great ensuing aria, "Ah! quand viendra l'instant," he sings that he cannot endure the agony of the final farewell. Yet he is determined to see her once again—to clasp her hands, to bathe her feet with his tears. The aria's concluding phrase, rising to a high B flat, is a cry of utter despair.

[*Scene Five*] Suddenly Aeneas staggers back, hearing a voice call his name. Then the ghosts of Priam, Coroebus, Cassandra and Hector materialize before him. Pointing accusing fingers, they warn him to leave Carthage at once ("Il faut vaincre et fonder"). Aeneas promises to go, but cries out in furious protest that the gods themselves will be to blame for the anguish he is causing Dido as the result of their divine commands.

[*Scene Six*] As the visions fade, an *agitato* variation of the "Trojan March" is heard. Aeneas gives orders to his fleet to sail at dawn. Then, turning toward the palace, he sings an impassioned farewell to Dido ("À toi mon âme").

[*Scene Seven*] Just as he concludes the refrain, Dido herself appears. A feverish colloquy ensues, beginning with the Queen's desperate entreaty. She sings ("Errante sur tes pas") that she has pursued him through night and storm to learn if his resolve to leave her is really true. Aeneas can only answer that he must obey the gods. Dido screams a curse at him and rushes away. Gazing after her in despair, Aeneas cries: "Italy!"

[*Scene Eight*] Dido's apartment in her palace. With her are Anna and Narbal. Distractedly the Queen asks them to help her persuade Aeneas not to leave her—at least to delay his departure for several days.

[*Scene Nine*] But at that moment Iopas dashes in to tell the Queen that the Trojan fleet has set sail. Beside herself with fury, Dido orders the Carthaginians to pursue Aeneas and burn his ships to the waterline ("Armez-vous, Tyriens! Carthaginois, courez!"). Then, realizing the futility of her rage, she subsides into the calm of despair. In measured, brooding phrases she recalls how she offered this treacherous adventurer a throne ("Et voilà donc la foi"). Bitterly she censures herself for not having exterminated this despicable race of Trojans . . . in revenge she should have forced Aeneas to feast on the flesh of his own son.

Then, in a paroxysm of fury, underscored by a harsh fanfare in the brass, Dido summons the priests of Pluto to officiate in a demoniac ritual of vengeance ("Du prêtre de Pluton"). She orders them to build a pyre and place upon it Aeneas' gifts to her—every memory of him must disappear in the avenging flames of hell. At her maniacal shout of "Sortez," the priests rush away to obey her.

[*Scene Ten*] Alone, Dido gives way to her madness, striking her breast and tearing her hair. Suddenly she stops, exhausted by her fury. In a grief-stricken plea she cries: "Venus, give me back your son" ("Vénus, rends-moi ton fils").

Now follows the lyrical conclusion of the monologue ("Adieu, fière cité"), marked by descending phrases of sorrow and hopelessness. Dido bids farewell to her sister Anna, to the city she founded and to her loyal subjects. Recalling Aeneas' passionate caresses, she repeats a fragment of the love duet! "Aux nuits d'ivresse." The great aria ends on a cadence that dies away into silence: "ma carrière est finie" ("my life is finished!").

[*Scene Eleven*] A terrace overlooking the sea. In the center is the funeral pyre surmounted by a couch and a bust of Aeneas, along with his toga, helmet and sword. The priests of Pluto and the Carthaginians are assembled. In a savage chorus they invoke the divinities of hell ("Dieux de l'oubli! Dieux du Ténare! Hécate . . . Érèbe . . . Chaos!").

[*Scene Twelve*] The crowd makes way for Anna and Narbal, who enter followed by Dido. She is veiled, with a chaplet encircling her brow. While the priests sing an invocation to Pluto, Anna and Narbal call down the curse of the gods on the Trojans. Dido mounts the pyre.

Throwing herself on the couch, she snatches up Aeneas' sword. But before she stabs herself she is transfixed by a vision of a conqueror who will rise from the soil of Africa to avenge her. "Hannibal," she cries, then plunges the sword into her breast. Yet even in dying she is tormented by another vision—that of imperial Rome. Gasping "Rome . . . eternal," the Queen dies in Anna's arms.

There is a great outcry from the people. In the turbulent chorus which closes the opera, the Carthaginians swear to eradicate the accursed race of Aeneas ("Haine éternelle à la race d'Énée"). But over their clamor for revenge come the sounds of the "Trojan March," symbolic of Rome's future triumph over Carthage. The curtain falls.

IL TURCO IN ITALIA

(*The Turk in Italy*)

by GIOACCHINO ROSSINI

(1792–1868)

Libretto by

FELICE ROMANI

CHARACTERS

Selim, the Turkish Pasha	Bass
Zaida, a gypsy girl in love with Selim	Mezzo-soprano
Fiorilla, a young Neapolitan wife	Soprano
Don Geronio, her husband	Bass
Don Narciso, the young lover of Fiorilla	Tenor
Prosdocimo, poet in search of a libretto	Baritone
Albazar, once Selim's confidant, now a gypsy	Tenor

Turks, gypsies, masqueraders

Place: In and around Naples
Time: Eighteenth century
First performance: La Scala, Milan, August 14, 1814
Original language: Italian

Rossini was twenty-two years old when he was commissioned by La Scala to write an opera for the opening of the 1814 season. The resounding successes of the *opera seria Tancredi* and the *opera buffa L'Italiana in Algeri*—both premiered in 1813—had set him on the road to international fame as an opera composer.

But the story goes that the Milanese at first were not very enthusiastic about *Il Turco in Italia.* They had expected something more from Rossini than an *opera buffa* with much the same plot formula as *L'Italiana in Algeri.* True enough, there was a reversal of plot: in *L'Italiana,* a suitor travels *from* Italy; in *Il Turco,* the suitor travels *to* Italy. But Rossini made many revisions, borrowing numbers from some of his other operas (*La Cenerentola, L'Italiana*) and including others (along with certain recitatives) he himself did not write. Cited as examples of this practice are Geronio's cavatina "Vado in traccia"; Albazar's Act Two aria "Ah, sarebbe troppo dolce"; the entire Act Two finale.

Despite confused and often inaccurate versions, the opera found increasing favor with the public in the early 1800s, and was performed all over Italy and in Europe and the British Isles. In Italy, there was a hiatus between 1855 and its revival in Rome in 1950 with a cast headed by Maria Callas. It was first heard in New York in 1826 and revived 122 years later by the Goldovsky Opera Company at Tanglewood, Massachusetts. The New York City Opera company staged a revival on September 24, 1978, and followed it with a number of performances.

It is worth noting that the post-World War II Rossini revival in Italy that restored *Il Turco in Italia* to the repertoire brought before the public contemporary singers who could handle the vocal pyrotechnics demanded by Rossini: artists like Callas, Stignani, Stabile, Valletti, Cossotto, Alva, Bruscantini and so on.

Il Turco is a frivolous, abstract work, with no deep soundings of musical thought or dramatic action, but it demands sophistication and charm in vocal execution. Despite the vagaries of musical score and libretto, the opera survives as one of Rossini's enduring masterpieces.

ACT ONE

[*Scene One*] An isolated place outside Naples. Farmhouses in the distance; the tents of gypsies in the foreground. On one side, the house of Don Geronio. Among the tents, the gypsies are busy at their tasks.

In the opening chorus ("Nostra patria è il mondo intero"), the gypsies sing lightheartedly about their carefree life roaming over the whole world. Zaida laments that she alone is unhappy because, once the favorite of Selim Pasha, she has incurred his displeasure and has been banished from his harem ("Hanno tutti il cor contento").

Albazar, who has befriended her, tries to cheer her up, urging her to forget her sorrows in a song. But at that point Prosdocimo enters, singing that he has been obliged by his patron to write a farce. He is at a loss to find a subject ("Ho da fare un dramma buffo"), although he has racked his brains for an inspiration. Some ideas seem too sentimental, others too dull. Then he hears the gypsies singing, and all at once an idea for a plot pops into his mind.

As the gypsies withdraw to their tents, Prosdocimo, in an ensuing aria ("Ah! se di questi Zingari l'arrivo"), reflects that perhaps they can provide this plot with a new twist. After all, a story involving Fiorilla—the capricious young wife, an aging ridiculous husband, a youthful lover and so on and so on—has been done to death. There *must* be something new.

He spies Don Geronio approaching—and presto, a character comes to life before his eyes. The unhappy Don is obsessed with having his fortune told—and here are the gypsies to accommodate him. Prosdocimo motions to them and they crowd around.

In the cavatina "Vado in traccia di una Zingara," Geronio sings that he is looking for a fortune-teller who can advise him how to manage his flirtatious young wife. He confesses he is completely baffled. Zaida steps forward and reads his palm. It reveals that he was born under the sign of the ram. A fatal constellation ("Che fatal costellazione"), she intones solemnly: it means that his wife, not he, is master in his house. This enrages Geronio. Sputtering over Fiorilla's caprices, he hurries back to his house, still pursued by the chattering gypsies.

Prosdocimo appears, elated over the preceding scene as new material for his plot, then questions Zaida and Albazar. In recitative, Zaida explains that she had been Selim Pasha's favorite slave. He wanted to marry her but jealous rivals told Selim that she was unfaithful.

Furious, he ordered his major-domo, Albazar, to kill her, but Albazar instead decamped with her to Italy, where both joined the gypsies. But Zaida pines for her royal lover who so cruelly rejected her. Prosdocimo raises her spirits by telling her that this very day a Turkish Pasha will arrive in Naples. *"A Turk in Italy!"* Zaida exclaims. Perhaps when he hears her sad story, Prosdocimo suggests, he will intercede for her with Selim Pasha. The three then leave.

Fiorilla enters with a group of her friends. In some versions of the score she now sings a gay cavatina, "Presto, amiche," in which she relishes the prospect of romantic complications. This is an alternate to the cavatina on the same theme: "Non si dà follia maggiore." Fiorilla and her friends watch eagerly as a ship sails into the harbor and Selim Pasha comes ashore with his entourage. The women sing a chorus of greeting ("Voga, a terra"); Selim responds with a florid cavatina ("Bella Italia") praising the glories of beautiful Italy.

Fiorilla welcomes him with tantalizing coquetry, Selim answers with Oriental gallantry. Romance immediately blossoms as they join in a long duet ("Serva . . . Servo. . . . È assai garbato!"). Already lovers —thanks to Fiorilla's practiced wiles—they leave arm in arm.

A moment later Geronio arrives with Prosdocimo and Narciso. Beside himself, as usual, Geronio begs the other two to extricate him from his connubial dilemma—"Amici . . . soccorretemi." His wife, he fumes, has invited the Turkish Pasha, Selim Damalec ("Maledetti tutti i Turchi"—"a curse on all Turks") to have coffee in her husband's own house.

To the angry surprise of Geronio and Narciso, Prosdocimo happily exclaims that this development will make his play a success: a flirtatious wife, a cuckolded husband, a handsome young lover. A perfect plot, Prosdocimo chortles ("Oh! che intreccio che si fa!").

The trio comes to a crackling climax as Geronio and Narciso

furiously warn Prosdocimo not to drag them into his plot and hold them up to ridicule. Prosdocimo blandly intones: "Act One, Scene One: wife, Turk, lover, shouting husband." The other two grimly retort: "Act One, Scene One: a meddling poet is thrashed by a husband and a lover!"

[*Scene Two*] The elegantly appointed apartment of Geronio, where Fiorilla and the Turk are drinking coffee. Both aware of each other's intentions, they engage in some amorous chatter in a brief duet ("Ammiro di questo gabinetto"). Fiorilla cuts short Selim's spurious compliments by observing that he, after all, is a Turk with a hundred wives—whom he buys and sells—and that she doesn't believe a word he is saying ("Siete Turchi, non vi credo"). This colloquy leads into a stormy quartet when Geronio and later Narciso enter.

The Don flies into a rage when he sees his wife with Selim, who—accustomed to being surprised in assignations—draws his dagger. Geronio recoils. Narciso takes in the situation at a glance: as the young lover, he already has been betrayed ("L'incostante già il Turco")—as destined in Prosdocimo's plot. Fiorilla restrains Selim from carving up the Don on the spot by saying that he has come simply to honor his eminent Turkish guest. Thereupon she forces Geronio into the indignity of kissing Selim's cloak.

As the quartet continues, Selim is cynically amused by the complaisance of Italian husbands; Fiorilla jibes at her spineless husband; Geronio rages against the interloping Turk; Narciso decries his role as a deceived lover, but at the same time denounces the Don's insulting behavior toward Fiorilla.

Glaring at him, Selim orders Geronio to show this upstart the door. The Don cringes, but does nothing. In an aside, Selim manages to arrange an assignation on the seashore with Fiorilla. The quartet concludes as Narciso urges Geronio to be firm with Fiorilla, while the luckless husband confesses he is much too afraid of the Turk to defy him. The others leave him pacing the room in frustration and despair.

Prosdocimo enters. Geronio implores him to explain why it is that an old man will make an utter fool of himself by marrying a young, beautiful woman. What is worse, he moans, she has a beast of a Turkish lover who wants to kill him. Very good, says Prosdocimo, notebook in hand: a *trio!* Bewildered, Geronio adds that his wife forced him to kiss the Turk's mantle. Fortunately, his friend Don Narciso came to the defense of a faithful husband insulted by a Turk with a dagger in his hand.

"What a scene!" Prosdocimo interjects. "Now it is a *quartet!*" ("Che quartetto prezioso!"). As Geronio, completely befuddled, stares at him, Prosdocimo casually remarks that he is making notes on a play he is writing. To Geronio's further confusion, Prosdocimo asks him what he will say to his wife about her latest escapade. If she were only like my *first* wife, the Don wails . . . reasonable and gentle. But *this* one . . . !

It's your own fault, Prosdocimo lectures. You are too easygoing. Geronio ruefully concedes that forbearance is the virtue of a jackass. Then in a pathetic attempt at bravado he declares that he has had enough: either this Turk goes, or he will turn Fiorilla out of the house.

As if to challenge his ultimatum, Fiorilla enters, and then ensues one of the principal duets of the opera in Rossini's inimitable satiric vein. It begins with an exchange in recitative. With true feminine guile, Fiorilla takes the offensive, accusing Geronio of not loving her enough.

The main section of the duet begins as Geronio sarcastically asks Fiorilla what she expects of him ("Per piacere alla signora") in the face of her scandalous behavior with the Turk. She admonishes him not to be a suspicious husband, to be blind and deaf to her faults and to love her as a husband should. When Geronio, driven to distraction, threatens unspeakable revenge on the Turk, Fiorilla plays her trump card, the classic female subterfuge: she bursts into tears. Geronio's ire melts away, and he overwhelms her with kisses.

Having reduced him to a burbling penitent, Fiorilla taunts that she will have a hundred lovers ("Mille amanti ognor intorno"). Geronio, utterly defeated, moans that this woman is mad and no doubt will die madder still ("E più matta morirà"). On these phrases the duet comes to its hilarious climax, after which the two storm away in opposite directions.

[*Scene Three*] The next scene changes back to the seashore, where Zaida and the gypsies are gathered. Zaida boasts of her fortune-telling prowess. Selim appears for his rendezvous with Fiorilla. Prosdocimo enters and stands at one side to comment on the progress of his plot. In a brisk refrain ("Per là fuggir è tutto lesto") Selim exults that everything favors his sea-borne elopement with Fiorilla: the wind is right, the sea is calm.

Prosdocimo, as the *deus ex machina,* comments on the actions of his characters. A delightful ensemble follows as the poet (and Rossini) ingeniously tie together the strings of this impish farce.

It is a charade of implausible plot manipulation. Zaida and Selim meet when Zaida offers to tell the Pasha's fortune. Prosdocimo observes that now there will be a confrontation, and somebody will faint. He runs offstage for a chair—and returns to find Selim and Zaida practically in each other's arms and rejoicing over their reconciliation ("Ecco il fin delle mie pene"). No one fainted, Prosdocimo grumbles; this is contrary to dramatic rules.

In some versions there now follows an amusing duet between Narciso and Geronio, who enter without recognizing Selim or Zaida. In conspiratorial tones they discuss how they will outwit their archenemy Selim ("Zitto, piano, senza strepito"). In other versions, the two come in looking for Fiorilla. Narciso wonders if she has betrayed him; Geronio vows to give her a piece of his mind.

At this point Fiorilla herself, veiled, comes in with a throng of merrymakers. For Selim's benefit she sings a romantic air ("Chi servir non brama Amor"), describing herself as the handmaiden of the God of Love. To Zaida's chagrin, Selim asks Fiorilla to unveil, which brings a shout of surprise from the merrymakers.

Pointing to Zaida, Fiorilla angrily accuses Selim of being unfaithful ("Infido! Ingrato!"). This touches off a long tumultuous ensemble involving all the principals. All express varying degrees of surprise, anger, frustration and confusion—except Prosdocimo, who sings that this confrontation is exactly what he is looking for to provide a grand finale.

During the melee, Fiorilla and Zaida turn on each other in jealous fury, each claiming that Selim belongs to her. They hurl insults at each other as the Pasha vainly tries to calm them. Narciso and Geronio also try to intercede, while Prosdocimo gleefully eggs the two on for the sake of making his finale more exciting.

Through the combined efforts of Selim, Geronio and Narciso, the screaming women finally are separated and calm is restored. The act ends as the onlookers sing that an eruption of Vesuvius would cause less upheaval than two females who are rivals in love ("Quando il vento improvviso sbuffando").

ACT TWO

[*Scene One*] A room in an inn. Geronio and Prosdocimo are seated at a table drinking. Selim enters. A striking duet follows as Selim and Geronio try to come to terms about who is to claim Fiorilla. Prosdocimo withdraws to one side and takes notes. Selim comes directly to the point by observing that it is an old Turkish custom for a husband to sell his wife if she becomes burdensome ("Il marito è venditor"). And it is an old Italian custom, Geronio retorts, for the husband to punch the prospective buyer in the nose ("Ma in Italia . . . il marito rompe il muso").

The verbal fencing becomes sharper as the two begin to lose their tempers. Selim ominously remarks that there is another Turkish custom, to wit: simply kill off the stubborn husband. It saves time. Geronio defiantly answers that the killer himself may be killed. Fuming with rage, the two ludicrously threaten each other—at a safe distance. At the climax of the duet, they shout that they will meet at another place to fight it out with knife and gun ("Ci vedremo in altro loco"). They storm off in opposite directions. Prosdocimo steps forward to sing that this quarrel has given a new turn to his plot: now he will need a new denouement—with a moral.

In a complete change of mood, Fiorilla and the gypsies enter to sing a melodious Mozartian chorus about the delights of love ("Non v'è piacer perfetto"). When the chorus leaves, Fiorilla reveals her plan to dispose of Zaida, this impertinent Turkish girl ("Che Turca impertinente"), once for all as her rival. She admits, with typical feminine illogic, that she really doesn't want the Pasha for herself. Nevertheless, she will invite both Zaida and Selim to the inn and then let the Turk decide between them. Zaida enters, and later Selim.

The dialogue ensues in a captivating trio. First Zaida demands that Selim make his choice at once. When the beleaguered Pasha demurs, she accuses him of faithlessness and flounces out of the inn. Fiorilla, hugely enjoying her strategic victory, dares Selim to follow Zaida, then begins to flirt outrageously with him. She finally beguiles him to the point where he swears he will love her forever. The two conclude the scene in a florid duet ("Tu m'ami, lo vedo") expressing their mutual adoration.

Prosdocimo enters, followed by Geronio, then Narciso comes in unobserved by both. While he eavesdrops, Prosdocimo tells Geronio that Selim is planning to abduct Fiorilla ("un rapimento"); the Don fumes helplessly. At this point Prosdocimo again takes over as *deus ex machina* for purposes of his plot.

There is to be a grand ball at which Selim, in disguise, will carry Fiorilla off to Turkey. When Geronio groans in despair, Prosdocimo discloses the surprise element of his plot: Geronio is to disguise *himself* as Selim—and presto!—Fiorilla's abduction is nipped in the bud. Geronio hurries off to find a Turkish costume.

Overhearing all this, Narciso frets that Fiorilla is deceiving him, but he decides to fall in with Prosdocimo's hocus-pocus to keep the girl from escaping him: *he* will disguise himself as Selim—thus hopelessly entangling the plot. Prosdocimo, in an aside, complacently remarks that now the play is completed ("Il dramma è già completo").

[*Scene Two*] The ballroom, where guests in masquerade costume are dancing. Fiorilla, disguised, enters looking for Selim ("E Selim non si vede!"), just as Narciso, disguised as Selim, comes in. Fiorilla greets him as Selim ("Eccolo qua, Selim") and asks why he has kept her waiting ("E tanto aspettar"). The two mingle with the guests.

The real Selim enters, sees Zaida (disguised as Fiorilla) and of course amorously greets her as Fiorilla ("Cara Fiorilla mia"). Zaida restrains her rage at being mistaken for her rival (her own disguise notwithstanding), and she and the Pasha also lose themselves in the crowd.

Geronio comes in. He is in a bad temper because of the frippery he is obliged to wear on Prosdocimo's orders, and vents his exasperation in cursing love and matrimony ("Maledetto l'amore e il matrimonio"). To make matters worse, he sees Fiorilla enter with Selim (Narciso in disguise). And to his consternation, he sees the *real* Selim and Zaida (disguised as Fiorilla) enter from the other side.

Now, Geronio wails distractedly, there are two Fiorillas, two Zaidas and three Selims. Which Fiorilla is his wife? ("Quale di lor la moglie mia sarà?"). An ensemble interlude ("Deh! seconda amor pietoso") follows. Selim sighs for Fiorilla, Narciso does the same. Fiorilla and Zaida pine for Selim. Geronio despairs of ever finding his real wife.

The scene ends in an uproar when Selim, Fiorilla, Zaida and Narciso try to leave the ballroom. Geronio blocks their way, shouting that he wants his wife—whoever she is—if he can find her in this insane confusion. The guests mock him as a madman as all leave the ballroom. Geronio is left standing alone.

[*Scene Three*] The beach as in Act One. In the background is Selim's ship preparing to sail. Fiorilla enters. Regretting the consequences of her romantic escapade, she wishes she could flee to Sorrento and forget about the ill-starred Turkish ship in the harbor. Prosdocimo enters with Geronio and urges him to approach Fiorilla ("Andate innanzi").

The Don does so, and then follows a lyrical colloquy in which the two describe their reconciliation in allegorical terms. Fiorilla sings that she is a clinging vine withering away for lack of the sturdy tree that has been its support ("Son la vite sul campo appassita"). Geronio responds that he is the tree that was deprived of the tender support of the vine. Prosdocimo adds that he is the gardener who can make these two loving plants grow together again as one. As Fiorilla and Geronio embrace each other, the poet remarks this reunion gives his play the final touch.

The proceedings need only the rest of the happy ending, which Prosdocimo now provides. Selim, Zaida, Narciso and the Turks crowd onto the beach. Prosdocimo, having complicated matters all along, is apprehensive over this meeting, but Zaida reassures him. Fiorilla and Geronio, she says, having been reconciled, are waiting to bid Selim Pasha a hearty bon voyage.

Zaida and Selim, ready to go back to Turkey, ask forgiveness of Fiorilla and Geronio for the misunderstandings. Narciso in turn asks forgiveness for his philandering and promises to reform ("Permettetemi, signori"). Prosdocimo is pleased with his happy ending and hopes the audience agrees. An exuberant chorus sings the theme of his play: "Be contented, be happy" ("Restate contenti; felici vivete"). The curtain falls.

THE TURN OF THE SCREW

by BENJAMIN BRITTEN
(1913–76)

Libretto by
MYFANWY PIPER

Adapted from the story by Henry James

CHARACTERS

The Prologue	Tenor
The Governess	Soprano
Miles and Flora, children in her charge	Treble, soprano
Mrs. Grose, the housekeeper	Soprano
Miss Jessel, the former governess	Soprano
Quint, a former manservant	Tenor

Place: Bly, an English country house
Time: Mid-nineteenth century
First performance: Venice Festival, September 14, 1954
Original language: English

The opera is based on a psychological horror story written in 1898 by the American novelist Henry James (1843–1916). It is one of Britten's twelve operatic works (counting his religious operas and parables) and is a mingling of fact and fantasy.

In a remote country house in England, spirits of the dead lay claim to the souls of the living, casting a pall of disaster over the house. The victims of the ghosts are two small children, a boy and a girl, in care of a governess and a housekeeper.

Both women are powerless against the demonic sorcery of the unquiet ghosts as they demand obedience of the children. The "turn of the screw" symbolizes the effect of the mounting tension (acting like a medieval instrument of torture) as the governess, driven to the brink of madness, attempts to keep the children out of the clutches of the dead. She fails: the girl's mind is poisoned against her; the boy dies in her arms.

Britten's work is in the form of a chamber opera, a form which he brought to a high degree of perfection. In a prologue and two acts with fifteen scenes, the opera calls for an orchestra of thirteen players and six singers.

The fundamental musical theme is established, following the Prologue, in a succession of rising intervals in fifths. Each scene then is linked to the next by extensive variations on this theme. There are fifteen variations in all.

The composer wrote his opera for—and dedicated it to—the English Opera Group, which followed its Venice premiere with performances in Europe and Canada. The first professional American performance was in Boston in 1961 under Julius Rudel, who also conducted the first New York City Opera performance in 1962. It was staged by the Opera Society of Washington, D.C., in 1969 and by the New York City Opera again in 1970 and 1978.

PROLOGUE

This is sung in front of the curtain by a tenor with piano accompaniment ("It is a curious story"). A young inexperienced governess has been engaged by the uncle and guardian of two small children. She goes to see him in London, where he explains her duties: she is to have complete responsibility—but she is never to write him about the children.

Although she is flattered by the guardian's trust in her, she is assailed by doubt. Will she be able to meet this challenge? The Prologue answers for her: " 'I will,' she said."

ACT ONE

[*Scene One*] The Journey. The Governess, in traveling dress, is in a carriage on the way to Bly. Trembling with anticipation and anxiety, she wonders what these two motherless children are like. Will they love her? Will she love them? But if things go wrong . . . what then? Who will help her? On the verge of panic she remembers the guardian's instructions never to write him . . . she must solve her problems alone. Somewhat recovering her composure, she reflects on the situation in recitative over the throbbing of tympani under orchestral phrases in fourths.

Variation I anticipates the lively mood of the welcoming scene which follows.

[*Scene Two*] The Welcome. The porch at Bly, where Miles and Flora are dancing around Mrs. Grose as they ply her with questions about the new Governess. The housekeeper good-naturedly scolds the two for pestering her, then makes them practice their bows and curtseys. They obediently comply, and continue practicing as the Governess timidly enters. Mrs. Grose welcomes her cordially, then introduces the children.

In an ensuing duet, the Governess enthuses about the charm of the children and the beauty of the stately mansion. Mrs. Grose sings that the children are good—but mischievous, like all children . . . too much for an "ignorant old woman." The duet leads into a quartet as Miles and Flora invite the Governess to come with them to show her the house. As they escort her out she sings happily that Bly is now her home.

Variation II, with its succession of rising and falling phrases in fourths, bridges into the next scene.

[*Scene Three*] The Letter. Again the porch at Bly, with part of the house itself visible, including a low window. Mrs. Grose enters and hands the Governess a letter. As the latter begins reading, there is the chime of the celeste—which later will be associated with Quint almost like a leitmotiv. For the first time a disturbing element intrudes as the Governess reads in dismay that Miles has been dismissed from school. No reason is given. The Governess wonders if Miles perhaps got into a schoolboy scrape with a classmate.

Mrs. Grose hastens to assure her that Miles is not a bad boy—wild, like all boys, but not *bad*. As if to substantiate her defense of him, he is seen through the window innocently playing a game with Flora to the tune of a traditional nursery jingle, "Lavender's blue, diddle, diddle." Their voices blend in a quartet with the two women, who marvel over these lovely children and agree that Miles's dismissal is wicked and unjust. When the Governess declares she will under no circumstances write the guardian about the matter, Mrs. Grose impulsively gives her an approving kiss.

Leading directly into the next scene, Variation III is a serene interlude, creating the atmosphere of a calm summer evening.

[*Scene Four*] The Tower. The house, with one of its towers visible. The Governess is walking about in the summer twilight. In a lyrical aria ("How beautiful it is") she reflects on her good fortune: the children are enchanting. She is no longer afraid—in spite of that mysterious cry in the night and those footsteps passing her door. She only wishes that the guardian himself could be here to see how well she is performing her duties.

But breaking in on her reverie comes the chilling sound of the celeste, whereupon the figure of Quint becomes visible in the tower. For a long moment he stares malevolently at her, then vanishes. Terror-stricken, the Governess first thinks it is the guardian. Impossible! One of the servants? No—she knows them all. An intruder . . . or perhaps a maniac locked away in some secret recess in the tower . . . ? In mounting hysteria, the Governess cries, "Who can it be?" as the scene fades.

Variation IV briefly introduces the sturdy rhythm of the nursery rhyme sung by the children in the next scene.

[*Scene Five*] The Window. The hall at Bly, showing the window. Flora and Miles ride in on a hobbyhorse and begin singing, "Tom, Tom, the piper's son." Still singing, they ride out again as the Governess comes in. To the ominous chant of the celeste, the figure of Quint appears at the window. For a moment the two stare intently at each other. Quint vanishes. Apparently hoping to confront him, the Governess rushes outside. Finding no one, she hurries back into the room just as Mrs. Grose enters.

In fear-stricken tones the Governess describes what has happened: a man she had seen before in the tower stared at her through the window. He was tall, red-haired, even rather handsome . . . but with sinister eyes that filled her with horror. Instantly the housekeeper screams, "Peter Quint!" Then she gasps out the story of the apparition. Quint was the master's valet and ruled the household in his absence. He was officious and insolent, forcing his attentions not only on the children but on the lovely Miss Jessel as well.[1]

When the Governess asks Mrs. Grose why she did not write the master she makes the excuse that it was not her place . . . she was not in charge of the children. She hated and feared Quint. Things went from bad to worse; Miss Jessel fled the household—and died. Quint himself was found dead on an icy road where he had fallen and struck his head. Mrs. Grose's story is interspersed by a recurrent descending phrase like an attenuated moan: "Dear God, is there no end to his dreadful ways!"

In a whispered aside, the Governess expresses her haunting fear of Quint's evil power. Now—in this quiet and beautiful place—there will be no peace: she is helpless against the satanic domination of this depraved creature. And yet . . . her first duty now, she tells Mrs. Grose, is to protect the children from him—and she must not fail. The housekeeper, bewildered and ineffectual as she is, promises to help.

Bridging to the next scene, Variation V is a complicated double fugue. Its rhythms and fundamental themes continue without pause.

[1] At this first mention of Miss Jessel a gong sounds deep in the bass. It is repeated when her name is mentioned later, an identifying sound similar to the celeste associated with Quint.

[*Scene Six*] The Lesson. The schoolroom. The Governess is hearing Miles recite his Latin lesson ("Many nouns in IS we find").[2] Flora, naïvely "helping," repeats some of his phrases. Finally bored with Latin, Miles asks the Governess to tell him about history, whereupon Flora mischievously chatters about Boadicea.[3] She is reproved by the Governess, who asks Miles to continue with his Latin.

In a sudden change of mood, Miles replies mysteriously in a minor refrain—"Malo I would rather be."[4] Puzzled, the Governess asks if she taught him this song. He replies vaguely: "No . . . I found it . . . I like it . . . do you?" He repeats his "Malo" refrain as the scene fades. The fugal pattern which underlies this scene is continued in Variation VI, which follows.

[*Scene Seven*] The Lake. The lake in the park. The Governess with her book, Flora with her doll. What follows briefly is another "lesson scene." The Governess asks Flora if she can name the seas in her geography book. On a simple repeated note, the girl glibly recites the names, and ends with a flourish: "The Dead Sea."

Pointing to the lake, she adds enigmatically: "This is the Dead Sea." The obvious inference to "death" is not lost on the Governess who—to maintain her composure—explains that a sea is called "dead" when nothing can live in it. She takes up her book; Flora sings her doll to sleep over an accompaniment in fourths and major thirds. As she sings her lullaby, her back to the lake, the Governess looks up from her book and sees the figure of Miss Jessel across the lake. The identifying gong sounds, then the figure vanishes. Panic-stricken, the Governess calls to Flora that they must go at once to meet Miles. He shouts at them from a distance, and Flora runs to meet him.

Alone, the Governess laments that the ghosts of Miss Jessel and Quint are in league to corrupt the souls of the children. She is convinced that Flora's apparent unconcern about the apparition means that the child has been completely mesmerized by Miss Jessel (she does not realize that Flora has not seen the apparition). In utter despair the Governess moans: "It is worse than I dreamed . . . they are lost . . . lost . . . !"

Variation VII, sounded mostly by celeste and harp, introduces the powerful climactic scene of the first act.

[*Scene Eight*] Night. The front of the house, with the tower, where Quint is seen. Miles, in his nightshirt, is seen in the garden below. In

---

2 Based on schoolboys' traditional rhyming Latin grammatical rules.

3 A British queen (circa A.D. 62) who is said to have attempted to lead a revolt against the Romans.

4 In this context, "Malo" has a double meaning: "bad," and "I would rather be."

eerie coloratura passages, Quint softly calls to Miles, who responds as though hypnotized. In insidious phrases he enmeshes the boy in a web of fatal magic: "I am all things strange and bold . . . the hero highwayman . . . King Midas, with gold in his hand . . . the two-faced Janus . . . the rascally Mercury . . . the keeper of secret desires. . . ." Spellbound, Miles cries: "I am here!"

Compounding the horror comes the wailing voice of Miss Jessel (signaled by the gong) calling to Flora. Like Miles, she eagerly responds. From this point the voices merge in a quartet. The ghosts and the children discourse in otherworldly terms, with references to bizarre dreams and creatures of mythology. There is a duet interlude ("On the paths, in the woods") in which Miss Jessel and Quint sing that they will wait patiently for the moment when they can claim the souls of the children —and in this they will not fail. The duet ends abruptly as the Governess and Mrs. Grose are heard calling to the children. When the two appear, the apparitions vanish. The housekeeper scolds Flora for being outside in the night. Miles, similarly admonished by the Governess, says simply: "You see, I am bad, aren't I?"

ACT TWO

The first scene is introduced by Variation VIII, which begins with a clarinet imitation of Quint's coloratura refrain in the preceding Scene Eight, in which he first calls to Miles. This prelude reprises the music of that scene.

[*Scene One*] Colloquy and Soliloquy. Quint and Miss Jessel, in the spirit world, continue their plotting to enslave the children. While Miss Jessel agonizes over being lured into this ghostly conspiracy by Quint, he himself sardonically describes the ultimate doom of the children: "The ceremony of innocence is drowned."[5] The two ghosts vanish as the Governess appears.

In one of the opera's major arias ("Lost in my labyrinth") she gives way to her fear of impending disaster. She despairs of finding a way out of the labyrinth of evil and corruption in which she finds herself. The aria is sung over a restless rising and falling ostinato accompaniment. Its conclusion leads into Variation IX, intoning the sound of church bells.

[*Scene Two*] The Bells. The churchyard, with a flat table tomb. Over the sound of the bells, Flora and Miles—unseen—are heard chant-

---

[5] From the poem "The Second Coming," by the Irish poet William Butler Yeats (1865–1939)—itself a requiem for a doomed world.

ing the *Benedicite* ("O ye works and days, bless ye the Lord"). The two solemnly march in like choir boys, continuing the chant partly in parody, partly in the traditional words. As they sit down on the tombstone, the Governess and Mrs. Grose approach. Mrs. Grose chatters aimlessly about the beautiful morning and the "dear children" singing so sweetly on the tombstone. The Governess morosely answers in monosyllables. While Mrs. Grose babbles on about how much the children love their Governess, Miles and Flora impishly mock her in terms of the *Benedicite*—"O Mrs. Grose, bless ye the Lord . . . may she never be confounded."

Finally the Governess, exasperated by the housekeeper's witlessness, takes her aside and tries to explain that the children are not innocently playing: they are possessed by the ghosts of Miss Jessel and Quint—and these demons can destroy them. Mrs. Grose, momentarily shocked into a sensible reaction, urges her to write at once to the guardian. The Governess flatly refuses to do so. In a brief trio she sings that the children are now "with" Quint and Miss Jessel; Mrs. Grose prattles on, while the children ironically continue the *Benedicite*.

Mrs. Grose then manages to hustle Flora into the church, but Miles hangs back to talk to the Governess. With insinuating slyness ("You trust me . . . but you think of us and the *others*") he plays on her doubts and fears to the point where she resolves to flee from Bly at once. As Miles casually walks into the church, the Governess rushes away crying: "Away from this poisoned place!" The somber theme in Variation X, which follows, echoes her distress.

[*Scene Three*] Miss Jessel. The children's schoolroom. Miss Jessel is sitting at her desk. The Governess enters.

Then follows the bizarre colloquy between the Governess and her ghostly adversary. The portent of disaster is in Miss Jessel's opening phrases: "Here my tragedy began. Here my revenge begins!" This in effect is a crucial encounter for possession of the souls of the children. Miss Jessel is calm, inexorable; the Governess furiously tries to exorcise her.

When the apparition finally fades, the Governess decides to write the guardian, and does so in one of the most lyrical interludes of the opera: "Sir, I have not forgotten your charge of silence . . . but there are things that you must know." As she finishes writing, the scene fades on a minor chord.

Variation XI starts with the theme (established during the Prologue) in canon form; this leads into softly flowing phrases introducing the next scene.

[*Scene Four*] The Bedroom. Miles, with his jacket and shoes off, is sitting on the edge of his bed. A candle dimly lights the room. As the murmurous accompaniment grows louder the boy begins the refrain he sang in Scene Six of Act One: "Malo than a naughty boy." He is interrupted by the entrance of the Governess. Somewhat disturbed by his secretive manner, she timidly reproves him for not being in bed. He replies casually that he was thinking—mostly about the way she constantly watches him. Perplexed, the Governess asks him why he has never told her what happened in this house before she came, then tells him she has written to his guardian. With a touch of insolence, Miles remarks that she will have much to tell him. So will you, the Governess retorts pointedly. Just as she tries to coax Miles into confiding in her, the ghostly voice of Quint—which only Miles hears—calls out, "Miles . . . I am here . . . waiting." As he looks around wildly, the Governess cries out that she is trying to save him. Miles shrieks in terror. The candle goes out and the room is plunged into darkness.

Variation XII is an agitated six-measure phrase that precedes the partly spoken and sung voice of Quint. Menacing, insistent, he demands to know what the Governess has written. Then he commands the boy to purloin the letter, which the Governess left on the desk. There is an interval of ominous silence.

[*Scene Five*] Quint. Miles, in his room, stands listening intently. Then comes Quint's ferocious whisper: "Take it!" Miles creeps across the room, picks up the letter and takes it into his bedroom. The scene ends as the "Malo" theme sounds in the orchestra.

Variation XIII, in fleeting arpeggios and chromatics, introduces a calmer, brighter mood that pervades the next scene.

[*Scene Six*] The Piano. Miles is playing the piano. Flora, sitting on the floor, is playing cat's-cradle. The Governess and Mrs. Grose, in a duet in fourths, effusively compliment Miles on his playing. His piece is in the style of an eighteenth-century sonata. The Governess manages to take Mrs. Grose aside and confide that her letter to the guardian is ready to be mailed. The housekeeper nods approvingly. Both women then continue to give their attention to the children, loudly praising them. The Governess hovers over Miles at the piano, while Mrs. Grose joins Flora in playing cat's-cradle. The two sing a childish ditty about the game.

Mrs. Grose begins nodding, then apologizes for being sleepy. Flora rises and quietly sings, "Go to sleep"—the same phrase she sang to her doll beside the lake in Scene Seven, Act One. But now it has a more significant meaning in the light of Flora's next action: she steals out of the house unobserved by the two women. The Governess, who has been enthusing over Miles's playing, suddenly stops him and calls out that Flora has left. Miles meanwhile hammers out the chords of his next selection (Variation XIV). The situation becomes clear to the Governess: Miles's virtuoso performance was simply to divert attention from his sister's escape. As the women rush out to look for Flora the music continues without pause into the next scene.

[*Scene Seven*] The Lake. Flora is looking intently out over the lake. Calling her name, the two women rush in, and both scold the girl for running away. Then to her horror, the Governess sees the apparition of Miss Jessel across the lake. When she hysterically calls attention to the figure, Flora and Mrs. Grose deny that anyone is there. The scene now builds into a powerful quartet. Miss Jessel implores Flora not to fail her now; when the Governess insists that Miss Jessel is visible, Flora turns on her, screaming in childish rage that she is cruel and hateful; Mrs. Grose sings that poor Miss Jessel is long dead and buried and that the apparition is "all a mistake."

The quartet storms to a climax when Mrs. Grose, at the Governess's frantic urging, rushes away with the still raging Flora. The vision of Miss Jessel fades. Alone, hopeless, defeated, the Governess sings that Miss Jessel at last has had her revenge—she has taught Flora to hate her Governess. She herself acknowledges that she has failed—failed in her mission to rescue the children from enslavement by the dead.

Variation XV begins with a twelve-note chord followed by sharply contrasting chromatic and sustained chords that sustain the mood of tension and doom.

[*Scene Eight*] Miles. The Bly house and grounds. Mrs. Grose and Flora, in traveling dress, appear on the porch. Flora carries her doll and a small bag. As the Governess approaches, Flora deliberately turns her back. Mrs. Grose agrees that the child must be taken away. Bursting into tears, she says she could not believe what Flora has told her—it was too horrifying.

The Governess advises her to take Flora to her uncle, who will understand the situation because by now he has received her letter. Your letter, Mrs. Grose tells her in an unaccompanied phrase, was never sent. Miles stole it. Nevertheless, go, the Governess answers . . . she will deal with the problem of Miles. Mrs. Grose and Flora hurry away.

Alone, the Governess resolves that she will yet save Miles. Now begins the dramatic trio that concludes the opera. When the boy casually strolls in, she greets him affectionately and promises to protect him at all costs. But he starts in terror as he hears the voice of Quint in its characteristic coloratura refrain: "Miles, you're mine . . . beware of her. . . ."

In mounting desperation she asks the boy if he stole the letter. Quint appears on the tower as Miles first denies then admits the theft. The Governess's insistent questioning as to why he stole mingles with Quint's relentless warning to be silent. Unseen by Miles, Quint now comes down from the tower, reiterating his threats. Miles stares around him in abject terror. The Governess fiercely pleads with him to speak the name of his tormentor.

With Quint's terrible warning ringing in his ears, he first refuses to comply. If he will only say the name, the Governess cries, he will be free of this demon forever. Miles suddenly screams: "Peter Quint, you devil!" With that he runs into the Governess's arms. She exultantly cries that together they have destroyed the ghost. As Quint slowly disappears, his voice is heard in a dying phrase of farewell to Miles.

The Governess looks at the boy in her arms and gasps in horror as she realizes he is dead. She lays him gently on the ground. Crushed by sorrow, she intones a plaintive repetition of his "Malo" song, which softly dies away as the curtain falls.

VANESSA

by SAMUEL BARBER

(1910–   )

Libretto by
GIAN CARLO MENOTTI

Based on an original story by Menotti

CHARACTERS

Vanessa, a lady of great beauty	Soprano
Erika, a young girl of twenty	Mezzo-soprano
The Old Baroness, Vanessa's mother, Erika's grandmother	Contralto
Anatol, a young man in his early twenties	Tenor
The Old Doctor	Baritone
Nicholas, the major-domo	Bass
Footman	Bass

The young Pastor, servants, guests, peasants and their children, musicians, dancers

Place: A "northern country" (Scandinavia)
Time: Circa 1905
First performance: Metropolitan Opera House, New York, January 15, 1958
Original language: English

Vanessa, Samuel Barber's first opera, was acclaimed at its premiere not only as the best American opera ever presented at the old Metropolitan but as a major contribution to the international operatic repertoire. As such, it represents the successful collaboration of two distinguished musicians whose association began when both were still in their teens. Music had brought them together from widely separated localities— Barber from West Chester, Pennsylvania; Menotti from Cadegliano, on the shore of Lake Lugano in Italy. Their operatic talents merged at "Capricorn," then Barber's home in Mount Kisco, New York, where they created *Vanessa.*

With all its dissonances and atonality, *Vanessa* is still in the grand opera *verismo* tradition. It has dramatic recitatives, interludes of soaring lyricism, resounding climaxes—although without massive choral ensembles. The plot itself is overlaid with a haunting mood of tragedy, at the core of which is a love triangle that culminates in disillusionment and despair.

Although infrequently staged in recent years, the opera has its firm place in the repertoire and finds favor with audiences in this country and abroad. One of the most noteworthy revivals was presented in a television simulcast of the new production on January 31, 1979, over WNCN presented by the Spoleto Festival in Charleston, South Carolina, in a co-production with FCE-TV, South Carolina Educational Television.

The brief but turbulent prelude begins with a thunderous orchestral outburst, followed by sustained passages marked by a striking four-note figure which will be heard again and again throughout the opera.

ACT ONE[1]

A night during a snowstorm in early winter, in Vanessa's luxurious drawing room. In a corner, a small table is laid for supper. All the mirrors and one large painting over the mantelpiece are covered. A large French window leads into a darkened conservatory. Vanessa, her face covered by a veil, is sitting by the fireside with her mother, the Baroness, who remains there motionless throughout the ensuing scene. In the middle of the room, Erika, notebook in hand, is giving instructions to Nicholas, the major-domo, and the staff of servants.

As she orders the dinner menu in French, the major-domo writes it down and repeats the items to the servants. Vanessa rather petulantly countermands some of Erika's suggestions and orders her own preferences. They finally agree on the wine—*Romanée Conti* and *Montrachet*. Vanessa adds that there must be a fresh camellia every morning on the dressing table of her long-awaited guest, Anatol. Finally, the gatekeeper is to ring the castle bell all night to guide Anatol's carriage through the storm. Acknowledging their instructions, the major-domo and the servants leave.

There is a sudden agitated orchestral interlude; Vanessa rises and paces the floor, fretting because Anatol has not arrived. Trying to calm her, Erika says he has probably decided to stay at an inn to wait out the storm. Vanessa fumes that if their coachman, Karl, has lost his way it will cost him his job. Melodramatically she cries that she will die if anything has happened to Anatol. From outside comes the tolling of the tower bell, which increases Vanessa's anxiety.

[1] Acts and scenes are presented here as indicated in the original score.

To distract her, Erika begins to read to her from the Greek legend of Oedipus: "Woe is me! Sorrowful that I am!"[2] Snatching the book from her, Vanessa jibes that she does not know how to read. She repeats the lines from Oedipus stridently in a higher key, then tosses the book away. Meanwhile, the Baroness looks on in stony silence. Erika leads her to the door, where a maid takes her to her room. Vanessa orders Erika to look carefully outside for a sign of the arrivals, then bids her goodnight. Alone, Vanessa laments the approach of winter in a melancholy aria, "Must winter come so soon."

As she concludes the refrain, the tower bell begins to ring faster, mingling with the sound of sleighbells. Lights are seen outside. Vanessa springs up and calls out orders to the servants, her excitement reflected in the agitated accompaniment. Erika re-enters, but Vanessa virtually pushes her out of the room, saying that she wishes to be alone with her visitor. Nervously pacing, she pauses in front of the mirror, starts to uncover it, but then turns away and turns off most of the lights.

Suddenly the door opens and the silhouetted figure of Anatol stands on the threshold as a swirling sextuplet figure sounds in the orchestra. Vanessa sits down by the fireplace, her back to the door. Struggling for composure, she calls Anatol's name and asks him not to speak or move. Then she gives way to her pent-up emotions in an impassioned aria: "I have waited for you." She recalls those endless bitter years of waiting . . . the agony of knowing that beauty withered and happiness faded day by day as she grieved in silence.

Rising, still without facing Anatol, she reaches back her hand. In a passionate outburst, she sings that she does not want to face him unless he can assure her of his love—"because all things change when love has died." She goes on to sing feverishly that if he does not love her he must leave her house at once.

In a quiet but trenchant phrase sung on a single repeated note, Anatol answers: "I believe I shall love you." At the sound of his voice, Vanessa whirls and faces him. In a frenzy, she screams that he is not Anatol . . . he is an impostor and a cheat. When she wildly calls for help, Erika rushes in. Raging that this unknown intruder is to be turned out of the house at once, Vanessa is helped upstairs by Erika. Anatol unconcernedly watches them go. Noticing Vanessa's handkerchief on the floor, he places it on a chair, then goes to the supper table and from the centerpiece selects a flower for his lapel.

Erika returns and brusquely asks him who he—who calls himself "Anatol"—really is, and why he has come. Anatol protests that he did not lie, and when his father died. . . . At that, Erika gasps in dismay,

2 Oedipus, King of Thebes, slew his father, Laius, and married his mother, Jocasta. Driven mad by remorse, he tore out his eyes and wandered away alone from Thebes.

realizing now that Vanessa's cherished dream has been shattered by death itself. But why, she asks, did he not write and let Vanessa know? In a brief refrain—"All through my youth"—Anatol recalls the course of Vanessa's tragic love affair. Her name, he sings, scorched his mother's lips and haunted his father. Now he himself has come here to meet, once for all, this woman: Vanessa.

Anatol casually ignores Erika's reminder that he has been asked to leave, and in turn asks her who *she* is. Vanessa's niece—but mostly her shadow, Erika replies. He approaches the table, notices the wine, *Romanée Conti,* and remarks that it was his father's favorite. Lighting the candles, he observes that he, like his father, loves good food and wine. His father, he adds, dreamed away his fortune while his mother poisoned his life with jealousy. With bland insolence, he invites Erika to join him at supper. Irritated—but still fascinated by his effrontery—she reminds him that the table was not set for her. Nor was *he* the expected guest, he retorts. With exaggerated gallantry he kneels before her, offers her the flower from his lapel and sings, like Dimitri in *Boris Godunof,* "I am the false Dimitri . . . be my Marina!"

Playing the romantic lover to the hilt, he leads her gently to the table, pours the wine and murmurs that she has never told him her name. Bemused in spite of herself by his spurious blandishments, she answers. They touch glasses. The music drifts away high in the strings.

ACT TWO

The same. A month later on a sunny Sunday morning. A breakfast table is laid in the conservatory. In the distance, snow-covered mountains. The Baroness and Erika, her head in her hands, are sitting in the living room.

At the curtain, Erika is making her "confession" to the Baroness: "He made me drink too much wine . . . I stayed with him all night. . . ." The Baroness listens incredulously, and a long colloquy follows. In *her* youth, the Baroness intones, her lover came to her like a proud conqueror. But this Anatol, she goes on with cutting scorn, this brazen interloper . . . who is he?

If she knew, Erika answers forlornly, she would also know why she hates and loves him at the same time. But will he do the "honorable thing," the Baroness queries relentlessly. Erika answers that she does not want his honor nor her own at the price of his love. Perhaps he will marry her, she adds, but she doubts if he knows what love is. In spite of their night of love, she cries in anguish, she still can hear his mocking laughter.

In a passionate outburst she sings that she loves "someone like him." The Baroness observes enigmatically that the beloved and the "image" of the beloved are never the same. At that moment the sound of the laughter of Vanessa and Anatol, outside, shifts Erika's concern to Vanessa. Has she herself the right to break the heart of the woman who loves Anatol "blindly"? The Baroness, returning to her place by the fireside, mutters contemptuously: "The fool!"

Laughing and chattering about skating, Vanessa and Anatol enter. Anatol's courteous greeting to the Baroness is met, as usual, with silence. The tension is broken by the entrance of the Doctor, who compliments the pair on their skating. Vanessa urges everyone to be on time for chapel. The Doctor reminisces about the gay life of the past. Thereupon, Vanessa promises that she will uncover all the mirrors and all the portraits and then give the most magnificent ball the county has ever seen.

Caught up in her enthusiasm, the Doctor invites Vanessa to dance one of the old country dances with him. Together they perform to the rhythm of a waltz tune sung by the Doctor—"Under the willow tree, two doves cry."

Looking on, Anatol compliments the Doctor on his dancing, whereupon the latter offers to teach him the steps. They dance together as the voices of Vanessa, Erika and the Doctor join in a charming trio in a continuation of the waltz tune. There is merry laughter as Anatol awkwardly tries to imitate the Doctor's dance steps. Out of breath, Anatol finally collapses on a sofa as the Doctor good-naturedly twits him about his dancing.

Vanessa announces that breakfast is being served in the conservatory. Anatol and the Doctor go out arm in arm. Watching them, Vanessa calls to Erika and happily exclaims that now she knows that *this* is the Anatol she has been waiting for: it is for him she has kept her youth because in him her lover has sent her his younger self. Ecstatically she whispers: "Anatol!"

Disconcerted by the intensity of Vanessa's emotion, Erika tries in vain to bring her back to reality. In agitated phrases over an accompaniment of undulating arpeggios, Vanessa describes what happened while she and Anatol were skating. They were flying over the ice, she sings, when suddenly he paused and looked ardently into her eyes and told her that now it is time for him to leave. He came as her guest, he said, but wants to leave as her "master." Erika questions incredulously: "He said that . . . and then . . . ?" With a mocking laugh, Vanessa twits Erika for her "curiosity."

The dialogue is interrupted by the arrival of the Doctor, Anatol and the young Pastor who is to hold chapel services. She invites them in for coffee and then, still in her euphoric mood, she leaves to get ready for chapel. Erika turns to her grandmother, who has been silently watching from her accustomed place at the fireside. Bewildered by Vanessa's amorous manner, she embraces the Baroness in a gesture of desperate appeal for an answer to the situation.

When the Baroness tells her she must fight for Anatol's love, Erika answers bitterly that—Vanessa or herself—it is all the same to him, yet she still cannot forget his kisses that night. What kind of a man is he . . . ? With devastating contempt the Baroness characterizes him as "the man of today . . . he only sees what is offered him . . . he will choose what is easier." Erika can only reply in desperation that she is dying of love for him.

At that point Anatol comes in flippantly remarking that he is escaping from the Doctor and the Pastor, who are deep in some completely boring theological discussion. Erika demands to have a talk with him. When he looks askance at the Baroness, Erika curtly assures him that she knows . . . they share their secrets.

A remarkable dialogue now ensues. Erika, in an unaccompanied phrase, asks him if what he told Vanessa (about being her "master") is true. When he hedges, she flares at him to stop lying. With an affable sneer, Anatol counters that the "little sphinx" now demands answers. Meanwhile, the Baroness, like a Greek chorus, interjects words of advice and warning to Erika. Anatol alternately plays on Erika's sympathy and blandly rationalizes his own conduct. To her utter confusion he asks—with the Baroness as witness—if she will marry him.

And what will he do, she asks in turn, if the answer is no? In that case, Anatol remarks facetiously, he might well be expected either to cut his throat or become a monk. Erika recoils angrily at this impudence.

Scoffing that she is much too sentimental, he says she belongs to a bygone age. The world has changed, he goes on with debonair cynicism, and "eternal love" has gone out of fashion. One must savor the pleasures of the moment. With assumed tenderness he declares that they could be very happy together. Taking her in his arms, he dazzles her with mention of the pleasure palaces of Paris, Rome, Budapest, Vienna . . . the romance of Spain . . . the glittering Grand Hotels for jeweled suppers, dancing—and goodbyes. All this, he says, will be hers if she accepts his love—and, who knows?—his love might last forever. Life, he adds whimsically, is so brief. Those words shatter Erika's moment of enchantment; as though waking from a dream she murmurs that now she knows him for the man he really is.

Unperturbed, Anatol asks if she will accept his offer. At that moment Vanessa comes in urging everyone to hurry to chapel. She fussily hands the Baroness her shawl and prayer book and asks the Doctor, who has just entered, to escort her to the service. Anatol offers his arm to Vanessa, addressing her as "Baroness." She archly replies that he is to call her "Vanessa."

Erika remains alone. To the accompaniment of a sonorous bass theme in the orchestra she walks despairingly around the room, collapses on the floor beside the sofa, then abruptly rises and goes toward one of the covered mirrors on the wall. The music crescendoes into wild discords as she tears away the covering. For a moment she stands in thought. Then she goes to the fireplace, climbs up on a chair and carefully pulls away the cloth covering a large frame. There is revealed the portrait of Vanessa, youthful and beautiful in a ball dress. Erika, her eyes riveted on the portrait, backs slowly away.

From the distance comes the sound of a hymn being sung in the chapel: "In the morning light let us rejoice." It continues during most of the action which concludes the act. Erika runs over to the mirror, stares intently at her reflection and compares it with the face in the portrait. In an impulsive motion she sits down on the sofa and pulls her blouse from her shoulders, baring them in imitation of the voluptuous décolletage of Vanessa's dress. As the "Amen" of the hymn fades away, Erika bursts out in anguish: "No, Anatol . . . let Vanessa have you . . . she who for so little waited so long!" Sobbing, she throws herself on the sofa as the music surges in a discordant crescendo.

ACT THREE

New Year's Eve. At right a stairway to upstairs rooms. At the back, a spacious archway opening into the ballroom. At left, the main entrance hall of the castle. The major-domo is arranging the wraps of the guests. A footman stands at the entrance to the ballroom, where couples are dancing. A graceful animated introduction sets the gay mood of the scene.

The major-domo gives instructions to the footman announcing guests, then turns to the rack where the women's furs are hanging. Sensuously rubbing his cheek against the furs, he sings amorously that, alas, this is all he will ever know about such beautiful women.

The Doctor, in a pleasant alcoholic daze, enters with a champagne glass in each hand. Weaving about, he describes to the openmouthed major-domo how he danced with a certain tantalizing blonde, carefully detailing her charms—naked shoulders and all. Almost losing his balance, he suddenly remembers that he is to announce the engagement of Vanessa and Anatol. Searching aimlessly through his pockets, he mumbles that he has lost his speech. The major-domo picks it up from the floor and hands it to him; he borrows the major-domo's comb and uses it with exaggerated care.

Suddenly Vanessa enters, magnificently gowned but obviously in a temper. She glares at the Doctor, who simply beams back and informs her that he has lost his engagement speech. But no matter, he knows it

by heart: "Ladies and gentlemen . . ." Vanessa fumes that Erika and
the Baroness refuse to come downstairs and begs the Doctor to use his
powers of persuasion. He lurches happily up the stairs, still murmuring
about dancing with the voluptuous blonde. Vanessa sits down on the
stairs and buries her face in her hands.

Anatol comes in from the ballroom and looks at Vanessa in alarm.
She whimpers that she feels weak and afraid, but then in a sudden outburst rages that Erika and the Baroness are sitting upstairs "like brooding harpies" who are trying to destroy her happiness with silence. Flinging herself into Anatol's arms, she asks if *he* can tell her why she has
waited in vain for a lover for twenty years.

His answer—"Love has a bitter core"—introduces one of the major
numbers of the opera. True to his amoral philosophy, Anatol urges her
to forget the past and to love as though their love was born today.
Vanessa sings that her love has always been waiting for him, and now
she will share its bitterness with him. He has come to her like a phoenix
soaring out of the ashes of shattered dreams. Then scatter the ashes to
the winds, Anatol sings in the vaulting climax of the duet, and follow
my flight. Their voices join in unison phrases as they clasp each other in
a passionate embrace.

The Doctor comes down to report that there is no cause for alarm—
Erika will be down directly. At Vanessa's instructions, the festivities
continue in the ballroom, where peasant children dancing to the tune of
a fiddler are entertaining the guests.

Suddenly Erika, in a white ball gown, appears at the top of the stairs.
Pale and distraught, she steps slowly down. Clinging to the railing, she
stands motionless as she hears the Doctor announce "the engagement of
the Baroness von . . ." Erika, clutching her stomach, faints and crumples at the bottom of the stairs. From the ballroom comes the gay chorus toasting the prospective bride and groom: "Prosit!"

The major-domo comes in, sees Erika and tries to revive her. After a
few moments she regains consciousness and asks him not to tell anyone
what has happened. He helps her to her feet and, at her request, leaves
her. As an ironic counterpoint to Erika's distress comes the singing of
the guests waltzing to the folk tune sung by the Doctor, Vanessa and
Anatol in Act Two—"Under the willow tree, two doves cry."

Erika, her hands clasped over her stomach, gasps in spoken words:
"His child . . . it must not be born!" Staggering to the entrance door,
she vanishes into the night, leaving the door open. The dancing continues; couples waltz in and out of the ballroom. The major-domo comes in
looking for Erika. Suddenly the Baroness, disheveled and excited, appears at the head of the stairs and calls Erika's name. Her despairing
cry is mocked by the careless laughter of the dancers. As the music and
laughter subside, she goes to the open door and once more calls Erika's

name into the blackness of the storm. Through the archway, Vanessa and Anatol are seen dancing, oblivious to the impending tragedy.

But a moment later, Vanessa and Anatol, having heard the Baroness's cry, hurry into the hall. The Baroness gasps that Erika has run out of the house toward the lake. Anatol snatches a cape from the rack, throws it over his shoulders and rushes out, followed by several men guests. Vanessa vainly tries to stop him.

ACT FOUR

[*Scene One*] Erika's bedroom. A brief orchestral interlude establishes the mood of tension and foreboding. The Baroness is seated by a small fireplace, her back to the audience. The Doctor peers anxiously through a window; Vanessa, in a dressing gown, is pacing restlessly. Outside, men's voices are heard, mingled with the barking of dogs. Beside herself with anxiety, Vanessa berates herself for being blind to Erika's unhappiness. She reproaches the Doctor for not being aware of the crisis in the girl's life. He ruefully admits that he not only is a bad doctor, but a bad poet as well: he does not know the human heart.

Vanessa turns on the Baroness, immobile as a statue, and furiously upbraids her for her eternal, frustrating silence. The Doctor sharply admonishes her for her outburst, then tries to calm her when she wails that Erika probably will be dead when they find her. The searchers, he says, found no footprints by the lake.

Tormented by remorse and fear, Vanessa gives way to her emotions in a dramatic refrain—"Why must the greatest sorrows come from those we love?" Subconsciously—haunted by feelings of guilt—she shifts the blame from herself to Erika: "Why have you done this to me? Erika, come back!" She sits down sobbing by the fireplace.

Suddenly the hunting horns of the rescue party are heard outside. Vanessa and the Doctor rush to the window and see the men carrying Erika. The Baroness rises and looks on silently. Anatol carries Erika into the bedroom, places her gently on the bed and leaves her in the care of the maids. Taking Vanessa in his arms, he describes, in a quiet, tender refrain ("On the path to the lake") how he found Erika: she lay in the snow like a bloodstained Christmas rose. He cradled her in his arms, felt the faint beat of her heart and warmed her against his breast. When he called her name she answered with a sigh. The Doctor interrupts to ask Anatol and Vanessa to leave the bedside until Erika is more fully recovered.

They withdraw to the far side of the room, where Vanessa, goaded by jealousy, begins to question Anatol: *why* did Erika do this . . . does she love you . . . do you love her . . . do not lie to me . . . ! The more evasively he answers, the more insistently she questions. He stops the inquisition point-blank when he tells her: "Ask Erika yourself. She never lies."

But in the next instant, Vanessa's mood changes. In a rapturous outburst she begs Anatol to take her away from this house where they are both enslaved by the sorrows of others. Anatol's voice joins hers in a brief, tempestuous duet as he exhorts her to trust in his love. The Doctor tells them that Erika is slowly recovering, and that she wishes to be alone with the Baroness. At his bidding, they leave.

There is a long silence, followed by a descending phrase sounded deep in the bass. From her bed, Erika asks the Baroness, sitting motionless by the fireside: "Do they know?" Speaking at last, the Baroness replies with a shrug that they lie not only to themselves but to each other. Then comes the crucial question: "And your child?" Erika answers simply: "It will not be born."

The Baroness, rapping savagely on the floor with her cane, rises and stalks toward the door. She goes out of the room ignoring Erika's anguished question: "Why are you leaving me?"

An intermezzo precedes the final scene of the opera. It begins with a rather plaintive theme sounded by the English horn, which is taken up by the cellos and builds up to a lyrical variation high in the strings.

[*Scene Two*] The drawing room as in Act One. The Baroness is sitting in her usual place. Anatol, in traveling clothes, is talking to the Doctor; servants are bustling about with trunks, boxes and other traveling gear. The scene continues in recitative. Anatol tells the Doctor that the new house in Paris will be ready by the time the newlyweds arrive. Vanessa, also dressed for traveling, comes in excited and happy and gives the servants last-minute instructions about packing the sleigh. She gives a farewell present to a maid, who bursts into tears.

In a touching refrain ("For every love there is a last farewell") the Doctor sentimentally recalls Vanessa's childhood—how he nursed her through chicken pox and scarlet fever and drove the goblins from her bedside. He is on the verge of tears when Vanessa gently but firmly tells him to go and help Anatol with the packing.

She turns to Erika, who has come in from the conservatory, and asks her to sit down for a final talk. In the ensuing colloquy, they try to resolve the emotional problems that have been haunting them. Vanessa begins by saying that she and Anatol will be living in Paris and may never again return to this house. She confides that she has willed the estate to Erika, who may live here as long as she likes. Erika firmly replies that she prefers to stay, adding—with a glance at the Baroness—that she cannot be left here alone. Vanessa, however, skirts that problem and goes on to chatter about household matters.

But then she comes to the point: she demands to know "the truth" about the night of Erika's disappearance. With forced composure Erika replies that she has told the truth: it was a foolish, unreasonable act . . . it was the end of her youth. Becoming annoyed at Erika's deceptive replies, Vanessa persists: was it because of Anatol? Managing a light laugh, Erika answers that it was simply a matter of loving someone who did not love her . . . in any case, it is all over now. With an air of mingled relief and lingering suspicion, Vanessa murmurs: "Perhaps he was not the man for you." With profound irony, Erika answers in an unaccompanied phrase: "I know now . . . he is not the man for me."

The tension is broken when Anatol comes in telling Vanessa to hurry. As though a heavy burden has been lifted from her shoulders, Vanessa quickly rises and goes into the hall, where she effusively bids goodbye to the servants, the major-domo and the Doctor. Anatol seizes the opportunity to tell Erika, rather fatuously, that he had hoped it would be with *her* he would be leaving this house.

Followed by the Doctor, Vanessa returns for a last farewell. There is a long silence as she looks around. The Baroness rises; all stand motionless. Then begins the magnificent quintet that climaxes the opera: "To leave, to break, to find, to keep." Its lyrical fugal design is dominated by the curving four-note figure first heard in the prelude, which seems to bring the musical and dramatic concepts of the opera full circle.

Each character in his or her own terms reflects on the sorrow of farewell, the shattered hopes, the lost love and the broken dreams that have enveloped this group of human beings in a remote castle in a tragic destiny. The ensemble concludes with a poignant trio phrase sung by Vanessa, Erika and Anatol: "May Death release you before . . . you cease to dream."

Goodbyes are said with kisses and embraces. Vanessa, Anatol and the Doctor quickly leave. The major-domo closes the door after them and Erika is left alone. She listens to the sound of sleighbells, then runs to the window and raises her hand in farewell. Over reverberating chords in the orchestra comes her last agonized cry: "Anatol!"

The Baroness slowly returns to her chair by the fireplace. Erika is about to ask her a question about Vanessa when she suddenly realizes that now—as it was with Vanessa—the old woman will never speak to *her* either. She summons the major-domo and orders him to cover all the mirrors, as before; she will receive no visitors; the gates to the park are to be locked permanently.[3]

---

[3] Like Lavinia's orders to the servant in the last act of Marvin David Levy's opera *Mourning Becomes Electra:* "Nail the shutters closed. I will never leave this house, nor will anyone ever enter it."

She watches the major-domo and the lackey drape the mirrors, then sits down next to the Baroness at the fireplace. In abysmal despair and resignation, she murmurs: "Now it is my turn to wait." The curtain falls.

I VESPRI SICILIANI

(Les Vêpres Siciliennes)

(The Sicilian Vespers)

by GIUSEPPE VERDI

(1813–1901)

Libretto by

EUGÈNE SCRIBE and CHARLES DUVEYRIER

CHARACTERS

Guido di Monforte, French Governor of Sicily for Charles of Anjou	Baritone
Siri di Béthune, a French officer	Bass
Conte Vaudemont, a French officer	Bass
Arrigo, a young Sicilian	Tenor
Giovanni da Procida, Sicilian physician and patriot	Bass
Elena, Duchess, and sister of Friedrich of Austria	Soprano
Ninetta, her maid	Contralto
Danieli, a Sicilian engaged to Ninetta	Tenor
Tebaldo, a French soldier	Tenor
Roberto, a French soldier	Bass
Manfredo, a Sicilian	Tenor

Sicilian men and women, French soldiers, pages, nobles, officers, monks, an executioner

Place: In and near Palermo
Time: 1282
First performance: Grand Opéra, Paris, June 13, 1855
Original language: French

(NOTE: As the opera is usually sung in Italian, the names of the characters are given in that language.)

Verdi's nineteenth opera is a product of his "middle period," which he began with the great trilogy of *Rigoletto, Il Trovatore* and *La Traviata,* composed between 1851 and 1853. *Les Vêpres* was commissioned by the Paris Opéra to be part of the Great Exhibition of 1855. To Verdi, who was then forty years old, this commission was important: it was to be his first real Parisian premiere. An Italian, he decided, could show the French a thing or two about opera. And so, in 1853, with Giuseppina Strepponi (his second wife, whom he married in 1859) he left his villa in Lombardy to write *Les Vêpres* on the spot in Paris.

But there he ran head on into problems. To begin with, he was dissatisfied with the Scribe/Duveyrier libretto because it not only showed the French being defeated but also portrayed the Italians in a somewhat unfavorable light because of the treacherous behavior of the Sicilian patriots. Verdi demanded changes; Scribe ignored him. What was worse, the musicians and the management disliked Verdi's music, while he himself resented the rigid, traditional requirements of five acts and a ballet. However, Verdi—always the professional—met all the conditions, and *Les Vêpres* was premiered with considerable success.

The opera continued in repertoire under various titles. During the Paris run, Verdi made an Italian translation. As *I Vespri Siciliani* it was premiered in Parma December 26, 1855. Because of censorship, which banned stories of foreign tyrants and patriotic rebels, the scene was shifted to Lisbon and the opera renamed *Giovanna di Guzman*, and thus presented at La Scala in 1856. It was staged at San Carlo, Naples, in 1857 as *Batilde di Turenna*. Performances were given in London and New York in 1859; there were modern revivals at the Metropolitan and the Paris Opéra in 1974, and it has since survived in the repertoire usually in the Italian translation.

The opera has a historical background in the occupation of Sicily by French troops during the thirteenth century and the efforts of the Sicilians to eject them. The overture, considered one of Verdi's best, is dominated by the cello theme which is heard during the Act Three duet between Arrigo and Monforte.

ACT ONE

The great square in Palermo. French soldiers are drinking and carousing while the Sicilians are sullenly watching them from across the square. The soldiers sing of their homeland ("A te, ciel natìo"); the Sicilians sing of their hatred of the oppressors ("Con empio desìo al suolo natìo").

The Duchess Elena crosses the square, coming from the chapel where she had been praying for the soul of her brother, Federigo (Friedrich of Austria), who had been executed on Monforte's orders for his patriotic activities. Monforte is now holding her hostage in his palace. In suppressed fury Elena sings about her brother ("O mio fratel, Federigo!"), then vows vengeance on the man who murdered him.

She stops suddenly as she is accosted by a drunken French soldier, Roberto, who orders her to sing ("Per mia fè! Canto gentile"). The Sicilians, who have gathered around her, are enraged, but Elena complies. Her song ("Deh! tu calma, O Dio possente"), however, is more than a reply to the soldier's insolence. It has a message (in metaphor) for the Sicilians: it tells of a vessel (Sicily) near shipwreck, saved by God's intervention and the courage of the sailors (Sicilian patriots). The long narrative *cantabile* line is followed by a wildly excited *allegro* —Elena's lyrical attempt to incite the dispirited Sicilians to action, telling them their destiny is in their own hands ("Il vostro fato è in vostra man").

The Sicilians lunge forward to attack the French, but Monforte suddenly appears and quells the incipient uprising. Soldiers and Sicilians alike flee the square in confusion, leaving Monforte faced by Elena, Ninetta and Danieli. The four express their reactions to the skirmish in a long unaccompanied quartet ("D'ira fremo all'aspetto tremendo").

Arrigo enters to tell Elena that he has been released from prison. Monforte orders the others to leave, saying he wants to be alone with Arrigo. A duet follows as the Governor questions him ("Qual è il tuo nome?"). His name, he replies, is Arrigo . . . he has no father . . . his mother is dead. . . . Glaring at Monforte, he fumes that his questioner certainly must know how much he hates him. Monforte, though aware that this angry rebel is his own son, controls his emotions.

He quietly says he has learned that Arrigo was in effect a protégé of Friedrich of Austria. Arrigo confirms this in a vigorous refrain ("I passi miei sorregger"), singing that Friedrich honored him as a soldier and that he would gladly have died for the King. In the duet that follows, Monforte sings that, in spite of the young Sicilian's defiance, he admires his spirit. The Governor, in fact, invites him to join the French. Arrigo scornfully refuses, whereupon Monforte warns him not to associate any longer with Elena. Arrigo turns on his heel and walks into the palace.

ACT TWO

A valley near Palermo. The exiled Giovanni da Procida lands on a beach near Palermo with a band of Sicilians to lead the revolt against the French. Here, in expressing his love for his homeland, he sings the opera's most famous aria, "O tu Palermo, terra adorata," then sends his men to alert the patriots.

He meets Elena and Arrigo—who were told of his secret arrival— and tells them he has Spanish support, providing the Sicilians will arm and revolt. He leaves the two alone, and they join in an impassioned duet ("Quale, o prode, al tuo coraggio"). She asks how she can reward his courage; he sings that her love is the only reward he desires. Elena promises she will be his if he will avenge her slain brother.

They are about to leave when they are intercepted by Siri di Béthune, a French officer, and a group of soldiers. He hands Arrigo an invitation to the Governor's ball ("Cavalier, questo foglio"). When Arrigo rejects the invitation point-blank, the soldiers disarm him and lead him away.

Procida comes back and learns of Arrigo's arrest. At the same time young couples arrive to celebrate their engagements at the seaside shrine of St. Rosalie. They dance a tarantella. Watching them, Procida concocts a bizarre scheme to arouse the Sicilians to revolt: he surreptitiously urges the French soldiers to carry off the Sicilian women. But the Sicilians still hesitate to act—even when a festive boatload of French soldiers and their Sicilian captives passes on the way to the Governor's ball.

The arrogant boasting of the French soldiers ("Viva la guerra! Viva l'amor!") and the frustrated rage of the Sicilians ("Su inermi tu stendi"), expressed in a combined chorus, bring the act to a tumultuous close.

ACT THREE

[*Scene One*] Monforte, alone in his study, reads a letter from the woman he had abducted eighteen years ago. He reflects remorsefully on his cruel treatment of her—this woman who bore his son Arrigo ("Sì, m'aborriva ed a ragion"). The boy never knew his father—in fact was taught to hate him. Monforte desperately hopes that a father's love may yet bring his errant son to his senses ("In braccio alle dovizie"). He orders Arrigo to be brought before him.

A fiery duet ensues ("Quando al mio sen per te parlava"), dominated by the cello theme heard in the overture. Monforte, handing Arrigo the letter from his mother, then reveals his paternity. He tries to win Arrigo over, but the son is horrified at the thought that his own father is his mortal enemy. The duet rises to a climax as Monforte begs Arrigo for understanding and love, while Arrigo prays to the memory of his mother.

[*Scene Two*] The ball at the Governor's palace. At this point, the action virtually is brought to a standstill by the interpolation of the long *Ballet of the Four Seasons* ("Le Quattro Stagioni"). It is usually omitted in contemporary stagings of the opera. Arrigo himself has decided to come to the ball; he is followed by Elena, Procida and other conspirators, all of whom are masked and are identified by a silk ribbon displayed on their cloaks. Elena and Procida make themselves known to Arrigo, but replace their masks when Monforte approaches.

Making their way among the dancers, the conspirators edge closer to Monforte. Suddenly Elena, dagger in hand, lunges at Monforte just as Procida himself is about to strike, crying: "This is the last day for the French! Sicily is ours!" ("L'ultimo dì per Francesi egli è! A noi Sicilia!"). Arrigo thrusts himself in front of his father, shielding his body with his own. French soldiers defend Monforte with drawn swords. Instantly the Governor orders all the conspirators, except Arrigo, to prison to face execution. The plotters, unaware that Arrigo is Monforte's son, curse him for his apparent treachery. The act ends with a vigorous concerted number.

ACT FOUR

Courtyard of a fortress. With Monforte's permission, Arrigo comes to visit the imprisoned patriots. In a somber E-minor aria ("Giorno di pianto"), he reflects on his predicament: he has been denounced as a traitor, hated by all his erstwhile comrades—and, above all, by Elena. When she emerges from her cell he tries to explain. At first she replies with furious scorn, ironically repeating his denial of treachery ("Non sei reo").

At length she understands, and expresses her pity and forgiveness in an enchanting bel canto *cantilena* ("Arrigo! ah parli un core").[1] Arrigo's voice then blends with hers in melodious avowals of love.

Procida, led in by guards, manages to hand Elena a note smuggled into the prison informing the conspirators that a Spanish ship laden with gold and arms is waiting offshore for the Sicilian revolt. When he catches sight of Arrigo he reviles him as a traitor, but is stupified to learn that he and the Governor are father and son. This, he realizes, will seal the fate of the Sicilians. In a brief phrase he bids farewell to Sicily—and to life ("Addio, mia patria, invendicato").

Monforte enters. When Arrigo pleads for mercy for his friends—or to be allowed to die with them—Monforte excoriates him as an ingrate. This leads into a quartet: Elena, Arrigo and Procida give way to despair, Monforte vows to execute the plotters unless Arrigo submits and acknowledges him as "father." Even though Elena implores him not to acquiesce, Arrigo finally utters the fateful words: "O padre!"

Meanwhile, four penitents, chanting the *De profundis* ("De profundis clamavi"), emerge from the Hall of Justice. With them is the executioner carrying his headsman's ax. When Monforte hears Arrigo's capitulation, he commands the grim procession to halt, then pardons all

[1] It is crowned with a brilliant chromatic cadenza, ranging from high C to F-sharp below the staff. Verdi thoughtfully provided a simpler optional one.

the conspirators on the spot ("Ministro di morte arresta! A lor perdono!").

He further declares that Elena and Arrigo are to be married this very
day—*at the hour of Vespers*—to seal the peace between the opposing
factions. The throng hails the Governor's magnanimity in a jubilant
chorus ("Risponda ogn'alma al fremito").

ACT FIVE

In the gardens of Monforte's palace, where the nuptials are to be celebrated. In a chorus ("Si celebri alfin") knights and ladies rejoice over
the end of hostilities and hymn the delights of love. Elena responds with
the stirring "Siciliana" (or "Bolero"), sung with choral interpolations
("Mercè, dilette amiche"). Arrigo joins her in a lyrical interlude ("La
brezza aleggia intorno carrezzarmi il viso").

When Arrigo briefly leaves to speak to his father, Procida slinks in
and approaches Elena. To her consternation, he sardonically congratulates her on the fact that her wedding will provide the signal for the
final revolt: at the sound of the wedding bells the Sicilians will cut
down the French. Horror-stricken, Elena declares she will not go
through with the wedding—and informs Arrigo accordingly, to his utter
stupefaction, when he returns.

This leads into the long, stormy trio which dominates the finale of the
opera, beginning with Elena's anguished cry: "Sorte fatal! O fier ci-
mento!" She laments her cruel dilemma: to save Arrigo's life she must
cancel her marriage; to save her countrymen she must go to the altar.
Arrigo denounces her for cowardice and treachery. Procida malevolently dares her to explain her repudiation. The trio climaxes in a wild
outburst of conflicting emotions.

Monforte now enters with knights and ladies of his French court. Arrigo rushes to him, crying that Elena has broken her troth. Virtually
dismissing this change of heart as a feminine whim, Monforte takes the
right hands of the pair in his own and announces: "I join you, noble
couple" ("V'unisco, o nobil coppia!").

Procida, standing apart, slowly raises his hand and with venomous
emphasis intones: "And you, happy signal, bells, echo!" ("E voi, seg-
nal felice, bronzi, echeggiate").

From every side, armed Sicilians—men and women—storm in and
hurl themselves upon the French with a thunderous chorus of "Vendetta! A morte, al terror!" The massacre is complete. The curtain falls.

WERTHER

by JULES MASSENET

(1842–1912)

Libretto by

ÉDOUARD BLAU, PAUL MILLIET and GEORGES HARTMANN

Based on the novel *Die Leiden des Jungen Werthers* (*The Sorrows of Young Werther*), by the German poet and novelist Johann Wolfgang von Goethe

CHARACTERS

Werther, a young poet	Tenor
Charlotte, daughter of the Bailiff	Mezzo-soprano
Sophie, her sister	Soprano
The Bailiff, a widower	Bass
Albert, fiancé of Charlotte, later her husband	Baritone
Schmidt ⎱ friends of the Bailiff	⎰ Tenor
Johann ⎰	⎱ Bass
Brühlmann ⎱ a young boy and girl	
Kätchen ⎰ who appear briefly	Treble voices

Younger children of the Bailiff (Fritz, Max, Hans, Karl, Gretel, Clara), servants, townsfolk

Place: Wetzlar, in Prussia
Time: About 1780
First performance: World premiere (in German), Imperial Opera, Vienna, February 16, 1892; first performance in French, Geneva, Switzerland, December 27, 1892
Original language: French

Werther, the ninth of Massenet's twenty-five operas, was his most popular with the exception of *Manon.* It was a favorite with French audiences, having been performed some thirteen hundred times at the Opéra-Comique in Paris following its premiere in Geneva.

In America, *Werther* was performed for the first time in March 1894. Subsequently, Mary Garden, while with the Chicago Opera Company, made the role of Charlotte one of her most memorable interpretations.

The Metropolitan presented *Werther* for the first time in April 1894 with a cast headed by Emma Eames and Jean De Reszke. In November 1909 and March 1910 revivals there, the cast was headed by Geraldine Farrar, Edmond Clémont, Alma Gluck and Dinh Gilly.

The San Francisco Opera staged the opera for the first time in November 1935 with the role of Werther sung by Tito Schipa, considered the finest Werther in the opera's later history. The most recent New York performance was given by the New York City Opera Company during its 1947–48 season. Abroad, the work was produced by Sir Michael Redgrave at Glyndebourne in June 1966. *Werther* was scheduled for the Metropolitan Opera's 1970–71 season for the first time in sixty years, with a cast headed by Christa Ludwig and Franco Corelli. It was again staged during the 1978–79 and 1979–80 seasons.

Massenet's craftsmanship, unerring musical instinct and sure sense of the dramatic give the opera a sound theatrical quality. The music ranges from unabashed romanticism to a kind of refined sensuality. There is a wealth of flowing melody combined with a fragile charm peculiarly French. Massenet makes effective use of identifying themes to heighten characterization, and the vocal line is supported by superb orchestration.

There is a brief, lyrical prelude, the themes of which reflect the realistic as well as the romantic elements in Werther's personality. The dominant theme is that heard later when the poet sees Charlotte's house for the first time.

ACT ONE

At left, the terrace at the entrance of the Bailiff's house; beyond, a courtyard with a fountain. At right, a garden. An afternoon in July. The Bailiff, seated on the terrace, is surrounded by his younger children, whom he is teaching Christmas carols.

Stopping them in the middle of a chorus, the Bailiff scolds them for singing too loudly, then asks them to begin again ("Assez! Recommençons"). The children do so, singing as loudly as before and without expression. Annoyed, the Bailiff asks if they would dare sing in such an unmusical manner if their sister Charlotte were there to hear them. This admonition impresses the youngsters, and they repeat the carol ("Jésus vient de naître") to their father's satisfaction. In fact, he is so well pleased that he ends the carol with them.

Schmidt and Johann appear and stand listening in the doorway. The children run to them affectionately. Johann twits the Bailiff for rushing the Christmas season by teaching the children Christmas carols in July.

The Bailiff answers rather testily that not everyone's artistic sensibilities are as easily offended as Johann's—and besides, it is not easy to teach children because they do not pay attention.

Their colloquy is interrupted by the entrance of Sophie. The scene continues in quasi-recitative and brief solo passages. Greeting Sophie, Schmidt inquires about Charlotte. Sophie answers that her sister is getting dressed for the family ball which is to be held at Wetzlar this evening. In a brief refrain ("Koffel a mis sa redingote") Schmidt describes how friends and neighbors are eagerly preparing for this gala event. Koffel is brushing up his frock coat, Steiner is hiring the brewer's horse, Hoffmann and Goulden are renting a coach and a buggy. Even that melancholy young poet, Werther, seems lately to be taking a more cheerful view of life.

The three men discuss Werther briefly. The Bailiff says he likes the young man, but the other two consider him too withdrawn and gloomy. When the Bailiff tells them that the Prince has even offered Werther a diplomatic post, Schmidt and Johann scoff that he is much too provincial for such a sophisticated position.

With that the two take their leave, telling the Bailiff they will meet him later at the Golden Grape—where they intend to collect the drinks he owes them. They add that the waitress has promised them lobster for dinner. The Bailiff jokingly calls them a pair of gluttons, then asks if they will not wait to see Charlotte. They answer that they will see her later at the ball.

Schmidt pauses to ask when Albert will return. He has not mentioned returning in his letters, the Bailiff replies, but he writes that his business is going well. Schmidt comments that Albert is a fine young man who will make an ideal husband for Charlotte. Finally leaving arm in arm, Schmidt and Johann sing a lusty duet in praise of Bacchus ("Vivat Bacchus, semper vivat!").

The Bailiff calls the children together again to rehearse the Christmas carol "note by note." He sends Sophie to bring Charlotte, then goes into the house with the children. Werther appears, accompanied by a young peasant who has shown him the way to the Bailiff's house. Walking slowly to the fountain, the poet sings the first of the opera's arias, a lyrical invocation to the pastoral beauty of this quiet spot ("Ô nature, pleine de grâce"). In an introductory recitative ("Je ne sais si je veille") he wonders if he is awake or dreaming, because this place is like paradise itself. In the aria, he hails Nature as the eternal mother, forever young and adorable ("Mère éternellement jeune").

A graceful arpeggio follows the conclusion of the aria, and then the sound of the children singing is heard. Listening, Werther murmurs that the bitterness of life cannot sully their innocence.

As he muses beside the fountain, Charlotte appears. The children, excitedly calling her name, rush out of the house to greet her. The Bailiff follows, and Charlotte asks him if he is pleased with their singing. Reasonably so, he answers, but the children assure Charlotte that Papa is "très content" with their performance. Gazing at Charlotte in her party finery, the Bailiff effusively praises her beauty. All their friends, he exclaims, will be jealous of her.

Modestly turning aside the compliment, Charlotte remarks that their "jealous" friends are late in arriving—and that will allow her time to give the children their supper. Thereupon she fetches a large loaf of bread and a dish of butter, then distributes the slices to her brothers and sisters.

At the sound of carriage wheels in the distance, the Bailiff tells Charlotte to hurry because the guests are arriving. At that moment he notices Werther approaching and welcomes him with pompous courtesy ("Vous venez visiter"). Introducing Charlotte, he explains she is mother to her brothers and sisters, who were left motherless by the death of his wife. Charlotte, somewhat embarrassed, apologizes to Werther for being remiss in her greeting. The children, she adds primly, refuse to eat their meals unless she herself serves them. Werther acknowledges with a gallant bow.

During a brief orchestral interlude, the guests begin to arrive. With them come Brühlmann and Kätchen, a young couple so wrapped up in each other that they pay no attention to the Bailiff as he greets them. Holding hands, they sigh ecstatically over "the divine Klopstock," whose poetry obviously has inspired them.[1] The Bailiff, with an indulgent laugh, advises the lad to save his rhapsodies until he gets to the ball, in order not to delay the proceedings at present.

A brief byplay follows. Approaching Werther with one of the youngest children in her arms, Charlotte tells the child to "kiss her cousin." Taken aback, Werther wonders if he is worthy of the name. Charlotte observes, rather enigmatically, that there are so many cousins that it would be unfortunate if he proved unworthy of the relationship. She then turns to Sophie and asks her to take charge of the children tonight in her stead. Sophie willingly assents, but remarks that the children would much rather be with Charlotte.

Deeply touched by the rapport between the sisters, Werther expresses his admiration in an impassioned refrain, "Ô spectacle idéal." It is at the same time a declaration of his love for Charlotte.

He and Charlotte then leave with the other guests. Brühlmann and Kätchen, still oblivious to everything, remain at the fountain for a mo-

[1] This is a reference to Friedrich Gottlieb Klopstock (1724–1803), a German poet. He was notable for his iconoclastic rejection of contemporary classic forms in favor of unrhymed odes expressing intensely religious emotions.

ment, then wander hand in hand after the others. The Bailiff, watching them with a smile, muses that the "divine Klopstock" and young love present a riddle beyond his understanding.

Sophie sends the children into the house. Then, hearing her father reprise a few bars of "Vivat Bacchus," she quietly brings him his hat and cane, mischievously reminding him that he promised to meet Schmidt and Johann at the Golden Grape. The Bailiff—somewhat abashed because Sophie knows he is anxious to join his convivial friends—at first demurs, then struts away, jauntily swinging his cane. Sophie accompanies him to the garden gate and closes it after him.

As she turns back to the house, Albert appears. With an exclamation of surprise, Sophie runs to him and they embrace. Their dialogue continues over a recurring six-note figure in the accompaniment. Albert's first question is about Charlotte. Sophie explains that this is one of the rare occasions when she is away from the house. Why, she asks, has he kept his arrival a secret? He replies that he wanted to surprise Charlotte, and now he wants to know if she thought about him during his six months' absence. Sophie assures him that Charlotte—who, after all, is to be his bride—thought of him constantly, as did everyone else in the house.

And meanwhile, Sophie goes on, she and the others have been busy preparing for the wedding—and she hopes there will be dancing. Albert promises that it will be a gay affair because he wants everyone to share his happiness. But for the present no one is to know that he has returned, he tells Sophie, then urges her to go into the house before they are discovered. With a tender "Goodnight, dear brother-in-law," she goes in and closes the door.

Alone, Albert expresses his happiness over his return in the melodious aria "Quelle prière de reconnaissance." He marvels how these familiar surroundings have taken on a new meaning, and looks forward with passionate longing to his first meeting with Charlotte after his absence.

As he slowly walks away, immersed in his thoughts, the scene gradually darkens and the moonlight glimmers through the trees. Here begins the exquisite music of the "Clair de Lune" scene, one of Massenet's finest creations. The sensuous theme, stated by the strings in elegant contours, is evidence of the composer's gift for orchestral effect. The music inevitably brings to mind Debussy's more impressionistic evocation of night in his own "Clair de Lune."

Charlotte and Werther, returning from the ball, walk arm in arm through the garden gate, then sing the great duet "Il faut nous séparer." Charlotte bids the poet goodnight; he responds with a passionate avowal of his love. She deprecates his extravagant praise of her beauty, saying that he really knows nothing about her.

In answer, Werther exclaims that their souls are linked together ("Mon âme a reconnu"). He declares that her own brothers and sisters will bear witness that she is the loveliest of women. Yes . . . the children know, Charlotte replies ("Vous avez dit vrai"), but that is only because these orphaned little ones see in her the image of their beloved mother. Even now, Charlotte goes on, they add to her own anguish by asking why "those men in black" carried their mother away.

But Werther, almost beside himself with ardor, scarcely hears what Charlotte is saying. In an impassioned refrain ("Rêve! Extase!") he again apostrophizes her beauty and reiterates his avowals. Disturbed by the violence of his emotions, Charlotte tells him he must go. At that moment, the Bailiff is heard calling out that Albert has arrived. Werther, staggering back in stunned surprise, repeats the name questioningly. In stricken tones, Charlotte tells him that Albert is the man she promised her dying mother she would marry.

Looking into Werther's eyes, she declares that when he was near she had forgotten that oath. Though crushed by despair, the poet tells her she must keep her promise—but if she does, he will die. As the "Clair de Lune" theme, in a minor key, sounds softly in the orchestra, Charlotte turns and leaves. Alone, Werther cries out in anguish: "She is betrothed to another!" The curtain falls.

ACT TWO

Before the curtain rises there is a brief prelude entitled "Les Tilleuls" ("The Lime Trees"), in the rhythm of a country dance. Its principal theme is associated with the convivial personalities of Schmidt and Johann.

The scene is the square before the Golden Grape at Wetzlar on a pleasant Sunday afternoon in September. Across the square is the Protestant church, next to it the parsonage. Schmidt and Johann are seated at a table outside the inn. Enjoying their wine, they sing a variation of their favorite tune, "Vivat Bacchus," in praise of wine, the weather and life in general.

They pause to listen to the sound of the organ in the church. Schmidt suggests they join in singing the service, whereupon they strike up an impromptu hymn of their own ("De bénir le Seigneur"). Sung in an ingenious imitation of the canon form, its burden is that each man should praise the Lord in his own way. At its conclusion, Johann tells his companion that on this day the rector is being honored for his fifty years of married life. Schmidt remarks that this is indeed an admirable achievement—but he himself could never have survived it. At that moment they both catch sight of Charlotte and Albert crossing the square on their way to the church. There, says Johann, are two people who were willing to take the risk of marriage. He and Schmidt gravely drink to the health of these two brave souls and then go inside the tavern.

Meanwhile, Charlotte and Albert sit down on a bench under a lime tree near the entrance of the parsonage. In a melodious duet ("Voici trois mois") they reflect on the happiness they have shared during the three months of their marriage. At the conclusion of the duet, organ music again is heard and the two enter the church.

As they do so, Werther appears on the other side of the square and grimly watches them. A sudden change in the orchestral accompaniment from the simple melody of the organ music to foreboding harmonies reflects his emotional turmoil. He gives expression to his thoughts in the dramatic recitative and aria "Un autre est son époux . . . J'aurais sur ma poitrine"—known as the "Désolation de Werther."

In the recitative he sings that if God had granted him this angel, he would have devoted his life to her. Now his love for her is blasphemy. But for a caprice of fate, he goes on in the aria, he could be holding this most glorious of God's creations in his arms, to be his own forever. In a climactic phrase of anguish, Werther sings that this dream is shattered. Staggering to the bench under the lime tree, he buries his face in his hands. The clamorous orchestral accompaniment gradually subsides.

As Werther remains motionless on the bench, Schmidt and Johann emerge from the inn leading young Brühlmann, who is beside himself as the result of a lovers' quarrel. The two men try to assure the lad that his Kätchen will come back to him, but Brühlmann is inconsolable. After all, Johann tells him, a seven-year courtship cannot possibly have been in vain. In any case, Schmidt adds gaily, taking the boy by the arm, he can forget his troubles at the rector's anniversary party. With that the men literally drag the distraught youngster away.

Albert, coming out of the church alone, sees Werther. Going to him, he impulsively puts his hand on the poet's shoulder in a comforting gesture. Werther, startled, leaps to his feet as though trying to avoid the other. A dramatic colloquy follows.

Restraining Werther, Albert sings that he understands his sorrow and is grateful to him for his abnegation. In an ensuing refrain ("Mais celle qui devint ma femme") he sings that he is aware that Werther and Charlotte once met, and that the poet dreamed of love. But now that dream has vanished, and he knows what agony this has cost. And to know, Albert adds, grasping Werther's hand, is to forgive.

In an equally moving refrain ("Vous l'avez dit") Werther answers that he has indeed tried to remain loyal. Rather than continue to harbor unworthy desires for what he has lost he will resist temptation and go away forever. When the storm of passion is over and the pain is gone, the consolation of true friendship will sustain him.

The scene is interrupted by Sophie, who comes tripping in to the accompaniment of a sprightly figure in the orchestra. Bubbling with happiness, she shows the two men a bouquet and sings that she has plundered the garden for the choicest flowers ("Voyez le beau bouquet"). Smiling up at Werther, she promises to ask him for the first dance at the anniversary party. Taking note of his crestfallen expression, Sophie exclaims that on this beautiful day everyone should be happy. She elaborates on this theme with joyous abandon in a sparkling aria, "Du gai soleil."

Werther, however, is unmoved by Sophie's gaiety. Albert, in order to be alone with him, tells Sophie to present her bouquet to the anniversary couple. With a significant look at Werther, Albert observes that while one looks far and wide for happiness, perhaps it is before one's very eyes—with a smile on her face and flowers in her hands. Werther's only reaction is stony silence.

Sophie comes skipping back, reminds Werther that he is to have the first minuet with her, then sings a reprise of her aria. Ending the number on an exuberant phrase, she hurries away followed by Albert.

Werther abandons himself to gloomy reflections to the accompaniment of somber chords in the orchestra. He asks himself if his love for Charlotte has been pure and untainted, then bursts out remorsefully that he has lived a lie: his love has been sullied by impure desire. Tormented by guilt, he cries out that he must go away to escape the consequences of his shameless weakness.

He is about to rush away when he sees Charlotte on the threshold of the church. He stands as though hypnotized as she approaches with downcast eyes, murmuring that prayer has given her new strength. Noticing Werther, she asks if he plans to attend the rector's anniversary party. He replies that it would mean only the torment of seeing her there with another man. Charlotte gazes at him compassionately.

Here begins one of the principal duets of the opera. As the "Clair de Lune" theme sounds in the orchestra, Werther recalls the day they first met ("Ah! qu'il es loin, ce jour") and the rapture they shared in that moment. Charlotte, determined not to weaken, coldly reminds him that she is now the wife of Albert—who loves her. "Who could help loving you?" Werther interjects wildly.

Trying to reason with him, Charlotte asks if there are not other women who could inspire his love ("N'est-il donc pas d'autre femme") . . . why must he love *her?* As well ask a madman the reason for his madness, Werther storms. When Charlotte resolutely tells him he must go, he wildly implores her not to send him away. The scene builds in intensity as Charlotte entreats Werther to have consideration for her own peace of mind. Her plea brings him to his senses.

In quiet resignation he sings that her peace of mind is all he desires—yet he cannot promise to go away forever. No . . . not forever, she tells

him fervently, but only for a little while. In fact, she adds, she will expect him back on Christmas Day. With that she leaves to the accompaniment of a descending chromatic theme in the orchestra which underscores Werther's emotional upheaval.

In a melodramatic soliloquy ("Oui! ce qu'elle m'ordonne") Werther resolves to act in accordance with Charlotte's plea for peace of mind. His self-sacrifice may cost him his life, but what does it matter! What is death but the drawing aside of the veil which separates the known from the unknown? Is it a sin to seek relief from suffering?

Werther continues his philosophizing in one of the opera's principal arias, "Lorsque l'enfant revient d'un voyage." When a wandering child returns home unexpectedly, he sings, his father greets him with joy and relief—not rebuke. By the same token, will not God, the Father of mankind, welcome back an erring son and pardon his sins? In the impassioned climax of the aria Werther cries that although he cannot claim to know the Almighty Father, he puts his trust in Him and implores His help in his hour of anguish. He ends the aria in a half-spoken phrase of desperate entreaty.

As Werther turns and walks slowly away, he meets Sophie, who tells him the anniversary procession is ready to start and is waiting for him. Werther brusquely tells her he is leaving. Staring at him in surprise, Sophie asks when he will return. Never, Werther snaps, then strides away. Calling after him, Sophie bursts into tears.

Charlotte, Albert and the other members of the party rush in, find Sophie weeping and excitedly ask what has happened. She sobs that Werther told her he was going away forever, then rushed away like a madman. Charlotte gasps: "Forever!" Albert, suddenly realizing what Werther's action means to her, says in a grim aside: "He loves her!"

As the gay music of the anniversary celebration blares out in ironic contrast to the tragic mood of the scene, the curtain falls.

ACT THREE

There is a brief prelude—mostly on the theme heard during the Letter Scene which opens the act. The curtain rises to show the home of Charlotte and Albert early on Christmas Eve. Albert is absent. Charlotte is sitting at a table reading a letter from Werther. Here follows another of the opera's famous arias, known as the "Air de lettres" ("Ah, Werther, qui m'aurait dit").

In recitative, Charlotte muses that Werther's absence has served only to bring him closer to her. Throwing the letters on the table, she murmurs that she cannot bring herself to destroy them. In an ensuing refrain ("Je vous écris") sung over a barcarolelike accompaniment in 6/8

tempo, Charlotte reads Werther's latest letter. It quite simply states the fact that he is alone.

Charlotte notes that there is no word of reproof, of love or regret, of blame or rebuke. This intensifies her feeling of guilt: she blames herself for her hardheartedness, for making Werther suffer in loneliness and frustration. This she expresses in an unaccompanied passage. In the letter, Werther adds that as he writes he hears the happy cries of children playing outside his window. They remind him of the tender care Charlotte lavishes on her brothers and sisters. They too will forget him. . . .

They never will forget him, Charlotte exclaims, and will welcome him when he comes back. But the tone of his letter disturbs her. He reminds her that when she set Christmas as the day of his return ("Tu m'as dit: à Noël"), his answer was: "Never!" When that day comes, it will become clear who was right—Charlotte or Werther. But if he does not return ("Mais si je ne dois reparaître") he asks only that she weep in memory of him. As the somber letter theme sounds in the orchestra, Charlotte finishes reading and sobs quietly.

Sophie runs in—effervescent as always—and chides her sister for keeping to herself while Albert is away. Father, she says, is unhappy about the situation. Noticing Charlotte's tears, Sophie asks if she is ill. Charlotte hastily assures her that she is merely tired but will soon regain her spirits and laugh again.

With childlike enthusiasm, Sophie responds in another characteristically lighthearted air ("Ah! le rire est béni") that laughter is a blessing. It is born of light and is as free as a bird, she sings in coloratura phrases. But suddenly she becomes serious, and the mood of the music changes with her. Leading Charlotte to a chair, Sophie kneels before her.

No longer prattling like a child, she says gravely that she is old enough to know the reason for her sister's tears, as well as for the general air of gloom which has settled over the household. It is all because Werther has gone away. At the sound of his name, Charlotte makes an involuntary movement; she tries to control herself but breaks into tears. The reaction is not lost on Sophie, who apologizes for mentioning Werther's name.

In an ensuing aria, "Va! laisse couler mes larmes"—known as the "Air des Larmes"—Charlotte sings that it is best to let tears flow unchecked. Unshed tears beat like waves upon the heart until at last it breaks. The aria ends on a descending phrase expressive of Charlotte's grief.

Alarmed by her despondent manner, Sophie begs her sister to leave her lonely house and come back to live with her family until Albert returns. Things will be merry at home . . . the children will sing their lovely Christmas carols to brighten the hours. The mention of Christ-

mas brings Charlotte's thoughts back to Werther's letter. In an aside, she repeats the phrase from his letter—"If I should fail to return." Fighting back her tears, she promises Sophie that she will come home. The sisters tenderly embrace.

After Sophie leaves, Charlotte sinks down at the table in utter despair. Then, in a moving prayer ("Seigneur Dieu! J'ai suivi ta loi"), she asks for strength to resist the temptation to surrender to Werther's love. The test is cruel, she cries, and her strength is failing. She implores God's help in her hour of trial. At the conclusion of the aria her voice dies away in a whispered plea.

As she sits hopeless and dejected, Werther suddenly appears in the doorway. Charlotte looks up and cries out his name over a thundering phrase in the orchestra. Werther, pale and haggard, stares at Charlotte as though on the verge of madness. There is a long pause as the two gaze at each other.

Then in broken phrases Werther says that every hour he was away he swore he would never come back to her. On her very threshold he fought against himself, but it was all in vain. Trying to hide her emotions and to calm him, Charlotte says that there was no reason for him to stay away—everyone was eagerly waiting for his return. Werther interrupts to ask if she too was waiting. Pointedly ignoring the question, she hastens to add that even in the house itself nothing has changed. Looking around, Werther murmurs: "Nothing . . . except the hearts."

Yes . . . everything is as he remembers it, he goes on (Charlotte repeats the phrase in a musical echo of his own). Werther notices the harpsichord and recalls how he and Charlotte sang together, then speaks of the books they read to each other. Suddenly he notices two pistols in a box on the table. Making a movement as if to pick them up, he murmurs ominously that these he also remembers. He held them once . . . when he was thinking of the final rest for which he longed.

His gesture is unobserved by Charlotte, who has turned to pick up a book from the harpsichord. She hands him a volume of verses by his favorite poet, Ossian, remarking that he had once asked her to translate them.[2] With a melodramatic sigh, Werther begins reading over a harp accompaniment. This introduces one of the most famous arias in the opera, "Pourquoi me réveiller."

Appropriately, it is a lover's lament, in which he asks why the voices of spring should awaken him, when the awakening will bring only sadness and desolation. The aria ends in an impassioned climax. Charlotte, realizing that Werther is describing his own feelings in terms of Ossian's verses, begs him not to go on reading.

[2] Ossian: a bard and epic hero of Gaelic folklore of the third century A.D. His poetry, flowery and romantic, was claimed to have been translated by James MacPherson in *The Poems of Ossian* (published 1760–62).

Believing she has at last betrayed her true feelings toward him,
Werther sings that now she understands ("Ciel! Ai-je compris?"). They
must throw off all pretense and submit to the divine decree of love. The
scene continues in duet form as Charlotte protests that she must not
allow herself to love the poet, while he reiterates his avowals. In momentary surrender, Charlotte yields to his embrace, then tears herself
from his arms. Crying that she cannot endure this anguish, she bids
Werther goodbye forever and rushes into her room, closing the door
behind her.

Imploring her not to leave him, Werther staggers toward the door,
then stops and listens. As dark harmonies reverberate in the orchestra
and then subside into a long, sustained chord, he murmurs that it is
goodbye at last . . . Charlotte has condemned him to death. Walking
slowly toward the entrance door of the house, he sings that now Mother
Earth may prepare to receive her son ("Prends le deuil, ô nature!"). He
must die, carrying his torment with him to the grave. Flinging open the
door, he rushes blindly away.

A moment later Albert walks in, his face grim. Told previously that
Werther had returned, he is puzzled at finding no one in the room and
the door wide open. Frowning darkly, he looks at the door of Charlotte's room and sharply calls her name. The door opens and she appears, gasping in surprise as she sees her husband. When Albert asks
her if anything is wrong she manages to answer that she was merely
startled at seeing him. With harsh insistence, Albert demands to know
who has been in the house. Confused and terrified, Charlotte is speech-
less.

At that moment a servant enters and hands Albert a letter. He looks
at it, recognizes Werther's handwriting, then glares at Charlotte. Slowly
and deliberately he reads Werther's message: he is going on a long
journey and wishes to borrow Albert's pistols. Charlotte wails that this
is an omen of disaster. In cold fury, her husband orders her to give
Werther the weapons. As though hypnotized, Charlotte walks to the
desk where the pistols are lying in the box. With Albert's eyes fixed on
her in a stare of icy hatred, she closes the box and hands it to the servant, who carries it away. Albert crushes Werther's letter in his hand,
hurls it from him in violent anger, then strides from the room.

As foreboding bass harmonies reverberate in the orchestra and then
flare up into a harsh chromatic figure, Charlotte frantically prays that
she may reach Werther in time. The curtain falls.

ACT FOUR

In the original score there is a long symphonic interlude called—with
a certain irony—*La Nuit de Noël,* which recapitulates some of the

themes heard in the previous acts. Its general character is dark and foreboding, heavy with Tschaikowskian gloom and the premonition of death. In some productions the interlude is omitted and the act is played as the second part of Act Three.

Werther's study. On the table is a three-branched candlestick, with books and papers scattered about. Through a large window at one side the snow-covered houses of the village are visible. Prominently seen is the house of the Bailiff, which is brightly lighted. In the study a ray of moonlight strikes across the floor and faintly reveals the form of Werther. He has shot himself and lies near death on the floor near the table.

As somber chords reverberate in the orchestra, the door is suddenly flung open and Charlotte enters. Looking around, she excitedly calls Werther's name. Then, going around the table, she comes upon Werther's form. With a cry of horror, she kneels and gently lifts him in her arms. Refusing to believe he is dead ("Non! Non! c'est impossible!"), she distractedly implores him to speak to her. This marks the beginning of the poignant death scene which brings the opera to its tragic climax.

Werther slowly opens his eyes. Recognizing Charlotte, he asks her to forgive him. Charlotte protests that it is she who must be forgiven, because she herself has shed the blood now gushing from his wound. Werther murmurs that because she had kept her love unstained she has spared him remorse in his hour of death. He sinks slowly back into her arms.

Panic-stricken, Charlotte calls for help. Reviving, Werther asks her not to call anyone ("n'appelle personne") . . . it is good to be alone at this moment when Death will allow him to say: "Je t'adore." In a flood of grief and passion, Charlotte bursts out into an avowal of her love: "Et moi, Werther, et moi je t'aime!" At last she confesses that from the day they first met she knew they were destined to love each other.

"And now," she goes on, as the "Clair de Lune" theme softly echoes in the orchestra, "take this last kiss as the seal of our love ("Ah! ton baiser") . . . and in this last kiss let us forget all our anguish." Over shimmering chords in the orchestra, the voices of the lovers die away together on the phrase "Tout, oublions tout!"

Suddenly from the Bailiff's house comes the sound of childish voices singing a Christmas carol ("Noël! Jésus vient de naître"). Charlotte recoils at the stinging irony of these sounds of joy in an hour of pain and death. Werther murmurs that these sinless children are singing a hymn of redemption. Now in the grip of delirium, he entreats Charlotte not to weep for him . . . this is not death . . . it is birth into new life. As though to add to Charlotte's torment, she hears Sophie's voice soaring over the children's chorus in an exultant phrase of the carol ("Dieu permet d'être heureux!").

Looking into Werther's face, Charlotte now realizes that he is at the point of death. As though to keep him from being physically taken away from her, she clasps him frenziedly to her breast, crying: "You shall live!" ("Tu vivras!").

For the last time, Werther opens his eyes. In serene phrases he asks Charlotte to grant him one final request ("Là-bas, au fond du cimetière"): he wishes to be buried under the two large linden trees at the back of the cemetery. But if the Church denies Christian burial to one who has taken his own life, then let him be buried in some secret, quiet place. And there, in the twilight, a woman will come and bless his last resting place with her tears.

As the theme of Ossian's poem ("Pourquoi me réveiller") surges through the orchestra, Werther dies in Charlotte's arms. With a cry of agony, she falls sobbing over his body. From outside comes the happy laughter of the children, mingled with the lilting chorus of the Christmas carol. The curtain falls.

DER ZIGEUNERBARON

(The Gypsy Baron)

by JOHANN STRAUSS

(1825–99)

Libretto by

IGNAZ SCHNITZER

Based on the novel *Saffi*, by the Hungarian novelist Mór Jókai

CHARACTERS

Ottokar, a young farm hand	Tenor
Lodovico Carnero, emissary of Empress Maria Theresa of Austria, Commissioner of Public Morals	High baritone
Sandor Barinkay, a young, impoverished Hungarian nobleman	Tenor
Czipra, an old gypsy woman	Mezzo-soprano
Saffi, a gypsy girl, supposed daughter of Czipra	Mezzo-soprano
Kalman Zsupan, a wealthy pig farmer	Baritone
Arsena, daughter of Zsupan	Soprano
Mirabella, mother of Ottokar and governess of Arsena	Soprano
Count Peter Homonay, Hungarian statesman and hussar	Baritone
Pali, a gypsy	Tenor

Peasants, gypsies, soldiers, nobles of the court, citizens of Vienna

Place: Hungary
Time: About 1750, during the reign of Maria Theresa
First performance: Theater an der Wien, October 24, 1885
Original language: German

This gay and tuneful operetta, rich in melody and fiery Hungarian rhythms, is second in popularity only to the composer's *Die Fledermaus*. Written about ten years after *Fledermaus,* it is another one of some fifteen works Strauss composed for the stage. While in Budapest to conduct one of his operettas, Strauss visited the Hungarian novelist Mór Jókai, who showed him his novel *Saffi*. It was a story of eighteenth-century Hungary—about the time when that province passed from Turkish to Austrian domination. Intrigued by its romantic and patriotic elements, Strauss saw in this subject the opportunity to unite—musically, at least—the ebullient spirits of the Hungarians and the Austrians. The result was a lusty, dashing, Hungarian gypsy piece, topped off with true Viennese *schmaltz*.

Strauss took two years to write *Zigeunerbaron,* making the most effective use of the dance forms which had made him the "Waltz King" of Europe. At the height of his fame as a composer of dance tunes (he wrote more than five hundred of them) he turned to light opera and operetta. With his incomparable talent for melody, he was highly respected as a musician by the great composers of his time—and these included men like Wagner, Richard Strauss and Brahms. His contemporaries said of him that he brought the spirit of the cafe into the opera house.

Zigeunerbaron opens with a typically Straussian overture, a collage of the major themes in symphonic style. First, a martial rhythm builds into the czardas theme, followed by the *andantino* of the finale of Act One. Then a wild marching rhythm leads into the gay waltz of the Vienna scene, with the theme of the "Werberlied" ("Recruiting Song") following. The overture then returns to the 6/8 tempo of the Boatmen's Chorus at the opening of Act One, and into a brilliant climax.

ACT ONE

A lonely clearing in the forest. In the background a stone tower rises above the ruins of a castle. In the foreground is a dilapidated, roofless hut; at right a gypsy cabin with a smoking chimney. Near stage front is a peasant house, trim and well kept, with a balcony. This is the home of Zsupan, the pig farmer, richest landowner in the region.

There is a brief orchestral prelude in a minor key, interspersed with bird calls. Then from behind the scenes comes the Boatmen's Chorus ("Das wär' kein rechter Schifferknecht"). In a barcarolelike rhythm they sing that anyone who is afraid of the water never will be a good sailor; the true seaman places his trust in his boat and oars. In a poetic turn, the sailors sing that they will sail the sea of life together with their sweethearts.

As the chorus ends, Ottokar appears, carrying a shovel and a pickax. He is vainly searching for buried treasure which, according to legend, had been hidden in the vicinity of the castle by its owner, Baron Barinkay, who had died in exile. Ottokar has been at this task for months and now he complains ("Jeden Tag, Müh' und Plag'") that he has been working like a slave to no avail. He curses his bad luck.

Czipra, the old gypsy woman, watches him and cackles in glee at his disappointment. She describes how she has seen Ottokar digging away day after day without finding anything ("Vergebens haben Sie gesucht"). Ottokar finally throws down his tools in disgust.

As the barcarole again is heard behind the scene, Czipra comes out of her hut. Spoken dialogue follows as she asks Ottokar what he is looking for—although she knows what it is as well as he does. Ignoring his rudeness when he tells her to mind her own business, she asks why he bothers to look for treasure when there is something more precious for him in a neighbor's house. When he asks what that may be, she answers that it is Arsena, the pretty daughter of Zsupan. With that she goes back into her hut.

Ottokar is dismayed because the gypsy woman knows about his secret love and—what is worse—probably knows he intends to meet Arsena at this very spot tonight. Suddenly hearing voices, he withdraws to one side.

Carnero and Sandor Barinkay enter, followed by officials and a crowd of villagers. In an amusing patter song ("Als flotter Geist doch früh verwaist") Barinkay describes his exciting adventures as he roamed the world over. He explains that he has been everywhere and has done everything. He traveled with a circus as an animal trainer, and all the animals simply adored him—giraffes, lions, tigers, hyenas, crocodiles and even alligators.

In a rousing waltz refrain, in which he is joined by the chorus ("Ja, das Alles auf Ehr'"), Barinkay boasts that he has done all this and more. And when you know what you're about, he sings, everything is easy. In a second stanza he modestly describes how he excelled as juggler, fire-eater, sword swallower, acrobat and magician.[1]

In ensuing dialogue it is explained that Carnero, as emissary of Empress Maria Theresa of Austria, has been assigned to reinstate Barinkay as lord of his ancestral land. This includes the ruined castle, a swamp under four feet of water and a nearby gypsy village. As Barinkay ruefully contemplates his inheritance, he notices the trim peasant house and asks whose it is. Carnero explains that it is the home of Kalman Zsupan, the "Prince of Pigs." His wealth includes not only thousands of pigs but a very pretty daughter, Arsena. Barinkay pricks up his ears.

Carnero leers amiably. Then, remembering his official position, he

[1] This paraphrase of Barinkay's couplet closely follows the translation of the original German. There are different versions—as is true of other patter songs in the operetta.

pompously declares that feminine beauty is of no interest to him. "Well then," says Barinkay, "let's get on with settling my affairs." They look around for witnesses to sign the necessary documents. First they knock on the door of the hut, bringing out Czipra. In answer to Carnero's questions, she says she lives here with the gypsies, who have gone to market but will return at sundown. Carnero introduces Barinkay to her as her lord and master, the rightful heir to this estate, who has just returned from exile.

Looking at him sharply, Czipra exclaims that her gift of prophecy did not desert her—she knows that this stranger is Barinkay. When Carnero suspiciously asks who told her she replies that she read the cards.

At that moment Saffi comes out of the hut and stares fixedly at Barinkay. She ignores Czipra's order to go inside and, with her eyes on Barinkay, murmurs that he casts a strange spell over her ("Bezaubernd wirkt auf mich sein Blick"). At Czipra's repeated bidding, Saffi re-enters the hut. Barinkay steps forward and asks the gypsy to tell his fortune. In a dramatic refrain ("Bald wird man dich viel umwerben") she prophesies a wonderful future—a treasure is waiting for him. He will find a loving wife who will be told in a dream on her wedding night where this treasure is hidden.

Carnero ironically compliments Czipra on her fortunetelling and asks her to prophesy for him. She mischievously obliges in a continuation of her aria ("Verloren hast du einen Schatz!"). The treasure *he* will soon find will be the sweetheart he lost, who was as scrawny as a sparrow but will come back to him as round as a barrel. And another prize will be restored to him—something that once was no bigger than his hand and now has grown taller than a beanpole. Czipra sings that Carnero will shortly discover these treasures. She chortles gleefully.

Embarrassed, Carnero blusters that this is all nonsense and orders Czipra to sign the documents. When she protests that writing is much too difficult for her, he tells her to draw a cross. After all, he snaps, this isn't a bargain with the devil. Sign, says Barinkay. "You command, I obey," Czipra replies. Seeing her mark, Carnero gasps that it is a drude's foot (*Drudenfuss*), a sign of witchcraft.[2] The onlookers comment with laughter. Saying that this is the only kind of writing she knows, Czipra shuffles away cackling to herself.

Zsupan, called out of his house, now strides up and asks what is wanted of him. When Carnero tells him that he is to sign a document as witness, the pig farmer replies in a patter song which is another of the comic highlights of the opera ("Ja, das Schreiben und das Lesen"), for

[2] *Drudenfuss*—the pentagram (five-pointed star), an ancient symbol against witches.

which Strauss wrote an earthy, bombastic melody quite in keeping with the character of the pig farmer.

Reading and writing, Zsupan sings, never were his long suit. From childhood on, pigs were his specialty. He knows nothing about poetry; his aesthetic fancies run to pig bristles and bacon. On the subject of fattening pigs, for example, he is the final authority. There isn't a skinny one in his drove of five thousand, which are known far and wide for their tempting sleekness. Strutting about, Zsupan brings his song to a bellowing climax.

An interval of spoken dialogue follows. Carnero informs Zsupan—who, in fact, had taken over the lands of the exiled Baron Barinkay, Sandor's father, and had become enormously wealthy—that the documents he is to sign as second witness will restore Sandor Barinkay to his rightful inheritance. Zsupan, outwardly cordial to Barinkay, fumes over his return but promptly marks the documents with his signature—a splotch of ink. A pig, he explains proudly, is his personal signature.

Barinkay, amused, remarks that he has heard about Zsupan's pretty daughter, Arsena. With such a father, of course she is pretty, says Zsupan. Thereupon Barinkay makes a startling offer: in order to avoid the nuisance of lawsuits over who is now the owner of the ancestral estate, he proposes to settle everything out of court by marrying Arsena.

Zsupan is flabbergasted but recovers quickly. He sends his servant into his house to fetch Arsena and her governess, Mirabella. He is to tell them that a suitor is waiting and that they are to bring a betrothal cake with them. A few moments later Mirabella comes rushing out of the house exclaiming she must have a look at Arsena's suitor.[3]

Suddenly she catches sight of Carnero and, much to his discomfiture, greets him as her long-lost husband. As the crowd stares in amazement, Carnero explains to Barinkay and Zsupan that it was at the Battle of Belgrade in 1718 that he became separated from his wife and child. Thereupon Mirabella drags Ottokar forward and tells him that here is his father. The young man jumps into Carnero's arms with a cry of "Vater!" The three then embrace to general exclamations of surprise from the onlookers. Carried away, Carnero also tries to embrace one of the young peasant girls, whom he calls "niece." Mirabella drags him away.

The scene is interrupted by the appearance of Arsena, veiled and dressed in bridal finery, with a group of peasant girls. A long ensemble begins ("Dem Freier naht die Braut") as the peasants hail the bride-to-be. Arsena sings that another suitor has come along—from whom, however, she will conceal her face for the time being. Barinkay, charmed,

[3] At this point in the sequence of musical numbers there is a couplet in which Mirabella relates how she was captured by a Turkish pasha at the Battle of Belgrade. This number is generally omitted.

tries to approach her but she demurely evades him. Zsupan impatiently tells her to drop her veil. Carnero interrupts to say that as Commissioner of Morals he will enforce the rules of propriety. He and Zsupan inform Barinkay that, according to custom, all parties concerned must first partake of the betrothal cake and wine; then the suitor's turn will come. The cake is brought in as the peasant girls invite all to share it as a symbol of a happy marriage ("Hochzeitskuchen bitte zu versuchen").

In a brief passage in quasi-recitative, Barinkay formally presents himself as Arsena's suitor. She herself is dismayed at being confronted by another swain when she is currently being wooed by Ottokar. Carnero announces that, as the betrothal cake has been eaten, the moment has come for the bride-to-be to drop her veil. The music continues in ensemble form interspersed with solo passages. Dropping her veil, Arsena resignedly sings that if Barinkay takes a fancy to her it means she will have to give up Ottokar.

Gazing at her, Barinkay enthuses over her beauty in a sensuous refrain ("Ach, sieh' da, ein herrlich Frauenbild"). Zsupan's voice blends with his as the pig farmer sings that Arsena's good looks are an exact copy of his own when he was a smart young lieutenant of twenty. Mirabella acclaims Zsupan as a veritable Apollo.

The voices of Barinkay and Arsena now blend in an obbligato to a choral passage, with the peasants singing Arsena's praises. Barinkay effusively compliments her on her beauty and asks her to marry him. But Arsena, quite unimpressed, sings that while his attentions certainly are flattering, his wife she will never be—and she will say it ten times over. On these various sentiments the ensemble comes to a rousing climax.

In a brief refrain ("Ein Falter schwirrt um's Licht") following the ensemble, Arsena sings that a suitor has been attracted to her like a moth to a flame. Whoever chooses her, she declares in a spoken phrase, must be—at the very least—a baron.

When Barinkay, shocked and infuriated by her snobbery, flares up at this implied insult, she calmly tells him to come back when he has proof of his nobility. With that she flounces off. Zsupan jokingly observes that he can't force his daughter to marry someone she doesn't want. In any case, he adds, she hasn't chosen *him*. He advises Barinkay to go to bed and then see to it, when he wakes up, that he is really a baron. Then Zsupan jovially invites everyone to come to his house and toast the "future" bride. Angry and chagrined, Barinkay watches him leave with the crowd.

As he is brooding disconsolately he suddenly hears Saffi's voice in the opening phrases of her gypsy song, "So elend und so treu ist Keiner auf Erden." This is the "Zigeunerlied," one of the most dramatic numbers in the opera. Its somber, haunting quality is focused in the ancient warning cry of the Hungarian gypsy—"Dschingrah, dschingrah!" No one on earth, Saffi sings as Barinkay listens fascinated, is so wretched and yet so loyal as the gypsy. When he is near, women must guard their children and men their horses.

At midpoint in the refrain, the mood changes with lightning swiftness from lamentation to defiance. When the gypsy appears, the song goes on, flee for your lives because the gypsy comes as an implacable foe. In the second stanza the mood shifts to one of calm reassurance: when the gypsy is your friend you can trust him. Give him your hand . . . he will never fail you. Saffi ends the "Zigeunerlied" with a defiant shout of "Heijah!" In spoken dialogue, Barinkay exclaims that he knows this song because his mother sang it to him long ago. Czipra, who has followed Saffi on the scene, tells him that his mother learned it from the gypsies when she and the Baron, Sandor's father, lived in the castle before their exile. The gypsies, who were allowed to encamp on the estate, made the Baron their Voyevode, or leader. Czipra then identifies Saffi as her daughter.

While they are talking, they suddenly become aware that Ottokar is cautiously approaching Zsupan's house and is calling to Arsena ("Arsena, es harrt auf dem Balcon"). He and Arsena pledge their love in a lyrical duet which marks the beginning of the long and stirring finale of Act One. Barinkay, furious at discovering that Ottokar is his rival for Arsena's love, swears revenge. Saffi and Czipra join him but warn him not to let his anger goad him into violence. Their voices blend in an accompaniment to the romantic phrases of the lovers' duet. As Ottokar gives Arsena a golden locket set with his picture, Barinkay, beside himself with rage, lunges toward the balcony. Saffi and Czipra restrain him. At that moment the gypsy chorus is heard in the distance. Arsena and Ottokar bid each other goodnight.

Barinkay, Saffi and Czipra listen in rising excitement as the voices come closer. During a brief orchestral interlude, the tribe crowds on the stage and all join in a choral reprise of the "Zigeunerlied."

As they stand facing Barinkay, who looks at them in bewilderment, Czipra says they have come to swear allegiance to him as their Voyevode—they are now his loyal subjects and he can trust them ("Du kannst dem Zigeuner getrost vertrau'n"). Turning to the gypsies, she exhorts them to pledge their faith to the new leader. They respond in a lusty chorus, "Er nimmt uns're Huldigung an." Barinkay acknowledges their homage.

As the cheers die down, Barinkay declares that now he will settle accounts with neighbor Zsupan. With that he strides over to Zsupan's house and knocks loudly on the door. Zsupan emerges followed by Arsena, Carnero, Mirabella and the crowd of villagers who have been celebrating with him. When he asks what the commotion is all about,

Barinkay answers that if he insists on having a baron for a son-in-law, he now has one. "I," says Barinkay, "am a baron." The villagers exclaim in surprise.

In a triumphant refrain ("Komm her und schau dir die Leute an") Barinkay bids Zsupan look upon the people whose Voyevode—Baron— he has now become. He is the Gypsy Baron. Saffi steps forward and in an equally exultant refrain ("Hier in diesem Land") hails the Hungarian who, inspired by the song of a poor gypsy girl, has returned to serve his fatherland. Her voice blends with Barinkay's and Czipra's in a brief passage commenting on the magical power of her song.

There is a moment of silence. Then the villagers burst into jeering laughter at the idea of a "Voyevode of the Gypsies." Ignoring the insult, Barinkay asks Arsena if she will marry him. A "gypsy" baron, she replies contemptuously, won't do. Thereupon Barinkay turns to Saffi and asks her to be his wife. When she protests that this is a cruel joke, Barinkay cries that her faithful heart has won his love and trust. Carnero steps forward and declares that Saffi cannot go with Barinkay because it is against the law of the land for a Hungarian to marry a gypsy. As Barinkay angrily defies him, the gypsies shout that they will protect their Voyevode. Zsupan roars that he will not allow his daughter to be spurned and made a laughingstock.

The scene builds up to a turbulent pitch as the two groups—Zsupan's villagers and Barinkay's gypsies—face each other and hurl insults. A fight finally breaks out as Carnero orders Barinkay's arrest. After a furious scuffle the voices of the combatants blend in the thrilling chorus which closes the act, with villagers and gypsies alike claiming victory.

ACT TWO

A gypsy encampment near the tower of the ruined castle, seen at one side. On the other, the gypsies' forge and smithy. Czipra, half reclining, lies in front of the tower. Saffi lies with her head on Czipra's lap. Above them in a ragged opening in the tower, Barinkay lies asleep. Czipra sings softly that she is keeping watch over this lovely child and her master's land ("Mein Aug' bewacht"). This marks the beginning of the Treasure Scene, sung in trio and duet form by Czipra, Saffi and Barinkay.

Slowly awaking, Barinkay wonders if his happiness is real or only a dream. Gazing tenderly down at Saffi, he calls to awaken her. When he fondly calls her "his wife," she somewhat sullenly asks if he still is jesting about marrying her. Barinkay answers in a passionate refrain ("In dieser Nacht voll herrlicher Pracht") that on this wondrous night he came to know that Saffi is his only love. Her beauty has completely enchanted him and his heart is hers. Overwhelmed by his ardor, Saffi yields to his embrace. They pledge their love in a lyrical continuation of the duet ("O Blick in Blick"), one of the loveliest numbers in the operetta.

At its conclusion Saffi remarks on the strange look on Czipra's face. In explanation the old gypsy says that last night she had a dream ("Ein Greis ist mir im Traum erschienen"). She saw Saffi's father, who told her where the ancestral treasure is hidden. The young suitor has only to lift a certain marble stone in the wall of the tower. Barinkay cries excitedly that the dream is true and that the treasure already is his. Czipra and Saffi urge him to begin the search at once. Barinkay's voice blends with theirs in a staccato trio as he strikes the stones with a hammer in time with the music.

Suddenly he shouts that one stone has a hollow sound. He pulls it away. In a triumphant phrase ("s'ist grandios! Der Schatz!") he sings that he has found the treasure as he brings out a large rough-hewn chest from the hollow behind the stone. Czipra and Saffi gasp in amazement as Barinkay opens the chest to reveal a glittering array of gold and jewels. The three express their joy over their good fortune in a trio ("Ha, seht, es winkt, es blinkt, es klingt") which is one of Strauss's finest waltzes.

This treasure, they sing, will buy all the things they have longed for—lackeys, fine clothes, wine, parties, masquerades, horses and palaces. Czipra cautions the lovers not to squander their wealth, so that its pleasures may last. Barinkay and Saffi, though dazzled by their riches, sing that love and trust still are more precious than gold.

It is now daylight and the gypsy camp is stirring to life. Hearing the sound of voices, Barinkay quickly puts the chest back into the hollow and replaces the stone. Pali, one of the gypsies, enters and calls on the tribe to go to work. The gypsies crowd in, the men going to their forges and the women watching. All join in the Anvil Chorus ("Ja, das Eisen wird gefüge"), which brings to mind a similar scene in Verdi's *Il Trovatore*. The theme of the chorus is that the gypsies will forge the iron into weapons with which they will strike their enemies blow for blow ("Schlag auf Schlag").[4]

Carnero now comes in with Mirabella, Arsena, Ottokar and a group of officials. He upbraids Barinkay for "living in sin" with a gypsy girl. When Sandor angrily retorts that she is his wife, Carnero asks who married them. Barinkay and Saffi reply in what is perhaps the most beautiful melody in the score, "Wer uns getraut?" It was the *Dompfaff*, the bullfinch, who married them under the blue cathedral dome of the sky,

---

[4] Here, in some versions of the opera, there is a comic byplay in dialogue involving Zsupan and a trio of gypsies—Pali, Ferko and Jozsi—who steal his watch and his moneybags.

the lovers sing. And then the nightingale serenaded them, singing that love is a power sent from heaven. Witnesses to the marriage were two storks, those symbols of a happy household, which clapped their bills loudly and wished the couple well.[5]

As the onlookers warmly applaud the lovers, they are startled by a shout from Ottokar, who meanwhile has been exploring the tower. He cries that he has found gold. When all rush toward the tower, Barinkay steps in their way declaring that this treasure is his own discovery and belongs to him alone. Carnero demands that it be turned over to him as a "war chest." Barinkay contemptuously rejects the idea.

The argument is interrupted by a fanfare offstage. A moment later Count Homonay enters, followed by his bodyguards, hussars and vivandières. Barinkay greets him with appropriate dignity as his noble patron. Homonay announces that he has come to recruit men to fight in the war against Spain. He himself, he adds, is too old to fight—but he still can sing the famous Hungarian recruiting song, the "Werberlied." He thereupon launches into the song, a call to arms in a thumping martial rhythm ("Her die Hand, es muss ja sein!"). It describes the traditional Magyar recruiting custom: a handshake, a glass of wine—and you're in the army. Then when the recruit exchanges his hat for the shako he is ready to fight for the fatherland. All onstage roar out the chorus, which bristles with martial spirit and defiance . . . victory or death . . . our blood will stain the earth before we surrender. The "Werberlied" ends with a fierce shout of "Strike hard!" ("Schlagt ein!").

Then the mood changes in a flash to one of wild abandon as soldiers and peasants sing and dance the czardas ("Wir alle wollen lustig sein"). It is a song in praise of the dashing hussar, who, next to fighting, loves wine, women and song.

After the czardas the recruiting begins. Zsupan and Ottokar unsuspectingly drink wine and shake hands, and find themselves in the army. Barinkay not only enlists but offers his treasure to Count Homonay to help pay for the war. As patriotic fervor rises to fever pitch, Count Homonay proclaims that the war will not last long, that victory is assured and that all will meet in Vienna to celebrate the triumph of the Hungarians. The crowd sings of the delights of Vienna in a sparkling Viennese waltz, "So voll Fröhlichkeit."

But during the merriment, Carnero, Mirabella, Arsena and Ottokar stand glumly to one side, eying the gypsies in disapproval. Disgruntled by his failure to get possession of Barinkay's treasure for his own use, Carnero complains to Homonay that, in spite of all the noble palaver,

---

[5] In the original score this scene is followed by a *Sittenskommissions* (Morals Commission) couplet, sung in unison by Carnero, Mirabella and Zsupan. It is usually omitted.

his authority has been flouted by this gypsy rabble ("Noch eben in Gloria"). The others join him in denouncing the gypsies as outlaws and thieves.

Suddenly Czipra, glaring at them, bursts out that she will no longer keep silent in the face of their insults ("Genug, nicht länger schweig' ich mehr"). Now they will learn that the gypsy girl whom they scorn as a hussy is far above them in rank and station. This child, Czipra cries, does not belong to her. The others gasp in amazement.

Thereupon she hands Homonay a document. In suspenseful phrases ("Ich hab' gewacht") she sings that while she watched over this child she also guarded the document she now entrusts to the Count. It will reveal the whole truth.

Reading it quickly, Homonay points to Saffi and declares that there stands the daughter of a prince. There is general consternation. Her father, Homonay goes on, was the last pasha of Hungary. Everyone present joins in a chorus acclaiming the newly discovered princess, "Ein Fürstenkind, ein Wunder ist gescheh'n!"

But Saffi's happiness is cut short when Barinkay tells her he must leave ("Ach, von Euch muss ich geh'n"). As she stares at him in dismay and unbelief, he says he is leaving only because he loves her. At that moment, as though to underscore the irony of the situation, the throng bursts into the "Werberlied." The voices of Mirabella, Arsena, Zsupan, Czipra and Ottokar blend with the chorus in contrasting expressions of disappointment over this turn of events.

Barinkay himself, despite Saffi's tearful protests, calls for the recruiting wine. He seals his decision by clasping Homonay's hand. After a momentary struggle with himself he declares that while he would gladly die for love, he first will die for the fatherland. He holds out his hand and Homonay grasps it, shouting: "Forward! On to battle—and then to Vienna!"

Now follows the great closing chorus of the act—a reprise of the *Werberlied*. All urge the hussars to go forward into battle and smite the foe for the glory of the fatherland. The curtain falls.

ACT THREE

Before the Kärntnerthor in Vienna. The populace is awaiting the arrival of the victorious Hungarians. Zsupan struts in and is welcomed by Arsena, Mirabella and Carnero. When Arsena asks her father about his exploits, he sums up the course of the war in a hilarious patter song. He begins by describing how the army returned after the campaign on the banks of the Tagus in Spain ("Von des Tajo Strand"), where they "taught the enemy manners." As for himself, he came through the war unscathed—except for a spot of sunburn. Next he launches into a nonsensical story of how he dealt with a Spanish soldier who tried to shoot him with an unloaded gun. Finally he brags about his scandalous flirtation with a pretty Spanish woman. He enchanted her, of course, and when he gallantly kissed her hand he managed to slip a diamond ring from her finger. He is now wearing it as a token of her affection.

There were many such beautiful donnas, Zsupan goes on, but none of them made him forget his duties as a soldier. At intervals during his recital his listeners comment admiringly in chorus.

There is a fanfare of trumpets announcing the return of the troops, led in by Barinkay and Ottokar. They sing the lusty Soldiers' Chorus ("Hurra, die Schlacht mitgemacht"). It expresses the usual operatic sentiments about the soldier bravely facing shot and shell and asking only a kiss from his beloved as his reward when—and if—he returns home.

As for Barinkay, he is awarded for his heroism in battle by being made a true baron. Zsupan hails the accolade, saying that Barinkay now can qualify as his son-in-law and marry Arsena. Then he will claim her now, Barinkay sings in a phrase which begins the closing ensemble of the opera ("Ich halte um deine Tochter an"). He amazes everyone by announcing that he claims Arsena not for himself but for the faithful Ottokar. The two young lovers rush into each other's arms.

Homonay asks Barinkay if he now intends to stay single. Before he can answer, the Count announces that the marriage of a certain Hungarian nobleman and a gypsy girl has been given legal sanction. Barinkay turns to Saffi and in a tender phrase sings that here is the queen of his heart. Gazing into his eyes, Saffi sings the phrase of her gypsy song— "give the gypsy your hand, for he comes as a friend." Barinkay, taking her in his arms, sings jubilantly that everything has turned out for the best—he has won both a victory in battle and a beautiful wife.

Then he swings into a reprise of his patter song in Act One, "Ja, das Alles auf Ehr'." The chorus joins him in the lilting refrain: "When you know what you're about, everything is easy." The curtain falls.

APPENDIX: AN OPERA GLOSSARY

A CAPPELLA: choral music sung without accompaniment of any kind.

APPOGGIATURA: an embellishment (*q.v.*), usually in the form of a note just above the principal note.

ARIA: a formalized vocal solo in an opera.

ARIA DA CAPO: typical of nineteenth-century opera. Its form is a first section, a contrasting second section, then a repetition of the first section.

ARIA PARLANTE: sung in loose rhythm closely paralleling rhythm of speech. Not to be confused with *Sprechstimme,* which is musical imitation of tones and rhythms of speech.

ARIOSO: a vocal solo between a recitative passage (*q.v.*) and an aria. It is not as declamatory as recitative nor as elaborate as an aria.

ATONALITY: music which has tone but is intended to sound free of any tonal center.

BALLAD OPERA: a musical play based on ballads or folk songs. An example is *The Beggar's Opera,* by John Gay (1728).

BALLET: a divertissement danced by a special corps of dancers between or during the acts of an opera. Example: "Dance of the Hours" in *La Gioconda.*

BARCAROLE: a boat song characterized by a pulsing sextuple rhythm. One of the most famous in opera is in *Les Contes d'Hoffmann.*

BARITONE: the adult male vocal range between bass and tenor.

BAROQUE: a period in musical history; also, a highly ornamental musical style. Baroque was infused into opera in the late seventeenth and early eighteenth centuries.

BASS, BASSO: the lowest range of the adult male voice.

BASSO CANTANTE: a lyric bass, particularly in the lower range.

BEAT: the *pulse* of the music. Not to be confused with tempo (frequency of beats), measure (grouping of beats) or rhythm (*q.v.*).

BEL CANTO: a smooth, beautiful style of singing, characterized by elegance of tone and delivery, developed by the Italians during the seventeenth and eighteenth centuries.

BOCCA CHIUSA: singing with mouth closed.

BRAVURA: great brilliancy and accuracy in execution.

BRINDISI: a drinking song.

BUFFO, BUFFA: denoting an operatic characterization which is humorous or comically grotesque. A *buffo* is an operatic clown.

CABALETTA: a short song set off by a triplet figure in the accompaniment; also, the second or third part of an aria.

CADENCE: final moment of a melody or phrase of music.

CADENZA: a florid passage in a song or aria—usually near or at the end—sung as a vocal embellishment.

CANTABILE: singing in easy, flowing style.

CASTRATO: an adult male singer whose boy's voice has been retained as the result of castration. During the seventeenth and eighteenth centuries some of the most famous singers in opera were the *castrati*.

CAVATINA: a solo shorter and less elaborate than an aria.

CHAMBER OPERA: intended for a small audience, or to be given in a small theater. Frequently without chorus and with a small cast.

CHEST VOICE, CHEST REGISTER: the vocal tone produced from the chest cavity, a distinguishing feature of big dramatic voices. It is in contrast to the head tone, which is lighter and more lyric. The concept of separate registers, however, has been questioned.

CHORAL OPERA: in which the chorus is predominant, as in most of the operas of Gluck, or in *Boris Godunof*. It has elements of the classic style of Greek drama.

CHORUSMASTER: the man who trains and rehearses an opera chorus.

CLAQUE: a small group of people sometimes hired by opera singers to lead the applause for them.

COLORATURA: florid vocal embellishments, chromatic runs, cadenzas and so on. Also, a soprano with a light, agile voice.

COUNTERTENOR: a male voice with an exceptionally high range.

DIATONIC: within the natural scale without altered notes; non-chromatic. Function is represented by the "white notes" of the piano.

DIVA: a female opera star. *Diva* is the Italian word for "goddess."

DIVISI: divided musical line. Passage in which individuals or choristers who have been singing in unison divide to sing different notes.

DODECAPHONISM: the theory of the twelve-tone scale—twelve equally spaced tones of the tempered system having equal harmonic value. The thematic structure is established as a series of twelve tones, with each tone used once. This is the harmonic system of Alban Berg's *Lulu*.

DRAMMA PER MUSICA: a more specific definition than *opera* for a drama in musical terms.

DYNAMICS: the contrasting action of loud and soft. As applied to opera, the rising and falling of emotional tension as the drama unfolds.

EMBELLISHMENTS: tones added to an essential melody for decorative effect, display or elaboration.

ENSEMBLE: a particular combination of three, four, five or more voices. Also, a chorus.

FALSETTO: a vocal tone minus resonance, produced with a high larynx position.

FINALE: the last scene of an act or of a whole opera. Earlier operas usually ended with a display aria for the star; after about 1750 composers began writing finales for ensemble or chorus.

FIORITURE: flowery embellishments.

FOLK OPERA: made up of folk songs or traditional material. The Spanish zarzuela is a good example.

GRAND OPERA: a term introduced in France circa 1820 to define an elaborate singing show without spoken dialogue, usually on a serious subject.

HABANERA: probably of African origin, this dance in duple rhythm was introduced in Spain from Havana, Cuba. Operatically, the most familiar is the *Habanera* in *Carmen*.

IMPRESARIO: the manager or director of an opera company.

INTERMEZZO: music played between the acts—a kind of bridge between the end of one act and the beginning of another. One of the best known is the *Intermezzo* from *Cavalleria Rusticana*.

KAMMERSÄNGER, KAMMERSÄNGERIN: in Germany and Austria, an honorary title conferred on virtuoso singers—both in concert and in opera.

LEGATO: a marking in music indicating notes that are to be given their full value, creating a smooth-flowing, continuous effect.

LEITMOTIV: a motif recurring throughout an entire opera, associated with a given character, situation or emotion. It was first developed and brought to its highest degree of effectiveness by Richard Wagner.

LIBRETTO: the printed text of an opera, usually available in booklet form.

LIRICO SPINTO: a voice combining the qualities of the lyric and the dramatic; usually applied to the male voice.

MEZZA VOCE: half voice.

MEZZO-SOPRANO: a voice in the range between soprano and contralto.

MISE-EN-SCÈNE: the manner in which a scene is staged (sets, costumes, lighting and so on).

OPERA BUFFA: low-comedy opera.

OPÉRA COMIQUE: opera (not necessarily comic) in which the dialogue bridging the plot situations is spoken instead of sung.

OPERA SERIA: serious or tragic opera.

OPERETTA: a light, amusing musical play, usually with a farcical plot, spoken dialogue and songs instead of arias.

OVERTURE: the technical term for an orchestral introduction or prelude of an opera, which in many cases states certain themes associated with different characters or sometimes plot motivations.

PRIMA DONNA: another name for *diva*.

PROLOGUE: a short or a long scene sung before the main section of an opera to explain the background of the drama. Because it is *sung,* it is different from a prelude or an overture.

PROMPTER'S BOX: a hooded installation at the center of an opera stage at the footlights, where the prompter, unseen by the audience, gives musical cues to the singers.

RECITATIVE: a passage in which the words are sung, but not to strict rhythm nor in the form of a flowing melody. The only accompaniment is an occasional chord played on a harpsichord or by the orchestra.

REFRAIN: a stanza which recurs in a ballad or a song. It may be a solo passage without the extent or elaboration of an aria.

RHYTHM: in a broad sense, "a steady flowing." It is the regular recurrence of grouped strong and weak beats, or heavily and lightly accented tones, in alteration; an arrangement of successive tones, usually in measures.

RITORNELLO: a term applied to instrumental interludes between scenes in baroque opera.

ROMANZA: a term describing an aria predominantly lyric in character.

RUBATO: literally, "robbed." In a rubato passage, the extra time given to one beat is made up by hurrying the other notes within the measure in order to maintain the tempo of the piece. It is used mainly for emphasis.

SCENA: an episode in an opera which integrates the music and the drama, making each equally important. It may be the extension of one of the principal arias of an opera.

SINGSPIEL: the German word for "song-play," spoken dialogue interspersed with songs or arias. It is closely allied to ballad opera and *opéra comique.*

SOPRANO: the highest range of the female voice—or boy's voice before mutation (voice change) occurs. Also designated as treble.

SOTTO VOCE: a kind of whispered singing.

TENOR: the highest range of the adult male voice.

TESSITURA: the prevailing range—not necessarily extremely high or low notes —of a song or aria.

TREMOLO: an uncontrolled wavy or oscillating tone with an unsteady pitch, mainly due to faulty breathing.

TRILL: prolonged singing of a note and the one above or below it in rapid succession. A difficult vocal feat which only the best singers can accomplish.

VERISMO: stark realism in opera, as first exemplified by Puccini, Leoncavallo and Mascagni. A prime characteristic of contemporary opera.

VIBRATO: a pulsating effect on a steady pitch—as distinct from tremolo— imparting a heightened emotional level.

BIBLIOGRAPHY

Billy Budd and Other Tales, by Herman Melville. A Signet Classic, New American Library, New York, 1961.

Bulfinch's Mythology, by Thomas Bulfinch. Modern abridgment by Edmund Fuller. Dell Publishing Company, Inc., New York, 1959.

Composers Since 1900, by David Ewen. H. W. Wilson Company, New York, 1969.

The Concert Companion, by Robert Bagar and Louis Biancolli, with introduction by Deems Taylor. Whittlesey House, New York, London, 1947.

Donizetti and the World of Opera in Italy, Paris and Vienna, by Herbert Weinstock. Pantheon Books, New York, 1960.

The Enjoyment of Music, by Joseph Machlis. W. W. Norton & Company, New York, 1955.

The Great Singers, by Henry Pleasants. Simon & Schuster, 1966.

Leoš Janáček. His life and work, by Hans Hollander. Translated by Paul Hamburger. St. Martin's Press, New York, 1963.

Life of Rossini, by Stendahl, translated and annotated by Richard N. Coe. University of Washington Press, Seattle, 1970.

Louise Homer and the Golden Age of Opera, by Anne Homer. William Morrow & Company, Inc., New York, 1974.

Massenet, by James Harding. J. M. Dent & Sons, Ltd., London, 1970.

Massenet and His Operas, by Henry T. Finck. John Lane Company, New York, 1910.

The Metropolitan Opera 1833/1966, by Irving Kolodin. Alfred A. Knopf, New York, 1966.

The Milton Cross New Encyclopedia of the Great Composers and Their Music, by Milton Cross and David Ewen. Doubleday & Company, Inc., Garden City, New York, 1969.

Mozart: a documentary biography, by Otto Erich Deutsch. Translated by Eric Blom, Peter Branscombe, Jeremy Noble. Stanford University Press, Stanford, Calif., 1966.

Music Lovers' Encyclopedia, compiled by Rupert Hughes, revised and edited by Deems Taylor and Russell Kerr. Garden City Publishing Company, Garden City, New York, 1939.

The New Encyclopedia of Music and Musicians, edited by Waldo Selden Pratt. The Macmillan Company, New York, 1924.

The New Kobbé's Complete Opera Book, edited and revised by the Earl of Harewood. G. P. Putnam's Sons, New York, 1976.

100 Great Operas and Their Stories, by Henry W. Simon. A Dolphin Reference Book, Doubleday & Company, Inc., Garden City, New York, 1960.

One Hundred Years of Music in America, by Paul Henry Lang. G. Schirmer, Inc., New York, 1961.

Poulenc and the Carmelites, by Edward Lockspeiser, 1905. *Opera,* London. Vol. 9, No. 1 (January 1958).

Secrets of Massenet's Workshop Divulged by the Composer Himself, by Herbert Peyser. *Musical America,* New York, 1912.

Stories of the Great Operas, by Ernest Newman. Blakiston Company, Philadelphia, Knopf, 1930.

The Turn of the Screw, by Henry James (1898). Dell, New York.

INDEX

Have you read *The New Milton Cross' Complete Stories of the Great Operas?*

CONTENTS

Der Rosenkavalier, *Strauss*
The Saint of Bleecker Street, *Menotti*
Salome, *Strauss*
Samson et Dalila, *Saint-Saëns*
Simon Boccanegra, *Verdi*
La Sonnambula, *Bellini*
Tannhäuser, *Wagner*
Thaïs, *Massenet*
Tosca, *Puccini*
La Traviata, *Verdi*
Tristan und Isolde, *Wagner*
Il Trovatore, *Verdi*
Turandot, *Puccini*
Wozzeck, *Berg*
Die Zauberflöte, *Mozart*
